Coast of Dreams

Coast
of Dreams

*A history of contemporary
California*

KEVIN STARR

ALLEN LANE
an imprint of
PENGUIN BOOKS

ALLEN LANE

Published by the Penguin Group

Penguin Books Ltd, 80 Strand, London WC2R ORL, England

Penguin Group (USA) Inc., 375 Hudson Street, New York, New York 10014, USA

Penguin Group (Canada), 10 Alcorn Avenue, Toronto, Ontario, Canada M4V 3B2
(a division of Pearson Penguin Canada Inc.)

Penguin Ireland, 25 St Stephen's Green, Dublin 2, Ireland (a division of Penguin Books Ltd)

Penguin Group (Australia), 250 Camberwell Road,
Camberwell, Victoria 3124, Australia (a division of Pearson Australia Group Pty Ltd)

Penguin Books India Pvt Ltd, 11 Community Centre,
Panchsheel Park, New Delhi – 110 017, India

Penguin Group (NZ), cnr Airborne and Rosedale Roads, Albany,
Auckland 1310, New Zealand (a division of Pearson New Zealand Ltd)

Penguin Books (South Africa) (Pty) Ltd, 24 Sturdee Avenue,
Rosebank 2196, South Africa

Penguin Books Ltd, Registered Offices: 80 Strand, London WC2R ORL, England

www.penguin.com

First published in the United States of America by Alfred A. Knopf 2004
First published in Great Britain by Allen Lane 2005

I

Copyright © Kevin Starr, 2004

The moral right of the author has been asserted

Printed in Great Britain by Clays Ltd, St Ives plc

A CIP catalogue record for this book is available from the British Library

ISBN 0–713–99846–6

For Sandra Dijkstra, Ashbel Green, Bruce Harris,
and Sheldon Meyer

CONTENTS

PREFACE

California on the Edge

As a writer who had dedicated the best part of his life and writing career to chronicling California, I became fascinated as the 1980s turned into the 1990s by the possibility—sometimes the probability—that California had gone seriously awry. I sensed this possibility most vividly in the epidemic of gang-related homicides and the attendant violence that seemed to pervade Los Angeles County. That foreboding became even more actualized as I lived through the Los Angeles riots of April and May 1992 and had my life altered by the Northridge earthquake of January 1994. As a more than occasional journalist and avid reader of newspapers, I became increasingly aware of the dark and somber picture of California that was emerging from California's coverage of itself. As someone attuned primarily to the imaginative dimension of social experience and to the moral drama of California as an American experiment, I became increasingly disturbed by the grim realities around me.

While a graduate student at Harvard in the 1960s, I had decided to devote my writing career to chronicling California as an essential and compelling component of the larger American experience. By the early 1990s, I was beginning to wonder whether I had chosen a dead end. Was California an aberration, a sideshow, or, worse, a case study in how things could go wrong for the United States? Such questions were of more than passing importance to me, in that I had invested most of my professional energies in California in the belief that the history of California was mainstream American history. Even more, I had extended, enhanced, even shored up, my personal identity by projecting my own hopes, dreams, and aspirations onto California. Had I made a terrible mistake?

Despite such reservations, however, I continued to enjoy and participate in many of the liberating aspects of life in the Golden State. Having been frequently attacked as a California booster, I did not—as so many others were doing at this time—become a California basher. As a classroom teacher at the University of Southern California and, later, as state librarian of California, I was encountering more than enough evidence that there was still something compelling about the California experiment: its ecumenism, for one thing; its embrace of the planet's peoples and traditions; its incomparable beauty, environmentally challenged yet persistent; the rich mélange of its syncretic culture, so full of hope for a diverse and renewed America. If it seemed at times to be the worst of times, it could also seem the best of times, especially as I found myself walking across a sunlit USC campus, surrounded by enthusiastic young people; dedicating a new library at Cathedral City on the edge of the great southeastern desert, a fully uniformed high school band in attendance; walking beneath the redwoods of Sonoma County on a mid-July morning; moving from painting to painting at an exhibition of California impressionism at the Santa Barbara Museum of Art; swimming in San Francisco Bay with the Dolphin Club; attending mass amid the comforting Gothicism of St. Dominic's Church in San Francisco; driving through the high desert of the Modoc Plateau en route to a remote county library.

It would be seductively easy, I realized, to join the naysayers and see California as one vast failed experiment. Do this, and I would be considered a deep thinker, like so many others of my tribe, called upon repeatedly by the press and television to say that California was over. But if I succumbed to this temptation, I would not be seeing the full truth about California and its people. And so, motivated in part by a fear that it was all going wrong, I was actively on the lookout for signs that it was also going right: this California of mine, where I was born as a fourth-generation citizen; this California, which had galvanized and coalesced the intellectual ambitions of my youth and absorbed the best writing energies of my middle age.

Chronicling California on the edge, I came to realize just how much of my life had been on the edge as well: on the edge of a vast and, I believed, nonmeretricious hope that I could make something out of the shattered fragments of my neglected and incoherent youth, that I could find in, with, and through California some measure of meaning. Pervading the facts and figures of this book, in and behind its incidents and stories, a reader can encounter the objectifications, the projections, of my own inner struggle to find California—that radiant golden vision that I had glimpsed so powerfully as a young man—as being still worth the living, the writing, the struggle.

This book is an effort to make an early, and certainly premature, report on this astonishing decade and the first two years of the new millennium. *Coast of Dreams* should not be seen as history—it is too early for history—but as a collection of snapshots and sketches, as notes from the field, as a preliminary effort to sort out a most extraordinary decade and millennial turn. A cinematic collage of facts and impressions, home footage from the video camera of an engaged participant, this book ranges across a variety of stories, statistics, interviews, and portraits in an effort to suggest the broad outlines and the complexity of a decade.

As of now, all evidence and impressions can only be partially assembled and interpreted. Historians of the future will have a clearer picture. They will be able to see with more certainty whether or not the period 1990–2003 was not only the end of one California but the beginning of another. In the meantime, contemporary Californians, caught in the midst of ordeals and transformations of great magnitude, can only gather fragmentary evidence regarding the ultimate significance of this end-of-the-century decade. California continues; but where it is going and what it will become—how, that is, it will handle the diversity of its people, the confusions of its values and culture, the global-colonial nature of its economy, the trade-offs between its militant environmentalism and concern for local well-being with the demands of its industrial infrastructure, and, most important, how it deals with the possible loss of one California and the ambiguous imposition of a new and uncharted identity—remains, like this book, on the edge, an open question.

Los Angeles, San Francisco, Sacramento
June 2003

PART I

Coast of Dreams

Surf's Up!

Most sunny afternoons in Newport Beach, Orange County, in the fall of 1997, Veronica Kay, a five-foot-eleven sun-bleached blonde Valkyrie, a junior at Newport Harbor High, could be found surfing toward shore on a killer wave. It may have cost Veronica $1,600 to do this bit of surfing—that's the fee she would collect that afternoon in Los Angeles after modeling for Union Bay jeans, J. Crew, Sunglass Hut, or any other company that was seeking a knockout blonde with the Southern California surfer look. Veronica Kay was certainly that: she had won *Seventeen* magazine's New Star Showcase (supermodel Niki Taylor got her start in the same contest), and was already the star of modeling sessions in Tahiti for *Wave Action* magazine and heading for Bali in May for another shoot. Kay was also a ranked surfer, obsessed with the waves since the age of thirteen, winning at the end of her sophomore year her first national competition at Trestles, a surf spot near San Clemente.

Without the surf, Kay might have been just another lost California kid. Her parents divorced when she was six. The split plunged Kay's mother and two siblings into poverty. Only contributions of groceries from friends kept them fed. Her brother and sister struggled with the drug culture. It was the same old California story, sadly, and at thirteen Kay might very well have been expected to follow the drill; but she picked up a surfboard instead, and in May 1996 was discovered by a modeling agency. ("She surfs," says her agent, "and it just so happens she's absolutely adorable and has an amazing figure.") Soon she had her first client, Oakley of Foothill Ranch, a maker of sunglasses, for whom she posed while continuing to surf competitively.

"The first image I saw of her," remembers surf contest promoter Allan Seymour of Capistrano Beach, "was a picture of her at Waikiki holding a board and kind of looking over her shoulder and laughing. So I figured, 'Oh, she's a model. She can't surf.' Then I found out she's one of the top short-board women in the world. I was like, 'Wow.' " With Kay's income, her brother and sister—to whom she remained devoted—got off drugs and into college. Her mother had no trouble with the groceries. "I'll model as long as it doesn't interfere with my surfing," Kay noted. "Modeling is just a real easy way for me to earn the money I need. Surfing is my life."[1]

California writer Jack London deserves as much credit as anyone for publicizing the Hawaiian sport after his 1907 visit to the islands on his yacht, *The Snark,* en route to Australia. That very same year, Pacific Electric Railroad magnate Henry Huntington brought surfing to the California coast when he hired an Irish-Hawaiian man by the name of George Freeth to give surfing demonstrations off Redondo Beach to promote the completion of the Los Angeles–Redondo Beach Interurban Electric. Another Hawaiian, Duke Kahanomoku, swimming gold medalist in the 1912 Olympics, continued to practice and teach the sport. Surfing grew steadily through the 1920s and 1930s as an elite pursuit, helped after 1932 when Tom Blake patented a hollow surfboard, halving the weight (up to 150 pounds) of the older redwood models, which were so heavy it often took two men to carry them to the waves. After World War II, Bob Simmons—a 4F aerospace engineer at Douglas Aircraft (a 1935 motorcycle accident had nearly severed his right arm) who had surfed through the war—lightened boards even more, using combinations of Styrofoam, resin, and fiberglass.

Through the 1950s surfing remained a quasi-outlaw occupation, or at least the rebellious pursuit at Malibu and San Onofre of such nonconformists as Tom Wert, who surfed under the *nom de surf* Opai, and Terry Tracey, a.k.a. Tubesteak. It was a James Dean sort of thing, Wert later stated, a way of proving that you and the other surfers—Mickey "Da Cat" Dora, Mickey Munoz, Kemp Aaberg, and the other guys—weren't into 1950s conformity and gray flannel suits. Both Tracey and Dora had tried it in the straight world, working as clerks at the Home Insurance Company in Los Angeles. Both were fired within the week. Better to stay out on the beach and surf, protected from the draft by the calcium deposits building up on your feet and kneecaps.

Then came the novel *Gidget* (1957), written by Frederick Kohner, based on the firsthand experiences of his surfing teenage daughter. Fleeing the Nazis in the late 1930s, Kohner could not speak a word of English when he arrived in Los Angeles. By the mid-1950s he was master not only of English but of teenage slang and surf argot. Columbia bought the film rights to *Gidget* for $50,000, and the resulting movie, released in 1959, followed in 1966 by the even more successful documentary *The Endless Summer,* reinforced by the surfing music of Jan and Dean and the Beach Boys, made surfing a primary emblem and ritual of California identity: a daydream, an idyll, of endless youth and an endless summer on the sunny shores of an endless sea. Young men and women went down to the shore in their teens, and sometimes—the men especially—they never came back. Like the central character in the film *Lifeguard* (1976), they stayed on, working for the county as lifeguards or running surfers' shops, lunching at Wahoo's Fish Taco in Costa Mesa, hanging out at Jack's Surfboards in Huntington Beach, hoping for a mention in *Surfer* magazine, never growing up, never leaving the beach.

You could live cheaply at the beach, provided you stayed single and didn't incur a lot of family obligations. That meant remaining a kind of boy well into middle age, perhaps for a lifetime, since surfing was a young man's game. If you were rich, like A. B. Spreckels III, scion of the great Spreckels family and stepson of Clark Gable, you could become a surfing legend under the beach name Bunker before your untimely death at the age of twenty-seven. And dying in the water was cool, too, if you had a death wish, as Bunker surely did.

It was even okay if you were kind of old—forty-nine, say, as of 1995— and had a Nobel Prize in chemistry, like Kary Mullis, living in a beachfront apartment in La Jolla and surfing and trying to score with chicks two years after winning the Big One as a staff scientist at Cetus for cracking the way that DNA replicates itself, thus making it possible, eventually, to reproduce billions of copies of a desired gene in a matter of hours. U.S. Patent 4,683,202 and the Nobel Prize had given Mullis fame and financial security, but he was still a Southern California sort of a guy: with three ex-wives and two sons, hanging out at the beach, an aging but still plausible surfer, trying at once to get and not to get a life. University of California at Santa Cruz undergraduate Daniel Duane, by contrast, was barely into his twenties when he spent a year surfing the California coast while keeping a journal, published in 1996 as *Caught Inside*. Although it was never stated as such, the model for Duane's year and the subsequent book was Henry David Thoreau's year on Walden Pond. Duane went down to the California beach to surf and to watch, and in surfing and watching to probe, like Thoreau, what it was all about and then to write it up in delightfully sinewy and tactile prose announcing the overnight presence of an important new California author. Guys like Daniel Duane, Kary Mullis, and the others—rebels, mystic seekers, Dharma bums—were fewer and farther between on the beach by the 1990s. They were really throwbacks to the wild and crazy guys of the 1950s: rebels without a cause, existentialists, and, as in Duane's case, developing writers.

By the mid-1990s, beach dreams and the search for surf, like every other sport in the United States, had gone big-time commercial. Surfware companies such as Quiksilver, Billabong, and Gotcha, selling their lines at places like the Waveline Surf Shop in Ventura, were doing $1.7 billion a year. In

March 1998, a newcomer, K2, stole Quiksilver's top rider, Tim Curran, the numero uno surfer in the United States, with a three-year, six-figure deal. Prominent surfers such as Veronica Kay and Shane Dorian could make hundreds of thousands of dollars endorsing or otherwise promoting lines of surfwear. When the Manhattan-based Tommy Hilfiger clothing company entered the surfwear business in 1997, it put an entire family on retainer: the legendary Paskowitzes, a multigenerational clan prominent in Southern California surfing circles for four decades.

Up and down the Southern California coast, from Carpenteria to La Jolla, at Malibu and Dana Point, Manhattan Beach and San Clemente, it seemed as if everyone under a certain age—every white kid, that is, and an increasing number of Asians, and the beginnings of a Latino set, but few blacks—was living on the beach or in the water as much as possible, using terms such as "raging" (stupendous), "stoked" (couldn't be happier), "barney" (stupid and annoying), "bettie" (a beach girl). Surfers knew their turf and their surf down to its ten- to twenty-yard specifics: the precise point on the beach—Old Joe's in Malibu, Super Tubes south of Point Mugu, Toes Over in Marina del Rey, and 150 precisely defined spots—where the waves were good. At Manhattan and Huntington Beach, you could find an abundance of "Newtons"—high, hollow waves. Down a steep hill near Laguna Niguel, at a little beach called Salt Creek, you could ride the tube on hard, consistent waves, not big, but clean and hollow. At the Wedge at the end of the Balboa Peninsula, just to the right of the jetty, the surf was pounding, pummeling, dangerous. For really ferocious surf, you had to travel north, up to Maverick's north of Half Moon Bay, where waves the height of a four-story building in 1994 took the life of Hawaiian surfer star Mark Foo, breaking his board and sucking him into a deep bowl called the Cauldron, where Foo's board leash jammed on an underwater rock spur and trapped him there until his breath ran out.

By September 1997, with El Niño in the offing, surfers were talking about three-story waves once again thrashing the Southland as well as hitting up at Maverick's. (When El Niño last came, in the winter of 1982–83, three-story waves were commonplace.) "Everybody's anticipating it," noted Randy Wright, owner of Horizon's West Surf Shop in Santa Monica, and a former professional surfer. "I'm working out more and not going out as much—not on a full party schedule. You gotta make sure your lungs can handle it."[2] Even if you didn't surf, there was always the beach, and the magic of it all, as six thousand times a day, every fourteen seconds, waves surged and came ashore. The beach was what Southern Californians had in common. It represented the first shared public space, the first county parks, the most desirable locations for real estate. Each morning, at the site of the original Muscle Beach in Santa Monica (the new Muscle Beach, founded in 1987, was further south at Venice), old-timers would gather for a light workout on the rings and bars and some schmoozing. Jean Claude Picard, sixty-eight, a transplanted Canadian who had been coming here for some forty years, could still do the flagpole, which is to say, suspend himself perpendicular to the beach from a monkey bar, his body held parallel to the horizon. Further south, at Hermosa Beach, a television crew from *Baywatch* was setting up its equipment to shoot a lifeguard competition. Growing up, noted *Baywatch* creator Gregory Bonann, himself a former lifeguard, the beach was the focal point of his life: "When I woke up in the morning, I had to get to the water to know what the day was really like. Was the surf big? Was the water flat? Was the wind up?" Thanks to his earnings from *Baywatch,* Bonann could now afford a home in Malibu.[3]

The very name *Malibu,* at once familiar and mysterious, identified not just surfing but the whole seaside lifestyle of Southern California. Many claimed that the mystic reverberations of Malibu came from the spiritual presence of the Chumash people, who had lived there in ages past. Geographically, Malibu was a mini Chile, twenty-five miles long and no more than three miles wide, running up the coast north from Santa Monica toward Ventura County. Malibu was a kind of city, in the legal and incorporated sense of the term—it was where entertainment people maintained homes—but Malibu was a state of mind, as well, and had been since Massachusetts millionaire Frederick Rindge had paid $300,000 for the Rancho Topanga Malibu Sequit in 1892 and made the shores of the sundown sea, as Rindge described his ranch, a private kingdom.

Rindge's widow, May, tried to keep it that way and spent more than twenty-five years (Rindge died in 1905) attempting to prevent the state of California from pushing what eventually became the Pacific Coast Highway through her property. By the early 1930s, however, strapped for cash, May Rindge began to sell off beachfront lots to Hollywood people, and Malibu Colony was created. Across the next half century and more, incrementally, an anti-city emerged along the Pacific Coast Highway between Topanga Canyon and the Ventura County line. J. Paul Getty built his museum there, a replica of a Roman villa, and the Church of Christ established Pepperdine University, in the form of a Greek village climbing up the hillsides; but in general, with the exception of the restaurants and retail along the highway itself, and the state beaches available to the public, residential Malibu kept itself hidden and private up along the canyons, each home enjoying a commanding view of the Pacific. If Beverly Hills were a Mercedes, noted one observer, Malibu was a Land Rover: rich but rustic, and with a touch of New Age.

Big Sur, the mystic midregion of the coast, lacked cities and towns of any size. The entire region supported a population of barely fifteen hundred permanent residents, although six million passed north and south each year on the scary eighty-plus miles of Highway 1, frequently skirting (just barely, it seemed) a multitude of thousand-foot drops into churning surf between San Luis Obispo and Carmel. The town of Big Sur, thirty miles south of Carmel (if this tiny settlement could be called a town), was little more than a cluster of grocery store, delicatessen, gift shop, and post office. No matter: Big Sur supported some of the most unusual resorts in the country—Esalen, Nepenthe, Tassajara, Ventana, the Post Ranch Inn, the Big Sur Inn—and these resorts were cities of a sort: idealized utopian places, such as the resort hotels that in the nineteenth century had given rise to Santa Barbara, San Diego, Coronado, and other coastal towns. Big Sur Inn, the earliest of these resorts, was built in the 1920s by the Norwegian-born Helmuth Deetjen. It was rustic, Adirondackesque; yet Chopin, Bach, and Beethoven were played as guests dined by candlelight.

Henry Miller settled in Big Sur in 1944, and began to write about it as the staging area of the new postwar bohemia. Miller's writings attracted the attention of *Life* magazine and, later, a pilgrimage by Jack Kerouac and aspiring Zen poet Gary Snyder, which Kerouac chronicled in the novel *Dharma Bums* (1958). In the 1960s, Big Sur became the refuge of choice for the psychedelic generation. At Nepenthe, a restaurant and bar on Highway 1 opened in 1949 on property once owned by Orson Welles and his wife Rita Hayworth, most employees were high on drugs at any given point of the day, the kitchen was painted in psychedelic colors, and waitresses breast-fed their children between orders. Opening in 1975, the nearby sixty-room Ventana Inn, perched atop a terraced mountainside twelve hundred feet above the Pacific like a Tibetan lamasery, brought a new note of luxury to the Big Sur experience. Within the decade, rooms at the Ventana Inn were being directly booked from New York and Europe.

Times were changing. Like Aspen, Colorado, Big Sur was becoming a haven for wealth. The California Coastal Act, passed by voters in 1972, made it impossible for anyone other than the very wealthy to build on a very restricted number of sites. Long gone were the days of Miller and his bohemian pals, reciting Rimbaud and drinking jug red around the fireplace in log cabins. It had now become an era of stunning homes owned by people such as David Packard, Ted Turner, and Steve Martin. Hotel and restaurant workers had to scramble for shelter or live in their cars or commute each day sixty-plus miles round-trip on the frightening highway from Monterey.

No place symbolized the new Big Sur better than the Post Ranch Inn, where rooms initially ranged from $290 to $1,500 a night and the dining room featured a wine cellar that would eventually list some 3,900 premium labels. Opening in May 1992, the thirty-unit establishment sat on a ninety-eight-acre parcel opposite the Ventana Inn on the Pacific Coast Highway and advertised itself as an environmentally sensitive luxury resort as much crafted as designed by architect G. K. Muenning. The units, each with a sweeping view of the Pacific, rose from their sites as if such cedar, pine, and glass modernity had been there forever. As might be expected, each detail—the wood, the glass, the stone fireplaces, the stylized Esalen Indian patterns on the fabric, the restaurant serving California cuisine, the extraordinary wine cellar—represented and fulfilled a certain dream of the good life on the coast of dreams.

Lest this all sound too restrictive, large portions of the coast had been set aside in city, county, state, or federal parks. Ten minutes from San Francisco, just north of the Golden Gate Bridge, were the Marin Headlands of the Golden Gate National Recreation Area (GGNRA), created by Congress in 1972 under the watchful eye of San Francisco's powerful Democratic congressman Philip Burton, whose statue now stands near the Marina Green in San Francisco. The GGNRA offered an astonishing, delightful juxtaposition: the densities of San Francisco, rising like Atlantis from the sea, linked by the Golden Gate Bridge, a structure worthy of comparison to the Parthenon itself, to wild headlands preserved by army occupation in a condition not far different from the time thousands of years earlier when the Coast Miwok hunted deer across the lion-colored hills or fished its foamy inlets. Hawks, turkey vultures, golden eagles flew overhead, sharing the sky with the ever more distant presence of 747s, gaining altitude after takeoff from San Francisco Airport. Nearby extended the Point Reyes National Seashore: a sea-surrounded peninsula, scooped by Drake's Bay, where the great explorer himself might have landed the *Golden Hinde* in 1579. By turns foggy and sun-drenched, Point Reyes Peninsula was protected through federal ownership and restored to pristine condition. Mule deer, tule elk, and pronghorn antelope loped through its dry sage savannahs or browsed beneath its forests of Douglas fir. Squadrons of brown pelicans patrolled the shoreline; egrets and heron—silent, solitary, as still as an Egyptian wall painting—stood watching for frogs and fish; and in December gray whales migrated offshore in stately procession. On the very edge, then, of the fourth largest metropolitan region in the United States was a necklace of park lands—the Marin Headlands, Mount Tamalpais State Park, Muir Woods, the Golden Gate National Recreation Area, Point Reyes National Seashore—attracting more than two million visitors a year to this mystic midregion of the California coast.

Zen California

O n December 10, 1968, the famed Trappist writer Thomas Merton met an untimely death in Bangkok while attending a conference of Buddhist and Christian monks. Electrocuted by a hotel fan, Merton, fifty-three, had recently been writing to friends that he was seriously considering relocating himself to a seaside hermitage on the north coast of California. There, Merton believed, where America ended and Asia began, the vibes were best for the kind of East-meets-West contemplative life he was more and more interested in. A writer, poet, and bongo-playing hipster from Columbia University, where he had absorbed the same ethos that later shaped John Clellon Holmes, Jack Kerouac, Allen Ginsberg, and other Beats, Merton had for some time been restive with the restraints of the Abbey of Gethsemani in Kentucky, which he had joined in 1941. Merton wanted into the coast of dreams, into Zen California, in the next phase of his life.

By 1990 the coast of dreams had truly become Zen California, energized by a hope for health, stability, and enlightenment. Zen California had at its foundation a feeling of integration, of mind-body well-being. At the Chopra Center for Well-Being in La Jolla, founded by Dr. Deepak Chopra, the best-selling author and television personality, arriving clients were debriefed about their physical, emotional, and spiritual health. The center's program was based on the five-thousand-year-old Indian healing tradition of Ayurveda, a cluster of therapies aimed at the detoxification of body and mind. Following the debriefing, clients undertook a weeklong program, consisting of such exercises as friction massage, followed by a hot-towel treatment (*abhyanga*); anointment with oil (*shirodhara*); a ninety-minute Bliss Facial; therapeutic yoga; daily counseling with an Ayurvedic physician for lifestyle assessment; daily meditation, gourmet vegetarian meals, and, if appropriate, holistic childbirth classes and special programs for cancer and cardiac patients. The Chopra regime, costing approximately $3,000 plus accommodations, was intended to bring those who completed the program into a new physical and mental zone. Given the big-ticket cost, it was

not surprising that Dr. Chopra's clients included some of the best-paid corporate executives in the nation.

Just a few miles away, on a high knoll with a distant view of the Pacific,
was the Marriott Health Club at La Jolla. Designed as a postmodernist neo-
Roman temple by postmodernist guru Michael Graves, the La Jolla health
club was in many ways a neo-Roman ruin in the making. Coming upon it a
thousand or so years hence, archeologists might mistake it for a place of
religious worship, which in many ways it was. On a particular Sunday
morning, the great central hall of the club was packed with young women in
Lycra Spandex pants or high-cut leotards and equally fit young men and a
phalanx of other middle-aged men and women, spending their Sunday
morning kneeling, bending, pumping one or another piece of Nautilus
equipment, like votaries in an ancient temple.

Behind them in time, extending back into the 1870s like the patristic and
medieval eras underpinning a theology of redemption through fitness,
extended the entire history of health culture in California. Critics such as
Aldous Huxley and Evelyn Waugh had satirized this preoccupation, depicting its more extreme edges and noting an almost Faustian rejection of time
and decay lurking at its core. At its best, such devotion to the flesh was a
healthy thing, if a little narcissistic; at its worst, it was an unholy defiance of
death. California was the place, it had to be remembered, where a company
in the Bay Area city of Emeryville deep-froze bodies on a long-range contract basis pending their eventual resuscitation; where UCLA sustained an
institute devoted to the study of longevity, and a professor there, keeping his
calorie count to approximately twelve hundred a day, considered himself a
prime experiment in undernourishment leading to longevity and looked forward to living to well past one hundred.

While some satirized, others praised coastal California for achieving a
revitalized relationship to the mind-body problem preoccupying Western
culture since ancient Greece. Here was the region that had promoted fitness
of mind and body—and had virtually ended smoking among the middle
classes as well. By January 1998 it was against the law for anyone to smoke
in a bar, restaurant, office building, or any other interior public place
throughout the entire state. Walk the campuses of the universities and colleges of California or stand at a strategic corner of the bayside Marina
Green in San Francisco and watch the joggers and soccer players in grace-
ful movement, and you had a sense of just how fit so many young Californians were, especially in the coastal regions. In contrast to their counterparts
in the East, the fit young women of California tended toward the muscular
and the sturdy. The social X-ray look satirized by novelist Tom Wolfe held
little appeal on the coast of dreams.

Young Californians pursued sports that, like California itself, brought nature and technology into new combinations. Surfing was not alone in employing innovative technologies through which one might align oneself with natural forces. Windsurfing also depended on a range of recently invented high-tech materials, and, as was evident from the figures moving across the waves at incredible speeds between the Golden Gate Bridge and Crissy Field in San Francisco, brought the human body to new levels of speed through windpower. "There is something very special about belonging to a community made up of men and women who are prepared to make a superior physical effort," Bill Abeel wrote in *American Windsurfer* in the spring of 1998, "[who] fall willingly into cold water, and choose winds a little beyond their ability to learn more about themselves." Known as the Flying Dutchman, Abeel—a successful oil investor and art, cigar, and martini connoisseur whose annual Wisteria Party in the garden of his Pacific Heights home was a premier San Francisco social event—was enjoying his fourteenth windsurfing season on San Francisco Bay, and his eightieth year on Earth.

At the Park Presidio Sporting Goods store in San Francisco, where Abeel purchased gear, a Plexiglas climbing wall, rising two or three stories from the main floor, invited rock climbers to try one or another of the new technologies that enabled them to move up smooth surfaces like Spiderman. Young Californians had long since mastered the sheer walls of the highest peaks in Yosemite, and over the previous twenty-five years climbers had made rock climbing a progressively cleaner sport, which is to say, a sport employing technology to work with existing crevices and footholds without resorting to hammer and chisel. Once again, Daniel Duane was on hand, this time climbing the northwest face of Half Dome and the Nose Route on El Capitan in Yosemite and writing about it in *Lighting Out: A Vision of California and the Mountains* (1994), published when he was still an undergraduate at UC Santa Cruz. Like John Muir and Gary Snyder, but without the booze-fueled transcendentalism of Jack Kerouac, Duane encountered in each rock, in each minuscule movement across an open face of granite, a quick way of cutting to the chase.

Less articulate perhaps but equally daring were the even younger dryland luggers hitting up to eighty miles an hour on Encinal Canyon Road off the Pacific Coast Highway in Los Angeles County, lying faceup on their eight-foot-long urethane-wheeled skateboards. Although they wore full-face fiberglass helmets and protective bodysuits, dryland lugging was still a dangerous sport. A lugger steered with his feet, and there was no braking system.

Such natural highs as Bill Abeel and Daniel Duane and thousands of others were experiencing depended on the most cunning arrangements of light metals and fabrics. What was a hang glider or a wind sail, after all, but a few ounces of fabric, plastic, and alloy? And what was a piton but a few ounces of metal passed between climber and the abyss? Yet the exhilarations of height and speed made possible by such arrangements had a peculiarly Californian reverberation, although these were sports that were being practiced in other parts of the country as well. Perceived as part of the pattern of Zen California, these pursuits—indeed, the entire physical fitness and holistic health movement—both celebrated and transcended nature.

Such events—celebration, transcendence, the flight from time into eternity—were at the psychological core of religion. When it came to religion, whether mainstream or wacky, Western or Eastern in inspiration, the coast of dreams proved a most hospitable setting. Orthodox Christianity was a perfect example. In one sense, Southern California—so Protestant, so Catholic, so Jewish—would hardly seem to be a center of Orthodoxy. Yet when His All Holiness Bartholomew I, spiritual leader of the world's 250 million Orthodox Christians, arrived in Southern California for a visit in October 1997, the region seemed to exfoliate in Greek, Romanian, Russian, Bulgarian, Lebanese, Serbian, and Ukrainian Orthodox events paying homage to the patriarch. On Sunday, November 9, more than eight thousand people jammed the Los Angeles Convention Center for a Divine Liturgy celebrated by the black-robed and bearded patriarch, followed by a youth rally. When His All Holiness entered St. Sophia Cathedral in the Pico Union district, he was greeted by a phalanx of Spanish-speaking youngsters and a mariachi band. The cathedral dean, the Very Reverend John Bakas, a robust, bearded former policeman, was part of an ecumenical coalition spearheading the reconceptualization of the Pico Union as the Byzantine-Latino quarter of the city—Byzantine because the Southern California Greek Orthodox community was refusing to abandon its ornate cathedral, constructed in 1952, despite changes in the neighborhood; Latino because the overwhelming population of the district was exactly that.

The practice of religion in California—Southern California especially—tended by its very definition to be ecumenical, cross-cultural, and keyed to faith-based social and educational initiatives. Harvard scholar Diana Eck almost had to restrain herself from including too many Southern California examples of interfaith influences and cooperation in her book *Religious America* (2001), in which she chronicled the growing multiplicity of religions in the United States. Eck certainly could have turned to the University of Southern California in Los Angeles, where the dean of religious life, Rabbi Susan Laemmle (of the motion picture family), issued a calendar of Hindu, Jewish, Catholic, Orthodox, Protestant, Muslim, Sikh, Baha'i, Mormon, and Native American days of observance.

Although a relative newcomer to the United States, as far as great numbers were concerned, Hinduism had something like a hundred-year presence in California and was experiencing rapid growth, given the increasing number of East Asian immigrants. More than fifteen hundred Hindus converged on the Fairplex cinema in Pomona in late June 2001 to attend a weeklong recitation of the Ramayana, the two-thousand-year-old epic and sacred text of Hinduism, by holy man Ramesh Oza, who, sitting on a white altar against an array of flowers, palm trees, statues, and religious panels, recited from memory the story of Lord Rama. Sponsored by the Radah Krishna Mandir Hindu Temple in nearby Norwalk, the reading by Ramesh Oza, a world-class master of such recitation, attracted Hindu Californians from across the state. Dominated by well-dressed middle-class professionals and their families, the reading attested to the flourishing condition of the Hindu population in California. Which was also the case in northern California, in Silicon Valley, where Umashankar Dixit, a Hindu priest at the Shiva-Vishnu Temple in Livermore, was in great demand by East Asian Hindu high-technology executives for traditional blessing ceremonies invoking the assistance of the wealth goddess Lakshmi at the opening of new companies or the start of new programs. As an honorarium, Dixit, one of a dozen Hindu priests in the Bay Area, was paid in both cash and stock options.

Among other things, metropolitan Los Angeles, with more than 519,000 Jews, was the third largest Jewish community in the world. Centered on Westside Los Angeles, including Beverly Hills and the San Fernando Valley but also extending west to Ventura County and south to the Palos Verdes Peninsula, Jewish life in the region embraced a multiplicity of social classes, countries of origin, and degrees of religious observance or nonobservance. Jewish life was one of the fundamental building blocks of the metropolitan Los Angeles identity: the key force for urbanism, one was tempted to say, in an otherwise suburban environment. By nature a communal people, synagogue and/or civic minded, Jews could never relinquish themselves completely to that suburbanized autism that represented the single greatest and most debilitating temptation in Southern California life. It was the Jewish population, in significant measure, that made Royce Hall on the UCLA campus a second cultural center for the city alongside the downtown Music Center. It was the Jewish population that flocked to the museums of the city, attended the opera and symphony, and kept flourishing an array of restaurants, delicatessens, and other eateries.

While Los Angeles abounded in smaller synagogues and sustained, in the San Fernando Valley especially, a solidly middle-class life and point of view, institutions of high Jewish culture—the Moshe Safdie–designed Skirball Cultural Center high atop its site near the Getty, the even more montane University of Judaism on Mulholland Drive, the Museum of Tolerance at the Simon Wiesenthal Center for Holocaust Studies on Pico Boulevard, the Hebrew Union College adjacent to the USC campus in the historic West Adams district—testified to the intrinsic internationalism of Jewish life in the City of Angels and environs. When it came to cross-cultural influences, Jewish life in California, while remaining centered on its own traditions, showed a Californian propensity to cultural eclecticism. The fact that Rabbi Laemmle was dean of religious life at the Methodist-founded USC spoke for itself, as did the fact that USC also supported the Casden Institute for the Study of the Jewish Role in American Life.

So, too, did Roman Catholicism, while remaining centered on its doctrinal and liturgical core, show an extraordinary range of variations. Catholicism in California had its foundations in the twenty-one Franciscan missions, which still stood, each of them by now icons of California's colonial era that cut across religious or nonreligious preferences. At Mission San Juan Capistrano in Orange County, perhaps the most beautiful and best known mission of them all, a group of volunteers of various religious backgrounds spent their spare time bringing the mission gardens to a condition of exquisite luxuriance. As in the case of the rest of the United States, Catholic culture in California had become dominated by Irish and Germans in the late nineteenth and early twentieth centuries; but now, with the repeopling of California by Latinos, it was regaining its Hispanic past: its love of public display and procession. More than one thousand Latino Catholics gathered at Union Station and Plaza in downtown Los Angeles in mid-September 1999 to welcome an accurately scaled digitized replica of the Our Lady of Guadalupe portrait from the Basilica of Guadalupe in Mexico City. After a three-month tour of some fifty parishes of the Los Angeles Archdiocese, the image—the primary icon of Mexican identity—was brought to the Los Angeles Sports Arena in December for a rally and prayer service.

Such attention to physical images of faith could be expected among Latino Catholics; but even Latino Protestants were altering the iconographic practice of their denominations. When the Salvadoran members of the Immanuel Presbyterian Church, a mainline congregation in midtown Los Angeles, petitioned pastor Frank Alton and the presbytery to have a statue of the Holy Savior (San Salvador), in Southern California on tour from San Salvador, placed on display in their church, the congregation departed from Presbyterian tradition and approved the veneration of the image.

At another midtown church, St. Agatha, Roman Catholic priest Ken Desy, a self-described "blond and blue-eyed surfer boy," was leading his largely African-American congregation in rousing masses at which Desy gave soul-fried sermons, a gospel choir sang, people danced in the aisles or swayed in the choir loft or clapped in the foyer, and cries of "Glory! Glory! Hallelujah!" could be heard throughout the service. Some sixteen hundred people were attending St. Agatha each Sunday for one of four standing-room-only masses. Even more impressively, Latinos and African Americans in the congregation were struggling for harmony, and a white flight in reverse was bringing hundreds of white parishioners into the church from across the region.[4]

Some might say that Father Desy was merely implementing the ages-old Catholic process of inculturation—the expression, that is, of Catholic belief and practice in local terms. Others, however, might see in the richly emotional ambience of St. Agatha the influences of Pentecostalism on other versions of Christianity. Tracing itself to the moments in the Acts of the Apostles in the New Testament when the Holy Spirit was said to have descended upon the disciples and they spoke in tongues, performed miracles, and were not afraid, Pentecostalism had become by 2001 a worldwide movement with a half-billion adherents. Because it avoided intricacies of theology or church organization in favor of an emotional, existential encounter with the Spirit, Pentecostalism seemed especially suited to California, where it was answering the needs of a disproportionate number of emotionally starved people, deracinated from elsewhere, cut off from their roots. In the case of Dyan Cannon, Pentecostalism fused with Hollywood when the beautiful and charismatic actress, in the religion's informal manner, began to preach at worship events known as God's Party. Dressed in her best Westside chic, a great choker of pearls around her neck, her blonde mane in free fall, Cannon moved among her congregation, preaching, comforting, extolling, touching and kissing the physically impaired, hugging the wheelchair-bound, dancing with members of the congregation, quoting scripture, praying, and (so some were claiming) healing—or at least lessening the pain—through her touch.

Not surprisingly, given all this religiosity, Southern California was experiencing by the late 1990s a building boom in church and synagogue construction. In 1997 permits for $30 million in religious construction projects were issued in Los Angeles County alone, much of it sponsored by the four-million-member Archdiocese of Los Angeles, the largest Roman Catholic archdiocese in the United States. Near UCLA, a $3.3 million

Newman Center was under construction. In Pacoima, Father Tom Rush of Mary Immaculate parish, whose congregation had grown to the point where 8,500 parishioners were attending one of ten masses every Sunday (seven in Spanish, three in English), was completing a $3.2 million renovation and expansion of the parish church and school. In downtown Los Angeles, work was under way on the Roman Catholic Cathedral of Our Lady of the Angels, scheduled for dedication in September 2002. Designed by Madrid architect José Rafael Moneo, the cathedral blended traditional Spanish and contemporary motifs and would at its dedication be one of the half-dozen most impressive church structures in the nation—the St. Patrick's Cathedral of the coast.

In Pacific Palisades, Congregation Kehillat Israel, which had added four hundred families within the decade, was raising and reconstructing its synagogue at a cost of $7 million. Further east, in Costa Mesa, Congregation Tarbut V'Torah was putting the finishing touches on a brand-new full-service K–12 Hebrew academy, whose architecture and bold use of primary colors was intended to convey a feeling akin to being in Israel. Most of the fifty Islamic *masjids* in Southern California did not involve new construction but the adaptation of existing warehouses, supermarkets, or similar structures. Similarly, in West Covina the interdenominational Faith Community Church was worshipping in a former Ralphs supermarket, pending the readaptation of a 165,000-square-foot Hughes Aircraft facility into a combination worship space and religiously oriented mall, where parishioners could enjoy cappuccino by the side of an indoor waterfall as well as shop for religious books and videos before or after services.

Further south, in San Diego, the Church of Jesus Christ of Latter-day Saints had in 1993 completed a $24 million 59,000-square-foot neo-Gothic temple on an eight-acre parcel overlooking the freeway. California now had three such freeway-oriented Mormon temples: in San Diego, overlooking the 405; in Westside Los Angeles, near the 10; and in Oakland, next to the 580. In each instance, millions of drivers-by were being presented via vivid architecture—especially at night, when the otherworldly structures were illuminated—proof positive that Latter-day Saints were flourishing on the coast of dreams.

Designed by Philip Johnson and completed in 1980, the 3,600-seat Crystal Cathedral in Garden Grove had been the first of such spectacular show-me structures. Higher, wider, and longer than Notre Dame, sheathed in ten thousand panes of mirrored glass, the Crystal Cathedral testified to the continuing vitality of evangelical Protestantism in the Southland. Its founder, the Reverend Robert Schuller (ordained in the Reformed Church of America, a mainline Anglo-Dutch denomination that has produced a number of American presidents), presided over an impressive interdenominational congregation for whom the cathedral—its worship services augmented and intensified by multisited giant screens; its concerts, lectures, seminars, and counseling; its day care and travel programs; its employment agency, its shut-in visiting services—constituted a full-service way of life. Each year during Passion Week and Easter, the Crystal Cathedral Passion Play and Easter Pageant featured dozens of actors. In one instance a caged tiger was fed raw meat by an actor playing Pontius Pilate. A number of Broadway-style showstoppers were sung variously by Mary the Mother of Jesus, Mary Magdalene, and other women from the Gospels, and, at the conclusion, as Christ rose from the tomb, six young women costumed as angels were lowered to the blaring of trumpets by invisible wires from the cathedral ceiling.

In suburban California, Southern California especially, evangelical Protestantism had successfully absorbed not just the techniques of showbiz, but its spirit as well. Critics who believed that evangelical Protestantism was doomed to fade away with the passing of rural America had another guess coming. In California this important American sensibility was making a successful end run into postmodernity. Each day, the Tustin-based Trinity Broadcasting Network was reaching more than seven hundred broadcast, cable, and satellite affiliates around the globe with a continuous array of religious broadcasting. Headquartered by the end of the decade in multimillion-dollar studios off the 405 in Costa Mesa, the Trinity complex featured a virtual reality re-creation of the Via Doloroso in Jerusalem and beamed high-definition video presentations of stories from the life of Christ and the apostle Paul. Trinity rivaled any of the secular enterprises—Disney, Fox, CBS, NBC, ABC—in its ability to span the globe and reach millions of homes. While lesser known than his colleagues in the secular media, Trinity mogul Paul Crouch was, in his own way, the evangelical equivalent of Rupert Murdoch or Michael Eisner. Among other programs, Trinity beamed the Reverend Schuller's *Hour of Power* telecasts from Crystal Cathedral and the salty homilies of the Reverend Doctor Gene Scott, pastor of the Los Angeles University Cathedral: a white-haired, cigar-smoking Stanford doctor of education who relished playing the shock jock of Protestant televangelism. Other Trinity regulars included Dale Evans, Efrem Zimbalist Jr., Carol Lawrence, and Gavin McCloud. In 1999, Crouch's son Matthew entered the Christian entertainment business with a surprisingly successful and relatively low budget ($7.2 million) thriller, *The Omega Code,* starring Michael York, Casper Van Dien, and Catherine Oxenberg. With a plot based on scripture and Christian theology, the thriller—a battle between good and evil set in modern times but inspired by the book of Revelation—soon became a cult classic among evangelicals following its release in the millennial year 2000.

Pentecostalism had first arisen in Los Angeles in the early 1900s, with the founding of the Assemblies of God and other denominations. Later, Orange County had nurtured the growth of two other important evangelical movements, Calvary Chapel and the Vineyard Christian Fellowship. Thus it was perhaps not too surprising that the single largest gay church in the world, the 52,000-member Universal Fellowship of Metropolitan Community Churches—314 congregations in sixteen countries—should also have Pentecostal and Southern California origins. In this instance, the Reverend Troy Perry, a defrocked (for being gay) Pentecostal minister, on October 6, 1968, in his cramped home in Huntington Park, assembled twelve congregants for the first worship service of what would turn out to be the start of a rapidly growing, gay-friendly denomination.

So much of the religiosity of Zen California on the coast ran through traditional channels, including Zen Buddhism itself; but so much of it as well, for the better part of the century, had sought more exotic mind-body, soul-body, or even star-body connections. Crystals, channeling, astrology, time travel, mental telepathy, cosmologies of every sort: California had long since been super-satirized for the wacky surreality of its New Age movements and cults. This was the state, after all, in which George Wyman, architect of the Bradbury Building (1893) in Los Angeles, one of the most avant-garde structures in the history of American architecture, received his inspiration, so he later claimed, from a Ouija board. Garry Trudeau might satirize the Malibu-based Boopsie for channeling Hunk-Ra, an ancient Egyptian prince, into present-day California; but actress Shirley MacLaine was making similar experiments, and no one seemed to notice. It seemed perfectly normal, therefore, in the mid-1980s, for First Lady Nancy Reagan to retain the services of her own in–White House astrologer, Joan Quigley of San Francisco, who helped with arranging the president's schedule. Quigley, a very proper San Franciscan reared on Nob Hill, was rather surprised by all the attention paid her when the story of her White House consultation hit the headlines. Didn't everyone have an astrologer on retainer?

Quigley considered herself a Roman Catholic as well as an astrologer. Religion on the coast of dreams, as in the case of ancient Alexandria, tended to be eclectic. Episcopal priest Matthew Fox, for example, was in the final stages of organizing his University of Creation Spirituality in a reconverted warehouse in a drab and grungy part of downtown Oakland. In and through Fox alone—a photogenic man in his late fifties, at once preppie and charismatic, a jeans-and-loafers sort of a guy, in top physical condition—there coursed and partially coalesced just about every strain of religiosity on the coast, from Native American to New Age. As a twelve-year-old in Wisconsin, Fox had been stricken with polio. Following a visit from a Dominican friar, he recovered. The experience set Fox upon his path. At the age of nineteen, he entered the Dominican Order, assuming the black and white robes worn by the friar who had presided over his healing. As a Dominican, Fox completed a seven-year course in philosophy and theology, capped with a doctorate from the prestigious Institut Catholique of Paris. As founder and director of the Institute for Creation-Centered Spirituality at Holy Names College in Oakland; as author of more than fourteen books, selling into the millions, including *The Coming of the Cosmic Christ* (1988), which many believed took up where Teilhard de Chardin had left off in the late 1950s; as the editor of *Creative Spirituality,* a review he founded in 1985; and as an inveterate preacher in season and out (the official name of the Dominicans was the Order of Preachers), Fox was soon leaving orthodoxy behind—or at least severely testing its limits. By the late 1980s, an understandably perplexed Joseph Cardinal Ratzinger, prefect of the Sacred Congregation for the Doctrine of the Faith at the Vatican, was making inquiries about why Father Fox had a witch named Starhawk on his faculty.

In 1988, Fox was silenced for a year by the Church, and was asked by his Dominican superiors, prompted by Rome, to reconsider the blend of creationist theology, Native American religion, Sufi mysticism, witchcraft, yoga, and other eclectic elements he was so busily propounding. Fox emerged from his year of silence only to reiterate that in his belief he was carrying on a time-honored Dominican tradition of cosmic theology as practiced by the Dominican theologian and mystic Meister Eckhart (c. 1260–c. 1328), who taught that Creation had been contained within God from all eternity, and hence God could not be separated from Creation, and hence Creation, as Native American and other mystical traditions understood so well, offered a pathway back to God himself. In Fox, the Vatican was coming face-to-face with Zen California, and it was difficult to tell who would be the first to blink. When Fox did get into real trouble with the Church, it was not for anything that he taught but, rather, for the fact that he was refusing reassignment back to his Dominican province in Chicago. Ejected from his order for disobedience, Fox remained a Roman Catholic priest and could have continued his teaching and ministry unattached to any order—except for the fact that he had by now discovered the Rave or Techno-Cosmic Mass, then being pioneered in England by Anglican priest Chris Brain.

In its basic identity, the Rave movement represented a revival of the ancient pagan cult of Dionysus, only this time the music was techno-pop and the liberating potion not wine, as in the case of the ancient Dionysian orgies, but the designer drug Ecstasy. Occurring at remote sites, Raves were already popular in California. Thousands of young people would converge on a remote location for a nonstop Ecstasy-fueled communitarian encounter: a techno-pop disco-be-in variously described as techno-shamanistic or cybertribal. After a day and a night of dancing to an insistent beat, popping Ecstasy, and performing various forms of communal ritual, something like transcendence was achieved by the hordes of young people, many of them with a plastic baby pacifier clenched in their mouth to ease the teeth-grinding side effects of the Ecstasy they had ingested. In his Rave masses, Brain sought to Christianize the neopagan aspects of Rave, building on its quest of community and transcendence. Swept away by the synesthetic power of the Rave Mass—rock music, slide projectors, song and prayer, gospel singing, Hebrew, Hindu, and Celtic hymns, ecstatic dancing, all of it so suggestive of the convergence of religious traditions—Fox began to find in the Episcopal Church a more congenial setting. He applied for and received acceptance into the Episcopal Diocese of California, and when his relationship to Holy Names College became increasingly strained, Fox made plans to move his syncretic flag to downtown Oakland, where former governor Jerry Brown lent him the use of his We the People auditorium for techno-masses.

For the past thirty years, California had been rife with experiments in community. They ranged from Delancey Street in San Francisco and Synanon in Marin (each of them eventually established Southern California operations) aimed at rehabilitating former or paroled felons, many of them with drug problems, to such centers of upper-middle-class communitarianism as Tassajara and Esalen in Big Sur, organized around the pursuit of holistic health, and the Zen Center in San Francisco, a pioneering Zen monastery. Animating these communes was one variation or other of the ancient quest—the dream, if you will—of truth, community, and self-esteem. While distinct from Zen California, the search for self-esteem, indeed the self-esteem movement, had become very much part of the coast of dreams. What other state in the nation, after all, had established its own Commission on Self-Esteem, as California had in the Jerry Brown era at the urging of Santa Clara County assemblyman John Vasconcellos, like Brown himself a Jesuit-trained visionary Democrat? Werner Erhard of San Francisco, founder of est, a self-actualization movement based on an almost fascistic concept of power and control, had only recently been capable of filling Madison Square Garden with a rally of est graduates. In the spring of 1991, however—his finances shattered, his employees suing him over a variety of charges, his daughter accusing him on national television of sexual abuse—Erhard fled to Russia, where he reinvented himself as a self-actualization guru for government bureaucrats.

Like est, the Church of the Movement of Spiritual Inner Awareness, MSIA for short, began with an upscale, conventional clientele. In 1963, Roger Delano Hinkins, a Mormon-born English teacher, awoke from a coma caused by a kidney stone operation. He was no longer Roger Delano Hinkins, he announced. He was now John-Roger, a prophet animated by the spirit of John the Beloved and suffused with Mystical Traveler Consciousness. By the early 1990s the MSIA movement owned properties throughout Southern California. John-Roger was himself dividing his time between luxury properties in Santa Barbara and Mandeville Canyon in Los Angeles. By now, the movement had spread to Canada, Chile, Mexico, Uruguay, and Spain and maintained its Peace Theological Seminary in Santa Monica, from which the teachings of John-Roger, the Traveler, on reincarnation and soul transcendence were disseminated.

The Traveler was only peripherally touched by sexual scandal throughout his thirty-year ministry. The same could not be said of Robert Burton, the fifty-seven-year-old founder of the Renaissance commune in Yuba County north of Sacramento. Based on the teachings of two turn-of-the-century Russian mystics, George Gurdjieff and Peter Ouspensky, Renaissance was dedicated to the pursuit of beauty, the good life, and culture as a way to the truth. By October 1997 more than four hundred devotees lived (permanently or on weekends) and worked (at farming, wine making, furniture repair, framing, and other specialized woodcrafts) on the thirteen-hundred-acre Renaissance property. Those holding outside jobs were required to donate a hefty portion of their salary to the commune. It was, for all practical purposes, the Abbey of Thélème as described by Rabelais in *Gargantua and Pantagruel* (1532), a monastery of affluent sybaritism whose motto was "Do what you will." As if to reinforce the Thélème comparison, the main house of Renaissance was an imitation French castle, surrounded by a rose garden. Manicured lawns, tennis courts, and agricultural fields fell away from the property. Three hundred and sixty-five acres of terraced hillside were devoted to vineyards producing prize-winning vintages. The castle itself was furnished with tasteful furniture and antiques, as in a first-class hotel: tapestries, oriental rugs, marble fireplaces, Steinway pianos, gilt chandeliers, displays of Sevres china, and authenticated baroque paintings. Among other activities, the commune maintained its own orchestra and chorus, a small opera company and theater troupe, and a private museum featuring a collection of seventeenth-century Chinese furniture. In 1996, when the movement was expanding into Eastern Europe and back taxes were owed on the property, the furniture was sold at Christie's for $11.1 million.

Less luxuriously, perhaps (although it would become rich in Hollywood), Buddhism was experiencing unprecedented growth throughout the 1990s. Everywhere one looked throughout the decade, California seemed to be in the process of becoming an increasingly Buddhist place. Each year, the Buddhist Sangha (Community of Monks) Council of Southern California—an association of monks representing the Buddhist traditions of Burma, Cambodia, China, Japan, Korea, Laos, Sri Lanka, Thailand, Vietnam, and Tibet—were organizing progressively larger public celebrations on the birthday of the Buddha. The May 1995 observance in Culver City, organized in part by the Venerable Havanpola Ratanasara, a monk with a doctorate in education from the University of London, then serving as president of the College of Buddhist Studies in Los Angeles, featured a speech by Robert Thurman, professor of Indo-Tibetan studies at Columbia. The 1997 observance, held at the ornate Wat Thai in North Hollywood, featured an elaborate procession of monks in orange, yellow, crimson, black, gray, or blue robes chanting in seven languages. Once again, Ratanasara was on hand, this time encouraging participants to "demonstrate Buddhist values, positive attitudes towards social problems, and virtues of loving kindness, compassion, and equanimity" in a strife-ridden world.[5] The May 1998 commemoration of the Buddha's birthday, held in Santa Ana, attracted an estimated twenty thousand people, most of them Vietnamese. The event was advertised as the largest observance of the Buddha's birthday ever to be held in the United States.

In Long Beach, at the corner of Ocean Boulevard and Redondo Avenue, at the Novice Buddhist Academy, the first such institution in the United States, boys and young men from California, the Far East, and Europe were beginning their studies and spiritual formation as novice monks under the guidance of the Reverend Heng Chang, a thirty-six-year-old refugee from Vietnam. Purchased in 1990 for $3 million by the Dharma Realm Buddhist Association, the thirty-five-room sand-colored building, facing the open sea, had previously been a cloister for Roman Catholic Carmelite nuns. The transfer of the building from one faith to another was in and of itself a cultural paradigm.

When the novice monks at Long Beach played their *taiko* drums, shedding their brown robes for gray T-shirts and loose black pants during the recreation period, the power of their drumming evoked the continuing presence of Zen Buddhism in its Japanese form in California. The leading poet of the state, Gary Snyder, had spent a long period of meditation in a Zen monastery in Japan before returning to California and creating a body of poetry suffused with the search for Zen in the California landscape. The Zen Center in San Francisco had long since become a world-renowned focal point for the study, teaching, and practice of Japanese Zen. In Yorba Linda in Southern California, more than 2,500 spectators turned out in mid-April 2000 to watch Buddhist priests in yellow and purple robes, filing in procession to the rhythmic beat of the *taiko* drums outside the Shinnyo-en temple en route to conducting the ancient *saito homo* fire ritual, being performed for the first time in the United States. "We believe that the fire carries these prayers to Buddha," noted temple official Naruhiko Yoshida, as priests, having purified an outdoor shrine by the waving of a special sword, set fire to a mound of cypress branches, then threw prayer notes on the flames.[6]

As usual, the Zen movement in California had resulted in multiple identities. In the 1930s, for example, Julius Goldwater—of the German Jewish clan that had produced the Arizona senator, his first cousin—had been ordained a Buddhist priest in Japan. Graduating from Yale in 1981, Erik Berall, a Connecticut-born Episcopalian, apprenticed himself to Korean Zen master Seung Sahn, the first of his order to live and teach in the United States. Ordained a monk in 1983 with the Buddhist name Mu Ryang Sunim (Infinite), Berall spent five years of study at various Buddhist centers in Korea, Japan, China, Thailand, and India. February 2001 found Mu Ryang Sunim living in the snow-covered Tehachapi Mountains as a contemplative hermit, spending his days in meditation or assisting in the construction of the forthcoming Buddha Hall Retreat Center.

Deborah Barrett of Newport Mesa in Orange County, meanwhile, was managing to be, simultaneously, an attorney at law, a licensed psychologist, a Roman Catholic nun, and a Zen monk. Growing up in Moline, Illinois, the fortyish Barrett had strongly admired her nun teachers in grammar school, high school, and St. Ambrose College. Taking a law degree at DePaul University in Chicago after completing a degree in philosophy and in classical languages, Barrett plunged herself into a social action career as a criminal law attorney. She also found time to earn a master's degree in theology. When she at last decided to become a nun, Barrett joined the innovative Sisters for Christian Community, a six-hundred-strong congregation that encouraged its members to maintain outside employment and to live in small self-supporting communities. Moving to Southern California, where forty members of her order were active, Barrett completed yet another degree, a doctorate in psychology, while studying Zen Buddhism at the San Diego Zen Center. In 1995 she established a Zen center in Newport Mesa offering a variety of religious, legal, counseling, and meditation services.

As a counselor also at the Donovan Penitentiary at the Otay Mesa border, Barrett developed techniques to teach meditation to convicts as a way of getting their minds, as well as their bodies, off drugs. In her Orange County practice, she found herself approaching her clients, at various times or simultaneously, from a Roman Catholic, psychological, or Zen Buddhist perspective.

Of all Buddhist paths, the most trendy, as far as the 1990s was concerned, was the Tibetan tradition. Behind its surface celebrity, however, particularly in the Hollywood community, was a more broadly based and impressive phenomenon. In Berkeley, Dharma Publishing, a nonprofit institute, was systematically editing, translating, and publishing the sacred writings of Tibet under the direction of Tarthang Tulku, an exiled Tibetan scholar-monk. By the mid-1990s Dharma had become an important force in worldwide Buddhism (paralleling the equally successful Roman Catholic Ignatius Press across the Bay in San Francisco) as its publication program made available a rich array of professionally edited text and artwork. "There's more Tibetan civilization here in Berkeley," remarked a scholar attached to Dharma Publishing, "than there is in many towns in Tibet."[7] HarperSanFrancisco, meanwhile, the religious-books arm of Harper-Collins, had by 1992 a best-seller, *The Tibetan Book of Living and Dying* (243,000 copies sold by April 1995) and equally inviting prospects for its forthcoming *Inside Tibetan Buddhism* by Robert Thurman, the Columbia University scholar and Buddhist monk. Such publishing programs were flourishing, most obviously, because of widespread interest in Tibetan Buddhism; but this interest, in turn, was developing because of the dense network of Tibetan Buddhist activism throughout the state, as *sangha* after *sangha* was established in private homes or communally acquired institutional buildings.

The average profile of a Tibetan Buddhist devotee was a white, educated baby boomer in his or her late thirties or forties. Boomers were attracted to Tibetan Buddhism because it offered an integrated way of life, subsuming many of the insights of Western psychoanalysis. It was also a fashionable political movement, in that Tibet—arguably one of the highest cultures in human history in terms of its spiritual nature—had been ruthlessly subjected by the People's Republic of China through the 1950s and was still being held in subjugation. The Shambhala Center in West Hollywood, one of the first of these centers, founded in the early 1970s, featured an aggressive program of Americanization. Its teachers wore Western dress, and the Tibetan new year was welcomed with a dinner dance at Hotel Bel-Air. "There will be a new generation of lamas," observed Lama Thupten Tulku. "Perhaps they wear suit clothes. Perhaps they wear blue jeans. They can

certainly have the name of the Dharma holder, and they can be enlightened—in blue jeans."[8] In June 1997 the seventy-one-year-old Dalai Lama
visited California, teaching and lecturing in San Francisco and Los Angeles. For various reasons—his notoriety as the 1989 Nobel laureate, his
worldwide acceptance as an emblem of nonviolent resistance, but also his
compelling personality and presence—the tour was a sensational success.
In San Francisco more than 100,000 devotees attended a two-day Free Tibet
concert in preparation for the Dalai Lama's visit. In Santa Barbara five hundred residents, with donations ranging from $10,000 to $50,000, established a Fourteenth Dalai Lama Professorship for Tibetan Buddhist and
Cultural Studies at UC Santa Barbara. At UCLA, a crowd of three thousand
came to the basketball pavilion to hear the Dalai Lama express his hopes for
a peaceful resolution to the Chinese-Tibetan conflict. At another event,
celebrities such as Richard Gere, Steven Seagal, Sharon Stone, and Shirley
MacLaine donated impressive sums after a private audience.

Very soon, Hollywood had two Tibetan Buddhist movies in the works:
Seven Years in Tibet, the story of the friendship between the youthful Dalai
Lama and his Austrian tutor, to be played by Brad Pitt; and *Kundun,* an evocation of the last days of Tibet before the Chinese occupation, to be directed
by Martin Scorsese. Tenzin Tethong, a lecturer in Tibetan studies at Stanford, served as a consultant to both projects. These films, Tethong believed,
would eventually find their way into China as videos, and in the long run
might exercise some influence on bringing the Chinese people to a more
positive stance vis-à-vis Tibet. Hollywood and Southern California were
forever dreaming of a clear-cut path to serenity and peace, beyond theology,
beyond dogma, which was perhaps one of the reasons why the Dalai Lama
made seven visits to the region within the decade. He was, so he told his
audiences, just a simple Buddhist monk; but His Holiness Tenzin Gyatso,
the Fourteenth Dalai Lama of Tibet, could never just be that. Spiritual
leader of an oppressed and exiled people, the Dalai Lama embodied the
sacred in a simple, universalized manner. For all the hype and celebrity posturing that could, and did, surround his visits, the Dalai Lama could not be
trivialized. Teaching with deceptive simplicity, he was quickening in the
minds and hearts of an eclectically burdened populace the best possibilities
of Zen California.

Mind Games

So much of the appeal of Tibetan Buddhism on the coast of dreams came from its profound regard for mental discipline. On an even more impressive scale—indeed, on an *epic* scale—the California coast had always nurtured dreams of technology and science and, more elusively, the fact and drama of human consciousness, the mind, as a biologically dependent process transcending biology itself. No city on the coast of dreams was more biologically oriented than San Diego. This affinity began with its rise as a health resort at the turn of the century and continued with the founding of the Scripps Institution of Oceanography in 1912. Not accidentally, the San Diego Zoo, which developed alongside Scripps, is among the best in the world. In 1963, Jonas Salk, creator and developer of the first vaccine for poliomyelitis, established the Salk Institute for biological studies in the San Diego district of La Jolla. By the 1990s, the University of California at San Diego, organized in the late 1960s as a science-oriented campus, ranked as one of the most important scientific universities in the nation.

Parallel to this academic growth and energized by it was the rise of the biotechnology industry centered on the posh suburb of La Jolla near the UCSD campus. A decade earlier, in the early 1980s, a biotech firm called Hybritech had first shown the possibilities of town and gown cooperation. Founded in 1978 by UCSD professor Ivor Royston, with local backing, Hybritech set out to develop and apply hybrid monoclonal antibodies for use in medical diagnostic kits. The company succeeded, and in 1986 Eli Lilly bought out Hybritech for $490 million in cash and securities. Since most of Hybritech's employees took a significant percentage of their salary in stock options, this represented a windfall for many a salaried worker. The man responsible for keeping the equipment clean (he half truthfully called himself a high-tech dishwasher) walked away with $500,000 in cash and securities. Ted Geisel, otherwise known as Dr. Seuss, lived in La Jolla, which was quite fitting, for very soon a coterie of companies bearing Seuss-like names—Amylin, Biosite, Cytel, Gensia, Lidak, Ligand, Mycogen,

Stratagene, Telios, Viagene—had ensconced themselves beneath the silvery green eucalypti and *Sui generis* pines of the Torrey Pines seashore.

No enterprise spoke more directly to the subliminal power of biotechnology on the coast than did the Salk Institute atop Torrey Pines Mesa on a high-rising bluff overlooking the Pacific. Initially financed by the National Foundation for Infantile Paralysis, better known as the March of Dimes, the Salk Institute had been designed by Louis Kahn as a complex of buildings, landscaping, and site which many critics considered one of the two or three most successful expressions of architecture in the nation. The institute had been intended by its founder and namesake to function as a monastery of scientific mandarins, devoted to science and philosophy and the reconciliations thereof. In many ways, the Salk Institute succeeded. It certainly paced the scientific and biotech development of San Diego and its UC campus and brought to the Kahn-designed complex numerous Nobel laureates and National Academy of Science members over the next forty years.

By the early 1990s, however, Jonas Salk, a lion in winter, was finding himself embattled on two fronts. First of all, like Rip Van Winkle awakening from a long sleep, Salk had come out of retirement (during which he had devoted himself to philosophical and humanistic writing) to take on another great plague, AIDS; but this new scourge was proving more resistant than the polio virus had in the 1950s. And besides: there were some who believed that Salk did not deserve the credit that he had initially received for the conquest of polio. A Harvard team headed by John Enders had done most of the scientific work, they claimed, and Salk had merely perfected the vaccine recipe, as proved by the fact that Enders received the Nobel Prize and Salk did not.

As he geared up to battle AIDS, Salk wanted more room; and that meant, so he claimed, building a wing across the open-ended western edge of Kahn's complex, which soared across a backdrop forest of eucalyptus trees, framed by the sky and the Pacific. When Salk announced plans to tear down the trees and seal off the vista with a third wing, the New York architectural elite—Vincent Scully, Bartholomew Voorsanger, James Ingo Freed, Richard Meier, Robert Venturi, and others—decried the destruction of Kahn's concrete and travertine masterpiece. By May 1993 the trees were gone, and bulldozers were grading the property.

The stress of it all perhaps shortened Salk's life. He died in June 1995. Yet the Salk Institute, even in reduced architectural circumstances, continued to serve dreams of science and philosophy facing the great Pacific. Each afternoon, DNA co-discoverer (with James Watson) Sir Francis Crick, a fellow at the institute, presided over an ongoing teatime seminar, open to neurophysiologists, geneticists, psychologists, computer scientists, and

philosophers. Its subject, examined each working day: the mind-brain problem, which is to say, the relationship between the physical brain and
mind/self-consciousness. Was mind or its result, self-consciousness, a
purely neurophysiological event traceable to physical causes, the gathering
asked, or did the duality of most philosophical and theological systems,
which considered mind a separate event from its physical basis, have validity? Crick favored a neuroscientific solution, linking brain cell oscillations
and, ultimately, consciousness. "You," he claimed, "your joys and your sorrows, your memories and your ambitions, your sense of personal identity
and free will, are in fact no more than the behavior of a vast assembly of
nerve cells and their associated molecules."[9] Philosopher Patricia Churchland, another regular at the institute tea parties, tended to agree—but with a
difference. Describing herself as a neurophilosopher, Churchland postulated the acceptance of the material basis of mind, but she advocated an
even more intense investigation of the borderlands between the physical
basis of thought and the functions and protocols of thought itself. Through
analytical philosophy, in other words, Churchland was searching for a back
channel to the physiological basis of self-awareness.

Barely a mile away, but on higher ground, at the Neurosciences Institute, Nobel laureate (for his work on immunology) Gerald Edelman was
dreaming the same dreams of solving the mind-body problem but taking a
different tack. Like Jonas Salk, Edelman had founded his institute to be, as
he and so many others had put it, a monastery of the mind: a community of
scholars devoted, like monks following the Rule of St. Benedict, to a way of
life organized around a central pursuit, in this case a conviction that the
brain was at the center of all future biological research. For Edelman and
his colleagues, the brain was not, as Crick contended, the result of forty-
hertz oscillations in the brain cells. It was, rather, a vast and complex ecological habitat that in its development recapitulated evolution itself as
evolution had progressed toward higher and more complex forms of behavior. The brain was not a machine, but a universe. Mind could not be reduced
to the sum total of its parts, but (and here Edelman agreed with Crick) mind
did not require the philosophical intervention of spirit to explain itself.

And so, at the Salk and Neurosciences Institutes, and other places as
well—at nearby UC San Diego, where Elizabeth Bates was studying the
relationship between the growing brain and language development; at
UCLA, where neuroscientist Mark Cohen was using a twenty-two-ton
imaging device to track brain waves; at Caltech, where Erin Schumann and
her colleagues were investigating the chemistry of brain cells; at UC Santa
Cruz and UC Berkeley, where philosophers David Chalmers and John
Searle were also tackling the problem of mind from a philosophical per-

spective—the search for the mystery of human consciousness continued on the coast of dreams. No matter how reductionist their solutions might be (and Sir Francis Crick was the most reductionist of them all), an element of the hierophantic—a sensing of other worlds beyond the physical, a testing of the mysterious alchemy of matter itself—clung to the quest. Californians were in search of mind, and that search, noted Chalmers, "is the last frontier of science."[10]

The coast was also nurturing another dream, closely related to finding the cause of consciousness: the dream of being wired, of using the new technology, originated in California, not only as a business, a way of making it big or at least getting by—but as a vision, a dream, a quest, and, for many, an almost total way of life. In certain instances this dream of being wired was dovetailing with other coastal dreams as well. San Francisco–based futurist Alexander Besher, for example, was envisioning the fusion of high tech and the spiritual/aesthetic traditions of Asia. Born in China to White Russian parents and raised in Japan, Besher was the author of *The Pacific Rim Almanac* (1991) and "Pacific Rim," a column syndicated by the *San Francisco Chronicle* focusing on business trends in the Asia-Pacific region. He was also a consulting futurist on Pacific Rim affairs for Global Business Network, an international research group specializing in corporate scenario planning, and a contributing editor to *InfoWorld* magazine. In a distinctly California-as-Asia sort of way, Besher—an ardent student of Buddhism, Zen, and Asian aesthetics—envisioned a future in which the human potential movement, as represented by Esalen, would blend with Asian traditions, and, most important, would be used by transnational companies as management techniques. In his futurist novel *Rim* (1994), Besher presented a world in which Tibetan Buddhism had developed its own software and the techniques of virtual reality would make it possible to take instruction from long-dead Zen masters. In the Virtualopolis of a future era, also known as Satori City, Virtual Reality would converge in the creation of a cybercity, a Shangri-la of shared consciousness, constituting a new modality for civilization itself. These were daydreams, of course, more science fiction than futurism (Besher's novel was set in San Francisco, Berkeley, Neo-Tokyo, and various virtual realities in the year 2027); yet Besher was the kind of consultant that could persuade companies to retain him to envision solar-powered passenger dirigibles (hotel operations by the Peninsula Group, catering by Chez Panisse) drifting across the South China Sea.

In contrast to Besher's wide-ranging Asian scholarship and Asia-oriented futurism, the condition of being wired had its cyberpunk dimension as well, as expressed in *Mondo 2000,* a Berkeley-based quarterly edited by R. U. Sirius, a.k.a. Ken Goffman, and Queen Mu, a.k.a. Allison

Kennedy, a thirty-nine-year-old former astrologer and anthropology student at UC Berkeley, where she had published papers on toad and tarantula venoms. Somehow this unlikely pair managed to convince fifty thousand people each quarter to shell out $5.95 for a distinctive blend of computer talk (reports on computerized break-ins at automated teller machines were a favorite item), together with articles on the implantation of electrodes in the human brain and brain-enhancing hormones, New Age speculation, homages to Frank Zappa and Timothy Leary, cyberkink, cyberart to include cyberperformance art, cyberfashion, virtual reality, smart drugs, and other items appealing to the rebellious instincts of punkish or crypto-punkish young communications and information workers in their late twenties who formed the bulk of *Mondo 2000*'s readership. More conventional than *Mondo 2000,* but equally expressive of the coast of dreams, was the San Francisco–based magazine *Wired.* If *Mondo 2000* bespoke the cyberage as a form of avant-garde rebellion, *Wired* released the dreams of a largely suburban generation of baby boomers and Generation Xers, college graduates dressed by the Gap, cyberpreppies as opposed to cyberpunks. Founded in 1993 by Louis Rossetto and Jane Metcalfe, a husband-and-wife team, *Wired* came closer to the *Rolling Stone* comparison claimed by R. U. Sirius for *Mondo 2000.* It was—in its stunning graphics, its hot info and well-researched stories, its sheer usefulness, its sense of mission—an impressive magazine by any standards, bespeaking, as all good magazines must do, a point of view, a way of life, an attitude instantly recognized by its 400,000 subscribers. Ironically for a magazine announcing the end of the print-to-pulp era, *Wired* made much more money than its allied company, Wired Ventures Inc., which failed in two public offerings. No matter: in early May 1998, S. I. Newhouse's Advance Magazine Publications of New York (*The New Yorker, GQ, Vanity Fair, Gourmet,* and other Condé Nast magazines) purchased *Wired* for a reported $80 million.

A collector of prime magazine properties, Newhouse was in no mood to change the essential strength of *Wired,* which is to say, its near-religious belief in the power of the new technology and the Internet to offer not only a living or a way of life, or even a dream, but a form of near transcendence. Just as fashion had meant more than fashion for the founders of *Vogue,* or New York had meant more than just New York for the founders of the *New Yorker,* so, too, for the editors, writers, and graphic designers of *Wired* did computer technology and the Internet mean more than mere engineering or applied science. Guy Kawasaki, it must be remembered, the director of software product management and super-salesman at Apple Computer in the go-go 1980s, had, with only the slightest touch of irony, described his job as "software evangelist"—indeed, he attended a four-day seminar offered by the Billy Graham School of Evangelism to upgrade his skills. In his best-selling *The Macintosh Way* (1989), Kawasaki outlined the faith he was preaching. Macintosh, he opined, was not only a product; it was a vision, a cause, a dream, a faith. Salespeople, Kawasaki contended, claimed that some things needed to be seen to be believed. Evangelists, by contrast, including computer evangelists, contended that some things needed first to be believed in order—later—to be seen.

Certainly, the communal belief in a vast and lavish future, together with a dream of perpetual youth, was at the core of Silicon Valley, where there thrived an abiding sense that it had all first happened here and that it had changed the world. These places—the Romanesque sandstone quadrangles of Stanford University, the venture capital complexes lining Sand Hill Road, the sprawling campuses of the now mythic companies that had brought the valley into being—rendered the region a type of enchanted, transformed place, another part of the forest, Shakespearean in magic, resistant to replication. Here, in this crowded portion of the coast of dreams, its housing prices soaring and its Porsche dealerships out of stock, had been nurtured not only the technology of the globe but also a dream of endless youth and creativity. It was not about the money, nor was it about the fame. It was about the thing itself—the dream, the thrill, the rush of being wired. Here was a dream of youth on the coast of dreams: high-tech surfers in search of the perfect wave, aspiring monks in search of a Zen connection. They worked together in their cubicles, side by side. They roomed together in the overcrowded housing of the valley, like monks in a monastery. Late into the night, they drank beer and watched horror movies together on their VCRs, as if they were still in college. At the entry levels of employment, they were mainly male, although women were also entering the field, especially as lawyers, accountants, and financial analysts. At Hewlett-Packard, they even danced together following the unexpected success of a company-based ballroom dancing program that earned its founder, Jennifer Zhang, eight hundred e-mail messages from otherwise shy engineers on the first day it was announced.

True, the whole youth thing (even when it was being faked by middle-aged CEOs) could get on some people's nerves or arouse their sense of injustice. "Take a reality check," wrote Claire MacElroy of Palo Alto in a letter to the *San Francisco Chronicle* protesting age discrimination in Silicon Valley, "and look at the parking lot at Oracle as the workers are going home. There won't be too many gray hairs in that crowd! Take lunch in a Palo Alto restaurant in the workweek. How many in the office crowd are over 40? Look to see how many older high-tech workers have been cycled through job placement agencies to low-tech positions."[11]

Employers, by contrast, themselves thirtysomethings, allowed such protests to fall on deaf ears, unless attached to a lawsuit. They and every affiliated activity in Silicon Valley and further south on the Digital Coast in Southern California wanted youth, youth, youth: people such as Nava Swersky, born in South Africa, raised in Israel, at twenty the youngest person to pass the Israeli bar exam, at twenty-one a captain in the Israeli army, at twenty-five a Swiss MBA, fluent in English, Hebrew, French, German, Italian; drop-dead beautiful (a daughter of Israel for whom any number of modern-day Jacobs might tend flocks for fourteen years), and now, at age thirty-two, a dynamic presence at Sanderling, a venture capital firm based in Menlo Park. Techno-MBAs, meanwhile, graduating from UC Irvine's pioneering high-tech-oriented MBA program, were starting life in their late twenties at an average of $84,000 annually, with a signing bonus of up to $20,000 in cash or stock options: young men such as Suvesh Balasubramanian, twenty-eight, born in India but thoroughly happy with his American prospects.

Obviously, as a techno-MBA, Suvesh was wired. All of a sudden, everyone on the coast of dreams wanted to be wired. A Bay Area company called Digital Interiors was making a fortune wiring new housing construction or rewiring existing properties for the information age. Running bundled strands of copper and coaxial wiring to link computers, television sets, VCRs, cable TV, and satellite dishes, Digital Interiors could transform a home into a comprehensive information system. Television moguls such as Barry Diller and Ted Turner were anticipating the day when some sixty-five million customers would be buying control boxes for such systems, and the home would become not just shelter but an integrated information, entertainment, and security system. People would literally be living inside their computers.

Being wired had its subliminal dangers, especially on the California coast, where science and science fiction were closely allied and where science, science fiction, and religion frequently intersected. Literary historians have long noted the proclivity of California writers for science fiction; indeed, the roll call of authors who have achieved distinction in this genre included such uniquely California figures as Ray Bradbury, Robert Heinlein, Frank Herbert, and the California-born and -raised Ursula Le Guin. Given the importance of science, given the dream of California itself, with its utopian/dystopian rhythms, it was perhaps not too far-fetched to see an affinity for science fiction at the very center of California culture with its blend of highbrow and pop. The whole *Star Trek* phenomenon, another California-based enterprise, showed the ability of science fiction, in this case a popular television series, to move into broad regions of philosophical discernment. In the case of Scientology, the coast had produced a religion whose theology read like a science fiction scenario. Seventy-five million years ago, taught Scientology founder L. Ron Hubbard, the tyrant Xemu released evil into the world as "body thetans," which prevent people from realizing their full potential. Scientology was a way of countering these destructive thetans through introspection and counseling and thereby enabling church members to move to new levels of existence.

The Los Angeles–based Church of Scientology seemed like mainstream Protestantism in comparison to a bizarre cult, Heaven's Gate, whose members, as March 1997 moved toward April, were busy at their headquarters in the exclusive San Diego County suburb of Rancho Santa Fe preparing to take themselves to the Next Level. When it was over, thirty-nine people lay dead in the cult's Rancho Santa Fe home, including cofounder Marshall Herff Applewhite, known to his followers as Do, as in *do-re-mi* (Applewhite was a former music teacher). It was the largest mass suicide on the North American continent. Here were thirty-nine Americans who believed strongly enough that they were scheduled to rendezvous with a spaceship trailing the Hale-Bopp comet that they actually—and with minimal signs of disturbance—killed themselves in order to make that celestial connection. In the days that followed this bizarre event, commentator after commentator, including many eminent academics, speculated about what possibly could be meant by thirty-nine Americans lying dead on their beds in black pants and Nike running shoes, covered in purple shrouds, after ingesting a pudding laced with phenobarbital, chased down with vodka, all of them believing they would soon be seeing each other on a spaceship.

The search for explanations soon led to a rising incidence of jokes on the Internet and then on late-night television. After Jonestown, Waco, and Oklahoma City, Americans were too tired to figure this one out and preferred instead to laugh it off. Naturally, California took its licks in the brief time that serious explanations were being attempted, before the laugh track was turned to high. The mass suicide of the Heaven's Gate members, it was agreed, was just another instance of the state's kookiness. Even a California booster, if he or she were being honest, might see some validity in such a claim. Did not the specific conjunction of forces that had formed the Heaven's Gate cult—the search for transcendence, the sense of science as religion and religion as science, the exaltations of being wired—constitute the vulnerable side, the noir dimension, of certain California obsessions? The members of Heaven's Gate, now departed, had made of high technology a bizarre cult. Crossing a borderland, they had become lost in a cyberspace of their own imagining.

Bon Appétit

The world could also be imagined through food, and food could be tied to affluence and education, even to generational ambition and identity. Once again, the trend began in the late 1960s when Joseph Coulombe, a Stanford graduate with an MBA, living and working in Pasadena, noticed how frustrated the educated but thrifty citizens of that city were becoming with Ralphs or Vons or the other chain supermarkets. No matter what their personal budgets, even out-of-work PhDs found their self-esteem affronted by stores that sold only packaged food, stocked a limited range of fruits and vegetables, and wrapped fish and poultry in cellophane. In 1971, Coulombe acquired control of a retail outlet, previously a convenience store owned by Rexall Drugs, on the Arroyo Seco Parkway in Pasadena. Keeping in mind the image of the thrifty PhD as his ideal customer, Coulombe traveled the United States, Europe, Latin America, and, eventually, the world in search of wine and food items that were at once tasteful and competitively priced.

Soon Trader Joe's, as Coulombe called his establishment, was featuring hundreds, then thousands, of wine and food bargains from around the globe, many of them personally discovered, selected, and annotated in *The Fearless Flier,* a whimsically written and illustrated newsprint catalog appearing five times a year. If the Hungarians were canning the best cherries that harvest season, Hungarian cherries would be on the shelf at Trader Joe's within the month. If the Germans were making the best pea soup, German pea soup could be found in the next aisle. Trader Joe's featured an opulent array of grain and nut products in packaged bulk form. Where else could one buy Turkish apricots by the pound, or macadamia-cashew butter, or wild rice, or extra-extra-virgin-virgin olive oil, or maple syrup from the forests of Quebec, or Stilton cheese from England, olives from Greece, pâté from Marcel and Henri, or low-fat gourmet turkey or chicken sausages from the Napa Valley, together with wines from California, Chile, France, and Australia, a dozen distinctive coffees, off-brand but elegant cognacs—and all this at competitive prices? No wonder *New York Times* reporter Joan

Cook compared Trader Joe's to a cross between Zabar's and the Job Lot
Trading Corporation. Over the next decade, Trader Joe's expanded throughout the state, opening new stores city by city, district by district, requiring
only that they possess the proper demographics of upscale trendy—and
thrifty—customers. In 1979 the Aldi grocery chain of West Germany,
owned by Theodore Albrecht and with twelve hundred markets in northern
Europe, bought Trader Joe's and asked Coulombe to continue on as CEO.
By the mid-1990s there were more than sixty stores throughout California
and Arizona, served by a 397,325-square-foot distribution center in Chino,
sixty miles east of Los Angeles.

Food had by the 1990s emerged as one of the most compelling
metaphors for the good life on the coast of dreams. Hundreds of California
cookbooks appeared in this period, and they could be cross-referenced to
any number of perspectives: wine-country cookbooks, California-beautiful
cookbooks, feminist cookbooks, ethnic cookbooks, and so forth. In *Aphro-
dite: A Memoir of the Senses* (1998), Chilean-born, Marin County–based
writer Isabel Allende offered a lyrical testimony to food as eros and vice
versa. It was no accident that California had produced the finest food
writer in American literature (which was exactly where she belonged, in
the upper-middle registers of literary evaluation): Mary Frances Kennedy
Fisher of Pasadena. Writing as M. F. K. Fisher across a half century of
books, Fisher had built upon distinctive California elements—the bookish-
ness of Pasadena, a Californian's special feeling for France, which had
equally nurtured her career, a Francophile Californian's love for wine and
food, a Californian's taste for a precise near-minimalist style, and a Californian's insight that great significance could be found in ordinary events—
to take the wine and food memoir into the realms of imagination and
literature. Despite its rich detail, there was in Fisher's work a quality of
indirection. It was not so much wine and food that she was writing about.
Here was not only food reportage and recipes. Here was also the memory of
wine and food as a way of recovering lost time or probing the otherwise
fugitive flow and patterns of life. For Fisher, on the other hand, food and
wine, eating and drinking, offered a pathway, a mode of approach, toward
philosophical understanding, a way of coping with the pity and terror of it
all. This was the Californian thing about her: her absolute courage to begin
with the most simple things and find out what they meant.

Fisher had turned to the writing of wine and food memoirs in the late
1930s and early 1940s as a way of recovering from a collapsed first marriage to aspiring poet Alfred Young Fisher, whose name she kept, and the
death of her second husband, artist-novelist Dillwyn Parrish. So, too, had
California's entire wine and food culture (building, of course, upon a previ-

ously existing hundred-year history) have psychological, even political, overtones. In Berkeley, for example, food and wine connoisseurship went hand in hand with a sense of oneself as belonging to a liberal elite. Let the rest of the country vote Republican and eat out of cans and packages. Berkeley would reform the world (or at least point it in the right direction) while dining on salads of dried cranberry, pecans, and arugula, free-range fowl from oak-fired ovens, fresh-baked whole-grain breads, and an appropriate white wine, with poached pears for dessert.

No one pursued this new philosophy of wine and food better or with more national effect than Alice Waters, a New Jersey–born, French-inspired and -trained, sensuously attractive (in a red-haired pre-Raphaelite sort of way) chef-restaurateur whose restaurant Chez Panisse, opening in Berkeley on August 25, 1971, soon emerged as a local, then state, then national, then international mecca and point of reference for the fact that young Californians were doing something new with food and that what they were doing constituted a cultural, even a political, statement. Alice Waters took the preparation of food back to basics: fresh and unprocessed ingredients; direct cooking techniques, centered on an oak-fired open grill; a skilled use of herbs and natural flavorings; and a flair for presentations based on juxtapositionings of untreated textures and colors. Hers was the New Left of cuisine: college educated, erudite, and privileged, but self-consciously seeking as well a reformed simplicity that was itself a species of elite metaphor. Located in a three-story neo-Craftsman structure on Shattuck Avenue, art nouveau in its furnishings and graphics, wine-country French in its plates, cutlery, and napery, abundant in floral presentations, Chez Panisse—even aside from the food and wine being served there—was making another statement as well, reprising a fin-de-siècle northern California ideal. Chez Panisse looked like tasteful northern California had wanted to look—and did look—at the turn of the century: at once European and Californian, or, more precisely, becoming more Californian through skillful employment of European metaphors.

The first wave of customers at Chez Panisse were what one might expect: Berkeley types, many of them still thinking of themselves as political radicals yet making the transition to new interests; faculty members; graduate students, out for a splurge; Trader Joe's people. In the early years, Waters kept her prices low, hovering around seven or eight dollars per entree. Ruth Reichl, soon to develop as one of the finest wine and food writers on the coast before moving to New York, was an early customer, finding, in part, her life's vocation in the course of these early dinners. Soon, the word spread.

Among other things, Chez Panisse was expressing the wine and food scholarship of Berkeley, especially in university circles, where since the 1930s people had been paying more-than-average attention to the niceties of food and drink. Alice Waters's friend Kermit Lynch, for example, opened an extraordinary wine store on San Pablo Avenue in 1972. Like Waters, Lynch was thoroughly committed to the scholarship of wine and food in dialogue with each other. The *Kermit Lynch Wine Merchant Newsletter* was in and of itself a source of satisfaction, given Lynch's pungent style, his knowledge of wine and food, his travels throughout Europe in search of suitable imports, his wining and dining in vineyard chateaus and London clubs. With friends and clients like this, how could Alice Waters lose? By the mid-1970s Chez Panisse had achieved near cult status, in part because Waters's friend Tom Luddy, director of the Pacific Film Archive in Berkeley, brought to the restaurant such film celebrities as King Vidor, Howard Hawks, Wim Wenders, Werner Herzog, Jean-Luc Godard, Martin Scorsese, Akira Kurosawa, and two who became regulars, Francis Ford Coppola and George Lucas. Such film folk mixed with an equally stellar group of food mavens—M. F. K. Fisher, Julia Child, Richard Olney, James Beard, Elizabeth David—and an increasingly upscale crowd of regulars. When Nixon's chief of staff H. R. Haldeman dined at the restaurant at the height of the Watergate crisis, he was punctiliously served but not allowed to pay for his meal. President Bill Clinton, by contrast, did pay for his dinner, and some five to eight hundred supporters cheered him in and out of the restaurant.

Something generational as well as political was going on. The baby boomers, in California at least, had turned to wine and food once politics, as they had encountered politics in their youth in the 1960s, had—for them—reached a dead end in the eras of Ronald Reagan and George H. W. Bush. Yet a political-generational subtext lurked beneath the surface of a wine and food culture that, paradoxically, was intended as an escape from politics but was always managing to reassert itself as a political-generational statement. Theirs was a generation of privilege: these men and women, now in their fifties, had been born at the takeoff point of the single most prosperous period in American history and, guided by Dr. Spock, had been cherished and cosseted through childhood and adolescence before being sent on to the best schools. They had traveled as no generation before them had traveled. Being against the Vietnam War had reinforced their privileged position with a conviction of personal and generational virtue that made it seem as if they had deserved all the good things that had come to them. For *New York Times* reporter R. W. Apple Jr. and his wife, Betsey, a pre-Thanksgiving rehearsal dinner at the Berkeley home of Alice Waters in November 1999 (a Diestel free-range turkey soaked in brine for seventy-two hours and slow-roasted for three hours over an open fire of California oak) offered the occasion for a ritualized celebration through wine and food of a generation feeling itself at the top of its game. Throughout the meal, the stereo played a new Cecilia Bartoli CD of Vivaldi songs. "The soprano's swooping vocal line," noted Apple, "prompted talk of opera at Salzburg, the director Peter Sellers, the Telluride film festival in Colorado, the Adelaide festival in Australia, and, somehow, eating in Naples."[12]

From this era, combining as it did food mania and boomer affluence, emerged a number of celebrity chefs (Jeremiah Tower, Joyce Goldstein, Judy Rogers, Wolfgang Puck) and restaurants (Chez Panisse itself, Star's, Massa's, Square One, the Zuni Café, and Postrio in San Francisco; Citrus, Fennel, Valentino's, Rex, and DC3 in greater Los Angeles) that survived through the austere early 1990s when such places as Trumps in Los Angeles, the Rex of Newport Beach, and Wolfgang Puck's Eureka closed their doors. By the late 1990s some of the Gongorism had left the movement (no more purple mashed potatoes, and, please, easy on the pumpkin-fennel sauce), and gourmet coffee was emerging as the next big thing, as indicated by the hilarious scene in the Steve Martin film *L.A. Story* (1991), in which everyone around the table orders a different variation of after-dinner coffee. After nearly a decade of nouvelle skimpiness, portions were returning to normal. Meatloaf was making a comeback. Hot restaurants now buzzed with excitement because of the celebrities who came rather than the food that was served. Yet as in the case of politics, in which Berkeley had helped transform attitudes toward power, the Berkeley-originated food movement had by the mid-1990s gone mainstream.

Even the Gallos were getting involved in the premium wine business. Matt Gallo, thirty-four, was planting pinot noir grapes in Sonoma County in 1997, preparing for a millennial vintage. His sister Gina Gallo, thirty, was introducing Gallo's first Napa label, Marcelina, at $16 a bottle. Already, E. & J. Gallo Winery had in its Turning Leaf label made a transition away from the bulk wine market to premium varietals. The upgrading at Gallo was proving once again that an essential element of the California formula—the dream of mass marketing of quality food pioneered by Trader Joe's—was still driving the California economy. In the early 1990s an outbreak of phylloxera erupted, but the vine-sapping louse was beaten back by a take-no-prisoners counterattack that saw entire vineyards uprooted and burned rather than yield to the destructive pest. In 1997 sales of California wine surged by 11 percent to an all-time high of $5.9 billion, much of it in reasonably priced premium vintages. Merlot was flying off the shelves, and Cabernet Sauvignon and Sauvignon Blanc were in short supply.

The lords and, increasingly, the ladies (Zelma Long of Simi, Gina Gallo, Carolyn Wente of Wente Brothers, and Jill Davis of Buena Vista, for exam-

ple) of this multibillion-dollar industry were, like their counterparts in Silicon Valley or Hollywood, youngish (or trim and fit in middle age), educated, and entrepreneurial, with a distinctive sense of going their own way,
dreaming the dream of wine at their own pace and in their own style. Thirty
years earlier, Jack Davies, the Harvard MBA who founded Schramsberg,
had pioneered the genre and established the paradigm. Successful in business, Davies left it all for wine making, as did Warren Winiarski, a former
University of Chicago faculty member, who founded Stags' Leap, which in
turn had won the gold medal at Paris in June 1976. Even Robert Mondavi,
another legend, began his career in business, working for his brother Peter
at Charles Krug. Frank Woods, founder of Clos du Bois, was a Cornell-
trained hotel and resort developer before he turned to wine in the 1970s. An
earlier generation, represented by Sam Sebastiani, had been born on the
land and had evolved into their success without losing the perspective of a
farmer. This new generation, by contrast, had to learn to become farmers
because they were, first and foremost, wine dreamers and entrepreneurs.

Fortunately, they had on hand the continuing services of wine consultant
Andre Tchelistcheff, who was turning ninety in 1992. Born in Russia,
raised in Bordeaux, Tchelistcheff had come to California in 1938, where he
became vineyard master and winemaker at Beaulieu Vineyards for the next
thirty-five years, playing a crucial role in the recovery of the California
wine industry from Prohibition and taking it into its new era. A generation
of winemakers learned their business from Tchelistcheff, although, in certain instances, it might take Vladimir Nabokov himself to grasp the full sub-
tlety of Tchelistcheff on wine. A Pinot Noir, for example, had according to
the master "the aroma of a dying black rose." Another wine, a Chardonnay,
had the bouquet of "the breast of a young woman in winter, wrapped in
fur."[13]

In the figure of Tchelistcheff, internationalism had come to California
wine. In the late 1980s and 1990s it went international. It began with a
French connection: the Mondavi-Mouton-Rothschild collaboration in Opus
One, released in 1985 and arguably one of the finest California wines ever;
and it continued as numerous French vintners—Moët & Chandon, Piper-
Heidsieck, Deutz & Gelderman, G. H. Mumm, Louis Roederer, and Tait-
tinger—began producing sparkling wines in Napa and Sonoma. Next came
the Italian connection, as California winemakers formed alliances with
their Italian counterparts and began making wine from California-grown
Italian varietals. Wente vineyards of Livermore, for example, joined the
Casa Vinicola Checchi to produce Insieme, a Chianti-type wine from the
Sangiovese grape. The Robert Mondavi winery, meanwhile, was releasing
the first vintages of its Luce della Vite wines—$55 a bottle—made from

Sangiovese and Merlot in conjunction with the Italian winemaker Marchesi de' Frescobaldi of Tuscany.

Having brought French and Italian wine-making skills and varietals to California, the wine entrepreneurs—so many of them backed, by the mid-1990s, by large corporations—turned their attention to offshore collaborations, most notably in the Maipo Valley of Chile, the California of South America, where Robert Mondavi, Freixenet USA (itself a Spanish-Californian collaboration), Kendall-Jackson, and Franciscan Estates began to grow grapes and make wine for the California market. By early 1998, Chilean wine—much of it with a California connection—ranked third behind Italy and France in imports to the North American market. Thus, California wine was returning to California and the rest of the nation with a Chilean accent, just as more than a decade earlier, in Opus One, Robert Mondavi and the Rothschilds had accomplished the dream of blending France and California together into one vineyard and one bottle.

Dumbing Down

In a bygone era dominated by jug wines and, even earlier, the use of false French labels, California wine could be seen as second-rate, even third-rate, in comparison to what it had become by the millennium—a wine culture approaching the great wine cultures of Europe. Alas, such a progress toward high standards could not be ascribed to every aspect of culture on the coast. True, wine and food were flourishing; but was not California, amid all the talk of surfing and Tibet, becoming a dumber place? And was not this dumbing down responsible for the growing vulgarization, even violence, of American life?

One of the reasons the coast of dreams was so frequently receiving such ambivalent responses from Middle America was the fact that the nation's primary dream machine, Hollywood, was putting forth so many destabilized and destabilizing messages. Twice before, in the early 1920s and again in the early 1930s, Hollywood had similarly pushed the envelope, provoking the creation of the Hays office and Motion Picture Code. The 1990s, however, exceeded these two earlier periods of rebellion against middle-American values on Hollywood's part; yet, aside from some political opposition from Dan Quayle, Bob Dole, Ross Perot, Patrick Buchanan, and certain religious groups, nothing like the anti-Hollywood movements of the early 1920s and early 1930s developed. Could it be that America itself had become so brutalized that it no longer differentiated itself from the sex and violence on the big screen but saw in them true reflections of how things were? Was the national permissiveness toward Hollywood merely masking, as some critics suggested, a growing indifference to traditional values on the part of grown-ups? Or was Hollywood merely losing its adult market and producing films primarily for an adolescent and young-adult audience who knew no better?

As prologue to the decade, His Holiness John Paul II asked Hollywood to clean up its act. On the morning of September 15, 1987, at the Registry Hotel near Universal Studios, Lew Wasserman, chairman of MCA, Inc., and one of the most powerful men in the business, introduced the pope to the Hollywood elite gathered in his honor. In his remarks, the pope, who had himself acted as a young man and written a number of successful plays, encouraged the audience to make films commensurate with the spiritual nature and aspirations of human beings, whatever their backgrounds. Tell good stories, the pope urged his audience (a local Paulist and a Washington-based Jesuit had helped him draft the speech), but tell them in a way that accrues to the dignity of each human being. "I thought he was going to be tougher on us, given some of the things we put out there," noted director Peter Bogdanovich. "One thing that rang a bell with me was the remark that even the smallest decision can affect millions for good or evil. I thought of decisions I've made, and would like to unmake."[14] As it was, in the years that followed the pope's visit, Hollywood had answered His Holiness's plea, if it heard it at all, with a decade-plus phantasmagoria of murder, mayhem, rape, incest, cannibalism—you name it. Cultural historians of the future will have their work cut out for them construing the exact significance of the pathologies pervading the silver screen in the 1990s, as Hollywood showed a growing taste for the perverse and mainstream audiences ate it up.

In *Hollywood vs. America* (1992), PBS film critic Michael Medved suggested a simple thesis: Hollywood had lost touch. Most Americans, Medved argued, believed in God, country, and marriage, did not like criminals, and adhered in general terms to Judeo-Christian values. More and more Hollywood films, by contrast, ridiculed religion, marriage, and patriotism and glamorized criminality of every sort, including bizarre sexual conduct. As a result, television had lost thirty million viewers over the past fifteen years, and movie attendance had dropped by half since *The Sound of Music* won the Oscar for best movie in 1965. Forty-five percent of all Americans went to movies infrequently. Thirty-three percent never went at all. Hollywood responded by pumping up ticket prices and by making more movies for those who did go, which is to say, for teenagers and the under-twenty-five crowd. Even so, this was not a winning strategy. Throughout the 1980s, Medved argued, R-rated films had jumped from 46 to 67 percent of the total Hollywood output; yet only one of these R-rated films, *Beverly Hills Cop* (1984), had made *Variety*'s list of top earners. PG films, by contrast, represented only 25 percent of all films released by Hollywood during the 1980s, yet they represented six of the ten films on *Variety*'s top earners list.

True, a classic and classy film producer such as Saul Zaentz was still in the business; but Zaentz—producer of *One Flew over the Cuckoo's Nest* (1975), *Amadeus* (1984), and *The English Patient* (1996)—was an older man working as an independent out of Berkeley. Still, *The English Patient* did prove that grown-up films could fill the theaters and run off with the prizes. But how much could one man be expected to do? Zaentz was making movies for adults, as opposed to adult films. Most producers, by contrast, were in their thirties in the 1990s, with some in their late twenties and a few senior figures in their early forties, and were producing films for teenagers and twentysomethings. In 1992 a UCLA survey revealed that nearly 60 percent of television industry professionals contacted believed that they had been discriminated against at some time in the recent past because of their age. As Neal Karlen pointed out in the *New York Times* on March 21, 1993, in the course of profiling a plethora of baby moguls in the process of seizing control of the film industry, Hollywood had never been younger or meaner in its history. The March 1995 issue of *Buzz,* the Los Angeles gossip magazine, featured an infant in sunglasses on its cover, announcing a story on the new baby moguls.

As movies became more controlled by younger filmmakers, aimed at younger audiences and keyed to video games, special effects became more important. Throughout the decade, blockbuster after blockbuster depended primarily on special effects, much of it coming from George Lucas's gated Industrial Light and Magic at Skywalker Ranch in Marin County. The climax of such films was *Titanic* (1997), a teenage-oriented $200 million special-effects extravaganza that more than recovered its costs in its first year of release and won eleven Academy Awards. Rather than be happy with his success, however, director and screenwriter James Cameron—who described himself as "king of the world" when receiving his Oscar, quoting the hero of his film—proved surprisingly thin-skinned when critics such as Mick LaSalle of the *San Francisco Chronicle* and Kenneth Turan of the *Los Angeles Times* pointed out the obvious: that from an adult perspective, *Titanic* was a dumb movie, devoid of complexity, subtlety, grace, or compassion, even though from a business perspective—in a business targeted toward teenagers—*Titanic* could be considered a work of genius.

The 1990s would not be an innocent decade, especially for the young. There would be no Ricky Nelson or Pat Boone lyrics for a generation watching Prince's new video for "Get Off," in which the singer realistically simulated various sexual acts, or tuning increasingly since the mid-1980s in to the pounding beat and staccato rhymes of rap. By 1991, rap accounted for roughly 9 percent, or $700 million, of the $7.8 billion American music market. The rapping of such figures as Queen Latifah, Ice-T, Ice Cube, Paris, Scarface and the Geto Boys, LL Cool J and Method Man, Tupac Shakur, and Notorious B.I.G. presented a world increasingly ominous in outright suggestions of street violence, embattled and angry self-esteem,

ferocious misogyny, and revenge. From even the most rap-sympathetic perspective, it had to be said that two Geto Boys releases—"Assassins" and
"Damn It Feels Good to Be a Gangsta"—edged into sociopathy. In "Bush
Killer," rapper Paris veered into outright criminality with a reference to an
assassination—claimed to be a figure of speech—of the president. On April
17, 1993, hundreds of concertgoers, their emotions charged by such lyrics,
ran riot through Magic Mountain and Santa Clarita in northern Los Angeles
County.

If rap music could be said to acknowledge an envelope, then certainly
Ice-T pushed through it with "Cop Killer," released as part of his *Body
Count* CD, in which he described how he was about to dust off some
cops with his twelve-gauge sawed-off shotgun, exclaiming, "Die, pig, die."
Needless to say: "Cop Killer" and Ice-T were denounced from coast to
coast by law enforcement officers. When *Body Count,* having sold 315,000
copies since its release in April 1992, began to slip in the charts, Ice-T (real
name: Tracy Marrow), then and only then, announced that he was withdrawing the offending lyric.

"Cop Killer" was not the product of some underground rap company.
The company for which Ice-T recorded, Warner Brothers Records, was
owned by Time Warner, and while uneasy with the lyrics, Time Warner had
stood by the rapper who had brought it so much profit. Here indeed was an
irony. The $700 million rap music industry, passing a billion dollars by the
end of the decade, was in and of itself the paradigm of big business. Even
more interesting, it was big business with a gangster-capitalist edge, as evidenced by the rise of Death Row Records, whose very name suggested its
origins and continuing connections with gang culture and the streets. As in
the case of so many rap lyrics themselves, enterprises such as Death Row
flourished on the edges of legitimacy and sustained their own underworld
connections. Rap stars and rap executives occasionally became members of
the criminal class or were themselves the victims of gang violence. Death
Row Records founder Marion (Suge) Knight, a talented entrepreneur in his
own way, was behind bars by 1997, sent to the California Men's Colony in
San Luis Obispo and barred from running his company after violating his
parole by getting into a fight at the MGM Grand Hotel in Las Vegas on September 7, 1996, just hours before Death Row rapper star Tupac Shakur was
assassinated. In addition to the two superstars, Tupac Shakur and Notorious
B.I.G., who fell in a hail of gunfire, other rappers went to prison for rape,
assault, and other offenses—just another way, it might be claimed, of living
the dream, of dancing to the music, of doing what rap lyrics were talking
about. The presence of such criminality within a billion-dollar business,
much of it controlled by Fortune 500 corporations, begged for an explana-

tion. Was this proof positive, radicals of various shades might ask, that American corporate life itself was a quasi-criminal enterprise? Or was rap allowing dissident blacks and dissident record executives to form an alliance against the mainstream and make big bucks in the process?

Music industry billionaire David Geffen of Malibu and Beverly Hills embodied the paradox. A quintessential outsider in one dimension of his existence, Geffen had faked a UCLA degree on his resume to secure a job in the mailroom of the William Morris Agency. Thirty years later—thanks to such stars and groups as the Eagles, Jackson Browne, Linda Ronstadt, Nirvana, Guns N' Roses, Don Henley, Aerosmith, and Peter Gabriel—Geffen was on the verge of donating $200 million to the UCLA School of Medicine, which would be named in his honor. Geffen was also leading a campaign against the growing violence and misogyny of gangsta rap, especially after the Geto Boys had in one of their releases extolled the pleasures of murdering women, cutting off their breasts, then performing necrophilia on their bodies. "I'm not going to put out records like that," Geffen stated. "Now they can call that racism if they want, but it has nothing to do with racism. It has to do with being a responsible person."[15]

Ocean Park

The 1990s witnessed a full and final authentication of an entire postwar generation of notable artists who had made their careers in California, sometimes at great risk. The decade opened with two events: a retrospective of the works of John Baldessari and Alexis Smith at the Whitney Museum of American Art in New York City, and in Southern California the emplacement of a phalanx of seventeen hundred twenty-foot-tall yellow octagonal umbrellas across the Tejon Pass by the Bulgarian-born Christo. Each represented high-water marks of 1970s- and 1980s-style conceptualism on the California coast.

Conceptualism itself, as represented by Baldessari and Smith at the Whitney and to a lesser extent by the Christo fence, paralleled the work of California composer John Cage in music. It was, in short, art driven by concepts. Cage died in 1992 at the age of eighty. Most of his music had been highly conceptual; as in the case of Arnold Schönberg, the idea behind Cage's music was often more satisfying than the music itself. Cage could be accused (and he frequently was) of producing not music but antimusic, as in his famous silent piece, *4'33"*, in which a pianist sat silently in front of a piano for four minutes and thirty-three seconds in an effort by Cage to communicate, through negation, the nature of music by presenting its opposite, silence—notions that Cage had absorbed from his Zen master, the celebrated D. T. Suzuki, and the white paintings of Robert Rauschenberg. In John Baldessari's case an almost platonic obsession with conceptual statement was the propelling and very necessary principle of unity. Baldessari created eclectic collages dominated by photographs whose realism became surreal or magical-real in various arrangements. What was Californian in Baldessari was the cinematic nature of his storyboards, as one critic called them, which at once discovered and presented storylines rescued from the multitudinous imagery of photographed life.

Alexis Smith, for whom the Whitney provided a midcareer survey extending through the winter of 1991–92, took as her material not only photographs but, seemingly, the entire composite of American visual life. Raised on the grounds of the Metropolitan State Hospital in Norwalk, where her father was psychiatrist and assistant superintendent, Smith became accustomed at an early age to a world in which reconfigurations of the ordinary, some of them only slightly askew, suggested intensities within, frequently disturbed and unresolved. As girl Friday to Los Angeles architect Frank Gehry, Smith had experienced aplenty how everyday objects and materials could be released through collage and positioning into new statement. In Smith's collages and assemblages, the multitudinous, the mass-produced, the everyday, even the banal—a *Life* magazine cover, a Foster Freeze ice cream cone, a high school graduation album, a newspaper headline, oversize piano keys, a swatch of belt fabric—played off one another as pulp fiction text, the whole suggesting psychic experience in a world of consumer objects and fragmentary statement. "I don't think that I'm specifically interested in Southern California," Smith once remarked, "but I'm a product of it."[16]

So, too, was Christo, ever seeking to arrange recognizable elements and materials—a white nylon fence running down the California north coast through Sonoma and Marin Counties to the Golden Gate in 1976; pink fabric surrounding the islands of Biscayne Bay in 1983; gold fabric wrapping the Pont Neuf in 1985; and now yellow umbrellas running alongside Interstate 5 through the Tejon Pass—in such a way as to make a transformed and startling new statement (which is to say, art) of engineering and/or landscape. In the case of the yellow umbrellas stretching for eighteen miles across the Tejon Pass, unfolded with great fanfare on October 9, 1991, thanks to the efforts of thousands of volunteers, Christo was seeking to say something about California and Japan. Parallel to the California umbrellas, Christo had also emplaced a line of 1,340 blue umbrellas in the rice paddies of Ibaraki Prefecture. (The events opened sixteen hours apart, so Christo could jet to each event.) What had Christo sought to express through this $26 million extravaganza, scheduled to remain in place for three weeks, aside from film rights and other franchises through which he hoped to recoup his expenses? Nothing less than an artistic probe into what made Japan Japan and California California, each of them different, yet linked in a powerful synergy symbolized by parallel runs of giant umbrellas. In Japan, for example, Christo needed the consent of 452 landowners to emplace his umbrellas. In California, he needed the permission of only twenty-five. In each instance, Christo meticulously assembled all documentary evidence regarding the permit process as a way of probing not only density and landownership but social imagination and value as connected to land-use planning.

Even in the matter of recouping his costs, Christo was seeking contrasting probes of capitalism in two different societies. Although drawn to the project for aesthetic reasons, Christo's volunteers were not technically volunteers at all. Christo insisted on paying each person some form of minimum wage, whether he or she wanted it or not. The artist regarded the business patterns and economic outcome of the umbrellas in Japan or California as essential components of his artistic statement. What better way was there to probe the nature of value in two differing capitalist societies than through the absurdity of making money off what one Japanese observer described as no-purpose umbrellas? Somehow, Christo's blue umbrellas, identical in design and construction to his yellow ones, managed to look Japanese in Japan, just as his yellow umbrellas managed to look Californian in California. Here on Christo's part was an effort to explore through public art on a grand scale the complex alchemies of topography, atmospherics, and imaginative overlay that make places so aesthetically distinct from each other.

When a volunteer was killed by a windblown runaway umbrella, Christo unintentionally achieved a prophetic probe of just how dangerous nature could be in Southern California. That one of these magical yellow umbrellas could turn into a killing machine underscored a persistent theme—the ominousness of the real—on the coast of dreams. Photo-realism, as a consequence, which so vividly explored the subtle disquiet that could lurk behind the ordinary, was a distinctively California style that was almost restricted to the state. In the works of such photo-realists as John Register of Southern California and Robert Bechtle of the Bay Area, photo-realistic depictions of suburban and urban landscapes brought with them, in Register's case, a sense of subliminal dread and, in Bechtle's case, a sense of isolation and loneliness begging comparison to Edward Hopper. At first glance, photo-realists such as Register and Bechtle seemed to be almost obsessively representational and certainly noninterpretive. The artist appeared to be trying to make his painting come as close to a photograph as possible. Yet look again and you find yourself in a world of allegorical intensity as everyday objects and places—patio furniture, swimming pools, backyard lawns, empty streets on Potrero Hill—emit the reverberations of a rapidly densifying dread. In Register's oil on canvas *The Riots* (1993), one of the most dramatic California paintings of the decade, the allegory becomes fully explicit as a bronzed and fit Los Angeles woman lazes in the nude by her pool, goddess of the California dream, while her husband stares into the distance and the smoke of a burning Los Angeles darkens three-quarters of the sky overhead.

While it was true that California art continued to nurture the work of a number of sublime serenicists—Lita Albuquerque, Terry St. John, Elmer Bischoff, Peter Alexander, William Brice, Joan Brown, Greg Kondos, and Wayne Thiebaud—each of them in search of harmony and reconciliation, an even larger body of California work was fraught with anxiety, whether expressed or displaced. Even David Hockney concealed behind his joyous colors and deliberately childlike figurism a world that seemed in the process of coming apart. Humorist Robert Arneson, who so loved to poke fun in his ceramic sculptures, cut so close to the bone, in his bust of assassinated Mayor George Moscone, the San Francisco Arts Commission rejected the work in favor of a more conventional bronze. The Benicia-based Arneson died in his hometown in November 1992 at the early age of sixty-two; and the mother of all comic ceramists, Beatrice Wood—"Mama of Dada," as she was called—died in Ojai at the age of 105 in March 1998. Thus the decade was bracketed with the departure of two California ceramists who were supposed to be having fun whenever possible but who were also giving release, increasingly, to the more ominous possibilities in pop-humorous, pop-happy California. When the San Francisco Arts Commission installed ten Keith Haring sculptures across the city in March 1998, the specter of Haring, dead from AIDS in 1990 at the age of thirty-one, could not help but qualify the buoyant humor of the dancing figures.

No wonder that in the sunset days of his life, living in the wine country in Alexander Valley in Sonoma County, Richard Diebenkorn seemed more and more a most necessary master. Nearing seventy, Diebenkorn and his wife of a half century, Phyllis, had moved north to Healdsburg from Santa Monica in 1988, to a home-studio set amid vineyards very much reminiscent of Claude Monet's retirement home in Giverny or Paul Cézanne's retreat at Aix-en-Provence. Critics had been increasingly comparing Diebenkorn to Monet and Cézanne ever since 1977, when the Whitney Museum of American Art had, in giving Diebenkorn a major show, admitted, with perhaps only the slightest sense of surprise, that one of the greatest American painters of the twentieth century had grown up, been nurtured and educated, and practiced his art in California.

Diebenkorn seems not to have played the artist as rebel at any point in his career. He had been, rather, a preppie sort of a guy, given to corduroy pants and button-down shirts and tweed jackets, like a stockbroker on his day off: a well-mannered gentleman who had gone to Lowell High School in San Francisco, graduated from Stanford in 1943, enlisted in the marines and been assigned to Officer Candidates School at Quantico, Virginia, where, on leave, he had haunted the Phillips Collection in Washington, seeing there the works of Picasso, Braque, Bonnard, and Matisse that would set the direction of his own creativity. Released from the military, Diebenkorn returned to San Francisco to enroll at the Art Institute, where he studied under Mark Rothko, Clyfford Still, David Park, and Elmer Bischoff. After graduation, he joined his teachers in the Bay Area Figurative movement. Initially, Diebenkorn had been attracted to abstract expressionism and was good enough in that genre to have a one-man show at the Palace of the Legion of Honor in San Francisco in 1948 when he was only twenty-six. In the mid-1950s, he returned to figuration. Airplane flights over the landscape of Southern California and the Southwest, however, kept him mesmerized with the abstract planes and patterns on the land. Nature herself, modified by mankind, was a kind of abstract painting.

In 1966, Diebenkorn accepted a professorship at UCLA and moved to Santa Monica. There, across the next twenty years, he produced his *Ocean Park* series, semiabstract depictions of the Ocean Park neighborhood in Santa Monica, fronting the Pacific, where Diebenkorn lived and maintained his studio. The result was an epic of line, plane, and color that critics such as Robert Hughes were soon calling the most impressive abstract landscapes done by an American artist in the twentieth century, to be ranked in the company of comparable works by Matisse, Cézanne, and Mondrian. By the mid-1970s, the developing *Ocean Park* series, together with Diebenkorn's earlier abstract expressionist work and his continuing Figurative painting, announced to New York—rather suddenly, for Diebenkorn had been working quietly in California these past thirty years—that a notable American painter was now, at age fifty-five, at the height of his powers (hence the exhibition, initially assembled by curators at the Albright-Knox Art Gallery in Buffalo, before moving on to the Whitney).

"Some landscapes were invented by painters and carry their names," observed *Time* art critic Robert Hughes, reviewing the Whitney exhibition. "The stone farmhouse on a lavender Provençal hill proclaims Cézanne; the shuttered hotel room with a blue glimpse of sea beyond a curlicued balcony announces Matisse. On a less exalted level, one cannot drive through rural Pennsylvania and not think of Andrew Wyeth. It happens in California, too, through the works of Richard Diebenkorn." Not that Diebenkorn was, Hughes continued, a California artist. He was, rather, an important talent arising out of California; and like everything else on the coast of dreams, his work sustained a paradox. "Diebenkorn's art is about sensuous pleasure," noted Hughes, "qualified and tightened by an acute sense of instability: through the paradise of paint, runs a San Andreas fault."[17]

When Diebenkorn died of heart failure at the age of seventy-one in 1993, the recognition by Hughes, first expressed in 1977, that the California-based artist was of world stature, was reiterated in countless obituaries. Californians, however, revered Diebenkorn beyond the accolades of art. Diebenkorn had become a foundational figure, one of the creators of California's consciousness and sensibility. Through art, Diebenkorn had reassembled the state, north and south, while continuing to acknowledge its tensions. In his work was blended, as in California itself, the sensuous color of the Mediterranean and the contemplative serenity of Asia. Echoing the French impressionists as distant music, Diebenkorn's Figurative work linked California to the inner dreams of southern Europe, while his *Ocean Park* series projected the state out onto a Pacific that was infinite in its beckoning possibilities. No art-aware Californian could ever again sit in the sunshine with a glass of wine, with the blue Pacific in the distance, and not have that moment in some way authenticated because Diebenkorn had painted it. No art-sensitive Californian would ever again experience the near-abstract encounters of sea, shore, and architecture on the coast of dreams without feeling the assurance that what he or she was seeing was truly there, for Diebenkorn had seen and painted it as well.

Frank's Kids

Diebenkorn's *Ocean Park* series was as much about architecture, urban planning, and landscape design as it was about sea and sky; for these arts had organized Santa Monica into the patterns he had perceived and presented. In the late nineteenth and early twentieth century, Americans had used architecture, gardening, and landscape design to create California—especially Southern California, which was semiarid and near treeless or outright desert—as a physical and imaginative place. South of the Tehachapi, just about everything could grow, provided there was water, which led to the dramatic questions: What to plant, and why? While the landscape history of Southern California remains to be written, it is already quite clear just how powerfully and self-consciously culturally—guided, that is, by cultural metaphors—were the horticulture and landscape design programs enacted at the turn of the century. Deliberately, through planting, Americans recreated Southern California from desert chaparral into a panorama of Mediterranean-Levantine lushness suggestive of southern Europe and the Holy Land, each region speaking so directly as metaphors for what Americans wanted out of Southern California: a new Italy, a new sacred place.

Even at its most lush, the Southern California garden was asserting itself against the desert. Eclectic boldness was evident in the landscape designs of Nancy Goslee Power, the Santa Monica–based landscape architect who was emerging in the 1990s as one of the half-dozen great figures in her field in the nation: as evidenced, among other things, by her winning in May 1999 the Henry Francis du Pont medal in landscape architecture from Winterthur. For Power and her associated designers, the essential Los Angeles/Southern California garden—whether the private gardens of clients in Beverly Hills or the grand public gardens of the Norton Simon Museum in Pasadena—began with a Zen statement of water, reed, and stone, then branched out from there to encompass parallel symmetries and serenities in classic Mediterranean design, as in the great gardens of the Italian Renaissance, with occasional indulgences in patches of wild English romanticism that played off the general austerity and also reminded everyone, in garden terms, that Southern California was a blend of Anglo-America, Latin America, the Mediterranean, and the Asian Pacific. Power's own home on a quiet side street in Santa Monica featured one of the most dramatically landscaped private gardens in the state: a tone poem of reconciled Spanish-southwestern and Asia-Pacific motifs, harmonized in sunlit hues of cinnamon, cactus green, and apricot.

In northern California, by contrast, the prelandscaped environment was itself the matrix of garden design. Hence, the deceptively simple (at first glance) landscape designs of the San Francisco–based Lawrence Halprin, who by the summer of 1997 was seeing to conclusion the greatest creation of his career, the Franklin Delano Roosevelt Memorial in Washington. As a student under Walter Gropius at Harvard in the late 1930s, Halprin had absorbed a conviction of totality and synchronicity in the arts. From this perspective, the landscape architect (as Halprin became after wartime service in the navy) sought primarily not to dominate landscape, but to intensify a landscape performance already in progress. An ardent outdoorsman, given to backpacking in the High Sierra, Halprin thus began with the premise that California itself was a garden, and it was the duty of the landscape architect, as subtly, indeed almost invisibly as possible, to enhance that existing identity. As the landscape architect for Sea Ranch, a second-home coastal development north of San Francisco, designed and constructed between 1962 and 1967, Halprin refused to allow housing to dominate the beach, as a Southern California landscape architect might have been tempted to do. Halprin, rather, working with such stellar architects as Charles Moore, William Turnbull, Donlyn Lyndon, Richard Whitaker, and Joseph Esherick, had kept ten miles of ocean frontage untouched and placed all housing elsewhere on the five-thousand-acre site, while sinking swimming pools and tennis courts beneath the horizon. In order to understand the land he was serving, Halprin camped out for several weekends, noting wind and weather patterns, shadowing and atmospherics. The result was that the rapidly weather-seasoned condominiums of Sea Ranch seemed as if they had been there from time immemorial, or as if nature herself had been Halprin's collaborator.

Like Diebenkorn, whom he equaled in achievement, and like architect Frank Gehry of Southern California, Halprin found himself performing increasingly on an international stage—designing the Walter and Elise Haas Promenade overlooking the Old City of Jerusalem, for example—while maintaining a flourishing California practice. By the 1990s so much of the significant public space in northern California—Sproul Plaza and the Student Union on the UC Berkeley campus, the Stanford Medical Plaza Gardens, Justin Herman Plaza in San Francisco, even the Visitors Reception Area at Alcatraz—bore the Halprin imprint. His selection in the mid-1980s to design the Roosevelt Memorial brought an internationalized northern Californian sensibility to national purposes. On seven and a half acres beside the Tidal Basin, Halprin emplaced a series of granite outcroppings, waterfalls, reflecting pools, and contemporary statuary that bespoke northern California and, like the Vietnam Memorial, made a quantum leap in the state of monumental art.

The very coastal edge of the coast of dreams, especially the fierce but beautiful region north of San Francisco, was quintessential Halprin territory. Eighty percent of the population of California, it must be remembered, lived within thirty miles of the coast. All things considered, Californians were a coastal people. Starting in the 1920s, the South Coast, from southern Orange County to Malibu and beyond, had become progressively lined with white-walled, red-tiled Mediterranean mansions and, after World War II, their high-tech modernist counterparts. By the late 1990s, Mediterraneanism—along with so much else—was back in style. With the recovery and globalization of the economy, Mediterranean villas on bluffs overlooking the Pacific were selling at escalating prices.

Interestingly, the second great era of Southern California architecture, 1950s modernism, was finding an equal appeal among the young. If Mediterraneanism spoke to Southern California as Europe, 1950s modernism represented the same region as the ultimate American place. In each instance, the affluent boomers of the 1990s were recognizing value in architecture enlivened by myths and dreams. In the case of 1950s modernism, which young buyers were snapping up, it was a way of recovering the optimism and sense of direction characteristic of the postwar era. For Kurt Andersen, writing in the special double California issue of *The New Yorker* in early 1998, the 1940s-, 1950s-, and 1960s-era getaway homes in Palm Springs, now so desirable to affluent boomers looking for a second address, bespoke a lost world "of cocktails, cigars, Sinatra, and poolside cha-cha-cha." To enter one of these low-lying sleek and horizontal constructions, made as much of glass as any other material, or to linger at poolside stretched on an aluminum and vinyl lounge, was to catch reverberations of the Rat Pack, perhaps even of JFK himself, in pursuit of Camelot as party time. "It's not just the buildings from the forties, fifties, and sixties that are remarkably well preserved," noted Andersen, "and that seem to 1998 sensibilities unwittingly hip. Human vestiges of the Rat Pack resort milieu survive as well, which is definitely part of the ironic-cum-anthropological attraction of the place: imagine Williamsburg, or Sturbridge Village if the actors in Colonial drag were real people from the eighteenth century."[18]

Having been told by the *New Yorker* that their city contained important modernist architecture by such California greats as Richard Neutra, Craig Ellwood, Donald Wexler, John Lautner, A. Quincy Jones, and Albert Frey (who died at the age of ninety-four in November 1998), Palm Springs began to re-regard itself architecturally and to take steps to preserve such structures as Frey's 1947 residence for industrial designer Raymond Loewy (the Coca-Cola bottle, the Studebaker Avanti), the 1952 city hall, and such a previously considered throwaway building as Frey's 1963 Tramway gas station, a hyperbolic paraboloid on the northern edge of town. Along with everything else, Rat Pack California was making a comeback. As Dean Martin might say, ain't that a kick in the head?

Lush or hard-edged, 1920s Mediterraneanism or postwar modernism, stucco and tile or steel and glass, or Rat Pack Palm Springs: California architecture, like California itself, bounced between polarities of soft luxuriance and machine precision. The verdant Napa Valley, for example, offered a dramatic contrast to the hard-edged desert modernism of Palm Springs. Here architects such as Ross Anderson (a bicoastal California-born New Yorker), Scott Johnson of Los Angeles, and Heidi Richardson of San Francisco (great-granddaughter of Henry Hobson Richardson, who established Romanesque revival as a dominant style and did the first designs for Stanford University before his premature death in 1886) offered their clients a variety of styles comforting in historical associations. In both the Mediterranean and modern styles that were enjoying such a retro revival in Southern California, clients subsumed their personal histories and dreams into architecture. Like Wallace Neff in prewar Southern California, Heidi Richardson was especially adept in using architecture to tell one or another story on behalf of her northern California clients. Richardson's patrons could pick and choose from dozens of metaphors—Greek or Roman classical, Japanese, Cape Cod, the South of France, each of them fitting so easily into the eclectic northern California mix—as a way of telling themselves who they were or who they wanted to be.

Yet Southern California also sustained numerous varieties of the genteel tradition and a more stately era. Take the Hancock Park district in Los Angeles, whose stately Edwardian and 1920s-era mansions baby boomers were also rapidly acquiring. Southern Californians felt equally comfortable not only in the steel and glass modernism of the Case Study era but also, or so it would seem, in the gritty realities of contemporary urbanism. Frank Gehry understood this perhaps better than anyone else, which is why he started an architectural revolution in 1977 when he expanded his own "dumb little house," as he called it, in an unpretentious part of Santa Monica. Deconstructing the house into its component parts, and leaving it significantly deconstructed, and using such materials as corrugated metal siding and chain-link fence, Gehry began a revolution of sorts or at the least established a style of architecture—cubist, deconstructed, plywood walls for interior spaces, corrugated iron and chain-link fencing for exteriors— that celebrated metropolitan Los Angeles as an unfinished city. Even Gehry's unorthodox sketching style (nonsketches, in fact, more doodles than renderings) testified to his reluctance to have anything fixed and static. Everything had to be in motion, including architecture.

From Gehry's Santa Monica studios, across a quarter of a century beginning in the early 1970s, emerged a circle of architects (Frank's Kids, they were called)—Michael Rotondi, Thom Mayne, Eric Owen Moss, Frank Israel—for whom all of Los Angeles, especially in the supercharged 1980s, was one vast process that architects should not try to fix in time and place but should seek only to keep pace with in breathless combinations of new construction, recycling, and industrial materials. How better to serve a city whose built environment had become, through the force of money, new people, and new uses, a shifting stage set? Reviewing an exhibition of Eric Owen Moss's work at the Harvard University Graduate School of Design in March 1993, Herbert Muschamp noted that Moss's Southern California work was as much about the process of architecture as about architecture itself. "Like writers who write to find out what they think," noted Muschamp, "Mr. Moss designs to see what kinds of information can be extracted in the making of a place."[19]

Frank's Kids loved deconstruction or partial construction, industrial materials, bright colors on metal surfaces, trusses, beams, cables, bold boltings, unadorned girders, pipes, and pillars. Their style was especially suited to a city in the process of repossessing and augmenting the industrial infrastructure of an earlier era. It was also a style that looked inward and away from the street toward soaring internal spaces protected from the dangers of the city outside. Here, safe from random violence and graffiti, subliminal or real, high-tech boomers and Generation Xers might work undisturbed before computer screens in a brave new techno-economic world of mixed media and information processing.

Was this a high-tech Disneyland or a reprise of the architecture of Fritz Lang's film *Metropolis* (1927)? The Lang comparison was especially appropriate to the outer edges of industrial chic as practiced by Frank's Kids. "Mad Science," Rob Braun of the Newport Beach office of Langdon Wilson called such architecture, in an effort to capture its futurist sci-fi fantasy. Were such buildings put-ons or the reentry points of sci-fi movie sets back into reality? In Southern California, the question was perhaps moot; for an entire generation was now absorbing its sense of architectural grandeur in architecture from the menacing sublime of Gotham in the *Batman* series or the stunning cityscapes of *The Phantom Menace* (1999).

Frank Gehry, meanwhile, like Richard Diebenkorn in art, had become a world figure, as his Los Angeles work—the Aerospace Museum in Exposition Park, the Temporary Contemporary Museum downtown, the Loyola Law School in the Pico Union, the Norton House and Chiatt/Day headquarters in Venice, the Wosk residence in Beverly Hills, the Frances Howard Goldwyn Regional Branch Library in Hollywood—attracted national and international attention. In 1989 Gehry received the Pritzker Prize, the Nobel of architecture. Despite such recognition, he kept to his casual, even offhand style. Like Diebenkorn he preferred windbreakers and open-neck shirts. Gehry smoked cigars, and his favorite sport, a holdover from his Canadian boyhood, was ice hockey, which he continued to play with some skill well into his sixties.

Born in Canada in 1929 and raised in Toronto and Timmins in eastern Ontario, Gehry had moved to Los Angeles in 1947 at the age of eighteen with his hardscrabble family, looking for a better life. A prophet, however, is not without honor save in his own country. Time and again, Los Angeles turned to other architects despite Gehry's growing reputation: to Arata Isozaki for the Museum of Contemporary Art, to Richard Meier for the Getty Center, to José Rafael Moneo for the Cathedral of Our Lady of the Angels. The one major Los Angeles commission Gehry won, for the Walt Disney Concert Hall, sat stalled for most of the decade as sponsors failed to reach their financial goals. No matter: by the 1990s Gehry was at work on his masterpiece, the Guggenheim Museum in Bilbao, Spain. As Disney Hall resisted efforts to restart it, the Bilbao project arose, assisted in significant measure by an aeronautical computer design program perfected in France that made Gehry's soaring spaces and sculptured shapes, flights of another sort, realizable. Dedicated in the summer of 1997, Gehry's museum—its sculptured shapes gleaming in titanium—was immediately hailed as a masterpiece. Even more gratifyingly, Gehry's Disney Hall atop Bunker Hill in downtown Los Angeles, first designed in 1987, was now, thanks to the dazzling success of Bilbao, restarted through the efforts of developer billionaire Eli Broad and Los Angeles mayor Richard Riordan. By the spring of 2001, Gehry himself was the subject of a retrospective exhibition at the Guggenheim Museum in New York, and Disney Hall, which *Los Angeles Times* architectural critic Nicolai Ouroussoff described as sensual and euphoric, was rising in its idiosyncratic grandeur atop Bunker Hill.

PART II

Catastrophe

Earthquake, Fire, and Flood

On October 17, 1989, at 5:04 in the afternoon, an earthquake measuring 7.1 on the Richter scale, centered in the Loma Prieta section of the Santa Cruz Peninsula, struck the San Francisco Bay Area. It was the most serious earthquake to hit the region since April 1906. It was also the most dramatically communicated; at the very moment it hit, the San Francisco Giants and the Oakland Athletics were conducting pregame ceremonies in Candlestick Park prior to the opening of the first game of the World Series. Millions of television viewers knew instantly that a major temblor had shaken the Golden State. Very soon, the news became even worse. A portion of the I-880 elevated freeway running through the Cypress section of West Oakland had collapsed just as commuter traffic was beginning. Forty-two motorists, it eventually turned out, had met horrible deaths beneath tons of falling concrete. The eastern portion of the San Francisco–Oakland Bay Bridge had split apart. Over in San Francisco, an entire district, the bayside Marina, created from the mud and shoals of the Bay as site of the Panama-Pacific Exposition of 1915, had been shaken like Jell-O. Hundreds of homes had collapsed on their foundations, killing a number of residents, and one apartment complex, its gas main severed, had burst into flames.

In the hours and days that followed, national television broadcast and rebroadcast a repetitive cluster of images, which, as bad as the Loma Prieta earthquake might be, made it seem even worse. The collapse of the Cypress Freeway was terrible enough, followed by equally chilling images of concrete being removed with heavy equipment and flattened automobiles, each bearing crushed human cargoes, being lowered to the street. Again and again, the nation was treated to the image of a lone automobile driving into the crevice created by a cracked Bay Bridge and being captured there, thus saving it from a fall into the Bay. (Miraculously, the driver survived.) Again and again, the Marina apartment building burst and reburst into flames. These repeated images, together with the severe damage at the epicenter of the quake sixty miles south of San Francisco, made the Loma Prieta earthquake seem even worse than its sixty-six deaths and $7 billion in damages already indicated.

Fortunately for San Francisco, the fires caused by the earthquake were contained by the prompt and effective action of the San Francisco Fire Department, which was ranked among the finest firefighting organizations in the nation. Two years later, as another catastrophe struck the Bay Area, the city of Oakland would not be so lucky. On a hot windy Sunday, October 20, 1991, embers from a brush fire that the Oakland Fire Department believed it had doused the day before burst into flame. Within the hour, a two-thousand-degree inferno, fed by oil-rich eucalyptus trees exploding like bombs in the heat, was devouring the exclusive Oakland Hills district. Wind driven and racing overhead as eucalyptus tree after eucalyptus tree spontaneously combusted, the firestorm advanced at incredible speed. At noon, Al and Gail Baxter and their guest Leigh Ortenburger had sat down to a preluncheon aperitif, waiting for architect Ian Mackinlay, delayed at San Francisco Airport, to join them. Within twenty minutes, fleeing in separate cars, Gail Baxter and Ortenburger were dead, and Al Baxter had saved himself (although he was burned horribly) by crawling into a drainage pipe running down a culvert.

Twenty-five Oaklanders lost their lives in the fire. One hundred and fifty people suffered serious injuries. Some 2,700 structures—single-family homes, condominiums, and apartments—were destroyed, and a total of eighteen hundred acres were burned to cinders. All in all, more than $5 billion in property was lost, making the Oakland firestorm one of the most expensive in the nation's history. Some five thousand people had been evacuated from their homes, and in the days following the fire, nearly twenty-five remained missing. Oakland Hills, one of the most privileged neighborhoods in the Bay Area—the neighborhood of choice for the UC Berkeley faculty (at least seventy-two of whom lost their homes)—had been left a scorched and barren desert.

California had had ample evidence in the twentieth century that, in building its most exclusive homes on the coastal heights, it was building them in the most dangerous places. While scenic, such sites were hot and dry and, equally dangerous, remote. Not surprisingly, there had been more than a half dozen home-destroying fires in coastal Southern California since 1970. The great Santa Barbara County fire of June 1990, for example, had killed two people and leveled 641 structures. Yet the Oakland fire of October 1991 was in a league of its own in terms of death and destruction. All such fires suggested the possibility of a wholesale conflagration sweeping down miles and miles of drought-parched canyons: of fires linking one to another across acres of dry sage and chaparral or moving like aerial napalm from one exploding eucalyptus or palm tree to another.

Such a grim scenario seemed on the verge of happening on October 27, 1993, as the entire South Coast—from Malibu to Thousand Oaks in Ventura County, east to Altadena and Sierra Madre nestled against the San Gabriel foothills in Los Angeles County, south to Laguna Beach in Orange County, east to Riverside and south to Escondido in northern San Diego County—erupted into a necklace of fire feeding on dry brush and parched grassland. Fanned by powerful Santa Ana winds, the various fires fortunately remained discontinuous. Raging ferociously, the Malibu fire destroyed eighteen thousand acres and razed more than two hundred homes. Pepperdine University came within a few hundred yards and a few shifts of wind to losing its new multimillion-dollar campus, and the old Getty Museum, modeled on the Villa dei Papiri at Herculaneum, also stood at risk.

The Laguna fire, destroying at least three hundred homes, including many in the Emerald Bay Estates, forced the evacuation of the entire city of 24,000, many of whom fled down to the Pacific Coast Highway like refugees from a war zone. Orange County novelist T. Jefferson Parker left in his Ford Bronco, packed with photos, books, manuscripts, three dogs, and five snakes. The Ventura County fire forced the evacuation of the Camarillo State Hospital as well as the removal of more than a hundred exotic animals, including three elephants, from the Amazing Animal Actors Ranch in the vicinity. The fire sweeping the brush-covered hills of northeastern San Diego County near Escondido likewise required the evacuation of the Wild Animal Park in the San Pasqual Valley, including the removal of twenty-six California condors. The Altadena/Sierra Madre fire forced a similar removal, with one resident, Caltech geophysics professor Barclay Camb, led off in handcuffs when he refused police orders to abandon his property. Throughout the long smoky day, as residents fled to safety and thousands of firefighters from throughout the state fought the various blazes, helicopters dipped their 150-gallon Bambi Buckets into the Pacific, then headed back into the blazing canyons like intrepid dragonflies. By Thursday afternoon, the full extent of the damage had revealed itself. A total of fourteen fires had ravaged more than 137,000 acres in six Southern California counties and destroyed 554 homes. Coastal Californians, especially those on the hot and dry coast extending as far north as the San Francisco Bay Area, enjoyed homes that were dramatically sited on heights, with commanding views of mesa, canyon, foothill, and sea. Yet within the context and atmosphere of such beauty, there also lurked a persistent insecurity that could, at the height of summer, edge into an active fear or, worse, the reality of a devastating fire.

Californians were still pondering the questions and lessons of the October fires when, less than three months later, at 4:31 on the morning of January 17, 1994, an earthquake 6.7 in magnitude, centered in the Northridge district of Los Angeles in the eastern San Fernando Valley, shook the city for ten terrible seconds. The Northridge earthquake was lower in magnitude than Loma Prieta and shorter in duration; but it was centered in one of the most populous and architecturally fragile districts of the city, and its pulses were characterized by a particularly vicious upward thrust.

From one perspective, the Northridge earthquake was not unexpected. First of all, there was the 1989 Loma Prieta earthquake. Second, in June 1992, a temblor of 7.5 magnitude had struck in Landers in rural San Bernardino County. Although it did minimal damage, the Landers quake, one of the largest on record, together with memories of the Loma Prieta earthquake of 1989 and the devastating Sylmar earthquake of 1971, heightened the seismic malaise of the Southland. If a magnitude 7.0 quake ever occurred along the Newport-Inglewood Fault, scientists reported that month, it could cause as many as 21,000 deaths in Orange and Los Angeles Counties.

From the perspective of the seismic volatility of Southern California, Los Angeles was fortunate. The Northridge earthquake struck when the city was asleep. Hence not 21,000 but fifty-seven people died, most of them from collapsing apartment houses (sixteen alone in the Northridge Meadows apartments), collapsing homes, collapsing freeways (including one officer speeding to his duty station), falling walls, bookcases, or other furniture, household accidents, and, in at least one instance, sheer terror. Accounting for nearly one-third of the dead, the collapse of the three-story Northridge Meadows apartment complex onto a pancaked first floor sent a chill of terror through the region. This building was typical of thousands of similar apartment structures throughout the Southland. Likewise did the collapse of the Santa Monica Freeway near La Cienega and Fairfax; the four-section collapse of the Golden State Freeway south of Newhall in the Santa Clarita Valley (leaving a truck, a mobile home, and two automobiles isolated in the sky); the collapse of the portion of the Antelope Valley Freeway, where Los Angeles motorcycle officer Clarence Dean was killed; and the collapse of a section of the Simi Valley Freeway in Granada Hills each underscore a frightening possibility. Had the earthquake struck at rush hour, hundreds of commuters would have been killed on the falling freeways. And had the earthquake been of greater magnitude or longer in duration, many more apartment complexes would have collapsed. As it was, more than five thousand structures were seriously damaged. Altogether, the Northridge earthquake destroyed more than $20 billion in property, displaced thousands, and impoverished untold others.

In and between this succession of earthquake and fire occurred a third component of biblical catastrophe: flood. In 1992, 1995, and 1998, California experienced its heaviest rains and worst flooding since the 1930s. (Ironically, during the previous six years, from 1986 to 1992, California had been suffering serious drought.) Beginning in late January and early February 1992, heavy rainfall caused the worst flooding Southern California had seen since 1938. The rains of February 1992 caused five deaths, three from drowning in a flash flood by the Ventura River, two from mudslide. At Point Loma and across the border in Tijuana, ruptured sewage mains poured millions of gallons of partially treated or raw sewage into the Pacific.

In January 1995, it was the turn of both the north and the south. In the south, rains poured down at the unprecedented rate of one inch an hour. Once again, the Ventura River raged, and Malibu was threatened by mudslides. Five people lost their lives. Further north, major flooding occurred along Highway 17 near Santa Cruz south of San Jose and at Guerneville on the Russian River. Napa-Sonoma also experienced serious flooding, parts of this region becoming a linked network of suddenly created lakes and waterways. North of Sacramento, the site in ancient times of a vast inland sea fed by a number of mighty Sierra Nevada–based rivers and creeks, something resembling that long-gone sea reasserted itself in the second week of January as the Great Storm of 1995, as it soon became known, overwhelmed dams and levees and put vast portions of farmlands, small towns, suburbs, even parts of downtown Sacramento, under water. South of Sacramento, a number of townships in the Delta sank beneath the rising waters.

By now, the Great Storm of 1995 had a more indigenous name: El Niño. And in January, February, and March 1998, El Niño returned with a vengeance. For three straight months, California, north and south, was pelted with lashing rains, the worst in a century. In Los Angeles County alone, February 2, 1998, from six a.m. to six p.m., the California Highway Patrol reported 338 accidents. Three weeks later, as El Niño continued to pound the California coast, six people were killed. In San Luis Obispo County, two California highway patrolmen were lost as, unaware, they drove across a portion of Highway 166 undermined by a sinkhole. The sinkhole collapsed, plunging the two officers into a torrent of mud created by an engorged Cuyama River. Mudslides became a common occurrence. In the Sea Cliff district of San Francisco, in Pacifica just south of the city, and in San Juan Capistrano, Laguna Beach, and Laguna Niguel in Orange County, homes slipped off their foundations—or, in the case of Pacifica, were bulldozed into the ocean as their back lots disappeared under the remorseless pressure of pounding surf. In Laguna Niguel, thirty households were evacuated because of the danger of mudslide; and in one early morning, March

19, 1998, seven of them, two houses and five condominiums, slid to oblivion. "I was jolted awake by a large popping sound, almost like a balloon exploding," Paul Gunther told the press regarding the loss of his home at Laguna Beach. "When I walked around the house to investigate, the whole structure was creaking and popping. I woke my wife, we grabbed the kids, and ran." Forty-five minutes later, the Gunthers' 3,600-square-foot home, valued at $600,000, plunged into a ravine, barely missing another house.[1]

When it was over, by late March 1998, El Niño had caused an estimated $500 million in damage. Dozens had died (the exact number remains unclear), and state and federal disaster areas had been declared in forty-one out of fifty-eight counties. For three long and tormented months, the nation had been perceiving California through the repetitive and cumulative imagery of rainstorms, flash floods, mudslides, accident-impacted freeways, blanket-wrapped refugees huddled in gymnasiums, or beautiful California homes, primary icons of the California dream, being bulldozed into the raging waters of an angry surf. The entire decade had witnessed recurrent onslaughts of earthquake, fire, flood, and mudslide. Two hundred Californians had died, and damages had easily passed the $25 billion mark. Hundreds of thousands had in one way or another seen their lives ruined, derailed, or severely tested. No state had more frequently appeared on the roll call of federal disaster areas. The image of President George H. W. Bush standing mutely before the collapsed Cypress Freeway, or President Bill Clinton inspecting the damage at Northridge, seemed to epitomize California's relationship to the federal government.

Recognizing these new dangers, Californians were being forced to reassemble for themselves a new and more sophisticated identity. No longer could California be considered exempt from the life-threatening possibilities of planet Earth: a place, that is, to escape from the blizzards, hurricanes, tornadoes, heatwaves, and other uncomfortable and dangerous aspects of life in the rest of the United States. True, nature had done its best in California to disguise such dangers, and what nature had not disguised, human engineering had glossed over. The 1990s, however, witnessed such dangers plainly revealed. Californians were being challenged to evolve for themselves a much more complex and nuanced sense of place.

Scene of the Crime

A long with earthquake and flood, Californians were also facing a catastrophic increase in violent crime. By the mid-1990s California was registering approximately a million crimes a year, one-third of them violent. California's reputation as a violent place was costing the state money in a leading element of its economy since the nineteenth century, tourism. The Los Angeles riots of April and May 1992 cost the city an estimated loss of $536 million in travel and tourist spending in just the first four months following the upheaval. The Japanese were proving increasingly cautious regarding travel to California, especially in the wake of certain well-publicized shootings of Japanese tourists. In the first part of the 1990s alone, spending by Japanese visitors in California had dropped by $225 million at a time when Japanese tourism was on the rise elsewhere in the United States and the world.

Californians, meanwhile, were buying and selling firearms at a frenetic pace. In the first six months of 1994 alone, 322,000 firearms were sold throughout the state—that is, eighteen hundred weapons a day, two-thirds of them handguns. And that was just the legitimate trade. As of January 1994, a staggering 266,065 firearms had been reported stolen throughout the state (and were, no doubt, in the wrong hands). In certain sectors of society, everyone had guns and was increasingly willing to use them. Guns were continually being drawn in the African-American community. In San Francisco, homicides dropped by half between 1993 and 1998 but remained stable among African Americans, who represented only 10 percent of the city's population but accounted for between 40 to 50 percent of its yearly homicides, mostly from firearms. For every killing there were between six and eight shootings or stabbings in which the victim, thanks to the first-rate emergency room facilities at the San Francisco General Hospital, survived. Not since Vietnam had emergency care for gunshot wounds reached such a state of effectiveness. So many California crimes, especially those committed in greater Los Angeles, seemed right out of a Robert De Niro film. Take, for example, the precision hijacking of an armored truck in Commerce, a business- and retail-oriented city adjacent to Los Angeles, on March 28, 1998. Three cars driven by men with walkie-talkies followed the bright red Dunbar Armored truck into the parking lot of a Wells Fargo bank. A few moments later, one of the men with a walkie-talkie was driving the truck, together with its $3 million cash cargo, toward the nearby city of Vernon, where they abandoned the vehicle and took the cash, leaving behind a wounded driver.

In June 1993 the Los Angeles office of the FBI released statistics showing that Southern California was the national capital of white-collar crime, most of it in financial scams of various sorts. Fully 10 percent of the financial fraud cases under investigation throughout the United States were pending in Southern California alone. Of these 1,003 cases, moreover, fully 797 were considered major, meaning that at least $100,000 had been bilked from unsuspecting victims. This was not surprising. Southern California, after all, had been the scene of the failure of the Irvine-based Lincoln Savings & Loan the previous year. All the bank robberies throughout the United States, noted Charlie Parsons, special agent in charge at the FBI's LA office, had amounted to only 3 percent of the $2.6 billion fleeced from elderly investors by Lincoln CEO Charles H. Keating Jr. and his staff, then serving time in the penitentiary. On both the macro and micro scale, Southern California could be considered the grifter capital of the nation. Daniel Ekman, senior customs inspector at the port of Los Angeles, spent the late 1980s and early 1990s scamming some $1.7 million in kickbacks for $5 million worth of false import reports. Investigators discovered $1.2 million in cash stored in file boxes in the garage of Ekman's unpretentious Whittier home. Another $500,000 was in safe-deposit boxes. An unassuming customs inspector, living modestly in Whittier, had pulled off the single largest bribery scheme in U.S. Customs history, without, it seemed, spending a nickel of the loot. Surely, this was a Hollywood script.

Reefer Madness

Thanks in significant measure to the Mexican Mafia, the 1990s witnessed a surge in the use of the designer drug methamphetamine, also known as crank, speed, meth, crystal, or ice. Discovering that it could make and distribute methamphetamine all by itself and thereby bypass its Colombian suppliers of cocaine and marijuana, the Mexican Mafia turned to the drug in the early to mid-1990s and soon drove the outlaw biker gangs and other small-time operators out of business. Another Mexican Mafia enterprise was black-tar heroin, which could also be produced locally in Mexico from poppies as opposed to having to be imported from Asia like white heroin. By 1996, an infrastructure of cooking and distribution of methamphetamine extended from the California-Mexico border to Alaska. A street dosage of methamphetamine, approximately ¹⁄₃₂ of an ounce, was selling for $50. A good cook could make between forty and sixty pounds of the drug every three weeks. Once again, a movie analogy surfaces: this time *The Godfather* (1972), with figures such as Jose Luis Begines, an otherwise ordinary and respectable bar, delicatessen, and restaurant owner-operator in the South Natomas district of Sacramento, playing a California-meth version of Don Corleone. Under surveillance for ten months across 1996 and 1997, Begines was suspected of being a big-time player in a methamphetamine production and distribution ring based in Mexico, North Hollywood, and Sacramento. Not for Begines, however, would there be Don Corleone's quiet death amid his tomato plants. On a morning in April 1997, Begines shot it out with six Department of Justice agents wearing navy blue combat fatigues, and died in sight of his three children.

The following October, a federal grand jury in Fresno indicted twenty-one members of a black-tar heroin ring based out of Mexico, with its California operations centered in San Jose. A task force of twenty DEA agents and San Jose police had spent fifteen months on the case. When the busts came down—in San Jose, Los Banos, Watsonville, Redding, and other places—some two hundred pounds of black-tar heroin, with a street value of more than $20 million, were seized, most of it in the Central Valley town of Los Banos. Despite such seizures, however, the problem only got worse. In 1992 seventy-three meth laboratories had been busted in the Central Valley. By 1999 the number of seizures in the Central Valley had tripled, to 261. At the time of the October 1997 indictments, DEA officers were investigating approximately sixty cases of methamphetamine manufacture and/or traffic in the Central Valley. By May 2001, more than eight hundred cases were under investigation in the same region. Forty pounds of methamphetamine, properly cut, could yield $1–2 million on the street. By 2001, since more than one million pounds of waste were being produced by meth labs, the Central Valley began to have yet another form of environmental pollution, as meth by-products such as red phosphorus, hydrochloric acid, hydriodic acid, and deadly phosphine seeped into the soil. By 2001 it was costing taxpayers $10 million a year to clean up seized or abandoned meth lab sites throughout the Central Valley.

With that much methamphetamine being produced in California, just exactly who was buying? Not just street people, as it turned out. On June 27, 2001, Kristin Rossum, a twenty-four-year-old alleged meth addict and the daughter of a Claremont McKenna College professor, appeared shackled in a San Diego courtroom. She faced charges of poisoning her twenty-six-year-old husband, who, angered over an affair that his wife was allegedly having with her supervisor, had threatened to reveal her alleged addiction and the fact that she was allegedly stealing the drug from the storeroom of the San Diego County Medical Examiner Office, where she worked as a toxicologist. The spectacle of Rossum, so obviously a daughter of upper-middle-class California, manacled in a prison jumpsuit and standing tearfully in court at her arraignment, could very well be linked, in part, to the influence of a drug worse than heroin, worse than cocaine in its effects, experts pointed out, cooked by Mexican crime families and assorted white trash in rundown shacks throughout central California.

Marijuana grower B. E. Smith of Trinity County, in the far north of the state, by contrast, had no intention of meeting a violent end. The marijuana community had spent the first half of the decade trying to go legitimate, in preparation for the passage of Proposition 215 in 1996, which authorized the medical uses of marijuana and allowed patients and caregivers with a doctor's prescription to use pot to control anxiety and pain. The very passage of Proposition 215 by the electorate underscored the deep-seated sympathy for marijuana by Californians of a certain age who had smoked pot in the 1960s and 1970s. In those days, growers such as Smith, a Vietnam veteran who had gone "from John Wayne to Timothy Leary" in the course of his psychological development, had retreated into the Emerald Triangle backcountry where Trinity, Mendocino, and Humboldt Counties met, to grow cannabis in remote, safe sites. For Trinity County, marijuana soon became the leading cash crop. The center of its pot trade was the hamlet of Denny, styled by drug enforcement officers in the early 1980s as "the most lawless town in America." There, Smith and his wife, paradoxically a born-again Christian ("It's one of God's miracles," said Mary Gale Smith of her marriage), lived in a rustic cabin crowded with law books. While Smith, in his own words, had "turned his back on the hypocrisy of society," he nevertheless felt it prudent to master society's laws. Better to be a grower-lawyer, Smith philosophized, than a jailhouse lawyer; or, as he put it even more succinctly: "I'm an honest criminal. I've never denied what I do." With the passage of Proposition 215, Smith was in the position to put himself forward as a caregiver. He had been arrested only one time in his life, for violating the motorcycle helmet law; and his marijuana had been featured in *High Times,* the pot smokers' magazine, with a photograph of Smith, tall, rangy, weather-beaten, mustachioed, standing proudly alongside his twelve-foot plants. And besides: Smith, now in his early fifties, had never had another drink of alcohol since, at the age of thirty-two, he had first smoked pot.[2]

Unfortunately, marijuana—despite the efforts of the marijuana lobby and such an appealing poster boy as B. E. Smith—was inextricably part of larger and interactive patterns of drug and alcohol abuse, especially among teenagers. Actor Robert Downey Jr., for example, who went to jail in December 1997 for six months for violating probation on a 1996 drug conviction and whose life was otherwise in a mess, had, like most drug offenders, begun his career smoking pot when barely into his teens. Marijuana was available in most high schools, public and private, throughout the state, and in many junior high schools as well. The early 1990s witnessed the arrival of an entire generation of teenage Californians who had started to smoke pot and drink alcohol on a serious basis when barely into high school, if not before. Lisa Parker of Covina, a west Los Angeles County suburb, began drinking vodka at the age of eleven, then went on to marijuana and cocaine. While still in junior high school, she was selling speed out of her locker and inhaling butane. At fourteen she committed her first burglary to support her habit. By eighteen she was an emaciated addict with an iron cross tattooed on her back, a legacy of hanging out with skinheads. By twenty, she was clean and sober and had recovered most of her good looks. How exactly Parker had found the courage—or the grace—to turn herself in to the Tustin Hospital Medical Center in June 1989 at age eighteen remained a mystery. But by November 1991 she was living clean, day by day, kneeling before her bed each night to say her prayers—though she was still a fan of punk rock.

Not everyone would get off so easy. Busted by Brea police in January 1998 for possession of methamphetamine, seventeen-year-old Chad Mac-Donald Jr. of Yorba Linda had worked—just once, police claimed—as an undercover informant in exchange for leniency, although the Brea police claimed that he was not working for them the day he and his sixteen-year-old girlfriend ran afoul of drug dealers Jose Ibarra, Michael Martinez, and Florence Noriega in Norwalk. "She'll take five bullets," Florence Noriega had said of MacDonald's girlfriend, who remained unidentified as a minor, "so load it all the way up." Miraculously, the young woman survived being raped, shot in the face, and dumped in a culvert near the San Gabriel Reservoir. Six days later, Chad MacDonald's body was found in an alley in Norwalk.[3] A state law was subsequently passed prohibiting the use of minors as undercover informants, unless authorized by a judge, and MacDonald's mother and stepfather sued the cities of Brea and Yorba Linda for $10 million on a charge of wrongful death. Convicted of first-degree murder, the three dealers were sentenced to life without possibility of parole when jurors deadlocked in the penalty phase over the death penalty. During the very time they were being sentenced in superior court at Norwalk, the trio chatted and laughed among themselves. "I see no remorse," a visibly frustrated Judge Dewey Falcone stated from the bench. "I see smiling and smirking. I have sentenced each of you to the maximum sentence possible. You are never going to get out. And if the death sentence could have been imposed, I would have imposed [it]."[4]

Chad MacDonald was a middle-class California teenager, as were most teenage marijuana users: youngsters such as the fifteen-year-old, recently bar mitzvahed Nick Markowitz of West Hills near Van Nuys in Los Angeles County. Raised in solidly middle-class circumstances, Nick adored his older half brother Ben, aged twenty-two, a drug dealer, and was himself an avid user of marijuana. Ben Markowitz owed other West Valley dealers a large sum of money for youthful street sellers, $36,000. Unable to get to Ben, the dealers, headed by a twenty-year-old thug improbably named Jesse James Hollywood, happened upon Nick one summer evening in August 2000 when they were heading toward the Markowitz family home to break windows in protest of Ben's nonpayment. The dealers, who had grown up with Ben, playing baseball together as kids, gave Nick a severe beating. A passerby, Pauline Ann Mahoney, driving home from church with her children, saw the incident and called 911.

Somehow, the police fumbled the call; and Nick was not only beaten but thrown into a van and driven north to Santa Barbara as a hostage against his brother's debt. Over the next few days, he was held in rather friendly circumstances by a growing group of druggies in their late teens and early

twenties, engaged in a nonstop drug and alcohol party at various locations
in Santa Barbara. Jesse James Hollywood's father, Jack Hollywood, found
out about the kidnapping and got in touch with a lawyer. The lawyer told
Jack Hollywood that his son had already contacted him regarding the kidnapping and that he had informed Jesse of the seriousness of the offense. By
this time, a number of young people in Jesse's circle were aware that Nick
Markowitz was being held hostage; yet no one said anything. Even Nick
himself did not seem to be that worried. But Wednesday morning he was
taken to a remote campsite outside Santa Barbara, bound and gagged, and
shot nine times with a TEC-9 pistol. Four young men were arraigned on
charges of kidnapping and murder. Jesse James Hollywood has remained at
large.

The cases of Chad MacDonald and Nick Markowitz underscored the
fact that doing drugs, by definition, meant dealing with dangerous people,
even if some of them had grown up playing baseball with your older
brother. MacDonald's drug of choice had been methamphetamine, which
most teenagers correctly considered more dangerous than marijuana, Nick
Markowitz's preferred narcotic; yet pot had a way of leading to hard drugs,
and by the end of the decade, in the Bay Area especially, heroin use had
reached epidemic proportions among the affluent and college bound. Such
scions of privilege, for example, as Nicholas Traina, the nineteen-year-old
son of best-selling novelist Danielle Steel, and Oscar Scaggs, the twenty-
one-year-old son of blues rocker Boz Scaggs, each lost his life in a heroin
overdose. By 1998 heroin was costing a mere five dollars a hit, down from a
hundred in the early 1990s, and had climbed in its purity from 5 percent to
between 60 and 80 percent. So powerful was late 1990s heroin that it could
be smoked, and thus not leave telltale arm tracks, which made it even more
appealing to upscale kids. It also made it easy to overdose on, as happened
to Traina and Scaggs, and the other sixteen San Franciscans who died of
overdoses in December 1998 and the first week of January 1999. By 1998,
some one hundred San Franciscans were dying each year from overdoses of
heroin, a fivefold increase from the early 1980s; and the BART station at
16th and Mission had emerged as ground zero of the Bay Area heroin trade.
"All I know is that whenever I walk down 16th Street," stated one resident
of the neighborhood, "it looks like a scene out of *Night of the Living
Dead*."[5]

Killing Time

The 1990s seemed a good time for murder as well as for drugs as Californians shot, stabbed, choked, bludgeoned, or otherwise dispatched each other in impressive numbers. In less than three months, in the first quarter of 1992, there were fifty-five homicides in the city of Oakland, prompting Mayor Elihu Harris to declare an emergency. In California, Southern California especially, even doing ordinary things, such as driving on the freeway, could prove dangerous. Many such freeway shootings (and there were enough of them to indicate a trend) had the earmarks of gangland and/or drug-related paybacks. Yet road rage could also be a factor. In most cases, innocent drivers became the victims of the drivers' road rage. In the case of Delfina Gonzales Morales, forty-two, a grandmother who had just dropped her grandchild off at school, road rage backfired. Incensed by being cut off on the Golden State Freeway near Sylmar one busy commute morning in January 1998, Morales tailgated and taunted the offending van, flashing her lights, honking her horn, and making obscene gestures, until she went into a spinout and crashed head-on into a truck, killing herself and her twenty-six-year-old daughter Maria Laura.

Being on the road could be dangerous for all Californians, including the privileged and the well-known. Ennis Cosby, a twenty-seven-year-old doctoral candidate in special education at Columbia University and the son of comedian Bill Cosby, pulled his Mercedes-Benz convertible to the side of the Skirball Center Drive off-ramp on the San Diego (405) Freeway at approximately one-thirty a.m., January 16, 1997, to deal with a flat tire. While changing his tire, Cosby was gunned down in a botched robbery attempt by nineteen-year-old Mikail Markhasev, who approached Cosby from a nearby park-and-ride lot, where he and two other friends had been using a pay phone to line up a drug transaction.

An epidemic of carjackings erupted in the first half of the decade. Between September 17 and October 23, 1992, thirty-five carjackings were reported in San Francisco alone, none of them, fortunately, involving fatalities. Other carjack victims were not so lucky. Terrence Booker of Gardena in south central Los Angeles County, a twenty-six-year-old pharmacy worker and the married father of three small children, lost his life to gunfire one Sunday morning in May 1994 in the course of delivering groceries to a housebound friend when two young men hijacked his customized Chevrolet Impala. The following November, eighteen-year-old West Hills college freshman Manuel Toste of Tulare was killed in a similar incident in the Fresno County community of Coalinga. "Don't you believe in God?" Toste had asked his six teenage hijackers before one of them shot him in cold blood.[6]

Equally cold-blooded was the execution of seven people gangland style, with a single bullet to the head, Saturday night before closing time at Carrillo's Club in Fresno by two gunmen in May 1993. The ruthless execution of nightclub owner Reyes Carrillo, his elderly mother, his half brother, a cook and his wife, a bouncer, and a lingering customer most likely had something to do with drugs. If so, the murders certainly set new standards for drug killings in California. (The famous Chicago St. Valentine's Day Massacre had also resulted in seven deaths.) But the Fresno killings seemed to pass almost immediately into oblivion. No culprits were ever apprehended or charged.

Where were such people coming from? Californians were asking themselves. These were not crimes of passion. This was killing for its own sake—killing way beyond the necessities of robbery, killing devoid of passion, devoid even of payback or revenge, devoid of any interpretive framework beyond the enjoyment of cold-blooded killing itself. Late one weekend evening in March 1991, two South Pasadena teenagers, David Adkins, seventeen, and Vincent Hebrock, eighteen, after a ten-hour beer and marijuana party at the home of Kathy Macaulay, eighteen, in the affluent hillside Annandale neighborhood of Pasadena, used a Mossberg twelve-gauge shotgun, appropriated from the Macaulay household (the parents were out of town), to execute (or smoke, as Vinny put it) Macaulay and two other girls, seventeen-year-old Danae Palermo and eighteen-year-old Heather Goodwin. In the days to come, the details of both the crime and the background of its perpetrators and victims—the broken homes, the early drug use, the early-appearing delinquency, the permissive parents, the bizarre and abusive relationships passing for social life—provided a scenario in which South Pasadena became not the Norman Rockwell place that it appeared (or pretended) to be, but a suburban enclave of drug- and alcohol-abusing teenagers and permissive, negligent parents. Two years later, after a painful trial, Adkins, now nineteen, was off to life in prison without possibility of parole, and Hebrock, now twenty, was given fifty-one years to life.

"Don't you believe in God?" Manuel Toste had asked his carjackers before they shot him point-blank on the road outside Coalinga. One might ask a similar question about belief in the devil when confronted by the rape-murder spree perpetrated by bartender James Daveggio and his girl-friend Michelle Michaud in the fall and winter of 1997. Michaud was a Pleasanton-based single parent, raising a daughter and a son. She was also a heavy-drinking part-time prostitute who dabbled in witchcraft. Daveggio was an outlaw-biker type who had already served time for sexual assault. Michaud and Daveggio were made for each other. They drank and took methamphetamines together. Michaud introduced Daveggio to witchcraft. She also trolled for other prostitutes to be put to Daveggio's service. Michaud and Daveggio drank and drugged and whored themselves into penury. Michaud sold her furniture on the lawn outside her home to pay for booze and drugs. Daveggio bilked his pals in the Devils Horsemen biker club out of $1,500. Sometime in early September, the pair, now evicted from Michaud's home, moved into their minivan and began a spree of abduction and bisexual rape, beginning with the thirteen-year-old daughter of a close friend. Two abduction-rapes later (the victims were a female college student and a twelve-year-old female relative of Michaud's), in late November, the couple found themselves cruising the Pleasanton area on the lookout for yet another victim. They found twenty-two-year-old Vanessa Lei Samson, walking to work. This time, Daveggio and Michaud added murder to abduction and rape, dumping Samson's body down a snowy embankment on Highway 88 in remote Alpine County.

All things considered, it seemed rather too easy to become a murder victim in California in the 1990s. Vanessa Samson did not know her abductors; she was merely walking to work. Eighteen-year-old Michele Montoya, a popular senior and cheerleader, was raped and murdered in the woodshop of Rio Linda High School, near Sacramento, by the substitute custodian, Alex Del Thomas. Thomas was a member of the 107th Street Hoover Crips gang in Los Angeles recently paroled from Folsom Prison, where he had served time for voluntary manslaughter and armed robbery. (Applying for the school job, Del Thomas had covered the gang tattoo on his forehead with makeup.) The slaying prompted a law barring the hiring of felons convicted of violent or serious crimes for nonteaching jobs at public schools.

School could be dangerous, and school parties as well, even on the college level, as in the case of the gunfire that broke out on the first Sunday afternoon of April 1992 at a fraternity-sorority picnic in Woodley Park in

Van Nuys in the San Fernando Valley. It was a UCLA affair, upscale, organized by the National Pan-Hellenic Council, an umbrella group representing African-American fraternities and sororities nationwide. Bad guys with
guns, however, crashed the fifteen-hundred-person event and began to
harass young women. When other young men asked them to leave, they
pretended to do so, but then returned from their cars with guns, firing indiscriminately into the crowd, killing Charles Wright, twenty-two, of Los
Angeles, and Eric Carver, twenty-three, of Carson, and wounding a number
of others.

It could be dangerous, in other words, even if you had made it into college. The danger was compounded if you were black; but even white university students lived in the constant presence of the possibility of street
violence. UC Berkeley sophomore John Mastny, walking home from campus through downtown Berkeley on a weeknight in late October 1992, was
shot dead on the street when he did not produce his wallet quickly enough
for the young man with a gun demanding money. By the 1990s, robbery and
murder, often for no apparent purpose or just to eliminate a witness, had
become an everyday event. Twenty-five-year-old Juan Mercado, delivering
pizza in Oakland from the Four Star Pizza and Deli Restaurant owned by
his family, was shot to death at point-blank range by street youths when
Mercado did not deliver fast enough through his car window the pizzas the
young men were demanding. Ana Yu, a jewelry store owner in Pasadena,
was killed by a fifteen-year-old gunman in April 1993 in the course of a
robbery. The teenage shooter then dispatched Yu's eleven-year-old son
Johnny with a bullet to his head. As Laurie Myles, thirty-four, of North
Hills, was exiting her car in front of the Shepherd of the Hills Baptist
Church in the San Fernando Valley, two young men demanded her purse.
Myles quickly complied, but one of the robbers shot her to death anyway, in
the presence of her nine-year-old son.

Self-slaughter, frequently following the slaughter of others, continued
through the 1990s at normal statistical rates in comparison to the rest of the
nation, although certain instances of self-immolation possessed a film-
scripted theatricality one is tempted to see as Californian. On the last day of
April 1998, Daniel Jones, a forty-year-old HIV-positive resident of Long
Beach, thoroughly dissatisfied with his HMO, decided to take his protest
public by committing suicide on the transition loop from the Harbor to the
Century Freeway in South Central Los Angeles. Unfurling a large banner
reading "HMO's Are in It for the Money!! Live Free. Love Safe or Die,"
Jones held police and traffic at bay, sitting in his Molotov cocktail–laden
pickup truck in the company of Gladdis, a seven-year-old Labrador-
whippet mix, as television helicopters whirred overhead. When his cache of

Molotov cocktails accidentally ignited, burning the dog to death, Jones jumped from his truck, his pants and socks in flames. Peeling off the burning garments, Jones wandered about for a spell, seemingly disoriented, as police watched cautiously. Finally, he retrieved a shotgun from the bed of his burning truck and turned it on himself as thousands of television viewers watched on live TV.

An even more certain means of self-slaughter during the decade was joining a gang. The 1990s witnessed a *Walpurgisnacht* of gang-related slayings: eight hundred for Los Angeles County alone in 1992, up from 771 the previous year. And this despite a truce arranged between the Crips and the Bloods in the aftermath of the Los Angeles riots. When a history of Los Angeles/Southern California street gangs is published, two memoirs, both written at the peak of the violence—Luis Rodriguez's *Always Running: La Vida Loca: Gang Days in L.A.—A Memoir* (1993) and *Monster: The Autobiography of an L.A. Gang Member* (1993) by Sanyika Shakur, a.k.a. Monster Kody Scott—will undoubtedly constitute classic sources and controlling texts. With precise, chilling detail, Rodriguez and Shakur chronicled how an entire generation of young men, African-American and Latino, became enamored of violence and entered a culture of death. While most young men were marking their progress through life via a sequence of first communions, confirmations, bar mitzvahs, and graduations, gangbangers most vividly knew only one ritual of passage: the funeral. One twenty-eight-year-old Crip attended thirty funerals in 1991 alone. Week in and week out, local neighborhoods witnessed elaborate wakes, funeral services, and cemetery interments as homeboys and relatives said good-bye to those who had fallen. A procession of more than five hundred accompanied the funeral cortege of James "Cadillac Jim" Shelton Jr., twenty-nine, a high-level Original Gangster, from the Angelus Funeral Home on Crenshaw Boulevard to the Forest Lawn Memorial Park in Glendale. Prior to interment, Cadillac Jim's body had rested in an open casket surrounded by blue garlands—blue being the color of the Crips. During the wake, many gangbangers, flashing hand signs, their colors held aloft, had themselves photographed by the open casket.

Florists in certain Los Angeles neighborhoods grew skilled in combining floral patterns with gang-color ribbons. Other vendors specialized in producing custom-made sweatshirts and T-shirts with stylized messages honoring the departed. James McCarty, chief embalmer at the Angelus Funeral Home, used a special putty to rebuild faces shredded by gunfire. Clergy such as the Reverend Modesto Leon, who had officiated at 106 gang wakes and funerals by March 1992, tried to use the occasion, subtly, to preach against gang violence. Over at the Dolores Mission, Jesuit Father

Gregory Boyle, while he allowed gang regalia, tried to downplay talk of revenge during the wake and following services. Funerals themselves could be the occasions of further violence. Gregory Williams's girlfriend and thirteen-month-old son were gunned down outside a liquor store when a drug deal in which Williams was involved went bad. Williams and his homeboys retaliated with their own spree of drive-bys. During the funeral of Williams's girlfriend and son (eight hundred people were in attendance, costing Williams $7,000 in drug earnings), a thirty-second barrage of gunfire erupted as the caskets were being lowered into the ground.

Whatever the causes of such repetitive violence (and there were many— poverty, racism, drugs, the normal desire of male teenagers to bond and gain peer acceptance, the absence of attentive fathers, the pervasive alienation in neighborhoods left behind in the rapid rise of Los Angeles, codes of honor rooted deeply in Mexican culture, comparable codes among American blacks), generations of young men, starting in the 1970s and continuing through the rest of the century, found themselves inducted almost beyond their will into a culture of turf-based gang loyalty, with an increasing capacity for violence that would leave the majority of them dead or serving prison terms before they reached twenty-one. A growing number of innocent bystanders, lingering on their porches, attending a baby shower, sitting or playing on their lawns, would also meet a violent end as, beginning in the mid-1980s and increasing steadily, drive-by shootings became the preferred tactic of gangbangers. By the time Luis Rodriguez had turned eighteen, he had lost twenty-five friends to gang shootings, overdoses, car crashes, suicides, and killings by police. Rodriguez's basic explanation for gang behavior among Latinos was the fact that they perceived themselves as outcasts in Anglo society, as he did growing up in the Las Lomas barrio east of Los Angeles: forbidden to speak Spanish in school as a boy, peeing in his pants when he did not know how to ask the teacher in English to go to the bathroom. Others might point to the fact that gangbanging, like all forms of evil, possessed its own distinctive thrill. "I lived for the power surge of playing God," remembered Monster Kody Scott, "having the power of life and death in my hands. Nothing I knew of could compare with riding in a car with three other homeboys with guns, knowing that they were as deadly and courageous as I was. To me, at that time in my life, this was power."[7]

Police attributed more than twenty 1991 murders, directly or indirectly, to one gang member: Cleamon "Big Evil" Johnson, leader of the 89 Family Bloods of South Central Los Angeles. As a gangland figure, Johnson, perhaps more than any other gang leader, embodied the power of gangbanging as an assimilative culture, possessed of its own distinctive attraction. Born to two attentive parents and raised in a three-bedroom home on 88th Street with a porch and a backyard and a pigeon coop, Johnson had belonged to Boy Scout Troop 374 and earned merit badges. Neighbors knew him as a cheerful, polite little guy who would help women tote their grocery bags into the house. In 1970, however, when Johnson was three, the Crips and the Bloods organized; and by the time Johnson was in the seventh grade, a mosaic of gangs, affiliated with either the Crips or the Bloods, had turned South Central Los Angeles into a war zone. When Johnson was eight, in 1975, on a sweltering summer afternoon, he received his first introduction to the new neighborhood order. He and an older friend were hanging out near a street-corner fire hydrant at 84th and Towne when a car pulled up. Two teenagers got out and opened fire with automatic weapons in retaliation for some gang-related offense that did not even involve the boys. Johnson escaped unhurt, but his friend was killed. Within a year, Johnson witnessed a second murder. His acculturation to gang life was well under way.

By the next decade, as leader of the 89 Family Bloods, Johnson was himself setting new records for mayhem. He had most likely personally murdered thirteen people, and had ordered the death of at least seven others. In 1994 the LAPD, the district attorney's office, and the FBI formed the 89 Family Task Force to deal, in effect, with Johnson alone. Frequently arrested and arraigned, Johnson was never brought to trial due to the absence of material witnesses. At least four potential witnesses were murdered. Not until 1997 was District Attorney Gil Garcetti capable of finding one cooperative (and living) witness to a Johnson murder, a certain Freddie Jelks, himself facing life in prison for homicide. Jelks testified that Johnson sat on the porch of his parents' home on the afternoon of August 5, 1991, and ordered the assassination, by Uzi, of two innocent, nongang young men as they waited at a car wash on 88th Street and Central Avenue. Why were Donald Ray Loggins, a cable company installer, married and the father of a five-month-old son, and his friend Payton Beroit killed? Because they lived east of Central Avenue in Crips territory, and Johnson wanted to provide a newly recruited Blood, Michael "Fat Rat" Allen, an opportunity to earn his gang membership. In December 1997, Big Evil Johnson and Fat Rat Allen received the death penalty for the murders.

Hundreds of Californians, many of them children, lost their lives just because they happened to be caught in fields of fire. Awareness that gang-banging constituted a danger to society at large crystallized in January 1988, when Karen Toshima, a twenty-seven-year-old Studio City advertising executive, window-shopping with a friend on Broxton Avenue, in the otherwise safe and supposedly gang-free Westside, was shot to death on the sidewalk by South Central gang member Durrell DeWitt "Baby Rock" Collins of the Rolling 60s Crips, one of the most violent gangs in the city.

At the time, Collins was busy shooting it out with a rival gangster, Tyrone Swain of the Mansfield Hustler Crips. Toshima's death forced Los Angelenos to face the fact that gang violence had jumped 50 percent over the past few years and was, for all practical purposes, out of control.

By the early 1990s, gang culture had spread throughout metropolitan Los Angeles, to include the Pomona-Claremont area in the eastern edge of the county. In South Bay, in a full-scale daybreak raid in early April 1998, police pulled in more than twenty suspects in a gang-affiliated stolen property ring. Some of the young men swept up in the dragnet were also suspects in various cases of armed robbery, carjacking, and grand theft. Needless to say, tensions ran high throughout South Bay in the following days, which was no surprise to mailmen on Route 4922 on and around Chadron Avenue, who were accustomed to being accosted, taunted, and sometimes even beaten by gang members. Eventually, the Los Angeles Sheriff's Department was forced to send one officer in a patrol car to accompany every mailman on the 4922 beat.

For the racially tense, poverty-stricken Oakwood district of Venice, the ascendancy of gang culture might be expected; but gang activity by its very nature was a moveable feast, and in October 1998 Santa Monica—a prosperous, liberal, largely white city—found itself the scene of a spate of gangland killings. On October 12, a fifty-year-old German tourist was shot to death outside the Loews Santa Monica Beach Hotel, and Omar Sevilla, a twenty-two-year-old former member of a Culver City street gang, was gunned down outside Santa Monica High School. The next weekend, in retaliation for Sevilla's death, Juan Martin Campos, twenty-eight, was killed in a liquor store; and the next day, Jaime Cruz, twenty-five, a former gang member now attending UCLA, was shot and severely wounded outside his home. A few days later, most horrendously, two non–gang members, Anthony Juarez, nineteen, and his brother Michael, twenty-seven, visiting Santa Monica from San Luis Obispo County, were shot in a hip-hop clothing store owned by their cousin in what police labeled a random retaliatory attack.

Homeboys

G ang culture, meanwhile, had solidly established itself in northern California as well, with similar patterns of gang formation and violence. By October 1992, Alameda County law enforcement officials were tracking 125 gangs, fifty-three of them in Oakland. Union City alone supported four rival gangs, for a total of some two hundred gang members. The recruitment process began early, as Union City police discovered when an eleven-year-old boy stabbed a motorist to death in an obvious effort to impress older gang members. Like the Mission district in San Francisco across the Bay, which also supported a number of active gangs, Union City was tough, gritty, and minority dominated. Gang activity was also expected in the teeming barrios of San Jose at the southern end of the Bay, the third largest city in the state, where Nuestra Familia and the Mexican Mafia vied for hegemony. These two rival gangs had been pitted against each other since the day in 1968 in the exercise yard at San Quentin when Nuestra Familia was formed as a northern California resistance to the Southern California–dominated Mexican Mafia. Each of these prison-based gangs had non-prison-based affiliates. Claiming the color red and the number fourteen, symbol of the Northern Star, Nuestra Raza (also called the Northern Structure) grew as a nonprison affiliate of Nuestra Familia throughout the 1980s. Nuestra Raza members dealt successfully in drug selling and related activities throughout the 1980s, until a three-year internecine war, beginning in 1990, claimed ten victims, and the Nuestra Raza leadership went into meltdown. Nuestra Familia gang leaders stood trial for these murders in June 1997.

One of the gangs to emerge in Long Beach in this period, the Asian Boyz, became especially active in Van Nuys. In April 1995, the Cambodian, Vietnamese, and Filipino members of the Asian Boyz, in an effort to win notoriety and hegemony for their gang, embarked on a one-year crime spree of heroic proportions. The Asian Boyz already had shown their capacity for mayhem when in 1993 two gang members shot a man to death at a Sylmar drag race because he had honked his horn in their direction. But this was insignificant compared to the gang's thirteen murders, dozens of attempted murders, assaults, robberies, and home invasions during their April 1995 to April 1996 reign of terror—crimes that yielded the gang a total of more than half a million dollars.

But hegemony as well as money was on their minds. Choosing Tet, the Vietnamese New Year, to begin their spree, the Asian Boyz on April 14, 1995, ambushed members of the Valerio Street gang in the mostly Asian-occupied Valerio Gardens apartment complex. The Valerio gang thought they were going to a fistfight, but the Asian Boyz opened up with an M-16 machine gun, killing two and wounding four, including a bystander. The following August, the Asian Boyz opened fire on rival gang members from one car to another on the Santa Monica Freeway. Leaning Hollywood style out their car windows, the Asian Boyz killed three rival gang members with their automatic weapons. They killed two others outside the Covina Bowl in the San Gabriel Valley. In the summer of 1995, the gang began to kill almost indiscriminately, just for the fun of it, just to achieve a reputation. Asian Boyz trailed two carloads of teenagers, for example, driving home from the Family Fun Park, and shot them up, killing one. When Asian Boyz member Cu Doung agreed to testify, it looked like the district attorney had finally built a case; but the gang killed Doung the day before his court appearance. Eight Asian Boyz, at long last, went on trial in September 1998, but the gang was still capable of having the father of one potential witness assassinated at his home in San Jose.

Chinatown Los Angeles was the turf of another ferocious group, the Oriental Lazy Boys. On February 25, 1996, the gang shot to death Oscar-winning Cambodian actor Haing Ngor in the carport of his Beaudry Avenue apartment. Ngor had already handed over his $6,000 Rolex watch but had refused to part with a gold locket containing a picture of his late wife, who had died in childbirth. The three Oriental Lazy Boys—Tak Sun Tan, Jason Chan, and Indra Lim—were high on crack cocaine at the time. Trained as a physician in Cambodia, Ngor had won an Academy Award for his role in the 1984 film *The Killing Fields,* which detailed the murderous rampage of the Khmer Rouge in 1975; this ensured that his death, in contrast to so many other gang-related killings, would receive more than passing notice in the newspapers.

In the aftermath of the Los Angeles riots in April and May 1992, leaders from the Crips and the Bloods announced a truce. For the time being at least, the agreement yielded a 50 percent drop in drive-by shootings, though the South Bureau of the LAPD still reported eighty-five drive-bys in the six weeks following the riots.

So many of these victims were African Americans, killed by African Americans; and that was terrible enough. But in the early 1990s a pattern of African-American gang retaliation against Latinos was emerging as well, especially in South Central Los Angeles, where the Latino population was rapidly becoming ascendant. Murderous conflict was especially noticeable in and around such South Central housing projects as Nickerson Gardens and Jordan Downs, where Latinos constituted about a third of the six thousand residents. The LAPD refused to list the race of either the crime victims or the perpetrators in South Central, claiming that the Southeast Division station did not have the resources to keep such statistics. Perhaps this was true, but it was perhaps also true that the LAPD did not want to exacerbate a near epidemic of violence against Latinos by African-American gang members in the terrible year of 1993, lest Latino gangs be encouraged to retaliate, and a full-scale gang war break out.

Interestingly, it was the very godfathers of Latino gang crime, the men of the prison-based Mexican Mafia, who tried to put a lid on things. On the afternoon of September 18, 1993, on orders from the Mexican Mafia, more than a thousand Latino gang members, representing sixty thousand Latino gang members organized into more than 450 gangs throughout Los Angeles County, converged on Elysian Park near Dodger Stadium for a summit. Present were members of the 18th Street gang, probably the largest Latino gang in Los Angeles County, and Mara Salvatrucha, the most powerful of the Central American gangs and a thorn in the side of their Mexican-American counterparts. Each gangbanger was frisked upon entering the park and asked to lift his shirt to reveal gang tattoos in order to screen out possible infiltrators. Throughout the afternoon, just a few dozen yards from the Los Angeles Police Academy, as unmarked patrol cars passed and repassed the gathering and police helicopters circled overhead, representatives of the Mexican Mafia, grizzled veterans in their forties and fifties, pounded home a simple message to clusters of teenage gangbangers: too many innocent bystanders were being killed in sloppy drive-by shootings. This was bad for business. If one gang had a beef with another, the two should face each other off in strictly gang circumstances, not shoot up an entire street. "They were saying," a gang member at the meeting later reported, " 'No more drive-bys. They're cowardly. We're killing our kids and grandparents. Anybody who does this is going to pay the price.' "[8]

The whole affair possessed a strong note of surreality. Here was La Eme (the Spanish pronunciation for the letter *M*), the Mexican Mafia, the mother of all gangs, with up to six hundred members in the California penal system and perhaps twice as many affiliates or sympathizers on the outside, intervening on behalf of innocent bystanders. In one sense, the Elysian Park summit represented a clash of generations; the leaders of La Eme were mostly middle-aged, and hence by definition veterans of the pre-Uzi, pre-drive-by era. Such men, though hardened and vicious, had lived their lives by a code in an organization founded behind bars in the late 1950s. They represented, in effect, organized crime, in contrast to the chaotic disorganization of the present generation of teenage gangbangers. If you must kill, La Eme was saying, kill competently, with honor and for a reason. Within two years, however, the Mexican Mafia would have its own problems, with twenty-two of its top leadership indicted under the RICO Act and twelve convicted in Los Angeles federal court on multiple counts of murder, drug distribution, extortion, conspiracy, and racketeering. Their transfer to federal prison upon their conviction and sentencing temporarily deprived the gang of its moderating role.

Gang truces, of course, however negotiated, were by definition temporary affairs; gangbanging had long since become a culture, and truces only addressed the symptoms of the underlying dysfunction. In the aftermath of the 1992 Los Angeles riots, Compton mayor Walter Tucker and former football star Jim Brown played key roles in negotiating a truce between the Crips and the Bloods in South Central. Most affected by the truce were the three largest housing projects in Watts: Nickerson Gardens, Imperial Courts, and Jordan Downs. For a few months gang members could move from place to place without fear of violating another gang's turf. In late May 1992, more than sixteen hundred gangbangers from mortal-enemy organizations converged on Imperial Courts for a love fest. They drank from common forty-ounce bottles of Old English 800 and traded high fives. Many confessed to being on another gang's turf for the first time in their lives.

Public high schools had long since become dangerous places. Robert Barner, principal of Manual Arts High School in Los Angeles, was estimating that by November 1991 he had some two hundred gang members in his school out of a student body of 2,500. Once again, there was the ever-present obsession with turf, as members of the 18th Street gang staked out the area near the student store as their own, while the Rolling 30s and the Hoover Crips marked their territories at opposite ends of the campus eating area. With some element of personal risk, Barner insisted that there be no gang clothes—no knit caps, no oversize baggy pants, no trousers with slits at the bottom—or insignia worn on campus. A student with a gang tattoo under one eye was told to cover it with makeup or withdraw from school. The student threatened to have his homeboys turn the place inside out, but the matter became moot when the boy violated his parole and was sent back to juvenile detention camp. Two uniformed LAPD officers, armed with nine-millimeter Baretta pistols, patrolled the campus along with six unarmed security guards.

A key problem with gangs in high schools was the fact that gang culture and high school culture interpenetrated and admixed to the detriment of the student body. Since football rivalries were connected to specific high schools in specific parts of town, they could become gang rivalries as well. Crenshaw and Dorsey High Schools were a few miles apart in South Central LA and had a longstanding football rivalry. Black Peace Stone, a gang of Bloods from the Dorsey territory, had it in for Crips in the Crenshaw area. In 1989 this double-layer rivalry had erupted into gunfire when the football teams met in Jackie Robinson Stadium. When a sixteen-year-old Dorsey student was shot to death in front of the school in October 1991 in a gang-related shooting, Banning High School, a longtime Dorsey rival, canceled its upcoming game, to the shock and embarrassment of the school district. Local African-American leaders, led by Councilman Nate Holden, considered the cancellation a racial slur.

Still, Banning officials had a point. In an era of gangs, teenage culture wasn't what it had been in the past. In the 1950s, for example, boys of a certain sort were always rumbling. But when twenty-four-year-old Artur Karapetyan, an Armenian immigrant experienced in mediation, tried to intervene in one such rumble at Sunset Boulevard and Western Avenue one Sunday night in April 1998, a fistfight erupted into gunfire, and Karapetyan—a graduate of Hollywood High School, a printer in a small shop in North Hollywood who had recently started his own custom printing company—fell dead to the asphalt. What would have been a rumble in the 1950s was now deadly mayhem. Throughout the decade, similar stories could be told of troublesome teenage activities raised to new levels by gang culture. Graffiti or tagging, for example, constituted a culture parallel to gangbanging, without the violence, although here too the lines were being blurred: more and more taggers carried guns, and some were beginning to use them. In February 1993 a Reseda High School student was gunned down on campus in what was most likely a tagger-related killing.

By the end of the decade, yet another gang activity was appearing in this same age group, this time on the Internet. Cybergangs, they were called; teenage hackers in cyberspace sharing information on site break-ins and other forms of cybernetic mischief. As in the case of gangs and taggers, the cybergangs had their own patois, their own rituals, and their own *cursus honorum* of hacker stunts. Like tagging, cyberganging attracted middle-class teenagers with access to equipment, time on their hands, and a sociopathic bent. Like the gangs, they also showed loyalty to their own. When FBI investigators seized two hackers' computers in Cloverdale, Mendocino

County, in a sudden sting, members of the Enforcers cybergang posted threats against the government. Serious espionage, however, was not the usual cybergang hacker m.o. What was preferred was a form of Internet tagging: invading a site, messing it up, and sharing the good news with other gang members on the Web.

From this perspective, tagging and cybergangbanging participated in the larger phenomenon of Gang Chic, which by the 1990s was pervading music, clothing, and the jargon of more teenagers than there were gangbangers. Gangsta rap, after all, was bringing the most murderous sentiments of the gangland ghetto into the homes of the mostly white teenagers who bought such CDs. This was the same constituency, starting at the preteen level, for hip-hop fashions and gang-related insignia, a multimillion-dollar market. By the early 1990s, gang language, hip-hop clothing, and gangsta rap CDs were all popular among a wide spectrum of teenagers, who called each other "bro" or "G" (gangster) and had even mastered a more ominous vocabulary relating to violence. "Everyone is totally into inner-city street language," noted Rory Laverty, a seventeen-year-old white from Manhattan Beach, just graduated in June 1992 from the exclusive Chadwick School on the Palos Verdes Peninsula and heading to Amherst College in the fall. "There is a lot of yearning to be black."[9]

Among grown-ups, Gang Chic received its most significant shot of adrenaline in the aftermath of the Los Angeles riots when two allegedly retired gangbangers, Li'l Monster from the Eight-Tray Gangster Crips and Bone from the Athens Park Bloods, took to the national TV talk show circuit. Flown to New York by TV host Phil Donahue and chauffeured to and from their Park Avenue hotel and the NBC studio by limousine, Li'l Monster and Bone, convicted felons each (first-degree murder and attempted murder for Li'l Monster, assault with a deadly weapon for Bone), mesmerized Donahue's thirteen million viewers with a mixture of class-conscious ideology and tough street banter. Not since Leonard Bernstein threw a party for the Black Panthers in the late 1960s—prompting Tom Wolfe's classic satire *Radical Chic & Mau-Mauing the Flak Catchers* (1970)—had New York gone so gaga for the real thing: real gangbangers, albeit inactive and on parole, preaching a philosophy of neighborhood empowerment. Ted Koppel also became a fan and was soon on a first-name basis with his guests. On television, Koppel admitted he was "only slightly embarrassed to say that I liked them very much and was extremely impressed with a great deal of what they had to say." Arsenio Hall and Larry King called about a show, and the Reverend Jesse Jackson sent his best.[10]

A year later, Monster Kody Scott's *Autobiography of an L.A. Gang Member,* published by the Atlantic Monthly Press, received the same star treatment. Given a six-figure advance, Scott had written the book while serving a four-year sentence for robbery at Pelican Bay State Prison, the Devil's Island of California. In April 1993, prior to publication, Scott's lurid chronicle of gangland mayhem was excerpted in *Esquire,* embellished by a photograph of a fearsome Scott, buffed, tattooed, naked to the waist, wearing sunglasses, and holding a semiautomatic weapon. The photo, which was included on the cover of the book, was obviously intended to reprise a similar photo of Huey Newton from an earlier generation. The following July the book received a rave review from the skeptical and demanding Michiko Kakutani, who in the course of her *New York Times* career had sent innumerable books into oblivion. Kakutani's review, as in the case of any prominent *Times* critique, set the tone for a spate of favorable notices to follow, and Scott's book—despite protests from certain African Americans that it was all about African Americans killing other African Americans for the most trivial of purposes—sold more than 100,000 copies.

Gangbusters

The LAPD was not amused. Here was a gangbanger bragging about taking down other young men ("the Blood made a last dash from the car to the porch. I raised my weapon and he looked back—for a split second we communicated on another level—then I laid him down") and receiving in return a large advance, best-seller status, the regard and grudging respect of the intellectual community, and a movie option. In September 1995, Scott was paroled with a contract to serve as a consultant on the screenplay of his book. The following February, police pulled him over in Moreno Valley, where he was living, and discovered a gram of marijuana in his car. Scott went on the lam rather than take a drug test and evaded parole agents for almost three months. When agents from the 77th Street Division Special Problems unit finally arrested him in May 1996 at his family's home in South Central Los Angeles, Scott was signing autographs of his book for friends and neighbors in the 'hood.

Being a police officer in the environment of violence created by gang culture was dangerous. In 1993 alone, nine Southland law enforcement officers were shot to death in the line of duty. The group included Compton police officers Kevin Michael Burrell, a twenty-nine-year-old African American who had been affiliated with the Compton Police Department in one way or another since his days as an Explorer Scout, and James Wayne MacDonald, a twenty-three-year-old white reserve officer serving his last day on active duty at Compton before accepting a permanent position with the San Jose Police Department. Toward midnight on February 22, 1993, MacDonald and Burrell made what should have been a routine stop of a red pickup truck for a possible traffic violation. As MacDonald and Burrell approached the vehicle, near Rosecrans and Dwight Avenues, the occupants emerged firing. Although the officers were wearing bulletproof vests, both fell to the ground, stunned. One of the occupants of the truck ran up to the fallen men and shot them in the head, execution style. If distinctions could be made in such a tragedy, the loss of Burrell was especially shocking to the community; raised in Compton in a stable and flourishing family, he was especially noted for his personal style of policing in this gang-torn city of ninety thousand.

In some instances, police were simply being outdone by firepower. On the morning of February 28, 1997, in North Hollywood, police found themselves outrageously outgunned as two robbers brazenly fought their way out of a Bank of America with automatic weapons. Unable to cope with the fusillade of automatic fire being unleashed by the pair, LAPD officers were forced to commandeer weapons from a local sporting goods store. Although no officer was killed, a number were seriously wounded. While one of the robbers shot himself to death on live television, the other, Emil Matasareanu, severely wounded, was handcuffed and left to bleed to death on the asphalt, in what was either an administrative snafu or indifference on the part of the police or a combination of both.

The question of technology, including weapons technology, was very much on the minds of police departments through the decade, as gang-bangers and ordinary robbers such as the North Hollywood pair armed themselves with automatic firepower. A key antigang initiative of the decade was the Gang Research Evaluation and Tracking (GREAT) interstate computer tracking system, which listed and followed the movements of some 250,000 known gang members in California, Nevada, and Hawaii. Police and sheriff's deputies in Fresno County were especially grateful for the system, since it allowed them to track the four thousand gang members responsible for a half-dozen or more homicides from mid-decade onward, rising to a quarter of seventy slayings in the city of Fresno alone by 1998. Later in the decade, Fresno County police and the sheriff's department organized a Multi-Agency Gang Enforcement Consortium (MAGEC), combining the efforts of a dozen or so police, sheriff's, and other law enforcement departments.

Another gang-suppression technique, worked out in conjunction with district and city attorneys, was court-ordered curfews or injunctions. In April 1993, the city attorney of Los Angeles secured a twenty-two-point injunction against the Blythe Street gang in Panorama City, with specific reference to some 350 identified gangbangers. The order prohibited such identified persons from possessing portable radios, high-powered flashlights, radio scanners, cellular telephones, or other devices used in the drug trade. Also banned were hammers, pliers, screwdrivers, and other instruments used to dismantle stolen vehicles, spray-paint cans used to apply gang graffiti, and a long list of items—crowbars, razors, belt buckles, not to mention firearms—used as weapons. The injunction also established an eight p.m. to six a.m. curfew for all juvenile gang members in a 112-square-block area. The American Civil Liberties Union opposed the measure immediately. Mark Silverstein, staff attorney for the ACLU in Southern California, said it "violates the most fundamental principles of due process." The ACLU took this and other antigang injunctions to court, but the California Supreme Court upheld the use of court orders to counter gang activity.

The following month the Los Angeles City Council seriously entertained a measure banning all gang members from public parks and beaches, but the proposed ordinance was rejected as being too far-reaching. Still, as the decade progressed, injunctions and curfews were increasingly used as a key strategy of the antigang crusade. In August 1997 a Los Angeles Superior Court judge approved a preliminary injunction against the Pico Union–based 18th Street gang, the largest in Los Angeles County. The injunction, argued attorney Michael Genelin and other lawyers assigned to the DA's Hardcore Gang Division, was designed to end the 18th Street gang's hold on the Pico Union area. Emerging from the hearing, defiant young gang members flashed gang signs as they left the courthouse, and in one instance threw rocks at a reporter. "Gangbanging is never going to die," defiantly stated one fourteen-year-old named in the preliminary injunction. A heavily tattooed Carlos Abaunza, forty-six, who had helped found the 18th Street gang thirty-four years earlier, agreed. "We're not taking [the injunction] seriously," he said.[11]

Still, law enforcement officials now had a powerful weapon in their arsenal: a name-by-name injunction against gang members. In March 1998, LA's district attorney Gil Garcetti launched an injunction effort against forty named members of the Hollywood branch of Mara Salvatrucha. The suit sought to ban any two members of Mara Salvatrucha from "standing, sitting, walking, driving, gathering, or appearing anywhere in public view in the target area unless the individuals reside in the same dwelling unit." In May 1998 city and county prosecutors moved once again against the 18th Street gang through injunction, this time seeking a court order to restrict the activities of named individuals in the zone surrounding MacArthur and Shatto Parks.[12] If the ACLU was disturbed by these antigang injunctions, it went positively apoplectic in March 1998 when Sacramento County authorities revoked the parole of and rejailed gangsta rapper Shawn Thomas when he released a CD, *Til My Casket Drops,* extolling guns, gangbanging, and hostility toward law enforcement and the judicial system. Despite protests that Thomas's First Amendment rights were being violated, the Sacramento rapper was returned to the slammer. In pulling such a unilateral preemptive strike, the Sacramento County authorities came into conflict with one of the most powerful forces of the decade: community resistance to what many considered overpolicing.

Nothing, however—absolutely nothing—could compare with what was going on among the officers of the CRASH unit of the Rampart Division of the Los Angeles Police Department. The story began to unfold in mid-September 1999 as ex-CRASH officer Rafael Perez, thirty-two, having pled guilty to eight felony counts stemming from the theft of eight pounds of cocaine from an LAPD evidence room in early 1998, began to sing like the proverbial canary to investigators in an effort to keep his sentence to five years. Fueled by fear, remorse, and ample servings of pizza, the macho ex-marine and disgraced street cop described to investigators, as part of a plea bargain struck just a few hours before he was scheduled to go on trial, how the equally macho young officers of CRASH (Community Resources Against Street Hoodlums) became, in effect, the most badass gang in the city.

Located on the edge of the midcity Pico Union district, the Rampart Division had as its responsibility the area bounded by the Harbor Freeway on the east, Sunset Boulevard on the north, Normandie Avenue on the west, and the Santa Monica Freeway to the south. The eight-square-mile area had the densest population, largely Latino, west of the Mississippi, comprising in the main the working poor, disaffected immigrants, and transients. In 1992, at the height of the homicide epidemic in Los Angeles, the Rampart Division policed the most violent of the eighteen divisions in the Los Angeles Police Department. Active in Rampart territory were two of the largest and most effective gangs in Los Angeles, the 18th Street gang and Mara Salvatrucha. In 1979 Rampart had inaugurated the CRASH squad specifically to take on the gangs. Over the next twenty years, CRASH became the most formidable gang in the region, its members fully armed, acting under color of authority, and having at their disposal—provided they were willing to plant evidence and commit perjury, which they were—the remorseless resources of the criminal justice system.

As Perez continued to give testimony through late 1999 and early 2000 (two thousand pages of testimony by February 2000), and as his testimony began to be corroborated by investigators, a pattern of social anthropological transformation emerged. The gangbusters had become a gang: the CRASH officers had their own code of silence covering an increasing number of illegal activities; their own lingo (especially useful for radio communication); and their own gestures, secret hand signs, and party pads. CRASH officers, Perez told investigators, kept a one-bedroom apartment near the Rampart station where they had sex with local prostitutes or their girlfriends during duty hours. Some officers even dated the girlfriend associates of gang members, taking them to parties held by the CRASH unit at the party pad, or in various hotel rooms rented in the area and in the San

Fernando Valley, or at the favored hangout of CRASH officers, the Short-stop Bar on Sunset Boulevard near Dodger Stadium. At one party in the San Fernando Valley, Perez described how one officer had chugged a bottle of vodka and vomited from the balcony onto an elderly lady below. A little later, two other officers discharged their guns from the balcony, and the group fled the apartment like fraternity boys on a caper. On another outing, CRASH officers headed for Las Vegas, where they blew $21,000 in a single weekend. Perez himself—who once sold some $10,000 worth of cocaine back to dealers—was especially fond of life in the fast lane: the Vegas vacations, the cars, the booze, the hundred-dollar cigars, the women. Some CRASH officers went so far as to get tattooed with grinning skulls, just like regular gang members.

Living up to its motto—"We Intimidate Those Who Intimidate Others"—CRASH officers, Perez testified, treated the streets and people under Rampart jurisdiction as if the police were soldiers in enemy territory—or gang members on another gang's turf. Cruising the region, often in unmarked cars, CRASH officers would roust suspected gang members from street corners, line them up on the sidewalk with their hands over their heads, pat them down, and verbally intimidate them, all the while deciding if and when to plant evidence. The officers especially liked to crash gang parties: busting in, holding several dozen gang members down on their knees, yelling and posturing and showing dominance before taking one or another gang member off on trumped-up evidence. In one case, apprehending a gang member who they believed had slashed the tires of a CRASH officer's car, an officer and his partner stripped the gang member naked and dropped him off in rival territory. No Los Angeles gang could have exacted a more stylized revenge.

Planting evidence was commonplace. A sergeant at Rampart—the quarterback of the operation, according to one LAPD investigator—encouraged the framing of gang members, and there was even, allegedly, a box with items in it that could be planted. Perez admitted that he and his former partners had framed a total of ninety-nine people in three years. In such an environment, violence was common, with CRASH officers favoring the potentially lethal choke hold. On February 26, 1998, for example, a CRASH officer arrested twenty-two-year-old Ismael Jimenez, an 18th Street gang member, outside a tattoo parlor. Having grown up in the neighborhood, Jimenez thought he knew what to expect—between 1992 and 1995, he had been detained, arrested, or jailed more than a hundred times by CRASH officers. This time, however, the officer in question seemed especially provoked and, back at the Rampart station, severely beat Jimenez, grabbing his neck, banging his head against a wall, striking his chest and stomach with his fist, and saying, "I could book you on anything. I'll put anything on you." Jimenez began to vomit blood. Released from the station, he sought emergency help, and the doctor who treated him reported the incident to the LAPD. A sergeant came to interview Jimenez on the matter. Jimenez was brought back to Rampart, where, he stated, two plainclothes officers threatened him if he didn't keep quiet. After the *Los Angeles Times* broke the story, Jimenez was awarded $200,000 on April 5, 2000, by the city council of Los Angeles, which feared a larger verdict if the beating ever went to trial.

CRASH officers also shot and killed people; and, at parties at places like the Shortstop, they awarded each other plaques in ganglike rituals: a plaque with a red two of hearts if the victim lived, a black two of hearts if he died. All in all, Perez testified, there were three incidents in which CRASH officers wounded or killed people. Even more chilling, Perez told how he and his partner Nino Durden cold-bloodedly shot a handcuffed Javier Francisco Ovando, nineteen, in the head, chest, and hip, on October 12, 1996, in an apartment building on South Lake Street in the Pico Union district. After the shooting, Perez claimed, Durden had planted an assault weapon with a banana clip on Ovando, and the two of them concocted the following story: They were staking out members of the 18th Street gang in the twelve hundred block of South Lake, Perez and Durden reported in a sworn declaration, when Ovando burst upon them brandishing an assault rifle. Durden then claimed to have shouted, "Police! Drop the gun!" Only when Ovando did not comply, Perez and Durden claimed, did they open fire. Although he wore the tattoos of an 18th Street gang member, and was uncertain in his immigration status, Ovando had no prior criminal convictions. Wheeled into the courtroom on a gurney, Ovando was quickly convicted on the basis of the evidence provided by Perez and Durden. Miffed by Ovando's apparent lack of remorse, the judge gave him an especially stiff sentence, of twenty-three years. Ovando's girlfriend, bearing his unborn child, later remembered how the LAPD officers in the courtroom sat there laughing and smirking as Ovando, now paralyzed for life, was wheeled out of the courtroom to prison.

On New Year's Eve 1996, Rampart officers working a gunfire suppression detail declared open season on the neighborhood. In the first instance, officers shot up a group of men ranging in age from eighteen to fifty-one, without provocation, falsely claiming that they were pointing guns at the officers. Two men were wounded. In a second and even more horrible incident, CRASH officers opened fire on another group of revelers, who were shooting bullets into the air to celebrate. As twenty-one-year-old Juan Saldana lay bleeding in the hallway of a shabby midcity apartment, CRASH officers intentionally delayed calling an ambulance while they concocted a story claiming that Saldana had leveled a gun at them. They also planted a gun near where Saldana lay. Saldana's condition deteriorated as the officers fabricated the story and planted evidence. Taken, finally, by ambulance to the County-USC Medical Center, the weakened Saldana died from two gunshot wounds, one in the chest, the other in his back. That night, Perez testified, he and other officers partied until six or seven a.m. at the Short-stop. The bartender closed the doors and let the CRASH cops ring in the New Year.

Was Perez telling the truth? LAPD, DA, and Department of Justice investigators, after cross-checking and investigating his story, believed that he was, despite one shaky polygraph test, and so did the criminal grand jury that took up the Rampart scandal in October 1999. By April 2000, a total of thirty former CRASH officers had been relieved of duty or suspended without pay, or had quit in connection with the growing scandal. Another forty LAPD officers, including two captains, were under investigation for allegedly knowing about the abuses, covering them up, or ignoring them. Los Angeles Superior Court judge Larry Fidler and his colleagues were sufficiently convinced to have dismissed, by May 21, 2000, more than eighty criminal convictions involving CRASH unit officers and ordering the release of numerous men, and at least one woman, from prison, beginning with the release September 16, 1999, of Javier Francisco Ovando, now twenty-two, who arrived in Los Angeles in a wheelchair, where he was greeted by his fiancée and nearly three-year-old daughter, Destiny.

The parade of those whose convictions were overturned or who were released from prison soon became a near blur. They were, in the main, Latino. Many were gang members. Some had done bad things in other instances. But all in one way or another had been falsely or illegally convicted through evidence planting, perjured testimony, or both. Not since the corruption of the Mayor Frank Shaw era in the late 1930s had such a scandal rocked not only the police department but the entire criminal justice system as well, including prosecutors who had convicted the innocent on tainted evidence and public defenders who had—unwittingly, it can be presumed—allowed their clients to be railroaded. The Rampart scandal suggested a systematic perversion of the entire criminal justice system. Up to three thousand cases could be affected, Gil Garcetti and public defender Michael Judge were admitting by mid-December 1999. "People who saw [the movie *L.A. Confidential*]," noted Judge, "and said it could never happen now—were wrong."[13]

Not surprisingly, Garcetti soon announced that he was reviving a previously canceled program in which prosecutors would respond immediately to the scene of any police shooting and conduct an independent investigation. Garcetti was especially embarrassed when it was revealed that one of his deputy prosecutors, Michael Kraut, had voluntarily refused to continue the trial of an alleged drug dealer in mid-June 1997, dropping all charges before the case went to the jury, when he began to doubt Perez's credibility. Kraut also had written a memorandum seriously questioning Perez's trustworthiness. Filed with his superiors in the DA's office and with the LAPD, the Kraut memo seemed to have provoked no response.

On September 21, 1999, Superior Court judge James Vascue temporarily suspended the permanent injunctions against dozens of 18th Street gang members. As it turned out, nearly half of the 140 alleged members of the gang covered by the injunction were listed there on the basis of sworn statements of Rampart Division officers currently under investigation. Also in question were some 62,000 names of alleged gang members (out of a total of 250,000 names in all) provided by CRASH officers to the much vaunted CAL/GANG computer database maintained by the California Department of Justice in Sacramento. Between 80 and 90 percent of the information in the CAL/GANG database had been provided by members of the CRASH unit. The very existence of the database had outraged the American Civil Liberties Union; it was, the ACLU claimed, a form of preemptive blacklist, a nonjudicial presumption of guilt against minorities. "I think it's outrageous," city councilwoman Jackie Goldberg had said of CAL/GANG. "It's probably every kid in some neighborhoods who wears baggy pants."[14]

Then there was the question of financial settlements. On January 26, 2000, defense attorney Steven Yagman, after a long struggle, secured from the LAPD the names of some five thousand people convicted in cases in which Rampart officers had offered testimony or in some way played a part. Yagman posted the names on his Web site and encouraged victims to contact him. Not surprisingly, some were speculating that damages from the Rampart case could eventually exceed $300 million. Within the year that figure had tripled to more than $1 billion. On July 28, 2000, LAPD officer Nino Durden was arrested and charged with attempted murder in the 1996 shooting of Javier Francisco Ovando. Already, lawyers on behalf of Ovando had filed a $20 million lawsuit against the city, which joined DeNovel Hunter's long-shot suit for $100 million, filed the previous December. Hunter, a Vietnam veteran with a prior drug record, had been one of Perez's first victims and had served a five-year term for felony possession of cocaine with intent to sell. By the time Hunter's lawyers filed their suit, the CRASH unit had been disbanded.

Doing Time

The officers of CRASH got away with what they were doing for so long, one suspects, in part because the 1990s were witnessing a hardening of attitude on the part of the people of California against crime. In 1972, California had reinstated the death penalty through initiative; but judicial delays throughout the 1980s, led most notably by California chief justice Rose Bird and a few of her colleagues on the state supreme court, had stalled its implementation for most of the decade. But by the early 1990s judicial delays had run their course, and California was ready to resume capital punishment.

Shortly after six a.m. on the morning of April 21, 1992, during a rising tide of crime and anticrime sentiment, Robert Alton Harris, thirty-nine, who in July 1978 had murdered two teenagers in San Diego in the course of a carjacking, was executed in the gas chamber in San Quentin. It was the first execution in California in twenty-five years; and its details—warring court orders in the final hours, with four stays quashed, one last-minute stay pulling a jaunty ponytailed Harris out of the gas chamber minutes before it would be too late, then returning a more sober Harris a few hours later to the chamber for execution; the demonstrations pro and con outside the prison—underscored the confusions and contradictions behind the change in attitude and penal culture represented by the resumption of the death penalty. By 1998, California had 504 condemned inmates on death row, the single largest such group in the world. (Texas had 425, Florida 368, Pennsylvania 216, North Carolina 199.) Persistent liberal sentiment, however, and an exacting attitude on the part of the judiciary kept executions to five; yet the sheer presence of so many Californians on death row suggested that at some point in the twenty-first century the state could very well become the execution capital of the nation. Still, it seemed dramatically divided on the issue, especially as it faced the foreseeable prospect of some thousand Californians on death row if prosecutors continued to ask for and receive the death penalty for first-degree-murder convictions.

It had to be admitted that in California, as elsewhere, murder often went unpunished. In Los Angeles County, for example, where some two thousand willful homicides were occurring each year by mid-decade, only one in three was leading to any form of punishment. Twenty-five years earlier, four out of five reported murder cases were solved by the police. Now only half of all murders were being solved. The difference: in the previous era people killed people they knew. They killed them, moreover, inside homes and for reasons—greed, jealousy, revenge—that left clues and enabled detectives to build cases. Now people on the streets were killing strangers in the course of gangbanging or robberies and at three times the earlier rate. Witnesses knew that if they talked, they were dead meat. Even if they talked at first, many disavowed their statements when it came to going to court, especially in the matter of gang killings, which accounted for four of every ten homicides.

Overworked homicide detectives just didn't have the time, much less the clues, to track down killers as they were able to do in the old days. In 1995 the South Bureau of the LAPD had so many unsolved murders on its hands that it had to call in the FBI. Veteran detective Paul Mize of the South Bureau confessed to the incoming FBI agents that they would be "appalled" at some of the leads that were "never acted upon." With such inadequate police work, hundreds of cases were dropped or dismissed for lack of evidence. Hundreds of others were plea-bargained down to lesser charges. Even hundreds of fugitives charged with murder, astonishingly, remained at large, with overburdened police just too busy to look for them. Michael Terry, for example, was charged with murder in 1981 but not apprehended until 1993, when he pulled a knife on his sister, who turned him in to the police. Prosecutors, however, had to drop the charges against Terry because of their inability to reconstruct the details of a twelve-year-old murder in a city in which murder was commonplace.[15]

Throughout the state, the parole system seemed equally shaky. By late in the decade there were some 100,000 Californians on parole. Like so many homicide detectives, parole officers were overwhelmed by their caseloads. California had a recidivism rate of 67 percent, the worst in the nation. In 1996–97, more than 82,000 prisoners admitted that year to the state and county system—or, in other words, two-thirds of all 133,000 new inmates—were parole violators or repeat offenders. Of the inmates released that year, more than half could be expected to commit a new crime, be convicted, and be resentenced within the next two years. This cycle of offense, parole, and reoffense was especially devastating to the African-American community. In 1993, one in three African-American male Californians in his twenties was either in prison, on parole, or on probation. A culture of crime was damaging this community unto the next generation; of every two children in the juvenile justice system, at least one had a parent who was incarcerated.

Not only was it costing taxpayers $246 million annually by 1998 to supervise offenders, it was costing another $1.51 billion to reincarcerate the parolees who either violated the conditions of their parole or committed new crimes. Overcrowded prisons, meanwhile, were releasing hundreds, if not thousands, of violent offenders back into society with little supervision and even less of a guarantee that they would behave: people such as James Porter, thirty-one, released on September 2, 1998, along with ninety-two other mentally disordered inmates, half of them high-risk rapists, when a ruling by the state court of appeal voided efforts to keep them behind bars beyond their parole dates. Within hours of moving from the Corcoran State Prison to the Flamingo Inn in Fresno, Porter, wearing an electronic ankle bracelet that would sound an alarm if he left the motel, raped a sixty-three-year-old woman who was living there.

Porter was now a three-time loser, which meant that he would be heading to prison for the rest of his natural life; in 1994, by both popular initiative and legislative action, Californians had passed three-strikes-and-you're-out legislation. The new law called for a mandatory indeterminate life sentence for anyone convicted of a third violent or serious felony. Parole would be possible only after a three-striker had served twenty-five years or three times the term that the current conviction would ordinarily warrant, whichever was greater. The law also had a two-strikes provision. A defendant convicted of a second serious or violent felony would have to serve a term of imprisonment twice the usual sentence provided for the second felony conviction. Two years after the passage of the three-strikes law, the California Supreme Court ruled that judges still retained the discretion to strike or dismiss prior felony convictions. Yet even with this modification, the three-strikes law was a time machine for convicted felons. And what the supreme court took away, it also returned: in May 1998, it ruled that a judge also had the discretion to count one violent conviction as a multiple felony. Thus a single carjacking could produce two strikes if the defendant were convicted of both carjacking and robbery.

The three-strikes legislation came at the climax of a decade of rising violent crime. Its theoretical underpinnings could be gleaned from the research and writing of such respected figures as Harvard and UCLA political scientist and philosopher James Q. Wilson, who in a number of books and studies had asserted what most Californians believed to be an incontrovertible fact: that a certain small percentage of the population committed most of the violent crime, and that such individuals tended to be repeat offenders. While the causes of violent crime might be argued, it was also true that violent offenders, kept for long periods behind bars, could not harm the general society during the period of their incarceration. Whether seen as punishment, societal self-protection, or both, the three-strikes law and its two-strikes provision would remove from the general population proven repeat offenders. The law also represented a retreat from any interest in the rehabilitative aspects of incarceration, or even in the sociological aspects of crime as an indicator of whether society was in good shape. The three-strikes law, by contrast, expressed a visceral reaction on the part of the California public and a growing group of legislators, led in the assembly by Fresno Republican Bill Jones, who were brushing aside considerations of criminology, sociology, or social justice and were unequivocally saying, *Basta!* Enough already with the killing, the robbing, the rapes, the assaults, the murderous gangland drive-bys, the drug dealing, the sexual offenses. Lock 'em up!

And lock 'em up they did. In 1980, California had fewer than 25,000 inmates in a dozen prisons. By January 1998 there were some 154,000 prisoners in thirty-three prisons, with the incarcerated population expected to reach 200,000 by 2003 and 401,000 by 2027—more prisoners than in all of Western Europe, Australia, Canada, Japan, and New Zealand combined. Another fifteen prisons, costing an estimated $5 billion, were scheduled for completion by the year 2000 to house incoming three-strikers. More than 101,000 felons were under parole supervision. At any given time, county-run jails contained another 72,000 inmates.

In 1996 a Rubicon was crossed when for the first time California spent more on prisons than it did on its two university systems. In terms of construction and job creation, prisons represented a growth industry for numerous remote places—Calipatria, Ione, Corcoran, Avenal, Blythe, Susanville—which might have otherwise succumbed to economic stagnation. California correctional officers were the highest paid in the nation—$44,676 a year after seven years on the job, with overtime frequently boosting that sum to $60,000. Overall, the state was paying its guards almost 50 percent more than the national average, second only to Alaska. Directed by Don Novey, a fedora-wearing, blunt-talking former prison guard, the California Correctional Peace Officers Association, with more than sixteen thousand members, had long since become a determining force in state politics, capable of pouring $1.5 million into the 1990 and 1994 gubernatorial campaigns of Governor Pete Wilson and a comparable amount into the 1998 campaign of Governor Gray Davis.

Even with the construction boom, however, California prisons and prison camps were by 1997 operating at 194.7 percent of capacity. In many institutions, prisoners were double celled, unless prohibited by court order. Gymnasiums and other larger spaces were converted into makeshift dormitories. The sheer scale of many penal institutions was mind-boggling. A number of them—San Quentin, Chino, San Luis Obispo, Susanville, Avenal, Jamestown, and Solano—held six thousand prisoners or more. Soledad had more than seven thousand. The Women's Correctional Institution at Tehachapi held six thousand.

A significant percentage of all prisoners were behind bars for drug-related offenses. They brought their addictions to prison, and that created a market. In a surprise raid in October 1994, correctional officers at Calipatria found heroin concealed in bars of soap, drugs in packages with a lawyer's return address, handmade hypodermic needles, and other paraphernalia. According to an August 31, 1997, report in the *Los Angeles Times,* drugs—black-tar heroin, crack, speed, marijuana—remained a problem at the Central California Women's Facility in Chowchilla. Opened in 1990 at a remote site forty miles north of Fresno, the very presence of such a large facility—fourteen squat dormitory buildings and two cell-block units housing 3,500, including eight death-row inmates—testified to the rising crime culture in California, so much of it connected to drug use, which was now bringing thousands of women into the penal system. The reputed use of dirty syringes, which transferred the HIV virus, compounded the problem. The combined problem of caring for aged prisoners from a previous era and the health problems of the younger population drove the health and mental care cost of the correctional system in 1994 to $372 million, more than thirty-six other states spent on their entire prison budgets. By June 1998 the figure had risen to $500 million, administered by a Health Care Services Division within the Department of Corrections that was among the largest HMOs in the state.

Some 6,500 inmates were enrolled in college courses at a time when the California State University system was in meltdown. Prisoners enjoyed a daily diet of 3,700-plus calories—15 percent protein, 55 percent carbohydrate, 30 percent fat—including a wide array of fresh meat, poultry, fruits, and vegetables. A typical breakfast might include stewed fruit, hot cereal, scrambled eggs, turkey ham, a muffin with butter, milk, and coffee. Lunch consisted of a turkey, bologna, or cheese sandwich, apple, chips, cookies, and a beverage pack. For dinner: salad, beef stew with noodles, canned peas, a roll, butter, cake, and a beverage pack. Many working Californians, it was pointed out, did not enjoy such a balanced diet; nor did they or their children possess comparable access to such well-stocked libraries. Each prison had an up-to-date library staffed by a professional. Prisoners were also allowed to purchase cigarettes, soda, vitamins, candy, ice cream, canned food, personal care products, stationery, and pens from canteens. Two mail-order firms specialized in sales to inmates, offering such corrections-approved items as clocks, small televisions, radios, tape players, and earphones. Prisoners were also allowed two plug-in appliances: an electric guitar, say, or an electric typewriter, a heating element for warming food, a fan, an electric shaver, a television or radio. Most prisons had cable television hookups, and the staff would regularly broadcast movies via cable to inmate sets. Exercise yards featured weights and other body-building equipment. There were also softball and soccer fields, handball and basketball courts, and running tracks.

No one could claim that life in a California prison was a piece of cake; yet the very standard of living made possible to most prisoners, especially in lower-security institutions, represented a reasonably high level of support in contrast to daily life in most Third World countries and, if the truth be told, to a disturbingly large number of Californians. Through no fault of its own, the Department of Corrections was finding itself on the horns of a dilemma. On the one hand, the department was guiding itself by the Inmate Bill of Rights—passed by the legislature and signed by Ronald Reagan in 1968, and expanded in 1974 by Jerry Brown—which guaranteed prisoners most rights enjoyed by free people, including the right to marry, to have conjugal visits (most prisons maintained facilities for overnight stays by spouses), to correspond confidentially with lawyers, and to have unrestricted access to all forms of reading material, including pornography. Society was sending the penal system more and more prisoners; yet it was also demanding that these men and women be fed, housed, medicated, educated, and recreated at a level comparable to that of outside society. This began to look like privilege when times got tough—as they did in the early 1990s—or when the crime and recidivism rate continued to rise at alarming levels. Confronted with a daily dosage of horror stories in their newspapers—murders, rapes, assaults, burglaries—Californians, so liberal in 1968, now grew hard of heart as far as doing time was concerned.

In early 1995, Governor Pete Wilson and the Department of Corrections launched an aggressive program of takeaways. Under this get-tough policy, prisoners were no longer allowed long hair or pornography. Lifers and many categories of sex offenders were denied conjugal visits. On the grounds that buffed prisoners represented a threat to guards, weight-lifting equipment was cut back, and weight lifting was allowed only as part of a specific exercise program. Access to reporters was curtailed, and prisoners could not accept payments for interviews or collect book royalties. By 1998 further restrictions included the removal of all weight-lifting equipment, the prohibition of packages sent directly to inmates from the outside, the substitution of white jumpsuits for blue jeans and blue shirts, random testing for drugs, and the reduction of the number of law books in prison libraries. "They're there to be punished," said Wilson spokesman Sean Walsh, "and hopefully rehabilitated. They're not there to be entertained and catered to."[16]

The worst prison scandal of the decade erupted at the Corcoran State Prison in the San Joaquin Valley north of Bakersfield off Highway 43, a five-thousand-prisoner facility (designed for three thousand) housing such high-risk celebrities as mass murderer Juan Corona, cult murderer Charles Manson, and Robert Kennedy assassin Sirhan Sirhan. There, throughout the first half of the decade and beyond, stated a federal grand jury indictment handed up in February 1998, guards and supervisors had systematically engaged in a program of prisoner abuse and cover-up under color of authority, culminating in the April 1994 shooting of prisoner Preston Tate. The indictment of eight guards and supervisors came as the result of a four-year FBI probe into civil rights violations at the maximum-security facility, reported by the *Los Angeles Times*. The investigation suggested that Corcoran, not Pelican Bay, a maximum-security facility in Del Norte County on the Oregon border, took top honors as the Devil's Island of California.

The indictments and the FBI report claimed that guards at Corcoran ran the maximum-security prison through a systematic program of intimidation and violence oddly reflective of the gang culture that had brought so many young men to this institution in the first place. It was perhaps the very existence of prison gangs—the Mexican Mafia, the Aryan Brotherhood, the Black Guerrilla Family—that motivated an equally youthful, newly recruited, and inexperienced correctional cadre at Corcoran, which opened in 1988, to adopt comparable gangsta tactics in dealing with inmates. In its first year alone, Corcoran listed a horrendous fifteen hundred fights and reportable altercations, sixty-two uses of gas, forty-seven instances of carbine fire, and 204 injuries by either bullet or rifle-shot woodblock, together with one death. It was an astonishing tally, suggesting an institution in deep turmoil.

When fifteen hundred of the most troublesome inmates of Corcoran were shipped north to Pelican Bay in 1989, things calmed down temporarily, but a pattern of organized guard violence against organized prisoner violence had been established. Gang culture had triumphed. The moment incoming prisoners stepped off the bus and were roughed up by guards, forced to lie spread-eagled on the hot asphalt, and pushed and punched as they moved from place to place, they were inducted into a culture of control through violence. The most egregious example of such a welcoming party, held in June 1995, subsequently became known as Ninja Day. In so many

ways, such an induction was an exact reflection of gang initiation techniques. A group of particularly tough guards, in fact, had a ganglike cog-
nomen, the Sharks, because they attacked without warning. If there were
gangs at Corcoran, and there certainly were, then the Sharks might very
well have been the biggest and baddest badass gang of all. The accusation
later surfaced that guards used Wayne Robertson, a murderer serving life—
also he was known as the Booty Bandit, for his proclivities as a rapist—as a
member of their suppression team, assigning Robertson to the cells of prisoners requiring punishment by sexual violence. One such charge made it to
trial in October 1999 after six years of investigations, but resulted in an
acquittal.

Corrections headquarters in Sacramento, meanwhile, had set in stone a
policy of integration. Small groups from differing gangs on the outside
were to be placed in the exercise yard at the same time in the belief that they
would learn to get along with each other as individuals, which would have
the effect of weakening gang culture in California prisons. The exact opposite occurred, as the epidemic of fights at Corcoran in the first year of the
program showed. A gladiator culture emerged. Guards, it was alleged,
would place rival gang members in adjacent cells to heighten hostility.
Fights were allowed in the exercise yard as long as specific rules were
obeyed: no weapons, no two on one, stop when the guard tells you to. Fighting, according to this scenario, became a form of spectator sport, administered and supervised by the guards. "I was written up six times for being in
fights," noted a former inmate of the security housing unit at Corcoran.
"Three of the six fights were set up by guards. They would come to me and
criticize my performance. They would laugh at what had happened."[17]

Political fallout from the Corcoran revelations continued throughout
1998, culminating in hearings that August by the state senate. The Corcoran
situation might have represented, first and foremost, a conspiracy by correctional officers; but it is difficult to understand how prison officials further
up the line were not alarmed by the growing number of exercise-yard shootings. From one perspective, the Corcoran situation was not specifically Californian, yet it must be remembered that the state's forty deaths of inmates
from guard shootings within a decade constituted more than the sum total of
all such shootings in the rest of the United States.

Corcoran represented, among other things, the triumph of gang culture
in the early to mid-1990s in a state increasingly overwhelmed by gang violence. If even some of the things that French social theorist Michel Foucault
had written about prisons were true—namely, that they represented repressive paradigms of society itself—then California, home state of most homeboys, should not be surprised that gang cultures could be found on both

sides of the barbed wire of its prisons. This, of course, was not universally the case. Corcoran, it could be hoped, was more of a warning than a pervasive paradigm. On the outside, as the Corcoran indictments were being handed up, Californians were trumpeting the decline of violence in the state; and certainly that was true, as far as it went, and worth trumpeting. But as recently as the six days between December 13 and 19, 1998, as Congress debated the impeachment of President Clinton and bombs and missiles fell on Iraq, eight young men fell dead in the streets of South Central Los Angeles, five of them in gang-related slayings, three in drug deals gone wrong. The deaths merited only a small story in the Metro section of the *Los Angeles Times,* so accustomed had the citizens of that city, and all California for that matter, become to the dangers and tragedies of gang culture as California catastrophe.

A Lost Generation

Ever since the reforms of the Culbert Olson administration (1939–43), California had maintained a strict distinction between young and adult offenders. Anyone tried and convicted as a minor could only be held by the California Youth Authority (CYA) until he or she reached the age of twenty-five. Youthful felonies, even murder, would not become part of a young offender's permanent adult record. The system presumed a formal line of demarcation between young offenders and adult criminals. It was also based on the premise that young offenders could be transformed into law-abiding adults if they were processed through a program of punishment, reform, and education.

Under the direction of CYA chief Francisco Alarcon and superintendent of education Dr. Dorrine Davis, the CYA maintained a system of eleven high schools offering a variety of academic and vocational programs that many smaller states in the nation or poorer counties in California might envy. The thing about the CYA schools—in terms of the quality and commitment of teachers, classroom space, libraries, and computers and other instructional equipment—was that they were so good, simply as schools. In flush times, the CYA school system could be seen as a symbol of hope. In difficult times, however, such as the early 1990s, not a few citizens drew the apparent contrasts between the well-equipped CYA high schools and the embattled public high schools up and down the state. In any event, educators such as Superintendent Davis and committed teachers such as Johanna Boss were capable of knowing what many of their students had done to get themselves incarcerated in the first place and also instinctively believing, hoping even, that youthful offenses need not permanently derail a life. A Dutch immigrant, Johanna Boss taught for twenty-nine years, class after class of convicted felons, without a single incident. It helped that she was rumored to have been in the Dutch Resistance during the war and to have personally dispatched a Nazi or two. In September 1997 the CYA named one of its high schools in Boss's honor, in recognition of her effective teaching and, more important, the reduced recidivism rate of her graduates.

As the 1980s, which had been bad enough, edged into the crime wave of the 1990s, Californians, along with most Americans, were beginning to lose faith in the liberal belief that youthful crimes were of a different order than adult felonies. First of all, crimes by young offenders—most notably, cold-blooded murder in the course of robbery or drive-by shootings—were growing more numerous and horrendous. Second, research was showing that violent criminals started their careers early and continued into adulthood. The crime wave, augmented by statistical and social science, was eroding the recently—as of the late nineteenth century—evolved theory that youthful crime and adult crime were not the same phenomenon. It was one thing to contemplate the kid gone bad, as in a Mickey Rooney movie from the 1930s, perhaps, with Spencer Tracy playing the priest who brings him back. It was another thing entirely to contemplate the murder and mayhem being wrought by teenagers through the 1990s. Gang slayings now ran into the thousands, and as the decade progressed, gangbangers attempting and committing murder were younger and younger. This wasn't a movie about kids throwing bricks who could be rescued; this was a culture of cold-blooded killers. What was one to say, for example, about the fifteen-year-old boy who asked a four-year-old to fetch him some cigarettes—this within a household of various unrelated adults operating a methamphetamine lab—and, when the boy didn't get the cigarettes, the fifteen-year-old shot him dead with a sawed-off shotgun belonging to the boyfriend of the victim's mother?

By the 1990s, not only were an increasing number of young people falling into criminal behavior, they were also the victims of crime—crimes that in most instances were perpetrated by young offenders. First of all, there were the gangs themselves. But there was also a second tier of organization: the posse, which, while not as territorially structured as gangs, nevertheless had a way of institutionalizing antisocial behavior. While Los Angeles County had more than 100,000 gang members by late February 1993, it had nearly a third that number affiliated with more informal organizations called posses, a term first used by Jamaican gangs in New York in the 1970s, which had in turn been taken from the sheriff's posses of the Old West, which had in turn come from the Latin phrase *posse comitatus,* meaning county power, or what the community was empowered to do. Posses, in many cases, could be harmless expressions of the desire of young men to hang out together and to form secret or semisecret organizations or clubs. In this category, there were basketball posses, skateboarding posses, snowboarding posses, rap or hip-hop music posses, or merely friendship groups from one or another junior or senior high school.

Even in such instances, there was always the danger of the alienation natural to adolescent and young adult males. Surfing, it should be remembered, had begun in part as a protest sport—an attitude even more characteristic of skateboarding in the 1990s. So often, kids tended to be skateboarding against society itself as they recklessly skated private property or public places that were off-limits, leaving behind, all too often, chipped or otherwise damaged surfaces. Quite naturally, skateboarding became tougher, meaner, more hard-edged as groups like the Santa Monica–based Dog Town saw themselves as outlaws. Skateboarding magazines such as *Big Brother* were filled with antisocial, antifemale, and other sociopathic imagery. An ad from one company, Bitch Skateboards, in a magazine by the same name, *Bitch,* depicted a male figure holding a gun to the head of a female. Such hard-edged attitudes, reinforced by skateboarding magazines and the general skateboarding cult, in which skateboards featured pictures of Charles Manson or women in lingerie bound and gagged, had eventually to have real-life expression, and this soon happened. In 1992 skateboarding champion Mark Anthony "Gator" Rogowski pleaded guilty to raping and murdering the girlfriend of his ex-girlfriend when his ex-girlfriend refused to reconcile.

Given the attraction of male teenagers to bonding and to misbehavior, it was not surprising that some posses turned sociopathic, even criminal. The destructive group Ace of Spades began with young men involved in junior ROTC at Polytechnic High School in Long Beach. The youths liked military drill and the protocols of military organization; they also became interested in stealing cars, vandalizing property, and committing assaults. "We love the way the military works," noted one member of the posse. "All of us just wanted to take it a little farther." On the night of February 1, 1992, members of the Ace of Spades took it very far indeed in the case of former posse member Alexander Giraldo, sixteen, who had cooperated with the police in a car burglary investigation. Over the previous two months, Ace of Spades members had been waging a systematic campaign of vandalism against Giraldo and his family, despite the family's frequent protests to the police. That night, they brought their campaign to a conclusion, garroting and stabbing Alexander to death, military style, then tossing his blood-soaked body off an oceanfront cliff.[18]

The Spur Posse of Lakewood attracted the most attention, including a profile by Joan Didion in the July 26, 1993, *New Yorker.* In its fifteen minutes of fame, the Spur Posse provided a perfect paradigm of dysfunctionalism and downward mobility among white working-class and lower-middle-class youth in the dead-end suburbs of recession-ridden Southern California. Lakewood, an aviation-dependent city of 73,500, had emerged in southern Los Angeles County following World War II. By the early 1990s, its economy under great stress, Lakewood was sliding into downward mobility. Nowhere was this more noticeable than in the dominant clique at Lakewood High School, the so-called Spur Posse of athletes, named in honor of the San Antonio Spurs basketball team. The members of the posse were white, athletic, and generally good-looking. They were also perhaps themselves recognizing, in the subliminal way of youth, that they were heading nowhere fast. A good number of their parents had been Lakewood High graduates and had stayed on in the suburb in blue-collar or white-collar occupations dependent in one way or another on the defense industry, now so obviously in the tank. For all their apparent arrogance, Spur members must have known that in terms of the declining economy, in terms of the talented and hardworking immigrants pouring into Southern California, and in comparison to the kinds of kids who were getting into good colleges, they were looking like losers. Forget sports skills. Forget good looks. High school would be all that they would have—and then the long years after high school replaying, as their parents were replaying, the glory years over and over again in memory.

Stories such as this had long been the staple of American fiction: the rhythms of realization, rebellion, and eventually acceptance by high school heroes who knew that they had already peaked. In the case of the Spur Posse, subliminal resentment edged into antisocial behavior, into ganglike patterns of vandalism, intimidation, and threat, and, most sociopathic, into the systematic seduction or outright rape of dozens of their female classmates. Each member of the posse kept score of his conquests, with the champion reaching sixty and the runner-up forty-four. Sheriff's deputies had already been alerted to the growing misbehavior of Spur Posse members, but it was only at a meeting at the high school in early March 1993 that certain parents began openly to suggest that their daughters had been raped by one or more members of the posse. Sheriff's investigators pursued these charges, and some two weeks later, in the middle of a Thursday schoolday, eight members of the Spur Posse were taken from the classroom and booked on a total of seventeen felony counts of rape, unlawful intercourse, and related charges.

At the end of it all, there was only one conviction: a pleading of no contest by one sixteen-year-old posse member to the sexual assault of a ten-year-old girl, who was perhaps claiming to be fifteen. What was fascinating about the entire case, however, was the fact that the Spur Posse became heroes of a sort, defended by parents and students alike. Released from jail, members of the posse posed defiantly for the *Los Angeles Times* and the *New York Times* in all their suburban machismo, unintimidated, unapologetic, neither asking for nor giving any quarter. Joan Didion saw in the episode a case study of California catastrophe in the early 1990s. The formula included a faltering economy and a recognition, however subliminal, on the part of both parents and their offspring that they might no longer be needed, or respected, by a changing society. In just two generations, a California suburb, created overnight in the aftermath of World War II, had become a wasteland of traditional values. Again and again, Didion quoted Spur Posse parents, themselves dysfunctional, as they defended the actions of their predatory offspring, repeating and repeating, almost mantralike, that the entire affair had been blown out of proportion, blown out of proportion, blown out of proportion. It was not so much that the Lakewood families had come under stress, Didion suggested, as it was that the entire structure and traditional value of family life had been swept away in the rise and fall of one California suburb across a brief quarter century. The death of dreams and the loss of values had made monsters of a disturbing number of Lakewood's children.

It could get even worse. Like figures from Greek myth, California parents—all of them for various reasons coming under special stress—seemed at times to be devouring their children. In Daly City, south of San Francisco, Megan Hogg, twenty-five, an account executive with AT&T in San Jose, living in her parents' home with her three children, was as of March 1998 wrestling with a variety of demons. For the past year and a half, Hogg had been treated for depression and was taking Prozac and nortriptyline. That January, an automobile accident had pushed her further into despondency, and she was placed on Dilantin and Vicodin to help her deal with pain and seizures. At some point on the evening of Sunday, March 22, 1998, Hogg methodically suffocated her three daughters, ages two, three, and seven, with duct tape.

Kids killed by parents—but also kids seeing their parents killed. In Los Angeles alone, by mid-decade, some two hundred children a year were witnessing the slaying of a parent, and a local cottage industry had arisen to help these children deal with post-traumatic stress. For thousands of kids, just living in certain neighborhoods was a life-threatening experience. Bianca Duran, ten, for example, was playing with her mother and her two younger brothers in Los Palmas Park in San Fernando when they were caught in gang crossfire. The entire family was riddled with shotgun pellets, but survived. In February 1991, Cristal Anguiano, twelve, was buying ice cream from a truck outside her home in South Los Angeles when a gang gunfight broke out. Cristal was shot in the heart, but managed to carry her two-year-old brother to safety. Miraculously, she survived.

Violence involving children, teenagers, and young adults—whether as perpetrators or victims—was, of course, not a problem confined to California. A 1994 report by the Charles Stewart Mott Foundation, *A Fine Line: Losing American Youth to Violence,* delineated the national extent of the problem. By 1992, homicide had become the second leading cause of death for fifteen to twenty-four-year-olds. For African Americans in that same age bracket, being murdered was the number one cause of death. Week by week throughout the 1990s, Californians were being reminded that the epidemic of violence characteristic of the decade, especially the first half, was taking down with it innocent children, teenagers, and young adults. In 1991, one-quarter of the 1,554 people shot to death in Los Angeles County were nineteen or younger. In April and May alone, three children under the age of ten were killed: Sabrina Haley, eighteen months, was killed by gang gunfire as she sat beside her father in his car stopped at a traffic light in South Central Los Angeles; Denise Silva, three, was shot through the heart in a drive-by attack as she walked hand in hand with her father to a corner grocery store in Boyle Heights; and Ramon Sanchez, nine, was hit in the head by a stray bullet as he sat in the kitchen of his family's home in Watts, drinking a glass of milk.

Most victims were young people of color. While their deaths were covered by the *Los Angeles Times,* at no point did they provoke a crisis of conscience, as one might reasonably assume. A terrible expectation, rather—that disadvantaged children of color existed in a condition of acceptable risk—seemed to pervade the larger society. When twelve-year-old Polly Klaas, however, a middle-class white child living in the picture-perfect community of Petaluma in Sonoma County, was abducted and murdered in October 1993, the entire state, even the nation, became riveted on the case. The city of Petaluma itself went into collective trauma. First of all, there was the unusualness of the case: a pretty and talented twelve-year-old, living in a community to which an entire generation of parents had moved seeking a better life for themselves and their children, abducted from her bedroom in the early hours of the morning as two of her friends and her parents were sleeping in nearby rooms.

In the weeks that followed, before her strangled body was found in an abandoned sawmill, thousands of posters were distributed throughout the region. Petaluma native Winona Ryder offered a reward for any useful information. Polly Klaas soon became a symbol of violated innocence and middle-class dreams turned to nightmare. Not even a middle-class youngster, sleeping in her own bed in Petaluma, was safe. But then again: all those children of color also died in innocuous circumstances, standing on lawns in front of their homes, sitting in their parents' station wagon at stoplights, drinking a glass of milk at their kitchen table, fixing a flat tire by the side of the road. But that was in Los Angeles, and this was Petaluma. More than a thousand people, including Governor Pete Wilson and other elected officials, attended Polly Klaas's memorial service; and a foundation, headed by Polly's father, Marc Klaas, was established in her name, which by 1999 had assisted more than fifteen hundred families searching for missing children. More than any other single case, the Klaas abduction and murder by a twice-convicted felon led to the passage of three-strikes legislation. It helped galvanize public opinion over the long life of the case that her abductor and murderer, career criminal Richard Allen Davis, only four months out of prison when he kidnapped and murdered Polly, seemed a monster from Hades itself. This perception was confirmed when Davis, upon his conviction in a San Jose courtroom in June 1996, winked at the Klaas family, blew them a kiss, grinned, and then extended two one-finger salutes with both hands to the courtroom, mouthing the words, "That was for everybody."[19]

School could be equally dangerous. Within one year, 1990–91, shootings at or near Compton and Centennial High Schools killed a student and a school janitor and seriously wounded two others. In April 1991, eleven-year-old Alejandro Vargas was struck below the eye and killed by a bullet fired by one of four gang members shooting at Compton school police, who had earlier driven them off the campus. Alejandro was standing on the front lawn beneath the flagpole of the Ralph J. Bunche Middle School in Compton, waiting for his mother to pick him up. He had specifically called his mother to come and take him home, because he had previously been harassed by gang members as he walked the eight blocks on Rose Avenue between his home and the campus. Just a few feet away from where Alejandro fell dead to the lawn was the school office and its sign, "Education—A Valuable Resource." Alejandro was a beautiful boy, "the sweetest thing this side of heaven," as one neighbor described him. He helped with household chores, including the ironing. A number of hours later, two teenage gang members, fourteen and seventeen, were booked for Alejandro's murder.

Then there was the question of racial tension, such as the fighting that broke out on October 27, 1992, at North Hollywood High School between African-American and Latino students, arguing about what kind of music would be played at the school's homecoming dance. Black students wanted hip-hop and rap. Latino students preferred techno-pop. It took more than a hundred LAPD officers to quell the melee, which at one point involved up to seven hundred students. The following day, fighting and shouting matches erupted between blacks and Latinos at two other Los Angeles Unified School District campuses, Hamilton High Schools Complex on the Westside and the Olive Vista Middle School in Sylmar, and once again the police were called.

No wonder that in two separate *Los Angeles Times* surveys, in March and September 1993, Los Angeles adolescents and teenagers were more than ready to express their fears about going to school. "I think about how I want to die," noted Gerri Washington, fourteen, an eighth grader at Foshay Junior High School. "I don't want to get shot, but if I do, I want to get shot in the head right here, so I die instantly." The photograph showed Ms. Washington pointing to the center of her forehead with her index finger.[20] "I am afraid of getting shot or getting killed," stated Alberto Cisneros, sixteen, a junior at Wilson High School in Long Beach. "I really want to live. And I want to be somebody, you know?"[21]

More and more preteens in middle school and teenagers in high schools were reporting to their parents that the schoolyard, the classroom corridors, the cafeteria, the bathrooms had become a nightmare scene of threat and intimidation. Large public schools had always been competitive, grinding, even hostile places, vulnerable to bullying and the psychological racketeering of cliques; and so from one perspective, it could be argued that everything was business as usual, only a little more so. Yet others were detecting a qualitative as well as quantitative amalgam of misbehavior and malaise. The acceleration of sexual activity, for example, resulted in girls being hit on as early as the sixth grade. Violent and obscene language—not coming from everyone, but loud and pervasive enough to be intimidating—was disturbingly the norm. Be average-looking or overweight, and you were in trouble. Be clumsy or ill-adept at sports, and you were in trouble. Raise your hand in class too many times, answer the teacher's questions too intelligently, and you were in trouble. At the John Adams Middle School in Santa Monica, music teacher Angela Woo kept her practice room open during the lunch hour so that sixth-grade girls, reluctant to enter the intimidating environment of the schoolyard, could spend the time safely among themselves.

By 1998, the Justice Department was announcing a nationwide decrease in violent crime. In metropolitan Los Angeles, the department revealed, violent crime had dropped by nearly 30 percent. Despite the statistics, however, it was difficult to feel overly optimistic as children continued to fall in the line of fire. Statistics regarding a falling crime rate offered little consolation to grieving parents such as Yolanda Morales. In September, in Highland Park, her twelve-year-old son, Steven Morales, a seventh grader crazy for sports (Little League, professional wrestling on TV) and devoid of any gangland associations whatsoever, was shot in the head—again, by gunfire from a nearby gang dispute—as he stood talking with friends in front of a neighbor's house. As soon as he heard the shooting, Steven had directed his playmates back into their houses before himself turning to face one of the gunmen, some 150 feet away, and was shot by him with a single slug to the forehead.

The automobile posed a distinctive threat to children in less privileged districts. The 1990s abounded with heinous instances of children being killed by automobiles, in many cases under hit-and-run circumstances. In December 1997, a speeding minivan coming out of nowhere struck Bobby Hobdy, sixteen, as he waited at a bus stop in Watts for his daily commute to Taft High School in Woodland Hills. Knocking Bobby thirty feet into oncoming traffic on Century Boulevard, the speeding van headed off into the anonymity of the city. And so it had continued down the decade, one incident after another, not ending, but peaking perhaps with the hit-and-run killing of eleven-year-old Alice Kang one Monday morning in Koreatown, in November 1998. Alice was walking across the street in a crosswalk to her school bus. She had the right-of-way when the blue Hyundai struck her down, then fled. For years, neighbors on a hilly stretch of Figueroa Street winding through the Highland Park section of Los Angeles had complained to city officials that the street had become a deadly speedway for cars racing downtown from Pasadena and Eagle Rock. On a Friday in October 1997, one such speeding car, swerving to avoid another vehicle, jumped a curb and plowed into a group of young children as they stood eating ice cream cones on the corner. Six-year-old Matthew Ruiz died in his mother's arms, and four other children were rushed to the hospital.

Not only were increasing numbers of children and young adults of California shooting each other as gangbangers, or being shot by gangbangers, or being shot or otherwise killed by their parents, they also were being abused or neglected in record numbers by an equally increasing number of malevolent or dysfunctional adults. In 1996, for example, fifty-three children were abused to death in Los Angeles County alone, an 8.1 percent increase over 1995. Police and autopsy reports revealed an absolute horror of head traumas, gunshot wounds, beatings to the abdomen and chest, suffocation, strangulation, drowning, fire, stabbing, poisoning, starvation, and shaken-baby syndrome. Some children survived, but at a cost. Each day in the Dependency Court of Orange County, superior court judge Richard Toohey, one of six judges on this court, was making scores of rushed decisions, some of them on minimal evidence, as to whether or not children were at risk by being left with their birth parents. Every now and then even Judge Toohey, a tested veteran promoted from the municipal court after a stint as a homicide prosecutor, confessed himself emotionally fatigued by the array of horrors coming before him in his courtroom.

Most distressingly, the number of cases coming under Dependency Court jurisdiction was increasing by a disturbing 220 families a month by May 1998, at a time when a total of more than 4,600 children had already been removed from their parents' care and placed with relatives or in foster or group homes. And this was Orange County, ground zero of upward mobility in suburban Southern California. It was also a county where more than 3,800 youngsters, up 45 percent since 1993, were by May 1998 living in court-supervised institutions or foster families. Statewide, some 22,000 children were in similar circumstances. Many of them were psychological and most often physical catastrophes, having been beaten, molested, starved, tortured, or variously abused since infancy. They were young Californians such as Jessica, eighteen, whipped by her methamphetamine-addicted mother's boyfriend at the age of three when he was in a drug-fueled rage, sexually abused at the age of ten by the father of another one of her mother's boy-friends while on a camping trip, a runaway by age twelve, an attempted sui-cide a few years later (seventy Prozacs in one gulp), a recalcitrant punker with a shaved head, promiscuous, intractable, moved by the court fourteen times in 1996 to different facilities, doped constantly on at least nine differ-ent psychotropic drugs: antipsychotics, antidepressants, anxiety suppres-sors, inhalers to control drug-induced shakes, and an injection of thorazine that flowed up her arms like fire. For most nights of her young life, Jessica cried herself to sleep. At eighteen, she was free to go out on her own, no high school diploma, no job prospects, no nothing. "My life sucks," noted Jessica. Few would dispute her assessment.[22]

Sexual abuse and the high probability of a youngster in turn becoming a sexual predator was just one aspect—albeit a horrific one—of the rampant child abuse so characteristic of the decade. In 1984, in the McMartin case, seven teachers at a Manhattan Beach day-care center had been indicted on 115 counts of sexual abuse of their charges. There was not one conviction, and to this day there remains a strong suspicion that the entire affair was an instance of mass hysteria. While the 1990s may not have yielded anything as surreal as the McMartin case (it had included charges of Satanic wor-ship), there was plenty of evidence to suggest that the sexual abuse of minors and young adults, frequently within the family, had revealed itself as an unsettling social problem. Equally terrible, abused children had a ten-dency to become abusers themselves. In early 1998, two California legisla-tors, Assemblyman Bob Hertzberg and Senator Adam Schiff, were calling for a dramatically expanded treatment program for the thousand or so young sex offenders in the custody of the California Youth Authority, in an effort to curtail the near-automatic production of another generation of sexual predators.

Most of the sexual abuse of children in California, including an epidemic of teenage pregnancies, was being caused by male adults. In one of the more gruesome events of the decade, as many as twenty men and boys gang-raped three young girls, ages twelve and thirteen, in a Fresno hotel in May 1998. "We've had gang rapes occur before, but not of this magnitude," noted Fresno police lieutenant Jerry Davis. "The crime itself is bad enough, but this was directed at children. It's mind-boggling." What Lieutenant Davis did not report was the fact that gang rapes were part and parcel of Fresno's gang subculture. In 1997 alone thirty-six group rapes had been reported to the Rape Counseling Service of Fresno, half of them gang related.[23]

There were still dangers in the matter of how California's teenagers were forming their sexual attitudes. Pornography of every sort was available to naturally curious teenagers in print and on the Internet. Those who argued that such pornography had no effect on behavior had to deal with the case of Jeremy Strohmeyer, a Long Beach teenager who was by his own confession an avid consumer of child pornography. On May 25, 1997, Strohmeyer raped and strangled seven-year-old Sherrice Iverson in a toilet stall of a Las Vegas casino, later telling police, "I just wanted to experience death."[24]

In the twilight hours of November 14, 1998, in a public restroom in Oceanside, San Diego County, nine-year-old Matthew Cecchi was strangled to death by Brandon Wilson, twenty-one. Matthew's parents had moved from Orange County to Oroville, seat of Butte County, seeking a safer environment in northern California, but had returned to the popular Oceanside beachfront for a family reunion. An avid fan of Nietzsche and shock-rocker Marilyn Manson, Wilson was also a heavy consumer of drugs and obsessed, after the recent divorce of his parents, with the idea of killing his mother with a knife. Passing up the opportunity to attend the University of Wisconsin (he had gotten A's in high school and had scored in the ninety-eighth percentile on his college boards), Wilson had left Wisconsin and headed out to California. Dousing himself with LSD and psilocybin while in the desert at Borrego Springs in eastern San Diego County, Wilson had gone to the coast looking for someone to kill: not anyone old, mind you, and so he passed up a number of potential victims because, as he later told the court, "when you offer a sacrifice, it's supposed to be a lamb, pure, without blemish."[25]

Such a bizarre scenario, heinous and demonic—where was it coming from? From the drugs? From Wilson's high school reading of Nietzsche, with its talk of supermen beyond good and evil? From Marilyn Manson? Many would also add the Internet to this list of contributing causes. The Internet, a growing anti-Internet lobby argued, was making available ferociously pathological pornography, which had to have some effect, if only as a matter of coarsening of attitudes, on its teenage consumers. But teenagers did not have to go to the Internet for titillation. Parents themselves could help out, as in the case of the suburban middle-class Pleasanton mother, age thirty-nine, who in November 1998 allowed her teenage daughter to organize and widely advertise a "Girls' Night Out" party at her home where a male stripper permitted the guests to fondle him beneath his G-string.

Was the rising rate of teenage suicide in part the result of such adult misbehavior and moral confusion? According to the Centers for Disease Control and Prevention, both the absolute numbers and the rates of suicides in the ten-to-fourteen age group doubled between 1979 and 1996. In 1998, seven children ages fifteen and younger took their own lives in Sacramento County. Two of them, boys, were only eleven. Experts were challenged to explain not only the epidemic of suicide, but its increasing youthfulness. Stress was certainly a factor, together with the availability of guns in the household; yet so many of the teenage suicides had hanged, not shot, themselves. Some teenage suicides achieved a level of statement, of deliberate protest, as in the case of the Romeo and Juliet deaths of Flor Zelaya and Marc Ballin, each fifteen, who hand in hand, on the morning of March 5, 1993, walked into the oncoming path of a commuter train in Sylmar. Flor had been raped and sodomized by her stepfather since she was a kindergartner. Marc had been raised by drug-addicted parents, and severely beaten by his father. Taken from his parents by the courts, Marc had been in eight living situations since he was seven. The couple met in a foster home. When Marc was moved to another foster home, he left it and sought out Flor. The two sat up all night talking in a pizza parlor. Later, Marc had shown up at Flor's school, and the two of them had taken their last walk on the railroad track.

The lower down the socioeconomic ladder an adolescent or a teenager was, the tougher it got. Ask those hundreds of children, some as young as four, working in the fields of California and elsewhere despite a roll call of laws prohibiting child labor. In 1997, Rutgers University labor economist Douglas Kruse, analyzing census and other data, estimated that there were 290,200 unlawfully employed children working the previous year throughout the United States. Some 59,600 of them were under the age of fourteen. And 13,100 of them worked in garment sweatshops.

Even when employed legally, American teenagers worked more hours per week than their counterparts in Europe or Asia. More than half of American high school seniors were working at least three hours a day after school. Not coincidentally, an equal amount, 54 percent, claimed they spent an hour or less a day on homework. The dream of universal high school education, fought for so valiantly in the late nineteenth and early twentieth centuries and fixed as part of American culture since the 1920s, was being eroded from within.

Many teenagers were working because they wanted the disposable income. Others were working because they had to. They got tired, thus distracted, at school. While their counterparts higher on the socioeconomic scale enjoyed afterschool sessions of track and field, lacrosse, tennis, soccer, or football, an increasing number of poor teenagers were flipping hamburgers or washing pots; and while their labor had a dignity in and of itself, what was happening to the dream of a high-school-educated population in all walks of life?

At school, counselors were in short supply. California had one of the highest ratios of students per counselor in the nation, which made it especially difficult on counselors in inner-city high schools. Marino Parada, thirty-six, was an El Salvador–born guidance counselor at Jefferson High School in South Los Angeles, where most of the 3,300 students spoke Spanish at home and came from families living on no more than $15,000 a year. Through long and harried days, Parada struggled to deal with the hundreds of his charges who were not going to school, not doing their homework, getting involved in, or running from, gangs, taking or being tempted to take drugs, and, cumulatively and worst of all, failing to recognize that Jefferson High School might very well be the opportunity or lost opportunity of their lives.

Finishing high school, even if in a state of fatigue or distraction, was especially hard for teenage parents. By the early 1990s, the United States had the highest teen birth rate in the developed world, with California in the lead. Most of these teenage mothers were poor and minority. Half would be on welfare within two years of the birth of their first child. By 1994, 42 percent of all families receiving Aid to Families with Dependent Children (AFDC) had begun their welfare dependency following a teenage birth. From this perspective, Veronica Velasquez of Nordhoff High School in Ojai was a notable exception. Married and a mother by the time she was fourteen, Velasquez maintained a B+ average in high school, worked on the yearbook staff, and won an academic letter for distinction in French. In her senior year, at the age of eighteen, she was elected one of four senior princesses for homecoming. Velasquez, on the other hand, was a stably married woman. Her husband, five years older, was steadily employed as a merchandise processor. Whatever her difficulties were in raising her daughter while completing high school, Velasquez did have the advantage of marriage and a working husband willing to help out with child care and household chores. Would Veronica Velasquez go on to college as she planned? Only time would tell.

David and Veronica Marquez of Long Beach, nineteen and seventeen respectively, were married with two children, a two-year-old and an infant, in September 1997. The couple had met in junior high school, when David was fifteen and Veronica thirteen. They married young, just as their parents had. Here was a crucial issue: the marriage age in the cultures that so many of these teenage California parents had come from—the various Hispanic societies most notably, but also various Southeast Asian societies—was based on a dramatically earlier entrance into marriage and childbearing than those of First World cycles. It was one thing, however, to marry and bear children in an agricultural or village community, surrounded by a supportive family and kinship structure, and quite another to do the same thing in 1990s California. And the Marquezes were having a tough time of it, despite their best intentions. Neither had finished high school. David wanted to work, and indeed had worked in the first years of his marriage, but it was difficult to make ends meet, given his intermittent employment. So the couple went on welfare, $673 a month (reduced from $700 a month after welfare reform) plus $300 a month in food stamps, supplemented by an allotment of dairy products for infant Michael under a special county program. Still, they were a family together and had hopes of better times.

By mid-decade, some 385 California teenagers each day were discovering that they were pregnant. Each day as well, some 140 of them delivered a child. As in the case of the crime rate, theories abounded as to the causes of this epidemic of births to unmarried girls, some of them not even technically in their teens. Community by community, the causes of this epidemic seemed to vary. In nearly all instances, however—whether in the ghetto or the barrio or among Southeast Asians or whites—the inability of girls to envision their future and to plan for it seemed a determinant cause. The majority of these girls were being made pregnant by young adults—young men over the age of eighteen. From this perspective, California was experiencing an epidemic of statutory rape as well as teenage pregnancies. Prosecutors rarely pursued statutory rape charges, lest the prison population swell into totally unmanageable proportions.

Part of the problem was the growing disjunction of sexuality and adulthood. Even in middle-class San Mateo, health officials were urging sixth graders to get shots for hepatitis B, a disease commonly transmitted through sexual intercourse. "We want them to do it before they become sexually

active," said county health officer Scott Morrow.[26] Planned Parenthood officials claimed that they had been kept out of the African-American community, since many black families, for historical reasons, considered the
organization just another technique of racist suppression. South Central Los
Angeles, which sustained some of the highest teen birthrates in the state,
was almost devoid of Planned Parenthood centers as late as 1993. Other
observers claimed that it was the anti–birth control, antiabortion Catholicism of Latinos that accounted for their high rate of teenage single parenthood. This was true as far as it went, but it did not take into consideration
that Catholics in developed nations, including upwardly mobile second-
generation Catholic immigrants to the United States, tended to have the
same number of children as everybody else. The lowest birth ratio in
Europe belonged to Spain and Italy.

Yet in the case of the outbreak of teenage births to Latina and African-
American girls, some form of life or pro-life dynamic was at work, whether
Catholic or not in inspiration: hundreds of thousands of black and Latina
teenage girls in the California of the 1990s did not see their future. They
were seeing, instead, their deaths—their *early* deaths—mirrored in the
many deaths of the young people around them. In Los Angeles County
alone, gang culture had by March 1993 pushed the birthrate among fifteen-
to seventeen-year-old girls to 40 percent above the national average. An
increasing number of these girls were telling counselors and social workers
that they were having these children because they wanted to. "As adults we
are horrified," noted Gayle Wilson Nathonson, executive director of the
Youth and Family Center of Inglewood, "but to children, their behavior is
logical. If you think your boyfriend won't live till he's nineteen, if you can't
go to college, having a baby at sixteen makes sense." Such a perception was
especially strong among Latina teens, who comprised 70 percent of all new
teenage mothers in Los Angeles County by March 1993, despite the fact
that they were only half of the female teenage population. While the desire
to give life amid death had noble aspects, it also had to be admitted that
Latina girls—whatever reasons lay behind their partial complacence—were
being exploited sexually by gang culture. "Does your boyfriend want a
child?" asked a social worker at the Valley Community Clinic in North Hollywood. "It doesn't make any difference to him," the girl replied. "He
already has three."[27]

As the 1990s ended and the new millennium began, experts throughout
the country and in California were divided about whether juvenile crime
was rising or waning. Dramatically conflicting testimony was available. A
study by the liberal-leaning Justice Policy Institute of Los Angeles was
claiming in March 2000 that juvenile felony arrest rates had dropped by

more than 40 percent through California from 1978 to 1998. The argument from the other side, coming mostly from prosecutors and law enforcement officials, accused the institute of playing games with comparative rates. The fact is, they argued, the raw number of arrests of juveniles for violent crime had risen by nearly 61 percent from 1983 to 1998. A study by the California Research Bureau of the State Library, issued in October 1999, painted an equally dire picture. Juveniles, the report stated, accounted for 18 percent of all felony arrests in California in 1997, including 16 percent of the homicides and 16 percent of all felony marijuana cases. It could be said that both sides were correct: while juvenile arrest rates might be falling in relationship to the total American population, juvenile crime itself—whatever its proportion of the total crime scene—was becoming increasingly violent and vicious.

The California Youth Authority had for some time been moving from its longtime program of rehabilitation and education to a more stark program of containment and punishment. CYA officials noted that the days of angels with dirty faces who could ultimately be reached were long gone. Gone as well were the days when delinquent boys and girls were housed by the CYA in cottage dorms designated by California-poetic names (San Simeon, Tamalpais, Shasta), with each dorm assigned a counselor, just like a prep school. Today's charges, CYA officials were noting—all 7,563 of them by the end of 1999, in eleven institutions and four firefighting camps—were increasingly violent felons (nearly two-thirds of them serving time for such crimes as rape, murder, and assault), a significant percentage of them mentally ill or made severely dysfunctional by long-term drug abuse.

Given the hardening of attitudes, it came as no surprise when Proposition 21 won the approval of voters in early March 2000. Officially known as the Gang Violence and Juvenile Crime Prevention Act of 1998, Proposition 21 enacted a tough, almost radical, change in the law affecting violent juvenile crime, especially when gang related. Prosecutors, for one thing, would be granted discretion about whether to prosecute a juvenile offender over fourteen as an adult, and would no longer have to ask for such permission from the juvenile court. Youths fourteen and over convicted of felonies as adults would now have to serve their time in adult prisons. Any gang member or former gang member convicted of a misdemeanor or even an infraction (truancy, underage drinking) would receive an automatic six-month prison term. All convicted gang members had to register with local law enforcement agencies. Vandalism resulting in more than $400 in damages was now a felony. Local police, finally, could now release the names of juvenile suspects to the press, even before they were formally charged with a crime.

Proposition 21 represented the most pervasive hard-nosed crackdown on juvenile crime, gang crime especially, in the United States. Defenders of Proposition 21, such as former governor Pete Wilson, argued that the initiative, if passed by the voters, would allow authorities to deal swiftly and summarily with violent offenders, hard-core cases, and recidivists and thus free up the juvenile justice system and the CYA to deal with nonviolent young offenders who could be rehabilitated. "The current juvenile justice system," Wilson argued, "does not work for violent, young, super-predators."[28] Opponents of the measure, such as Cardinal Roger Mahony of Los Angeles, speaking on behalf of the Roman Catholic bishops of California and the National Conference of Catholic Bishops, argued that Proposition 21 unfairly targeted minorities, despaired of rehabilitation, ignored social and economic factors contributing to youthful crime, and represented a form of vengeance in its willingness to send young offenders into adult prisons where they would be at high risk of rape, violent abuse, and suicide. "In 2004," Mahony said, "we'll be going after twelve-year-olds, then ten-year-olds. Where does it end?"[29]

As in the case of so many other cutting-edge and sweeping initiatives passed in the 1990s, Proposition 21 was no sooner approved by the voters than it came under legal challenge in San Diego, Los Angeles, San Francisco, and Contra Costa Counties. Interestingly, one of the most conservative of the California appellate courts, the Fourth District Court of Appeal in San Diego, was the first to act, ruling in February 2001 that a key provision of Proposition 21, transferring authority from the juvenile judge to the prosecutor in decisions relating to trying juvenile offenders as adults, violated state and federal doctrines of the separation of powers by giving judicial power to prosecutors. A significant number of district attorneys throughout California implicitly or explicitly agreed with the ruling. Supporters of the measure began the process of taking their case to the California Supreme Court.

There was little doubt that juvenile judges, whatever the final legality of Proposition 21 might turn out to be, would almost automatically view certain juvenile crimes as matters for the adult court. No one was surprised when the decision was announced by the San Diego Superior Court that Charles Andrew Williams, fifteen, would be tried as an adult for the killing of two of his fellow students and the wounding of thirteen others at Santana High School in Santee, a middle-class suburb outside San Diego, on the morning of March 5, 2001. Coming in the aftermath of the Columbine High School killings, in suburban Denver, Colorado, Williams's rampage with an eight-shot .22-caliber revolver destroyed two lives—senior Randy Gordon, seventeen, a cross-country runner with plans for joining the Navy SEALs upon graduation, and Bryan Zuckor, fourteen like Williams himself, a freshman whose mother had been so suspicious of public education that she had home-schooled him through the eighth grade—and blasted their families' hopes, and wounded thirteen other people, including a school security guard.

Just a few weeks after the Santee killings, Jason Hoffman, eighteen, a senior at Granite Hills High School in nearby El Cajon, another San Diego suburb, armed with a revolver and a shotgun, took up a sniper position outside his 2,900-student school and opened fire. Fortunately, school security officers and local police responded promptly and efficiently, and although five were wounded, no one was killed in the exchange. Hoffman himself was severely injured after what was described as a running battle with police. "Everybody knew it was going to happen," noted freshman Giovanni Gomez, fifteen, of the incident. "We were waiting for it." Hoffman later hanged himself in his prison cell.[30]

Whether any of this had a specific California dimension could be debated. If anything, it could be argued, California was merely showing—yet again—an intensification of a more pervasive American problem. Yet one could not help but glimpse in the fragmented story of Charles Andrew Williams, as it emerged in the press in the immediate aftermath of the Santee rampage, something approaching a probe into distinctive California circumstances. Here was a boy, as *Los Angeles Times* columnist Sandy Banks pointed out in a brilliant and compelling article, who for all practical purposes was flourishing in the small Maryland town where he was born and grew up. He was an honors student who loved theater and sports, played board games with his father, and was respected by his peers as a peacemaker capable of breaking up a fight. Then came the parents' divorce, and the move with his father (his mother remaining behind in Maryland) to a blue-collar/middle-class suburb on the other side of the country—a place where everybody was from someplace else, where hordes of white people lived on the margin in near anonymity in quickly and shabbily built rental properties indistinguishable one from another.

Santee was a city of 58,000 that, after the shootings, portrayed itself as a Norman Rockwell kind of place that had been unexpectedly violated by heinous violence. Others might have another opinion: marine lance corporal Carlos Colbert, an African American, who three years earlier had been severly beaten by five young white men because of his race; or another black man and his sister who, just that November, had been persecuted by a white resident, who referred to Santee as Klantee; or the young African-American female student, recently moved to Santee from Japan where her parents were in the military, who faced an onslaught of racial slurs en route to school, in the hallways, in class. ("I feel more like a foreigner here," she noted, "than I did in Japan.") Just before the killings at Santee, in January, Mayor Randy Voepel had asked a local pastor to serve as the human relations advisor for the city when swastikas and racist literature surfaced at Santana and another local high school.

Santee, in short, was showing the tensions and brutalizations of a society thrown together overnight: of white people who were, simultaneously, arriving at better circumstances but also leveling out in their mobility and experiencing the paranoia and anger that comes from being at a dead end. Charles Andrew Williams's father was a computer programmer dropped in the middle of a lower-register San Diego suburb, like everybody else around, who kept guns in his house. Motherless, unsupervised, his son began to be formed—or rather de-formed—by the society and culture around him. In Maryland he had been respected by his peers, and for a fifteen-year-old, this means everything. At Santana High he had become the butt of aggressive bullying by older boys, who took the money out of his wallet and taunted him because he was skinny and a geek and did not fit in. "He should have started fighting people to get respect," said a sophomore after the killings. "Even the people who got picked on, picked on him."[31]

Williams's refuge, such as it was, became a nearby local park, where he hung out with other neglected and marginalized young people, uncertain even in these relationships, skateboarding, experimenting with alcohol and marijuana, brooding over his treatment at school. Whatever criminal he was soon to become, however horrible would soon be his actions, Charles Andrew Williams was at that moment just another trashed kid, unsupervised, uncared-for, surrounded by danger. He told his ragtag confederates that he would soon be bringing his father's .22-caliber revolver to school and getting even. They mostly did not believe him, although one adult—the boyfriend of the mother of one of the kids at the park—hearing of the threat, did make a halfhearted effort to contact Williams's father, one telephone call, but no one was at home to answer. And so the youngster from Gaithersburg, Maryland, tiring of the effort of fitting in—of becoming a Southern Californian, one might say—put the pistol in his backpack and went to school, just another trashed kid, now on the verge of killing and trashing others. He was crossing a line here, an adult line, between two evils: the evil he had endured and the evil he would now perpetrate. Quite correctly, society would soon be judging him as an adult. Yet the question lingered: Was society, in judging Charles Andrew Williams, also obliged to judge itself?

Send In the Marines

As far as urban theory was concerned, the decade opened with the publication of Mike Davis's *City of Quartz* (1990), an evocation of Los Angeles as an oligarchical conspiracy. Brilliantly written and forcefully argued, *City of Quartz* soon became the Los Angeles book of the decade and, with the exception of a Raymond Chandler novel or two and Reyner Banham's *Los Angeles: The Architecture of Four Ecologies* (1973), one of the most influential books on Los Angeles to appear in the second half of the twentieth century. Like Chandler, Davis wrote from an interior bleakness that found in the City of Angels much to corroborate his inner vision and emotional landscape. Powerfully seizing upon every noir aspect of the rise of Los Angeles in the twentieth century—and there was much to seize upon—Davis, a working-class intellectual shaped by the British labor movement and the social scientific insights of the Frankfurt school, argued a complex and compelling case for his vision of Los Angeles as grim, conspiratorial, racist, repressive, and squandering of land, water, and people. Even the Roman Catholic Church, so closely held in the affections and imagination of those Latinos with whom Davis intensely sympathized, was presented not in terms of the dynamism of the Virgin of Guadalupe devotion or even the theologized fatalism of Mexican culture, but in terms of Cardinal Roger Mahony's long and bitter war with the Latino gravediggers in his archdiocesan cemeteries.

Davis had special contempt for the work of the Los Angeles 2000 Committee chaired by Bank of America vice chairman James Miscoll. Meeting through the middle years of the previous decade, taking thousands of hours of testimony from hundreds of community figures, the blue-ribbon committee had in 1988 produced a report abounding in optimism for the Los Angeles future. Davis considered the report the last gasp of a booster decade that had opened with the Los Angeles Olympics and was now assuring one and all that an expanded oligarchy, this time including upwardly mobile minorities and minority oligarchs, working in conjunction with megadevelopers and the haute intelligentsia, would continue the good times well into the twenty-first century.

Against the booster feel-goodism of the Los Angeles 2000 Committee, Davis touted the insights of the neo-Marxist postmodernist Los Angeles school based in UCLA, USC, and to a lesser extent in other local faculties. Los Angeles was far from being the comforting world-class city rich in diversity, the theorists of the Los Angeles school opined. It was not the crossroads entrepôt of the Far West, vibrant and jazzy, as claimed in the committee report. Los Angeles was, rather, the city of dreadful night or, as Davis put it, quoting UCLA geographer Alan Scott, a "new Dickensian hell of underclass poverty."[32] For various reasons—in part because some aspects of Davis's critique were sadly true—*City of Quartz* became an instant cult classic and the dominant gloss on Los Angeles for the rest of the decade. Virtually every other interpretation of the city was pushed aside. The Los Angeles 2000 report was filed and forgotten. Academics and journalists from around the world besieged Davis with requests for interviews or personal tours of this new Dickensian hell on the Pacific.

Whatever the merits of Davis's analysis—and even admirers of the book winced at its exaggerations—the sheer popularity of *City of Quartz* was in and of itself a symptom of the psychological condition of the city, at least among its book-reading public. The very fact that such an unmitigatingly bleak view of Los Angeles should be so immediately accepted as the final word said something very important about the psychological state of the city in the early 1990s. Davis's apocalyptic vision, filtered and structured through a variety of postmodernist prisms, had become the norm. The Los Angeles of *City of Quartz* was one vast prison, one dead-end system, one ash heap, an already happened disaster waiting to repeat itself. Even those who disagreed with the fundamental thesis of the book had to acknowledge that something violent needed to be said about this violent city. If only because of the deaths of the gangbangers and those they took down with them, if only for the wounded, abused, or killed children, if only for the extremes of poverty and wealth, if only for the loneliness and the terror, something like *City of Quartz,* however incomplete and one-sided, had to appear. As the decade opened, Los Angeles was entering into some dark and fearsome region, and for the time being, Mike Davis's explanation was as good as anyone's, and better than most.

And so Los Angeles continued to build toward explosion, not in a process of cause and effect, necessarily, but more in terms of a scattershotting of symptoms that revealed a city in trouble in a number of differing ways that were somehow beginning to coalesce. In February 1991 an air traffic controller at LAX landed a USAir jetliner on top of a SkyWest commuter plane. Thirty-four people were killed. The subsequent investigation revealed a long list of glaring deficiencies: an aging, malfunctioning ground radar system, glare from ground lights, poor staffing patterns, deviations from standard operating procedures (switching runways at the last moment, permitting planes to land and take off in opposite directions, holding waiting planes dangerously close to active runways), and prior complaints, including a negative red star rating from the International Federation of Airline Pilots. The Crossroads City described in the Los Angeles 2000 report did not have its airport in order.

The following month, slightly after midnight, March 3, 1991, the California Highway Patrol, joined by the LAPD and one car from the school district police, ran down a speeding white 1988 Hyundai on the Foothill Freeway in Sun Valley. Its driver, twenty-five-year-old Rodney King, a part-time Dodger Stadium groundskeeper from Altadena, recently paroled after serving two years for second-degree burglary, was ordered to take a prone position on the asphalt. King, an African American, was a big man—six feet three inches tall, 225 pounds—and he had been drinking. Later, it was claimed that he might have been on PCP, but tests revealed no presence of this drug. A beating by four LAPD policemen ensued, fifty-six baton blows in all, caught on video camera by George Holliday, a resident of the apartment complex adjacent to the spot where the police had brought King to ground. According to emergency-room physician Dr. Edmund Chein, who treated King immediately after the beating, the victim had a broken leg, a shattered eye socket, and a fractured cheekbone. Fillings had been knocked from his teeth, and his flesh was a maze of bruises. There was also evidence of concussion and serious facial nerve damage that compounded the pain of the other injuries.

In late March 1991, at the Empire Liquor Market Deli on South Figueroa in South Central Los Angeles, storekeeper Soon Ja Du, a middle-aged Korean female, got into an argument with a fifteen-year-old black teenager named Latasha Harlins over a $1.79 plastic container of orange juice the storekeeper accused the girl of trying to steal. Harlins placed the container of juice on the counter and turned to leave. As a video camera recorded the event, Soon Ja Du shot Latasha Harlins twice in the back of the head, killing her instantly. When the case came to trial, Los Angeles Superior Court judge Joyce Karlin—youngish and very blonde—placed the woman on probation. The outcry—was this all that a black teenager's life was worth?—resulted in the removal of Karlin from criminal court, but the incident remained a stinging point of contention in the black community. A few weeks later, at Chung's Liquor Market near Western Avenue and 79th, another Korean grocer shot and killed a black man in dubious circumstances. No charges were filed. In Glendale a man was sentenced to thirty days in jail for killing a cocker spaniel.

Over the weekend of April 19–21, 1991, while the videotape of the Rodney King beating continued to be played throughout the world, fifteen citizens of the city were lost to violence, the majority of them gunned down on the sidewalks in one or another gang ambush. Most were young, with the exception of fifty-six-year-old Tommy Lee Jordan, who lost his life because two younger men wanted his 1987 Chevrolet Monte Carlo.

Already, the city was edging into an unusual level of introspection. Hundreds had already died in gangland warfare without so much as a moment of interpretive commentary; but the Rodney King beating and the subsequent uproar, together with the eventual indictment of the four offending officers on felony charges, was forcing Los Angeles to think about itself, and not in a very flattering way. Los Angeles had become the Selma, the Birmingham of the West Coast. "You think of Los Angeles as this advanced, open society," noted Sharp James, mayor of Newark, New Jersey, "and all of a sudden it's behaving like some Southern backwater."[33]

Then there was the question of whether history was repeating itself. Los Angeles, after all, was where, in the early 1940s, seventeen young Mexican Americans had been framed for murder in the Sleepy Lagoon case, and where, as in the case of the Rodney King beating, police officers had been standing by impassively for decades while other police officers beat minority heads. For Robert Towne, screenwriter of *Chinatown* (1974), the Rodney King beating, like the story of *Chinatown* itself, offered a sinister view of the power structure of the city. The beating, Towne noted, reminded him of comparable events that preceded the 1965 Watts riot. Not that he was predicting a riot—he was not, Towne insisted—but as in the case of the pre-Watts incidents, the King beating revealed that something was festering in the City of Angels.

Los Angeles was not a violent city, Mayor Tom Bradley was telling the Japanese in Tokyo in late April 1991. Despite the gang warfare, the Rodney King beating, the freeway shootings, the bizarre street incidents, the impression that Los Angeles was dangerous to tourists was, the mayor argued, a myth. Drive-by shootings and gang activity, Bradley noted, occurred only in limited areas of the city and involved only black or Hispanic gangs. To date, no tourists had been threatened. "I can tell you with authority," the mayor stated, "that when there is a drive-by shooting—and they do occur from time to time—and when there are conflicts between gangs—and they do occur—in no case will you have found that those involved or threatened tourists."[34]

The following fall, Mayor Bradley proclaimed Friday, September 13,

1991, Freddy Krueger Day in Los Angeles, in honor of the serial killer in the latest installment of the *Nightmare on Elm Street* film series. Many protested the fact that one of the nation's most violent cities was honoring a mass murderer, albeit a fictional one. "It's unbelievable," stated Jerry Rubin, director of the Los Angeles Alliance for Survival, an antiviolence group based in Venice. "Does that mean you can celebrate by going out and stabbing and killing someone?"[35]

Many would say yes, for by then Los Angeles had become an armed camp. Everyone, it seemed, had a gun. Judges had guns under their robes as they held court. Salesmen had guns in their sample briefcases. Housewives had guns in their purses. And gangbangers had guns, lots of them, many of them automatic. In 1991 alone, a record 1,554 people were slain with firearms in Los Angeles County—four times the combined number of those who were killed through other means, and not including the 489 who shot themselves to death voluntarily or the thirty-two who died in accidental shootings. At least 8,050 people had been rushed to local hospitals with fatal or nonfatal gunshot wounds. More than three thousand licensed gun dealers were feeding this hunger for weaponry. Between 1987 and 1992, 46,453 handguns were sold legally in Los Angeles County alone, one for every nineteen residents. Deaths from stray bullets were becoming commonplace. In 1991, gangbanging and drive-bys were moving toward yet another record year.

Awareness that Los Angeles had deep-seated problems was manifesting itself everywhere as 1991 lurched toward 1992. In the aftermath of the Rodney King beating, attorney-entrepreneur Richard Riordan had given a dinner party at his Brentwood home for a group of friends and civic leaders. Riordan was active in a half-dozen civic causes and charities, and his network was diverse. One of the topics of conversation that came up that evening was how rarely the disparate leaders of the various Los Angeles communities got together. In times past, Riordan believed, Los Angeles had shown that it was especially sensitive to oligarchical guidance. The Municipal League had reformed the city charter in the mid-1920s; and recently, in the go-go growth years of the 1960s, a Committee of Twenty-Five had exercised a decisive and stabilizing influence. What was needed, Riordan argued, was a Coalition of One Hundred, tapping leaders from every background; and so in late October 1991 he sprang for an initial gathering, in the City Club high above the downtown, of what he hoped would become a new and healing force in the city. Together in one room, at least for one evening, was the multiethnic leadership of the city—Riordan himself, Stewart Kwoh of the Asian Pacific American Legal Center, African-American attorney Gilbert Ray, Rand Schrader, a municipal judge and gay activist, Monsignor

Terrance Fleming, vice chancellor of the Archdiocese of Los Angeles, Watts activist Sweet Alice Harris, and all the others, hoping against hope that they could hold it together. "If heaven is like that," said Harris of the luxuriant City Club, "I will be more than satisfied."[36]

One of the things Sweet Alice was talking about that evening was the debilitating shortage of retail shops, including grocery stores, in her part of the city—Watts, Baldwin Hills, Ladera Heights—and this, too, was part of the tension that was building. Approximately a million people in South Central Los Angeles, the majority of them African-American and Latino, were retail deprived. They paid high prices, often for shoddy merchandise, and they had to travel long distances, frequently by bus, to do their shopping. The entire region lacked supermarkets, drug stores, discount stores, and restaurants, with the exception of McDonald's and Kentucky Fried Chicken. When a Denny's opened in Willowbrook, a South Central community, it rated coverage in the local press. Retail food chains that were still doing business in the area—Boys, Viva, ABC, all owned by the Food 4 Less supermarket company—charged higher prices, which the company justified by citing the increased costs of doing business in these regions, including security expenses and losses from theft.

Sheer economics could be seen as the cause of this scarcity. Median family income in this part of the city hovered around $20,800, which was 32 percent less than that in the rest of Los Angeles County. And there were continuing problems with theft, especially from the young. "A lot of kids come in and take things and run away," noted one owner of a South Central food shop. "We can do nothing. When we're busy, they come in and take everything."[37] Many stores in the region, especially the larger supermarkets, were by now fenced and arms-guarded camps. A number of them had elaborate electronic security systems. Customers, for their part, complained that Korean grocers could frequently be abrupt, even rude. Behind the shooting of Latasha Harlins by the elderly Korean-American grocer simmered more diffuse and subterranean tensions between Korean-American shopkeepers and their minority customers.

If one were to look for further evidence of tension, this time in a highbrow setting, Los Angeles playwright Reza Abdoh's new play *Bogeyman*, then playing at the Los Angeles Theatre Center on Spring Street, would more than suffice. Few theaters would find it necessary, as the Los Angeles Theatre Center did, to post a sign in the lobby warning theatergoers that they might find parts of the play offensive. Which parts? All parts, it could be argued; for *Bogeyman* was a nonstop plotless progression of horrors. Blacks and gays were violently tortured; women were relentlessly beaten. There was a castration by chain saw and other selected atrocities, including a scene where a nude green-haired punk—rings through his tongue, nipples, stomach, genitals, and anus—was suspended from his feet into a fish tank. Many viewers found themselves grateful for the relatively noncontroversial scene of two nude men having sex in a shower. At least no one, in this case, seemed to be suffering. All this occurred, incidentally, in one single set depicting a three-story, fourteen-room apartment house. "I'm not in the business of pandering to the audience," said Abdoh, in a rare moment of understatement.[38]

Further artistic evidence of the torment and noir at the center of the Los Angeles imagination could be witnessed that January with the opening of curator Paul Schimmel's "Helter Skelter: LA Art in the 1990s" at the Temporary Contemporary annex of the Museum of Contemporary Art in Little Tokyo. As in the case of *Bogeyman,* the museum posted a warning sign at its entrance: "This exhibition contains imagery and language that some people may find offensive. Viewer discretion is advised." The exhibit's title was taken from the repertoire of mass murderer Charles Manson in a deliberate effort to shock. (Schimmel also made central to the exhibition narrative drawings by Jim Shaw chronicling the career of a serial killer.) Too many of the artists with international reputations, Schimmel complained—David Hockney and Sam Francis, for example—presented an image of Los Angeles as pastoral idyll and beachfront. In this new show, by contrast, the work of sixteen contemporary Los Angeles artists would be presented as a netherworld of sex, violence, perversity, and alienation spread through 45,000 square feet of exhibition space.

Nowhere were the growing tensions felt more keenly than in the always problematic matter of police-community relations. The four LAPD officers who had savagely beaten Rodney King were now standing trial for felony assault under color of authority in Simi Valley in Ventura County, where the case had been moved at the request of the defense. For most minority communities in Los Angeles, especially the African-American and Latino, the King beating was far from being an isolated incident. It represented, rather, the tip of the iceberg. In 1986, when last such statistics were available, LAPD officers were killing three persons a year and wounding more than eight per one thousand sworn officers, the highest rate in the nation. Between 1986 and 1990, thanks to more than three hundred lawsuits alleging excessive force on the part of the LAPD, the city had to shell out another $20 million in judgments, settlements, and jury verdicts.

In the aftermath of the King beating, the mayor and city council had convened a special commission, chaired by lawyer Warren Christopher, an assistant secretary of state in the Carter administration, to investigate misbehavior in the LAPD. Presented personally by Christopher to chief of police Daryl Gates in July 1991, the 228-page *Report of the Independent Commission on the Los Angeles Police Department,* subsequently known as the Christopher Commission report, offered a soberly written but scathing indictment of the attitudes and policies of the LAPD. Because the LAPD was small in terms of the city it covered—two officers per thousand residents, the lowest ratio of any big city in the nation—it had developed a highly mobile, proactive response to crime. Like an elite commando force, the LAPD practiced a program of mobile response, proactive action, and, if necessary, deadly fire. Writing in the *New York Review of Books* on October 24, 1991, novelist John Gregory Dunne pushed the military metaphor even further. The LAPD was not just a commando or marine unit, Dunne suggested, but a heavily armed Panzer division with its own helicopter air force. Indeed, throughout the 1980s and early 1990s, LAPD helicopters had been droning over the city, their spotlights tracking fleeing suspects in scenes reminiscent of the opening sequences of Francis Ford Coppola's Vietnam epic *Apocalypse Now* (1979).

From one perspective, it was comforting: a crime-ridden city had necessitated the creation of a mobile defense force—SWAT teams on the ground, helicopters overhead, squad cars capable of being deployed at a moment's notice—in response to both the crime rate and the sheer size of the city. Like any elite unit, the paramilitary LAPD trained its officers in the most demanding police academy in the nation. Like marines graduating from boot camp, newly sworn LAPD officers emerged lean and mean, well trained, gung ho. The good news was that the LAPD was not corrupt, in the sense of cash payoffs and the like. It was, rather, a constabulary, a praetorian guard, proud of its uniform and its traditions. But too often, proactive action involved an assumption of guilt on the part of minorities, which led to a tendency toward false arrests, many of them involving rough treatment and a pervasive us-against-them attitude on the part of white working- or lower-middle-class cops and the city's minorities. The LAPD officers, moreover, were not afraid to fire their guns. The department possessed the highest kill-per-officer ratio in the nation.

Perhaps the most damaging part of the Christopher Commission report was not in the report itself but in its verbatim listing in an appendix of some 693 transcribed radio messages. Here, in the officers' raw humor, was revealed the inner psychic life—the life of the street—in which the men and women of the thin blue line lived and worked. Like all barracks banter, it was profane and visceral and gave no quarter. This was a culture of them-against-us, a contempt for large sections of the population being policed, and a love of the chase and the "stick work" that inevitably followed when the culprit was run to ground, as in the case of Rodney King. Only when middle-class citizens asked questions, for example, when stopped for a speeding ticket or when they otherwise failed to show subservience when confronted by the LAPD, did they also join the ranks of the despised, becoming, in cop parlance, assholes, meaning middle-class citizens with complaints.

The Christopher Commission called for an end to this culture and—indirectly perhaps, but it was there as a subtext of the entire report—for the resignation of Chief Daryl Gates. Therein lay the rub, for Gates—the leanest, meanest, most representative cop on the beat—wasn't having any of it. Forget former mayor Sam Yorty or any comparable figure. If you were looking for someone to epitomize the hardscrabble Los Angeles of the 1930s, it would be Daryl Gates. Although he wore four stars on his collar, Gates was as much an outsider as the people he policed; Gates's Los Angeles—white, evangelical Christian, migrating to the coast from the South and Midwest in the 1920s and 1930s—had never really achieved its place in the sun (with the exception of Yorty's tenure as mayor), and it was now on the way out before it had found its way in. Raised in Glendale in the 1930s, his father out of work, his mother working six days a week as a dress cutter in the garment industry downtown, Daryl Gates came from another coast: not the coast of glamour or even the coast of dreams but the coast of recently uprooted hardscrabble dirt farmers in the first generation of suburbanization or urbanization, people who had focused their hopes in the 1920s and 1930s on the Foursquare Gospel of Aimee Semple McPherson and who were by the 1950s seeing the diminishing, if not the end, of even their little piece of the LA pie.

Finishing his service as a navy seaman in the Pacific during World War II, Gates, twenty-one, married with a pregnant wife, joined the LAPD and continued a part-time college course at USC. Excelling at the police academy, he was assigned to the personal staff of legendary Chief William Parker as chauffeur and bodyguard. There, in the eighteen months that followed, Daryl Gates, like a young priest serving as a bishop's secretary or a lieutenant serving as a general's aide, saw the inside workings of the agency he would one day head. At the time, Parker was taking the LAPD out of its prior existence as a corrupt force and refashioning it into more than just a department. It would be an institution, a government within the government, its chief unremovable (so said the city charter) by either mayor or city council.

Resign, as the Christopher Commission report suggested and as city councilman Mike Woo was now openly calling for? Forget it! Not Daryl Gates, not the man who had worked his way up the ranks into the best job someone from his background, with his education, could ever get. What did he care if they didn't like him? He had as much contempt for the bleeding hearts on the city council and the press, for the downtown suits, as he had for the scum on the streets. (Gates had once suggested that a huge section of the Mojave Desert be cordoned off and up to 500,000 criminal misfits be segregated there.) True, he had been appointed by the mayor (Sam Yorty in Gates's case, another poor white man who had struggled to the top) and confirmed by the city council; but according to the Los Angeles charter, once the chief was in, that was it until retirement, provided there were no criminal convictions. And however stone-faced and laconic he might be on the outside—and impassivity was his best defense—Gates had felt sick to his stomach at seeing the videotapes of the Rodney King beating, or so he would later claim in his autobiography. These four guys—Stacey Koon, Laurence Powell, Theodore Briseno, and Timothy Wind—had brought disgrace to the LAPD, and for Daryl Gates the honor of the department was more precious than life itself.

As soon as the officers were indicted Gates suspended three of them without pay and fired the fourth, Timothy Wind, who had been on probation. The chief had already survived one effort of the LA Police Commission to get rid of him by putting him on a sixty-day paid leave, and was even now playing off the city council against the commission in a skilled effort to save his own job. The very day Gates suspended or fired the four indicted officers, commission president Dan Garcia, disgusted that the council was thwarting the commission's efforts to oust Gates, resigned in protest. One Los Angeles had gone eyeball to eyeball with another, in that Garcia—a highly decorated Vietnam veteran, a brilliant attorney, a civic leader frequently mentioned as a future mayor of the city—represented, at its best, Latino Los Angeles in its politically emergent phase. It was Garcia, however, not Gates, who blinked; or, at least, he got fed up with the efforts of pro-Gates council members to keep the chief in his job.

Troubles continued to mount. In August 1991 two sheriff's deputies shot and killed—nine shots to the back, together with numerous head, mouth, elbow, and knee injuries inflicted before the shots were fired—a mentally disturbed African-American male, Keith Hamilton, thirty-three, in Ladera Heights. Later that month, a city garbage-truck driver, Vernell Ramsey Jr., forty-one, an African American, filed a $50 million suit against the LAPD, claiming that on August 16, officers had gratuitously beat him, shattering his right kneecap and leg, when they stopped him at eleven-thirty p.m. outside a food stand at the corner of Van Nuys Boulevard and Tamarack Avenue on suspicion, so the LAPD later said, of possessing cocaine. No drugs had been found on Ramsey's person.

In late September 1991 a team from Amnesty International traveled from London to Los Angeles to investigate the mounting charges of police brutality against the LAPD. Amnesty had been monitoring Los Angeles, its spokesperson told the press, long before the Rodney King incident, and had prepared itself for its investigation by a meticulous study of the Christopher Commission report. It now had a dossier of some fifty alleged cases of brutality on the part of the LAPD or sheriff's deputies. "We are here to look at the question of police brutality," Amnesty spokeswoman Anita Tiessen told the press on the first day of the team's visit. "We are going to be looking at the questions of when is force used, under what criteria is the use of force justified, what are the rules?"[39] Although he agreed to meet with the Amnesty team for an hour, Daryl Gates was furious at the depiction of Los Angeles as a Third World city in a banana republic dictatorship.

And so it continued into 1992, as the Rodney King trial got under way in Simi Valley, and the city waited. On Sunday, the first of March, police shot and killed a man in full view of spectators gathered at the finish line of the Los Angeles Marathon. The dead man, Daryl Montgomery, thirty, of Inglewood, an African American, had attacked two LAPD officers, almost as if he had wanted to die. Although the police were judged justified in their response, the trauma of the event and the sight of Montgomery's body lying in front of the Los Angeles Memorial Auditorium in Exposition Park during one of the most celebratory events of the year hardly soothed the nerves of an increasingly jittery city.

Sociologically, the trial under way in Ventura County was a case study in ethnic and class conflict. The four indicted officers embodied the white middle class that made up 70 percent of the LAPD and that also represented, in diverse ways, a psychologically embattled sector of the population: an embattlement that could only be exacerbated and intensified by the day-to-day work of a police officer. Koon had once threatened to shoot a neighbor's dog if it came back into his yard. Powell, the most conspicuous assailant in the King beating, with as many as forty-five strikes with his baton, had already been involved in charges of excessive force with that instrument, breaking one arrestee's elbow so severely that it had to be pinned back together. Briseno's first wife once charged that he had beaten her severely about the head, and in 1985, he had received a citizen's complaint for excessive force, which was later repeated to the Christopher Commission. In 1987 he had been suspended without pay for sixty-six days for beating a handcuffed suspect on the head with his baton.

For whatever reasons—their backgrounds, the stress of their jobs, the streaks of violence and racism in their nature—the four white cops had lost their minds—or at least their control—completely in the early-morning hours of March 3, 1991; yet their Simi Valley jury, made up of white, middle-class, suburban men and women, found it difficult to convince themselves, individually or collectively, that the four officers had acted with criminal intent. Even so, no one—or very few, at the least—could have expected the verdict that came six days later, on April 29, at four p.m.: not guilty. Not guilty despite the videotapes. Not guilty despite the medical reports of King's post-beating condition. Not guilty.

News of the verdict raced through the city. "I was speechless when I heard that verdict," Mayor Tom Bradley told a hastily assembled press conference. "Today this jury told the world that what we saw with our own eyes is not a crime."[40] Many would later claim that Bradley's remarks and the visible distress of the otherwise impassive mayor constituted an implicit license to riot. Yet the demonstrators outside Parker Center, the LAPD headquarters, needed no one's permission as they began to pelt the plate-glass doors of the building with rocks and call for the resignation of Daryl Gates.

Nor was any permission needed for the crowds forming at 71st and Normandie and at Florence and Normandie a block away, where two hundred people were already hurling chunks of pavement at passing cars and dragging light-skinned motorists into the street to be robbed and beaten. Then, as a television crew covered the action live from a hovering helicopter, Reginald Denny, thirty-six, rolled his eighteen-wheeler into the intersection, hauling twenty-seven tons of sand toward a cement-mixing plant in Inglewood. Slowing down to avoid the overturned trash cans in the street, Denny was yanked from the cab of his truck by one of several black men who had surrounded his rig. Now, on live television, ensued a beating— blows, kicks to the head when Denny was down, the bashing of his skull with a fire extinguisher taken from his truck, hands lifted in triumph by one of the assailants—that mirrored the horrible ferocity of the Rodney King assault, only this time the LAPD was not in sight.

At this very moment of horror, with a white man being beaten so savagely by four young black men in an orgy of racial revenge, some element of future redemption and reconciliation appeared—even as the riot was only beginning, even when the deaths and burnings had hardly begun. Two African-American men who had been watching the beating on live television, together with another African-American man who had stepped from the crowd and an African-American woman who lived in the neighborhood, spirited Denny to safety, saving his life. "You're going to make it," the woman kept telling Denny. "You're going to be OK."[41]

For the next three days, however, whether or not Los Angeles would make it remained an open question. For three nights and two days, Central Los Angeles burst into flames. Later, when the looting, burning, and killing had stopped, the Los Angeles riots—the worst civil disturbance in contemporary American history—would, like Los Angeles itself, be open to various interpretations. Most immediately, the riots were a protest against the Rodney King verdict and everything the beating and the verdict stood for. This was perhaps the easiest and the most complimentary way to interpret the disturbances. An oppressed people, in such a scenario, had risen against the oppressors.

But it was a consumer riot as well—an orgy of wholesale looting motivated, most immediately, by the simple pleasures of theft and the more long-range resentments of consumers, many of them recent immigrants, others third-generation prisoners of the ghetto, as they looted, then torched, stores that contained the consumer goods that had for so long tantalized their welfare incomes or their working poverty. And so, one saw the spectacle of women carrying armfuls of Pampers and household utensils out of stores, and young men carrying off designer sneakers, and middle-aged men liberating caches of liquor. The deliberate burning of so many Korean-owned stores underscored the racial tensions of this particular seller-consumer relationship, and the name of Latasha Harlins was now and then heard from anyone who felt a vague impulse to justify the looting or torching of a Korean-owned shop.

The predominance of looting as a riot activity would later trouble those who wished to view the riots as the rising up of the oppressed masses. The riots, after all, did not involve to any significant degree the Latino communities of East Los Angeles, where people were hardworking and owned their own homes. Its epicenter was the great center of the city—South Central moving north into Pico Union and south toward San Pedro and Long Beach—where more than one million people, the majority of them renters, lived in conditions of economic stress that would make them, despite their lack of criminal background, vulnerable to this sudden free-for-all, this unexpected *mercado*. An uprising planned and executed by a paramilitary or otherwise organized group from an earlier era—the Black Panthers, say—would have shown discipline and concentrations of force. It would have sought to seize the city. The Los Angeles riots, by contrast, displayed a spontaneity within certain sectors of the city (not the Westside, not Beverly Hills, not Los Feliz, not Silver Lake, not Mt. Washington, not East Los Angeles) that made it seem, rather, a kind of mirror image or reverse paradigm or grotesque parody of a folk festival, a market festival run amok.

For certain critics, the riots were primarily the result of police mismanagement: despite the growing tensions of the city and the impending verdict in the Rodney King case, Daryl Gates and the top brass had no real plan for coping with widespread civil disturbance. On the day of the verdict, much of the LAPD's top hierarchy was either on vacation, out of town, or driving home when the violence began. Two-thirds of the department's eighteen patrol captains, the frontline commanders of the force, were attending a training seminar in Oxnard. Hundreds of officers were released to go home from the afternoon shift despite the stunning Simi Valley verdicts. Gates himself had continued with plans to attend a Brentwood fund-raiser that evening, even after the verdict was announced. Later, Gates would claim that Lieutenant Mike Moulin at the 77th Street division, in deciding not to regroup his officers and rout rioters from the intersection of Florence and Normandie—flashpoint of the riot, and where the televised assault on Denny had occurred—failed to cut off the riot at its inception. Moulin, however, was unapologetic. "I didn't want them killed," he said of the officers under his command. "It's really that simple. And I didn't want the incident to escalate. And I didn't want to go into that area without sufficient forces."[42]

Others blamed an ill-prepared and ill-equipped California National Guard, which had bungled the deployment of two thousand troops into the city, losing a full day by keeping soldiers in barracks because they did not have the ammunition, batons, protective shields, or even the training to carry out the required antiriot deployments. A subsequent report, prepared by the acting Guard commander after the adjutant general had stepped down in the aftermath of the riots, noted that the Guard had deemphasized training for urban civil unrest during the 1980s. Nor had the Guard leadership been alerted that their services might be necessary as the Rodney King verdict approached. It was on April 29, after conferring with Tom Bradley, that Governor Pete Wilson ordered two thousand Guardsmen into Los Angeles. The men should have been on the streets before dawn. They were not deployed until the evening, however, twenty-four hours after the governor had ordered the intervention. The effective deployment of the Guard by daybreak of the first full day of rioting might have saved the city from two more days of murder, arson, looting, and disorder.

As it was, President Bush was forced to authorize the commitment of 4,500 federal troops into the city on Friday, May 1. A rioting city had now come under federal jurisdiction. It would eventually take, by Sunday evening, nearly 8,500 Guardsmen, army, soldiers and marines to bring order to the City of Angels. By Sunday evening, May 3, a smoky haze hung over the city from the multiple fires that had been set throughout the region. Forty-five bodies lay in morgues under the supervision of the coroner. Guardsmen and marines in camouflage stood guard on street corners or behind gunnysack emplacements. Jeeps and Humvees patrolled the city.

PART III

Diversity

Viva Mexico!

Just as the most important ethnic question facing Americans in the 1960s was civil rights for African Americans, the most important ethnic question facing the United States in the 1990s was how exactly the nation would adjust to its developing Hispanic identity and how Hispanic immigrants would be adjusting to their new country. The megastates New York, Florida, Texas, and California were on the cutting edge of this experiment. In August 1993 the Census Bureau released a report indicating that there were 22.1 million Hispanics in the United States. Forty percent of these were immigrants. At 63.6 percent, Mexicans constituted the single largest group, followed by Central and South Americans (14 percent), Puerto Ricans (10.6 percent), and Cubans (4.7 percent), with the remaining 7 percent consisting of other Hispanic groups, including European Basque, Portuguese, and Spanish. In terms of income, Cubans ranked highest, with a median household income of $26,593, and Puerto Ricans, at $17,967, ranked lowest. But both Cubans and Puerto Ricans, as well as the other Hispanic groups, were located primarily on the East Coast. Mexican Americans and recent Mexican immigrants, by contrast, had settled mainly through the western half of the Sun Belt and in California, although by January 1998 a gradually extending seven-million-strong Mexican diaspora had ranged as far north as Maine and Alaska.

In Santa Ana in Orange County, immigrants had been arriving from the village of Granjenal in northern Michoacan for thirty-five years, beginning in the twilight years of the bracero program. Gradually, in this three-decade period, Santa Ana made the transition from an English-speaking Anglo-American town to an overwhelmingly Spanish-speaking settlement—population 305,000, of whom 69 percent were Latino—dominated by ex-villagers from Granjenal. This process was accelerated after 1986 when the federal government granted amnesty and legal residency to three million undocumented immigrants nationwide, including some 140,000 residents of Orange County, who could then bring their family members north. Francisco Lopez, for example, a construction worker, settled in Santa Ana in 1962 and eventually brought his wife and eight children to Southern California. Like so many men from Granjenal, Lopez supported his family by building the housing tracts and new towns—Mission Viejo, Irvine, Rancho Santa Margarita, Leisure World—rapidly transforming Orange County. By August 1997, Lopez, now fifty-nine years of age and tiring, was nevertheless reporting each morning at six to the hiring hall of Laborers' Union Local 652 (350 Granjenal immigrants made up more than one-tenth of 652's membership) for a cup of coffee and perhaps a game of cards as the men waited for their names to be called for a day of employment. By the second generation, Granjenal Santa Anans included not only construction workers but also two doctors, two attorneys, a psychologist, and a sprinkling of secretaries, court interpreters, police officers, teachers, real estate brokers, and small-business owners. Village associations had tended to remain intact for more than thirty years, as evidenced by the presence of not one but three Granjenal soccer teams. Immigrants from a single village, moreover, were most often interrelated or at least shared a village identity akin to kinship itself. Such associations softened the terrors of transition by maintaining, as far as possible, the values and folkways of one's native village in a new setting.

By 1993 a new pattern was asserting itself. Urban dwellers, including *capitalinos,* natives of Mexico City, were also moving north in significant numbers. While village immigrants tended to regroup by village in El Norte, *capitalinos* and other city dwellers—already uprooted from village life—tended to gravitate toward metropolitan Los Angeles, which was in its own way a reflection of Mexico City. Very soon, Broadway in downtown LA was transformed as a matter of retail, appearance, and a certain pedestrian rhythm and beat into a Mexico City street. With the rise of urban immigration came an increasing diversity as urbanites of some education made the trek north. Even among urban immigrants, however, the village was still present; for many neighborhoods of Mexico City were themselves transported rural villages, and when *capitalinos* came north they still preserved, in remembering their Mexico City barrio, the even more distant and displaced memory of an earlier ancestral village.

Suggestions of village life were also evident in a proclivity to keep chickens and roosters as pets and to fight gamecocks. Although there were laws in Los Angeles about keeping roosters and chickens, no one seemed to mind in the 1990s, and establishments such as Elia's Pet Warehouse in the Florence-Firestone area near Huntington Park were by August 2000 selling approximately four hundred chickens and roosters a month, most of them kept as egg producers and pets. Chickens and roosters, Latino immigrants said, reminded them of former times on the farm or in the villages of Mexico or Central America. (Other backyard pets included goats, although these tended to wind up on holidays as pungent plates of *birria*—shredded, marinated goat meat.) Cockfighting, also illegal, was a flourishing underground sport throughout metropolitan Los Angeles, with an estimated ten thousand people involved as breeders and trainers, pit masters, impresarios, and bookmakers.

At the same time, the Latino population of Southern California was becoming increasingly middle class, as social analyst Gregory Rodriguez documented in an October 1996 report issued by the Institute for Public Policy at Pepperdine. Half of all United States–born Latinos in Southern California, Rodriguez wrote, enjoyed economic near parity with the overall Southern California population, a remarkable feat for such a large and heterogeneous first-generation-American group. United States–born Latinos, in fact, were setting the pace for their Mexican- or Central American–born counterparts in such matters as total family income, home ownership, and other socioeconomic indicators. All in all, there were nearly four times as many United States–born Latino households in the middle class as there were in poverty in the five-county area; and more than half of these middle-class households, 58.6 percent, earned a combined total of over $50,000 a year. Latinos, Rodriguez argued, whatever the difficulties immigrants might be experiencing, had to be perceived as a rising middle-class group. Certainly, he continued, the Latinos of Southern California perceived themselves that way, registering high levels of satisfaction with their upward mobility and the general conditions of life in the United States. The fact that Latinos in the five-county metro Southern California area made up 21 percent of the total Latino population of the United States indicated a developing middle-class future for Latino America.

Where to find priests—and soccer fields—to serve this stable, home-owning middle-class population? Providing the priests, at least, was the problem of Cardinal Roger Mahony, archbishop of the Archdiocese of Los Angeles, in which 65 percent of the estimated four million Roman Catholics in the three-county archdiocese (Los Angeles, Ventura, Santa Barbara) were Latino. The same held true for the neighboring Roman Catholic Diocese of Orange, although to a lesser extent. Each week at Our Lady Queen of Angels Church in downtown Los Angeles, in the church known as La Placita near the historic plaza where Los Angeles began in 1781, some three hundred children were baptized. Eleven masses were celebrated each Sunday. On Christmas and Easter, chairs and loudspeakers had to be set up in the plaza because of the overflow crowds. Mahony recruited priests from Mexico, and mandated that all seminarians, whatever their ethnicity, pass a competency test in Spanish before ordination.

Providing enough soccer fields was equally challenging. The World Cup soccer championship playoffs, for both men and women, held in Pasadena in 1994 for men and in 1999 for women, only intensified a growing passion for soccer in the Southland. For Latinos *fútbol,* like baseball in the United States, was more than just a game. It was a national and local obsession, an energetic and ritualized expression of sport, individual prowess, team and community identity. By the late 1990s, largely due to middle-class Latino teams enlisting children, adolescents, young adults, adults, the middle aged, and, in certain cases, the near elderly in a labyrinth of leagues and teams— each of them with special uniform and colors—a scarcity of soccer fields throughout the Southland was becoming a problem. The rage for soccer, moreover, spilled into the Latino community as yet another instance of interculturalism. In the five-county area alone, approximately 145,000 youngsters, ages four to eighteen, played in leagues run by the American Youth Soccer Organization. On weekends in park-scarce Los Angeles, most publicly owned open spaces were ablaze in soccer colors. The proverbial soccer mom and soccer dad had become significantly Latino, and the emotional investment of parents ran deep: too deep upon occasion, it soon turned out, as sheriff's deputies were noting in the spring of 2001 when they were called in to break up two separate melees of quarreling soccer parents.

Soccer, however, was not on the minds of most California farmworkers, at least not immediately, given the long and difficult hours they worked. In rural California, Mexican immigration was by the mid-1990s becoming increasingly Indian, as Mixtec from Oaxaca and other indigenous peoples—some fifty thousand by 1995—became more noticeable in the farm labor force. Where once Spanish predominated, the sounds of nine Indian languages—Cakchiquel, Chatmo, Kanjobal, Nahuatl, Otomi, Tlapaneco, Trique, Mixteco, and Zapoteco—now echoed throughout the state's fields and orchards. A 1993 survey of migrant farmworkers at nineteen labor camps in northern San Diego County revealed that 40 percent of the workers spoke an Indian language. Coming to the same realization, the Madera school district hired a bilingual aide to help communicate with Mixtec children and parents. The aide spoke only Mixtec and Spanish but was also taking English lessons. Mixtecs were the dominant group, and Mayans the lowest on the totem pole. Many Mixtecs obtained amnesty in 1986 and were thus free to come and go as they pleased. Like most rural people, however, they preferred to associate with their fellow villagers.

Even as Indian-language speakers, supervised by Spanish-speaking foremen, began to replace Spanish speakers in the fields of California, the most prominent Mexican American of them all, César Chávez, died peacefully in his sleep at the age of sixty-six while on union business in Arizona. Himself a migrant worker in his youth and early manhood, a navy veteran of World War II, a family man, and, increasingly, as he grew older, a contemplative and mystic, the Arizona-born Chávez had thirty years earlier unionized California farmworkers and, after a long and bitter boycott, achieved a number of pioneering farm labor contracts for the United Farm Workers of America. "He was our Gandhi," stated Democratic state senator Art Torres from the east side of Los Angeles. "He was our Dr. Martin Luther King."[1] On April 29, 1993, 35,000 mourners, marching in a column estimated to be more than three miles long, followed Chávez's white-pine coffin through the Central Valley town of Delano, where Chávez had begun the grape boycott nearly thirty years earlier. Former California governor Edmund G. Brown Jr. served as one of the pallbearers, as did the Reverend Jesse Jackson and three sons of Bobby Kennedy. Ethel Kennedy herself walked behind the casket. Cardinal Mahony, vested in a serape, presided over the funeral, reading a message of condolence from Pope John Paul II. Thus ended the earthly pilgrimage of the single most influential Mexican American in the history of the United States, a man whose stature and meaning would, like Gandhi's, take a generation and more to construe. "He belongs forever to California," wrote Richard Rodriguez, "in ways deeper than memory. He brought from Mexico a spirit of resilience; he planted a challenge on the land. He stood under an unforgiving sun. The cloudless sky does not forget such people."

And yet, in a number of ways, Rodriguez—himself a highly educated San Francisco–based urbanite with a growing reputation as an essayist and television commentator—considered Chávez a Gandhi without an India; for California was changing, and so was its Mexican-American population. "The last time I saw him," Rodriguez remembered, "was at a black-tie affair at the Fairmont Hotel in San Jose. He was not in black tie. We were—we the new generation of middle-class Mexican-Americans. He was seated at a table with movie stars and fat cats and stuffed shirts. We applauded him, so small in that ballroom. He reminded us of our grandparents."[2]

The process suggested by Rodriguez, seeing in Chávez, barely into his midsixties, a figure from an earlier era, could be reinforced from the 1990 census. Nearly half—46 percent of the 3,306,116 Latinos in Los Angeles County were American born, thus citizens equal in their citizenship to any other group. Of the remaining immigrant population, some 1,072,825 had arrived prior to 1982 and were eligible for the amnesty provisions of the Immigration Reform and Control Act of 1986. Only 7 percent of the total

Latino population in the county could be considered undocumented or illegal. Most Latinos, moreover, were working in the private sector; and while their average household income tended to be lower than that of any other group, Latinos, immigrants especially, were by far the least likely to be on any form of public assistance. Virtually half of immigrant Latino households consisted of stable couples with children. Only 3.7 percent of immigrant Latino households were headed by a divorced householder. In category after category, immigrant Latinos in Los Angeles County were comparing favorably with in-migrant Anglos as documented in the 1940 census. Like the Anglo in-migrants of the 1930s, arriving in California from the Dust Bowl and surveyed in 1939–40, Latino immigrants were hardworking, struggling out of poverty, and possessed of strong family values— and, sadly, they showed a high rate of high school noncompletion. Later research would show that Latino immigrants enjoyed surprisingly good health and longevity and a high rate of home ownership.

Likewise symbolic were the Fiesta Mexicana evenings presented by the Los Angeles Philharmonic at the Hollywood Bowl under the sponsorship of such indicative organizations as *La Opinión,* the leading Spanish-language newspaper in the Southland, a lineup of Spanish-language AM and FM radio stations (KTNQ-AM, KLVE-FM, and others), and various cultural organizations such as Artes de Mexico. At the Hollywood Bowl, ground zero of the turn-of-the-century Anglo-American Protestant tradition of choral music, and reinvigorated in the 1930s by the European Jewish passion for the performing arts, Mexican-American Southlanders now gathered toward twilight in the great amphitheater with picnic baskets as Enrique Diemecke, music director of the Orquesta Sinfónica Nacional de México, led the Los Angeles Philharmonic in lush renditions of such national classics as Ponce's "Concierto del Sur," Chavez's "Sinfonia India," and Revueltas's "Sensamaya," the latter presented with a grand display of fireworks.

A vivid and compelling body of writing, meanwhile, was making its appearance as Hispanic Californians, mostly of the second generation but some of the first, began fashioning a body of interpretive commentary, fiction and nonfiction alike. Rudolfo Anaya's *Bless Me, Ultima* (1972), a magical, mystical novel about a young Mexican boy and a wise old woman, sold more than 275,000 copies, testifying to the presence of a Latino book market as well as the acceptability of Latino fiction among Anglo audiences. In November 1996, San Francisco–based author Victor Martinez won the National Book Award for his first novel, *Parrot in the Oven: Mi Vida* (1995), a lyrical work of magical realism set in the Central Valley. Fresno-born and working in the fields alongside his parents as a boy, Martinez had made it into Cal State Fresno, thanks to the intervention of an involved high school guidance counselor, and later enrolled in the creative writing program at Stanford, founded by Pulitzer Prize–winning novelist Wallace Stegner. The next year, a Latino writer living in the Mission district of San Francisco, Alfredo Vea Jr., won comparable praise for *The Silver Cloud Cafe* (1997), another magical realist novel (two angels have speaking parts) set in Stockton and San Francisco.

Closely allied to the magical realist novelists were such memoirists and cultural theoreticians as Octavio Romano-V and Jose Antonio Burciaga. While Romano-V's *Geriatric Fu* (1990), an autobiographical reminiscence of the author's first sixty-five years in the United States, struggled toward simplicity and acceptance through a minimalist narrative depicting how life in its fundamental essence remained good, even for the marginal and oppressed, Burciaga's *Drink Cultura: Chicanismo* (1993)—an eclectic, postmodernist exploration of inner landscapes and identities, myths and symbols—sought to replicate Octavio Paz's classic *Labyrinth of Solitude* (1950) for Mexicans living north of the border. The point was that Mexican California was interpreting itself in a variety of modes. A literature was forming that sometime in the twenty-first century might provide a source of insight into the cultural dynamics of Latin America, as it was advancing, however reluctantly, the unfinished dialogue between Mexico and the United States.

More gritty, contextualized commentary continued to pour forth from Oakland-born Al Martinez, a former combat correspondent writing a column for the *Los Angeles Times* since 1984. While Latino fiction might show a proclivity for magical realism, Martinez's down-to-earth commentary brought a Latino flavor to a well-established journalistic genre practiced most notably by Mike Royko of Chicago and Jimmy Breslin of New York: the columnist as voice of the city, close to the beat of the street, sympathetic to the little guy being screwed by the system. Terse and impassioned, Martinez was a crossover figure, a native-born Mexican American, a veteran of the Korean War, literally born on the Fourth of July. While proud of his Latino heritage, Martinez did not confine himself to Latino topics. He was at once a throwback to a more assimilated pre-*la raza* style and a look-forward to that rapidly approaching time when Mexican Americanness would be as American, as universal, as any other ethnic identity in the nation.

Even the most vociferous critics of undocumented immigrants admitted that they were hard workers; indeed, whether undocumented, documented, or multigenerational Americans, Latino immigrants had long since proved themselves as the fundamental labor pool in many sectors of the California economy. Construction in Orange County was an example. Sometime in the 1980s, Mexicans of varying immigrant status began to replace the Irish, German, and other white European ethnic groups as construction workers, especially in the hard, dusty task of fixing large sheets of drywall to the interior frames of the thousands of homes being built, almost overnight, in and on the hillsides and valleys of Orange County. Most of these Mexican drywallers did not belong to the United Brotherhood of Carpenters—until, that is, they launched a countywide strike in late 1991 and early 1992 and brought the Pacific Rim Drywall Association to its knees, despite the fact that they were not a union but a wildcat organization. Suddenly, the union became interested.

Thousands of Latino men remained largely unorganized, however, like Salvadoran immigrant Pedro Ortiz and his friends, who gathered each morning, some twenty-five to a hundred of them, at the corner of Slauson and Fairfax in Ladera Heights, hoping to be hailed by a passing car and truck for the opportunity to earn $20–50 for cutting grass, hauling furniture, busting concrete. Juan Carlos Ruiz, thirty, was one of the Ladera Heights morning "size-up" regulars, commuting by bus from his apartment in Inglewood. When neighborhood merchants protested the growing size of the gathering to the police, Ruiz was outspoken in its defense. Coming to the same spot each morning, he noted, gave the men the conviction that they were working at a regular job. And individual workers, having done good work, built up a clientele among employers, who knew exactly where to go when they needed trustworthy men. At best, Ruiz was making $50 a day. Although he showed up five, even six days a week, in some weeks he would be hired as few as three times. "I'm not going to do anything against my moral principles," Ruiz told an interpreter. "We prefer to work—even if it's only for $30–40 a day—rather than stealing."[3]

Numerous immigrants, in Los Angeles especially, took to street vending. They peddled fruit and flowers at freeway entrances. Dora Alicia Alarcon, thirty-nine, a Salvadoran, sold knit caps, lacy underwear, scarves, whatever her wholesaler supplied her, from a cart, which she preferred to park at the corner of Santa Monica Boulevard and Western Avenue, some eight blocks away from the apartment she shared with five other immigrants, each of them paying $125 in rent a month. On a good day, Alarcon might gross up to $30, half for her, half for her suppliers. In El Salvador, Alarcon had grown up with an impression of street vending as an honorable occupation. In Los Angeles, by contrast, she had to keep an eye open for the police. In one year alone, 1989 to 1990, some 2,700 street vendors had been arrested in Los Angeles, with penalties ranging up to six months in jail and a $1,000 fine. (Fortunately, the city council relaxed anti-street-vendor restrictions in January 1992.) As little as she made, Alicia Alarcon still sent part of it back each month to her parents, who were raising her four children in El Salvador.

As difficult as their lives might be, street vendors enjoyed a degree of autonomy and entrepreneurial possibilities. Among domestic workers, by contrast, there continued to exist a practice of exploiting Latino help, particularly if the employee was undocumented. Throughout Southern California especially, there existed a formidable if uncounted cadre of Latina domestic workers whose lives were but a few steps above peonage. Alejandra (not her real name), for example, thirty-one, an undocumented Nicaraguan, was by August 1997 traveling three hours each day by bus, round trip, from the one-room West Adams apartment she shared with her boyfriend, her mother, her daughter, and her sister, to an upper-middle-class household in Pasadena, where, for $200 a week, she cleaned house and cared for three young girls. Alejandra's bus fare ran $21 a week, and because her employers' refrigerator was off-limits, she brought along her own lunch of rice and beans or tortillas. All things considered, Alejandra thought her present conditions were excellent in comparison to her past experiences with other employers and the horror stories she had heard: stories of Latina women being physically violated by their employers, or forced to sleep in an unheated garage, or, in one instance, being made to sleep overnight on the lawn on a rainy night after being locked out when missing the employer's ten p.m. curfew. Just once, Alejandra tried the experiment of bringing her own daughter to work, but she immediately realized that the child was not welcome. "It's ugly taking care of other people's kids," Alejandra admitted, "and feeding them when you don't even know if yours is eating." Undocumented, thus fearful of moving about the city lest she be picked up by immigration authorities, Alejandra spent her days off largely confined to the one-room apartment (a crib, two beds, a small color television set, no room for a kitchen table). If she felt brave, she would occasionally take her daughter for a weekend visit to the beach or a trip to the neighborhood market. Small spaces, overcrowding, a fear of the streets: hardly the Southern California dream of popular imagination.[4]

For immigrants, California could be a dangerous place, whether in terms of crowded apartments or equally crowded vans and trucks on the highways. In rural areas, immigrant workers and their families tended to pack vans and trucks to a dangerous level. They also tended to go fast—and not too skillfully—whether driven by the need to make size-ups in the foggy early-morning hours or showing the recklessness of a village people in control of fast-moving machines. In any event, newspaper headlines from the 1990s chronicled a succession of horrendous crashes involving immigrants in vans and trucks.

Wherever recent immigrants were working or living, credit and banking services remained problems. An estimated 25 percent of the California population—with Latino immigrants forming the majority of this disenfranchised group—did not have credit cards or checking accounts. Sensing a market in these unbanked and perhaps unbankable Californians, whom mainline banks avoided, New Yorker Gary Cypres formed the Central Financial Acceptance Corporation in 1995. The mission of this company, which went public the following year, was to provide Latino immigrants with loans and ATM services. Once a Latino was granted a loan, he or she could draw upon it from some seventy-seven locations throughout metro Los Angeles. By January 1998, CFAC had acquired 150,000 customers, who had taken out $133 million in loans, and was negotiating with Kmart to bring its cash machines to four other western states. That was the good news. The bad news was that Central Financial Acceptance Corporation, in which Wells Fargo and the Union Bank of California also held partial interest, charged its customers a crushing 26 percent interest, just 4 points beneath the 30 percent maximum allowed by state law. At 26 percent, the principal had a way of remaining on forever, given the fact that immigrants were also forced to pay taxes on the meager income they were making, on which they would have to live from day to day as well as use to pay back the loan. Cypres admitted that he wore a bulletproof vest when he visited CFAC offices in poorer neighborhoods.

The closer one got to the border, the tougher life became. Los Angeles was, after all, a significantly Latino city in which, for all the difficulties experienced by Hispanics, there was at least a sense of continuity and development. Likewise in the smaller cities and towns of the state, from San Bernardino, Riverside, and Orange Counties northward, there existed Latino communities in which some sense of identity and stability was beginning to coalesce. The border, by contrast, was volatile, shifting, and ambiguous. Of all California's cities, San Diego was most dramatically resisting Mexicanization, especially through illegal immigration. In March 1990, residents of Greater San Diego, representing such organizations as the Citizens for Border Control, the La Jolla Republican Women Federated, the Submarine Veterans of World War II, and the Democratic-Republican Consortium for Border Sovereignty, lined up nearly five hundred cars side by side facing south across the border and, at nightfall, turned on their headlights to illuminate the undocumented aliens crossing into the United States.

This Lights Across the Border Campaign, organized by radio talk show host and former mayor Roger Hedgecock, clearly underscored the anxieties being experienced by white San Diegans as their city became a sieve for illegal immigration. At the border crossing itself, undocumented workers would sprint in and between cars toward El Norte, and it was a common sight in the Robinhood Homes Development in the city of San Ysidro, bordering the Tijuana River, to see undocumented workers, wearing knockoff versions of designer tennis shoes, sprinting down residential streets, heading north. Frustrated residents, edging into vigilantism, laid out their own concertina walls of barbed wire and purchased guard dogs. Border Patrol vehicles roared through the night, and the walkie-talkies of neighborhood patrols squawked. On the morning of April 19, 1992, San Ysidro resident Harold Ray Bassham, nineteen, pursued with a .25-caliber pistol five border crossers who had run through his family's backyard and shot and killed one of them, Humberto Reyes, twenty-three, as Reyes was trying to climb a wall in a cul-de-sac.

Illegal border crossing was a dangerous business, as documented by the National Commission for Human Rights in a widely publicized 1991 report. At each stage of the journey north—dealing with exploitative Mexican police, equally exploitative smugglers, border vigilantes such as Harold Ray Bassham, the Border Patrol, and police and sheriff's deputies further north—illegal immigrants experienced chance after chance of being shaken down, raped, beaten up, even murdered. Mexican bandits operating on the border killed nine people and robbed and raped numerous others between January and August. A gang of nine young men, armed with tire irons, hammers, a nightstick, a baseball bat, and a knife, was preying on illegal immigrants, just for the fun of it. An edgy local policeman, patrolling the scrubland along the border, shot and killed one of the group.

As illegals tended to come more from the big cities, they also tended to come from the urban criminal class. Between 1989 and 1990, assaults by undocumented immigrants or bandits against Border Patrol agents increased from 60 to 217. Naturally, agents were growing increasingly on edge, as were police and sheriff's deputies further north. Hot pursuit of smuggling vans and trucks by agents became commonplace. In June 1992, agents pursued a Chevrolet Suburban camper filled with thirteen suspected illegal immigrants through the city of Temecula in Riverside County north of San Diego. As the stolen Suburban sped past the Temecula Valley High School at seven-thirty a.m., it crashed into an Acura Legend, killing three people—a father driving his son and his son's friend to school—and also killing a brother and sister standing nearby on the sidewalk. Horribly, the woman sent to cover the crash for the local newspaper learned that it was her two children who had died on the sidewalk. All five crash victims were Mexican-American legal residents.

High-speed chases such as this, so fraught with danger, tended to put Border Patrol agents, police, and sheriff's deputies into an adrenaline-pumped mood of near hysteria. On April 1, 1996, Riverside County sheriff's deputies, after an eighty-mile high-speed chase, stopped a truck carrying nineteen Mexican illegals as a helicopter bearing a television cameraman hovered overhead. Despite the lack of resistance on the part of the driver and his passengers, a sheriff's deputy repeatedly billy-clubbed two illegals, a man and a woman. Broadcast over local, state, and national television, the beatings initiated an uproar comparable to the beating of Rodney King earlier in the decade.

The illegal immigrants, including those being beaten on the side of the freeway in Riverside, were young, in their late teens, twenties, or early thirties. A distressingly large number of them were juveniles, some crossing the border on their own when as young as eight or nine. In 1990 alone, American authorities returned more than three thousand unaccompanied minors to Mexican officials in Tijuana. Once across the border, it was easy for these children to get into trouble in one or another of the dozens of teenage barrios peopled by *abandonados* in Southern California cities—disturbing replications of similar settlements in Mexico City, Rio de Janeiro, and elsewhere throughout the Third World. In Westminster, a Barrio Huerfanos (Orphans' Barrio) emerged in the early 1990s in the shabby neighborhood wedged between the Garden Grove and San Diego Freeways. To this barrio in mid-1991 came Jose Morales, fourteen, an illegal immigrant of Mixtec descent. On his back was a soiled bedroll. In his pocket were forty-two cents and a scrap of paper with a cousin's address on 15th Street in Westminster. It had been a long and difficult journey. In Tijuana, Morales had been taken in by a compassionate prostitute who found him late one night curled up in a gutter, covered with trash and stinking of urine. Finding the Westminster address listed on the slip of paper, Morales discovered that his cousin was long gone. The youngster sat on the pavement outside the house and wept.

In early 1991, pressed by a growing arrest rate of illegal juveniles, the counties of Los Angeles, Orange, and San Diego, in a program called the Border Youth Project, began repatriating illegal juvenile offenders directly to Tijuana. Malnourished, violently treated or sexually abused or both, unschooled, addicted to drugs, soon to join the more than five thousand homeless children roaming the streets of Tijuana—here were truly the wretched of the earth. Illegal youngsters who evaded the police or the Border Patrol continued their nightmare life sleeping under freeways, selling drugs, inhaling Octane Booster—a gasoline additive and makeshift drug—from Coke cans, bolstering their courage as well with fanciful names such as Squirrel, Little Dracula, Karate Kid, the Russian, or, in the case of a colony of immigrant children living under a freeway overpass in San Diego's Balboa Park, prostituting themselves to pedophile men who came cruising in business suits and BMWs, from whom they might earn from $20 to $40 per trick.

Approaching the two million mark because of internal migration and economic growth, the city of Tijuana was, for better or worse, a California city, with all that implied. Baja California, it must be remembered, had been part of the Californias since the Spanish colonial era. No mere line on the map could permanently disjoin the affinities and interactions of a border culture whose fundamental nature, despite all difficulties, was legal and coping. The majority of crossings and recrossings of the border between San Diego and Tijuana, Tijuana and San Diego, were routine, legal, and commonplace. True, Tijuana had its nightmare sections, such as the shanties near the trash heaps, from which the flickering lights of San Diego could be seen in the distance, where trash pickers and their families lived in Sisyphean squalor. And there was crime aplenty. In June 1993, Mexican police discovered a fourteen-hundred-foot underground tunnel between Tijuana and the outskirts of San Diego built by drug traffickers to near-professional standards, including two large air-conditioning units with generators. Mexican authorities speculated that the tunnel was constructed by the same drug ring that had recently shot to death Cardinal Juan Jesus Posadas Ocampo, the archbishop of Guadalajara, outside the city's international airport. (The shooters mistook the archbishop for a rival drug lord, because the prelate was riding in a white 1993 Grand Marquis with tinted windows, the vehicle of choice among Mexican drug traffickers.) In March 1994, presidential candidate Luis Donaldo Colosio, the nominee of the dominant PRI party, and therefore the next president of Mexico, was assassinated as he spoke on a Tijuana street.

For the first half and more of the twentieth century, Tijuana had one and only one reputation: it was sin city, an open border town, noted for its bars and brothels and little else. As it passed the million-person mark in the early 1990s, however, the point at which urban historian Lewis Mumford claimed that cities start to take themselves seriously and are able to do something about it, Tijuana began to yearn for respectability. By the year 2000, it would be bigger than San Francisco, San Jose, Portland, Seattle, and Vancouver. It was also developing its own distinctive urban culture, mirroring San Diego on the other side of the border in a blend of Latino and Yankee elements. Tijuanans said *bye* instead of *hasta la vista* and sprinkled their

Spanish with numerous Americanisms. They rooted for the San Diego Padres and Chargers and celebrated Halloween as well as the Day of the Dead. Affluent Tijuanans—and there were thousands of these—preferred nothing better than a day across the border in San Diego, shopping, dining, visiting a doctor or dentist, catching a football or baseball game.

All things considered—with the exception of the extreme edges of poverty, which were horrific—Tijuana was functioning as well as a number of Mexicanized communities north of the border. As in the case of El Norte as well, Tijuana was filling with Mexicans from the south attracted there by hopes of a better life and the unleashing of an entrepreneurial spirit. In 1948, Justina and Rafael Brambila, migrants from Jalisco, opened a side-street taco stand on Avenida Revolucion. Fifty years later, the Brambilas were owners of a 180-seat restaurant, and their son Alfredo was a success-ful Tijuana gastroenterologist. "Tijuana is the American dream for Mexi-cans," noted Nick Inzunza in January 1998, a member of an affluent family prospering on both sides of the San Diego–Tijuana border. "It means jobs. People come here to work hard and get ahead. It is the land of opportunity." Proudly, Inzunza and others were pointing to a 1 percent unemployment rate in a city where less than half of the population were natives.[5]

As in the case of Los Angeles, Tijuana supported a vibrant retail and street vendor culture on Avenida Constitucion, which by the latter part of the 1990s was developing an affluent binational clientele. Newcomers to Tijuana praised its can-do spirit, its lack of snobbery, and the conspicuous absence of a privileged leisure class communicating the notion that hard work was something performed only by social inferiors. Tijuana could seem rootless and unsettled, an unstable amalgam of pieces from every component of Mexican culture—but so could Southern California. With the Latinization of Southern California proceeding apace, Tijuana was en route to becoming a full-fledged California city, with connections and synergies linking it more to Southern California than to Mexico.

Each day more than forty thousand Tijuanans and San Diegans crossed the border to go to work. Each month, there were more than 200,000 cross-ings north to San Diego by Tijuanans, mostly to shop. Thousands of affluent Tijuana high school students passed the border each school day to attend private high schools in San Diego. There was even a cross-border singles scene, and a noticeable number of cross-border marriages. North of the bor-der, the gender ratio was 56 percent Latinos to 44 percent Latinas. Socializ-ing in Tijuana, north-of-the-border Latinos found themselves doubly admired by the young women of Tijuana. They were affluent, successful Americans, and they were Latino. Nick Inzunza, for example, son of a prominent border family, working for the San Diego County Board of

Supervisors, married a young Tijuana woman, Olga Martinez. "It's like going back to the Old Country to get married," Inzunza, twenty-seven, noted. "Except the Old Country is just twenty minutes away."[6]

Matters became even more integrated when Mexico changed its constitution to permit, after March 21, 1998, millions of Mexican-born American citizens and their American-born children to reclaim their Mexican nationality, hold Mexican passports, and, eventually, vote in Mexican national elections. Leticia Quezada had immigrated to the United States at the age of thirteen and later became the first Latina to serve on the school board in Los Angeles. By February 1998, Quezada was serving as the director of the Mexican Cultural Institute of Los Angeles. "It is important to me," noted Quezada of the possibilities for dual nationality. "I never stop feeling Mexican. I have become a United States citizen because this is where I live, where I have made my professional life. I have made a commitment, but it's sort of an intellectual commitment, whereas emotionally I am Mexican. I want to be Mexican. I feel very close to the country of my birth."[7]

Asian Attitudes

California was Asian, as well: Asian in heritage, Asian in its ethos and aesthetic tastes, Asian at the core of its most financially dynamic and flourishing population sector, increasingly Asian in attitude. In a postmodernist scheme of interpretation allowing for multiple states of consciousness in one place, it could be claimed that the San Francisco Bay Area, portions of central California, and metropolitan Los Angeles, embracing most of the population of Southern California, were in some very important way Asian commonwealths coexisting, spatially and psychologically, on the land and within the political framework of California USA. Conversely, non-Asian California had been eating Asian, dressing Asian, driving Asian, speaking Asian, and marrying Asian in growing numbers and intensity. By the millennium, Asian Chic had long since migrated out from California and become a national phenomenon.

While California was not exclusively responsible for this phenomenon, it had once again, as in so much else, helped fashion the national trend; over the past quarter century, so many Californians—Amy Tan, Wayne Wang and Maxine Hong Kingston, Kristi Yamaguchi and Michelle Kwan, among others—had played a crucial role in extending the Asian-American sensibility to a national audience. The first and most vital connection between Anglo California and Asia was established between California and Japan. The very letter of introduction to the shogun which Commodore Perry brought to Japan in June 1853 made reference to the fact that the Americanization of California had now made the United States an Asia-Pacific nation, and therefore a neighbor of Japan. During the Meiji restoration, American technology and certain aspects of American culture gave Japan the tools with which to transform itself into a modern nation. In California, the newly founded Stanford University in Palo Alto, whose president was the ardent Nipponophile David Starr Jordan, educated an important cadre of Japanese academics and civil servants.

In matters of art and aesthetics, a profound connection was eventually

established between California and Japan. The Bay Area artist Theodore
Wores spent long periods of time in Japan in the 1890s and was decorated
by the government there for his depictions of Japanese scenery, architecture, and daily life. California architects such as Bernard Maybeck inserted
Japanese architecture and wood-building techniques into regional California design. A generation of Japanese immigrant gardeners brought to the
developing domestic landscape of Southern California the spatial arrangements and serenity of Zen. California hostesses of the upper classes entertained in kimonos. The San Francisco department store Gump's imported
Japanese objets d'art and helped create a style of interior design blending
European and Japanese motifs that would last for a century. In 1905 a Japan
Society devoted to the study and appreciation of Japanese culture was
founded by David Starr Jordan and attorney Henry Pike Bowie, a wealthy
savant living in a Japanese-style Burlingame estate, married to a Japanese
woman, waited on by Japanese servants, and conducting his domestic life in
Japanese.

Japanese immigrants, meanwhile, building on the legacy of Chinese
California, expanded and revitalized California agriculture, especially in
such fields as potatoes, strawberries, and flowers. Immigrant George Shima
not only became the potato king of California, he also wrote exquisite
poetry in both English and Japanese. The story of Japanese California—the
steady increase of population, especially after the arrival of the "Picture
Brides" in the 1920s; the insults and deprivations of the White California
movement; the Alien Land Acts of 1913 and 1920, which banned Japan-
born Japanese from California land ownership; and, finally, the roundups
and imprisonments of 1942—was central to the rise of California in the
twentieth century. By the 1990s, Japanese California had surpassed even
the accomplishments of the pre–World War II generation in terms of education, affluence, noncriminality and nondelinquency, home ownership, and
mental and physical health—whatever criteria one might employ to suggest
success. The fact that Japan was California's number one trading partner in
the first half of the decade and most significant offshore investor only reinforced the Japanese identity of the Golden State.

Was this Japanese-ness merely a matter of California's high-achieving
and prosperous Japanese-American population (the third largest Asian
group in California as of 1990, dropping to sixth by 2000), so many of them
in medicine or allied health sciences? After a hundred years of social and
cultural interaction, California had incorporated within itself a strong element of Japan. One encountered it in the resorts of Big Sur, with their great
outdoor hot tubs. One saw its aesthetic sensibility in the poetry of Gary
Snyder, the leading poet of the state, who had spent time as a student in a

Zen monastery in Japan. It was there by the shores of the Golden Gate when the *taiko* drums were played triumphantly by a group of Japanese and Anglo Californians: the great drums of Old Japan, pre-Meiji Japan, and twenty-first-century Japan as well, thundering across the waters of the strait and through the cables of the Golden Gate Bridge as through an aeolian harp.

Asia-California was a varied place. It embraced extremes ranging from Hmong people in the Central Valley living a thousand-year-old lifestyle to the hippest kids in LA gathering by night in one or another Asian-American dance club. It included cops, firemen, pharmacists, Matt Fong—the elected treasurer of the state of California—and some of the most brilliant scholars in higher education. The 1990 census revealed that the three top ethnic Asian groups in the nation were the Chinese (1,645,472), the Filipino (1,406,770), and the Japanese (847,562). Other than Native Americans, Filipinos were the Asian group with the longest lineage in the Golden State. Filipinos—then called Luzon Indians or Manila Men by the Spanish—first visited California with the exploring expedition of Pedro de Unamuno in 1587 and served as crew members of the Manila galleons traveling between the Philippines and California from the late sixteenth to the early nineteenth century. Filipino sailors were aboard the galleon *San Augustine* when it shipwrecked near Point Reyes near San Francisco Bay on November 6, 1595. In the Spanish and Mexican eras, Luzon Indians or Manila Men lived in Los Angeles. In 1898 the United States acquired the Philippines from Spain, although Philippine patriots bravely resisted the American takeover on the field of battle. In the ensuing years, once the Philippines had become a United States–affiliated and, to a certain extent, United States–administered nation, Filipino men were recruited to California as farmworkers, especially after 1924, when the United States shut its doors to Chinese and Japanese immigrants and the farmers of California and Hawaii turned to some fifty thousand Filipinos as a new source of cheap labor. Larry Dulay Itiliong, for example, the sixteen-year-old son of a Pangasinan rice farmer and sari maker, arrived in Seattle in 1929 having never slept in a bed or used a toilet. Over the next two decades, Itiliong worked in the lettuce fields of Washington State, the canneries of Alaska, the sugar beet fields of Montana and South Dakota, and the Central Valley of California. In 1956 he formed the Filipino Farm Labor Union. Ten years later, Itiliong joined with César Chávez to form the United Farm Workers. Itiliong died in February 1977 at the age of sixty-three.

By that time, the Filipino presence in California had become not a matter of single, lonely men working in the fields, but urbanized families in the San Francisco Bay Area (the suburban enclave of Daly City just south of

San Francisco had by 1990 become a Little Manila) and metropolitan Los Angeles (223,276 Filipinos in Los Angeles County alone, according to the 1990 census), branching out into nearly every phase of American life. The claim could be made that, of all Asian peoples, Filipinos were already the most profoundly Americanized, given the shaping influence of American culture on the Philippines in the first four decades of the twentieth century. Most Filipinos spoke English. Many had served in the American armed forces. Migrating to California represented a continuity rather than a departure. Americanized and English-speaking, Filipinos—a million or more by 1996—fit easily into the work life and social infrastructure of the state. Relishing steady employment and able to pool their salaries through family unity, Filipinos prospered in civil service, middle management, hospitals, health care, and convalescent homes, and were able to find employment in such previously Filipino-friendly sectors as restaurant and hotel work, agriculture, and private resorts and clubs. There was also a rising Filipino professional class, equally divided between men and women, with degrees from universities and institutes in the Philippines and California. (Fred Quevedo, for example, a gynecological surgeon practicing in Burbank, had grown up following with his family the seasonal crops up and down the San Joaquin Valley.) Higher education in nursing and allied health sciences flourished in the Philippines; and so it was not surprising that, beginning in the 1980s, a large number of Filipino nurses emigrated to California, lured there by annual wages of $40,000 and higher, beyond the wildest dreams of most nurses in the Philippines. By March 1991, the Philippine Nurses Association of Ventura County listed some five hundred Filipino nurses working in the area. Many of them had come to the United States as wives of servicemen stationed at the Naval Air Station at Point Mugu or the Naval Construction Battalion Center at Port Hueneme. Like most Asians, Filipinos were family oriented. It was common for Filipino Americans to send "remittance dollars" back to the Philippines long after they had left their homeland. "I still send back a few hundred dollars every month," noted Artemio Pagdan, a Pomona physician, thirty-two years after he emigrated in 1962. Remittance dollars from the 1.4 million Filipinos living in the United States constituted an important part of the Filipino economy. Payments from Filipinos working around the world, in fact, were by August 1994 returning $2 billion and more (perhaps as much as $6 billion, given the fact that much of the money came in undocumented cash) to the Filipino economy.[8]

Centered, like Filipino culture, on the San Francisco Bay Area, including Sacramento and metropolitan Los Angeles, Chinese California was as venerable as California itself. In the frontier era, Chinese workers had constructed the trans-Sierran half of the transcontinental railroad, a Sino-public work worthy of comparison to the Great Wall of China itself. Having accomplished this, the Chinese had turned to agriculture, and in their collective subdual of the Sacramento flood plain had helped agriculture replace mining as the leading element in the California economy. By the 1990s there were many Chinese families—especially in the Sacramento and Delta regions, where Lok was the only exclusively Chinese city in North America—who were fourth- and fifth-generation descendants of these pioneers. Chinatown San Francisco, which each year hosted the largest Chinese New Year parade in the nation, likewise nurtured fourth- and fifth-generation Chinese Californians, marching behind the 160-foot golden dragon down Kearney Street toward Columbus Avenue to the staccato cackle of 600,000 exploding firecrackers.

Most Chinese Californians, however, were first- or second-generation immigrants: women such as the Taiwan-born Nai-Chang Yeh, the only female physics professor at Caltech; or Madame Sylvia Wu, born to the upper-class family Cheng in the city of Jiujiang on the Yangtze River and educated in convent schools before meeting her future husband, King Yan Wu, a government official, in Hong Kong at the outbreak of World War II. By 1961, displaced by the war and the revolution, Sylvia Wu and her husband found themselves in Los Angeles. With a bank loan of $2,000 and no experience, Madame Wu went into the restaurant business on Wilshire Boulevard in Santa Monica. Soon, the customers—Cary Grant, Frank Sinatra and Mia Farrow, Grace Kelly, Mae West, and Irving Lazar, among others—came; by the 1990s Madame Wu, restaurateur to the stars, elegant in horn-rimmed glasses and driving a Rolls-Royce Silver Cloud, had become a Hollywood legend.

Between 1973 and 1993, the Chinese population in Southern California multiplied nearly sevenfold. Most recent immigrants came from Taiwan and Hong Kong, and most of them had money: $200,000 per family, ran one report from the 1980s. Soon, they tended to make even more money in the dynamic economy of Southern California. Many of those who arrived with few resources managed to make up for lost time. William Mow, immigrant and founder of the trendy Simi Valley–based Bugle Boy clothing company, for example, was doing $400 million a year in sales. In 1990 the federal government inaugurated a program giving immigrant status to foreigners promising to invest $1 million in American businesses and create at least ten full-time jobs. More than a third of the 488 millionaires who came to the United States under this program originated from China, Taiwan, or Hong Kong. Many Hong Kong–based corporate executives and entrepreneurs—*tai hung wan,* they were called, or "astronauts"—located their families in

such posh enclaves as San Marino or Pacific Palisades while they continued
to commute back and forth across the Pacific. David Wong, for instance,
worked out of a boxlike two-bedroom apartment in a high-rise block in the
bustling Mongkok district of Hong Kong while his family lived in a spacious townhouse in Rolling Hills on the Palos Verdes Peninsula. Many
astronaut fathers such as Wan were known to keep in touch with their children by having them fax their homework to them on a daily basis.

While the rest of the state plunged into recession in the early 1990s, the
Chinese were prospering. "The high visibility of Chinese wealth in Southern California is something I feel very concerned about," noted Wellington
Chan, a professor of history at Occidental College in Los Angeles in October 1993 at the depth of the recession. "The local economy is bad, and you
have a small group of the population driving expensive cars and buying up
malls. I think there could be a backlash if there is communal strife in the
future."[9] Despite Professor Chan's fears, Chinese Californians continued to
create wealth through hard work and to invest it, helped along by the
twenty-eight Chinese community-owned banks in the state. One such
investment, San Gabriel Square in the San Gabriel Valley, became a prime
paradigm of how Chinese investment was revitalizing the Southland.
Developed in the late 1980s and early 1990s on a twelve-acre site, the forty-
store complex, with a thousand-car parking lot, spoke the language of a
Southern California supermall in a Chinese-American accent. The 99
Ranch Market, part of a successful chain of Asian-oriented supermarkets
originating in the Sino-Vietnamese enclave of Orange County, was at once
an American-style Southern California supermarket and a purveyor of
Asian foods in bulk, live fish and crustaceans, and other Asian delicacies.
Many customers of the 99 Ranch Market came from Monterey Park, just
east of Los Angeles, the first predominantly Chinese-American suburb in
the country. In 1960, Monterey Park was 85 percent Anglo. By 1990,
Asians made up 60 percent of the population, Anglos had declined to 12
percent, and Latinos constituted the remaining 28 percent. Lily Lee Chen,
who came to Southern California from Taiwan in 1958 to study social work,
stayed on to become the first Chinese-American mayor of Monterey Park
and was typical of the highly educated émigrés who began pouring into
Southern California in the 1960s. Married to a Taiwan-educated aerospace
engineer turned venture capitalist, Chen herself was the chairman of a
Pasadena-based export company active in China trading.

As impressive and influential as the influx of Chinese immigrants into
California since the 1960s was, it could not fully displace the lingering
reverberations of nineteenth-century Chinese California, especially in San
Francisco, Sacramento, and the Gold Country. In Weaverville in Trinity

County, there survived a great joss house built in the early 1850s by the more than five thousand Chinese miners who were wont to gather there once a year for games and festivals—and in certain cases to settle old scores or new conflicts. Legacies such as this, together with the levees of the lower Sacramento Valley and Delta, which still functioned as the prime vehicle of flood control in these regions, or the trans-Sierran railroad, or the older districts of Chinatown in San Francisco, reverberated with imaginative associations. In some fundamental sense, American California had always been, in part, Chinese; and as the millennium approached, it was not so surprising that this should continue to be the case.

Koreans, by contrast, were relatively recent arrivals on the scene. They had come to California in the early 1900s, but in very small numbers. As of 1910 there were only 461 Koreans in the entire United States. In the ensuing half century, San Francisco and Los Angeles supported small Christian Korean communities. Not until 1970 did Koreans begin to migrate to the United States in large numbers, averaging more than twenty thousand per year through that decade. Many settled in Los Angeles, where over the next two decades Koreatown developed west of the Harbor Freeway that ran through the center of the city. By the early 1990s, the 600,000 in Southern California constituted the largest population of Koreans outside of Korea itself, and metropolitan Los Angeles, with more than 400,000 residents, had emerged as a ranking Korean city.

The April-May 1992 Los Angeles riots not only cost the Korean community lives and property, it also traumatized their sense of security and identity. Koreans, after all, had been the quintessential American immigrants. They had come in great numbers, established businesses, and prospered. They prized education and barely appeared on any charts chronicling crime or juvenile delinquency. As a people they had been traditional allies of the United States since the Korean War in the 1950s and had been an important trading partner since South Korea became an economic force. By 1996 trade with the United States was topping $55 billion a year, making South Korea the fifth largest U.S. trading partner. California alone was responsible for 35 percent of this trade, and in 1996, South Korea replaced Mexico as the third largest foreign consumer of California products. More than 270 South Korean businesses had offices in California, and these companies had directly invested approximately $1.2 billion in the state.

For such a population to be burned, trashed, shot at, and killed by rioting Los Angelenos seemed to Korean Californians a grave affront. As in the case of the pogroms of Eastern Europe, Korean Californians felt both dishonored and angry that they had been singled out for trashing strictly because of their ethnicity and prosperity. In the immediate aftermath of the riots, many Korean Californians petitioned the South Korean government to demand of the State Department a formal apology from the United States for the way that South Koreans had been treated in the riots. Their very willingness, they noted, to conduct small businesses, such as corner grocery stores, in otherwise marginal or even redlined zones of the city had made the Koreans of Los Angeles especially vulnerable.

For the rest of the decade following the riots, it became the special responsibility of the "1.5 Generation"—Koreans in their twenties and thirties, born in Korea but raised in the United States—to assist their immigrant parents, many of them speaking limited English, all of them still attached to the old ways, to reconstruct their sense of place and participation in the American scheme of things. Bilingual, bicultural, highly educated, energetic, and totally hip, the 1.5ers had law degrees and PhDs, beepers and cell phones, and a fierce determination that Korean Californians would never again be victims of anyone's pogrom. As far as internal matters were concerned, the 1.5ers had to deal with a work ethic and a near addiction to higher education that could energize parts of the Korean California population but become a straitjacket for others. An emotional void afflicted many Korean immigrants. They had left their homeland. They had confronted a language that many of them could never fully master. They had opened stores and cleaning establishments in dangerous neighborhoods and run them fifteen hours a day, seven days a week. Aside from the insult and rejection offered by the riots, they were also asking themselves: What did it mean? What had it amounted to?

Due in part to various strands in Korean culture itself, Korean Americans fixed upon education as the means and the answer. Getting their children into an Ivy League school, Harvard especially, soon reached the point of a debilitating mania. Despite the ironclad class system in Korea, even the poorest of farmboys could get ahead if he could pass the *gwaguh gupjae,* a competitive examination offered by the government whose origins and emotional texture was profoundly Confucian in its emphasis on learning and academic prestige as both the fact and the primary symbol of success. Translated to 1990s Southern California and further reinforced by the immigrants' emotional need to see their success symbolized in the United States, that meant getting into Harvard or, failing that, into less than a half-dozen other prestigious institutions. Metropolitan Los Angeles abounded in Harvard-oriented cram academies. Some of them even used the Harvard logo. Promising students—and many not so promising (and herein lay the tragedy)—were steered toward Harvard as early as the seventh grade. High school students were kept at their studies until ten in the evening. No time for sports; no time for hanging out at the mall.

No wonder, then, that Banana Man—the outrageous, politically incorrect anonymous Korean-Californian columnist appearing in the monthly *KoreAm Journal* (circulation 12,000)—took special pride in mocking such values and playing the role of the outsider. Although his identity was never revealed, Banana Man was most likely a twentysomething 1.5er subject to all the pressures of his generation. Satirically, Banana Man turned the world inside out. Even his moniker was an insult (an Asian yellow on the outside and white within, like a banana) turned to his advantage. Among other things, Banana Man cautioned 1.5ers about being too obsessed with education or feeling that they had to marry Korean. He suggested that young Korean Americans might wish to become writers and artists and bohemians as well as doctors and lawyers and businessmen.

Although he eventually toned down his role as satirist, even protected by anonymity (some of his columns, after all, had provoked death threats), Banana Man offered evidence that Korean culture in California was being transformed by the American experience. Already, Korean-language radio, especially KBLA-AM, the most popular such station in the region, KWIZ-FM, a Santa Ana–based adult contemporary station, and KFOX-FM, an alternative talk show station based in Redondo Beach, was playing an important role in assisting Korean Californians to deal with what was, by its very definition, a culture in transition. Banana Man, it must be noted, was not anti-Korean, merely anti any overly rigid definition of what being Korean meant. Even as they were being driven to gain admission to Harvard, the American-born generation following the 1.5ers was becoming taller, more good-humored, and hipper, although young women still tended to live at home, even after marriage, until they could afford to buy their own place, and young people still revered their elders. And besides: the number one hero of the Korean community was, after 1994, not a lawyer who had gone to Harvard but Chan Ho Park, the six-foot-two, 185-pound Korean-born pitcher for the Los Angeles Dodgers and the first Korean to play major league baseball in the United States. Even the older generation was impressed. After all, Park had started his career at the age of twenty with a $1.2 million contract. An alumnus of Hanyang University in Seoul, Park adhered to the Confucian ethic. "Basic education," he told his young fans, "has to be fulfilled in order for a person to be a good ballplayer. Otherwise, you can't be considered a true gentleman athlete."[10]

Still, there could be chilling reminders and tragic consequences of inter-Asian animosities brought to Southern California that could have used the good humor of Banana Man or the reconciling presence of a flourishing Korean-born pitcher for the Dodgers. When Myung-Sub Mike Lee, thirty-nine, hanged himself in the fall of 1999, a longtime animosity between

Japanese and Koreans stood revealed as translatable to Southern California. A Korean immigrant to Southern California, Lee had gone to work for the Japanese-owned Nippon Express, a freight-forwarding company, and, being of a sensitive nature, had severely internalized and begun to brood upon certain anti-Korean remarks made by some of his Japanese employers. Lee kept a diary, made public after his death, in which he struggled to cope with the jokes and insults leveled against him as a Korean: the way he spoke Japanese, the smell of *kimchi* (pickled cabbage) on his breath after lunch, the virtue of his wife, the size of her breasts. Reverberating through the entire encounter were the overtones of the longtime colonial dominance of Korea by Japan and the sense of superiority felt by so many Japanese over Koreans. When Lee lodged a discrimination complaint in 1998, he was interviewed by the human resources manager from the Nippon Express headquarters in New York, an Anglo. In the course of being interviewed, Lee told the manager that he was sometimes so angry with his employers that he felt like killing them. The company turned the threat over to the police, and Lee found himself facing felony charges. His job, his newly purchased home, his chances of American citizenship—everything seemed lost. And Mike Lee hanged himself, leaving his wife, Junko, to raise their children Amanda, ten, and Sky, eighteen months, alone.

The Korean-American community of metropolitan Los Angeles was galvanized by the entire affair, which represented, it believed, a chilling importation of negative Asian attitudes to the United States. A Committee for Justice for M. S. Lee was formed, demanding a public apology from Nippon Express, punishment for those who had harassed him, and financial compensation. Already, the company had sent Junko Lee a check for $25,000 at Christmas, which she had returned, and she refused to accept her share of a $50,000 settlement her husband had agreed to before his death. "I believe the company sent him to trap my husband," said Junko Lee of the human resources manager from New York. "I cannot forgive them."[11]

More promising as a California paradigm was the experience of Asian Indians in the Silicon Valley. Throughout the 1990s the Asian-Indian population in Santa Clara County, part of the Silicon Valley, tripled. Overall, Asian-Indian residents of California doubled over the same decade, reaching 314,819 by 2001. The success of the Silicon desi, as Asian-Indian immigrants called themselves, testified to the almost immediate transferability of immigrant peoples to California, provided that they bring skills with them. In the case of the Asian Indians, their talents as English speakers and writers only accelerated their adaptability. A veritable brain drain had brought to the Silicon Valley throughout the 1990s a rising number of highly trained and educated college graduates, together with their parents, members of their extended families, and a less skilled but equally necessary cadre of service personnel, looking for opportunities outside India and finding them in an industry in which Asian Indians had played a leadership role from the beginning.

To leaf through the advertisements of the 150-page *India West* weekly was to encounter a near-complete India successfully translated to California circumstances: Indian restaurants galore, Indian grocery stores, sari shops, travel agencies specializing in California-India connections, information regarding upcoming festivals and parades. "They can find whatever they find in India," noted Raj Bhanot, cofounder of the Hindu Temple and Community Center of Sunnyvale. "They're not missing anything, basically." Amenities included a cinema complex in Fremont that showed only films from South Asia and hosted guest appearances by noted Indian performers, for whom Silicon Valley had now become a regular stop. Established in a converted electronics warehouse in 1994, the Hindu Temple and Community Center of Sunnyvale was serving a congregation of approaching five thousand by the end of the decade. The Sikh Gurdwara, or temple, in San Jose, was planning a new facility on its forty-two-acre property.

Of course, there were problems. *India West* documented, among other things, the outrage experienced by Asian Indians over the fact that certain fast-food chains cooked their french fries in animal fat or used beef flavoring. On a more positive note, Asian brainpower and academic orientation were transforming the public schools of Silicon Valley and the adjacent East Bay. More than three hundred students were taking a college-level statistics course at the Mission San Jose High School north of San Jose in the East Bay, where sixty-one percent of the student body was minority, much of it Asian. Fully one-third of the entire student body of two thousand had been identified as gifted through standardized testing. While some Asian Indians decided to return to India, the deflation of the dot-com industry in 2000 and 2001 showed no signs of disestablishing the California-as-India that had emerged in the 1990s. "The Silicon Valley," noted Palo Alto management consultant Vish Agarwal, "values your talent more than your race, color, sex, or religion."[12]

The pervasive and generally successful emergence of California as Asia had to be noted, respected, evaluated, and learned from by non-Asian Californians. Chinese, Japanese, Filipino, Korean, Asian Indian, Pakistani, Vietnamese, Cambodian, Laotian, Thai, Indonesian, Samoan, Hawaiian, Guamanian, Asian and Pacific Islanders: everywhere one looked in census 2000, evidence of California-as-Asia asserted itself. Behind the presence of each group stood one or another shift, slight or cataclysmic, in recent world history. In certain cases—the Samoan communities in Compton, Gardena, Carson, and San Pedro; the Hawaiian communities in Westchester, Gardena, and Carson; the Guamanian enclaves in Carson, West Long Beach, and Tustin; the Asian and Pacific Islanders in Daly City in the north and Thousand Oaks, Calabasas, Glendale, Whittier, and Anaheim Hills in the south—the presence in California of a community simply expressed the Americanization of these peoples, temporary or otherwise, beginning in the 1890s and continuing through World War II, as the United States pushed into the Pacific. In the cases of other communities present on a lesser scale—the Asian Indians in Silicon Valley in the north, Granada Hills and Diamond Bar in the south; the Pakistanis in Diamond Bar as well; the Indonesians in El Segundo, Alhambra, and Diamond Bar—one or another war, civil war, coup d'etat, or other political adjustment lurked somewhere in the profile of why these people had come to California.

In the case of the Southeast Asians—the Vietnamese in Orange County and San Jose, the Cambodians in Long Beach, the Laotians in Santa Ana, the Hmong in the Central Valley—their presence was the direct outcome of the traumatic and failed involvement of the United States in Southeast Asia through 1975. Camp Pendleton, the marine corps training base in northern San Diego County, had served as one of the key processing centers for Vietnamese refugees. Although it was U.S. policy to settle such refugees throughout the country, the Vietnamese liked Orange County—its climate, its opportunities for work and entrepreneurialism, and, it must be said, its generous welfare programs—and through the late 1970s and early 1980s they reconsolidated there, centering themselves on a cluster of strawberry fields, used-car lots, and marginal shopping centers that eventually developed into Little Saigon. With a population of forty thousand, Little Saigon was now the largest Vietnamese community in the world outside of Vietnam. Although less dramatic in numbers, the Vietnamese of metropolitan San Jose, spinning off from an introduction to this region from the Moffett Field Naval Air Station, where refugees also were processed, represented a second Little Saigon.

By the 1990s a generation akin to the Korean 1.5ers—arriving, that is, in the United States as children and coming of age in American circumstances—was creating the first Vietnamese-American wave: people such as the San Francisco–based journalist Andrew Lam, an editor with Pacific News Service, who in the mid-1990s began to write reflectively on his experience and that of his Vietnam-born, American-raised peer group, especially as those reflections were triggered each year on April 30, the day in 1975 that Saigon fell to the North Vietnamese. As a boy of eleven, Lam flew out with his parents to Guam in a crowded C-130 on April 29. As a teenager, Lam lived in a culture in which his parents and elders were obsessed by the defeat and, even as they made their adjustments to Little Saigon in San Jose, dreamt of making an exile's return. By the time Lam reached early adulthood, however, the world of his elders began to seem a cluster of outdated passions. Lam's older brother, who had grown up wanting to be a freedom fighter in a heavily rumored U.S. reinvasion of South Vietnam, became instead a prosperous civil engineer. Lam himself startled his parents one morning with the highly unusual announcement that he wanted to become a writer. "When did this happen?" Lam asked himself. "Who knows? One night, America quietly seeps in and takes hold of one's mind and body, and the Vietnamese soul of sorrows slowly fades away. In the morning, the Vietnamese American speaks a new language of materialism: his vocabulary includes terms like career choices, down payment, escrow, overtime." By the mid-1990s, Lam and his Vietnamese American friends had evolved their own April 30 rites: getting together and watching *Gone With the Wind,* seeing in the defeat and fall of the American South a mirror image of their own social experience.[13]

Like Vietnamese Californians, Laotian and Cambodian Californians tended to be concentrated in metro Los Angeles and Orange County and scattered up and down the Central Valley. By 1997, the city of Fresno in the Central Valley had three thousand Vietnamese-Californian residents. On March 15, 1997, Mayor Jim Patterson, speaking in front of the new red, white, and blue–painted Vietnamese Buddhist temple on South Elm Avenue, proclaimed March Vietnamese Association of the Central Valley Month in honor of that organization. The national anthems of Vietnam and the United States were played, and Vietnamese food was served. Many of the women and children attending the event were dressed in traditional costumes. "It's not a small achievement to have a temple of this size in Fresno," noted one speaker, Sudarshan Kapoor, the India-born chairman of the Fresno Human Relations Commission. "I came to Fresno in 1967, and our community did not have a temple."[14]

Not all Southeast Asian immigrants were from the educated classes. Many were rural people who had been recruited into American service by the armed forces or the CIA. Coming to California, they set themselves to the task of making a living, sometimes in unusual ways. The Cambodian refugees settling in the Little Phnom Penh section of Long Beach, for example, beginning with Ted Ngoy, got into the doughnut business. Taking his training with the Winchell chain in the late 1970s, Ngoy became rich by opening small doughnut shops, then selling them off to other Cambodians. Like another Southern California self-made Cambodian millionaire, Kim Kethavy (gas stations and automotive spare parts), Ngoy eventually returned to Cambodia to get into politics—but not before he had helped launch a significant percentage of the more than 2,400 doughnut shops in California. Cambodians liked running doughnut shops in part because, in contrast to liquor stores or gas stations, they were not as susceptible to armed robbery. A doughnut shop took about $80,000 to open and could support a family of three to five, provided that each person worked a shift. And it was a business that even the most uneducated Cambodian refugee could master. Fleeing the slaughter in Cambodia in 1982, Ly Yiv arrived in Southern California speaking no English. That was two in the afternoon. By midnight, he was learning how to bake doughnuts with a Cambodian friend, sorting through the intricacies of twist, glazed, jelly, chocolate, buttermilk, and old-fashioned. "Some people can't write and can't tell the name," noted Ly Yiv, by now the owner of the Good Time Donuts in Diamond Bar, "but they can smell the flour and make the doughnut. This is a good business for people who don't speak too much English. They can say, 'Good morning' and 'How are you?' and count the money."[15]

Many Cambodians, together with other Southeast Asian refugees, became ensnared not in doughnut dough, but in the welfare culture. Of the more than 200,000 Cambodians reaching the United States in the late 1970s and early 1980s, more than half settled in California, many of them attracted by the welfare benefits offered by the state. A family of three on welfare in 1991 would receive $663 a month in California, together with Medi-Cal health coverage and $170 a month in food stamps, as compared to $577 a month in New York, and $184 a month in Texas. Even families wanting to get off welfare, such as the Say Vann family of Stockton, found it next to impossible to detach themselves from such benefits, especially health care. A foreman in a sugar factory in Phnom Penh, Say Vann moved his family to California from Pennsylvania specifically for the benefits, and by December 1991 was living with his wife and five children in a small but comfortably furnished home in Stockton on welfare benefits totaling $899 a month. Vann was not a lazy man. Since arriving in the United States, he had mastered English, earned a high school diploma, and was only one unit short of a junior college degree; but if he left welfare and took the $1,150-a-month job he had been offered in Stockton as a teacher's aide in a bilingual education program at Charterhouse, a refugee agency, how could he pay out-of-pocket monthly expenses of $136.77 per dependent for health coverage and $17.58 per dependent for dental coverage, for a total of $600 a month, on such a salary? Going to work was strictly not competitive with staying on welfare; and so Say Vann, with the best intentions in the world of making it in his new environment, languished in limbo as his twenty-three-year-old son, Smey Reak, his nineteen-year-old daughter, Sophorn, and his eighteen-year-old daughter, Sophreap, attended college at Temple University, the University of the Pacific at Stockton, and UC Davis, respectively, heading toward careers in engineering and pharmacy. "Nobody can steal it," Say Vann said of his children's education. "No fire can take it away. Knowledge is inside your body."[16]

Of the 110,000 Hmong refugees brought to the United States after their ferociously loyal service with the American military and CIA during the Vietnam War—in which they suffered casualty rates ten times as high as those of American soldiers in South Vietnam—nearly half had settled in northern and central California. Like Laotians and Cambodians, the Hmong had been distributed throughout the country by the U.S. government, but since they were accustomed to a tightly knit village life, they had soon reconsolidated themselves in California. Here was an ancient and proud people—fiercely antiauthoritarian, without a written alphabet, ignorant of electricity, accustomed for thousands of years to living in the highlands of Laos on their own terms, their supreme imperative being *Hmoob yuav tsum hlub Hmoob,* "Hmong people look out for their own," together with *mab sua,* "Everybody else can kiss my ass"—now being thrust into the complexities and contradictions of 1990s California, including its welfare culture. A Hmong refugee father, unable to find a job in Sacramento, was apprehended for hunting small game within the city limits. Social workers also had a problem with the man's proclivity to put a gun to his terrified son's head and say: "If you don't listen to me or get A's and B's in school, I'll kill you." Back in Laos, the Hmong guided themselves by the principle that if you love your children, you must beat them, and if you hate them, just praise them. In California, they found themselves in front of the court for child abuse, in many cases reported by their own children.[17]

The most serious point of contention between Hmong and the larger culture was their marriage practices. Hmong men married early, in their late teens or early twenties, and preferred even younger brides—as young as thirteen. Marriage was a simple ceremony, with the bridegroom-to-be bringing his intended bride to his father's home, where the father performed a thirty-second ceremony blessing the new couple with a live chicken. Later, over tea and whiskey, elders from both sides argued over the payment due the bride's clan, which could range from $2,000 to $5,000. Obviously, such impromptu arrangements, involving at least the appearance of kidnapping and sexual intercourse with female minors (and this sometimes with at least an outward show of force) ran counter to the false imprisonment, rape, and statutory rape laws of California. Although Central Valley district attorneys were loath to bring felony kidnapping and rape charges against Hmong bridegrooms, a serious clash of cultures was in evidence.

Hmong young women rarely resumed their education after bearing three to four children while still of high school age, and Hmong custom allowed a young male to take a second wife if his first could not bear him a son. According to the *Los Angeles Times,* polygamy—which the law called bigamy, a felony—was common among the Hmong of the Central Valley into the early 1990s, and young husbands with childless or girl-baby-only wives commonly were on the lookout for other women. Understandably, Hmong women who had grown up in American circumstances began to grow restive. At Cal State Fresno, there were seventy Hmong women out of a total of 270 Hmong students enrolled by May 1993, up from a dozen females five years earlier. An increasing number were resisting early marriages. "I was supposed to marry my uncle's son," noted one seventeen-year-old senior at Merced High, who was planning to go on to college. "He had been chosen for me a long time ago. I told my parents, 'Forget him. He's not my type.' There is a lot of good in our culture. You know there's no such thing as a Hmong convalescent home or a Hmong homeless person. So I want to keep my language. I want to keep my customs and music. But this early marriage stuff has got to change."[18]

Multiple Identities

B y the early 1990s, Californians had long since recognized that their state had changed and was now an immigrant-dominated commonwealth. Library signs in Long Beach were printed in English, Spanish, Vietnamese, and Cambodian. Visit the public high school in San Marino, a once Anglo-elite enclave near Pasadena rapidly becoming Asian, and you would find not only Asian teenagers on the track team, but Latina Anna Maria Munoz as well. Visit Belmont High School in Los Angeles, about a mile west of downtown near the Pico Union district, and you would find in February 1994 not only the largest high school in California, with 4,200 students, but teenagers from around the world, speaking more than thirty languages, with Spanish predominating. Metro Los Angeles had the second largest concentration of Japanese, Taiwanese, Koreans, Filipinos, Armenians, Thais, Vietnamese, and Mexicans outside their respective homelands. At lunchtime, the line into the cafeteria snaked around the campus. Nearly three-fourths of the student body were poor enough to qualify for free or reduced price lunches. Classes averaged fifty students, and only the most aggressive of them—such as Chris Van, class of 1993, who went on to MIT—could extract the instruction and tutoring they needed. SAT scores averaged 378 in math and 299 on verbal aptitude, far below the national average. The dropout rate hovered between 25 and 30 percent.

Visit the southern portion of San Francisco, and you found the highest concentration of Samoans outside Samoa. At Woodrow Wilson High School, there was a Chinese majority, with Filipinos and Latinos not far behind, but also assorted Cambodians, Ethiopians, Samoans, Vietnamese, Laotians, Fijians, Yemenis, Palestinians, and Koreans, equally trendy in their jeans, sweatshirts, and running shoes. The Mission district of San Francisco had become the home of some 150,000 Central Americans. The North Beach district, once the center of the Italian community, was now only defiantly Italian (with something like less than three thousand Italians actually in residence) while becoming increasingly an annex of Chinatown.

What did all this mean? For many commentators, the diversity of California—despite all the problems—implied the economic revitalization of California itself. Immigrants had come to work, and their work was necessary for the state's economic recovery. Everywhere one looked, immigrants were starting businesses, washing dishes, teaching classes in theoretical physics, cleaning high-rises by night, staffing pharmacies, waiting tables—doing the business of California. Without its Latino workforce, writer Joel Kotkin argued in March 1996, the Los Angeles economy would collapse. "In Los Angeles County," Kotkin noted, "Latino workers now constitute nearly two-thirds of all the production workers in such key manufacturing industries as textiles, metal-working and medical instruments. The now predominantly Latino 'neglected areas' of the county contain a manufacturing economy that has a total net worth of more than \$54 billion and some 360,000 employees, more than the industrial economies of thirty states."[19]

"All day," wrote essayist Richard Rodriguez of a visit to a Los Angeles hotel in August 1993, "I saw Mexicans working, busily working, to maintain California's legendary 'quality of life.' The common complaint of Californians is that the immigrants, whether legally or illegally here, are destroying our quality of life. But there the Mexicans were—hosing down the tiles by the hotel swimming pool, gardening, everywhere gardening. The woman who could barely speak English was making beds; at the Yuppie restaurant, Mexican men impersonated Italian chefs."[20]

Polyglotism was prevailing—at work and school, and in athletics, social life, and religious practice. The United States had once, rather easily, been described as a Protestant nation. That designation had been modified to a Judeo-Christian nation, to accommodate other groups. Then Buddhism arose as a force, especially on the West Coast. Now the formula was requiring even further modification, as Islam as well—with strong help from California—found its home in the republic. While Islam represented a religion rather than a single nationality, immigration to California by Muslim groups—Egyptians, Syrians, Lebanese, Palestinians, Iraqis—proceeded at a competitive pace. By the mid-1990s, California was ground zero of Islamic America, with half a million Muslims in Southern California and almost half that number scattered elsewhere throughout the state. The first generation of Arab-American immigrants to the United States had been 90 percent Christian. The generation to arrive after the immigration reform laws of 1965, however, was predominantly Muslim. A distinction had to be made, obviously, between Muslims and Arab Americans. Muslims in California also included Sudanese, Filipinos, Bosnians, Albanians, Asian Indians, Pakistanis, Bangladeshis, Kurds, Turks, Somalis, Indonesians, Sri Lankans, ethnic Chinese from various Muslim countries, and other groups;

but the majority—and the predominant image—of Muslim California was Arab-American.

It did not take much investigation to note that by the mid-1990s, California nurtured the largest concentrations of Arabs outside of the Middle East and the largest Muslim community outside dar al-Islam, the sprawling house of Islam embracing three continents, dozens of nations, and a significant portion of the people of the world. Increasing their national number by 21 percent between 1986 and 1996, until it was passing 800,000, Arab America, including Arab-American California, was among the most educated and prosperous of all immigrant groups. Twenty-two percent of Arab-American adults held bachelor's degrees; 15 percent had advanced to the master's level. In every other indication of adjustment to the United States—home ownership, low crime and juvenile delinquency rate, low divorce rate, low rate of bankruptcies—Arab Americans were highly competitive with other groups.

There was also a growing observance of Ramadan, the Muslim holy season, throughout California, and in Southern California especially. Along with almsgiving, prayer, pilgrimage to Mecca, the profession of the unity of God and the prophethood of Mohammed, Ramadan constituted one of the five pillars of Muslim faith. Formed in early 1995 to coordinate the interests and concerns of an estimated half-million Muslims in the region, the Islamic Shura Council of Southern California (*shura* is Arabic for "mutual consultation") orchestrated larger and larger Ramadan observances throughout the 1990s. By February 1996, as many as ten thousand Muslims were expected to gather at three Southern Californian sites for the three-day holiday ending Ramadan. Southern California Muslims pointed with pride to the fact that the precise start of Ramadan was being scientifically determined with the help of scientists and astronomers from Caltech and the Jet Propulsion Laboratory. "This is part of what I call the United States' gift to the rest of Islam," noted Shabbir Mansuri of Fountain Valley, director of the Council on Islamic Education.[21] Even more revealing of the progressively Californian nature of the Islamic experience was the fact that the previous December, Marine Corps brigadier general Robert Magnus, commander of all marine air bases on the West Coast, at the request of his Protestant chaplain, navy captain Tom Atkins, had authorized the use of a vacant blimp hangar at the Tustin Marine Air Base by seven thousand Muslims for the end-of-Ramadan observances.

Another immigrant group, Assyrian Californians—approximately ten thousand in number, settled in the mid–Central Valley between Modesto, Ceres, and Turlock—were experiencing more ambivalent feelings toward the U.S. Marine Corps in January 1991 during the Gulf War. Descendants of a great people that had once ruled the Middle East, 400,000 Assyrians survive these days in Iraq, out of a population of 24 million, as a Christian minority, speaking Aramaic, the language of Jesus Christ. Few of the Assyrian Californians in the Central Valley were without relatives in Iraq as the U.S. Army, Marine Corps, Air Force, and Navy pounded their homeland in a hundred-hour blitzkrieg. At least one family suffered the tension of having a son in the American army as part of the Gulf forces and several cousins serving in the army of Saddam Hussein. Despite this stress, however, Assyrian Californians might look with pride upon what they had accomplished over the past sixty years. Like so many other groups, they represented one of the largest enclaves of their people outside their homeland. They had preserved their religion, Assyrian Orthodoxy, and through their church had preserved their language and culture into the third generation. And they had prospered in business. William Lazar, for example, had moved north to San Francisco and by the 1980s, as president of the elite Luxor Cab company of that city, had organized the San Francisco Taxicab Association and had seen to the erection of a great bronze statue of the ancient Assyrian emperor Sargon outside the San Francisco Public Library.

Like Assyrian Californians, Armenian Californians could not be considered a new immigrant group. For nearly a century, the Armenian community, centered on Fresno in the Central Valley (and later in Southern California, where the Armenian population exceeded 350,000), had been at the forefront of that region's development. By the 1990s, the Armenian community was in its third or fourth generation: an ancient people, skilled in the ways of trade and negotiation, significantly prosperous. Armenian American George Deukmejian had served as governor of the state through the 1980s; and another Armenian American, Armand Arabian, sat on the state supreme court. An Armenian vintner, Robert Setrakian, was president of the Bohemian Club in San Francisco. Cal State Fresno and UC Berkeley supported endowed professorships in Armenian studies. The William Saroyan Papers were at Stanford University, and the image of Saroyan, author and playwright and the most famous Armenian Californian of them all, graced a U.S. stamp.

Equally resonant were the Russian reverberations of California, dating from the visit of Count Nikolai Rezanov of the Alaska-based Russian-American Company in April 1806. Dropping anchor in San Francisco Bay, Rezanov dreamed of extending the arc of Russian influence southward from Alaska to California. In 1812, five years after Rezanov himself had died in the middle of a terrible Siberian winter en route from California to St. Petersburg, the Russian-American Company established Fort Ross a hundred miles north of San Francisco Bay. For twenty-seven years, until the company was disbanded in 1839 and sold in 1841, the onion-shaped spires of the Fort Ross chapel suggested the possibilities of an enlarged Russo-California. Such possibilities quickened once again to life after the 1917 Russian Revolution and ensuing civil war, as thousands of White Russians made their way cast through Siberia and China toward San Francisco.

Now, in the early 1990s, a new wave of Russian immigration was under way, much of it likewise San Francisco–bound. Legal immigrants from the former Soviet Union (some 69,212 in all) outstripped all other groups—Mexicans (66,890), Vietnamese (65,455), Guatemalans (56,420), Filipinos (52,997), and Chinese (47,203)—in the busy immigration year of 1992. For various reasons—and these reasons were not hard to find amid the ambiguities of a Soviet Union deconstructing itself, with the ever-present possibilities of a resurgent anti-Semitism lurking in and behind the social chaos—Russian Jewry had been in the process of reducing its numbers by half since the late 1980s as, each year, some 120,000 or more Russian Jews left for Israel, Canada, or the United States. Not all these immigrants wound up in San Francisco or Los Angeles. They also settled in Brighton Beach in New York and Rogers Park in Chicago; but they were arriving in the Bay Area at an estimated rate of twenty thousand a year from the mid-1980s on, adding their considerable numbers to the existing Russian-American community of some fifty thousand. Most of these immigrants from Russia and the other former Soviet republics were Jewish—80 percent of them, according to legislation passed by Congress in 1985 and 1990. The rest were Pentecostal Christians and other persecuted religious minorities. Only a sliver of them were Russian Orthodox Christians, whom Congress did not consider a persecuted group.

Russian-Jewish immigrants to San Francisco and the surrounding communities of the Bay Area included many engineers and administrators who, despite the lingering anti-Semitism of Soviet society, had risen in their professions. Their immigration to the United States had been expressly authorized by congressional legislation and sponsored locally by the Jewish community, which saw as much as possible to their rapid adjustment through a variety of social agencies and programs. Still, it was tough: a new society and a new language, the necessity of reearning one's credentials and licenses in medicine, dentistry, and engineering, the fall in status from being in the managerial and professional elite of one society and apprentices in the next, or cabdrivers, or hospital technicians with a temporarily inactive MD degree. Russian-Jewish immigrants of blue-collar background seemed to have the easiest time of it. Within a few short years a significant percentage of San Francisco cabs were being driven by them, a pattern also being repeated in Los Angeles.

Ethnic Russian Orthodox illegals, by contrast, were having a rough go. Even legal immigrants from this group, and there were very few, came into an unprepared environment. If you were an illegal, such as Yuri and Olga Popov were, living in June 1993 in a homeless shelter in San Francisco with their six-year-old daughter, Tanya, the American bureaucracy might more than occasionally and more than a little chillingly resemble that of the Soviet Union. The Popovs, who had come to California on a business visa, were claiming political asylum on the intriguing argument that during the Soviet era each of them had suffered because of numerous run-ins with the KGB over their political views, and now, as Yuri put it, "the same KGB Communists who had given me trouble always were still in power." Fortunately, the Popovs were granted temporary work permits. Both of them were trained engineers. Artur Belokonov, by contrast, another illegal ethnic Russian applying for asylum, had primarily to his credit that he was the founder and editor in chief of *Soul & Body,* a pioneering Soviet sex magazine. Wearing his hair in a Russian version of dreadlocks, the twenty-six-year-old Belokonov hardly seemed a victim of persecution. No matter: even before the authorities had made up their mind, or Belokonov's English had advanced to more than rudimentary, this physical fitness buff, a daily jogger along Ocean Beach, was promoting helicopter tours of the North Pole. "This is a wonderful country," Belokonov noted joyously. "It is a dream."[22]

PART IV

Wedge Issues

Backlash

Whatever they were taking out of the system, immigrants were putting back more than their share: this according to Richard Rodriguez and such other pro-immigrant commentators as Professor Julian Simon of the University of Maryland, author of *The Economic Consequences of Immigration* (1989), and Joel Millman, author of *The Other Americans: How Immigrants Renew Our Country, Our Economy, and Our Values* (1997). Simon and Millman were especially skilled at marshaling statistics asserting that immigrants generated more than their fair share of wealth and paid more than their fair share of taxes. At the University of Southern California, demographer Dowell Myers, comparing and contrasting census data on some 850,000 Southern California residents from 1980 and 1990, argued that not only were immigrants working hard, they were also getting ahead. Latino immigrants, especially males, lagged behind in educational attainment, but their average income had managed to climb 27 percent, from $14,890 to $18,899, over the past decade. Even more comfortingly, American-born Latinos were moving up the ladder more rapidly than their Latino immigrant counterparts. Being in Southern California, in other words, had a way of making things better. English-language skills seemed central to the process. The earlier one learned English, the faster one got ahead. Sadly, nearly 80 percent of the Hispanic immigrants who came to California between the ages of twenty-four and thirty-four failed to master English, and hence failed to achieve the expected upward mobility.

It was on this issue of assimilation, symbolized by English-language skills, that much of the anti-Latino immigrant critique first focused. As early as 1984, the Virginia-based American Immigration Control Foundation published a pamphlet entitled *The Coming Triumph of Mexican Irredentism* predicting the breakup of the United States by the year 2080 into an Anglo-American north and a Spanish-speaking south realigned with Mexico. In both its pamphlet series and its newsletter *Border Watch* (later changed to the less aggressive *AICF Report*), the foundation maintained throughout the 1980s an assertive anti-immigrant line of argument. In one of its pamphlets, *Sociobiology and Immigration: The Grim Forecast for America,* husband and wife authors Glaister and Evelyn Elmer argued: "Taken together, current trends, history, sociological research and sociobiological theory suggest that the United States has thoughtlessly placed its future in peril by embarking upon an unprecedented experiment in the large-scale mixing of multiple peoples with highly diverse cultures in a democratic society. If present immigration policies continue, a great nation 'indivisible' seems less likely in the next century than cultural chaos, political instability, and economic deterioration."

New York writer David Rieff spent parts of 1989–90 in Los Angeles, observing the immigrant scene. The results of Rieff's sojourn, *Los Angeles: Capital of the Third World* (1991), painted a dire portrait of the City of Angels well advanced into a *Blade Runner* scenario of cultural fragmentation and mutual incomprehensibility. There was no way that the new immigration, as evidenced by Los Angeles, Rieff argued, could be compared to previous American experiences. Rather than serve as a matrix for assimilation, Los Angeles was being colonized. It had become, in fact, the capital of the Third World. Rieff's book caused controversy but remained on a level of disciplined cultural analysis. With the recession worsening in 1991, 1992, and 1993, rarefied cultural questions were rapidly yielding to more gut-level issues as more and more Californians began to blame immigrants for the tough times and the pervasive perception that the quality of life had declined in the Golden State.

At this point, in 1993, anti-immigration sentiment began to surface among environmentalists. Respected Bay Area environmental writer Harold Gilliam, basing his argument on the population statistics presented in the pamphlet *50,000,000 Californians?* by Leon Bouvier, published by the Center for Immigration Studies in Washington, D.C., wrote that there were too many people in California for the good of the environment, and, more pointedly, immigrant Californians were having too many children. A year before Gilliam's article first appeared in the *San Francisco Chronicle,* the Los Angeles–based *Wall Street Journal* writer Tim Ferguson had noted that the immigrant debate was coalescing around the issues of immigrant fertility, birth control (or lack thereof), and public assistance to pregnant illegals. Latino culture revered children, Ferguson reported, and large families were common. American-born Latinos, or those long resident in the United States, tended to have as many children as their American counterparts. Immigrants, by contrast, whether legal or illegal, had a higher rate of reproduction, not only because of the usual joy in children common to Latino culture but because children constituted a form of wealth in families in which there would have to be many workers for the family unit to survive.

By the fall of 1997 the Sierra Club was struggling with a nationwide anti-immigration referendum that had already driven more than one thousand members to quit the organization in protest of an argument they considered racist, elitist, and divisive. "The upcoming Sierra Club ballot," wrote commentator Alexander Cockburn in October 1997, "may not have the aroma of a Klan rally, with burning crosses and white hoods. In fact, it's something much more sinister and dangerous, a middle-class, do-gooder movement with public credentials paddling in the most polluted waters of American political life."[1]

Equally insulting was the parallel notion that Latino immigrants, especially those coming from Mexico, were not only burdening American society but also were lowering its tone. Worse, the argument ran, they were most likely inassimilable, or not worth the social costs of bringing them up to speed. Arguments such as this, stated or implied, hurt and alienated Latinos, whether legal immigrants or longtime Americans, for they represented, ultimately, an implicit harsh judgment not just against illegals but all Hispanics. Issued in September 1997, a RAND report written by demographer Kevin McCarthy and urban planner Georges Vernez argued that high-tech California, home to more than one-quarter of all recent immigrants in the United States, had no need for the continuing influx of low-skilled, poorly educated immigrants from Mexico and Central America. The California economy had shifted toward higher-skilled industries. What low-skilled jobs remained could be more than met by the present population, immigrant or native-born. Immigration, the report stated, had always been a balancing of benefits versus cost, and now for California, more than any other state, the balance was shifting to the cost side. It was just too expensive, if not impossible, to educate the first generation of immigrants, and even their children were proving such a strain on the system that Congress should reimburse California for doing the nation's work in educating and otherwise assisting immigrants. Congress, McCarthy and Vernez argued, should dramatically reduce legal immigration to something between the 300,000 annual average of the 1970s and the 800,000 annual average of the 1990s. Future quotas should be adjusted in accordance with projected needs. In all instances, the RAND team concluded, the criteria of education levels and English-language skills should bear much more weight than the current preference system based on family ties.

Illegals

In his analysis of the alleged pressures posed by immigration on the California environment, Harold Gilliam made no distinction between legal and illegal immigrants. The federal government, Gilliam argued, should stop both, if the water, topsoil, trees, open space, and other natural resources of California were to be preserved. Gilliam's failure to distinguish between legal and illegal immigrants—legal immigrants, after all, had the same moral right to be in the United States as Gilliam—underscored the tangled nexus of legitimate concern, cultural disconnect, and even racism, subtle or otherwise, at the core of the immigration debate. At this point, anti-immigration forces, especially in California, began to shift their arguments in the direction of illegal immigrants, especially the expenses attached to their imprisonment when necessary, their education, their health needs, and, an ever-present concern, their reproductive vitality.

Certainly, there was a problem. By 1993 the rate of illegal immigration in the United States was three times greater than its legal counterpart. According to statistics released by Senator Dianne Feinstein, there were 2.83 million illegal immigrants living in California, which made the state the home to 52 percent of the illegals in the United States. According to the Immigration and Naturalization Service, 95 percent of all illegal immigration was taking place across two hundred miles of the southern border of California. In 1992 alone, a fourteen-mile segment south of San Diego was crossed by an estimated 1.2 million illegal aliens. In August 1993, Governor Pete Wilson released new figures claiming that the overall cost to California taxpayers of illegal immigration should be set at $2.3 billion annually. The city of Los Angeles alone, Wilson argued, was home to more than one million illegal immigrants and their children. Facing a reelection campaign in 1994, Wilson led the charge underscoring the rising costs of public assistance of both illegals and those legalized by the Immigration Reform and Control Act of 1986. Programs such as Medi-Cal and Aid to Families with Dependent Children (AFDC), together with the cost of maintaining illegals in California prisons, Wilson noted, was now adding up to a $1.5 billion yearly price tag. Dramatically, Wilson sent a bill to the federal government for that amount. It was never paid.

Altogether, California was by 1993 educating approximately 45 percent of all immigrant schoolchildren in the United States, and so it came as no surprise when the Los Angeles Unified School District estimated that 23 percent of its $6.5 billion school budget was being allocated to the education of recent immigrants, both legal and illegal. Approximately 12,750 undocumented immigrants, meanwhile, were serving time in state prisons at an annual cost of more than $20,000 each. Together with illegals in county jails and juvenile facilities, they were costing the state more than $400 million a year.

In California, crime was an equal opportunity employer. The Russian mafia made its debut in San Francisco. In Los Angeles a ring of Armenian immigrant mobsters was rounded up for plotting the assassination of a United States Secret Service agent investigating their activities. Mexican drug cartels operated throughout the state, adding their corrupting presence to hundreds of mom-and-pop methamphetamine laboratories, which appeared and reappeared in remote locations like gypsy camps. The smuggling of illegal immigrants from Central America and Mexico via the Mexico-California border, from China via Baja California, or even the direct offloading of illegal Chinese immigrants onto the California coast— continued as a lucrative enterprise for organized crime. According to a 1992 U.S. Senate report, smuggling illegal immigrants had become a $3 billion a year national industry. By April 1993, it was estimated that approximately 100,000 Chinese were being smuggled into the United States annually, more than three times the thirty thousand who came legally. The production and sale of false documents—birth certificates, green cards, Social Security cards, driver's licenses—had risen to the status of an impressive business.

Many Chinese illegals were landed from overcrowded ships by Mexican fishermen on one or another remote inlet on the Baja California coast. Hiding out for a day or two at staging sites (one successful bust in the inlet village of Maneadero twenty-five miles south of Ensenada revealed 306 Chinese packed into two tiny sheds), they were smuggled by their contractors into the United States at one or another point along the California-Arizona border. Once in the United States, Chinese illegals spent the next five years or more paying off the $20,000 to $35,000 owed their smugglers. All in all, the entire experience of *toudu* (to steal passage, to be smuggled) was harrowing and demeaning. Aside from overcrowded conditions in passage, smuggled Chinese were often victims of physical brutality and exploitation as they crossed the Pacific. In one instance, in the fall of 1992, crew members systematically raped all thirty-seven women on board the ship. When at last working in the United States, smuggled immigrants owed an enormous amount of money to one or another underworld organization of snake heads, as smugglers were called. They became, in effect, indentured servants, working inhuman hours, six, even seven days a week in restaurants or sweatshops, living in crowded rooms where dozens of men might share a half-dozen beds among them, sleeping in shifts.

Illegals were not just on the margins of the California economy. They were at its center, doing the work no one else wanted to do. Nowhere was this more true than in the fields. California had long since anchored its agricultural economy on the seasonal availability of low-cost labor, much of it migrant and 92 percent of it, by 1996, foreign-born. Senator Pete Wilson and other congressional leaders from farm states had in 1986 intervened in the Immigration Reform and Control Act to add a provision legalizing more than one million farmworkers (a third of all the immigrants who were granted amnesty), provided they had been in the country a mere ninety days before passage of the act. This provision was intended to stabilize a large pool of documented farm labor. Unfortunately, both the demands of agriculture and the tendency of documented immigrants to find urban employment meant that almost as a matter of course, despite the intentions of the act, agriculture in California involved the hiring of undocumented workers. Jorge Garcia Mejia, eighteen, his brother Angel, twenty-five, and Jose Luis Miranda, thirty-one, were undocumented immigrants from the village of San Miguel in the state of Michoacan, Mexico. Working in a vineyard near Linden in San Joaquin County in early 1996, the three men raised aloft an irrigation pipe when a jackrabbit ran into it. The metal pipe touched high-tension wires overhead, and the three men were immediately electrocuted. Local workers raised $4,500 from among themselves to send the bodies of the three young men back to Mexico.

Some estimated that as of early 1996 nearly half the 700,000 farmworkers in California were undocumented; yet employer fines and penalties were only infrequently leveled by the Immigration and Naturalization Service. Between 1989 and 1994, the INS fined a mere forty-nine farm labor contractors and forty-six farm operators. Waging a reelection campaign that would soon mutate into a race for the 1996 Republican presidential nomination, Governor Pete Wilson consistently rejected the notion that the farmers of California should be held primarily responsible for the documentation of their workers. It was just too easy, Wilson argued, for undocumented workers to obtain forged documents; and how or why should farmers be held liable for sorting legals from illegals when, at harvest time, it was necessary to hire hundreds, even thousands, on quick notice? Wilson favored tighter federal control of borders and a federally administered program of farmworker identity cards. And besides: it was not only the farmers of California who were hiring illegals. Through the first half of the 1990s, the INS had fined such firms as the Walt Disney Company, Avis Rent-a-Car, the San Francisco Press Club, the First Korean-American Presbyterian Church of San Francisco, and Seton Medical Center, a Roman Catholic hospital complex in Daly City, for putting undocumented workers on their payrolls.

In most instances—and with the definite exception of adolescent labor in the fields—the jobs for which these companies were being fined, while onerous and low-paying, remained within the boundaries of free labor, unlike the case of garment manufacturing, a growing sector of the Southern California economy, in which metro Los Angeles was surpassing New York City by the mid-1990s. By its very nature, garment manufacturing lent itself to the wholesale employment of both documented and undocumented immigrants, who were often willing to do exhausting piecework for less than the established minimum wage. Martha Morales of Los Angeles stitched collars on blue sport shirts for an average net of $176 for a six-day, sixty-hour week. Jose Cortez pressed fabric at Santa Fe Finishing, another LA company, standing all day in his T-shirt before a hot pressing iron for similarly low wages.

Labor activists and union organizers were appalled by the poor pay, the long hours, the lack of benefits, the unsafe and unsanitary working conditions, the sheer drudgery of piecework, always racing against the clock. Defenders of the system pointed out that the majority of the 125,000 workers in the garment industry in metro Los Angeles were doing better than they would be doing in their home countries for similar work. Such jobs, however arduous, allowed immigrant families who pooled their incomes to establish themselves on the first rung of the American ladder. So, too, it was argued, had Jewish immigrants labored nearly a century earlier in the sweatshops of the Lower East Side. While demanding, garment work was not, finally, inhumane. It led to better things.

No one made any defense, however, when officials of the California Department of Labor and INS agents swept down on a squalid garment factory in El Monte, a suburb twelve miles east of downtown Los Angeles, in the early hours of August 2, 1995, and liberated seventy-two Thai garment workers living and working in conditions of involuntary servitude akin to slavery. As early as 1988, certainly by mid-May 1991, at least one INS agent, Philip Bonner Jr., who was married to a Thai woman and spoke Thai, had been highly suspicious of the El Monte compound, ringed with rolls of barbed wire and a six-foot-high brick wall topped by metal spikes, its first-floor windows covered with thick iron bars and its second-floor windows blocked by plywood sheets nailed from the inside. By day, a guard sat in front of the compound, forbidding passersby to talk to the women workers, many of them teenagers, who intermittently took the air in a tightly moni-tored open space, occasionally singing songs in their native language. Bon-ner got nowhere with his investigations, nor with several memoranda he wrote proposing raids on five other establishments in addition to the El Monte compound. All in all, his contacts were suggesting that up to two hundred illegal immigrants were being held against their will at six separate sites. The INS, however, deemed that it did not have sufficient evidence for a federal warrant. But when a Thai woman escaped from the El Monte com-pound and was put in contact with a lawyer, and the lawyer got in touch with the INS, Bonner was brought back on the case, along with agents of the California Department of Labor. It was the state agents who secured the legal instruments for the raid, which the INS only joined at the last minute.

The El Monte sweatshop still remains a sore point in the garment indus-try of Southern California and with the Los Angeles Chamber of Com-merce. A proposal by the Smithsonian Institution to mount an exhibit depicting the sweatshop and to bring the exhibit to California created an outcry in the Chamber of Commerce and other circles. Distilling all the evils and abuses inherent in the employment of undocumented workers, the El Monte compound served as a chilling paradigm of just how bad things could get. Seventy-two Thai women, brought into Southern California ille-gally by an organized crime ring, were kept as prisoners, some for as long as seven years, forced to work off their $4,800 passage at the rate of $300 a month. If they protested, they could be, in one dramatic instance, severely beaten and returned to Thailand. Even worse, reputable American compa-nies were receiving goods from the El Monte operation.

Almost within the year, the eight principals running the compound were indicted, tried, convicted, and sentenced to terms ranging from six to seven years; but the El Monte episode left a lingering anxiety. It was operating on the extreme margin, yet garments and labels found at the site, indicating such retailers as Macy's, Hecht's, Filene's, J. C. Penney, Robinsons-May, Dayton Hudson, Montgomery Ward, and others, suggested a pattern of complicity, however unknowing, in an operation that underscored larger patterns and enduring realities of First World consumerism and Third World labor, now brought to the United States itself. "I figured slavery went out years ago," noted Chuck Lieder, manager of the Rolling Homes Manor Mobile Home Park next door to the compound, after the raid. But shortly after the bust of the Thai compound, federal labor investigators were admitting that routine inspections of some fifty garment contractors in metro Los Angeles had turned up wage and overtime violations at forty-six sites, representing the shortchanging of some six hundred workers of more than $500,000 in wages—and this in legally registered factories.[2]

Rising Tensions

Certain points of contention in California were part of a larger pattern. In April 1992, Hungarian-born Georgia Gabor, sixty-two, a survivor of the Holocaust, was suing the San Marino Unified School District, where she had taught mathematics for twenty-one years, for what she considered the district's lackadaisical attitude toward anti-Semitic attacks leveled against her. After she published an autobiography in 1981 entitled *My Destiny: Survivor of the Holocaust,* postings of swastikas and anti-Semitic slurs and obscenities appeared on her classroom door or on nearby lockers and desks. Gabor also began to receive late-night hate phone calls at her home. Stopping at the San Marino post office one day, she returned to her car to find that someone had scrawled with a marker on it, "Jew, get out of San Marino." To her horror, despite repeated requests, the school district failed to investigate the matter and took its time removing the anti-Semitic graffiti.[3]

Such, sadly, was an instance of classical anti-Semitism—most likely perpetrated by teenagers. More complex was the reaction of African-American teenagers brought to the Grand Lake Theater in Oakland on Martin Luther King Day in 1994 to see Steven Spielberg's *Schindler's List.* A sizable group of students laughed throughout the film. Finally, the theater manager stopped the movie and ordered the laughing students to leave the theater. Some members of the audience applauded the manager's action. Defenders of the students claimed that the entire outing had been ill conceived from the beginning. It would be, they claimed, as if Jewish students were forced to commemorate the Holocaust by watching *Roots.*

Tensions between African Americans and Koreans in Southern California had been rising since the 1980s. Between March and September 1991, two Koreans and three African Americans were killed in Korean-owned stores in the course of holdups or other disputes. Tensions were exacerbated in September when two Korean storekeepers in Lynwood were shot and severely wounded by two African-American gunmen. Black community leaders, meanwhile, were calling for the boycotting of Korean-owned stores for being generally disrespectful of African-American customers. Black-Latino relations in this same region were likewise going downhill. Once predominantly African-American, South Central was now in the process of becoming Latino, and the process was fraught with conflict, especially on the more embattled margins of an already marginalized and embattled part of town. The huge (2,500 residents) South Central public housing project of Jordan Downs was now one-fifth Latino. Early on the morning of September 7, 1991, three young men—whom witnesses identified as African Americans (in fact, one was Latino)—doused the front door of a Jordan Downs apartment housing a Latino family with gasoline or another flammable liquid and set it ablaze. Martha Zuniga, twenty-two, her two children, Juan Carlos, five, and Claudio, four, and their great-grandmother Margarita Hernandez, seventy-eight, all perished in the flames. The following November, a huge brawl broke out between hundreds of African-American and Latino students at Gardena High School. Ironically, the melee at the 2,800-student school had erupted in the course of its annual International Assembly when some black and Latino students began booing the dances of other cultures.

Despite the fact that minorities, most of them immigrants, made up 54 percent of public school students as of 1992, 82 percent of their teachers were white. Controlling eruptions such as that at Gardena remained difficult. At Carlmont High School in Belmont, a prosperous suburb south of San Francisco, racial problems had been endemic since 1976, when the Sequoia Union High School District closed the Ravenswood High School in the predominantly African-American community of East Palo Alto and began busing the bulk of its students to Carlmont. So problematic was the enforced juxtapositioning of blacks and whites at Carlmont, the high school served as the real-life model for a racially troubled school in the film *Dangerous Minds* (1995). By October 1997, after some easing of tensions in recent years, troubles flared when someone broke into the car of a white student and stole his stereo, and the boy's friends in retaliation kicked in the headlights of a Latino student's car. An estimated sixty students were soon involved in a standoff that only narrowly avoided violence.

In the aftermath of the Los Angeles riots, *Los Angeles Times* literary editor Jack Miles had tried to make sense of this growing tension. Writing in the October 1992 *Atlantic,* Miles speculated that African Americans subliminally and even consciously understood that they were being replaced by Latinos as an acceptable minority in the minds of Asians and whites. In the past, however tangled the relationship, whites and blacks had shared a certain intimacy that, even in the era of slavery, had extended into the family itself. Generations of whites, after all, had been wet-nursed and raised by African-American women; and, before slavery and after, in the South and elsewhere in the United States, it was not uncommon for white and black youngsters to play together as children—either privileged white youngsters and the black children of family dependents, or more casual and less hierarchical associations among the less privileged—until the realities of a racially segregated culture caught up with them. As late as the 1930s, in other words, Our Gang had been integrated. In recent years, ran Miles's argument, African Americans were being increasingly kept at a psychological, even physical, distance by whites and Asians and were being replaced by Latinos as the minority of choice. Worse, blacks were being demonized as a violent people. Once intrinsic to the American scene, they were now being regarded as the Other. A generation of prosperous white and Asian Southern Californians was now turning to Latinos as housemaids, nannies, gardeners, family retainers of every sort. The old intimacy had been transferred to another group.

Not that the relationship was always that cozy. In March 1993, three Latino candidates presented themselves for the presidency of Long Beach City College. Each held a doctorate in higher education and had extensive experience in community college administration. The board of trustees, however, chose an Anglo woman who had dropped out of her PhD program at UCLA and was currently heading a small, overwhelmingly Anglo community college in Livermore, with only five thousand students. "How qualified do Latinos have to become before we can equally compete?" asked Margie Rodriguez, a member of the Long Beach City College staff.[4]

Then there was the leaf blower crisis. The majority of gardeners in Los Angeles were Latino. In the course of their work, they used gasoline-powered leaf blowers, which created an infernal racket. So powerful and continuous were the protests against them coming from prosperous, politically influential neighborhoods, the Los Angeles City Council was initially considering in late 1997 not only banning the blowers but making their use a misdemeanor subject to a $1,000 fine, even a jail sentence. The Association of Latin American Gardeners, an ad hoc group formed to counter the measure, saw in it a form of socioeconomic, even cultural warfare— gasoline-powered leaf blowers made their job easier and more efficient.

Residents, on the other hand, had a point. Neighborhoods filled with gardeners running high-decibel leaf blowers throughout the day were certainly being deprived of the quiet enjoyment of their premises. Since most of these residential owners tended to be affluent Anglos and Asians, cultural lines were being drawn. Despite the fact that the city council reduced the misdemeanor penalty to an infraction and the fine from $1,000 to $270, a group of gardeners, mostly Mexican immigrants, went on a hunger strike in early January in front of the city hall. In the days that followed, Mayor Richard Riordan, practicing a form of localized shuttle diplomacy, moved back and forth between the fasting gardeners and the city council, trying to negotiate a compromise. Riordan even offered a free meal at his downtown restaurant, the Pantry, for protesters coming off their fast. Finally, on January 10, 1998, the fasters ended their strike when the city council delivered written pledges to hold hearings on technological alternatives to gasoline-powered blowers. A crowd of some five hundred gardeners and their families, holding vigil in the rain in front of city hall, waving hundreds of brooms in protest, greeted the news with cheers.

On February 13, the ban on gasoline-powered blowers took effect. That morning at roll call, police officers were reminded that it was now illegal to use gasoline-driven leaf blowers. Many gardeners, such as Israel Belasco, fanning his rake in front of a home in Pacific Palisades, were complying with the new ordinance, although Belasco claimed that without his leaf blower he would be down from fifteen to ten jobs a day. In many areas throughout the city, one could still hear the high-decibel roar of leaf blowers as gardeners took their chances on the $270 fine. "I'm not afraid," noted Joel Martinez, using a leaf blower to clean the poolside area in a San Fernando Valley backyard. "The boss pays. If my boss tells me to use it, I'll use it. I'm violating the law. I understand that. But I'm not doing anything wrong. I'm trying to earn a living." That very day, state senator Richard Polanco, a powerful Los Angeles Democrat, introduced legislation in Sacramento to override the Los Angeles ordinance by placing leaf blowers under state regulation and standards. Los Angeles city councilwoman Cindy Miscikowski attacked the Polanco measure as an assault on home rule.[5]

The leaf blower crisis revealed yet another disconnect in a society in which people could look at the same matter in mutually incomprehensible ways. Take the question of soccer. On Sunday, February 15, 1998, the United States lost to Mexico, 1–0, in the Los Angeles Coliseum before a largely Mexican-American crowd of 91,000. During the playing of the American and Mexican national anthems at the beginning of the game, the crowd drowned "The Star-Spangled Banner" with boos and blowing horns. Throughout the game, it cheered Mexico and jeered the United States. Worse, the crowd pelted the American team as it left the field with a hail of plastic bottles, beer-filled cups, fruit and fruit rinds, nachos, and other debris. What's going on here? many commentators asked. "Why," asked sports commentator Bill Plaschke in the *Los Angeles Times,* "would those who attend U.S. schools and receive U.S. medical care feel it necessary to pelt any U.S. player running near the stands with water and beer?"[6] Mexican-American commentators such as Sergio Munoz and Gregory Rodriguez tried to make light of the event. After all, it was only soccer. Yet an uneasiness lingered in the minds of many.

Chinese Californians were disturbed by what they considered an anti-Asian bias arising from the scandals connected to the fund-raising activities of the Democratic Party in the 1996 elections. In general, Asian Americans in California had tended to stay out of politics. Although they were one in every ten Californians by the 1990s, they accounted for only one in every twenty registered voters, and for only three out of every one hundred votes cast. California was the home of 40 percent of all Asian Americans in the United States, yet there were no Asian Americans in the state senate and only two in the assembly. (In 1994, Matt Fong, son of longtime California secretary of state March Fong Eu, was elected treasurer.) Local representation, with the exception of such places as San Francisco and Monterey Park, was also sparse.

Some analysts suggested that Chinese Californians were by culture and tradition disinterested in elective politics. The implications of such a judgment tended to position Asian Americans as second-class citizens who were culturally, even temperamentally, indifferent to the democratic process. Hence it came as no surprise that, as the 1996 presidential campaign approached, certain Chinese-American political activists in California saw an opportunity to showcase an emergent Asian-American political power. Asian Americans, these advocates reasoned, had been the second most donating ethnic group, after Jewish Americans, in the presidential campaigns of 1988 and 1992; but unlike the Jewish community, they had received little credit and even less clout for their generosity.

And so, spurred on by political activists from within their own community, Chinese-American Californians gave, and gave generously, to Republican and Democratic candidates alike. Imagine their chagrin, then, when a congressional panel began televised hearings in mid- and late 1997 looking into the fund-raising activities of two prominent Los Angeles–based Chinese-American Democratic fund-raisers, Maria Hsia, an immigration consultant, and businessman Johnny Chung. On February 18, 1998, Hsia, forty-seven, was indicted in Washington on charges of laundering money through a Hacienda Heights Buddhist Temple in order to make disguised, illegal campaign contributions to the Clinton-Gore campaign and various candidates in the Los Angeles County supervisor's race. The federal grand jury also named the Hsi Lai Temple as unindicted coconspirator in the alleged scheme. Less than a month later, on March 5, 1998, Johnny Chung, investigated for delivering an illegal $50,000 campaign contribution to the White House, agreed to cooperate with Justice Department investigators as part of a plea bargain arrangement. A mere five days later, Representative Jay Kim, a Republican from Diamond Bar, a suburb outside Los Angeles, and the first Korean American to serve in the United States Congress, was sentenced to two months' house detention and one year probation for accepting more than $250,000 in illegal campaign contributions. These political scandals embarrassed and angered many Asian Californians. The televised congressional investigations—with a gray-robed Buddhist nun describing how checks and other records were shredded—had been bad enough. But in the case of Chung's activities, there had been more than a suggestion that offshore Chinese money had been involved, which compounded the seriousness of the charges.

And so a sense of disconnect gathered strength and persisted through the decade as Californians—many of them, at least—grew increasingly hostile to or oblivious of each other. The decade opened with the sentencing of nineteen-year-old San Diego County resident Kenneth Kovzelove, who said he hated Mexicans, to fifty years to life in prison for shooting to death two Hispanic men. By October 1995 a special *Los Angeles Times* report captured dozens of moments of hostility and disconnect. A Latino construction worker, wanting to buy a silk tie, waited and waited in a Beverly Hills men's store as the staff stared through him like glass. An African American living in Pacific Palisades, out on his nightly walk, grew somewhat accustomed to the honking horns, jeers, and thrown objects coming from passing motorists. A homeless, obviously deranged white woman stood on a street in the Pico Union district, slapping at young Latinos and telling them to go back to Mexico. Between 1995 and 1996, hate crimes in California jumped 17 percent.

Traveling the state through the middle decade, Pulitzer Prize–winning reporter Dale Maharidge, a journalism instructor at Stanford, found a high level of alienation on the part of California's soon-to-become white minority. Maharidge was especially intrigued by a pattern of white flight to the north, whether that north be the Antelope Valley north of Los Angeles or the nearly unsettled top tier of upstate California north of Sacramento. What Maharidge did not point out, but was equally true, was the fact that California was merely pacing the nation in a continentwide white flight north. As any demographic map of the United States would show by the mid-1990s, the farther north one went, the whiter it became; with the exception of Detroit, a White Pale ran across the top tier of the nation from Seattle through Boise, through Fargo and Bismarck, Minneapolis and St. Paul, to Portland, Maine.

Beginning in the 1960s, the top tier of California had become increasingly the refuge of those fleeing the cities. First it had been the hippies and the marijuana growers; now it was larger and larger numbers of whites escaping the racial complexity and perceived dangers of the cities, even the suburbs, south of Sacramento. By February 1991, Nevada County north of Sacramento had become the whitest county in the state—94 percent—and had been made that way by refugees from the south. To travel north of Sacramento was to encounter a world dramatically different from the Bay Area and Southern California, even central California, where minority workers were much in evidence. In the northern tier, white people were the janitors, truck drivers, waiters and waitresses, deliverymen, mail carriers and postal clerks, health care workers, and holders of all the other jobs held by Asians in the Bay Area and Latinos further south. Looking toward the future, Dr. Elias Lopez, a demographer and economist at the Research Bureau of the State Library, was noting in September 1997 that Californians were clustering according to ethnicity throughout the state, and that this would profoundly affect the next California. By 2040, Lopez speculated, the Los Angeles basin, indeed most of Southern California, would be Latino dominated, and the Bay Area would be predominantly white. Central California would become a mosaic of ethnic groups, with each group tending to coalesce around its own territory, as would the Asian communities in both northern California and the Southland.

Wedge Issues

As early as 2020, the population of California would reach the 47.5 million mark, larger than the combined populations of New York and Texas, paving the way for what many feared would become the Balkanized megastate of 2040. Californians were finding themselves at the center of a titanic process of change and transformation, so much of it connected to the dynamics, possibilities, and, some would argue, limitations of immigration. Such transformations had to have political consequences. Politics—or, more correctly, politicians—needed issues through which the larger process might be glimpsed and confronted. Some of them needed wedge issues through which to win tough races. Three issues, distinct but related—illegal immigration, affirmative action, and bilingual education—offered a prism into the future as well as wedge issues with which to leverage the vote.

By September 1993 a *Los Angeles Times* poll was revealing that an overwhelming majority of Californians—86 percent—believed that illegal immigration had become a moderate to major problem confronting the state. Only the economy and crime ranked higher, and these three issues were related in the minds of many. Already, a political response to the problem was shaping up. In early 1992, the Placer County Board of Supervisors had passed a resolution calling for a sharp reduction in immigration. In June 1993, the Orange County grand jury went even further, calling for a three-year ban on all immigration to ease burdens on government services. In Sacramento, more than thirty immigration-related bills, most of them restrictive, especially in the ability of undocumented immigrants to receive state services, were being heard by the legislature. In the halls of the state capitol, an advocacy group, Californians for Population Stabilization, was more active than ever.

On the national scene, Representative Elton Gallegly, a Republican from Simi Valley, was proposing a constitutional amendment denying citizenship to children born in the United States to illegal immigrants. Senators Barbara Boxer and Dianne Feinstein were suggesting the use of California

National Guardsmen as supplements to the Border Patrol. Feinstein was also advocating the expansion of the Border Patrol, the bringing of the Immigration and Naturalization Service under the direct supervision of the attorney general, and an increase in federal penalties for smuggling illegal immigrants into the United States, together with the deportation and home-country imprisonment of illegals convicted of crimes. In the June 1992 presidential primary, Republican candidate Pat Buchanan stumped the state with the idea of digging an impassable border trench along the entire California-Mexico border.

No elected official was more outspoken in the anti-illegal campaign than Governor Pete Wilson. A former assemblyman and longtime San Diego mayor, Wilson had gone to the U.S. Senate as a moderate Republican, and he had played an important role in adding a million Mexican farmworkers to those granted amnesty by the Immigration Reform and Control Act of 1986. This suggested—correctly, as anyone who knew Wilson would immediately agree—that the governor was not personally hostile to Latinos or other minorities. And in fact, Governor Wilson would appoint numerous Mexican Americans to high positions in his administration and place an African-American woman on the state supreme court. Wilson was, however, facing a formidable challenger in the forthcoming 1994 gubernatorial election in state treasurer Kathleen Brown, the politically bred daughter of one gover-nor and the sister of another, a lawyer and fiscal expert, attractive, articulate, and favored by the press. Brown had gotten her start in the family busi-ness—politics—as an elected member of the Los Angeles community col-lege district. Marrying Van Gordon Sauter, an equally charismatic television executive, she had moved to New York when Sauter became head of CBS News. There she completed undergraduate and law degrees at Fordham and began a career in law, banking, and finance. Returning to Los Angeles when her husband joined Fox Television News as a senior consultant, Brown won election as state treasurer in 1990 and almost immediately focused her ambition on becoming the third Brown to sit in the governor's chair.

In his first run for the governorship in 1990, Wilson had faced an equally compelling female politician, former San Francisco mayor Dianne Fein-stein, whom he had barely beaten. Three years later, Wilson found himself trailing Kathleen Brown in the polls by as many as twenty-three points a full year before the election. As governor, Wilson had done a brilliant job seeing California through three years of revenue shortfall. He had also helped set into motion government policies and programs that would facili-tate the economic recovery of the state within the next four years. None of this achievement, unfortunately, seemed immediately relevant to the upcoming election. Voters could as easily blame Wilson for the recession as they could praise him for negotiating the state through it. And by reducing the state budget by 40 percent, as he was forced by law to do (California required a balanced annual budget, with no deficit financing from the general fund), Wilson had not only made enemies, he had strengthened the hand of the Democrats, since most cuts he had enacted had come from Democrat-inspired social programs.

If he were to have a chance against the charismatic Brown, Pete Wilson needed an issue—a big issue, a wedge issue with which to separate Brown from her early lead. He found it in illegal immigration, specifically its cost to California in terms of health and welfare programs, K–12 education, and imprisonment. The illegal issue would allow Wilson to wedge his way between Brown and the electorate; as Wilson correctly estimated, Brown could not join him in the anti-illegal crusade without alienating liberals, Latinos, and other traditional sectors of Democratic support. Wilson's strategists rightly intuited that Brown—a Roman Catholic educated in convent schools and the Jesuit-staffed Fordham University, the daughter of the most effective and beloved liberal Democratic governor in the history of the state, the sister of a former Jesuit seminarian turned governor and political prophet in his own right—would have no gut instinct for any sort of anti-illegal crusade that of necessity would draw upon masked anti-immigrant, anti-Mexican attitudes. Recalling her own father's anguish at enforcing the death penalty, Brown had even declared her personal lack of belief in capital punishment, although she promised to enforce it evenhandedly as governor. Thus, despite her twenty-three-point lead, Brown was cut off from the one issue that was on the minds of 86 percent of Californians, the issue that was joined at the hip to three other important matters on the minds of Californians: welfare reform, the anticrime crusade (the death penalty, three-strikes legislation), and the revitalization of K–12 education.

By mid-1993, Pete Wilson had emerged as the primary spokesman of the anti-illegal crusade. Among other things, he was calling for a $1.5 billion reimbursement from the federal government for costs associated with illegal immigration; arguing that the North American Free Trade Agreement should not be approved unless Mexico came up with a specific program to curb illegal immigration on its side of the border; and seeking congressional action on a constitutional amendment to deny American citizenship to children born to illegal aliens. He was also advocating the cessation of all federal and state welfare benefits to illegals. Proposition 187 provided Wilson the lightning rod, the wedge issue, for his reelection campaign.

Subtitled the Save Our State initiative (SOS), Proposition 187 put before the voters five major provisions. First, illegal aliens could no longer attend public schools, from kindergarten through public university. Schools would have to verify the citizenship or residential status of students, effective January 1, 1995, and, effective January 1, 1996, that of their parents. Second, all public providers of nonemergency health care services would have to verify the citizenship or residential status of their clients. (Emergency health care, however, would continue to be offered to legals and illegals on the same basis.) Third, no illegals would be entitled to cash assistance or other benefits in welfare programs. Fourth, all service providers—school personnel, clerks in welfare offices, anyone ascertaining the illegal status of someone seeking public benefits—would be required to report suspected illegal aliens to the office of the attorney general of California and to the Immigration and Naturalization Service. Fifth, making, distributing, and/or using false documents to obtain public benefits or employment would now (with the exception of teenagers using false documents to buy alcohol or cigarettes) be a felony, punishable by fines and prison terms.

Proposition 187, in short, was draconian, and having it on the ballot sent a shock wave through the state. The American Civil Liberties Union, among others, was appalled by the reporting requirements, which it claimed would turn California into a nightmare nation of snitches. The Roman Catholic bishops of California were distressed by the warfare waged by Proposition 187 against expectant mothers and their children, who would be American citizens when born. Most profoundly, a significant percentage of the Mexican-American community saw in Proposition 187 an assault not just on illegals but on the very presence of Mexicans in California, legals and illegals alike.

As September edged into October, Proposition 187 subsumed the gubernatorial campaign. Governor Wilson pounded away, again and again, at the cost of illegals to California and their subversion of American law and institutions. Kathleen Brown, by contrast, refused to endorse 187, characterizing it as just another eruption of xenophobia in California, comparable to the anti-Chinese agitations of the 1870s, the anti-Okie sentiment of the 1930s, and the antiblack and anti-Mexican agitations of World War II and after. Nonsense, Wilson replied: there was an important distinction to be made between legal immigrants who had played by the rules, filled out their forms, and waited, sometimes for years, for their visas, and those who slipped across the border illegally, thereby corrupting their entire relationship to the United States. It was an insult, Wilson argued, to conjoin legal and illegal immigration. The United States was built upon the one, and it could be destroyed by the other.

Senate candidates Dianne Feinstein, the Democratic incumbent, and the Republican challenger, Santa Barbara congressman Michael Huffington, were outdoing each other to get on the Proposition 187 bandwagon, despite the fact that they both, millionaires many times over, had admitted to having hired illegals: in Feinstein's case as a housekeeper in her Presidio Terrace mansion in San Francisco when Feinstein was serving as mayor in the early 1980s, and in Huffington's case as a nanny for his children in the late 1980s and early 1990s at his equally grand Santa Barbara estate. (Ironically, it would later be revealed that Wilson and his first wife had employed an illegal housemaid in the 1970s.) Anxiety over these past indiscretions only intensified the efforts of Feinstein and Huffington, locked in a race too close to call, to pound away at the illegal problem and seek to outdo each other in pushing for Proposition 187.

Anti–Proposition 187 forces did themselves no good in the final days of the campaign when they encouraged large numbers of Latino high school students in Los Angeles to walk out of their classrooms and, waving Mexican flags, demonstrate against the measure. Nor did it particularly win over undecided voters when on the eve of the election some 700,000 opponents of Proposition 187, the vast majority of them ethnic Mexicans, paraded through downtown Los Angeles in the single largest demonstration in that city's history, also waving Mexican flags, as if to confirm in the minds of many the charge that Mexicans represented an irredentist intrusion in California, resistant to taking on an American identity.

The Mexican government also entered the fray. President Carlos Salinas de Gortari denounced Proposition 187, as did incoming president Ernesto Zedillo. However well intended, these criticisms further polarized the California electorate and made Proposition 187 even more dramatically a referendum not only on the question of illegals, but also increasingly on the social and cultural nature of California itself. Such polarization frightened many Republicans—such as former cabinet members William Bennett and Jack Kemp, who came out against the measure—who believed that Proposition 187 was driving a psychological wedge between the Republican Party and a Latino community that in its love of family, its work ethic, and its religious orientation might otherwise prove fruitful ground for Republican recruitment. (Kemp and Bennett would later help prevent the Republicans from putting a strong anti-immigration plank in its 1996 platform.)

Rarely before in its history had California faced such a divisive measure on the ballot. The state was acting out a drama of acceptance or rejection on behalf of the entire country. Congress, after all, had found itself stymied in the case of immigration policy. From one perspective, the Immigration Reform and Control Act of 1986, with its generous amnesty program and its last-minute incorporation of nearly one million farmworkers, had not been a policy at all, but a retreat from the problem by making most illegals legal and hoping the problem would go away. Nor had Congress yet come to terms with the future of welfare in the nation. By conjoining questions of both illegal immigration and welfare reform, Proposition 187—so it would soon turn out—was pacing the nation.

But that would prove to be its only contribution; as soon as it passed, 59 to 41 percent on November 8, 1994, Proposition 187 became tied up in the courts. The day after the election, San Francisco Superior Court judge Stuart Pollack issued a temporary restraining order, as did Los Angeles Federal District Court judge Matthew Byrne Jr. Even more effectively, a second temporary restraining order was issued in Los Angeles on November 21, by U.S. District Court judge Mariana Pfaelzer, after hearing a plea from the League of United Latin American Citizens. At the time and in later rulings, Judge Pfaelzer cited a number of constitutional problems intrinsic to the measure. Her injunction blocked all but two of Proposition 187's provisions: those dealing with higher education, which she saw as a state program and hence a state prerogative, and the use of forged documents, which was already covered by federal law. In the question of denying K–12 educational benefits to illegals, Judge Pfaelzer expressed concern that Proposition 187 seemed to run directly counter to *Plyer v. Doe,* a 1982 U.S. Supreme Court decision blocking efforts by the state of Texas to exclude children of illegals from public schools as being, among other things, a violation of the Fourteenth Amendment. Writing in the *New Republic* on January 30, 1995, legal commentator Jeffrey Rosen predicted that constitutional questions would keep Proposition 187 tied up in court for many years to come.

Rosen was right. A year after she issued her first restraining order, which had remained in effect, Judge Pfaelzer ruled that a central requirement of Proposition 187—the banning of elementary and secondary education for illegal immigrants—was unconstitutional. She also demanded that state attorneys provide her with a complete description of how the ban on social and health benefits would be implemented before she decided on that issue.

Predictably, Wilson and the other supporters of Proposition 187 howled at what they considered this unwarranted interference of the federal judiciary in state affairs. Throughout 1995 and the first half of 1996, Wilson, now in his second term and eyeing the 1996 Republican presidential nomination, continued to hammer away at the cost of illegals to California and, by implication, the entire United States. In January 1996, accompanied by reporters and television cameras, he personally escorted a twenty-five-year-old convicted drug dealer, Eliseo Gonzalez de la Cruz, an undocumented alien serving time in a California prison, to an INS detention center in El Centro, and demanded that federal authorities take charge of him and that he serve the remainder of his sentence in federal custody at federal expense. As the cameras whirred and reporters took notes, INS officials informed Wilson that they did not have the authority to incarcerate a felon convicted under California law. If Gonzalez de la Cruz were left on their doorstep, they would have no option but to deport him to Mexico. Realizing that if Gonzalez de la Cruz were deported to Mexico he would most likely go free, Wilson backed off and returned him to state custody. The entire event had been a highly staged and choreographed photo op, and Wilson had theatrically made his point, as Proposition 187 languished in the courts.

In the months that followed, Wilson dispatched several letters to Attorney General Janet Reno complaining that the state of California was currently incarcerating, at a cost of $400 million a year, twenty thousand illegal aliens who should be in federal custody. In March, the governor himself went to court, filing a suit on behalf of California in the U.S. District Court for the District of Columbia, asserting that the Clinton administration was refusing to abide by a 1994 federal law that required the federal government either to reimburse states for the costs of incarcerating alien felons or to take custody of them. Reno and other spokespersons for the Clinton administration, meanwhile, were claiming that Congress had appropriated only $130 million in 1995 and $300 million in 1996 for reimbursements to states for the incarceration of illegal aliens. Should California be fully reimbursed, they claimed, there would be no money for anyone else.

However justified in fiscal terms, Wilson's campaign for reimbursement was tricky business. By focusing attention on the twenty thousand undocumented felons in California prisons, Wilson was making a legitimate point, but it was a double-edged sword that dramatized illegals as criminals as well as welfare recipients, and these negative judgments had a way of seeping over into the image of legal immigrants, who were, however indirectly, being conjoined with their welfare-dependent and undocumented felon counterparts.

Certainly, tensions were running high in a state in which Proposition 187 had been passed but not enforced. In April 1996, these tensions coalesced around the televised beating by Riverside sheriff's deputies Donald Franklin and Tracy Watson of Andrian Flores Martinez, twenty-six, and Leticia Gonzalez-Gonzalez, thirty-three, after an eighty-mile chase, frequently reaching one hundred miles per hour, that began in Riverside County and ended in the city of El Monte in Los Angeles County. The incident got started near Temecula when Border Patrol officers noticed that a dilapidated pickup truck had left Interstate 15 to avoid a checkpoint. The Border Patrol officers called the Riverside County sheriff's department, which dispatched Franklin and Watson, who then began pursuit north on

Interstate 15, then west on the Pomona Freeway toward Los Angeles. En route, occupants of the truck—there were twenty-one of them—threw beer cans at the pursuing patrol car and also pieces of a metal frame affixed to the truck bed. At least twice, the driver, Martinez, sideswiped other cars in an effort to distract the pursuing deputies.

When the deputies finally ran the truck off onto the side of the road in south El Monte, about twenty miles east of downtown Los Angeles, its twenty-one occupants bolted across a fence into a nearby field and scattered. At this point, Martinez and Gonzalez-Gonzalez were beaten on the back and shoulders with nightsticks as they emerged from the vehicle. Hovering overhead, a helicopter news crew from television station KCAL filmed the entire episode. Martinez suffered bruises and a hairline fracture of an elbow and was taken to Riverside General Hospital pending booking on multiple charges. Gonzalez-Gonzalez was not immediately hospitalized. Like the Rodney King beating, the assault on Martinez and Gonzalez-Gonzalez ignited a controversy that further polarized an already tense situation. Demonstrators protested in English and Spanish outside the federal building in downtown Los Angeles, and the FBI began an investigation. The Mexican consul general in Los Angeles, Jose Angel Pescador, encouraged the victims to sue for damages, which one of them did, filing a lawsuit against Riverside County for $10 million.

Two weeks later, incensed by the lawsuit and galvanized by a remorseless anti-immigrant commentary on talk shows, some five hundred counter-demonstrators in Riverside listened to speaker after speaker, including Daryl Gates, now the former police chief of Los Angeles, support the deputies and bash the immigrants and the press. In his remarks, Gates said that he did not want to see happen to the Riverside deputies what happened to the four Los Angeles police officers in the Rodney King case in 1991— which is to say, that they be acquitted on state charges but convicted in federal court on civil rights violations.

"Latinos were very offended by the beating," observed Gregory Rodriguez, a research fellow at Pepperdine University. "It was almost a delayed reaction to Proposition 187."[7] The same might have been said regarding the anger on the other side, for Proposition 187 had been in court almost from the day it was passed. Yet however hobbled by the courts, Proposition 187 had been helping create a climate of opinion in a Washington now rapidly approaching the presidential election of 1996, with lawmakers, Republicans and Democrats alike, clearly reading from its passage that the issue of benefits to immigrants, both legal and illegal, was coming to a head in such states as California, Texas, Florida, New York, and New Jersey, which had the largest immigrant populations. Galvanized to action,

Congress passed a bill even more stringent than Proposition 187 had ever dared to be. (Proposition 187, after all, was only directed at illegal immigrants.) On August 9, 1996, President Clinton signed into law the Personal Responsibility and Work Opportunity Reconciliation Act, which made illegal immigrants ineligible for all state and federal benefits, with the exception of emergency medical care, immunizations, and emergency disaster relief. No state could offer benefits to illegals unless it enacted a new state law expressly providing such benefits to them. Even more draconian, legal immigrants would now lose their eligibility for food stamps, disability assistance, and other benefits. And individual states now had the right to cut off Medicaid to legal immigrants as well as illegals.

Buoyed by the passage of the federal bill, Wilson moved aggressively to implement a program tied up in the courts the previous two years. On August 27, 1996, he signed an executive order ending access by undocumented immigrants to a long list of benefits, including public housing and prenatal care. He could not bar them from public primary and secondary schools, as Proposition 187 had intended, because the federal law had not included such strictures and Proposition 187 was still tied up in court. Federal law had, however, taken from legal immigrants their eligibility for food stamps, disability assistance, and other benefits—programs from which illegals were already barred. All in all, the month of August 1996 represented an unprecedented attack on benefits for immigrants.

Wilson's banning of the prenatal care then being given to seventy thousand undocumented women, effective January 1, 1998, was especially galling to Latino, Democratic, and Roman Catholic activists as an attack on the unborn, who would be American citizens. The governor had held no public hearings on the matter and was thwarting Democratic efforts to fund the program by redlining the $83.7 million cost out of the state budget. In June 1997, eight pregnant illegal immigrants, backed by the Mexican-American Legal Defense and Educational Fund, took the matter to the federal courts, alleging that Wilson—by continuing to block all efforts by Democrats to pass legislation allowing prenatal care to illegal immigrants—was violating states' rights by denying an option guaranteed in the federal legislation. On December 16, 1997, Wilson won his case when U.S. District Court judge Susan Illston dismissed the suit.

Wilson's victory had its ironies. The federal government, against which he had so dramatically set himself, was now making possible what state law could not allow: the denial of benefits to illegals. On November 14, 1997, a month before Wilson's victory, Judge Mariana Pfaelzer had issued a thirty-two-page opinion declaring Proposition 187 unconstitutional. The measure usurped federal prerogatives to regulate immigration law, Pfaelzer opined, and, irony of ironies, it was in direct conflict with the 1996 Personal Responsibility and Work Opportunity Reconciliation Act denying welfare benefits to undocumented immigrants. Wilson immediately announced that he would appeal Pfaelzer's decision to the Ninth Circuit Court of Appeals "so the will of the people can be upheld"; but here he was, anyway, empowered by the federal government to do what Proposition 187 had intended.[8] Backers of Proposition 187 should call it quits, editorialized the *Los Angeles Times* on November 17, 1997. Judge Pfaelzer was correct. Regulating immigration was a federal prerogative.

Nor was the federal Immigration and Naturalization Service, under the direction of Doris Meissner, reluctant to exercise its prerogatives. Throughout 1997, illegal immigrants in California—having lost all public benefits—now found themselves on the receiving end of a concerted federal campaign to rid the United States of illegal residents and to seal the porous Mexico-California border. Between October 1996 and October 1997, more than 111,000 illegal immigrants (46,000 of them from California alone), nearly half with criminal records, were deported by federal authorities. Galvanized by augmentations under Operation Gatekeeper, the Border Patrol targeted the fourteen-mile San Diego–Tijuana border with new energy, and by March 1998, Meissner was declaring that section of the border, which shortly before had accounted for 25 percent of all illegal border crossings from Mexico, under complete control. Future operations, she announced, would concentrate on border crossings to the east of this once gaping section.

INS offices throughout Southern California were thronged by long lines of illegals hoping to clarify their status. The new federal legislation required undocumented immigrants with pending green card applications to return to their native country while awaiting processing. A loophole, however, in previous (1994) federal legislation, which had been extended to October 1997, allowed green card applicants to await processing in the United States provided that they pay a $1,000 fine. As the deadline for the expiration of this extended provision approached, thousands of undocumented immigrants, many of them longtime residents, scurried to find the money, stand in line, and fill out the forms.

For the 1.7 million illegals estimated to be in the state, California had quickly become a shadowy and fearsome place. Once cared for by the state welfare system, they were now without health benefits, except in emergency circumstances. Once surviving in a live-and-let-live world prepared to ignore their presence because it needed their labor, they were now at risk of being scrutinized at every turn. Each point of contact with society—driving an automobile, applying for a job, sending a child to school—was fraught with peril. Showing up at an emergency ward with a broken arm had risks. A ticket for an illegal left turn could rapidly lead to deportation.

Not that all illegals avoided the California Department of Motor Vehicles. In August 1997 investigators were uncovering a ring of DMV employees who had sold up to 25,000 fraudulent driver's licenses to illegals for bribes of between $200 and $1,000 each. Seventy-nine employees were eventually dismissed, and investigators estimated that up to 250 of the eight thousand employees of the DMV could have been involved in the scam. Charges were brought in some cases, and two employees received prison sentences. It was perhaps the most widespread scandal involving state employees in California history.

Even sending one's child to school, which federal legislation had specifically not prohibited, became a point of dangerous contact, and by mid-1997 educators from throughout the state were reporting the disappearance of many Latino students from their classrooms. For some time now—since the Proposition 187 campaign of 1994—teachers such as Laura Simon, a fourth-grade instructor at Hoover Elementary near the USC campus in the West Adams district of Los Angeles, was noting a rising anxiety in her undocumented students, who—in that mode of subliminal apprehension, swift and sure, so characteristic of children—now felt themselves the object of statewide scrutiny and hostility. "They don't like us," one boy told her. Another Latino youngster confessed his fear that the police would be taking his parents away. Still others merely failed to show up at school, either kept at home by their parents or returned to Mexico, Guatemala, or El Salvador. Borrowing a video camera, Simon began to record the entire ordeal. Her resulting documentary, *Fear and Learning at Hoover Elementary,* was aired on PBS television nationwide and honored at the Sundance Film Festival in June 1997.[9]

Affirmative Action

A ffirmative action was based on a theory of race, ethnicity, gender, even sexual orientation—and a theory of history. In the first instance, affirmative action postulated that people were primarily who they were—in their fundamental moral and legal selves—because of their gender, their racial and ethnic descent, their sexual orientation. In such a scheme, no one could postulate any other aspect of identity as being more powerful, more determining, than biological or ethnic profile or sexual orientation. From a number of perspectives, this was an innovative assumption, very much at the center of postmodernism. Prior schemes might give precedence to a theory of a transcendent self, in which the individual as person, as moral being, was primary. Other theories might see one's religious identity as paramount. Even others might see vocation, work, or social class as the determining elements. But ever since the civil rights movement in the 1960s Americans—to the dismay of many—had begun increasingly to define themselves in terms of race, gender, and sexual orientation. Suddenly, the landscape of the nation was proliferating with hyphenated Americans.

These classifications involved a moral reading of history. Certain groups, ran this theory, had been formally suppressed in the past, and, even after the civil rights movement had rectified many of the formal instruments of such suppression, such groups—African Americans, most noticeably, but also Native Americans, Asians, and Hispanics—continued to feel the effects of the prior suppression. Government, moreover, had an obligation to atone for past and continuing injustices by establishing, as extensively as possible, participatory quotas in every phase of American life. Through such programs of affirmative action, equity would eventually be reestablished, after which, presumably, affirmative action, no longer necessary, would go away.

While not logically dependent upon such a notion of equity and its reestablishment, affirmative action was also based on another assumption:

diversity. In this theory, affirmative action sought not only the redress of past injustices and alleged continuing debilitations but the strengthening of society through its diversification. According to this theory, the more diversified an organization or an enterprise might be along lines of race, ethnicity, gender, and sexual orientation, the more vital it became. While logically distinct from the equity argument, equity and diversity were psychologically conjoined in most affirmative action programs. Affirmative action, from this perspective, was not only fair because it redressed past and present grievances, it was also socially enhancing because a diverse society was by definition a better society. Affirmative action was thus at once a theory of identity, a moral judgment of history, a corrective program, and a vision of the good society. Since the mid-1960s, affirmative action had been in effect throughout the nation; and even its detractors had to admit that it had profoundly transformed American society.

Yet it had also engendered growing resentment on the part of those who were being required to pay for the sins of the past. Only the most primitive of racial and ethnic theories, critics of affirmative action claimed, could hold individuals from one group personally responsible for what had been done in previous generations. Sensing this resentment, as well as disagreeing philosophically with the continuing of affirmative action as a permanent requirement in California, Governor Pete Wilson, returned to office in November 1994, set about to dismantle the program. His most important ally in this campaign, so psychologically linked to the anti-illegal drive, was—paradoxically—Wilson's African-American friend of more than thirty years, Sacramento businessman Ward Connerly.

Born in Louisiana in 1939, Connerly had been raised in Sacramento by his grandmother after the divorce of his parents in 1941 and the death of his mother the following year. Graduating from public high school, Connerly went on to American River Junior College and Cal State in Sacramento, becoming the first member of his family to receive a college degree. Connerly's ambition at the time was a good job in civil service; and so he went to work for the Redevelopment Agency of Sacramento before moving on to the California State Department of Housing. Through his work there, Connerly met a young assemblyman from San Diego, Pete Wilson, chairman of the assembly's Housing Committee. Wilson hired Connerly as chief consultant to the committee, and the two became friends. By the mid-1990s, Connerly was a balding, mild-mannered African-American Republican who had somehow remained aloof from a heavily racial interpretation of his own experience and identity. When Wilson became governor, he offered Connerly a place in the administration, but Connerly did not want to leave the private sector to which he had migrated as a consultant. He accepted instead a twelve-year appointment to the board of regents of the University of California, which would allow him to continue a business career.

In the summer of 1994, Connerly was visited by Jerry and Ellen Cook of San Diego. Their son, the Cooks told Connerly, was a Phi Beta Kappa who had been accepted into the combined Harvard-MIT health sciences program and the Johns Hopkins Medical School. He had wanted to attend medical school at UC San Diego, so he could be close to his parents and ailing grandparents and save money on tuition. But UC San Diego had turned him down, while accepting less qualified minority candidates. Medical school admission was a sensitive matter in California. In 1973, Allan Bakke, a white man, had been rejected by the UC Davis medical school in favor of a less qualified African American, Patrick Chavis, for affirmative action purposes. Bakke appealed all the way to the Supreme Court, and in its 1978 decision *Bakke v. Regents of the University of California* the Court had split the difference. Bakke was ordered enrolled, but racial preferences were not negated. This confusing and contradictory decision—you may not violate any student's rights but you can practice affirmative action—shakily guided University of California affirmative action programs for the next decade and a half.

Alerted by the Cooks, Connerly queried Jack Peltason, president of UC, regarding the university's admissions policies. Peltason reported that affirmative action policies were necessary in medical schools to ensure medical service to minority communities and because diversity equaled excellence. Digging further, Connerly obtained a screening matrix in use at UC Berkeley that explicitly scored applicants on the basis of race. Initially, UC officials, when confronted by Connerly, denied that they were using such a matrix, but when Connerly produced the screening form, they backtracked. Connerly then came up with evidence of Chinese-American students with perfect 4.0 grade point averages being denied admission to UC Berkeley or UCLA in favor of African-American or Latino students with a 3.0 average or lower. Connerly was offended by these practices. Affirmative action might have been necessary in the 1960s, he suggested, and even the 1970s; but it had now become a permanent program based on the assumption that certain minorities could never be admitted to UC without set-asides and would always remain in second-class status.

Almost single-handedly, Ward Connerly ended race- and gender-based preferences at UC. The first thing he did was to take the problem to Pete Wilson at the beginning of the governor's second term. "Let's fix it," Connerly later reported Wilson as saying; and between the two of them they did so in rather rapid order. Wilson did most of the lobbying of the regents; and on July 20, 1995, meeting in San Francisco, the board voted 14–10, with one abstention, to end all racial or gender admission preferences at UC, effective in 1998.

It was a coup d'etat that sent shock waves throughout the academic community both at UC and in the rest of the nation. The faculty and administrators running academia were by and large products of the 1960s. They had grown up with affirmative action as accepted practice, and they believed in diversity as a self-evident good. And here was this obscure Sacramento businessman, a Republican, and his hard-nosed governor pal, already doing his best to end public assistance to illegal immigrants, striking down a central tenet and protocol of the world as they had known it for the past thirty years. Understandably, defenders of affirmative action reacted strongly. In the eyes of many of his fellow African Americans (and this was their mildest judgment) Ward Connerly became a traitor to his race. In no time, in liberal circles, Connerly was the Man You Loved to Hate, the Erich von Stroheim of the affirmative action debate. But Connerly, nonplussed, was only beginning his crusade. He now turned his attention to the banning of gender or racial preferences throughout the entire public sector. His vehicle for this bold program was Proposition 209.

Proposition 209 began as the California Civil Rights Initiative (CCRI). The initiative was conceptualized and initially organized by two disgruntled late-fifties white professors, Glynn Custred and Thomas Wood, who were tired of seeing ethnic preferences run rampant in the California State University system. As of August 1994, however, the CCRI was getting nowhere. When Wood and Custred were invited to testify before an assembly committee in August 1994, they asked Ward Connerly to join them. "He stole the show," Wood later remembered. "Glynn and I started plotting immediately on the drive back to the Bay Area about how we could get him on board."[10]

Initially, Connerly rejected Custred's and Wood's invitations to join the movement; but by late 1995, fresh from his success with the UC resolutions, he took another look at the matter. The CCRI was in trouble. It had next to no cash and only a shadow of an organization. It also had little more than three months to secure another 700,000 signatures to add to the 200,000 it had on hand to qualify for the ballot. Signature gathering, however, had been suspended. Once again, Custred and Wood went to Connerly. This time, he listened and agreed to come on board. He also brought Pete Wilson with him. Almost immediately, Connerly became the spokesman for the initiative and Wilson its chief fund-raiser. The once faltering CCRI made it onto the November 1996 ballot as Proposition 209.

It was a simple statement, a mere thirty-seven words in length—"The state shall not discriminate against, or grant preferential treatment to, any individual or group on the basis of race, sex, color, ethnicity, or national origin in the operation of public employment, public education, or public contracting"—but it is hard to imagine a more revolutionary or counter-revolutionary reversal of a program of entitlements and preferences that had now become, in the public and private sector, an American way of life. The opposition howled in protest. Already the recipient of telephone threats because of his work on the UC resolution, Ward Connerly became *the* number one negative poster boy for the anti–Proposition 209 forces. Custred and Wood, who might very well have been attacked as two white guys getting even, were ignored. Even the establishment opposed Proposition 209. After thirty years, affirmative action had become part of the establishment. The Ford, Rockefeller, and Carnegie Foundations donated $1.5 million to programs indirectly bolstering the anti–Proposition 209 campaign. The CEO of the mega-utility Pacific Gas & Electric came out against the measure, as did Mayor Richard Riordan of Los Angeles and Cardinal Roger Mahony. Only Wilson's personal intervention kept other prominent Republican CEOs from following suit.

A month before the November 1996 election, Proposition 209 was leading in the polls. On election day, it passed by 54 percent, losing only in Los Angeles County, the city and county of San Francisco, and five other counties surrounding San Francisco Bay. Once again, as in the case of Proposition 187, the defeated forces headed immediately to the courts. On November 27, a San Francisco–based federal judge, Thelton Henderson—a Carter appointee and an African American who had once served on the board of the American Civil Liberties Union of Northern California—granted a temporary restraining order, arguing that there was "a strong probability" that Proposition 209 was unconstitutional. Less than a month later, on December 23, Judge Henderson followed his temporary restraining order with a preliminary injunction claiming that Proposition 209 violated the equal protection cause of the Fourteenth Amendment because it was eliminating only programs benefiting women and minorities and not, for example, programs benefiting military veterans or other designated groups.

Once again, Governor Wilson and Republican attorney general Dan Lungren found themselves back in court fighting an adverse injunction from a federal district court. This time they won. With almost unprecedented swiftness, on April 8, 1997, a three-judge panel of the U.S. Court of Appeals for the Ninth Circuit overturned Henderson's injunction. "A system which permits one judge to block with the stroke of a pen what 4,736,180 state residents voted to enact as law," read the decision, written by court of appeal judge Diarmuid O'Scannlain, "tests the integrity of our constitutional democracy." Mark Rosenbaum, the American Civil Liberties Union lawyer acting as lead attorney for the Proposition 209 opponents, claimed that the appeal court decision defied decades of decisions by the Supreme Court. "It doesn't just force women and minorities to the back of the bus," Rosenbaum charged. "It boots them off altogether." On August 22, the full eleven-member U.S. Court of Appeals rejected Rosenbaum's appeal that it reconsider the three-judge panel April 8 ruling. Rosenbaum immediately appealed to the Supreme Court.[11]

On August 28, 1997, the day Proposition 209 took effect, the Reverend Jesse Jackson led thousands across the Golden Gate Bridge in a March to Save the Dream protesting Proposition 209. (The rally almost collapsed when the chronically late Jackson failed to show up on time, and San Francisco mayor Willie Brown gave orders to start the parade without him.) In October, as appeals were being heard in the Supreme Court in Washington, Jackson brought his March to Save the Dream crusade to Sacramento. Once again late—(by two hours)—Jackson addressed a crowd of two thousand protesters gathered before the state Capitol, denouncing both Proposition 187 and 209. On the back steps of the Capitol, meanwhile, some fifty California College Republicans staged a smaller counterdemonstration, listening to a broadcast of Martin Luther King Jr.'s famous "I have a dream" speech.

As the ACLU's appeal of the Ninth Circuit's decision wended its way to the Supreme Court (which would issue its decision the following November), the debate on affirmative action in California—and whether or not to comply with the court-upheld Proposition 209—continued. Following the decision of the court of appeals and the enactment of Proposition 209, Governor Wilson issued an executive order and a number of follow-up directives prohibiting race or gender preferences in state government. Wilson's order was almost universally obeyed. Local jurisdictions, however, especially in the San Francisco Bay Area, continued to resist. Connerly himself founded the Sacramento-based American Civil Rights Institute to monitor compliance with Proposition 209 in the fifty-eight counties, five hundred cities, and more than five thousand special districts in the state. Unlike Proposition 187, Proposition 209 had only passed narrowly. Californians seemed equally divided on the issue.

On November 3, 1997, the U.S. Supreme Court let stand the decision of the Ninth Circuit Court of Appeals upholding Proposition 209. The decision was without comment—that is, the Supreme Court did not take up the issue of the constitutionality of the California proposition. Thus the path seemed left open to future challenges on specific executive orders, statutes, or ordinances enforcing the measure. Opponents of Proposition 209, now

the law in California, watched anxiously as the 1998 deadline to end affirmative action in admissions to UC, voted by the regents in July 1995,
approached. Many African Americans were already looking to other
options. Fisk University, Wilberforce University, Morehouse College, and
other African-American institutions saw an opportunity to attract qualified
and ambitious African-American high school graduates from California,
and stepped up their recruiting efforts. African Americans, recruiters
claimed, would not be welcomed at UC in a post–Proposition 209 era,
whereas they would be highly prized at predominantly black colleges and
universities. Certainly, such a message—that they would not be welcomed
at UC—seemed to be in operation in September 1997, when none of the
fourteen black students admitted to the Boalt Hall School of Law at UC
Berkeley that year accepted admission. Only one black student, who had
been admitted the previous year but had deferred, was in the entering class.
Critics of this argument pointed out that of the fourteen who rejected admission to Boalt, four had gone to Harvard, two had gone to Yale, two had gone
to Stanford, and the rest had found berths at such prestigious institutions as
Columbia, Duke, and UCLA.

Asian-American Californians were especially conflicted by the impending affirmative action ban because so many of them could see both sides of
the issue. On the one hand, newly arrived Asian groups like the Cambodians, Laotians, and Vietnamese might see in affirmative action an enhanced
opportunity to attend a UC campus. UC Berkeley chancellor Chang-Lin
Tien, among others, confessed himself deeply disappointed by the regents'
vote to end affirmative action and, even after that vote, remained outspoken
in his defense of affirmative action at Berkeley, based on his own experiences in 1956 as a penniless twenty-one-year-old immigrant from China
with a limited grasp of English. No matter how accomplished Chinese
Americans might be, in other words, Tien believed that they should not
break solidarity with other minority groups. "I think that affirmative action
should be a temporary measure," Tien wrote in the *New York Times* in
March 1996, "but the time has not yet come to eliminate it." With the majority of regents believing differently and Proposition 209 being upheld in the
courts, Chancellor Tien saw UC heading in a different direction. On July 9,
1996, he unexpectedly resigned. During his tenure, Tien had proved himself
immensely popular with students and faculty alike and had brought millions of dollars of gifts and endowments to UC Berkeley from Asian and
Asian-American sources, and his departure was a great loss.[12]

Other Chinese-American Californians had other opinions, or were at
least ambivalent. Both UC Berkeley and UCLA had informal caps on the
number of admitted Asian Americans, fearing that if they were enrolled

strictly on the basis of academic performance, UC Berkeley and UCLA would become predominantly Asian-American institutions. Although Asian Americans made up only 10 percent of California's population, they constituted nearly a third of all undergraduates in the nine-campus UC system. Critics compared such policies to the cap on Jews in Ivy League and other prestigious universities two generations earlier, and for much the same reasons.

As the 1998 deadline approached, UC administrators scrambled for ways to observe the letter of the law while maintaining diversity. They had a problem. Latinos, even with a vigorous affirmative action program in place, represented just 4 percent of the 155,000 students enrolled at UC. The end of affirmative action could be expected to reduce that number to near negligibility. In September 1997 a specially convened Latino Eligibility Task Force chaired by Eugene Garcia, dean of the School of Education at UC Berkeley, recommended that UC stop using SAT scores in admissions to its nine campuses. Such a move, the task force claimed, would more than double the number of Latinos eligible for admission to the UC system. Applicants to the California State University system, the task force pointed out, who had a B average or better in high school did not have to submit standardized test scores, although most did so. The *Los Angeles Times* editorialized against the proposal, and a faculty committee came out strongly against it; and—for the time being, at least—the recommendation went nowhere.

In February 1998, a second proposal surfaced, this time from UC president Richard Atkinson. Every UC campus, Atkinson submitted, should reserve space for the top 4 percent of graduates of every public high school in the state. That way, inner-city schools with large minority populations could send their top students to UC without a judgment being made about race, gender, or ethnicity as prohibited by Proposition 209. Atkinson's proposal was ingenious, for it would allow the top students in rural, mainly white high schools in northern California to have the same advantages as minority students from inner-city schools.

Even as Atkinson made his recommendation, however, UC admissions officers, faced with a record number of applications, were admitting their first freshman class on a race-blind, gender-blind basis. For backers of affirmative action, the news was bad, but not as bad as they expected. While the number of underrepresented minorities—primarily African Americans and Latinos—accepted as freshmen at UC Berkeley fell by 54.7 percent, at UCLA by 36 percent, and at UC San Diego by approximately 43 percent (the three most desirable campuses), the number of minorities at five other undergraduate campuses held steady, and, as in the case of UC Riverside, which admitted 42 percent more African Americans and 52 percent more Latinos, it increased. Underrepresented minorities may have been experiencing a 50 percent cut at three of the most competitive public university campuses in the nation, but they were not disappearing from the UC system entirely, as some had predicted. In terms of the overall nine-campus system, minorities were embattled, but they were managing to hold their own, thanks to the willingness, among other factors, of UC Riverside to increase its overall admissions by 28 percent—and because UC president Atkinson wrote personalized letters to thirteen thousand promising minority and low-income students urging them to apply to the UC system. Early in the next millennium, Atkinson would have even more creative solutions in mind.

Hasta la Vista!

Even as the affirmative action controversy continued down an uncertain path, another related battle, the banning of bilingual education, was surfacing. Once again, the debate was focused on a statewide initiative, in this case Proposition 227. Sponsored by Silicon Valley multimillionaire Ron Unz and longtime Orange County teacher Gloria Matta Tuchman, Proposition 227, which qualified for the June 1998 ballot by gathering 433,000 signatures, called for the disestablishment of California's over $400 million bilingual education program in favor of a one-year immersion in English-language proficiency. Whether or not this English for the Children Initiative could be construed as an anti-Latino measure, as was being claimed by, among others, Teresa Bustillos of the Mexican American Legal Defense and Education Fund, was a matter for debate. Ron Unz had been an outspoken opponent of Proposition 187 in the 1994 gubernatorial primary when he challenged Pete Wilson for the Republican nomination. Gloria Matta Tuchman was herself a Latina, with long experience teaching Latino children.

Certainly, no one would dispute that California had a problem. Between 1987 and 1997, the number of students in California with limited English proficiency had tripled. By 1997 it stood at 1.4 million. California had 43 percent of all limited-English-speaking students in the United States, followed by Texas, New York, Florida, and Illinois. Although there were some eighty languages spoken by California schoolchildren, and although some communities differed from the dominant profile—Glendale, for instance, where the leading first language of limited-English students was Armenian—nearly 80 percent of limited- or non-English-speaking students were Spanish-speaking; and this, in effect, gave Proposition 227 the possibility of functioning, if only on a subliminal level, as a pro- or anti-Latino measure. In 1984, municipal court judges in heavily Latino Huntington Park had ruled that their clerks could speak to each other only in English during work hours. The clerks countered with a lawsuit, which reached the

Supreme Court, where it was declared moot because the plaintiff had changed his job. In 1986, California voters had approved Proposition 63, backed by the U.S. English organization in Washington, D.C., declaring that English was the official language of the state. Many considered Proposition 63 to be an explicitly anti-immigrant measure.

On the other hand, there were real educational issues involved. Defenders of bilingual education claimed that it was unfair to penalize non-English-speaking students in their early education by instructing them in basic subjects, so crucial to their future development, in a language that was foreign to them. Such instruction had a built-in factor of alienation between the student and the classroom; and this in turn fostered low self-esteem, which led to an educational bad start, which contributed to the distressing high school dropout rate among Latinos and their low graduation rate from college. If a Spanish-speaking child was taught initially in Spanish, by contrast, he or she had the chance at an equal start in basic subjects.

As Proposition 227 approached election day, the Los Angeles Unified School District, which ran the largest bilingual program in the state, promoted two studies, one by itself and the other by the Tomás Rivera Policy Institute at Claremont, claiming that non-English-speaking students fared better by the fifth grade if they began their classroom instruction in Spanish. UC Berkeley School of Education dean Eugene Garcia was equally supportive. Bilingualism, Garcia argued, even trilingualism, was rapidly becoming a way of life in California. Soon the majority of Californians, like so many Europeans, would be able to handle two or three languages; and one of them would invariably be Spanish.

Unz, Tuchman, and other supporters of Proposition 227 expressed concern for disadvantaged Spanish-speaking children under present bilingual programs. It was one thing for the affluent to master two, even three, languages. It was quite another matter, however, for a poor Spanish-speaking child who heard only Spanish both at home and at school. At what point could such a child be expected to enter the mainstream? Thirty minutes of English a day, Unz argued, was dooming 1.4 million children, fully a quarter of all children in K–5 programs in public schools throughout the state, to second-class status. Latino parents knew this. Many parents were especially angry that their children, born in the United States, were being confined to a linguistic barrio at such an early age. Public opinion surveys, including a 1997 *Los Angeles Times* poll, consistently showed a massive distrust—between 80 and 85 percent—of bilingual programs on the part of Latino parents. In February 1996 seventy-one poor immigrant Latino families had organized a boycott of the Ninth Street Elementary School in Los Angeles until their children were removed from Spanish-language programs and placed in classrooms where the language of instruction was English. A poll taken that year by the Center for Equal Opportunity, a Washington, D.C., think tank, found that 81 percent of Latino parents wanted their children to learn English as soon as possible.

The real engine behind bilingualism, Unz argued, was economic. There were thousands of bilingual teachers in California, backed by some $400 million in programs. In Los Angeles, bilingual teachers were getting up to $5,000 a year in bonuses, and school districts were receiving hundreds of dollars for each child who was designated as having a limited proficiency in English. "This generates," Unz argued, "the worst sort of perverse incentive, in which administrators are financially rewarded for not teaching English to young children or pretending that they haven't learned the language."[13]

Going even further, the *Economist* reported on September 5, 1997, that Latino children and other ethnic minorities were being railroaded into bilingual classes, even if they spoke English at home, in order to maintain support for bilingual teachers. Bolivian-born Jaime Escalante, whose skill at teaching calculus to Latino students was celebrated in the film *Stand and Deliver* (1998), agreed. As young parents recently arrived from Bolivia, Escalante and his wife had refused to allow their children to be enrolled in Spanish-only programs. Escalante's sons grew up to be engineers, speaking fluent English and Spanish, and proud of their Bolivian heritage. "Let's not confuse things," Escalante argued. "Culture you learn at home. You educate at schools."[14]

Given the complexities of bilingual education, which was basically Spanish-language education through the fifth grade, with some English instruction, it is not surprising that Latino politicians and gubernatorial candidates tended to avoid the issue. In Sacramento, a measure sponsored by state senator Dede Alpert, a Democrat from Coronado, called for the decentralization of bilingual programs on a district-by-district basis. Alpert's measure was opposed by both supporters and opponents of Proposition 227. In March 1998 the state board of education endorsed its own version of the Alpert measure, notifying school districts that they would no longer need to petition Sacramento to disestablish Spanish-only instruction in favor of English-intensive methods. Meeting in April, the board reaffirmed its earlier decision on a voice vote without dissent. Although its measure was only advisory and did not have the force of law, it was obviously intended to dissipate a polarized debate along ethnic lines as the June vote approached.

Already, there were signs that the issue was on the verge of becoming polarized. Meeting in Anaheim in September 1997, California Republicans endorsed Proposition 227, despite pleas to the contrary by Ernesto Feliciano, leader of the Latino caucus at the convention. "Now it's up to the Republican Party to let [the measure] stand on its own merits," Feliciano noted wearily after the vote, "and not use it as a wedge issue heading into the 1998 [gubernatorial] campaign."[15] Certainly none of the gubernatorial candidates, including Attorney General Dan Lungren, the presumptive Republican nominee, were showing any sign in April 1998 of wanting to use Proposition 227 as a wedge issue, as Pete Wilson had recently used Propositions 187 and 209. Far from it: all four gubernatorial candidates— Lungren, businessman Al Checchi, Lieutenant Governor Gray Davis, and Representative Jane Harman—seemed anxious to avoid the entire issue, although the three Democrats were on record as opposing the proposition.

True, opposition to Proposition 227 was mounting as June approached. It gathered strength from the resistance of the San Diego, Los Angeles, and San Francisco school districts against compliance with a recent law, passed reluctantly by the legislature and signed by Governor Wilson, requiring all districts to test only in English in the upper grades and to report the results of such testing on the Internet. Wilson had strong-armed the measure through the legislature, using as leverage the release of other education funding, including a cost-of-living increase. In February 1998 the Los Angeles Unified School District went to court to oppose the state mandate. Governor Wilson, claimed Jose Velasquez, principal of Miles Elementary in East Los Angeles, the largest elementary school in the nation, was "an unfriendly, unbending, openly hostile governor, whose battlefield for this confrontation is a Latino child's education."[16]

In June, Proposition 227 passed with 61 percent of the vote. Although there were a few affiliated legal cases, 227 was not immediately put into administrative limbo by any successful court challenge. The law contained an exemption waiver, moreover, intended to relieve pressure on any group for whom English immersion would constitute an undue hardship.

As the school year began the following fall, the question was: Would there be a wholesale request for waivers? There was not. Most requests for waivers seemed to come from school districts—Oakland, San Francisco, Los Angeles, Santa Ana—in which bilingual teachers encouraged parents to request such waivers. Even in the Los Angeles Unified School District only 11,809 requests for exemptions were received. In more than half of the campuses of the school district, not one waiver request was forthcoming— and this despite an energetic campaign by the United Teachers of Los Angeles's Bilingual Committee. Throughout the fall, pro-bilingual teacher groups continued to oppose the measure and achieved some victories. After thirty days of English-immersion classes, for example, parents of some

3,400 students in the Hueneme Elementary District in Ventura County were asking for waivers. This many parents could not have come to this conclusion in such massive numbers without teacher encouragement. And yet, despite the strong resistance by the pro-bilingual coalition in the teachers' union, English-only immersion managed to take hold—even in Los Angeles, where by late October only twelve thousand students were remaining in bilingual education, at their parents' request, compared to the 107,000 students who were in formal bilingual classes at the time Proposition 227 was passed.

The majority of teachers and Spanish-speaking parents were embracing Proposition 227 as best they could, despite a shortage of English-only instructional materials. Cuban-born Zoe Garcia, twenty-nine, a first-grade teacher at the Thomas Jefferson Elementary School in Anaheim, had initially opposed Proposition 227, but when it passed, she decided not to resist but to throw herself as enthusiastically as possible into the program, despite start-up difficulties. Every now and then Garcia would use a Spanish phrase or two to help a struggling child, but by and large she remained in English, despite the difficulties of teaching students to master new sounds for words to which they were only now being introduced. Garcia would lie awake at night long after her husband and her five-year-old son were asleep, concocting in her mind ways of teaching English in English, with only an emergency use of Spanish. "It's going better than I thought," Garcia remarked some ninety days into the program. "It just amazes me."[17]

However intense the debate, and however fiercely resisted in certain school districts by certain groups of teachers, Proposition 227 had not become a wedge issue—had not, that is, been perceived on a wholesale basis by the Latino community as a form of insult or rejection. Throughout the campaign, proponents of Proposition 227 went out of their way to extol Spanish as an invaluable parallel language—not a second language, a *parallel* language—for Latino Californians. Full participation in the society and economy of contemporary California, however, they had argued, demanded competency in English. Youngsters who were instructed in Spanish-only classes, which is what most allegedly bilingual classes turned out to be, were not being tracked for success in the larger culture.

In an effort to dispel any notion that Spanish was being downgraded as a language, the public libraries of California, assisted by federal funds administered by the California State Library, made a concerted effort to buy more Spanish-language books, especially children's books, and to encourage Spanish-language story hours for Spanish-speaking children. The goal of all these programs, whether English-only immersion classes or Spanish-language story hours, was to assist in the creation of an educated bilingual generation connected to its own heritage through Spanish and to the common culture through English. Significantly, traffic was also in the other direction, and by the dawn of the millennium an increasing number of Anglo and other Californians were learning and speaking Spanish.

Accommodations

Could it be that Californians were becoming reconciled to each other, or, at the least, were growing wary of offering offense to other ethnicities, despite the fact that Proposition 227 could so easily be construed or employed as an anti-Latino measure? San Francisco–based writer Richard Rodriguez had long since come out against affirmative action and the Spanish-only approach to early childhood education. In three compelling memoirs, *Hunger of Memory: The Education of Richard Rodriguez* (1982) and *Days of Obligation: An Argument with My Mexican Father* (1992), followed by *Brown* (2002), together with innumerable articles in national magazines and newspapers, Rodriguez had probed the complexities of Mexican-American identity as Latinos entered the middle class. Educated in the Catholic schools of Sacramento, at Stanford, the Warburg Institute in London, Oxford, and UC Berkeley, where he took a PhD in Renaissance literature, Rodriguez had turned down a tenure-track appointment to the English department at Yale because he believed it to be tainted by affirmative action.

No matter how politically correct it might be, Rodriguez could not see himself as a victim. His Sacramento boyhood, he claimed, had been more Tom Sawyer than Huck Finn, and the Irish Sisters of Mercy at his parochial grammar school had drilled him assiduously in the basics of English grammar, spelling, and composition. In later years, Rodriguez would see in these Irish nuns, especially in their passion to communicate to him the precision and elegance of good English, a genuine commitment to him as an individual whose God-given talent should be given every opportunity to prosper. Now and then, Rodriguez would experience disquieting reminders of his Mexican identity. The sight of Mexican field workers at stoop labor on farms in the vicinity of Sacramento triggered memories of the one summer he spent in such activity, and provoked an eerie combination of destiny and revulsion. To be Mexican was to be in struggle with the land, at once to love and to hate the sun and the soil, or to escape them as Rodriguez did, enrolling, not at Cal State Sacramento or even a UC campus, but at Stanford, a rich kids' school, to which he had won an academic scholarship.

As an adolescent, entering the complexities of social and sexual identity, Rodriguez had been ambivalent about his dark Indian skin, which so differentiated him from the other kids at school. As time went on, he discovered that his beaked nose and Indian face (as if he had just stepped off the frieze of a pre-Columbian temple) was his destiny as well—and not a bad destiny, at that. The older Rodriguez got, the more he gloried in his Mexican Indian identity. It was great to be brown and even better to be brown in dialogue with other people who were of another color. The more he meditated upon California, the more he experienced life there as a working journalist—with continued connections to New York, Paris, and London—the more Rodriguez saw that the peoples of California, all of them, in their total diversity, were becoming increasingly like each other.

Take the border as an example. Nowhere in California did the ethnic tensions of the new society reveal themselves more dramatically than along the San Diego–Tijuana border, especially in the early years of the decade. Yet this region, more than any other place in Southern California, was during this same period the most mediated, hence accommodated, through photography, painting, collage, and sculpture. In November 1989 the Museum of Photographic Arts in Balboa Park, San Diego—working with such groups as the Border Arts Workshop, the Centro Cultural de la Raza, and the Taller de Arte Fronterizo—mounted an exhibition of border-related photographs and videotapes in color and black-and-white that announced to San Diego and Southern California in general that the number one item on the social agenda in the 1990s would be Anglo-Latino relationships on the borderlands. Legitimately, critics made comparisons to the previous work of Lewis Hine, Jacob Riis, Dorothea Lange, Margaret Bourke-White, and other American photographers who had in the past similarly alerted the public through equally stark images, by turns compelling and repugnant.

Across the decade, the border became increasingly the point of contact between Mexican, Mexican-American, Anglo-Californian, and European artists. In 1990, sponsored by the Centro Cultural de la Raza and the San Diego Museum of Contemporary Art and funded in part by a $250,000 grant from the National Endowment for the Arts, eight border artists, some of them with roots on both sides of the line, traveled the full length of the border between Brownsville, Texas, and San Diego. The result: a real-time artistic presentation combining art, documentary, performance, spontaneous theater, and other forms of expression which, in the manner of Christo, tried to make of the border itself a work of art.

In June 1991, one of the best known of these border artists, Guillermo

Gomez-Peña, a Mexico City–born resident of San Diego, received a MacArthur Fellowship. A performance artist and writer, Gomez-Peña had taken as his theme nothing less than the entire relationship between pre-Columbian society and Spanish civilization. In March 1993, the San Diego Museum of Contemporary Art sponsored the exhibition "La Frontera/The Border," featuring paintings, drawings, sculptures, photographs, prints, and installations by more than thirty-five border artists. The exhibition, observed *Los Angeles Times* art critic Christopher Knight, offered "pervasive evidence of the way in which pressing social and cultural tensions can be transformed into resonant works of art, and how the conflicted border region has emerged as a principal metaphor."[18] By 1997, San Diego and Tijuana were mounting a joint city, binational exhibition called inSITE97 featuring the work of forty-three artists at various sites each side of the border. While one cannot claim too much for these exhibitions in terms of their immediate social effect, the very emergence of a border art tradition bespoke the possibilities not just of conflict, but of resolution as well. After all, the most analogous event had been, earlier in the decade, the Light Up the Border flooding of the Tijuana River by hundreds of massed headlights by angry San Diego residents.

In January 1993, Mexico City itself entered the dialogue with a "Mexican Faces in California" exhibition of photographs in the National Museum of Anthropology and History covering more than one hundred years of Mexican-Californian history. In separate ceremonies but connected to this exhibition, President Carlos Salinas de Gortari presented the Order of the Aztec Eagle, Mexico's highest honor, to Los Angeles County supervisor Gloria Molina, Clinton cabinet member Henry Cisneros, and Raul Yzaguirre, director of the National Council of La Raza, for defending the culture and human rights of Mexicans and Mexican Americans in the United States.

Again and again, Southern California seemed more than willing—on the level of art and performance, at least—to come to terms with its Mexican heritage. Throughout the decade Mexican-oriented popular festivals proliferated, beginning with a yearly *Artes de Mexico* Los Angeles festival featuring performances throughout the city. By August-September 1993, the citywide Los Angeles Festival, under the direction of Peter Sellars, was turning the entire city into a performing arts extravaganza for the better part of a month. Embracing as it did a global range of cultures, the festival celebrated through film, dance, drama, painting, choral music, and solo performance Los Angeles's image of itself, not yet a year after its devastating riots, as an ecumenopolis, a world city, in acceptance as well as fact.

In October 1997, at the Dorothy Chandler Pavilion, the Los Angeles

Opera Company produced a sumptuous version of Mexico City–based composer Daniel Catán's *Florencia en el Amazonas,* with libretto by Marcela Fuentes-Berain, based on a story by Gabriel García Márquez. A romantic feast of lush and sumptuous Latin American–inspired music, Catán's score and the impressive Los Angeles Opera staging of a diva's journey down the Amazon into her past seemed bent upon returning opera forward to the future as an engaged and engaging art form possessed of broad appeal. Of equal importance in social terms was the fact that a five-year-old organization, Hispanics for Los Angeles Opera, partially under-wrote the production and organized festivities for the opening-night premiere, with tickets selling between $375 and $405 apiece. Placido and Marta Domingo were much in evidence as honorary cochairs. On hand as well were the consuls general of Colombia, Chile, Peru, Argentina, and Mexico, and the Mexican ambassador to Canada.

The very next month, Bernard and Edith Lewin, who had arrived in Los Angeles in the late 1930s as refugees from Nazi Germany and had pros-pered in the furniture business, donated their collection of more than eigh-teen hundred works by Mexican artists—among them Diego Rivera, Rufino Tamayo, José Clemente Orozco, Frida Kahlo, Carlos Merida, and David Alfaro Siqueiros—to the Los Angeles County Museum of Art. Conserva-tively valued at $25 million, the Lewin Collection was one of the largest of its kind in the United States; and it made LACMA the premier museum for Mexican modernist painting in the United States.

And so the struggle toward understanding, dialogue, accommodation, even reconciliation, continued through the decade in ways large and small. The city council of Long Beach named a new eleven-acre park after César Chávez. In Sacramento, the state board of education called for textbook writers to address the diversity of peoples who had made California. Purdy Tran became the first Rose Parade Queen of Asian descent. In Oakland, at the Madrone Hotel for low-income tenants, the East Bay Local Develop-ment Corporation, which owned and ran the hotel, fostered dialogue among its ethnically diverse residents through a series of mutual help projects and social programs. In 1996 consultants Philip Harris and Robert Moran issued the fifth edition of *Managing Cultural Differences: Leadership Strategies for a New World of Business* (1979), which had been adopted in graduate business programs at more than two hundred colleges and universities across the country. How does one deal with Iranian poetic exaggeration, with Asian reticence, with the Filipino's reluctance to complain, with the Latino's need for dignity—and do so without stereotyping any one individ-ual? Difficult questions, but, increasingly, managers at every level of soci-ety were being forced to come up with the answers.

Directed by sociologist Chuck Nathanson, the UC San Diego–based San Diego Dialogue, a working committee of representative community leaders, took on as its special charge the present and future of metro San Diego and Baja California, from San Diego to Ensenada, from Tijuana to Mexicali, and produced a series of working reports and papers that underscored problems and challenges but also envisioned a unique binational, bicultural prosperity for the region. Developer C. Samuel Marasco was pushing to conclusion Las Americas, a retail, cultural, resort, and entertainment complex on both sides of the Tijuana River, which Marasco hoped to cross with a bridge that would unite the complex and symbolically conjoin Mexico and the United States. In Los Angeles, retired UC Berkeley Spanish professor Luis Andres Murillo, now returned to his native Pasadena, wrote a key to Spanish pronunciation for use by the California Highway Patrol, the Los Angeles Police Department, and the Los Angeles County Sheriff's Department. A highly decorated fighter-bomber tail-gunner in World War II, Murillo knew from personal experience the value of quick, concise, two-way radio communication. It was important, he believed, that the police be able to take emergency calls in Spanish or, conversely, to give emergency instructions in that language over the radio or telephone.

The Los Angeles–based Mexican American Legal Defense and Education Fund, faced by the fact that more than half of the Anglo community had some degree of negative stereotypes regarding Latinos, was commissioning a series of television ads aimed at an Anglo audience, showcasing the mainstream American values and ambitions—work, family, home ownership, education, community involvement—of Latino Southern Californians. Students at San Francisco State University had at least one stereotype shattered by the fact that the biology department had five Latino tenure-track professors. Interestingly enough, biology was becoming a popular major for Latino students at San Francisco State and elsewhere. Jose Trejo, eighteen, for example, went from a mobile home park in Banning to Stanford University, entering in the same class as Chelsea Clinton. Trejo hoped to study biotechnology, his way to Stanford financed in part by the Vikki Carr Scholarship Foundation, founded by the Latina singer. Cynthia Rios, Tony Toledo, Jewely Lopez, and Karina Mendoza, meanwhile, were unpacking their bags in a freshman dorm at USC, just a few blocks from their homes, thanks to a Neighborhood Academic Initiative Program sponsored by USC, which had been tracking them since the sixth grade.

Los Angeles KABC radio talk show host Dennis Prager started a program in which whites and minorities would have dinner in each other's homes—just that and nothing else—as a way of fostering understanding. When bus driver Ruben Hernandez, part Latino, part Apache, who also went by his Native American name Running Wolf, was transferred from his Hollywood-Pasadena route, his riders gave him an impromptu party in Old Town Pasadena. In a brief six months on the route, the thirty-six-year-old ponytailed driver had made his bus the mobile equivalent of the bar in *Cheers*. Hernandez knew everyone on Line 180—the immigrants en route to their night jobs, the partying kids, the lonely who rode the bus just for company—and they knew him. It was not uncommon for a passenger to let one bus pass by until Hernandez's bus came along. On Friday nights, passengers were known to distribute pizza, buffalo wings, chips and salsa, or chocolate-chip cookies to other passengers.

Ironically, Census 2000 revealed that immigration, far from destabilizing California, had actually steadied the basic social structures of the state. During the 1990s, 1.8 million of the 6.9 million immigrants arriving in the United States settled in California, giving the state 26.1 percent of all immigrants, and making it, as demographer Ali Modarres put it, "the Ellis Island of the late 20th century."[19] At a time when the traditional family was in a condition of meltdown among so many groups (834,716 single-mother families in California by 2000; 292,346 single-father families), immigrants showed a marked preference for traditional family life. While American-born groups talked family values, they were actually in the process of getting divorced, having children out of wedlock, or not having children at all whatever their marital condition. Immigrants, by contrast, census 2000 showed, were marrying, having children, and staying married.

Immigrants were also accommodating themselves to other immigrant and nonimmigrant groups of various ethnicities in some twenty-four California cities in which white flight was not occurring. Throughout the 1990s in Southern California, the number of cities showing a mosaic of three or four ethnic or racial communities coexisting in one urban polity, albeit in ethnic neighborhoods, grew by more than 50 percent. No one group, in other words, was driving any other group out. The relative absence of white flight, furthermore, was occurring in a context in which white people had made the transition from three-quarters of the population to less than one-half. Hispanics made up nearly one-third of the state's population. That figure climbed to 43 percent in the under-eighteen category.

Census 2000 revealed a California almost equally divided among the young, adult, middle-aged, and elderly. Demographically, the state was best represented by a column, minus the great bulge in the center that Census 1970 and Census 1980 revealed as the baby boomer generation passed through the population like a heifer swallowed by a python. And yet Census 2000 was not without significant revelations as far as generations were concerned. Take the young (under-eighteen) Millennial Generation as an example. First of all, as befitting the columnar demographics of the state, the total population of under-eighteen Californians stood at 9,249,829, 27.3 percent of the total population. Yet this one-quarter of the population, this young California, was only 34.8 percent Caucasian. The majority of the under-eighteen category comprised African Americans (6.7 percent), Asians (9.6 percent), Hispanics (43.8 percent), and others, including American Indians and Alaskan Natives (0.5 percent), and Native Hawaiian and Pacific Islanders (0.1 percent). It did not require a doctorate in mathematics to see that millennial California would have a strong Hispanic majority, a secondary sector of whites, a significant Asian-American community, a declining African-American population, and a very small percentage of people in other categories. These statistics were not fully stable, however. They were capable of floating upward to other percentages, because 7.3 percent of Californians under the age of eighteen were claiming two or more racial/ethnic identities.

The future of California, in other words, as judged from its youngest generation, would not look like a scene from *Gidget* or the cover of a Beach Boys album. It would look, rather, like a Benetton commercial, with young people of every color singing "We Are the World." It would, in cultural terms, be predominantly Hispanic and Asian. All this could change, should there be a surge in immigration from one part of the world or another into California; but there was little chance that this surge would be coming from Ireland, Norway, or Sweden. If it came at all, it would most likely come from Mexico, Central America, or Asia and would thus intensify even further the Hispanic-Asian dominance in the culture of the Golden State.

Young California, Hispanics and Asians especially, would most likely sustain a certain bipolar cultural identity and style. Since there was a less powerful white culture to assimilate to (as was the case when whiteness dominated the mainstream), Millennial Generation California would most likely not experience the pressure to assimilate that young second-generation Irish, German, Slavic, Italian, Greek, and Jewish Americans experienced in an earlier era. Their cultural styles and identities would most likely remain rooted in their prior culture and heritage. Nearly everyone— and this included a growing number of whites—would be bi- or even trilingual.

Mainstream culture itself would not only reflect the diversity of the population, it would also reinforce this growing condition of bipartite or tripartite identities. In the mid-1990s certain Anglo–Southern Californians had been shocked when Mexican Americans cheered for the Mexican team, as opposed to the American team, at the World Cup games in Pasadena. For the Millennial Generation, such dual or even triple loyalties would be commonplace.

Would there be a common culture, a common California? Yes—but it would be on a different model. Interacting cultural identities would affect and flavor each other. Already, Southern California could boast Korean-American bagpipe players, Japanese-American surfer dudes, white homeboys, Latinos who did stand-up shtick. Already, as Richard Rodriguez was pointing out, Californians were beginning to resemble each other. Even bloodlines were coalescing, as indicated by those young Californians who saw themselves as blending racial and ethnic identities. Census 2000, in short, revealed a California in the process of making accommodations.

PART V

Turnaround

For the Good Times

During World War II, California went on defense steroids. Dependency was severe and lasted fifty years. Coming off these drugs in the early 1990s—which California did only of necessity—the Golden State, so cocky, so sure of its destiny, lost its revenues and, almost overnight, came close to losing its self-confidence. For fifty years, California had mistaken the rush of military spending as merely the exhilaration of its own intrinsic economic strength, and now, like an addict going clean and sober, the state was forced to acknowledge its dependency and face the future, shaped up and chastened. Defense spending—a raging torrent in the blood of people, growth, construction, and self-congratulatory ballyhoo—had helped transform California into the seventh largest economy on the planet by the end of the 1980s. Yet so many of its dollars were cold war dollars, and in 1990 the cold war was ending, and within a year or two California would find itself profiled, even taunted, as the Vanishing Dream by *Time* magazine. Losing money and people—more important, losing its essential myth: that it was bigger, brighter, and more untouchable than other American regions—California hit bottom, then almost as swiftly began to reassemble from the materials of its pre–World War II economy the program and tool kit of its recovery.

Californians were tempted to ask whether time was growing denser as it reached the millennium. It had all happened so quickly: the high tide of Defense Department spending in the late 1980s under the jurisdiction of two Californians, President Ronald Reagan and his secretary of defense, Casper Weinberger (a spending spree that would economically bomb the Soviet Union into oblivion); the collapse of the Soviet Union; the fall of the Berlin Wall; the Gulf War (with Desert Storm providing the United States with an after-the-fact dress rehearsal of the European land war with the Soviet bloc it would never get to fight); the collapse of the California economy, the downward spiral of the early 1990s, the dawn of recovery in 1994, and the reassertion of a world-class trillion-dollar economy by 1997. All this had unfolded in less than a decade: it was as if time itself were becoming more compressed, and each year sustained the historical impact of a half decade. One way to explain this dilemma is to say that the collapse was not a collapse at all, but merely a temporary adjustment. At no time in the first half of the 1990s, it must be remembered, did California fall from the ranks of the half-dozen or so top economies in the world; and as impressive as it might have been, defense spending had accounted for only 5 percent of the total California economy as of 1990. Yet no such qualifications could devalue the impact of the 40 percent falloff in tax revenues experienced by the state government in the early years of the 1990s, the hundreds of thousands of jobs lost, the businesses closed, the out-migration, and, most important, the willingness of even sympathetic observers to speculate that perhaps the California economy, like the freakish muscles of a steroid-pumped bodybuilder, was an artificial, unnatural thing, destined not to last.

Not true. Even at the height of the cold war, when Reagan and Weinberger were spending a fifth of their $120 billion defense budget in California, the state enjoyed a diversified economy. Agriculture, the leading economic element since 1879, now comprised more than two hundred commercial crops and represented (as of 1986) a $14 billion a year enterprise, which made California the number one agricultural state in the nation. On the other end of the spectrum, more than a third of the nation's high-tech employees, including skilled technicians in computers, software design, robotics, space science, and telecommunications, were living and working on the California coast. Nor was manufacturing absent. In Fremont, on the eastern side of San Francisco Bay, Toyota and General Motors were operating a $300 million state-of-the-art production facility employing twenty-five hundred, and a second assembly line was being staffed. Pohang Iron and Steel, one of the top five steel manufacturers in Korea, and U.S. Steel had recently announced a $300 million joint venture to renovate steel-production facilities in Pittsburg in the north Bay Area.

Japanese investors seemed especially enamored. California was Japan's second leading trading partner, second only to the United States itself. Each year California exported more than $7 billion worth of goods to Japan. These exports constituted the leading element in California's participation in the $3 trillion Pacific Rim trading market, which was growing at the rate of $3 billion a week. By 1986, California was doing more than $65 billion worth of trade with Pacific Rim nations. Fifteen leading Japanese banks maintained strong California operations or secondary connections. More than 180 Japanese-owned companies were operating in Orange County alone. Among them was Toshiba, which had recently announced the impending construction of a 350,000-square-foot facility for the manufacture of X-ray instruments. According to a California State Department of Commerce report, of the $2 billion invested by Japan in the United States by 1983, an estimated 30 percent had been invested in California enterprises.

Nor was small business absent from the scene, whether mom-and-pop operations owned and operated by recent immigrants or high-tech or biotech start-ups in Silicon Valley and Orange and San Diego Counties. According to a report released in 1983 by the Wells Fargo Bank, California led the nation in small-business start-ups and expansions. In the first three years of the 1980s alone, small business had created more than 400,000 new jobs in the state. Among Californians—a population that had grown by 600,000 in 1982—per capita income averaged $14,487, higher than the national average and among the top two or three averages on the planet. Californians were spending more than $125 billion on consumer goods each year, more than the retail sales of Texas, Arkansas, Louisiana, and Oklahoma combined.

Property values, meanwhile, were soaring, especially in the coastal regions where the major cities and suburbs were located. While homes in the interior remained competitive with the rest of the nation (averaging $89,000 for the Inland Empire, $77,000 for the Central Valley, $61,000 in rural northern California), homes in the coastal cities and suburbs bought for $40,000 in the 1950s tripled, quadrupled, even quintupled their value as home owners experienced (as Mike Davis was fond of pointing out) the single most dramatic financial windfall—in terms of home prices and the extent of the population affected—in American history. An existing home in San Diego County valued at $104,000 in 1980 would be worth $224,000 by 1989. A newly constructed home costing $119,000 in 1980 would sell for $259,000 nine years later. No wonder that San Diego builders, contemplating the 1990s, were predicting an average price of $1.5 million for new homes by the end of 1999. An entire generation of 1940s and 1950s home buyers were suddenly being presented with a retirement nest egg, while throughout the state the staple of cocktail- and dinner-party conversation frequently (and rather drearily) became how this or that Californian had made a killing just by owning a house. Nor were newcomers to California unwilling—after a period of psychological adjustment—to pay these prices, judging from the rising rate of housing starts across the state.

Critics were not oblivious to the present and future possible costs of such success. Quality-of-life issues had also been on the state's collective mind since the smog crisis of the mid-1950s and the increasingly burdened freeway system beginning in the 1960s. Ever since the Santa Barbara oil spill of 1969, environmentalists had been making dire diagnoses of California's stewardship of its environment and resources. By the 1990s, millions of Californians were commuting to and from work, hundreds of thousands of trucks were spewing exhaust fumes, and factories and other manufacturing installations, especially furniture manufacturing enterprises such as Wisc's Furniture Profiles of Los Angeles County, were emitting even more particles into the atmosphere. Battle lines were being drawn between environmentalists—the majority of them affluent, educated, and white—and immigrants such as John Enriquez, an Arizona native raised in Guadalajara, who by the age of sixty in 1989 had worked himself up to a $50,000-a-year foremanship at Wise's in charge of sixty-eight furniture makers, most of them immigrants from Mexico. Claiming that he had invested hundreds of thousands of dollars in equipment designed to prevent stains and lacquer from polluting the air but was still unable to satisfy the Southern California Air Quality Control Board, Wise's chairman, Carl Schulman, sold his home in Woodland Hills and set up a new plant in Tijuana, where emissions standards were more permissive.

And while Californians might comfort themselves with anecdotes of exploding real estate values—especially if they owned the home in question—a certain doubt clouded the statistics. How many Californians could afford such prices? Were not an increasing number of Californians being priced out of their own market? Only 19 percent of existing San Diego householders, for example, could afford by the late 1980s to purchase their present home at current prices. Throughout the 1980s, the rate of home ownership, stated the California Association of Realtors, dropped more than in any similar period since the Great Depression. By December 1988, in Los Angeles and Orange Counties, only one in five households owned its own home. For a growing number of middle-class residents, home ownership meant the purchase of a modest tract in an outlying region and a 150-mile round-trip commute to work.

Government services, most noticeably public schools, were showing signs of stress. A rising crime rate was diminishing both the quality of life and the national image of the state. Even more ominous, there were signs that California was creating an economy whose jobs were beyond the education, or even the ability, of a growing sector of the population. California was creating more jobs, but a growing percentage of the population, unable to read, write, add, or subtract at a satisfactory level, could not fill the positions. By December 1989, Kaiser Permanente had some three thousand job openings in its health care system, because it could not recruit a workforce sufficiently skilled in English, mathematics, and critical thinking. "The worst-case scenario for me," noted Kaiser personnel vice president A. D.

Bolden, "is that if this were to continue for fifteen or twenty years, the entire entry-level work force would be largely untrainable."[1]

California was in danger of not being able to staff the economy it was creating. The problem could be solved in part by immigration laws favoring skilled and professional workers, but what of the existing populations? Were they to be relegated to an expanding underclass, minimally employed (if at all) in a sweatshop or *campesino* economy? High-tech employment was one thing—but what about the thousands of workers in underground sweatshops, or the undocumented men standing on street corners each morning available for a day's work, or, worse, the younger Californians—African Americans disturbingly represented in such high numbers among them—who were not even getting a start in the economy?

And then there was the question of attitudes toward work among the employed. Did Californians really want to work that hard? "In California, I had to interview thirty people to find one questionable employee," noted Russ Gurstein, who worked for his parents at U.S. Products, a small company making carpet-cleaning machinery in Agoura, Los Angeles County. "They had an attitude problem. And when the surf's up, you said good-bye to half your employees." In 1988 the Gursteins, native Californians all, moved their company to Coeur d'Alene, Idaho, where, among other benefits, workers' compensation rates were only $2.60 for each $100 in salary, compared to $7.90 in California. "Officials listen to you here," Gurstein noted of his new environment. "Even the Governor came out to welcome us when we arrived."[2]

Free Fall

A ll these ambiguities—an overreliance on defense and aerospace spending; the tension (soon the clash) between growth and environmental legislation; high taxation and bureaucratic interference; the rising costs of housing; deteriorating schools; a growing sector of marginal workers—flashed into full-scale crisis when the California economy went into free fall following the end of the cold war. In the first four years of the decade, more than half a million jobs evaporated. Between July 1990 and July 1991 alone, California lost 100,000 jobs, and the pace continued at an accelerated rate. Three-quarters of these jobs were in defense. A significant percentage of the remaining quarter came from the removal of companies to states (or nations) in which the tax and environmental regulatory climate was more favorable. A survey conducted by the California Business Round-table in mid-1991 revealed that 14 percent of California business leaders were looking to relocate outside the state, and another 41 percent were planning to expand elsewhere than in California. In August 1991, General Motors announced the closure of its Van Nuys plant, which had employed two thousand.

The loss of jobs could be traced most vividly in the most vulnerable industry, aerospace. In August 1991 the air force chose Lockheed of Georgia over Northrop of Southern California for the $72 billion program to replace its existing lead fighter. Loss of its share of the contract cost Southern California 21,000 jobs over the next decade. In September 1992, Northrop announced that it would be losing an estimated 6,500 jobs due to the winding down of the B-2 bomber program. The following year Northrop reported the elimination of another 2,400 jobs, due to the continuing decline of B-2 stealth bomber and jetliner production. In March 1993, Hughes Aircraft said it would close its Canoga Park missile facility due to an unfavorable working environment, and move nineteen hundred engineering-related positions to Tucson. The following year, in March 1994, Northrop continued its cutbacks, announcing the loss of another three thousand jobs from its plants in Pico Rivera, Hawthorne, El Segundo, and Palmdale. The St. Louis–based McDonnell Douglas, a leading Long Beach employer, entered the 1990s on the ropes. In November 1991, the company said it had sold 40 percent of its commercial aircraft business for $2 billion to a Taiwanese consortium (an agreement the company had to defend before a suspicious Congress). Still, despite the infusion of Taiwanese cash, the company was forced to lay off two thousand employees at its Torrance plant the following year.

Laid off or unable to follow their job to a new state or to Mexico, the unemployed soon emerged as a new kind of representative Californian. Photographs of the unemployed lining up for the few jobs available at private companies or queuing outside the offices of the Employment Development Department to register for their unemployment compensation provided a reverse paradigm of the California job scene a few short years before. By September 1991, close to 10 percent of the 318,000 Americans who had exhausted their twenty-six weeks of unemployment benefits could be found in California: people such as Bruce Garnier, fifty-nine, of San Gabriel Valley, former facilities engineer for McDonnell Douglas in Long Beach. For nearly thirty years, Garnier had enjoyed the good life as a well-paid employee in aerospace. Now, his unemployment benefits exhausted, he was beating the bushes along with 36,000 other Californians in a similar condition, looking for a job, any kind of a job—an electrician perhaps, a warehouse worker, a truck driver—to no avail.

Valiantly, such organizations as the California Chamber of Commerce and the Economic Development Corporation of Los Angeles County fought to counter the out-migration of jobs to Colorado, Nevada, Utah, Arizona, Oklahoma, Oregon, and Idaho. (Such efforts were ironically compromised in August 1991 when it became known that Wilford Godbald, chairman of the Zero Corporation, a Los Angeles–based manufacturer of aircraft cargo containers, camera cases, and industrial cabinets, then serving as chairman of the Chamber of Commerce's Task Force on Saving California Jobs, had recently shifted part of his business and three hundred positions from Pacoima to Salt Lake City, soon to be followed by the 450-job Zero plant in Burbank.) By August 1991, Southern California Edison was estimating that sixty manufacturers in its service area had either moved or expanded to Nevada, forty-four had moved to Arizona, and 284 had moved to Mexico.

Such companies were no longer paying California taxes; nor, obviously, were the unemployed. By April 1991, California state government was facing a $12.6 billion gap between what it was committed to spend in the remaining fiscal year and the next and expected revenues in the same time period—this in a state that in 1987 had developed a $1 billion surplus, which Governor George Deukmejian had returned to taxpayers. The $12.6 billion shortfall was larger than the entire budgets of all but four other states in the union: New York, Massachusetts, Illinois, and Texas. Even if every prison and state university in the state were closed, noted Governor Pete Wilson, and all state employees were laid off, the gap could not be closed. Desperately, the governor and the legislature scrambled to make the necessary cuts. Through various forms of fiscal jury-rigging, state government stumbled through the next three years on 60 percent or so of its cylinders.

Hardest hit, with the exception of state government itself, was California's three-tier publicly sponsored higher educational system, the pride of the state since the adoption of the Master Plan for Higher Education in 1960. The plan had envisioned California as an educational utopia meeting the educational needs—hence the employment possibilities—of every citizen of the state through more than fifty two-year community colleges, twenty campuses of the California State University, and nine campuses of the University of California. For thirty years California had paraded this higher educational system before an admiring nation. Now it went into serious decline, especially the CSU campuses, entrusted with the education and upward mobility of a third of the high school graduates in the state. At San Diego State University, for example, 550 part-time instructors were let go, and 662 classes were canceled, which meant that more than thirteen hundred students could not get the classes they needed to graduate. At San Francisco State University, students would sit on the floor outside classrooms, hoping for admission, or crash classes despite the absence of their names on enrollment sheets, hoping for mercy from the instructor. Even the prestigious and more insulated University of California system was not exempt, although its budget was cut by only 1.1 percent, in contrast to the 3.2 percent taken from CSU. Nevertheless, UC was forced to offer early retirement to nearly 3,500 employees, including 672 senior faculty members, and to raise student fees by 40 percent, to $2,274 a year, which was still a bargain, although many, long accustomed to the luxury of a world-class education at public expense, howled in protest.

And so the decline continued through 1990, 1991, 1992, and 1993. The editors and writers of *Time* ended their November 18, 1991, special issue on California with dire predictions for the state on economic, fiscal, ethnic, and environmental fronts. They were correct in their prognostications. Nineteen-ninety-two was a catastrophe, the nadir year of the decade. In early 1992, Wall Street—first Standard & Poor's, then Moody's Investors Service, then Fitch Investors Service—downgraded California's bond rating from AAA to AA-1, just as state treasurer Kathleen Brown was making a record $1.3 billion bond offering, with most of the money slated for prison construction. Jobs continued to leave the state by the tens of thousands, and in Sacramento the fiscal crisis continued as Governor Wilson and the legislature confronted a $10.7 billion gap between revenues and near-fixed expenses. By July 1992, California was without a budget for the second straight summer and was paying its bills with IOUs as Republicans and Democrats argued about what should be sacrificed.

In Los Angeles County the grand jury, in a rare move for this body, opened an investigation—some two weeks before the riots—into the flight of businesses and jobs from the region. Perhaps the jurors were especially piqued by the announcement that Froxx, a manufacturer of Lycra bodysuits for women, was moving its operation to Dade County, Florida. If Los Angeles could lose such a successful and regionally appropriate three-year-old start-up as Froxx—whose president and workforce of nearly one hundred were largely Latino—the city was truly in trouble. Following the April-May riots, Douglas Aircraft of Santa Monica announced that it would lay off five thousand workers by the end of the year. Hughes Aircraft, another leading Los Angeles County employer, stated that it expected to lay off twelve thousand within the next eighteen months. Even the Times Mirror Company was losing money: a total of $66.6 million for 1992, the first loss of the Los Angeles–based media megastar since 1964, when its stock was first listed on the New York Stock Exchange.

It seemed impossible that things could get worse, but in 1993 they did. As the rest of the nation showed signs of pulling out of the recession, California remained in free fall. Unemployment stood at 9.4 percent, the highest in the nation. More than 1.51 million Californians were out of work. (Even the city and county of San Francisco, an epicenter of public employee featherbedding, was talking of laying off fifteen hundred employees.) More than 19,500 California businesses failed that year, four times the rate of the nation. Business failures were up 73 percent over 1991 in Los Angeles, 23 percent in San Francisco. All in all, between May 1990 and April 1993, California lost an estimated 820,000 jobs. Forty percent of these were in aircraft, missiles, or defense electronics. Even more chilling was that up to a half million defense jobs were expected to be lost nationwide in the following two years, and 40 percent of these would be in California. By December 1992, California had accounted for 38 percent of all job losses in the United States since June 1990. Employer dissatisfaction, meanwhile, kept rising over such matters as high taxes and an inadequately educated and motivated workforce. Pacific Bell, among others, was complaining that six out of ten entry-level job applicants were failing examinations keyed to the seventh-grade level.

Commercial real estate continued to plummet, especially in Los Angeles. Even before the riots, the city had had a problem leasing the Japanese-, European-, and pension plan–financed skyscrapers that had been thrusting themselves toward the heavens throughout the 1980s. By August 1991, downtown office rents had sunk by as much as 25 percent, and building values had declined by up to 35 percent. The Dai-ichi Mutual Life Insurance Company had paid $530 per square foot in late 1989 for a quarter interest in the First Interstate World Center atop Bunker Hill, the tallest building west of Chicago. By August 1991, the going price had dropped to $400 per foot. Seven months after its opening, the 777 Tower on Figueroa Street was only one-third leased. Companies such as Dai-ichi, Mitsui Fudosan, and the Shuwa Group (which in and of itself had plowed nearly $2 billion into twenty-five Southern California properties) knew that they were in big and long-term trouble. "We've written off downtown for the next decade," pension investment advisor Sol Rabin of TCW Realty Advisors told the *Wall Street Journal.* "No one will make any money here."[3] By April 1993, California was leading the nation in commercial and residential foreclosures. Housing starts were down 30 percent. Not surprisingly, Robert Parry, president of the Western Regional Bank of the Federal Reserve Board in San Francisco, stated in March 1993 in testimony before the Senate Committee on Banking, Housing, and Urban Development that the current recession in California had been the longest and most severe since World War II. While states less dependent upon defense spending were rebounding, Parry noted, California remained in trouble.

"Can an entire state have an identity crisis?" asked the *Wall Street Journal* on November 16, 1993. "Yes—if it's California." The *Journal* was referring to Assembly Bill 3, sponsored by Assemblyman Stan Statham, a Republican from Shasta County in the northern Central Valley, that proposed to divide California into three states. AB 3 was passed by the assembly by a 48–27 vote on June 10, 1993, and was sent to the state senate. Given the wide margin of its passage in the assembly, there was some chance that AB 3 could win the senate. In the foreseeable future, Californians could be faced with the prospect of voting on the unthinkable—the division of the state into Southern, Central, and Northern California. Statham's bill, despite the fact that it went nowhere in the senate, underscored the fact that California itself seemed up for grabs. "Call it a crisis of identity," wrote Frederick Rose of AB 3 in the *Wall Street Journal* on November 16, "a psycho-economic complex. The nation's most populous state—now floundering in its fourth year of economic distress—is at odds with itself, with nearly 32 million people divided ever more visibly by region, race, language and economic fortune."

No one could be more dislocated than the unemployed—especially aerospace and defense workers, who had once believed that they had found lifetime security, and construction workers, who had harbored similar expectations, given the long building boom. In March 1993, the *Los Angeles Times* commenced a series called "Starting Over," which chronicled the efforts of the unemployed to recover from the shock of receiving pink slips. Not surprisingly, many, such as the Ebarb family of Yucaipa, a suburb of San Bernardino, decided to leave California altogether. Native Californians in their early thirties, Philip and Michelle Ebarb had met while working at a General Dynamics Corporation missile factory in 1987. A high school graduate with some college credits, Michelle was working as a lab technician. Philip, who had never finished high school, began his career at General Dynamics hoisting parts and materials. It was the good life: a joint income of $47,000 by 1989, weekend trips with the company ski club, Saturdays at the car races followed by a night of country and western music and dancing, Sunday mornings at the Green Valley Foursquare Church, and a day-to-day life in a funky 1920s clapboard house, where they lived with their one-year-old daughter Brianna—not bad for two blue-collar kids with limited educations.

Then came the pink slips. With her slight educational advantage, Michelle Ebarb got by as a temporary census employee, followed by a stint with a mortgage company, before landing an apprenticeship with the International Brotherhood of Electrical Workers paying seven dollars an hour—when there was work. Philip drove snow-grooming equipment at night at the Ski Hill resort thirty miles away for six dollars an hour, half his pay at General Dynamics. When the ski season ended, he found a spot stretching upholstery in a small nonunion factory making La-Z-Boy recliners. Philip had difficulty keeping up with his coworkers from Mexico and Central America, many of whom were undocumented. Fortunately, he was transferred to another job, building arms for the chairs at seven dollars an hour. On a good day, Philip Ebarb, Anglo American, a recently unionized employee, got to the point where he could finish more than two hundred arms, and thus keep pace with his immigrant colleagues.

Selling their home, the Ebarbs first moved in with Michelle's mother, then into a fourteen-foot trailer that they had, in better days, bought for family vacations. By January 1993, the Ebarbs had had it: had it with Michelle's intermittent employment and Philip's stoop labor at the La-Z-Boy factory, had it with life in the trailer park, had it with the gunfire they could hear at night and the police helicopters whirring overhead and the bullet casings found scattered on the playground of a nearby primary school. One day, at a local shopping center, Philip and Michelle watched two robbers shoot out the front window of a liquor store as they made their escape. For the Ebarbs, California was over.

Already the couple had been talking of moving to Alabama, where Michelle's sister Barbara and her husband lived. And so—in an ironic reversal of the migration of Steinbeck's migrants fifty-five years earlier— the Ebarbs, themselves of the same Anglo-American stock as the Joads, packed their belongings into a Ryder rental truck and headed east, "back-trailers," Hamlin Garland might call them, on the California border. "We know we are going to miss people here, Lord," Philip Ebarb prayed at a farewell luncheon (pizza on paper plates) at the Green Valley Foursquare Church before the family departed. "We thank you for the time we have spent in this place." In Alabama, Philip Ebarb found work driving a bull-dozer, but his employer demanded that he cut his shoulder-length hair and get rid of his earring.[4]

The Ebarbs left in a Ryder rental. More affluent émigrés hired movers. In 1992, Allied Van Lines and United Van Lines reported that 63 and 58 percent, respectively, of their California business was with clients leaving the state. Between 1990 and 1993, some 600,000 émigré Californians packed up and left. Many were young blue-collar workers such as the Ebarbs, but the majority tended to be white, educated, and high-wage earn-ers. They flooded into Washington, Oregon, Colorado, Arizona, Nevada, and Texas, creating real estate and retail booms and, in certain instances, instigating crises in suddenly overloaded local public school systems. Yup-pie émigrés—such as Brian Burns, a San Francisco attorney in his late twenties in 1992, or Paul Patterson, a psychotherapist in his mid-thirties from Camarillo—showed a strong attraction to Colorado. In the case of Burns and Patterson and the other 21,000 Californians who emigrated to Colorado in 1992, the motivation was not so much that they had lost a job at a defense plant as it was that as young urban professionals they were increasingly finding California, north, south or central, too crowded, too polluted, too competitive, too dangerous, and too expensive.

Despite the loss of these Californians, the state was not losing its overall population, although Los Angeles did decrease by 68,000 between 1991 and 1992, the single largest annual decline in the history of the city. Yet in 1992 alone California gained 654,000 residents, due in great part to the largest influx of foreign immigrants in twenty years. Documented immigra-tion increased by 22 percent between 1990 and 1991. There were no precise figures for the hundreds of thousands of undocumented immigrants, the bulk of them from Mexico and Central America. California was losing, however, many of its affluent retirees, many of its engineers and technicians, and the descendants or kin of those Dust Bowl folk who had migrated to California in the 1930s.

Those who remained in California, especially blue-collar workers and the lower rungs of the middle classes, found themselves in the grips of a constant and pervasive anxiety that had its origins in more than just the immediate crisis. The entire American economy had been in the process of globalizing and restructuring over the past decade. The industrial heartland had long since surrendered suzerainty to Asia or closed its plants entirely. Fewer and fewer Americans were pouring molten steel, assembling television sets, or making shoes, pants, or dresses, much less missiles and radar, and more and more were finding themselves squeezed out of good-paying union jobs into marginal employment.

Long-range economic forces were at work, and they were striking at the very core of well-being in an entire class of working Americans. Between 1947 and 1973, the median family income in the United States had doubled, from $17,765 to $35,474. Provided they were willing to work, Americans could now enjoy the good life. For the first time in industrial history, working people were functioning as primary consumers. Nowhere was this more true than in California, where entire suburbs sprung up—Newark, Union City, Hayward, and Vallejo in the north; Downey, Commerce, Lynwood, and Fontana in the south—designed to house and service working white people with high school degrees. The homes may have been smaller in these suburbs than those in Lafayette or Brentwood, and the shopping centers were not so lavish. But there were small swimming pools and barbecues in every backyard, a Ford or Chevrolet in the garage, and the kids were attending brand-new public schools; and their mothers were there when they got home, and dads were commuting no more than an hour a day to work, and violent crime was the exception, not the rule.

Then, in the 1970s, median family income began to stagnate, and it dipped during two recessions in the early 1980s. By January 1992 it stood at $35,353, $19 less than it had been eighteen years earlier. To maintain the same lifestyle, American households had long since had to have two incomes. Through the 1960s, only a quarter of American women with children had jobs outside the house; by January 1992, two-thirds of American mothers were working full-time. At this point, it was beginning to dawn on many—as a fear, if not a proven economic idea—that, if things continued the way they had been going the past eighteen years, even two working parents might not be able to make it in the future.

The pervasiveness of such fears in California represented a local instance of a national malaise; but because California had offered—and delivered—so much to working Americans during the go-go defense years, the malaise seemed to strike with a special force. The city of Fontana, an hour east of Los Angeles in San Bernardino County, was Southern California's one unambiguously blue-collar town, a onetime service center for citrus growers and chicken ranchers, jump-started into industrialism during World War II when Henry J. Kaiser built there the first comprehensive steel plant ever to be constructed in California. The plant had closed in 1983; but by that time Fontana had enjoyed forty years during which to evolve its own special version of blue-collar culture under the sunny skies of the Southland. In contrast to the beach towns of the coast or the cities that had grown up around hotels and resorts, Fontana was an unpretentious, even rough-and-ready, sort of a community, the birthplace of the Hells Angels, a town recently gentrified (but not too much) by an influx of younger families looking for housing bargains.

But as George H. W. Bush gave what turned out to be his last State of the Union message to Congress on January 27, 1992, Fontana had become an uneasy place—Kaiser gone, GM and IBM announcing layoffs—filled with working people fearful of the future: San Bernardino County deputy sheriff Marcia Mesa, for example, whose stepson and two daughters, in their twenties and high school graduates, were still living at home with her and her husband, a construction worker. "Even if they could get a job," Mesa complained, "they are $6–$7 an hour jobs. How are they going to have a car, pay for insurance, find a place to live? No way." Or Arlen van Vuren, an aircraft worker in his early thirties, who was commuting with his wife each morning to their jobs at Hughes Aircraft in Fullerton, forty-five miles away, where their shift began each morning at six a.m. Leaving their three-month-old daughter with a babysitter, the van Vurens would take their nine-year-old son with them to Fullerton, where he attended an elementary school near his grandmother's house. "I'm surviving," van Vuren noted of his life, "but what about my kids? The way it is now, the American Dream seems to be just for the rich."[5]

Turnaround

Throughout 1992 and 1993, Governor Pete Wilson, assembly speaker Willie Brown Jr., and senate president pro tem David Roberti led the effort to keep state government afloat across the two-year, $12 billion shortfall, an attempt that involved two late budgets and the issuing of state IOUs in lieu of checks. State treasurer Kathleen Brown led the campaign to keep the state's bond rating from further erosion on Wall Street. To do this, she insisted that it was time for California to take a come-to-Jesus look at its embattled economy and come up with a vision for the future.

Wilson, whom Brown would challenge in the next election, thoroughly agreed with the notion that California should rethink itself, economically at least. Already, on December 18, 1991, he had announced the Council on California Competitiveness, a sixteen-member panel of top representatives from business and labor chaired by Peter Ueberroth, the former baseball commissioner who enjoyed near-legendary status for his successful chairmanship of the 1984 Los Angeles Olympic Games. The report issued by the council on April 23, 1992, under the title "California's Jobs and Future," cannot be viewed as just another governmental report, to be filed and forgotten. It must be regarded as the Magna Carta of California's economic revival, which can be symbolically—and substantively—dated to its appearance. Somehow, this composite panel—Republican and Democrat; white, black, brown, and yellow; male and female; ranchers, labor leaders, corporate CEOs, and a sausage maker—saw to the center of California's economic dilemma and discerned the main pathways of recovery.

"A biting economic wind is blowing in California," the report opened poetically. "It brings with it a feeling of personal threat, broken promises and a sense of crisis. The economy is stagnating, while government appears immobilized." What was wrong with the California economy, besides the jobs being lost by the cutbacks in defense? Plenty. Small business, the true creator of wealth, was being "discouraged, harassed, shut-down, and driven off." Excessive regulation was making manufacturing near impossi-

ble. The state-sponsored workers' compensation system was a miasma of
fraud and abuse. The educational system was failing to prepare young men
and women for the modern workplace. California, in short, had grown lazy
and inefficient. What was needed was nothing less than the refounding of
the California economy, or better, its liberation into the future. Pervading all
the recommendations of the report—reform workers' compensation, clear
away the regulatory and bureaucratic jungle, encourage small businesses
and start-ups, bring a customer-service attitude to government, key education to the future economy—was a sense that one California was over and
another was struggling to be born.

In describing California as a bloated bureaucracy in the public sector
and much of the private as well, the Ueberroth report cogently expressed a
discontent that so many were feeling throughout the state. What was the use
of being California if it meant only to repeat on an even more deadly scale
the sins of the national government and economy? California had always
functioned best when it functioned as a trendsetter, a pacemaker, a creative
alternative. In the Ueberroth report, and in other venues as well, 1992
became the year of rethinking California through to first premises. Los
Angeles–based economic commentator Joel Kotkin, who had been almost
single-handedly waging a battle against California bashing over the previous two years, welcomed the report's optimistic tone, its bipartisanship,
and, most important, its refusal to overemphasize defense cutbacks and
business flights to other states as fatal, unbeatable causes of decline. Kotkin
also agreed with the emphasis on small businesses, believing that they were
already on the front line of the California comeback.

The Ueberroth report signaled that ideas, even difficult and challenging
ideas, were once again in good taste. Even such liberal observers as Werner
Hirsch, a retired economics professor at UCLA, believed that austerity and
cutbacks had their usefulness. The recession, Hirsch wrote, as painful as it
was, was forcing California to take up the long-overdue task of restructuring
itself. "After the recession," he argued in January 1992, "labor will be
more productive. We will be more competitive. The private sector will be
lean, and the public sector will also be more productive and responsive."
Paradoxically, Hirsch believed, this restructuring would bring California
forward into history by reconnecting it with the energies of the Earl
Warren–Goodwin J. Knight–Pat Brown era, 1942–66, in which California
tripled its population and extended the vision and practice of the good life
to millions of upwardly mobile Americans, native-born and immigrant
alike.[6]

Even in the megacorporate sector, as judged by the annual list of the
One Hundred Best Performing Companies in California, published by the

Los Angeles Times, corporate California was on the mend. Defense-oriented companies no longer dominated the list (although Northrop still ranked fortieth, and Lockheed remained, barely, in the money at number ninety-two), but a new California economy—organized around computers, entertainment, food products, financial services, insurance, banking, pharmaceuticals, and retail conglomerates—was not only in the making; it had already arrived. A state in which Frederick's of Hollywood, purveyors of exotic lingerie, could rank among the most profitable enterprises in the apparel industry—and which also included the Gap, Mattel Toys, the Walt Disney Company, the Good Guys, Williams-Sonoma—was a state that had more than defense on its economic agenda. When it came to ranking absolute profits, moreover, California—with Chevron in first place, Bank of America in second, followed by such behemoths as Pacific Gas & Electric, Pacific Telesis Group, Hewlett-Packard, and Occidental Petroleum—still had more than its fair share of old-fashioned megacorporations, many of them on the comeback trail (as were Occidental, Advanced Micro Devices, Genentech, and Atari), now doing business in a new-fashioned way and creating profits and jobs.

The renewed vitality of the 1993 economy was evident in the fact that the top-ranked company in the *Los Angeles Times* list of one hundred for that year, Total Pharmaceutical Care of Torrance, was only now making its first appearance on the list and had completed its initial public stock offering just two years earlier. Companies ranking in the top twenty-five in both absolute profits and profit margins showed a healthy mix of oil and gas, banking, public utilities, entertainment, department stores, insurance, clothing, financial services, medical equipment, computers (always and increasingly, computers), and defense. Intel Corporation of Santa Clara, the world's largest semiconductor company, had soared—and this in 1992—to more than $24 billion in value.

At Newport Beach that summer a meeting of the California Business–Higher Education Forum—an annual assembly of university and college presidents and CEOs from the private sector, founded by UC president Jack Peltason—heard treasurer Kathleen Brown fine-tune her economic and governmental restructuring remarks of the previous year. By now something approaching a California consensus had emerged, as could be seen from the fact that Brown's and Wilson's analysis and programs were 90 percent identical, an overlap that would prove troublesome to Brown one year later when she challenged Wilson for the governorship. The recession had driven most of public and private life toward a reforming center, although, as usual, the Democratic and Republican Party machineries were each controlled by the ideologically intense wings of their constituencies.

The Perceptronics Company of Woodland Hills was getting serious, for one thing—and in a most revealing way. Seven years earlier, Perceptronics was making high-tech army tank simulator modules designed to train tank crews. By 1993 it was using the same technology to manufacture simulators designed to train truck drivers. Defense conversion was asserting itself. Northrop had just signed an agreement with a Canadian company to build light-rail cars for the Metro Green Line in Los Angeles County. But so also were emerging new ways of doing defense business. The Whittaker Corporation of Los Angeles, a small, embattled defense contractor averaging $160 million in annual revenue, had recently acquired the equally embattled Dowty Avionics, a manufacturer of electronic submarine detectors based in Arcadia, and Ocean Technology, a Burbank-based supplier of parts for Trident submarines. With some restructuring, these three companies, now unified, were emerging as continuing competitors for the defense dollar. All in all, some one thousand or so small contracting firms in Southern California were in the process of such mergers or realignments. Former suppliers, even bottom feeders, were now networking, forming partnerships, or merging assets. As the *Los Angeles Times* pointed out on December 26, 1993, the defense industry in Southern California—with more than three hundred thousand jobs, the state's biggest manufacturing employer— was down, but not out.

Aerospace brainpower was not about to migrate from Southern California. Although there were only three large aircraft assembly lines still in operation—the F/A-18 Northrop plant in El Segundo, the B-2 Northrop facility in Pico Rivera and Palmdale, and the C-17 McDonnell Douglas factory in Long Beach—the research, development, design, and engineering of aircraft remained solidly centered in the Southland. Planes might be assembled elsewhere by blue-collar workers, but Southern California would do the brainwork. Even under the worst-case scenario, the consulting firm of McKinsey & Company predicted in a 1993 report to the Los Angeles Chamber of Commerce, "the aerospace industry will continue to be an important factor in California's economy, supporting over 700,000 direct and indirect jobs."[7]

This good news also brought some bad news: Southern California, which had the highest dependence on defense industries, was lagging slightly behind the recovery rate of the rest of the state; and California, having the greatest dependency on defense of any state in the nation, was lagging slightly behind the recovery rate of the nation. Within Southern California, the recovery rate of Los Angeles County, which had the highest dependence on defense in Southern California, was lagging slightly behind the recovery rate of the rest of the Southland. In each instance, the more the dependence upon defense, the slower the recovery. Still, movement was in the right direction.

Even émigrés were returning, having found that California was not that bad a place after all. U-Haul Corporation was announcing that outbound rentals exceeded inbound rentals by a mere 1 percent during the one-year period ending March 31, 1993, down from a high of 15.3 percent in 1990. Fed up with San Diego, Janet and Tom Wing had sold their home in August 1992 and moved to Coeur d'Alene in northern Idaho, population 29,000. Within a few weeks, they were asking themselves: "Where's the theater? The symphony? The Chinese takeout? How much country-fried steak and mashed potatoes can a person eat?" Reading the daily newspaper, Janet Wing counted seven or eight pages of ads for firewood, four to six pages for livestock, and six to eight pages for firearms. Within two years, the Wings went back to San Diego.[8]

Shortly after their return, California, like the rest of the nation, was heading toward full recovery. Even McDonnell Douglas, at ground zero of the embattled aerospace industry, was reporting a record net profit of $142 million in the third quarter of 1993. Oracle was announcing an alliance with Bell Atlantic. In Southern California, reported the *Economist* on January 15, 1994, the six most common family names among home buyers were Lee, Nguyen, Garcia, Rodriguez, Martinez, and Wong. As defense cutbacks continued, however, it now became northern California's turn to absorb the hits. The closure of the Mare Island Naval Yard, the Alameda Naval Air Station, Fort Ord on the Monterey Peninsula, and numerous other military, medical, and supply operations loomed on the horizon.

On the other hand, northern California also had Silicon Valley, and by 1994 it was apparent to everyone that the California economy had recovered itself in this region. Just a year or two back, most talk of economic recovery centered on aerospace. In 1993, however, Hewlett-Packard saw its sales surge to $21.4 billion. Only Chevron, a traditional oil and natural gas company, showed higher sales. Electronic start-ups, meanwhile, were flourishing. In 1989, Solectron, a manufacturer of computer circuit boards, was reporting sales of $140 million; in 1994, five short years later, it had reached the billion-dollar mark and was operating subsidiaries in France, Scotland, Malaysia, North Carolina, and Washington State.

Certain key categories of reform, which had been put forth two years earlier by the Ueberroth committee and which by now possessed the stability of a statewide consensus, remained open questions. The public infrastructure of California continued to languish, with only 5 percent of the state's budget being allocated to highways, water systems, and educational plants. According to the Research Bureau of the State Library, California now ranked forty-sixth among the fifty states in the per capita value of its infrastructure stock, and forty-ninth in the average annual growth rate of its infrastructure investments. The workforce remained dangerously unprepared for the new economy, and most new businesses—highly competitive start-ups with budgets on the razor's edge—were stating their reluctance to embark on expensive training programs to augment a weak educational system. "Jobs are getting more and more complex," noted Susan Daniel, vice president for human resources at the Sunnyvale-based Advanced Micro Devices, "and they require more thinking, reasoning and organizational skills, but we are just not seeing that in graduates. We just see too many people who don't have the basics." Within the year, in 1995, California would be sinking $30 billion into its K–12 system.[9]

Quality-of-life issues, another emphasis in the Ueberroth report, continued to prove troublesome. Affordable housing remained at a premium; a 1992 study by the California Senate Republican Caucus had argued that the cost of housing relative to wage levels was twice as high as the national median. The California Business Roundtable reported that an estimated 82 percent of major employers were citing the high cost of housing as having a negative effect on their businesses. Violent crime continued to soar; and this above every other factor, whether taken as a matter of statistics or perception, tarnished the state's reputation and determined the attitudes of voters.

Nevertheless, the economic comeback continued, spearheaded and stimulated in significant measure by Governor Wilson. As controversial as he might be regarding certain issues—aid to illegal immigrants and affirmative action, for instance—Wilson's performance as architect and enabler of California's economic recovery was a tour de force of leadership, governmental reform, and salesmanship to the private sector (including trips by Wilson to the East Coast, where he personally recruited companies to California and argued the state's case for economic recovery to the New York–based financial press). By October 1995, for the first time in more than four years, California was creating jobs at a faster pace than the nation. As recently as April 1993, job growth had been 3.2 percentage points below the national rate, and now economist Howard Roth was predicting a 6.1 percent rise in personal income throughout the state for 1995. In November 1995, *Forbes* magazine trumpeted the California comeback: "*Forbes* was among the first to note that California was committing economic suicide," wrote business journalist Tim Ferguson. "We are happy to be among the first to report that things are finally looking up in the Sunshine State." Most important, Ferguson noted, "For what may be the first time since World War II, California isn't growing on steroids. Neither Pentagon spending nor tax-and-inflation bred real estate expansion is leading the recovery."

An important factor in the recovery, Ferguson argued, was the fact that state government was finally getting its act together. Workers' compensation was being tightened up. No longer could a worker go out on disability because 10 percent of his job was causing him stress. The legislature had softened its 6 percent tax on the purchase of new equipment by allowing that sum to be deducted against corporate income taxes. This alone had made some $500 million available for reinvestment purposes. In Southern California, the Air Quality Management District had lifted its van and car-pooling requirements, which had proved so onerous to start-ups and mid-size companies. Silicon Valley—where $450 million in venture capital had been invested in the second quarter of 1995 alone, $100 million more than had ever been invested before in a comparable period—continued to enjoy the lowest ratio of public-to-private-sector workers in the nation, setting a model for competitive government for the rest of the state.

Film and television production, which had been doubling in receipts every five years for the past two decades, now accounted for 15 percent of the $238 billion Los Angeles County economy. In Burbank, Warner Brothers had just announced an $800 million expansion program for its studios and the tripling of its local payroll over the next twenty years. On the small-business front, forty-three of the two hundred best small companies in America, as selected by *Forbes,* were in California, nearly three times as many as any other state. Even Wilford "Woody" Godbold Jr., CEO of the Los Angeles–based Zero Corporation, the man who in 1991 had closed his Burbank plant and sent four hundred jobs to Utah, had stopped complaining. His workers' compensation costs down 25 percent, his permit approvals from the Air Quality Management District coming in record time (two months, as opposed to a year or more), Godbold and Zero were happy and hiring. "There's been a change," Godbold told *Forbes,* "in how we see job creation in California."[10]

Immigrants to the Rescue

Very quickly it was becoming apparent that economic recovery was significantly in the hands of California's recent immigrants—an irony not lost on a state that had lately been so busy about the business of immigrant bashing. No one could be happier regarding this newfound awareness than a small but ultimately prophetic band of revivalists who were resisting the notion—precisely because of its immigrants—that California was an economic basket case. The group included Joel Kotkin of Pepperdine University, Los Angeles attorney and business writer David Friedman, and economists Dennis Macheski of the Yarmouth Group, David Hensley of Salomon Brothers, and Stephen Levy of the Center for the Continuing Study of the California Economy in Palo Alto. What united these commentators was a resistance to the growing *Blade Runner* scenario of the neo-Marxist Los Angeles School of academic commentators and others which saw Southern California, Los Angeles especially, in a state of de-evolution toward a future of polyglot helotry and lost quality of life.

To counter the *Blade Runner* image, Kotkin and Friedman, who in the fall of 1992 formed New Visions, a nonprofit regional think tank, began to formulate a counterscenario in which California, Southern California especially, was rebuilding itself through start-ups and small and midsize businesses, many of them owned and operated by immigrants. As early as March 1992, as California was showing signs of a growing anti-immigrant, antiforeign investment phobia, Kotkin and Friedman outspokenly defended foreign investment in California—such as the recent anxiety-producing major investment (or was it a quasi takeover?) in McDonnell Douglas by Taiwanese interests, and the growing Japanese participation in the film industry and Southern California real estate—on the basis that not only did California need the capital, these offshore investors, Japan and Taiwan especially, were important consumers of the goods and services produced by California's three largest industries: agriculture, aerospace/high tech, and tourism. Two-thirds of all citrus consumed in Japan, Kotkin pointed out as one of many examples, came from the giant California-based Sunkist Cooperative; and Japanese tourists were spending almost $1 billion each year in the state.

On the local, even micro level, Kotkin was arguing in April 1994, immigrants were spearheading the revival of the California economy through small or midsize involvement in the food-processing, textile, electronic components, medical equipment, and software industries. In Silicon Valley, roughly one in three engineers were immigrants. In Orange County, electronic manufacturers depended so heavily on Vietnamese technicians that one Anglo executive claimed that he was setting up an affirmative action program for people whose first language was not Vietnamese. Nowhere was the immigrant-driven recovery more noticeable, Kotkin averred, than in Southern California, a recovery apparent in such enterprises as California Capital, founded in 1989 by the Espinoza family to make loans to Hispanic home buyers. Organized in 1988 by six Chinese immigrants, Kingston Technologies, a manufacturer of computer components, was by 1994 showing sales approaching $1 billion annually and employing a three-hundred-person workforce that included immigrants from at least twenty different countries. By 1994 there were more than twelve hundred Chinese-owned computer firms in Southern California.

Nor were Mexican Americans absent from this entrepreneurial picture. In Los Angeles, Richard Gomez and Jose Sahagun, owners and operators of Transportes InterCalifornias, were by October 1997 bringing in revenues of some $3 million a year, transporting five hundred passengers daily by bus from metro Los Angeles to the Mexican border. Out in Pacoima, Miguel DeLeon, owner of DeLeon Enterprises, Inc., a manufacturer of custom electronics, was recalling with satisfaction that day in 1994 when, forced to oversee the closure of a defense manufacturing firm where he was quality-control manager, he had decided instead to buy the company with help from a nonprofit business development agency and move it in a new direction. In January 1998, twenty-eight employees had jobs at DeLeon Enterprises, and annual sales were pushing $2 million.

It was precisely to help such Latino start-ups that Daniel Villanueva and Guillermo Bron launched the Bastion Capital Fund in June 1994. Cited by *Hispanic Business* magazine as the eleventh richest Latino in the United States, Villanueva, a native of Calexico on the California-Mexico border, the ninth of twelve children in a tightly knit immigrant family, had graduated from New Mexico State University, then joined the Los Angeles Rams as a placekicker while also doing a five-day-a-week newscast in Spanish and weekend newscasts in English for KNBC-TV. In 1968, Villanueva left pro football for full-time involvement and an equity position in Spanish-language television. His station, KMEX-TV, was sold to Hallmark Cards and First Chicago Venture Capital for $301 million in 1987 and became the anchor station of the newly formed Univision television network. Villanueva decided to go into the business of helping other Latinos move into the entrepreneurial class by creating an $80 million venture capital fund aimed in their direction. His partner in this venture, Costa Rica–born Guillermo Bron, a graduate in electrical engineering from MIT with an MBA from Harvard, had earned his spurs doing thirty-two corporate finance transactions at the Los Angeles branch of Drexel Burnham Lambert for an aggregate value of $4 billion.

None of the companies Villanueva and Bron helped finance, or the thousands and thousands of other similar enterprises—with the notable exception of Kingston Technologies—were especially impressive, if one judged merely from gross sales and the bottom line. Taken cumulatively, however, these immigrant companies were moving California in a new direction. California, David Friedman argued, had become captive to a technocratic definition of itself that held that two enterprises—large aerospace and publicly held computer companies—accounted for the essential vitality of its economy. When the cold war ended and aerospace came under threat, California seemed doomed to a low-tech, low-wage service or menial assembly economy. Not true, Friedman rejoined. Only 5 percent of California's economy, it should be repeated, had ever been defense dependent. And as far as computer, other high-tech, or biotech companies were concerned, the publicly owned megacompany was the exception, not the rule. Most Californians employed in the high-tech or biotech industry worked for smaller, privately held enterprises. Small to midscale manufacturing, meanwhile, was employing hundreds of thousands of workers and producing billions of dollars in income.[11]

Why were such companies not being recognized? The problem came, Friedman argued, from the fact that university theorists and other opinion makers downgraded such enterprises or cavalierly dismissed them as unable to create wealth. Fixated on mega-enterprises, so many of them defense related, and unable to see the value or present vitality of manufacturing and service industry employment, economists and other business commentators quite naturally veered toward apocalyptic scenarios and jeremiads when the defense industries came under assault. When the world they best understood—megacompanies with links to the universities and big-ticket research and development companies—became embattled, establishment-oriented business analysts remained blind to the small-scale renewal all around them. Academics might denigrate service industries, but for immigrants working for, say, Smith Friday Enterprises of Los Angeles (a janitorial service company cofounded in 1982 by Errol Smith, a Harlem-born son of Afro-Caribbean immigrants), the jobs created by providing building maintenance services to smaller office, retail, and industrial facilities across Southern California constituted the bright beginning of their California dream.

It was perhaps the pervasive presence of this new economy, as Kotkin and Friedman described it, that gave such poignancy to the announcement in November 1997 that the San Francisco–based Levi Strauss & Company was closing eleven plants—in Arkansas, Tennessee, Texas, and New Mexico—and laying off 6,395 unionized workers. For better or for worse, California had by now made a transition in its economy to the point that there were few such unionized workers in manufacturing enterprises left for downsizing companies such as Levi Strauss to cut. And those who were left were vulnerable, such as the eighteen thousand unionized employees at the Hughes Aircraft plants in El Segundo and Fullerton. The facilities had been acquired by Raytheon in December 1997 at the height of the revival of the California economy, only for workers to learn less than a month later that the new owner would be eliminating an estimated five thousand to ten thousand jobs in its defense and aerospace operations nationwide, including many of their own. It was déjà vu all over again, as these last employees of a prior California economy at long last came under the knife.

By January 1998, Los Angeles and Orange Counties had recovered some 11,500 aerospace jobs since the low point of the fall of 1995. As the 1990s came to an end, there were some 203,000 aerospace workers in the two counties—a not inconsiderable workforce. On the other hand, restructuring and its inevitable consequence, job loss, showed signs of continuing. The Raytheon cutback not only meant the possible loss of some 5,200 jobs in Southern California, but also the elimination of an equal number of positions—perhaps even as many as 7,800—among second- and third-tier aerospace suppliers. Lockheed Martin was negotiating an $11.6 billion purchase of the Los Angeles–based Northrop Grumman, which might mean further job cuts. The Douglas Products division of Boeing in Long Beach was still manufacturing the MD-80 and the MD-90 jetliners, but what would happen when these projects were completed? Would Boeing produce its hundred-seat 717 (formerly the MD-95) in Long Beach or seek a more competitive labor situation?

For the rest of the decade, the debate continued. Had the new economy led California into new realms of job-creating entrepreneurialism, or, as far as jobs for ordinary Californians were concerned, was the state rapidly becoming one vast sweatshop of immigrant labor? In July 1996, the Public Policy Institute of California, a San Francisco–based think tank endowed in

1994 by computer magnate William Hewlett, issued a study asserting that the gap between rich and poor was wider in California than in the rest of the nation and was growing. The causes for this gap, the study asserted, included a decline in unionization, the erosion of the value of the minimum wage, the increasing numbers of the population unemployable in high-technology industries—and loss of the jobs to low-wage countries.

Swords into Ploughshares

For many—most notably national, state, and local Democrats—the answer to aerospace cutbacks was defense conversion: the beating, as was so often stated, of swords into ploughshares. California, it should be remembered, had faced a similar challenge after World War II; indeed, as early as 1944, a special commission appointed by Governor Earl Warren was already at work exploring civilian uses for the state's shipyards, aircraft factories, and other defense-related industries. *Los Angeles Times* business columnist James Flannigan made a specialty of covering the conversion of defense industries to peacetime uses. In October 1992, Congress appropriated $1.7 billion to assist areas whose economies had been damaged by military base closures and defense contract cutbacks. If California were to receive its fair share of these funds, Flannigan reported, $336 million would eventually be available for defense conversion and military base reuse programs.

Indeed, as early as November 1992, Los Angeles County received a $5.6 million grant from the Department of Commerce to assist conversion programs. In a speech given that same month in Anaheim entitled "Defense Technologies to Reignite American Competitiveness," C. Michael Armstrong, the recently appointed chairman of Hughes Aircraft, led the first wave of the defense conversion rally. "We can turn military air defense into civil air traffic control," Armstrong exhorted. "Sensors that warn of chemical warfare can be used to detect pollutants; signal processing can yield digital telephone systems; cruise control radars and infra-red night vision can lead to automotive safety systems."[12]

Even as Armstrong was speaking, certain companies, such as the Leach Corporation of Orange County (five hundred workers, annual revenues of $50 million), were successfully making the transition. By September 1992, Leach, which had previously done 70 percent of its business supplying aerospace components to the Pentagon, was making 65 percent of its sales to nondefense customers, most notably civilian aircraft manufacturers.

Aside from an obvious turn to that area, the first wave of defense conversion discussion centered upon a series of ambitious proposals to redirect aerospace toward the design and manufacture of high-speed rail and electric cars, buses, and trains. By March 1992, Northrop, Lockheed, McDonnell Douglas, Hughes Aircraft, and Teledyne were each seriously considering major conversions to commuter rail. Such vehicles, after all, resembled aircraft.

In the second wave of conversion, entrepreneurs and theorists turned to the adaptation of defense technologies for medical equipment. Natel Engineering of Chatsworth, which had previously manufactured electronic components for Stinger anti-aircraft missiles, turned under the guidance of its Indian-born CEO Sudesh Arora to the making of heart pacemakers and implantable defibrillators. While still continuing to do some missile work, Natel also supplemented its medical devices with electronics for space satellites, computer workstations, and telecommunications equipment. By February 1996, Natel was employing more workers than it had at the height of its defense contracts. Experts Systems (XXsys) Technologies of San Diego had previously specialized in ultrasound testing for composite materials in the manufacturing of military aircraft wings. Under the direction of its chairwoman, Gloria Ma, a PhD in molecular biology from UC San Diego, XXsys turned to the analysis of damaged highway structures, and the company flourished in the post-1994 earthquake-driven highway and bridge retrofitting boom.

By 1997, some defense-converted companies were, ironically, finding their way back to military contracts. Illusion Inc. of Westlake Village was a spin-off of a defense company that had manufactured tank training simulators before shifting to such high-tech virtual reality entertainment attractions as the Grand Prix Racing Center at the Sahara Hotel and Casino in Las Vegas. By October 1997, Illusion, together with similar companies like Viewpoint DataLabs, Paradigm Simulation, and Cinebase Software, was back in dialogue with the Department of Defense on a number of simulator training projects.

Like everything else, defense conversion had its critics, especially in the Kotkin-Friedman wing of economic analysts and forecasters, who considered it a federally funded boondoggle designed to stabilize and keep in place, as far as possible, the cold war cozy accommodations among subsidized corporations, federal bureaucrats, unions, and their journalist and academic champions. For such critics, a better model was already at work in the smaller to midsize companies that, without federal subsidy, were responding to new markets: companies such as Rotary Technologies in Gardena, which had shifted from tool work for military aircraft to civilian auto-

mobiles; or Fadal Engineering in the San Fernando Valley, which had made
a similar transition without federal subsidy and was now outperforming its
nearest Japanese competitor.

But even critics of defense conversion had to admit that base closures
provided a challenge that could not immediately be met by small to midsize entrepreneurial enterprises. As University of North Carolina historian
Roger Lotchkin so vividly demonstrated in *Fortress California* (1990), the
very pattern of urban-suburban density in California had been shaped not
only by shipyards and aerospace but by the very locations of these defense
installations. Sacramento, despite its being the state capital since the 1860s,
had remained a minor agricultural market town until such behemoths as the
Mather, McClellan, and Travis Air Force Bases and the Sacramento Army
Depot helped boom the metro region past the one million mark by the
1990s. For a half century and more, California had been a Gibraltar on the
Pacific; now, beginning with the first base closures in 1993, not only an era
but for many thousands of Californians an entire way of life was ending.

The closure of Fort Ord on the Monterey Peninsula meant not only the
loss of 16,500 jobs for that job-scarce region but the loss of a dominant
civic institution. The shutdown of Norton and George Air Force Bases in
San Bernardino County cost more than the twelve thousand jobs that were
lost, or even the 48,000 that might also eventually vanish in the multiplier
effect; it meant also the loss of the core industry of the county for the rest of
the decade. And even the San Francisco Bay Area—for all the diversification of its economy, for all the vitality of Silicon Valley and the city of San
Francisco as a financial center—could not help but be severely impacted in
certain sectors of its economy by the closure of a ring of defense installations: Moffett Field in Sunnyvale, the Presidio and Hunters Point in San
Francisco, Treasure Island Naval Air Station, the Alameda Naval Air Station, the Oakland Navy Supply Center, and the Mare Island Naval Shipyard.
Thousands of blue-collar and lower- to midmanagement jobs would now be
lost to the Bay Area: it was the social, economic, and psychological equivalent of the jobs being lost in Southern California to the aerospace cutbacks
and closures.

The Bay Area would continue to thrive, but increasingly at only the
most competitive and global levels. The region would mint millionaires by
the dozen in Silicon Valley. Nor would other aspects of the immigrant-
entrepreneurial world so favored by Friedman and Kotkin be lost. As with
Southern California, the Bay Area likewise enjoyed a vibrant, immigrant-
driven economy of small to midsize businesses. What would be lost, however—in the city of Vallejo especially—was a way for working whites and
a smaller number of blue-collar minorities to enjoy the good life. The soon-

to-close naval shipyard at Mare Island off the city of Vallejo had been in operation since 1852. During World War II, more than forty thousand men and women had found work there. In September 1993, officials in Vallejo were talking desperately, without much conviction, of the economic potential of converted military golf courses and a bed-and-breakfast industry in former military housing.

By June 1994, the Defense Department had scheduled eighteen military bases for closure and four for serious downsizing or realignment. As in the case of the aerospace cutbacks, these moves would cost up to 250,000 civilian jobs. Altogether, California would experience a loss of 70 percent of all positions lost in the nation due to base closures. As with aerospace, these figures only further emphasized to what extraordinary degree contemporary California had been created by military spending during the cold war.

The Defense Base Closure and Realignment Act of 1990 governed the process whereby California closed its eighteen installations. By 1993, the Defense Base Closure and Realignment Commission had made its recommendations for the state. Over the next five years, an alphabet soup of joint authority commissions, funded by millions of federal dollars, struggled with the problem of transforming vast acreages, millions of square feet of buildings, long-standing employment patterns, and established economies to postdefense uses. The easiest option was realignment. Thus the March Air Force Base Joint Powers Commission, faced with the challenge of recycling its facility in Riverside County, after some discussion of civilian uses began to court Marine Corps aviation units scheduled to leave the Miramar Air Station in San Diego. Most proposals for former air force bases moved at a snail's pace toward a civilian adaptation of existing facilities. Once a home to B-52 bombers, Mather Air Force Base outside Sacramento was in March 1997 a struggling civilian air cargo and private aircraft hub.

An even easier option, taking far less time and reestablishing some cash flow, was the commercial leasing of vacant defense properties to private companies. Some of this leasing was short-term, even haphazard, as commissions responsible for a facility showed themselves anxious to reestablish cash flow. Vallejo rapidly leased 700,000 square feet (out of the 10.5 million square feet available) on Mare Island to tenants paying as little as fifteen cents a square foot. Pacific Bell, encouraged by the fact that fiberoptic phone lines were already in place, leased a terminal half the size of a football field at Castle Air Force Base in Merced County for a four-hundred-job customer service message center. In May 1997, Packard Bell NEC was employing 3,800 workers at the former Sacramento Army Depot.

In general, however, results were mixed. By the millennium, no one could honestly say that a uniform picture of positive base transformation had emerged in the state that had absorbed nearly two-thirds of all national base closures. True, the California State University was in the process of transforming the buildings of Fort Ord into a college campus, the Presidio of San Francisco was en route to becoming a hybrid national park and real estate development, and there were definite successes, like Mather and Castle Air Force Bases. But the picture remained confused, despite the millions of dollars being spent on conversion efforts. It was not so easy for California to leave one world and enter another—at least as far as its military bases were concerned—within a single decade.

By this point, the entire question of the decline of the defense industry—the closure of bases, the loss of jobs, the conversion or recycling of bases and industries—was verging on the passé. Such was the prodigality of the new California economy. Many had been claiming all along that defense spending had been in decline relative to the California GNP long before the end of the cold war. The ultimate destiny of California, such critics had argued, was not the static condition of federally subsidized industries producing wasteful weaponry for a cold war that was becoming increasingly irrelevant. California was much too dynamic a society to depend forever on such a vassal relationship to the federal defense establishment. It was time to reinvent the California economy: time to beat swords into ploughshares.

The Comeback Kid

By 1997, California was talking about itself in a manner radically different from the discourse of four years earlier. That summer, as its economy reached (and perhaps passed) the trillion-dollar mark, the Center for Continuing Study of the California Economy released a report predicting that the state, outpacing the nation, would be racking up double-digit growth in jobs, income, and population over the next ten years. "It is hard to think of a high-growth sector in which California is not an industry leader," noted Stephen Levy, coauthor of the report.[13] In October 1997, Governor Wilson signed a package of tax cuts passed by the assembly and the senate in the previous month, with just two dissenting votes, that would return nearly $1 billion in taxes to the taxpayer in 1999. At the beginning of the decade, in the first three years of his administration, Wilson and the legislature, faced with a 40 percent falloff in tax revenues, had been unable to pay the bills. Now, sitting outdoors at a temporary desk in a cul-de-sac in the 1950s-era bedroom community of Temple City east of Los Angeles, the governor signed a tax cut intended, he noted, for the working people of the state. A *Los Angeles Times* poll taken the following month revealed that most residents believed that California—Southern California especially—was heading in the right direction. Most interesting, given the antibusiness attitudes noted in April 1992 by the Ueberroth report, most of those polled believed that California was now a good place to do business.

In late December 1997, the California Employment Development Department released statistics showing that the jobless rate had in November fallen to a seven-year low of 5.8 percent. In November alone seventy thousand Californians had found work. In December, the Employment Development Department later reported, another 40,600 jobs were created. All in all, California now enjoyed 800,000 more jobs than it had in 1990 when the recession began. Even real estate was improving, noted the *Los Angeles Times,* for the first time since 1990. By the end of 1997, home prices in Southern California had regained a third of the value they had lost earlier in the decade. The number of home owners forced to sell at a loss had been cut in half. Mortgage defaults were down for the first time in the decade. There was also a 1.3 percent growth in population, due, in part, to more people moving to California and fewer moving out.

What was driving this recovery? It was certainly not defense, nor even defense conversion technologies. As important as the latter might have been, they were still in the developmental stages. Redirected military bases were not a factor; most conversion efforts, with a few exceptions, were still in the planning phases. It was, rather, the diversity and entrepreneurial nature of the economy that was making California the Comeback Kid. The state still had its large corporations, but the boom was coming from other sectors: computers, entertainment, apparel, agribusiness, tourism, and exports, much of it organized on a smaller scale. California had returned, in short, back to the future: to the mixed economy it had evolved in the pre–World War II era. Computer technology and biotechnology now surpassed aviation in the formula; but California, as it had sixty and more years earlier, had returned to a balance of industries. It had also become a transportation, shipping, and receiving hub for the entire nation. The importance of the California comeback was that it offered the rest of the country a paradigm of a multifaceted inclusive economy rather than one based upon overreliance on any one industry.

Most exhilarating, perhaps, was the resurgence of the entertainment business. The industry, after all, had played a key role in defining twentieth-century California in the first place. Even at the depth of the recession, in 1991, motion pictures were seemingly recession proof. As in the case of the Great Depression, Americans craved, rather than forswore, entertainment in hard times. In the fall of 1991 nearly fifty new screens were added to the eight hundred already in existence in Los Angeles and Orange Counties. Altogether in 1990 and 1991, more than one hundred new screens were added throughout Southern California. Between 1993 and 1996, jobs in the movie industry increased by 40 percent. The decade opened with some 143,000 people in Greater Los Angeles working in films. By 1998, the figure had reached 262,000, which represented an 83 percent increase since 1991. And these figures did not include up to fifty thousand affiliated jobs— in multimedia, the record industry, film promotion and advertising, and theme parks—nor the numbers of lawyers, accountants, caterers, and the like dependent on motion picture and television production for their incomes. The Southern California–based entertainment industry showed every sign of being a $40 billion annual business by 2000.

As a matter of people and places, entertainment was moving into the terrain and social structures of aerospace. As the boom developed and continued, the industry initially repossessed or refurbished existing studio spaces in Hollywood and other parts of Los Angeles and Santa Monica. The Hollywood Center Studios off Santa Monica Boulevard were refitted with more than twenty miles of cable and fiber-optic wires linking up to four thousand computers. Seventy years earlier, Warner Brothers had crossed the Santa Monica Mountains into Burbank, where its studios and, later, the studios of NBC television, existed side by side with Lockheed, Weber Aircraft, Pacific Airmotive, and hundreds of other affiliated businesses through a simultaneous golden age of aviation-aerospace and motion pictures. With the pullback in aerospace, Burbank witnessed both its real estate infrastructure and many of its workers subsumed by an equal variety of companies—Outside Sunrise Sets, Innovative Design Technologies, Lexington Scenery & Props, CenterStaging, Preferred Media, Shades of Light Studios—serving one or another aspect of the movie and television explosion. Former aerospace buildings, for one thing, were low-lying and spacious. Many of them were well wired or, if not, did not offer significant obstacles to the high-tech rewiring that was now so vital to a digital-based entertainment industry.

As Burbank filled up, the entertainment industry edged eastward into Glendale and westward into West Los Angeles and Santa Monica. In the West Los Angeles area alone, more than one million square feet of industrial space was being devoted to film production and related businesses by January 1997. Later that year, the industry—in this instance, a partnership between Shamrock Holdings of Burbank, owned by the Roy E. Disney family, and FN/Flesch & Neuhauser of Los Angeles—reached the coast of dreams itself when construction commenced on the $77 million Manhattan Beach Studios project: 550,000 square feet divided into fourteen soundstages, an office building, a commissary, and parking for eighteen hundred cars, all of it equaling, if not surpassing, the glory days of studio construction.

The industry iself was flying past aerospace at the speed of sound in the growing intricacy of its corporate arrangements. No aerospace company— not Hughes, not Lockheed, not McDonnell Douglas, not Northrop, even at the height of the cold war—approached the comprehensive corporate power represented in the purchase, in late July 1995, of Capital Cities/ABC by the Walt Disney Company for $19 billion in cash and stock. The leading television distributor in the nation, the leading television network, and the leading producer of movies were now one company, with combined annual sales of $20.7 billion. The entire industry, in fact, was consolidating itself at the top. Viacom International owned Paramount Pictures, MTV, and Blockbuster Entertainment. Rupert Murdoch's News Corporation owned the Fox TV Network, 20th Century Fox, and a string of newspapers. Time Warner owned Warner Brothers, Time-Life Publishing, and the largest music company in the United States. For nearly sixty years, the Department of Justice had been fighting such vertical integration in entertainment but had lately relented. Congress was now allowing film, television, publishing, recording, cable, and satellite distribution entities to be coalesced under single ownership.

Was this sheer fatigue on the part of the federal government? Or a realization, proceeding at the profoundest levels of techno-social revolution, that the antitrust notions of another era were impossible to impose on industries that were becoming increasingly unified through digitalization and electronic transmission? Newspapers were now published on the Internet hours before their printing presses rolled. Joint Internet and television news programs had made their debut. Ahead lay the possibility that all this integrated media might be fused with telephone technology so that a single line into a single home attached to a single, as yet vaguely defined, device would provide radio, television, Internet, motion picture, music, retail, banking, credit, computer-accounting, and other telecommunications services.

It came as no surprise when in October 1997 Universal Studios announced that it was selling its television assets to the Home Shopping Network conglomerate being assembled by Barry Diller. Already, Diller had shown himself capable of creating from scratch a television network, the Fox Broadcasting Company, and in a few short years pulling it alongside ABC, NBC, and CBS in national competition. Universal, meanwhile, had watched as Disney and Warner Brothers, now empowered by the regulatory changes that allowed studios to own broadcast networks, began to put together their own television empires. By teaming itself with the Home Shopping Network into a new entity, to be called USA Networks, Universal had entered the television business with a vengeance. It would now enjoy instant access to nearly 100 million American households and a growing (some claimed $50 billion a year by the year 2000) electronic commerce market. It was also in the business of selling tickets for the Los Angeles–based Ticketmaster, the largest ticket operation in the nation, valued at $600 million, which was also part of the Home Shopping Network deal.

No aerospace mogul, even at the height of the cold war, had ever come remotely close to the corporate power and financial remuneration being experienced by the titans who owned and/or controlled these rapidly consolidating enterprises. The workforce of this new industry, furthermore, was not the stable, unionized, workforce of aerospace, which, for all its advanced technology, was basically bound to a conventional industrial model. So, too, had the studios been organized industrially for most of the twentieth century, with each maintaining a large permanent workforce, heavily unionized. While the entertainment conglomerates maintained stable administrative and support staffs at headquarters, most production and postproduction work was subcontracted to small companies, such as those proliferating throughout Hollywood, West Los Angeles, Burbank, and Glendale. Nor did the making of films themselves, whether for motion picture or television distribution, involve more than the smallest cadre of administrative staff. Up to five hundred workers might come together for a single film, remain on salary for less than a year, then find new employment.

Film workers, even those in the highly unionized lighting, electrical, and sound crafts, tended to be entrepreneurs of their own employment. If they had a benefit package at all, it was likely to be with the union; otherwise they were responsible for their own health and pension benefits. Even in the matter of health insurance, entrepreneurs entered the field, making temporary health care benefits available through a specific production. As films became more technical, highly trained architects, graphic designers, and computer experts joined the more conventional boom operators, gaffers, best boys, grips, sound mixers, script supervisors, carpenters, and caterers in the entertainment industry workforce. Architects with computer design skills, capable of creating visual effects such as the computer-generated Gotham City skyline for the film *Batman Forever* (1995), were especially prized.

The $200 million *Titanic* from 20th Century Fox, well on its way by January 1998 to becoming one of the highest grossing films in Hollywood history, epitomized this new production culture, including the effects of NAFTA evident in the facility built by 20th Century Fox near Rosarito Beach in Baja California for the construction of a replica of the doomed ocean liner. Even before this Baja California option was exercised, the industry had been looking beyond metro Los Angeles for expansion. Because of real estate and labor costs, 20th Century Fox decided to locate its new $100 million animation studio in Phoenix. Other studios were looking to Canada, Florida, North Carolina, even New Jersey, directly across the Hudson River from Manhattan, where the American film industry had first begun in the early 1900s.

Then there was the question of trained production talent, especially in the field of computer design. One of the first programs inaugurated by the School of Cinema-Television at the University of Southern California in the early part of the decade, after USC received a $120 million grant from media mogul Walter Annenberg, was a program to retrain defense workers for the entertainment industry. In 1997, Governor Pete Wilson allocated $6.5 million in state funds for a similar program. Santa Monica College opened the cutting-edge Academy of Entertainment and Technology. Yet highly skilled jobs still went begging for want of qualified personnel.

Despite such retraining efforts at USC, Santa Monica College, and a state-assisted program at Technicolor, the entertainment industry had not entirely absorbed the aerospace workforce. The blue-collar and lower-middle-class, and predominantly white, culture of aerospace could not easily make the transition to the entrepreneurial entertainment industry. The hundreds of techies, caterers, gaffers, best boys, even skilled carpenters and electricians who coalesced to make a film and then repositioned themselves into a dozen other enterprises when the film was in the can, were falling into temporary patterns like the stones of a kaleidoscope. They did not see themselves as doing one job for the rest of their lives, protected by long-term union contracts. Nor were they interested in buying tract homes in the suburbs, with recreational vehicles parked out back. These younger people—at least the American-born among them—tended to remain single through their thirties and early forties (and future demographics might indicate even beyond that), wear jeans to work, live in rented apartments, and generally take each day as it came. Theirs was a postmodernist, postindustrial world, eclectic and nonlinear. Overnight, they had become the representative worker—even the representative Southern Californian—in the post–cold war era.

The vitality of the entertainment industry, furthermore, helped in 1999 to put Los Angeles County at the top of the nation in the rate of growth of private-sector businesses. Newly elected governor Gray Davis even had high hopes of revitalizing the aerospace industry. On November 15, 1999, Davis convened some three hundred company and public officials in Los Angeles for an aerospace summit, at which he outlined a series of tax credits and a congressional task force in Washington aimed at bringing aerospace business back to California. Davis came to the conference buoyed by the good news that California would finish 1999 with at least a $2.6 billion surplus in state coffers.

Legislative analyst Elizabeth Hill publicly stated that she believed California was at the beginning of a five-year growth cycle as far as tax revenues were concerned. In Marin County the unemployment rate had dropped to 1.7 percent, which Michael Bernick, the Harvard- and Oxford-educated director of employment development for the state, described as a near statistical impossibility. San Mateo County was reporting an unemployment rate of 1.8 percent; Santa Clara 2.7 percent; and San Francisco—despite its inner-city problems—only 2.9 percent. The western side of the Bay Area, in short, was arguably the most prosperous stretch of urbanism in the nation. In Marin County, where the per capita income averaged nearly

$50,000, the main problem now facing the economy became one of finding service employees for upscale groceries, restaurants, retail outlets, and boutiques. Brian Wilson, co-owner of Sam's Anchor Café in Tiburon, was offering his employees a free membership in a local health club to keep them motivated. In the last week of October 1999, Mark Rudy was one of the very few people—and the only Marin County resident—waiting in line at the state unemployment office in San Rafael, while David Canepa, co-owner of the super-upscale Mill Valley Market, was concerned about the lines in his store. Customers, Canepa told the *Los Angeles Times,* were beginning to grumble about having to wait too long for Kadota fig jam, fresh venison, and ahi tuna.

Valley Talk

As a matter of people and shifting corporate structures, another engine driving the California comeback, computer and computer software design and manufacture, shared many characteristics with both aerospace and the entertainment industry. As in the case of aerospace, Silicon Valley south of San Francisco, ground zero of the computer industry, went into recession in the early 1990s. *Time* magazine reported in November 1991 that the boomtown had become Gloomy Gulch as the end of the cold war, together with rising competition from Japan and Singapore, had driven such giants as Apple, National Semiconductor, and Advanced Micro Devices into the doldrums. No longer did fuzzy-cheeked genius entrepreneurs roar down the streets of Mountain View and Sunnyvale in their BMWs; the streets of Silicon Valley were eerily empty. Layoffs numbered in the thousands, and some 8,700 homes (median price: $226,500) languished on the market.

As in aerospace, however, there were those who were managing to see the future. For Regis McKenna, the leading marketing consultant in the computer industry, the current falloff was just another one of the half-dozen recessions Silicon Valley had experienced since its emergence in the early 1960s. "Every three years we go through these cyclical changes," McKenna noted. "In the course of them, people predict that the Valley is changing or coming to an end."[14] C. Richard Kramlich, the managing general partner of New Enterprise Associates, one of the largest venture capital firms in the nation, was equally unfazed. As a young MBA out of Harvard, Kramlich had mastered his calling under the tutelage of the legendary Arthur Rock, the San Francisco–based investor who invented the practice and coined the term venture capital and had grown up with the valley. All one had to do is to inventory the resources of Silicon Valley, Kramlich argued. The existing infrastructure, built up over the course of thirty years, was first-rate. Local governments were efficient and supportive. There was easy access to air, sea, and surface transportation. The enduring presence of such unshakable companies as Fairchild, Intel, Hewlett-Packard, Applied Materials, 3Com, and National Semiconductor—each of them closely linked to the scientific and technological resources of Stanford University—together with the largest concentration of venture capital in the country, conferred range, depth, and stability on the underlying economy. The town-and-country lifestyle available in Palo Alto, Portola Valley, Woodside, Atherton, and the competitive suburban lifestyle of San Mateo, Sunnyvale, and Mountain View made the region among the most desirable places to live in the nation. Most important, the human resources, the schooled brainpower, so much of it young and filled with entrepreneurial ambition, which had in-migrated from the rest of the United States or immigrated there from South Korea, Taiwan, and India, gave the valley its final competitive edge.

What was not necessarily noted in the Silicon Valley recession of the early 1990s, but what became clear as the decade unfolded, was the central-ity of the valley to the rise of the American West as the economically dom-inant region of the United States. As social critic George Gilder and others correctly pointed out, the most important invention in the second half of the twentieth century was the microprocessor, first announced by Intel in late 1971. Fueled by venture capital from such firms as the Menlo Park–based Sequoia Capital, Arthur Rock, and others, Silicon Valley went into over-drive. A global revolution had been launched, and the technology and eco-nomics of it all had been hardwired into Silicon Valley, just as the stock market was hardwired into Wall Street, and the entertainment industry, no matter how it diversified itself, would always be hardwired into Hollywood.

Sure enough, by the mid-1990s the crisis was over, thanks in great measure to a new invention, the Internet, which, like the microprocessor a quarter of a century earlier, threw the valley into warp speed. Twenty-five years earlier, a generation of young geniuses translated the microprocessor to scores of new uses. The most revolutionary of these was the personal computer, invented in a Sunnyvale garage by two college dropouts in their twenties, Stephen Wozniak and Steven Jobs, a computer eventually reach-ing the market as the Apple, a product that defined an era. So, too, did the Internet now challenge an entirely new generation of inventor-entrepreneurs, many of them born just before the dawning of the Age of Apple, in the mid-1970s.

In the mid-1990s, the Internet had become a chaotic world calling for access and organization, lest it evolve into an intergalactic junkyard. As in the case of the scholarly editions of Hellenic literature prepared at the great Library of Alexandria three centuries before the Common Era, or the classi-fication schemes of Melvil Dewey two millennia later, an entire field of information was demanding arrangement, classification, and retrieval. Search engines and super-servers had to be invented, combining hardware capacity and software programs, if seas of information were to be even navigated, much less organized. The new hardware, moreover, required sophisticated software programs in order to do real work, be useful, and turn a profit. All this meant that a generation of hardware inventors was now being augmented by a younger generation of software programmers active on two fronts (and these fronts frequently coalesced): the organization and navigation of the Internet, and the harnessing of computer technology through software programs to the world of real work.

In its first phases, starting in the late 1950s, Silicon Valley, like aerospace, to which it was then intimately linked, was organized on an industrial model. Pioneering companies such as Memorex and IBM were smokeless factories where long lines of industrial workers produced or assembled equipment. While this industrial culture remained operative for thirty years, with hundreds of assembly lines functioning in numerous tilt-up structures throughout the valley, it was succeeded in prestige and leadership by a research and development model—collegial, entrepreneurial, nonhierarchical, with long hours and no frills—as most dramatically established by Robert Noyce, co-inventor of the silicon microchip, at the two corporations he headed, Fairchild Semiconductor and Intel. The ambience and ethos of such companies resembled that of a university research laboratory, with a senior professor heading the team, which consisted of equally brilliant and thoroughly unintimidated graduate students and postdocs who would soon be the professor's professional equals and were equally invested in the outcome of the project. So persuasive was this collegial model, Silicon Valley companies began to resemble college campuses, not factories. Ed Zschau, later a congressman and Senate candidate, came of age in this second-stage culture. "I see my role as providing a vision to the employees," Zschau noted in April 1993, when he took over as chairman of Adstar, a $6.1 billion subsidiary of IBM based in San Jose, "and then creating a culture that allows people to pursue entrepreneurial opportunities."[15]

The first generation of baby boomers entering the valley, being products of the late 1960s, tended to add a dash of high touch to the already pervasive high tech. Nat Goldhaber, for example, a multimillionaire computer entrepreneur born in 1948, preferred to live in the Berkeley Hills and was heavily involved in transcendental meditation. A disciple of Maharishi Mahesh Yogi, Goldhaber had helped found the Berkeley Transcendental Meditation Center and later played a key role in the establishment of the Maharishi International University in Fairfield, Iowa. In September 1992, Goldhaber assumed the reins at Kaleida Labs, a joint venture of Apple and IBM for the development of multimedia software. "Everything I've learned about business," Goldhaber claimed, "I learned working for the Maharishi."[16]

Ed Zschau was born in 1940 and belonged to the Silent Generation. Nat Goldhaber was a baby boomer. In the mid- and late 1990s, it was now the turn of Generation X. Internet search companies such as Yahoo, Excite, Lycos, and Infoseek were the creations of twentysomethings recently out of college. Excite cofounders Joe Kraus and Graham Spencer, the twenty-five-year-old computer whiz who designed the company's search engine, had been roommates at Stanford. Jayson Adams had started and sold four companies since graduating from Stanford in the late 1980s. When their companies went public, they and their employees, including secretaries with stock options supplementing salaries, were becoming overnight millionaires. Montgomery Securities, a brokerage firm based in San Francisco, counted 120 Silicon Valley companies going public between January 1995 and September 1996. Tens of billions of dollars of market capitalization were created, as were hundreds of millionaires. And once companies went public, they tended to attract further private capital. In the summer of 1997, Intuit bought 19 percent of Excite for $40 million. Established companies such as Cisco Systems (8,500 employees and an annual revenue of $4.1 billion for the fiscal year ending July 1997), a maker of computer networking equipment that had gone public in the early 1990s and had a market capitalization of $36 billion by the fall of 1996, brought more than five hundred employees to millionaire status because of stock options.

By 1997 it was estimated that some sixty millionaires a week were being created in Silicon Valley, many of them Generation Xers. In August 1997, Netscape Communications Corporation held one of the most successful initial public offerings (IPOs) in Silicon Valley history. With just $17 million in annual sales, Netscape sold more than $3 billion in stock, creating dozens of multimillionaires within the company. What the market gave, however, the market could also take away. Technology stocks took a beating in late October 1997, and companies such as Lycos, Excite, Yahoo, Infoseek, and Netscape dropped anywhere from 7 to 24 percent in value. Still, given the fact that all this capitalization had been created virtually from nothing in the IPOs, some adjustment could be expected. (On a less grand scale, but equally revealing, Brian Pinkerton, a University of Washington graduate student, sold his still unfinished doctoral thesis on Internet search engines to America Online for $1.4 million.)

Once again, the streets of the valley were filled with Mercedeses, BMWs, and Lamborghinis. Selling his fifth company to Netscape Communications, Jayson Adams, at twenty-nine, celebrated with a new $80,000

Porsche Carrera. Draeger's supermarket in Menlo Park reported an increase in the sale of $1,200 magnums of Chateau Cheval Blanc. Housing prices soared. Homes in Hillsborough and Atherton reached a median sale price of $1.1 million by August 1996—$400,000 more than the median sale price in Beverly Hills. Multiple offers, many of them in cash, became the norm in Palo Alto, Menlo Park, Los Gatos, Woodside, and Portola. The rental vacancy rate dropped below 1 percent. It was another Gold Rush, and a global one at that. The elementary school district in Cupertino reported fifty-two languages and twelve dialects in its student body, with Hebrew, Russian, and Farsi among the top ten. Taken together, the eight hundred brokers of Cornish & Carey Real Estate of Foster City, desperately searching for properties throughout the San Francisco Peninsula, commanded approximately forty different languages on its salesforce.

The layoffs of the early 1990s now yielded to a competition for trained programmers. Silicon Valley personnel directors, the *Wall Street Journal* reported in August 1997, were allowing programmers to bring pets to work (including, in one instance, an eight-foot python). At one feature animation firm, a solitary programmer, who preferred to work in the nude, was allowed to work the late-late shift. A Silicon Valley job fair, Westech, attracted 416 employers to the Santa Clara Convention Center in September 1997. Quantum Corporation was among them, hoping to fill two thousand openings. Cisco Systems was looking for four hundred employees.

In the aerospace era, government and corporations formed a nexus of value overshadowing engineers and certainly production workers. Even the entertainment industry, which had managed to restructure itself, held to many of its time-honored hierarchies. In Silicon Valley, by contrast, it was more or less acknowledged by the late 1990s that the fundamental asset of any company, whether an established corporation or a start-up, was its intellectual capital, its employee brainpower. At any point, after all, the keys to the future were most likely being held by someone just out of college. A new literary genre, the Silicon Valley novel—represented by Douglas Coupland's *Microserfs* (1995), Pat Dillon's *The Last Best Thing* (1996), and Po Bronson's *The First $20 Million Is Always the Hardest* (1997), together with such astute nonfiction analyses as Robert Cringely's *Accidental Empires: How the Boys of Silicon Valley Make Their Millions, Battle Foreign Competition, and Still Can't Get a Date* (1997)—investigated this brave new world of computer programmers, still living like college kids, ever in search of the hardware and software engines that would create the future.

By the late 1990s, the emergent Web portal culture of Silicon Valley had defined itself. The companies—Yahoo, Netscape, Lycos, Infoseek, Excite,

CNet—embodied a social and cultural paradox. On the one hand, these were firms well into billions of dollars in post-IPO assessed value. Never before in the history of capitalism had so much capital flooded into so few companies in such a short time. Each day, each hour, minute by minute, second by second, millisecond by millisecond, millions of visitors were being navigated through the swirling galaxies of the Internet by companies that hadn't even existed a few short years earlier—in the case of Yahoo, a company that did not even own its own building. In times past, plutocrats such as Andrew Carnegie, J. P. Morgan, John D. Rockefeller, and even Henry Ford (who tended to have a style of his own), having acquired their wealth, withdrew—or were withdrawn—into some Valhalla of the megarich. And even the great corporate bureaucrats of the postwar era had been absorbed into a separate sphere, in their case one modeled on the command and general staff structures of World War II. Now, however, on-paper billionaires such as David Filo and Jerry Yang, cofounders of Yahoo while graduate students at Stanford, strode through the open-cubicled rented spaces of their company in jeans and T-shirts, with Filo continuing his propensity for hundred-hour workweeks, which meant sleeping overnight in his cubicle, sacked out under his computer like any other obsessed programmer.

Already, business writer AnnaLee Saxenian, in her book *Regional Advantage: Culture and Competition in Silicon Valley and Route 128* (1994), had shown how an innovative, flexible, idea-driven culture had allowed Silicon Valley to outperform the bureaucracy-burdened, inwardly focused companies of Route 128 in Greater Boston; but even Saxenian would have to marvel at the flexible, innovative, entrepreneurial companies of Silicon Valley. Part of the new Silicon Valley style was generational pose: it's fun to wear jeans to work and hack all night when you're under thirty and worth a billion dollars. When the employees of Yahoo, young and, many of them, surprisingly rich (on paper, at least), praised Filo and Yang for their "lifestyle leadership," they were obviously reinforcing this generational statement. A generation of twentysomethings had become Masters of the Universe.

By the millennium, the Internet and the companies that served it had made the transition from revolutionary innovation—solitary, eccentric, cyberlibertarian—into a mainstream and commanding position in the American economy. Some 54 million Americans were now using the Internet on a fairly regular basis. Serving such an extensive market demanded something more stable than the wild and crazy times, with their millenarian beliefs and mysticisms. Joe Kraus, cofounder of Excite, compared the process to the Big Bang and its aftermath. "The universe was one big mass of little teeny companies," Kraus said of the early 1990s. "Then gravity started taking hold, and now you are starting to see a greater condensation of the Internet business into larger, denser areas where you have a couple of major players and smaller players orbiting around them."[17]

Southern California, meanwhile, was reaching for as much high-tech business as it could accommodate, whether existing corporations, start-ups, or spillovers from Silicon Valley. The valley could only absorb so much expansion. Commuting traffic in the Silicon Valley and metro San Jose region had long since reached nightmare proportions. The Sierra Club and the Greenbelt Alliance argued that open space was disappearing at too swift a rate. In November 1996, Sun Microsystems announced plans to build a one-million-square-foot, $230 million R&D complex in Santa Clara on the site of a former state facility for the developmentally disabled. Shortly thereafter, Sun was opening facilities in Broomfield, Colorado, and Burlington, Massachusetts. Hewlett-Packard, Intel, 3Com, and National Semiconductor were all busy relocating facilities around the world, from Malaysia to Ireland. Southern California could not have been happier. As early as 1984, the Irvine Company had made a bid for high-tech business with the creation of the 3,600-acre Irvine Spectrum High Technology Industrial Park in Orange County. Aside from construction costs, the Irvine Company had poured more than $227 million into infrastructure, including palm-lined streets and a privately financed freeway clover leaf. By May 1997, Irvine Spectrum was almost completely leased, with an array of major tenants—Western Digital, AT&T, Mazda Motors, Motorola, Toshiba—as well as midsize companies and start-ups requiring as little as one thousand square feet.

Although the numbers were impressive, "Tech Coast," as the Los Angeles–Orange County computer, software, and multimedia industry began to call itself in the late 1990s, had trouble, like Rodney Dangerfield, getting respect. "Oddly enough," observed Joel Kotkin, "Los Angeles, the legendary home of hype, has been exceptionally poor at marketing its technological prowess." This failure, Kotkin continued, hurt most in the question of attracting venture capital. What Tech Coast needed was its own Regis McKenna, the Silicon Valley marketing genius, to take its case to the public.[18] What Kotkin and other champions of Tech Coast failed to note, however, was the fact that in Southern California no one industry—not entertainment, not technology, not biotechnology—could dominate the region as Silicon Valley dominated the Bay Area. Southern California could never become a one-company town (although Los Angeles found itself dominated in the late 1990s by entertainment). Like the entertainment industry, high technology, whether based in Silicon Valley or Tech Coast, had come forward to drive the economic engine of the state in the post–cold war 1990s. Certainly, there were winners and losers. An entire generation of Silicon Valley residents found to their distress that their children could no longer afford to live in the valley, unless they too became computer whizzes. "My son is in construction," Palo Alto store manager Judy Rohlfes remarked sadly, in early October 1996, "and his wife is a nurse. They can't afford anything here. They went to Sacramento, and I told them not to move back."[19]

Genes to Work

By the millennium, almost 40 percent of all American biotechnological research and manufacturing was located in California. The San Francisco Bay Area, which led the nation in this industry, supported as many as a thousand biotech firms. San Diego stood fourth in ranking, and the combined Los Angeles and Orange Counties sixth. By the end of 1997, biotech industries in California were employing some 210,000 workers and paying wages totaling $8 billion. By 2000, the Bay Area was employing as many as 122,000 individuals in various aspects of biotechnology research, development, and manufacturing. The Los Angeles and San Diego regions were each employing more than fifty thousand people in this field. With almost a quarter of a million jobs in place by the year 2000 and revenues approaching $6–10 billion, biotechnology held a substantial position in the new California economy.

Amgen, Inc., of Thousand Oaks in Ventura County, was the largest biotech company in the world. Specializing in genetically engineered treatments for kidney disease, cancer, and hepatitis C, Amgen reached more than $3 billion in annual sales by 2000. Its 120-acre campus (with forty-one buildings), however, stood in relative isolation, in agricultural and suburban Ventura County. Most biotechnology companies tended to cluster in dedicated suburban office parks, with the Bay Area and San Diego in the lead. Yet Orange and Los Angeles Counties were also nurturing biotech ambitions. Biotech clusters, as they were called, included a university, an adjacent corridor of campus sites, housing opportunities for the highly paid biotechnology workforce (average earnings of $50,000 a year), and access to airports.

The clusters were recapitulating the model first established by Stanford and its surrounding communities in the 1950s during the rise of the computer tech industries. Throughout the second half of the 1990s, the research universities of California began to position themselves as centers of biotech and biomedical research, with an emphasis on usable products with entrepreneurial possibilities, and profits to be shared between the sponsoring university and the faculty researcher-entrepreneurs. By 2000, California was receiving twice as many federal research dollars as any other state—a total of $14.4 billion annually—with a growing amount of it available for biotech and biomedical research. Through its BioSTAR program, UC actively solicited private-sector backing for biotech research on its campuses that could result in entrepreneurial possibilities, with BioSTAR backers given first option for development. UC San Francisco, already a leader in the field, was developing a forty-three-acre biomedical research campus in the Mission Bay district of the city. The CSU board of trustees had plans under way for an $80 million biotech research park on twenty-eight acres of the Northridge campus in the San Fernando Valley. This venture was in partnership with biomedical entrepreneur Alfred Mann, who had already donated $110 million to USC for a biomedical research lab on campus and was planning to do the same thing on behalf of UCLA.

Starting with the administration of Governor Pete Wilson and continuing through the first term of Governor Gray Davis, the state government was especially eager to foster biotech ventures. In 1998, in fact, the state doubled state tax credits for any company working in affiliation with UC. Thus empowered, UC president Richard Atkinson guided his campuses to a closer alignment with the emergent biotech industry. The day of the great corporation-sponsored research laboratory such as Bell Labs, Atkinson argued, was over. The new model was an alignment between university research centers and a host of smaller entrepreneurial companies, each side moving as rapidly as possible to discover and develop new products, get them approved by the Food and Drug Administration, and then move as rapidly as possible to market. If UC and other research universities did not offer these services, Atkinson pointed out, biotech start-ups would move elsewhere.

With approximately 170 biotech and medical tech companies in its immediate vicinity, and $77.4 million in private donations in 1998 alone, UC San Diego led the UC biotech initiative. The new UC San Diego Center for Molecular Genetics opened in 1998, and ground had already been broken for the Howard Hughes Medical Institute for Molecular Biology. UC Irvine was developing an eighty-five-acre University Research Park, hoping to foster a cluster of biomedical companies in Orange County. Already, more than 20 percent of the total UC Irvine undergraduate student body was majoring in one or another aspect of biology. In early December 2000, Governor Davis announced a $300 million subvention by the state to create three UC-based Institutes for Science and Innovation: UCLA and UC Santa Barbara would work on nanotechnology; UC San Diego and UC Irvine would concentrate on telecommunications and information technology; UC San Francisco, UC Berkeley, and UC Santa Cruz would cooperatively conduct the California Institute for Bioengineering, Biotechnology, and Quantitative Biomedicine. USC's Keck School of Medicine was in the process of creating a one-hundred-acre biomedical research park at its health sciences campus in East Los Angeles.

Initially, the California Institute of Technology in Pasadena had reservations about the openly entrepreneurial aspect of so much biotechnological and biomedical research. Caltech, after all, bristled with Nobel laureates who had made notable advances in pure science. One such laureate was David Baltimore, the president of Caltech; Baltimore was still lamenting that MIT had not patented Baltimore's 1970 discovery of an enzyme that allows retroviruses, such as HIV, to replicate, for which Baltimore had won the Nobel Prize in medicine in 1975. "It was a great loss to MIT," noted Baltimore, "because MIT would have had one of the basic patents in biotechnology." MIT had thereby forfeited a heroic amount of potential royalties—a mistake Baltimore wanted Caltech to avoid. Said Baltimore: "I want to make sure that doesn't happen here."

Baltimore was especially sensitive to the ongoing federally funded Human Genome Project, which was intended, by 2003, to map the three billion genetic letters determining individual heredity. Such a detailed mapping held enormous possibilities for medicine as a matter of pure research, as well as of clinical practice. Baltimore wanted Caltech to be part of the action, just as the institute had been on the forefront of previous developments in chemistry, physics, and pure and applied engineering. In May 1998, Baltimore launched a $100 million biological sciences initiative called Beyond the Genome. Caltech trustees Camilla Chandler Frost of the Los Angeles Times Company and Ben Rosen, chairman of Compaq Computer, each contributed $5 million, and Eli Broad, chairman of SunAmerica Inc., kicked in $18 million. "The rock stars of this century may be computer nerds," noted Rosen, "but the next group will be biologists." As a longtime developer, Broad was especially interested in the creation of a Pasadena-based corridor of biotech companies in the vicinity of Caltech, turning the university and/or jointly sponsored research into profitable ventures.[20]

By September 1998, the San Francisco–based $350 million Biotechnology Value Fund was busy making long-term investments in development-stage biotech companies throughout the state. Managed by investment banker Mark Lampert, the San Francisco hedge fund already held positions in nineteen biotechs in expectation of a fivefold increase in the value of the initial investment: companies such as Corvas International of San Diego, developing drugs related to blood-clot formation, strokes, inflammation, and

hepatitis C; Protein Polymer Technologies of San Diego, developing genetically engineering protein compounds; SIBIA Neurosciences of La Jolla,
pursuing treatments for Alzheimer's dementia and Parkinson's disease; and
Microcide Pharmaceuticals of Mountain View, developing drugs to counter
the growing problem of drug-resistant infections. Neither Lampert nor other
major investors in biotechnology, however, had any truck whatsoever with
the flamboyant and iconoclastic youth-oriented culture of high technology at
comparable times of start-up in the late 1980s and early 1990s. In contrast to
high technology, the culture of biotechnology was not about brilliant kids in
jeans sleeping beneath their computers. Biotechnology involved expensive
laboratories and intricately managed research by highly trained staffs. A
hacker sitting at his computer could make a major breakthrough with minimal overhead. Biotechnology, by contrast, demanded tightly controlled, and
extremely cost-conscious, corporate structures and practices.

Still, lightning could strike; and that kept some glamour in the industry.
In December 1998, after researchers at Calypte Biomedical Corporation in
Berkeley announced the creation of a urine test that could screen for HIV at
approximately three dollars per test, the NASDAQ registered a 72 percent
increase in shares of Calypte, from $1.63 to $3.83. That September, the
Bayer Group of Germany paid $1.1 billion to buy the clinical diagnostics
division of the Chiron Corporation of Emeryville, and Chiron sales rose 56
cents, to close at $17.44 on NASDAQ. Biotechnology might be more staid
and corporate than high technology, but there were still dazzling prospects
of sudden wealth.

Frequently, especially in the area of prosthetics, biotechnology and high
technology coalesced. Unlike high technology, which was left to the judgments of the free market, biotechnology was heavily regulated by the FDA
and an alphabet soup of other federal and state public health agencies. By
October 1997, Advanced Bionics had already spent $30 million researching
and developing a cochlear implant for the deaf or hearing impaired, yet had
not received permission to market the device from the various regulatory
agencies. By the late 1990s, well over a thousand clinical trials of new
drugs and biological agents—most of them intended for cancer or cancer-
related conditions, and one out of seven of them relating to AIDS or HIV-
related conditions—were being tested in California's biotechnological
laboratories.

A generation or two before, this work would have taken place in the
university; but with the economic stakes so high—what, after all, would be
the dollar value of a cure for cancer?—biotechnology had migrated out
from the university and into such for-profit companies as Cetus,
BioGrowth, XOMA, Triton, Cal*Bio, Glycomed, BioProbe, Ideon, Gilead,

and Synbiotics. Here the very building blocks of life were being engineered not for the sake of pure science, although the spirit of science pervaded the enterprise, but for the sake of putting marketable products before the public. Gilead Sciences of Foster City, for example, devoted itself to pioneering a new class of potential human therapeutics, based on nucleotides, the primary molecules of life and intended for a broad range of diseases, including viral infections, cardiovascular disease, inflammatory disease, and cancer. In contrast to the Silicon Valley software boom, with its sudden and breathtaking breakthroughs and overnight riches, biotechnology was a more patient process: a process that had taken hundreds of millions of years in the evolution of animal and human biology. As in the case of evolution, biotechnology took time. Genentech, the founding company of biotechnology in California, only reached $1 billion in annual revenues for the first time in 1997, more than twenty years after it began.

As far as venture capitalists were concerned, the risks in biotech were more subtle and extended across a longer period of time than in other forms of comparable investment. Still, when faced with the dazzling humanitarian and financial prospects that biotech could very well make possible—cancer control through new pharmaceuticals or gene therapy; the creation of artificial organs; the development of new vaccines; the improvement of animals and plants; the cleanup of toxic spills and military bases through new biotechnological agents; the linking of biotechnology and microelectronics; the containment or outright curing of cancer and AIDS; the mitigation of heart attack and stroke; the biotechnological, indeed bioelectronic, supplementing of hearing and sight—venture capitalists were willing to take a chance on an industry whose golden age was only just beginning. Like so many investors, then, Californians were eager to wear genes to work.

Foreign Trade

A nother powerful engine in the California economy—$1.3 trillion, by 2000—was foreign trade, which, directly and indirectly, accounted for approximately a quarter of the state's GNP. Like everything else, foreign trade showed signs of recession in the early 1990s, due to a decline in air-craft exports; but by late 1993, foreign trade was once again surging for-ward, with 1.5 million workers, approximately 11 percent of the state's workforce, serving the exporting of $110 billion of agricultural products, merchandise, and services to the rest of the world, most notably Japan, Canada, Mexico, Taiwan, South Korea, and Singapore.

Key to California's success as a foreign trade mart were the cargo con-tainer ports of Los Angeles, Long Beach, Oakland, San Diego, and Port Hueneme. As the largest port on the Pacific Coast, the port of Los Ange-les—blasted by dynamite from the rocks and shoals of San Pedro Bay in the early twentieth century—was a masterpiece of civil and mechanical engi-neering and an economic engine that barely sputtered, if it sputtered at all, in the recession-ridden early 1990s. In fiscal year 1991–92, the port of Los Angeles, administered by the Los Angeles Harbor Commission, was directly supporting 203,000 jobs in its five-county area. Under the executive direction of Ezunial Burts, a protégé of Mayor Tom Bradley and the only African-American port director in the nation, the port of Los Angeles was an empire unto itself. Crafted at the height of the Progressive movement, the Los Angeles City Charter had given the Harbor Commission near autonomy, in order to insulate it from political interference. While techni-cally part of city government, the Harbor Commission enjoyed wide-ranging authority and control over its own profits. The port maintained thirteen overseas offices, and its sales personnel roamed the world in search of business.

In 1992, the Los Angeles Harbor Commission began a $2 billion, thirty-year capital improvement program that over the next five years would invest more than $100 million a year in upgrading, modernizing, and expanding its facilities. Another $200 million was budgeted for the creation of the pro-posed Alameda Corridor: a clear-path rail link running through a half-dozen cities on the axis of Alameda Boulevard and directly joining the port with major railroad transfer points further inland. The Alameda Corridor would supplement the freeway system, which already linked the Los Ange-les and Long Beach ports to the region. At some early point in the new mil-lennium, container cargo would enter or exit the ports by freight train or truck swiftly and with no interruption. One longshoreman perched eighty-five feet in the air atop one of the many towering hammerhead cranes lining the wharves could reach into the hold of a cargo ship and, with the assis-tance of a computerized blueprint, pluck a specified twenty-five-ton cargo container, lift it from the ship, place it gently on a truck chassis or railroad car, and send it on its way. The entire process, which a skilled operator could perform in approximately ninety seconds, was reversed for the load-ing of ships. Taken together, the ports of Los Angeles and Long Beach, served by the same infrastructure, would form the largest and most compet-itive deep-sea port on the planet.

Between 1992 and 1998, foreign trade increased by 45 percent through-out the state. (Had California been an independent nation in 1998, it would have replaced Canada at the annual G-7 meeting of the world's largest eco-nomic democracies.) At the level of state government, the Trade and Com-merce Agency maintained ten overseas foreign trade bureaus and was planning five more. These offices were supplemented by others maintained by the larger California cities and ports. In terms of trade matters, Califor-nia was maintaining something approaching its own foreign policy, or at least a strong consular presence. Located on the fourteenth floor of a down-town high-rise, with an excellent view of the snowcapped Popocatepetl vol-cano, the twelve-person Mexico City office of the Trade and Commerce Agency served the $10 billion in exports California businesses did with Mexico each year, the third largest foreign market for California behind Japan and Canada.

Nor was such business strictly a matter of large companies. The 1990s was an era of start-ups. Nick Renner, for example, owner of NESS Inc., a three-person computer software company in Madera, had no clue about how it should be done. Flying to Mexico City, Renner was briefed at the California trade office, which also scheduled for him four days of appoint-ments with prospective clients. Three weeks after his return, Renner was doing $40,000 in monthly business with Mexico, was looking forward to doing $1 million annually, and was planning to expand his software line elsewhere in Latin America.

Foreign trade was interactive—which is to say, it involved binational and multinational patterns of development. Howard Marguleas, chairman of Sun World International, a giant fruit and vegetable grower based in Bakersfield, wanted in the early 1990s to grow mangoes in the California desert. He turned to the best desert agriculturalists in the world, the Israelis, and hired the Volcani Agricultural Research Institute near Tel Aviv to give him assistance. Already, Marguleas had been working with Israeli researchers on efforts to give his tomatoes a longer shelf life, to make his red sweet peppers even bigger, and to grow strawberries in winter. As a regular part of its operation, Intel Corporation maintained a design center in Israel to work on a line of advanced microchips, which it manufactured in California.

While the U.S. Constitution reserves the right to conduct foreign policy to the president and the Congress, the foreign trade power of California possessed more than a Chamber of Commerce dimension. In many parts of the world, doing business with California companies—which, in one way or another, meant doing business with the government of California—was crucial to a national economy. There was also the question of the enormous influence of the foreign investments of California's two major public pension funds: the California Public Employees' Retirement (CalPERS) and the California State Teachers' Retirement System (CalSTRS). At any one time, a good chunk of the $280 billion in combined assets of these two funds was in offshore investments. (By specific mandate, $5 billion had to be invested in developing nations.) The teachers and public employees of California, in short, were leading players in world finance.

Until 1999, when it was surpassed by Mexico, California's leading trade partner was Japan. Like the Mexico-California connection, the Japan-California relationship, in all its achievement and ambivalences, stood at the core of the California identity. In the 1980s, Japan began to invest heavily in the United States and Europe in an effort to sidestep a rising tide of protectionism in each region. Between 1980 and 1989, Japan doubled its investment in the United States, in real estate, manufacturing, high technology, stocks, bonds, even in the federal debt, in which Japan became a big investor. By 1989, Japan had more than $7 billion invested in California property and enterprises. Between 1989 and 1992, however, it began to pull away from the United States and direct its investments to Asia. By 1992, Japanese investment in California had dropped to $2.6 billion.

This falloff involved an irony; for it was in the recession-ridden early 1990s that anti-Japanese feeling surfaced most vividly in California. Was the resentment because Japan was too much on the scene, or because Japan was looking elsewhere? Everywhere one looks in these years, both in California and nationwide, there is Japan bashing, subtle or overt. On December

7, 1991, the *Los Angeles Times* concluded a three-part series on Pearl Harbor in a jingoistic vein, juxtaposing on its front page an ominous article regarding the possibility of Japan reemerging as a belligerent military force. Pointedly, the *Times* ran a photograph of the entry into Pearl Harbor of the USS *Missouri,* on whose deck Japan had signed surrender documents on September 2, 1945.

Tensions came to a head in October 1991 when the Los Angeles County Transportation Commission announced its intention to award a $115 million contract for high-tech subway cars to the Sumitomo Corporation of Tokyo. William Agee, chief executive officer of Morrison Knudsen of Boise, Idaho, a manufacturer that had not only not been chosen but had had its engineering expertise criticized, launched a ferocious counteroffense, directed by its local lobbyist Maureen Kindel, Mayor Tom Bradley's top fund-raiser and a former president of the Board of Public Works. Meeting with Bradley, Agee claimed that Morrison Knudsen could assemble the cars at the soon-to-be-closed General Motors Corporation facility in Los Angeles County, hiring local people. Still, the Transportation Commission held fast; in December 1991 it adhered to its earlier decision. Agee called for an investigation of the commission staff. The anti-Sumitomo campaign continued through the first half of 1992, led in this second phase by Catherine O'Neill, wife of the syndicated columnist Richard Reeves. The campaign gained momentum with President George H. W. Bush's inconclusive, indeed ill-fated, visit to Japan, which ended at an official banquet with a flu-ridden Bush vomiting into the lap of the Japanese prime minister.

A week later, Yoshio Sakurauchi, the seventy-nine-year-old speaker of the lower house of the Japanese parliament, stated in an interview that the root of America's economic troubles lay in its lazy and illiterate workforce. One-third of American workers, Sakurauchi claimed, were illiterate. Affronted, Assemblyman Richard Katz and City Councilman Zev Yaroslavsky put an initiative on the June 1992 ballot granting most favored nation status to local goods and services in city contracts. It passed, strengthened by both anti-Japanese feeling and the Rebuild LA effort launched after the April-May riots. The Southern California–based Michael Crichton's best-selling novel *Rising Sun* (1992) probed the noir and tensions of the U.S.-Japan industrial relationship.

Certainly the war was not over for the anti-Sumitomo forces. Although they had no authority in the matter, the Los Angeles City Council and the state assembly and senate passed resolutions opposing the Sumitomo deal. When Morrison Knudsen won a $380 million contract from the Illinois Metropolitan Rail Authority to build new transit cars and refurbish old ones, Agee felt further vindicated in his continuing battle with Sumitomo.

Finally, on January 22, 1992, the Transportation Commission, although it complained of "gutter politics" and "irresponsible Japan-bashing," changed its vote. "He scared them into signing," noted transportation commissioner Jackie Bacharach of the Agee-led campaign.[21]

It was all dumb show; or, more correctly, it was political theater, giving vent to American fears of Japan. It was difficult to say whether or not William Agee had even been for real in his opposition. Despite the reverse vote in January 1992, Morrison Knudsen refused to enter the second round of bidding, claiming involvement with its other contracts. Having backed down on its original choice, made after competitive analysis, the Transportation Commission found itself with no new bidders—not one—capable of meeting its specifications. Nine months after its first vote, the commission returned, hat in hand, to Sumitomo and negotiated a new agreement.

The California economy, it was evident—indeed, the American economy—could never again consider itself a stand-alone affair. Whatever the tensions might be, Japan and California, and Japan and the United States, were inextricably linked in their economies. True, the United States, including California, had much it could object to in the matter of Japanese protectionism and the continuing trade imbalance; yet four out of every ten dollars of American trade with Asia was with Japan; even with the early-1990s falloff of Japanese investment in California, Japan could not be ignored in any economic profile of the state. When the Japanese electronics giant NEC chose Roseville as the site for its new semiconductor factory in the early 1990s, that decision translated to a $1 billion investment, and provided two thousand jobs at a time when California needed every job it could get.

In Fremont, the New United Motor Manufacturing (NUMMI), a joint venture between General Motors and Toyota, managed by Toyota, was flourishing as the last active automotive assembly plant in California. Opened in 1962 by General Motors to produce Chevrolet cars and GMC trucks, the facility soon racked up a devastating reputation for high absenteeism, low productivity, and poor-quality vehicles. Unable to make the plant work, General Motors closed it in March 1982, a living symbol of declining American productivity and industrial integrity. In 1984, GM made an agreement with Toyota to form an independent California corporation and bring the plant back into production. Initially, GM thought it would primarily acquire from Toyota advanced technology, including robotics. What it learned instead was how to ensure quality control and productivity by motivating the workforce—insights that GM later took to its new Saturn plant in Spring Hill, Tennessee. Entering into dialogue with workers and their union, Toyota brought to the Fremont plant *hoshin kanri* (management policy) aimed at four goals: first, stabilizing a cooperative relationship among all team members, particularly between labor and management; second, ensuring quality in the production process itself; third, establishing and maintaining a long-term and stable relationship with qualified suppliers; and fourth, maintaining a cooperative, friendly relationship within the community by being a fair employer and a good neighbor. Central to *hoshin kanri* was *ringisho,* or decision by consensus. It was the job of management at NUMMI not to boss people around but to facilitate the work, quality control, and innovative thinking of employees, who were designated "associates" or "team members."

By September 1997, some 4,700 Californians, most of them represented by the United Auto Workers Local 2244, were producing Chevrolet Geo Prizms, Toyota Corolla sedans, and Toyota Tacoma compact pickup trucks in a spotless, state-of-the-art, four-million-square-foot assembly plant that resembled a think tank as much as it did a factory. Visitors to NUMMI encountered an almost serene industrial culture. Along the great assembly lines, assisted by gleaming and spotless equipment, NUMMI team members (43 percent Caucasian, 28 percent Hispanic, 17 percent African-American, 12 percent Asian, 0.7 percent Native American; 81 percent male, 19 percent female) moved at a steady, not rushed pace. Associates moved autonomously about their tasks, or in self-directed teams. Management seemed conspicuous in its absence. Not only was NUMMI spending $1.3 billion in annual California purchases and payroll and keeping vital some thirteen thousand jobs connected with suppliers, it was helping to forge the industrial culture of the future, in which teamwork replaced hierarchy and each worker was viewed as a creative individual and a profit center.

The Rim

The fusion of Japan and California so evident at the NUMMI plant suggested another possibility on the minds and imaginations of Californians since the 1980s: the dawning Asia-Pacific culture, in which California
would play an important role on behalf of itself and the rest of the United
States. As in the case of the Japanese relationship, the Asia-Pacific dream
went to the very core of the California identity. In the Senate debates connected to the admission of California to the Union in September 1850,
Daniel Webster touched upon the topic, as did President Fillmore in his
1853 letter to the shogun of Japan. One of the most fervent believers in the
Asia-Pacific dream was Lincoln's secretary of state, William Seward, the
key figure in the purchase of Alaska. "Henceforth," Seward believed,
"European commerce, European politics, and European activities, although
becoming actually more intimate, will nevertheless sink in importance,
while the Pacific Ocean, its shores, its islands, and the vast regions beyond,
will become the chief theater of events in the world's great hereafter."[22]

In nineteenth-century California, intellectuals such as Benjamin Parke
Avery, editor of the *Overland Monthly* and first United States minister to
China, and Anson Burlingame, another American minister to the Celestial
Empire, established a body of doctrine and commentary dealing with the
emergence of a transpacific community and the role to be played therein by
California. In Frank Norris's novel *The Octopus* (1901), one of the most
impressive and thematically comprehensive novels ever to deal with the
California experience, the San Francisco capitalist Cedarquist discourses
on the role to be played by California in the Asia-Pacific Basin. Cedarquist's vision, of course, was imperialistic, as might be expected from a fictional character in the era of American expansion into the Pacific. Eighty
years and five Pacific wars later, such strident imperialism, however poetically expressed, had been severely qualified. Yet Californians, many of
them, at least, still dreamed of an Asia-Pacific destiny, based on high-tech
communication, jet travel, and growing trade and commerce.

This Asia-Pacific awareness—variously called the Asia-Pacific Basin, the Pacific Rim, or just the Rim—surfaced most strongly in the mid-1980s, the direct result of the fact that by 1985 California was doing more than $65 billion worth of business with Pacific Rim nations and that more than half of all American trade with Rim nations was passing through California ports. In 1984 the Futures Research Division of the Los Angeles–based Security Pacific National Bank issued a white paper entitled "Pac Rim 2010," almost novelistic in its descriptions of what life in California and on the Rim would be like some twenty-five years into the future. Once a barrier, "Pac Rim 2010" stated, the Pacific Rim would by 2015 be a busy pathway of trade and communication. The California lifestyle would have long since become transnational and cross-cultural in its values and perspectives. Culturally, the Rim could be centered—if it could be centered at all—in Honolulu. Financially, its center would be the Los Angeles metroplex, Greater Los Angeles, by then an electronic nerve center for a multitude of transnational financial deals and transfers.

Since the Security Pacific Bank was headquartered in Los Angeles, the city won out as capital of the Pacific Rim in futurist projections. Hong Kong, after all, was scheduled to revert to the People's Republic of China in July 1997 and thus had an uncertain future. It was not yet clear whether or not Singapore would become an investor-friendly city, and Tokyo had always remained impenetrable to outsiders. Los Angeles, by contrast, was open, prosperous, on the Rim, and available. Already, more than thirty Chinese banks were operating there. Eight of the nine leading Japanese automakers and five of the thirteen largest Japanese banks headquartered their American operations there as well. More than six hundred Japanese firms were in or near the city. The population of metro Los Angeles was becoming increasingly Asian. Of equal importance, the nations of the Rim liked LA, indeed were fascinated with all things Southern Californian, whether athletic footwear from LA Gear or California Colors lipstick and nail polish from Beauty Products International. San Francisco, meanwhile, was making its case for Pacific Rim hegemony. In February 1982, in *San Francisco Magazine,* Frank Viviano, Far Eastern editor of the Pacific News Service, chronicled how an infusion of Asian wealth was transforming San Francisco. That August, after a seven-month tour of the Rim, Viviano returned with a report on how the economic future of the world was being shaped by the city-states of New Asia: Tokyo, Seoul, Taipei, Hong Kong, Manila, Bangkok, Singapore, Jakarta, and San Francisco. Viviano failed to mention Los Angeles.

As in the case of the opposition to Sumitomo, resistance to the Pacific Rim, whether as a fact or as a metaphor, came primarily from liberal and conservative commentators wedded intellectually and emotionally to an industrial order centered in the United States. The lethal suppression of student dissenters in Tiananmen Square in 1989 further galvanized hostility to China in such prominent figures as Congresswoman Nancy Pelosi, a liberal Democrat from San Francisco; and without China playing a central role, there could be no discussion of a realistic Pacific Rim community. When in late October and early November 1997, People's Republic president Jiang Zemin visited New York, both Governor George Pataki and Mayor Rudolph Giuliani refused to meet with him. Arriving in Los Angeles in early November, however, Jiang was feted by a luncheon crowd of some 750 business and community leaders (Rupert Murdoch, futurist Alvin Toffler, dancer Cyd Charisse) at the Beverly Hills Hotel, who were drawn there, in part, by the fact that China had become LA's second largest trading partner. (From California as a whole, $19 billion in goods had been shipped to the People's Republic in 1996 alone.) In New York City, Jiang had been snubbed by the governor and the mayor; in Los Angeles, he sat at the head table alongside former secretary of state Warren Christopher, Governor Pete Wilson, Mike Bowlin, president of ARCO, and Los Angeles mayor Richard Riordan. But then again, visiting New York City, Jiang had been in a foreign country. In California, he was still in Asia-Pacific territory. He was safely on the Rim.

NAFTA

By 1999, Mexico had become California's leading trading partner. To cite this fact is to glimpse only one facet of the powerful and growing connection between California and Mexico in the last three decades of the twentieth century. It was a matter, most fundamentally, of colonial history. Even after it became an American state, California stood in relationship to its initiating culture, Mexico, the vice-royalty of New Spain and later the republic, in much the same way that the states of the Atlantic East stood to England. Even in its most Americanizing of eras, California could not detach itself from the nation, culture, and people who had served as its founders. As the late twentieth century progressed, and immigration intensified, California was becoming once again Mexico, and Los Angeles a ranking Mexican city.

In the late 1940s, a young Mexican diplomat with literary instincts, Octavio Paz, found himself posted to the consular office in Los Angeles. "At first sight," Paz later recalled in *The Labyrinth of Solitude* (1961), "the traveler is surprised by—besides the pureness of the sky and the ugliness of the dispersed and ostentatious constructions—the vaguely Mexican atmosphere of the city, impossible to capture in words or concepts. This Mexicanness—a taste for adornments, carelessness and splendor, negligence, passion and reserve—floats in the air. And I say floats because it does not mix nor is it joined with the other world, the North American world, made of precision and efficiency."[23] Paz was talking about what could be considered the second largest Mexican city on the planet. The Mexican connection of California was a matter of people and money, food and music, ambience and culture. It was a matter of social and political value. It was, in all its dimensions—trade, immigration, politics, and social policy—the overriding California connection, and the big California story of the late twentieth century.

As far as business and foreign trade were concerned, three factors dominated the California-Mexico connection in the early 1990s: first, the efforts of President Carlos Salinas de Gortari, an economist and urban planner by training, to privatize the Mexican economy; second, the increasing economic interdependence between Mexico and the United States, especially in border states such as California; and, third, the debate in Congress on the North American Free Trade Agreement (NAFTA), which would establish free trade among Canada, the United States, and Mexico—from the Yukon to the Yucatan, as one slogan put it.

What Margaret Thatcher and the Conservative Party did for the United Kingdom in the 1980s—privatization of publicly owned companies and assets—became the goal of other nations in the 1990s. Nowhere was this more evident than in Mexico, as two Harvard-trained presidents from the long-ruling Institutional Revolutionary Party (PRI)—Miguel de la Madrid, who took office in late 1982, and Carlos Salinas de Gortari, who took office in late 1988—sought to take Mexico from its highly protectionist, semisyndicalist past into a free market future. By September 1991 the Mexican government had sold nearly nine hundred of the 1,155 companies it owned. Beginning in the administration of de la Madrid and continuing more intensely under Salinas de Gortari, a new kind of technocrat—polished graduates of prestigious Mexican universities with advanced degrees from the Ivy League—began to take hold of the reins of government and direct the divestiture process.

Encouraged by these developments and by the Thatcherite rhetoric emanating from the presidential palace in Mexico City, American companies began to look to Mexico, especially its northern states, as convenient and inexpensive offshore sites for manufacturing. Aside from northern Mexico's low wages, available workforce, and ready access to U.S. markets, Mexican law, through its *maquiladora* program, had established free trade zones for goods made or assembled in Mexico for shipment back into the United States. Throughout the 1980s and early 1990s, *maquiladoras* attracted thousands of Mexicans into the northern states, which began a process of urbanizing the border from Texas to California.

Nor was American or other offshore investment in northern Mexico confined to simple assembly plants. By 1993—attracted by, among other factors, the availability of a trained, even professional, labor force willing to work for a quarter of what engineers and technicians were demanding in the United States—Ford, Zenith, Whirlpool, AT&T, Nissan, and Sony each maintained technologically sophisticated factories in the region, which, together with the *maquiladoras,* employed some 600,000 Mexican workers.

A subtle but powerful adjustment of industrial culture was evident. On the one hand, companies such as Ford could have automated their factories at great expense. What Ford chose to do, however, was to relocate to Chihuahua in northern Mexico and build a semiautomated factory, making up the difference with the availability of trained Mexican engineers and technicians. A graduate engineer in northern Mexico was willing to work for $1,400 a month and, if necessary, to function as a foreman, which most American engineers refused to do. This was a long way from the image of Mexican workers as serape-clad *campesinos* grinding corn with American stone. "The technological superiority that retained the most advanced production in the United States is disappearing," noted UC San Diego labor economist Harley Shaiken in 1993, "so that northern Mexico is now almost a fifty-first state in terms of production. Boeing might still have a hard time making jet airliners in Mexico, but Mexican workers can match the skills of 70 percent of the labor force in the United States."[24]

These transformations in industrial culture clashed, most obviously, with Mexico's onetime protectionist point of view and the previous self-sufficiency of American industry, in which manufacturing and markets were contained and protected primarily within the United States. Thus there was growing support for NAFTA, which would remove most barriers to the flow of goods and services among the three leading nations of North America. Thoroughly in tune with the Thatcherite future, the Reagan and first Bush administrations favored such an agreement, as did the Canadians, who had to import and export in order to maintain their standard of living. Salinas de Gortari and the technocrats of the PRI, for their part, welcomed the agreement with open arms; it was estimated that by May 1993 the Mexican government had already spent more than $25 million lobbying for NAFTA in Washington and elsewhere in the United States.

In December 1992, Presidents Bush and Salinas de Gortari and Prime Minister Brian Mulroney signed the NAFTA treaty. Throughout the presidential campaign of 1992, President Bill Clinton supported it as well. Once in office, Clinton opened negotiations on side agreements on labor standards, environmental protection, and import surges prior to submitting the NAFTA agreement to Congress for approval and implementation in January 1994. The years of the NAFTA negotiation, but especially the year 1993, as the Clinton administration negotiated its side agreements, brought the NAFTA debate to the center of American, and Californian, political life. NAFTA was a litmus test asking powerful questions: What do you think about yourself? it asked Americans. What do you think about your employment and your prospects? Do you trust or mistrust the developing multinational economic order? And, even more pertinent, what do you think of Mexico? What do you think of Mexicans?

Here was a people whom Americans had conquered in 1846, and whose country's top third they had seized. The war and the lands Mexico lost remained a continuing trauma whose wounds had never fully healed. Following the conquest, the United States had withdrawn its troops from Mexico City and, faced with the half-century task of developing the conquered Mexican territories, all but turned its back on its neighboring republic. In 1990, 144 years later, the American-Mexican dialogue was being reopened at a time when the United States had within its borders some 22 million citizens of Mexican descent. Mexico itself—its intellectuals at least—frequently showed anxieties about closer ties. For most Mexicans, the sheer opportunity to find better employment to the north—and this in a nation that by its very demographics and socioeconomic structures could not provide full employment for its people—helped offset any sense of cultural anxiety or displacement.

Border culture, despite the deep anxieties and protests in California regarding an influx of illegal aliens, had already proved its sustainability. By 1994, the U.S. Immigration and Naturalization Service was estimating approximately three hundred million legal crossings a year—in both directions—between the United States and Mexico. Whatever points of contention might surface, especially in California, the border had emerged as its own cultural region. Mexico and the United States were interacting. Families were maintaining themselves on either side of the line. In many public sectors, transportation, criminal justice, urban and regional planning, health care, even the envisioning of a binational international airport south of the border in Baja California—officials were building a body of practice and precedent that constituted the diplomatic underpinnings of a new transnational relationship.

Mexican companies were continuing their growing export to the United States of nonpetroleum products, with trade increasing 20 percent annually between 1982 and 1989. This involved chemicals, iron and steel products, glass, cement, and also beer—by 1991, Corona held second rank among imported beers in the United States. Other Mexican companies were creating north-of-the-border subsidiaries or joint ventures more directly to serve American markets, and Mexican or Mexican-American companies were being founded in the United States to meet combined American and Mexican needs. Fortunes were being made on both sides of the border, as salsa replaced catsup as the leading American condiment, and the largest supplier of tortillas to northern Mexico emerged in East Los Angeles.

Spanish, the fourth most spoken language in the world, was now the second language of the United States, heard and spoken daily on radio and television, used by millions in personal and family life, increasingly taught in high schools and colleges, and being mastered by non-Hispanic Americans. As in everything else, language itself was showing the effects of the permeable border, and by the mid-1990s certain academic purists were complaining that a hybrid Spanglish—*lonche* (lunch), *yonke* (junk), *los taggers, los punks, los hard coreros, los raves, techno, wanna-bes, pozers, get-a-life, dame un quebrazo* (give me a break!)—was compromising the language of Cervantes and Unamuno. No American audiences, however, had trouble understanding Bart Simpson when he exclaimed *Ay caramba!*, or misinterpreted the intention of Arnold Schwarzenegger in *Terminator 2* when he dispatched an opponent with *Hasta la vista, baby!*

Once signed and enacted on September 14, 1993, NAFTA had almost immediate effects. Samsung, the South Korean consumer electronics giant, announced the establishment of a $100 million plant in Tijuana to make television picture tubes. Samsung already maintained a large television assembly plant in Tijuana but imported most of its components from Asia. Since the NAFTA agreement stipulated that computer and television monitors had to be made in the United States, Mexico, or Canada if they were to remain duty free, Samsung would be manufacturing as well as assembling at its Tijuana site. By 1996, Tijuana alone was attracting $1 billion a year in *maquiladora* investment; further east along the border, Mexicali, population 750,000, at the southern end of the Imperial Valley, was also being transformed by American and offshore investments, from the Japanese electronics giants Sony and Daewoo. In September 1997, Mitsubishi and NEC announced plans to invest more than $300 million in Mexicali plants, employing 3,100 workers. Rapidly, the Baja California–California border—Tijuana, Tecate, Mexicali—was urbanizing. Some demographers predicted that if present growth patterns continued, the second largest city in California after Los Angeles by the 2030s would be the binational metropolitan region formed by San Diego, National City, Chula Vista, Imperial Beach, San Ysidro, and Tijuana.

Business—or so it would seem from statistics—was more important than politics, and it ran on its own separate track. Despite the wedge issues that had surfaced in the 1990s—the controversies over illegal immigrants, affirmative action, bilingual education—trade between California and Mexico continued to grow. In 1994, which could be considered the nadir of California-Mexico relations, with 60 percent of the voters passing Proposition 187, Mexico nevertheless bought $7.7 billion in Californian goods. By 1997 that figure had climbed to $12.1 billion. By 2000, California was selling some $15 billion of goods and services to Mexico.

Still, it did not do well for California to remain politically alienated from a nation that would soon be its leading trade partner. Realizing that wedge issues can cut both ways, Democratic primary candidate Lieutenant Governor Gray Davis had repeatedly stated in his campaign that he would make reconciliation with Mexico one of the first goals of his administration. Davis realized it did no good to keep the state government alienated from a nation with which private-sector California was doing so much business. Barely a month in office in 1999, Davis embarked on a three-day self-described healing mission to Mexico City, taking with him an entourage of corporate, cabinet, educational, and union dignitaries, together with the conspicuous presence of such Latino officials as Lieutenant Governor Cruz Bustamante, the first Mexican American to hold that office in more than a hundred years, assembly speaker Antonio Villaraigosa, state senator Richard Polanco, and state assemblywoman Denise Moreno Ducheny. Wearing a lapel pin with entwined American and Mexican flags, Davis called on President Ernesto Zedillo and openly sought reconciliation between the two commonwealths that—although this was not openly stated—had continued to do business with each other despite California's affronts to Mexico's self-esteem. "I think it is time," said the governor, "for a new compact between my great state and the great people of the Republic of Mexico."[25] The trip represented a personal triumph for Davis and for the Mexican-American officials who accompanied him and were feted by the Mexican press. Davis returned to Sacramento with a commitment from Zedillo to visit California as soon as possible. Three and a half months later, Zedillo made good on his promise, becoming the first Mexican president to come to California since Carlos Salinas de Gortari had slipped into Los Angeles in 1991, and only the second Mexican president to visit in more than thirty-five years.

The month before Zedillo's arrival, Davis had made a controversial decision not to drop California's appeal against the injunction of the federal court against Proposition 187, but to send the matter to the federal court for mediation. That way, he would not have to carry on the pro–Proposition 187 appeal launched by his predecessor, Pete Wilson, and offend a core Democratic constituency. At the same time, he would not have to ride roughshod over the intentions of 60 percent of the voters who had passed the measure in 1994. In sending the matter to mediation, in which proponents and opponents of Proposition 187 could argue their case before a federal appellate court panel, Davis was also banking on the fact that newly passed federal immigration laws had subsumed the constitutional provisions of 187. He was hoping, in short, that the whole matter would burn itself out and go away. When asked by a reporter in Sacramento to comment on Davis's mediation strategy, Zedillo replied: "I trust Governor Davis. And I hope and trust and know that in the end there will be a good solution regarding this issue."[26]

The visit of the forty-five-year-old Mexican president to California in mid-May 1999 was, like Davis's earlier visit to Mexico, a triumphal progress of goodwill and healing gesture. At the Capitol, Davis welcomed Zedillo in Spanish, and Zedillo addressed a joint session of the legislature in Spanish after being introduced by Bustamante and Villaraigosa, also in Spanish. Zedillo's speech was carried live statewide on Spanish-language television. Yet he returned to Mexico to face the end of his administration (and, more dramatically, the defeat of the PRI, which had governed Mexico since 1929), by the National Action Party (PAN) candidate, Vicente Fox, a fifty-eight-year-old businessman-rancher from Guanajuato and former chief executive for Coca-Cola in Mexico. The men made a dramatic contrast: Zedillo was a Yale PhD in economics who had come up through the technocratic ranks of the PRI and fully accepted the centralized and state-oriented philosophy of his party; Fox had barely managed to finish his bachelor's degree the year before he ran for president, and was a self-made man with an orientation toward private enterprise who was also capable of appointing the brainy, left-of-center theoretician Jorge Castañeda as his foreign minister. While personable, in his way, Zedillo conducted himself with the reserve of a grand academic and spoke in measured phrases. Fox, tall and ruggedly handsome, was outgoing, plainspoken, gregarious, and given to wearing jeans and size-twelve cowboy boots. While Zedillo, in the tradition of the PRI, remained scrupulously secularist in utterance and attitude, the Roman Catholic Fox made open references to his faith and the devotion of his nation to the Virgin of Guadalupe.

Davis was on hand in Mexico City for Fox's inauguration on December 1, 2000, part of a large delegation headed by Secretary of State Madeleine Albright. Fox began the day praying on his knees at the Basilica of Guadalupe, followed by a tamale breakfast with sixty street children in the rough-and-tough Tepito section of Mexico City. In his inaugural address, Fox promised an end to corruption in Mexican politics, justice for the Indians of Chiapas, social and educational programs for the young, health care for the elderly, environmental action, a renewed war on the drug trade, and a curbing of Mexico's all-too-powerful central intelligence service (Fox's own telephone calls had been monitored during the campaign)—nothing less than the reform and modernization of Mexican society.

For however long this mood of renewal would last, or however successful it would turn out to be, Vicente Fox began his six-year term full speed ahead as far as Mexico and California were concerned. When he visited California in late March 2001, it seemed as if he contained within himself the hopes of California as well as of Mexico. It was a dazzling performance, a charismatic progress across the state. In Sacramento, Fox addressed a joint session of the legislature, stressing themes of trade and commerce and mutual understanding. Far from being a mere petitioner, Fox pointed out that Mexico was not only California's number one trading partner, but was also selling electrical power to the state to help offset its energy crisis. He urged California to offer in-state tuition rates to the children of noncitizen Mexicans living and working in California and seeking citizenship. Why should such children, he asked, be prevented from enhancing their future—whether that future be in California or Mexico—through higher education?

From Sacramento, Fox flew to San Jose for tours of Silicon Valley businesses and talks about bringing high technology to Mexico. Most movingly, he met in Fresno with a crowd of some 2,500 Mexican and Mexican-American farmworkers; he praised them for the dignity, quality, and productivity of their labor, told them Mexico was proud of what they had achieved for California north of the border, and cited them as representatives of Mexican culture and the Mexican people's strong work ethic. "You are the cultural engine, the permanent ambassadors of Mexican culture," Fox told the jean-clad farmworkers in their John Deere hats, the women in simple dresses, many of whom were raising the black Aztec eagle flag of the United Farm Workers along with the tricolors of Mexico. "In addition to missing you, we are very grateful to you."[27]

At this point could be found the moral core of Vicente Fox's mission to California. True, the levels of trade between California and Mexico had now moved past $15 billion. True, Fox was in search of high technology, water technology, and management expertise, and an educational Marshall Plan for young not-yet-citizens of Mexican descent. And true, Fox would soon be meeting with elite groups of academics at UCLA and investors at a banquet at the Century Plaza Hotel in Beverly Hills; but the time he spent with the 2,500 farmworkers in Fresno underscored a deeper and more impressive relationship between California and Mexico: an acknowledgment that the stoop labor of Mexican people for most of the twentieth century had been the fundamental premise and moral center of the lead element, agriculture, in the California economy. Behind these bronze-faced men and women gathering in the Fresno City Exhibit Hall in the early-morning hours, awaiting the arrival of Mexico's president, was the palpable presence of millions of Mexican workers and the interminable hours under a merciless sun they had spent in the creation of California. A new note had been struck, and it could be hoped that it would be sustained, whatever the difficulties facing the Mexican economy might be. At some point in the 1990s, California had experienced a transformation of value and attitude. It now knew itself to be, in significant measure, a Mexican-American commonwealth, linked to Mexico by economic ties, by trade and commerce, but also by the even more binding ties of shared culture and bloodlines. Mexico and California, along with the other states of the border, now shared a people in common. In turning against Mexico, if that ever happened again, or against the Mexican people, California would be turning against itself.

PART VI

Cities, Suburbs, and Other Places

How Should We Live?

When it came to the question of how they should live, Californians had long since opted for suburban density. The point could be made that throughout its 150-year existence as an American commonwealth, California had always favored density in its built environment. Again and again, Californians had expressed their preference for the sub/urban way of life: in the Gold Rush towns; in San Francisco, the tenth largest city in the nation by 1870; in the suburbs fanning out from San Francisco, starting in the 1860s; and in the almost overnight suburbanization of the Los Angeles basin in the first three decades of the twentieth century. The year 1990 found California, according to the Census Bureau, the most intensely suburbanized state in the nation: 92.6 percent of all Californians were living in a city, a suburb, or a township of some density. (At the other end of the spectrum, Vermont had 68 percent of its population living in rural areas.) A number of cities that did not even exist in 1980—Santa Clarita and Moreno Valley, for example—had passed the 100,000 mark. Bakersfield had jumped fifty-five places, from 152nd to 97th.

The midsize suburban communities of California, meanwhile, fueled by the economic growth of the 1980s, available and inexpensive land, and access to interstate highways, were burgeoning. During the 1980s, Rancho Cucamonga had grown by 83.54 percent. Escondido, Oceanside, Bakersfield, and Chula Vista were all experiencing growth rates in the sixtieth percentile. Ontario, Santa Ana, Stockton, and Pomona were growing by 42 to 50 percent. San Bernardino, Santa Rosa, Thousand Oaks, and Salinas had each increased their populations by more than a third. Traditional cities, suburbs, and towns, edge cities, suburban new towns, golf and country club leisure developments, exurban developments of every sort: Californians were developing every type of suburban possibility. Urban theorists could find corroborating examples, for better or for worse, for their theories without having to leave the state. Jane Jacobs, author of *Death and Life of Great American Cities* (1961), might very well revel in the densities and traditional neighborhoods of San Francisco, a mid-nineteenth-century city constructed on an orthodox urban grid. Despite his general distaste for things American, on the other hand, London-based urban theorist Leon Krier, mentor in these matters to the Prince of Wales, might find in such places as Carmel, Palo Alto, Sausalito, Napa, Sonoma, St. Helena, Mount Shasta, Santa Barbara, or Del Mar sufficient densities, downtown activity, and social interaction to dispute his own claim that American settlements lacked intimacy and social complexity.

Throughout the decade, as in the case of most metropolitan centers in the Far West—Phoenix especially, but also Denver, Albuquerque, Las Vegas, and Salt Lake City—the cities and suburbs of California were almost universally in a condition of sprawl. Theorists on both sides of the question argued about just how damaging such sprawl might be to the environment or to quality of life. While most academicians condemned sprawl as being environmentally damaging as well as unable to pay for itself, USC professors Harry Richardson and Peter Gordon were making a spirited defense of dispersion as a fulfillment of Frank Lloyd Wright's concept of Broadacre City. And besides, Richardson and Gordon argued, the jobs/housing balance was continually correcting itself as more and more jobs migrated out to where the most coping and competitive Californians were living. Commute times, they argued, were growing shorter as a result. A rising number of workers were telecommuting during part of the week; indeed, the very nature of the city was being transformed through telecommunications into a cyberentity that represented a new modality of urbanism.

From this perspective, cities could increase their complexity and activity through communications without a massive expansion of the built environment. Or, conversely, new cybercities could form themselves with minimum impact. That is what the Sierra Business Council was setting out to do: assist residents of the Sierra Nevada to form separate or integrated telecommunications-based economies that constituted, in effect, a new city in the Sierra Nevada that was making next to no demands on the environment while supporting some 485 businesses in a population of 563,000, expected to double by 2020.

The new communications environment, suggested Joel Kotkin, was actually creating a new opportunity for the inner city. The more routine business was done in cyberspace, he stated, the more opportunity there was for cities to take up the specialized tasks of trade, commerce, and culture that had revived cities in the first place in the medieval and Renaissance eras. Cities, Kotkin advanced in *The New Geography: How the Digital Revolution Is Reshaping the American Landscape* (2000), no longer had to do everything: process the paperwork, ship and distribute goods, house workers by the hundreds of thousands. Edge cities could bear the burden of administration; and even this function could be further dispersed through telecommunications. Cities, in turn, could now specialize, even re-elitize themselves, as in the case of the Renaissance cities of Italy or the jewelry district in downtown Los Angeles or the entertainment industry spread throughout the metropolitan region.

Surveying these trends in January 1997, New York University urban historian Thomas Bender saw a difficulty. The city, Bender argued, was becoming the City Lite—a consumerist theme park for visiting suburbanites, as opposed to its own centered economy and value system—and nowhere was this more true than in California. What, after all, were Pier 39 and Universal CityWalk but idealized theme park replications of San Francisco and Los Angeles respectively? And was it only accidental that in Irvine the South Coast Plaza shopping mall and the Orange County Performing Arts Center faced each other? Both, after all, were "merely sites of upper-class consumption." Cities, Bender said, had through the first half of the twentieth century served as "engines of wealth and incubators of creativity—from politics to the arts. But since mid-century, growing suburbanization, as decentralization of populations and as a cluster of values celebrating the privatization of life, has eaten away at the spirit of urbanity. Suburban values also resist the essential qualities of the city: diversity, the chance encounter, the unpredictable story, the unprogrammed space and activity."[1]

Perhaps no development corroborated such trends and the fears behind them more dramatically than the gated community, with its privatized streets and controlled access, its home owners' association constituting the de facto local government. By 1997, urban scholars Edward J. Blakely of USC and Mary Gail Snyder of UC Berkeley were reporting in *Fortress America: Gated Communities in the United States* (1997) that there were more than twenty thousand gated communities, encompassing more than three million units, throughout the United States. And nowhere was the gated community more in evidence than in California. In 1988 alone, Blakely and Snyder said, fully a third of the 140 projects being developed in Orange County were gated, representing a 100 percent increase over the past five years. In California gated communities ran the gamut from the ultra-exclusive Black Hawk in the hills of Contra Costa County and the equally expensive Palm Desert, Rancho Mirage, and Indian Wells in Riverside County, to more affordable communities like Redwood Shores in Redwood City and the Silver Creek Valley Country Club in San Jose. As Blakely and Snyder encountered them throughout the United States, but in California especially, gated communities, whatever their precise niche within a general sector of affluence, represented a desire to withdraw from urban society, or to better control it. Gated communities were utopias of a sort, or at least brought with them a utopian intent. They also stood for a triumph of private over public value, taking care of communal needs through a home owners' association or, if the community were incorporated as a city, subcontracting municipal functions—police, fire, garbage—to a private operator.

A significant percentage of California's gated communities were retirement oriented. In them, a number of factors—increased longevity, a general rise in real estate values allowing retirees to cash out at the conclusion of their working lives, the wholesale spread of pension benefits and investment programs for the middle classes following World War II—had resulted in growing populations of tanned and fit men and women in their late fifties, sixties, seventies, even eighties, gathered into gated enclaves that had become, over the past thirty years, a virtually new form of city. One such community, Leisure World, fifty miles south of Los Angeles in Orange County, incorporated itself as the city of Laguna Woods in 1999 in order to cope better with questions of growth, especially efforts to transform the nearby El Toro Marine Corps Air Station into a commercial airport, which Laguna Woods residents opposed. Orange County now had a city of eighteen thousand residents living densely on three square miles. The average age was seventy-seven, which made Laguna Woods an anthropological experiment of the first order.

Not only did gated retirement communities represent a new development in urban form, they also were provoking equally impressive innovations in urban programming. The things that occurred more or less spontaneously in ordinary cities and townships—the formation of friendships, voluntary associations, recreation, and entertainment—now became formally structured and choreographed activities, most of them administered by professional staffs with backgrounds in physical therapy, dietetics, recreation, and other aspects of occupational science and therapy. The monthly calendars of many such communities showed a variegated and well-planned program of lectures, golf and tennis, aerobics, swimming and aquathenics classes, book groups, field trips, pinochle, bridge and poker, potluck dinners, calligraphy and ceramics, painting and language instruction, country and western dances, and at least in one case—that of the Summerset Life Community in Brentwood in Contra Costa County—a regularly scheduled toga party.

The gated retirement community represented, then, a new and entirely coherent way of handling old age. It was one thing to talk about seniors remaining in their homes, surrounded by adoring grandchildren and an appreciative community. It was quite another matter to see these same seniors becoming isolated if they tried to maintain themselves in the communities where they had raised their families or pursued their careers. Whether the elderly remained in their homes or cashed out and moved to retirement communities (the majority of them offering some form of convalescent care when the time came), affluent California was growing older and older. Across California, wealthy communities—San Marino, Rolling Hills, Carmel, Sausalito, Beverly Hills, Palos Verdes Estates, La Cañada Flintridge, Ross, Atherton—were declining in population as children grew up, moved away, and left behind aging parents. The city of Ross in Marin County refused to believe it when the Census Bureau told it in 1990 that it had lost nearly a quarter of its population. The Palos Verdes Peninsula Unified School District, which had seventeen thousand students in 1973, had only nine thousand in 1990, forcing the closing of five elementary, two intermediate, and two of three high schools. In Atherton, on the San Francisco Peninsula, the population had grown so elderly that the city supported a computerized system that automatically telephoned seniors to check on their well-being. If no one answered, the police paid a visit.

Holy Land or Plains of Id?

Southern California and Metro Sacramento

The question of aging in the suburbs was very much on the mind of
Lakewood official D. J. Waldie in 1996. That year, Waldie's *Holy
Land: A Suburban Memoir* appeared. Not since Joan Didion delved into the
context and meaning of California suburbia in the 1960s had there been a
more searching and sometimes painfully truthful evocation of both the
American Mean and the American Gothic that could exist side by side in a
California suburb. In Waldie's case, it was the blue-collar suburb of Lakewood, near Long Beach, in southern Los Angeles County. Waldie's father
had brought his family there in 1950, and Waldie himself remained on as a
city employee, living alone in the same home in which he had grown up,
haunted by both the promise and expectation of Lakewood as it had been
developed in the years following World War II.

Waldie's *Holy Land* instantly, and deservedly, became a cult classic. In
bare minimalist language (the language of choice for the best of Southern
California writing, from Raymond Chandler to Joan Didion), Waldie
evoked in fewer than two hundred sparse pages worlds within worlds of
aspiration, achievement, and disappointment across a half century in boxlike homes on fifty-by-hundred-foot lots, eight homes to an acre, eleven
hundred square feet per home, the one repeating the other, $7,575 for a two-
bedroom, $8,525 for a three-bedroom. Homes such as these had symbolized
to an entire generation its hopes for the good life. On a cloudless Palm Sunday in April 1950, some 25,000 people had lined up before the sales office
in hopes of making a purchase. Nearly fifty years later, Waldie remained in
one of these homes, haunted by ghosts from the past and by a sense of time
that in less than five short decades had achieved an unexpected density and
weight. Here in this California suburb, one might encounter hundreds of
houses of seven gables, each of them reverberating with the traces and

memories of lives accomplished or lives that had been stillborn or gone awry. Still, Waldie, who might have gone to other places, chose to remain, living and working in Lakewood, owning and renting a second home in this suburb to the woman whom he once might have married before she married someone else. What Waldie accomplished in *Holy Land* was the linking to ancient and immemorial human association each detail of Lakewood—the homes themselves, the nearby mall, the day hundreds of moving trucks arrived en masse and were photographed for *Life* magazine, the excitement of television in the early 1950s, the jobs in defense that supported so many families, the fifty-year efforts to customize mass-produced houses—until this otherwise nondescript suburban community achieved the imaginative density of a New England village as described by Nathaniel Hawthorne.

The strength of *Holy Land,* however, lay in its depiction of the past, even in its burden of tragedy and defeat. Covering the sexual racketeering of Lakewood's teenage *posse comitatus* for *The New Yorker* in 1993, Joan Didion depicted a Lakewood far removed from the spontaneous dignity of the first generation to occupy these homes. What, then, was this suburb of Lakewood? Was it an imaginatively recovered Holy Land, or was it a present-tense wasteland of vulgarity, downward mobility, and multiple mis-behavior? Closer inspection of both Waldie's and Didion's view might reveal an equally disturbing instance of class division in the California and America of the 1990s. Lakewood was intended for working people of the lower ranges of the middle class: engineers and plant managers, skilled craftsmen, defense workers with some skills and union protection—the very kind of people who were being squeezed out of California in the early 1990s and were, as both the cause and effect of such marginalization, disin-tegrating in their personal and family integrity. The white people who in Waldie's memoir were dressing in the 1950s in coat and tie on Sundays, their children in starched pinafores or short pants and flat caps, were by the 1990s covered in tattoos, wearing T-shirts and jeans, the men in long hair and earrings, the young people tending to slobdom or punk. What, one might ask, had happened to those self-respecting Lakewoodites of yore? What had they lost? What had been taken from them?

Whatever the answer was, it could not clearly be called the fault of the suburbs; other populations were experiencing an even more accelerated downward mobility in the inner city. And besides, the more prosperous sub-urbs of California—and these were in the majority—were doing quite well, including in the delicate matter of decorum and civility. If you were edu-cated and affluent, you tended to be doing well in the California of the 1990s. Any deficiencies, however, any dimensions of noncompetitiveness, showed themselves instantly in questions of public behavior and taste. Few residents of Palo Alto or San Marino smoked Kools, were fiercely tattooed, or if they were male, wore ponytails. The more affluent the suburb, the more it had the look of a backdrop for an L. L. Bean or Talbots catalog. Wealth and education had migrated to the suburbs just as Lakewood was welcoming the middle classes. By the 1990s, most affluent Californians lived in suburbs, leaving the cities, in general, to the less affluent and the outright rich. Suburban affluence and education was also multicultural, leavened by millions of educated immigrants drawn to California as a high-tech mecca. By the end of the decade, European travel companies were organizing tours to Silicon Valley that included extensive exposure to the elegant suburbs— Saratoga, Los Gatos, Los Altos, Los Altos Hills, Palo Alto, Atherton, Menlo Park, Woodside, Portola Valley—bordering the region.

By and large, as both a *Los Angeles Times* poll and the one-hundredth anniversary of *Sunset* magazine were emphasizing, Californians were enjoying their suburban lifestyle. For more than seventy years, ever since Laurence Lane bought the magazine in 1928, *Sunset* had achieved the highest levels of circulation in California and the Far West promoting the suburban ideal. As USC journalism scholar Bryce Nelson pointed out, "*Sunset* has been able to figure out better than the editors of our major newspapers what the readers want. It's about life's pleasures, like sitting on the patio and watching your garden grow. It's not about the rich and trendy, it's about the real."[2]

A poll taken by the *Los Angeles Times* in the fall of 1999 revealed that the fundamental ideal of *Sunset*—a responsible and cultivated domestic life in suburban circumstances—was alive and well throughout Southern California. Some 2,385 respondents stated that by and large they liked their suburbs—88 percent in the San Gabriel Valley, 91 percent in Orange County—and, perhaps surprisingly, that they approved of the fact that their suburbs now supported many Asians, Latinos, and other nonwhites who believed in the suburban ideal as well. An exception to this general sense of well-being was the eastern San Fernando Valley, one of the oldest suburban communities in the Southland; but here the bête noir was not the suburb itself but the fact that the valley was part of Los Angeles, hence vulnerable to all the problems plaguing the less affluent inner city. Crime, of course, remained a concern, with one in four of the polled residents living in a gated community and one in every four households having a gun. On the other hand, 57 percent of the suburbanites surveyed ate dinner at home most evenings, in the company of their family—an impressive statistic in an era of family dysfunction and fast food.

And yet, as the dissatisfactions registered by residents of the less affluent regions of the San Fernando Valley underscored, the less affluent suburbs could still be considered—as the English urbanist Reyner Banham first dubbed them—the Plains of Id, vast reaches of settlement ungraced by the institutional or cultural life of urbanism. So disaffected were they with their conditions—poor police and fire protection, poor schools, poor public transportation, a sense of being an afterthought in the minds of the power structure—many residents of the San Fernando Valley, heartland of the Plains of Id, organized as Valley VOTE to take the valley out of Los Angeles entirely. Valley VOTE managed to secure millions of dollars from state and local sources to study the implications of such a breakup, which would have to be approved by voters of the entire city of Los Angeles in the November 2002 election. Thus the City of Angels, because of deep discontent in its suburban regions, stood in danger of becoming an anomaly: an important world city, the second largest in the United States, finding itself in the preliminary stages of voluntary dismemberment.

The Valley VOTE secessionist movement sprang from a variety of causes, among them a determination on the part of local political leaders and wannabes to break free from the control of an indifferent Los Angeles City Council and form their own governing body, with careers open to talent. At the same time, Valley VOTE could not be totally dismissed as a rump quorum of ambitious politicos. Discontent was high in the valley, as the *Los Angeles Times* suburban poll indicated; and nowhere was this more evident than in the dismay and distrust residents felt for the 710,000-student Los Angeles Unified School District, the second largest in the nation, which was ending the decade as a kind of political football in a power game being played out by the Latino and Jewish communities. By late 1999, Valley VOTE had decided to concentrate its energies on the dismantlement of the school district as a necessary first step.

How had it all become so desperate? How had so many residents of the San Fernando Valley, the first among equals of all Southern California suburbs, become so disaffected with their circumstances and, most revealingly, so hungry for a renewal of local institutions? Part of the answer was in the nature of suburbs themselves, in the valley or elsewhere. Just how much of a civic fabric—the weaving together of local institutions and loyalties in definable environments—could be expected to develop amid such suburban sprawl? The answer was of significance not only to the valley but to all the other overnight suburbs—north, south, and central—California was creating, not to mention such shopping-mall-dominated cities as Irvine and Newport Beach in Orange County, Fresno in the Central Valley, San Jose and the cities of Contra Costa and Alameda Counties in the Bay Area, and metropolitan Sacramento. Even such a staid old-fashioned city as Palo Alto was in the process of reconfiguring itself around the megapresence of the

Stanford Shopping Center, one of the most upscale malls in the nation—a Shangri-la of tasteful consumerism. For some fifty years now, California had been developing itself, primarily, as planned suburban developments with shopping malls and adjacent parking as the central public space. Was this enough to make a city? Could an evident decline in citizenship—as judged, say, by voter participation, volunteerism, or other forms of public service—be linked to a suburban environment that was devoid of value-enhancing public spaces and institutions beyond the local shopping mall?

Malls could certainly make for a culture of sorts, as evidenced in the San Fernando Valley, and as interpreted by such films as *Fast Times at Ridgemont High* (1982), *Valley Girl* (1983), *Scenes from a Mall* (1991), and *Encino Man* (1992). Each film underscored the importance of the mall as center of civic and personal life. In *Scenes from a Mall,* the entire life cycle, from birth to death, occurs within the confines of a single mall on a single day. It was in the mall that teenagers congregated and hung out. Families went to the mall on Sundays for an outing. A significant amount of daily or weekly nutrition was taken at the mall, either from fast-food outlets or more ambitious restaurants. During the holiday season, it was the mall—decorations abounding, Christmas carols sounding, Santa Claus available for the kids—to which one repaired to get into the holiday spirit.

The decade opened with twenty-three-year-old Priscilla Butler of Laguna Hills serving as the poster girl of the shop-till-you-drop syndrome. "Gluttonous consumption" was the way that San Bernardino County deputy district attorney Michele Elizalde-Daly described it; for by this time, May 1991, Butler was in the county jail on charges of pursuing the greatest shopping spree—$1.4 million over a two-year period—in Southern California history. The problem was that the money had been embezzled, beginning with $10,000-a-month increments, but growing bolder as time went on, taken by her bookkeeper mother from her employer and funneled to her daughter in a kind of reverse paradigm of tough love by a guilt-ridden parent. Accepting the money from her mom, Butler brought consumerism to near-metaphysical heights. When her mother was discovered and the scam was over, it took an entire team of deputy district attorneys and investigators to locate and retrieve the harvest of Priscilla Butler's two years of nonstop shopping before she and her mother were convicted and sent to state prison. The home in Laguna Hills was easy enough, as was the Mercedes, the Porsche, the Saab, and the Jeep Cherokee; and the closets stuffed with designer clothes could also be expected (a $4,000 Chanel suit was at the dry cleaner's); but what could you say about the four rented storage units stuffed with shoes, purses (Butler had a thing for purses, especially expensive leather ones, and Louis Vuitton and Michael Cromer leather luggage), and other items? None of the purveyors in South Coast Plaza in Costa Mesa, where she did most of her shopping, found it odd that a young woman in her early twenties would plunk down $1,200 for four pairs of shoes, buy a $70,000 car with cash, or come within one day of closing escrow on a 3,800-square-foot, $488,000 mansion in Laguna Hills with limestone flooring and its own library. "Maybe it's unusual in San Bernardino," one retailer told the DA, "but this is Orange County."[3]

It was not reported whether Priscilla Butler spoke Valley Talk—jamming words together rapidly, ending the last word of each sentence with a singsong uplift that sounds like a question, punctuating each sentence with such interjections as *like* or *for sure* or *totally* or *ohmygosh*—but this distinctive patois, alleged to have originated in the malls of the San Fernando Valley, had by the early 1990s become the lingua franca of not only Valley Girls but young women throughout suburban America, including Olympic gold medalist Kristi Yamaguchi of Fremont in northern California, another mall suburb, and teenage tennis star Jennifer Capriati from suburban southern Florida. Rock musician Frank Zappa and his daughter, Moon, had first satirized Valley Talk in their joint song hit "Valley Girl" (1982), and comedian Julie Brown perfected a routine in which she played the ultimate Valley Girl, but by the early 1990s such phrases as "gag me with a spoon" and "grody to the max" were already, like, retro, totally. Yet Valleyspeak had taken hold with such ferocity that speech therapists were making a reasonable living breaking teenagers of the habit, lest their way of speaking prevent them—ohmygosh!—from getting into a good college.

Anthropologists and linguists had a field day dissecting the implications of Valleyspeak, particularly after Winona Ryder brought the genre Valley Girl to perfection in the film *L.A. Story* (1991); and most interpretations were linked to the suburban lifestyle and the mall, especially as encountered by female teenagers. On the one hand, Valley Girls might easily be dismissed as consumerist airheads, which they frequently were. On the other hand, Valleyspeak was so pervasive—including in the college classroom, where undergraduates with good board scores lapsed frequently into it—the phenomenon was clearly a linguistic response to the mall as public culture and space. In the absence of competing institutions—that is, competing voices and dictions—Valleyspeak spread from mall to mall, starting in the San Fernando Valley and sweeping across America, as a way for teenagers to bond with each other, through a specialized vocabulary, mantric patterns of interjection, and singsong intonation.

Even as the mall emerged triumphant, however, it was experiencing decline. In 1999 the Sherman Oaks Galleria, the first and major mall of the San Fernando Valley and scene of both *Valley Girl* and *Fast Times at Ridge-*

mont High, closed for lack of business. The closing provoked a flurry of speculation about whether the era of the mall was ending, first in Southern California, and then, later, throughout the rest of the United States. By the late 1990s, the trouble being experienced by such malls as the Plaza Pasadena, the Long Beach Plaza, Huntington Center in Huntington Beach, and Anaheim Plaza indicated that the era of the mall was in a process of transformation. Mere retail in an enclosed space was not enough to remain competitive; and this in and of itself was a form of social and cultural statement—a looking back, or, more correctly, a looking back to the future, toward the needs and satisfactions of a more sophisticated urbanism. Those megamalls that were doing well—the Glendale Galleria, for example, or the South Coast Plaza in Orange County, the Stanford Shopping Center in Palo Alto, and Stonestown in San Francisco—were offering not just shopping but a full variety of pedestrian-oriented retail and entertainment options, including quality restaurants and multiplex movie theaters. It was not enough to fill an enclosed space with bargain goods and teenagers. Adolescents possessed minimal spending power, for one thing, and bargain goods could only pay for themselves in specialized outlets in the low-cost hinterlands beyond the city and suburb.

Something akin to the old pedestrian-oriented retail zone, even the variety and intrinsic urbanism of the old-fashioned department store, was in order. Urbanologist Charles Lockwood was discerning a national trend based on "Americans' hunger for community," and their desire "to create a public realm, a sense of place and identity out of anonymous suburban sprawl." Such efforts could already be seen in the recasting of the enclosed mall into a quasi-open suburban galleria, as in the case of the 1993 Valencia Town Center, which discouraged roaming packs of teenagers and elaborated its retail presentations through an interplay of indoor and outdoor options on a traditionally scaled pedestrian Main Street, national stores and local shops, restaurants, a multiplex movie theater, and a hotel. To add further to the quasi-urban mix, the developers of Valencia, the Newhall Land and Farming Company, also located an office complex nearby (Princess Cruises was an early tenant) and several hundred apartment units on the nearby Town Center Drive. Lockwood considered the Valencia experiment a key example of how new development was beginning to avoid its prior fixation on malls in favor of a recreated urbanism.[4]

Mark Baldassare, a professor of urban planning at UC Irvine, dubbed this phenomenon the New Urbanism, by which he meant not only a reappreciation for the pedestrian city, but also the desire to bring classic urban values to the suburb. In California, the UC Berkeley–based urban planner Peter Calthorpe served as the leading theoretician and practitioner of the

New Urbanist movement, which sought to bring pedestrian city values to the suburbs by public transit and walking-oriented urban villages in developing suburbs. The New Urbanism also advocated downsized neighborhoods, smaller streets, networks of alleys and walking trails, even old-fashioned porches. Older homes in the suburbs, many of them dating back to the era of Craftsman and Progressive bungalows (which had been considered marginal housing in the postwar era, the near-abandoned remnants of an earlier identity), were being snapped up by New Urban gentrifiers anxious to live in what one buyer termed "homes with attitude."[5]

The creation of the Third Street Promenade in Santa Monica in 1989 revitalized a lackluster retail street through the deliberate re-creation of a public pedestrian culture emphasizing not just food and entertainment but necessary retail services such as drug stores and dry cleaners for the local community. Spearheaded in the late 1980s by Douglas Stitzel, a UC Berkeley–trained Sanskrit scholar turned developer, Old Town Pasadena represented a similar effort to restore pedestrian culture, with an entire neighborhood, down and out through the 1980s, being brought back into a competitive array of shops, restaurants, theaters, bookstores, and other retail, all of it keyed to pedestrian traffic. Before his untimely death at age forty from leukemia, Stitzel also completed Two Rodeo Drive in Beverly Hills, an off-street pedestrian enclave at the otherwise automobile-dominated corner of Wilshire and Rodeo.

Traditional suburban communities such as Walnut Creek in Contra Costa County, in the East Bay, were revitalizing their central shopping districts, long since neglected in favor of outlying shopping centers and malls, with quality retail that reintroduced the older central portions of the city to its residents. In Walnut Creek, along Locust and North Main Streets, a pedestrian-oriented shopping culture emerged that became competitive with Chestnut or Union or Sacramento Street in San Francisco. Even the East Bay community of Emeryville, recreating itself as a big-box shopping center (Borders, Home Depot, Ikea, Trader Joe's, Pak 'n Save, Ross), made sure that these big boxes were packed tightly adjacent to each other, with pedestrian pathways and open green space down a central outdoor mall, and that cinemas, restaurants, and a nightclub also were part of the mix.

Sacramento developer Philip Angelides and his architect-planner Peter Calthorpe, meanwhile, had taken the reurbanization efforts of the decade to even greater lengths with their whole-cloth creation of Laguna West, an eight-hundred-acre new town twenty miles east of downtown Sacramento. With a population (eventually) of thirty thousand in 3,400 housing units, Laguna West represented a neotraditional city that would have no trouble pleasing neocon advocates such as Prince Charles or Leon Krier. Organized around pedestrian pockets and a traditional street grid, with housing fronting sidewalks in an urban manner, Laguna West featured a direct light-rail connection to downtown Sacramento and devoted 14 percent of its space to parks and man-made lakes. It also offered clusters of condominium complexes for sale and an array of apartment rentals intended to foster density and an inclusive economic mix.

Within a decade, a brand-new metropolitan region had emerged in central California, extending north from Davis to Woodland in Yolo County and eastward into the Sierra Nevada foothills of Placer, El Dorado, Calaveras, and Madera Counties, whose populations jumped by more than 20 percent between 1990 and 1996. Developer Norman Jarrett was even planning a Disneyland North for the region: a $300 million Gold Rush City theme park celebrating the 1850s Mother Lode. But was Sacramento a city, or even a city in the making? Yes and no. Certainly, metro Sacramento was divided and subdivided into a number of independent governments; yet from the air, or even from Highways 99 and 50 or Interstates 5 and 880, the region looked like a city in its continuous weaving of shopping-center-oriented suburban communities. There were other characteristics of a maturing metropolitan region as well: a first-class research university at UC Davis; an important teaching institution at CSU Sacramento; a respected medical school in Sacramento, run by UC Davis; the McGeorge School of Law, an arm of the Stockton-based University of the Pacific; an impressive array of parks and public golf courses; the notable Crocker Art Museum, housing a collection of nineteenth-century European and American paintings; the state-sponsored Railroad Museum and Golden State Museum; the ARCO Arena, home of the Sacramento Kings, a professional basketball team; an international airport, with direct connections to the Midwest and the East and chartered flights abroad; and, of course, the state Capitol park and administrative complex. These and other amenities—a growing hotel and restaurant culture, for example—bespoke the developing urbanism of the metro Sacramento region. Still, in terms of its social-spatial arrangements, metro Sacramento was most fundamentally a mall- and shopping-center-oriented kind of a place, with the Arden Mall at the intersection of Interstate 80 and Arden Way serving as the de facto civic center of the region.

Despite its public identity as the state capital, Sacramento had had the embarrassment of seeing its symphony orchestra go under in the mid-1990s. At the same time, however, the Sacramento Kings had received a $50 million–plus subvention. Yet metro Sacramento seemed unembarrassed by either development; the region still represented a triumph of middle American values. It was an intensely private place, with people relating most directly to their own homes and families, secondarily (if applicable) to their places of religious worship, thirdly to the schools their children attended, and fourthly to a life of outdoor enjoyment. Metro Sacramentans liked big homes on big lots, with big garages, where they could park their sport-utility vehicles, their boat, their camper, their motorcycles, their mountain bicycles, skis, Jet Skis, John Deere lawn mowers, Black & Decker tools, and other stuff. More than 20 percent of the homes sold in the Highland Reserve subdivision of Roseville, north of Sacramento, in 1999 had four-car garages, many of them one thousand square feet in extent, larger than the average urban apartment.

Suburbs were not cities, true; they lacked the ancient structures and synergies of urban life so eloquently praised, in the main, by professors of urbanism at prestige universities in or near established cities. For upscale elites, cities could provide the portal to an enhanced experience of life. But for the middle classes, cities, including those of California, too often meant nonresponsive institutions, questionable public schools, and a growing sense of danger based on the realities of rising crime statistics. Ever since the 1920s, Americans had been increasingly choosing the suburban option. In the 1950s, suburban California was based on white flight. By the 1990s, the suburbs were as mixed in their ethnicities as the rest of California. Suburban Californians owned their own homes (57 percent), with their own swimming pools (32 percent), and their own home offices with Internet connections (34 percent), and they loved their churches, synagogues, mosques, temples, and soccer leagues.

The one thing they did not like—crime—most believed they had left behind by moving to the suburbs, with the exception of the San Fernando Valley, where crime had been rising since the 1992 Los Angeles riots and where 53 percent of adults felt, in late 1999, that their most important local problem was gangs, drugs, and crime. In contrast to the happy talk coming from the other suburbs, valley residents were talking about having knives held to their throat when someone took a fancy to their Thunderbird at a local gas station or seeing dead bodies on the front lawn just down the street after a Fourth of July altercation—this in contrast to the Fourth of July parade and pancake breakfast held each year in Huntington Beach. Even people in the safer suburbs said they were glad they lived in a gated community or in a development that was patrolled by a private police force.

Plains of Id, urbanophiles might sniff. Can anything good come from suburban Nazareth? Yes, suburbanites were responding. Everything good was coming from this Holy Land: a house, a job, the quiet enjoyment of one's premises, good schools, available tennis courts and golf courses, friendly police and responsive firemen, a city council that listened, a wonderful public library with story hours for the children, park and recreation programs (Little League games, soccer, gunnysack racing and face painting), a supermarket with offerings equal to any gourmet grocery store in upscale cities, Fourth of July parades, a menorah in the window at Hanukkah, block lightings at Christmas time, barbecues on the back lawn nine months a year, ministers, priests, and rabbis who knew you by name—and family, family, family. In suburb after suburb younger respondents to the *Times* poll in late 1999 were saying that one of the things that made them happiest about their suburb was its proximity to the suburb where their parents or other family members were living.

Research by the Fannie Mae Foundation showed that by the summer of 2002 an increasing number of suburbs were growing denser, more walkable, more centered on their downtowns. Half of all such "boomburbs," as the Fannie Mae study called them, were in California, in places like Oxnard, Simi Valley, Thousand Oaks, Corona, Fontana, Moreno Valley, Ontario, Rancho Cucamonga, Anaheim, Costa Mesa, Fullerton, Irvine, and Santa Ana—Southern California suburbs in search of a city, looking for that transition that had already been made in northern California by Moraga, Concord, Walnut Creek, Lafayette, Newark, Hayward, and Mission San Jose. As suburbs developed, the most vital of them were converging on social, psychological, and spatial centers. The ancient values of the city—community, the drama of everyday life, the shaping presence of institutions—were returning to the Plains of Id.

Staying Time

Santa Barbara and Palm Springs

S anta Barbara and Palm Springs offered affluent Californians, permanent and seasonal residents alike, a way of staying time—of arresting
the remorseless progress of devouring years—by offering the stylized
pleasures of an urban resort. Ordinary life—the passing of time, the
demands of daily work, the gains and losses of each day—was also characteristic of these places. The ordinary can never be banished, even in Palm
Springs or Santa Barbara. No one knew this better than the gardeners, waiters, busboys, hotel maids, firemen, and cops who kept these resort cities
operative on a day-to-day basis. Much of the work in Santa Barbara was
being done by Mexican immigrants, many of them supporting families in
Mexico. Up to a dozen people could share one apartment, sleeping in shifts.
It was common for Mexican workers to put in up to seventy hours a week,
holding down two jobs, which could also be in agriculture; the Coachella
Valley, especially around Indio, abounded in dates, citrus, melons, peaches,
nectarines, table grapes, and vegetables, while the Santa Barbara hinterlands supported one of the best developed organic farming economies in the
state. Santa Barbara even had a manufacturing company, Santa Barbara
Creative Foods, which each year shipped millions of pounds of salsa to a
grateful nation.

Each community had thousands of middle-class residents willing to take
their place in the economy that outside money, or money that was already
made, or dividends that were continuously yielding, was making possible in
Santa Barbara and Palm Springs. From this perspective, each metro region
was a job-creating machine: every kind of job, up and down the labor market, from gardener's assistant to busboy, from tax accountant to plastic surgeon. Even in bad times, you could go to these places and make a living;
and the people who did so, the ordinary people, the working people, pro-

vided the vitality for the grade schools, the high schools, the community colleges, the churches and synagogues, of the region. It was a testimony to the success of each place that people who grew up in metropolitan Palm Springs or metropolitan Santa Barbara most often wanted to stay there. If they left, they tended eventually to drift back home. The natives, too, were interested in staying time.

Successful resorts are utopias of a sort. They stylize experience through metaphor and storyline. In each instance, the fundamental metaphor of Santa Barbara and Palm Springs, the story they told of themselves, was that time could be stayed: that whether coming early or late, affluence and leisure—like the Rapture of Final Days so ardently believed in by evangelical Christians—could seize one from the conditions and cares of daily life in favor of a timeless realm of beauty, pleasure, and, through philanthropy, serious purpose. Metropolitan Palm Springs did this in a predominantly masculine way, as appropriate to a network of desert cities wrung from resistant nature by sheer force of will. Santa Barbara, by contrast, had a decidedly feminine element, nurturing and mystical, as appropriate to a seaside region of beaches, rolling hills, oak trees, morning mists yielding to midmorning sunshine, that had been prized as magical and salubrious since the days of the Spaniards. For all its many charities and good causes, Palm Springs was about golf, nightlife, swimming pools, with a Frank Sinatra soundtrack in constant play. Santa Barbara was about gardens and roses, Mediterranean villas perched on Riviera hills, and some golf, but also a lot more talk about spiritual values.

In each case, you had to have had the struggle of life, meaning the economic struggle, behind you if you were to enter fully into local myth. Each region, metro Palm Springs especially, was fueled by outside capital: the money earned elsewhere, the pensions and portfolios, the income-yielding investments of every sort. Each place had developed in the first instance as a seasonal resort: Santa Barbara at the turn of the twentieth century, catering to wealthy elites from the East and Midwest searching for winter sunshine; Palm Springs in the 1930s, offering Hollywood a place to play in the desert. Throughout the 1990s, despite the changes that were under way, Santa Barbara still sustained a subliminal connection to the Anglo-American Midwest and East in its elite phases: a daydream of polo and black-tie dinner parties with servants in livery in Mediterranean villas, cross-references everywhere to the Hamptons and Newport, Rhode Island. Palm Springs, meanwhile, continued to nurture a show business metaphor at the center of its DNA code, still idolizing Bob Hope, Dinah Shore, Frank Sinatra, America since the 1940s as refracted through entertainment.

Such values, such stylization of experience, a moralist might argue, were merely the delusional and distracting comforts of those who had mastered (or whose forebears had mastered) the Darwinian struggle of American life. But such judgments, even if true, missed the point. An oasis such as Palm Springs could by definition be a mirage in the desert, and frequently was; and one of the main streets of Santa Barbara was named Anacapa, which in the language of the Chumash people meant a pleasing illusion, a magical realm rising from the waters of the Santa Barbara Channel. Each city, then, was ready to concede the point. A lot of what went on was illusional, but who cared? Faced with the extraordinary materialized urban fabric of either region, one could not deny that mirages and pleasing illusions had brought into being two of the most intriguing urban cultures of California in the 1990s. As resorts, as stylizations of value and social experience, Santa Barbara and Palm Springs yielded insights about what was on the mind of California, hence on the mind of America, as the twentieth edged into the twenty-first century. Resorts are useful that way, almost from an anthropological perspective.

Each place was at once an initiating city, the core of the metaphor, and an extended metropolitan region. Seized from Mexico in 1846, the presidio settlement of Santa Barbara on the channel was developed as an American town in the 1870s and a resort city at the turn of the twentieth century. To the northwest was the more recent suburb of Goleta, site of the University of California at Santa Barbara. To the south, the metropolitan region included Montecito, Hope Ranch, Summerland, Carpinteria, and Ojai in adjacent Ventura County. Highway 101 ran like a spine through this network of communities. Santa Barbara was also a county, but the other communities and townships of the thinly settled north coast and wilderness interior did not participate in the resort metaphor. Even nearby Goleta, because it was a university town, with thousands of students crammed into quick-turnover apartment buildings and professors getting by in suburbia, did not fully participate in the metaphor either, although the 1990s did witness a continuing closure of town and gown tensions as Santa Barbara philanthropy turned its attention, increasingly, to its nearby university.

Incorporated in 1938, the city of Palm Springs was by the 1990s the gateway to an axis of communities running southeast along Interstate 10 and Highway 111 in the Coachella Valley of Riverside County. Moving in a southeasterly direction, these communities included Desert Hot Springs (incorporated in 1963), Cathedral City (1981), Rancho Mirage (1973), Indian Wells (1981), Palm Desert (1973), La Quinta (1983), Indio (1930), Coachella (1946), and the unincorporated Bermuda Dunes and Thousand Palms. As the incorporation dates suggest, metro Palm Springs was a decidedly post–World War II creation. Despite the multiplicity of cities and

townships, both metro Palm Springs and metro Santa Barbara could be considered contiguous and integrated communities, although Santa Barbara
and Montecito, with their long histories and long-achieved lifestyles, would
resist such a notion. In each case, Mother Nature herself—in the form of a
surrounding desert and the Pacific Ocean and the wilderness backcountry—
sealed each community into cohesiveness, despite the resistant nature of
Indio, which remained a no-nonsense agricultural town, and Goleta, a university suburb struggling to escape the downsides of an academic ghetto.

Each community had its fears of the college crowd, which might be
interpreted as the anxieties of one generation against another, especially in
metro Palm Springs, where a significant percentage of the population was
made up of retirees. Santa Barbara, it could be argued, had real cause for
grievance; on the night of February 25, 1970, at the height of anti–Vietnam
War resistance, rioting UCSB students had torched the Bank of America in
downtown Goleta. Palm Springs, by contrast, had only the 1986 spring
break riots to point to, when the city had been flooded with ten thousand
party-mad students. Local police had been forced to call in the California
Highway Patrol and the Riverside County Sheriff's Department to deal with
drunken collegians and coeds in thong bikinis crisscrossing the city on Ves-
pas and motorbikes.

And besides: young people were not a crucial element of the Palm
Springs formula, except on spring break weekends. Metro Palm Springs
was a much more middle-aged and late-middle-aged kind of place. Metro
Santa Barbara, because of UCSB and elements of a dot-com industry,
remained a young-adult-friendly place, especially on the beaches—and this
could be seen, doubly especially, during volleyball season, which was most
of the year. On any given weekend, on East or West Beach in Santa Barbara
or on the beaches of Goleta, up to 250 young people—the men in colorful
swimming trunks, the women in bikinis—gathered to play volleyball across
the long day in festive celebration, so it seemed, not only of the sport itself,
but of their own youth as well, their time of bodily health and the joy of life
under the sun. Over the years, metro Santa Barbara had developed as the
West Coast epicenter of beach volleyball, which differed from the indoor
variety, and it was no wonder that some of the great players of all time—
Rich Riffero, Henry Bergmann, John Hanley, Olympian Karch Kiraly, the
twins Lisa and Kelly Strand, Kathy Gregory (by the 1990s the volleyball
coach at UCSB)—had developed their skills on Santa Barbara beaches.

The beach also informed the day-to-day men's couture of metro Santa
Barbara, which consisted of jeans or Bermuda shorts and floral patterned
short-sleeved shirts, such as those available at Gary's Island in Paseo
Nuevo. A variation of the Hawaiian shirt, these Santa Barbara shirts

instantly bespoke the beach and by the early 2000s had become popular throughout coastal Southern California, wherever the water was in sight. Palm Springs, on the other hand, favored a more mature adult golfing look for men, although Gary's Island had recently opened an outlet in Palm Desert, and floral shirts had started to be seen around the swimming pool. Santa Barbara also preferred what might be described as the safari look, as sold by the Territory Ahead on State Street in downtown Santa Barbara. Founded in 1989 by Bruce Willard—a Middlebury College graduate and veteran of L. L. Bean, where he had learned the catalog business—the Territory Ahead was by the late 1990s employing some two hundred and doing a brisk $30 million business in catalog sales.

What the beach was to Santa Barbara, the swimming pool was to Palm Springs: the emblem of time-defying leisure. Santa Barbarans loved the beach and spent a lot of time on it. In the annual Coastal Project, two hundred regional artists would converge on Leadbetter Beach for an arts festival celebrating the relationship of Santa Barbara to the sea through a variety of art installations centered on flag emplacements and other forms of environmental art. Santa Barbara had also been a center of surf culture since the 1930s. The Palm Springs swimming pool offered a more artificial and engineered equivalent to the Santa Barbara beach, with pool designs growing more and more intricate across the last two decades of the twentieth century. While the younger women on the beaches of Santa Barbara favored the bikini, the poolside women of Palm Springs specialized in high-fashion swimsuits, as sold in the Palm Desert store Everything But Water: swimsuits edging into haute couture and releasing a message of stylized artifice that was so typical of Palm Springs culture as a whole.

What was being enjoyed so spontaneously by the beach volleyball players of Santa Barbara—health, fitness, the prospect of time without end—was a matter of deliberate effort in Palm Springs, in so many ways a retirement community (the Joslyn Cove Community Senior Center in Palm Desert had more than one thousand participants in its wide array of programs); hence the flourishing of an extensive spa, gymnasium, and medical culture. The city of Palm Springs itself was a center of spas—mud baths, massage, chiropractic therapy—including the spa opened in 1996 by French designer Hubert de Givenchy. Gold's Gym and the Oasis Health Club had brought personal training to a point of high art; indeed, trainers were themselves celebrities, courted and well paid, their names dropped in cocktail-party conversations as a sign of status. The hospitals of the region—the Eisenhower Medical Center and the Desert Hospital most notably—were world-class. The Betty Ford Center for Drug and Alcohol Rehabilitation was in and of itself an institution of international importance, with celebrities of every sort checking in, publicly or discreetly, for treatment. Metro Palm Springs was also a world center for cosmetic dentistry and plastic surgery, cosmetic or otherwise, most conspicuously at the Morrow Institute on the campus of the Eisenhower Medical Center, where the noted plastic surgeon David Morrow presided over an extensive staff and a wide variety of surgical services.

All this—the workouts, the spa treatments, the occasional surgery—had visible results. Metro Palm Springs abounded in very fit and very attractive people of a certain age who seemed to be winning the struggle with time. Each Memorial Day weekend, in the restored Plaza Theater, there was produced a revue entitled *The Fabulous Palm Springs Follies*. Aside from looking good in their showgirl attire, the volunteer chorus girls of the Follies had one other requirement: no one could be under the age of fifty-five. Founded in 1989 by retired television actor Riff Markowitz, who served as master of ceremonies, the Follies had by the late 1990s developed into a local institution, with 125 employees on its $2 million annual payroll. During its sixth season, more than 145,000 had come to Palm Springs to see the revue, bringing in an estimated $15 million to the local economy.

Metro Santa Barbara also abounded in tanned and fit people, although the age spread of the population was more inclusive. Samarkand, one of the great estates of the region, had been recast as a retirement community keyed to senior citizens, but in general in metro Santa Barbara one tended to retire early in life, in mid-middle age mostly, in order to devote oneself to philanthropy, spirituality, and the good life; but that meant that you had to stay active and fit. Montecito tycoon and business philanthropist Paul Glenn, for example, a good friend of Dr. Nathan Pritikin, was fascinated by the question of longevity. In 1965, while still in his thirties, the dapper Princetonian, already semiretired, founded the Glenn Foundation for Medical Research, which meant, primarily, research into longevity, for which the foundation each year dispensed substantial grants.

Most particularly, metro Palm Springs was about the people who had survived, the World War II generation, now in its final maturity but still enjoying life, still playing golf, attending black-tie benefits, giving dinner parties, reminiscing about the old days—but without a debilitating nostalgia, for they had brought the old days with them. Metro Palm Springs had been brought into being by the first flush of postwar affluence, embracing a middle-class view of the good life, which was why entertainment celebrities were so important. They embodied the history of the past half century. In surviving and thriving, entertainers, even those of minor or fleeting reputation, had transcended time and in a very real way had given metro Palm Springs its history. If it were not for the movie stars, went a local witticism,

Palm Springs would be indistinguishable from Banning. In founding the Racquet Club in the late 1930s, retired movie star Charles Farrell had done more than open a tennis and swimming spa for Hollywood. He established the very DNA code of the city. Since 1989, Palm Springs had had an annual international film festival and a sidewalk of stars in the downtown. Each issue of *Palm Springs Life* teemed with photographs of entertainment celebrities at one or another golf tournament, black-tie soiree, gallery opening, or benefit.

The entertainment industry and the legacy of entertainment—the recognition of specific stars and the memory of the innumerable movies and television shows they had appeared in since the 1940s—was the way metro Palm Springs defined its public culture. Streets were named after Bing Crosby, Fred Waring, Dinah Shore, Ginger Rogers, George Burns, Gracie Allen, Danny Kaye, Jack Benny, Barbara Stanwyck, Greer Garson, Claudette Colbert, George Montgomery, Bob Hope, and Frank Sinatra: some thirty-three streets in all with the names of Hollywood celebrities, most of them dating from the 1940s and 1950s. Remembering these stars metro Palm Springs retirees had found a way of both defining the present and remembering their lives. The history of entertainment had been fused with the history of the area, and the two had become one.

Based in his Rancho Mirage compound, Frank Sinatra merely had to sing "Fly me to the moon," and millions of Americans believed they could get there. Associated with Palm Springs since the late 1940s, Sinatra and his wife Barbara stood at the apex of the Palm Springs celebrity pantheon, along with Bob Hope, a near equal, and Dinah Shore, a close third. Each of them—Sinatra, Hope, and Shore—had his or her own annual golf tournament, and they were regulars on the cover of *Palm Springs Life*. Shore had gotten her start as a big-band singer in the early 1940s, and her husband, actor George Montgomery, a furniture designer and fabricator whose work was featured in the Palm Springs Museum, had also been a highly involved local resident. During the 1960s, in the central years of the World War II generation, Shore had dominated Sunday-night television. Entering her seventies in the 1990s, she seemed ageless as she welcomed the great professional women golfers of the nation to her annual tournament. Bob Hope was in his nineties in the 1990s, and would reach one hundred by May 2003. He and his wife Dolores were enjoying their sixth decade of desert life. In Bob Hope—his wit and humor, his longevity, his love of golf, his entertainment of the armed forces across a half century, his outspoken patriotism and friendship with presidents—metro Palm Springs could find the essence of its generational style as expressed and celebrated through entertainment.

Frank Sinatra, by contrast, standing at the heart of the metro Palm Springs celebrity culture, embodied the other side of the post–World War II generation—the booze, the cigarettes, the take-it-or-leave-it charm, the edgy restlessness of the cold war—that Sinatra had so cleverly orchestrated as leader of the Rat Pack. Sinatra's Rat Pack days may have been long behind him, and Barbara Sinatra, along with Betty Ford and Dolores Hope, was among the most respected and revered celebrities in the region; but there was still to Frankie, even as he entered his eighties, an ambience of very late nights (sunrise, he said, was his favorite time of day) and a party that had been in progress, as one Palm Springs wit put it, since both Sinatra and the city were in bobby sox.

When JFK had been in the White House, Sinatra had been a Democrat. In later years, however, starting with his close friendship with Nancy Reagan, Sinatra explored his inner Republicanism. Both he and Hope had known, and were to a degree befriended by, nearly every president since FDR. In office and in retirement, Dwight Eisenhower was the first president to embrace Palm Springs. Leaving office, Ike spent part of the year at the El Dorado Country Club, playing golf there and at Thunderbird and Indian Palms. Among other amenities, Eisenhower appreciated the fact that Palm Springs was, despite its Hollywood orientation, a solidly Republican sort of place. On his first Palm Springs weekend, in February 1954, he had stayed at the Smoke Tree Ranch, the favored resort of the Anglo-American oligarchy of metropolitan Los Angeles, with hardly a Democrat in sight.

In time, Palm Springs—or, more precisely, Rancho Mirage—would have its own presidential couple in residence, Gerald and Betty Ford. The Fords had first come to Palm Springs in the early 1960s during a congressional recess, invited there by Earl "Red" Blaik, former football coach at West Point and a longtime Ford friend. The Fords stayed at La Quinta Country Club, enjoying golf with Blaik and director Frank Capra. After that, they were hooked on Palm Springs, arriving there each Easter week. In 1975, the Fords were the guests of Fred and Vonnie Wilson at the Wilsons' home in Thunderbird Heights, again during the Easter recess. In 1977, following the victory of Jimmy Carter, the Fords took up residence in Rancho Mirage and were soon enjoying the good life at the heart of the metro Palm Springs establishment whose Republican doge in residence was Walter Annenberg, also of Rancho Mirage, the former ambassador to the Court of St. James, who was spending more and more time on his luxuriant estate in the desert. Here each year during the 1980s, Nancy and Ronald Reagan would fly in on Air Force One for Walter and Lee Annenberg's annual New Year's Eve party, which constituted the celebration par excellence of the region's Republican identity.

Even the mayor of Palm Springs, Sonny Bono, who won election in 1988, was a Republican celebrity. Retiring from show business, Bono had operated a restaurant in Palm Springs before his election and, despite his goofy-guy image as Cher's consort and straight man, was by all reports doing a good job as mayor through the first half of the 1990s. This led to his election to the 104th Congress in 1995, where he also—to the surprise of nearly everyone—turned in a credible performance, despite the skeptical, openly satirical attitude of the national press. When Bono died in a skiing accident in 1998, his photogenic and brainy wife Mary, a USC graduate in art history, was appointed to the vacant seat and won reelection. Congress-woman Bono's counterpart in Santa Barbara was Democratic congress-woman Lois Capps, an equally attractive and intelligent widow who had gained her husband's congressional seat after his death. Tall, angular, younger looking than her six decades might suggest, Congresswoman Capps epitomized the persistent Anglo-Americanism of Santa Barbara, which during the 1990s was undergoing both political and ethnic diversifi-cation.

Throughout the 1990s, despite so many social and cultural changes, the Santa Barbara region, especially the core cities of Santa Barbara and Mon-tecito, managed to emanate a mood of Anglo-American ascendancy, as rep-resented by, among others, the Hollister clan, which traced itself to Santa Barbara's leading citizen of the 1870s and 1880s, and the Firestone family, which epitomized eastern money arriving on Santa Barbara shores. Santa Barbara even had an eastern-style prep school tradition, as represented in the nearby schools of Cate and Thacher, where masters such as Marvin Shagam, a tweedy Oxovian and former army intelligence operative during World War II, throughout a career of teaching literature at Thacher, kept alive a local version of the Mr. Chips/Powlett-Jones tradition. And as far as the Anglo in Anglo-American was concerned, the Duke and Duchess of Norfolk remained part-time Santa Barbarans during the 1990s, with the duke, a retired army major general, feeling totally at home in a community that had always had its resident English, part- or full-time, since the early twentieth century. Julia Child—in so many ways the very paradigm of a certain kind of Anglo-Americanness—retired to Santa Barbara in the 1990s. As a girl, growing up in Pasadena, Child had vacationed there during the summer. Since the late 1970s, she and her husband had found refuge there from the winter gloom of Cambridge, Massachusetts, and now she had in the Channel City the perfect place for retirement: sunny and civil, with a bountiful downtown farmer's market, where she could shop each weekend for organic produce, and the Santa Barbara Girls Club, where she delighted in giving cooking lessons to local youngsters.

In the mid-1920s, Anglo America had elected a Spanish-themed Santa Barbara as its mise-en-scène of choice, rebuilding the city after the earthquake of 1925 in varieties of Spanish Revival design. It was the aristocratic style of the early Spanish Santa Barbarans, most likely, real or imagined, that spoke most powerfully to the desires of Anglo-American Santa Barbara to see itself as possessed of comparable panache. The region still nurtured ninth- and tenth-generation descendants of pioneering Spanish families that had long since melded Hispanic and Anglo lines. Superior court judge Frank Ochoa, for example, was a direct descendant of Santa Barbara presidio commandant Jose Francisco de Ortega. The judge's wife, KEYT news anchor Paula Lopez, also a ninth-generation Santa Barbaran, was a direct descendant of Pablo Cota, a lieutenant in the Spanish army stationed at the Santa Barbara presidio as well. In Santa Barbara terms—indeed, in California terms—the Ochoa family was living proof that neither Santa Barbara nor California was a Johnny-come-lately kind of place.

Palm Springs, by contrast, had not been settled by either Spain or Mexico and could hardly imagine a past beyond the founding of the Racquet Club in the late 1930s, which gave special significance to the fact that the Cahuilla Indians, residents of the region since time immemorial, had survived so robustly into the present and were emerging into new prominence in the 1990s as entrepreneurs and casino operators. The Cabazon Band of the Cahuilla operated the Fantasy Springs Casino complex in downtown Palm Springs and held commanding portions of Palm Springs real estate. While less involved economically—on such a scale, at least—the Chumash people of the Santa Barbara region were equally significant as survivors and avatars of indigenous value. Mary Yee, who died in 1965, was the last person to speak the Chumash language in its full range and variety. Yee also kept meticulous notes and made recordings of spoken, chanted, and sung Chumash in the 1950s, which were eventually housed in the Santa Barbara Museum of Natural History, where scholars such as Ernestine McGovran, Yee's daughter, were painstakingly reassembling the lost language from recordings and notebooks.

As a class, Santa Barbarans revered something they called spiritual value, which was in part connected to the Native American traditions of the region. Perhaps it was the lingering influence of the Chumash shrines in Oak Park and Sycamore Canyon, or the persistence of Santa Barbara Mission itself atop a knoll overlooking the city and the channel, where Franciscan Father Virgil Cordano, the longtime pastor of the mission and a lifelong Santa Barbara resident, displayed more than a touch of its elegance, along with the equally compelling statement emanating from the brown friar's habit, which Father Virgil wore everywhere, even to black-tie events. Once a year, the amiable Franciscan conducted an annual Blessing of the Bikes, in which a leathered and hirsute cavalcade of motorcyclists roared by the mission to be sprinkled with holy water. Since the 1920s, Ojai had been an important spiritual center, starting at the point when the spiritual master Krishnamurti had established himself there in 1922. In 1924 the Krotona Institute of Theosophy had moved to Ojai. By the 1990s, the 118-acre institute housed the largest collection of theosophical literature on the planet. *Ojai* was the Chumash word for moon, which was appropriate, given the dreamy, mystical nature of the place. (Interestingly, the Ojai Valley had been used as the mise-en-scène for Shangri-la in the film *Lost Horizon* [1937].) Over the years, figures as similar and diverse as Aldous Huxley, Jonas Salk, Jerry Brown, Eric Clapton, and William Buckley Jr. had traveled to the Oak Groves complex of the Krishnamurti Foundation in search of enlightenment. Joseph Campbell had not been a Santa Barbaran, but his myth and journey-inspired discourse was very much at the center of the Pacifica Graduate Institute on the former Max Fleischmann estate in the foothills of Carpinteria, where students studied depth psychology, myth studies, and literature from a Campbell-inspired perspective.

Santa Barbarans old and new, including Oprah Winfrey, were quick to cite the spiritual reverberations of the region—the fact that, with your place in the world financially secured, with the struggle for survival behind you, you had now come to Santa Barbara to become more spiritual, whatever path that quest might take. So many people, like Winfrey, arrived with their money already made: people such as Paul Orfalea, founder and former CEO of Kinko's, who came to Santa Barbara with his wife, Natalie, to run the Orfalea Family Foundation and to teach an occasional class at UCSB. Don Gevirtz of Montecito, the retired chairman and CEO of the Foothill Group, a multibillion-dollar venture capital group based in West Los Angeles, also fit the mold. He and his wife, Marilyn, gave $1 million to the UCSB Graduate School of Education and founded the Gevirtz Research Center at UCSB. In 1996, Gevirtz's friend Bill Clinton appointed him ambassador to the island nations of the South Pacific. So developed was the foundation scene in Santa Barbara that by 2000 the Foundation Roundtable of the region included some thirty-five foundations representing millions of dollars in assets and annual giving. Those who saw these organizations as an emergent aspect of community governance in California might easily have looked to Santa Barbara for corroboration.

Much of this spirituality was Earth-centered, which made environmentalism an important component of the Santa Barbara identity. The great Santa Barbara oil spill of January 1969 was the Original Sin implied in the theology of environmentalism—the tragic fall from grace. Cleaning up their coastline from the muck that had engulfed it and destroyed flora and fauna alike, Santa Barbarans had vowed: Never again. Gradually, since that time, the Channel Islands had come under the protection of the Channel Islands National Park, which still allowed for a few working cattle ranches to continue operations. Cross over to the Channel Islands or travel into the wild and rugged Santa Barbara County backcountry, and you encountered places truly out of time. Confident of a receptive audience, Jean-Michel Cousteau made an annual pilgrimage to Santa Barbara to raise funds for the Monte Carlo–based research institute founded by his father.

At any one time during the summer, some fifty to a hundred blue whales were moving through the channel. In 1994 the California gray whales, also abounding in the channel during migration season, had been taken off the endangered species list, but they still, occasionally, got caught in fishing nets or discarded cables. Troubled whales were monitored by volunteers at the Santa Barbara Marine Mammal Center. If necessary, crews would jump into rubber boats and speed out to assist an encumbered whale. Wearing scuba gear, the volunteers would dive into the water to cut away the nets or cables, and would try to make eye contact with the endangered whale, which seemed to have a calming influence. No one was afraid of being bitten by a whale; that had not, as of yet, happened. Being hit by a whale's tail, however, was a more pressing possibility.

Onshore, at UCSB, the National Center for Ecological Analysis and Synthesis had been established in 1995 with funds from the National Science Foundation. Using satellite images and high-tech computer technology, scientists at the center monitored the world's environments in terms of rainfall, the condition of the polar ice caps, global warming, flora and fauna food balances, and other signs. Over in Montecito, in a Spanish Revival estate designed by George Washington Smith in the 1920s, Diane Simon, wife of Herb Simon, one of the country's most successful developers of shopping malls, was serving as president of Global Green USA, an affiliate of Green Cross International founded by Mikhail Gorbachev, who had personally invited Simon in August 1993 to head his American environmental effort.

Santa Barbara, of course, had always loved to party, right from the beginning, at places like the Coral Casino Beach & Cabana Club opposite the Biltmore in Montecito, the counterpart of the Racquet Club in Palm Springs. As was common in the upper strata of Anglo America, costume parties were a perennial favorite, with the likes of Vincent Price and, later, George Hamilton judging the costumes, and Ernie Heckshier and his orchestra—the Peter Duchin/Lester Lanin counterpart on the West Coast—flying down from San Francisco to play for the event. Then there was the annual Concours d'Elegance, established in the mid-1970s and second only to its counterpart at Palm Beach, which each September brought to the Santa Barbara Polo & Racquet Club an array of classic automobiles for display and the occasion of parties characteristic of the lifestyles of the rich and famous. The annual Casablanca Ball benefited children's programs at Transition House; the annual Santa Barbara Wine Auction weekend raised funds for the Santa Barbara Museum of Natural History.

If there was one display of conspicuous upper-crust activity that each community had in common, it would have to be polo. Santa Barbara County was still ranch country, albeit with a Santa Barbara twist, as in the case of the fourteen-thousand-acre oak-dotted Spanish land grant Rancho San Julian, where cattleman Jim Poett, a local blueblood, was busy raising organic beef. In the nineteenth century, the cattle ranches of the coast and the interior had accustomed Santa Barbarans to horsemanship. Combine this equestrian orientation with eastern wealth, and it is no surprise that Santa Barbara became polo country as early as the mid-1890s, with the Santa Barbara Polo & Racquet Club, the third oldest continuing operating polo club in the nation, dating from 1911. The club offered a late-spring, summer, and fall season that brought to Santa Barbara champion polo teams from across the world and offered opportunities galore for social life. Polo was so popular that an excursion via private jetliner to Argentina was organized each year for local fans wanting to see Argentine matches.

The Coachella Valley was also horse country, albeit more in the dude ranch mode as opposed to working cattle ranches. Each year, the annual Desert Circuit in Indio saw 2,500 horses, ridden by two thousand riders, enter into a full array of equestrian competition running across two full months, from January to March, one of the biggest events of its kind in the country. Polo had come to Palm Springs in 1928 with the establishment of a club at Smoke Tree Ranch. Next came the Palm Springs Polo Club, and the Empire and El Dorado clubs in Indio on the eastern edge of the valley. In the mid-1990s the Empire and El Dorado combined forces to form the Pacific Coast Polo Center, where actor-restaurateur William Devane was especially active as a player and a polo entrepreneur.

It was not surprising that Devane should be active in Palm Springs polo. After all, celebrity actors and actresses were everywhere. By the 1990s, however, and continuing through the decade, it was evident that metro Santa Barbara was also in the process of becoming Hollywood-friendly. It began with Fess Parker, the onetime television Davy Crockett turned Santa Barbara developer and hotelier. In the late 1980s, Parker had developed the Doubletree resort on Cabrillo Boulevard and was correctly seen by many old-line Santa Barbarans as bringing a new element, the vacationing middle classes, into the city, to a hotel resort that depended on size and volume for its profitability, as opposed to the more elite-oriented Four Seasons Biltmore, Miramar, and San Ysidro Ranch. Needless to say, such old-liners opposed Parker as best they could, but they lost. President Ronald Reagan, meanwhile, had brought a new kind of attention to Santa Barbara County through frequent sojourns at his 688-acre Rancho del Cielo in the Santa Ynez Mountains northwest of the city. All in all, while president, Reagan spent some 345 days on the ranch—nearly a full year of his presidency— riding horses, chopping wood, communing with nature.

Certain Santa Barbarans were not so sure that they appreciated the attention President Reagan was bringing to their city. In times past, a certain element of Hollywood, those with old-line connections—Joseph Cotten, for example, or Claudette Colbert—had always been welcomed to parties at the Coral Casino Beach & Cabana Club, where Hollywood mixed with local bluebloods, to the benefit of each. Likewise the San Ysidro Ranch in Montecito, where John and Jackie Kennedy honeymooned in September 1953, showed itself capable of harmonizing noted English writers, Hollywood stars, local families, and East Coast money. By the 1990s, however, Hollywood was gaining ground on the patricians. Comic Jonathan Winters was a longtime Santa Barbara resident, as was Oscar-winning film composer Elmer Bernstein. Johnny Carson bandmeister Doc Severinsen and his wife, Emily, had a ranch in the Santa Ynez Valley. Robert Mitchum, Tab Hunter, and Jane Russell moved to Montecito, to be followed, in time, by Jeff and Susan Bridges; Chris Carter, creator of the *X-Files,* and his wife, Dorie; and Michael Douglas and his then wife, Diandra. Douglas had gotten his start as an actor while an undergraduate at UCSB. His parents, Kirk and Anne Douglas, had moved to Santa Barbara in 1999 after a forty-two-year connection to Palm Springs. Bo Derek, star of the iconic *10* (1979), and English comic actor John Cleese and his wife, Alyce Faye, settled in on nearby ranches. In early 2001 came the most momentous move of all: that of Oprah Winfrey to a forty-two-acre, $50 million Montecito estate. Arriving cold, as it were, but loving the beauty of the place, Oprah fell almost immediately into the Santa Barbara groove. She loved the socializing, for one thing, and Santa Barbara in turn prized Oprah for her value-oriented intellect. Very soon, Oprah and Kirk and Anne Douglas were on the forefront of an emergent and increasingly acceptable Santa Barbara identity: that of an alternative to Palm Springs, or even Beverly Hills, as a place of contemplative rustication for entertainment superstars.

Loretta Young and her husband, designer Jean Louis, however, moved in the opposite direction, decamping from Santa Barbara, where Jean Louis had long had a house (Young felt the climate was too damp and cold) in favor of Palm Springs, where they reestablished their life. Another bi-city Palm Springs–Santa Barbaran was actor George Hamilton, who was highly accepted in both places. In Santa Barbara, Hamilton presided over black-tie gatherings at the casino and was a prize guest at local dinner parties. In Palm Springs, he palled around with Sonny Bono, and enjoyed the nightlife and the opportunities for tanning. A Palm Springs tan, Hamilton told *Palm Springs Life,* was the best winter tan in the hemisphere, provided that you kept it moisturized.

A comparable change in resident clientele—the arrival of the gay community—was also being experienced in the 1990s by Palm Springs and the adjacent Cathedral City. Liberace had lived out the last two decades of his life in the ornate Casa de Liberace at the foot of Mount San Jacinto, a former private hotel that he restored to neobaroque grandeur. Liberace, in fact, must be given major credit for bringing the glamour back to Palm Springs in the late 1960s, when the city was in decline. Slowly, through the 1970s and 1980s, Palm Springs became increasingly attractive to the gay community. By the mid-1990s the city had thirty-three hotels catering to gays. Each Easter weekend, the gay community flocked to the annual White Party at the Marquis Crowne Plaza Resort and Suites, everyone wearing spring white. A total of 2,300 guests attended the 1994 event. The gay-oriented Desert Business Association had more than three hundred members. By mid-decade, it was estimated that fully a quarter of the homes in Palm Springs and Cathedral City were owned by gays. City councilman Greg Pettis of Cathedral City was the first openly gay politician in the metropolitan region. The biggest social club in Palm Springs was the Prime Timers, keyed to gay men over the age of fifty-five. By 1995 it had over six hundred members.

As in the case of so many people in metropolitan Palm Springs, the gay community liked to go out: to dine in restaurants or otherwise to enjoy the scene. Not surprisingly, metropolitan Palm Springs was a restaurant mecca in the state, with celebrity chefs represented in the hundreds of establishments chronicled in an annual special issue of *Palm Springs Life.* Santa Barbara, though, had for decades been about dinner parties in the home and hence had remained a restaurant wasteland—until 1979, when Penelope Williams, a local heiress and former fashion model, with a longtime residence in Paris, where she had taken courses at Le Cordon Bleu, opened Penelope's, earning rave reviews in the November 1980 issue of *Gourmet.* That gave Doug Margerum courage to open the Wine Cask in 1981, followed by Steven Sponder's Palace Café in 1985. By the 1990s, Santa Bar-

bara was showing full and encouraging signs of catching up with the cuisine movement that had emanated from Berkeley under the influence of
Alice Waters.

Each metropolitan region, then, had its similarities and differences, its
cross-references, its divergent aesthetics. Literary life was sparsely represented in Palm Springs, most noticeably by two East Coast expatriates, Sid-
ney Sheldon and Herman Wouk, writers of the World War II generation
who continued to be productive into their seventh and eighth decades. Santa
Barbara had always been something of a literary subregion in the annals of
American letters in California. Before his death in 1999, Robert Easton had
been productive as a writer of fiction and environmental history. Through
the 1990s, John Sanford, age ninety in 1994, continued to produce his idiosyncratic but highly regarded novels and memoirs (he died in 2003). Writing under the name of Ross Macdonald, novelist Kenneth Millar, who died
in 1983, had helped make of Santa Barbara not only a center of detective
fiction, but the subject—under the name of Santa Theresa—of fiction, as his
detective Lew Archer peeled away the various layers of the city uncovering
the buried past. Santa Barbara had its real-life Lew Archer in private detective Mike Kirkman, who had earned his skills as a homicide investigator for
the Santa Barbara County Sheriff's Department. Charging $80–100 an
hour, Kirkman had cracked such important cases as the fatal stabbing of
Montecito millionaire Lester Berman and the murder of thirty-five-year-old
Montecito trust-funder Rick Klaus, a case that Kirman solved before
Klaus's body was even discovered in July 1991 in the Los Padres National
Forest north of Ojai. In another notable case, screen mogul Harry Warner's
granddaughter Desiree Telstar had hired Kirkman to nab her husband,
David, who had decamped with $1.6 million of family funds. Kirkman
caught him as he tried to enter New York State from Canada.

These were Ross Macdonald kinds of stories, based on the premise that
murder and other heinous impulses could not be banished from Santa Barbara, no matter how spiritual the ambitions of the community were. Sue
Grafton, creator of the detective Kinsey Millhone series, took up where
Macdonald left off, starting a series of novels whose titles began with the
successive letters of the alphabet. Kenneth Millar's wife, Margaret Millar,
had been herself a distinguished novelist, fully equal to her husband in talent. A successor was novelist T. Coraghessan Boyle, who moved to Santa
Barbara in the early 1990s with his wife and two teenage children after fifteen years in the Woodland Hills section of the San Fernando Valley. Buying and restoring a Frank Lloyd Wright house in Montecito, Boyle, a USC
professor, said that he had grown tired of Los Angeles—the crowds, the
pollution, the traffic—and preferred to commute twice weekly to the uni-

versity campus. By the late 1990s, Boyle had become the best known and respected writer living in the region.

Each year, the genial and talented Barnaby Conrad, a former San Franciscan and the author of some thirty books, including *Matador* (1952), based on the life of Manolete, brought some four hundred aspiring writers to Santa Barbara for a week of conferences and workshops on the campus of Westmont College. Graduating from Yale in 1943 after prepping at the Cate School, Conrad—rejected by the draft because of an athletic injury— had served as vice consul in Seville, Malaga, and Barcelona through World War II. There he became interested in bullfighting, later making forty-seven appearances in the bullrings of Spain and Mexico as the California Kid. Each year, for the Santa Barbara Writers' Conference, Conrad assembled a stellar cast of instructors, being the sort of person who knew everyone worth knowing, a trait that had made Conrad's El Matador bar the crossroads saloon of San Francisco throughout the 1950s.

Provided you had the means, you did not have to be starved for cultural life in either Santa Barbara or Palm Springs, and this despite the fact that metropolitan Palm Springs was playing catch-up in this dimension of its civic life. For such a small city, Santa Barbara sustained an impressive array of formal institutions: an excellent art museum, an equally impressive museum of natural history, and a zoological garden on forty acres overlooking the Pacific with seven hundred animals in first-rate settings, considered by many to be the most beautiful zoo in the world. (The annual Zoofari, which raised funds for the zoo, gave Santa Barbarans yet another opportunity to dress up, this time in safari clothes and other forms of outdoor gear.) Ever since the 1920s, the Lobero Theater had been maintaining its reputation as one of the most ambitious regional theaters in the country. UCSB English professor Homer Swander, meanwhile, was directing a program that brought noted stage stars from London directly to the region. A perennial favorite was Patrick Stewart of the Royal Shakespeare Company, better known to some as Captain Jean-Luc Picard of *Star Trek: The Next Generation.*

Founded in 1947 by Santa Barbara resident Lotte Lehmann, the noted soprano who had fled Nazi Germany, the Santa Barbara–based Music Academy of the West kept a steady stream of trained vocalists available for performances in places such as the Santa Barbara Bowl, a Greek-style amphitheater hewn out of sandstone, a miniversion of the Hollywood Bowl, hosting outdoor performances since 1936. In 1997, mezzo-soprano Marilyn Horne accepted the directorship of the voice program at the academy, headquartered in Miraflores, a private estate donated to the organization in 1951. Each summer the academy offered a festival bringing noted performers to the region, as did the Libbey Bowl in Ojai, where figures such as John Adams and Pierre Boulez came to conduct. Santa Barbara had its own opera company, civic light opera company, and two symphonies: the Santa Barbara Symphony, conducted by Uruguay-born Gisèle Ben-Dor, playing in the historic two-thousand-seat Arlington Theater, and the West Coast Symphony, a private orchestra under the direction of its underwriter, Christopher Story, a wealthy music lover retired from the insurance business.

Located on Fred Waring Drive in Palm Desert, the 1,125-seat McCallum Theatre at the Bob Hope Cultural Center featured some 150 performances annually, most of them touring shows of national and international rank. The Desert Town Hall of Indian Wells, with Gerald Ford as the honorary chairman, brought a steady succession of writers, pundits, and talking heads to the region. (President Ford was also active at the Bighorn Institute in Palm Desert, which was devoted to animal care and research.) Each metropolitan region had its own international film festival, which because of the strong Hollywood connections showed continuing strength. Each also enjoyed a vigorous gallery scene, with Santa Barbara having the edge in terms of a usable art history and a presently practicing painting community. Like Santa Barbara, Palm Springs also had an ambitious art museum, opened in 1958.

Architecturally, each region was a center of fine design and interior decoration: metropolitan Santa Barbara in terms of Spanish and Mediterranean Revival—the work of such important figures as Bertram Goodhue, George Washington Smith, Reginald Johnson, Gordon Kaufmann, and Lutah Maria Riggs, from the 1910s through the 1920s; and Palm Springs with pre- and postwar modernism, as represented in the steel and glass modernism of Richard Neutra, John Lautner, Pierre Koenig, and Albert Frey, a European-trained modernist, born in Switzerland, who since the late 1930s had completed some two hundred projects in all, including the Palm Springs city hall. Interestingly, it was Frank Sinatra who had helped fix modernism as the preferred style of the region when in 1947 he commissioned architect E. Stewart Williams to design a home for him on Alejo Road in Palm Springs. The clean lines of steel, brick, and glass, and the swimming pool (Williams had worked for Raymond Loewy in the late 1930s) of the Sinatra residence had helped fix in mind over the next four decades what Palm Springs should look like when it was seeking architectural distinction. Williams's other buildings included the Palm Springs High School and the Desert Museum, his masterpiece. More than any other architect, with the possible exception of Frey, Williams had established the classic Palm Springs look of 1950s modernism.

From this perspective, metro Palm Springs was about the future, and metro Santa Barbara was about the past, although by the 1980s Palm Springs was supporting its own version of Desert Mediterranean in its new developments. The modernism of Palm Springs bespoke a brave new world being created in the desert. The Mediterraneanism of Santa Barbara celebrated California as historical place. As fussy and expensive to maintain as they were, the great estates of Santa Barbara and Montecito—so real-estate agent Steve Slavin, estates director of Previews, the exceptional-properties division of Coldwell Banker, would tell you—were more than holding their own. Multi-multimillion-dollar prices were everyday events. Santa Barbara even had its own Trust for Historic Preservation, headed by USC-trained scholar Jarrell Jackman, which through the 1990s restored the venerable Spanish presidio, the adjacent chapel, and the Casa de la Guerra adobe.

In terms of interior design, Palm Springs sustained a tendency toward eclectic modernism. Deprived of historicity in a classic and comforting sense, the desert demanded clean lines and smooth surfaces. Santa Barbara was about the mixing of classic new furniture and antiques. Paris born and bred, Helene Aumont, daughter-in-law of the French actor Jean Pierre Aumont, was doing a landslide business through the decade at Europa in El Paseo, featuring the furniture and antiques of Europe, Spain and France especially, which the Aumonts secured on biannual buying expeditions. In 1987, Paige Rense, the longtime editor of *Architectural Digest,* semi-retired to Montecito. Her favorite weekend hobby was touring the elegantly decorated homes of the region.

This meant enjoying the gardens as well, for Santa Barbara was in so many ways one of the garden capitals of all California, recognized as such since the 1920s, when Elizabeth and Lockwood de Forest had helped create a landscaping tradition of stately Mediterraneanism cross-referenced with the more hardy assertions of the Spanish Southwest. By and throughout the 1990s, this older tradition, while remaining characteristic of many of the grand estates in Montecito, was giving way to a more eclectic tradition combining Mission, Southwest, Japanese, and dry tropical design. These gardens—the style was sometimes called Mission Japanese—reconciled the California-as-Mexico and California-as-Asia motifs that were so characteristic of the decade. Spearheading the movement for this distinctive landscaping style was, among others, Carl Noss, president of the County Horticultural Society. Where else but in Santa Barbara, garden fanciers might ask, could you bring together cactus and dwarf banana into the same landscape, or combine Japanese-garden Jupiter with roses and rosette-forming succulents, and this against a classic Mediterranean palette of acacia, palm, and olive trees?

While Palm Springs had its gardens—and some of them were quite impressive—the poetry of this region could mainly be experienced through one predominant mode of landscape design: the golf course. Golf—not only the game itself, but its rituals, its lore, its postgame socializing, and the entity it engendered, the country club—was the heart and soul of metro Palm Springs as resort. In the 1980s alone, thirty-three country clubs were established in the region, with a golf course opening on an average of one every hundred days. By the early 1990s, there were seventy-three courses in the region, each of them Elysian fields of a sort, assertions of green against the desert, gardens that promised a kind of paradisiacal timelessness as men and women spent the better part of each day following a luminous little white ball across cighteen holes. Without golf, what would Palm Springs do? Yet here was the paradox. The very consumption of time that golf offered was also an escape from time itself.

In its postwar phase, country club life began with the establishment of the Thunderbird in Rancho Mirage: a golf course, country club, housing development, and dude ranch initiated by Frank Bogert and candy manufacturer Joe Edy at the suggestion of amateur golf champion Johnny Dawson. Opening on January 8, 1951, the Thunderbird Country Club established the paradigm for the golf-focused development of the Coachella Valley in the half century to come, stimulating almost immediately the creation of the El Dorado and La Quinta clubs. Phil Harris and Alice Faye bought the second home in the development and raised their children there. King Hassan II of Morocco was an early Thunderbird devotee, sponsoring Thunderbird-oriented tournaments in his kingdom. Thunderbird golf pro Jimmy Hines invented the motorized golf cart, based on similar vehicles being used for the handicapped. Member Ernest Breech, later the chairman of the board of the Ford Motor Company, received permission from the club to name Ford's new sports car after the establishment.

Presided over by club manager Edgar Schill and restaurateur Ron Fletcher, with Werner Simon serving for nearly thirty years as the maître d', the bar and dining room of the Thunderbird was ground zero for social life in the region into and through the 1990s. When Gerald and Betty Ford left the White House in 1977, Leonard Firestone, an early Thunderbird home owner, offered them an adjacent property overlooking the thirteenth hole. The Fords built their retirement home there, and could frequently be seen dining at their favorite table at the club.

Betty Ford had her own invitational golf tournament, a sure sign of celebrity status in the region. Played at the Indian Wells Country Club, the annual Bob Hope Desert Classic, later the Bob Hope Chrysler Classic, benefiting the Eisenhower Medical Center, dated back to 1960 at Thunderbird, moving on to El Dorado, then Indian Wells. It drew every living Republican president, past or present, and Joe DiMaggio. In 1995, President Bill Clinton added a Democratic note to the proceedings, joining former presidents Gerald Ford and George H. W. Bush on the links. Golf icon Arnold Palmer, a resident of Bermuda Dunes and the designer of the courses for Indian Ridge and Mission Hills, played every Bob Hope Chrysler Classic since 1960, winning five of them. The annual Nabisco Dinah Shore tournament and the Celebrity Pro-Am, a benefit for the Desert Hospital, brought such champions as Nancy Lopez and Vickie Goetze to the Rancho Mirage event.

But it was the Frank Sinatra Celebrity Invitational Tournament, held since 1989 at the Desert Falls Country Club and Marriott's Desert Springs Resort and Spa in Palm Desert as a benefit for the Desert Hospital and the Barbara Sinatra Children's Center at the Eisenhower Medical Center, that attracted the most entertainment celebrities and constituted the high point of metro Palm Springs's 1990s definition of itself as a fusion of golf and show business. Of course, such nonentertainment figures as Gerald Ford and Alan Shepard were on hand, together with athletes like Steve Garvey and Bruce Jenner, but the real action came from the multiplicity of entertainment celebrities of past and present notoriety who joined Frank and Barbara on the links and for the tournament's gala. Here was Palm Springs at its apex: the golf, the celebrities, the galas, the photographs of Frank and Barbara on the cover of *Palm Springs Life,* and, above all else, the illusion that in Palm Springs you could escape time alongside celebrities who had kept you company throughout your life.

The Upper Left

Berkeley, Santa Monica, West Hollywood

The spiraling housing costs in San Francisco were at once putting at risk and intensifying that city's status as Capital of the Upper Left, a Hanseatic League of cities and suburbs that included Davis, Berkeley, parts of Marin County, Santa Cruz, Santa Monica, and West Hollywood. Upper Left cities were educated, affluent, progressive in politics (as the Upper Left preferred to put it), angry at an unjust and unprogressive world, but more or less convinced that their community represented a saving remnant. Davis, Berkeley, and Santa Cruz were university towns, which meant that they came by their Upper Left status easily. Davis, a city some fifteen miles west of Sacramento, was so politically correct that a serious effort was made in December 1998 to strip the name Sutter from all streets and public places on the basis that Captain John Sutter, the pioneer mid-nineteenth-century landowner who had first developed the region, was a chauvinist, a bounder, a racist, and a sexual exploiter of Native American women. The city council, however, found the anti-Sutter campaign too extreme—even for Davis—and voted the proposal down.

To the south, the city of Berkeley remained, even more than San Francisco across the Bay, the true psychological, emotional, and imaginative capital of the Upper Left, although even Berkeley was by the 1990s showing signs of moderation. The upheavals of the 1960s, after all, were still very much on Berkeley's collective mind, despite the passage of time and the rise of Alice Waters's Chez Panisse in the 1970s as the icon of a transpolitical, lifestyle-oriented sensibility. Not that activism was showing any signs of disappearing in this city, where housing was highly rent controlled, and where, under the Berkeley Cares Voucher Program, the homeless were given vouchers that could be used at local stores for anything but alcohol or cigarettes. Among other things, Berkeley condemned economic sanctions against Iraq, declared the Gold Rush of 1849 racist and hostile to the environment, transformed Columbus Day into Indigenous Peoples Day, and banished Styrofoam.

Because of various boycotts on environmental or geopolitical grounds, no Berkeley city vehicle could use the services of Mobil, Texaco, Chevron, Arco, Shell, or Exxon. By the spring of 2001, the city council was seriously considering meeting most of its delivery needs, including mail, with Pedal Express, a Berkeley-based bicycle delivery company. One Pedal Express vehicle, the trihauler, pedaled by a recumbent cyclist, could haul up to seven hundred pounds of freight on its trailer and was already in use delivering organic student lunches from local restaurants to Berkeley High School. For a brief time when the city council was mad at the soft drink industry, it was difficult to get vending machines supplied. When the Boy Scouts banned gays and atheists from their organization, the council cut off all public subsidies for the two Sea Scout boats docked at the Berkeley Marina.

Such a sensibility was, by the late 1990s, coexisting with the emergence of Berkeley as a world center of cuisine, in the course of which, as one wag put it, the counterculture had become the counter culture: as in the case of the counter at Bette Kroening's Oceanview Diner on Fourth Street, famous for its scones and pancakes. In February 1998, Kroening was one of five Berkeley restaurateurs chosen to represent the city in its booth at the International Fancy Food & Confection Show in the Moscone Convention Center in San Francisco. Nouvelle Berkeley, this sector of the community called itself. Its headquarters and central shrine was Chez Panisse on Shattuck Avenue, of course, but it also included Andronico's across the street, a gourmet grocery store featuring a world-class inventory of vintage wines, a dozen types of lettuce, and organic and/or miniature vegetables that were hand-polished before being put on display for sale. The Acme Breads bakery on San Pablo Avenue had become so famous that its owners were considering an IPO. Next door to Acme was Kermit Lynch Wines, and Alice Waters had opened Café Fanny, a much more casual place than Chez Panisse, serving pizzas and sandwiches. The Fourth Street Grill was celebrated for its mesquite-grilled meats, and Bette's Oceanview Diner boasted the best breakfasts in the region.

But Nouvelle Berkeley was not without its activism. Alice Waters herself had started a vegetable-growing project at the nearby Martin Luther King Jr. Middle School, designed to encourage students to grow their own vegetables on school property and substitute organic produce for their fatty, fast-food lunches. Activism remained a Berkeley trademark; but it had taken a kinder, gentler, more holistic emphasis in this city of some 103,000, whose population was augmented each weekday by commuting students, faculty, and staff of UC Berkeley. The city that had functioned as ground zero of the anti–Vietnam War protest now was one of the few communities in the state to have its own Vietnam veterans memorial, thanks in part to the efforts of Berkeley resident Country Joe McDonald, singer, activist, and Vietnam-era veteran, and Berkeley mayor Lonnie Hancock. (Hancock was first elected in 1985, and stated as her goal a desire to lead Berkeley out of its antibusiness culture and transform the city into a model of progressive development and social compassion, an effort continued by Hancock's successor, Shirley Dean.) Founded in 1969, the Berkeley Ecology Center remained the oldest ongoing recycling program in California. Three highly placed Berkeley housewives—Sylvia McLaughlin, Kay Kerr (the wife of Clark Kerr, the longtime UC Berkeley chancellor and president), and Esther Gulick—had in the 1960s single-handedly stopped the filling in of San Francisco Bay, a crusade that led to the formation of a Bay Conservation and Development Commission, with regulatory authority. Berkeley had also established the greenbelt Eastshore State Park, extending from the Bay Bridge to Marina Bay in Richmond along the waterfront.

FM radio meant a lot to Berkeley as a source of news and entertainment, but primarily as a means of establishing community on the progressive left. Ever since it was founded in 1949 by left-leaning pacifists in reaction to the rightward turn of American society at the opening of the cold war, Berkeley radio station KPFA-FM (94.1) had been broadcasting a steady stream of left-oriented programming and commentary; indeed, one could not understand Berkeley—which is to say, one could not understand the entire 1960s antiwar radical movement—without reference to the community created by KPFA, the oldest public radio station in the nation. In April 1999, trouble broke out between the staff of KPFA and the nonprofit Pacifica Foundation, which owned the station. Restive with the autonomy of the KPFA staff, the foundation sought to exercise tighter controls over broadcasting, policy, and costs. The popular station manager Nicole Sawaya was fired, together with two veteran broadcasters who mentioned her firing on the air. In mid-July 1999, radio host Dan Berstein, discussing the crisis on his show, was pulled from his broadcasting booth by security guards. The sounds of scuffling and shouting were broadcast live to shocked listeners. Some two hundred demonstrators converged on the now-padlocked station in protest. The two weeks that followed witnessed a replay of the 1960s, as hundreds of demonstrators—many of them aging radicals from the Vietnam era—demonstrated in front of KPFA, demanding the return of the former broadcasters and staff who had been locked out. Some demonstrators tried to occupy the studio. Helmeted and baton-wielding police were called into action. It was a classic Berkeley confrontation, this time between an aggrieved local community and a foundation owning five listener-sponsored stations with sixty-five affiliates.

This was 1999, however, not 1969, and so local KPFA supporters took to the Internet with their campaign as well as to the streets, drawing the ire of progressives throughout the country toward the board of directors of the Pacifica Foundation. Unable to sustain the withering irony of a left-liberal foundation being cast as a corporate ogre, Pacifica in late July 1999 rehired the fired staff and tentatively agreed to a higher degree of local control. Still, there was something poignant in the whole affair, however successfully concluded: the poignancy of time itself as evidenced in the bald heads and graying beards of the protesters, the way that the men's midsections bulged against their sloganeering T-shirts, the 1960s-style long hair on women with late-middle-aged faces.

Still, it had been a good fight, just like old times. Those old times were memorialized in April 1998 when UC Berkeley alumnus Stephen Silberstein, a 1964 graduate of the college and a 1976 graduate of the School of Library and Information Science, made a $3.5 million gift to the university to commemorate the Free Speech Movement. Over the years, Silberstein, after a decade of library work, had taken his library and information science skills into the field of software development and became a self-made multimillionaire, perhaps the only librarian in the nation ever to achieve this status. Never could he forget, however, the drama of the Free Speech Movement of his undergraduate days. His gift was divided into three parts: $1.4 million for the Mario Savio/Free Speech Movement endowment fund in the UC Berkeley Library; $500,000 for the Free Speech Movement Archives at the Bancroft Library on campus; and, most unusual and very Berkeley, $1.6 million to build a cafe adjacent to the library that would feature rotating exhibits of Free Speech materials. Mario Savio's widow, Lynne (Savio himself had died of a heart attack in 1996), and their son Nadav were on hand when Berkeley chancellor Robert Berdahl announced Silberstein's gift.

The Free Speech Movement Cafe was a fitting memorial to the momentous events of the 1960s. Berkeley, after all, had practically introduced the coffeehouse and espresso (as well as the foreign film, thanks to impresaria Pauline Kael) to the United States in the 1950s; and by the late 1990s the coffeehouse culture of Berkeley, now spread through some twenty establishments, was flourishing. Berkeley's cafes—the Mediterranean, the Caffe Strada, the Wall Berlin Caffeehaus, the Au Coquelet, the Odyssia Caffe Bistro, and the others—stood for something beyond the coffee, rolls, and pastry they served. These establishments were preserving the lingering

1950s bohemianism, with its existential engagement with high literary culture, its dream of Europe, its sense of contemplative leisure and university life arriving in the United States.

This Berkeley could be found as well in the many new and used bookstores of the city, most notably Cody's Books on Telegraph Avenue, where, since 1946, in a total of three progressively larger locations, five decades of students, professors, and avid readers could find exactly the title they were looking for, or, serendipitously, stumble on a title they only just then knew they needed to read. Cody's was more than a bookstore. Like Lawrence Ferlinghetti's City Lights Books in San Francisco's North Beach, Cody's was a forum for free speech, a shrine to liberal-bohemianism, and an evocation of world culture through the array of European, Latin American, Asian, and African writers on display for sale in quality trade paperbacks, which Cody's, again like City Lights, had helped introduce to the American public in the 1950s.

Cody's and the other Berkeley bookstores had also nurtured a community of writers and a mini-climate of literary attitudes, as revealed in 1997 when Heyday Books of Berkeley issued the anthology *Berkeley! A Literary Tribute,* edited by Danielle La France. Showcasing a progression of writers from Jack London, to Irving Stone, to Jack Kerouac, to Dorothy Bryant, Bobby Seale, and Maxine Hong Kingston, the *Berkeley!* anthology offered proof positive of the distinctive hold Berkeley had had upon the intellectual and imaginative culture of northern California literary life. Heyday Books, publisher of *Berkeley!,* was itself an important Berkeley phenomenon. Founded in 1974 by the Harvard-educated Malcolm Margolin, Heyday Books was to regional publishing what Chez Panisse was to regional cuisine: a blend of tradition, innovation, and style. In his own writing career, Margolin had produced the California classic *The Ohlone Way* (1978), and in his own values and lifestyle the fiercely bearded Margolin represented a fusion of Native American scholarship, New Age idealism, a highbrow Harvard education in history and literature, an easy Berkeley bohemianism, a rabbinical conscience, and an equally rabbinical belief in the transforming power of the written word. Just as Alice Waters's cookbooks and restaurant practice offered a deep core cut into the geology of post-1960s Berkeley, so too did the publication titles of Heyday Books offer a comparable probe into a sensibility that, while rooted in Berkeley, extended itself out to the larger world of California, the West, and the international avant-garde.

Headquartered in Berkeley as well, the University of California Press shared with its colleagues at Heyday Books and the other small presses in the city a comparable sense of California-based internationalism: a sense, that is, of the world radiating in and out of California and of Berkeley in particular as an international capital of intellect fully worthy of being ranked alongside Los Angeles and London, the two other cities listed on the title page of UC Press imprints. Even more than Heyday Books, however—which published only fifteen books a year—the publication list of the UC Press was mapping in the 1990s, title by title, the intellectual and imaginative landscape of California. At the same time, with the special encouragement of longtime director James Clark, the press was publishing a growing list of California-oriented titles in natural history, environmentalism, history, sociology, art, literature, and novels of regional importance.

In publishing terms, Berkeley was showing how a small city could be a capital city as well. And it could also be a capital of Jewish thought, thanks to the founding in Berkeley of *Tikkun* magazine in 1986 by Rabbi Michael Lerner and other members of the Berkeley-based Institute for Labor and Mental Health, established in the 1970s to research the interactivity of work, belief, value, and political behavior. After taking a PhD in philosophy from UC Berkeley in 1972, and a second PhD, in clinical psychology, from the Berkeley-based Wright Institute, Lerner had completed his training at the Jewish Theological Seminary in New York. If Chez Panisse, Heyday Books, and the University of California Press represented a distinctive blend of tradition and innovation, so too did *Tikkun;* for the writers it published bore witness to an upgrading and reintensifying of Jewish values through, simultaneously, a return to traditional spiritual values with an assimilation of contemporary developments in psychology and a wide array of Berkeley-based initiatives in philosophy, theology, mysticism, and historical scholarship.

Berkeley was about understanding the world, but also about redeeming it, making it better, even if such an ambition, as in the case of the city council, might occasionally lead to unintentionally humorous boycotts. But Berkeley could have an ugly side as well. Cody's owner Andy Ross, in the summer of 1998, was harassed by street people whom he had discouraged from camping out in front of his store. Ross is Jewish, and the harassment took an ugly anti-Semitic cast in the graffiti, fliers, and hate calls targeted at him. It got so far as a swastika and a Star of David being chalked on the sidewalk in front of his store. Skinhead punks were part of the Berkeley scene as well, it had to be remembered, as anyone emerging from the BART station on Shattuck Avenue where they congregated knew full well. "There is no room here for more Kristallnachts," Ross protested to the Berkeley City Council.[6] Even lovers of Berkeley had to admit that the city had a decidedly noir dimension: not only the anti-Semitic attacks, but also the long roll call of young people, many of them in grammar school, who had succumbed in one way or another to drugs over the past three decades; the chilling record of street murders and assaults; the persistent problem of the homeless and vagrants on the streets; the smell of feces and urine in so many downtown doorways.

Santa Monica, another capital of the Upper Left, had experienced a similar crisis of public misbehavior in the 1980s and 1990s, when the well-known tolerance and civic compassion of that oceanside city had yielded an influx of vagrants and the homeless, who had camped out along the public spaces beneath the Palisades, effectively creating a no-man's-land between Santa Monica and the sea. Santa Monica was a liberal place—very liberal, as evidenced by the fact that it was represented in the state assembly and, later, the state senate by Tom Hayden, a surviving icon of 1960s resistance. As in the case of Davis, Berkeley, San Francisco, and Santa Cruz, the Santa Monica City Council frequently voted against one or another international evil—nuclear weapons, apartheid—as well as against any agenda being pushed by Republicans. But despite its leftward tilt, Santa Monica was also a prosperous city graced by fine homes, a wealth of art deco architecture, and many of the best hotels and restaurants in the region.

By the early 1990s, Santa Monicans were growing tired of their city as People's Republic, at least the dimension of it that had turned so much of its waterfront park into a camping ground for the dysfunctional and dispossessed. As far as its public life was concerned, Santa Monica spent the 1990s restructuring its identity. It remained a community of the Upper Left, to be sure; but it also fostered the development of a highly successful retail promenade on Third Street and began to crack down on the vagrant and homeless encampments that had brought Santa Monicans to a state of compassion fatigue. The City College–based radio station KCRW (89.9 FM) continued to keep vital Santa Monica as a forum for progressive values and inquiry. Radio host Warren Olney's daily show "Which Way LA?" was so successful, thanks to Olney's intelligent guests and his own ability to upgrade the talk show format into true debate, that it provided one of the few unifying forums for public discussion in the metropolitan region. By the millennium, Santa Monica stood sparkling white and pastel by the seashore, an art deco Atlantis, reborn from the Pacific, that had somehow turned itself away from that public squalor that seemed invariably to accompany an overdose of Upper Left compassion.

The gay- and senior-citizen-dominated city of West Hollywood, by contrast, had never lost sight of its ambition, since its incorporation in 1984, to be not only the most tolerant and open but also the best-run city in the state. In times past, before incorporation, the gay community had gravitated to the unincorporated West Hollywood region partially in the belief that the Los Angeles County Sheriff's Department did not harass patrons in gay bars as much as the Los Angeles Police Department did. Because the region was unincorporated, building permits were easier to obtain, and an apartment building boom began, drawing numerous seniors to the area. When West Hollywood became a city, its predominant population, gays and seniors, was made up of two groups ever vigilant on behalf of their individual rights. A city of 36,000 (only four thousand of them registered Republicans), packed into 1.9 square miles and set, like Beverly Hills, in the midst of metropolitan Los Angeles, West Hollywood immediately joined the Hanseatic League of Upper Left California cities. Like other cities of the Upper Left, West Hollywood had a foreign policy. No business in the city could do business with Myanmar (Burma), because of human rights violations in that country. A 1996 resolution demanded that the Japanese government observe international whaling agreements. Another resolution that year condemned the hanging of political opponents in Nigeria. West Hollywood also had its own progressive domestic policies. It was the first city in California to ban Saturday night special handguns and spent $250,000 defending the ordinance in court. When Nabisco allegedly denied sufficient bathroom time to its female employees at its Oxnard food processing plant, the city council called for a boycott of the company's Grey Poupon mustard. Quite soon, Nabisco "clarified" its existing policy.[7]

Like the other cities of the Upper Left, West Hollywood had a high level of self-esteem. This attitude also expressed itself in a passion for effective municipal administration. West Hollywood was a very well run city. On New Year's morning 2000, street-cleaning crews were at work before dawn. Residents also prized the ambience of tolerance found there, the welcome result of the eclectic origins of the city and its gay-senior détente. Governor Gray Davis and First Lady Sharon Davis were quite happy as West Hollywood residents, as were the city's Republicans. Among other things, the city had solid control of its growth policies, which was totally appropriate to such an Andorran–like enclave. Like Kansas City in the musical *Oklahoma!* (1944), West Hollywood had gone about as far as it could go.

Booming Places

Ventura, Los Angeles, San Bernardino, and San Diego Counties

In contrast to West Hollywood, Los Angeles, Orange, San Diego, and Riverside Counties were still growing at what many considered frightening rates. These four counties, in fact, were the fastest growing in the nation through 1996 and 1997, according to the census. Riverside County alone was experiencing a 24 percent rate of growth. Other Southern Californian counties—Ventura (8.5 percent), San Bernardino (14 percent), Santa Barbara (6 percent), and Kern (15 percent)—were also in a state of rapid development. As in the case of all the fastest growing U.S. counties, the increase in Southern California was centered on a new urban form, the edge city, which urbanologist Joel Garreau had profiled earlier in the decade in his pathbreaking study *Edge City: Life on the New Frontier* (1991). Otherwise known as urban villages, technoburbs, or postsuburban outer-cities, these settlements—created *a novo* over the previous twenty years—represented, in effect, an overnight society whose founders were such developers as the Kaufman & Broad Home Corporation, the largest home builder in the Southland, Lennar Homes of Mission Viejo, the Lewis Home Group of Upland, and others (the *Los Angeles Times* listed ninety of them as being of significance in the Southland) who were, through development, fast-forwarding history itself. Not only was this happening in Southern California, but also on the eastern shore of San Francisco Bay in such edge cities as Milpitas, Fremont, Newark, Union City, Hayward, and, further north, Fairfield. Cities that once took a hundred years to create through diverse hands were now being actualized in short order as fully realized planned communities appropriating the ancient and complex designation *city*.

Put the video history of any of these communities on fast-forward, and one saw a similar story. First, there would be agricultural fields, with a small market town somewhere in the region. Very rapidly, a generation of agriculturalists were making real estate their last cash crop, selling out to developers. Then came the construction of a great interstate or state highway—Interstates 5 and 10 in the south, pushing east and south from Los Angeles; Interstates 880 and 680 in East Bay San Francisco, pushing north and south—together with an intersecting network of ancillary interstates, state highways, and county roads. Next would come housing developments, with homes laid down by the hundreds (Kaufman & Broad built 2,117 single-family homes, 179 apartment buildings, and forty-four condominium buildings in Southern California in 1997 alone), and, almost simultaneously, shopping centers at strategic intersections. Industrial and office development was proceeding on a parallel track, as was the construction of K–12 schools and a CSU campus (CSU Hayward, CSU San Marcos, CSU Dominguez Hills, CSU Channel Islands), places of worship, and other (however rudimentary) amenities. In the second phase of economic development, office parks supplemented warehouses and other forms of industrial space, and a franchised and restaurant hotel made its appearance. Voilà, the edge city!

In the 1940s and 1950s, the San Fernando Valley had formed the cutting edge of suburban and exurban development, which largely remained within the city boundaries of Los Angeles. In the 1960s, 1970s, and 1980s, Orange County had led the way in the edge city–izing of Southern California and was still maintaining impressive growth rates, for a total of 2.67 million residents by March 1998. In the 1990s, Los Angeles County and the Inland Empire—Riverside and San Bernardino Counties—led the way.

With a population of 9.5 million by March 1998, however, Los Angeles County still remained the center of development. Growth was in four directions: northwest along state highway 101 into Ventura County; north along Interstate 5 toward Santa Clarita; northeast along state highway 14 to Lancaster and Palmdale; and east along Interstate 10 and state highway 60 toward Ontario in southeastern San Bernardino County and the rest of the Inland Empire. Previously centered on such venerable nineteenth-century cities as Ontario, San Bernardino, Redlands, and Riverside, which also functioned as market towns for the agriculture of the region, the Inland Empire had gone into development overdrive in the 1990s, with the 10 and 60 freeways and the Ontario International Airport at once serving and fueling growth. In a region of edge cities, Rancho Cucamonga served as first mover and DNA code. Incorporated as a city as recently as 1997 from the small ranching towns of Etiwanda, Alta Loma, and Cucamonga, Rancho Cucamonga adopted a master plan in 1981 calling for the systematic development of its thirty-six square miles across the next two decades. Through-

out the 1980s, Rancho Cucamonga maintained its place as the second
fastest growing city in the United States. By 1999, a newly built Ontario
International Airport stood at the center of what was, in effect, an important
new metropolitan region: a confederation of edge cities suddenly rivaling
Orange County, eastern Los Angeles County, East Bay San Francisco, and
metropolitan Sacramento as an overnight place.

Growth to the north was equally impressive. By November 1999, northern Los Angeles County, so recently empty, supported more than a half million people—a settlement roughly the size of Cleveland—and was expected
to increase by 169 percent by 2020, according to forecasts by the Southern
California Association of Governments (SCAG). Settlement centered on
Lancaster and Palmdale in the northeast county and on Santa Clarita and
Valencia along Interstate 5. Kaufman & Broad was doing 40 percent of the
development in the Antelope Valley; and the Newhall Land & Farming
Company was continuing to develop Santa Clarita. The Tejon Ranch Company, which controlled more than 270,000 acres in northern Los Angeles
and southern Kern Counties, was in the process of planning a four-thousand-
acre development that would rival Santa Clarita. The total population of Los
Angeles County was expected to grow by 33 percent, to 12.2 million,
between 2000 and 2020.

Nor was Santa Clarita intended to be a mere bedroom suburb of Los
Angeles. It was, rather, like Rancho Cucamonga and its satellites in the
Inland Empire, a fully developed edge city, which Newhall Land & Farming chairman and chief executive Thomas Lee was determined to make a
livable, workable, pedestrian-friendly community. Incorporated in 1987,
Santa Clarita reached the 142,000 mark in 1997. At incorporation, 92 percent of Santa Clarita was white, and the average age was twenty-nine. This
was a city of young white suburbanites in search of something very much
resembling what D. J. Waldie described as being at work in Lakewood forty
years earlier: home, Holy Land.

Because everyone in this edge city had come from somewhere else, concern for the evolving reality and image of Santa Clarita was high. Residents
wanted it to be a Mayberry RFD–type community—an edge city, that is,
touched by the values of the New Urbanism. Santa Claritans prided themselves on being down-to-earth and friendly. At the opening of the decade,
the city council, wanting to find out what was on people's minds, invited
fifty hairstylists from the region for a symposium and free lunch, on the
basis, as one council member put it, that people say what's on their minds to
their hairstylist. While basically a Republican law-and-order community
(by 1992 it was enjoying the third lowest reported crime rate among 179
American cities of its size), Santa Clarita also liked to think of itself as a

fun-loving place. On Halloween, city workers were encouraged to come to work in costume.

Northern San Diego County, meanwhile, was showing comparable development throughout the decade, again along Interstate 5 (Del Mar, Solana Beach, Encinitas, Carlsbad, Oceanside), and inland along state highway 78 (Vista, San Marcos, Escondido). By 1999, with a population of 2.72 million, much of it in the newly developed northern area, San Diego County ranked as the second most populated in the state. As in the case of southern Orange County, which it bordered, northern San Diego County was elegant and upscale; indeed, it would be difficult to find more impressive homes in as many spectacularly sited communities anywhere else in the state, other than Santa Barbara or coastal Orange County itself. Orange County, now into its second half century of development, had even begun to acquire the patina of elegance and age, especially on its sun-drenched Riviera coast, in such places as Newport Beach, Laguna Beach, Laguna Niguel, San Juan Capistrano, and San Clemente.

All this growth, in one way or another, was motivated by the desire to create an alternative to Los Angeles and thus to leave that city behind. It was the old and persistent American ambivalence to cities all over again, this time with a vengeance. Los Angeles, after all, had in its 1992 riots confirmed in the minds of just about every Southern Californian that there were more desirable places to be. In the emotion-charged aftermath of the riots, Congress was contemplating something between $9 billion and $12 billion in emergency funding for LA; instead, the city received only part of a $1.1 billion package that included summer jobs, flood relief for Chicago, and small business loans. Coverage on national television profiling the problems of the inner city increased to thirty-seven stories (up from three the previous month) in early summer 1992. By August, it was back to seven.

Neither presidential candidate seemed interested that year in discussing the inner city. Even with the riots, Los Angeles was not going downhill as fast as Philadelphia; but neither was it recovering itself at the same rate as Boston, New York, or Chicago. A generation of distinguished commentators—Lewis Mumford, Jane Jacobs, William Whyte—had done their best to make the classic city an inviting prospect; but in Southern California at least, and to a certain extent in the north, Californians were not buying it. They were preferring suburbs and edge cities, as far away from the inner city as possible. Only rarely were large-scale developments turned down or postponed in the 1990s, so remorseless was this rage for growth. Even the city of Napa, at the southern edge of the Napa Valley, embarked on a massive project of expansion and redevelopment, much of it spearheaded and financed by winemaker Robert Mondavi, designed to transform that workaday city of seventy thousand into an international wine and food resort. Mondavi estimated that 300,000 tourists a year could be expected in downtown Napa by 2001.

Old-time residents of Napa were worried about the impact of Mondavi's plans for the American Center for Wine, Food, and the Arts—an amphitheater for concerts, an exhibition hall, cooking and tasting facilities, a world-class restaurant, a residential art school on the opposite side of the Napa River, the restoration of the city's historic opera house into a performing arts center—but were willing to go along with it anyway, given the overall high quality of the project. Not so the citizens of the Tassajara Valley to the south. In May 1998, landowners dropped plans to develop 5,330 new homes in the still rural and scenic Tassajara Valley in Contra Costa County because of opposition from environmentalists. In Ventura County that fall, anti-sprawl activists put a measure on the ballot that made it necessary for each Ventura city to go to the voters whenever it wished to expand its boundaries. The measure passed, thereby making the electorate the de facto planning commission of the county.

Talk to the residents of the city of San Bernardino about the benefits of such growth, and they would tell a different story. The suburbanization of San Bernardino County had in two decades left the city of San Bernardino reeling on the ropes. In 1976 this foothill community had been ranked as one of the top ten All-American Cities in the nation. By the mid-1990s, some 40 percent of its 185,000 residents were on welfare; and Zero Population Growth, an environmental advocacy group, was ranking it at the very bottom of the list of places to raise children in the United States. *Money* magazine described San Bernardino as the most dangerous city in the state and the sixth most dangerous in the country, based on 1993 statistics. Local police sold and wore T-shirts depicting two vultures sitting on a bullet-riddled "Welcome to San Bernardino" sign, with the population figure scratched out and lowered as a result of the murder rate. More than ten thousand shirts were sold. The city's economic fortunes were already in steep decline even before the closing of the nearby Norton Air Force Base in 1994 and the removal of the hundred-year-old Santa Fe Railroad's repair yard, which had employed more than four thousand workers, to Topeka, Kansas. Even the federal district court moved from downtown San Bernardino to Riverside to escape the crime-ridden streets. San Bernardino, had become a classic example of an abandoned inner city and, ironically, a magnet for welfare recipients from the Los Angeles area, from which so many residents of San Bernardino County were fleeing. Nearly 70 percent of the schoolchildren in the city qualified for free breakfasts and lunches (the figure was 31 percent statewide); the rate of babies born to drug- or alcohol-abusing mothers was the third worst in the state. On most days, smog hung over the city; the sound of gunfire was frequent. "You just have to put the kids on the floor until [the gunfire] stops," noted welfare recipient Pam Waggoner, who, along with her boyfriend, an unemployed tree trimmer, were raising eight children between them on public assistance.[8]

These were the very conditions most residents of San Bernardino County would say they had tried to escape in coming there, although they would most likely visualize and objectify the problem as being in some way connected with inner-city Los Angeles. Suburbs and edge cities could not guarantee utopia. In and amid all this upscale growth were poor communities that had been left behind, just as the inner city had been abandoned. Many of these places—Santa Ana in Orange County, as well as San Bernardino—were struggling because that was where lower-end workers lived, the majority of them immigrants, who remained necessary for the region's economy. No suburb or edge city, in other words, could fully banish the fact, much less conceal it, that it took a lot of working poor to keep a region thriving: to run the fast-food outlets, to make the beds in hotels, to clean the office buildings in the business parks, to do the heavy lifting in hospitals and nursing homes. From this perspective, the myth of suburbia and the edge city was based on denial about just exactly who was doing the work of society that others preferred not to do.

The suburbs and edge cities were about denial as well as control. Knowing the dangers of American life, and its ferocious possibilities for downward mobility, people went to suburban, exurban, and edge city neighborhoods in an effort to escape what they feared: the debris-ridden streets of the inner city, its teeming and tumultuous population, its mean streets of violence and crime.

In the ultra-elite suburban community of San Marino, the effort to control could reach comic proportions. San Marino was the most regulated city in the country, according to its vice mayor Paul Crowley, a lifelong resident, who had written a book to guide home owners through a maze of do's and don'ts. No home can cover more than 40 percent of its property. A fifth bedroom required a three-car garage. No kitchens above the first floor. (Even the president of USC was denied a permit to construct a kitchen on the second floor of his university-owned estate.) No resting of bicycles against trees or on park grass. Business signs must be at least 80 percent in English. No watering down of sidewalks. No removal of trees without city approval. A badly trimmed tree may require a home owner to attend tree-pruning classes. No neon signs, no mortuaries, no used car lots. No basketball hoops or other forms of recreational activity visible to the street.

As far as anyone could tell, San Marinans liked it that way; and, while the city represented an extreme case, it also underscored a more pervasive attitude. For social commentator David Friedman, California was increasingly coming to resemble the society described by science fiction writer Isaac Asimov in *The Naked Sun* (1957). At a future time, Asimov wrote, the earth would be populated by two distinct classes: Solarians, a pampered and technologically developed elite, living in their own enclaves; and the Robots, the working, sweating, tumultuous residents of the cities. But then again, Friedman admitted, this was a national situation, and California was only part of a larger picture: a conspicuous part of the picture, of course, with the income gap between rich and poor showing, according to the California Public Policy Institute, the greatest spread since the 1920s.

Even worse, the visible signs of just exactly what side of the divide you were on were becoming increasingly apparent. Dennis and Martha Mendoza, for example, Honduran immigrants with high school educations—she a caregiver to an elderly housebound man; he a truck driver for a company paying no benefits; the two of them making $27,000 a year—scrimped and saved to be able to rent a two-bedroom apartment in a better section of San Mateo, so their children would not be bothered by nighttime gunfire on the other side of the tracks and could attend better schools. They still were driving their beat-up Oldsmobile, however—which meant that they were frequently being pulled over by the police. Scrimping and saving even more, the Mendozas bought a twenty-year-old repossessed Mercedes sedan for $500 and repaired it with junkyard parts. "I don't get stopped by the police anymore," laughed Martha Mendoza, standing beside her restored and gleaming white Mercedes. Still, the Mendozas had their dream: once a month, they would take their nine- and ten-year-old daughters out to a restaurant, so they could learn the social graces. "The girls need to know how to behave," noted Martha Mendoza, "what to order in a nice restaurant, because someday they are going to have that in their lives."[9]

Tough Love

Jerry Brown's Oakland

The Mendozas' search for a better life was exactly the kind of upward mobility Oakland mayor Jerry Brown wanted for the residents of his own city. The whole phenomenon of suburban and exurban development, exploding like a supernova across the state, was based on the desire to get out of town, to leave the older inner cities behind as fast as possible—and this in California, where even the inner city tended to be a twentieth-century development! By seeking and gaining election as mayor of Oakland, Jerry Brown had not only taken a reduction in rank from his previous status as governor of California and presidential contender, he had also taken responsibility for the most embattled California city of them all.

In the nineteenth century, Oakland had developed as a Brooklyn to San Francisco's New York. Thanks to its Progressive oligarchy in the early twentieth century, Oakland was one of the best planned cities in the nation and one of the first to exploit fully the possibilities of greenbelts and public transit. Throughout most of the century, Oakland was dominated by an Anglo-American Masonic elite: the kinds of people who—like Earl Warren, who was one of them, or U.S. senator William Knowland, son of the publisher of the *Oakland Tribune*—were Old Blues from Cal in rimless glasses and double-breasted suits. Oakland did share its controlling elite with the city of Piedmont, set independently in the Oakland Hills like the republic of San Marino in central Italy; but the cumulative presence in Oakland across the century of California Progressives, college educated and with civic ambition, had helped the city develop, especially in its mountainous regions, into a place of Mediterranean villas and sylvan charm. Downtown Oakland, meanwhile, dominated by the Tribune Tower and centered on Lake Merritt, was a wonderland of public spaces and art deco architecture, most notably the I. Magnin department store and the Paramount Theater (1930), designed by Timothy Pflueger, who had stylized the towers of the San Francisco–Oakland Bay Bridge. At the Athenian-Nile Club, oligarchs sank into sumptuous leather chairs amid the incense of good cigars, comforted by the fact that all was well with their Bayside city.

World War II changed Oakland forever, although the Old Blue oligarchy managed to hold on through the 1950s. As almost a last gasp of its prior identity, the city in 1969 opened an art museum, designed by Kevin Roche, notable simultaneously for its innovative design and for its pioneering collections of California art and historical items. Soon, the Oakland Symphony would be performing in a renovated Paramount Theater, and the Oakland Ballet Company—perhaps the last, last, last gasp of the old city—would be offering serious competition to its sister company across the Bay. By then, however, Oakland had become a distinctively African-American city, its flatlands populated by former shipyard workers or their descendants who had come to the Bay Area from Texas and the American South during the war. As in the case of most American cities, there had always been a small black population in Oakland through the nineteenth century, augmented in the early 1900s by a strong presence of hotel workers from San Francisco and sleeping car porters. C. L. Dellums, cofounder of the Brotherhood of Sleeping Car Porters in 1925, was an Oaklander. By the mid-1990s, African Americans made up 43 percent of Oakland's population (the same percentage of white people who had left the city between 1970 and 1995) and were entering their third decade of political power.

In 1977, Judge Lionel Wilson became the first African-American mayor of Oakland, breaking the long Republican-Masonic control of the city. Reelected in 1981 and 1985, Wilson—New Orleans–born, a professional-level tennis and baseball player, a liberal-to-moderate Democrat in his politics, with a pro-business orientation running concurrently with his commitment to affirmative action and civil rights—presided over the rise of the port of Oakland, which included a highly competitive international airport (headquarters for World Airways, the largest charter carrier in the country), and some $1 billion worth of construction, including the new City Center complex, a downtown hotel and convention center, federal and state office buildings, and the redevelopment of Jack London Square. In developing City Center, urban renewal artist Glenn Isaacson had brought to Oakland the city-building skills he had acquired under Justin Herman, the Robert Moses of San Francisco. Throughout the 1980s, Isaacson—who had also completed the Embarcadero Center project in San Francisco—never tired of repeating, almost mantralike, his belief that, strategically and in other ways as well, Oakland was better sited than the waterbound San Francisco to function as the shipping and transportation matrix of the Bay Area. Witness the fact that the port of Oakland was thriving, while the port of San Francisco was a memory. To corroborate further its big-city status, Oakland had an American League baseball team, the Athletics; a pro football team, the Raiders; and a pro basketball team, the Golden State Warriors, performing at the newly constructed Oakland Coliseum. For transportation the city was more than adequately serviced by the Bay Area Rapid Transit system (BART). Oakland, in fact, had more stops than any other city in the Bay Area, and was the core of the BART network of subways, elevateds, and dedicated pathways.

Its crossroads status, together with its first-rate housing stock, made Oakland, especially in the highlands, the residence of choice for many of the Bay Area's intelligentsia, professionals, and bourgeois bohemians. The Oakland Hills were especially favored by writers, artists, Berkeley professors, gallery owners, and professionals with aesthetic and/or bohemian instincts. Running north into Berkeley, College Avenue exfoliated with fine restaurants, bookstores, and other university-oriented establishments. On Birch Court, off Chabot, the Dominican Order maintained an exquisitely beautiful Tudor Gothic theological college designed in the 1920s by Arnold Constable, a student of Ralph Adams Cram. The Rockridge district was home to a significant number of UC Berkeley and other faculty commuting to colleges and universities throughout the Bay Area. Gleaming high above the city was the Edwardian elegance of the Claremont Hotel, flourishing since 1904 as both a hostelry for the public and a country club for locals.

According to a study released by the University of Wisconsin, Oakland was by the 1990s the most ethnically diverse city in the nation—even more so than Los Angeles—with eighty-one languages and dialects spoken within the city limits. All this diversity was occurring, moreover, within a matrix of African-American dominance. Not only was the mayor—Wilson and his successor, Elihu Harris—black, the president and CEO of the port was black as well, as was the head of the convention center and the director of the chamber of commerce, retired rear admiral Robert Toney, one of the first African Americans to reach flag rank in the navy. African-American Oaklanders could point with pride to such entertainment figures as the Pointer Sisters, Earl "Fatha" Hines, Sly Stone, the Edwin Hawkins Singers, the Whispers, Marla Gibbs, en Vogue, and other entertainers and entertainment groups as Oakland natives, all of which made the city something of a Motown West. Yoshi's in Jack London Square was ground zero of the Bay Area jazz community. Presiding over the jazz scene was Al "Jazzbo" Collins, the all-knowing spinmeister who for nearly forty years, on shows migrating across a half-dozen radio stations, delighted listeners (until his lamented passing, at age seventy-eight, of pancreatic cancer, in 1997), with

his encyclopedic knowledge of jazz past, present, and future on three continents.

As befitting Jack London's hometown, flatland Oakland nurtured a blue-
collar community offering a counter-paradigm to the gentility of the Hills.
Oakland remained an urban industrial, hence working-class, city long after
San Francisco had succumbed to wine-and-cheese tourism and financial
services. The Hells Angels motorcycle club had been founded in Oakland
in April 1957 by Ralph "Sonny" Barger and others, and its Oakland chapter
remained dominant for three decades. Before the drug culture corrupted it,
Hells Angels could be justified—at least in part—as a reasonably legitimate
response by white, working-class men to their impending obsolescence. So
too did the Raiders football team cultivate a tough-guy outlaw image. While
the 49ers across the Bay were featuring the cerebral play of quarterback Joe
Montana and wide receiver Jerry Rice, Raider stars—Kenny "the Snake"
Stabler, Ben Davidson, and Willie Brown—played a kind of no-holds-
barred, kick-ass game thoroughly appreciated by their working-class fans.
When owner Al Davis took the Raiders to Anaheim in 1982, thousands of
Oakland and East Bay men lost something akin to religion: lost, at the least,
an image of themselves out there on the football field, playing like heroes,
showing the fancy-pants team on the other side what it was all about.

In 1995, however, the Raiders came back to Oakland, although many
claimed that the multimillion-dollar package the city assembled for them
was ruinous, given other needs. No matter: the Silver and Black was back in
the Oakland Coliseum, and the glory days would return. The port was also
back, redredged and made shipshape. The Claremont Hotel and Resort was
under new ownership and renovation. Developer John Protopappas was
talking about refashioning the Tribune Tower, empty since 1992, into office
and live/work loft space for urban professionals. The Oakland Hills, devastated by firestorm in 1991, sprouted with reconstruction. Even Hells Angel
Sonny Barger was back—paroled after a four-year term in the Federal Correctional Institution in Phoenix. A thunderous bash had been arranged to
welcome Barger in November 1992 at the Mountain House near Livermore
outside Oakland. Two thousand leather-clad bikers—some from as far away
as Canada, France, Germany, and Russia—were on hand to welcome
Barger as he rode in with his wife, Sharon, on a seven-hundred-pound
Harley-Davidson FXRT, Sonny's hog of choice. Barger was returning to his
middle-class house near the Oakland Zoo, which he had bought in the mid-
1960s. He settled in with his wife of twenty-one years, an attractive former
model, and reopened Sonny Barger's Oakland Custom Motorcycles, a
repair and parts shop. If Barger were coming in from the cold—working at
his shop, living a quiet life with Sharon, marketing Sonny Barger's Cajun

Style Salsa—Oakland could truthfully be described as getting its act together.

And, to a great extent, it was—except for the violence that proved the Achilles' heel of the Oakland experiment. "Oakland," noted commentator Richard Rodriguez in April 1992, "is on its way to becoming a symbol of evil, a metaphor for hopelessness, and for all that we no longer acknowledge as ourselves. Oakland is Detroit and Bedford Stuyvesant and the other side of the tracks."[10] Rodriguez's remarks were prompted by the fact that Oakland had sustained 165 homicides in 1991 and 56 (in a city of only 372,000) in the first quarter of 1992, 7 of them in one day. What was causing this? The answer was simple: drugs. Or, more precisely, the money that could be made from drugs, and the turf battles over who would control the trade. This was not surprising. It was the drug trade, methamphetamines mostly, that had corrupted the Hells Angels in the 1960s and early 1970s. So, too, in the same era, did drug consumption and trafficking help to corrupt whatever was legitimate in Oakland's Black Panther Party.

By the early 1990s, the drug trade had made a homicidal wasteland of the flatlands of West Oakland. Crack cocaine was proving especially vicious, both in terms of the drug traffic itself and the instant and debilitating addiction it offered. Oakland novelist Ishmael Reed, an African American, considered crack cocaine an instrument of genocide, so devastating was it on the world he had known and loved throughout his life. "It's not just a criminal justice problem," noted Oakland police chief George Hart in March 1992, as the homicide rate increased in epic proportions. "It is part of society that is getting very, very sick in some quarters. There are people who are willing to do absolutely anything with absolute abandon."[11]

Two Oakland-set novels appearing that year—*Buffalo Nickel* by Floyd Salas and *Way Past Cool* by Jess Mowry—memorialized the mean streets of the flatlands with mesmerizing power. Growing up on the streets of West Oakland, packing an army .45-caliber pistol when he left school after the eighth grade (he continued to read ambitiously, thanks to his hard-reading father, who operated a scrap-yard crane), Jess Mowry, of equal white and black descent, knew the mean streets of Oakland firsthand. Mowry's fiction was about how kids ("Little Rascals with Uzis," he called them), mostly black, got corrupted early by the drug trade and had their very virtues—their resilience, their loyalties, their entrepreneurial spirit—turned against them. Unlike most embattled writers, who make it big and then get out of the downwardly mobile circumstances they write about as soon as they can, Mowry stayed put. Each morning he wrote in an abandoned 1959 bus parked near his apartment, which served as his office, and stayed close to the kids he was writing about, the kind of kid he had been himself once, despite his Farrar Straus & Giroux imprint, the $100,000-plus advance, and the movie option for *Way Past Cool.* Even when his eight-year-old son was shot in the shoulder on his way home from school, Mowry was reluctant to leave his neighborhood, which for him would mean leaving Oakland itself, leaving the kids behind, washing his hands of the entire city.

Was that the answer? To stay and make Oakland work? By the mid-1990s, the most improbable figure of Jerry Brown, now living in something resembling a commune in a reconverted industrial warehouse near Jack London Square, was saying that this *was* in fact the answer: stand fast, stop running, make Oakland work. Independently wealthy, Brown had moved to Oakland in 1992 and sunk $2 million into a waterfront warehouse, equipping it with living quarters, a radio studio, and a five-hundred-seat auditorium. The reconverted nineteen-thousand-square-foot facility served as headquarters for the former governor's We the People movement, a vaguely defined populist left-of-center reform campaign spearheaded by Brown's daily talk show on the Pacifica Radio Network and town hall meetings in his auditorium, where everything from urban planning to natural childbirth was discussed. As the 1990s wore on, however, Brown's interests, which were always mercurial, began to focus on the question of sustainable cities and urban culture. By the summer of 1996, he was helping sponsor a School of Sustainability in his We the People warehouse. As the mayoral election of June 1998 approached, Brown was increasingly interested in Oakland politics. He asked Mayor Harris for an appointment to the port commission but was turned down—surely a humiliating blow for someone who as governor, twenty years earlier, had selected Oakland as the test case for his Urban Strategy for California program and pumped millions of dollars into rehabilitation, transportation, and social programs for that city.

So Jerry Brown decided to run for mayor, declaring in late October 1997 in front of his warehouse complex, wearing his accustomed black attire, including his trademark collarless shirt. Initially, the press made fun of the man in black: this former Jesuit seminarian, this failed politician, Governor Moonbeam, near sixty and over the hill and a white guy in a black town. But Brown leapt instantly into the lead of all declared candidates, with between 42 and 57 percent support in most predominantly black communities and some 40 percent support among whites. It was never even a contest because, among other things, the black community remembered Brown favorably from his treatment of Oakland when he was governor, his appointment of the first black state cabinet officer and a raft of black judges, and, before that, the way that Brown's father, Governor Edmund G. "Pat" Brown, had nominated the first black judge in the state and pushed through the Fair Employment Practices Act of 1959 and the Rumford Fair Housing Act of

1963, two pathbreaking state-level pieces of civil rights legislation. A handout from Blacks for Brown listed hundreds of African Americans Jerry Brown had appointed while governor, ranging from members of the Acupuncture Board to judges on the California Supreme Court. And besides: wearing his trademark black attire (now relieved, intermittently, with a collarless white shirt, giving him the look of the Jesuit priest he almost became), Brown took his campaign household to household, coffee shop to coffee shop, bar to bar, jazz joint to jazz joint, church to church.

What was Jerry Brown's message? The basics: safety, schools, economic development. The other candidates were pursuing similar themes. Ed Blakely, an African American and longtime professor of urban planning and development at UC Berkeley, was saying these same things in the context of highly articulated programs. Brown rather was saying them, as he said nearly everything, in a series of mantralike utterances that went to the core of what Oakland had to do—clean up its act, make its streets safe, get business to trust Oakland once again—without insulting the African-American stewardship of the city. Brown was also pushing for Measure X, which he had helped place on the ballot, junking Oakland's weak-mayor system, in which city government reported to the council as a whole, in favor of the direct administration of the city by the elected mayor through a city manager.

In June 1998, Jerry Brown was overwhelmingly elected mayor of Oakland, and Measure X passed. The city, which twenty years earlier had ushered in an era of African-American mayors across the United States, had now signaled that race was not enough in urban politics: that the African-American people of Oakland would vote for anyone, regardless of race, who talked in a clear and understandable manner about stopping the crime, improving the schools, and bringing in jobs. For all his flaws—his challenged attention span, his aloofness and occasional arrogance, his tendency to posture—Brown had helped unleash a compelling hope that Oakland could get its act together. Almost instantly, the new mayor bonded with city manager Robert Bobb, an African American already in place; and the two of them—with the shadowy presence of longtime Brown guru Jacques Barzaghi now and then in the background—became inseparable in their efforts to reform and fine-tune the city administration.

Brown—having ousted the first African-American police chief in Oakland's history—turned to another African American for police chief, Richard Ward, a thirty-seven-year-old captain, who, like Brown, had grown up in San Francisco and come through the Catholic school system there, and who had the support of the black ministers of the city. The grandson of a San Francisco police captain, Jerry Brown had always liked cops. Now, as mayor, he rode with them on patrol in the early hours of the morning, went with them on drug busts, hung out with them after hours in their favorite waterfront bar. Personally checking out a reputed drug house in East Oakland a few weeks after his election, Brown came across an addict shooting up and had the police officer at his side put the man under arrest. If, on his rides, Brown saw suspected drug dealers on a corner, he would have the car stopped, get out, and go over to talk to them—to sort out, as he put it, the drug dealers from the street-corner socializers.

How all this would work out remained uncertain as 1999 became 2000, and Oakland remained a volatile city. A rap concert at the Oakland Coliseum in mid-January 2000 erupted in a melee that took 250 Oakland police and California Highway Patrol officers to contain. Shortly thereafter, coliseum and arena officials were seriously considering banning all hip-hop and rap programs from these venues. Yet Jerry Brown had helped Oakland articulate to itself a better path. For better or for worse, as one commentator put it, "power in Oakland is now embodied in one man's character, and an unusual character at that."[12]

"The Brown and Bobb era," noted Heather MacDonald in *City Journal,* the magazine of the Manhattan Institute, "might turn out to be Oakland's fourth seismic shift, as momentous for the city as the Gold Rush, World War II, and the black revolution of the 1960s and 1970s." If Brown succeeded, MacDonald concluded, it would not be just because he was a star. "It will also be because, for all his far-left pronouncements, he understands cities' basic needs for order and private development, and he is willing to beat down all opposition to achieve them."[13]

Midway through his first term as mayor, it was becoming clear that Brown's plan for Oakland was working. Oaklanders thought so, at least, and gave him an unprecedented 80 percent approval rating after his first year in office. Jacques Barzaghi had caused Brown some embarrassment and cost the city $50,000 to settle a sexual harassment claim; but overall the direction of the administration had defined itself. First of all, Brown spearheaded an effort to bring new tenants and businesses into the downtown. Initially, he went after government clients. The investigations unit of U.S. Customs and the regional offices of the National Park Service and the Federal Emergency Management Agency (FEMA) were lured to Oakland from San Francisco, attracted there by more competitive costs. Then the San Francisco–based Shorenstein Company, the privately held flagship real estate giant that had acquired the 1.1-million-square-foot City Center in 1996, announced plans for a 487,000-square-foot office building in an adjacent location. To lure dot-com companies, Oakland helped transform the historic hundred-year-old Rotunda Building into the Communications

Technology Cluster, where start-up dot-commers could find low rent, high-speed fiber-optic connections, and even furniture.

In his second year as mayor, Brown held a conference for three hundred high-tech executives promoting Oakland as a business center, then made a similar pitch the following month in Las Vegas to a convention of shopping center developers. To attract companies, Oakland offered ten-year deals on business and property taxes—or cut better deals, if necessary. Oakland was flexible. To get Zhone Technologies there, city officials offered a discount on a large parcel of undeveloped waterfront in exchange for 100,000 shares of Zhone's pre-IPO stock. The city went so far as to rename a nearby freeway exit Zhone Way. "I've never seen a city government move that fast," Zhone executive Mory Ejabat told *Newsweek*. By April 2001, when *Newsweek* was profiling Oakland as one of the hot new tech cities, more than three hundred dot-com and biotech companies had located there.[14] The more San Francisco companies relocated in Oakland, the more acute the need for housing became. Brown launched an initiative to create more than six thousand housing units, many of them live/work lofts, that he hoped would attract ten thousand new residents to downtown by 2003. Housing activists began to charge that Brown would soon be pricing many low-income African Americans out of their own city, through what was now being called the Jerrification of Oakland. Was Oakland to remain a welfare city? Brown countered. Why not have a rising tide lift all boats?

In 1999 only twenty-nine African-American males, less than 10 percent of all of Oakland's graduating black male high school students, had completed the courses necessary to apply for UC or CSU. Initially, Brown tried to get the entire public school system under his authority. Failing that, he secured the right to appoint three school board members. He also helped create a number of charter schools in Oakland: publicly funded schools, chartered by the state of California, locally managed by parent, teacher, and community alliances. To reach young people who were falling through the cracks because of a lack of a supportive home and family environment, Brown, with the help of his former chief of staff Governor Gray Davis, got through the state board of education a charter for an Oakland Military Institute to open in the fall of 2001 on a former Oakland army base. Staffed in part by California National Guard personnel, the institute would put uniformed students through a rigorous six-day week of Outward Bound–style physical and mental training and an academic program of college preparatory studies, all of it structured by military courtesy and the honor code. Opening with 162 seventh graders, the institute planned to add a grade per year until there were one thousand students in grades seven to twelve.

Left-liberals were appalled. Was this the Jerry Brown, they asked, who just a short time ago was inveighing on his national radio program against corporations, big government, and militarism? The Reverend Ken Chambers, however, an African-American Baptist pastor and economic development executive, had another opinion. The Oakland Military Institute, he argued, would provide an opportunity for "regular citizens to participate in the kind of school usually open only to the elite."[15]

Despite his newfound pragmatism, Jerry Brown still remained in touch with his previous identities as Jesuit seminarian, student of Zen, volunteer with Mother Teresa in Calcutta, and all-round gadfly. Guru Barzaghi might be in disgrace, but no matter; Brown was bringing historian and philosopher Ivan Illich to his warehouse loft near the Oakland waterfront twice a year to moderate six-week sessions of what Brown called the Oakland Table: lectures, discussions, and seminars, open to the public, dealing with various aspects of urbanism and community building in a philosophical context. The Republican Party, meanwhile, was sponsoring expeditions by bus into African-American neighborhoods under the auspices of a "Republicans in the 'Hood" program sponsored by the statewide party. "Largely black cities like Oakland," noted Ron Nehring, chairman of the San Diego Republican Committee, "are fertile grounds for ideas; now we need to make them fertile ground for Republican candidates." Mayor Jerry Brown was making a difference. And tough love was part of the answer.[16]

Downtown

The Reurbanization of San Jose

J erry Brown's program was running parallel to the tough-love philosophy of another California reformer, San Jose police chief Joe McNamara, a onetime New York City cop with a Harvard doctorate. Like Brown,
McNamara believed that you began the governance of any city, however
troubled, with a basic respect for its residents, even if they were not con-
forming to the middle-class values of the suburbs. Appointed police chief of
San Jose in 1976, McNamara initially found the minority-dominated city
council hostile to the police, so bad had been relations in the past. McNamara, who wrote detective novels on the side, put into effect a distinctive
brand of community policing based on a number of simple premises. First
of all, the police worked for the people. Second, it was not the job of the
police to judge the people derogatorily as far as their values and way of living were concerned, provided that no laws were being broken. Third, the
community had to participate with the police in the policing process, which
involved a recognition on the part of the police that the community wanted
them there and felt better because they were on hand.

In neighborhoods bothered by prostitution, the streetwalkers themselves, the cruising johns, the menacing pimps, the whole volatility of it,
were making certain parts of the city unusable by night. Some downtown
San Jose residents would actually go out and try to make citizen's arrests or,
in other instances, take Polaroid photographs of streetwalkers, pimps, and
johns and tell these individuals that they were going to turn the photographs
over to the police. This was irregular, even dangerous; but McNamara was
impressed by the desire of these largely Hispanic communities to take back
their sidewalks and street corners after dark. He invited community representatives to accompany armed officers on pedestrian patrol in these areas
to create a counterpresence. The American Civil Liberties Union was ini-

tially suspicious; and the mayor at the time, Janet Gray Hayes, the first woman to be elected mayor of a major American city, did not want the spectacle of burly cops running girls into the pokey by the squad-car-full when their pimps and johns were equally part of the problem. (As mayor, Hayes had fired McNamara's predecessor and hired McNamara, but before doing that, she had invited the U.S. Civil Rights Commission to come into her city and monitor her police force.) But the program worked.

In his first years on the job, McNamara, charismatic and formidable in his blues, spent many an evening in the homes of minority residents of San Jose, showing them respect, as he put it, hearing their complaints. On Saturdays, McNamara and groups of his officers would barbecue hamburgers and hot dogs for the people of neighborhoods that were especially at risk. Within four years, the Civil Rights Commission was complimenting the San Jose Police Department for its community-based policing. In 1984, San Jose was voted the safest large city in the United States. A Mexican-American city was confronting the culture of crime that was in the process of destroying so many other minority-dominated urban places.

In 1991, McNamara stepped down to accept a research fellowship at the Hoover Institution in Palo Alto. By that time, San Jose was not only the third largest city in California, it had become, thanks to its relationship to Silicon Valley, thoroughly competitive with Los Angeles, San Diego, and San Francisco as a center of urban influence. A de facto triumvirate—Tom McEnery, elected in 1982 to succeed Hayes; McNamara; and Redevelopment Agency director Frank Taylor, appointed by Mayor Hayes in 1979 and lasting in office into the millennium—played key roles in creating an environment in which San Jose reversed the almost universal American process of inner cities becoming the hole in the center of the doughnut. McNamara's job in this process, most obviously, was to sustain an atmosphere of law and order alongside citizen satisfaction, especially in the minority community, lest San Jose, like Oakland, see its reputation as a business-friendly environment devastated.

To this process Tom McEnery, who was only in his late thirties and early forties through most of his mayoralty, brought the passion, the commitment, and the political skills, and the sheer love of San Jose that was equally necessary. Born into a prominent local family of affluent Democrats (McEnery's father had once brought Harry Truman to San Jose for the first visit of a sitting president to that city), educated at the nearby Jesuit-founded Santa Clara University, McEnery stood for the city council out of a mixture of noblesse oblige, a deeply emotional involvement with San Jose (as an amateur historian, he would later make important contributions to the history of his city), and the Camelot idealism of someone who had been profoundly influenced by the Kennedy era.

An aerial photograph of downtown, McEnery later remembered, taken in the late 1960s, revealed San Jose's problem. Like Fresno, the city was spreading out to the horizon. It would eventually encompass 176 square miles and leave its center behind. In the 1950s alone, San Jose had annexed nearly fifty square miles of adjacent orchards and farms. Would San Jose itself be lost as a definable city in this process? Would it, like Fresno, disappear into the very sprawl that was dissolving its center? Here was a city—founded by the Spanish in 1777 (the first city in Alta California, to be given full *pueblo*, or civic, status), briefly the capital of California in 1849, a charming market and college town for most of the next century, with fewer than 100,000 people living there as late as 1947—that was now passing the half-million mark. True urbanism, McEnery realized, would not have a chance if this situation continued. "If San Jose wasn't the center of anything," he later said of this period, "downtown wasn't even the center of San Jose."[17]

Redevelopment director Frank Taylor, a planner and an architect, agreed. San Jose, Taylor feared, was actually ashamed of itself as a city; and the wasteland at its center was both the cause and the symbol of that disquiet. Within a very short time, given the fact that only its attached mall- and freeway-centered suburban developments offered opportunities for pride and civic identification, San Jose would in effect cease to exist as anything other than a provider of police and fire and other services to the suburbs. As mayor, McEnery resolved to fill in the doughnut hole, the center of San Jose, through redevelopment. This was something he had the power to do, as the city council had in 1975 declared itself the Redevelopment Agency's governing board, and hence had direct control, with the mayor sitting as board chairman. The city government, in other words, had control of the governance of redevelopment, which was in most cities a quasi-autonomous agency. Across two decades, San Jose grew, largely from forces beyond its control—the rise of Silicon Valley especially—and leveraged this growth through bonds and incentives in the private sector to re-create it as the eleventh largest city in the United States, the third largest in California, and, most important, a city centered on its downtown and an array of classic civic institutions and utilities.

All together, the Redevelopment Agency spent more than $500 million on buildings and $300 million on infrastructure in transforming downtown, and entered other joint ventures with the private sector totaling more than $1 billion: office high-rises (Adobe software located more than 2,600 employees in two office towers, jointly financed with redevelopment), hotels (a Fairmont, a Hilton, a restored St. James), a Children's Discovery Museum, the Tech Museum of Innovation, a convention center, a 2,665-seat Center for the Performing Arts, a repertory theater, a sports arena with a professional hockey team, an airport, a light-rail transit system, affordable housing, redeveloped and usable parks, even street toilet kiosks in the Parisian manner. In 1999 the agency announced plans to landscape the banks of the Guadalupe River into a twenty-mile regional park and launched the seven-square-block San Jose Civic Plaza project, which over the next ten years would foster the construction of a new city hall, a new symphony hall, a new main library, an elementary school, a renovated supermarket, a parking structure, and fifty housing units.

Each month the city magazine *San Jose: The Magazine for Silicon Valley* grew thicker with listings for restaurants, jazz concerts (at the Mountain Winery amphitheater in the hills overlooking the city), and social and athletic events. In 1992, San Jose made a brave attempt to lure the Giants from San Francisco, but voters balked at the $250 million cost for a stadium package. No matter: the Sharks hockey team was drawing large crowds in the arena. Brandi Chastain, America's first female soccer superhero, was from San Jose, and had learned her game in part playing in the many leagues in the area and at the nearby Santa Clara University, which *U.S. News & World Report* consistently ranked as the best private smaller university in the Far West. San Jose State University, meanwhile, the oldest in the CSU system, remained among the most popular of the CSU campuses. The intelligently written and edited *San Jose Mercury News,* a Knight Ridder newspaper, dominated the Southern Bay Area–Silicon Valley market. Thanks to the efforts of managing partner John Charles Stein, the sixty-five-year-old Boccardo Law Firm, one of the largest plaintiffs' firms in the state, closed its San Francisco branch office and consolidated its entire operation in downtown San Jose.

By the end of the decade, following two terms by another woman mayor, Susan Hammer, San Jose had its first Latino chief executive in the American phase of its existence, Ron Gonzales, who earlier in his life, before moving to San Jose, had served as mayor of Sunnyvale. Unlike Jerry Brown in Oakland, Gonzales was dealing with a very opposite range of problems: namely, the fact that rising prosperity was also booming housing prices beyond affordability for most workers (million-dollar homes were commonplace) and causing terrible traffic congestion.

The answer to such congestion, according to the Redevelopment Agency, was to create more and denser housing downtown. San Jose, with a population of more than 900,000 by the millennium, had less than 1 percent of its residents living downtown. The answer was to build eight thousand downtown units by 2010. The first of these projects was the 104-unit Paseo Villas condominium complex and a 320-unit apartment complex known as 101 San Fernando, a cluster of apartment complexes with seven separate entrances and interior courtyards reminiscent of Italy or Spain. These buildings created concentrations almost unknown in California cities outside of upscale San Francisco and the downscale portions of Los Angeles. "These are densities that are comparable to those in Berlin and Vienna," noted Daniel Solomon, the San Francisco–based UC Berkeley architect who had designed 101 San Fernando.[18]

All this—the office complexes, the hotels and housing, the light rail, the museums, the sports and cultural centers, the new library, the restored Roman Catholic cathedral, the parks and plazas—had coalesced by the millennium to create in San Jose a vibrant downtown, where, a mere twenty years earlier, there had been a wasteland of parking lots. Because it was the capital of the Silicon Valley, San Jose was seeing its statistics go off the graph. According to figures released by the Redevelopment Agency, the median household income had by January 2001 risen to $73,818, making San Jose the second most affluent market in the nation. (Median household income in San Francisco, by contrast, was $54,724.) Not surprisingly, when the Grill, a Beverly Hills power restaurant, decided in 1999 to make its first expansion, it chose downtown San Jose, following in the wake of the E&O Trading Company from San Francisco and Il Fornaio. Some two million people had attended a total of 181 downtown festivals in 1999. By the millennium, 75,000 people were coming downtown for social events each week. Over all, 6.2 million visitors were showing each year that they knew the way to downtown San Jose.

Play Ball!

San Diego in the Major Leagues

Whatever else might happen to San Diego, the sixth largest city in the United States, it had always been and would continue to be a tourist town of great beauty sited on a grand bay: a city that had developed in the late nineteenth century as a health and hotel enclave and would always have the resort metaphor close to the core of its identity. San Diego abounded in places to visit: Balboa Park, the San Diego Zoo (the most comprehensive and distinguished zoo in the United States), the San Diego Wild Animal Park, SeaWorld, the Birch Aquarium at the Scripps Institute of Oceanography, the Mission Basilica San Diego de Alcala, the stately Hotel del Coronado, the redeveloped Gaslamp Quarter in the downtown, and a newcomer, Legoland. Such attractions would continue to bring millions of tourists into San Diego each year. It was a fun town, a family town, perfect for mid-cost vacations.

It was also a navy and Marine Corps town. San Diego had deliberately joined the navy in the 1920s, and it had paid off. The city sustained the largest naval complex in the free world, with nearly one-fifth of the fleet and the Marine Corps stationed in San Diego County. The Naval Training Center and Marine Corps Recruit Depot in the city itself, a network of naval stations around the bay, Camp Pendleton north of the city, the Miramar Naval Air Station: nearly 22 percent of the gross regional product of San Diego County, estimated at $42.1 billion in 1987, was connected in one way or another with defense spending, augmented by the paychecks of countless retired naval and Marine Corps personnel.

In 1991, when some fifteen military bases were under consideration for closure in California, the San Diego establishment, the private sector and elected officials alike, went into overdrive. When the Base Closure and Realignment Commission held public hearings in mid-June 1991, it was bombarded with telling testimony regarding the pivotal nature of San Diego's navy and Marine Corps facilities and the devastating economic impact disestablishment would bring to the region. With a few exceptions—the Miramar Naval Air Station, for example, was downsized for the Marine Corps—San Diego won its case. Still, defense spending was dramatically curtailed, and by the summer of 1993, the worst year of the slump, unemployment hit 9.2 percent in San Diego, the highest rate in the decade. In mid-September, however, the navy awarded $1.3 billion to the National Steel and Shipbuilding Company to build as many as six supply ships. As far as the navy was concerned, San Diego was back in business.

The trouble was, while San Diego held on to the navy and the Marine Corps, it was not holding on to its large corporations. Already, by March 1990, eight of the fifteen largest publicly held businesses in San Diego County had been taken over and moved, or were facing the threat of acquisition. By mid-1990, Pacific Southwest Airlines, the major commuter airline in the state, had been acquired by USAir. Fisher Scientific, with revenues close to $1 billion, merged with the Henley Group and moved to New Hampshire. Oak Industries relocated its electronics components company to Boston. Other publicly held high-tech companies—Pancretec, Gen-Probe, Monitor Technologies, Sintro—also left the region. Great American Bank, the eighth largest thrift in the nation, went on the ropes (federal regulators had already taken over the San Diego–based Imperial Savings), and there was a serious possibility that the San Diego Gas & Electric Company would soon be merging with Southern California Edison Corporation, thus moving control of the city's utilities to Los Angeles.

A whole new wave of high-tech and biotech start-ups, however, would eventually find in San Diego exactly what they needed: available office space, a beautiful and pleasant city and county to live in, the scientifically oriented UC San Diego campus, perhaps the best weather in the nation—everything except a major international airport. The public and private sectors would spend the entire 1990s debating, proposing, and rejecting various airport sites—the downsized Miramar Air Station, Otay Mesa near the border, even a transborder facility in northern Baja—to replace the over-burdened and boxed-in Lindbergh Field. Talking about a new airport soon became a sort of therapeutic mantra for San Diego County: something that allowed the region to envision itself in its next stage of development, but not really, deep down, to be taken all that seriously, given the fact that each proposed site had its own bloc of naysayers.

Yet San Diego had more than an airport on its mind. The loss of so many local companies threatened both the fact and the financing of civic identity. Where was the new oligarchy to come from, the new philanthropy, the next generation of civic projects? One of the reasons everyone was so worried about the possible acquisition by outside investors of the Great American Bank, with $16.1 billion in assets by 1990, was the fact that its founder, Gordon Luce, a former member of Governor Ronald Reagan's cabinet in Sacramento, whom Reagan had tried to lure to Washington with a cabinet appointment and later an ambassadorship, was the key giver ($1 million a year to a wide range of social and civic programs) and civic leader of the region. To whom should the San Diego Symphony, the San Diego Opera, the Old Globe Theater turn, now that the city, like Los Angeles, was losing its corporate headquarters?

The navy and Marine Corps, and to a lesser extent their civilian employees and retirees, represented a world unto themselves. For such people, their uniformed service, and not metropolitan San Diego, constituted their primary culture and mode of self-identification. High-tech and biotech start-ups were bringing an extraordinarily well-educated cadre of young people into the city (San Diego had more PhDs per total population than any other metropolitan region in the nation); but this talented group, committed to the time-consuming development of cutting-edge products in highly leveraged companies, were hardly the types to form a reservoir of either civic sentiment or cultural involvement.

Thus San Diego spent the first half of the 1990s in a condition of lowered mobility as the city experienced its worst economic downturn since the Great Depression. As in the case of the Depression, San Diego was filling, once again, with the homeless: an estimated nineteen thousand in the county, with seven thousand of them in the city itself. The situation became so bad that the city council was entertaining in the fall of 1992 a controversial proposal, eventually rejected, to build tent cities for the homeless throughout the city. Between 1991 and 1993, San Diego lost fifty thousand jobs, which represented a 5 percent drop in total employment. It had managed to save the navy and the Marine Corps; yet the very fact that 20 percent of its regional economy had been dependent on defense spending meant that San Diego was not exempt from the overall cutbacks in this area. The city was cutting it so close to the economic bone that the absence of sailors and marines from the region during Operation Desert Storm in 1991 resulted in sagging retail sales. Even defense workers who managed to get retraining and reenter the workforce were experiencing a 20 percent drop in pay. San Diego was the sixth largest city in the nation, but Nelson Media Research was ranking it by October 1994 as a dismal twenty-seventh of all national media markets. Even the tourist business, a mainstay since the early twentieth century, was off, due, in part, to a sharp decline of Japanese tourism. By January 1993, hotel occupancy had plunged to 65 percent in a region that had 44,500 rooms in support of its tourist and convention economy.

Matters came to a head in July 1994 when General Dynamics announced that it would stop making commercial jetliner fuselages in San Diego, close its Convair division by the end of 1995, and move its operations to Denver and Tucson. Aside from a loss of nineteen thousand jobs, the departure of Convair constituted a trauma at the very core of the San Diego identity. It was as if General Motors were announcing it was leaving Detroit. In 1935, Major Reuben Fleet had relocated Consolidated Aircraft from Buffalo to San Diego. For fifty-nine years, Consolidated Aircraft—later Consolidated Vultee and still later Convair—had embodied in its harborside plant, on property leased from the port of San Diego, the preeminence of the city as Gibraltar of the Pacific. During World War II, Consolidated Vultee had built B-24 Liberator bombers in this plant. After the war, Convair had continued on with a steady stream of military and civilian contracts.

Its parent company, General Dynamics, by 1961 had 46,859 employees at several plants throughout the county—15 percent of the total San Diego County workforce—busy making such cold war necessities as the eighty-foot Atlas Intercontinental Ballistic Missile and, later, the all-purpose Tomahawk. As recently as the late 1980s, General Dynamics San Diego was employing nearly twenty thousand workers. No wonder that the saying around City Hall had for so many years been "What's good for General Dynamics is good for San Diego." A company that at the height of its power employed nearly a third of the workforce in San Diego County had ceased to be something private. It had become, rather, a bedrock of public identity. Missile Park, a twenty-seven-acre enclave maintained by General Dynamics at its plant on Kearny Mesa, was second only to the publicly supported Balboa Park in popularity. Most of the families using the baseball fields, the horseshoe pits, the swings and picnic tables at Missile Park, taking their children for rides on the carousel or miniature train, playing tennis, or enjoying the community meeting halls, most likely thought, if they thought about it at all, that the palm-tree-guarded, lawn-lavish park was a public amenity.

By July 1995, General Dynamics had fewer than one thousand employees on its local payroll. To add insult to injury, the chief executive officer who was moving the company from San Diego was a native son: William Anders, an *Apollo 8* astronaut, the very person who in 1968 had taken the famous photograph of Earth rising that had become a primary icon of the space age. Native son or not, Anders wanted Convair out of San Diego as quickly as possible, no retraining programs, no job counseling, no nothing.

In mid-November 1995, San Diego was treated to a most melancholy spectacle: the auctioning off of all machinery in the harborside Convair factory.
As the equipment was sold, crated, and shipped—the milling and turning
machines, the grinders, borers, drillers, rooters, brakes, lathes, shears, fabri-
cators, arc welders, hydraulic-feed reciprocating surface grinders, all of it,
some of it in use since 1935—one era of San Diego came dramatically to a
close. Already, the departure of General Dynamics had had a ripple effect
on such affiliated companies as Teledyne Ryan, Loral, and Rohr, for a net
loss of 41,000 jobs.

How could San Diego regain its civic self-confidence, economic
momentum, and public life? The answer involved, in various degrees and
with various levels of success or failure, telecommunications, professional
sports, and the San Diego Symphony. Tracing its origins to 1912, the symphony hardly seemed in 1995 a candidate for the promotion of civic identity
and self-esteem. By mid-decade, it was en route to bankruptcy, despite the
fact that the city council had in 1995 advanced a whole year's worth of
funding ($418,000) to stave off the impending disaster. Things got worse,
and on January 13, 1996, Maestro Yoav Talmi gave a farewell concert in
Copley Symphony Hall. A few last-minute gifts, however, postponed bankruptcy until the end of May. For two and a half years, the symphony
remained silent, yet one more blow to the identity and self-esteem of the
city, especially since the bankruptcy had been so messy, with the bankruptcy trustee at one point on the verge of selling Copley Symphony Hall
itself, even the orchestra's musical library, to assuage creditors.

Enter the telecommunications giant Qualcomm, which in and of itself
seemed capable of ushering in the new San Diego. Founded by a group of
UC San Diego computer scientists in 1985—among them, Irwin Jacobs—
Qualcomm filled in the second half of the 1990s the void created by the
defense cutbacks, the savings-and-loan debacles, the departure of General
Dynamics, and the falloffs in affiliated companies. Qualcomm built its fortune on a complicated digital telecommunications technology for mobile or
wireless telephones. Known as code division multiple access, or CDMA,
the technology was a commercialized version of a defense communications
strategy in which digital signals were compressed and coded to maximize
over-the-air capacity and security. CDMA, in short, compacted sound digi-
tally and sent it swiftly and safely through the airwaves. Few companies in
the nation could match the rapid rise of this telecommunications phenomenon, especially after it legally secured rights to its technology against the
claims of a Swedish competitor. By March 1998, Qualcomm had a workforce of ten thousand. By early 1999, its stock had risen to $4 billion. A
year later, it stood at $108 billion. Many people were becoming millionaires

from Qualcomm stock, including a thousand local employees known as Quillionaires. By 2000, Qualcomm was the largest employer in San Diego County. By January 2002, it was enjoying $2.7 billion in annual revenue. Locals affectionately dubbed Qualcomm the Q, as in "What's good for the Q is good for San Diego."

In historical terms, a gamble had paid off. The University of California had specifically established its San Diego campus in the mid-1960s as a science- and technology-oriented research center. By the 1990s, UC San Diego was appearing on all the expected lists as one of the ten best science, engineering, and technology universities in the nation. Quite literally, in terms of its entrepreneurial professors, UC San Diego can be said to have founded Qualcomm in 1985—certainly, at least, to have established the culture for such a development. So, too, was San Diego's developing biotech industry driven by UC San Diego. A lot of things had gone wrong with San Diego, but not its UC campus—and not Qualcomm.

Money like this was exactly what San Diego needed. Irwin and Joan Jacobs, whose worth in cash, property, and stock options was estimated at $4 billion by the millennium, were generous people, as was Qualcomm vice chairman Andrew Viterbi, also a billionaire a few times over. In 1993 the Jacobses gave $500,000 to improve Copley Hall. This was followed by gifts of $2.2 million to the San Diego Foundation, $5 million to the La Jolla Playhouse, and $15 million to the UC San Diego School of Engineering, which was renamed in their honor. The San Diego Symphony, meanwhile, was preparing for a comeback, thanks in part to help from the Jacobses and the Barona Band of Mission Indians, who operated a casino east of San Diego and sent along a check for $200,000 to underwrite a Truly Tchaikovsky pops festival, held on Navy Pier in July 1998. Following the success of that concert, the symphony, now under the interim direction of its former associate conductor, Jung-Ho Pak, also music director of the USC Symphony Orchestra, edged itself gingerly back into the consciousness of the city with a concert series accompanying silent movies, a series of family concerts on Sunday afternoons, and a regular series of classical music at Copley Hall.

Two other events, meanwhile—Super Bowl XXXII in January 1998 and the 1998 World Series, each of them held in San Diego—were also promising to add lustre to a renewed city. Hosting the Denver Broncos and the Green Bay Packers for the Super Bowl, San Diego came to national attention to a degree only approximated two years earlier when the city had welcomed the Republican National Convention. And when the Padres reached the World Series that October, San Diego's cup ran over. So recently embattled in its civic identity, San Diego was now facing the great New York Yankees—the Bronx versus the Beach—and bringing to San Diego a measure of equality with the Big Apple itself, the biggest big-time city in the nation. When the Padres returned from New York for the final game of the series, a navy band led the parade, and thousands of cheering fans lined the downtown streets.

All this fervor fed into Proposition C on the forthcoming November ballot. That July, Mayor Susan Golding had announced a deal with the Padres to build a 42,500-seat ballpark modeled on Camden Yards in Baltimore and Jacobs Field in Cleveland. It would cost $411 million. The city and the Redevelopment Agency would give up to 70 percent of the money, and the Padres would provide the other 30 percent. In exchange for this generous support, the Padres promised to remain in San Diego until 2024 and to develop the area around the ballpark, on the neglected eastern edge of the downtown, with hotels, retail, and housing. The ballpark would thus function as the catalyst and cornerstone for the largest downtown redevelopment project in San Diego history. The entire city seemed to rally to the project. The campaign committee alone had listed two thousand names, with 119 cochairs. That November, voters approved Proposition C by a 60 percent vote.

The new Padres stadium would not be ready until the 2002 season. In the meantime, work had been completed on a $60 million expansion of Jack Murphy Stadium, approved by voters in 1995. The project called for the addition of ten thousand seats, pushing capacity to 72,000, as both the Chargers and the National Football League were requesting. (The NFL required stadiums seating seventy thousand or above for Super Bowls.) When the $60 million fell short of the full refurbishment, Qualcomm donated $18 million to complete the expansion project. And so the name of Jack Murphy, late sports editor of the *San Diego Union,* was taken from the stadium and assigned to the field; and both Super Bowl XXXII and the 1998 World Series were played at Qualcomm Park.

Stockton developer Alex Spanos, owner of the Chargers, however, said that he did not like Qualcomm Park, even after $78 million had been spent on its refurbishment, and by 1998 Spanos was talking about moving the team to the Rose Bowl in Pasadena. Nor had the Padres liked Qualcomm Park, for that matter. Principal owner John Moores, a computer magnate, wanted something like the new Giants ballpark in San Francisco. And even as refurbishments were being finished, Moores was talking about the difficulties of extracting enough income from Qualcomm Park to meet the skyrocketing salaries of his ballplayers. Moores, of course, could look forward to the new Padres park the voters had authorized in November 1998—

except for the fact that this project had become, immediately and devastatingly, the object of nearly a dozen lawsuits, most of them orchestrated and energized by former city councilman Bruce Henderson, a Republican lawyer in his late fifties, independently wealthy, with strong libertarian tendencies leading him in the direction of a devoted opposition to the lavish public subsidy the city had promised the baseball team. (A lawsuit by Henderson had also threatened to stop the improvement of Jack Murphy Stadium, until Qualcomm had come up with the extra $18 million in exchange for naming rights.)

Henderson's eleven suits were more than nuisances. They were making it impossible for the city to sell bonds to meet its $70 million obligation for the Padres stadium, now in the first stages of construction. If all this were not bad enough, a federal grand jury was in the process of investigating city councilwoman Valerie Stallings, a respected Democrat in her early sixties, known for her work on environmental and mass transit issues. The cause of the investigation: Stallings had made an $11,200 profit on stock purchased in an IPO recommended to her by Padres owner John Moores. She had also accepted the use of Moores's home in Carmel, had eaten lunch at a Pebble Beach country club at his expense, and had received such gifts as an answering machine, a camera, and assorted Padres souvenirs and autographed baseballs. Poignantly, Moores had also given Stallings airline tickets so that her sister and her sister's daughter, Stallings's niece, could fly to San Diego from Kansas to be with Stallings during a mastectomy and the chemotherapy that followed. Moores had also flown Stallings's mother up from Florida for the same purpose.

It was not so much that she had received these gifts that got Stallings in trouble, as it was the fact that, with the exception of the stock purchase profit, she failed to disclose them while voting for and ardently championing the ballpark project. For concealing this $2,300 in gifts, Stallings was now the target of a federal investigation; and while this was under way, the city could not sell the $299 million in bonds necessary to continue construction on the Padres park. Ironically, it was Stallings who had defeated Bruce Henderson for the city council in 1992. Now it was her turn to stall the project.

Throughout the second half of 2000, as the Stallings investigation continued, a cloud hung over City Hall as the downtown ballpark came closer and closer to a shutdown. In June 2000, the money ran out, and the council advanced $10 million in interim financing, which the Padres matched with $20 million. Late in September 2000, however, the handwriting was on the wall when Padres president Larry Lucchino drove out to the construction site to inform three hundred workers that the ballpark project, now being kept alive by interim financing from the city, would be out of money and shut down by early October. Bruce Henderson could not have been happier.

As if all this were not enough, San Diego was losing its shirt to the Chargers. In 1995 the team had made it to Super Bowl XXIX, losing to the San Francisco 49ers after a well-fought game. They were a hot team, and San Diego, still in the midst of its recession, desperately needed something first-rate with which to identify. It was in this mood that the city had signed a contract authorizing the improvements to the stadium. Even more improbably, the city had promised to reduce rent in Qualcomm Park for every Chargers game that did not exceed sixty thousand in attendance, and agreed to buy all unsold tickets to every Chargers game, should that ever be necessary. It seemed a good idea at the time, a necessary move to keep the team in San Diego and the city pumped in its self-esteem. Unfortunately, the Chargers went into decline. By May 2002, they were in limbo, having finished 1–15 in 2000 and 5–11 in 2001. By 2000, attendance at Chargers games had for some time been declining, and the city was shelling out $7 million a year for unsold tickets and receiving no rent on Qualcomm Park. By May 2002, San Diego had bought a total of $25.3 million in unsold tickets, many of them given away free to youth groups.

Naturally, the Chargers were blaming San Diego and not themselves, and so were the Padres. (This seems to be the custom of professional sports franchises all over America: Ask for more, and do even less.) Finishing the 2000 season in last place, their second consecutive year in the cellar of the National Football League West, the Chargers front office seemed to feel no embarrassment in openly talking about looking for another town, where they could find a better deal. In 1960 the team had come to San Diego from Los Angeles. Now they began talking about going home. Their 1995 contract, after all, had reserved the right to leave San Diego after 2004, should its players' salaries exceed the NFL cap. This was the leverage that owner Alex Spanos was using to look toward Los Angeles, and LA was listening.

As a first step, the Chargers announced in May 2002 a five-year deal in which they would conduct their six-week preseason camp, starting in 2003, at a sports complex being built by Denver billionaire Philip Anschutz on the campus of Cal State Dominguez Hills in Carson in southern Los Angeles County. Anschutz was also working with his fellow Los Angeles Staples Center investors Ed Roski, Casey Wasserman, and Ron Burkle to finance and build a $450 million stadium on public land near Staples Center in downtown Los Angeles. Not only did these investors have the Chargers in mind, they were also talking about a two-team stadium, with either USC or UCLA sharing the turf. San Diego, which had invested so much in each of its teams, could very well find itself without a baseball or football franchise—and with one, and possibly two, empty stadiums.

In January 2002, the San Diego Symphony announced the largest single gift ever to be given to an American orchestra—$100 million, from Qualcomm CEO Irwin Jacobs and his wife, Joan. A year earlier, Valerie Stallings, now removed from office, had pleaded guilty in superior court to two misdemeanors (prosecutors had agreed to file misdemeanor rather than felony charges against Stallings because she had resigned from public office). Because of Stallings's record of public service, superior court judge Wayne Peterson, while imposing a $10,000 fine, spared her any jail time. Prosecutors did not indict John Moores, however, because there was no proof that his gifts to Stallings were intended as bribery for a specific outcome. Dazed and aggrieved by her fall from grace, Stallings seemed more a symbol of San Diego now than she had while serving on the city council. Meeting the press in front of her home after sentencing, the devastated former councilwoman was wearing a rumpled Padres sweatshirt.

PART VII

A Tale of Two Cities

Los Angeles and San Francisco

People

In the aftermath of the April-May 1992 riots, an ad hoc group of Latino leaders, believing that the Latino future of Los Angeles was not being fully recognized in the Rebuild LA effort, organized the Latino Coalition for a New Los Angeles. Within the year, they issued a startling and prophetic report, *Latinos and the Future of Los Angeles: A Guidebook to the Twenty-first Century* (1993). Prepared by the Latino Futures Research Group and written and edited by UCLA professor David Hayes-Bautista, the document correctly predicted what had become obvious by 2002: the emergence of Los Angeles as a Latino city, the second most important Mexican city on the planet. The majority of Latino residents, the document insisted, did not participate in the riots; indeed, they were as horrified as anyone by the misbehavior and devastation. Los Angeles Latinos, the report argued, tended to be home-owning, churchgoing family people, believing and practicing a traditional conception of marriage and childrearing. Latinos were essential to the stabilization of Los Angeles, and they constituted the largest single matrix of reliable working people on whom could be based the rebuilding of what the report described as "a new and even grander city on the Pacific Shore, a twenty-first century City called Los Angeles."

Seven years later, in his third thought-provoking book of the decade, *Magical Urbanism: Latinos Reinvent the US Big City* (2000), urbanist Mike Davis forcefully argued that such a new metropolis on the Pacific was showing every sign of having arrived. Far from deconstructing American cities, Davis pointed out, Latinos were creating a new urban matrix with a special proclivity for public life. The big urban story of the 1990s, Davis said, especially the big Los Angeles story, was how Latinos had brought to the abandoned inner city a vibrant street life and a passion for public culture. Far from being abandoned, downtown Los Angeles, the East Side, Pico Union, and even the South Central portions of the city were witnessing Latino immigrants in the process of repossessing streets, parks, playgrounds, public squares, public libraries, and other places previously left behind by white flight. Los Angeles, in short, was being reinvented in its central district as a Latino public place, and this process, occurring as well in Houston, San Antonio, Dallas, Phoenix, and San Diego, was restoring to the American city a public identity and civic value resistant to the debilitating provincialization that came from obsessive privatization.

For Joel Kotkin, the teeming Pico Union district was reprising New York's Lower East Side of one hundred years earlier, when equally embattled Jewish immigrants from eastern Europe had poured into the city and created a ghetto that bore within itself the possibilities of an eventual, and much more sophisticated, urbanism. Poverty and crime were evident in Pico Union, Kotkin admitted, but it also had to be recognized that in 1906 fully one-third of the juvenile delinquents in the children's court of New York came from the Jewish immigrant population. Already, within five years of the riots, 90 to 95 percent of all damaged properties in Pico Union had been restored or rebuilt. Firms such as Giroux Glass, the Western Badge, and the electronic mart La Curacao had resisted pressures to relocate. Not that Pico Union was on the edge of fashionability, Kotkin conceded; but it was holding its own, and its population of Latinos, notably Central American in origin, like the Jews of the Lower East Side one hundred years before, were headed for better things.

Mike Davis's notion of Los Angeles as a magical realist city received corroboration by a series of increasingly ambitious Cinco de Mayo festivals, the well-attended Latino nights at the Hollywood Bowl, and the Latino revitalization of a previously abandoned Broadway Street downtown. In November 1996 the Getty Museum presented an exhibition by documentary photographer Camilo Jose Vergara abounding in images and words depicting the transformation of Los Angeles into a magical realist place, including the blazingly colorful re-creation of East LA tract homes in the style of Acapulco. In what other city, after all, could members of mariachi bands, resplendent in *charro* suits, be found standing on the corner on any given evening in East Los Angeles, available to play at parties or other impromptu gatherings, after a quick curbside negotiation with prospective customers? Then there were the *vendedores,* the street vendors, three thousand of them, selling everything imaginable: hand-crocheted baby clothes, ornately dressed dolls, bootlegged cassettes of Spanish-language hits, oranges, flowers, balloons, cotton candy, coconut, mango and watermelon slices, hot dogs wrapped in bacon, Latin American drinks such as *tejuino, atol, piña,* and *tamarindo.* Expressly outlawed in 1974—with the exception of vendors specializing in newspapers, steamed hot dogs, pretzels, and poppies sold by war veterans—the *vendedores* refused to be banished from the city's streets. Beginning with efforts by Councilman Mike Woo in 1991, Los Angeles grew increasingly permissive of the street vendors, who were doing so much to enliven the sidewalks of the city and, of even greater importance, to bring retail products and refreshment to churches and parks, street corners and playgrounds, to Latino Los Angelenos who were spending a significant part of their lives in public, and on the street.

How were African Americans coping in this process of Latinization? Not so well in San Francisco, although in that city gentrification, not Latinization, was the problem. Through the 1990s, the African-American population of San Francisco dropped from 79,039 to 60,515. By Census 2000, African Americans constituted a mere 8.6 percent of the city, most of them living in the toxic and gang-ridden Bayview Hunters Point. During World War II, San Francisco had experienced an explosion of its black population when thousands of African Americans came west from Louisiana and Texas to get defense jobs in the naval shipyards. Centered on the Fillmore district of the central city, soon known as Harlem West, the African-American community, with many of its residents living in surviving nineteenth-century Victorians, enjoyed a vibrant social, church, and musical life that made the Fillmore a center of jazz performance and nightclubs.

By 2002, however, the Fillmore was becoming an upscale neighborhood of expensive apartment buildings, refurbished Victorians, trendy restaurants, and antique stores. The transforming agent was the Redevelopment Agency of San Francisco, which had, over the previous forty-five years, torn down many of the Victorians and set in motion a process of gentrification that was transforming Harlem West into the Upper West Side of San Francisco. Still, the African-American community did maintain a political clout way beyond its numbers, as symbolized by the election and reelection of Mayor Willie L. Brown Jr., the longtime speaker of the California Assembly and now one of the few African-American chief executives of a major American city. Community leaders such as businessman H. Welton Flynn and the Reverend Cecil Williams, pastor of the downtown Glide Memorial Methodist Church, wielded plenty of clout; yet a certain despondency was in the air as African-American San Francisco went into demographic decline.

Most basically—although this fact was never fully acknowledged—the black community was losing its upwardly mobile middle class to the suburbs. Secondly, there remained the problematic question of the horrific condition of the Bayview Hunters Point district. In 1997, Mayor Brown had spearheaded a successful $100 million bond issue to build a new stadium for the 49ers football team in the district, together with a megamall. The legal troubles of 49ers owner Eddie De Bartolo Jr., and the consequent management shake-up of the team, however, kept the project on hold. The Redevelopment Agency, meanwhile, was pursuing plans to run a light-rail system along Third Street from the downtown to Bayview Hunters Point, and to rezone Third Street to commercial in the hopes of creating a transportation and retail corridor that would join the isolated district to the rest of the city. Understandably, residents of Bayview Hunters Point, having watched the agency remove them from the Fillmore, had strong reservations about the project.

The African-American community of Los Angeles, by contrast, while embattled, was far from declining in terms of numbers, upward mobility, or political influence. Its candidate for mayor—James Hahn, the white city attorney with strong ties to the black community through his father, a long-time county supervisor—was successfully elected in June 2001 in a telling testimony to the continuing political clout of the black voters in Los Angeles. The Baldwin Hills/Ladera Heights district in southwestern Los Angeles supported an extensive mosaic of middle-class and upscale African-American home ownership. In 1995 retired Lakers star turned entrepreneur Earvin "Magic" Johnson, in partnership with Sony/Loews Theaters Corporation, opened a twelve-screen Magic Johnson Theatres complex in Crenshaw Plaza. Over the next seven years, the entertainment center became a flourishing nexus of local life.

The more the success of the Magic Johnson Theatres was analyzed, the more intriguing it became as a fact and symbol of African-American coalescence and civic well-being in this part of Los Angeles. The complex represented a major investment by both a black entrepreneur and a mega-corporation in an area previously boycotted by such development. It offered local residents a way of being themselves in a pleasant public context. It was not uncommon, for example, for audience members to call out advice or admonishment to the screen, as if responding to a well-delivered sermon. Films with an African-American orientation—the Afro-Brazilian classic *Black Orpheus* (1959), Steven Spielberg's *Amistad* (1997), Quentin Tarantino's *Jackie Brown* (1997), George Tillman Jr.'s *Soul Food* (1997), Timothy Chey's *Fakin' Da Funk* (1997), together with the movies shown as part of the annual Los Angeles Pan-African Film Festival—had a powerful hold on audiences. At times, the response could be humorous, as in the case of the scene in Forest Whitaker's *Waiting to Exhale* (1995), in which Angela Bassett, playing the role of a devoted wife whose husband has left her for another woman, gathers together all his clothes, stuffs them into his BMW, pours lighter fluid on the mess, lights a cigarette, and thinks it over.

"Burn it! Burn it! Burn it!" shouted the women in the audience, while many of the men shouted, "No!" Bassett lights up the clothes and car, walks away, and it explodes. The women in the audience applauded. The men sat silently, pondering the message.[1]

Athletics had long since been in the process of creating a Los Angeles–based black elite. When the Lakers returned home with the National Basketball Association title in June 2000, more than 1.5 million Los Angelenos, the majority of them people of color, lined the parade route on Figueroa to welcome home champions who, in the main, were people of color as well. Cultural critics might complain that the Lakers' multimillion-dollar salaries were sending the wrong message. Inflated income and celebrity status, after all, could only enable a chosen few to attain a better life. Yet athletic ability and performance had played an important part in the lives of those African-American leaders—Jackie Robinson, Tom Bradley, Woody Strode, Ralph Bunche—who in a previous generation had used the opportunities offered them by athletics at UCLA to distinguish themselves from the crowd and launch themselves, eventually, into important careers as diplomats, politicians, professional athletes, and actors. Like Robinson and Bradley, Woody Strode had grown up poor in South Central Los Angeles before going on to UCLA, where he integrated football and, after graduation, the National Football League, before becoming an actor. Less conspicuous, but equally effective, was the career of Compton civic leader Jessie Lee Robinson, another UCLA athlete, who, like football star Burl Toler of San Francisco, became a leader in his community at a level of influence that went beyond public office. These were all figures to whom the community could relate as emblems of black achievement and civic value.

Still, a poignancy clung to the many young black men who were dead from gunfire long before they had a chance to prove themselves on the basketball court. And this worried the Reverend Cecil "Chip" Murray, the charismatic senior pastor of the First African Methodist Episcopal Church in South Central: a leader almost beyond conventional politics in his ability to connect with the deeper aspirations and tragedies of his congregation, the largest African-American church in the city, and the portion of Los Angeles it served. In the immediate aftermath of the 1992 riots (or "civil unrest," as he preferred to call it), Murray played a pivotal role in calming the agitated city and calling for a renewal of civic purpose. "The white power which could wage a devastating war against Iraq," Murray said shortly after the riots, "or put a telescope in space to peer into the genesis of the universe, claims it can't do anything for the inner cities of America. It can't find a way of opening up a few thousand jobs in Los Angeles. The situation must be changed." Empowered by a $1 million grant from the Disney Corporation, Murray set about fostering the economic and moral renewal of his community.[2]

A decade later, things had gotten better in South Central, thanks in part to a new generation of African-American politicians at the local and state levels who were proving themselves adept at serving their multi-ethnic constituencies. The rib masters of the region, meanwhile—Joe Robbins at Mr. Joe's Bar-B-Que, Woody Philips at Woody's, Foster Phillips at Phillips, Eric Walker at Big Daddy's Q House, together with those at Warren's, Mr. Jim's, Hardin's, and Jay Bee's—were keeping their communities ethnically ecumenical by attracting to their establishments people of all colors from throughout the region. Still, for all the positive things that were happening—the good ribs, the skilled politicians—the persistent problem of gang- and drug-related homicide, cast a pall over the civic hopes of the region. Between January and December 2000, seventy-six people were killed within the precincts of the Los Angeles Police Department's Southeast Division, twenty-three of them twenty-one years old or younger. South Central was now a mixed Latino and African-American community, which too often translated into an exacerbation of existing tensions. "Southeast and adjacent neighborhoods," noted *Los Angeles Times* contributor Jocelyn Stewart, "are shared territory, claimed by those building dreams and by those constructing nightmares."[3]

A nightmare would be the description of Los Angeles given by the Korean community in the immediate aftermath of the April-May 1992 riots, in which Korean-owned stores had been the chief target of arsonists and looters. Awaiting the outcome of the second Rodney King trial in April 1993, Korean Americans flocked to the Western Gun Shop, the largest gun store in Koreatown, and purchased rifles and semiautomatic pistols with which to defend themselves against a possible repeat of the 1992 riots, which had done some $400 million damage to Korean-American properties. Jay Shim, owner of a Koreatown liquor store, had a complete arsenal in his establishment, together with bulletproof vests for himself and his employees. Between February and December 1993, forty-two Korean Americans were either killed or wounded in the course of robberies in Los Angeles County. Thirty such incidents occurred in Central Los Angeles. A year after the riots, nearly half of the Korean-American businesses that had been damaged or destroyed had not yet reopened. Nearly a year after the riots, Jae Yul Kim, for example, was still making up his mind whether to reopen his liquor store in South Central. Twice before the riots, he had been held up at gunpoint. One robber had fired a shot at his chest, but a shield of bulletproof glass in front of the cash register had saved Kim's life. Myung

Suk Lee did decide to return to her doughnut shop near Florence Avenue and Figueroa Street, pending loan discussions that would allow her to move to another neighborhood. In the middle of those negotiations, in July 1993, Lee was shot in the course of a robbery, and died after three months in a coma.

In time, the situation stabilized; many Korean Americans reopened their establishments, and the robbery/homicide rate remained at lower levels. But the damage to the Korean-American psyche, compounded by the continuing danger of doing business in certain neighborhoods, still had a debilitating effect. How soon could Korean Americans trust Los Angeles? Throughout the decade and into the millennium, they remained even more privately centered than other ethnic groups in the City of Angels. There were, for example, no Korean Americans in citywide elective office or even seeking such office. The focus of the community seemed to be on rebuilding businesses and staying safe.

Convenience stores in the Bay Area were owned and operated by a wider variety of ethnic groups. All kinds of people, a cynic might say, now had the opportunity to be shot to death in their places of business. Asian-American life in the Greater Bay Area had a decidedly collegiate/yuppie texture, reinforced by the large number of Asian Americans in the region's universities and workforce. Kelvin Yip, a market analyst in his twenties from San Francisco, was by August 2001 at the helm of the Drink Club, a mobile weekly party moving from San Francisco nightspot to nightspot and attracting as many as six hundred young Asian Americans from a two-thousand-member e-mail list. The pan-Asian-American nature of the Drink Club, which gathered Korean-, Chinese-, Japanese-, Indonesian-, Filipino-, and Indian-American young people in their twenties and thirties, represented a new development. To a certain extent, a shared American identity was bringing together otherwise disparate Asian groups.

And then there was the fact of San Francisco itself, the most Asian-American city in the nation—where, as Vietnamese-American writer Andrew Lam pointed out in August 2001, one in three residents of the city had an Asian face. By 2017, if not earlier, San Francisco would become the first major city in the nation to have an Asian-American majority. "The Far East has come very near San Francisco," Lam wrote, "and is beginning to subvert the age-old black-white dialogue about identity and race, in fusing it with an even more complex model, one informed by a transpacific sensibility." Non-Asian architects and interior designers in San Francisco, Lam noted, were careful to incorporate feng shui, the Chinese art of spatial arrangement. HMOs accepted acupuncture as legitimate therapy. And Vietnamese fish sauce was being stocked at Safeway.[4]

Already, the Chinese-American community, which accounted for 60 percent of Asian Americans living in San Francisco, was exercising decisive political clout. No one was riding the wave of this influence more successfully than the Fang family. Arriving in San Francisco from Taiwan in 1960, John Ta Chuan and Florence Fang initially supported themselves as publishers of a newspaper sponsored by Taiwan's then ruling party, the Kuomintang. Expanding into job printing and the restaurant business, the Fangs created a business and publishing empire that included, among other properties, *Asian Week* magazine and a chain of free community-oriented newspapers. Of equal importance, the Fangs accumulated an extraordinary amount of political influence, beginning with close ties to Representative Philip Burton, the powerful San Francisco Democrat, and continuing through friendships with Mayor (later Senator) Dianne Feinstein, Mayor Frank Jordan, whom the Fangs helped put in office, and Mayor Willie L. Brown Jr., whom the Fangs helped stay in office. Brown and other political connections helped the Fangs obtain from the Hearst Corporation a sweetheart deal when the company, purchasing the *San Francisco Chronicle* for some $660 million, literally gave the *Examiner* to the Fangs, together with a three-year $66 million subsidy. (Hearst considered it worthwhile to make such a donation, since the Justice Department saw the move as the only fair way to extract itself from a 1965 joint operating agreement that had allowed the *Chronicle* and the *Examiner* to combine facilities, even their Sunday edition, and remain exempt from antitrust laws as long as the editorial pages maintained their distinctive identities.) Political consultant Clint Reilly tried to prevent the Fangs' acquisition of the *Examiner* but lost his case in federal court, despite the skeptical attitude of federal judge Vaughn Walker, who heard the case without a jury. Even if the *Examiner* failed to make it as a newspaper, the Fangs stood to make, at minimum, $10 million in exit subsidies.

What the Fangs' situation boded for the civic spirit of San Francisco only time could tell. Could the overwhelmingly immigrant Asian-American community of San Francisco blossom, suddenly and gloriously, into a coherent and civic-minded force concerned for the welfare and identity of a city that had so recently kept them in their place? Critics who claimed that the Asian-American community lacked philanthropic spirit had to deal with the fact that Seoul-born Korean-American businessman Chong Moon Lee, founder and chairman of Diamond Multimedia, a leading manufacturer of graphics and accelerator cards for personal computer systems, had donated the $15 million needed to move the Asian Art Museum from Golden Gate Park to a reconverted San Francisco Public Library building in the Civic Center. Thanks to Lee's generosity, San Francisco would now, at long last, enjoy a proper site for its Avery Brundage Collection, the single finest comprehensive collection of Asian art in the nation.

By this time, San Francisco had become the leading Asian-American city in the nation. Thanks to its sponsor, Southwest Airlines, the colorful Chinese New Year's parade organized each year by the Chinese Chamber of Commerce was being enjoyed by millions on television. Chinese Americans had long since been serving on the board of supervisors. Fred Lau was chief of police. Schoolyards were teeming with Asian-American children. Public high schools, including the rigorously academic Lowell High School, and the private high schools of the city as well, were sending generations of Asian-American students on to colleges and universities. When state regulation of insurance collapsed in California due to the shenanigans of the elected insurance commissioner, who soon resigned, Governor Gray Davis turned to a prominent Chinese American from San Francisco, retired court of appeal judge Harry Low, to straighten out the mess.

Payday

The city of Los Angeles did not do itself an economic favor by rioting in 1992. The turmoil caused an estimated $1 billion in damages in a city that could not afford such a loss. Even before the riots, in July 1991, the *Economist* was worrying about the job-producing capacities of metropolitan Los Angeles, given the increasing overregulation of business. "In Los Angeles a business person is guilty until proven innocent," argued one furniture maker, chafing at the excessive air quality control restrictions of the region.[5] The following January, USC economists and planners Harry Richardson, Peter Gordon, and Genevieve Giuliano warned in a forthright report, *Los Angeles: At an Economic Crossroads* (1992), prepared for the Los Angeles Headquarters City Association, that an overabundance of local regulation was driving businesses from the city into the suburbs and even out of California altogether.

The authors of this report belonged to the free-market-oriented Adam Smith Gang at USC, and so some might dismiss it as recycled Reaganomics. But then came the riots, and following the riots came the question: How best to rebuild? Through the free market? Through government intervention? Through community-based politics? Through a combination thereof? Not surprisingly, Mayor Tom Bradley chose the last answer, and established Rebuild LA, a public-private coalition officially designated "an extra-governmental task force," separate from city government—but not, as it turned out, from city politics.

To head Rebuild LA, Bradley turned to Peter Ueberroth, paladin of the Los Angeles establishment. Born in 1937 in Evanston, Illinois, and graduated from San Jose State University in 1959, Ueberroth was well on his way to multimillionaire status before he was thirty, taking a small travel consultant firm and developing it into one of the biggest travel companies in the nation. In 1980, Mayor Bradley had appointed Ueberroth to head the Los Angeles Olympic Organizing Committee. Not only did Ueberroth spearhead the organization of the successful 1984 Olympics, bringing to Los

Angeles a triumphant sense of having arrived as a world city, he turned in a $215 million surplus. In 1984, *Time* named Ueberroth Man of the Year. That year as well, Ueberroth became the sixth commissioner of major league baseball. In 1991, challenged by the recession, Governor Pete Wilson asked Ueberroth to head his Council on California Competitiveness, and the recommendations of this committee became the blueprint for the economic recovery of the state. Polished, assured, arguably the one person in California with the best connections to the nexus of public and private power, Ueberroth embodied the notion, the hope, that Los Angeles could recover itself through a focused crusade of public-private partnership.

Almost immediately, it became apparent that Rebuild LA was in danger of being torn apart by the same ethnic tensions that had recently destroyed large portions of the city. Korean-American groups wanted reparations. The Korean community was also demanding a dominant position on the board of Rebuild LA, since its community had been most affected by the riots. African-American groups wanted Rebuild LA to assume the entire burden of restructuring, reforming, and revitalizing South Central Los Angeles. Latino leaders, led by City Councilman Mike Hernandez, sought a big piece of the action—at least half of the upper- and executive management positions with policy- and decision-making responsibility—in recognition of the fact that the Latino community was now a major player. Very soon, the board of directors of Rebuild LA had swollen to eighty members, many of them unsure about their exact role.

Ueberroth, meanwhile, working with his cochairs Bernard Kinsey, a former Xerox executive, Tony Salazar, a housing expert, educator Linda Wong, and Barry Sanders, a lawyer with Latham & Watkins, began the arduous task of persuading the private sector to reinvest in inner-city Los Angeles. Already, Robert D. Taylor, a principal with McKinsey & Company, had told Rebuild LA that it would take $4–6 billion in investment to create the 75,000–94,000 jobs necessary to stabilize the inner city—and this in the middle of a rapidly expanding recession that had already cost Los Angeles County 240,000 jobs in the private sector between 1988 and 1992, and a predicted falloff in tourism that could cost the region as much as a billion dollars in revenues.

Ueberroth and his team were able to extract certain promises—a $100 million pledge by Vons Cos., $35 million from Southern California Edison, $31 million from IBM, $11 million from Chief Auto Parts, $7 million from Atlantic Richfield, $2 million from the Bank of America, and $1 million from ARCO—but in most cases these came in the form of investment pledges or promises of loans and not cash grants. This was still a long way from the minimum of $4 billion in public-private assistance cited as necessary by McKinsey. Within a year, many of these pledges remained unreal-ized. All in all, Rebuild LA claimed nearly $1 billion in future rebuilding commitments, yet by December 1992 the *Los Angeles Times* was reporting that fully a quarter of these companies really had no plans to invest heavily in inner-city Los Angeles. By this time as well, the sharks were beginning to circle around Ueberroth. He was criticized for, among other things, being a white Orange County multimillionaire with minimal connection to the inner city. African-American elected officials such as Representative Max-ine Waters and City Councilman Mark Ridley-Thomas, together with Joe Hicks, executive director of the Southern Christian Leadership Conference, were vocal in their criticism. On May 21, 1993, a little more than a year after joining the council, Ueberroth, dispirited by the squabbling—tired, in the words of one of his colleagues, of serving as a lightning rod for discon-tent—resigned.

Ueberroth's successor, Linda Griego, a former deputy mayor of Los Angeles, promised a community-savvy, bottom-up approach as opposed to the top-down style of her predecessor. A skilled administrator with entre-preneurial experience in the private sector, Griego kept Rebuild LA active until 1997, when it went out of business. Its main accomplishment during these years was to continue documenting the economic challenges facing metropolitan Los Angeles: the census tracts in the inner city and in other satellite areas, with 20 percent of the populace below the poverty line; the dearth of manufacturing enterprises in these regions; the avoidance of the inner city by certain manufacturers; the persistence of brown fields and empty lots; the scarcity of supermarkets; and the damaged properties still awaiting repair.

By June 2001, the $352 billion economy of Los Angeles County ranked sixteenth in the world, greater than the entire economy of Russia. What had happened? California had recovered, for one thing, along with most of the United States, and metropolitan Los Angeles was participating in this recovery. Yet when the camera zeroed in for a close-up on the exact nature of this comeback, Los Angeles, city and county alike, revealed itself to have gone through an extraordinary transformation. Here was no Fortune 500–based recovery, the *Economist* was reporting by late May 1997. Rather, a myriad of companies employing fewer than one hundred people were now responsible for half the jobs in the county: immigrant-run firms, in the main, doing business in new activities like textiles, toys, and high tech.

Corporate Los Angeles had virtually disappeared in the decade, or had been colonized through mergers and acquisitions. Toshiba and C. Itoh of Japan had in 1991 sunk $1 billion in a 12.5 percent stake in Warner Brothers Studios, owned by Time Warner, making Warner Brothers the fifth major studio with significant offshore ownership. The embattled Bank of Credit and Commerce International, a Luxembourg bank convicted of laundering drug money, was the actual proprietor of the Independence Bank of Encino, although Saudi Arabian tycoon Ghaith Pharaon was claiming ownership. It mattered little, however, since the Federal Reserve Board ordered BCCI to sell the Encino-based bank, the largest in the San Fernando Valley, to another institution. The very next year, in April 1992, the largest and most historic bank in Southern California, Los Angeles–based Security Pacific, was acquired by the San Francisco–based BankAmerica Corporation, itself an impending takeover victim.

Even such revered institutions as the Los Angeles Dodgers and the *Los Angeles Times* were no longer locally owned. On March 19, 1998, Rupert Murdoch's Fox Group acquired the Dodgers for $311 million, and on March 13, 2000, the Chicago Tribune Company bought the Times Mirror Corporation. The removal of the O'Malleys from the Dodgers ended one of the most successful and respected franchise ownerships in major league history. Walter O'Malley had brought the Dodgers to Los Angeles in 1958, actualizing the aspirations of the city, literally and figuratively, to major league status. His son Peter stood at the very center of the Los Angeles establishment. The Chandler family, owners of the Times Mirror Corporation, were the mega-oligarchs of the region; the family had, through the *Los Angeles Times,* helped the city invent itself. In so many ways, the *Times* was the one commanding institution of the Southland. Now, it belonged to Chicago.

No wonder the eighty-member board of directors of Rebuild LA had proved ineffective. Not even the very able Linda Griego could fuse its roll call of prominent names into a movement. For all its inclusiveness, Rebuild LA was a top-down organization in a city whose economic vitality was percolating from the bottom up, and whose entrepreneurs—so many of them recent immigrants—were deeply suspicious of government boards, even quasi-government boards, however well intended. Were they not able to achieve growth on their own terms? And was not the growth they were so successfully achieving—with next to no governmental or public assistance—the very thing Rebuild LA was seeking to effect? Why get involved talking the talk when you are already walking the walk?

The one exception to all this was the extraordinary relationship forged by the 28,000-student University of Southern California, a private institution, and its adjacent communities in the West Adams and Exposition Park districts. With a budget of $1 billion a year, USC was the largest private employer in the city, with more than seventeen thousand full- and part-time people on its payroll. During the riots, USC had remained unscathed, despite the fact that it was on the immediate periphery of the disturbances. Following the riots, many in the USC community were tempted to ask whether the university had made an error in declining to move to Malibu in the 1950s, when property there had been offered. Opposed to such hand-wringing, the USC's newly appointed president, Steven Sample—an electrical engineer with proven track records at Purdue and SUNY Buf-falo—pointed in another direction: a renewed engagement by the university with its neighboring communities. Although the Sample initiative was threatened with derailment by a number of painful labor negotiations across the ensuing decade, the general goals of his program were realized, in part because of the social entrepreneurial skills of Jane Pisano, dean of the school of public administration and senior vice president for external rela-tions, whom Sample had recruited from Rebuild LA. Among other things, USC adopted neighborhood outreach as an essential premise for its strate-gic plan. Programs included down payments on houses in the neighborhood for USC workers, most of them minorities; scholarships to grammar school, high school, and USC for their children; a community safety program; and the expenditure of almost $1 million a year in local projects, the majority of it donated by USC faculty and staff. By 2000, *Time* was naming USC Col-lege of the Year, not only because it had entered the ranks of the top ten pri-vate research universities in the nation, based on federal research and development support, but because it had established a community relations and improvement program that *Time* considered a model for inner-city uni-versities in challenged urban areas.

In general, however, with the exception of USC, most of the recovery of Los Angeles from the riots had been under Rebuild LA's radar, despite the group's continuing orientation toward involving Fortune 500 companies. It took an explosion, killing three and injuring twenty-five, on November 5, 1997, in a downtown plant built in 1913 by Henry Ford to assemble auto-mobiles, to alert Los Angeles to the fact that it had a thriving $3 billion toy industry, much of it run by Chinese immigrants with close connections to the home country. The clothing and textile industry, mostly Latino and Korean, the largest in the United States, was employing more than 100,000 who were producing such well-known labels as B.U.M. and Rampage and generating more than $10 billion in annual sales. The eleven hundred food-processing companies of the region had more than fifty thousand people and were realizing over $12 billion a year in sales. Despite air quality restrictions, Los Angeles was second only to the High Point area of North Carolina in the manufacture of furniture, with six hundred firms and more than thirty thousand workers. The multimedia and high-tech industry, most of it centered in smaller companies, was employing some 133,000, more than in New York City and Silicon Valley combined. There was even some concern that too many downtown buildings were being used for high-tech equipment, to the detriment of pedestrian retail and a vibrant street life. Hollywood itself had evolved into a federation of 4,400 tightly staffed firms that, from film to film, employed and reemployed some 100,000 free-lancers. Devastated by the 1992 riots, when only five conventions made reservations at the Los Angeles Convention Center, the tourist industry, an economic standby of the region since the early twentieth century, was experiencing in 1997 its best convention business since 1979. Conventions and individual tourism were bringing some $26 billion into Los Angeles by the end of the year.

San Francisco was also continuing to do well as a convention and tourist destination. The lead element in the city's economy since 1962, tourism was continuing to bring in an average of $14 million a day by 1997. Sixteen million tourists were visiting San Francisco annually, pumping billions into the local economy and $80 million into city coffers. Hundreds of small multimedia companies, many of them clustered in the Multimedia Gulch south of Market, were by 1997 employing 35,000, generating $2.2 billion in revenues. Less than a decade old, the multimedia industry already had half as many on its payroll as the more established financial, insurance, and real estate sectors. Most multimedia companies were small start-ups, one-third of them reporting annual revenues of $300,000 or less. Only 6 percent of them had one hundred employees. Nearly half had ten or fewer on staff. Multimedia start-ups paid well: $31,000 for entry-level clerical help, $70,000 and above for entry-level programmers. They sucked up available office space, creating a vacancy rate of less than 3 percent by February 1998. Even marginally located properties could be reconfigured as Telco Hotels, as they were called, warehouses crammed with telecommunications equipment.

At the same time, San Francisco remained the headquarters city of an impressive number of national and international corporations. Some were privately owned, like the 150-year-old Levi Strauss & Company, which had bought back its publicly traded stock. San Francisco–based companies that continued to flourish through the 1990s included respected names in banking (BankAmerica, Wells Fargo, UnionBanCal, Sumitomo, Pacific Bank, First Republic); energy (Pacific Gas & Electric, Chevron, HS Resources); financial services (Transamerica, Hambrecht & Quist, PMI Group, Charles Schwab); clothing (Gap, Old Navy, Banana Republic, Levi Strauss, Esprit); quality retail (Williams-Sonoma, Sharper Image); Internet, software, and telecommunications (AirTouch, CNET, Genesys, Digital Generation Systems, Micromuse, Advent); real estate development (Catellus, Shoren-stein); mining (Homestake); pharmaceuticals (McKesson); and even fertil-izers (U.S. Home & Garden).

While BankAmerica remained the eight-hundred-pound gorilla in this corporate lineup, San Francisco–founded companies such as Charles Schwab and the Gap were the most socially and culturally interesting. Like another San Franciscan, A. P. Giannini in the early twentieth century, Schwab had brought a whole new range of financial services to ordinary consumers. Giannini had taught his customers how to use banking services previously reserved for elites. Schwab placed in the hands of his growing clientele the tools and techniques of investment and portfolio management. Another company founded in San Francisco, the Gap, like Levi Strauss in an earlier era, had franchised fashion to an unprecedented degree, allowing a hitherto untapped mass audience to enter the world of style at affordable prices.

Founded by San Franciscans Don and Doris Fisher—two Lowell High School and UC Berkeley graduates—in August 1969, as a store specializ-ing in blue jeans, the Gap was by the late 1990s a multibillion-dollar phe-nomenon: 1,590 (as of 1998) stores across the world selling clothes in various formats: Gap, Baby Gap, Gap Kids, Old Navy, and Banana Repub-lic. The success of the Gap was due to the Fishers themselves—who remained living in their pre-Gap home in Pacific Heights and were an active part of the San Francisco social and philanthropic scene—and to the mar-keting guru they had hired to run the company, Millard "Mickey" Drexler. Not only did Drexler know how to market, he knew how to manage talent, as in the case of the Old Navy label, which reached $1 billion in annual sales in three short years. Still, the rag trade, even on the scale of the Gap, remained volatile. The more Drexler chased an upscale and trendy market, the more the Gap was leaving behind its core constituency: people in search of serviceable bargains, who were now beginning to drift over to Target and Wal-Mart. Through 2001, Gap stock fell by 53 percent; by late May 2002, Drexler was saying good-bye to the 4,200-store empire he had assembled in happier times.

Yet even as the Gap was planning—earlier, in better days—its lavish Robert A. M. Stern headquarters at 250 Embarcadero, some changes resem-bling those in Los Angeles were already under way. In the mid-1970s Baron Edmond de Rothschild had acquired stock in the venerable Bank of Califor-nia, whose roots went back to the 1860s. In 1988, Rothschild, who now held a commanding interest in the bank, sold it to Mitsubishi Bank Ltd. for $282 million amid allegations from shareholders that the baron and his associates had acquired control of the Bank of California in violation of banking laws.

Whatever the merits of the case (one claim was eventually settled through a private court-supervised agreement), upper-crust San Francisco, initially so dazzled by the baron, had witnessed its prized possession migrate to Europe, depressed stock sale by depressed stock sale, then sold, after secret negotiations, to Tokyo, to the great profit ($39 million, tax free) of the baron and the embarrassing loss to a local elite that had perhaps been fatally charmed by a suave and crafty Frenchman with a Napoleonic title.

In 1988 another signature San Francisco property, I. Magnin, with comparable roots in the frontier era, was acquired by R. H. Macy of New York. For generations of San Franciscans, I. Magnin's on Union Square, a building modernized by architect Timothy Pflueger right after the war, embodied all that was smart in couture and sophisticated about San Francisco. In March 1993, Macy's announced the closing of five I. Magnin stores in California (San Mateo, Los Angeles, Santa Barbara, Sherman Oaks, La Jolla) and the layoff of six hundred employees. In due time, the flagship San Francisco store was shut down and absorbed into the adjacent Macy's.

Gump's, meanwhile, the legendary luxury retailer founded in 1861, was acquired in 1989 by a Tokyo conglomerate, Tobu Credit Company. For nearly 140 years, Gump's had offered to San Franciscans and affluent Far Westerners a unique array of furniture, jewelry, and Asian objets d'art. It was Gump's that inspired in San Francisco a juxtapositioning of classic European furniture, Asian screens, and art objects that became by the second half of the twentieth century a preferred mode of interior design. In May 1993, however, Tobu Credit sold Gump's to Horn & Hardart, a New Jersey–based distributor of mail-order catalogs. The sale included Gump's landmark sixty-thousand-square-foot store at 250 Post Street. Some 165 local jobs were lost.

The merger of the San Francisco–based Wells Fargo and the Minneapolis-based Norwest Corporation, which created the seventh largest bank in the United States, with branches across twenty-one states in the West and Midwest, was advertised as a win-win deal for San Francisco. First of all, the bank kept its Wells Fargo identity, which dated back to the 1850s, and remained headquartered in San Francisco. Secondly, it kept San Francisco a big-bank town; already, in April 1998, BankAmerica had announced that it was moving its headquarters to Charlotte, North Carolina.

The announcement of the merger of NationsBank of Charlotte and BankAmerica initially emphasized that the union was a merger, not an acquisition. It made good sense, it was said, to merge the two banks and thereby create a vast network extending from coast to coast through twenty-two states. Neither service area—the Far West for BankAmerica, the Southeast and Midwest for NationsBank—overlapped, so there would be little redundancy. The merger, moreover, fulfilled the lifelong dream of Bank of America founder Giannini to establish a national network of interstate banking. Ever since federal law was adjusted in 1994 to allow for such networks, NationsBank CEO Hugh McColl had been looking for an opportunity to break through to the West Coast. Now he had in motion a merger that would create the biggest bank in the United States, with $570 billion in assets, serving twenty-nine million retail customers.

At the New York press conference announcing the merger, and in subsequent press briefings, McColl, sixty-two, and Bank of America president David Coulter, fifty, did everything possible to present the deal as a merger between equals. In the days to come, however, it soon became apparent that Coulter—a slight and diminutive Ivy Leaguer, bald and owlish behind horn-rimmed glasses—was no match for McColl, a lean, brush-cut ex-marine and take-charge southerner who kept deactivated hand grenades on his desk and had climbed Mount Kilimanjaro on his sixtieth birthday. San Franciscans were shocked that their great bank, the longtime substance and symbol of the city's preeminence as a center of finance—the single greatest corporation, in fact, in the 150-year history of the city—should have been, for all practical purposes, hijacked to what many San Franciscans would consider a third-tier city, where people preferred hominy grits to brie and stock car races to opera.

San Francisco commentators were either sneering or defensive, or both, about the so-called merger. Charlotte might have the Bank of America, *Chronicle* business writer Peter Sinton argued, but San Francisco still outstripped Charlotte as a banking center. The city was, after all, headquarters to 339 banks and 137 savings-and-loan institutions, in contrast to the ninety-five banks and twenty-two thrifts in the entire state of North Carolina. San Francisco had twelve Federal Reserve regional banks, the Pacific Stock Exchange, and such prestigious brokerage and security firms as Montgomery Securities, Robertson Stephens, and Hambrecht & Quist. It remained the headquarters of nine major corporations. The more Sinton argued, however, the more one was tempted to ask: If all these things are true, why is the headquarters of the newly constituted Bank of America leaving the city, and why are the layoffs of duplicate staff showing a decided tilt in the direction of San Francisco?

Former city chief administrative officer Roger Boas, who had presided over the re-creation of South of Market as a corporate and convention center, openly described the movement of the Bank of America to Charlotte as "a maiming blow" to the power and prestige of the city. "The growth of downtown's retail sector is flat," Boas noted, "as epitomized by the nearly empty Emporium building. Maritime activity is non-existent. With the exit of the Bank of America, San Francisco is frighteningly dependent on a single sector: tourism."[6]

David Coulter never bought that house he had promised to buy in Charlotte, North Carolina. Sixteen days after the merger became final, McColl—angry that the new institution's profits had fallen by half as a result of losses incurred by the then San Francisco–based administration—fired Coulter unceremoniously. Not that Coulter or any of the other sacked executives seemed to mind. The skies over the Bank of America building on California Street were filled with golden parachutes. H. Eugene Lockhart, the former chief executive of MasterCard International, who had headed the bank's Global Retail Bank subsidiary for a mere eleven months before the merger, was the first to open his chute: a severance package worth close to $23 million. Then Martin A. Stein, vice chairman and director of technology and operations, an eight-year veteran, hit the silk beneath a $10 million package. When it came his time to leave, Coulter floated gently to Earth with $30 million in stock, a $5 million annual pension, and lifetime medical and dental benefits for himself and his family. "This is one of the most munificent severance plans in the history of the universe," compensation consultant Bud Crystal had said at the time of the merger. "If Coulter stays on, he should be fired for stupidity."[7]

Poor

Beneath their descending golden parachutes, the Bank of America executives could look below and see hundreds of ordinary workers already on the street looking for work. Not only did the loss of such flagship banks as Security Pacific and Bank of America cause stress to Los Angeles and San Francisco, the mergers put great sectors of the rank and file out of a job. This, of course, was the pattern on the national scene as a whole. The year 1997 alone witnessed a trillion dollars' worth of mergers and acquisitions. If you were young enough and skilled enough, you could most likely find work. If you were older, however—even if you were highly educated and older—you might be in trouble. If you were a minority, you stood a strong chance of not being fired—because you hadn't been hired in the first place.

There was another trend as well: throughout the 1990s—throughout the nation, but especially in California—the rich got richer and the poor got poorer. In the 1980s, the number of households in California earning $75,000 a year or more had grown by 800 percent. Hidden Hills and Rolling Hills on the Palos Verdes Peninsula were reporting median incomes of $150,000. Census data released in May 1992 indicated, however, that 12.5 percent of Californians were living beneath the poverty line. That contrasted favorably with the national poverty rate of 12.8 percent. But this was California. It was supposed to be better in California.

Even more alarming was the rate at which Californians were becoming poor through the 1980s, as revealed by the 1990 census, which stated that the number of poor families in California had increased by 28 percent, a figure that rose to 32 percent if the head of the household was female. The number of elderly poor had grown by 21 percent. Children under eighteen living below the poverty line had increased by 41 percent. These trends would continue throughout the decade. People on blue-collar and lower-middle-class incomes were also losing earning power at a significant rate and finding it increasingly difficult to get by. (Alarmingly, Global Exchange, a San Francisco–based nonprofit organization, was taking in

$1 million a year organizing tours to poverty-stricken locations in Third World countries—and California.)

It was tough to be poor wherever you lived, but it was especially galling in cities like San Francisco and Los Angeles, where there was so much urban beauty and grace. If you were poor in inner-city Los Angeles, in Pico Union and South Central especially, you were in an area that, all things considered, was as of 1990 even more deprived than it had been in the time of the 1965 Watts riots. Ironically, Washington had refused to declare Los Angeles a federally funded empowerment zone in 1994, despite the fact that the 1992 riots had inspired the controlling legislation, because the federal reviewers had found the city's application vague and incomplete—which was probably the case. The Clinton administration, however, grateful for Los Angeles's overwhelming support in the 1992 election, provided $430 million in grants and loan guarantees, which the city used to create the Los Angeles Community Development Bank. Ably administered by C. Robert Kemp—a burly African American in his early sixties who took pride in running the bank out of a pink stucco walk-up at 54th and Vermont, the heart of the 'hood—the bank had by February 1998 closed some $25 million in loans to local businesses hiring local people. That year as well, Los Angeles at long last got its empowerment zone designation, which, among other things, meant that any company employing local workers in designated inner-city areas could receive up to $3,000 in federal tax credits per employee. Since more than 300,000 people were working in inner-city Los Angeles, and since the empowerment zone would last for ten years, that meant a major influx of federal dollars.

That was the good news. The bad news was the continuing difficulty posed by life on the margins for the unemployed and working poor. Barbara Lott-Holland, for example, had a job in Torrance on the southwestern edge of metropolitan Los Angeles. She lived near USC. By automobile, this would be a thirty-minute commute, at most. But it took Lott-Holland an hour and forty-five minutes each way, because she had to take the bus. Public-transit-dependent workers in metropolitan Los Angeles lived in the inner city, which they could afford, but were often forced to take long bus rides to reach their places of employment in more affluent areas.

Approximately 72 percent of all students in the Los Angeles Unified School District came from beneath the poverty line—and they often came to school hungry and ragged. The lack of proper clothes had become an impediment to learning for thousands of Los Angeles schoolchildren. Children were known to arrive at school in their pajamas. Tattered sneakers were commonplace. In one case, two brothers alternated days attending class because they had one pair of pants between them. Underwear was unwashed and frequently nonexistent. Many children stayed away from school because they were ashamed of their clothes or got in fights when other children taunted them. Krista Lombard, a counselor at Magnolia Avenue Elementary School in Pico Union, estimated that 90 percent of the two thousand students in her school required some form of clothing assistance.

Alvaro Perez, thirteen years old as of February 2000, lived with his impoverished parents and four younger siblings in Canoga Park, where the family took turns sleeping on the bed and the floor, using old curtains for blankets, and on many evenings ate only tortillas for dinner. He often stayed away from school on cold days because he only had a T-shirt. When it rained, he would sometimes miss classes at Parkman Middle School in Woodland Hills because of his leaky tennis shoes. Scrounging an extra five dollars, Alvaro's mother bought him a pair of shoes. His classmates laughed even more. They were girl's shoes. "I've been in Mexico and in Thailand and Central America," observed Sylvia Poareo, a counselor at Middleton Elementary, "and I've seen a lot of poverty. But you don't expect to see poverty as bad as this in the United States—especially so close to Beverly Hills."

Providing needy children with secondhand clothes became the specialty of a Hollywood-based charitable group calling itself Operation School Bell. Raising more than $220,000 each year in gifts, together with scads of donated clothing, the volunteers at the Sunset Boulevard headquarters of Operation School Bell provided 4,400 needy children with underwear, shoes, socks, a hygiene kit, and five outfits. Youngsters were especially delighted if they were given such cool clothing as Rugrats raincoats and Old Navy cargo pants. "They just keep trying the clothes on over and over," noted one mother, "and admiring themselves and asking me, 'How do I look, Mommy?' "[8]

Fortunately, most schools in the inner city had breakfast and lunch programs. A survey taken in South Central Los Angeles in 1993 revealed that more than a quarter of the population, 27 percent, lacked money to buy food an average of five days a month. Even when there was money for food, it was difficult and expensive to shop in a region so lacking in supermarkets. Without transportation, the poor found it next to impossible to buy in bulk from discount outlets. Some supermarkets, such as Numero Uno, ran shuttle buses for people spending a minimum of $30 in the store.

Housing was always a problem. The inner-city poor were paying exorbitant amounts out of their meager weekly paychecks for crowded apartments, rooms even, in rundown buildings that frequently erupted into killing fires. More than a quarter of a million people, it was estimated, were by the early 1990s living in rented garage space throughout the metropolitan area. Los Angeles operated twelve public housing developments, most of them built in the late 1940s before the city decided that such projects represented a form of creeping socialism. The second largest city in the United States, Los Angeles ranked twelfth in its number of public housing units. Altogether, there were some 26,000 residents in public housing scattered from the San Fernando Valley to the harbor, and another twenty thousand on the waiting list.

The health needs of the poor were the essential responsibility of the 2,045-bed County-USC Medical Center in East Los Angeles, a towering structure built in the early 1930s, looming over the Santa Ana Freeway. By the early 1990s, County-USC was serving an average of fifteen thousand patients a day. Nearly three million residents of Los Angeles County had no medical insurance, and the pool was growing by twenty thousand people per month by late 1999. A county facility whose medical programs were run by USC, the medical center was chronically underfunded. Over the years, County-USC, one of the largest acute-care hospitals and medical teaching facilities in the nation, had grown into a maze almost beyond management. There were some 157,000 different door keys on registration. Antiquated two-thousand-horsepower Southern Pacific locomotive engines served as backup generators. There was at least a mile of pneumatic tubes carrying blood samples and lab specimens throughout the building, and more than a million color-coded files in a cavernous underground storage space.

The medical treatment offered at County-USC was frequently praised for its challenged excellence. Lack of funds, however, overcrowding, and long delays in treatment qualified the performance. In January 1992 the *Los Angeles Times* ran an investigation of the shocking delays patients frequently experienced in the overcrowded and understaffed facility. Nearly ten years later, in June 2001, the *Times* published a similar series—and this despite a 1995 federal bailout that had helped keep the hospital afloat. The time spent by the uninsured poor waiting for free medical services at County-USC had reached epic proportions. Twenty-hour waits were common, and the record for the decade was eighty-four hours—that is, a half a week.

Early in the decade, room 1050 at County-USC, where emergency patients were sorted in triage by attendant doctors, had become an especially tense place. In six months of 1991 alone, some fourteen hundred incidents of violence or threatened violence against staff were logged. "It's like a war zone in there," noted clerical worker Ruby Brown, describing how an angry patient had assaulted an emergency-room doctor with a telephone.

Ken Wong, an emergency-room nurse, had a female patient come after him with a shard of glass. It came as almost no surprise, then, when slightly after noon on February 8, 1993, forty-year-old Damacio Ybarra Torres shot and seriously wounded three attending physicians and held two women hostage for five hours before surrendering to the police.[9] Disgruntled with the treatment he had been receiving at County-USC, Torres had deliberately planned his attack, during which he was reported to have screamed: "Goddamn, give me something for my pain! Can't you give me something for my pain?" One of the critically wounded doctors, forty-five-year-old Glenn Rogers, an internist, had deliberately chosen to work at County-USC prior to volunteering to practice medicine in a Third World country.[10]

Embattled health care, going hungry, not having the right clothes to wear to school: these were three ways of being poor. Looking for shelter was another. Even the employed were having trouble surviving in the competitive California housing market; housing was a limited commodity that was expensive and was growing ever more so. Across the state, housing values, after the mid-decade economic recovery, were rising at an average of 10 percent per year by the late decade. Even urban Los Angeles properties in middle-class and working-class districts, devastated by the recession and riots of the early 1990s, were in the process of first recovering, then exceeding, their 1990 value. By mid-2001, such unpretentious communities as Bell, Paramount, Compton, Pomona, and the less affluent sectors of Orange County were reporting value increases of 17 percent or more.

The Bay Area market, San Francisco in particular, was spiraling upward out of control. Luxury homes were averaging $1.25 million by the end of 1997. Then, in May 1999, a two-bedroom home in the working-class Crocker Amazon district on the southern edge of the city, listed in a probate sale for $261,000, prompted a take-no-prisoners bidding war among some sixty-one prospective buyers that showed signs of increasing the value of the property by 50 percent. Crocker Amazon, after all, was where for nearly seventy years the working people of San Francisco had lived in blue-collar contentment. But bidding wars had become commonplace in the overheated Bay Area real estate market. Agents would deliberately offer properties for sale after underpricing them from 10 to 20 percent to attract a large pool of buyers. The home-buying market was so hot that the Palo Alto–based E-Loan, one of a new breed of online mortgage information and brokerage firms (others included HomeShark of San Francisco and Intuit of Mountain View), was doing a land-office business.

In most markets, such increased demand would result in an increased supply. But for various reasons it was difficult to build housing in California. In June 1998, Bruce Karatz, chairman, president, and CEO of the Los

Angeles–based Kaufman & Broad Home Corporation, the largest builder in California and the third largest in the United States, put the matter succinctly. "Communities have become more and more restrictive in the amount of development that they will permit," Karatz stated. "As restrictions pile on top of each other, the end result is less new development in the areas where the demand is greatest, and therefore prices tend to go up and out of the reach of first-time buyers or even first-time move-up buyers." Ironically, Karatz had recently been awarded the Legion of Honor by the French government for his home-building activities in France, apparently a much easier market.[11]

Until his tragic death in 1996 in the plane crash in Croatia that also took the life of Secretary of Commerce Ron Brown, I. Donald Terner, a bold and charismatic builder, president of the Bridge Housing Corporation of San Francisco, was busy showing California a possible way out of its dilemma, provided that urban Californians were willing to live in smaller attached units in previously neglected or recycled urban properties. Terner held three degrees from Harvard and was the vice president of a private construction firm, and he had distinguished himself as the California state director of housing and community development in the Jerry Brown administration between 1978 and 1982. In 1982, an anonymous donor contributed $670,000 in IBM stock to the San Francisco Foundation to explore ways to develop affordable housing in San Francisco. The chair of the task force was Alan Stein, former state secretary of business, transportation, and housing under Brown. Stein chose Terner, who had worked for him in Sacramento, to lead a new kind of housing venture: a public-benefit section 501(c)(3) nonprofit corporation that would build or rehabilitate housing for low- or limited-income clients. The program involved the acquisition of properties, the financing of construction, and the evolution of new building typologies.

For some time, a movement had been growing among architects and housing theorists favoring the creation of smaller, more compact attached housing for urban, even suburban, settings. Witold Rybczynski, professor of architecture at McGill University in Montreal, was among the leaders of this crusade to encourage developers and architects to consider alternatives to the single-house-on-its-lot model that had dominated construction for so much of the twentieth century. San Francisco architect Donald MacDonald was another leader in this movement. So was Don Terner.

But where would the lots come from? The cities and suburbs of coastal California, Terner believed, were filled with unused properties, most of them in marginal locations and, more importantly, many of them under one form or another of public control. Negotiating with local governments, the

Bridge Housing Corporation, Terner's venture acquired permission for higher densities and other land use concessions and in many cases partnered with the public sector in developing housing on neglected or ill-used public properties. Functioning as a private developer, Bridge participated in joint-venture arrangements with for-profit and nonprofit developers and the public sector, to include developing turnkey projects for public agencies. The projects created by Bridge through the rest of the 1980s—family garden apartments in Livermore, Fremont, and Mill Valley; studio condominiums in Vallejo; condominiums and garden apartments for the elderly in San Francisco and Pacifica, together with clusters of condominium townhomes and midrise apartment buildings in multiple San Francisco and San Francisco Bay Area locations—represented in each instance a distinctive public-private partnership, the use and/or reuse of neglected or recycled properties (the site of the Old Polytechnic High School, just south of Golden Gate Park, becoming the Parkview Commons), and a drive toward new rhythms of density and open space.

In terms of land use, architecture, and public-private financing, Bridge projects were anticipating the California future: the time when, around 2040, there would be more than sixty million people in the state; when only the entry of the public sector, in partnership with the private sector, into the housing market could create affordable housing for the millions of Californians priced out of the mid-range and upscale market. By November 1999 in Southern California, some 140 nonprofit housing development groups were busy creating 400,000 units of affordable housing. The Esperanza Community Housing Corporation, as an example, headed by two laywomen and a Roman Catholic nun, had just completed the redevelopment of the derelict Budlong Apartments in South Central Los Angeles into spiffy three- and four-bedroom family apartments, with a park across the street, which it also improved with a new playground and a basketball court.

An increasing number of Californians, especially those with a bohemian streak, were choosing to live on their boats, since boat dwellers could get by on fees ranging from $150 a month for small boats to $600 a month for larger vessels. Teachers, nurses, social workers, and other middle-wage earners were having an especially difficult time securing rentals near their places of work. Lincoln High School faculty member Chuck Manthe was basing himself temporarily out of the back seat of his car, parked behind a Motel 6 in San Jose until he found a room in a house in a marginal neighborhood for $600 a month, sharing a bathroom with five other people. Most younger single teachers at Lincoln were recruiting roommates to share expenses. They were also moonlighting. Art teacher Kevin O'Kane was waiting on tables to pay his rent. Special education teacher Kevin Collins drove a beer truck as a second job to meet his mortgage.

In San Francisco, where the vacancy rate hovered around 1 percent, a Darwinian struggle had developed, pitting prior renters against dot-commers with good incomes. In 1997 alone, there were approximately 2,700 evictions from rental properties, double those in 1995. The trend continued down the decade, adding to the volatility of the politics of that ever-volatile city. Yet even the yuppies and dot-commers searching for rental properties in San Francisco had difficulties. As in the case of the housing-for-sale market, each vacancy had multiple candidates, many of them brought to the property by e-commerce rental search agencies. Bidding wars were common, given the fact that empty apartments in San Francisco were exempt from rent control and could float to market value.

In an environment such as this, up and down the state, especially in the more expensive coastal regions, it was not surprising that a growing number of Californians—the unemployed, the working poor, single mothers with children, welfare recipients, and those made dysfunctional by mental illness, substance abuse, or generalized sociopathology—should be homeless. By 1993, in the city of Los Angeles alone, an estimated forty thousand were on the street on any given night, the majority of them on the gritty avenues of Skid Row bounded by Third and Seventh, Main and Alameda. Statistics from a 1996 survey by Shelter Partnership indicated an estimated 84,000 homeless throughout Los Angeles County. Other advocates believed the figure to be higher.

In a desperate effort to accommodate this population, especially in winter, the Homeless Services Authority of Los Angeles County maintained twenty-four facilities with about 10,800 short-term shelter beds across the region. One shelter alone, Weingart Center near the downtown, provided six hundred beds. Most of the homeless—64 percent, according to one 1991 study—were single adult men, many of them minorities. By 1993, however, a growing presence of homeless couples, some with pets, was being noted. Cindy and Charles Drafts built a treehouse near Blaine and Eighth Streets. Christine and Darryl Scott lived beneath the Hollywood Freeway near the Men's Central Jail. Eri Burns and her companion, Bill Matthews, were living, as of October 1993, in an elaborate partition shelter on Golden Avenue in sight of downtown high-rises, prior to moving into one of eighteen fiber-glass domes being built at Ninth and Golden by homeless activist Ted Hayes, a dreadlocked African American, himself homeless, who had wrangled the money for the Genesis I encampment from ARCO and other corporate sponsors. That December no less a personage than His Royal

Highness Prince Edward visited Genesis I for a personal tour. "The prince and the pauper," noted Hayes after the prince had gone from dome to dome and chatted amiably with many residents.[12]

As the homeless population grew, it also became more intrusive, dangerous even, which was not surprising, given the high levels of drug and alcohol abuse, mental illness, and other modes of dysfunctionalism that had put so many younger men on the streets. Tired of being aggressively panhandled in the downtown, Los Angeles city councilman Joel Wachs, a liberal from the Westside, sponsored an ordinance making it a misdemeanor for panhandlers to intimidate passersby by blocking their path, touching them in any way, or using profane or hostile language in the course of asking for money. The ordinance also forbade panhandling near ATMs, asking motorists for money at traffic stops, or washing windshields without permission. In July 1997, Mayor Richard Riordan signed the ordinance enthusiastically. The ACLU opposed the measure, however, and it languished in the courts.

A significant percentage of the homeless—25 to 30 percent, according to a study in 1990—were mentally ill. In times past, society would have institutionalized such people in one way or another, or they would have remained safely hidden in supportive circumstances, whether urban or rural. The increasing stratification of American society, however, had flushed the mentally ill from cover. With no place to hide, they had alighted, like frightened quail, on the streets. How many of the mentally ill on the streets were, to use an old-fashioned term, criminally insane, hence posing a threat to society? And how many were, at best, sociopaths, men—it was almost always men—who for one reason or another had never made a personal connection to society or seen themselves as functioning participants in the social order? Always, throughout American history, there had been such men. In untold numbers they had taken to the road as vagrants and hobos in the nineteenth and twentieth centuries. But they had not, except for in times of extreme economic distress, camped out en masse in the streets of American cities, as they were now doing.

Then there was the question of alcohol and drug abuse, an epidemic that was washing up significant sectors of an entire generation onto the streets. There had always been Skid Rows in most American cities, places where men and some women with chronic drinking problems could fade into anonymity. Now, the sheer numbers were making anonymity impossible. Drug abuse, however, was a new form of epidemic, and it seemed capable of filling the streets even more rapidly than alcohol. It was hard to reach the homeless, activists and social workers were admitting, hard to penetrate the nexus of ills and disorders that were keeping them on the street.

No city in California suffered more from this dilemma—wanting to do something for the homeless, but not knowing what to do—than San Francisco. Not that the raw numbers were as great as those in Los Angeles, city and county; but San Francisco was a compact place, less than forty-eight square miles, and its downtown region was even more compact. And San Francisco thought itself to be a cut above other California cities: Baghdad by the Bay, Queen of the Golden West, lovely and civil in its bay-guarded site, liberal, compassionate, tolerant, with a special regard for the suffering and downtrodden.

It was also a very expensive city, in which only one family in ten could afford to buy a new home; a city whose 1997 eviction rate, already at an all-time high, jumped by another 40 percent in 1998; a city in which California's minimum wage—$5.75, as of 1999—made no sense, given the cost of living; a city with so many poor that it had, in 1996, witnessed the creation of its own poverty-oriented magazine, *Poor,* edited by a mother-and-daughter team who had once been homeless and described themselves as still being on the home-endangered list. San Francisco was a city where even a graduate of Cornell Medical School, such as Dr. Shannon Morgan, sixty-seven in 1997, could find herself homeless, living on the streets, after a run of bad luck: a divorce, an ill-advised move to California in the early 1980s to care for a mentally unstable daughter, followed by three strokes and forced retirement with no pension, and the loss of her job as a live-in caregiver.

Shelter beds were scarce in San Francisco and remained that way throughout the decade. There were, on average, an estimated sixteen thousand homeless in the city through the 1990s, but municipal shelters accounted for an average of only eight hundred beds. Nor did San Francisco have the highly developed street mission culture of Los Angeles, where, on Skid Row, the Union Rescue Mission in January 1992 opened a $25 million, twenty thousand-square-feet, 306-bed shelter that included a racketball court, a weight room, and a gymnasium on the roof. The closest thing San Francisco had to such a shelter was the municipally supported Mission Rock Homeless Shelter in China Basin, which could handle, in a pinch, two hundred homeless more than its official four-hundred-person capacity; but in September 1999 this shelter was closed when the warehouse that housed it reverted to the San Francisco Giants, who needed the space and the facility for a five-thousand-car parking lot for its new Pacific Bell Park stadium.

It came as no surprise, then, that in the spring of 1998, Sister Bernie Galvin, a Roman Catholic nun, and a coalition of homeless advocates, including members of the clergy and city supervisor Leland Yee, began to covet the nineteen hundred units of former army housing in the Presidio, now a national trust charged by Congress to become self-supporting. Putting a nonbinding proposition on the June ballot, Galvin and her coalition unsettled the Presidio trustees and Congresswoman Nancy Pelosi, who had played a key role in negotiating the restructuring of the Presidio. The prospect of the Presidio as home to thousands of previously homeless street people hardly squared with the need to make the Presidio self-supporting.

Society for the Prevention of Cruelty to Animals (SPCA) director Richard Avanzino had an even more startling proposal: he offered to have a homeless shelter in the SPCA's brand-new $7 million pet adoption center, built from the bequest of a wealthy patron and from donations raised by Avanzino, under whom the SPCA was pulling in $11 million in donations per year from more than eighty thousand contributors. (That meant that one in three households in the city was donating to the SPCA.) It was incongruous, Avanzino argued, that the SPCA Adoption Center in San Francisco should have a day-care program ($20 a day to drop off your dog while you were at work), kitty condos where cats could watch videos of songbirds on television, a dog apartment with doggie furniture and a television playing *101 Dalmatians,* and a feral-cat-neutering program (eleven hundred a year), when so many people were living on the streets. Avanzino meant well, but homeless advocates were insulted by what they considered a demeaning proposal.

The continuing problem of the homeless, meanwhile, had defeated, or at least stymied, the efforts of three mayors. Art Agnos, a social worker before entering politics, had in August 1989 issued a well-researched and elegantly reasoned white paper entitled *Beyond Shelter: A Homeless Plan for San Francisco,* emphasizing a social service approach to the problem. Despite his efforts to enact a comprehensive and compassionate program, however, Agnos suffered the embarrassment of having the Civic Center in front of city hall turned into a sprawling encampment of homeless, which his political opponents quickly dubbed Camp Agnos. The next mayor, Frank Jordan, a former police chief, initiated a program called Matrix, in which the police were encouraged to cite aggressively such previously overlooked misdemeanors as panhandling, blocking sidewalks, and urinating in public. Police also began to confiscate shopping carts filled with belongings when their owners were arrested, tossing the carts into hydraulic garbage trucks, where they were crushed. The American Civil Liberties Union took Matrix to court and had it stopped. Initially, Mayor Willie Brown had wanted to avoid a Matrix-like approach to the homeless problem. Confronted with the growing unusability of Golden Gate Park, however, where thousands of homeless had established camps, Brown, a classic liberal, ordered a crackdown in October and November of 1997, going so far as to have his police chief request, unsuccessfully, the use of Oakland's helicopter-borne thermal imaging system to buzz the park in search of homeless encampments.

There was no doubt that the quality of life in San Francisco was deteriorating. Aggressive panhandling seemed rampant in the downtown area, especially in the hotel and shopping district. By day, the homeless ensconced themselves on the downtown streets, many of them establishing elaborate settlements, complete with begging signs and pets. Churches in the downtown or midtown areas were favorite spots for nighttime sleeping, and by dawn anyone walking along Mission Street, Market Street, Van Ness Avenue, Polk Street, or elsewhere in the downtown encountered numerous prone figures tucked into their sleeping bags. By midmorning, United Nations Plaza adjacent to the civic center remained, despite the efforts of Supervisor Amos Brown, a Baptist minister, to clean it up, crowded with disheveled homeless and other shaggy people who might have had rooms in the nearby Tenderloin but whose true home was the streets. This culture of the visibly distressed and dysfunctional continued down Market Street to Sixth and was especially intense at the intersection of Golden Gate Avenue and Jones in the Tenderloin, where for fifty years the Franciscans from the nearby St. Boniface Church had been dispensing free meals in St. Anthony's Dining Room.

Desperately, the city purchased 150 self-cleaning pay toilets from a French company and scattered them through heavily trafficked downtown and tourist zones. Pay toilets in certain areas soon became the favorite haunts of prostitutes and drug addicts (a man was found inside one, dead of a heroin overdose), and were frequently pried open so people could sleep or share drugs within. San Francisco, in short, had a problem—a very visible and human problem—that stood in stark contrast to its reputation as one of the most beautiful and desirable cities in the nation. No amenities of site, climate, or architecture, no charm of sidewalk flower stands or cable cars, could mask the truth that it contained within its population thousands of citizens who were losing what English novelist Evelyn Waugh once described as the unequal struggle with life.

Politics

As the 1990s progressed, metropolitan Los Angeles could be considered the true capital of California. Governors Pete Wilson and Gray Davis had their homes in the region. Twenty-five of the state's eighty assembly members represented one or another district in Los Angeles County. In times past, when Sacramento was a twenty-four-hour train ride from Los Angeles, legislators stayed put in that quiet and leafy town. Through the 1950s, San Francisco functioned as the shadow capital of the state. Now, with Southwest Airlines running a frequent and low-cost shuttle service (made even less expensive through special rates for state officials) into the Burbank, Los Angeles, Ontario, and John Wayne (Orange County) Airports, elected officials from Greater Los Angeles tended to think of themselves as being permanently based in their home districts and only on temporary assignment in Sacramento three or four days a week during the legislative session. Come Thursday afternoon, the Southwest terminal in the capital city was crowded with legislators making their way southward. Governor Davis, Lieutenant Governor Cruz Bustamante, assembly speaker Antonio Villaraigosa and his successor, Robert Hertzberg, Secretary of State Bill Jones, and Attorney General Bill Lockyer often spent the beginning and end of each workweek in the Ronald Reagan State Building in downtown Los Angeles. Lockyear, in fact, had more lawyers and paralegals in Los Angeles than he did in Sacramento. State controller Kathleen Connell maintained offices in Culver City, where she worked a good part of each week, commuting to Sacramento when necessary. Southwest Airlines, faxes, e-mail, and the process of video-teleconferencing had respatialized and relocated exactly what it meant for a city to be a capital. Like most state capitals, Sacramento had been an arbitrary imposition in the late 1850s when the natural capital had been San Francisco. Now the natural capital, metropolitan Los Angeles—natural in terms of size, wealth, media buzz, and glitz—was asserting itself.

Not that San Francisco was totally out of the picture. The California

Supreme Court and the Public Utilities Commission were headquartered in San Francisco. For fourteen years assembly speaker Willie L. Brown Jr., representing an inner-city San Francisco district, had wielded decisive influence not only over the assembly but over all state government. Now, San Francisco state senator John Burton had comparable authority as president pro tem of the senate, and other San Francisco–based legislators—Kevin Shelley, the assembly Democratic whip, Carole Migden, chair of the Appropriations Committee, and state senator Jackie Speier—were playing notable roles as well. San Francisco was a very political town, and its skilled politicians could never be considered out of the Sacramento picture, no matter how important Los Angeles was looming on the political power horizon of the state. With the exception of real estate mogul Walter Shorenstein, however, the oligarchy of San Francisco had long since lost interest in local politics. In times past, the major corporations of the city—Bank of America, Pacific Gas & Electric, Fireman's Fund Insurance, Schlage Lock, Crown Zellerbach, Matson Lines, Hills Brothers, MJB, Schilling Spice, and the Southern Pacific—were locally owned and managed, and their corporate leadership was itself homegrown and locally involved in politics. Now, San Francisco companies tended to be owned and operated by people from elsewhere, many of them on temporary assignment, and the old oligarchy—while maintaining an active involvement in the arts (the opera, the symphony, and museums)—were otherwise loath to stray beyond the confines of clubs and social circles established, many of them, in the late nineteenth century.

National politics was another matter. San Francisco's small but potent Republican community, around 15 percent of the city's 450,000 registered voters, sustained excellent connections with the national party power structure. Ever since the nineteenth century, San Francisco had been colonized by Ivy League graduates from Harvard, Yale, and Dartmouth especially. Founded in 1873, the Harvard Club of San Francisco was one of the oldest and largest Harvard clubs in the United States. The rise of Stanford University to Ivy League levels of prominence, moreover, had also nationalized the influence of a large number of Stanford graduates living in the city. Into the 1980s, at least, the San Francisco oligarchy was Republican, UC Berkeley, Stanford, or Ivy League, essentially private, except when called to national office. Such San Franciscans, who in general expressed amusement at the eccentricities of local politics, lived in a few select neighborhoods (Pacific Heights, Presidio Heights, Telegraph Hill, Nob Hill, Russian Hill, Sea Cliff, St. Francis Wood), belonged to the same clubs, sent their children to the same local schools. The dominant portion of this establishment had long since been suburbanized to Burlingame and its annex, Hillsborough, south of the city and had either cashed in its civic interests or was involved in investments on a national and international level and preferred to exercise its influence on that playing field.

The oligarchy of Los Angeles, by contrast, was democratic, self-made, politically engaged locally as well as nationally (Los Angeles investor Brad Freeman was among the chief fund-raisers for George W. Bush), and rich—very rich. Since its emergence in the early twentieth century, Los Angeles had been a city in which the oligarchy exercised decisive influence; indeed, the oligarchy that emerged in the early 1900s lasted, in one form or another and in successive variations, through the 1950s and 1960s, when Pacific Mutual Life Insurance president Asa Call served as shadow doge of the city. The essential political stability of Los Angeles in those years had come from a détente among the oligarchy, the proprietary municipal departments they dominated (harbor, water and power, the airport), the *Los Angeles Times,* a family-owned newspaper, and the Los Angeles Police Department, which kept a lid on everything.

A million or two in the bank could maintain well-bred San Franciscans in the best of circles, provided they had secured their real estate in an earlier era. Los Angeles, by contrast, abounded in self-made billionaires and multimillionaires too numerous to count: political activists such as Ronald Burkle, who had begun his career, Horatio Alger–style, as a supermarket box boy before going on to become a millionaire by age twenty and a billionaire supermarket magnate by early middle age. Billionaire Eli Broad, founder of Kaufman & Broad and SunAmerica Builders, was the close friend of self-made millionaire Richard Riordan, mayor of the city. Each year, the two of them vacationed together, concocting civic projects: raising funds for Disney Hall, getting a pro-football franchise, building Staples Center for the Lakers and other athletic events, reforming the school system, securing the 2000 Democratic National Convention for Los Angeles, advancing the opera, the museums, the symphony. The oligarchy also included lawyer and investment banker Bill Wardlaw, an omnipresent Mr. Fixit, an éminence gris whose power seemed to come not so much from money but through behind-the-scenes maneuverings. In a class by himself was Warren Christopher, managing partner of the historic law firm of O'Melveny and Myers, secretary of state in the Clinton administration, respected arbiter in times of crisis. Christopher was a wise and steady man, modest, meticulous, measured. In significant measure he embodied whatever was left of the gentlemanly circles that had once run the city.

Christopher's counterpart in San Francisco, the single most powerful person, that is, in the private sector—although the comparison represents a stretch—was real estate mogul Walter Shorenstein. From one perspective,

Shorenstein fit more clearly into the self-made up-from-nowhere pattern of Los Angeles. The son of a Long Island haberdasher, a self-made multimillionaire, Shorenstein was an oligarch more than willing to mix it up politically on a local, state, or national basis. Obviously, he preferred his national connections: the frequent visits from Al Gore and Bill Clinton, the long telephone calls with Senate majority leader George Mitchell, the deference paid him by the national Democratic Party as one of the leading political fund-raisers in the nation. In all directions from Shorenstein's forty-ninth-floor office in the Bank of America building on California Street (which he had bought from the bank in 1985, reselling it to them in 1989 for an estimated profit of $57 million) there unfolded a panoramic view of a city that was in its activist political culture even more liberal than Shorenstein himself. With the exception of the Dartmouth- and Harvard Law–educated state senator Quentin Kopp, a feisty independent who represented whatever was left of the pre-1960s city, nearly the entire political cast of characters in San Francisco during the 1990s—mayors, members of Congress, members of the assembly and state senate, district attorneys, members of the board of supervisors, even judges in a city in which sitting judges were frequently challenged for reelection—was liberal to left in its orientation. The epithet San Francisco Democrat had long since become a code word in national circles for far-out liberalism, including (but not confined to) the campaign for gay rights.

The Los Angeles City Council could be fractious, especially in its ongoing battles with Mayor Richard Riordan, but it rarely took what could be construed as ideological positions. The San Francisco Board of Supervisors, by contrast, was forever voting ideological resolutions, many of them having to do with foreign policy. Matters reached a crisis in November 1997 when, at the insistence of board president and longtime gay activist Tom Ammiano, the board shelved a motion, introduced by Supervisor Gavin Newsom, to commend General Colin Powell, former chairman of the Joint Chiefs of Staff, for raising $1.4 million for programs affecting San Francisco schoolchildren. Ammiano's hostility to Powell was based on Powell's refusal to endorse gays in the military. Embarrassed by the national scandal that ensued, Mayor Willie Brown did his best to do damage control, apologizing personally to the general.

While not formally political, entities such as the Glide Memorial United Methodist Church and the Delancey Street Foundation helped reinforce the liberal ethos of the city. In his thirty-five years as pastor of Glide, an endowed church on the edge of the socially challenged Tenderloin, the Reverend Cecil Williams transformed his congregation into a bastion of federally supported community programs and liberal activism. The Sunday service at Glide combined gospel music, sacred and secular sermonizing, and celebrity appearances up to and including President Bill Clinton. Though not holding elective office, the Reverend Williams was second only to Shorenstein in political influence held by a nonelected private citizen. The Delancey Street Foundation, founded in 1971 by former addict John Maher and his associate Mimi Silbert, who held double doctorates in criminology and psychology from UC Berkeley, had pioneered an innovative residential rehabilitation program in which ex-cons, alcoholics, and ex–drug addicts counseled paroled cons, recovering drug addicts, and alcoholics, guiding them to clean-and-sober productive lives. By the early 1990s, the foundation was ensconced in a complex of apartments and businesses, including an award-winning restaurant in the redeveloped South Bay waterfront district, and was opening a Los Angeles operation in the defunct Midtown Hilton on Vermont Avenue near the Hollywood Freeway.

Drug addiction became a big issue in Los Angeles on August 21, 1997, when city councilman Mike Hernandez, forty-four, who represented a string of Latino neighborhoods in and around Dodger Stadium, was arrested in Pacoima for possession of cocaine. Tipped off anonymously, the police had been investigating Hernandez for weeks prior to the arrest. He had been going steadily downhill: drinking a quart of tequila a night, snorting $100 worth of cocaine each day, chain-smoking menthol cigarettes, showing up late and disheveled for events, leaving his wife, taking up with an aide. Entering a court-supervised diversion program, Hernandez avoided a felony conviction, provided that he stay off drugs and alcohol for three years. Still, he had been charged with a felony, and some city council members and Mayor Riordan demanded that he resign. Hernandez refused, and when he returned to city hall the first time after his arrest he was applauded by a large gathering of supporters. In the course of his long and very public ordeal, no one charged Mike Hernandez with being corrupt. Weak, perhaps, boozy, careless, and drug addicted, but never with his hand in the till, and he never lost the support of his core constituency. Hernandez's survival, moreover, constituted a transition in the political culture of Los Angeles. A 1999 federal study showed that Mexican-American men had the highest rate (33 percent higher) of alcohol abuse of any ethnic group in the United States, including Native Americans. And certainly, cocaine usage was rampant throughout metropolitan Los Angeles, which was why the courts had diversion programs that allowed first-time offenders to avoid a felony conviction. For many, then, Hernandez was fighting a representative battle against addiction, which conferred on him a kind of reverse power based on the recognition that he was wrestling with demons that were, sadly, all too familiar in his community.

Rent, not drugs, was pacing the San Francisco political agenda. With the rising cost of housing and rate of evictions, a growing number of San Franciscans were fearing that their very way of life—being San Franciscans, that is—was coming to an end. Almost 65 percent of San Franciscans rented, and, not surprisingly, San Francisco was a strong rent-control city. In 1992 voters approved Proposition H, limiting annual rent increases to 60 percent of the federally determined consumer price index, which meant increases of no more than 1 to 2 percent per year. Running for mayor in 1995, Willie Brown promised voters a tenants' bill of rights. In 1996, early in his administration, Brown spearheaded a $100 million bond issue to finance the construction of affordable housing in the city. Landlords went along with the Brown proposal on the basis that the mayor would, in turn, restore the rate of rent increase to 100 percent of the consumer price index. Brown agreed. Landlords, not renters, wrote the checks to political campaigns. Without landlord support, Brown's affordable housing bond issue would not have made it on the ballot. By mid-1998 landlords were saying that the deal was off because Brown had not come through with the payback mechanism. Sure enough, another bond issue backed by Brown—to refurbish the De Young Museum in Golden Gate Park—went down to defeat along with the affordable housing measure. Even worse, he now seemed thoroughly in the pocket of landlords.

Enter Tom Ammiano, a former San Francisco schoolteacher and stand-up comic in his mid-fifties. He had burst onto the San Francisco political scene in the Lavender Sweep of November 1990, which saw two lesbians, Carole Migden and Roberta Achtenberg, elected to the board of supervisors and Ammiano elected to the board of education. Ammiano, Migden, and Achtenberg had won support outside the gay community—and this in a city that twenty years before had been deeply divided on the issue of gay political power, culminating in the assassination of San Francisco's first openly gay supervisor, Harvey Milk, and Mayor George Moscone by native son Dan White, a former cop turned fireman turned city-county supervisor. Non–San Franciscans, or even San Franciscans themselves, tempted to dismiss Ammiano as a local eccentric were missing the point. First of all, as a graduate of Seton Hall with a master's degree in special education from San Francisco State, he had been a compassionate, popular, and notably successful teacher of the handicapped during his twenty-three years with the school district. Of blue-collar New Jersey origins, the witty and quick-tongued Ammiano had an instinctive empathy for people who were oppressed or who, for one reason or another, weren't cutting it. Elected to the board of supervisors in 1994 and reelected, this time as president, in 1998, Ammiano built a growing constituency outside the gay community, including renters facing eviction and various tenants' groups; the retired elderly, so many of them insecure in their housing; the working poor; aging radicals who, like Ammiano, had arrived in San Francisco in the 1960s looking for utopia; neighborhood activists hostile to the downtown corporate sector; and the young, who tended to like Ammiano precisely because he was such a skilled stand-up Seinfeld figure, outrageously parodic and even self-parodic, capable on one occasion of describing himself as a Jesse Ventura in pumps.

Willie Brown, meanwhile, was coasting toward a second term, well ahead of former mayor Frank Jordan and political consultant Clint Reilly. Three weeks before the primary, however, an Internet-fueled write-in campaign for Ammiano took fire; and Brown found himself running neck and neck with Ammiano in the runoff. Ammiano's campaign was said to be coming from the far left; but so many of the things he was talking about, a growing number of San Franciscans were talking about as well: taking back San Francisco from developers and corporations, opposing gentrification, putting a moratorium on the construction of live/work lofts catering to upscale professionals, making the city friendly for families, children, and seniors, deregalizing City Hall (*Chronicle* cartoonist Phil Frank was wont to depict Mayor Brown as the King of San Francisco), and, above everything else, keeping rents down and fighting evictions. Holding his own against Brown in televised debates, Ammiano spoke of wanting to "pay back San Francisco because it has allowed me to be just about everything I want to be."[13] Brown won his second term, but he had to go to the local Republican Party to ensure victory, since Republicans held a crucial 15 percent of the votes in the city. The irony was not lost: one of the leading liberals in California turning to San Francisco's small and often derided Republican establishment to hold off a challenge from his left. Attorney Donald Casper, chair of the Republican Party in San Francisco, soon found himself chair as well of the all-powerful civil service commission.

Not rent but race, meanwhile, was emerging as the shaping issue in Los Angeles. The establishment would deny this, and to a certain extent, such denials had some plausibility. From one perspective, Los Angeles was successfully sustaining the most ambitious juxtapositioning, if not integration, of the most diverse human community ever assembled into one large American city. That was the good news, and, as far as it went, it was true. Yet Los Angeles had experienced in 1992 one of the worst riots in American history, and, in its aftermath, many Angelenos were asking themselves whether or not they wanted to stick around. As *Los Angeles Times* reporter Elizabeth Mehren asked, "Would they remain in a city that trumpets diversity and exudes a glorious—if sometimes delusional—aura of possibility? Or would they leave a metropolis where racial disharmony, economic decline, and disintegrating schools and deteriorating air have now been joined by an overriding sense of distrust of government and the city's institutions?"[14]

In the week after the riots, real-estate agents in suburban Ventura County north of the city reported a large influx of prospective clients from Los Angeles, including a notable number of Korean Americans. In the year following, real-estate values in Los Angeles County collapsed, and the property tax bills of an estimated 240,000 home owners were reduced due to a $14 billion decline in the assessed value of Los Angeles County real estate. Property values in Santa Monica were down by 37 percent. Still, these trends had little effect on the continuing willingness of first-time Latino buyers to purchase homes in Los Angeles, most notably in the South Central district, where the riots had begun. For hardworking Latino home buyers, the prospect of a two-bedroom house for $120,000—a bargain in Southern California—was worth the risk of the neighborhood. So, too, was there stability in such affluent enclaves as Los Feliz, Hancock Park, Beverly Hills, and Pacific Palisades. As far as housing was concerned, the wealthy and the newly enfranchised were finding it worth their while to ride the problem out; but middle-class home owners were more tempted to translate their equity, even at a loss, from Los Angeles to safer suburbs.

Safer from what? From crime, of course; but could the perception of Los Angeles as a dangerous place be totally extracted from the question of race? Many African-American residents, demographers were noting, were moving out of inner-city neighborhoods, out of their own communities, because of the safety issue and heading for such suburban places as Moreno Valley in Riverside County, where blacks soon constituted 15 percent of the population and where Bill Batey had become the first black mayor of the city— and this in a town where 55 percent of the residents were white and 20 percent Latino. African Americans were moving to Moreno Valley, quite simply, because they were tired of the dangers of inner-city Los Angeles.

The acquittal in April 1992 of the four LAPD officers charged with beating Rodney King had touched off one of the worst urban riots in American history. Now, exactly a year later, the same four officers were standing trial in the federal district court of Los Angeles on charges of depriving King of his civil rights: charges for which, if proven guilty, the previously acquitted officers could face up to ten years in jail and fines of $25,000. As Rodney King 2, as it was called, moved toward its conclusion, Angelenos braced themselves for a possible Riot 2, should the officers be acquitted, as some lawyers thought was inevitable, given the difficulties of proving conscious intent to deprive King of his civil rights. The verdict that was rendered on April 17, 1993—Koon and Powell, guilty; Wind and Briseno, not guilty—

and the stiff sentences that followed for Officers Koon and Powell may have been sufficient to prevent the expected riot. Yet Los Angeles was continuing to reveal itself as a city far from the image being projected by the twenty billboards erected as part of Tom Bradley's Neighbor to Neighbor program, depicting black, brown, yellow, and white hands clasped in harmony above the downtown Los Angeles skyline.

And even as Rodney King 2 was being heard, another case fraught with overtones of racial animosity—the trials of three young African-American men charged with the near-fatal assault on white trucker Reginald Denny during the riots—had gone through its preliminary phases. The Rodney King beating was about white cops under color of authority beating a black man; the Denny case was about black men beating a white man in the course of a riot. Both beatings were caught on videotape and broadcast repeatedly, exacerbating to excruciating intensity a physical and subliminal drama of racial animosity. As a television helicopter hovered overhead, broadcasting live, the defendants in the Reginald Denny case—Damian Monroe "Football" Williams, nineteen, Antoine Eugene "Twan" Miller, twenty, and Henry "Kiki" Watson, twenty-seven—were caught in various acts of violence, Williams especially, who had thrown a brick at Denny while he lay prostrate on the ground after being kicked and hit with an oxygenator and a hammer. Following this assault, Williams had performed a victory dance, like a football player who had just made a touchdown. Before, during, and after the Denny beating, the trio had been involved in other attacks and robberies in the vicinity of Florence and Normandie, which had led to their indictment on multiple felony counts, with Williams being charged with the especially grave crime of aggravated mayhem, which could lead to a life sentence. On October 18, 1993, a Los Angeles jury acquitted the defendants on most charges. Williams was convicted of simple mayhem, a felony, for his attack on Denny, and misdemeanor assault charges in four other attacks. Watson was guilty of a mere misdemeanor assault for holding Denny down so that Williams could better aim his brick. The jury clearly had bought the defense's argument that the rioting had created a mob psychology in which the defendants were not capable of the premeditation and intent demanded for conviction on the more serious charges. The score now stood one to one in terms of crimes of whites against blacks and blacks against whites, convictions and acquittals; for it was hard not to see in the Denny case the strong presence of political forces, subliminally internalized, in the willingness of jury members to buy the mob psychology argument. "Riot used to be an offense," noted Paul Robinson, professor of law at Northwestern University. "Now it's a defense. No other state or country has ever recognized such a defense."[15]

Then, one year later, came the grisly discovery of the butchered bodies of Nicole Brown Simpson and Ronald Lyle Goldman, followed by the trial for murder of Nicole's estranged husband, football star and television commentator O. J. Simpson, that scholars will be analyzing for decades to come as a case study in race relations. The King and Denny beatings had occurred within narrow sectors of society, the world of LA cops and street people. The Simpson case, by contrast, coalesced and brought into focus every sector of Los Angeles life. Working from the facts of the case alone, followed by the trial, a social analyst might very easily extract the full sociology of the city, to include an inventory of its ethnicities and types: the defendant himself, a football and television celebrity; his brutally murdered wife Nicole, so suggestive of all those good-looking women with uncertain talents who filled the city; Ronald Goldman, one of LA's countless young and handsome waiters preparing for a better future; the Goldman family, so representative of the Jewish middle class of Southern California; the up-from-the-streets defense attorney Johnnie L. Cochran Jr., who had come up the hard way, case by case, without ever losing the street smarts and shrewd intuitions of earlier years; Judge Lance Ito, patient to a fault, representing the strong presence of Japanese Americans in almost every aspect of the city; prosecutor Marcia Clark, bristling with the assertive feminism of a newly arrived generation of professional women; her brooding and uncertain colleague, Christopher Darden, the African American as preppy boomer; Rosa Lopez, the Latino maid, and Allan Park, the limousine driver, the two of them representing the working people of the city; detective Mark Fuhrman, a pulp-fiction LA cop, who saw his career as a screenplay, which he was busy writing; and Brian "Kato" Kaelin, Simpson's more-or-less-permanent houseguest, a quizzical figure caught between a life not yet started and a prior life that had never gotten off the ground.

For sixteen months, from June 12, 1994, when the bodies were discovered, to October 3, 1995, when the jury announced its verdict, the O. J. Simpson trial mesmerized the world; it fused into the alembic of one criminal case a paradigmatic story of love and lust, celebrity and obscurity, cops and lawyers, centered on a celebrity defendant at once brutal and amiable, like Los Angeles itself. There had also been—at bottom, constantly—the never-ending drama of race. Whatever else Simpson and his wife had been to each other, in the good times and in the final horror, they had been playing out what Swedish sociologist Gunnar Myrdal had in 1940 correctly described as America's enduring dilemma—race. And this was not just in terms of the Simpsons' marriage, and what went wrong, but in terms also of how Simpson, however compromised, however repellent, became a subliminal antihero for so many of his people: a figure of payback, of tables being turned, of chickens coming home to roost. From this perspective, the very dueling of Cochran, African American, and Darden, African American, for the guilt or innocence of O. J. Simpson, African American, had its own representative drama within the larger drama of the trial. As the verdict approached, some African Americans began openly to suggest their identification with O. J.—especially after Mark Fuhrman's racist comments on tape to a screenwriter were played in open court, without the jury present. Here was what seemed to many African Americans proof from hell: proof that the cops and the white society the cops served held them with the contempt seething through Fuhrman's obsessive repetitions of the "n" word. After the playing of the tape on August 29, 1995, what was implicit in the Simpson case—race—became explicit and on the table.

And race burst even more openly into view on Tuesday, October 3, 1995, when a predominantly African-American jury acquitted Simpson, and a predominantly African-American and Latino crowd of four to five hundred people broke into joyous cries and applause when they heard the verdict, a scene repeated throughout the city among African-American and other minority groups. Whites, whether individually or in groups, tended toward stunned silence. "That's how it should be," noted one Simpson supporter, " 'cause white folks been doing stuff to black folks for all these years. I don't care if he did it or not. There's been a lot of injustices done to the black community. So what if he did it and got away with it? Hey, that's life. He had the money to get the good lawyers."[16]

"If you haven't been pulled over and patted down," noted *Los Angeles Times* columnist Robert A. Jones, a white man, "the O.J. verdict doesn't make sense. If you have, it makes all the good sweet sense in the world. A huge divide separates those two groups. Usually, the everyday world works in such a way to hide the divide. Yesterday, the opposite happened. For a brief hour or two, until everyone got themselves composed, the verdict pulled back the curtain and showed us the divide in all its breadth and depth."[17]

In terms of the relationship between the Jewish and the Latino communities, such a divide showed itself in June 1998 in a bitterly and narrowly contested state senate primary battle between termed-out assemblyman Richard Katz and city councilman Richard Alarcon. In the course of the election, state senator Richard Polanco, a Los Angeles Democrat backing Alarcon, sponsored a mailer to eighteen thousand newly registered Latino voters in the San Fernando Valley. The mailer associated Katz with a 1988 Republican-backed effort in Orange County posting guards at twenty voting sites allegedly to keep illegals from voting, but also intimidating legal Latino voters. The mailer was grossly unfair, but it could not be said to be explicitly anti-Semitic. The Anti-Defamation League, the American Jewish Committee, and the American Jewish Federation, however, protested the mailer on the basis that it attacked a highly respected Jewish politician as being anti-Latino. Winning the primary by a mere twenty-nine votes, Alarcon later offered to apologize for the flier, but Katz refused his apology, and the matter festered, especially when Alarcon won the general election in November and Katz, a highly respected former assemblyman, was out of public life.

In October 1999, Jewish-Latino relations soured further in the controversy surrounding the de facto removal of Los Angeles Unified School District (LAUSD) superintendent Dr. Ruben Zacarias. The ostensible cause of Zacarias's removal from the control of the 700,000-student district (500,000 of them Latino) was a scathing report released in September by a special investigations unit of the LAUSD. The report discussed the chain of events and bureaucratic responsibilities that had led to the district sinking $200 million into the Belmont Learning Complex, which stood incomplete and unusable on Second Street, just west of the Harbor Freeway in the downtown, because it had been built on a former oil field toxic with methane gas and other chemical by-products. The problem was that the people leading the campaign to oust the superintendent were Jewish, as was Zacarias's proposed successor, and Zacarias—a handsome dignified man of seventy, impeccably tailored, who had worked his way up the ranks of the LAUSD—was Latino, as were most of his students. Throughout October 1999, the drama played itself out, with Zacarias—the beloved "Dr. Z" of the Latino community—fighting for his job, speaking to spirited rallies of parents and students, announcing his own plans for the reorganization of the district into twelve semiautonomous units. In Sacramento, the Latino Legislative Caucus and the Black Legislative Caucus, and locally key Latino civil rights organizations across the city, were rallying to Zacarias's side. *Times* columnist Al Martinez was especially appalled by the way that Zacarias was being made into a public spectacle. Commentator Gregory Rodriguez was disconcerted by the fact that the LAUSD coup had bypassed, even trumped, the local Latino political and cultural establishment. It took a number of noisy and tension-ridden meetings and a lot of behind-the-scenes shuttle diplomacy by assembly speaker Antonio Villaraigosa before Zacarias agreed to accept a $750,000 buyout of the remaining twenty months of his contract. It also helped that Zacarias's interim replacement was another Latino, respected school administrator Ramon Cortines.

Hot-button issues such as the anti-Katz mailer and the Zacarias controversy fortunately did not lead to violence. They did, however, provoke hurt feelings in both the Latino and Jewish communities. Commentators and community leaders such as Gregory Rodriguez, Joel Kotkin, Rabbi Gary Greenebaum, Arturo Vargas, executive director of the National Association of Latino Elected and Appointed Officials, and Steven Windmueller, director of the Irwin Daniels School of Jewish Communal Service at the Hebrew Union College, initiated a body of bridge-building dialogue between the two groups. Jews and Latinos alike, it was suggested, had too much to lose in a *kulturkampf*. Each group was an outsider, now politically enfranchised in Los Angeles, tended to vote Democratic, and, if getting along, could form a powerful and stabilizing political and cultural coalition.

And besides, there were more pressing issues at hand, such as whether or not Los Angeles wanted to remain a city at all.

Starting in 1997, a drive by an organization calling itself Valley VOTE was making plausible the possibility that the San Fernando Valley might sometime early in the new millennium take its 1.4 million people and form a new city the size of Philadelphia, thus reducing Los Angeles by a third. Initially, the Valley VOTE crowd seemed NIMBYism personified, its not-in-my-backyard point of view easy to dismiss as so much suburban selfishness. As the 1990s turned into the 2000s, however, Valley VOTE and its secessionist program began to gain credibility and respect, and it succeeded in persuading the state to create an autonomous Local Agency Formation Commission preempting the veto authority of the city council, which was understandably hostile to the breakup of the city. Valley VOTE also secured sufficient signatures to authorize a formal study of just exactly what the fiscal and organizational implications of breaking off the valley into an independent city were. The Local Agency Formation Commission could then use this plan for putting a secessionist measure on the ballot as early as June or November 2002. In late May 2002, the commission did exactly that, placing the matter on the November 2002 ballot. Los Angeles now had the opportunity to become the first world city voluntarily to deconstruct itself. Appalled by this prospect, five city council members, spearheaded by first-termers Wendy Greuel, herself representing parts of the valley, and Janice Hahn, representing the San Pedro and Harbor area, scrambled to place a countermeasure on the November ballot calling for the creation of a borough system on the lines of New York, London, Paris, and Berlin.

The prospect of breaking Los Angeles apart provoked a torrent of argument and commentary, ranging from the practical to the philosophical. Where would the proposed new city get its water? How were the propri-etary agencies of Los Angeles—its department of water and power, its harbor, its airport—to be divided up? What about the city's debt? Its police and fire departments and other city services? How were they to be divided without a crippling loss of efficiency? A 925-page analysis of these problems, released by the city in June 2001, insisted that secession would create two fiscally strapped municipalities. Other commentators questioned the motives of the secessionist advocates, sensing a barely disguised effort by middle-class activists to exempt themselves from the problems of the inner city. Mayor Richard Riordan was especially emphatic on this point, seeing in secessionism a willful withdrawal of the haves from the have-nots. Other groups similar to Valley VOTE, meanwhile, were organizing secessionist movements for the Wilmington–San Pedro area, the Eagle Rock district, Hollywood, and West Los Angeles. Thus all classes and conditions—the working people of Eagle Rock, the middle classes of the San Fernando Valley and Wilmington–San Pedro, the bohemians of Hollywood, and the upscale trendies of the UCLA-centered Westside—were erupting in secessionist sentiment. While these movements at first seemed marginal, so had Valley VOTE seemed in 1997.

Hot-button issues in San Francisco, by contrast, did not involve the slightest suggestion of the city dismembering itself. In 1912, at the very time Los Angeles was putting the finishing touches on the reservoir and aqueduct system that would allow it to annex neighboring communities and expand across the plain, San Franciscans were specifically voting down a ballot proposal by the Greater San Francisco Association to create a boroughlike system of regional government throughout the Bay Area. In time, various Bay Area–wide jurisdictions did evolve (twenty-two agencies, for example, had one form or another of jurisdiction over San Francisco Bay), but none of them involved any significant surrender of sovereignty on San Francisco's part or the absorption by the city of neighboring entities, such as had happened in Los Angeles. Self-contained and self-regarding on its 46.38-square-mile peninsula, San Francisco was suffering, if anything, from an overdose of civic self-esteem in contrast to Los Angeles's flirtation with dismemberment. Throughout the 1990s, raging issues tended to reflect the eccentric, even quirky, political culture of a city that conservative columnist George Will mocked as "this caricature by the bay."[18]

San Francisco, for example, cared about marijuana—cared very much about marijuana, if the truth be told; indeed, in certain neighborhoods, the sweet smell of cannabis frequently mingled with the sea breezes on the streets of the city. In 1996, Dennis Peron, founder of the nonprofit Cannabis Buyer's Club, had placed on the ballot Proposition 215, a statewide initiative authorizing the sale and use of marijuana for medical purposes. To everyone's surprise, the measure passed. Three months before the initiative won, however, state agents had raided the Cannabis Buyer's Club and shut it down. After Proposition 215 became law, the San Francisco Superior Court ruled that the club should be allowed to reopen and sell marijuana for medical purposes. A year later, the state court of appeal overruled this decision, ordering instead that clubs such as the one run by Peron were not health-care providers and thus could not legally sell pot. By this time, Peron—described by one reporter as "a chain-smoking, pot-toking, commune-living, gay, vegetarian, Buddhist Vietnam veteran"—was running for governor, as a Republican, against state attorney general Dan Lungren, who had ordered the initial raid on the club.[19]

While the Los Angeles Unified School District was worried about firing its Latino superintendent, or fretting over $200 million squandered in the Belmont Learning Complex, the San Francisco Unified School District was debating the imposition of a formal quota, proposed by two African-American school board members, that more than half the books on high school required-reading lists be books written by nonwhite authors. Only 13 percent of the students in the public high schools of San Francisco, they pointed out, were white, and the largest group was Chinese, so why not require reading lists to reflect this diversity? As in the case of Peron's effort to unseat Lungren in the Republican primary, the proposal attracted much scorn and satire in the national press and a surprising amount of support on the home front, including endorsements or quasi endorsements from such Bay Area writers of color as Maxine Hong Kingston, Ishmael Reed, Cecil Brown, Terry McMillan, and a host of reading advocates. No other school district in the nation, opponents argued, had racial quotas for books. Wasn't this a form of literary apartheid? In the end, the school board compromised. While not requiring a formal quota, the board voted that works of literature read in high school "must include writers of color which reflect the diversity of culture, race, and class of the students." Students, however, would still be required to read books appearing on SAT exams. Thirdly, "writers who are known to be lesbian, gay, bisexual, or trans-gender shall be appropriately identified in the curriculum."[20]

San Franciscans also cared about taxicabs, streetcars, buses, and cable cars, more or less in that order. None of these seemed to be working—properly, at least. For a city priding itself on its sophisticated urbanism, it was a constant source of frustration not to be able to flag down a cab on any but a narrow corridor of streets serving downtown hotels or Fisherman's Wharf. Many cab drivers did not have a sufficient command of either English or the city streets to work the radio effectively. And besides, with rental gates often exceeding $100 a shift, it hardly paid drivers to answer radio calls to remote portions of the city to serve the poor and the elderly on short trips. When a cab slammed into a cable car near Union Square in late June 1998, injuring three of the fifty tourists aboard, two icons of San Francisco's valued urbanism came into conflict. As in the case of cabs, cable cars had become almost exclusively the prerogative of the tourist economy. Basically, cable cars were an efficient means of transportation up and down San Francisco's hilly topography, which is why they had survived since their introduction in 1873. The California Street cable car, for example, offered an exhilarating and convenient ride across the top of Nob Hill down into the financial district. Yet San Franciscans, except in the off-hours, could not find room on the overcrowded, tourist-laden cable cars careening through the densest parts of the city.

At least the cable cars were moving, which was more than could be said of San Francisco's multibillion-dollar Municipal Railway system, whose fixed-rail streetcars, electric trolley buses, and gas-driven buses had by mid-decade reached a point of crisis, despite the completion of two decades of underground excavation along Market Street designed to turn that thoroughfare into a swiftly moving transit corridor. With BART fixed-rail serving the entire region on the first level, Municipal Railway light-rail serving San Francisco on the second level, more light-rail serving the Embarcadero from Fisherman's Wharf to South Bay, and restored antique streetcars on the surface adding color and charm to the cityscape, it was an ambitious program, and the city had put nearly twenty years, and billions of dollars, into preparing it. By the mid-1990s, however, a chorus of complaints was surfacing that human error and mismanagement were blunting the bright promise of the Boeing-built streetcars. In one case, two *Chronicle* reporters proved that a person could walk from Civic Center to the Embarcadero on Market Street faster than a streetcar could travel the same distance beneath the surface. (A few days later, Mayor Willie Brown, resplendent in a Panama hat for the occasion, made the same trip and was happy to be beaten by the Muni Metro.) Running for mayor in 1995, Brown had promised to shape up the Municipal Railroad within a hundred days of taking office. It took him most of his first term to make good on his promise, but Da Mayor (as he was called) came through. By late in the decade, the trains and buses of the Muni were running on time.

Brown was a big-city man to the core of his being, and, along with Richard Riordan of Los Angeles, was doing his best to fight a rising tide of factional NIMBYism and other provincializing forces. In their respective cities, Riordan and Brown bestrode the civic stage through the second half of the 1990s and early in the new millennium with the full force of contrasting yet similar personalities. The contrast, in point of fact, could not have been more pronounced than that between Riordan, an Irish American born in Flushing, New York, in 1930, the son of a successful department-store executive and a graduate of Princeton, where he had studied with the philosopher Jacques Maritain, and Brown, an African American born in Mineola, Texas, in 1934, the child of sharecroppers, growing up amid all the cruelties and indignities of a segregated society. After service as an artillery officer in Korea, Riordan had graduated at the top of his class at the University of Michigan Law School and had come to Los Angeles in 1956 as a member of the blue-chip law firm of O'Melveny and Myers. Arriving in San Francisco as a teenager, Brown had worked his way through San Francisco State and the Hastings College of the Law and, with no offers in hand, had started a solo practice in the then largely African-American Fillmore district. His first client was a prostitute. For most of his adult life, Riordan remained in the law and investment finance, founding his own law firm and becoming a multimillionaire by investing in, and turning around, troubled companies. So, too, did Brown stay with the law throughout a lifetime, taking advantage of special dispensation that allowed state legislators to remain in legal practice.

But it was politics, politics, and more politics that provided Willie Brown with his true education and calling. It was in the assembly that he won his campaign medals. Becoming Speaker in 1980, Brown soon became the second most powerful figure in state government, which he remained for fourteen years. It was said, legitimately, that the voters passed term limits in 1990 partly in an effort to get rid of Willie Brown, just as the FBI was said to have been probing state government for a number of years in an effort to snare Brown in one or another irregularity.

Each man, Riordan and Brown, was brilliant, albeit each in a visceral postintellectual way: smart, that is, through a fundamental intuition that in many cases moved too swiftly for ideas. Brown, however, possessed the verbal facility of an eloquent preacher, while public speaking was difficult for Riordan, although he was quite effective in private conversation. As he grew older and more successful, Riordan became more contemplative, an inveterate reader, and, eventually, the proud possessor of a large and distinguished personal library. Brown, by contrast, absorbed ideas orally rather than through reading; indeed, he seemed to inhale ideas from the very political atmosphere he moved in. He also saw innumerable first-run movies, ducking into theaters for the last showing after a night on the political circuit. A member of *Chronicle* columnist Herb Caen's inner circle, Brown loved the good life—the sharp suits, the restaurants and night life, the company of beautiful women—while Riordan preferred to socialize at home or to read a good book. There was in Riordan, moreover, something that Brown lacked—indeed, could never have acquired, given his early circumstances—a formal sense of culture, that is, which Riordan shared with one of Brown's predecessors as mayor of San Francisco, Joseph L. Alioto, a polymath of encyclopedic learning and avid cultural interests.

Each man, however, Brown and Riordan, was shrewd and prized loyalty. Each possessed the ability to render his enemies distraught when they were contrasting, as they frequently did, so many manifest deficiencies in either of them—their egos, their arrogance, their willingness to bypass accepted procedures, their abbreviated attention spans—versus a growing catalog of acknowledged accomplishments as their administrations unfolded. Riordan was especially distinct in this regard; unlike Brown, he was not a practiced politician, but was sometimes painfully blunt, even misspoken, and often unafraid to say the unsayable.

Brown had come into office by defeating Frank Jordan, who had gained the mayoralty by defeating Art Agnos. One figure—political consultant Jack Davis—ran both the Jordan campaign that defeated Agnos and, four years later, the Brown campaign that defeated Jordan. A preppie and gay activist in his late thirties, Davis was nothing short of a political genius when it came to engineering successful campaigns in San Francisco. Davis was also flamboyant, mercurial, profane, and meticulous when it came to his craft. His crony was columnist Warren Hinckle, a one-eyed, black-patched Brooks Brothers–clad gonzo journalist in his late fifties, founder and former editor of the radical magazine *Ramparts,* and a flamboyant throwback to the Front Page era. Hinckle tended to use the blue-collar and bohemian bars of the city as his office. Working together as behind-the-scenes operatives, their business conducted in the late evening and early hours (until the bars closed at two a.m., and sometimes after that), Davis and Hinckle managed to play a decisive role in persuading Jordan to run against Agnos, who in 1990 had helped indict Davis on misdemeanor charges of violating campaign laws. That case was soon thrown out of court, but now it was payback time. Dee Dee Meyers, scheduled to join the Clinton presidential campaign a few months later, worked as Jordan's press secretary. To everyone's surprise, Jordan upset the sitting mayor.

As mayor, Jordan ran a cautious administration, marred only by the appointing and subsequent firing of former sheriff Richard Hongisto as police chief, which lost Jordan whatever support he had on the left. Then, in one of those inexplicable acts of self-destruction, Jordan had his picture taken in the nude, showering in the company of two radio shock jocks from Los Angeles. From that point, his hold on the mayoralty progressively weakened. Four years later, after falling out with Jordan, Davis and Hinckle (basing themselves out of Hanno's in the Alley, south of Market, Tosca and Spec's in North Beach, and miscellaneous watering holes in the Mission, West Portal, Sunset, and Richmond districts) successfully masterminded the Brown campaign, just as they would later be instrumental in the acquisition of the *San Francisco Examiner* by the Fang family.

Richard Riordan, in turn, had had his mayoral campaign against City Councilman Mike Woo masterminded by another notable San Francisco political consultant, Clint Reilly, a mercurial ex-seminarian, who devised for Riordan the campaign-winning slogan "Tough Enough to Turn LA Around." Certainly, Los Angeles in the post-riot year of 1993 needed turning around; and there could be no better choice of who was to do it—and according to what ideology—than the two leading candidates: Republican Riordan, playing the turnaround-artist-outsider, and Michael Woo, a UC Santa Cruz–educated Chinese American with a graduate degree in planning from UC Berkeley and a solid record of liberal activism as a two-term city councilman. Each candidate was offering Los Angeles, in effect, a clear-cut alternative to the long reign of Tom Bradley, which had come so painfully to its conclusion with the riots. Bradley had worked his way up the hard way—to police lieutenant, nighttime law school, the city council—and was, in his heart of hearts, possessed of a fundamental caution that did not always sit well with his more liberal supporters. Woo, like Riordan a child of the prosperous upper middle class, was offering the city a clear-cut liberal alternative, which his fellow boomer politician, President Bill Clinton, enthusiastically endorsed. Riordan, by contrast, played the tough guy, promising to shake up City Hall and put a thousand more cops on the street. Riordan won.

As mayor, Brown the liberal Democrat had moved toward the center. Likewise, Riordan the Republican revealed a liberal streak, together with an ability to get along with liberal politicians—including his good friend Senator Dianne Feinstein—that would make him vulnerable in 2002 when he had left office and was seeking the Republican nomination for governor. Early in his first administration, Brown was photographed wearing a baseball hat inscribed with "Da Mayor"; this suggestion, whether accidental or deliberate, this evocation of an East Coast–style, big-city mayor, emerged as the motif of his two terms in office. Not since Alioto in the late 1960s and early 1970s had San Francisco had a mayor who reveled so openly in the symbols and accoutrements of power. Brown loved to roar about the city under motorcycle escort, sirens blaring, if only returning from a 49ers game at Candlestick Park. The city payroll swelled with personal assistants to Da Mayor appointed outside the civil service system. Department heads who pleased Brown saw their salaries climb well past the $100,000 mark. Department heads who displeased him were soon returned to private life. Brown loved to give, and, if it was necessary, to take away. Until the reestablished district elections brought in a slew of neighborhood activists, he maintained control over the board of supervisors. No one could ever criticize Brown for being lazy. His days at city hall were long, his nights were filled with up to a half-dozen civic events at which he was scheduled to make an appearance, and he often ended the evening with a late-night movie. Loving the pomp and circumstances of being Da Mayor, Brown almost single-handedly transformed San Francisco's monumental city hall into a city museum and venue for civic receptions, private parties, and weddings. Like Joe Alioto before him, Brown believed in jobs and growth, and very soon San Francisco found itself sprouting new hotels and office highrises and, in the case of the Mission Bay project of the Catellus Development Corporation (apartment complexes, retail, and research facilities for the UCSF medical campus), redeveloping an entire section of the city. You could do business with Willie Brown, noted Nelson Rising, president of Catellus. Da Mayor kept his word.

By the end of his first term, Brown—the onetime outsider, the shoeshine boy from Mineola, Texas, the solo practitioner in the Fillmore district—had subsumed unto himself and dominated just about every aspect of mainstream political life in the city. A lifelong advocate of the dispossessed, Brown was now even capable of taking on those who were coming into San Francisco to make welfare a way of life. "San Francisco touts itself as a city where people can come from all over the world for HIV or AIDS treatment," Brown remarked of a group of able-bodied male welfare recipients who were resisting work requirements in the city's welfare program and disrupting public meetings. "But when a few people come across the Bay Bridge to get benefits, we slam the door."[21]

In the long run, San Francisco was lucky to have Willie Brown as mayor, whatever his faults and vanities; for the city was—in its basic identity—politically dysfunctional. Too many clashing and contradictory agendas had been imported for the system to work. In their diversity, San Franciscans wanted, almost simultaneously, a supportive welfare system and a dot-com boom, preservationism and the creation of new housing, traditional culture and Halloween every night, a reputation for tolerance and a taste for blasphemy, an established button-down city, an immigrants' haven, a corporate and financial capital, a nurturing place for artists, a redeveloped metropolis with slow-growth policies, the running of red lights, and bicycle lanes throughout the city. Even with Brown as Da Mayor, San Francisco stood in constant danger of political implosion, of having every legitimate and wayward impulse clash with, and cancel, its opposite, as in particle physics. In a city stymied by such an agenda impasse, only the most persistent of solo performers fueled by ego, brainpower, and a love of glory and the game—the sheer fun of it all, the hell of it—had a chance of getting anything done.

Richard Riordan, by contrast, had come into power in a city of tightly defined council districts and a city council authorized by charter to exercise administrative vetoes or sanctions. After thirty successful years in the private sector, innocent of politics until his sixty-third year, Riordan was at an even further disadvantage because of the city's weak-mayor system. And besides, so many city council members were themselves formidable political figures, whether permanently on the council or en route to higher office. Each of them was supreme in council districts that would in other jurisdictions constitute fair-size cities. Riordan wasted a lot of time quarreling with council members, and these disputes constituted the central weak point of his two mayoral terms.

At the end of it all, neither side had either broken or convinced the other. Riordan remained an effective solo performer, and the city council sustained its prerogatives. On the other hand, the mayor lost nothing truly essential, nothing that he truly wanted; within the narrow bandwidth allowed him by the city charter, he performed brilliantly on a number of fronts. He was, after all, an experienced businessman, a turnaround artist; and slowly, in a number of sectors, across the eight years of Riordan's two terms, Los Angeles turned around. Reporting for duty as mayor, Riordan spent one day a week working at a succession of city jobs, including garbage collector, to get a feel for how government functioned at basic levels. Eventually, he would play a significant role in getting voters to approve a new city charter that was intended to make Los Angeles run more efficiently as a business.

When the 1994 Northridge earthquake hit early in his tenure, Riordan was masterful as chief executive. Within sixty-six days, the collapsed Santa Monica Freeway was up and open for business. At the beginning of his first term, construction of Frank Gehry's Disney Hall stood stalled atop Bunker Hill, and the city desperately needed a major new indoor arena. By the time Riordan left office, the Disney Hall was rising over the skyline, and Staples Center had opened its doors. True, he had the support of his fellow oligarchs in accomplishing these projects—Eli Broad at Disney Hall, Ron Burkle and Ed Roski at Staples Center—but that was exactly the point. An oligarch among oligarchs, Riordan was capable of galvanizing and focusing his circle on a variety of projects. Friendly with Bill Clinton and Dianne Feinstein, Riordan brought to Los Angeles more than its fair share of federal funds. He persuaded the Democrats to hold their 2000 national convention in Los Angeles, raising part of the necessary funds from his friends in the oligarchy and contributing a million dollars of his own money. Hosting the convention, Riordan believed, would announce to the nation that Los Angeles was back—fully back—from the flames of 1992.

As in the case of Rudolph Giuliani of New York, whom he most resembled in his efforts to turn around a great city, Riordan breached the barrier between the mayor's office and the K–12 educational establishment. Picking three reformers and one reformer-incumbent, he fashioned a slate of candidates, raised sufficient funds, and all but took over the board of the school district. A father and a grandfather who had lost two offspring to early deaths, he was passionately devoted to children. His official portrait showed him with schoolkids. A lifelong reader, he loved books and libraries; during his tenure, support for the Los Angeles Public Library was increased, cumulatively, by more than 20 percent, and the city passed a $66 million library construction bond issue. When he stepped down, the Central Library was named in his honor. Although Riordan could not control the exodus or acquisition of major Los Angeles corporations, he did facilitate, through cutting red tape, the rebuilding of the city's economy as a linked network of small to midsize businesses. By means of a near-imperial Asian tour and continuing contacts with Asian investment, he helped keep offshore money flowing into the city.

Richard Riordan was not smooth; he was famous for his corny jokes and flubbed lines. His critics were driven to distraction by what sometimes seemed his arrogant indifference or, at the least, his absentminded insensitivity to the world around him (munching on a hamburger when greeting hunger strikers on the steps of city hall, or touring the wine regions of France by bicycle when the city's public transit workers were out on strike). But whatever his deficiencies, Riordan was a leader, someone not afraid to be out ahead of the crowd. As mayor, he was much more than the sum of his parts. Like Dwight Eisenhower, whom he admired and more than a little resembled, Riordan possessed in a distinct degree the general consent of the governed, no matter what his current gaffe or minicrisis might be. Like Brown, Riordan loved the performance dimension of being mayor: biking in the LA Marathon, playing piano for noontime workers in the California Plaza, or donning hockey garb to inaugurate the rink at Staples.

Although most cops supported him in the election, Riordan, like many a Los Angeles mayor before him, discovered that the LAPD was more than just another agency reporting to the mayor. The thin blue line had its own private compact with the city. At some point in the 1920s, as Los Angeles ballooned to mega-urban proportions, taking in some 662,000 newcomers, the city made an implicit agreement—more precisely, a covenant—with its police. Among those 662,000 was a majority of respectable and self-respecting people, whose values and lifestyle dovetailed with the pervasive Anglo-Protestant rectitude of the city, its condition, as Willard Huntington Wright described it in 1913, of being chemically pure. But also arriving were hordes of the rootless, the destabilized, the marginal, the actually or potentially criminal, and this group was linking up with its undesirable counterparts in the existing city. Respectable Los Angeles, fearing that such an alliance would make the city unlivable, said to its developing police department, in effect: You run it, you take care of it, and we will cut you as much slack as we can. It was the Progressive era, still, and that meant that there was yet in operation a philosophy of municipal management that wanted city agencies to be run by the experts, not the politicians. So the police, being the experts in managing crime, should be insulated from politics as far as possible. Hence, the LAPD developed over time as a quasi-autonomous entity, both psychologically and administratively, with its own continuing covenant.

The police departments of New York, Chicago, and San Francisco, by contrast, were part of the political structure of their cities, and cops were, most fundamentally, people of the city, citizens in uniform. As such, they were part of their communities and in most cases no better or worse than the people they served. The San Francisco Police Department embodied this kind of close connection. Cops, a significant percentage of them Irish Catholics into the 1960s, tended to be born and raised in San Francisco, lived and raised their families in San Francisco, vacationed with other San Franciscans in places favored by working San Franciscans, and saw their lives in San Francisco terms. Even when the demographics of the department changed, this identification with the city still lingered. Homicide inspector Earl Sanders (whom Brown appointed chief of police in 2002) and his partner, Napoleon Hendrix, for example, were pioneering African-American detectives in the SFPD. Their fedoras and double-breasted suits, however, their sharp neckties, their connections with local politicians, union leaders, restaurant owners, bartenders, and other assorted civic celebrities and characters, testified to the fact that Sanders and Hendrix were carrying on the traditions of their department. They were San Francisco cops—no better and no worse than the city they served, proud of their identities as successful homicide detectives, dedicated to the city and the SFPD, despite the fact that African Americans had only begun to come into their own on the force in recent decades, and had to cope with a prevailing atmosphere of antiblack sentiment.

The LAPD, by contrast, could be best symbolized by its helicopters patrolling the endless expanses of the Plains of Id, nocturnal dragonflies scanning the inky blackness below with powerful searchlights. Whether by day or night, the staccato chop of the LAPD helicopters, seen or only heard overhead, reminded one and all that the City of Angels was under the jurisdiction of an authority—flying overhead, moving through the city in patrol cars and on motorcycles—that at once was, and was not, part of the city.

To suggest that the San Francisco Police Department was a little more *gemütlich* than its counterpart in the Southland was not to imply that San Francisco did not have crime, or that its cops were not called upon, all too frequently, to put themselves in harm's way. San Francisco had gangs and gangbanging, murders, rapes, and robberies in ample measure. Whole areas of the city, in fact—Bayview Hunters Point, Ingleside, Western Addition, the outer Sunset—could be just as dangerous as any of the mean streets of Los Angeles. San Francisco had a mass murder in this period: the gunning down of eight victims in one law firm in a high-rise at 101 California Street on July 1, 1993, by a fifty-nine-year-old dissatisfied client, Gian Luigi Ferri, armed with semiautomatic assault weapons. It was the worst mass killing in the history of the city. San Francisco even had what could be termed a terrorist attack: this against the Pacific Gas & Electric Company in late October 1997, which left one-third of the city dark through the night and into the early-morning hours. Yet San Franciscans liked to think that their crime problems more typically consisted of such wacky events as the poisoning of pigeons with strychnine-laced birdseed by some anonymous pigeon hater or the time, on November 7, 1998, that Mayor Brown, holding a press conference in the civic center, was hit from the front and both sides in a three-pronged pie attack—cherry, tofu crème, and pumpkin—by members of the Biotic Baking Brigade, an informal collective of homeless advocates protesting evictions and Brown's alleged continuing of his predecessor Frank Jordan's Matrix program against the homeless.

San Francisco's sense of itself as a lovable and fun place, however, suffered a setback on January 26, 2001. That day, a most gruesome killing occurred in the fashionable Pacific Heights district: the mauling to death in the corridor outside her apartment of Diane Whipple, thirty-three, a lacrosse coach at St. Mary's College across the Bay in Moraga, by a Presa Canario–English mastiff owned by a husband-and-wife team of lawyers, Marjorie Knoller and Robert Noel, living on the same floor. Knoller and Noel had been keeping two Presa Canario crosses in their apartment for some months, and the animals had already terrified many in the neighborhood. As lawyers, Knoller and Noel had been representing convict members of the white supremacist Aryan Brotherhood prison gang confined to the maximum security facility at Pelican Bay. One of these convicts, Paul Schneider, whom Knoller and Noel had adopted, was the actual owner of the two animals, Bane and Hera, which Schneider had bred and trained as attack dogs through outside contacts, as both a business and a cultish activity centered on the viciousness of the animals. So brutal had been the attack on Whipple, police responding to the scene had requested counseling.

In the weeks that followed, as the case went before the grand jury, Knoller and Noel showed no remorse: indeed, they faced the press with arrogant assurance and went so far as to suggest in a nationally televised interview that the victim was at fault because the perfume she was wearing had enraged the dogs. Indicted on charges of second-degree murder (Knoller) and involuntary manslaughter (Noel), the pair continued to protest their innocence and even to compare themselves, when their home was searched under subpoena, to other Jewish victims of police persecution. The trial, in any event, while remaining under the jurisdiction of the superior court of San Francisco, was moved to Los Angeles and tried before a local jury. On March 21, 2002, Marjorie Knoller was convicted of second-degree murder and her husband of involuntary manslaughter. Each was facing stiff prison sentences, although Judge James Warren later reduced Knoller's conviction to involuntary manslaughter, which carried a maximum sentence of four years. Would other cities have allowed Knoller and Noel to parade such vicious animals up and down the streets without there being some form of intervention? Was the much-vaunted tolerance of San Francisco just another name for indifference?

The crimes of Los Angeles, up to and including homicide, came in three categories: gang related, robbery related, and *L.A. Confidential*—which is to say, pulp-fiction crimes that seemed to be writing themselves as set-in-LA detective stories or movie scripts. Metropolitan Los Angeles, among other things, had always been about murder, whether in fact, fiction, or on the silver screen. The year 1991 alone witnessed 2,401 corpses wheeled into the county coroner's office, an average of 6.6 a day, all victims of homicide. The next year, in one weekend in late August, twenty-seven citizens met their deaths within a sixty-hour period. The causes of death ranged from gangbanging (instances too numerous to mention); robbery (Tony Proxmire, forty-three, for example, shot to death on the floor of his restaurant in Long Beach); domestic disputes (including a quarrel at a Little League game in Eagle Rock Park); and the hard-to-classify case of Edward Kislo, fifty, an off-duty LAPD detective fatally shot while investigating reports of a prowler in his neighbor's backyard in Palms. Gang-related killings continued down the decade, most of them so accepted as part of daily life that they only rated two or three lines in the back pages of the newspaper, although some killings did deserve and sometimes get more ink. Even a twelve-year-old girl, abducted off the street by men in a van while walking with both grandparents in South Central, warranted only a half-dozen lines; and it took the slaying in Inglewood of three brothers—none of them gang members—in two separate incidents in early October 2001 to rate seven inches of type.

On the other hand, there were the made-for-movies crimes from real life that seemed to blend the lines between truth and fiction: the death by gunfire in January 2000 of international career criminal Daniel Walcott, seventy-three, and his Miami attorney, Richard Reynolds, seventy-two—two over-the-hill guys who should have known better—shot to death in a dead-end street off the Avenue 43 exit in Montecito Heights northeast of Chinatown, as they were frantically trying to make a U-turn, by much younger Latino men in a drug deal gone awry. A former airline pilot with an aristocratic manner, speaking several languages and knowing his wines, Walcott had been moving in international jet-set circles ever since the 1950s. He had been profiled in *Time* magazine in 1996 as an international wheeler-dealer straight from a movie script. By 2000, he should have long since retired. But Walcott was looking for one last score, and he and his partner met a swift end near Pasadena, following a freeway chase.

The line between street violence and film street violence was getting more difficult to discern. In February 1997, the two bank robbers who held police at bay in North Hollywood with high-powered assault weapons had motivated themselves, in part, by viewing a video of the movie *Heat* (1995), a very violent film about bank robbers carrying assault weapons. In the initial phases of the North Hollywood shootout, a passerby could understandably assume that a movie was being filmed. On any given day, after all, films depicting various degrees of mayhem were being made on the streets of Los Angeles. Moviemakers were specifically exempted by the city council in December 1997 from an ordinance restricting the use of assault weapons within city limits. And, conversely, many Hollywood types were, to put the matter simply, gun-crazy. "I would feel very naked," noted actor Charlton Heston in May 1992, "without a 12-gauge shotgun under my bed and a .38-caliber revolver in the drawer of my night table."[22]

So, too, was the LAPD intrinsically cinematic. Perhaps it had begun with the *Dragnet* series, starring Jack Webb, in the 1950s and 1960s, which Chief William Parker had enthusiastically sponsored as presenting an image of the LAPD as fair, tough, incorruptible. Given the intensities of LA noir—meaning criminal Los Angeles, fact and fiction—the image established by Webb as Sergeant Joe Friday was replaced in the 1990s by a near obsession with the LAPD as some form of corrupt conspiracy. Throughout the decade, Hollywood released a number of films—*Devil in a Blue Dress* (1995), *Mulholland Falls* (1996), *L.A. Confidential* (1997)—in which the LAPD was starring in one way or another as the villain. Films were only reflecting the steady decline in reputation of this once elite and reputable force, as in the era of Chief Parker and Sergeant Friday.

Slowly, through the late 1960s and 1970s, the covenant between the LAPD and the people of the city had begun to unravel. The citizenry, for one thing, had changed. They were no longer a predominantly white population preferring to let the LAPD keep undesirables—too frequently, that meant minorities—in check. Now the people were minorities themselves, and the LAPD was increasingly being staffed by white officers living in the suburbs. The covenant, the mandate to keep LA in check, did not totally disappear, but it grew contradictory and at cross-purposes. The 1991 Christopher Commission report revealed an LAPD riddled with contempt for significant portions of the city—the minority portions, that is; "gorillas in the mist" was one especially offensive epithet used by officers over the radio—and a grinding, cynical attitude toward the populace at large. Then came the riots of 1992, in which the LAPD failed to live up to a fundamental tenet of the covenant, to keep the city from destroying itself, which had been a fear of Los Angeles since the 1920s. Even worse, the minorities whom so many frontline officers held in contempt had in the course of the riots, initially at least, outperformed the LAPD, forcing the police withdrawal from Florence and Normandie in South Central, and allowing the riot to spread to the rest of the city.

Even deputy chief Matthew Hunt was willing to admit, shortly after the riot, that the initial deployment of the LAPD at the riot flashpoint was something right out of *The Gang That Couldn't Shoot Straight*. Fire chief Donald Manning complained bitterly about the lack of police protection for firefighters. Even a justice of the state supreme court, Armand Arabian, breaking precedent, openly criticized the police. "Where was the protection and service?" the justice, a longtime Los Angeles trial judge, asked. "Any slower response and we would have seen photos of policemen pasted on milk containers and listed as missing."[23]

In 1992, LAPD chief Daryl Gates took his retirement under less than favorable circumstances, and Mayor Bradley and his police commission turned to an outsider, Willie L. Williams, an African American from Philadelphia, to head the department. Inheriting a force alienated from its constituency, Williams embarked on an ambitious program of community-based policing emphasizing foot patrols, an increase in female officers, systematic liaison with neighborhood groups, and even, in the San Fernando Valley, the Volunteer Surveillance Program, in which community members, perching in the dark on rooftops or crouching in vacant apartments, peering through shrouded windows, recorded drug deals in progress with cameras, camcorders, and notebooks, and, if appropriate, radioed patrolling officers to make arrests. The very technique that had recorded the Rodney King beating—a handheld camcorder—was now being used to document drug deals and facilitate arrests.

While committed to community-based policing, Chief Williams also pursued another technique—a massive show of force—to deal with a volatile city approaching the second Rodney King verdict. The 1992 riot had gotten out of hand because the department could not deploy itself rapidly and in concentrated formations. But when the second verdict was announced, Williams had 6,500 officers on the street. It was the biggest show of police force in Los Angeles history, and had the verdict gone against the prosecution, this massive deployment would have most likely saved Los Angeles from a second riot. Displays of force in such numbers, as evidenced in the response of the LAPD to the King verdict, were a double-edged, Janus-faced paradox. They offered comfort that there was no riot. But they also brought back, even more powerfully, an awareness that Los Angeles was a volatile entity that only a paramilitary force could control.

Richard Riordan understood that his paramilitary force had reestablished its covenant with the majority of the city, who had no desire to see Los Angeles go up in flames. Running for mayor against Woo, Riordan promised that one of the ways he would be tough enough to turn Los Angeles around would be to put a thousand more cops on the streets. Unfortunately, almost the first thing the police did after Riordan became mayor was to go out on strike. On the first day of the strike, 248 officers—45 percent of the 548 scheduled to report to day watch duty—called in sick. Nearly a third of the traffic officers assigned to the San Fernando Valley failed to show up for work. The Rampart division had one of the highest sick-out rates—the Blue Flu, it was called—in the department. When Riordan spoke to a gathering of striking officers at the Wilshire-Ebell Theater, he was interrupted with boos and shouts. He wanted to give them a raise, Riordan tried to say, but "the city is facing the gravest financial situation since the Great Depression."[24]

Chief Williams, meanwhile, remained an outsider within the department. He also lost the confidence of Riordan and the police commission and was not renewed for a second term. In 1992, Riordan and the commission appointed an insider as chief, Bernard C. Parks, an African American, who represented the best possibilities of the LAPD in its finer days—when Parks, a thirty-two-year veteran of the department, had begun his career. In appointing Parks, Riordan and the commission were going, in a certain sense, back to the future. Parks embodied the minority nature of Los Angeles and the increasingly minority nature of the LAPD. Tall, lean, command-

ing, voted by *People* magazine as one of the fifty most beautiful people in
the nation, a graduate and postgraduate of the USC School of Public
Administration, Parks was in public relations terms straight from central
casting. While a backer of community-based policing, he also embodied the
austerity and esprit de corps of the Parker era. In time, his detractors would
describe him as a black Daryl Gates, by which they meant that Parks was
first, last, and always a department man, playing it by the book. There was
much truth to this claim; but Parks was better educated than Gates and better able to conceal, behind a demeanor restrained to the point of iciness,
whatever resentments he had picked up along the way. That such a chief, so
devoted to the LAPD as an institution, should have the CRASH scandal at
Rampart station surface on his watch was indeed a tragic irony. But it got
even worse, in a way that underscored the fundamentally dangerous nature
of the city. Parks's own granddaughter, a college student one day short of
her twenty-first birthday, was shot to death on a Sunday evening in late May
2000 by a gang member targeting her companion as she sat next to him in a
car parked in front of Popeye's Chicken & Biscuits at La Brea Avenue and
Jefferson Boulevard.

Parks spent the last three years of the decade struggling to deflect what
he considered a growing number of intrusions into the longtime autonomy
of his department. In this rearguard action he was joined by the mayor, who
refused, despite Rampart, to break openly with the LAPD. Riordan had
been good to the department, buffing its budget with federal funds, bringing
its strength to 9,760 sworn officers. As the Rampart scandal unfolded, however, Parks himself came under attack. Day after day, columnists and editorial writers were hammering away at Parks and the department, calling for
reform. The Justice Department sent out investigators from Washington and
began dropping less-than-subtle hints that it was planning to sue the city in
federal court for systemic and repeated violations of civil rights by the
LAPD. The inspector general of Los Angeles, Jeffrey Eglash, received
complaints of police misconduct, which Parks claimed Eglash had no
authority to get. City Attorney James Hahn backed Eglash, as did the police
commission, which saw in the city attorney's opinion an opportunity to
regain control of the department from Parks, who, like Horatio at the
bridge, had been fighting off any and all efforts at a civilian takeover, even
an investigation of the LAPD. Parks was convinced that the department
could clean its own house, and Riordan backed Parks in the belief.

The U.S. Justice Department, meanwhile, continued to press its case for
a court-supervised consent decree that would allow it to monitor the LAPD.
Riordan and Parks resisted this proposal and insisted that it was the prerogative of the LAPD to investigate the Rampart scandal. At the least, Parks

argued, the LAPD should be allowed to complete its own inquiry before Justice Department investigators entered the case. Parks and Riordan, as they saw it, were fighting a rearguard action on behalf of the autonomy of not only the LAPD but of Los Angeles itself. What could be more humiliating, more provincializing, than to have the Justice Department take over the single most powerful agency in city government and, by implication, bring all of Los Angeles into receivership?

At this point, almost as if by design, the LAPD—plagued by the Rampart scandal, bedeviled by a number of shocking shootings, castigated by pundits as an out-of-control department no better than it was in 1991 when the Christopher Commission report disclosed its shortcomings—was given a chance by the Democratic National Convention, held in Los Angeles in mid-August of 2000, to make a show of force that, among other things, re-reminded the people of Los Angeles just exactly who, when the chips were down, was in charge. For the better part of a week, beginning on August 13, 2000, downtown Los Angeles and the area surrounding the nearby Staples Center was empty of ordinary life. In its place ensued an almost choreographed encounter between protesters and phalanxes of helmeted LAPD legionnaires in full riot gear. In the weeks before the convention, Parks, determined not to repeat the mistakes of his counterpart in Seattle when anarchists disrupted a meeting of the World Trade Organization, brought his department to full-scale riot alert for an entire week.

Just how prepared the LAPD was for mass action became evident Saturday morning when a handful of activists, unloading 553 wooden crosses at the First United Methodist Church on Flower Street near the Staples Center (each cross representing an immigrant who had died in the desert trying to get to California), found themselves suddenly surrounded by fifty police officers in twenty-five police cars. Fortunately, the demonstrators had a lawyer with them, who convinced an arriving police captain that they were acting within their constitutional rights. Not so fortunate was Sean Biener, a protester from Salt Lake City dressed as a pig. As supporters stood nearby chanting "Meat is murder," Biener unloaded a dump truck of manure in front of the Wilshire Grand Hotel on Figueroa. A handcuffed Biener, still wearing his pig suit, was hauled off for booking on suspicion of felony vandalism.

It was a humorous image, a man in a pig costume being cuffed by two determined LAPD officers; but there was little humor in the days that followed as, time and again, LAPD riot squads went into action against protesters. Especially violent was a Monday-night confrontation after a Rage Against the Machine concert directly across from Staples Center, after which some protesters tried to storm a chain-link fence being used to create a cordon sanitaire in front of the convention center and were repelled by riot police using pepper spray and rubber bullets. In defense of the police, it had to be noted that certain bandanna-wearing, black-clad anarchists in the crowd, in addition to charging at the fence, were throwing garbage and pieces of concrete at the police. Yet it also had to be said that, whether justified or not, phalanx after phalanx of officers in riot gear asserted and reasserted continuing and continuous authority over every demonstration, whether disruptive or peaceful, throughout the four days of the convention. Backers of the police could point to the provocative behavior of the so-called anarchists. Critics of the police, including a reporter or two who were beaten, could also see a display of uniformed dominance that virtually eliminated any legitimate protest. In the context of the Rampart scandal, moreover, it could also be speculated that the LAPD was welcoming an opportunity to reassert itself through a show of force: to remind citizens of the city—who were staying away from downtown and the convention area in droves—that the LAPD might be down, but it was still an awesome institution demanding and commanding obedience. Deploying platoons of baton-wielding legionaries in riot gear, emptying the city of demonstrators, turning the area around the convention center into a moonscape, the LAPD reminded one and all that, Rampart notwithstanding, the long blue line still ruled.

The triumph of the LAPD, however, was brief. Four months later, Richard Riordan signed a consent decree with the Department of Justice. The LAPD was now under the supervision of a federal judge.

Place

San Francisco spent the 1990s in an epic of construction centered on its waterfront and downtown, an epic whose planning premises could be traced to the 1950s. San Francisco had a clear idea of itself as a city classically centered on its waterfront and downtown spaces. Los Angeles, by contrast, spent the same decade struggling to recover—if only on the level of planning—a renewed sense of downtown identity. In 1957 the city repealed its long-standing thirteen-story height limit on new construction, which had been designed to keep the twenty-eight-story city hall the dominant downtown building. The removal of this restriction made possible something that Los Angeles had never had: a high-rise district downtown. Over the next twenty-five years, a cluster of steel and glass towers, both commercial and residential, rose to the west of the existent downtown, culminating in the seventy-three-story First Interstate World Center at the southern base of Bunker Hill, the tallest building west of Chicago and the eighth tallest high-rise in the nation. Just as city hall had served as the signature building for the television series *Dragnet* in the 1950s and 1960s, this new skyline was featured prominently in the opening credits of the television show *L.A. Law* as the new signature image of the city.

As so frequently was the case in the development of Los Angeles over time, however, the existing downtown was not rebuilt. It was merely left behind in favor of the new high-rise district to the west. The migration of professional and commercial enterprises to the towers at the base of, and atop, Bunker Hill left the old downtown—centered on Main, Spring, Broadway, Hill, Olive, Grand, between Pershing Square and the Civic Center—an increasingly abandoned place, as building after building, so many of them architecturally distinguished midrises in the Italian Renaissance style from the 1920s, became progressively empty above the first floor, with the first floor itself occupied by marginal enterprises or merely boarded up. To do business in the early and mid-1990s in the eastern part of downtown Los Angeles—much less to live there, as a number of loft-dwelling artists were trying to do—was, according to Tracy Lovejoy, director of the Central City East Association, similar to living in a Third World country (although such a comparison might be unfair to much of the Third World). "On the corner of Fifth and Crocker Streets, at any time of the day," Lovejoy noted, "you can find anywhere from 50 to 100 people milling about. Open trash bins have turned into bonfires. People have created a sort of tent village. There are tents or cardboard homes leaning against the sides of buildings. You have people walking by selling drugs. You have prostitutes trying to make money. There is a sense of unreality that you are in the downtown of the city of Los Angeles."[25]

Nor was the nearby Civic Center any safer. The homeless were especially fond of the lawns in front of city hall, and sneak thieves, whether homeless or housed, entered the building and roamed its corridors. In 1992 an estimated $250,000 worth of property—computers, cell phones, vacuum cleaners, cameras, briefcases, and other forms of personal property, even unopened bottles of liquor from the press room—disappeared from the city's central administrative complex. Panhandlers were known to wander the corridors, putting the touch on civil servants working at their desks.

In the mid-1980s the California Redevelopment Agency spent $27 million creating the Los Angeles Theatre Center in a reconverted office building on Spring Street in hopes that it would serve as the catalyst for other theaters, together with restaurants, cafés, and bookstores, to locate nearby. But the center closed its doors in mid-October 1991, and Spring Street grew more forlorn than ever. The nearby Clifton's Cafeteria on Olive had in the 1950s served between ten thousand and fifteen thousand meals per day to workers and shoppers at the nearby Robinsons and Bullocks department stores. Now these stores were empty, and Clifton's stood silent behind a wall of concertina wire.

Ironically—and quite significantly, in a sociological sense—immigrant Los Angeles found in these midrise buildings exactly what it was looking for: space, plenty of space, at cheap rates for the manufacturing of clothing and toys. While more ambitious and subsidized proposals faltered, immigrant-owned companies, mostly Asian and Latino, moved into these former office buildings and started to cut, sew, and make things. The sixty-seven-year-old Financial Center Building on Spring Street, once known as the Wall Street of Southern California, filled up with sewing shops. Certain critics, as might be expected, were abashed that what they considered little more than sweatshops should be proliferating through the downtown, and there were a number of efforts to regulate the area, and, more importantly, to contain the growth; but in the 1990s the garment district evolved into an officially recognized fashion district, with its own Fashion Institute of Design and Merchandising in brand-new buildings at the corner of Ninth and Grand. So, too, had a jewelry district and a toy district arisen in the central and eastern downtown: a multiplicity of smaller immigrant-owned enterprises that the existing stock of aging but serviceable midrises suited to a T.

In the fall of 1993, the Community Redevelopment Agency of Los Angeles issued a Downtown Strategic Plan that envisioned the downtown, not as something to be redeveloped through grandiose top-down schemes, but as a zone to be nurtured as authentic local life reinhabited and revitalized the district. The downtown, taken totally—from Chinatown through the El Pueblo Historic Park district, the Union Station transportation and transfer district, the Civic Center, Little Tokyo, Bunker Hill, the financial district, the jewelry district, South Park, and USC/Exposition Park on the Figueroa corridor—remained, for all its problems, a formidable urban complex that required localized revitalization as opposed to big-concept development. The downtown, noted USC dean of architecture Robert Harris, was an assemblage of patches that required stitching into a quilt.

Tax revenues allowed state of California real estate official Daniel Rosenfeld to lead a $245.9 million effort to bring 3,500 state workers into the center of downtown Los Angeles along Fourth Street between Broadway and Spring. Rosenfeld proposed the buying and refurbishing of three historic buildings in the vicinity of the Ronald Reagan State Office Building on Main Street and the construction of one new office tower. "I'm very impressed," noted Linda Dishman, executive director of the Los Angeles Conservancy, of the state proposal, which was ready by the year 2000. "The state seldom takes the long view of things. In this, they have not only the sense of saving individual buildings, but of how to make this a more livable city."[26] Public funds also made possible the half-billion-dollar, 870,000-square-foot Los Angeles Convention Center on fifty-four acres along Figueroa, designed by James Ingo Freed of New York and opening in 1994. The gigantic center, which spurred the construction of fifteen hundred new hotel rooms in the adjacent area, was intended, in part, to function as the first phase of a connection along the Figueroa corridor between downtown and the USC/Exposition Park coliseum complex.

The next extension down the Figueroa corridor, built with private funds, was Staples Center: a twenty-thousand-seat sports and entertainment arena, home to two basketball teams, the Lakers and the Clippers, and to the Kings hockey team. Opening with a Bruce Springsteen concert on October 17, 1999, and a hockey game between the Kings and the Boston Bruins on October 20 (Mayor Richard Riordan had already suited up and tested the ice), the Staples Center, a state-of-the-art complex and eerily beautiful in a *Star Trek* sort of way, was soon attracting large crowds into downtown for more than 230 events a year.

Encouraged by the success of the center, its owners, including billionaires Rupert Murdoch and Philip Anschutz, organized a development company and secured permission from the city council to develop around the center what the group described as a Times Square West. The proposed $1 billion complex would include two hotels, with a total of eighteen hundred rooms, a seven-thousand-seat theater for live performances, 250,000 square feet of office space, eight hundred residential units, shops, restaurants, nightclubs, and parking for 7,500 cars in a number of structures. In the spring of 2002, an overlapping affiliated group of investors won city council approval for a $450 million football stadium, to be built with private funds on public property near Staples Center. Shortly thereafter, the stadium proposal fizzled; yet on the level of proposals and permissions, at least, some very major investors were betting on the notion that sports and celebrity entertainment, together with the adjacent convention center, could not only bring people to downtown Los Angeles, but keep them there as well.

Bringing people downtown and keeping them there: for years, that was what promoters of downtown Los Angeles had been trying to do, with mixed results. Downtown needed between 150,000 and 300,000 new permanent residents to ensure vitality on its streets. True, the convention center and Staples Center were bringing people downtown, just as Dodger Stadium had been bringing people to Chavez Ravine for nearly four decades, but was anyone sticking around after the game or the show? The Music Center, opening in 1964 atop Bunker Hill, had long been attracting large crowds to the Dorothy Chandler Pavilion, home of the Los Angeles Philharmonic and the Los Angeles Opera Company, the Mark Taper Forum, and the Ahmanson Theater. Yet there had been little discernible effect on the surrounding neighborhood of dreary government buildings and parking lots. One restaurant served the entire complex, and after performances the underground parking lot became an Indianapolis Speedway of roaring engines and screeching tires as arts lovers, facing a long drive home, raced each other to the exit gates.

Still, the notion that art—as either design or performance, or a combination thereof—could center a city in its downtown and reurbanize abandoned or lifeless urban places was a notion that did not die easily, for it was connected in some deep and compelling way with the power of art in public places as revealed in the great cities of Europe and, to a lesser extent, in other leading American metropolises. Pershing Square, for example, was where Los Angeles had localized itself in the 1870s and where downtown had remained centered into the 1950s. To revive the forlorn and gang-ridden area in the early 1990s, the city turned to Mexican architect Ricardo Legorreta, who redesigned the square into a bright and colorful postmodernist Mexican plaza whose flamboyant aesthetics represented an eruption—welcomed by some, not by others—of Mexican sensibility in the second largest Mexican city.

The forthcoming Walt Disney Concert Hall, designed by Frank Gehry, argued Joanne Kozberg, president and chief executive officer of the Music Center, had to be seen in the context of all Bunker Hill development—not only Gehry's Walt Disney Concert Hall, future home of the Los Angeles Philharmonic, but also the Roman Catholic Cathedral of Our Lady of the Angels designed by Spanish architect José Rafael Moneo, on time for its dedication in September 2002; the Museum of Contemporary Art, designed by Arata Isozaki, further down Grand Avenue; the restored and expanded Richard J. Riordan Central Library at the base of Bunker Hill; and the Spanish Steps leading up into the California Plaza; and just down Bunker Hill, Civic Center itself, with its array of public buildings, including the newly restored city hall, the *Los Angeles Times* building, and the Japanese-American National Museum in the adjacent Little Tokyo. What was needed, Kozberg believed, was a scheme unifying all these facilities into one compelling urban place. After preliminary studies were completed by urban designer Doug Suisman, setting forth the general direction of the plan, a team of international heavyweights that included Gehry, Isozaki, Moneo, and Laurie Olin (responsible for the landscaping of Getty Center) gathered in the summer of 2000 for a charette leading to the production of, on paper at least, one of the boldest proposals for integrated open space ever to be launched in the history of the city. Among other things, the plan, costing approximately $50 million in its first phase, would reconfigure Grand Avenue into a serpentine pedestrian-friendly Avenue of the Arts, integrating a network of cultural, public, and, in the case of the cathedral, religious structures. The first floor of the Music Center, now a street-deadening wall of concrete surrounding a parking level, would be blasted through, and an entirely new area of restaurants and retail would be created, together with a new lower plaza and performance space. Most breathtaking of all, a twenty-acre urban park, graced by fountains, trees, plazas, and clusters of public seating, would sweep down from Bunker Hill through the Civic Center to city hall.

But would people come? Yes, Kozberg argued. The performing arts were already accounting for most of those arriving downtown after five p.m. But would they use the public spaces evoked in the Music Center proposal? Yes, if they were there in the first place. The solution was housing, up to 300,000 units. Then pedestrian traffic would come from downtown itself. Developer Tom Gilmore, a charismatic visionary from New York—a foolhardy visionary, some would say—was committing himself to buying as many old downtown buildings as he could get financing for ($170 million by the summer of 2001) and reconverting them into lofts and apartments, hoping that if he built them, they would come.

The Los Angeles–based architect and urban planner Jon Jerde believed they would come—if they had fun once they got there. As a designer (Horton Plaza in San Diego, a raft of temporary structures and spaces for the 1984 Olympics, CityWalk at Universal City, the Mall of America in Minnesota, Canal City in Fukuoka, the Beursplein in Rotterdam, the Bellagio in Las Vegas), Jerde was the preeminent Los Angeles master of managed urban spaces. Opening in 1992 on a hilltop in Universal City overlooking the Hollywood freeway, Jerde's Universal CityWalk, a $100 million venture of MCA Development, part of a larger Entertainment City that the company planned to build over time, was taken to task by a number of highbrow critics as a faux Los Angeles, a Los Angeles lite. It was, they argued, little more than a gated theme park pretending to offer an authentic Los Angeles experience. Precisely, defenders of Universal CityWalk replied. The four-block strand of shops, restaurants, theaters, and offices was exactly that: a managed and safe City of Angels.

Pedestrian values and downtown orientation came more easily in San Francisco, given the relative intimacy of its 1847 grid. The design team at Johnson Fain Partners—interestingly enough, a Los Angeles–based firm—were taking the fifty-*vara* lot of mid-nineteenth-century San Francisco (the Spanish *vara* equaled thirty-three inches) and using this pedestrian- and density-friendly divisional unit as the basis for their plan for Mission Bay, a 313-acre, $4 billion project intended to transform long-neglected Bayside properties of the Southern Pacific Railroad into an entirely new master-planned district of a proposed six thousand housing units, commercial space, retail and restaurants, a biotechnology park, and a forty-three-acre campus for the University of California. The idea of using the fifty-*vara* lot as the basis of Mission Bay had first been proposed by UC Berkeley architecture professor Daniel Solomon in 1987 after more large-scale modernist proposals by John Carl Warnecke (1980) and I. M. Pei (1985) had been rejected for their sheer gigantism.

Two forces—scale and intimacy—were coalescing to create the Mission Bay prototype. Scale came from the publicly traded Catellus Corporation, the largest private landowner and developer in California, formed in 1990 from the Santa Fe Pacific Corporation, which transferred to Catellus the combined land assets of the Santa Fe and the Southern Pacific Railroads in California. Headed by Nelson Rising, a lawyer-developer from Los Angeles, Catellus was in many ways *the* development game in California, with Mission Bay, the 840-acre Pacific Commons Business Park in Fremont, some ninety-five acres in downtown Los Angeles, centered on Union Station, and a fourteen-acre development property adjacent to the Santa Fe Depot in downtown San Diego. So, too, did the design firm chosen by Catellus, Johnson Fain Partners, possess a comparable capacity for large-scale projects, many of them in the Far East, climaxed by its master plan for an entirely new five-hundred-building central business district for Beijing. Whereas Warnecke and Pei had each proposed triumphant statements of mega-modernism centered on high-rise towers of steel and glass, Johnson Fain advocated a multifaceted urban village, rarely more than ten stories high, integrated through linked parks, squares, commons, and green pathways.

The same values of pedestrian intimacy were dominant in architect Joseph Spear's designs for the new Pacific Bell Park at Third and King in the adjacent China Basin that opened in April 2000. Working with a cramped 12.5-acre Bayside site, Spear fashioned for the San Francisco Giants a tight, intimate ballpark reminiscent of Wrigley Field in Chicago or Fenway Park in Boston. As in the case of Mission Bay, the emphasis was on intimacy and pedestrian access. Special permission had to be secured from baseball's National League to allow seats to be so near to the field. A right-field home run only had to travel 306 feet from home plate. If the ball went any farther, it would drop into the bay. Pac Bell Park was the only major league baseball stadium in the nation to be served directly by ferry boats and to have a yacht harbor adjacent to its parking lot.

The intimacy and pedestrian values of Mission Bay and Pac Bell Park were generally sustained in the entire pleasure zone south of Market that had taken nearly twenty years to design and construct. Not that scale was lacking: the George Moscone Convention Center was as capacious as any convention center in the nation. Yet most of it was underground, its great exhibit hall sustained by soaring arches that were themselves kept tense by cables in bow-and-arrow configurations that would allow the center to ride out even the most formidable earthquake. Atop the center flourished Yerba Buena Gardens, an urban resort—a theater, a small concert hall, a children's museum, parks, playgrounds, a nearby cinema complex—inspired by the Tivoli Gardens of Copenhagen. To house the collection of the San Francisco Museum of Modern Art, Swiss architect Mario Botta, working in conjunction with the firm of Hellmuth, Obata & Kassabaum, designed a $60 million, 225,000-square-foot structure, one of the largest museums devoted solely to modern art in America. Merely to walk into Botta's museum, just to ascend or descend its multiple stairways, to cross the transparent bridge that hovered over the great skylit atrium, was to experience a source of delight competitive with the art itself.

Each of these new public places you could get to and enjoy by walking. Such were the gifts of topography and grid in San Francisco. As in the case of downtown, however, what came easily in San Francisco—in this case, the street itself—had to be theorized, planned, designed, and promoted in Los Angeles. The major boulevards and intersecting streets of Los Angeles remained vital in terms of automotive traffic. The challenge was to keep them vital as urban spaces. Wilshire Boulevard, for example—the ur-avenue of Los Angeles, first developed in the 1890s on an east-west axis that had served rancheros and cattlemen since the eighteenth century, not to mention countless generations of Native Americans before them—had in the 1930s developed into the so-called Miracle Mile. Wilshire Boulevard conjoined a newfound delight in the swiftness of automotive travel with the off-street urbanism of such quintessentially pedestrian places as Bullocks Department Store, the May Company, the Park La Brea apartment and townhouse complexes, and the Farmers Market. Indeed, since the 1930s, the Farmers Market, a plazalike open space off Wilshire at Fairfax, had, like the Grand Central Market in the downtown, been offering in its intricate array of eateries, stores, open-air food, and floral stalls a vividly dissenting argument to the notion that Los Angeles was a purely automotive city.

By the 1990s, however, the apartment culture of Wilshire had migrated further west as blocks of ultraluxurious apartment/condominium buildings. The more modest apartment houses in the thirteen square blocks just north of the Miracle Mile, many of them built in the 1920s and 1930s, were being bulldozed at an alarming rate by developers who believed they could re-create in mid-Wilshire the luxury culture of Wilshire West. Late in the decade, plans were announced to dismantle the Farmers Market in favor of a $100 million office and high-end theater, retail, and restaurant complex. Inner Wilshire, just west of MacArthur Park, had already witnessed the closing of the Ambassador Hotel in 1989, the Sheraton Townhouse in 1993, and Bullocks Wilshire in 1993, and had in general been engulfed by the crime-ridden scuzziness of MacArthur Park. Wilshire, in short, was being whiplashed—like Los Angeles itself—by violent juxtapositions of high end and low end, luxury and poverty, Los Angeles as glitz and glamour versus Los Angeles as city of dreadful night.

Adolfo Nodal, meanwhile, general manager of the Los Angeles cultural affairs department, was pushing his Wilshire-related revitalization effort: the relighting of dozens of neon signs along what Nodal had designated the

Historic Wilshire Neon Corridor. Neon had come to Los Angeles in 1923 in the form of three orange and blue signs saying PACKARD atop the dealership owned by Earle C. Anthony, who had first seen neon in Paris in 1922. Over the next two decades, until the neon signs were turned off because of the war, Wilshire Boulevard and the Hollywood area exfoliated in pathways of light that, like Los Angeles itself, were taking simple materials, a glass tube filled with argon gas, and making of them an electric landscape of dreams. Born and raised in Cuba, Nodal had grown up with the magic of nighttime neon in that city and through his LUMENS project (an acronym for Living Urban Museum of Electric and Neon Signs, but also a play on the Latin word *lumen,* meaning light) had convinced the city, for a relatively minor cost of $400,000, to relight dozens of signs along the historic Wilshire neon corridor. In June 1996, the mayor, city council members, and redevelopment officials gathered to throw the switch on twenty-five restored neon signs along the Wilshire corridor. The LUMENS project then moved on to Hollywood, where forty-three surviving relightable neon signs had been located. It was one of the most imaginative and cost-effective redevelopment schemes in Los Angeles history. By 2002, Wilshire Boulevard, Hollywood Boulevard, and Sunset Boulevard were transformed into nighttime pathways of light glowing with the magic of the city and the promises of the night.

Sunset Boulevard, especially the Sunset Strip section in West Hollywood, did not require assistance from the LUMENS project to keep its neon aglow; for the magic had never left this primal boulevard of dreams. Frequented by café society in the 1950s and by trendy young people since that time, Sunset Strip had never lost its glamour or its notoriety, thanks to films such as *The Graduate* (1967) and the 1960s television series *77 Sunset Strip,* or even the 1966 hit song by Buffalo Springfield, "For What It's Worth." Over the years, such places as the Crazy Horse twist club, Sneaky Pete's, and Whisky a Go-Go (the discotheque and performance space that launched the careers of the Byrds, Cream, the Doors, Jimi Hendrix, Otis Redding, the Who, and Led Zeppelin) had kept the Strip at the center of youth consciousness across the world. In 1977 the Comedy Store opened, and the Strip was launched on a twenty-year career as a center of stand-up schtick. In 1982 an Austrian immigrant chef, Wolfgang Puck, opened Spago's on the Strip, and another cycle of celebrity restaurants was launched.

But Sunset was more than the Strip. It was a boulevard that extended between the central city and the sea. Even here, the glamour persisted: the sense of Sunset Boulevard as a street of dreams, cycled from the silent film era into the 1950s in Billy Wilder's *Sunset Boulevard* (1950) and recycled through the 1990s in Andrew Lloyd Webber's musical of the same name. To drive from west to east down Sunset Boulevard via that pathway of neon light was to drive, if only subliminally, into the very heart of the mystery of Los Angeles in all its magic and noir.

Reaching midcity, Sunset Boulevard encountered less glamorous but even funky and still compelling portions of the city. The Echo Park district, with its Angelus Temple, reverberated with memories of Aimee Semple McPherson and the Folks she ministered to. Here also, the Episcopal diocese had decided to make its stand, bringing to completion in the 1990s a cathedral and administrative complex on Echo Lake. A few times a week, the erudite Episcopal bishop of Los Angeles, the Right Reverend Frederick Borsch, a noted scripture scholar and former dean of the chapel at Princeton, would make his way up the few blocks to Sunset Boulevard to do his official entertaining at the Brothers Taix, a restaurant with taproots in the 1890s. Here the cuisine, French provençal, was steady and certain, and the wine cellar one of the best in the city.

The nearby Silver Lake district off Sunset was centered in part on Millie's at 3524 Sunset Boulevard, a 1940s-style eatery famous for its meatloaf, chili, Devil's Mess (spicy scrambled eggs), extra-strong coffee, three-inch-thick slices of fruit pie, and bread pudding, together with rude waitresses wont to ring a cowbell and shout at demanding patrons, "Problem customer!" and a jukebox blasting rockabilly and reggae. The conjunction of city workers, movie lot techies, punkers, bohemians, and Silver Lake residents (these last two were often one and the same) in this unaccountably popular un-air-conditioned café testified (as did Taix a few blocks to the west) to the persistence of community in a city that could so often be such a lonely place.

How to bring back vitality like this to an embattled district was the essential question facing Hollywood through the decade. Hollywood was not a city. It was a district of Los Angeles, although there were those wanting to follow the San Fernando Valley into secessionism and, it was hoped, civic independence. Yet even as a part, not the whole, of Los Angeles, Hollywood was making a subliminal statement on behalf of the entire city as a place of glamour and dreams; and so when it devolved, beginning in the 1980s, into a shabby war zone of T-shirt stores and substandard honky-tonk, it became a matter of concern for the entire city. Some twenty million tourists a year came to Hollywood in pursuit of glamour and dreams, and, after reading the names of the stars on the Walk of Fame in front of Mann's (nee Grauman's) Chinese Theatre and perhaps buying a T-shirt, they were being prompted to ask, à la Peggy Lee, is that all there is? True, the restaurant Musso & Frank sustained the ambience of the old city, and Paramount still had its studios there; but it had become increasingly difficult to reconcile Hollywood the dream with Hollywood the semi-slum.

The revitalization of Hollywood that began in the 1990s involved a variety of approaches, many of them imported from New York City. First of all, a coalition of business owners organized the Hollywood Entertainment District in 1996 and began privately to police and clean up the streets, taking back Hollywood Boulevard from the assorted sociopaths who had held it hostage during the previous decade. By 1998 violent crime had dropped 38 percent, the streets were clean, and graffiti abated. The next step was redevelopment.

Enter David Malmuth, a veteran of the revitalization of Times Square properties, including the New Amsterdam Theater, by the Disney Corporation. A patient, persistent, unpretentious developer-politician of extraordinary skill, Malmuth had a mantra: Bring the Academy Awards back to Hollywood, where they had not been since 1960. Malmuth's goal embodied a metaphor of all that was lacking in Hollywood, its onetime glamour as the center of the film industry. Rebuffed by Michael Eisner of Disney, who saw the Hollywood challenge as a real estate challenge and not an entertainment one (and besides, Disney was also in the process of redeveloping the El Capitan Theater), Malmuth linked up with the megabuck San Diego–based, Canadian-owned TrizecHahn Corporation, a builder of malls worldwide, and—with the support of City Councilwoman Jackie Goldberg, who represented the blighted district—patiently assembled a $615 million development package, including $90 million of public funds ($60 million for a six-level, three-thousand-car underground parking garage, $30 million toward the Kodak Theatre). By the end of the decade, TrizecHahn was constructing a shopping and entertainment center at the corner of Hollywood Boulevard and Highland Avenue that included the 640-room Renaissance Hollywood Hotel, decorated in the style of the 1950s, sixty shops and restaurants, a fourteen-screen movie complex, and the sumptuous 3,600-seat Kodak Theatre, built expressly to house the Academy Awards. Opening in early November 2001, Hollywood & Highland, as the development was officially named, greeted visitors via a grand staircase ascending toward a replication of the Babylonian gates from D. W. Griffith's *Intolerance* (1916), including its two gigantic elephants.

Other Hollywood developments included the restoration of the nearby Pantages Theatre, which opened with *The Lion King* at the end of the decade, and the refurbishing of the Egyptian Theatre as the American Cinematheque, featuring a full program of classic films dating from the invention of the medium. Art galleries started moving to Hollywood from the crime-ridden arts zone downtown, beginning with Los Angeles Contemporary Exhibitions, which relocated to Hollywood Boulevard in April 1993. The Metropolitan Transportation Authority (MTA) was doing its best to enhance public art in the region with the installation in the Red Line Hollywood Station of commuter shelters in the shape of the now vanished Brown Derby restaurant, a tiny Chinese theater, and a stretch limo. The entrance to the subway elevator was designed to resemble a 1920s movie palace.

Terminating in North Hollywood on the other side of the Santa Monica Mountains, the MTA Red Line linked Hollywood with its transmontane sister district, which was in the process of recasting itself as NoHo, the Los Angeles equivalent of the artsy SoHo district in New York, including the formally designated NoHo Arts District intended to attract some of the flourishing little-theater companies in the region. For years, the California Redevelopment Agency had been planning big things, and spending millions of dollars in the process, in hopes of revitalizing North Hollywood centered on the intersection of Lankershim and Magnolia Boulevards. Of all the CRA proposals—the hotel, the office buildings, the street-level mall, the creation of pedestrian walking and shopping zones, the construction of seven hundred residential units including twin towers with 320 units for seniors—little, if anything, had been realized by the millennium. But North Hollywood was on the mend. Younger people, many of them employed in motion pictures, had decided that they wanted to live there: wanted, that is, to purchase one or another of the charming and serviceable homes in he area, built between the 1930s and the 1950s and ranging in price, until late in the decade, from an affordable $100,000 to $200,000. Those resettling North Hollywood, many of them couples with children, wanted to repossess for themselves the very same dream of life in one's own home, with a front and back yard, in a tree- and hedge-laden district, that had made North Hollywood so popular with the middle class in the years following World War II.

It took people, in short—people living there, walking there, relating to others there—to revitalize a district. Including people coming to party. That is what made the English-born Chris Breed a key player in the effort to revitalize Hollywood. The founder in 1990 of the world-famous Roxbury on Sunset Strip, perhaps the hottest nightclub in the nation since Studio 54 (and inspiring frequent mentions on the television program *Saturday Night Live,* together with a spinoff movie), Breed brought his expertise to Hollywood in the late 1990s with the opening of the Sunset Room and, in early 2001, the Pig 'n Whistle on Sunset Boulevard. There were already a number of flourishing spots in the area (the Garden of Eden, Lucky Seven, the Opium Den, the Knitting Factory, the Room, the Burgundy Room, El Camino, the Beauty Bar), but the arrival of Breed—a former model in London and Paris, a rugby blue with a business management degree from King's College, Cambridge (married to an equally glamorous former model), a man known variously as the King, the social mayor of Hollywood, the party pal of filmdom—was providing both the evidence and the symbol that the onetime glamour of Hollywood, hence its user-friendly urbanism, had returned. Chris Breed was partying for an evening, and the places he was helping revitalize had, perhaps, the shelf life of a decade. But no matter: other places would follow. Successful cities would forever need the night.

In San Francisco and Los Angeles alike, preservationism had attained great force not only because so much of the urban fabric had already been lost but also because a new generation of San Franciscans and Los Angelenos had discovered the complexity and value of California as a cultural legacy and continuing force. So many of them had chosen to come to these cities precisely because they believed them to be mythic and sustaining places, and they did not want their choice to be devalued by the ongoing destruction of the built environment. By the 1990s, moreover, a generation of architectural historians had established the preeminence and continuing vitality of architecture in the Golden State. Architecture, like wine and food, emerged as one of the key means through which a new generation of urban Californians defined the value and meaning of California to themselves and the world. In 2000 the Getty Trust launched a grant program to support either the planning or the implementation of preservationist projects in Los Angeles. By July of that year places and institutions such as the Wilshire Boulevard Temple, the Griffith Observatory, the Church of the Blessed Sacrament in Hollywood, the Baldwin Hills/Village Green Owners Association, the Christ Faith Mission in Highland Park, the Craftsman Alpha Gamma Omega house in the historic West Adams district (one of the oldest graduate chapters of the first African-American sorority in the nation), and the 1900 Victorian-era chapel at the veteran's center in West Los Angeles were receiving grants either to plan or to implement preservationist projects. In Los Angeles, however, distinctions among high-brow, middle-brow, and low-brow places were porous and uncertain. Thus, the Los Angeles Conservancy was equally interested in preserving Coffee Shop Modern diners—such as Pann's at La Cienega and La Tijera—that had survived from the 1950s as it was more formal structures. Here, after all, were surviving buildings storing the style and optimism of the postwar era.

An entirely different category on the must-save list of the conservancy consisted of buildings prominent in the fiction of Horace McCoy, James M. Cain, Raymond Chandler, Mickey Spillane, James Ellroy, and other writers, past and present, of the LA hardboiled school. Detective stories and film noir, the conservancy pointed out, had—considered cumulatively—formed a meta-narrative for the city, and this overriding story had endowed building after building throughout Los Angeles with the transformative powers of legend, nostalgia, and art. The Pacific Bank building at Hollywood and Cahuenga, for example, could never be the same once detective Philip Marlowe had maintained his office there. (San Franciscans felt a similar regard for Burritt Alley, atop the southern entrance to the Stockton Street tunnel, where Sam Spade's partner Miles Archer had been gunned down by Brigid O'Shaughnessy.) Since these same places also had a tendency to reappear in filmed versions of novels, or to be chosen as settings for original films in the noir tradition, a multiple interaction of Los Angeles the novel, Los Angeles the movie, and Los Angeles the place endowed even the most ordinary sites with cinematic grandeur.

Scouting the city in late 1996 in his 1947 four-door Packard sedan, director Curtis Hanson had little trouble coming up with locations to shoot *L.A. Confidential* (1997), a film noir redux dealing with the Los Angeles Police Department in the 1950s. Among other places, there was the neon-lit Formosa Cafe, at the corner of Santa Monica Boulevard and Formosa, where Johnny Stompanato might actually have hung out with Lana Turner; or the Frolic Room on Hollywood Boulevard, with its movie star murals by Al Hirschfeld; or the art deco former bank nearby, used in the film to depict a nonexistent glamour spot, the El Cortez, which, once the film was released, had people asking Hanson how they could find that particular hot spot.

Not surprisingly, given the preservationist impulses animating each city, San Francisco and Los Angeles spent a total of $600 million in the 1990s restoring their respective city halls. Each building evoked its city in a manner that had made it irreplaceable as a civic icon. Designed by the École des beaux-arts–trained John Bakewell Jr. and Arthur Brown Jr. in 1913 for a 1915 opening, the San Francisco city hall—an ambitiously domed (higher than the national Capitol itself) French Renaissance palace extending across two city blocks—perfectly expressed San Francisco's daydream of itself as the Paris of the Pacific, a city seeking to be thought of, at least in aspiration, alongside the capitals of Europe. The Los Angeles city hall, by contrast—a movie-set mélange of beaux-arts classical, Byzantine, Moorish, and art deco elements, designed by John Austin, John and Donald Parkinson, and Albert C. Martin for a 1928 opening—expressed Los Angeles's subliminal knowledge of itself as an eclectic fantasy, a city imagining itself into Arabian days and nights.

Each restoration paced and energized a number of associated projects. In San Francisco, the refurbishment of city hall was part of a larger $1 billion renewal of the entire Civic Center that included the construction of a county courthouse, a supreme court building, the upgrading of an existing state building, a new $150 million main library, and the multimillion-dollar transformation of the old (1917) main library into a museum of Asian art. At the beginning of the decade, the Civic Center had devolved into the campground of choice for the homeless. Now it stood re-revealed in all its beaux-arts grandeur as one of the finest legacies of the City Beautiful movement in the nation. Across town, a $100 million program (from state bonds, passed by only 866 votes) was under way to restore San Francisco's second most powerful public space: the plaza facing the venerable Ferry Building (1898), which architect Arthur Page Brown had modeled on the Giralda Tower in Seville. With the Embarcadero Freeway torn down in the aftermath of the Loma Prieta earthquake, it had now become possible to create in front of the Ferry Building a grand palm-guarded plaza served by light rail.

In little more than a decade, Los Angeles, a city notorious for what cultural critic Norman Klein described as its tendency to erase memory from the built environment, had managed to preserve and bring back to glory its most important architectural icons, including the Powell Library (1929) in the UCLA Quadrangle, a luxuriant Italian Romanesque palace, designed by George Kelham and dedicated in honor of longtime university librarian Lawrence Clark Powell, and the equally ornate Edward L. Doheny Jr. Memorial Library at USC, designed by Samuel Lunden of Los Angeles and Cram and Ferguson of Boston from original renderings by Ralph Adams Cram and dedicated in 1932 as a memorial to the murdered Doheny heir. Also restored, with a new wing added, designed by Hardy Holzman Pfeiffer Associates, was the downtown Central Library (1926), renamed the Richard J. Riordan Central Library in June of 2001. The restoration and expansion of three large-scale libraries brought back to full glory three Alhambran palaces redolent of the confidence and optimism of 1920s Los Angeles.

Central to this decade-long epic of restoration was the architectural firm of Levin & Associates, headed by Brenda Levin, a longtime Los Angeles resident from New Jersey who, by 2002, had been personally and professionally at the center of the city's effort to reinvent itself through the restoration and/or adaptive reuse of such architectural icons as the Bradbury Building (1893) on Broadway, the Wiltern Theater (1931) on Wilshire, the Grand Central Market on Broadway, the Oviatt Building (1927–28) on Olive Street, the Fine Arts Building (1925) on Seventh, and the Griffith Observatory (1930), scheduled for a $63 million upgrade in 2002.

In San Francisco, meanwhile, the Presidio Trust was in the process of planning a city within a city, to be developed on the 1,480-acre Presidio headlands fronting the Golden Gate. Under terms of legislation passed by Congress in 1996, the Presidio army base was reconstituted as a federal trust under the supervision of a board of trustees. Their challenge: to make the Presidio a self-sustained enterprise by 2013, generating $36.4 million a year. In late March 1998, the trust released plans for the development of the Presidio into a mini-city of housing, restaurants, more than three million square feet of commercial and nonprofit office spaces, a movie theater, bed-and-breakfast inns, and a health club, all this involving the adaptive reuse of army structures together with the maintenance of large amounts of public open space. In August 2001, after two years of intense negotiations, came the first big commercial score for the Presidio: an agreement with Lucasfilm Ltd. for a twenty-three-acre Letterman Digital Arts Center at the site of the Letterman Army Hospital, which would be razed, at the eastern entrance to the Presidio. The 800,000-square-foot facility would include a production studio, the George Lucas Educational Foundation, the Visual Effects Archive, a digital arts museum, and other amenities.

In Southern California, by contrast, plans for the expansion of the Los Angeles International Airport were going nowhere, especially after the terrorist attacks of September 11, 2001. Outgoing mayor Riordan and the city council had spent more than $78 million across six years to plan for the expansion of LAX, increasing its capacity by a third (some were arguing for a 50 percent increase) to meet the needs of the new millennium. In the aftermath of September 11, however, usage of LAX began what promised to be a 35 percent decline in the fiscal year—a falloff of some 25 million passengers. Not surprisingly, incoming mayor James Hahn put all expansion plans—forty-two new gates, a new terminal, a new perimeter ring road—on hold in favor of expanded security programs.

Fortunately for San Francisco, the $1.5 billion project linking BART with the San Francisco International Airport, the seventh busiest airport in the world, was nearing conclusion by September 11. And the ambitiously conceived Alameda corridor—a sweeping railroad and truck pathway linking the ports of Los Angeles and Long Beach with major railheads and trucking depots on the periphery of the city—was proving resistant to cutbacks following the terrorist attacks and, unlike plans for LAX, continued in various stages of planning and construction. Whatever problems Los Angeles might experience with its air cargo and passenger traffic, it would soon have a direct connection of its port to the railway and trucking lines of the nation.

What a ride it had been! What an epic of construction, renovation, and adaptive reuse. At some point in the new millennium, the people of each city might very well be asking themselves: Was all that built in so short a time? Did these two metropolitan regions, amid so many countermovements and distractions, reurbanize themselves so resolutely through so many construction projects, public and private? In a decade that began and ended in recession—ten years of earthquakes, riots, bitter quarrels and shuddering adjustments to immigration, epidemics of crime and other forms of social misbehavior—was it not truly the stuff of history for these two cities to have struggled so valiantly to reconnect themselves to place?

Talk of the Town

Neither city was a particularly easy place in which to be a child, especially a child low on the socioeconomic scale, which increasingly meant a minority child. This was the main reason—raising children—why so many Californians had fled to the suburbs. In the 1990s, the 2000 census revealed, San Francisco had grown by 52,774 people but had lost 4,081 children. The percentage of residents under eighteen had been in decline since 1960. Zero Population Growth, however, a Washington-based non-profit organization, ranked San Francisco the fifth most kid-friendly city in the nation. Los Angeles, although it was not losing its children, was ranked nineteenth. This meant that for affluent San Franciscans, the city was an okay place to raise children. Los Angeles, by contrast, presented distinct challenges to middle-class families, and its overall rating of C−, according to Zero Population Growth, was dragged even lower by its communities of underserved immigrants.

On the other hand, *Dog Fancy* magazine rated San Francisco the number one city in the nation in which to be a dog—this in a city with formally designated dog parks and an SPCA adoption center whose dogs were kept in pet condos. There were, quite possibly, more dogs in San Francisco than children, one per seven San Franciscans. The city had the lowest pet euthanasia rate in the nation and three times as many volunteers as any other SPCA organization. San Francisco also featured an annual blessing of pets, dogs included, at Grace Cathedral atop Nob Hill, St. Boniface Church in the Tenderloin, and the Shrine of St. Francis of Assisi in North Beach. Then there was the city's annual Animal Wingding, which claimed to be the largest pet street fair in the world, and the certainly one-of-a-kind Pets in Drag contest in the Castro.

Each city was proving attractive to young single people, although, once again, San Francisco showed the most startling statistics. At the height of the dot-com boom, fully 62 percent of the city was under forty-four, and of all age groups only 34 percent were married. Thus San Francisco was more discernibly a city of single people under forty-four, both straight and gay, while Los Angeles, whose population in this regard was greater in raw numbers, tended to have its image significantly adjusted by its large population of married-with-children immigrants and second-generation Americans.

Gay or straight, each city prided itself on being open-minded as far as sex was concerned. San Francisco was a city, after all, in which District Attorney Terence Hallinan was openly in favor of legalized prostitution and each year there was held a Hookers' Ball under the sponsorship of activist and local celebrity Margo St. James, herself a former member of the profession. One would have to travel to Amsterdam, perhaps, to witness the kinds of wild costumes and uninhibited behavior this event engendered. AIDS and the epidemic of sexually transmitted diseases had by the 1990s toned down San Francisco's previously more reckless behavior in matters erotic, and its topless bar and pornography culture, which had seemed so innovative in the 1960s and 1970s, had receded to a seedy sideshow at a few furtive and shabby locations. This decline was symbolized most horrifically on February 27, 1991, when pornmeister Jim Mitchell shot and killed his brother Artie, a sad event that seemed to end an era.

Yet for all its sexual flamboyance, San Francisco was also a place in which most of its young straights eventually married and had children—and left the city for the suburbs—by their fortieth birthday. The singles scene in San Francisco tended to be a moveable feast capable of many definitions. Wednesdays were for volleyball games on the Marina Green near the St. Francis Yacht Club. On Fridays after work in the financial district and SOMA, as the south of Market district had been dubbed by resident artist Sam Provenzano, the sidewalks of certain streets were made impassable by crowds of Thank-God-It's-Friday celebrants.

Getting a date, however, could be a problem. For so many singles, San Francisco or Los Angeles could be Lonely Town. Cherry Norris, a Los Angeles filmmaker, went for eight years without a date before turning to an Internet-based dating service. Being a filmmaker, Norris made a film about it, *Duty Dating,* shot at twenty-eight locations around the city. In the movie, a career woman—good-looking, well educated, successful—makes a mess of her love life by being too aggressive. Seeking the help of a counselor, she learns the art of dating, in part by dating as many men as possible, considering it her duty if she is going to meet Mr. Right. At the premiere of Norris's film, some five hundred singles, many of them subscribing to online dating services—Match.com, Matchmaker.com, Jdate.com—paid $25 each for both the screening and a chance to hear Pat Allen, a therapist specializing in singles, with offices in Brentwood and Newport Beach, tell them:

"Duty-dating is when you go out with people whom you hope die on the way to the bathroom. I don't care if they're not eligible for the gene pool you're creating—you will duty-date!"[27]

In Los Angeles, because it was a much larger city with so many more options, one could remain a swinging single (at least in one's own mind) for a lifetime without incurring social pressure. At the Marina City Club condominium and apartment complex in Marina del Rey on the Westside, for example, some two thousand residents could remain happy singles for life in a complex featuring three swimming pools, its own lively bar and restaurant (happy hour started at six), a gym, a spa, and tennis courts. Featuring a nonstop round of social events, Marina City Club was like a cruise ship that forever stayed in port. "Being married and living in Brentwood," noted one divorced resident, "I never went to a bar. In my former life, I never knew anybody. I went home to my wife every night. Here, I feel like I know everyone."[28]

Community, certainly, was what the Castro district in San Francisco and West Hollywood represented for many gay Californians, with these two cities continuing to function on the cutting edge of gay culture and society, as they had been doing since the 1960s. The yellow brick road, however, could sometimes be treacherous. Nationwide, attacks on gays reached record highs in 1992, with some 435 antigay incidents reported in San Francisco alone. Still, despite these attacks, no one could deny that, in each city, gay America had come into its own. Gay San Francisco had become an almost mythic place due to the continuing notoriety of Armistead Maupin's *Tales of the City* novels and their popular television adaptations. The June 2001 issue of *San Francisco* magazine was devoted to showcasing gay men and women influential in every sector of the city.

In January 1995 the Houston Grand Opera was preparing a production of the opera *Harvey Milk* by composer Stewart Wallace and librettist Michael Korie, commemorating the life and times of San Francisco's first openly gay supervisor. In its sweep and tragedy, the situation was intrinsically operatic: a Wall Street stockbroker, Jewish and Republican, galvanized by the 1969 Stonewall resistance of gays to police harassment in Greenwich Village, accepts himself as a gay and a Jew, moves to San Francisco, becomes a public figure, is tragically assassinated, and in death assumes the power of a near-mythic figure in the worldwide gay liberation movement. It was perhaps in dramatic contrast to Milk's assassination— and in testimony to how accepted gay people had become in California— that when Los Angeles city councilman Joel Wachs almost casually announced in November 1999 that he was gay to the openly gay moderator of a public affairs television talk show, it barely caused a ripple.

Passing Proposition 22 in June 2000, Californians joined twenty-seven other states in restricting legal marriage to male-female couples. This vote, however, only intensified the drive toward a statewide domestic partner bill, which passed the legislature and was signed by Governor Davis on October 14, 2001. Already, cities such as San Francisco and West Hollywood had in force highly articulated domestic partner benefit arrangements. Even more, starting in 1997, San Francisco held an annual same-sex wedding ceremony officiated by the mayor and other city officials. By then, up to one million people a year were attending San Francisco's annual Lesbian, Gay, Bisexual, and Transgender Pride Parade, which marked the Stonewall uprising. A lesbian motorcycle group calling itself Dykes on Bikes traditionally led the march.

In the course of the parade, it was frequently pointed out that the award-winning San Francisco Gay Men's Chorus had lost between 160 and 190 members to AIDS. Dressed in black shirts, two men led a saddled horse with no rider as a symbol of all those who had been lost. New drug therapies—protease inhibitors combined with older AIDS medications like AZT and 3TC—had slowed down, even temporarily stayed, the death rate from AIDS (there was a 44 percent decline in deaths in 1997 alone), but the disease still provided a tragic undertone to so much of what was witty and, literally, gay in the gay communities of each city. No city, perhaps, had suffered more proportionately from the AIDS epidemic than San Francisco, as an entire generation of the city's young men succumbed to the disease between 1981, when it was first encountered at the San Francisco General Hospital, and the mid-1990s. Such a rate of death, past ten thousand by the early 1990s, from one community in one relatively small city, brought to San Francisco as a whole a tragic dimension that belied the overt frivolity of its public culture. At San Francisco General Hospital during these years—a first-rate county facility operated in close conjunction with UC San Francisco Medical School—physicians such as Paul Volberding and Donald Abrams attained national reputations in their fight against the AIDS plague; but they also witnessed, as did so many in San Francisco, a harrowing loss of young life. Not surprisingly, raising funds for AIDS research became an obsession in each city, although in this matter San Francisco could not match the power (toward $3 million per benefit) of the annual AIDS Project Los Angeles's Commitment to Life benefit, which throughout the 1990s drew a host of stars and whose doyenne was Dame Elizabeth Taylor, the grand dame literally and figuratively of AIDS activism.

Condoms, together with drug therapy, had by mid-decade significantly slowed the visible effects of the AIDS epidemic. Such was the accomplishment, but also the problem; by the mid- to late 1990s, a new generation of young gay men was engaging in sexual activity without personal experience of the horrendous effect of the first phase of the AIDS epidemic. A decade earlier, the Castro, West Hollywood, and other gay enclaves had teemed with emaciated men marked with the dark blotches of Kaposi's sarcoma. Everyone knew someone who had died or was dying. Now, almost overnight, few young gay men knew anyone who had died or was dying, and those they knew to be HIV positive seemed to be getting along, thanks to the new drug therapies. A mood of carelessness—reckless defiance, even—crept back into the gay community, to the dismay of older AIDS activists who had seen an entire generation destroyed. Even more subtly, suggested reporter Erica Goode, writing in the *New York Times* on August 19, 2001, there appeared to be in some young gay men a semiconscious flirtation with AIDS, as if to get the matter over with once and for all, to end the fear of the unknown by contracting the disease. Gay men suffering from one form or another of depression were especially vulnerable to this syndrome.

This did not mean that either city, San Francisco or Los Angeles, gay or straight, ceased to be fun. Pleasure as well as pain and peril, after all, was at the core of the urban experience. Each city remained justifiably noted for its restaurants, bars, dance halls, and clubs, its continuing ability to sustain the appetite for life through pleasure and distraction. San Francisco remained a restaurant capital of the nation, with one for every 230 residents of the city, which translated to about two thousand establishments, and a new generation of first-rate kitchens—Charles Nob Hill, Aqua on California, Gary Danko on North Point, Postrio on Post, Betelnut on Union, Eos on Cole, Hawthorne Lane (Bill and Hillary Clinton's favorite restaurant when they were in town) on Hawthorne opposite the Museum of Modern Art, Rose Pistola on Columbus, Moose's on Stockton—coming online in the 1990s as competitors to such well-established places as Fleur de Lys, Bix, Boulevard, Massa's, Campton Place, the Zuni Café, and others. A number of once venerable establishments, meanwhile—Ernie's, Jack's, the Blue Fox, L'Etoile, Trader Vic's—were closing their doors in that inevitable cycle of appearance and disappearance so characteristic of the restaurant business in general. In Los Angeles, revered establishments such as Musso & Frank's in Hollywood were flourishing more than ever. Chasen's, however, the legendary Hollywood hangout, shut down in January 1995.

The San Francisco club scene—in such places as Club V/SF, the Paradise, the Holy Cow, the DNA Lounge, Slim's—tended to be young, electronic, loud, and south of Market, which gave rise, just before the dot-com bust, to growing tensions between loft owners in that district and clubs whose music was being amplified through the night. Los Angeles, however, displayed more sophisticated tastes in contrast to the huddled dark places and air-splitting amps of San Francisco, although at the Tempest in Hollywood loud rock was still the norm. The Los Angeles club scene had wit, style, and an almost scholarly range of decorative reference. It was theatrically more aware of itself, even self-parodic. At Tigerbeat on Santa Monica Boulevard, the sound was disco and pop, with more than a touch of the go-go spots of the 1960s. The Garden of Eden on Hollywood Boulevard was fulsome and luxurious, like a nightclub from the 1940s. A raft of new Los Angeles places—the Balboa in the Grafton Hotel on Sunset, Dominick's on Beverly, the Lucky Duck on La Brea, the Hollywood Canteen on Seward Street, the Little Door on West Third, Vine on Vine—deliberately replicated the supper club culture of the 1930s.

Each city maintained flourishing opera companies, with lavish opening nights, although in San Francisco the hoopla in early September had long since surpassed the opera itself in importance. Each month the illustrated tabloid *Nob Hill Gazette* chronicled countless parties, most of them benefits for one cause or another. There was now and then a self-consciously zany side to San Francisco, as in zany-respectable: the long-running satiric revue *Beach Blanket Babylon,* for example, which celebrated its twenty-fifth birthday in June 1999 at the Herbst Theater, with former secretary of state George Shultz playing Clark Kent, and his wife, Charlotte, chief of protocol for the city, playing Wonder Woman, for an audience of celebrities who had paid between $300 and $1,000 for an evening that ended, as ever, with singer Val Diamond belting out the song "San Francisco" while balancing atop her head an outrageously oversize papier-mâché pastiche of the city skyline.

If one were to judge from the social columns of each city's newspapers, social life in San Francisco—the social life that got reported, anyway—had an infinitely more narrow base than it did in Los Angeles, and this said something about the differences between the two cities. For more than a half century, *San Francisco Chronicle* columnist Herb Caen had exercised a near monopoly on just exactly who was in and who was out, although Caen's colleague at the *Chronicle,* society editor Pat Steger, also exercised some influence and maintained whatever contact could be maintained with the older wealth that, among other things, owned the newspaper and signed the paychecks. After Caen's death in 1997 and that of Steger in 1999, San Francisco suffered a crisis of identity, both in terms of the aging of its increasingly narrowing cast of café society characters and the absence of chroniclers to replace Steger and Caen. Los Angeles—that is, the social coverage of the *Los Angeles Times*—represented a much more inclusive approach. Although celebrity figures from the Industry could always hog the scene in a celebrity-obsessed culture, the *Times* did manage to cover, in any given week, a wide range of people and places. *Times* social reporters such as Ann O'Neill, Patt Diroll, and Ann Conway went out and covered the city with enthusiasm and open-mindedness. The City of Angels column, moreover, was gloriously illustrated with color photographs that would one day provide researchers an album of the faces and figures, in all their attractiveness and occasional pathos, of celebrity Los Angeles entering the millennium.

Each city had its privileged neighborhoods—Pacific Heights, Presidio Heights, Nob Hill, Russian Hill, Sea Cliff, the Marina in San Francisco; Hancock Park and Bel Air in Los Angeles, Beverly Hills, Pasadena, San Marino. But it was also interesting to note, as far as upper-class life in Los Angeles was concerned, that Hancock Park, ground zero of the old Anglo-American establishment, was being successively transformed into an Asian-American and showbiz enclave as a generation of boomer actors, actresses, producers, directors, and others in the Industry found themselves attracted to the dignity and historicity of its stately mansions. Old-time residents were increasingly willing to rent their homes to the studios as locations for compelling fees. In and of itself, Hancock Park incorporated the transformation of Los Angeles from a city dominated by an Anglo-American elite that did not like movie people into a more fluid environment in which Asian Americans, film folks, and old families lived beside each other congenially. So fascinating was this conjunction of real estate and show business, the *Los Angeles Times* ran a weekly column called "Hot Property" chronicling the latest purchases or sales of real estate by entertainment celebrities.

And yet, in Los Angeles, everyone was a celebrity. Local couture—youth oriented and hypereclectic through variations of punk, rockabilly, neo-disco, slinky sirens, the near naked, tattoos provocatively in evidence—seemed keyed to making everyone the star of his or her own premiere. In nearly every case, the fashion boutiques of the city were producing a look that, however eclectic, tended to showcase each client as the star of her own movie-in-the-making, a dancing queen at the hottest club in town, just waiting to be discovered. Not surprisingly, an increasing number of young people were maintaining their own Web sites.

The internal combustion engine continued to tell Los Angelenos—and others—just exactly who they were. For Los Angeles, the internal combustion engine was a Jungian archetype, subsuming and construing value and identity. In May 1993, just for the hell of it—following the riots, with the recession still on—125 owners of Rolls-Royces organized a cavalcade through Beverly Hills, thus winning a place in the *Guinness Book of World Records* by surpassing the previous record, set in 1991 in Hong Kong, of a mere eleven Rolls-Royces. The Rich Urban Bikers (RUB) movement got its start in Los Angeles during the same period, as hundreds of doctors, lawyers, executives, and other professionals, resplendent in denim and leathers, took to the road on customized Harley-Davidsons, the Rolls-Royce of the motorcycle world. Rapidly, the RUB movement spread north to San Francisco, east to New York, and emerged as a trend in Europe and Japan as high-performing professionals—including actors Dennis Hopper and Jeremy Irons, and supermodel Lauren Hutton—became addicted to the exhilaration of the open road.

You could be there, out on your own, or so it seemed, more easily in Los Angeles than San Francisco, and, if you were an artist, you could even make it big, which stood in contrast to the dwindling cadre of San Francisco artists being driven out of the city by housing costs. Tony and Karen Barone of Venice, for example, could hardly be described as a conventional urban professional couple. The dining-room table of their three-story loft, for one thing, was the lowered shell of a 1958 Cadillac. Karen circled her eyes with eyeliner, like a raccoon, and often took her early-morning walk in full makeup and pigtails. Yet Tony's bright and optimistic paintings sold—and only this cliché could describe it—like hotcakes, at some $12,000 a canvas, and the graduate of the Chicago Art Institute did a comparably lucrative business in commercial art. A poster by Tony Barone for a sausage company featured godly hands, à la Michelangelo's Sistine Chapel, bearing gigantic sausages. And then there was Karen's cosmetic line, which Macy's, Bloomingdales, and Fred Siegel carried and which the Barones marketed in Japan through their own string of boutiques.

Across town, Jackie Kallen could be found standing in stiletto heels ringside at the downtown Los Angeles Boxing Club, one of the few female boxing managers in the nation. An attractive woman in her late forties, Kallen had gotten her start as a prizefight manager twenty years earlier in Detroit, making the transition from fight publicist. In the mid-1990s, a series of life crises and a costly divorce returned her to the fight game. Just a few years earlier, Kallen had been driving a Ferrari and owned more than one hundred pairs of shoes and a wardrobe so extensive it had to be stored and indexed electronically in a closet the size of a bedroom. Now she was living in a two-bedroom apartment just outside Beverly Hills and was devoting her time to up-and-coming prospects at the club and reveling in the good reviews accorded her recently published *Hit Me with Your Best Shot* (1997), a combination autobiography and self-help book aimed at helping people who, like herself, had known some tough times.

What Tony and Karen Barone and Jackie Kallen had in common—guts, style, panache, a taste for life lived outside the box—was not exclusive to

Los Angeles, but was certainly well represented there, and more so than in San Francisco, which for all its vaunted bohemianism had a strong streak of conformity. And this was ironic, given the bohemian past of San Francisco, literary and artistic, down through the Beats, the hippies, the Fillmore Auditorium, the Grateful Dead, the rock poster and underground comics movement as represented by the work of R. Crumb. Yet the hippies had long since left San Francisco for upstate marijuana fields, and Haight Ashbury was by the mid- to late 1990s a deplorable place, with hundreds of runaway youth encamped in nearby Golden Gate Park and Haight Street itself lined with forlorn and dysfunctional young people, most of them deeply into the buying, selling, and consumption of illicit pharmaceuticals. In place of the peace-and-love hippies of yore, Haight Street now abounded with alienated youth in black leather who called themselves Goths and formed street groups with names such as the Fallen Angel Society. When Mayor Willie Brown cleared Golden Gate Park of homeless encampments in the summer of 1998, the situation got even worse, and the remaining bank, pharmacy, and copy center on Haight Street closed down.

All this was a long way from the stated ideals of the long-gone Summer of Love of 1967. No wonder, then, that the organizers of the Burning Man movement fiercely resisted any comparison to the hippies. In 1986 arts entrepreneur Larry Harvey and a group of friends had built and burned an eight-foot-tall Burning Man effigy on Baker's Beach as part of a midsummer celebration. Fifteen years later, some 25,000 Burning Man aficionados were doing the same thing, albeit on a larger scale, at the annual encampment in the Nevada desert near Black Rock City. Burning Man was many things: a revived neopagan ritual and festival, a 1990s version of the Summer of Love keyed to college-educated professionals willing to pay the $100 admission fee, an arts festival, and a stylized summer saturnalia where people could get naked (as Wolf Man Jack used to say), wear costumes, play communal games, race camels, take mud baths, construct impromptu and fantastic encampments lasting a week, put on pageants, burn the Burning Man (now a highly stylized seventy-foot-tall effigy), and test whatever constraints had survived the 1970s. It was also a commercialized, hence democratized, projection of San Francisco as bohemian place.

Technically speaking, San Francisco still had its bohemia, which is to say, the North Beach district, centered on Lawrence Ferlinghetti's City Lights Bookstore on Columbus at Broadway. Here, forty, nearly fifty, years earlier, a postwar generation of writers and poets, comics (Mort Sahl) and musicians, had in a fusion (or confusion) of radicalism and orthodoxy created, if not an enduring body of literature, then at the least an intriguing moment in the unfolding consciousness of post–World War II America.

Ferlinghetti, who had served as a naval officer in that war before taking his doctorate in literature at the Sorbonne on the GI Bill, remained in North Beach into the millennium, a continuously publishing poet, successful publisher, bookseller, and painter, and poet laureate of the city by official designation of Mayor Brown in August 1998, his name adorning a street as well. So, too, did novelist Herb Gold, another veteran of that war (a Russian-language intelligence specialist), remain productive in the general vicinity of North Beach, keeping a residence and studio above the Broadway Tunnel. Yet by the 1990s the enduring bohemianism of North Beach had become not so much a matter of literary production, although that was continuing, as it was in the subliminal suggestions of the place itself, organized around City Lights, Washington Square, and a slew of inviting coffeehouses, bars, and restaurants.

Indeed, it was in its restaurants, together with the Italian-language bookstore of A. Cavalli & Company and the imposing Saints Peter and Paul Church facing Washington Square, staffed by priests of the Salesian Order, that the onetime Italian environment of North Beach survived. These restaurants ranged from the unpretentious—the US Restaurant, the New Pisa, Capp's Corner, the Golden Spike, Little City, Buca Giovanni, the Stinking Rose—to more ambitious enterprises such as the North Beach Restaurant, presided over by owner-impresario Lorenzo Petroni (an immigrant from Lucca who had become a key political kibitzer in the city through sheer force of personality and a late-night pasta-and-wine association with hungry pols converging on his establishment), and the Fior d'Italia facing Washington Square, founded in the mid-1880s and advertising itself as the oldest continuously serving Italian-American restaurant in the nation. Interweaving themselves throughout the district were a dozen of the most colorful bars and hangouts in the city: Tosca on Columbus, favored by café society, featuring opera in its jukebox; Vesuvio's across the street, adjacent to City Lights, where reverberations of the Beat era managed to survive, and Spec's in a nearby alley, where gonzo journalist Warren Hinckle gathered gossip for his column, his ever-attendant beagle Bentley at his feet, munching on a hamburger.

For most of the 1980s and the first half of the 1990s, the lead hangout for café society and bohemian San Francisco in North Beach had been the Washington Square Bar & Grill on Powell and Union facing the Square. It was owned and operated by Sam Deitch, an in-the-know local restaurateur, and Ed Moose, a longtime St. Louis political activist turned San Franciscan, with first-rate connections in the national media. Moose's cuisine-savvy wife Marietta supervised the menus, Dianne Feinstein's sister Lynne Kennedy kept the books, and mixmeisters Cyril Boyce, Gene Baskett, Ray

Hagen, and Michael McCourt tended bar. The Washington Square Bar & Grill reigned supreme across two decades of North Beach bohemia; at nearly any time of the day, legendary drinker Glenn Dorenbush could be found at the bar, fresh from his morning appearance in the Herb Caen column. There as well, at lunch or dinner, could be found *Chronicle* columnists Stan Delaplane and Charles McCabe, actor and classical disc jockey Scott Beach, actor-playwright Sam Shepard, local fund-raiser Tom Jordan, then in the process of making the American Ireland Fund an important force in Irish culture, Jordan's good friend the Irish poet Seamus Heaney, assorted Giants and 49ers, opera singers, the Democratic (and Republican, for that matter) establishment, ink-stained wretches from various newspapers and magazines, media celebrities from New York, friends of Ed Moose's (Walter Cronkite, Tom Brokaw), and tourists soaking up the atmosphere.

Malvina's, Caffé Trieste, Caffé Greco, Caffé Puccini, Caffé Roma, Mario's Bohemian Cigar Store, the North End Caffé: North Beach abounded in atmospheric espresso bars, the majority of them in the Italian style, serving pastry in the morning and sandwiches later through the afternoon. As Herb Gold pointed out in his charming mid-decade memoir *Where Art, Angst, Love, and Strong Coffee Meet* (1993), and, indeed, as Joseph Addison and Richard Steele had already observed in the early eighteenth century, coffeehouses were places where people came to hang out, to schmooze, to keep company together or alone, entering a certain kind of conversational—or silent, for that matter—dream time. Former mayor Joseph Alioto loved the Cappuccino Circuit, as he called it, especially Saturday mornings at the Caffé Puccini when, quietly battling the prostate cancer that would soon defeat him, he would sweep in, his wife, Kathleen Sullivan (of the New England Patriots family), and assorted friends in tow. There, for the next hour and a half or so, he would drink coffee, swap stories with local artists and poets, play operatic selections on the jukebox, and discourse on the poetry of Dante and Robert Browning, the novels of Stendhal and Manzoni, the operas of Verdi and Puccini, the wines and cuisines of Tuscany, where the family maintained a villa and spent part of each year, and—a recurrent theme—the glories of the Cappuccino Circuit in North Beach, which, for him, entering the final battle of life, embodied the exuberant vitality of the North Beach he had known and loved his entire life and had embodied the Mediterranean magic of his native city. Alioto's reading of "The Ballad of My San Francisco"—a long rhymed poem he had written over the years, recounting the history of the city—at the North End Caffé at Grant and Green attracted a crowd so large that loudspeakers had to be placed on the sidewalk, and friendly cops closed the street to traffic for the rest of the evening.

Presumably, then, San Franciscans and Los Angelenos, gathering in coffeehouses—or, for that matter, in homes, classrooms, bars, and restaurants, wherever people met and conversed—might be expected, occasionally, to discuss the comparative state of the arts in the two metropolitan regions. Just a few decades earlier, such a conversation might have been one-sided and brief. San Francisco represented civilization, it was assumed, and Los Angeles represented Hollywood. By the 1990s, however, such a facile distinction—never true in the first place—had long since been out of date. For many, such as creative writing professor Tobias Wolff of Stanford, any excessive concern with regional identity was in and of itself provincializing. The question was further complicated by the pervasive internationalism of the Bay Area and metropolitan Los Angeles in the late twentieth century. Not only had the peoples and the cultures of the world come to California, an increasing number of creative Californians were sustaining one or another mode of offshore connection and identity.

This was especially true of writers in the Bay Area, not just university-based writers and academics, who had long since joined the circuit described by David Lodge in *Small World: An Academic Romance* (1984) of jet-setting scholars globe-trotting from conference to conference, but a growing number of independent writers as well. Memoirist Olga Carlisle, granddaughter of Victor Chernov, leader of the Socialist Revolutionary Party and member of the provisional government prior to the Bolshevik takeover, was by definition an internationalist, fitting into the longtime identity of San Francisco as a post-czarist Russian enclave. Novelist Diane Johnson spent portions of each year in Paris, where she and her physician husband maintained an apartment, and her most well-received novel, *Le Divorce* (1997), had a Parisian setting. Carol Field's preoccupation was the culture—wine, food, hill towns—of Italy, and another San Franciscan, San Francisco State professor Frances Mayes, had her breakthrough with the success of *Under the Tuscan Sun* (1996), a memoir chronicling how she and her husband, a poet and professor at Santa Clara University, restored an ancient Tuscan villa over five years. Herb Gold sustained his offshore identification not with the sweet softness of Italy but the grim realities of Haiti, where he sojourned for intermittent periods, returning to write about Haiti in San Francisco, as he had once covered the civil war in Biafra, being, like Graham Greene, drawn to mise-en-scènes of intense suffering. Orville Schell, dean of the School of Journalism at UC Berkeley, had China for his beat, which he covered for *The New Yorker.*

The dominant mood of literary San Francisco in the 1990s was solidly Tory bohemian, upper middle class in style and value, with exceptions, of course. Ernest Gaines (before his departure for Louisiana) preferred the bars and neighborhoods of whatever was left of African-American San Francisco. Ensconced in Monte Carlan splendor in the Spreckels mansion—with twenty-six automobiles registered to her Pacific Heights address—best-selling novelist Danielle Steel was a fixture in café society. Although only in his early thirties, children's writer Daniel Handler, a native San Franciscan who wrote under the name Lemony Snicket, was rapidly taking on the demeanor of a donnish man of letters.

Which threw into relief such a writer as Darcey Steinke, who viewed San Francisco in terms of its underground. The daughter of a Lutheran minister, her mother a descendant of the founder of the Seventh-day Adventist church, Steinke, a willowy blonde, given to hip-hugger jeans and thrift shop op-art blouses and dark Ben Franklin sunglasses, had been improbably discovered and later edited by Jacqueline Onassis for Doubleday. In contrast to the general upper-middle-class comfort of so much San Francisco–based writing, Steinke preferred as her mise-en-scène—as was thoroughly evident in her novel *Suicide Blonde* (1992), the story of a stripper/whore dominated by a lesbian hooker named Madison—the world of strip joints, sex bars, porn shops, peep shows, and other assorted sites of sleaze and degradation as encountered in the Tenderloin district of the city. The great big San Francisco novel of the decade, in fact, all 780 pages of it—*The Royal Family* (2000), by William Vollmann—was an obsessive, gongoristic epic, set in the Tenderloin, of drugs, prostitution, squalor, disease, and violence that made even readers with open minds and strong stomachs yearn for the days of Kathryn Forbes's *Mama's Bank Account* (1943), taken to Broadway as the play *I Remember Mama.* On the other hand, those who knew the Tenderloin would not accuse Vollmann of exaggerating.

Even the most casual survey of the Los Angeles novel during the 1990s would reveal such mayhem, degradation, dysfunctionalism, perversion, marginalization, sadomasochism as the norm, not the exception. At some future time (provided that people are still interested in such things), literary scholars will have their work cut out for them assessing the validity of the social and psychological critique at the core of Los Angeles. Could any city on the planet, they might ask, be so dark, so foreboding, so lonely, so dysfunctional as the city revealed in these novels?

In contrast to the more staid pace of San Francisco, Los Angeles was throughout the 1990s a hotbed of novel writing. In its February 6, 1998, issue, *Los Angeles Weekly* profiled eighty-four Los Angeles–based writers, the majority of them novelists, most of them with a credible bibliography of nationally published works. In a city in which every other person was working on a screenplay, it was not surprising that a disproportionate part of the population should be writing novels as well. New York editors had long since learned to regard Los Angeles as an intriguing setting for fiction. The engine that was driving film and television was also driving a by-product, the novel, at least among younger Los Angeles writers. Everyone, even the most established writers, seemed to be producing alternative fiction, stories filled with marginal and alienated people, most frequently doing or enduring shocking things, usually involving violence, deviant sex, drugs, or combinations thereof.

A preliminary sorting of the Los Angeles novel in the 1990s revealed some continuities and persistent patterns and genres. The city that had nurtured Raymond Chandler remained vividly connected to the crime novel. Many Los Angeles novels appearing in the 1990s were in one way or another detective fiction. Los Angeles for such writers remained a subterranean, disconnected city in which things were never what they appeared, and only the detective had a chance of finding the truth, hence keeping the City of Angels marginally coherent. This Chandler tradition had, like Los Angeles itself, gone multicultural. The prolific Walter Mosley—ten books in ten years, including *Devil in a Blue Dress* (1990), successfully adapted in 1995 to the screen, starring Denzel Washington as the reluctant detective Easy Rawlins—used his novels to explore the African-American experience in Los Angeles from the postwar era through the 1960s. Bruce Cook, while not himself a Latino, introduced a Boyle Heights barrio-based detective, Antonio "Chico" Cervantes, in *Mexican Standoff* (1988), and continued the series through the 1990s. In *The Killing of the Saints* (1991), a lush, violent, erotic thriller, Alex Abella introduced Cuban-American private detective Charlie Morell, an attorney who had fled South Florida for Los Angeles under mysterious circumstances. Later in the decade, writers Paula Woods and Karen Grigsby-Bates introduced an African-American heroine, Charlotte Justice, an LAPD detective, and Alex Powell, an African-American newspaper columnist and occasional private eye. From one perspective, Mosely, Cook, Woods, Grigsby-Bates, and the other LA-based novelists who were introducing minority shamuses were crossing the detective story with the novel of manners, in that the communities these heroes and heroines represented had been woefully unchronicled in decades past.

Then there was the John Fante–Charles Bukowski tradition: the perception of Los Angeles as belonging, primarily, not to the film celebrities or the downtown swells but to the hordes of little people, near nobodies, whose obscure and desperate lives were made even more obscure and desperate by running headlong into the great big golden myth of LA. Fante pioneered this genre in *Ask the Dust* (1939), and this novel in turn galvanized the writing career of Bukowski, German-born but living in Los Angeles since the age of three (and dying there of leukemia at the age of seventy-three in

March 1994). At once a poet and an autobiographical novelist, Bukowski can be considered the best-known and most influential Los Angeles–based writer, and writer on Los Angeles, since Chandler.

This is strange to say, in one sense, for Bukowski lived and wrote in an almost antiliterate underground of hardscrabble working people and the compulsive drinkers, smokers, fornicators, and layabouts who were dropping into and beneath blue-collar status, Bukowski included. Was all this a literary persona, a way of Bukowski transcending being a nobody by writing about nobodies, or was it a sincere projection of Bukowski's oft-stated belief that everybody was the same, even the most wasted people, that all the beautiful people and big shots, all of the barflies and working stiffs, all the aging broads and beaten people, everybody was the same, and dying the same at the end of it all? It was probably a mixture of both—sincerity and an artfully constructed persona—and it worked; at the time of Bukowski's death, this deliberately marginalized figure, published by the little-known Black Sparrow Press in Santa Rosa, had achieved a cult status akin to that surrounding J. D. Salinger—even more than Salinger, perhaps, because you could only relate to Salinger when you were young, whereas you could grow up, grow old, get beaten down, and still find something that spoke to you in the defiant fiction of Charles Bukowski.

There had, of course, been a lot of anger and disenchantment in Chandler, a sense of Los Angeles as having once promised something, then turning bleak, violent, and ugly. James Ellroy was continuing this tradition in spades, including the literary minimalism. Ellroy, master of the one-word sentence, was reducing this to a condition of antimatter. In June 1958, when he was ten, Ellroy's divorced mother, a fun-loving redhead overly fond of Early Times, was found beaten and strangled to death, her body dumped in some bushes in El Monte. Ellroy was raised by a dysfunctional father, whose deathbed advice to his seventeen-year-old son was: "Try to pick up every waitress who serves you."[29] Ellroy spent the next ten years doing what sometimes could seem a requirement for Los Angeles novelists: living on booze and drugs, supporting himself as a petty thief, being thrown into the county jail twenty-five to thirty times, getting abscesses on his lungs, slipping in and out of pneumonia and auditory hallucinations. Reviewing Ellroy's *White Jazz* (1992), Cynthia Robins gave a capsule summary of the developing Ellroy oeuvre. *White Jazz,* Robins wrote, "makes previous detective fiction, including [Ellroy's] own, read like Dr. Seuss. Pared down to the verbal equivalent of Gillespie-Kenton rebop, Ellroy's prose scans nervous, jittery, polyphonic, and blood-soaked. A fugue for tinhorns, hookers, extortionists, dopers, window peepers, porno kings, crooked cops, vicious Feds, millionaires, mobsters, murderers, and molesters."[30]

Even such a formally literary novelist as Robert Ferrigno, whose *Horse Latitudes* (1990) and *Cheshire Moon* (1993) won high praise in the national media for their literary quality, seemed to live and move in this Chandler-Ellroy world of bleakness, danger, violence, and contempt. And when such violence and bleakness was crossed with the gay protest novel, as in the case of James Robert Baker's *Tim and Pete* (1993)—in which two men with AIDS go on an assassination spree against selected enemies of the gay movement—things could really get depressing, as might be expected from a mid-forties writer who (one is tempted to say, as was the usual case with so many Los Angeles writers) spent his formative years on speed and booze in rebellion against his conservative Republican Long Beach origins before sobering up and going, temporarily, into the movie business as a screenwriter. Baker satirized the film industry in *Boy Wonder* (1998), whose antihero Shark Trager makes Sammy Glick seem benevolent. So tortured, so outrageous, was the landscape of Baker's fiction, it seemed a case of life imitating art when in November 1997 Baker decided to end his life.

So much of Los Angeles was a normal place, one might speculate. Why had all normality been banished from the Los Angeles novel in the 1990s? Still, there were exceptions, or at least partial exceptions, for even UCLA professor Carolyn See, the closest thing to an old-fashioned novelist of manners in the city, crossed her *Making History* (1991), the story of a Pacific Palisades family in meltdown, with elements of magical realism. Readers were grateful, ultimately, for whatever social connections the novelists of Los Angeles were making: grateful for the sociology of T. C. Boyle's *Tortilla Curtain* (1995), itself a primary document regarding the symbiosis of Anglo Southern California and its illegal immigrants; grateful for Janet Fitch for her *White Oleander* (1999), whose emotionally abused child becomes a payback adolescent and a coping adult, missing little detail around her in the process. And then there were the two most improbable novels, *Shop Girl* (2000) by Steve Martin and *Lying Awake* (2000) by Mark Salzman, the two stories seemingly so disparate—a Beverly Hills salesgirl sleeping with a rich older man; a cloistered Carmelite nun in a Los Angeles convent, assessing the validity of her vocation—yet joined in the theme of being alone in Los Angeles and similar to each other as well in the precise realization of the city not as a nightmare, or a conspiracy, or an engine for the destruction of human hopes, but as a place in which the deepest longings of the human heart were still possible.

The poetry of Los Angeles showed higher intensities of social extension; but, then again, the poetry and sustaining presence of Charles Bukowski, a legend whether living or dead, underlie the fundamental premise of poetry in Los Angeles, namely, that it is a popular as well as a high art, and as many people as possible should be encouraged to practice it. Where else, after all, could there be such a thing as the early-1990s weekly poetry readings in the Launderland laundromat in Silver Lake, where, over the hum of twenty-two Speed Queens, the scent of Clorox in the air, aspiring poets from the neighborhood gathered on Saturday mornings, did their laundry, and read their work: poems about everyday life, gangbanging in the 'hood, Dizzy Gillespie, the angels overlooking the City of Angels, the barrio girl still surviving within the life and demeanor of a Latina lawyer, and X-rated confessions that usually drew hoots and catcalls from the audience.

Poetry was flourishing as a popular vernacular art throughout the decade, which pleased Bay Area poet Robert Hass. In the course of his two terms as poetry consultant to the Library of Congress, from 1995 to 1997, Hass, a St. Mary's College and, later, a UC Berkeley English professor, devoted his best efforts to promoting poetry as part of everyday life, once again published in the daily newspaper and plastered across bus stops and kiosks. For poet and poetry critic Dana Gioia, a Los Angeles native who had gone on to Stanford and Harvard, made his career in New York, then retired at fifty to Sonoma County to lead the life of a man of letters, this ubiquity was exactly the problem. California, Gioia claimed, had democratized poetry at the cost of its cumulative quality. Without a coherent critical community, he argued, and with such a pervasive atmosphere of poetry as therapy and as self-expression for everyone, poetry as high art was languishing in the Golden State. Gioia's accusations provoked a slew of angry responses, many of them published in *Poetry Flash,* a Berkeley-based bimonthly, and even led to late-night debates on talk radio.

Gioia's challenge rankled so intensely, perhaps, because it contained within itself the age-old California question: Could California nurture excellence? And who was in charge of authenticating excellence anyway, hundreds of published California poets might reasonably ask (especially after Gioia became head of the National Endowment for the Arts in early 2003)? Los Angeles had been alive with poetry throughout the decade, not only at Launderland, but also in the metropolitan region, as evidenced in *Grand Passion: The Poets of Los Angeles and Beyond* (1995), edited by Suzanne Lummis and Charles Harper Webb. A number of poets in the anthology—David St. John, Carol Muske-Dukes, Robert Mezey, James Ragan, Aleida Rodriguez, Timothy Steele, Webb himself, Cecilia Woloch, Kate Braverman, and, of course, Bukowski—were as accomplished and as nationally published as Dana Gioia. And there was throughout *Grand Passion*—a point underscored by Webb in his afterword—a most extraordinary connection between poetry and life, between poetry and the daily facts of

Los Angeles, in contrast to the phantasmagoric world of the LA novel. Someday, someone would figure out why the LA novel went one way while poetry took another path.

The architects of Los Angeles were traveling the same path as its poets. In contrast to the dark and chaotic world so frequently portrayed in the LA novel, the buildings erected in the 1990s radiated a joyful and stylish confidence in metropolitan Los Angeles as an urban civilization and, secondly, the continuing vitality of modernism, now that it had become deconstructed and playful, and, thirdly, the intrinsic power of industrial materials. Were one to select an icon from the 1990s suggesting the festive success of architectural design in the region, it would be, perhaps, the Temporary Powell Library at UCLA, designed by the Santa Monica–based husband-and-wife team of Craig Hodgetts and Hsin-Ming Fung. The Temporary Powell Library—or the Towell, as it was soon dubbed—was a temporary structure of declassé steel, fabric, and Plexiglas, intended to serve as a temporary campus library while the Lawrence Clark Powell Library itself underwent restoration. Standing for five years, from 1992 to 1997, the Powell was an immediate sensation because it fused—pushed to the limit, in fact—a sense of Los Angeles as temporary place while also suggesting the permanence that comes from a useful and distinguished building. Indeed, the Powell could have served—and may very well do so in some future time—as a new kind of Southern California architecture, suspended midway between classicism and a Bedouin tent, appropriate to an oasis city rising in the midst of a semi-arid plain.

When it came to more large-scale construction, the preeminent Los Angeles architects in this field—Scott Johnson and William Fain, David Martin, Jon Jerde, Rick Keating, Ruble Yudell—were busy building an international practice, exporting Los Angeles on a global scale. The Japanese were especially appreciative of the Los Angeles style, whether in large buildings, housing developments, or restaurant design. In the previous decade, Arata Isozaki had brought a Japanese-flavored modernism to Los Angeles with his Museum of Contemporary Art (MOCA) on Grand Avenue. MOCA struck a chord because it went to the core of the identity of California as Asia. Now California as Asia, the Los Angeles architectural style, was returning to Asia through a host of commissions in Japan, China, Guam, Indonesia, and Malaysia being awarded to Los Angeles architects.

As far as commercial art was concerned, San Francisco continued to lead the field, with the work of Walter Landor and Primo Angeli. Arriving in San Francisco as an expatriate from Germany, Landor founded the design firm of Landor Associates in 1941. Since 1964, the company had been headquartered in the *Klamath,* a reconverted Southern Pacific auto ferry boat, docked at Pier 5. By the time of Landor's death in 1995, his firm had created many of the best-known brands and logos of the second half of the twentieth century. This tradition was further amplified by the younger Primo Angeli, a protégé of Buckminster Fuller. Over the years, Angeli's clients had included DHL Worldwide Express, Transamerica, Standard Oil of California, Christian Brothers Winery, Bank of America, E. & J. Gallo, Hills Brothers Coffee, Henry Weinhard beer, Dreyer's Ice Cream, Boudin Bakery, and Banana Republic. Angeli was also a master of poster art, best known for his Vietnam War–era poster depicting a line of headstones in a military cemetery above the caption "The Silent Majority."

Each city was increasingly supportive of ambitious public murals, although Los Angeles, as a Mexican-American city, outpaced San Francisco as it monumentally adorned itself with such superscale murals as Kent Twitchell's photo-realist *LA Marathon* on the San Diego Freeway near Century Boulevard and *Harbor Freeway Overture* on the Harbor Freeway downtown, each done early in the decade, together with dozens of striking murals by Mexican-American artists on the city's Eastside. Whether through the formal work of such mural masters as Twitchell, Richard Wyatt, Terry Schoonhoven—even non–Los Angeleno Frank Stella, whose art swept across a multistoried facade downtown—or all the work in the Mexican-American community, some of it formal and ambitious, some of it arising from the twilight zone just above graffiti, Los Angeles was picturing itself to itself through mural art beyond any other city in the nation.

A decade of museum building and enhancement in each city was most singularly summarized by the design, construction, dedication, and instant success of the Getty Center in Brentwood. Since 1974 the J. Paul Getty Museum, devoted to classical art, had been flourishing in Malibu in a re-creation of the Villa dei Papiri in Herculaneum, a city buried when Mount Vesuvius erupted in A.D. 79. When John Paul Getty died in 1976, he left $700 million in oil stock to the museum. The only requirement laid down by the Southern California–born and –raised London oilman was that the income from the trust be spent "for the diffusion of artistic and general knowledge." By the mid-eighties, the Getty Trust was initiating a number of curatorial and educational programs, based in various sites in Santa Monica and West Los Angeles.

Trustees such as former UCLA chancellor Franklin Murphy, chairman and chief executive officer of the Times Mirror Corporation, and Getty executive Harold Williams, a lawyer who had risen to the presidency of Norton Simon's Hunt Foods, had even more ambitious plans in mind. Under the U.S. tax code, the Getty Trust was required to spend slightly more than 4 percent of the market value of its total endowment three out of every four years. That meant disbursing something like $90 million a year by the late 1980s, a figure that grew dramatically in the 1990s as the endowment pushed past $3 billion. The sheer magnitude of such funds demanded the envisioning of an entirely new kind of institution in terms of its programs and architectural setting. Under the guidance of Williams, president of the trust, plans emerged for an institution that would cluster a number of research institutes devoted to conservation, art history (a library of 750,000 books, an archive of primary sources, two million photographs), art technology and management, education, and a research grant program around a major museum open to the public.

Patiently, starting in the early 1980s, the trust embarked on the acquisition of acreage atop an empty mountain in Brentwood adjacent to the San Diego Freeway. In late 1983, the trust announced plans to move to the Brentwood site. By February 1984, three world-class architects—Richard Meier of New York, James Stirling of London, Fumiko Maki of Tokyo—were announced as finalists. Shortly thereafter Meier was chosen, and for the Getty Center, as the entire complex was called, the Pritzker laureate and his associates designed a glimmering white Acropolis, eventually costing $1 billion, for the 110-acre promontory. As the center moved toward its December 1997 opening, it was becoming increasingly apparent that Meier had accomplished a masterpiece of monumental modernism, at once classical in its open spaces, massing, and other arrangements, and romantic in its shimmering poetry of place.

What was not predicted, however, was the popular success of the Getty among ordinary Los Angelenos. Here, after all, was an institution that constituted a monument to Alexandrianism: to rigorous scholarship and impeccable taste. Here was also a monument to the sheer power of money compounding and recompounding itself as stocks doubled and tripled in value. What did this Acropolis have to say to the common people, a number of critics were asking as the opening approached? Plenty, it turned out, as—following the usual A-list inaugural party on the evening of December 9, 1997—the people of the city poured into the complex in unprecedented numbers, despite the fact that Brentwood neighbors of the Getty had rigidly restricted parking to twelve hundred spaces in an underground structure, to be booked in advance. Within a year of opening, toward two million visitors had made the pilgrimage to the Getty mountaintop to enjoy—for free, there was no admission charge—the art and exhibits, the architecture, the views, and landscape architect Robert Irwin's Central Garden. The reasons for the success of the Getty—the art, the architecture, the extraordinary array of lectures and programs open to the public, the interactive learning centers throughout the museum, the welcoming restaurant, café, and cafeteria, bookstore and gift shop—were easy to understand. More subtly, the Getty offered Los Angeles an experience of traditional urbanism at the very center of a deconstructed city. Through Getty Center, Los Angeles could daydream of itself as a classical city, condensed, balanced, and dense, released from the burdens of hyper-horizontality. At the Getty, Los Angeles became a city on a hill.

In terms of the things that the intelligentsia were interested in, or at least tended to measure their community by—bookstores, libraries and museums, art and foreign film houses, theater, restaurants, available universities, newspapers, opera and symphony—metropolitan San Francisco and metropolitan Los Angeles were evenly balanced. Each had nationally ranked symphony orchestras, with noted conductors—Michael Tilson Thomas in San Francisco, Esa-Pekka Salonen in Los Angeles—and was experiencing equal anxieties regarding an aging audience and a failure to bring boomers into regular subscription series. The opera companies of each city pushed the envelope, ever so slightly, in an effort to make this venerable—and very expensive—art form appealing to younger audiences. San Francisco Opera general director Lotfi Mansouri commissioned André Previn to write an original opera based on Tennessee Williams's *A Streetcar Named Desire* (1947). The performance was released by Deutsche Grammophon and was scheduled for reprises with the San Diego Opera, Opera Pacific in Orange County, Australia, and the Welsh National Opera.

The Los Angeles Opera, first under its founding director Peter Hemmings, then under his successor, tenor Placido Domingo, brought to its productions an attitude of assertive theatricality. Designed by such artists as David Hockney and Gerald Scarfe, directed by such bold personalities as Peter Sellars, conducted by, among others, Zubin Mehta, Esa-Pekka Salonen, and Kent Nagano, lit with the skill of a high-tech movie studio, and costumed like Cecil B. DeMille productions, the Los Angeles Opera modernized and intensified the entertainment value of this sometime cumbersome and improbable art form. Productions—and they included such ambitious efforts as the second-only American performance of Hector Berlioz's multihour epic *Les Troyens,* John Adams's *Nixon in China,* and Daniel Catan's *Florencia en el Amazonas*—were, in the main, boldly theatrical, well acted by physically attractive artists, and skillfully staged and directed. The LA Opera, in brief, was showing the influence of the Industry.

Placido Domingo took over direction of the opera in 1999 and recruited as his principal conductor Kent Nagano, a Japanese-American Californian who was also serving as principal conductor for the German Symphony Orchestra of Berlin and the Berkeley Symphony, and who had previously had successful stints at the Lyon Opera in France, the Hallé Orchestra in

Manchester, and the London Symphony. The recruitment of Nagano—a UC Santa Cruz and San Francisco State graduate, charismatic in gesture and manner, musically erudite, one of the most noted conductors in the profession despite the fact that he was not yet fifty—offered proof that Domingo was looking not only for new audiences but for a new generation of musical talent. And a new generation of musical patronage as well, for Domingo's good friend, investor Alberto Vilar, a Cuban American in his forties and a noted opera lover, made over an attention-grabbing pledge of $24 million, to be shared with the Mariinsky Theatre in St. Petersburg, to be used for new productions.

In defining and implementing the style, even the status, of a metropolitan region, perhaps no institution or agency—not opera or symphony, not little theater, not libraries or museums, not even universities—possessed the impact of a newspaper. Recasting itself in the 1950s under the editorship of Scott Newhall as a daily magazine of feature columnists—Herb Caen, Stanton Delaplane and Charles McCabe, society writer Pat Steger, arts and cultural critics Terrence O'Flaherty, Kevin Wallace, Robert Commandy, Al Frankenstein, Ralph Gleason, John Wasserman—the *San Francisco Chronicle* rode the wave of postwar Bay Area growth by offering its readers news lite and a daily dose of chatty commentary, sustained by an assumption that San Francisco and its environs was the most privileged place in America. In doing this, the *Chronicle* not only saw its circulation soar, it also anticipated a number of national trends: first-person celebrity journalism, the local lifestyle magazine, a general shift from hard news to feature commentary, the increasing importance of food and entertainment coverage, the newsworthiness of fashion, architecture, interior design, and, on a more serious note, science reporting. To read the *Chronicle* from the postwar era into the 1990s was to encounter the power of a newspaper as a daily magazine in the service of regional ambition.

The *Los Angeles Times* lacked the sparkle and style of the *Chronicle* and was much more overtly interested in politics, power, and sport. Its lead columnist, Jack Smith, in contrast to Caen, offered a much more folksy view of things, a kind of easygoing Midwesternism that saw humor, hence affirmation, in the routines and stories, including the shaggy-dog stories, of ordinary life. While the *Chronicle* was content to dominate its region, the *Times* had national aspirations, if only in terms of reputation. Under publisher Otis Chandler, the *Times* attained a national, even international, reputation by the 1980s, thanks to a strong Washington presence and a number of overseas bureaus.

To foster its ambitions, the *Times* began in the 1970s to recruit a rising generation of journalism school graduates with respected bylines, some of them, like Robert Reinhold, coming from the *New York Times.* Imagine the shock, then, when it was discovered in the fall of 1999 that a special issue of the *Los Angeles Times Magazine,* covering the dedication of the newly completed Staples Center, involved a secret profit-sharing agreement between the center and the newspaper. Already, for some time, the writers and editors of the *Times* had been highly suspicious of the efforts of Mark Willes, CEO and chairman of Times Mirror, who had come to the newspaper from the General Mills cereal company, and publisher Kathryn Downing, another product of the corporate world, to make the paper more "advertiser-friendly," which is to say, to write stories that made advertisers feel more comfortable, hence more willing to advertise in the newspaper. Shock among the staff—the very value of their bylines being under threat—led to a collective rally on November 4, 1999, in the newsroom, during which a letter by the retired Otis Chandler denouncing the Staples Center agreement as the greatest threat to the integrity of the *Times* in more than half a century was read to the staff by city editor Bill Boyarsky, who had rejected the request of three superior editors that he not read the letter. When it was all over, Willes and Downing were gone (not without their golden parachutes) and the *Times,* late that December, published a fourteen-page insert by Pulitzer Prize–winning David Shaw exhaustively chronicling the entire controversy. Within two years of each other, both family-owned, big-city California newspapers—longtime pillars of the state's establishment—had passed to non-Californian ownership: the *Los Angeles Times* to the *Chicago Tribune,* the *San Francisco Chronicle* to the Hearst Corporation of New York.

PART VIII

Growth and the Environment

Heartland

L ike Caesar's Gaul, all California could be divided into three parts, north, south, and central. In the nineteenth century, central California—more commonly known as the Central Valley or even the Great Central Valley because of its scale and geographical unity—took a far, far third place to coastal northern California and, later, coastal Southern California in the collective identity of the state. Throughout most of the twentieth century, in fact, the north California/south California dichotomy seemed sufficient to explain the entire California experience. By the 1990s, however, no one could evaluate California past, present, or future without reference to the newly emergent third force.

Here was the heartland: four hundred miles long, forty to sixty miles wide, the size of a respectable nation. It was divided into three components: the San Joaquin Valley in the south, the Delta country in the center, and the Sacramento Valley in the north. The Sierra Nevada mountain range delineated the Central Valley on its eastern flank, and various coastal ranges marked its western edge. More than five million Californians, governing themselves through eighteen county jurisdictions, were by the mid-1990s scattered across its 24,000 square miles, which made up two-fifths the land mass of the state. Agriculture—a $16 billion annual economy by 1996, producing a quarter of all the food consumed in the United States—was the main enterprise, followed by oil; but every other aspect of the California economy was represented in the Central Valley as well; in economic matters, as in so much else—diversity, growth, transformations of culture and value—central California contained within itself the representative formula, the paradigm, of the entire state. After a hundred years of irrigation and agricultural development, central California had become an Invented Garden of boundless magnitude. The San Joaquin Valley alone, were it a separate state, would be larger in area than ten other states in the nation and would rank thirty-first in population. Only the entire states of California and

Texas would have more residents of Mexican origin. Only seven other states would have more people of Asian ancestry.

In ancient times a spacious inland sea, with 2,100 miles of shoreline and adjacent wetlands, filled the region. When the seas receded, a vast Serengeti Plain teeming with bunch grass took its place. Herds of grazing elk extended as far as the eye could see. Overhead, in what became known as the Great Pacific Flyway, birds of every description darkened the sky. In time, baked by incessant heat, the grasslands receded to the periphery, where the wetlands also survived; and the southern regions of the Central Valley, over the centuries, were baked into a hard and resistant semi-arid desert awaiting the conquests of irrigation. The Sacramento Valley to the north, meanwhile, remained a flood plain periodically inundated by the inland sea that had vanished only to appear and reappear at cyclical intervals.

By the 1990s, the Central Valley had long since become the most productive unnatural landscape in the world, a triumph of irrigation technology. Only technology could have made the valley fertile. There was little humus or topsoil, next to no worms, and very little water. From one perspective, the entire valley, at least the dry southern regions, represented an extensive experiment in hydroponic gardening: a thoroughly artificial conjoining of heat (an average of 86 degrees, day and night, in the summer, three hundred growing days a year), soil, water, farm technology, and transportation. On the west side of the valley, Interstate 5 moved through a flat landscape that extended in every direction as far as the eye could see. And yet the signs of irrigation and agriculture were everywhere—canals, silos, orchards, and planted fields—and engendered an atmosphere of remote power, as if an absent race of giants had planted this great garden, then stole away into the distant Sierra Nevada or Coast Ranges to watch it grow.

Mesopotamia, the rice fields of China, the Po Valley: the Central Valley stood in a long line of irrigated cultures which had, in turn, given birth to civilization itself. From the air, the valley revealed itself most fully for what it truly was: an imposition of will—of pattern and abstract organization—on endless stretches of resistant, heat-hardened clay. Across a century, great public works, ferocious machines, and the back-breaking labor of millions now forgotten had brought into being a place that nature never intended, a place, like so much of California, possessed of an instability, a fault line, just beneath the tranquilly patterned landscape.

In older societies, technology and environment tended to reach a point of balance, hence stability. There are agricultural regions in Europe and Asia that have been under cultivation for more than one thousand years. In the Central Valley, technology—the early irrigation districts, the Fresno scraper, the tractor, dams and canals without number, railroads, roads and highways, an interstate, and, finally, mass-produced housing—had for more than a century been in relentless motion, as if technology had a mind of its own and was making every effort to dominate a region almost too immense to be contemplated and too resistant to be subdued.

In human terms, from the beginning, the Central Valley had diversity. In ancient times, snowy white egrets left the wetlands to forage for horned toads in the southern deserts, elk roamed the plains, and grizzly bears rose in anger or inquisitiveness to their full height. The Native Americans of the valley belonged to some eighty (some claimed a hundred) separate language groups. Then came the Chinese, 10 percent of the population by 1852, building the levees of the Delta region, showing that agriculture could be performed, creating their own subculture and towns, such as Locke in Sacramento County. By 1900, 40 percent of all Chinese living in California were engaged in Central Valley agriculture. Arriving next were the Anglos, many of them ex-Confederates looking for a new start, then the Sikhs, and African Americans (gathered into their own township, Alansworth, in the south Central Valley), followed by Armenians fleeing genocide and successive waves of Mexican field workers and hundreds of thousands of refugees from the Dust Bowl in the 1930s, then more Asians—Vietnamese, Laotians, Cambodians, one-half of all the Hmong to be settled in the United States after the fall of Saigon. By 1990, Anglos made up 60 percent of the valley's population (although they were 82 percent of those voting). Of incoming groups, 45 percent were Hispanic and 31 percent Asian. By the year 2000, central California had a majority of minorities, as residents at least, if not in economic or political power.

Of all three areas, central California was the most stratified. Nonresident ownership, much of it corporate but much of it still in private hands, topped its six-tier social structure. Resident rich constituted the next stratum, many of them descendants of nineteenth- or early-twentieth-century families living on the land in baronial structures or in one or another of the Central Valley cities but owning as well an apartment on Nob Hill in San Francisco or on the Upper East Side of Manhattan or in London, and a getaway in Aspen, Vail, or Sun Valley. The middle classes held to the cities. On the fourth tier were the lower-middle and employed blue-collar classes, who could be found in both the larger cities and the townships and hamlets up and down the valley. Tier five comprised the upwardly mobile poor—the poor, that is, who were working, whether in the fields or in allied activities, or in the many low-tech manufacturing enterprises throughout the valley, or as service workers in the cities and towns. Tier six was a large underclass.

The lower-middle and working classes, so many of them second- or third-generation descendants of Dust Bowl migrants, represented the heart of the heartland. Bubba was alive and well in central California, happy in a world of country and western music and bars, county fairs, good old boys and girls, driving pickup trucks, wearing jeans and T-shirts, cowboy or John Deere hats, or, on more formal occasions, a short-sleeved white shirt or a sweatshirt with something funny on it. Bakersfield, headquarters for Buck Owens, Merle Haggard, Dwight Yoakam, the Maddox Brothers, and Sister Rose, prided itself in the Oklahoman and Texan origins of so many of its residents, and was the second national capital of country and western music after Nashville. In the first part of the century, Bakersfield had also produced the greatest Californian of them all (or so many thought), Earl Warren, governor and, later, chief justice of the United States.

Over the years, the Central Valley had by and large sent forth its most ambitious sons and daughters into the world. This was what the Modesto-based film *American Graffiti* (1973), written and directed by Modesto native George Lucas, was all about: the repetitive need of American youth to leave home to make it big or, conversely, the limitations of remaining a hometown boy or girl. Singer-actress Cher left, as did actor Mike Connors, another Fresno Armenian (his real name was Krekor Ohanian), and director Sam Peckinpah, another Fresno lad, and actors Jack Palance, Annette Funicello, and Jan-Michael Vincent of Kern County, and Janet Leigh of Stockton. Military careers had claimed World War II marine air ace Gregory "Pappy" Boyington and Admiral Elmo Zumwalt of Tulare, who rose to be chief of naval operations. Athletes with a Central Valley background included Rafer Johnson, Bob Mathias, and Mark Spitz, each winners of Olympic gold. There were artists like the Fresno-born Maynard Dixon, one of the leading figures in California painting in the first half of the century, sculptors Clement Renzi and Varaz Samuelian, and Wayne Thiebaud and Greg Kondos, who lived and painted in Sacramento through the 1990s. Thiebaud found his subject matter in the pop surfaces of contemporary life. Kondos discovered in the sun-baked landforms of the valley a landscape suggestive of another sun-baked, color-splashed land, his ancestral Greece. The valley was here and now, suggested Thiebaud. It was a pair of sunglasses, an ice cream cone. It was also, claimed Kondos, enlivened by immemorial association. It was a canal set against an orchard and a distant grain field, as Homer—or Kazantzakis—might have seen it in another land of the sun.

If there were one word to describe the Central Valley in the 1990s, however, it would not be art but growth, growth, and more growth. California was the fastest growing state in the nation, at twice the national rate, and the Central Valley was the fastest growing portion within California, at twice the rate of the state. Metropolitan Sacramento was approaching two million, and similar rates of growth were evident in metropolitan Fresno, which now sprawled across a hundred square miles, a city one-third the size of Los Angeles, metastasizing across vineyards and fields. Demographers were predicting another ten million in population within the next ten to fifteen years, bringing the Central Valley to fifteen million.

The problem was agriculture. Since 1964, seven million acres of farm land had been lost to development. The ease with which this had happened proceeded directly from the very structure of California agriculture. The Spanish and Mexicans had made large land grants, which had, in turn, been even further consolidated in the first phase of American ownership. As San Francisco economist Henry George and others were noting by the 1870s, the consolidation of preexisting land grants, already extensive in and of themselves, together with a too-generous policy of grants to the Central Pacific Railroad by the federal government, had placed the majority of Central Valley properties under the control of a small number of individuals or corporations. Henry Miller, for example, a German-born ex-butcher who had landed in San Francisco in 1850 under the name of Heinrich Alfred Kreiser with six dollars in his pocket, by the end of his life owned more than 800,000 contiguous acres in Santa Clara County and the San Joaquin Valley.

Arriving as a naval officer in 1846, Edward Fitzgerald Beale consolidated four Mexican land grants in southern Kern County into the Rancho Tejon. By the late twentieth century, having passed to the control of the Times Mirror Corporation, the 270,000-acre Tejon Ranch, the largest contiguous privately owned property in California and the sixth largest in the nation, was beginning to approach half the state of Rhode Island in terms of its total acreage. By the 1990s such agribusiness giants as Castle & Cooke, JG Boswell, and Salyer American controlled equally impressive acreages. Even the descendants of Henry Miller were still in the business, specifically his great-great-grandsons Philip and Corky Bowles, whose Bowles Farming Company owned and operated fourteen thousand acres in Merced County, strategically placed alongside the San Joaquin River, to which it held extensive riparian rights, and Nickel Enterprises, under the direction of Miller's great-grandson George W. Nickel Jr., which held eight thousand acres in Kern, Fresno, and Merced Counties.

Although there still existed throughout the valley numerous smaller holdings and enterprises, the key characteristic of the region's agriculture was its century-plus organization as large-scale agribusiness. The water economy of the state, in which the federal and state governments delivered millions of acre-feet to Central Valley growers at hypersubsidized prices, reinforced such a polity. For nearly a hundred years, critics had been railing against the government-subsidized corporate structure of valley agribusiness, but to no avail. Even such late start-ups as the E. & J. Gallo Winery of Modesto, founded in 1933 by Ernest and Julio Gallo, ran to Herculean proportions: seventeen thousand acres under family and corporate titles, its own trucking fleet, a 265-million-gallon tank farm and twenty-five-acre warehouse for storage, and control by 1993—the year that Julio Gallo, eighty-two, drove his Jeep down an embankment and died from a broken neck—of a third of the wine, brandy, and wine-cooler business in the United States.

Given their well-defined ownership and clear lines of authority, such large-scale enterprises were perfectly capable of becoming equally large-scale housing, office, and retail developments. In a state in which by 1987 a mere 1,012 landowners controlled fifteen million acres or 49 percent of all agricultural land, the decision to develop portions of such properties did not have to endure a painful and expensive assemblage of acreage, farm by farm. Thus the Newhall Land Company could develop the thirty-thousand-resident suburb of Valencia on one corner of its fifty-eight-square-mile ranch in the Santa Clarita Valley as part of an integrated corporate program; and the Tejon Ranch Company could have on its drawing boards resort and suburban development for many parts of its 270,000-acre spread. Even in the case of smaller holdings, ranchers making at the most $2,500 a year per acre could quite easily be persuaded to dispose of such acreage for, say, $30,000 an acre. Thus in the 1960s neophyte developer Angelo Tsakopoulos of Sacramento was able to assemble acreage in the Pocket district on the American River in South Sacramento from a handful of Portuguese-American farmers long settled in the area—this in the opening phases of a career that would see Tsakopoulos, alone or in various partnerships, develop over the next thirty years five thousand acres of farm land into housing, office parks, and retail malls.

By the 1990s, a traveler moving north through the Central Valley on Highway 99 would encounter city after city—Bakersfield, Visalia, Fresno, Merced, Modesto, Stockton, Sacramento, Yuba City, Marysville, Oroville, Chico, Red Bluff, Redding—which had over the previous twenty years ballooned out from its earlier identity into a highly repetitive interlocking scheme of suburban housing enclaves, industrial parks, and shopping malls. The same thing was true of even the smaller townships in between—Selma, Madera, Chowchilla, Atwater, Delhi, Turlock, Tracy, Manteca, Elk Grove, Rio Linda—which were either metastasizing as independent townships or developing into bedroom communities for nearby cities. By the 1990s, the time seemed not far off in the future when a continuous metropolis would run north on Highway 99 from Bakersfield to Yuba City.

All this, among other things, suggested a loss of farm land. In a report issued in October 1995, the American Farmland Trust projected the loss of more than a million of the remaining seven million acres of productive farm land between Yuba City and Bakersfield over the next two generations. An additional 2.5 million acres would come under risk because of urban encroachment. The Central Valley, noted the trust, was one of the most threatened agricultural regions in the nation. As might be expected, the trust study, researched and written over a two-year period by consultants from the Institute of Urban and Regional Development at UC Berkeley, met with the sympathy of economists, urban planners, and government officials who had long since become concerned that sprawl could not pay for itself. The year the report appeared, the Bank of America issued a white paper entitled *Beyond Sprawl* (1995), based on data supplied by the Department of Finance of Governor Wilson's administration, which argued that low-density sprawl drained local government coffers without generating comparable taxes, hence weakened public services and, in lowering quality of life, eventually drove away investment and jobs. Not only that, sprawl reduced agricultural productivity by billions of dollars. In conclusion, the trust study envisioned the dystopian possibility, by the year 2040, of a congested and smog-choked spine of sprawl running up the Central Valley, unable to pay its bills and taking billions of dollars out of a once flourishing agricultural economy. Fresno, for example, had been debt free in the early 1980s. By 1999, it had taken on $329 million in bond debt to pay for its infrastructure. Local taxes were spiraling upward as the city struggled to maintain services between its ever-expanding boundaries.

Already, many observers pointed out, one could see signs of a dystopia in the making as tax-devouring sprawl and income-producing agriculture proved more and more incompatible. In Merced County, home owners living next to still-productive fields complained of the noise of farm machinery operating into the early hours of the morning, the sound of biplanes roaring overhead, nighttime and early-morning spraying, the scent of pesticide in the air (and, worse, the effects of pesticide on automotive paint), the pungent smells of livestock and fertilizer, the slow-moving tractors and farm vehicles on the roadways at the height of the commute hours, the flies, the dust, the stink. Was this, they asked themselves, why they were commuting four hours each day into the Bay Area? Was this their California dream? When residents took their complaints to city and town councils, the farmers fought back. Ranching, farming, cattle raising, they pointed out, was dirty business. In county after county, farmers and ranchers launched a counterattack and succeeded in having numerous right-to-farm ordinances passed. One popular measure required that real estate agents describe in writing for prospective clients the realities of living adjacent to agriculture.

Critiques of the Highway 99 situation were coming from many quarters. Agriculturalists decried the loss of prime farm land. Environmentalists protested the headlong consumption of natural resources. Architectural critics and urban planners lamented the repetitive mazes of suburban tracts and shopping centers filled with chain stores, all of it so indistinguishable and undistinguished. Planners also criticized the low density of development, which by its very nature pushed sprawl further into the heartland, as if Frank Lloyd Wright's Broadacre City were running amok. Traffic planners noted the reappearance of the very same gridlock so many residents had fled coastal cities to escape. Social commentators denounced the debilitating effects of the daily commute on family life, the reduplication of gang culture, the drugs, the crime, the alienated young.

Nothing symbolized the growth ordeal of central California more than smog. For decades the Los Angeles basin was the smog capital of the nation, but by 1991 Bakersfield was the second smoggiest city in the United States, and Fresno was the third. Ozone was choking crops. In the case of certain products—cotton, table grapes, Valencia oranges—ozone was reducing yields by 20 percent and more. In the case of other crops—black-eyed peas, dried beans, alfalfa, almonds, sweet corn, and tomatoes—damage was lower but still significant. All this, together with other related smog losses, meant a $200 million setback to growers by the early 1990s and $184 million in higher prices at the grocery stores.

In October 2001, the U.S. Environmental Protection Agency designated the 25,000-square-mile San Joaquin Valley a severely polluted ozone region, one of the eleven most polluted, urban or rural, in the United States. Even more shocking was the added note that the San Joaquin Valley–based Sequoia National Park had the worst smog of any national park in the country, with higher ozone levels than those of Los Angeles and New York City combined. Naturally, officials of the San Joaquin Valley Air Pollution Control District, now being forced to submit a revised antismog program by May 31, 2001, that would bring the valley back to federal standards by 2006, went onto red alert. Much of the pollution, they claimed, was drifting in from the highly populated Bay Area and South Coast, pushed there by prevailing west to east winds. Yet despite this legitimate claim, it had to be faced that the sheer growth of the valley was also taking its toll.

Fresno—one hundred square miles of continuous and interlocking subdivisions and shopping centers extending endlessly to the horizon—provided the most dramatic example of runaway sprawl in the valley. In the 1980s, Fresno's population had expanded by 63 percent, as acre after acre of prime farm land was paved over to create housing and malls, malls and housing for more than 400,000 Fresno residents. Longtimers looked on with horror as a city famed through the 1950s for its quality of life became, in terms of sprawl, smog, crime, and various forms of social dysfunction, a reverse paradigm of its former self. Downtown Fulton Mall, created in the 1960s to attract shoppers to the central city, sat almost deserted under the hot sun, its sidewalks lined by marginal retail outlets advertising their wares through handpainted signs. With almost no planning (or so it seemed), Fresno had spread out from its center in a near frenzy to reach the horizon. As many as 25,000 acres of vacant land had been left behind in this obsession to expand: enough land, that is, to house 100,000 residents without plowing under even one more acre of farmland, pulling up one more vineyard, or extracting one more fruit tree. At many points throughout the city, malls stood adjacent to empty acres only recently under cultivation, and tracts of housing spilled through inactive or partially active industrial sites.

Sprawl brought with it a declining quality of life as social and community ties weakened and civic and religious institutions lost their ability to keep connected. In reviewing the CBS miniseries *Fresno* on August 4, 1986, the *New York Times*'s Stephen Farber pointed to the fact that in one national survey Fresno had been rated the least desirable American city in the United States to live. Gang activity and drive-by shootings rivaled those of Los Angeles. Entire neighborhoods now featured barred windows and iron security doors. Graffiti was rampant. At one point in 1994, Governor Pete Wilson had to send in the California Highway Patrol to help local police deal with gang-infested neighborhoods. "Our juvenile hall now is basically for murderers and attempted murderers," noted one Fresno resident. "These kids are not afraid of anything. They are not even afraid of dying. If you choose to raise your children here, you are really gambling."[1] One in six residents of Fresno County was on welfare, the highest rate in California, twice that of Los Angeles. The Aid to Families with Dependent Children program was rising annually by 30 percent, more than the population growth itself. Writing in *Time* on November 18, 1991, Garry Wills accused the federal government of dumping on Fresno more than its fair share of Southeast Asian refugees, which was not a sprawl issue but did pertain to quality of life, in that these new populations showed a high and steady rate of welfare dependency.

As far as the sprawl was concerned, what had happened? How had things gotten so out of hand? Among those asking this question were the IRS, the FBI, and a federal grand jury, which by mid-decade had launched

Operation Rezone, probing the relationship between developers and elected officials on the Fresno City Council and various county boards. In time, agents uncovered an almost Byzantine pattern of connections between developers and officials, including outright payoffs, in addition to more subtle schemes of political fund-raising, which had, in effect, given developers carte blanche to metastasize the city and the county. Two forces, greed and political corruption, had conjoined to bloat Fresno beyond its carrying capacity. But even as nine politicians, lobbyists, and developers pled guilty and were sent off to prison, and two former councilmen and a leading developer came under indictment, the damage had been done: to the urban culture of Fresno, first of all, but also to the environment and to the fertile farm land now lying dead under tons of asphalt and concrete.

Each of the major cities and towns of the Central Valley had once represented—and were still struggling to maintain—some very powerful and important dimensions of the California formula. From this perspective, the cities and towns of the valley were too good to be lost. For those who knew, loved, and lived in the valley, these places were not just stops along Highway 99 or Interstate 5. They were communities with founding myths and legends, stories to tell about revered pioneers, high school heroes, young men who had gone off to war and returned or not returned, county fairs, high school football games, dragging the downtown main, as in *American Graffiti*. Sprawl overwhelmed and dissipated these identities, erased these memories. Sprawl pushed the physical fabric of the city beyond the ability of a dilated culture to hold social attachments and institutional loyalties together.

The Central Valley led the state in rates of poverty and unemployment, which remained in the low double digits in eight valley counties, over 9 percent in three more, and 8.5 percent in San Joaquin County, even as the economy of California recovered in the second half of the decade. As late as June 1997, when coastal California, north and south, was feeling the full force of recovery, more than 20 percent of the population in Fresno, Merced, and Tulare Counties were on welfare, with unemployment hovering between 12 and 16 percent. As late as November 1998, eleven of the fifteen counties with the worst unemployment rates in the state were in the Central Valley. Of the 5.5 million people living there, only 2.1 million had jobs. In the town of Orange Cove in Fresno County, half of the eight thousand residents were on welfare. When adult residents worked, they averaged about $4,000 a year in wages, the lowest per capita income in the state.

Some explained this appalling disparity between the Central Valley and the recovering California economy as resulting from the seasonal nature of farmwork, in which long bouts of unemployment were expected. Others saw a more grim scenario: one involving a decline in marketable skills in an increasing sector of the Central Valley workforce, an advancing high school dropout rate, drug use, and other forms of criminal behavior, together with personal and family dysfunction—the sum total, that is, of all the social shocks and downward mobility of the recent era—took their toll. When a manufacturer announced jobs affixing decals and buttons to Coke machines for seven dollars an hour in Fresno in October 1998, 835 job seekers showed up at the Ramada Inn where applications were being taken. Still, the company was barely able to fill 120 openings, since most applicants could not pass tests for literacy, work experience, drug use, or criminal histories.

Poverty, born of dysfunction, was an equal opportunity employer. Statewide, more Anglo families received financial aid, food stamps, and other forms of public assistance in 1991 than any other racial or ethnic group, and, overall, this rate remained steady for the rest of the decade, especially in the Central Valley. In Stanislaus County, for example, in 1991, some 8,349 Anglo families were on welfare, compared to 3,124 Latino families, 533 Asian families, and 528 African-American families. In trailer courts and shabby slums, in isolated shacks or rundown apartments in town, in cars parked on riverbanks or near roadside restrooms, thousands of poor whites (exact figures were unavailable) lived a *Grapes of Wrath* existence reminiscent of the 1930s. Some were the working poor. The majority were on welfare. Drugs, alcohol, and teenage pregnancy, most of it out of wedlock, were recycling portions of white California back onto Tobacco Road.

As tough as times were for so many whites, it was not enough to drive them into the fields as migrant farmworkers. Here at ground zero of the Central Valley economy, in agriculture, were the toughest jobs in the state, and they were getting tougher. In 1975, César Chávez and his associates had achieved what had long seemed an impossible breakthrough: the organization of the previously unorganizable, and the creation of some semblance of an industrial culture structured by rights and obligations on either side, as set forth in the California Agricultural Labor Relations Act signed that year by Governor Jerry Brown. The act had been the first—and only—legislation ever to give farmworkers the right to bargain collectively. Two Republican grower-oriented administrations had followed in Sacramento, however (becoming governor in 1982, George Deukmejian had cut the budget of the Agricultural Labor Relations Board and named a conservative Republican as general counsel); and by the time of Chávez's death in 1993, the United Farm Workers Union had shrunk from 100,000 to 10,000 working members organized and under contract.

If anything, times—and the work—were even tougher than they had been in the 1960s. The short-handle hoe might have been outlawed in 1975, but California Rural Legal Assistance activists were reporting by the early

1990s the growing appearance of the short-handle knife, a tool that was also illegal and, like the short-handle hoe, caused crippling back injuries. California agriculture, valued at $25 billion by 1996, had long since shifted from the cultivation of mechanically harvested crops—hay, oats, barley—in favor of a whole new inventory of berries, fruits, nuts, specialty lettuces and other exotic vegetables, cut flowers, and ornamental plants, which demanded excruciating stoop labor at harvest time. Strawberries alone (the "devil's fruit," farmworkers called them, because of the back-breaking work they demanded) had increased fivefold in acreage in the first seven years of the decade. All in all, the strawberries, kiwi, culinary herbs, arugula, endive, radicchio, romaine, artichokes, nuts, mushrooms, table grapes, and other specialty products, 250 in all, required more and more seasonal labor, 22 percent more since 1970.

Such an expanding, volatile labor market as California had become could not be contained within the organizational structures hammered out by the United Farm Workers in 1975. By the late 1990s, only a minuscule portion of the farmworker population in California (barely ten thousand out of 342,102 as of March 1997) were working under union contracts. Much of this labor force, moreover, had arrived long after the UFW-led boycott and strike of the late 1960s and 1970s. Ten percent of the harvesters in the field were recently arrived Mixtecs, an Indian people from the state of Oaxaca in southern Mexico. Other Indian peoples—Zapotecs and Triquis, also of Oaxaca, and various groups from Guatemala—had joined them. Indian farmworkers spoke little Spanish, let alone English; and, if they regarded the United Farm Workers at all, they tended to consider the union as being dominated by the more elite mixed-blood Mexicans who had caused them such grief for the past few hundred years in their homeland. Besides, many of the old-line *mestizo* Mexicans had left the fields to become labor contractors and, as had been the case in Oaxaca, were brokering Mixtec and other Indian labor. In the early 1980s, farmers personally hired their own workforce. By the late 1990s, most farmers were dealing with contractors, who had replaced union leaders as middlemen and advocates.

By the opening of the decade, many California farmworkers were earning less than their counterparts in Mexico. A group of some one hundred asparagus pickers near Stockton, for example, were paid $67 for fifteen days of work in September 1991. Even then, the labor contractor was deducting $8.50 a day for lunches and $2.50 per can of beer, having refused to provide water in the fields. Contractors frequently charged workers for tools and accommodations. In one case, a farmworker earned $35 picking garlic for two days. After he had paid $27 for tool rental and $5 a day for rides to and from the fields, he ended up owing the contractor $2.

Accommodations, always a problem, devolved to levels even below those reached prior to the Progressive reforms of the late 1910s. Workers slept in cars and trucks, beneath abandoned camper shells, in tool sheds or chicken coops, in makeshift plywood huts waterproofed with plastic sheeting or in tents made from plastic garbage bags. They slept under trees and, frequently blanketless, on mattresses in the backyards of contractors' houses (fifty farmworkers in one Madera backyard alone, each of them paying the contractor $20 a week for the space). Some workers literally dug themselves into the earth, living in hillside caves or holes scraped in the ground. They cooked their food over open fires, washed in nearby rivers, drank from irrigation flumes. As in the case of the 1930s, public health officials—if and when they made contact—were reporting a rise in nutritional problems, anemia, urinary tract infections, and other side effects of unsanitary living conditions.

Farm labor towns such as Huron in Fresno County were at lettuce harvest time filled with farmworkers carrying razor-sharp lettuce knives in stapled cardboard sheaths stuck in their hip pocket. Huron did not have a high school, or a newspaper, or even a Burger King. It did have, however, four labor camps, and was the poorest town in California. Not surprisingly, it was also known as Knife Fight City. Methamphetamines proved a special temptation to farmworkers anxious to maintain their productivity and cope with killing back pain. While the quality of life in Huron represented the outer edge, it was not irrelevant as a paradigm. Throughout California, central California especially, life in rural areas lagged significantly behind the rest of the state. In its *Report Card for Rural California* for 1995, the U.S. Department of Agriculture gave rural California barely passing grades, D+ in economic vitality, fiscal capacity, and housing; a C– in transportation; and a C+ in health. Only in two areas—a B– for education and a B for environment—did rural California edge into the honors category. In certain instances—the quality of drinking water, for example—the heartland ranked in the bottom category.

Rural California, agricultural California, was thus participating in that decline of economic vitality and quality of life being experienced throughout the United States by agricultural and ranching regions in the 1980s and 1990s. Indeed, there were some theorists who were speculating that the entire Great Plains region running down through the central United States, with the exception of certain urban areas, was being progressively and steadily abandoned and was en route to devolving back to being the Great Steppes of the nation. Could it be that the very steppe nature of the Central Valley, vast and arid, against which the cities of the interior had been forced to assert themselves, had also made the region especially vulnerable to suburban sprawl? In a region in which very few metaphors of settlement and nurture had been imposed on the landscape, had it become relatively easy for bulldozers to clear away the instances of cultivation that had been accomplished—the fig trees, the fruit trees, the crop lands—for developers to pave over?

People just kept coming. Exactly how many more would come remained an open question, but many agreed on a figure of at least ten million over the next two decades. Carol Whiteside, executive director of the Great Valley Center in Modesto, accepted the ten million figure. Started by a $1 million grant from the Hewlett Foundation, the Great Valley Center was intended to function as a central California think tank and grant-making foundation. A daughter of the valley, Whiteside was a gregarious middle-aged Republican politician of consummate talent and one of the smartest people in central California as far as land use planning was concerned. The mayor of Modesto from 1987 to 1991, she had served as a brain truster on the staff of Governor Pete Wilson, concentrating on issues of land use, finance, rural development, and economic restructuring, before leaving in 1997 to found the center. As mayor of Modesto, Whiteside had already taken the lead in encouraging a Central Valley–wide vision. Because she was a local girl made good, Whiteside had a chance to be heard. By the end of the decade, the center was sponsoring scores of environmental and planning initiatives. Among other things, Whiteside was offering $100,000 in prize money for the best suggestions on how California could cope with its next ten million residents. By May 1999, ideas were pouring in from across the world to Whiteside's interdisciplinary competition, formally known as "Housing the Next 10 Million: Envisioning California's Great Central Valley." Proposals ranged from dense Italian-like communities of four- to six-story buildings surrounded by farmland to a linear city running up along the entire length of Interstate 5. The purpose of the exercise was not necessarily to come up with one enforceable solution—it was too soon for that—but to begin the dialogue by suggesting alternatives to sprawl.

Was it too late? Perhaps. The example of Tracy suggested a spilling over of the crowded Bay Area into the western flank of the San Joaquin Valley over the Altamont Pass. A quiet agricultural town for more than one hundred years, Tracy ranked second in the state in its rate of growth, after Cupertino in the Silicon Valley, for cities of more than fifty thousand. As of May 2000, some 25,000 new homes were being planned for subdivided agricultural properties now covered in orchards and alfalfa. There was talk of Tracy expanding north to Stockton, east to Manteca, and south to Modesto over the next decade, eating up agricultural properties with row upon row of oversize McMansions and creating, eventually, a solid block of urbanization along this portion of Highways 5 and 99. From this perspective, this region, just east of the Bay Area across the Altamont Pass, was another Fresno in the making.

On the other hand, people liked it that way. A poll taken by the Public Policy Institute of California on behalf of the Great Valley Center in November 1999 revealed that three out of four residents of the Central Valley were by and large pleased with their lives. Given the growth of the valley, this was not surprising. Why else would people be flocking into the valley in the first place, if not to find a better life? Here was a paradox of success. Middle-class Americans, edged out of the expensive housing markets of the coastal regions, were willing to commute to and from such Central Valley towns as Tracy, Manteca, and Merced because they could afford a home there, even if it were located alongside an alfalfa field. Sure, the commute to jobs in the Bay Area was long. It could start as early as four in the morning and not be over until past seven at night; but train service had been inaugurated between Tracy and San Jose, and this in its way prefigured the possibilities of a more sophisticated integration of the mideastern Central Valley, where so many people lived, and the Bay Area, where so many people worked.

Was density being ignored? While sprawl clearly appeared to be in the ascendancy, there was another side to the argument. A report by the Solimar Research Group of Ventura, released in mid-July 2001 by the Brookings Center on Urban and Metropolitan Policy in Washington, D.C., revealed the startling news that California was using its newly urbanized areas—an average of 5.76 people per acre—at higher rates of density than similar areas in New York, New Jersey, and Pennsylvania. "The West is putting three times as many people on any new urbanized acre as anywhere else in the country," noted Bill Fulton, president of Solimar and one of the authors of the report. "In California, you have six to seven houses per acre being built on the metropolitan fringe. That doesn't happen anywhere else."[2]

Fresno, Davis, Visalia, and Lemoore had by August 2001 each completed model infill housing developments intended to show a more dense way of life to the heartland. Given the anti-growth attitudes of the city of Davis, its Aggie Village, a downtown infill development, came as no surprise; but the arrival of infill density in Fresno—including plans for accommodation for 25,000 in the nearly abandoned downtown, one thousand new homes in older neighborhoods, the refurbishment of another one thousand homes, and the consideration of a revolutionary new ordinance that would allow people to live over first-floor retail—made one almost giddy with hope that density and a more prudent policy of land use might find its way into the heartland.

Waterworld

A s far as water guru David Carle was concerned, the only way to contain sprawl, or, more precisely, runaway growth, was to cut off its water supply. In *Drowning the Dream: California's Water Choices at the Millennium* (2000), Carle argued that there had never been enough water in California precisely because an open-ended water calculus progression had been used to develop the state dangerously beyond what Mother Nature had intended. Every twenty-five years or so, Carle claimed, the California water community—spearheaded by developers, but also by farmers and officials from various water districts, and the legislators who wanted to please them—would predict a catastrophe if more water were not available. That alleged catastrophe, however, was merely a way to leverage new growth. Californians had been loath to ask, much less act upon, a much more simple question: If water development were stabilized, would growth stabilize as well? Was not water the fundamental premise of the Golden State?

Ever since the Gold Rush, Carle said, California had been inventing itself through water. Without human intervention on a massive scale in water allocation and management, California would not have existed in its present condition. Nature alone, or even nature with some modification, might have made possible a society of less than ten million clustered on the coast. What Californians did, however, was spend one hundred years and billions of dollars to create a federal, state, and county public works infrastructure of dams, aqueducts, reservoirs, and pipelines to capture, store, transport, and distribute an ever-growing percentage of the 193 million acre-feet of water that fell on California each year as precipitation, two-thirds of it in the northern third of the state. (An acre-foot equals enough water to cover one acre of land, roughly the size of a football field, to the depth of one foot, or 326,000 gallons.) Another 4.4 million acre-feet were brought in from the Colorado River by an equally impressive public works infrastructure radiating westward from the Hoover Dam, while cities such as San Francisco and Los Angeles maintained their own aqueduct systems, bringing water in from rivers to the east. Another 16.6 million acre-feet were pumped annually from the ground, most of it for agricultural irrigation.

To fly over California by the 1990s was to behold a statewide water infrastructure of titanic proportions. Made manifest in hundreds of dams, reservoirs, aqueducts, and canals was a century of consistent effort to capture the waters of California and distribute them proportionately as needed throughout the state. The agriculture of the region depended on the Central Valley Project (CVP) of the Federal Bureau of Reclamation. Extending from Shasta Dam on the Sacramento River north of Redding at the northern limit of the valley to Bakersfield at its southern boundary, the CVP was delivering seven million acre-feet of water annually, 90 percent of it intended for the three million acres of farmland on the valley floor. The State Water Project, meanwhile—twenty-nine dams and reservoirs linked by more than six hundred miles of aqueducts, approved by the voters in 1960 and under continuous construction for the next thirty years—was delivering another 2.5 million acre-feet annually to farmers in the San Joaquin Valley and the urban populations of the Bay Area and coastal Southern California. If all this were not enough, another six hundred cities and local agencies—among them, the Hetch Hetchy Project of San Francisco, the East Bay Municipal Utility District, the Los Angeles Department of Water and Power—were serving their populations with millions more acre-feet. Delivering nine hundred billion gallons of water a year to some seventeen million Southern Californians, the Metropolitan Water District (MWD), created by the California legislature in 1928, with two thousand employees, a multibillion-dollar infrastructure, and an annual budget of $800 million, was by the 1990s the largest water agency in the nation.

This infrastructure—colossal, intricate, a wonder of the modern world—was based on the assumption that, as far as California was concerned, there would always be enough water. Precipitation, after all, averaged approximately 193 million acre-feet per year, of which only 72 million acre-feet was run off. The rest was lost to evaporation, percolation into the ground, or transpiration by native plants. If worse came to worst, more of this lost water could be recovered. Between 1987 and 1993, however, California experienced a severe drought. By the winter of 1989–90, rainfall across the state had fallen by 55 percent, and most reservoirs were down by a fourth. The drought was a catastrophe comparable to the collapse of the economy, the Loma Prieta earthquake, or the Los Angeles riots, also happening in these drought years.

As in the case of other disasters, the drought forced a rethinking of the entire question of water allocation and, of equal importance, the relationship of water to growth and conservation. In 1952 the board of directors of the MWD had adopted its so-called Laguna Declaration, a two-paragraph statement that said that when additional water was required in Southern California, the district would be prepared to deliver it. And for forty years, it did. In August 1991, however, the MWD announced a shortfall of 250,000 acre-feet, enough water to serve half a million households for a year, and was projecting a shortfall of 500,000 acre-feet in 1992. Even if the drought ended immediately, the MWD was reporting, the agency would fall behind demand in six of the next ten years. Like defense jobs, acre-feet were drying up.

The first and most obvious effect of the drought was to raise consciousness about just how precious a resource water was. In the nineteenth century, the arid West had known this instinctively. Beyond the hundredth meridian extended an encompassing dryness that demanded the most careful possible use of water resources. California, however, had forgotten this lesson. Not only did rainfall and snowfall in its mountains and northern tier exempt California in part from the larger aridity of the Far West, the state had successfully defied the dryness through water-bearing public works of a heroic order of magnitude. What were the golf courses of Palm Springs, after all, or the millions of acres of lawn throughout the semi-arid Southland, much less the dense metropolitan populations of Los Angeles and the Bay Area, but dramatic witnesses to the fact that in California water had been captured and stored, allocated and distributed, conspicuously used and more than occasionally wasted? The entire civilization of California rested on arrogant assumptions of water appropriation. Now it was time to conserve.

Just how deeply conservation awareness penetrated the collective consciousness of California during the drought years remains a matter of debate. A significant percentage of the population was, as always, oblivious to the crisis. On the other hand, the seventeen million residents served by the MWD were certainly getting some sort of message: their property taxes increased to reflect rising costs; their water rates were raised by 14 percent; and there was serious discussion of a 40 percent water rate hike over the next few years if the drought continued. New sources of water were also being discussed. The long proposed Auburn Dam on the American River thirty-five miles northeast of Sacramento was once again brought before Congress for consideration. At 508 feet, larger than Hoover Dam, the Auburn Dam was intended to protect the floodplain below, where some 400,000 people were living, and to function as a mega-reservoir. Site preparation had begun in 1967, but the project had stalled when a 5.7 magnitude earthquake shook the area in 1977 and forced a redesign. In 1992, lobbied

intensely by environmentalists, Congress voted down the $1 billion pro-
posal, even in the face of the drought. Like Dracula, however, the Auburn
Dam refused to die. It remained the favored cause of Congressman John
Doolittle (R-Auburn) for the rest of the century.

Los Angeles County supervisor Kenneth Hahn, meanwhile, was discussing the feasibility of building a fourteen-hundred-mile ocean-based
pipeline capable of bringing water in from Alaska at the rate of five thousand cubic feet a second, or four million acre-feet a year. Alaska governor
Walter Hickel was an enthusiastic backer of the project, as was the engineering firm Fluor Daniel, which estimated the cost of the proposed Alaska-
California Subsea Water Pipeline, as it was called, to be hovering around
the $110 billion mark. The MWD joined with Southern California Edison
to study the feasibility of erecting a $1.5 billion desalination plant in Mex-
ico, to be constructed by the Bechtel Corporation of San Francisco, capable
of producing five hundred megawatts of electricity and one hundred million
gallons of water a day. Seventy-five percent of the processed water would
be shipped north from Baja to Southern California. The rest would remain
in Mexico. The cities of Santa Barbara, Morro Bay, and Avalon on Santa
Catalina Island each brought desalination plants online in the early 1990s.
The Santa Barbara facility was intended to meet a third of that city's needs.
Numerous recycling proposals surfaced, including an ambitious program in
Los Angeles to sell recycled water for car washing, lawn watering, and con-
struction work.

Observance of water-saving measures was especially strong in the
conservation-oriented Bay Area. As the drought entered its fourth year, the
Santa Clara Valley Water District was reporting a 31.5 percent cutback;
the East Bay Municipal Utility District, a 29.5 percent reduction; San Francisco, an impressive 38 percent savings; and the Marin Municipal Water
District, an astonishing 48 percent cutback from predrought 1986 levels.
Even Southern California, which was supposed to be less conservation
minded, was showing a 25 percent savings in San Diego and an impressive
31.5 percent in Los Angeles. The majority of these drought-responsive cutbacks had been mandated by the various water authorities and agencies.

One thing was certain: the drought had deconstructed water in California. Before, water possessed a fixed meaning and social scenario: Thanks to
public works, California had maximized its resources and was moving
water to where it was needed. There would always be enough for everyone:
suburbanites and farmers, lettuce fields, vineyards, and golf courses. California had constructed its identity on water. That identity remained stable.
If more water was needed, it could be obtained. But following the drought,
the water identity of California had become destabilized on a number of

fronts. The old formula said that the great water projects would allow California to correct shortfalls of location. Water could be moved from the north to the south or in from the Colorado River or from other places, and there would always be enough. Under the new formula, Californians knew that a prolonged drought could prevent there being enough. Even more important, the drought suggested that California had outpaced its multibillion-dollar water system, that the shortfalls of the early 1990s were not merely a matter of drought but were based on long-range deficiencies of water as a resource and the ability of the public works infrastructure to deliver it. The drought had underscored long-range changes of climate and water availability. Even in the wettest years, the public works infrastructure of California—however impressive, however worthy of comparison to the pyramids of Egypt and the aqueducts of Rome—was falling far short in its ability to service growth. California was outrunning its water delivery system.

The State Water Project, which had been delivering water since 1973, had by 1990 fallen 50 percent behind the deliveries it had promised in 1960 when construction began. Now that Arizona and Nevada were using their full entitlements, the MWD's share of Colorado River water had fallen by 50 percent, which represented a nearly 20 percent drop in its total annual deliveries. In 1982 the voters had overwhelmingly defeated Proposition 9, which would have constructed a peripheral canal around the Sacramento–San Joaquin Delta in order to move northern California water more efficiently into Southern California; thus the waters of northern rivers, like those of the Colorado, were not going south at the rate they were needed, that is, at the rates determined by current growth and usage. The drought and its aftermath had destabilized California's water identity with the knowledge that even after a century of heroic construction there was no way that the state could keep up with the water needs being created by its growth rate and lifestyles. There was a built-in shortfall, and something had to give.

Even as the drought ended, in cotton fields outside Bakersfield, in cattle pastures near Red Bluff, from the coastal sageland in Chula Vista to the floodplains of Sacramento, subdivisions were being planned or were already coming under construction. Their names—Pacificana, Celebrity City, Liberty New Town, Diablo Grande, New Jerusalem—bespoke a headlong expectation that the future as growth would once again happen and there would be plenty of water for everyone: 600,000 acre-feet a year, to be precise, or 10 percent of what urban California was already using, for the subdivisions on the drawing boards by August 1995 alone. These subdivisions envisioned two million residents, thirty thousand acres of commercial, industrial, and office space, and, at the minimum, forty-four golf courses. The projects moved toward reality, furthermore, at the very time that the California Department of Water Resources was warning of an impending 2.7 million acre-foot shortfall. What use was it to put a brick in your toilet tank or a governor in your shower or let your lawn go brown when Kern County alone had by August 1995 approved fourteen new subdivisions, which meant 256,000 more people using 150,000 more acre-feet of water?

As water-subdivision awareness intensified, so did the political climate surrounding election to local water boards. Control a water board and you controlled growth, one way or another. (An average California household was by then using one-half to one acre-foot of water per year.) By November 1997, the race for seats on the once-obscure Newhall County Water District board had become a referendum, if not a possible moratorium, on the subdivision of that region by the Newhall Land and Farming Company, a publicly traded real estate partnership that had developed the cities of Valencia and Santa Clarita and was now proposing Newhall Ranch, a 25,000-home development. If there was one thing developers feared, it was a moratorium on growth implemented by water policy. Gary Cusumano, president of Newhall, went on the counterattack as vice chairman of the Water Resources Committee of the California Chamber of Commerce. Why not store water by creating reservoirs in dry canyons, Cusumano argued, and hence not interrupt an existing stream? Why not allow the transfer of water rights from marginal agricultural enterprises to flourishing subdivisions?

This last idea—and it was a precedent-shattering proposal: to permit cities and suburbs to use agricultural water—became official state policy with the establishment by Governor Pete Wilson of an Emergency Drought Water Bank in the first year of his administration. The idea was simple. The Department of Water Resources would purchase water at $125 per acre-foot from agricultural jurisdictions in which there was a surplus, then bank the water for resale to urban and suburban agencies experiencing shortfalls. In 1991 the Water Bank brokered 205,000 acre-feet. By the time the water was purchased, banked, stored, resold, and redistributed, it naturally rose in price. Pistachio grower Doug Anderson, for example, was paying $260 per acre-foot for Water Bank water by June 1991. High prices like this hurt, Anderson admitted, but the water got him through another season. Conversely, many farmers whose allotments more than met their needs were discovering that surplus water had now become their leading cash crop.

In times past, under the predrought rubric and identity, farmers would have found it unthinkable to transfer water rights, even for a profit, to urban areas, just as cities would have considered it unimaginable to transfer their water rights to farmers. But the drought had deconstructed these hard-and-fast rules, and something resembling a water market was emerging. In addition, the knowledge that the federal, state, and local water systems of California could not meet urban and suburban needs in the decade to come, drought or no drought, made the competitive pricing and transfer of water rights, either through resale or through reallocation, inevitable. By May 1998, river-rich Yuba County in the Sacramento Valley, population 62,000, which had earned some $30 million selling water rights to the Water Bank in the early 1990s, was continuing to do a multimillion-dollar business shipping thousands of acre-feet to the farms and cities of the San Joaquin Valley.

California congressional members, many of them from water-scarce urban or suburban districts, were quick to grasp the implications of transferring federally supported water, most of it intended for agricultural use, to districts serving densely populated areas. Passed by Congress and signed by President George H. W. Bush in 1992, the Central Valley Project Improvement Act (Public Law 102-575) specifically authorized the federally supported CVP to sell its excess water to users outside the system, provided the water transferred from the CVP represented no more than 20 percent of what was on hand with the local supplier. (The federal government did not want to become the dominant supplier through the CVP for water-scarce local districts, hence the 20 percent limit.) Over the next few years, an intricate water market involving spot transfers, option transfers, and core transfers, including compensation formulas for water wheeling by third-party agencies moving water from one part of the state to the other, developed between the CVP and various clients. Previously, 85 percent of CVP water had gone, invariably and inevitably, to agriculture. Now the CVP was serving urban and suburban growth.

What did agriculture think of all of this? On the one hand, the good news was that agricultural districts could now sell federal water to urban areas. The bad news, for farmers, at least, was that a free market was being created that had broken agriculture's long monopoly on federal water. In time, that free market could very well turn the CVP into an urban- and suburban-oriented water agency. Certainly, such a transformation was on the minds of many elected officials backing the 1992 bill. Senator Bill Bradley (D-New Jersey), chairman of the Senate Subcommittee on Water and Power, who along with California representative George Miller (D-Martinez), chairman of the House Interior Committee, was cosponsoring the Central Valley Project Improvement Act, had stated during hearings that California had a $760 billion economy, yet agriculture represented only $20 billion of that total sum. Why should 85 percent of federal water in California, Bradley and Miller asked, continue to go to agriculture when there were so many other pressing needs? Each year, they pointed out, the rice crop of California alone—600,000 acres, second in the nation after Arkansas and representing a quarter of all rice grown in the United States—consumed more water than all the households of Los Angeles and San Francisco put together.

The Central Valley Project Improvement Act also further enabled another issue and set of players—environmentalism and environmental activists—in the California water game. The act provided for the restoration and protection of fisheries and wildlife habitat, including wetlands, by earmarking up to 800,000 acre-feet a year from the CVP for environmental uses. Nine years earlier, in 1983, Californians had been shocked by an epidemic of dead and deformed waterfowl due to water pollution at the Kesterson Reservoir in the western San Joaquin Valley. The key offenders were pesticides and other agricultural chemicals, especially selenium, poisoning agricultural drainage water. Three years later, voters passed Proposition 65, the Safe Drinking Water and Toxic Enforcement Act, prohibiting the discharge of toxic chemicals into state waters.

Californians had always been justifiably proud of the purity and taste of their drinking water. The San Francisco Water Department had long since claimed that its water—from the Hetch Hetchy in the Sierra Nevada near Yosemite National Park, where the sheer granite cliffs of the reservoir walls prevented soil erosion into the water supply—was the purest and best-tasting water in the nation. Southern Californians were making comparable claims. In 1995, in the annual Toast to the Tap Water Tasting sponsored by a number of national food and beverage magazines, MWD water from a faucet in the Beverly Hills home of actor Kirk Douglas placed sixth in national competition. Two years later, in the same competition, the MWD had edged upward to fourth place overall and to first place among thirty-eight comparable systems.

It had to be remembered, however, that even after a century of water project development, about 40 percent of all California water, including drinking water, came from groundwater sources as opposed to precipitation runoff, and this groundwater was most vulnerable to pollution in a society so totally dependent on industrial solvents. In 1991, for example, the U.S. Justice Department and Environmental Protection Agency were on the verge of forcing the Lockheed Corporation to spend up to $80 million cleaning up polluted groundwater in Burbank when the Defense Department stepped in and agreed to pay the bill. Lockheed had been building aircraft at this site for more than a half century and the havoc it had caused could be taken as a paradigm of the damage caused to California groundwater in highly populated areas after a century or more of industrial use.

To make matters worse, the drought had seriously depleted groundwater aquifers or underground basins, and this, too, posed dangers to water quality. Brackish water, trapped in layers of rock beneath freshwater, seeped into the water supply when pumping went deeper and deeper. In the Salinas Valley, excessive pumping of groundwater allowed briny seawater to contaminate municipal and agricultural underground reservoirs. Even worse, in the 97 percent Spanish-speaking Salinas Valley town of Chualar, the poorest town in Monterey County, nitrate-contaminated groundwater was blamed for causing birth defects and blue baby syndrome (methemoglobinemia), which inhibited the ability of newborn infants to absorb oxygen into their bloodstream.

Not only was groundwater becoming polluted, it was also in short supply. Although there were an estimated 250 million acre-feet of usable water beneath the surface of the state, six times the amount of water stored in state reservoirs, excessive pumping could still run out ahead of the replenishment process. In the San Joaquin Valley, for example, more than 1.3 million acre-feet of groundwater were being pumped each year than were replenished by rain or runoff. The statewide figure approached two million acre-feet. Nature could not keep up with California's insatiable desire for water as its number one engine of growth.

If there was one place—one site, one source—in which the water formulas and water future of California coalesced in all their possibilities and problems, it was in the San Francisco Bay/Sacramento–San Joaquin Delta Estuary, more succinctly known as the Delta. Like a body being fed by major arteries, here converged the two great rivers of California, the San Joaquin running south to north and the Sacramento running north to south. Into these two rivers, in turn, flowed many of the great rivers of the state: the Fresno, Merced, Tuolumne, Stanislaus, Mokelumne, and Cosumnes into the San Joaquin; the McCloud, Pit, Feather, Yuba, and American into the Sacramento. As the largest estuary on North America's west coast, the Delta was nature's reservoir, located at the very heart of California. Surrounding the Delta, again like major arteries, a network of canals, aqueducts, and pumping plants received and transferred Delta waters to the southern portion of the state. Reservoir-like, the Sacramento–San Joaquin Delta was, however, not a reservoir in the true sense of that term, but a fragile water environment and ecosystem flowing remorselessly into San Francisco Bay. When water was scarce, salty Bay tides had the advantage, and the Delta grew saline and brackish on its western boundary, despite the fact that the Napa River, flowing southward, entered the Delta at that point and helped reinforce its freshwater barrier against the waters of the Bay. But most times, the westward flow of the Delta was so great, not even the tidal waters of San Francisco Bay itself—pushed in turn by the Pacific outside the Golden Gate—could compromise the freshwater integrity of what was, in effect, an inland freshwater sea. The most logical way to preserve the environment of the Delta, many believed, was to construct a canal that would move water north to south on the eastern edge of its periphery. Even green-leaning governor Jerry Brown bought into this solution and became its outspoken advocate; but in 1982 voters overwhelmingly defeated Proposition 9, which would have authorized the peripheral canal. An alliance of conservationists, claiming that the canal would despoil the Delta of its freshwater, and anti-growth advocates, obsessed with the mushrooming and water wastefulness of Southern California, helped defeat the measure.

In September 1991, the Environmental Protection Agency informed the Water Resources Control Board of California that its plan for protecting fish and wildlife in the Delta was inadequate, because it did not leave enough freshwater in the region. Correcting this deficiency meant that even less freshwater could be taken from the Delta for shipment to the Southland. The EPA gave California ninety days to come up with tougher standards. For the next three years, an intricate and continuing battle ensued across many fronts and in dozens of agencies regarding environmental conditions in the Delta. Finally, in June 1994, Water Resources secretary Douglas Wheeler, a savvy and respected environmental lawyer, announced the creation of a seven-agency federal-state committee specifically established to address questions of endangered species, water quality, and CVP Improvement Act environmental requirements in the Delta Estuary. These discussions, in turn, led to the Bay-Delta Accord, calling for the creation of the permanent CALFED Bay-Delta program, serviced by its own support staff. CALFED, however, was not just a federal-state governmental system. Nongovernmental stakeholders, including conservationists and water-users groups, also had a place at the table. At long last, relevant agencies and interest groups were being brought together to discuss the preservation and proper use of the Delta. Whatever the final outcome, this was a new and reconstructed California formula; these agencies and interest groups had by and large been at each other's throats since the 1960s.

In November 1997 California voters passed Proposition 204, otherwise known as the Safe, Clean, Reliable Water Supply Act, which authorized $995 million in bonds, much of it slated for Delta improvements. Without the creation of CALFED in 1994, and thus the implementation of a common statewide forum on Delta and related issues, Proposition 204 might not have passed. Nor would it have succeeded without significant support from immigrant voters. For the first time in history, California voters of every background and political persuasion had authorized a comprehensive program based on adjustments and compromises between human and environmental needs. Proposition 204, in other words, drove no one component of

California out of the formula. Although the path was not yet clear, voters had stated that they somehow wanted to respect both the endangered Delta smelt and the immigrant buying his first home in San Bernardino County.

Even Southern California, whose insatiable thirst for water had driven it to a century of appropriation and, frequently, to an arrogant disregard of the environment, began to show some modification in its behavior, whether as the result of court decisions or enlightened choices or combinations thereof. The pivotal point of transition in this process—the watershed, one might say—was the Mono Lake crisis. In 1941, an ever-growing, ever-thirsty Los Angeles had pushed into the Mono Basin above its existing Owens Valley diversion system and began diverting tributary streams toward the Los Angeles Aqueduct, which since 1913 had been making the growing metropolitanization of the city possible. The problem was that these streams— Lee Vining, Rush, Parker, and Walker—flowed directly into Mono Lake, a cobalt-blue million-year-old lake and ecosystem, white alkali ringed, on the eastern base of the Sierra Nevada in Mono County. As the diversions of the LA Department of Water and Power increased, rising to appropriations of 100,000 acre-feet or greater, the water level of Mono Lake subsided, and an ecosystem began to die. Previously, millions of gulls had nested on islands of tufa towers jutting from the briny water. Now, coyotes loped across the shallows toward the rookeries and dined on gull eggs. For eons past, Mono Lake had been an important stopover on the Pacific Flyway used by migratory birds passing between South America and Canada. With the decline of freshwater in the lake, the population of brine shrimp and flies declined, and the Pacific Flyway lost an important feeding source.

In 1978 student David Gaines and a handful of concerned biologists formed the Mono Lake Committee. Joined by other environmental groups, the committee took the Department of Water and Power to court. The case was heard through a variety of environmental lawsuits in fourteen different courts; but the most important victory came on February 17, 1983, when the California Supreme Court introduced a new notion—public trust—into water law. Whatever past allocations the state had made, the supreme court decided it could adjust those allocations, however historic, if the public trust were involved. The concept of public trust, moreover, was a dynamic concept that could develop over time. It now included environmental awareness, and could be applied in the case of Mono Lake, in which the concept of public trust superseded the prior rights of Los Angeles to Mono Basin water.

Under the leadership of Martha Davis, a graduate of the Yale School of Forestry and Environment with a Greenpeace background, the Mono Lake Committee fastened itself onto the thigh of the Department of Water and

Power like an enraged pit bull. By the early 1990s, Mike Gage, the former deputy mayor of Los Angeles then serving as the president of the Water and Power Commission, admitted that the entire process had been "a learning experience for us, albeit not a pleasant one. We're changing the way we look at all water as a resource."[3] By 1998 the water level at Mono Lake had reached 6,384 above sea level, a dozen feet higher than its 1982 low point. Coyotes could no longer lope out to the rookeries, and the brine shrimp and flies were making a comeback. Of universal importance, the public trust doctrine had inserted itself into each and every water contest. In the matter of water negotiations, concern for the environment was now an equal player at the table.

Endangered Species

It sometimes seemed that Californians had a disturbing amount in common with the other endangered species across the state. In agricultural counties that were in the process of being suburbanized, residents complained frequently about the omnipresence of agricultural pesticides. At the Rio del Valle Junior High School in Oxnard, Ventura County, teachers constantly pointed out that pesticides used on nearby strawberry fields were causing an epidemic of asthma, pneumonia, respiratory ailments, headaches, nausea, dizziness, skin rashes, watery eyes, runny noses, and hand and leg tremors among teachers and students. In one incident in 1996, six teachers went home ill after a nearby farmer sprayed; in another situation, twenty-two teachers sought medical attention, and two were briefly hospitalized. That same year, operators of a Ventura child care center were forced to evacuate a dozen youngsters after a farmer sprayed his strawberry field with the powerful fumigant methyl bromide.

Then there was the question of toxic waste. It could be expected, perhaps, in such places as Hunters Point in San Francisco, a 522-acre property on the southeastern edge of the city, owned by the U.S. Navy. For nearly 120 years, Hunters Point had been a private, then, after 1939, a naval shipyard facility. In 1990, following a recommendation by the Base Realignment and Closure Commission, Congress closed Hunters Point and directed the navy to lease it to the city of San Francisco for a thirty-year period. Development was delayed throughout the 1990s, while an effort was made to clean up toxins and hazardous waste materials from the site. Nearby was the predominantly African-American community of Bayview Hunters Point. In October 1997 the San Francisco Health Department released a study showing that among that population, hospitalization rates for asthma, congestive heart failure, hypertension, diabetes, and emphysema were off the graph: 138 per 10,000 residents, as opposed to a statewide average of 37. In assessing the causes for such rates, together with a life expectancy of 59.9 years for African-American men in this neighborhood, as compared to

64.6 nationwide, and high rates of breast cancer among women, health officials could not overlook the seven hundred hazardous waste material sites, the 325 underground petroleum storage tanks, and the two sites eligible for Superfund cleanup by the EPA.

A University of California Policy Research Center report by UC Santa Cruz professor Manuel Pastor Jr. released in 2001 documented the sad fact that a significant percentage of the poor minorities of the state lived in environmentally unfavorable circumstances, despite the passage in 1999 of Senate Bill 115, which mandated the Office of Planning and Research to develop and coordinate a new environmental justice program for the state. Los Angeles County alone, Pastor documented, had between 1960 and 1990 placed forty-four high-capacity toxic storage and disposal facilities in or near minority neighborhoods. But what could one say of what some alleged to be a near epidemic of Hodgkin's disease in the prosperous Los Angeles community of La Cañada? A number of women from this suburb who developed this virulent form of cancer in the 1990s believed they had found at once the answer and the culprit: the nearby Jet Propulsion Laboratory, which had been polluting the area since the 1940s and in 1992 had also been placed on the Superfund list.

Residents of the small desert town of Hinkley were shocked to discover in June 2001 that hexavalent chromium, a carcinogen capable of altering DNA and mutating cells, was creeping back into their water. In July 1996, the Pacific Gas and Electric Company had paid 650 Hinkley residents a total of $330 million to settle claims arising from the fact that PG&E had between 1951 and 1982 pumped chromium-laced wastewater into disposal ponds that had leaked into the community's drinking water. Legal investigator Erin Brockovich had uncovered the dumping. (In March 2001, actress Julia Roberts won an Oscar for her portrayal of the dogged investigator.) Now it was local farmers who were causing the damage by irrigating their fields with nonpotable water, which was releasing unacceptable levels of hexavalent chromium into the air.

The city of Willits in Mendocino County, meanwhile, was wondering whether a longtime hydraulic equipment plant in its midst, dumping chromium and other highly toxic chemicals into its groundwater and air, had caused the epidemic of tumors, birth defects, bladder and kidney infections, and cancers that seemed to plague this otherwise idyllic community. John and Pam Arlich had raised their family three blocks from the plant and remembered the smell coming from there after heavy rains. They developed sinus problems. Their oldest son had asthma. Their younger son, born prematurely, had a bad stutter and rarely talked. Their daughter developed bladder and kidney infections and required a hysterectomy at age twenty-two. (Her son was also a near nontalker with a stutter.) "This is five people all living in the same house," Pam Arlich said. "You should have at least one healthy person."[4]

Hinkley and Willits were inland cities. Almost 75 percent of the population of the state lived within thirty miles of the shore. In 1976 the state had passed the California Coastal Act establishing a commission with a broad mandate to regulate development, conserve wetlands, and otherwise care for twelve hundred miles of coastland. But try swimming in Santa Monica Bay in May 1998. El Niño had doubled the rainfall that year in Los Angeles and Ventura Counties, flushing pesticides, animal waste, motor oil, and some 120 million gallons of raw sewage into the bay. Only five of sixteen recreational beaches along the Santa Monica coast were safe for swimming that month—this in a county in which going to the beach was central to the local way of life. The next three years witnessed, if anything, an intensification of the problem, especially at Santa Monica Bay, polluted as it was by runoff from the canalized Ballona Creek with its burden of bacteria, pesticides, hazardous metals, viruses, and other pollutants. Enteric viruses, causing diseases of the intestinal and respiratory tract—the runoff result of faulty sewer lines, septic tanks, toilet waste dumped from recreational vehicles, fecal matter on streets from pets and the homeless—were especially troublesome to swimmers and surfers.

Oil spills continued to pose a threat, or become a reality, as in the case of the 5,100 gallons spilled into Humboldt Bay in Eureka in early 1997 by the Hong Kong–owned, Panama-registered, Japanese-crewed 639-foot bulk freighter *Kure,* which slammed into a concrete piling, piercing a hole in its fuel tank, and gushed oil for some thirty minutes before the flow could be stopped. The slick stretched for about five and a half miles across the northern portion of Humboldt Bay, the biggest oil spill in the history of the state. In June 1998, the state took delight in announcing a ten-year extension of the ban on new offshore drilling initiated by President George H. W. Bush in 1990. Going even further, Governor Pete Wilson was urging President Clinton to sign a permanent ban on drilling off the coast, not just a ten-year extension.

Clinton and Al Gore were in Monterey for the first National Ocean Conference. More than five hundred scientists, business leaders, top-ranking military officers, and environmentalists had converged on the Naval Postgraduate School for two days of conferencing. Clinton and Gore announced federal subventions: $12 million to map the ocean floor within U.S. coastal waters; another $12 million to place hundreds of monitoring buoys to track world climate and global warming; an executive order to protect coral reefs, the marine equivalent of rainforests; and, to that end, $6 million through

2002 for the restoration of eighteen damaged coral reefs off the American coast; and, of course, a ten-year ban on offshore drilling. The goal of these programs was twofold: save the environment and, by so doing, save the species living there.

For nearly forty years, Americans had been increasingly concerned that so many species were making it to the endangered list or, even worse, passing into extinction. To prevent such disasters, Congress had passed the Endangered Species Act of 1966, which had been broadened in 1969, and even further enlarged in 1973. Signed by President Nixon, the 1973 act was the most comprehensive legislation for the protection of endangered species ever enacted by any nation, and the Supreme Court upheld it in 1978. California's own Endangered Species Act went on the books in 1970, followed by the Native Plant Protection Act of 1977.

All this was coming a little late for the white abalone, a once abundant coastal mollusk now on the verge of extinction. Found at offshore depths of eighty to three hundred feet, the white abalone, an exquisite delicacy, had been heavily harvested throughout the twentieth century. In 1972 the harvest peaked at sixty-five metric tons. Unfortunately, that brought the population down to such low levels that the white abalone lost its critical mass for reproduction. To counter the decline of a population reduced from 4.24 million to fewer than 2,300 adults by 2001, UC Santa Barbara biologists, working with state and federal conservationists, initiated a captive breeding program that produced an estimated six million baby mollusks. This batch was expected to yield a harvest, eventually, of at least ten thousand four-inch survivable adults that could then be taken from their temperature-controlled tanks at Port Hueneme and reintroduced into the ocean at safe sites more than one hundred feet beneath the surface.

Since the Pleistocene, the mighty condor, distantly related to the stork, had been soaring on ten-foot wings, borne aloft by thermal currents, survivors from an era when woolly mammoths and saber-toothed tigers roamed the savannahs below. By the mid-1980s, the California condor was all but extinct. Its special vulnerability—aside from being shot at, which had been happening since the Gold Rush—was flying into or landing on high-tension wires. Certain purists argued that the condor should be allowed to go out of existence. They wanted, perhaps, one compelling tragic symbol of what costs were involved in the hyperdevelopment of California. The Audubon Society, however, together with Cal Walters, CEO of the Tejon Ranch Company of southern Kern County, where the few surviving condors often roosted, backed a captive breeding program to be conducted at the Los Angeles Zoo, the San Diego Wild Animal Park, and the World Center for Birds of Prey in Boise, Idaho. By the winter of 1998, the condor population had increased to 150: still a tenuous hold on the planet for an entire species but a move in the right direction. Fifty-seven condors bred in captivity had been released into the wild. Not for sixty years had there been that many condors crisscrossing the skies of central and Southern California.

A paradox was asserting itself. Human beings had caused the problem, but in so many cases only intervention by human beings could save the species. Sometimes, decisions could be difficult. Protected sea lions and seals, for example, wrought havoc on salmon and steelhead. Pursuing steelhead and chinook salmon, these saltwater mammals became adept at moving up into freshwater streams flowing into the ocean. Given the fact that there were some 180,000 California sea lions on the West Coast—a population growing at 5 percent a year—and another 75,000 harbor seals, this behavioral adaptation, the pursuit of spawning steelhead and salmon into their upstream freshwater breeding grounds, posed yet another level of danger to two already threatened species by two other species that human protection had allowed to make a comeback.

Equally protected, equally on the comeback trail—and equally hungry—was the California sea otter. Covered in luxurious golden fur and weighing up to seventy pounds, a sea otter could eat twenty pounds of shellfish a day. The sight of a sea otter floating on its back, prying open a clam or mollusk of one sort or another, was like the sighting of a panda bear in the highlands of China or a California gray whale off the coast: a highly epiphanic moment, filled with a sense of the wonder, charm, and beauty of animal life on the planet. Before Europeans arrived in California, sea otters swam offshore in abundance. Between 1812 and 1841, however, Aleut hunters in kayaks decimated the herds for their pelts, which the Russian masters of the Aleuts traded with the Chinese for tea. After being placed on the Endangered Species list by the U.S. Fish and Wildlife Service in 1977, sea otters made a comeback. Interestingly, part of their resilience was due to the availability of an introduced exotic species, the mitten crab. Thus an introduced species, which in and of itself might have proved dangerous, helped an indigenous species recover. By the spring of 1995, the population had passed the two thousand mark. By the late 1990s, sea otters were being spotted in San Francisco Bay, from which they had been absent for more than 150 years.

Other introduced species could prove troublesome, such as the northern pike brought in by parties unknown to Lake Davis in Plumas County, 220 miles northeast of San Francisco. If anglers were responsible for their introduction, it was most likely because they considered this hardy Minnesota game fish good sport. The problem was that no other fish—indeed, no other living creature—could stand up to the feisty pike flourishing in the shallow and nutrient-rich Lake Davis. State biologists were concerned that the pike might migrate from Lake Davis to the Feather River to Lake Oroville and ultimately the Sacramento River, which would mean curtains for migrating salmon. In October 1997 the California Department of Fish and Game eradicated the non-native predator pike by poisoning the mountain lake. Everything in the lake died, which destroyed the angler-dependent tourist economy of the nearby community of Portola. Plumas County district attorney James Reichle was so angry at the poisoning, he filed misdemeanor charges against three fish and game officials for violating the state water code. The charges went nowhere, but they did testify to the profound alienation felt by Portola residents.

More positive were the efforts of the MWD of Southern California, the mega-agency serving seventeen million customers, which through the 1990s spent $30 million making the creeks and tributaries it controlled in northern California more salmon friendly by modifying its dams and intakes. In times past, thousands of adult spring-run chinook salmon would hurl themselves to death against concrete dams or be sucked into irrigation pipelines. In 1999 the federal government listed the spring-run chinook salmon as a threatened species under the Endangered Species Act. Now, by November 2001—thanks to the removal of many of the dams, the construction of fish ladders on others, and screening programs at intake points—spring-run chinook salmon were making it successfully up the six streams, including Butte Creek, controlled by the MWD.

No comeback was more formidable in terms of sheer size and grandeur than that of the humpback and blue whales summering off the Southern California coast. Once hunted to near extinction, these creatures were now increasing in population 5 to 6 percent each year. They wintered off Mexico and Hawaii, summered off Southern California, and moved north to Oregon and Washington as the summer progressed. By their very nature—the power of their presence, their developed intelligence and signaling systems—whales forced human beings to acknowledge the fact that they shared this planet with creatures of comparable grandeur. Whales touched something mystical and communal in Californians, as evidenced by the fact that, when a starving and disoriented female calf, its umbilical cord still attached, washed up on the shores of the Marina del Rey district of Los Angeles, a spontaneous crowd of rescuers sprang to its aid, pouring water over it from buckets as a rescue truck, notified by 911, rushed north from SeaWorld in San Diego, the only facility in the state capable of handling such a creature.

At SeaWorld the week-old calf—a mere thirteen feet, eight inches long and weighing an emaciated 1,670 pounds, her ribs and skull visible beneath her skin, her heartbeat faint, her blood sugar low—was put immediately into intensive care, although veterinarians were not optimistic about the comatose, dehydrated, malnourished creature, so obviously near death. Still, the calf had survived the 120-mile trek to San Diego, which many had doubted she could do. During the trip, warm water, dextrose, and antibiotics had been pumped into her stomach to keep her alive. At SeaWorld, this treatment continued until the calf—now named JJ after the recently deceased Judi Jones, director of the Marine Mammal Rescue Center in Laguna Beach—could be put on a formula of cream, vitamins, and pureed fish intended to resemble whale's milk. Within sixty days, JJ was eating squid. Within fourteen months, she had grown to thirty feet and was devouring a daily diet of 475 pounds of white bait, capeline, herring, squid, krill, sardines, and small shrimp. She now weighed eighteen thousand pounds and was gaining up to two pounds an hour. SeaWorld now had another problem: the largest mammal in human captivity—and she had only begun to grow. Her estimated adult size—up to forty-six feet and seventy thousand pounds at maturity—made keeping her a nonoption. And so, on the last day of March 1998, JJ, now thirty-one feet long and weighing nineteen thousand pounds, was trucked on a bed of foam rubber in an open-topped eighteen-wheeler to the Navy Pier on San Diego Bay, where she was hoisted aboard a Coast Guard cutter via crane and sling. Throughout the journey, handlers had sprayed her with water mist, and a CD of comforting whale sounds had been played and replayed. Wired for radio and satellite tracking, JJ was returned to the sea via her specially fitted red canvas sling. "Release the whale!" bellowed Chief Boatswain's Mate Thomas Young. (It was the first, and perhaps last, time such an order would ever be given by a serving chief petty officer.) The Coast Guard had selected a release point near a pod of migrating whales. JJ joined them. When last seen, she was heading where she should have been heading—to the north.[5]

On so many levels, the endangered wildlife of California bespoke—most often positively, but sometimes negatively—the endangered possibilities of California itself. Each year at the Joshua Tree National Park in the Mojave Desert outside Palm Springs, members of the Park Association sponsored a census of desert tortoises across the 800,000 acres of protected habitat. This usually happened in April when desert grasses and wild flowers began to bloom after winter and spring rains. Placed on the threatened list in 1994 by the federal government, desert tortoises once lived in great density throughout the region, as they had for millions of years. In 1997 a mere eight tortoises were surveyed during the spring count. The following year, researchers had found seven tortoises by mid-April and were hoping for as many as forty. This was good news, since the availability of tortoises above ground—like a canary in a mine—was a sure indicator of how the entire desert ecosystem was doing. Each recovered tortoise was affixed with a computerized radio collar so it could be monitored via satellite.

Suburbs and wildlife were coming increasingly into conflict, whether before, during, or after the suburbs were built. Consider the case of the gnatcatcher, a small blue-gray bird, which mewed like a kitten and inhabited the coastal sage districts of Southern California. The problem was that the gnatcatcher's mating population was down to 2,500 pairs, and their habitat in the seaside hills of San Diego and Orange County was exactly the place that developers planned to be constructing homes with a view of the sea. Some builders, fearing that the gnatcatchers stood between them and construction permits, bulldozed their habitats in preemptive strikes. In March 1993 the federal government declared the bird a threatened species as defined by the Endangered Species Act. That meant no more bulldozers, no new construction, no nothing, on thousands of acres of some of the most valuable real estate in the country—and all because of the tiny songbird. It could have been a confrontation of destructive magnitude. Developers had borrowed millions from the banks, and over the past three years they had spent millions more trying to prevent the federal declaration. Fortunately, state officials in the Wilson administration, working with the U.S. Department of the Interior, had for the previous eighteen months been negotiating a plan. Called the Natural Communities Conservation Planning program, it provided for a negotiated settlement, tract by tract, between developers and wildlife officials. In each instance, developers were responsible for setting up dozens of gnatcatcher preserves in the coastal sage scrub habitat. For their reward, they could bulldoze the rest. Depending on one's point of view, it was either a win-win or lose-lose situation; yet, as in the case of water compromises, the gnatcatcher agreement made a feeble gesture toward some form of accommodation between growth and wildlife preservation.

Not so in the case of the spotted owl. Here was an instance of endangered species as winner taking all. The spotted owl controversy provoked a ban on logging that brought to California its most impassioned environmental crisis of the decade. In May 1991, Judge William Dwyer of the U.S. District Court in Seattle issued an injunction halting timber sales in national forests inhabited by the spotted owl. Since the federal government owned and leased 54 percent of all commercial timberland in California and since many of these national forests—the Shasta, Trinity, Klamath, Mendocino, Six Rivers, Siskiyou, and Rogue River—contained the spotted owl, the logging economy of northern California was in serious trouble as millions of acres of timberland became suddenly off-limits. Forty percent of California's one hundred million acres are forested, and from the nineteenth century onward, logging had been the staple of the upstate economy. Lumberjacks and mill workers were seeing their incomes endangered by the work of college-bred activists, and all in the name of a bird few people had ever seen.

Even before the spotted owl decision, however, environmental activists had been effectively using the courts to block what they considered overcutting that destroyed not only trees but entire ecosystems. Eroding hillsides, denuded of trees, were silting up streambeds vital to salmon migration and spawning. The spotted owl decision climaxed more than a decade of bitter skirmishes that had brought about a 79 percent reduction in timber harvests between 1985 and 1991. A bumper sticker favoring loggers underscored the intensity—even the class conflict—behind the logger versus environmentalist debate. Indirectly but vividly, the bumper sticker predicted a shortage of toilet paper manufactured from forest products. WIPE YOUR ASS, it taunted, WITH A SPOTTED OWL.

North Coast Redwoods
and Other Trees

In the course of officially listing the northern spotted owl as an endangered species, the U.S. Fish and Wildlife Service stressed the importance to the owl of large blocks of "unentered old-growth" forest, which translated to forty-acre or larger stands of trees that were at least two hundred years old and had never been harvested. The tree best fitting this description was the redwood, which could almost stand alone as a symbol of California found and lost, lost and found. Combined with the spotted owl, the symbolism became even more potent.

In pre-European times, a continuous redwood forest extended four hundred miles up the coast of California from Big Sur to the Oregon border. Now the forest was gone, and only 4 percent of its original two million acres remained, most of it in state or federal jurisdiction. For nearly one hundred years, loggers had been felling these ancient trees, some of them more than two thousand years old, to build the homes, fences, wharf pilings, railroad ties, chicken coops, lawn and patio furniture, and vineyard stakes required by a growing population. Tightly grained and resilient, redwoods stood up to water, wind, and weather. Redwood pilings pulled from the water after a hundred years remained unrotted. Equally compelling was that redwood was beautiful. It could be sanded and polished to a glassy gleam. In the era of the great Victorians and the ensuing time of the Craftsman bungalow, redwood interiors glowed with the promise of California itself.

As California's population increased exponentially in boom after boom, however, redwood became the victim of its own desirability. By the 1990s redwoods were either in public hands or no more. One notable exception was a three-thousand-acre stand in the Headwaters Forest near Eureka in Humboldt County. Owned by the Pacific Lumber Company, the Headwaters Forest was the last stand of old-growth redwood in private hands in the

United States. Here, along foggy, fern-carpeted canyons, soared a cathedral complex of ancient trees. The most spectacular examples were two millennia old and rose as high as a thirty-story building.

Founded in 1869, Pacific Lumber had once—socially and environmentally—come the closest a company could come in a competitive free enterprise environment to being a social democratic organization. Many considered Pacific Lumber a kind of corporate utopia. Environmentally, it practiced selective harvesting rather than clear cuts. It literally owned the town of Scotia—every house, the school, the store—and for decades had practiced a form of benevolent corporate socialism, subsidizing workers in their housing and health care, the education of their children, their vacations and retirement. Generations of workers, content with their lot, remained with the company. Sociologists studied the Pacific Lumber way of life as a unique instance of corporate socialism.

All that, however, was in the past. In December 1985, Charles Hurwitz, chairman and chief stockholder of Maxxam Inc. of Texas, acquired Pacific Lumber for $874 million in a hostile takeover financed with junk bonds arranged by Michael Milken of Beverly Hills. If novelist Tom Wolfe ever needed corroboration for Charlie Croker, the country-boy developer anti-hero of *A Man in Full* (1998), Hurwitz would be a good candidate. Born in the pass-through town of Kilgore, Texas, Hurwitz had begun his career as a small-time mutual fund dealer. By the go-go 1980s, when the art of the deal was in the ascendancy, Hurwitz had developed excellent connections with the junk bond traders of Wall Street. Savings-and-loan banks, suburban office parks, downtown real estate: Hurwitz's portfolio grew steadily, financed and leveraged by short-term easy money and his own sky's-the-limit expectations. By 1985, he owned more than two thousand years of biological history in the Headwaters Forest. The problem was that Hurwitz had to cut, and cut quickly, if he was to be able to service his highly leveraged debt. This need became even more dire in 1988, when the savings-and-loan operation controlled by Hurwitz, the United Savings Association of Texas, went belly-up. Taxpayers financed the $1.6 billion bailout, but the FDIC and the Office of Thrift Supervision wanted repayment. Meanwhile, there were those millions of dollars in junk bonds heading toward their up-front, drop-dead doomsday redemption.

For the first half of the 1990s, Pacific Lumber was content to leave the old-growth redwoods alone. After all, such trees could be found on only three thousand out of sixty thousand acres. But by mid-decade, Hurwitz was doing a Texas two-step around the edges of the redwood forest. These old-growth trees, after all, were worth more than $100,000 each in marketable timber products. In March 1996, Hurwitz announced that, under an agreement brokered with the California Board of Forestry in accordance with state law, the following September Pacific Lumber would begin to harvest 10 percent of the dead and diseased trees from the old-growth grove of the Headwaters Forest and five other old-growth locations. Here it was, then: the imminent possibility of what many considered a barbaric intrusion into the ancient groves. Washington, Sacramento, Earth First! headquarters in Arcata, and the Environmental Protection Information Center in nearby Garberville all went onto red alert. "These places are cathedrals," said Cecelia Lanman, programs director for the center. "They are irreplaceable. No one has the right to destroy the irreplaceable."[6]

Over the next six months, Senator Dianne Feinstein, deputy interior secretary John Garamendi, also a Californian, and California secretary of resources Douglas Wheeler, together with representatives from the Clinton administration, tried to arrange a swap. What would it take for Hurwitz to give up his legal right to the grove? An exchange of properties? (At one point in the negotiations, Treasure Island in San Francisco Bay was briefly on the table.) The withdrawal of the FDIC/Office of Thrift Supervision claims and lawsuit? Hurwitz wasn't buying. He wanted $500 million—the value put on the forest in 1993 by the U.S. Forest Service—and pronto. It was worth no more than $200 million, countered Secretary Wheeler. Then there was the question of the coho salmon and the northern spotted owl and a diminutive seabird known as the marbled murrelet, three endangered species that called the Headwaters Forest home. Pacific Lumber could not legally begin to log even dead and diseased trees until after the nesting season of the murrelet was over. In May 1996, Hurwitz filed a takings lawsuit in federal court. The government, he claimed, was stripping him of the value of this land. Pacific Lumber, meanwhile, had already announced plans to harvest every live old-growth redwood from the Headwaters Forest by 2007. Garamendi and Wheeler were now talking about trading $380 million in government assets for 7,500 acres, including the Headwaters Grove and a smaller stand nearby. The result was a temporary cease-fire agreement. Pacific Lumber would keep its lumberjacks out of the Headwaters for at least ten months while it negotiated a logging plan for all of its 200,000 acres in northern California.

On September 23, 1996, nesting season was done for the marbled murrelet. The next day, salvage logging—the harvesting of fallen trees—began in the three-hundred-acre Bel Lawrence Grove a few miles east of the three-thousand-acre Headwaters Grove. Technically, Pacific Lumber was observing the ten-month moratorium. There was a distinction to be made between hauling out fallen redwoods and cutting down standing trees. Garamendi and Wheeler, however, each of them caught off guard, were disturbed, as

was Dana Stolz of the Environmental Protection Information Center in Gar-
berville. "We're mostly concerned," she noted, "that they're going to dese-
crate the forest even before they develop a habitat-conservation plan
provided for in the agreement."[7]

Frustrated by these dickerings and delays, Earth First! activists burst
into Representative Frank Riggs's office in Eureka on October 16, 1997,
terrorized the staff, ransacked the furniture, and left the office blanketed in
six inches of wood chips, sawdust, and pine needles. As a farewell gesture,
a one-ton tree stump was dumped from a truck before the entrance to the
office building, to which four other Earth First! activists—not the ones who
had ransacked the office (they had fled)—chained themselves. Then sixty or
more Earth First! demonstrators, converging from out of nowhere, surrounded the tree stump and its four chained witnesses—three women and a
sixteen-year-old girl—chanting slogans, even trying to reenter Riggs's
office, before being dispersed, with some arrests, by the Eureka police.

Unfortunately for their reputations, the Eureka police officers and sheriff's deputies, arriving in riot gear, used Q-tips to apply pepper spray directly
to the eyes of demonstrators who refused to leave the site. Videotapes of the
burly officers swabbing the eyes of recalcitrant female demonstrators, with
the women crying out in pain, went out over national television and generated criticism from across the country. The FBI announced it was beginning
an investigation to determine whether or not the use of the pepper spray
Q-tips had, in fact, constituted a criminal act by the police.

A year of further demonstrations and pepper spray followed as Washington and Sacramento continued to negotiate with Charles Hurwitz. The
key issue in the negotiations was how much cutting of old-growth redwoods
would be allowed. The government was admitting that some of these trees
would be lost, reduced to $100,000 worth of boards in two hours by sixty-
foot band saws wielded by Pacific Lumber lumberjacks. That's why an
Earth First! Bonnie Raitt concert could draw some eight thousand of the
faithful, and why Green Party candidates came to control the town council
of Arcata on Humboldt Bay. Both the government and Hurwitz were talking
about cutting down two-thousand-year-old trees. Sure enough, when the
next agreement was announced, in addition to paying Pacific Lumber $380
million ($250 million from the federal government, $130 million from the
state), the settlement allowed the company to cut a half a billion board feet,
or 16 percent of its old-growth redwoods, ranging in age from several hundred to several thousand years, including one cathedral grove in the Headwaters Forest the size of Central Park. Hurwitz had gone eyeball to eyeball
with the federal government and the state of California, and they, not he,
had blinked.

On December 10, 1997, Julia "Butterfly" Hill ("Butterfly" was her Earth First! forest name, taken as a nun would assume a new name upon pronouncing vows), aged twenty-three, ascended a thousand-year-old two-hundred-foot redwood, which she named Luna because she first saw it by the light of a full moon on a hill overlooking the Eel River in Humboldt County on Pacific Lumber property. Butterfly remained on Luna for the rest of the millennium. As the months wore on, more and more reporters were willing to make the steep two-hour climb from the nearest paved road above the southern Humboldt County town of Stafford to interview Hill by cell phone in her habitat or even (some of the more agile members of the Fourth Estate) to climb up for a visit with her. If requested, Hill would take pictures of herself with a reporter's camera, then lower it back by rope. By October 1998, she was giving several cell phone interviews a day and was writing up to one hundred letters a week to supporters and friends, together with handwritten petitions to state and federal officials. Some ten months into her stay, photographs of Hill revealed an underlying fatigue, although no lack of continuing purpose, in her determined gaze. Just about this time, Earth First! activist David Chain was killed by a tree felled by a Pacific Lumber logger. In one sense, Chain's death was the natural outcome of increasingly violent confrontations between loggers and demonstrators, and it brought to Julia Hill even more notoriety and a renewed sense of commitment.

Caught in the middle of the entire affair, Richard Wilson, director of the California Department of Forestry and Fire Protection and chief forester of California, pleaded for a comprehensive and integrated program not only for the Headwaters Forest but for all forests in the state. A longtime rancher in Covelo in Mendocino County, Wilson argued for a philosophy of replenishment and prudent use, such as that which had brought back in less than fifty years the Jackson Demonstration State Forest in Mendocino County from a logged wasteland to a commercially flourishing source of forest products, prudently logged, and a successful recreational resort. Early in the decade, in the Plumas County town of Quincy, local environmentalists and representatives of the Sierra Pacific Industries, meeting in the Quincy Public Library, had hammered out a model agreement about what could be cut and what would be left alone. The Quincy Library Group, as it was called, continued to meet on a regular basis throughout the decade, and Plumas County was significantly free of conflict.

Was there not a point, many were beginning to ask, at which society had the right to question the right of any individual, even Charles Hurwitz, to cut down two-thousand-year-old redwood trees to make patio furniture and pay off junk bonds? There were other ways of doing things. In October 1998 the Trust for Public Land paid an estimated $43 million for the Coast

Dairies and Land Company, a seven-thousand-acre ranch, which included redwood forests and five miles of shoreline, along Highway 1 on the north coast of Santa Cruz. The trust was able to make the purchase thanks to a $20 million gift from the David and Lucille Packard Foundation. This coastal property was owned by the grandchildren, now living in Switzerland, of the Swiss immigrants who had first developed the dairy ranch in the early 1900s. It was a family-owned property, and there was no junk bond debt.

Like the redwood, the California live oak was an icon of place and regional identity. These great trees, many of them hundreds of years old, carpeted the coastal hills and the foothills of the interior. Strong, thick, assertive, cleaving to the earth through growth patterns balancing the horizontal with the vertical, the oak, unlike the redwood, had survived the nineteenth century, even the first half of the twentieth century. But now two factors, fungus and human expansion, were placing the tree in jeopardy. Forest pathologists at UC Davis were wondering late in the decade just exactly how the fungus *Phytophthora ramorum* had entered California, but however it had arrived, it was killing off thousands of coastal oaks from Monterey to Sonoma County in the form of sudden death that could see a one-hundred-year-old oak die within three months of an initial attack. The pathogen was clever, creeping up along lesser plants, shrubs, and trees before launching its attack and sucking out the life of the live oaks.

The oak trees of California, like so much else in the ecosystem, were also coming under increasing threat in the growth that followed World War II. In the 1990s, the oak became pitted against the vineyard, which was ironic, given the fact that vineyards were also enhancing the California landscape. In their own way, like Pacific Lumber, many of the wineries were overfinanced and overhyped, having been bought, in many instances, from their founders at outrageous prices in the 1980s. Now, vineyard owners were being forced to expand exponentially in an effort to produce more wine and service their debt. Matters came to a head in November 1997 when the Santa Rosa–based winery Kendall-Jackson felled more than nine hundred oaks on its new six-hundred-acre Camelot vineyard near Los Alamos, some fifty-five miles north of Santa Barbara. To Kendall-Jackson's credit, the winery had spared 90 percent of the oak trees on its thirteen-hundred-acre ranch and promised to plant hundreds of seedlings in more convenient locations; yet the loss of a three-hundred-year-old oak, while not as vivid and painful as the loss of a two-thousand-year-old redwood, still had a way of suggesting that there was something threatening the environment in the overwrought segments of the California economy.

Richard Sanford, owner and founder of the Sanford Winery in northern Santa Barbara County, owned his property, and it was not heavily leveraged, and so it was perhaps not irrelevant that Sanford, a devoted follower of Taoism who had served as a naval officer in Vietnam, was leading the effort, on his own ranch and as an environmental activist, to head off the growing clash between vineyards and oak trees. Sanford was fully aware that the county was the hot new place in winery expansion and that vineyard acreage would be tripling to 45,000 acres over the next decade, putting Santa Barbara on a par with Napa and Sonoma. This meant the possible loss of thousands of oaks and the oak woodlands and riparian systems they formed: the most biologically diverse ecosystems in the state, supporting nearly 2,400 species of plants and animals and four thousand species of insects. Between 1996 and 1998, an estimated two thousand oak trees had already been decimated and bulldozed, then hauled away, in the developing vineyards of the region. If even more oaks went, so too would go the hawks, the eagles, the deer, foxes, and bobcats. If oak woodlands and hundred-year-old vineyards could coexist in France, Richard Sanford was asking, why could not the same pattern be sustained in California?

The same question could be asked of California's olive trees. Introduced by Franciscan missionaries in the early nineteenth century, the olive tree evoked those Mediterranean associations, that sense of California as a new Italy and a new Spain, that served as such a powerful metaphor for development at the turn of the century. By the late twentieth century, numerous groves of olive trees, some of them more than one hundred years old, were yielding rich fruit and bringing to the rural landscapes of California the texture of time and history. But the highly subsidized olive industries of Spain, Morocco, and Greece were crushing the California market. True, the American market for olives was better than ever—$150 million in fact, especially with the growing popularity of pizza (and, it might be hoped, the resurgence of the martini). But unfortunately, Mediterranean growers could get their olives to the East Coast of the United States by boat more cheaply than their California counterparts could get them there by train. So in 1999, an estimated seven hundred of the 35,000 acres of olive trees in California were ripped out in favor of oranges or other products, and an additional thousand acres were scheduled to be removed by January 2001. On Corfu, by contrast, there were olive groves that had been yielding fruit for nearly a thousand years.

A tree, an increasing number of Californians were recognizing, was not just a tree. As California's chief forester Richard Wilson was fond of pointing out, a tree was part of an ecosystem. Clear the land of trees, and you cleared it of everything else as well: birds in the sky, flora and fauna on the forest or woodland floor. But a tree was something else as well, a living entity with a life of its own. As such, trees had standing before the law and in the minds and moral imagination of the people sharing the planet with them.

Even when trees offended, as in the case of the eucalyptus, they were cherished and forgiven. Imported from Australia more than a century ago, planted by the hundreds of thousands throughout the central and southern portions of the state to create windbreaks or delineate paths and to confer historical credibility on new neighborhoods (the eucalyptus could grow from ten to fifteen feet a year in the early stages of its life and reach heights of two hundred feet within decades), the eucalyptus had become by the 1990s an aged, troublesome, and occasionally dangerous citizen. Yet it still kept its stateliness and its ability to intensify and articulate a landscape. What would the campuses of UC Berkeley, Stanford, or UCLA be without their great stands of eucalypti? Large portions of Southern California would be nearly treeless were it not for the Australian import. When the wind blew through the silver-green eucalyptus leaves and caused them to shimmer in the sunlight, you could almost forgive them for being so messy and dangerous. Eucalyptus branches had a way of falling precipitously to the ground, smashing automobiles and sometimes causing death; literary critic T. K. Whipple of UC Berkeley met his end this way, crushed by a branch falling from one of the hundreds of eucalyptus trees on campus. Then there was the fact that eucalypti stored thousands of pounds of oil. When these trees burned, as in the case of the great Oakland fire of 1991, they became thermal bombs exploding into flame, tree to tree, spreading the firestorm at a rate too rapid for effective containment.

And yet Californians loved their eucalypti, whether or not these trees had any real right to be there in the first place, and even though they were reaching the end of their natural life cycle and were growing messy and dangerous. When the Dana Woods Homeowners Association in Dana Point, Orange County, decided to remove hundreds of eucalyptus trees for being too old and too dangerous, home owners spontaneously rebelled. Lining up their cars on both sides of the street, they prevented tree cutters from bringing their equipment into play—this despite the fact that at least four properties had been damaged by falling limbs and trees in recent months. "All of these trees don't have to be chopped down," noted one protesting resident. "Why not take only the ones that have to go? Why turn this special place into a logging mill?"[8]

Going Green

In their own way, these Dana Woods homeowners had gone green, and so had many Californians. Going green characterized Republicans and Democrats alike and was making particular headway among the intelligentsia. No figure better epitomized this sensibility—educated, affluent, liberal, upper middle class—than did Stanford man of letters Wallace Stegner, author of some thirty books, history, memoirs, novels, naturalist essays, and the undisputed spokesperson for environmentalism in his generation. Stegner entered the decade—his last; he died following an automobile accident in New Mexico in June 1993—with more than even his usual levels of green, given the runaway growth he was seeing all around him. As he watched the spreading suburbs beneath his hilltop home in Los Altos, Stegner took little comfort from the fact that over the years he had become one of the most respected writers on the environment in the country. What good were his books, he was tempted to ask, if things kept getting worse?

If traces of the apocalyptic could be discerned in Stegner's voice—this successful historian, nature writer, and Pulitzer Prize–winning novelist, this preeminent Stanford professor, balanced and sane—then a measure could be taken of just how aggrieved the environmental community was feeling. Already, David Brower, the former executive director of the Sierra Club, had long since left that organization to found the more militant Friends of the Earth. A decorated combat infantry officer in World War II, Brower was the equivalent in activism to Stegner's literary witness. He and Friends of the Earth were already green, whatever they called their organization, which was why the Green Party of California, once it was founded in the early 1990s, looked to Brower as the prophet and avatar of this movement, along with actors Peter Coyote and Ed Begley Jr., singer Bonnie Raitt, and former Democratic congressman Dan Hamburg of Ukiah.

Globally, the 1990s witnessed the continuing theologization of the green movement, building on the pangaian theories of an earlier decade and the poetic insights of French Jesuit scientist and mystic Teilhard de

Chardin. Pangaian theories, which had emerged in Cambridge University in the 1960s and 1970s, advanced the notion that the Earth was one integrated and self-regulating system: a living entity, that is, an All-Earth. In the 1980s, thanks to such thinkers as Catholic priest Tom Berry, building on the work of Teilhard Chardin, pangaian thinking was integrated into an even larger biophysical evolutionary pattern in which the universe was perceived as a unified entity evolving toward higher forms of integration, perhaps even to consciousness itself. Drawing on the mystical traditions of the Dominican Order, maverick cleric Matthew Fox pushed these theories even further, giving to them a distinctive California spin. For Berry, Fox, and others of this proto-pantheistic school, Earth was not merely integrated and self-regulatory, it was also a holy living Being with a capital B, akin to (or even identical with) Divinity.

While it would be false to ascribe such religiosity to all green activists, such as those in the Earth First! movement, one could not ignore the evangelical faith of these environmentalists, so many of whom, like the early Christians, seemed willing to die for their beliefs. Dressed in jeans, muumuus, parkas, and plaid shirts, the women with their hair long in the style of the 1960s, the men with beards, men and women alike with beads and feathers galore, the Earth First! demonstrators had the look not only of a time warp, a replay of the 1960s, but of members of a millenarian sect. Theirs was more than a political movement. It was a commune, a community, a way of life, a commitment akin to joining a monastic order or the Salvation Army. Some Earth First! activists considered themselves in a state of holy crusade against the logging industry and went so far as to drive spikes into trees to stop them from being logged. Lumberjacks with chain saws and small mill owners using band saws were frightened of hitting one of these hidden spikes, which could not only destroy the saw, but could ricochet and do serious damage to the operator.

Despite such guerrilla tactics by extremists, however, the Green Party of California was edging toward respectability. In 1998 the party ran Dan Hamburg for governor. Hamburg was planning a million-dollar budget for his campaign, which was chaired by Peter Coyote. In the election, the Green Party won thirteen local seats and—surprising to all—put a Green in the state assembly, Audie Bock, from the prosperous Oakland Hills enclave of Piedmont. A crisp professional in a tailored suit, Bock hardly fit the profile of the typical Earth First! protester.

The green movement in California had need that year of the pert and presentable Bock, a Harvard graduate, for the state was only then recovering from the trial in Sacramento of confessed Unabomber Theodore

Kaczynski, another Harvard alumnus, who across a solitary eighteen-year campaign had killed three people and maimed another twenty-eight by sending them bombs in the mail as a protest against modern technology. Kaczynski's last victim had been California Forestry Association lobbyist Gilbert Murray, killed on April 24, 1995, when a package bomb mailed by Kaczynski exploded in the association's Sacramento office. A onetime assistant professor of mathematics at UC Berkeley, Kaczynski had spent the last fifteen years of his life living in a remote shack in Montana. Five of his victims had been Californians. The threat posed by Kaczynski to the green movement was one of guilt by association. During the Sacramento trial in federal court, Kaczynski's lawyers had done their best to portray the accused bomber as a paranoid schizophrenic. Kaczynski resisted this line of defense and midway through his trial sought to fire his lawyers and represent himself. Finally, however, rather than have himself portrayed as a nut case as opposed to a man of principle, he pleaded guilty to all counts—which is to say, he took both responsibility and credit for what he had done—and in May 1998 was sentenced to four life terms in federal prison.

Still, not even Kaczynski's extremism could halt the growing desire of mainstream California to preserve its environment, wildlife, and ecosystems. Even though he was himself a member of the same political party as the president, Governor Gray Davis filed a lawsuit in September 1999 to block the Clinton administration from granting extensions to offshore oil leases that Davis believed would dramatically expand production off the central coast. The lawsuit pitted Davis against Interior Secretary Bruce Babbitt, a national icon of the conservationist movement, on grounds that Babbitt was not acting in conformity with the federal Coastal Zone Management Act of 1972. "If California had been consulted," noted state secretary of resources Mary Nichols, "we would have insisted that many, if not all of these leases, should be allowed to expire immediately because there is no way they can be developed in an environmentally sound way."[9] Two years later, Davis would veto a bill allowing oil companies to leave their aging offshore platforms in the ocean as ecosystem sanctuaries.

At the same time, environmentalists were keeping a steady watch on the new secretary of the interior, Gayle Norton, as she began assessing on behalf of the George W. Bush administration the oil resources of the Carrizo Plain in remote eastern Kern County. Known as the Serengeti of California, the Carrizo Plain represented the last remnant of the grassland that had once covered the San Joaquin Valley. Jointly operated by the federal Bureau of Land Management, the California Department of Fish and Game, and the Nature Conservancy, a nonprofit foundation, the fifty-mile-long, eight-mile-wide corridor abounded in antelope, bison, elk, kit foxes, giant kangaroo rats, and other endangered creatures. It was also, the U.S. Geological Survey reported, most likely a rich source for oil and natural gas. President Clinton had declared the area a national monument just a few days before the inauguration of his successor, putting the plain off-limits to oil and gas drilling; but Secretary Norton was, as of May 2001, taking a second look.

However mainstream the green movement was becoming, it had yet fully to confront the thorny issue of class—namely, the fact that most of middle-class and blue-collar California was in no mood for green values when it came to their lifestyles. Each Memorial Day, for example, toward 48,000 Californians showed up on a 5.5-mile stretch of beach at the Oceano Dunes State Vehicle Recreation Area near Pismo Beach in San Luis Obispo County. They came in SUVs, Jeeps, all-terrain vehicles with souped-up engines, and jacked-up trucks with monster tires. They brought along their dirt bikes and their dune buggies. They were middle-American Californians, camping over the weekend in tents and recreational vehicles. Their goal was to tear hell out of the dunes in their various vehicles, in what one observer described as a scene from the movie *Mad Max* (1979). The drivers of these vehicles—churning the sand with their Super Swamper Bogger tires, their vanity license plates saying things like Hog Pull, with skull and crossbones pirate flags flying—were hardly worried that the snowy plover, long accustomed to nest on this beach, had by June 2001 been reduced to 976 birds on the entire Pacific coast. "The Sierra Club is hell bent on getting us off the beach," noted Ed Waldheim, president of the California Off-Road Vehicle Association. "They have 1,100 miles of beach and what do we have? Five miles left." Dunester Wes Hoagland—his Ford F-250 truck jacked up over eighteen-inch-wide tires—perfectly embodied this play of one California against another. "If we don't fight for our land," Hoagland noted, "we're going to lose it." Ironically, Hoagland was sounding like an environmentalist.[10]

For the time being at least, both sides of the question were remaining relatively civil. But would it last, especially in a time of population growth and increasing class divisions? On Saturday morning, December 18, 1999, after 728 days aloft, Julia "Butterfly" Hill, having come to an agreement with the Pacific Lumber Company, descended from Luna and, unsteady on her feet, walked two miles to a press conference. Pacific Lumber had agreed, Hill announced tearfully, not to destroy Luna or any other tree in 2.9 acres of the immediate environment. Hill would be allowed to visit Luna any time she wished, provided that she give the company forty-eight hours' notice. The environmental group supporting Hill in turn would pay Pacific

Lumber $50,000 for lost revenue. The company, however, would donate this sum to Humboldt State University for forestry research. Hill spent the following year writing a book about her experiences. At some time in late November, parties unknown took a chain saw to the thousand-year-old, two-hundred-foot tall Luna and cut a gash thirty-two-inches deep around the base of its trunk. Tree specialists did not expect Luna to survive.

Open Space

The vengeful attack on Luna underscored the class warfare implicit in so many conservationist controversies. Ranchers in eastern San Bernardino County, for example, had for nearly one hundred years been able to graze their cattle through lease arrangements on properties owned by the federal Bureau of Land Management (BLM). Then came the Endangered Species Act—and the Mojave Desert tortoise, an endangered species. The result was that the BLM banned grazing and closed roads on some 1.3 million acres of tortoise habitat. Cattle ranchers, as might be expected, went apoplectic. "There is no endangered species in the United States of America," noted cattle rancher Dave Fisher, owner of a sprawling 155,000-acre spread southeast of Barstow, "that generates one red cent for the economy. . . . They are exalting the tortoise above mankind."[11]

In times past, it had never been easy for BLM employees in this part of California. They never felt safe when wearing their uniforms in public and were frequently refused service in local restaurants. Now, because of the desert tortoise, matters took a decided turn for the worse. The San Bernardino County Board of Supervisors canceled a prior agreement to allow the BLM free use of the county dump to deposit trash collected from the desert by environmentally minded volunteers. County sheriff Gary Penrod revoked permission for BLM rangers to function as local law enforcement officers in such matters as vandalism and drunk driving. Even more stressful, some BLM employees were so fearful of violence from locals that a Sacramento-based group, Public Employees for Environmental Responsibility, requested an investigation by the San Bernardino County grand jury and the state attorney general.

Of the many strategies employed by environmentalists, the acquisition and preservation of open space by land trusts like the Nature Conservancy, the Big Sur Land Trust, the Santa Monica Mountains Conservancy, and the 116 others operating in California by 1999 was perhaps the most simple and effective. Hence the staggering effect of the $175 million conservation grant announced by the David and Lucille Packard Foundation in March 1998. Even before making this grant, the Packard Foundation—itself valued at nearly $9 billion, the third largest philanthropic foundation in the country—had awarded a number of multimillion-dollar grants for conservation purposes. Packard Foundation money, for example, had allowed the Nature Conservancy to purchase development rights to a large cattle ranch in Lassen County near Redding and had enabled the Big Sur Land Trust to protect a critical drainage area into the Elkhorn Slough in northern Monterey County, the second largest estuary in the state.

In October 1999 the Packard Foundation, its assets by then pumped to $12.3 billion due to a rising stock market, turned its attention to the Central Valley. In 1995, foundation officials had been galvanized by a report from the American Farmland Trust stating that, unless something were done, the best farmland along Highway 99 would by 2020 be one continuous corridor of strip malls and housing tracts. Entering the Central Valley in a bold way, the Packard Foundation promised to spend more than $175 million by 2002 to conserve farmland and other vulnerable areas on the California coast and in the Sierra Nevada. A third of this money would be paid directly to farmers to make up the differential in selling their farmland to other farmers rather than to developers. "For years," noted Carol Whiteside, president of the Modesto-based Great Valley Center, "farmers have been saying, rightfully so, that the only way I can retire is to sell my land to a developer. Well, suddenly, that farmer has a new option."[12]

In embarking on this strategy, the foundation was following in the footsteps of the Marin Agricultural Land Trust, founded in 1980 by dairywoman Ellen Straus and Mill Valley educator and environmentalist Phyllis Faber to protect agricultural lands in West Marin through a similar strategy. By 2000 some 26,000 acres of farmland had been preserved. Despite its proximity to San Francisco and to the urbanized and suburbanized eastern and southern portions of the county, West Marin, thanks in significant measure to the Marin Agricultural Land Trust, entered the new millennium as an idyllic landscape of grasslands and rolling hills, dairy farms and grazing cows, oak trees, and farmyard fences, moistened by marine mists in the morning, sunny by day, clean-aired and fragrant with the salt of the nearby sea: a far cry from the suburbanization that might otherwise have long since devoured this strategically placed region.

Since 1980, Southern California had benefited from the activities of a unique entity, the Santa Monica Mountains Conservancy, a state agency charged with acquiring parkland for the Santa Monica Mountains National Recreation Area and the hills and mountains encircling the San Fernando

Valley. Between 1980 and 1998 this agency, public in charter, private in support, had acquired and preserved more than thirty thousand acres that would have otherwise been lost to growth. A major donor was Barbra Streisand, who in 1993 gave twenty-two acres of montane ranchland. In September 2001 biomedical entrepreneur and philanthropist Alfred Mann—motivated, in part, by the gargantuan tax bill he was facing for the recent sale of one of his companies, MiniMed Inc., an insulin pump maker, for $3.8 billion—donated a thousand acres of prime open space overlooking the Malibu shoreline to the conservancy.

Further north, in Carmel, actor-director Clint Eastwood and his former wife and continuing business partner Maggie Eastwood presented the Big Sur Land Trust with their jointly owned Coast Ranch. This stunning 130-acre property at the mouth of the Carmel River was at once a dramatic guarantee of open space in a growth-threatened region and a promise of clean water to the Carmel community. The gift yielded the Eastwoods a significant tax break; but, as in the case of Streisand's beneficence, no talk of tax breaks could obscure the fundamental conservation and public-mindedness of the Eastwood bequest or its value as a conservationist paradigm. Altogether, by mid-1999 California's land trusts had acquired and preserved 536,922 acres of environmentally significant property.

William Randolph Hearst's San Simeon estate in San Luis Obispo County had long since become a state park, although the Hearst Corporation maintained extensive portions of the original property. By late 1997, Hearst management was announcing plans to build a resort complex—a dude ranch, two hotels, a twenty-seven-hole golf course, restaurants, and related retail buildings—along the shoreline and at the base of San Simeon Point. Under the terms of William Randolph Hearst's will, the $5 billion Hearst Corporation was not being run as a family enterprise but by nonfamily directors and professional management, although a few of Hearst's thirty-five adult heirs sat on the board. The Hearst Corporation, then, was exactly that—a corporation. The Chief had wanted it that way. But most corporations are in business to maximize profits, not to conserve the scenic shores of San Simeon. A number of Hearst's heirs opposed the project; but they were not members of the board and could do little to thwart, or even scale down, the proposal. In order to go ahead with the project, however, Hearst needed an easement from the California Coastal Commission. After a long day of testimony in January 1998, the commission turned down the Hearst proposal as presented, recommending instead that the development be reduced from 650 rooms to 375, that the oceanfront golf course be eliminated, and that all building be concentrated on one site at the base of San Simeon Point.

It is difficult to determine just exactly what the Hearst Corporation was offering the state of California, other than the $3 million in taxes the resort would generate for San Luis Obispo County. Only the most affluent could have used the resort as it was being outlined before the coastal commission. And did California really need another Pebble Beach? From the start, it could be argued, Hearst was doomed to lose the battle. There was no way that the publicly appointed state officials on the commission would give away that much pristine shoreline without some hugely appreciable benefit to the public, especially now that California was going so green.

No matter: Hearst had another strategy in reserve as far as development rights were concerned, one that could very well allow it to subdivide its 83,000-acre ranch into 279 parcels, including oceanfront subdivisions. They were called certificates of compliance, and they had been discovered by a Las Vegas land speculator named Brian Sweeney. In 1997, Sweeney had taken an option on a seven-thousand-acre property running along nearly seven miles of coastland in Santa Cruz County. The option was costing Sweeney $1 million a month. The environmentalists were, as might be expected, resisting his plan to develop the property. Hiring a slew of attorneys and land surveyors, Sweeney discovered that the property in question had been assembled from 139 underlying parcels. Under the law, he was able to file for certificates of compliance that restored to each of these parcels development rights. "I have 139 buyers ready to build monster homes," Sweeney announced to the environmental community. Very soon, he was pocketing $43 million from funds amassed by the Save the Redwoods League, the Trust for Public Land, a number of other foundations and nonprofits, and local taxpayers.

Taking his act down the coast, Sweeney purchased—for a mere $2 million—the 1,226-acre Big Sur ranch of the late Allen Funt, creator of the *Candid Camera* television program: prime property overlooking the Rainbow Bridge on Bixby Creek. This time, Sweeney's researchers produced certificates of compliance for nine parcels. Sweeney thereupon prepared plans for nine McMansions on the Big Sur coast. The Trust for Public Land paid Sweeney more than $26 million for the property—a profit of approximately $24 million. "This is a new kind of environmental terrorism," complained Representative Sam Farr (D-Carmel).[13] Perhaps it was—but the Hearst Corporation certainly liked the idea. Among other things, certificates of compliance might very well allow the corporation to build the hotel resort the commission had turned down, especially since development rights from such documents could be consolidated on oceanfront properties.

If all politics were local, as Tip O'Neill once observed, nothing could be more local than the politics of growth. Most of the funds pouring into the campaign coffers of locally elected officials came from developers. In Fresno County, where developer–elected official relationships edged into outright corruption, growth had metastasized; but even when there was no claim of illegality, the relationship between developers and local officials often spoke for itself. In 1978, Los Angeles County had unveiled a plan to preserve the Santa Monica Mountains through guided development. Twenty years later, those limitations had been exceeded sevenfold, which is to say, by 700 percent: decision by decision by officials, donation by donation by developers, the left hand claiming that it didn't know what the right hand was doing. Between 1981 and 1991, the Santa Monica Mountains growth plan had been altered in favor of developers thirty-seven times, or an average of nearly once every three months. In one instance, 204 homes were approved for a tract earmarked for 37; in another, 2,200 homes rose on land designated for 1,000. Not that density is a bad thing, but these homes were not condominiums or apartment buildings. They were individual tract homes, sitting next to each other, side by side, up and down the hills, as far as the eye could see. If such were the case with a population of 32 million, 16 million in Southern California, what would become of the landscape when the population reached 40 or 50 million within the next two decades?

There had to be a better way. In the November 1998 election, voters in Ventura County passed Measure B, put on the ballot by SOAR, an acronym for Save Open and Agricultural Resources. Measure B stripped the elected county board of supervisors of its power to approve new subdivisions on land zoned for open space or agriculture. In the future, all such variances could be granted only by county-wide ballot on a case by case basis. This was radical populist politics, the land-use equivalent of Proposition 13, which twenty years earlier had put a severe statewide cap on property taxes. The voters of Ventura County had taken land-use management into their own hands.

In contrast to Ventura, the supervisors of Orange County—supposedly the most conservative county in California—had acted proactively and creatively in response to the growing green sentiments of their constituencies. Orange County was the essence of the postwar suburbanized development of Southern California; hence the special drama in early 1996 when the board of supervisors created a 38,000-acre reserve stretching from the coast at Laguna Beach to the base of Saddleback Mountain, from Costa Mesa in the north to San Juan Capistrano in the south. The Irvine Company, which had practically invented suburbanized Orange County in the first place, contributed 21,000 acres. County and state parks, together with other private entities, provided the rest. Designated the Nature Reserve of Orange

County, this network of undeveloped land would forever protect the landscape flora and fauna of the region; indeed, it would keep at the very center of the county a pristine example of what the region had looked like in ages past.

Further south, the San Diego City Council was developing a plan whereby, instead of fighting endangered species issues site by site, entire landscapes—integrated ecosystems—would be set aside by developers in exchange for exemptions on their remaining properties. Whether such a proposal was legal under the Endangered Species Act—whether, that is, endangered species on one site could be protected in exchange for the sacrifice of species on other sites—remained dubious; yet the proposal did show an effort on the part of government to head off confrontations such as that unfolding over logging redwoods in the Headwaters Forest. Orange County, for example, was by 1998 in the process of crafting patterns of trade-off—what could be developed, what could not—for a 131,000-acre portion of the county, with both developers and environmental activists seated equally at the table. This meant that developers were recognizing that they had to become part of the environmental solution, and environmentalists were acknowledging that there had to be some possibility for development.

Nature and settlement, city and environmental preserve: were they each so antithetical to each other? As of yet there was no clear-cut answer, but a dialogue had begun. Things, moreover, had a way of getting complicated. In Huntington Beach, when city and county officials announced plans in March 1998 to turn a fifteen-acre strip of park into a wild sanctuary reprising the ecological past of the region, local sports organizations legitimately asked: What about baseball? What about football? What about soccer? Already there was a growing shortage of soccer space in sub/urban Southern California, giving the existing popularity of the sport among Latinos and its rising popularity among middle-class boys and girls of every ethnic background, watched over by their devoted soccer moms. "In the best of all possible worlds," noted Mark Baldassare, professor of urban planning at UC Irvine, "there should be both types of parks. But with the cost of land in California, it sometimes becomes an either/or situation. The tension between those who want recreational space and those who want it left in natural settings is going to grow with increased urbanization."[14]

The U.S. General Accounting Office estimated that there were roughly 450,000 brownfield sites throughout the nation. California had more than its fair share, possibly as many as 45,000. The collapse of the aerospace and defense industries, the closure of military bases, the decline of the timber industry in upstate California, corporate downsizing, the flight of jobs and housing to newer suburbs: these and other factors had left the brownfields behind. Languishing empty and deserted, their buildings tumbling, their windows broken, magnets for drug dealing and other criminal activity, brownfields were blights on their cities and suburbs. In Richmond, a gritty waterside region, filled with abandoned or marginally used sites, was redeveloped as Marina Bay, a complex combining commercial, light industrial, parkland, residential units (apartments, condominiums, townhouses, single-family detached homes), and restaurants, rivaling Tiburon in Marin County across the bay. Under the leadership of Mayor Rosemary Corbin, the city next took on a former Santa Fe Railroad right of way in the center of town and began its redevelopment. Across the bay in San Francisco, Catellus Development Corporation was in the process of transforming a three-hundred-acre brownfield at Mission Bay into an urban complex and UC San Francisco Medical Center that would eventually produce $1 billion in property taxes. In Los Angeles, Venice-area city councilwoman Ruth Galanter was spearheading the cleanup and reconversion of an unused oil pumping facility into a roller skating park. The Southern Pacific Railyards in Sacramento, the Kaiser Steel Plant in Fontana, and the Revere Copper facility in Commerce were other sites in the process of being rescued and recycled. Conservation, in short, was not just a matter of endangered species or trees. It involved endangered urban neighborhoods as well. In a society increasingly integrated by technology, distinctions between urban, suburban, exurban, and rural were blurring. Conservation, reclamation, recycling, and reuse were needed everywhere.

Fixed Rail

For environmentalists, fixed rail was as much an environmental as a transportation strategy. Fixed rail, in fact, has to be seen as the most ambitious—and, as it turned out, the most ambiguous—of all sub/urban-oriented efforts to cleanse the environment. In seeking to unravel the mystery of how and why the Los Angeles County Transportation Commission and Southern California Rapid Transit District, later fused into the Metropolitan Transit Authority (MTA), first proposed the multibillion-dollar fixed rail program and succeeded in having the voters twice approve of it, reference must be made to the power of environmental arguments. Since 1943 residents of the Southern California basin had suffered from smog: a thick brown haze in the atmosphere formed from the combination of ozone and particulates derived from diesel soot, road dust, smoke, auto and industrial emissions, sulfates, and other compounds. By the 1960s, the smog of the Los Angeles basin had achieved a near-mythic quality. No other region in the country was so dependent on the automobile, and no other region had such smog. In 1976 alone Greater Los Angeles had 102 days of smog alerts. Medical scientists, such as USC pathologist Russell Sherwin, conclusively documented the risks posed by smog. One report claimed up to five thousand smog-related premature deaths a year. Another report estimated that by the late 1980s health costs related to air pollution in the Los Angeles basin were exceeding $10 billion a year. Metropolitan Los Angeles had the worst air quality in the United States, with ozone and carbon monoxide levels at nearly three times the national ceiling for health maintenance. Each month, by 1990, the burning of petroleum was dumping into the atmosphere the pollution equivalent of the *Exxon Valdez* oil spill.

No wonder, then, that both planners and voters saw fixed rail as a salvific solution to the Southland's pollution problems. (To the bitter end, the Sierra Club of California would defend fixed rail as an environmental strategy.) As the MTA rose to unprecedented power and authority in the fixed-rail-oriented 1990s, it swept into comparable acceptance the South

Coast Air Quality Management District, responsible for managing the atmosphere across the 13,350 square miles of Los Angeles, Orange, Riverside, and San Bernardino Counties, where more than twelve million residents were operating more than eight million motor vehicles. The district, its publicists claimed, was struggling to prevent metropolitan Los Angeles from becoming another Mexico City in terms of atmospheric pollution. Announced in March 1989, the Air Quality Management Plan of the South Coast Air Quality Management District launched an all-out attack on sources of atmospheric pollution in the Southland. Since cars and trucks accounted for more than half the pollution, they obviously bore the brunt of the agency's attack. As in the case of the fixed rail solutions, the focus was on lessening the number of automobiles on the road. Companies employing more than one hundred workers were required to come up with van pool programs or face stiff fines. The district also enforced 123 separate pollution control measures in industrial and commercial areas. As in the case of the MTA, the South Coast Air Quality Management District was by the mid-1990s one of the most powerful governmental entities in the Southland, with its authority, empowered by the sanction of fines, reaching into just about every dimension of industrial and transportation life in the region. As in the case of the MTA also, the district derived much of its psychological authority from the demonization of the automobile.

From one perspective, this assumption of authority by the district paid off. By 1996 the Los Angeles basin was experiencing the lowest levels of smog in forty years, with only seven days of alert. By 1997 the basin was enjoying its cleanest air in fifty years, with only one smog alert. Nearly everyone admitted, however, that most of the cleanup was due not to the draconian requirements of the district but to the increase in the use of unleaded gas and the improved emission technologies of the newer automobiles. Under the provisions and requirements of the 1990 amendments to the federal Clean Air Act, California was running an effective smog check program at more than nine thousand licensed locations. The best way to fight air pollution in the Southland, many were now saying, was not to take cars off the road but to make sure that those on the road were as emission efficient as possible.

As early as the 1970s, planners and public policy wonks were taking a hard look at the automotive dependence of metropolitan Los Angeles, especially the city proper. Like San Francisco, Los Angeles contained within itself the lingering memory, now the myth, of a time when public transit was predominant, in Los Angeles's case the early-twentieth-century era of the Big Red and Big Yellow Cars. (The Yellow Cars served the city; the Red Cars the region.) This myth of a lost urban Eden, like the biblical myth, had a villain: General Motors, which was alleged to have conspired and bribed the Big Red and Big Yellow Cars out of existence. The majority of Southern Californians believed this myth—that General Motors had deliberately, conspiratorially, eliminated fixed rail transit—despite the repeated efforts of scholars to assert a simpler, if less mythic, truth: namely, that the Big Red and Yellow Cars had gone out of business because they ceased to be competitive with the automobile, and that signs of this noncompetitiveness could be seen as early as the late 1920s and certainly by the 1930s. At the core of most stories about Los Angeles is a tale of urban growth as a fall from grace. In the film *Chinatown* (1974), growth linked to water is the villain. In the Big Red and Yellow Car story, growth linked to the automobile did the damage. In each instance, the myth claimed, a finer Los Angeles was lost.

In the 1970s, Los Angeles, with growing force, began to repossess its near-lost mythic memory of the Big Red and Yellow Cars. The city began to reenvision itself in terms of nonautomotive mass transit. The motivation for this was twofold. First, the problems of the automotive era were apparent; Los Angelenos were spending too much time on freeways. Second, the city seemed to be losing its identity along with the dilation of its physical space. In the era of the Big Red and Yellow Cars, all carriers had converged on downtown, bringing some fifty thousand commuters into the central city each day. Through World War II, downtown Los Angeles had been a glorious place: a mise-en-scène of American Renaissance office buildings, splendid movie palaces along Broadway, clubs, picturesque restaurants and assorted hangouts, newspaper plants, surviving adobes from the Spanish and Mexican eras, St. Vibiana's Cathedral (dedicated in 1876 and one of the oldest surviving buildings in the city), and Civic Center, one of the largest assemblies of government buildings in the country. Even after the war, downtown had held on as the center of commerce and power. Clubs such as the California, the Jonathan, the University, and the Los Angeles Athletic continued to cater to a cohesive civic elite. The streets teemed with well-dressed people. When it came time to build a new stadium for the Dodgers, recently acquired from Brooklyn, downtown beat out all other alternatives. It was still the heart of the city.

For a variety of reasons, however, most of them shared with other American cities—the flight to the suburbs, the dispersion of retail, the rise of edge cities, the decentralization of white-collar work through technology, together with the abandonment of public spaces for fear of crime, increasing vagrancy, and dysfunction—downtown Los Angeles was also experiencing a loss of population and civic influence. And thanks to the automobile and the freeway system, Greater Los Angeles now had many downtowns, perhaps as many as fourteen, each complete in its array of office and retail spaces, entertainment, and other amenities.

By the 1970s, the downtown establishment (and despite depredations, it still existed) was coming to the conclusion that it would need more than redevelopment to keep itself vital. It would have to bring people back. And that would require public transit. The downtown establishment, with the assistance of transit planners and anti-automobile activists, began to reenvision a new transit future for the region, one drawing on memories of the Big Red and Yellow Cars and, of equal importance, tapping into the desire of Los Angeles to consider itself, and to be considered, a world city. London and New York, it was argued, were defined by their subway systems, and, with its Bay Area Rapid Transit (BART), San Francisco was following suit. In reenvisioning itself in terms of public transit, Los Angeles was turning its back on fifty years of automobile-oriented development. A city that had crisscrossed itself with freeways—had invented itself, in fact, through freeways, beginning in 1940 with the Arroyo Seco Parkway—now began to dream of tunnels and swift subway trains crossing great distances, of light rail retracing the roots of the Big Red and Big Yellow Cars, of commuter trains pouring into Union Station from the hinterlands.

No one possessed this dream more powerfully than Mayor Tom Bradley. Despite his hardscrabble origins as the son of a Pullman porter and a housemaid, Bradley—and this could be said of most of his pioneering generation of African-American mayors—was a man of downtown, a downtown insider who in his rise to power had forged a classic old-style Democratic coalition of labor, inner-city minorities, and the establishment. It might have happened, but it was a long shot for an African American to become mayor of Los Angeles when the city was predominantly white; indeed, Bradley had lost his first run against incumbent Sam Yorty when Yorty played the race card. The new Bradley coalition, however, would not be between downtown and whites, for, with the exception of the Westside and a rapidly diminishing presence in the San Fernando Valley, whites no longer predominated in the city. The Bradley connection was with the big entities: big labor, big blocs of minority votes, big wheels downtown. In 1984, when Los Angeles hosted the Olympics, Bradley had shown triumphantly to the world the power and cohesion of this new coalition. Planning for the Olympics, especially getting people to and from sites by the hundreds of thousands in their automobiles, had more than ever convinced Bradley that Los Angeles needed to move forward with mass transit on a countywide scale.

Already, in a number of votes, the citizens of the city had expressed their support of Bradley's plans. In 1976 the legislature had authorized the cre-

ation of the Los Angeles County Transportation Commission (LACTC) as
the sole transportation authority in the county. In 1980 county voters had
approved Proposition A, a half-cent tax increase for transportation programs, including mass transit. The tax began to be collected in mid-1982,
and by 1990 was bringing in approximately $400 million a year. Thirty-five
percent of this money was set aside for rail construction and the operation
of a fixed rail rapid transit system. In November 1990 county voters
approved a virtually identical measure, Proposition C, which by the following year was generating another $400 million in yearly funds. If all this
were not enough, state voters in June 1990 passed three transportation
measures. Two of them, Propositions 108 and 116, provided $1 billion and
$2 billion respectively for fixed rail bonds. Los Angeles County, mean-
while, was receiving another $150 million per year from the federal govern-
ment for subway construction.

All this money was flowing into Los Angeles County or being collected
there in response to an awesome public transit program developed by the
LACTC through the 1980s and endorsed by the commission in 1990 as a
thirty-year plan, priced at approximately $184 billion. The Metro system,
as it was named, called for the construction of subway tunnels from downtown to East Los Angeles, from downtown to Santa Monica along the
Wilshire Corridor, and from downtown to the San Fernando Valley via the
Hollywood Hills. There would also be light rail lines linking downtown
with Long Beach, Glendale, and Pasadena. Another light rail line would
sweep across the southern tier of the county from Norwalk to the Los Angeles International Airport. From LAX another light rail connection would
run north to the city of San Fernando in the valley. Light rail would also run
south from LAX toward the Palos Verdes Peninsula, then move west to Signal Hill north of Long Beach. Elevated busways would run east to west
from El Monte to Union Station downtown and north to south from the
Santa Monica Freeway through Lynwood, Compton, Gardena, and Lawn-
dale in the southern portion of the county. The plan also included electric
trolley bus service for significant portions of the city and shuttle buses
downtown. All this would be fully linked to the five-county Metrolink commuter rail system of the Southern California Regional Rail Authority,
which by 2010, it was planned, would be carrying a half a million commuters a day into Union Station from Orange, Riverside, San Bernardino,
and Ventura Counties.

Here was being envisioned through public transit an entirely new organization of the Southland; and no one played a greater role in fashioning
and implementing this vision, alongside Bradley, than Nick Patsaouras. A
self-made millionaire in electrical engineering and banking, the Athens-

born Patsaouras had been appointed to the Southern California Rapid Transit District in the early 1980s by county supervisor Michael Antonovich, whom Patsaouras had endorsed in the general election of 1980, after challenging him in the primary. With its fleet of 2,600 buses, its 1.3 million boardings per day in more than eighty cities, the RTD was the largest transit district of its kind in the nation. Here, truly, was an empire to shape, and Patsaouras was an empire builder. Here, also, were the tools with which to bring into being—through transportation—the next stage of Los Angeles's development, and Patsaouras was a bold dreamer, desirous of bringing Los Angeles to world prominence as an achieved urban environment. Whatever its eventual format (and fixed rail may very well make a comeback), no one will be able to write the history of public transit in Southern California—its successes and failures alike, its relevance or irrelevance as social experiment, its utopian and dystopian dimensions—without reference to Patsaouras. Like Robert Moses of New York, Patsaouras exercised a species of appointed authority beyond that of elected government. Like Moses, Patsaouras sought, sometimes single-handedly, to use public works to bring into being a highly personal, deeply felt vision of regional urbanism.

Transportation systems and public works, Patsaouras believed, had more than a functional importance to metropolitan Los Angeles. Like the Eiffel Tower or the skyline of Manhattan, transportation expressed, perhaps better than any other form of public activity, the particular genius of the region. As fact and symbol, metropolitan Los Angeles was about the mobility of people in society across space and, as Patsaouras knew from personal experience, as movement across classes and social conditions. Transportation was the one thing everyone had in common, and it offered a compelling symbol of civic aspiration and unity. Transportation also needed to be more efficient, and it needed to be more public. Freeways and the automobile alone could not fully satisfy Patsaouras's notion of a collective civic ideal: his vision of metropolitan Los Angeles as an integration of urban nodal points. Fixed rail was a necessity.

From the start, Patsaouras knew he was fighting a battle of metaphor and identity as well as the more gritty realities of day-to-day politics. Metropolitan Los Angeles—indeed, all of Southern California—had built its social identity around the automobile. It was an intensely suburban model, one prizing individual choice, point-to-point transportation at will, good roads and the monumental freeway system, and, above all else, privacy: the right to choose where to go and when to go, and with whom, the right to be alone in one's car, the expectation that one could live anywhere and work anywhere one chose, as long as one could afford an automobile. This vision of reality, this cluster of preferences, demanded a certain level of affluence.

The miracle was that Southern California had been providing millions of citizens this level of economic well-being since the end of World War II. If asked what were their civic or communal symbols, millions might readily answer: their roads and freeways, the long processions of automobiles in which they joined daily. For all its disassociation, its emphasis on the solitary choosing self, this infrastructure—cars, roads, freeways—constituted for millions one of their most primary and fundamental experiences of society and civilization as a larger force.

With the assistance of Doug Suisman, director of Public Works Associates, a public-interest urban-design group, and Michael Wester, a senior urban designer and project manager at Kaplan McLaughlin Diaz, Patsaouras launched an assault on the notion that current arrangements, as far as transportation was concerned, were inevitable. The suburban era, meaning the automobile and freeway era, Suisman and Wester suggested, was coming to an end. It was too polluting, for one thing, even though the worst days of smog were over, too time-consuming, too expensive for ordinary commuters, and (this argument was made subtly but persistently) too promotive of fragmentation and disunity. Hostile to pedestrian values, the automobile-dominated transit culture of metropolitan Los Angeles had emptied downtown, swept clean the streets of pedestrians, encouraged building after building to turn its back to the streets, and, in so doing, not only to empty the streets, but to destroy civic culture in the bargain.

Mass transit, Suisman argued, would reintroduce Los Angeles to public spaces and value. Stations on the proposed subway lines, through which thousands would be coming and going each day, would serve as the nucleus of urban villages, supporting dense housing, plazas, restaurants, theaters. Michael Wester was especially eloquent in evoking the urbanization that would occur around subway stations and light rail transfer points: the plazas and *paseos,* the colorful vending carts, the outdoor cafés: the Manhattanization, in short, the Parisizing and Londonizing of the now empty, ominous, deserted streets of the City of Angels.

And so the work began. On July 14, 1990, the twenty-two-mile light rail Blue Line opened between Los Angeles and Long Beach, the first installment on the more than three hundred miles of light rail, heavy rail (subways), and commuter rail (Metrolink) scheduled to be in operation by 2020. Construction was already under way on the second light rail project, the Green Line between Norwalk and LAX. Work had also begun on the tunnel that would bring the Blue Line underground between Twelfth and Pico Streets to Seventh and Flower, where it would connect with the heavy rail Red Line, also under construction. Starting at Union Station, the Red Line tunnel pushed toward Seventh and Flower, from which it would move west-

ward into Hollywood, then out to the San Fernando Valley under the Hollywood Hills. On Valentine's Day 1991, Bradley and assorted dignitaries
were on hand to welcome the first Blue Line train into the Seventh and
Flower Streets station. Total cost for the project: $900 million.

Construction on the Red Line out to the San Fernando Valley had been
under way since June 1988. The first phase of the project consisted of 4.4
miles of underground tunnel, beginning at Union Station and looping
through downtown along Hill and Wilshire with stops at Civic Center, Fifth
and Hill, Seventh and Flower, Wilshire and Alvarado. The second phase
would push the Red Line tunnel north and west under Vermont and Hollywood Boulevard with eight stations en route. In the third phase, the tunnel
would bore through the Hollywood Hills to Universal City and North Hollywood. From there, the Red Line would head on the surface into the valley.

On January 30, 1993, after some four years of tumultuous tunneling
through downtown, at the cost of $1.4 billion, the first Red Line trains
began to operate on the 4.4 miles between Union Station and the West-
lake/MacArthur Park Station at Wilshire and Alvarado. In ceremonies
opening this first phase of Red Line service, Bradley made explicit reference to the eleven hundred miles of streetcar lines that had served Los
Angeles in the Big Red and Yellow Car era. From an aesthetic point of view,
at least—the gleaming stainless steel railcars traveling at seventy miles an
hour, the sumptuous stations embellished with vivid murals and other artwork, the pedestrian-friendly escalators, the user-friendly ATM-like ticket
dispensers—this first phase was an apparent success.

But already, even as Bradley made his comparisons to the Big Red and
Yellow Cars, dissenting voices were being heard. Was it really worth it,
these critics asked, to spend $1.45 billion on a seven-minute subway ride
serving a minuscule portion of the population? Would not this money have
been better used to improve bus service, which served more than 95 percent
of commuters? "I think we will eventually abandon our rail plan," noted
USC planning professor James Moore. "We'll sink a lot of money into it,
but in the end voters are going to decide to call an end to it."[15]

Moore's opinion was diametrically opposite to that of Gary Hausdorfer,
chairman of the Orange County Transportation Authority board. "The
future of transportation in California," Hausdorfer was insisting, "is rail."[16]
The previous year, on October 28, 1991, Hausdorfer and fellow members of
the authority had borne witness to their belief in this fixed rail future by voting through a $4.4 billion rail proposal to link Orange and Los Angeles
Counties. Under the plan, an elevated urban rail system would tie into the
Los Angeles Metro Rail system at connection points in Norwalk and Long
Beach. It would also push eastward into Riverside County. A year later, on

October 26, 1992, Hausdorfer helped inaugurate Southern California
Regional Rail Authority Metrolink commuter rail service into Los Angeles.
That day, 114 miles of fixed rail routes to and from Los Angeles were put
into service, the first installment on a proposed 450-mile web of train tracks
linking Los Angeles with its suburban hinterlands. Comparisons to the Big
Red Cars were multiple as some five thousand passengers boarded the silver
and blue double-decked commuter trains. A Roman Catholic priest blessed
the cars, and a high school band played. Hardly noticed were two solitary
protesters denouncing Metrolink as an unjust subsidy of affluent suburban
commuters at the expense of less affluent transit-dependent bus riders.

Two years later, these protesters had been joined by thousands of other
bus riders, predominantly minority or working class. Organized as the Bus
Riders Union, a project of the Labor/Community Strategy Center, and
backed by the NAACP Legal Defense and Educational Fund, the Bus Riders Union filed suit in September 1994 in federal court charging that the
MTA was violating the civil rights of hundreds of thousands of minority
plaintiffs by operating separate and unequal bus and rail systems that discriminated against low-income people of color in violation of Title VI of
the Civil Rights Act of 1964. The suit had been precipitated when the MTA
attempted to raise fares and eliminate monthly passes on its dilapidated and
inefficient bus system, which served an overwhelmingly minority and poor
ridership, while simultaneously spending billions on a rail system that
served a disproportionately affluent white ridership.

Meanwhile, as the suit was being argued in court, the MTA showed no
signs of pulling back. As construction continued on the Red Line tunnel,
now nearing Hollywood, the MTA, spearheaded by Nick Patsaouras, was
pushing its Union Station Gateway Intermodal Transit Center toward a September 1995 opening. Connected to Union Station—an imposing Spanish
Revival–Modern structure opened in 1940, the last of the great stations of
the railroad era—the transit center brought together in one terminal the
Amtrak line, running north from San Diego along the coast, the commuter
trains of Metrolink, the light rail Blue Line from Long Beach, the Red Line
subway, and the regional and local bus lines using the El Monte Busway
that extended eighteen miles to the east. These all terminated at the Gateway Center, which was also intended to serve a convergent network of van
pools, taxis, and shuttle services.

The investment of hundreds of millions of dollars in the MTA headquarters high-rise and the Gateway Center (the headquarters alone, financed and
refinanced through the rest of the decade, would eventually cost $480 mil-
lion over a thirty-year period) testified, if anything, to the power of the
vision of metropolitan Los Angeles reshaped by rail-oriented public transit,

as advocated by Patsaouras and his allies at the MTA. Yet national and local trends were pointing in the other direction. Voters in Los Angeles, for example, were being forced to acknowledge by 1993 that the $900 million light rail Blue Line to and from Long Beach was carrying 35,000 passengers each weekday, but one of the bus lines running parallel to the light rail had nearly the same amount of people at a fraction of the cost. The Blue Line, moreover, was making the trip more slowly than the express bus service it had replaced. Add all this to the fact that the Blue Line had originally been estimated to cost $200 million, and one had the makings of a disturbing situation.

In October 1996, buses won with a court-approved consent decree in which the MTA agreed to invest approximately $1.3 billion over the next ten years to improve its bus system. In terms of the dollar value of the settlement, it was the largest civil rights case in American history. NAACP attorney Robert Garcia made extensive use of the statistics and arguments compiled by the anti-rail academic group. This was one immediate and telling effect of their work. Yet in other ways as well, the academic critique had been devastating. The very integrity of the MTA had been questioned. "Whether they're building subways or office towers," USC planning professor Peter Gordon told *Forbes,* "what the MTA does has very little to do with transportation. It has everything to do with giving out money and letting contracts."[17]

Beyond such academic critiques, an even more powerful indictment was surfacing. The MTA, it was claimed, was a runaway, even rogue agency: a colossus for tax consumption, a program of public works long since devoid of social meaning, a bureaucracy bedeviled by more than one thousand lobbyists (more on duty than in Sacramento) out to get their share of the pork. The MTA played to and reinforced this developing anti-identity with a growing crescendo of accidents, indictments of officials for bribery and kickbacks, and other fiscal faux pas. On June 22, 1995, most scandalously, tunnelers under Hollywood Boulevard created a sinkhole, seventy feet deep and a half a block in diameter. For Mike Davis, the Hollywood Sinkhole, as it was called, "has become the taunting symbol of the biggest transportation fiasco in modern American history." After the expenditure of billions of dollars, Davis pointed out, the Los Angeles subway was carrying less than a quarter of the 61,000 daily riders using the 204 Vermont line alone, which served a fifteen-mile corridor between Gardena and Hollywood.[18]

Still, the tunnelers pushed on, despite the Hollywood Sinkhole and other accidents that claimed the lives of two workers, despite the departure of two MTA officials to jail, despite the growing bad press, despite the academic attacks. For a year and a half, the great boring machine pushed through the

2.4 miles of hard rock and soft shale beneath the Santa Monica Mountains, advancing foot by foot one of the longest and deepest public transit tunnels ever built in the United States. Their destination: North Hollywood, 17.4 miles from Union Station. By this time, however, the Brobdingnagian public work was proceeding almost autonomously as, above ground, the MTA sank further into administrative confusion. When construction workers punched through into North Hollywood on October 23, 1997, the MTA was in meltdown. Neither its new chairman of the board, Mayor Richard Riordan, nor its new CEO, turnaround artist Julian Burke, attended the ceremony. By now, moreover, Riordan had replaced Patsaouras as the dominant voice in MTA affairs.

Even as the Gateway Center opened, the MTA was collapsing from within. No amount of impressive architecture could conceal the growing knowledge that the agency was in big trouble—financial and political trouble, and construction trouble in terms of cost overruns. In the spring of 1997, Riordan ordered an independent audit of the MTA's finances. Pressure to get its house in order was coming from the federal government, which was paying for nearly half of the subway construction project, by now the single largest public works project in the Far West. Along with MTA inspector general Arthur Sinai, Washington was also concerned that Joseph Drew, the previous MTA chief, had exceeded his authority the prior January, just before leaving office, in approving retroactive merit raises totaling more than $1 million.

As scandalous as such pork barreling might be, however, a million dollars was chicken feed in comparison to the multimillion-dollar debt uncovered by Riordan's team of City Hall auditors, led by budget director Christopher O'Donnell, Riordan's chief assistant Lorenzo Tyner, and Julian Burke. The Riordan team found a $29 million debt of which the MTA management seemed hardly aware, together with an operating deficit that would soon be pushing $58 million. By November, as the audit proceeded under Burke, now interim CEO, the news had become even worse. Having discovered the operating deficit, Burke and his team had gone after the question of long-term debt. A five-year spending spree, auditors reported, together with the habit of financing and refinancing its growing debt, had put the MTA $2.8 billion in arrears. That figure could reach $5.2 billion by 2007, at which time the MTA would be unable to service its debt.

The next year the news got even worse. By June 1998, *Los Angeles Times* writer Jeffrey Rabin was reporting that the cumulative MTA debt now totaled $7.01 billion. Debt service was absorbing more than 30 percent of the MTA's annual $1.2 billion operating budget. Rabin should have won a Pulitzer Prize for the clarity with which he outlined the Ponzi schemes the

MTA had financed itself with across a decade-long spending spree. The intricate financing of its new headquarters, which included short-term borrowing from its own workers' compensation reserve account and a refinancing at fixed interest rates in 1996, would drive the total cost of the building to more than $480 million by 2026. Between 1995 and 2006, all payments on this debt would be interest, none principal. The key underwriter of MTA bonds had been the now defunct Grigsby Branford & Company of San Francisco, once the largest African-American investment banking firm in the nation. It did not help the reputation of the MTA when in January 1998 Calvin Grigsby was indicted (but later acquitted) in Miami–Dade County, Florida, for bribery, money laundering, and conspiracy after being videotaped allegedly offering a commissioner a $300,000 kickback for obtaining a piece of the county's bond business.

In assuming the interim directorship of the MTA, Burke opted immediately for the time-honored turnaround technique of the layoff, announcing that the agency would be cutting 2,100 nonunion positions in planning, construction management, and public relations from its 7,900 budgeted positions. Burke went so far as to try and save $159,000 by replacing sidewalk stars on the Walk of Fame along Hollywood Boulevard with less expensive versions, but was reversed by the Cultural Heritage Commission. By December 1997, it had become apparent that only one strategy could save the faltering MTA: the immediate suspension of the Blue Line to Pasadena (budgeted for $804 million), the canceling or at least the postponement of the extension of the Red Line to East Los Angeles (budgeted at $1 billion), and the suspension of construction on the Red Line from North Hollywood through the San Fernando Valley to Warner Center (budgeted at $682 million). Already, Los Angeles County supervisor and MTA board member Zev Yaroslavsky was calling for such a moratorium; and Richard Riordan, once an enthusiastic backer of the San Fernando Valley subway, was now talking more and more about buses.

In the course of his career, Julian Burke had turned around some $30 billion worth of companies. Now, at seventy, he was facing his greatest challenge. The surfacing of the operating deficit had been bad enough; but then came the news that the Hollywood segment of the Red Line had exceeded its budget by $79.1 million. While Burke might call for the suspension of all rail projects, numerous investments and purchases had already been made. More than $200 million had been spent acquiring the Pasadena Blue Line right-of-way and preparing for construction. A $13 million bridge had been built across the Los Angeles River to take the line to Pasadena. The MTA had purchased seven thousand tons of rail at the cost of $5 million and some 34,000 concrete railroad ties for $12 million for the Pasadena project. Fourteen subway cars for the Eastside extension of the Red Line were being completed in Italy at the cost of $28 million and were due to begin arriving by the summer of 1998 for final assembly. It could be claimed that the entire Green Line was an incomplete project, for it had stopped a half mile and a half billion dollars short of its final connection to LAX. Pushing the Red Line toward North Hollywood, meanwhile, was costing money, some $300 million a mile. By January 1998, Burke realized he was $727 million short for scheduled rail construction. Even if the MTA never laid another track, it was facing a projected $465 million shortfall just to maintain its existing bus and train operations over the next six years. No wonder that Federal Transit Administration head Gordon Linton was saying: No more money until you get your house in order.

On January 14, 1998, the MTA directors voted ten to three to suspend, for at least six months, all scheduled work on its Eastside, Mid-City, and Pasadena rail lines. The Red Line would be allowed to be finished as far as North Hollywood. Already, Yaroslavsky was in the process of placing an even more draconian measure—the suspension of all rail construction in Los Angeles County for the foreseeable future, if not forever—on the November 1998 ballot. A longtime subway backer, Yaroslavsky had by the end of the decade become a leading anti-subway crusader. Within six years from the triumphant announcements of 1992, the subway idea was on the verge of being closed down forever. Fiscal conservatives, including Supervisor Mike Antonovich and the Howard Jarvis Taxpayers Association, enthusiastically supported the measure. Pro-subway forces included prominent Latino and African-American officials, among them Supervisors Gloria Molina and Yvonne Brathwaite-Burke, the Sierra Club, construction trade unions, and Eastside activists, who saw the largely Mexican-American Eastside getting the short end of the deal. Interestingly enough, the Bus Riders Union initially opposed the measure but later changed its mind.

No prominent supporters, however, weighed in with pro-subway arguments in the voters' handbook. On election day November 1998, Proposition A passed overwhelmingly—66.4 percent of the vote in the city of Los Angeles alone—throughout the county. In Hollywood, through which the subway had been snaking for the past half decade, 74 percent of the voters said no to the new rail systems. In South Central, already being served by the Blue Line and by the Green Line, 59.9 percent said no. In downtown and adjacent neighborhoods, which the subway was supposed to benefit so dramatically, 60.5 percent said no. In the Eastside, where elected officials and other activists had argued that the subway would link the Latino population more conveniently to the city, 69.3 percent said no. Los Angeles

County was no longer envisioning itself in terms of fixed rail. We already know what the Los Angeles of 2017 will look like, argued USC planning professors James Moore, Harry Richardson, and Peter Gordon; and it has nothing to do with the straight lines drawn on the map by the MTA. "The Los Angeles metropolitan area of the future will become even larger and, on average, less dense than it is now," the trio wrote in the *Los Angeles Times* in their moment of triumph, as Burke was calling for the immediate halt of all rail projects. "Employment will be more dispersed. Fewer areas will qualify as employment centers, and job densities in those that do will diminish. Downtown will become even less relevant to the region's lifestyle and economy, though the ideal of a quaint, walkable, 24-hour downtown experience will doubtless remain the eternal pipe dream of downtown boosters."[19]

As historian Scott Bottles had already pointed out in *Los Angeles and the Automobile: The Making of the Modern City* (1991), Los Angeles had turned to the automobile precisely because fixed rail had failed to fulfill its needs. Once that process had occurred—once metropolitan Los Angeles had respatialized itself through the automobile—it could never go back to the future. Los Angeles had become a new type of city, a new range of options, a new set of spatial solutions. In choosing the multiple and deconstructed over the unitary and centralized, it had become the first postmodernist city in the country. It had deconstructed itself into multiple identities and options. For all the problems such a choice involved—crowded freeways, smog, four-hour daily commutes—no fixed rail system, however well intended, seemed able, at least for the time being, to reverse this choice. Like a half-built medieval cathedral interrupted by plague, famine, or war, the fixed rail system in operation by 2002 only fragmentarily expressed the vision that had so exhilarated Nick Patsaouras and an entire generation of advocates. Yet medieval cathedrals, even when interrupted, had a way of getting finished. For those who still kept the faith, fixed rail remained a certainty for some future time in the dawning millennium.

PART IX

Back on the Edge

Bill and Barbra

He was president of the United States, the forty-second in succession to George Washington, and she was a living legend as singer, actress, and film director. The friendship and political alliance they formed through the 1990s said much about each of them, the culture of Hollywood that had brought them together, and the state of California that provided him his start, his continuing support, and his final victory lap. What brought them together, William Jefferson Clinton and Barbra Streisand? What was the nature of their political alliance? What did this alliance say about the developing role of California in national politics?

On a surface level, it was easy to see how they were attracted to each other. She was, arguably, the most powerful woman in Hollywood, certainly one of the best known show-business personalities of the late twentieth century. For nearly forty years, she had set performance standards that would rarely be equaled, and she had become an extraordinarily wealthy woman in the process, living, at the opening of the decade, on a twenty-four-acre estate in Malibu. She had also remained a ferociously liberal Democrat, which was connected to her way of being Jewish and wanting to do *tikkun olam,* to repair what was broken, to heal the world.

Over the years, she had backed numerous liberal Democratic candidates. Early in her career she had sung for Presidents Kennedy and Johnson. In April 1986 she had joined with lyricist Marilyn Bergman ("The Way We Were") and others to form the Hollywood Women's Political Committee. Constructing an amphitheater on her Malibu property, she had invited the Hollywood elite to her estate that September, at $5,000 a couple, for a concert of seventeen songs that raised $1.5 million for Democratic senatorial candidates. It was the first time she had sung in public, or quasi public, since receiving a death threat, allegedly from the Palestine Liberation Organization, during a concert in Central Park, in 1967. Thanks in part to the money raised by Streisand, five of the six Democratic senatorial candidates she backed won their races that November. From that point on, the Hollywood Women's Political Committee and Barbra Streisand were in the fund-raising game, big-time. She met Bill Clinton early in the 1992 presidential campaign at a political fund-raiser at producer Ted Field's home in Beverly Hills. By the time of the November election, she had raised nearly one million dollars on his behalf.

It was easy, then, to understand how the presidential candidate, soon to be president, would very much like the charismatic megastar, with her proven talents as a fund-raiser and her formidable presence at the center of the Hollywood establishment. For his part, Clinton could not help but be intrigued, flattered even, by the attention being paid him by a woman whom, over the years, millions of fans had found an equally compelling presence. Barbra Streisand, in turn, could not help but be flattered by the president-to-be, so charismatic in his own way and so willing to take her seriously not only as a fund-raiser, but as a spokesperson for liberal Democratic values.

Aside from politics, they had a lot in common. Each had lost a father early in life and had endured, in one case, an indifferent and, in the other, a hostile replacement. Each had had mothers who were— in the differing ways of a Brooklyn yenta and a fun-loving, occasionally hard-luck Arkansas nurse—life forces who had at once energized their offspring and left them strangely incomplete. Almost immediately, Streisand became good friends with Clinton's mother, Virginia Kelley, with whom she shared a high regard for Elvis Presley. (And the Elvis connection was significant, for Streisand and the King had been friends, and Bill Clinton, in so many ways, was an Elvis impersonator.)

Many divorced or otherwise parent-deprived children love movies, and Bill Clinton had loved movies all of his life, wolfing them down—in shabby little cinemas in Hope, Arkansas, at Georgetown, Oxford, and Yale, in countless hotel rooms when on the campaign trail, in the governor's mansion in Little Rock, in the White House, on Air Force One—with the same gusto he wolfed down cheeseburgers and french fries. It was the movies that had showed each of them the possibilities of a better life, inflamed their imaginations, propelled them into shortcuts to destiny: he in Hope and Little Rock, she in Brooklyn, finishing high school and going to work as an usherette so she could see movies all day long and still earn a living.

Without this connection to Barbra Streisand, Bill Clinton would have still discovered Hollywood, but perhaps not in such an immediate and overwhelming way as took place during the 1992 campaign, when liberal Hollywood was climbing aboard the Clinton bandwagon. Not since the Kennedy era had there been such a vital and clear-cut connection between a presidential candidate and the entertainment industry. Whether Republican or Democrat, most presidents since Kennedy had not been starstruck or particularly congenial to the Hollywood way of perceiving reality. Even Ronald Reagan had only a few Hollywood friends—Bob Hope, Claudette Colbert, Charlton Heston, Senator George Murphy—to hang out with when he reached the White House, and these few, like the president himself, were from another era entirely. But now, young Hollywood, which is to say Boomer Hollywood, was making its own connection with a candidate who was one of them in thought, word, and deed. Nor was this Hollywood connection irrelevant to Clinton's larger California connection, for the liberal values and beliefs of Hollywood were the values of liberal California as well, and liberal California in the 1990s was, despite some setbacks early in the decade, in the ascendancy.

By 1999, there would only be one Republican in statewide office, Bill Jones, the secretary of state, a straight-talking, churchgoing rancher from Fresno, married to his high school sweetheart, and not a Hollywood kind of guy. Even the fact that Clinton had dodged the draft by pretending to enroll in ROTC, then withdrawing from the program after he received a safe lottery number, was, for the majority of Californians, a nonissue; no state had supported opposition to the Vietnam War more vociferously, and this one-time generation of collegiate naysayers and nonservers was now at the center of just about every form of authority, public or private, in the state. From this perspective, it could be argued, Boomer Hollywoodites were the ultimate Californians, setting the pace and values for the rest of the state, which, in turn, was having more than its share of influence on the national value system and mind-set.

And so Streisand sang at the first Clinton inauguration (and the second one as well), and the stars flocked to Washington in great numbers for the festivities. Within the next few years, she would be singing again for the president, this time at a concert in the USAir Arena just outside Washington, at the beginning of her first concert tour in twenty-eight years. She acknowledged the president from the stage, accompanied him to the annual Gridiron Dinner, stayed overnight at the White House in the Lincoln Bedroom, dined with Attorney General Janet Reno, rubbed elbows with the chairman of the joint chiefs of staff, examined the basic documents of the republic at the National Archives, attended weekend parties with Václav Havel at Madeleine Albright's Virginia farm.

Bill Clinton, meanwhile, was expanding upon his Hollywood/California connection. As president-elect, he took his first vacation at the Summerland beach home just south of Santa Barbara of his longtime friends Harry Thomason and Linda Bloodworth-Thomason, Arkansas natives who had prospered as television producers. (The local tavern kept a saxophone at the ready.) Clinton's transition team, headed by Los Angeles attorney Warren Christopher, was dominated by Californians, and, not surprisingly, some seventy-three high-level jobs in the administration went to people from California. In his first term alone, Clinton would average a trip to California once every seven weeks, a pace he held during his second four years. His half brother, Roger, moved to California, and his daughter, Chelsea, chose to attend Stanford, which brought him and Hillary to that campus on a number of occasions.

When in the Bay Area, Clinton tended to stay with real estate mogul Walter Shorenstein, happy to roar up and down the hilly narrow streets of San Francisco in presidential motorcade, a phalanx of motorcycle police in attendance, traffic stopped at every corner. Yet it was Southern California he most favored, as his press secretary Dee Dee Myers, herself a Californian, once pointed out. He loved the restaurants in Beverly Hills, the Westside, and Santa Monica. He loved to run in the morning on the beaches of Malibu. He loved the parties, the movie stars. Los Angeles was the kind of place where he could go to the House of Blues on Sunset with Al Gore and James Belushi, the three of them wearing shades, as in the film *The Blues Brothers* (1990), mugging for the camera as if they were guys back in college, singing the Elvis song "Viva Las Vegas!" and in so doing celebrating their boomer identity, young enough to be hip, old enough to be in power.

Clinton loved the glamour and glitz of the Southland, the way it treated him like a star (although he was pushing matters in May 1993, when Air Force One stood idle on a LAX runway while he had his hair cut by Beverly Hills stylist Christophe, causing the fifty-six-minute closing of two LAX runways); and he loved the money he could raise on California weekends from such show-business pals as Steven Spielberg, Jeffrey Katzenberg, and David Geffen. By April 1996, Spielberg and Geffen alone had raised one-sixth of all campaign funds available to the president. That year, four of the top corporate donors to the Democratic National Convention—Seagrams/MCA, Disney, DreamWorks SKG, and MCI—were from the entertainment business. Across two administrations, the Industry would raise and donate to the Democratic National Committee more than $50 million.

What did Hollywood want from the president? Political commentator Alexander Cockburn has suggested that Hollywood wanted to get Clinton on the side of easing restrictions against its films in European Union countries. Such a motivation, of course, would be perfectly appropriate to someone like Jack Valenti, the longtime president of the Motion Picture Association of America, but it is doubtful that it was very much on the minds of the Hollywoodites who flocked to the Spielberg, Katzenberg, Geffen, Streisand galas bringing Clinton back again and again to the coast. Hollywood's Clinton mania was, rather, the glamour of being on the national scene after such a long banishment from presidential corridors. Politics was show business for ugly people, one wag had said, yet hanging out with Bill Clinton was a definite rush.

It was also a way of warding off the unwanted attentions of the other half of American society, who did not like Hollywood's product, finding it banal or subversive or violent or all the above. Every so often, Hollywood knew in its heart of hearts, the American people were wont to rise up, as they had in the mid-1920s, the early 1930s, and the late 1940s, and call Hollywood to task for its immorality and dubious politics. From this perspective, Clinton was the righteous gentile who might protect them from the other Baptists of America, people from places like Arkansas and Texas, should those Baptists and others get angry and come calling via repressive legislation.

Then there was the question of respect: intellectual respect. Everybody respected the money of Hollywood, the profits taken, the salaries paid. Everyone respected, even envied, the physical beauty of the stars. But never, even in its heyday, had Hollywood been looked to by the American people for intellectual leadership, for ideas. Boomer Hollywood was a college-educated Hollywood. Most of the leading personalities had gone to college, many of them to nationally ranked schools, where they had taken courses in political science and political philosophy as well as cinema and television. Now that one of their generation was running things in the White House, they wanted in on the action. Streisand was especially eager for such intellectual respectability, for she was a brilliant woman—her directing showed this—who had missed college and hence sustained the sensitivities of the autodidact.

Clinton gave Boomer Hollywood the respect and the recognition it thought it deserved, and Hollywood was grateful for its place at the presidential seminar table. Which perhaps accounted for the double, even triple, shock Hollywood went into when Clinton faced impeachment. Were Hollywood to lose Clinton as president, it would lose its growing hold on the national discourse, which was why it immediately went into a two-pronged defense. On the one hand, no one—except for a few far-out rap singers—defended the president's sexual conduct. On the other hand, the Industry went into overdrive in raising money for the president's defense and described the entire impeachment crisis as an attempted coup from the right. Once again, Spielberg, Katzenberg, and Geffen rounded up the usual suspects, and the Clinton defense fund reached $1.5 million by late September 1998.

Barbra Streisand was especially outspoken in Clinton's defense, contributing the $10,000 maximum to his fund. On the weekend of October 22–24, 1998, a beleaguered Clinton did four fund-raisers in California, including a dinner party in Bel Air, at which Streisand spoke passionately on his behalf, attacking independent counsel Kenneth Starr, and describing the impeachment proceedings as an "attempted coup on our government."[1] On December 16, Streisand and Jack Nicholson organized an anti-impeachment rally in West Los Angeles, at which Streisand, describing herself as "stupefied" by the impeachment proceedings, spoke in praise of Senator Edmund Ross, the Kansas Republican whose dissenting vote against impeachment had kept Andrew Johnson in office in 1868. Despite the sometimes excessive nature of Streisand's rhetoric, the majority of Californians agreed with her. Throughout the crisis, sentiment in California in favor of impeachment hovered around 30 percent, perhaps because California had long since been considering Clinton as in some way an honorary Californian, and because most Californians agreed with Streisand that Clinton's perjury, arising out of sexual misconduct, had to it an element of entrapment.

Clinton also had been very good to the Golden State, just as California had been good to him. Even Republican mayor Richard Riordan had been basking in the funds coming from the federal government during two Clinton administrations. As a presidential candidate, Clinton had in 1992 toured the burned-out sectors of Koreatown and South Central and called for an expanded federal relationship to cities. While Riordan was bitterly disappointed the following year when Los Angeles was not chosen by the federal government as an empowerment zone, relations were soon improved as other streams of federal dollars flowed into the city by the end of Clinton's first term. Later, toward the end of the second term, Riordan almost single-handedly secured the August 2000 Democratic National Convention for Los Angeles, persuaded the city council to spend $33.5 million on its behalf, and raised an equal amount of money from the private sector.

That convention provided Bill Clinton with his victory lap. Despite the scandal over his relationship with Monica Lewinsky (a California girl) and the impeachment trial in the Senate, in California the president had remained a favored son: feted, once again, as he had been feted for the past eight years by an admiring Southland, beginning with a big Hollywood party at the Robert Taylor ranch on August 12, 2000, presided over by Gregory Peck. This party launched a week of high-profile events for Clinton and his wife, Hillary, now a candidate for the Senate from New York, including a bash on the set of NBC's *The West Wing,* in which the television version of the White House staff mingled with the real-time version of the Clinton staff, and few people could tell the difference.

When Al Gore won the popular vote, lost in the electoral college, and failed in the Florida recounts and before the Supreme Court, Hollywood, especially Barbra Streisand, once again went into shock. In late March 2001, she wrote a blistering three-page memo titled "Nice Guys Finish Last or Where Do We Go from Here: A Case for the Democrats" to Democratic leaders, castigating them for abandoning the Clinton legacy, and defending his last-minute presidential pardons as having "no impact on the health and welfare of the American people." Above all else, Streisand excoriated President George W. Bush for stealing the election, poisoning the air and water of America, and advocating laws that benefited corporations and the privileged few. "How could such a destructive man be so popular with the American people?" Streisand asked.[2]

Then came September 11, and Hollywood bent over backward to show its patriotism in, among other things, a lavish television special raising funds for the families of terrorist victims while positioning itself, as usual, at the head of the patriotic parade. Streisand took down the anti-Bush material from her Web site and replaced it with statements such as: "This indomitable American spirit has always carried us through the darkest of days and strengthens our determination to create a brighter tomorrow."[3] The following month, describing herself as in semiretirement, she was spending a lot of time on her Malibu estate, where she was preparing a new Christmas CD, and devoting her best energies to being at home with those she loved. With his wife in the Senate, Bill Clinton did not settle in Southern California, as so many had expected, and take a job in the entertainment industry. He ensconced himself, rather, after some controversy, in offices in New York City's Harlem, where, like so many aging baby boomers who had done well, he was deciding what to do with the rest of his life.

Dot-Com Debacle

These were the good times, the mid- to late 1990s, as the dot-com industry brought a new Gold Rush to California. As in the case of the 1849 version, a generation of young people flocked into California to strike it rich. Their mother lode was the Internet, through which they would find new ways of doing business, new ways of buying and selling insurance, scheduling construction, selling groceries, wine, toys, books, CDs, and real estate, finding jobs, staffing companies, managing portfolios and bank accounts, taking university courses, even getting a degree, booking travel or tickets for a Broadway show, and, of course, communicating megabytes of data at high speeds. The Internet, the dot-commers believed, was the matrix for an entirely new economy—and an entirely new way of doing business and living life—and they would design the hardware and software tools for this new way of life, and organize the companies to deliver the services, which would then go public and make everyone, even the receptionist, rich.

As in the case of 1849, 1850, and 1851, the streets of San Francisco—the very same streets of the Gold Rush, south of Market—were filled with young people who could barely suppress a swagger as they moved along the sidewalk, talking into their cell phones, or crowded into restaurants at the end of long and exhilarating days at dot-com start-ups, sitting around the dinner table as their predecessors had sat around campfires, gossiping, in their case, about technology and IPOs over nouvelle cuisine and very expensive bottles of wine, with nary a necktie in sight. They were living a 24/7 pace, for the rush was on, and there was no time to lose. In San Francisco, but elsewhere as well, they swarmed into previously marginal industrial spaces and transformed them into high-tech hives. They paid each other top dollar, together with stock options, and they had plenty of money to burn, and they were willing to burn it on upscale apartments with views, SUVs and foreign imports, restaurants—anything, it seemed, except expensive clothes, in a culture in which even CEOs prided themselves on dressing down seven days a week.

Each year, starting in 1996, dot-commers in San Francisco, the center of the start-up movement, gave their annual Webby Awards bash, the equivalent of the Academy Awards, for the best Web sites. The city went so far as to block off streets to facilitate the event. After all, the Webby event—the awards themselves, the various exhibition booths, the food stalls, the dancing atop Nob Hill or at the Veterans Auditorium, the send-up costumes—celebrated an industry rapidly becoming an ATM for municipal revenues. These young people were taking San Francisco out of the economic doldrums, City Hall believed, and jump-starting it, once again, into a hip place to be. Older residents of San Francisco were hostile to, even despised, them. They did not like the way they crowded onto the streets outside their favorite bars on Friday night, blocking the sidewalk; did not like the way they drove up the cost of rental apartments, the way their SUVs hogged all the parking spaces, the way they sped up and down jogging paths on their high-speed bikes, the Lord-of-the-Universe look in their eyes. The media, however, staffed by journalists of their own generation—and ever on the lookout for a good story—loved to cover them, seeing in the dot-commers the next great wave, the entrepreneurs of the new economy, the makers and finders of the future.

Throughout the 1990s, especially the middle and later years, these bright, ambitious, college-educated young people flocking into California created a boom. In April 2000 the NASDAQ peaked at 5,048. Then, over the next eighteen months, a steady, then precipitous, decline ensued. By mid-August 2001, the NASDAQ index had dropped to 1,930, and by the fall of 2001 some 129,310 workers had lost their jobs at Internet-based companies. Why had this happened? It was, first of all, part of a larger economic pattern. During the same period, more than one million American workers had received pink slips as the global economy—that is, the off-loading of American business and manufacturing to offshore sites—took its expected toll on American jobs. But the collapse had other causes as well, more elusive, even mysterious causes, relating to the bursting of a bubble, the end of an illusion, the rude awakening from a collective dream state.

One could divide the entire industry into two categories: the design and manufacturing of hardware, and the writing of software programs. The two did not function apart from each other. Programs were dependent on hardware capacities, and hardware was designed and manufactured with appropriate programs in mind. Most start-ups, however, were in the program side of the industry—the application of the Internet, that is, to some new phase of American life. Here is where the big money, the sudden overnight money, was to be made. Yet the very speculative nature of such start-ups obscured the forces that were gathering toward collapse. Speculative ventures, after all, are expected to fail. Not every salmon struggling upstream is destined to spawn. One paid attention to the successes, not the failures, especially when initial IPOs made millionaires, and a few billionaires, of recent college graduates and, more to the point, a notable number of college dropouts.

Yet the failure of a manufacturing enterprise could not mask itself, for hundreds, even thousands, of jobs were inevitably lost. The overture to debacle was presented in early November 1999, when the owners of Packard Bell NEC, the NEC Corporation of Japan, and Groupe Bull of France pulled the plug on fourteen hundred workers at the Packard manufacturing site at the former Sacramento Army Depot, which had been launched with such fanfare in late 1994. Hailed as a model for the conversion of military properties and a boost to the sagging California economy, the arrival of Packard Bell in Sacramento had created five thousand jobs and had encouraged Apple Computer to locate a manufacturing facility there as well. The closing, moreover, virtually ended Packard Bell as a player in the manufacturing of computers.

Gateway, meanwhile, was also having troubles. Just how many computers, after all, could the economy absorb? What rate of obsolescence would consumers tolerate? In terms of personal computers, only the most avid of wonks would agree to the necessity of an upgrade every eighteen months. Like a good Packard or a Hudson car, a good computer should last. But then again: Packard and Hudson—as well as Nash, DeSoto, Studebaker, Oldsmobile—had all gone out of business because their products had lasted and lasted, and people did not have to buy new cars. So, too, could computers go on forever. In late August 2001, the San Diego–based Gateway announced that it was laying off 4,700 employees, or 25 percent of its global workforce, which translated to some 2,200 Americans losing their jobs, about half of them in California. Nor were the manufacturers of telecommunications equipment exempt from the same paradox, namely, the good equipment they manufactured tended to last, and new orders were not rolling in. Cisco Systems saw its quarterly earnings plunge a traumatizing 99 percent between 2000 and 2001. Cisco was forced to write off $2.2 billion in inventory in the third quarter of 2001. Its product was there in the warehouse, ready to go, but it was not moving.

Hewlett-Packard of Palo Alto, meanwhile, was in close consultation with Compaq Computer Corporation of Houston regarding a possible merger. On September 4, 2001, Carleton "Carly" Fiorina, the CEO of Hewlett-Packard, and Michael Capellas of Compaq announced the intended merger and $25 billion stock swap, designed to combine two struggling manufacturers into an entity big enough to take on IBM, Dell, Sun

Microsystems, and Gateway. The problem was that mergers like this cost jobs—fifteen thousand, in this case—as duplicate staffs suddenly had to be cut. Investors, moreover, were wary of having their stock decline in value as it was being merged or traded, as was soon evident when Hewlett-Packard stock plunged 22 percent and Compaq stock sank by 14 percent in the aftermath of the announcement. Fiorina, a Texas-born Stanford MBA with an undergraduate degree from Stanford in medieval philosophy, and the highest-ranking female in the computer industry, argued that Hewlett-Packard and Compaq fit like two sides of a zipper. Others in California, however, feared a repeat of the Bank of America takeover of April 1998, in which Hugh McColl Jr. and the boys from North Carolina gutted a premier California institution. Was Fiorina a Margaret Thatcher saving two companies through tough love (as proved to be the case), or would the boys from Texas wind up taking over yet another California property?

And so the downward tumbling continued among big companies and small. ExciteAtHome Corporation, the result of a $6.7 billion merger in April 1999, then trading for almost $95 a share on the NASDAQ, was closing at forty-seven cents a share by late August 2001. In 2000 alone, ExciteAtHome had lost $7.4 billion. The Beverly Hills–based Global Crossing, a telecommunications company in the process of creating a worldwide fiber-optic network for voice and data traffic, saw its stock value fall more than 95 percent through 2001, as the task of finishing its system was eating up its cash reserve by the billions.

Companies like Global Crossing, even ExciteAtHome, represented sophisticated applications of technology beyond the interest of ordinary consumers. The dot-com Gold Rush, however, had also sought to apply the Internet to everyday functions as well: buying groceries, furniture, toys, pet supplies. Many eventually went under, as did Webvan.com, which offered a case study for the debacle. Founded by Louis Borders, the highly successful book retailer, Webvan.com of Foster City was intended to do for groceries what Federal Express had done for packages: deliver the product, safely and conveniently and in record time. The concept was simple: Webvan would list a complete inventory of grocery products, stored in a network of highly automated warehouses. People would order their groceries from Webvan over the Internet. The groceries would be rapidly assembled at the warehouses and delivered to the customer in colorful trucks by cheerful uniformed drivers. No longer would anyone have to go to the store. The astonishing thing about Webvan was how quickly the idea was taken up by big-time investors such as Softbank Corporation, Amazon.com, and Sequoia Capital of Menlo Park. In almost a year, some $1.2 billion was raised from public and private investors. In November 1999, Webvan stock rose to $34 a share, which gave the firm a value of more than $10 billion—on paper, at least. Shortly thereafter, the company acquired its major rival, HomeGrocer.com, in a stock swap worth $1.2 billion.

Paper, however—specifically, toilet paper and other cheap and bulky products—soon proved a problem. At its best, the grocery business allows for only a few cents of profit on the dollar. Buying, storing, and delivering not only expensive groceries but bulky inexpensive household products as well cost money. Webvan was delivering groceries in seven markets—San Francisco, Los Angeles, Orange County, San Diego, Seattle, Portland, and Chicago—but it also was hemorrhaging money, losing almost $524.4 million in 2000 alone, its stock value sinking from an all-time high of $34 per share to an abysmal six cents in July 2001, when it shut its doors and put some two thousand employees on the street.

By now the auctioning of assets of failed dot-com companies had become a near art form in California and had accounted for the emergence of yet another such company, the San Francisco–based Webmergers.com, a clearinghouse for buyers and sellers of now available assets of these companies. By the first half of 2001, Webmergers.com had completed one hundred such auctions or sales. Webvan sold its surviving assets in three separate auctions in Atlanta, Baltimore, and Oakland. Grocery chains and restaurant supply houses had a field day acquiring its state-of-the-art equipment. When Wine.com went under in the summer of 2001—the New York Times Company had been among its lead investors—more than a million bottles of inventory went on the auction block in a Napa Valley airport hangar, in what was advertised as the wine auction of the century. More than one thousand bids—$2,000, for example, for a 1921 Château d'Yquem sauterne—were made online.

As myriads of dot-com companies went under, the publications that tracked them—*Upside, Access, Family PC, Feed, Red Herring, T3, Wired, Business 2.0*—came under stress or ceased publication. In mid-August 2001, the San Francisco–based *Industry Standard* shut down. At the height of the dot-com Gold Rush, the magazine had employed more than six hundred and had been valued at $200 million. It had been sassy and full of dot-com attitude. ("Going Public, Everybody's Doing It," ran one article. "B-School, Skip Class, Get Funded," ran another.) The Friday-night parties on the roof of its building at 315 Pacific Street had evolved into a downtown happening in which those who could not get inside partied on the street. "Success was coming very easily," noted staff writer Gary Rivlin. "We had the hubris. We looked down on the established media. Then when it all turned, we were slow to trim back our sails, despite articles in our own magazine making fun of others for not trimming their sails."[4]

Rivlin found out he had lost his job when he came back to the office from jogging. Suddenly, thousands of young people who had been riding the wave for more than a half decade, many of them millionaires on paper at one point or another, were now seeing their lives collapse beneath them. In the early 1990s, as defense industries declined, blue-collar workers had gone through the same experience. Now it was the dot-commers' turn to be out of a job. Once again, rental truck companies in San Francisco were reporting record numbers of one-way reservations.

Others remained, holding on to marginal jobs, dot-com casualties, their hopes deflated, preferring to hang on in any way possible rather than go home and admit defeat. This, too, had been a characteristic of the Gold Rush of the nineteenth century: the truncation of a life when the big bonanza evaporated. "Now I'm thirty years old," rued Wendy Wedlake as she volunteered nights at the San Francisco Food Bank to keep herself net-worked. "I have no job. I haven't had a date in months; I mean, who'd want to date me? I'm living at my aunt and uncle's house, sleeping in my cousin's old bedroom under a Laura Ashley bedspread." San Francisco exfoliated with newly formed support groups—ProMatch, Layoff Lounge, Recession Camp—for out-of-work dot-commers. Some sessions reminded one of Alcoholics Anonymous. ("Hi, I'm Kelly. I got laid off from two dot-coms in six weeks.") Rather than partying at bars and restaurants on Friday nights, young people gathered for pink slip parties that frequently exuded an ambience of hormonal overdrive as dot-commers, in a panic, turned to temporary relationships for support.[5]

Not surprisingly, the San Francisco real estate market, commercial and residential, dropped from warp speed as first-tier rentals crashed by 44.76 percent in the area south of Market in the first half of 2001 and second-tier properties declined by nearly 60 percent. Fine printer Andrew Hoyem, for example, had his Arion Press evicted from its south of Market location when the owners of the building wanted to cash in on the dot-com market. It took Hoyem two years, half a million dollars in moving costs, and another half a million in lost revenues to move his company—one of the finest print-ing houses in the nation—to new quarters in the Presidio. By the time that was accomplished, however, his old building stood empty, and "Available" signs dotted other buildings on this once busy block. Some dot-commers had perfected the art of moving from their properties early in the morning, with no notice, in order to avoid months of overdue rent. Landlords were known to come into an abandoned space and find no tenants in sight, with half-eaten cartons of Chinese food everywhere in evidence.

Had not the whole dot-com boom, after all, especially in San Francisco, been, like the earlier Gold Rush, a kind of collective frenzy? Did anyone truly believe that an entire generation was destined to become millionaires by thirty-five, tooling around Telluride in SUVs for the rest of their lives? (The average forty-niner was lucky to make $1,000 in the mines. And one out of ten died in the effort.) And it had been fun, all of it: fun to be young and to dream dreams of impossible wealth and feel the exhilaration of creating new ways of doing business and a new information economy. What was good and salvageable from the entire frenzy would survive. The workable ideas would reappear in more stable companies. And the entrepreneurial spirit of the dot-commers—their conviction that they could make the world anew—would survive as well and would reappear, most likely, in future enterprises. The Gold Rush of 1849, after all, had transformed California and made of it, precipitously, an American state.

Report Card

O ver the decades, California, like the United States itself, had always been able to import skilled workers—physicians, scientists, engineers, technologists of every sort—when there was a shortage. In the agricultural sector of its economy, almost from the very beginning, American California faced a shortage of people to do the necessary work and relied on a seasonal influx of migrant workers. Throughout the 1990s, this process of labor recruitment continued, whether legally, in the case of federally authorized special immigration quotas, or illegally, in the case of undocumented workers. In this same decade, however, a perplexing question was clarifying itself. How long could this pattern continue, given the growing population of native-born Californians? Census 2000 had revealed that more than half of all Californians—50.2 percent, to be precise—had been born in the state. The immigrants of California were busy creating an entire generation of native sons and daughters. If California were to continue to import outside labor to meet its needs, especially in the skilled categories, what did that mean for the resident population, increasingly California-born? More importantly, why was the resident population not competitively available for these jobs? Maybe there were two Californias: the one more and more complex, requiring higher and higher levels of skills, recruiting globally to meet its labor needs, and a native-born California, more and more noncompetitive, sinking further and further into the underclass. If that were true, what were the causes of such dysfunction?

The answer most immediately given was education. By the 1990s it was becoming apparent that California stood in real danger of not being able to provide itself with an educated and skilled workforce. True, it could always import such people, as it had in the past; but then there was the danger of those being left behind developing into a problematic (and growing) portion of the California population whose primary experience of the state was downward mobility. A rising portion of Californians, in short, were being dumbed down, or dumbing themselves down, into economic marginality.

Obviously, this was not a problem exclusive to California. For years, companies across the country were being forced to mount elaborate training programs, frequently connected with the teaching of basic math and verbal skills. In late 1997, for example, the Boeing Company of Seattle announced a $1.6 billion draw against future earnings, due to its need to train unskilled workers and to offset the production delays such training necessitated. The penalties of being unskilled or poorly educated, noted Michael Milken, the onetime junk bond king, now a leading philanthropist and educational activist, were being compounded by the general loss of earning power being experienced by workers in most sectors. Seventy percent of American workers, Milken claimed in January 1998, were, given inflation, earning about a third of what they had twenty years earlier. A lack of ability to compete in the new economy because of poor math and verbal skills would only compound the problem.

There were, however, some hopeful signs. Young people were learning skilled trades at high schools and community colleges—welding, carpentry and cabinetmaking, automotive repair, electronics, medical technology, culinary arts, specialized secretarial work (medical, paralegal)—and were acquiring good jobs after graduation. But such training was also dependent on a rising level of reading and math skills. Technology and the skilled trades were upping the ante as far as educational attainment was concerned. It took so much more to be a welder working on high-tech equipment than it might have thirty or forty years earlier. Office work now involved a significant level of verbal, computational, and computer skills. Office equipment, manufacturing and production equipment of all sorts, medical technology, advanced ordering for food and beverage service, driving a BART train, ticketing passengers via computer for a complicated airline trip: modern society demanded a high level of technical skills, even at an entry level. Police and firefighters had long since been drawn from college graduates. To be uneducated in America was to find an increasing number of jobs beyond attainment.

Hence the horror, the scandal, of California's declining educational statistics and scores: its bad report card. In 1993, for example, fourth graders in California, taken cumulatively, were vying with fourth graders in Mississippi for the dubious distinction of being the worst readers in the nation. That year, California ranked fortieth in per capita spending per student. A year later, the fourth graders of California were outperforming only Mississippi and Louisiana in math and reading skills. By 1997 the tenth and eleventh graders of California were scoring from ten to fourteen points below the national reading average, which was fifty. In high school science, California placed three states (Hawaii, Mississippi, and Louisiana) from the bottom of the barrel. Fifty-four percent of entering California State University freshmen in 1998 needed remedial work in math. Forty-seven percent needed remedial courses in English. And these were students from the top third of their high school classes.

Confronting such statistics, many observers, whether hostile or sympathetic, cited immigration as the problem. After all, they argued, in the era of Anglo-American ascendancy, the 1950s through the 1970s, the California educational system had been nationally ranked: had, in fact, been one of the key factors attracting people to the state. Now, California was taking on the task of educating more than a third of the immigrant children in the United States, whose primary language was not English. Given this task, what kind of statistics did one expect? Sort out the nonimmigrant from the immigrant population, they suggested, and California became, if not competitive, then at least not abysmal. In June 1998, a San Francisco judge, responding to petitions from the Berkeley and Oakland school districts, ordered state officials not to release the test scores of students who were not fluent in English but had nevertheless been tested in English, since such linguistic difficulties gave an inaccurate measurement of the immigrant students and tended to stigmatize them.

There was some truth to this defense. In the 1970s and 1980s, the public schools had done more than their share of assimilating an entire generation of Vietnamese and Central American children, many of them witnesses to horrific violence in the wars that had ravaged their countries. From this perspective, it was the remorseless testing of public school children that was at fault, in that the true educational process under way was the long-range scenario of immigrant children making the transition into productive American lives, which the majority of them would do eventually, no matter what their current scores. And, besides, native-born white children from dysfunctional backgrounds—and dysfunction was sadly becoming the norm in California—did even more poorly on standardized tests. The adults of California, ridiculing scores, were in effect blaming kids for the culture they themselves had created. What if roles were reversed, and the California kids were asked to evaluate the performance of the adults upon whom they were dependent? What kind of report card would the adults receive?

It would be grossly unfair, furthermore, to stigmatize low-income immigrant Latino students as incapable of standard to better performances when Latino students in Catholic grammar schools were going on to high school at the same rate as non-Latino students. An impressive 97.4 percent of Catholic high school graduates in California, 29 percent of them Latino, were matriculating at two- or four-year colleges. Serving middle- to low-income families living along La Brea Avenue in Los Angeles's Fairfax district, Daniel Murphy High School was noted for its high graduation rates, college success stories, and public service careers, including those of Bernard Parks, later chief of police, William Bamattre, later fire chief, and Craig Chretien, later the third highest ranking official in the federal Drug Enforcement Administration. Fernando Amarillas, a senior at Dan Murphy in the spring of 1998, who commuted from South Central, had been accepted by UCLA and other top colleges.

Which was precisely the point, noted defenders of the public school system. Catholic schools were free to refuse admission to severely handicapped students, to expel troublemakers, and in general to enforce a rigorous code of conduct, even to demand uniforms in the primary grades and a strict dress code in high school. From this perspective, Catholic schools resembled public schools in times past—schools, that is, animated by a supportive social ethos—and were showing the results that public schools used to show before being overwhelmed by a variety of factors, including hundreds of thousands of students with a minimal command of English. As test scores were demonstrating, the educational advantage remained strongly tilted in the direction of private schools, whether Catholic, Protestant, Jewish, or nonsectarian. Such schools could control their internal culture in a way that public schools could not, or at least could not to the same degree.

Hence it was unfair to bash public schools when they were taking on the ills and challenges of a frequently dysfunctional society. Wherever and whenever it could, affluent America—which once had used the public sector—was withdrawing into a controlled privacy. In times past, for example, the local public high school (as revealed in scores of notable novels, plays, and films) brought together all classes in a common curriculum, which in turn implied a quasi-leveled playing field for the talented and upwardly mobile and a sector of common culture for all graduates, no matter what their pathway in life. Now, for a variety of reasons—including the marginalization, if not elimination, of the middle, lower-middle, and blue-collar classes—kids were getting tracked early into either the public or the private sector. If a youngster was being processed through the private sector, his or her deficiencies could be mitigated by tutorial programs. Already, in fact, California was experiencing a boom in private after-school math and reading tutorial centers, where parents, including many public school parents, were willing to pay between $2,000 to $4,000 a year for supplemental instruction.

Then there was the question of social, even moral, value. Private schools did not in general pursue aggressive programs of sex education, or, if they did, taught sexuality within a defined moral and cultural context. Public

schools, by contrast, such as those in San Francisco, offered graphic programs of sex education, including same-sex sexuality, starting in middle
school. The Los Angeles Unified School District made condoms available
to public high school students in order, it was stated, to prevent the spread
of AIDS. Sex education programs were among the most frequently cited
reasons, especially among religious groups, that led parents to choose private schools.

Furthermore, many believed, there were fiscal reasons why public
schools remained at a disadvantage. In times past, local school districts
were supported by local property taxes. That meant that support was
unequal, of course, yet the state could target poorer districts with supplemental state and federal funds. In 1971, however, in the lawsuit *Serrano v.
Priest*, brought by the Western Center on Law and Poverty, it was argued
that the different levels of spending across various school districts violated
the equal protection clause of the Fourteenth Amendment. The courts
agreed and ordered the state to equalize all revenues in every district. The
problem was that seven years later California voters passed Proposition 13,
which drastically capped current property taxes and shifted control of the
tax from school districts to the state. California now had to treat all districts
equally but with woefully depleted revenues. Prior to *Serrano* and Proposition 13, it was suggested, California's public school students did as well on
standardized tests as any of their counterparts in the nation. Once the full
effect of *Serrano* and Proposition 13 made itself felt, by the mid-1980s,
scores began to decline. The state government was being told, on the one
hand, to equalize school revenues. On the other hand, it was being forbidden to raise property taxes. Affluent school districts could deal with the
resulting falloff in revenues more effectively because their communities
were more controlled, more education oriented, and more supportive. If a
community were troubled, however, no matter what the source of trouble
might be, those troubles tended to invade a marginally supported school
system and destabilize it.

As a counterpart to James Q. Wilson's broken windows theory, one
could advance a broken bathroom theory to determine the overall health of
a public school. If bathrooms were vandalized, graffiti-ridden, and dangerous, such as they were at the Whaley Middle School in Compton in February 1993, the school could immediately be seen as troubled in other aspects
of its programs, as was the case at Whaley. On February 25, 1993, some
three hundred Whaley students broke into a spontaneous demonstration
protesting the squalid state of their graffiti-strewn nonfunctioning bathrooms (sans soap, paper, sanitary napkins, even trash cans), the dried mud
and bird dung caking the benches in their outdoor eating area, the litter-

strewn playing field, the battered lockers (the boys' locker room had been closed entirely due to vandalism). Administrators had tried to do something, as best they could, but were short of funds. After the school had been recently painted, it was very soon, once again, covered in graffiti. Paradoxically, the students were demonstrating in part because three administrators, including a popular assistant principal, had been transferred by the Compton school board in an effort to break the cycle of trashing in the economically depressed, gang-ridden school. Trashed bathrooms, from this perspective, equaled substandard math and reading scores, kids dropping out, and dangerous, dysfunctional schools.

California public schools, especially high schools, could be tough places. In more prosperous suburbs, such toughness consisted mainly in a brutal culture of snobbery and exclusions based on looks, wealth (as manifested in clothes and material possessions), class, and social status: a reflection, alas, of the society the students came from. Then there was the question of actual violence that had made so many inner-city schools so dangerous. Teachers in California, especially at the high school level, were forced to be concerned for their physical safety during the school day.

Throughout the 1990s, there were a number of programs keyed to improving public education. In 1992, California became the second state in the nation to allow for charter schools, which meant publicly supported schools with their own charter, functioning outside existing school systems. The 1992 law allowed for one hundred such schools, but by 1998 there were 132 of them, due to waivers granted by the state board of education. In early May 1998, Governor Wilson signed Assembly Bill 544, sponsored by Assemblyman Ted Lempert (D-San Carlos), allowing the number of charter schools to be increased to 250 within the next year, and by one hundred annually thereafter. Charter schools could be formed by parent groups, teacher groups, parent-teacher groups, or other communities. If half the tenured teachers agreed, an existing school could revert to charter status. The theory behind charter schools was that they would allow all the cohesion, community support, parental involvement, and work ethos of private schools but would be available to families who could not afford private school tuition. Visiting the 270-student charter Accelerated School in South Central Los Angeles in June of 2001, *Los Angeles Times* columnist Steve Lopez was impressed not only by the better-than-average test scores of the school but by the intensity of parental involvement among the almost exclusively immigrant parent group. Teachers at Accelerated, moreover, who were nonunion, frequently stayed on campus up to two hours after the end of the school day and, when necessary, were known to make house calls on behalf of students kept home by sickness. Another growing program through the 1990s was the magnet high school, allowing for an orientation or specialized curriculum—foreign languages, math and science, the arts, computer sciences, medical technology—in the belief that such coherence stimulated the creation of a better motivated, better behaved, better performing student body.

In the legislative session of 1996 three bills were passed authorizing nearly a billion dollars to be spent on reducing class sizes throughout the state. In 1997 the state board of education, thus funded, launched its Class Size Reduction (CSR) program, which had as its goal nothing less than keeping the average size of a California public school classroom in the lower grades to twenty to twenty-two children. This meant the hiring of thousands of new teachers, which very soon made teaching a growing career choice for college graduates and a second or third choice for people wanting midcareer adjustment. Some complained that too many inexperienced, untrained teachers were being thrown into the classroom. On the other hand, an increasing number of midcareer candidates were entering the profession, bringing with them their seasoned talents and life experiences.

A significant percentage of second-career teachers coming into the program were retired military personnel, most of them with the ability to teach mathematics, which was the specialty of Jaime Escalante of Hiram Johnson High School in Sacramento, where he had been instructing since 1991. In the 1980s, teaching at the Garfield High School in East Los Angeles, the Bolivian-born Escalante had won national fame, including a movie based on his life, *Stand and Deliver* (1987), for his ability to motivate and educate Latino mathematics students into national ranking in second-year calculus. Between 1986 and 1991, an average of 61 percent of all Garfield students who took the advanced placement exam in calculus passed. Ironically, Escalante was finding Hiram Johnson—with its working-class white, Asian, black, and Latino student body—a more formidable challenge than he had faced at Garfield, with its focused, upwardly mobile Latino student body, which said something about the culture of California in the 1990s as a barrier to classroom success. If such a master teacher as Escalante was experiencing difficulty motivating his blue-collar students, then the question of how exactly teachers should be prepared, rewarded, or punished quite expectedly surfaced as a statewide issue. Superintendents were showing themselves willing to penalize or reward principals depending on the test scores of the schools they led. In September 1998, Los Angeles superintendent Ruben Zacarias handed out $5,000 bonuses to sixty-eight school principals with improved scores and put another thirty principals on notice that they stood in danger of being removed if their students did not do better in the next round of testing. Later, when times were flush, Governor Gray Davis extended such a bonus program to the entire state.

For most of the decade, education remained the number one political issue in California, if one were to judge this according to the amount of state funds expended. When Governor Wilson was forced to cut back on education early in his first administration, he found himself in a firestorm of protest. As soon as things got better, Wilson, with the assent of the legislature, set new standards for K–12 spending in California. His last budget allotted $23.5 billion for K–12 programs—43 percent of the entire state budget. Much of this outlay, of course, was mandated by the passage of Proposition 98 in 1988, which each year stipulated the percentage of general fund revenues that had to be spent on K–12, based on enrollments, per capita personal income, and projections of state tax revenues. But in many of his last budget programs—$240 million for new math textbooks, $230 million for library books and science equipment, $60 million for summer reading and math classes, $45 million for supplemental teacher training—Wilson was going well beyond the call of duty.

In the election to replace Wilson, the candidate who won, Lieutenant Governor Gray Davis, stayed on an educational message throughout his initially underdog campaign. Among his other talents, Davis could count. There were 5.5 million students in the public schools of California, he noted. "Each of them has two parents who care about them. They may not be living together, but they care about the well-being of their child. Fixing the schools and offering hope and opportunity will influence voters. The candidate who is most compelling and persuasive on education has a big leg up."[6] When it came time for the Los Angeles Unified School District (budgeted at $8 billion a year) to replace Interim Superintendent Ramon Cortines in June 2000, it turned not to a seasoned educational administrator but to Roy Romer, former governor of Colorado and onetime chair of the Democratic National Committee. Romer declined to run for the U.S. Senate to take the position. In so many ways, he later stated, being superintendent represented a more formidable political challenge.

As was the presidency of the University of California, constitutionally established in 1879 as the fourth branch of state government, and the chancellorship of the sprawling California State University (23 campuses and 388,734 students as of the fall of 2001), whose governance had been formalized by the Higher Education Master Plan of 1960. Reigning as CSU chancellor through the first two-thirds of the decade was the skilled and dapper Barry Munitz, a diplomatic up-from-Brooklyn Princetonian who by the time he stepped down in late 1997 had become the most trusted and admired public administrator in the state: a Democrat with strong possibilities for either the U.S. Senate or the governor's chair in Sacramento. Instead, Munitz assumed the presidency of the J. Paul Getty Trust and headed the transition team for the newly elected Davis.

To replace Munitz, CSU trustees hired Charles Reed, the mid-fifties chancellor of the ten-campus, 225,000-student Florida State University system. There were many contrasts between Munitz, fresh from the pages of *GQ,* and the hefty, rumpled, plain-talking Reed, a onetime football quarterback at George Washington University. During his tenure, Munitz had seen the CSU system through the devastating first half of the decade and had left it in the best political shape of its existence. Equally skilled politically, Reed built upon his predecessor's success, forging a special alliance with senate president pro tem John Burton, a fierce champion of the underdog and a graduate of San Francisco State, thus a natural ally of the CSU system, which was in so many ways the Rodney Dangerfield of public higher education, charged by the Master Plan of 1960 with the education of the majority of California's publicly educated college students. While the constitutionally established University of California drew from the top ten percent of the state's high school graduates and was granted a monopoly on doctoral and professional degrees, the CSU system was expected to draw its students from the top 33 percent of each graduating high school class and was prohibited from offering degrees beyond the master's level. CSU professors, moreover, when all was said and done, were expected to spend more than twice as much time in the classroom as their UC counterparts. CSU professors were expected to teach. UC professors were expected to do research, along with a light teaching load.

Maintaining a two-tier system was always difficult in such public circumstances. First of all, over the years, CSU graduates soon dominated the legislature. While UC was highly aware of itself as one of the world's great research universities, the CSU system tended to regard itself not institutionally, but in terms of the extraordinary upward mobility it was offering the middle, working, and immigrant classes of California. CSU Los Angeles, for example, had over the years graduated Garland Burrell, a pioneering African-American federal judge, calculus teacher Jaime Escalante, tennis champion Billie Jean King, entrepreneur-investor Tom Condon, Los Angeles County sheriff Sherman Block, Clippers owner and real estate magnate Donald Sterling, astronaut Samuel Durrance, novelist Joseph Wambaugh, artist Frank Romero, and a host of Latino and African-American representatives, supervisors, assembly members, and state senators. The same story could be told in just about every one of the CSU campuses: a story of young Californians from ordinary or less-than-ordinary backgrounds working their way through college, using their CSU degree as an entry point into careers as teachers, public servants, local business people, elected officials.

It was a great story to tell, and both Munitz and Reed told it well; yet for all of CSU's success, its institutionalized restraints and second-tier status rankled, bothering faculty especially, as the system grew to maturity. So many of the CSU campuses, after all, had reached true academic distinction. Had they been the first or second campuses of any smaller state, they would have been able to develop more easily on their own terms. Hence the problem with the 1960 Master Plan, which capped the academic development of each CSU campus and insisted that it be governed by a strong central bureaucracy in Long Beach. Was this democratic, many asked? Was it good public policy to cap the academic growth and development of publicly supported CSU campuses, which were doing the bulk of the teaching in higher education? And besides, faculty argued, even in its teaching mission the CSU system was being unfairly served. Between 1995 and 2001, part-time nontenured faculty, the so-called "freeway fliers," had risen from 39 percent to 48 percent of the CSU teaching faculty, while during the same period the percentage of tenured professors had dropped from 47 percent to 35 percent. Nearly half of all CSU students, in short, were being taught by a subprofessorate class, second tier within the second-tier system, forced to eke out a living, semester by semester, as freelance lecturers speeding by freeway from campus to campus.

Even the usually insightful Barry Munitz was taken aback by the depth of alienation in the full-time CSU faculty. A significant percentage, it should be pointed out, had formed their attitudes in the 1960s and 1970s and were estranged from authority as a matter of routine. That was, in part, why they had become academics. Yet there was more than generational anger and/or academic attitude in the CSU faculty resentment as it surfaced in mid-decade against Munitz's proposal to form a consortium with Microsoft, GTE, Fujitsu, and Hughes Electronics, in which these companies would lend the system $300 million to buy their products, which the companies would in turn service and, eventually, replace. From the perspective of Munitz and, later, Reed, the proposal was a win-win proposition. The CSU campuses got the equipment, and the companies got the business. From the point of view of the faculty, however, it was the 1960s all over again: the sellout of a public institution to private corporate interests. Across two years of acrimonious debate, the proposal went into meltdown, starting in 1998 with the elimination of the corporate ogre Microsoft from the package.

Reed, meanwhile, was being pummeled for the consortium proposal and a variety of other offenses, chief among them his suggestion that the campuses be put on a twelve-month operational basis as a way of absorbing the 140,000 increase in students expected in the next decade. Almost affably, Reed took the punishment like the quarterback he had once been and, ironically, secured from the legislature faculty salary increases two years in a row and an overall 27 percent rise in funding. Reed even achieved the impossible: a joint doctoral program in education between CSU and UC: the camel's nose in the tent, many suggested, for the eventual uncapping of the CSU system.

Reed's counterpart at UC—Richard Atkinson, who had at first opposed the joint doctoral proposal as being contrary to the Master Plan—was busy solving the dilemma facing his system by the statewide ban on affirmative action. As test scores were showing, many minority students from public schools, for whatever reasons, were at a disadvantage when it came to taking tests. Whatever their individual potential as human beings might be, their scholastic aptitude test (SAT) scores were below the mark. Working patiently across the late 1990s in conjunction with the faculty Academic Senate, Atkinson, himself a highly respected cognitive psychologist, took a hard look at the SAT I requirement that was causing so much trouble. Was not, Atkinson challenged, the SAT II examination—testing competency in writing and mathematics and a third subject of choice—more relevant than a generalized testing of aptitude? High schools in California, after all, varied in quality from district to district, as did student circumstances. The SAT I test presumed a universalized California that translated into the California of the affluent and well instructed. The SAT II exams tested students on the basis of courses they had actually taken. Atkinson did not just say these things. He embarked on an extensive program of research in conjunction with the Academic Senate in order to open this line of inquiry in an academically responsible manner.

Then there was the question of evaluating each student comprehensively and in his or her local context. Ivy League schools had long since adopted this technique as crucial to its admission procedures. (Harvard had had its boondocker category for rural students of merit, however sketchy their preparation.) Likewise, Ivy Leagues took into consideration such factors as an individualized analysis of high schools and prep schools, indications of leadership or community service, athletic ability, or any other sign of academic and/or personal promise. Why, Atkinson asked, should not UC be doing the same?

And besides, UC enjoyed a unique relationship with more than fifty-eight community colleges throughout the state. Why not inaugurate a program of dual admissions, in which students would be admitted to UC, pending a successful completion in specified subjects in freshman and sophomore years at community colleges? And finally, in order to balance the whole procedure, Atkinson asserted that a certain percentage of admissions should be based on raw scores, lest high school high achievers be penalized, as had been the case in the past when students with high SATs and 4.0 grade point averages had been rejected from UC or sent to a campus not of their choice because of the need to achieve ethnic balance. Even more adroitly, Atkinson proposed that the top 4 percent of graduates from California high schools be admitted to UC. Such a policy would level the playing field without ignoring signs of academic promise. It would also ensure an ethnic mosaic of incoming freshmen. Finally, Atkinson was willing to allow each of the nine university campuses to structure its specific admission policy within certain guidelines so as to create variety and flexibility within the system.

As the 1990s edged into the new millennium, Atkinson achieved approval from the Academic Senate and the regents for his program. A generation of young Californians that had previously been tested and found wanting—thus entering UC primarily through quotas—was now being tested, albeit in new ways, and found up to the mark. Six years after voting to ban affirmative action, the regents in mid-July 2001 voted through the various components of Atkinson's formula. In achieving this, Atkinson had not only kept the University of California politically and academically viable; he had established the possibilities of a paradigm for California itself—all of it—in its diversity and discontinuities. If UC could be made to be inclusive and fair, so, too, could California.

Even as the regents finished their momentous July meeting, the latest round of test scores were announced. Taken cumulatively, the elementary schools of the state had shown gains, even in the immigrant-challenged Los Angeles district. When it came to high school tests, however, problems persisted, with Los Angeles County ranking fifty-seventh out of fifty-eight counties in the percentage of ninth graders passing language arts, and fifty-fifth out of fifty-eight in the percentage (35 percent) of students passing in math.

An immigrant generation, nevertheless, was still being prepared for survival in California, and the state was willing to work with each and every student to achieve the best possible results, whatever they might be. No student, however faltering, would be tested into permanent marginality. Whatever problems of language, poverty, distracted or dysfunctional parents, or harmful cultural values the students of California might be facing, the bulk of them were being given some chance, and the best performing of them— no matter how relative was their achievement—were heading to community colleges, to the California State University, and to the University of California. They would not be tested into the trash bin. They would be given, rather, a first, second, third, and fourth chance to be the best they could be. Some would not make it, but many more would, and in the educations they received, and in the lives they would soon be leading, one could glimpse the possibilities of a California that had been able, increasingly, to make room for everyone.

The Boys from Texas

If it ain't broke, don't fix it. So goes the folkloric adage, and like most observations of this sort, it makes sense. In the mid- to late 1990s, however, California fixed its long-standing energy regulatory culture—or so the state thought. As things turned out, the deregulated system was in a state of catastrophic crisis by June 2000, and by 2002, California was preparing to sell $12.5 billion in bonds to pay for electricity it had already used. Even worse, investigations by Congress and by state attorney general Bill Lockyer revealed a conspiracy by private companies such as Enron to manipulate the energy market to the detriment of the state.

How did it happen? Why did California, so recently recovered from the recession of the early 1990s, voluntarily deconstruct its energy culture and turn itself into an ATM for the boys (and some gals) from Texas (and North Carolina): the crafty operators behind the energy companies with the day-glow names—Enron, Sempra, Reliant, Mirant, Dynegy, and Duke—that turned California, almost overnight, into a dependent colony where unexpected blackouts had become a way of life? The answer to such questions involved the hyper-abstruse economics of energy. But the answer was political as well, for it was the politicians who had authorized the revamping of the system. The answer was also cultural; more precisely, it represented cultural expectations and social psychology. California also revealed, this time through electricity, what it had previously revealed through banking in the case of the Bank of America takeover: namely, that the state contained within itself the mind-set of a resort—a society, that is, with little room for the trade-offs, the nitty-gritty, the ambiguities of a real-time American place. California was a society that wanted the good life but was not prepared to deal with the environmental trade-offs the good life demanded. The state was also prepared to surrender its autonomy, its vaunted condition as a coherent and cutting-edge commonwealth, if that was the price it had to pay to sustain its resort identity and cherished pastoralism. In short, the state preferred to let the boys from Texas do its dirty work, and Texas would soon be eating California's lunch.

It began, as disasters frequently do, as a perfectly logical piece of business. For nearly a hundred years, California had been evolving a public utilities culture that seemed to work. Some three-fourths of all residents received their electricity from three flourishing and highly regarded publicly regulated investor-owned utilities: Pacific Gas & Electric in the north and central regions, Southern California Edison in the mid-central and southern regions north of San Diego County, and San Diego Gas & Electric in the lower tier of the state. The remaining 25 percent purchased their electricity from municipally owned and operated utilities in Los Angeles, Sacramento, Palo Alto, Santa Clara, Lodi, Riverside, and a few surviving companies in rural areas that had maintained their independence. Regulating this entire system was the Public Utilities Commission (PUC), headquartered in San Francisco.

Students of California's political history could see in these arrangements the direct and continuing legacy of the Progressivism that had reformed and restructured the state in the early 1900s: a balanced trade-off, that is, between public and private interests. For those growing up and living their lives under the jurisdiction of one or another of the three mega-utilities, they embodied, like the state itself, the very paradigm of achieved public interest. They were a total and compelling way that the citizens of California had organized themselves socially and economically. The municipally owned utility companies also embodied the ongoing identity and stability of California, but they celebrated their cities as assertive communities that had chosen public power as a key component of urban identity.

This system had reached out to the Colorado River in the Hoover Dam project. It had bored tunnels through mountains, and constructed dams, aqueducts, reservoirs, and hydraulic generating systems. It had raised great oil- and gas-driven generating plants at strategic locations throughout the state. At Diablo Canyon in San Luis Obispo County and San Onofre in San Diego County, it had constructed two nuclear power plants that by the mid-1990s were providing the state with 20 percent of its electricity. The system had come into being, in various phases, when California had fewer than five million people. It had grown over the years with the state—through the mobilizations of four wars, the influx of millions of new Californians, the transition of an agricultural state into the high-tech capital of the world—and by the mid-1990s was providing some thirty-three million people with the two sources of energy necessary for modern life: natural gas and electricity.

The problem was—or so certain manufacturing interests, cement and steel especially, were beginning to say in the early 1990s—it was a system designed for domestic use and for equity, which is to say, it was designed to ensure that virtually every Californian, even those in marginal economic circumstances, would have access to electricity. It was the very opposite, then, to an open market system, and industrial users were growing restive with the necessity of being confined to an energy economy keyed, finally, to the electrical needs of millions of residential rate payers on limited budgets. Somebody had to pay for the ability of everyone, regardless of income, to be guaranteed enough electricity to run his or her household, and that somebody, they were complaining, was the big-ticket industrial user, prevented under the current system from going out and buying its electricity in bulk from sources outside the system.

Two factors fed into the discontent of large-scale industrial users: the general tendency toward deregulation and the desire of Governor Wilson and the legislature to do everything they could do to help bring back the California economy and thereby create jobs and lives for unemployed workers and hope for the future. By the 1990s, furthermore, trucking companies, airlines, and telecommunication companies had each been deregulated with apparent success or at least without catastrophic collapse. (Savings-and-loan banks were another matter.) In the aftermath of the deconstruction of the cold war economy, moreover, the emphasis of society had shifted toward empowering the private sector rather than regulating it. The Wilson administration was especially proud of its program of public/ private partnerships, its recruitment of big-payroll companies to California, and its willingness to cut through governmental red tape on behalf of job-producing, thus tax-producing, companies, whether newly recruited or long established.

As far as energy was concerned, the federal government got the ball rolling on October 24, 1992, when President George H. W. Bush, himself one of the boys from Texas, signed the Energy Policy Act welcoming independent power companies into the electricity market by exempting them from the constraints binding regulated utilities, and authorizing the Federal Energy Regulatory Commission to allow independent wholesale energy companies access to the nationwide grid. At this point, Texas companies naturally cast a covetous eye in the direction of the Golden State. The problem was that under the system presently in force in California, which the federal Energy Policy Act did not abrogate, they could not compete with the regulated utilities or the municipally owned companies. This especially bothered cement and steel producers organized as the California Large Energy Consumers Association: companies such as the Hanson Permanente

Cement company in the foothills above Cupertino in Santa Clara County. By the early to mid-1990s, the monthly $900,000 electrical bill Hanson was paying PG&E represented some 25 percent of its total production costs, three times what the same amount of electricity would cost in Idaho. Not surprisingly, executives such as Earl Bouse at Hanson were looking, following the passage of the federal Energy Policy Act, to enter into what they believed would be cost-saving long-term contracts with energy wholesalers outside California. Otherwise, it was implied, moving to Idaho might prove a necessary alternative.

Pete Wilson did not want companies such as Hanson moving to Idaho. His most important achievement through two terms of office had been to rebuild the California economy. Wilson also appointed the members of the PUC, and they tended to be private-sector and efficiency-oriented Republicans. In 1993 the PUC issued a two-hundred-page report arguing for deregulation in order to benefit industrial customers and keep the publicly regulated utilities efficient. The next year, the commission issued an even more comprehensive report favoring deregulation. On December 20, 1995, after three years of reviews and hearings, the PUC authorized the restructuring of electricity markets in California, to include direct sales from non-regulated wholesalers, effective January 1, 1998.

What would this new system look like? While the PUC could authorize deregulation, only legislation signed by the governor could make it law. Thereupon ensued in Sacramento an absolute epic of lobbying and counter-lobbying, maneuver and countermaneuver, argument and counterargument, as the various components of the electrical community—public, private, and publicly regulated—jockeyed for position in the forthcoming deregulated universe. The big-ticket industries wanted the right to buy wholesale from nonregulated energy companies. They got it. The regulated public utilities wanted the right to recover some of the billions of dollars they had spent on nuclear plants and federally mandated alternative energy programs, even if it meant selling off assets, including generating plants, to nonregulated wholesalers. They got it. Environmentalists wanted some $450 million for the research into and construction of renewable and alternative energy projects. They got it. Large-scale users such as BART, the University of California, and agribusiness wanted some $200 million in price breaks in the new system. They got it. Labor wanted a multimillion-dollar program to retrain workers for the new system. It got it. Municipally owned utilities wanted to preserve their independence in the new order. They got it. Residential and small business users wanted a 10 percent rate cut for four years. They got it.

The bill authorizing the new system, the Electric Utility Industry

Restructuring Act, introduced on February 24, 1996, by Assemblyman James Brulte (R-Rancho Cucamonga), grew into a sixty-seven-page document as it moved its way through the legislature. The heavy lifting of seeing the bill through the legislative process was done by state senator Steve Peace (D-El Cajon), an occasional filmmaker (the 1978 low-budget horror flick classic *Attack of the Killer Tomatoes*), who across eighteen days of hearings in mid-August 1996—the so-called Steve Peace Death March—hammered out the intricate array of compromises necessary to create a brand-new energy culture. Peace later stated that he had severe doubts about deregulation (and offered film clips to prove it) but had stepped in when he saw that deregulation was inevitable and that someone in the legislature had to take responsibility for brokering the new system. In any event, Peace, a skilled and experienced legislator, did his job very well, for the bill passed unanimously through both houses, so convinced were all Californians that this was the right thing to do, and was signed into law by Governor Wilson on September 23, 1996, with a target date of March 1998 for start-up.

Over the next eighteen months, the new system was set in place. All long-distance high-voltage power lines now came under the supervision, but not the ownership, of a nonprofit entity named the California Independent System Operator (ISO), located in Folsom, northeast of Sacramento. A centralized open electricity market called the Power Exchange (PX), working from offices in Pasadena and the suburb of Alhambra east of Los Angeles, was also created, as was an Electricity Oversight Board (EOB), responsible for monitoring the entire system. The theory was simple: Using computer software, consumers would log into the PX to see what was for sale, when, and for what price. Prices would fluctuate hourly. Orders would be filled by computer on a spot-market basis, followed by an equally computerized billing system. The power would then be wheeled to its consumer via the ISO-supervised grid. Ideally, the new system would allow for a competitive free market buying and selling of electricity that was intended, given the California market, to flood the state with electricity providers anxious to do business at competitive prices. On March 31, 1998, the system went into effect. Some $87 million, passed on to rate payers, was spent educating Californians via a TV, radio, and print blitz regarding their options under the new system.

It took little more than a year for the new system to show signs of stress. Significantly, it happened in San Diego. Publicly regulated utilities were now allowed to sell off their gas- and oil-fired power plants, which San Diego Gas & Electric was more than happy to do. For some time, all three regulated investor-owned utilities had been worried that the sunk costs they had expended in building generators, including nuclear generators, would

become stranded costs that they would be unable to recover from rate payers, given the caps previously enforced by the PUC. Under the new system,
however, the generator plants instantly made the transition from sunk costs
to saleable assets. The new system encouraged the selling off of generating
plants to multiple ownerships so that no one producer could dominate the
market. Hence, the very month deregulation went into effect, San Diego
Gas & Electric sold its forty-six-year-old gas-fired generator plant at Carlsbad, in addition to eighteen small combustion turbines scattered around San
Diego County, for $365 million, four times their book value. A buying and
selling frenzy ensued, in which the three regulated public utilities sold to
private energy companies a significant portion of their generator assets at
prices—$3 billion in all—that delighted investors, who were happy with
increased dividends. These were straight sales, moreover, with no long-
term contracts for future electricity involved. Ownership of the ability to
generate electricity, hence to call the shots in terms of pricing, had now
passed from regulated California companies to unregulated Texas companies and a private California company or two, such as Calpine.

With its debt wiped out, thanks to the sale of its generators, San Diego
G&E, under the provisions of Assembly Bill 1890, returned to the PUC in
June 1999 for permission to charge market rates, now that their stranded
costs had been recovered. Permission was granted. Over the next year, San
Diego rate payers, homes, and small businesses saw their utility bills double, then triple. Nor could San Diegans turn to other options for competitive
relief. Almost immediately, the Texas companies, led by Enron, had
become uninterested in serving the small-time California consumer at rates
capped by the PUC when they could be getting into the much more profitable business of buying the generators that would soon allow them to corner the California market.

By June 2000 a number of causes had coalesced to precipitate a perfect
storm. Sparse rainfall had lessened the hydroelectric capacity of California
and its suppliers in the Northwest. The price of natural gas (the majority of
electrical generators in California were gas fired) increased sixteenfold
between December 1999 and December 2000. A number of important generators went off-line for maintenance, much of it connected to meeting rigid
emissions standards. The growing needs of Arizona (Phoenix), Nevada
(Las Vegas), Oregon (Portland), and Washington (Seattle) were siphoning
off electricity that had once, almost automatically, flowed into California.
In-state consumer demand had grown by 24 percent since 1995. No new
generating plant, meanwhile, had been built in California within the past ten
years, largely due to environmental barriers; and nuclear energy, which had
the potential to meet the needs of a significant portion of the state, had long

since been demonized, and thus was restricted to two existing facilities. Suddenly, almost overnight, California was being forced to purchase its electricity in an increasingly difficult market: electricity that was now significantly in the hands of private companies.

Electricity is the essence of real time. Electricity has no past or future. It cannot be stored. So when electricity falls short, even by a small percentage, the entire system falls short. Electricity cannot draw upon reserves. It has to be generated as needed. Nor can a grid tolerate a sudden overabundance of electricity or a sudden shortage without causing major damage to the system. Hence transmission grids must be keyed in real time to the amount of electricity they have to transmit, nothing more, nothing less. The slightest shortage of electricity, as California began to experience in June 2001, meant blackouts, either localized or rolling, as the engineers at the ISO control room in Folsom kept the grid in equilibrium by lessening its service areas. In June 2000, as summer (meaning air conditioning) kicked in, California experienced blackouts on a scale unknown since World War II. In January 2001 a ten-day power emergency was declared, with the public encouraged to watch the Super Bowl in groups so as to minimize the number of television sets in use. In late May 2001, in an effort to cope with a predicted second emergency in June, Governor Gray Davis announced a three-tier program of warnings forty-eight hours in advance for the rolling blackouts that were expected to occur throughout the summer.

The cost of electricity, meanwhile, spiked, to put it mildly, as the private companies who now owned both the in-state and nonstate generators sold power to California in an unregulated spot market. Between May and November 2000, officials from the ISO reported, power suppliers reaped a total of $505 million in extra profits from the California spot market. In the summer of 2000 alone, California saw its electric bill increase by $10.9 billion over the previous summer, with most of this money going to the boys from Texas. Houston-based Reliant Energy alone experienced a 600 percent increase in profits during this period, $100 million of it coming from California.

The question was—and it was a question that was soon being asked by the governor, the attorney general, and the legislature—whether such profits were merely the legitimate result of the free market system California had established, or the boys from Texas were manipulating the market. In July 2001, three former workers from a Duke Energy power plant in San Diego testified under oath to a state senate investigating committee that Duke had taken its plant on- and off-line to manipulate availability and prices. Two other former employees later corroborated their story. Duke spokespeople, however, soon produced evidence that the ISO had ordered the shutdowns, and the case remained ambiguous.

Unambiguous, or seemingly so, was the fact that in January 2001 the Charlotte, North Carolina–based Duke had been (albeit briefly) charging consumers $3,880 per megawatt hour. Once again, Duke pointed to the ISO, claiming that it had directed Duke to start up a nonoperative power plant in Chula Vista and to sell power to San Diego G&E, Southern California Edison, and Pacific G&E on an emergency basis. These sales, Duke claimed, represented less than one-tenth of 1 percent of the business it had done in the state that year. Overall, Duke argued, it had averaged $136 per megawatt hour, up from the $76 they had been charging throughout 2000.

By January 2001, the entire system was approaching collapse. The price of natural gas had quadrupled from its last-year all-time high. On January 10, PG&E, saying that it was running out of cash, asked Governor Davis for state assistance in buying natural gas. PG&E and Southern California Edison, having divested themselves of their generators, were buying electricity at three to four times the cost they could ever hope to recover from consumers, and were edging closer toward bankruptcy. Not surprisingly, Wall Street assessed its bond credit that month at one level above junk bond status. Increasingly, the boys from Texas, North Carolina, and elsewhere were finding themselves reluctant to sell electricity to either Southern California Edison or PG&E, given their openly admitted financial troubles. On January 11, 2001, the ISO announced a Stage Three alert, which lasted for thirty-two days, and warned that the state stood in danger of having some two million residents deprived of power in an upcoming series of rolling blackouts. Six days later, the ISO, fearing that the state grid was verging on a crash, ordered rolling blackouts statewide.

At this point, Governor Davis declared a state of emergency. Already, in his state of the state address on January 8, Davis had denounced deregulation as a "colossal and dangerous failure" and proposed a new public power authority to re-regulate the system and crack down on the price gougers.[7] Four days later, Davis, together with the governors of Oregon and Washington, urged the federal government to impose price controls on the out-of-control wholesale power market in the Far West. On the seventeenth, Davis got the state of California back, in a big way, into the power business, authorizing the state Department of Water Resources to buy power on behalf of the embattled utilities from the very companies he had, nine days earlier, denounced as gougers. For the time being, Davis had nowhere else to go, since California had largely sold off its generators.

The federal government, meanwhile, in the final days of the Clinton administration, for the fourth time extended an emergency order by Secretary of Energy Bill Richardson requiring energy companies to sell power to California through the twenty-second of the month. Richardson also issued a similar order to out-of-state natural gas suppliers. These orders were extended by the new secretary of energy, Spencer Abraham, when the Bush administration assumed control of the federal government. California's much-vaunted experiment with private-sector energy supply had now reverted almost entirely to the public sector.

Caught in the greatest crisis of his public career and one of the most dramatic crises ever to afflict California, Davis embarked on a six-step program of corrective action. First, he had to use public funds to buy enough electricity to keep California functioning. Second, he had to stimulate the construction of new power plants and the bringing online of shut-down facilities. Third, he had to encourage Californians to conserve electricity, since only a 10 percent reduction in usage could stabilize the system in terms of blackouts. Fourth, he would try to persuade the federal government to bring the nonregulated power suppliers under control through price caps and, even more boldly on Davis's part, to force them to repay California companies for their price gouging throughout 2000. Fifth, he would work with the legislature to come up with an acceptable bailout program for PG&E and Southern California Edison. Sixth, and most important, Davis and the legislature would have to fix the presently broken system with a new program of public/private cooperation or, as some were suggesting, a major entry of California into the power business.

In declaring a state of emergency, Davis simultaneously directed the Department of Water Resources to start buying power from suppliers on behalf of PG&E, Southern California Edison, and San Diego G&E. Within two weeks, the department had spent $400 million on electricity. By June, it had either spent or encumbered some $8 billion from the general fund for purchases, initially, on the spot market and, later, for long-term contracts with suppliers. Such a depletion of the general fund could not continue. California had already devoured a $4 billion surplus. Once again using his emergency powers, Davis in late June authorized state treasurer Phil Angelides to negotiate a $4.3 billion interim loan for future purchases, pending a $12.5 billion bond issue later that year. Angelides secured the loan from J. P. Morgan Chase ($2.5 billion), Lehman Brothers ($1 billion), Commerzbank ($500 million), Bayerische Landesbank Girozentrale ($300 million), and State Street Bank & Trust ($250 million), which came in later, after the loan had already been negotiated. The interest required for the loans began at a reasonable rate, approximately 4 percent, but contained stringent interest penalties calling for a jump to 7.5 percent if the loan were not repaid by October 2002. "In essence," said Angelides of the loan, "it stops the general fund bleeding." True enough, and it also temporarily allayed fears concerning California's credit rating, which Standard & Poor's had downgraded the previous April. At the same time, however, California now owed more than $4.3 billion for electricity it had already consumed. Where would it end? How long could the state continue to finance its day-to-day energy needs on credit cards?[8]

Clearly, something had to be done on the supply side of the crisis. That meant generators, and more of them—which was ironic, because all three of the investor-owned utilities had done everything they could, and as quickly as possible, to reap windfall profits by getting out of the generator business. For Gray Davis, it was not so much a matter of who owned the generators, but whether or not they were operating and how many new ones—especially the so-called peaker plants, designed to be brought online during peak hours—could be activated as quickly as possible.

Building generator plants in California, whether before or after the deregulation crisis, had always been a problem, which was why none had been built during the 1990s. The fierce environmentalism and NIMBYism of California hardly created conditions favorable to the gritty realities of building oil- or even gas-fired plants. In the deepest part of its collective psyche, California had all but banished the industrial metaphor, although it remained overwhelmingly dependent on the most fundamental industrial product and enabler of modern society: electricity. Even the investor-owned utilities had been ambivalent, not wanting, perhaps, the hassle of building plants. When the PUC in 1995 ordered the three investor-owned utilities to join with private companies and construct new plants capable of generating fourteen hundred megawatts of power to meet expected growth, Southern California Edison appealed to the Federal Energy Regulatory Commission on the basis that it would "not need this power until 2005," and won its case.[9]

Even before the energy crisis, the California Energy Commission, preparing for a deregulated environment, had come up with a streamlined one-stop-shopping process for new plant permits. Nine power facilities were authorized between 1996 and 1999 under this revised fast-track system. Six were under construction by January 2001. At this point, however, in a deregulated environment, yet another factor hampering the creation of power plants—competition among energy suppliers—was added to the already impacted situation. Some private companies, it was alleged, had gone so far as to make alliances with environmental groups to sink or delay plant proposals from their competitors. In any event, Governor Davis wanted those peaker plants online, and so in the crucial month of June 2001, in yet another executive order, he lifted air emission limits on new natural-gas-fired power plants, if they sold their electricity in the state. Within the month, Davis was throwing the switch at new power plants in Bakersfield and Pittsburg. Within the year, he was taking credit for some thirty new generating plants in the state.

Even in such emergency circumstances, California sustained its environmental ambivalence to the very power plants that were intended to keep it functioning as the fifth largest economy in the world. In the Coyote Valley near San Jose, for example, the unlikely trio of Cisco Systems, the Santa Theresa Swim & Racquet Club, and Mayor Ron Gonzales joined forces to oppose a six-hundred-megawatt plant being proposed by the San Jose–based Calpine Corporation. The swim and tennis club, understandably, did not want a nasty plant nearby, nor did Cisco, which was planning a corporate campus in the vicinity, and the mayor was backing two out of three locals. Further south, at Moss Landing on the coast, where Duke Energy was planning to expand the warhorse plant it had acquired from PG&E, state wildlife authorities were requiring Duke to comb the region for any signs of the Santa Cruz long-toed salamander, and, later, to build a "salamander fence" to keep the creatures, if they were in the vicinity, from the construction site. Duke also pledged $1 million to local environmental groups for continued monitoring and research. All in all, Duke paid out more than $12 million to governmental and environmental groups in its effort to get the Moss Landing plant modernized.

Neighborhood groups, meanwhile, were opposing power plant construction or expansion on Potrero Hill in San Francisco, Rio Linda and Elverta in the Delta south of Sacramento, the largely African-American community of Baldwin Hills in Los Angeles, and the mostly Latino town of Santa Fe Springs to the southeast. Neighborhood and environmental groups were even questioning the construction of a plant on the outskirts of the California Institution for Men prison near Chino in southwestern San Bernardino County. In northeastern San Diego County, environmental activists were opposing a $270 million, 500,000-volt, thirty-one-mile transmission line from Temecula to Romoland being proposed by San Diego G&E. No wonder that Sempra Energy, parent company of San Diego G&E and Southern California Gas, was making plans to build its next big operation: a $400 million liquid natural gas terminal, on the coast of Baja California, sixty miles south of the border. Even here Baja environmentalists were grousing and preparing a possible resistance. Oddly enough, according to a Field Poll taken in May 2001, Californians were backing off their quarter-century-long opposition to nuclear power, with 59 percent of those polled saying they would support the construction of new nuclear power plants in the state. The following month, the second nuclear generator at San Onofre, put out of commission by a fire in February, came back online. The two San Onofre generators were now powering some 2.2 million households, supplying between 3 to 4 percent of the state's total electricity.

When it came to the third point of Gray Davis's anti-blackout campaign—conservation—Californians proved themselves more than willing to go along, since conservation had long since established itself as part of the green mind-set of the state. There were exceptions, of course. The municipally owned power companies—the small Central Valley city of Lodi, for example—had not participated in the rolling blackouts of 2000. But in general the conservation habits that had been encouraged during the drought years of the late 1980s and early 1990s carried over into the new crisis, reinforced by Davis's promise of rebates up to 20 percent on monthly bills for conservation up to 20 percent—the so-called 20/20 program— reduced to a 15/20 program in the San Diego area because San Diegans had already been practicing conservation for a year. Up and down the state, newspapers ran articles and special supplements on ways to conserve electricity. Unplug computers, stereos, television sets, and telephone answering machines when not in use, since they consumed power by merely being plugged in. Use the microwave oven, rather than the electric stove, during the summer months. Replace incandescent lighting with fluorescent lighting. Content yourself with single pools of lamplight rather than lighting the entire room. Use air conditioning only when absolutely necessary, and, if at all possible, use it only in the room you are in. Reduce commercial neon lighting after business hours.

Simple suggestions such as these, followed by a sufficient number of Californians, reduced energy use by 12.3 percent in June 2001 and an overall 7.1 percent across the summer of 2001; and since the difference between a Stage Two alert and a Stage Three alert with rolling blackouts was a mere 3.5 percent of total reserve electrical capacity, and since the supply of electricity held steady across the summer months, the summer of 2001, with no rolling blackouts, stood in dramatic contrast to 2000. In June 2001 the state granted some $65 million in rebates to energy-saving rate payers, rising to $90 million in July. By this time, Californians were accustomed to moving through dimmed airports and public spaces during evening hours, as well as seeing a general dimness descend, after hours, on business districts.

Earlier, Vice President Dick Cheney, one of the boys from Texas, had rejected, almost mocked, conservation as an effective technique in the energy crisis, whether in California or elsewhere, which tended to underscore the fact that the gulf between Sacramento and the George W. Bush White House—which is to say, the gulf between California and Texas—on the entire energy question could not be wider. Texas had given its electoral votes to Bush. Californians had voted for Al Gore. Each state had a colorful heritage, a robust economy, and high self-esteem; but while Texas had remained, more or less, hard-nosed and realistic, California had, by the very nature of its being, remained tempted by the resort alternative. The myth of Texas was about making money, about wrestling a resistant environment into submission, about the extraction of oil and gas. The myth of California was, among other things, about how pleasant life could be, or should be, on the shores of the sundown sea.

By spring 2001 there had emerged a rapidly developing energy show-down: a shootout at the energy corral, if you will, with Governor Davis demanding wholesale price caps and refunds from the boys from Texas and their cohorts in the energy business. The whole energy crisis, Davis told *Time* magazine, represented "a massive transfer of wealth from the ordinary citizens of California to rich energy barons in Houston, Charlotte, and Atlanta."[10] Perhaps these were the same boys who were meeting with Cheney that spring, helping to formulate the Bush administration energy policy: something that might be suspected, but never known for sure. Later that summer, Cheney was refusing, on the basis of executive privilege, to turn over documents detailing any meetings or deliberations he had held with energy companies as he, a former energy executive from Texas, played the key role in formulating the energy agenda of the Bush administration.

It came as no surprise, when the White House released its supply-side-oriented energy plan in May 2001, that it made no provisions for California, although in discussing the plan both Bush and Cheney frequently referred to the state as an example of how not to conduct energy policy. The answer to America's energy needs, Bush argued, was, among other things (there were some 105 recommendations in all), a federally monitored national grid, more nuclear generation, the spending of $2 billion on the development of clean-coal technologies, the streamlining of the regulatory process for power plants, and the opening of a portion of the Arctic National Wildlife Refuge in Alaska to oil and gas exploration. As Congressman Brad Sherman (D-Thousand Oaks) put it, the Bush energy plan could be summed up quite simply: "Bush to California—Drop Dead!"[11]

Which was not an unfair characterization. Already, the previous February, FERC had not renewed its emergency order requiring suppliers to sell electricity to California. A Stage Three alert and two days of statewide rolling blackouts followed in mid-March. On April 5, 2001, Davis had made a statewide televised address in which he blasted the federal government for its refusal to take action on California's behalf. On April 25, FERC, on a divided vote, had offered a highly qualified temporary cap on wholesalers only, not producers, and only in emergency circumstances. On May 7, rolling blackouts reappeared for the first time since March.

The stage was set for Bush's first postelection visit to California on May 29. The trip, Bush adviser Karen Hughes told reporters, was intended in part to show California that the president cared; yet even as Hughes was meeting with reporters, Cheney was castigating California for its refusal to bite the bullet and take the unpleasant steps necessary to make its deregulated system work. Nor could Davis get any response from the White House regarding his campaign for permanent and inclusive caps. "The last time I looked," Davis told reporters in anticipation of the president's visit, "California was still part of the United States of America. We have contributed disproportionately to the economic growth of this country. There is no reason why a president should not respond to a legitimate request [for caps] from the chief executive of the largest state in the union."[12]

As soon as Air Force One discharged its passenger on the tarmac at LAX, the lobbying began, initially by Congressman Sherman. Following a speech to the World Affairs Council in Century City, Bush met with Davis for forty minutes. For Bush, the meeting was a big mistake. Photographs of Davis greeting Bush just before his speech were worth the proverbial thousand words: each man in his dark suit and power tie, Davis trying for eye contact, Bush making eye contact once, askance, then lowering his head and looking across Davis's shoulder, a look of displeasure on his face. All day long, prior to the meeting, Davis had been maximizing contact with the press, arguing and rearguing the need for caps and a refund, citing a letter he would hand to the president by leading economists arguing for caps, making and remaking his version of California's case. Surprisingly enough, after all this, Bush agreed to a private meeting with Davis in his hotel room. The meeting was inconclusive, but its very imagery—the president of the United States meeting with the governor of California as a near equal—represented a public relations triumph for Davis and a public relations gaffe for Bush.

And besides, congressional Republicans, not wanting to alienate the fifty-four-strong California delegation, were drifting toward Davis's point of view. California senator Dianne Feinstein, a Democrat, and Oregon senator Gordon Smith, a Republican, had already introduced bipartisan legislation calling for price controls. In mid-June, Governor Davis did not get exactly what he wanted—comprehensive caps—but he did get something from FERC: the extension of the existing soft cap from peak hours to twenty-four hours a day. This concession represented a break on the part of the Bush administration from its hard-line stance, and thus a personal victory for Davis.

No sooner had these soft caps been announced, however, on June 19—literally, the very next day—Davis was in Washington testifying before the Senate Committee on Governmental Affairs to ask the Senate's help in California's effort to secure from FERC some $9 billion in refunds. Six days later, on June 25, administrative law judge Curtis Wagner Jr., acting as a mediator on behalf of FERC, began hearings on California's claims. Judge Wagner's initial opinion, issued two weeks later, was highly skeptical. Whatever suppliers might owe California, Wagner pointed out, could be equally offset by the money the cash-strapped utilities owed them. Wagner's comments had a particular relevance. On April 6, 2001, Pacific Gas & Electric had filed for Chapter 11 bankruptcy protection against the $9 billion in wholesale energy debt it had incurred over the previous year. Nine billion dollars—the same amount of money that Davis was claiming had been overcharged—was what PG&E owed wholesalers who, under bankruptcy law, would most likely be receiving, eventually, only cents on the dollar in repayment. By going into Chapter 11, PG&E had already secured its refund.

By early 2002—as California sought a market for $12.5 billion in bonds to pay for electricity already consumed, saddling a future generation with debt; as the state struggled to cope with long-term contracts it had signed in haste at much higher rates than it now deemed fair; as residential rate payers in investor-owned utility service areas found themselves adjusting to an 18 percent increase in the cost of electricity and even higher multiples in the cost of natural gas—it could be legitimately asked: Why had all this been done in the first place? The economic answer to such a question, as has been suggested, was simple. Industrial users had grown tired of carrying domestic rate payers on their backs in the old system.

But was there something deeper involved? Some exercise in willful deconstruction, creative destruction, as some might call it? Had California disassembled and brought its energy arrangements to the brink of collapse as a way of testing the very nature of California itself? Was it merely economic incentive that had put the state in bondage to such a shameless company as Enron? Or was California, in deregulating itself, deliberately flirting with creative destruction on behalf of better arrangements?

Perhaps. But perhaps California was merely growing tired of what it took to remain coherent, comprehensive, and autonomous in its institutions. Like the resort, the unreal place it was always tempted to be, California had turned over the nitty-gritty of its industrial infrastructure to the boys from Texas, signing $45 billion in long-term contracts and, by late February 2002, appealing to the Federal Energy Regulatory Commission to cut these contracts by $21 billion, on the claim that twenty-two energy companies had gouged California during the crisis.

How embarrassing for a state that so prided itself as being the bellwether of the nation, to find itself admitting to the federal government that it had been so duped and bullied by the boys from Texas, especially after the rogue nature of one such company, Enron, stood so shockingly revealed. It was high time, it would seem, for California to start thinking of once again generating its own electricity and re-regulating its own energy culture: high time to step back, that is, from looking for the easy way out and accepting the responsibilities and trade-offs of an energy-hungry economy and lifestyle. Better to be a nation-state with its own generators than an energy colony dependent on the boys from Texas.

9/11

The morning of September 11, 2001, subsequently referred to as 9/11, galvanized the nation, California included. Two of the hijacked aircraft were en route to California, and many Californians lost their lives in the New York and Washington, D.C., attacks and the Pennsylvania crash. Ironically, California had almost become a main event. On December 14, 1999, Ahmed Ressam, thirty-three, as he sought to enter the United States from Canada, was arrested at the ferry depot in Port Angeles, Washington, when an alert customs officer, suspicious that Ressam, an Algerian émigré living in Montreal, should be so nervous and sweating so profusely on an otherwise chilly day, searched his rental car and uncovered a 130-pound cache of explosives and timing devices. Ressam, it was later discovered, was en route to the Los Angeles International Airport, where he hoped to detonate a suitcase bomb in a crowded terminal on the eve of the millennium. Had Ressam succeeded in exploding his bomb at LAX, it would have been the first and last major terrorist attack on the United States; for one cannot imagine the various agencies of the federal government continuing in their slipshod and uncoordinated policies and procedures that led up to the 9/11 attacks, had there been an earlier assault on Los Angeles.

As the United States geared up its military to take on the Taliban and al Qaeda in Afghanistan, San Diego County found itself in a condition of heightened mobilization. Eleven percent of the 2.8 million people living in the county—108,000 active duty military, 2,800 naval reservists, 128,000 military family members, 59,000 military retirees, and 21,000 civilian employees of the Department of Defense—were directly part of the military establishment. Another 200,000 residents were veterans. With numbers such as these, San Diego County went into red alert as marine, naval, and SEAL units packed up and deployed to the Middle East. Not since the Gulf War had there been such a mobilization.

Yet during the Gulf War, there had been no fear that the city of San Diego itself would be attacked. Now, according to a poll conducted by the

San Diego Union Tribune, 84 percent of all San Diegans feared that the city, given its garrison status, would be an almost certain object of a terrorist attack. Two days after the New York and Washington assaults, on September 13, the navy alerted the city that naval intelligence had information that its world-famous zoo was in danger. The zoo was immediately evacuated. In the days that followed, the streets of downtown San Diego, the shopping malls and the beaches, were eerily empty, and attendance dropped by five thousand at the Chargers game at Qualcomm Park.

Still, Representative Barbara Lee of the Ninth Congressional District, embracing Oakland and Berkeley, had cast the sole vote in Congress against granting expanded war powers to the president. Lee's vote, while singular, did express the dominant ultraliberalism, edging into pacifism, of her district. Then, on September 19, the Berkeley city manager ordered firefighters not to fly oversize American flags from their fire trucks lest they inflame some three thousand protesters at a National Student Day of Action rally to stop the war held on the Berkeley campus. On September 25, the city council voted unanimously to commend Representative Lee for her antiwar vote. The following month, on October 16, the council passed a five-point resolution that, among other things, called for a nonmilitary response to the al Qaeda attacks on New York and Washington and an end to the bombing in Afghanistan. The Peace and Justice Commission of the council announced a program to counsel eighteen-year-olds required to register for the draft, active-duty military seeking discharge for reasons of conscience, and conscientious objectors.

John Walker Lindh, twenty, a former resident of Marin County, was not in this category. He was, in fact, a rifle-carrying foot soldier with Taliban forces operating against the Northern Alliance on the frontline trenches in Takhar, Afghanistan. In November 2001, Lindh's unit had surrendered to the Northern Alliance and been imprisoned in a medieval-era fortress at Mazar-e-Sharif. There, Lindh had been briefly questioned in late November by CIA operative Johnny "Mike" Spann, an interview caught on videotape, with Lindh, posing as a Pakistani, remaining mute for most of the interrogation. Shortly thereafter, the Taliban prisoners revolted, killing Spann, and after their defeat and surrender, CNN cameras focused in on one of the wounded prisoners, the bearded and distressed Lindh, by now identified as an American. When Lindh did talk, he spoke in a heavy Arabic accent, having lived in that language for nearly two years. Perhaps it was the morphine that he had been given for his wound. In any event, Lindh allegedly told interrogators that, while he had nothing to do with the revolt, being in the basement the entire time, he did approve of the Islamic jihad and the 9/11 attacks.

California now had its 9/11 poster boy, although he stood in total contrast to the Californians who lost their lives on the hijacked planes, in the
World Trade Center, at the Pentagon, or on the battlefields of Afghanistan.
The story of what had brought Lindh to Afghanistan constituted almost a
caricature of life in Marin County, with its affluence and indulgence, its
broken families, its follow-your-bliss experimentalism, its syncretic religiosity. Born, baptized, and haphazardly raised a Catholic, Lindh—by all
reports a shy, sensitive boy, an only child, learning to play the flute, hardly
guerrilla material—had gone into psychological and religious free fall
when his parents divorced, as was so frequently the case in Marin. Already,
Lindh had shown a taste for role playing, passing himself off as an African
American in chat rooms on the Internet. His mother, a convert to Buddhism, tried to interest him in American Indian and/or Buddhist philosophy, but by age sixteen, Lindh, a student at the progressive Tamiscal High
School in Marin, had read *The Autobiography of Malcolm X* and converted
to Islam.

Taking the name Suleyman al-Faris, donning white Muslim robes and a
skullcap, and growing a beard, Lindh began attending a mosque in Mill Valley with the full approval of his mother, who would drive him to services,
and his father, a lapsed Catholic, who believed that Islam and Catholicism
were comparable belief systems and ways of life. Continuing his prayer life
and studies at two San Francisco mosques, Lindh decided in 1998, at age
seventeen, to spend a year learning Arabic in Yemen, where it was most
purely spoken. Following that year, he returned to live with his mother in
the Marin County township of Fairfax for about eight months before returning to Yemen.

At this point, in one of their last communications, Lindh e-mailed his
father that he approved of the attack on the destroyer USS *Cole,* which had
cost the lives of seventeen American sailors. At some point, whether in the
radical environments of the San Francisco mosques or in Yemen itself,
Lindh had been converted to a more militant version of Islam, which
brought him to Pakistan in 2000, where he studied at a religious school near
Bannu on the northwest frontier, then, at some point, slipped over into
Afghanistan, his name now changed to Abdul Hamid and his associates
consisting of, so a later federal grand jury indictment would allege, the
Taliban, al Qaeda, and the Pakistan-based terrorist group Harakat ul-
Mujahedeen.

Nor was John Walker Lindh the sole California role player, pro or con,
in the aftermath of the 9/11 attacks. If one were to judge from the alleged
hate crimes against Muslims, Arab Americans, and others being investigated within nine days after the terrorist offensive—seventy by the attorney

general of California, fifty by the Los Angeles office of the FBI, thirty-seven by the city attorney of Los Angeles—a number of Californians were involved in jihads of their own, which could be dangerous in a state that had more than a half-million Muslims out of an estimated national population of six million. The robbery-murder on September 15, 2001, of San Gabriel shopkeeper Adel Karas, forty-eight, a Coptic Christian from Egypt, was being investigated as a possible hate crime, which is what his grieving family believed to be the case.

Role playing, whether subliminal, deadly serious, or a combination thereof, was in the air. Was it merely the three glasses of red wine he had drunk before boarding an Air Canada flight from Los Angeles that prompted the Iranian-born Woodland Hills businessman Javid Naghani to start smoking in the lavatory once the jumbo jet was in the air, and, when reprimanded by stewardesses, to mumble threats, it was later alleged, about killing Americans? The Air Canada crew, in any event, took Naghani's remarks seriously, and the jet was escorted back to Los Angeles by two American fighters, with Naghani now returned to his seat. A SWAT team boarded the plane when it reached the tarmac, and very soon Naghani was in front of federal magistrate Jennifer Lum, who ordered him held without bail prior to formal charges.

Something more than midair threats, but equally disconcerting, was the one-man crusade by self-styled Muslim fundamentalist Emad Ibrahim Saad, thirty-five, a Los Angeles family man with a veiled wife and five children, to eliminate as many statues of the Virgin Mary in Los Angeles–area Roman Catholic churches as possible. Before Saad was finished with his one-man jihad, five Catholic churches in the area had found their statues of the Virgin Mary decapitated or otherwise maimed, and a statue of Father Junipero Serra belonging to one parish had been carted off to the nearby King Fahd Mosque in Culver City. Although Saad was alleged to have been a member, spokesmen for the mosque denied any involvement in the vandalism or the fliers proclaiming "Allah is the only true God" that Saad had left behind.[13]

Even more bizarre was the arrest by federal authorities in early December 2001 of Jewish Defense League (JDL) national chairman Irv Rubin, fifty-six, of Monrovia, and his colleague Earl Krugel, fifty-nine, on charges of plotting to blow up the King Fahd Mosque and the Los Angeles offices of Representative Darrell Issa (R-Vista), a Lebanese American. Arrested some forty times in the course of his JDL career, Rubin—a big, beefy man, given to disrupting meetings he disapproved of with either his bullhorn or fists or both—had nevertheless managed to stay out of jail. This time, however, the disciple of the late New York rabbi Meir Kahane was facing a mandatory thirty-year sentence, should a jury return a guilty verdict. News of the alleged plot and the arrests, moreover, exacerbated Muslim-Jewish tensions in the Southland. The alleged JDL plot, charged Aslam Abdullah, vice president of the Council on American-Islamic Relations, proved that "Jewish terrorism is just as dangerous as Muslim terrorism." Abdullah also suggested that airport authorities start profiling people who looked like Irv Rubin, just as they were now profiling Arab Americans.[14]

Suddenly, the very success of California as a center of Islamic-American settlement was reversed in its implications as hundreds of FBI agents fanned out into Muslim-American communities and began their investigations. Tensions ran especially high in the San Diego area, where three of the 9/11 terrorists—Nawaf Alhazmi, Khalid Almihdhar, and Hani Hanjour—lived and/or attended flight school before the attack. Two of them, in fact, had boarded with the India-born Dr. Abdussattar Shaikh, a respected retired college professor and cofounder of the San Diego Islamic Center. The prominence of Dr. Shaikh and the extensiveness of the greater San Diego Muslim community—100,000 strong, fourteen mosques, participation in practically every level of society—had offered the hijackers, and possibly even head hijacker Mohamed Atta, who was suspected of visiting San Diego to coordinate the attacks, the cover they needed. The success of Islamic San Diego, in this regard, also made it, following 9/11, a prime arena of suspicion, engendering more than three thousand leads in the aftermath of the attack. Not only were three, possibly four, hijackers residents there, another five Middle Eastern men living in the area were taken into federal custody as material witnesses. In December 2001, eleven Middle Eastern students, ten men and one woman, were detained for visa violations.

North and south, in matters great and small, the much vaunted success of Islamic California had suddenly reversed. As if to symbolize the abrupt halt of the Islamic California that had been so successfully in the making, construction stopped immediately on the $11 million Masjid Al-Rahman in Garden Grove, whose Orange County congregation had been in the process of erecting an architecturally distinguished two-story structure, sandstone on the exterior, dazzling white within, facing northeast to Mecca, as part of a larger complex that would also include a school, two libraries, lecture and meeting halls, kitchen and dining facilities, and an outdoor basketball court. Suddenly, Dr. Riad Abdelkarim, an Orange County resident and internist with the Southern California Permanente Medical Group in Anaheim, was thinking twice about going to the local shopping center with his Palestinian-born wife, Wijdan, and two children, Rasmieh, twelve, and Zuhdi, nine, who were reporting harassment. "It's so hard, because I'm proud to be a

Muslim," noted Wijdan, thirty-three, of her trips to the nearby mall, wearing the traditional Islamic head scarf, since the terrorist attacks. "Now I can't go out because everyone looks at me like I'm an enemy."[15]

California Sikhs, meanwhile, present in the state since the 1890s, were earning more than their fair share of hostile stares (and one hate-crime murder in Arizona), together with temple vandalism, harassment of Sikh children at school, racial profiling at airports, and, in San Diego, the stabbing of a Sikh woman. All this was engendered by the fact that Sikh men wore beards and turbans that made them resemble the well-known photograph of Osama bin Laden and his al Qaeda and Taliban followers, although the fiercely egalitarian monotheistic Sikh religion, founded in 1469 in northern India, was totally distinct from Islam. Anti-Sikh sentiment was particularly hurtful to Sikh Californians, for their community (half a million strong throughout the nation) had been especially adaptive to the Golden State, where they had first come as agricultural workers and later percolated upward into the professional ranks.

On campus, evidence of conflict emerged almost immediately, as might be expected, at UC Berkeley, where an antiterrorist cartoon in the *Daily Californian* incited violent reaction. The cartoon depicted two bearded terrorists, a flight manual at their feet, finding themselves in hell just as they were saying: "We made it to paradise! Now we will meet Allah, and be fed grapes, and be serviced by 70 virgin women, and . . . " Some one hundred students stormed the offices of the *Daily Californian* demanding an apology for the cartoon, which they said was a racist insult to Arab Americans, encouraging violence against them.[16]

In the Southland, political science professor Ken Hearlson, fifty-seven, a former marine and a convert to evangelical Christianity, was put on leave at Orange Coast College when four Muslim students complained that he called them Nazis, terrorists, and murderers during a classroom debate. "You killed five thousand people," the Muslim students alleged Hearlson to have said. In the weeks that followed, tensions ran high on the community campus as the students pursued their charges and Hearlson was defended by his teachers' union and, among others, a group of Arab-American Christian students. After a seventy-three-page report by an outside investigator cleared Hearlson of the charges in early December, he was reinstated for the following semester, although what Hearlson described as a letter of reprimand by college president Margaret Gratton was put into his file.[17]

Despite such difficulties, California, along with the rest of the nation, had avoided anything resembling the anti–Japanese American sentiment of early 1942, which had led to the incarceration of Issei immigrants and American-born Nisei alike. In San Diego County, which could have been ground zero for continuing conflict, given the activities of the terrorists there, the Muslim community, in a rare display of ecumenism, invited non-Muslims to attend services during Ramadan, especially on Eid al-Fitr, the joyous holy day ending the Ramadan month of fasting. Some fourteen thousand Orange County area Muslims felt secure enough in their citizenship to gather at the Orange County Fairgrounds in Costa Mesa on Eid al-Fitr for prayers and celebration. To move through the crowds, so many of them in traditional attire, was to experience a Muslim version of a typically California gathering.

The 100,000-strong Afghani community of California, meanwhile—two-thirds of all Afghanis living in the United States—was being almost overwhelmed with sympathetic media attention. Even before 9/11 and the subsequent focus on the anti-American, anti-women, anti-everything Taliban, Afghanis in California were perceived by the larger public (when they were perceived at all) as victims, not perpetrators, of the abuses of Islamic fundamentalism. This was true enough. The majority of California Afghanis had arrived in the aftermath of the antiroyalist coup of 1973, the Soviet invasion in 1979, and the bloody civil war that followed the withdrawal of the Soviets. As was the case with so many émigré movements, the Afghani refugees were in many instances members of the educated and affluent classes in their home country—the people, that is, with the wherewithal to get out. Of course, there was also repeated the scenario of émigré downward mobility—doctors and engineers driving taxis, a former foreign secretary running a liquor store, a high-ranking army officer operating a gas station, a generation of professionals now managing snack shops and pizza parlors, in one instance a former provincial governor selling hot dogs from a cart—yet in the main the Afghani community, buoyed by its respect for education and hard work, was notably prosperous and successful by the time of the 9/11 attack. Afghanis' regions of choice within California centered on the city of Fremont on the southeastern edge of the Bay Area and Orange County, with further sprinklings throughout Los Angeles and San Diego Counties. Downtown Fremont had its Little Kabul district, largely Tajik in tribal origin, hence supportive of the Northern Alliance. Orange County tended to be more Pushtun and royalist in its political orientation.

From one perspective, 9/11, coupled with the dot-com debacle, was returning California to the economically challenged conditions of the early 1990s. The immediate falloff in tourism and travel was noticeable. Most of the major cities of coastal California financed themselves in part from sales and hotel taxes, which now declined. Post-9/11 San Francisco, doubly traumatized by the dot-com bust, seemed a ghost town. Hotel occupancy fell to 59 percent, and three thousand hotel and restaurant workers were laid off.

The slump in hotels and restaurants, in turn, together with the dropoff in food purchases by airlines, sent agriculture into decline. Even Hollywood was having troubles, as some $200 million worth of already produced motion pictures—most notably *Collateral Damage,* starring Arnold Schwarzenegger—were held from release due to their sensitive subject matter. Combine the energy crisis with the dot-com problems and the post-9/11 slump, and it was easy to understand why state government was facing a $23.6 billion shortfall by the spring of 2002 in its projected 2002–03 revenues.

On the other hand, if the slump represented a reprise of the early 1990s, the suddenly hot war on terrorism, beginning in Afghanistan but promising to continue across decades, represented a booster shot for local economies in garrison-rich areas such as San Diego County and defense industries that had been looking for other things to do since the end of the cold war. Ceradyne of Costa Mesa, for example, had been scrambling for some time to find civilian outlets—diesel engines, orthodontics—for its primary product, an ultra-hard high-tech ceramic, which the company had during the cold war produced for nuclear weapons, combat helicopters, and fixed-wing aircraft. Now, however, Ceradyne was busy filling orders for 28,000 ceramic body armor plates to be used by infantry in Afghanistan, while the price of its shares rose more than 55 percent on the New York Stock Exchange. General Atomics Aeronautical Systems of San Diego—whose pilotless Predator aircraft was performing so well over Afghanistan as a provider of real-time television intelligence and a deliverer of air-to-ground missiles with pinpoint accuracy—was adding one hundred employees to its six-hundred-person workforces in San Diego and San Bernardino Counties, to keep up with new orders from the Defense Department.

In El Segundo, Flyer Technologies, a manufacturing start-up spearheaded by Oded Nechushtan, an Israeli émigré with a background in desert warfare, was showing every sign of beating out DaimlerChrysler for the contract for the next generation of lightweight, air-transportable fighting vehicles. Should Flyer Technologies win out over DaimlerChrysler, California would once again be back in the military vehicle business. And it would be in the counterbiological warfare business as well, given the sudden onslaught of research into this field going on at the Lawrence Livermore Laboratory in the Bay Area, where the anthrax mailings and the looming possibilities of bioterrorism had turned the attention of scientists and engineers at the laboratory in the direction of anti-bioterrorist technology, including a handheld nucleic acid analyzer that could identify pathogens in record time.

In November 2001, the FBI and two other government agencies

reported that terrorist attacks might be expected against bridges in California. Acting immediately, Governor Davis on November 3 sent the National Guard and the California Highway Patrol to the major bridges of the state. Some criticized Davis's decision as hasty, but approval of the governor's action was near total within the general public. Newspaper photographs of rifle-toting Guardsmen and CHP motorcycle officers patrolling the Golden Gate Bridge subliminally linked one of California's major icons with the towers of the World Trade Center in a manner that offered identification (California also was under attack), atonement (California had not been attacked), and envy (California should be important enough to be attacked) in an acting out that said much about the state of mind of California in the aftermath of 9/11.

Los Angeles seemed especially preoccupied with comparisons of itself to New York. The 9/11 attacks and the admirable response of New York firefighters, policemen, emergency medical technicians, public officials, and ordinary citizens underscored the love and pride held by New Yorkers for their city. Did the people of Los Angeles love, and take pride in, their city to a comparable degree? Would they behave as well in the face of a similar attack? Openly discussed on talk show radio or indirectly approached by politicians and newspaper columnists, such questions possessed increased significance in that the image of Los Angeles in some form of catastrophic collapse—whether by earthquake, fire, volcano, or extraterrestrial attack—had been a fixed point of imaginative identity since early in the last century. Here was a city, moreover, in the midst of a secessionist movement that at the very moment of the 9/11 attacks was seriously considering making Los Angeles the first great world city voluntarily to disestablish itself. Here also was a city that had pulled the plug on its developing subway and light rail system, that remained ambivalent about expanding its international airport, and that in the aftermath of 9/11 had brought all airport plans to a halt, with a near-audible sigh of relief on the part of Mayor James Hahn, a suburbanite from San Pedro, who had opposed LAX expansion from the beginning. Whatever New York City was—gritty, uncomfortable, challenging—it was not suburban. It was a city: one of the greatest cities in human history, and it was behaving that way in the aftermath of the 9/11 attack. Los Angeles understood and applauded this response and the highly developed urbanism it represented. But there was also an element of envy in this admiration; for Los Angeles, beset by the rising power of the secessionists, was wondering whether or not it even was a city in the first place.

Reviewing the post-9/11 debut of the Emmy-winning television series *Sex and the City, Los Angeles Times* television critic Howard Rosenberg used the occasion to launch an elegiac love song to New York as captured by the series. Neither *Law & Order* nor *Seinfeld,* Rosenberg wrote, could match *Sex and the City* in capturing the majestic urbanism of New York and the equally urban belief of its citizens that the Big Apple was the center of the known universe. In the opening installment of the series for the 2001–02 season, Rosenberg noted, filmed just before the 9/11 attacks and now functioning as an unintended but effective tribute to the city, one of the four protagonists, the publicist Samantha, knows someone who is moving to Napa, California. "I'm always surprised when anyone leaves New York," notes Samantha. "I mean, where do they go?"[18]

The difference between New York and Los Angeles, some television critics were noting, could be found in the difference between the late-night ruminations in the aftermath of 9/11 of David Letterman out of New York and Jay Leno out of Burbank. Disconnected in Los Angeles, Leno could be respectful of the catastrophe but could also soon get back to being generically hilarious, functioning in a line of direct descent from Bob Hope. Letterman, by contrast, was a New Yorker by place, adoption, and prior temperament. The attacks touched him deeply, bringing out not only the noir dimensions of his quirky, irony-laden sensibility but also his love of his adopted city and his own willingness openly to participate, along with Mayor Rudy Giuliani and other guests, in the grieving and healing process following the catastrophe.

Giuliani, in fact, would come to California in early spring 2002, both in person and in paid political television advertisements, and play a role in convincing Republican voters to turn from two quintessentially Californian and politically experienced figures—Secretary of State Bill Jones and former Los Angeles mayor Richard Riordan—and give the Republican nomination for governor to Bill Simon, a New Jersey/New Yorker in his early fifties who had worked as an assistant U.S. attorney for Giuliani, had been in California for slightly more than a decade, and had frequently failed to vote. Giuliani, of course, could not be given full credit for Simon's primary victory in his first run for elective office. Governor Gray Davis spent $10 million in the primary attacking Riordan, whom he regarded as the stronger opponent, and the strategy worked, handing Riordan a stunning and unexpected defeat. Yet neither could the ringing endorsement, television ads, and active campaigning of the highly popular former mayor of New York City be discounted. Some portion of Giuliani's New York charisma had proved transferable to Simon, who began the race with single-digit possibilities and ended up winning the nomination, in part because he was the gubernatorial candidate bearing the imprimatur of New York.

Epilogue

Déjà Vu All Over Again

By the third year of the new millennium, a growing number of Californians were saying that the early 1990s seemed to have returned with a vengeance: soaring crime rates, failing schools, trashed kids, endangered species, urban disorders, persistent homelessness (most notably in San Francisco), police-community disconnect, conflict over the harvesting of redwood trees, an economy on the ropes, leading to a fiscal meltdown in state government. Energy, meanwhile, remained a problem, and there was serious talk in the legislature about re-regulating the deregulated energy culture, returning it to the early 1990s. Even nature was repeating itself as, ten years from the great Malibu fire, no less than eleven wildfires raged out of control in the last week of October 2003 across Ventura, Los Angeles, San Bernardino, Orange, Riverside, and San Diego Counties, scorching 744,754 acres (an area larger than Rhode Island), destroying 2,817 homes, and taking twenty lives.

The disintegration of the returning shuttle *Columbia,* which began over California at 5:52 a.m., Pacific Standard Time, Saturday, February 1, 2003, was a national, not a Californian, event. Yet because of the state's close connection to the space program, many Californians were tempted to see in the tragedy yet another example of how things could go wrong, even amid the most advanced of circumstances. From this perspective, the loss of the *Columbia* and its crew over California, Arizona, New Mexico, and Texas—due to something as simple as wing damage caused by a detached piece of foam insulation weighing a mere 2.67 pounds—underscored the fragility of technology itself and the inherent instability of societies, such as California, structured and propelled by technological advance. The *Columbia* was in part a product of the very same half century of cold war federal spending that had revolutionized California.

The predatory northern pike of Minnesota, introduced into Lake Davis in Plumas County in the early 1990s, refused to die. In 1997 state officials had spent $10 million to poison the lake to no effect, save for the destruction of the local tourist economy. The hardy pike would not be intimidated. It kept breeding, and it kept eating other fish. By 2002, state biologists were using nets, explosives, and electroshock waves, costing a half-million dollars a year to dispose of 17,635 northern pike pulled from the waters of Lake Davis. Should the pike get into waters downstream, noted state fish and game official Patrick Foy, the results would be catastrophic, as the predatory pike, with its crocodile jaws and powerful tail fins, would wreak havoc on the trout, salmon, smelt, and other fish of the lower rivers and Delta. "Our greatest fear," noted Foy, "is a malicious person who places them in some other lake."[1]

Throughout the 1990s, a captive breeding and release program had kept the California condor from extinction. In late February 2003, the U.S. Fish & Wildlife Service reported that the last female condor to have been born in the wild—a majestic creature with a wingspan of 9.5 feet—had been shot to death by a poacher. Captured in 1986, AC-8, as she was known, had spent fourteen years in captivity, during which time she had produced twelve chicks. Released in 2000, the great condor matriarch, anywhere from between thirty to forty years old, perhaps the oldest condor surviving on the planet, was killed for no reason except that she was there, soaring the skies of California. "This is a senseless death," noted Governor Davis, "that strikes a blow at our efforts to bring these great birds from the edge of extinction."[2]

Earth First! and other activists were determined that such destruction would not be leveled against the redwood trees owned by the Pacific Lumber Company in Humboldt County. The 1999 agreement between Julia "Butterfly" Hill and Pacific Lumber seemed to settle the impasse between the company and conservationists by allowing the harvesting of some old-growth redwoods under certain conditions and the purchase by the state of the most important of the redwood groves. In mid-2002, however, the paradigm provided by Hill proved too compelling for activists distrustful of Pacific Lumber, and eighteen of them took to the tops of old-growth redwoods in continuing protest. As in the case of Hill, these activists renamed both themselves and their trees. A demonstrator calling herself Annapurna, for example, was living in a tree called Robin; Lodge Pole inhabited a redwood called Poseidon; Remedy named her tree Jerry; and so forth. Securing the necessary court order, Pacific Lumber sent specially trained tree-climbing agents up these redwoods to remove the tree sitters from their plywood platforms. They, in turn—after hot showers—promptly returned to their arboreal habitats, switched on their cell phones, and continued their anti-logging campaign.

Things got worse for Pacific Lumber in late February when the district attorney of Humboldt County sued the company for allegedly using fraudulent data in the Environmental Impact Report required by the 1999 agreement. Then, on May 19, superior court judge John Golden, sitting in Eureka, threw out the entire agreement between Pacific Lumber and the state Forestry Department on the grounds that the plan had no provisions to protect watersheds and endangered species. If Judge Golden's ruling was upheld on appeal, it would be back to the drawing board for everyone: lumber executives, state and federal officials, and tree sitters. The original tree sitter, meanwhile, Hill, was leading a campaign to put on the California ballot in March 2004 a proposition that would prohibit the logging of any tree alive in California as of 1850, the year in which it became a state. Hill was joined in her campaign by Susan Moloney, who in the fall of 2002 had spent fifty-two days fasting on the steps of the state Capitol in support of the Campaign for Old Growth.

Another problem resurfacing in the early 2000s was gang-related homicide, so epidemic in the early 1990s. Mayor Jerry Brown was bringing his tough love program to Oakland with some success; yet 113 Oaklanders, the majority of them young black men, died from drug- and/or gang-related homicides on the streets of the city in 2002, the highest number since the epidemic year of 1995. By late October 2003, the figure stood at one hundred and rising. As far as homicide was concerned, Oakland seemed headed for another banner year, and this distressed the children and teenagers of the city, who were quite realistically asking themselves just exactly who would be next. From the perspective of 2003, Brown admitted he could now see that it had been a mistake twenty-five years earlier, when he had been governor, to put an end to California's indeterminate sentencing law. Under this program, violent felons were sentenced to a set number of years plus life. The "plus life" part of the sentence meant that after felons had done their time, they could only be released after they had convinced parole boards that they had a program—a job, a place to live, a network of personal support—that would prevent them from returning to prison. Brown now complained that Oakland was teeming with paroled felons, adrift in the city, accounting for one in five of the homicide victims and 14 percent of the arrested suspects.

No one, however, could blame the volatility of Oakland and some of its nearby suburbs exclusively on paroled felons. There was in the very DNA code of the city a restlessness, a proclivity to antisocial behavior, in many of the young and unattached males of the city: a trait that Oakland shared with any number of economically embattled communities across the nation, but one that took on a special intensity in the East Bay, given the fact that it was frequently reinforced by the left-to-anarchistic sloganeering, ideology, and mind-set peculiar to the region. The Oakland Raiders professional football team, for example—more precisely, the Raider Nation, as fans collectively called themselves—gave release to the anxieties of dispossessed or quasi-dispossessed young men. When the Raiders lost Super Bowl XXXVII to Tampa Bay in January 2003, Oakland erupted into a dangerous melee, which police were forced to confront with tear gas, rubber bullets, and flash-stun grenades. "Raiders rule! Fuck the police!" was the rallying cry along International Boulevard as some sixty officers confronted groups of bottle-throwing, window-smashing, auto-overturning, fire-setting Raider fans. All in all, some four hundred police officers, sheriff's deputies, highway patrol personnel, and mounted police from nearby Vallejo were necessary to keep the mayhem in check.

Across the bay in San Francisco, the Norteno and Sureno gangs were fighting it out for control of the streets of the southern part of the city. Their murder rate might seem minor in comparison to Oakland's but tell that to the parents of seventeen-year-old Hugo Enrique Ireta—a soccer player, not a gang member, getting his money from working in the kitchens of local restaurants—shot to the sidewalk near his home at 21st and York Streets on February 14 by one or another of the gangs because he had his name tattooed on his back (a gang member had demanded that Ireta remove his shirt and show him his tattoo before he shot him), dying shortly thereafter at the San Francisco General Hospital.

In Los Angeles, the homicide rate among gang members was regaining its momentum: nothing like the rate of the early 1990s, but alarming enough to have new LAPD chief William Bratton compare the gangs of Los Angeles to the Mafia of New York City, where he had previously served as police commissioner. The appointment of Bratton in October 2002 by Mayor James Hahn, who bypassed internal and local candidates, a number of them minorities, could be seen in the context of the New York envy that had been seeping through Los Angeles since 9/11. Outspoken, politically ambitious, Bratton proceeded to upstage the self-effacing Hahn as soon as he arrived in the Big Orange and was being touted as a future mayor by the featured speaker at the annual St. Patrick's Day dinner, twelve hundred strong, of the Friendly Sons of St. Patrick, held in the Beverly Hills Hilton. Bratton himself, meanwhile, was acting, increasingly, like the Doge of the City, demanding more and more police from the city council, which, quite soon, cured itself of New York envy and began to oppose Bratton as a brash New Yorker lecturing longtime Angelenos about what was good for their city.

The city council, in turn, knew that while Chief Bratton was overstating his case with the Mafia comparison, vast portions of Los Angeles, especially South Central, remained known primarily as killing zones. On April 9 the council voted to change the designation South Central Los Angeles to South Los Angeles in hopes that the southern tier of the city could be detached by a name change from the street gang legacy that Bratton was using as a scare tactic, so many council members believed, as leverage for the recontrol of the city by the police department, as in times past.

As far as police matters were concerned, San Francisco seemed in melt-down in early March when a grand jury indicted the SFPD command struc-ture—the chief, two deputy chiefs, an assistant chief, a captain, a lieutenant, and a sergeant—on conspiracy charges, alleging that the brass had con-spired to obstruct justice in the case of three younger officers, one of them the son of the assistant chief, charged with an off-duty assault and battery in the Marina district. District Attorney Terence Hallinan, who had had his troubles with the police since his rebellious teenage years, stood by the indictments; and San Francisco seemed a surreal place as its top officers— Chief Earl Sanders in full uniform—showed up at the Hall of Justice for booking. Within weeks, superior court judge Kay Tsenin tossed the grand jury indictments out of court, and all but Sanders, who was suffering from high blood pressure, returned to duty. Still, the playing out of such a goofy (there is no other word for it) melodrama—the bizarre indictment (some of it not even typed but handwritten, as if in haste), the spectacle of the SFPD brass being booked and arraigned, Hallinan's obvious distaste for the cops, the screaming headlines in local newspapers—showed San Francisco at its most unstable: more unstable, in fact, than any self-respecting American city could allow itself to be and still be considered capable of self-governance.

Just two weeks later, these very same San Francisco cops—directed by the very same brass who had been so arbitrarily and flimsily indicted by a grand jury that obviously did not like or trust police—were busy protecting the city streets from an influx of thousands of demonstrators protesting the impending invasion of Iraq. It was comforting—almost like old times—to see Joan Baez on the streets when the demonstrations began, greeting well-wishers and singing songs of peace; but that was in mid-February. By mid-March, as the antiwar rallies entered their second month, crowds had grown to more than 65,000 and had become ugly. Few were listening to Baez as Seattle-style demonstrators, dressed in black and other forms of intifada costuming, began to trash downtown. Assistant police chief Alex Fagan Sr., recently under indictment but now acting police chief of the city, had no trouble reclaiming the moral high ground as he directed efforts to contain roving bands of protesters, many of them clandestinely armed, as they stopped cars and harassed motorists, broke windows or otherwise vandalized the financial district, or brazenly rumbled with the police.

Even after San Francisco had been cleaned up, however, its downtown remained in shabby condition, due in part to the hordes of homeless and other feral people living on the streets. By November 2002, the problem of what to do about the homeless had become the number one political issue in the city. That month, San Francisco voters approved Proposition N, calling for the reduction of welfare payments to three thousand homeless people from $395 to $59 a month, the difference to be made up in food, shelter, and related services. Sponsored by mayoral hopeful Gavin Newsom, a city supervisor, Proposition N passed handily at the ballot box but, as was the case with so many of these sweeping measures, was voided by the court the following June on the grounds that under state law only the city/county board of supervisors, and not the voters acting directly, could enact or retract welfare programs. Faced with the lack of a legal mandate, the San Francisco Welfare Department suspended the Care not Cash program. On an almost daily basis, the letters to the editor columns of local newspapers were filled with accounts of panhandling and unhygienic behavior by the homeless. A vividly emblematic example of how bad things had become occurred in late May when Dr. Geetha Jayaram, an associate professor of psychiatry at the Johns Hopkins School of Medicine, visiting San Francisco to attend the annual meeting of the American Psychiatric Association, was struck from behind on a street near her hotel in midday by a mentally disturbed homeless man. Dr. Jayaram spent a week in recovery at the San Francisco General Hospital. Even before the attack, attendees at the convention were discussing the fact that the streets around their downtown hotel were disturbingly full of people obviously in need of psychiatric care.

So many of the problems occurring in the early 2000s were repeating problems of the prior decade or disestablishing the strategies used to overcome them. Children were being trashed at alarming rates in the early 1990s. Was the situation improving, or was it getting worse? San Francisco, a special task force reported in February 2003, had become a shocking center of child prostitution, with up to three thousand girls—most of them illegal immigrants smuggled into the country—selling themselves on the streets. Those tempted to disbelieve these statistics, released by the End Youth Exploitation Task Force, would have to deal with similar statistics released by the State Department in Washington, which was asserting that between 50,000 and 75,000 children were being brought into the United States each year for purposes of sexual exploitation, with the Bay Area a key point of entry.

Proposition 227, on the other hand, the English-only measure passed in 1998, was, five years later, functioning smoothly and on schedule according to statistics released in March 2003 by state superintendent of public instruction Jack O'Connell. By the fall of 2002, O'Connell announced, 32 percent—for a total of 862,000—of all California students learning English in English-only immersion classrooms were now speaking the language proficiently as measured by the California English Language Development Test. Thus, California seemed to be avoiding the alleged and predicted irredentism on the part of immigrants that had caused so much political turmoil, insult to Latinos, and personal pain in the early 1990s. As of Census 2000, moreover, 32 percent of the total population of California was now Hispanic, and as of July 2001, according to a study released by the Center for the Study of Latino Health and Culture at UCLA, more than half of the babies being born in California were Hispanic as well. California was en route to becoming, rather soon, a center of Hispanic-American people and culture. Far from being irredentist, Hispanic California—speaking English as well as Spanish, owning homes, advancing up the socioeconomic ladder—was permeating the entire fabric of California life, including its politics. Very soon, predicted Harry Pachon of the Tomas Rivera Policy Institute, 50 percent of Hispanic California would be marrying non-Hispanics. As a matter of culture and bloodlines, then, a new California was in the making: a recovery forward, historians might claim, of the Hispanic origins of California in the eighteenth century.

Californians had need of the comforting news that English-only immersion was working in the public schools; for the task of integrating immigrants into American life (whatever the exact nature of that life and culture turned out to be), while at the same time coping with a multitude of social problems affecting the classroom—poverty, dysfunctional parents, a lack of pro-educational values reinforced by family structure—was still proving a challenge to the K–12 establishment. All in all, by 2003 the state superintendent of public instruction had been forced to take control of six local school districts facing financial and academic meltdown. The largest and most recent was the Oakland Unified School District—$82 million in debt, its academic scores declining—taken over in June with a $100 million bailout. Even in coping school districts, moreover, the much vaunted panacea of the late 1990s—small class sizes, twenty students or less—was proving too expensive a burden to bear, now that state revenues were decreasing. The California State University system, meanwhile, was announcing in January 2003 that it had expelled 8.2 percent of its 2001 freshman class for failing to master basic English and math skills.

Anxiety over test scores, however, did not constitute a case study in déjà

vu all over again. Californians, after all, had been concerned with this problem for some time now. The collapse of the economy, by contrast, was
another matter. The downswing of the economy in the early 1990s and its
recovery in mid-decade had been the big story of the millennial fin de siè-
cle. A state that was going broke in the early 1990s was awash in a $12 bil-
lion surplus by the end of the decade. Prudence dictated that these excess
revenues be put aside for a rainy day or, at the least, be expended on one-
time-only improvements. Instead, the annual state budget jumped from $67
to $97 billion between 1998 and 2002 as windfall revenues were ploughed
into a wide array of ongoing educational and social programs.

Still, even during the flush times, there had been the energy crisis, which
had put a great strain on the California economy. Between 1999 and 2000,
spending for electricity quadrupled from $7 to $27 billion. This money
came from consumers in the private sector and, as the crisis deepened, from
state government, the buyer of last resort, which by 2000 was spending billions in spot purchases and long-term contracts to keep California operational. Then came in rapid order 9/11, the dot-com collapse, and a
complexity of causes bedeviling the American economy in the early 2000s.
The State of the Region 2002, issued by the Southern California Association
of Governments (SCAG), revealed a distressing falloff in incomes for the
entire region, starting in the year 2000. The top two hundred companies in
the San Francisco Bay Area, so the *San Francisco Chronicle* reported in
May 2003, had lost nearly $85 billion in net income through 2001 and 2002
and had seen their total market capitalization fall by 31.6 percent.

All this translated to slashed payrolls. Unemployment insurance tax filing data suggested that California had lost some 205,000 jobs since the dot-
com collapse. In San Francisco the venerable and prestigious law firm of
Brobeck, Phleger & Harrison shut down in January 2003. At the height of
the dot-com boom, the firm, specializing in high-tech IPOs and related
forms of business, had increased its staff from four hundred to nine hundred
attorneys and was paying graduates of prestigious law schools $135,000 a
year. Partners were averaging $850,000 annually. Now there was a padlock
on the door. As was the case in the early 1990s, economists at UCLA were
predicting a long and steady agony of recovery for the economy, with a job
growth rate of a mere 0.4 percent predicted for 2003.

The higher paying the job, the more likely it was to be one of those to
have been lost, especially in the field of high tech. (Intel alone was in the
process of laying off ten thousand workers.) Hardest hit was the tax bracket
of $100,000 a year or more, from which the state derived a significant per-
centage of its revenues; hence, by early 2002, state revenues were going
into free fall. By the spring of 2003, the governor and legislators were grap-

pling with a $38 billion shortfall, if the present level of state services were to be sustained.

Where was this money to come from? True, the Federal Energy Regulatory Commission in late March, after scrutinizing a thousand-page brief filed by the state, ruled that Enron and five other energy companies had manipulated energy markets against California at the height of the crisis. FERC, however, also stated that California was owed a mere $3.3 billion in refunds. California was asking for $9 billion. The unkindest cut of all was when FERC decreed that California was obligated to pay energy companies the $3 billion in unpaid bills it was withholding in protest. That left the state with a moral victory as far as the gouging was concerned and a net gain of a mere $333 million, which would hardly resolve the fiscal crisis.

By the summer of 2003, the budget crisis had reached a point of intractability that was more than a mere repeat of the budget crises of the early 1990s. The very viability of state government itself was coming into question. The 2002–03 state budget totaled $98.9 billion, of which $78.8 billion was general fund monies for state operations. The remainder of the budget was for debt service and other mandated obligations. Although the governor and the legislature successfully extracted $3.3 billion from the current budget in March, when it came to dealing with the $38 billion shortfall in revenues being predicted for the 2003–04 budget—if something approaching the current level of services were to be preserved—elected officials found themselves in a condition of intractable impasse. Cut services, Republicans urged—and no new taxes. Cut some services, Democrats countered—raise some taxes selectively, and borrow money from Wall Street to get through the crisis.

Announcing his 2003–04 budget of $96.4 billion in January, calling for $62.8 billion in general funds for state operations, a reduction of $16 billion over the previous year of general spending (increased by later cuts to $20 billion), Davis spent the winter and spring watching it come under ferocious opposition from Republicans and Democrats alike. First of all, because so much of the budget was in mandated health and education programs, the total budget did not look that different from its predecessor. There was only one place that Davis could cut, and that was state operations and general fund–supported programs. Within that narrow sector of permissible cuts, however, Davis's proposed budget involved a pandemic level of layoffs. As required by state law, advance layoff notices went out to thousands of state employees, teachers, and state-supported health, social service, and fire and safety personnel, even the sacrosanct California Highway Patrol, which received 469 notices. The educational and social service sector of the state went into collective shock. Layoffs such as those being proposed exceeded, proportionately, the rates of the Great Depression. By April, Davis was back at the cutting board, ordering state agencies to prepare plans for another overall 10 percent reduction in personnel, this in part to gain leverage against militant unions, protesting the proposed layoffs and an ongoing wage freeze already implemented. Republicans, meanwhile, were calling for $25 billion in cuts, which together with the $20 billion already proposed by Davis, would reduce state government by a third. Assembly speaker Herb Wesson (D-Los Angeles), however, was quick to point out that the state could lay off every one of its quarter of a million employees and still not close the budget gap.

Throughout the spring, some 117 bills and proposals were debated in the state assembly and the senate calling for up to $28.8 billion in taxes: on beer and cigarettes ($1.97 a pack, the highest in the nation), and license fee increases of every kind, which might be expected, but also proposed taxes on such disparate items as bottled water, diapers, cell phones, dry cleaning, mercury lamps, and satellite dishes. Democrats opposed Davis's plan to raise vehicle license fees, while Senator James Brulte, the Republican leader, threatened to work against the reelection of any Republican who voted in any way whatsoever to raise taxes. Desperately scrambling for funds, Davis asked the sixty-one recognized Native American tribes of California to renegotiate their gambling agreements with the state, which the tribes rejected. (Why had the agreements been so favorable in the first place, critics of Davis asked?) Davis also pleaded with Congress for bailout funds on the grounds that California had spent billions of dollars since 9/11 on homeland security programs that were basically a federal responsibility. And besides, Davis pointed out, California was not alone in its difficulties. Forty-seven of fifty states were facing budget deficits, although none so threatening as California's. Like the casino operators, Congress initially remained impervious to Davis's plea, although President George W. Bush—who had lost California in the 2000 election but saw prospects of winning it in 2004—did send along $2.4 billion in relief in the summer of 2003.

Across the winter, spring, and early summer, the notion of using borrowed money to bail out the state was also coming under attack. It was one thing, critics noted, to issue bonds for capital construction (although Davis's proposal to put a $220 million bond issue on the ballot to build a new death row met with withering scorn and soon disappeared from the radar screen); it was an entirely different matter to issue bonds to pay for ongoing expenses. Already, the state was trying to borrow against a $3.2 billion tobacco settlement that would eventually come its way. (As of then, the check was not even in the mail.) Other lawmakers, even some assembly

Republicans, were talking about issuing $10 billion in deficit bonds, to be paid off across the next five years, as a way of avoiding a tax increase.

Issuing a thousand-page report, the nonpartisan legislative analyst Elizabeth Hill opposed the idea of using debt to get California through its fiscal crisis. The state, Hill pointed out, was already paying $2.6 billion a year in debt service. Should it go further into debt, that figure would rise to $5.6 billion by fiscal year 2007–08, which represented the equivalent cost of the entire community college budget. And besides, Hill noted, piling on debt did nothing to deal with the continuing structural imbalance between revenues and fixed expenses that, if not corrected, could drive California into insolvency.

Wall Street agreed. Already, in the fall of 2002, Standard & Poor's had dropped California to the bottom of its risk assessment list, ranking it alongside Louisiana. In February 2003, Moody's Investors Service also lowered California's creditworthiness to the lowest possible tier, alongside New York and Louisiana. In June, Moody's further tightened the rein on California, and this warning barely allowed the state to borrow the $11 billion state controller Steve Westley said was necessary to get California through the summer. The lower the rating, the higher the interest rate paid to Wall Street.

The state seemed to be in a condition of political meltdown as well, as a petition to recall Gray Davis from the governorship gained momentum through the summer of 2003. Under a little-known and never-before-used provision of state law, the legacy of Progressive reforms early in the twentieth century, a recall election against a sitting governor could be implemented by petition, provided that signatures on the petition reached a certain percentage of the total vote in the election that had brought the governor into office, which translated to slightly less than 900,000 signatures in Davis's case. Any registered voter, moreover, provided that he or she had been a resident of California and a U.S. citizen for at least five years, could place himself or herself on the ballot as an alternative to the sitting governor for a filing fee of $3,500 and the signatures of sixty-five registered voters from the same political party. In January 2003, three Republican activists—outgoing state party chairman Shawn Steel, former GOP assemblyman Howard Kaloogian, and Ted Costa of an antitax organization called People's Advocate—announced that they were initiating such a recall petition. Davis, the trio charged at a noontime press conference held outside the state Capitol, had dilly-dallied for more than a year during the energy crisis before coming up with a responsive plan, had squandered a $12 billion surplus, had spent the majority of his time fund-raising, and in general had brought the state of California to the brink of fiscal collapse.

In late February, the state Republican Party endorsed the recall measure. Many Republicans were still affronted by the fact that Davis had spent $10 million on hard-hitting television ads against Richard Riordan in a successful effort to deny the popular former mayor of Los Angeles the Republican nomination in favor of Secretary of State Bill Jones or investor William Simon, the other two Republican contenders. Once Davis had broken the long-standing agreement that a primary was the business of the party involved, all bets were off. For this reason alone, many normally cautious Republicans felt entitled to back the drastic recall measure, despite the fact that it could be seen as a fatal blow to representative government, turning California once and for all into a populist free-for-all ruled by special interest lobbyists and daily polls.

Initially, the recall effort seemed to be getting nowhere. Then, Republican congressman Darrell Issa of San Diego County donated nearly $700,000 to finance the effort (Issa later matched this sum with a second donation); by mid-June 2003—as recall spokesmen said that they had already collected more than 700,000 signatures—newspapers that had once given the recall back-page treatment were running headlines saying that Davis was in trouble. On the Republican side, Issa declared that he would have his name on the ballot as an alternative to Davis. Republican activist Arnold Schwarzenegger, former secretary of state Bill Jones, and investor Bill Simon, whom Davis had barely defeated in November, also expressed interest. In Democratic circles, the names of Senator Dianne Feinstein, Lieutenant Governor Cruz Bustamante, Attorney General Bill Lockyer, Treasurer Phil Angelides, Insurance Commissioner John Garamendi, California Senate president pro tem John Burton, and former White House chief of staff Leon Panetta were being discussed as possible alternatives to Davis if the recall petition successfully reached the ballot.

A perfect political storm was brewing. When the legislature passed, and Davis signed, a tripling of the vehicle license tax in August, netting the state $4 billion (much of it intended for local subventions), malaise and anxiety quickly sharpened into focused resentment. In California, everyone drives an automobile. There were more than twenty million of them on the road as of fall 2003. With little warning, millions of Californians were now being alerted in the most painful possible way—hundreds, even thousands, of dollars suddenly taken from their pockets—that state government was in big trouble. Thanks to the Internet and talk radio, meanwhile, the recall petition was gaining strength. Inspired by incessant anti-tax, anti-Davis talk radio, Californians were downloading the recall petition from the Internet and circulating it locally. The recall petition thus had millions of points of dissemination. Thanks to the Issa funds, paid agents were fanning out into

shopping centers, gathering signatures. On July 23, Secretary of State
Kevin Shelley certified that the recall petition had qualified for the ballot.
The next day, Lieutenant Governor Cruz Bustamante set the recall election
for October 7, 2003.

For Davis to be recalled, however, Republicans needed a strong candidate. Already, Congressman Darrell Issa and Senator Tom McClintock, a
respected conservative from Thousand Oaks in the Simi Valley of Ventura
County, had declared, but each of these candidates had limitations: Issa
from a troubled past involving a charge of car theft, later dismissed, and
McClintock because of an array of conservative opinions, including an
unapologetic pro-life stance, considered outside the political mainstream.
Paradoxically, Issa and McClintock each epitomized the controlling force
behind the recall—anger at the fiscal mess California was in, together with
anger over the car tax—but neither of them showed any sign of being able
to move beyond his immediate political base.

Nevertheless, the perfect storm continued to gather force, with Davis
showing only a 22 percent approval rate by the summer of 2003. If only
they had the right candidate, Republicans began to agree among themselves, they had every chance of reclaiming the election Davis had hijacked
from them in 2002. Was that candidate Richard Riordan? Perhaps. But
Riordan was still reeling from the shock and awe television campaign
unleashed against him by Davis in the Republican primary: attacks later
characterized as "puke politics" by Attorney General Bill Lockyer, a Democrat, who warned Davis that he would support him in the recall campaign
only if the governor, this time around, eschewed such tactics. And besides,
Riordan was showing no inclination to run, although he was flattered by the
attention. If not Riordan, then who?

A cadre of Republican professionals, led by former governor Pete Wilson's chief of staff, Bob White, sixty-one, knew exactly who—Arnold
Schwarzenegger. Leaving office in 1998, White had formed California
Strategies, which in short order became the leading planning and political
advocacy partnership in the state. A top client of California Strategies was
Arnold Schwarzenegger. Within a few months, many in the press would be
treating Schwarzenegger as if he had come out of right field, a political
novice, to enter and win the recall race. Not true. For virtually his entire life,
Schwarzenegger, now fifty-six, had been dreaming of a political career and
edging into one, in fact, by heading physical fitness programs at the federal
and state level, and, in November 2002, successfully leading an initiative,
Proposition 49, mandating after-school programs.

In years to come, historians and cultural critics will have their work cut
out for them aligning the social, psychological, and cultural mind-set of

California with that of Arnold Schwarzenegger. He is an immigrant, first of all, in a state dominated by immigrants. A fierce hunger for something more—something big, something he could barely name it was so grand and compelling in its possibilities—had in 1968 brought him, near penniless, from his native Austria. In *Moby-Dick,* the narrator Ishmael describes the whaling ship *Pequod* as his Harvard and his Yale. Schwarzenegger's Harvard and Yale was Gold's Gym in Venice Beach, where the young immigrant from Austria, pumping iron, built his body to the Michelangelo grandeur that would win him the Mr. Universe title in 1968 and seven Mr. Olympia crowns. Schwarzenegger's assault on the universe—standing before a mirror, pumping iron for hours at a time, alone with the image of himself and his dreams—said something about California's proclivity to nurture the redesigned self, to encourage big dreams even when the chances for success were slim. What were the possibilities, after all, for a small-town Austrian boy, speaking English in an impenetrable accent, to achieve more than a modest success in his new circumstances? Within three decades, Schwarzenegger had long since become a world champion body-builder, a real estate multimillionaire, a top-ranked movie actor, a member by marriage of the Kennedy clan, and a respected Republican activist. He accomplished all this through sheer force of brainpower and will. As a teenager in Austria, he later remembered, he had been appalled when some of his friends, not yet into their twenties, were discussing job prospects in terms of pension plans. He wanted out of such a preplanned, predigested life. He wanted freedom, glamour, upward mobility, big challenges. He also wanted money, the freedom and power of it, and from the beginning of his California life, he paid attention to business. While still a bodybuilder, he began to invest in real estate. He would eventually own a diversified portfolio valued at over $200 million. Motion pictures brought him the fame he had dreamed of as a youngster. He starred as himself in his first successful film, *Pumping Iron* (1976). In an earlier effort, *Hercules in New York* (1970), his Austrian accent was so thick his lines had to be dubbed. By 2003, he had appeared in twenty-seven movies grossing more than $1.6 billion.

Still, he wanted more. As a European, Schwarzenegger instinctively knew the strength that can come from an alliance with an established family: an insight that few American motion picture stars—ricocheting from marriage to marriage with one or another of their own kind—have ever learned. In 1986, at the Kennedy compound in Hyannis, he married Maria Shriver and hence became a Kennedy by assimilation. In slightly more than fifteen years, this penniless immigrant, now a multimillionaire and international film star (and a college graduate), was an adopted member of America's most formidable political clan. Troubled in his relationship to his own father, he now had for in-laws Sargent and Eunice Shriver: the sister of a beloved president and, in his father-in-law, the first director of the Peace Corps, a onetime vice presidential candidate, and one of the leading knights of the Camelot roundtable.

The perfect storm of the summer of 2003 also included Arnold Schwarzenegger's realization that, four years from sixty, it was time for him to make the transition from action movie star to serious political candidate. Critics had been kind to *Terminator 3,* released in the summer of 2003, but it was apparent to everyone that Schwarzenegger was approaching a point in his film career in which he had either to evolve into a character actor, which is always a difficult transition for a featured star to make, or get out of films entirely. Significantly enough, at a sneak preview of *Terminator 3* in June in Santa Monica, people were coming up to Schwarzenegger and urging him to run for governor. Up until the last minute—to the moment he announced on the Jay Leno show on August 6—not even Schwarzenegger's closest associates knew his intentions.

Disinterested in state government—indeed, in politics in general—Californians, along with the rest of the nation, had long since begun to take their governance, psychologically and subliminally, from entertainment. A Hollywood wag had once observed that politics was show business for ugly people. Now show business had become politics for the good-looking. From this perspective, whether from the left or the right, activists such as Charlton Heston, Barbra Streisand, Bruce Willis, Sean Penn, Warren Beatty, and Arnold Schwarzenegger had long since become politicians. Schwarzenegger understood this better than most. He was, after all, a Kennedy by assimilation and specific instruction from his wife and in-laws, and the Kennedys had helped invent entertainment politics. When the recall unexpectedly offered Schwarzenegger an opportunity to avoid the conservative-dominated Republican primary that he could never win, given his rowdy behavior (as he would later describe it) in the past, or his laissez-faire attitudes toward sexual and lifestyle issues, he and his advisors knew that he now had the chance to make an end run around the traditional pathway to the governorship. He could avoid debates, hardball interviews with print and television journalists, the issuance of policy wonk white papers, and town hall meetings, and effect instead a direct subliminal connection with each voter through friendly talk-radio interviews and highly orchestrated celebrity appearances with Jay Leno, Oprah Winfrey, Howard Stern, Larry King, and other friendly folk. Gray Davis offered to debate him one on one. Schwarzenegger wisely declined. When Schwarzenegger did speak, he stayed on message, and this message—about a young immigrant who achieved everything because of California and wanted to give back to the people of California—was based not on any strident Republicanism (indeed, Schwarzenegger ran a virtually party-neutral campaign), but on the assumption that he could speak, and was speaking, to each Californian on an individual basis.

The early American theorists of film—Hugo Münsterberg, Vachel Lindsay, William Dean Howells—had each noted the particularly personal relationship audiences had with the characters on the screen. Even more powerfully than Ronald Reagan, who was not as well known as an actor, Schwarzenegger tapped into, instantly, this near-primal relationship and never strayed outside of its confines. When the *Los Angeles Times* published multiple allegations of groping just days before the election, the charges could not sever this subliminal connection, even among women, who voted for him in significant numbers, as did Latinos, union members, independents, and run-of-the-mill Democrats. Schwarzenegger apologized for his behavior just before embarking on a four-day bus tour of the state, culminating in a rally on the steps of the state Capitol, with the candidate holding a broom in his hands and promising to clean up Sacramento.

And so a naturalized Austrian immigrant was overwhelmingly elected (4,203,596 votes, 48.6 percent of the total votes cast) to replace Gray Davis as chief executive of California and hence, by definition, to embody California values. In casting their vote for Schwarzenegger, Californians were going beyond the mere facts of the fiscal crisis or whatever other reasons were being given for the recall. They were voting in one of their own: someone who had assembled a big-time life from small-time beginnings, an immigrant who could now drive his Hummer straight down the highway to Sacramento. Arnold Schwarzenegger was a Californian who had spent most of his life, even the successful parts of it, on the edge, pushing the limits, defying the odds, making an end run around his formative circumstances.

Was California the Great Exception, as Carey McWilliams had described it—a better place for ordinary people—or had that belief gone by the wayside? In times past, Americans had come to California, the coast of dreams, in search of a better life, and that was still happening. But the California of 1990–2003 had grown incredibly complex, competitive, and cold, in comparison to the dreamy lotus land that had once been imagined, even believed in, by many. No longer was California to be found first in its myth and then in reality. California had become, rather, a reality in search of a myth that had once been believed in, had been lost, but never fully repudiated. That dream, in fact, had been the first and only premise of the Schwarzenegger campaign.

Fewer and fewer people were speaking of the California dream these days. Like the newly elected governor, more were talking about the challenges facing California, especially in the matter of growth, the state budget, and the once-again-embattled economy. And many were predicting disaster. For a good part of the twentieth century, California had been building its regional institutions, public and private. Now, its private institutions—its banks, generators, newspapers—were being put, increasingly, up for sale, and its public culture, in the field of energy at least, had been deconstructed and made retail. Still, the public sector—the universities and colleges, the high schools, libraries, museums, parks, recreational facilities of every sort—remained, even when embattled, a sustaining reminder of Progressive California and the sweeping optimism and can-do attitude of the postwar period. The question: Could Californians continue to pay for all this? Even more precisely: Were Californians willing to pay for all this, even if they had the revenues in hand? And if not, what were they *willing* to pay for? What was the California they wanted to hold in common?

Once, Americans had come to California to get away from it all. Now the peoples of the world were arriving, as Arnold Schwarzenegger had, to take their chances with life on the edge. For many, that edge was dropping off into nowhere. For others, it offered a toehold, at least a road sign, and sometimes even a lottery ticket, in the direction of a better way of life. In times past, California had advertised itself as offering the highest possible life for the middle classes. Now, the state was becoming increasingly divided among the very rich, the merely rich, the affluent, the embattled middle and blue-collar classes, a growing number of the downwardly mobile, the poverty stricken, the marginalized, and those who had fallen completely below the graph. Once, people retired to California. Now, they were retiring *from* California, selling their homes at inflated prices, taking their money, and going to kinder, gentler places.

But for those whose tickets were punched, or were otherwise competitive or, better yet, fiercely competitive with nothing to lose, California remained a rewarding place in that it continued to be dynamically expressive—perhaps still on the cutting edge—of the American Dream, with all that that implied. Being fiercely competitive in California could take many forms and could be found in many sectors of society. An entire generation of immigrant Californians had proved itself in its capacity for hard work, its devotion to family, its determination to fit into American society, while a smaller sector of affluent Anglo California had proved itself by taking one or another mode of slacking off or opting out; indeed, by the early 2000s, the California Slacker—young white people going nowhere and caring even less—had become a recognizable stereotype.

Whatever the dangers and disappointments of California, however, people were still coming. The political television ad of the 1994 gubernatorial election, telling Californians that still they were coming, coming, coming, had gotten it exactly right. When legal, they were coming by plane, train, bus, and car. When not legal, they came anyway, by foot across deadly deserts, by ship in suffocating containers, in the trunks of cars, beneath the floorboards of trucks, or merely by overstaying their visas. This was not commendable, perhaps, in terms of those who had legally waited their turn, but testimony nevertheless to the persistent dream of a better life—now being measured against a growing global violence and deprivation—that had always been peopling California. In their frequently clumsy and inconclusive way these newcomers were raising American culture to new levels of effective ecumenism. By 2003, if and when the United States wanted to see and know itself as a successful world commonwealth, an ecumenopolis, all it had to do was to look to California as it remained the coast of dreams, even if so many of these dreams were, increasingly, on the edge.

ACKNOWLEDGMENTS

Bruce Harris of Random House first suggested that I write this book. My literary agent, Sandra Dijkstra, placed it with Alfred A. Knopf, where Ashbel Green took charge of the project. Sheldon Meyer, my good friend and editor for life, helped me pare down the manuscript to acceptable length. I dedicate this book to these four professionals with pleasure and gratitude. Without them, this book would still be lost on the Coast of Dreams.

As state librarian of California, I have had the pleasure of being associated with the scholars and research analysts of the California Research Bureau. In so many instances, CRB publications have helped me understand contemporary California. Dean Misczynski, bureau chief of the CRB, and Paul Smith, general counsel to the State Library, generously read the manuscript in draft and made valuable suggestions. The reference librarians of the California History Room at the State Library, especially John Gonzales, have been most helpful. Retired Santa Clara University professor of history Peter O'Malley Pierson kindly read the galleys of this book. Sarah Ereira of London prepared a masterful index. In each and every phase of writing this book, I have benefited from the research and editorial skills, the judgment and good sense, of my wife, Sheila Starr, with whom I have shared life's journey these past forty years.

NOTES

FREQUENTLY CITED NEWSPAPERS

Associated Press	AP
California Research Bureau	CRB
Daily News of Los Angeles	*Daily News*
Fresno Bee	*FBee*
Los Angeles Times	*LAT*
New York Times	*NYT*
Orange County Register	*OCR*
Sacramento Bee	*SacBee*
San Diego Union-Tribune	*SDUT*
San Francisco Chronicle	*SFCh*
San Francisco Examiner	*SFEx*
San Jose Mercury News	*SJMN*
United Press International	UPI
Wall Street Journal	*WSJ*
Washington Post	*WP*

PART I / Coast of Dreams

1. Kathryn Bold, "Her Big Break," *LAT*, 4 Dec. 1997.

2. D. James Romero, "Having a Swell Time," *LAT*, 17 Sept. 1997.

3. Amy Wallace, "Waves of Feelings," *LAT*, 6 Sept. 1993.

4. Matea Gold, "Miracle Workers," *LAT*, 27 July 1998.

5. John Dart, "Birth Rite," *LAT*, 5 May 1997.

6. Deepa Bharath, "Ancient Buddhist Fire Ritual Draws Thousands," *LAT*, 16 Apr. 2000.

7. Jim Doyle, "Restoration of the Sacred in Berkeley," *SFCh*, 26 Oct. 1996.

8. Edward Silver, "Finding a New Path," *LAT*, 11 Apr. 1995.

9. John Cornwell, "Is Mind Merely Matter?" *Sunday Times* (London), 15 May 1994.

10. Robert Lee Hotz, "The Brain: A Work in Progress," *LAT*, 16 Oct. 1996.

11. Claire MacElroy, "Age Bias in the High-Tech Industry," Letters to the Editor, *SFCh*, 27 Apr. 1998.

12. R. W. Apple Jr., "In a Berkeley Kitchen, a Celebration of Simplicity," *NYT*, 17 Nov. 1999.

13. Alan Goldfarb, "Living with the Wines," *Image, Sunday SFCh and SFEx*, 11 Oct. 1992.

14. Thomas Rosenstiel and Stephen Braun, "Entertainment, Media Leaders' Power Cited," *LAT*, 16 Sept. 1987.

15. Alan Citron, "The New Adventures of the Barefoot Billionaire," *LAT*, 7 Mar. 1993.

16. Hunter Drohojowska, "A Cut Above: Alexis Smith Has Expanded Collage to Monumental Proportions, Mixing Pop Culture Images with Snippets of Fiction," *LAT,* 22 Mar. 1992.

17. Robert Hughes, "California in Eupeptic Color," *Time,* 27 June 1977.

18. Kurt Andersen, "Desert Cool," *The New Yorker,* 23 Feb. and 2 Mar. 1998, 135.

19. Herbert Muschamp, "An Enterprise Zone for the Imagination," *NYT,* 14 Mar. 1993.

PART II / Catastrophe

1. Tini Tran, "Laguna Beach House Slides Down Wet Hill into Ravine," *LAT,* 10 Mar. 1998.

2. Phil Garlington, "Pot Grower Insists Others' Medical Needs Let Him Flaunt Weed," *OCR,* 11 May 1997.

3. Richard Marosi, "Three Guilty in Death of Informant, 17," *LAT,* 19 Oct. 1999.

4. "Three Get Life Terms in Informant's Slaying," *LAT,* 8 Jan. 2000.

5. Kevin Fagan and Neva Chonin, "Young, Rich, and Strung Out," *SFCh,* 8 Jan. 1999.

6. AP, "Details of a 'Senseless' Coalinga Carjack Killing," *SFCh,* 1 Nov. 1994.

7. "Sanyika Shakur, a.k.a. Monster Kody Scott," *Esquire* (April 1993), 87.

8. Robert Lopez and Jesse Katz, "Mexican Mafia Tells Gangs to Halt Drive-bys," *LAT,* 26 Sept. 1993.

9. Anne Roark, "It's Dope, So Chill. For the Young, Slang's Mad New Words Are Straight Off the Streets of Los Angeles," *LAT,* 18 Aug. 1992.

10. Amy Wallace, "Li'l Monster and Bone Offer Nation New Image of Gangs," *LAT,* 18 May 1992.

11. Richard Lee Colvin, "Judge Issues Sweeping Injunction Against Gang," *LAT,* 8 Apr. 1993.

12. Michael Krikorian, "City Seeks Injunction Against 40 Hollywood Gang Members," *LAT,* 6 Mar. 1998.

13. Henry Weinstein, "Rampart Probe May Now Affect over 3000 Cases," *LAT,* 15 Dec. 1999.

14. Anne-Marie O'Connor, "Massive Gang Member List Now Clouded by Rampart," *LAT,* 15 Dec. 1999.

15. Fredric Tulski and Ted Rohrlich, "Only One in Three Killings in LA Lead to Any Punishment," *LAT,* 1 Dec. 1995.

16. Dan Morain, "More Inmate Privileges Fall in Get-Tough Drive," *LAT,* 9 Feb. 1998.

17. Mark Arax and Mark Gladstone, "Grand Jury Indicts Eight for Abuses in State Prison Case," *LAT,* 27 Feb. 1998.

18. Dean Murphy, "Ace of Spades—Unlikely Clique of Militaristic Teens," *LAT,* 22 June 1992.

19. Dianne Griego Erwin, "Killer Showed Us His True Nature," *SacBee,* 20 June 1996.

20. "The World of Fear," *LAT,* 18 Mar. 1993.

21. "Everyone Should Be Scared," *LAT,* 26 Sept. 1993.

22. Tracy Weber, "Systematic Child Abuse," *LAT,* 21 May 1998.

23. "Fresno Shaken by Gang Rape of Three Girls," *SFCh,* 7 May 1998.

24. Nora Zamichow, "Strohmeyer Parents Sue County over Adoption Process," *LAT,* 16 Oct. 1999.

25. Tony Perry, "Drifter Testifies God Led Him to Kill Boy, 9," *LAT,* 22 Sept. 1999.

26. "6th Graders Encouraged to Get Hepatitis B Shots," *SFCh,* 12 Jan. 1999.

27. Laurie Becklund, "I Wanted Somebody to Love," *LAT,* 14 Mar. 1993.

28. Rene Sanchez and William Booth, "California Toughens Juvenile Crime Laws," *WP*, 13 Mar. 2000.

29. Larry Stammer, "Bishops Urge Wide Justice Reform," *LAT*, 15 Nov. 2000.

30. Jeff Adler and William Booth, "Five Wounded in Month's 2nd Calif. School Shooting," *WP*, 23 Mar. 2001.

31. Sandy Banks, "The Suburb That Closed Its Heart to a Newcomer," *LAT*, 11 Mar. 2001.

32. Mike Davis, *City of Quartz* (1990), p. 86.

33. Frank Clifford, "Has Police Beating of King Taken the Luster off LA?" *LAT*, 14 Apr. 1991.

34. Sam Johnson, "LA a Safe City, Bradley Assures Japanese," *LAT*, 24 Apr. 1991.

35. Bob Pool, "Sharp Edge," *LAT*, 13 Sept. 1991.

36. Frank Clifford, "Coalition Looks for Ties That Bind a Diverse City," *LAT*, 26 Oct. 1991.

37. John Mitchell, "Gleaming Mall Struggles to Attract Tenants, Clients," *LAT*, 25 Nov. 1991.

38. Daniel Fromstein, " 'Bogeyman' Overkills," *Daily Trojan*, 17 Sept. 1991.

39. Greg Krikorian, "Amnesty International Ends LA Visit in Probe of Brutality Allegations," *LAT*, 29 Sept. 1999.

40. *LAT, Understanding the Riots*, p. 45.

41. Ibid., p. 50.

42. Ted Rohrlich and Richard Serrano, "Riot Found Police in Disarray," *LAT*, 6 May 1992.

PART III / Diversity

1. George Ramos, "Cesar Chavez Dies at 66," *LAT*, 24 Apr. 1993.

2. Richard Rodriguez, "Cesar Chavez: He Belongs Forever to California and to the Mexican Past," *LAT*, 2 May 1993.

3. "Toil and Trouble," City Times insert, *LAT*, 27 Feb. 1994.

4. Kevin Baxter, "Domestic Policy," *LAT*, 31 Aug. 1997.

5. Anne-Marie O'Connor, "Mexico City of Promise," *LAT*, 26 Jan. 1998.

6. Anne-Marie O'Connor, "Marriage Made in Tijuana," *LAT*, 1 Mar. 1998.

7. Jonathan Tilove, "Rise of the 'Ampersand American,' " *San Francisco Sunday Examiner and Chronicle*, 15 Feb. 1998.

8. Karl Schoenberger, "Living Off Expatriate Labor," *LAT*, 1 Aug. 1994.

9. Karl Schoenberger, "Breathing Life into Southland," *LAT*, 4 Oct. 1993.

10. Jake Doherty and Sean Waters, "Dodgers to Debut with 'Chan Ho-Mania,' " *LAT*, 3 Apr. 1994.

11. K. Connie Chang, "Suicide a Symbol of Workplace Prejudice," *LAT*, 27 Mar. 2000.

12. Bettina Boxall, "Asian Indians Remake Silicon Valley," *LAT*, 6 Jul. 2001.

13. Andrew Lam, "Goodbye Saigon. Finally," *NYT*, 30 Apr. 1993.

14. Donald Coleman, "Vietnamese Celebrate Formation of Association," *FBee*, 16 Mar. 1997.

15. Seth Mydans, "From Cambodia to Doughnut Shops," *NYT*, 26 May 1995.

16. Jane Gross, "Poor Seekers of Good Life Flock to California," *NYT*, 29 Dec. 1991.

17. Stephen Magagnini, "Refugee Parents Face Conflict with Kids," *SacBee*, 16 Dec. 1996.

18. Mark Arax, "The Child Brides of California," *LAT*, 4 May 1993.

19. Joel Kotkin, "Urban Renewers," *Inc.* (March 1996).

20. Richard Rodriguez, "Closed Doors," *LAT,* 15 Aug. 1993.

21. John Dart, "New Muslim Panel Decrees a Date for Start of Ramadan," *LAT,* 20 Jan. 1996.

22. Robert Collier, "Russians in the Richmond," *SFCh,* 13 June 1993.

PART IV / Wedge Issues

1. Alexander Cockburn, "A Big Green Bomb Aimed at Immigration," *LAT,* 2 Oct. 1997.

2. Kenneth B. Noble, "Thai Workers Are Set Free in California," *NYT,* 4 Aug. 1995.

3. Denise Hamilton, "A Long Lesson in Hate," *LAT,* 23 Apr. 1992.

4. Jill Gottesman, "Selection of College President Stirs Anger," *LAT,* 13 Mar. 1993.

5. Bettina Boxall and Anne-Marie O'Connor, "Gas Blower Ban Takes Effect; Results Mixed," *LAT,* 14 Feb. 1998.

6. Bill Plaschke, "Star-Spangled Banter," *LAT,* 17 Feb. 1998.

7. Kenneth B. Noble, "Sympathies Sharply Divided on Beatings of 2 Immigrants," *NYT,* 6 May 1996.

8. Michael Dougan, "Judge's Final Say: Prop. 187 Unenforceable," *SFEx,* 18 Dec. 1997.

9. Stephanie Elizondo Griest, "Immigrant, Teacher, and Now Filmmaker," *NYT,* 30 June 1997.

10. Rich Lowry, "Rolling Back Quotas," *National Review,* 2 Sept. 1996.

11. Tim Golden, "Federal Appeals Court Upholds California's Ban on Preferences," *NYT,* 9 Apr. 1997.

12. Chang-Lin Tien, "A View from Berkeley," *NYT,* 31 Mar. 1996.

13. Ron Unz, "Bilingual Is a Damaging Myth," *LAT,* 19 Oct. 1997.

14. Bob Sylva, "Getting Through," *SacBee,* 18 Mar. 1998.

15. Cathleen Decker and Mark Barabak, "State GOP Backs Anti-Bilingual Education Drive," *LAT,* 29 Sept. 1997.

16. Amy Pyle, "LA Schools to Fight English-Only Testing," *LAT,* 18 Feb. 1998.

17. Liz Seymour, "Following the Letters of the Law: Zoe Garcia, Who Opposed Prop 227, Is Making a Concerted Effort at Immersion with Surprising Results," *LAT,* 16 Nov. 1998.

18. Christopher Knight, "Exploring the Border Experience," *LAT,* 13 Mar. 1993.

19. Ali Modarres, "Two Decades of Immigration: Has the Sky Fallen Yet?" *State of Immigration* (Pat Brown Institute of Public Affairs, CSU Los Angeles, 2000), p. 4.

PART V / Turnaround

1. Jonathan Peterson, "The Trouble with Success," *LAT,* 17 Dec. 1989.

2. Robert Reinhold, "California Is Not Laid Back Anymore When It Comes to Holding On to Jobs," *NYT,* 12 Aug. 1991.

3. Ralph T. King Jr., "Real Estate Experts See the Next Disaster in Central Los Angeles," *WSJ,* 27 Aug. 1991.

4. Frederick Rose, "The 'New Joads' Hit the Road," *WSJ,* 9 Jan. 1993.

5. Ronald Brownstein, "Crisis of Confidence Grips US," *LAT,* 27 Jan. 1992.

6. Werner Hirsch, "The California Dream Is Far from Over," *LAT,* 15 Jan. 1992.

7. James F. Peltz, "Down but Not Out," *LAT,* 26 Sept. 1993.

8. Robin Clark, "Expatriate Californians Finding 'Elsewhere' Isn't What They Want," *Daily News,* 27 Nov. 1993.

9. Gus Koehler, "New Challenges to California State Government's Economic Development Engine" (CRB, 21 Mar. 1994), p. 5.

10. Tim Ferguson, "California Comeback," *Forbes,* 20 Nov. 1995.

11. David Friedman, "The Myth That Threatens to Eat California's Future," *LAT,* 20 Feb. 1994.

12. James Flannigan, "Let Defense Cash Flow Nurture New Business," *LAT,* 22 Nov. 1992.

13. Robert Rosenblatt, "Strong Growth Projected for California," *LAT,* 29 Jan. 1997.

14. Scott Brown, "How Gray Is My Valley," *Time,* 18 Nov. 1991.

15. Tom Abate, "Zschau Takes the Helm at Adstar," *SFEx,* 27 Apr. 1993.

16. Jonathan Weber, "In Search of Computing's Holy Grail," *LAT,* 27 Sept. 1992.

17. Greg Miller, "Computer Age Enters Maturity," *LAT,* 28 Dec. 1998.

18. Joel Kotkin, "High Tech Hype," *Techno Manifesto* (Summer 1997).

19. Quentin Hardy, "Digital Gentry," *WSJ,* 8 Oct. 1996.

20. Kenneth Weiss and Paul Jacobs, "Cal Tech Joins Rush to Foster Biotech Spinoff Companies," *LAT,* 16 Sept. 1998.

21. Frederick Rose, "How a US Company Used Anti-Japan Mood to Help Reverse a Loss," *WSJ,* 22 Apr. 1992.

22. David G. Timberman, "In Search of a Pacific Basin Community," *Asian Survey,* May 1981.

23. Octavio Paz, *The Labyrinth of Solitude* (1961), p. 13.

24. Louis Uchitelle, "America's Newest Industrial Belt," *NYT,* 21 Mar. 1993.

25. Dave Lesher, "Davis Arrives in Mexico to Start Mending Fences," *LAT,* 2 Feb. 1999.

26. George Skelton, "Zedillo's Visit a Kodak Moment for Governor Davis," *LAT,* 20 May 1999.

27. James F. Smith and Mark Arax, "Fox Barnstorms Across State," *LAT,* 23 Mar. 2001.

PART VI / Cities, Suburbs, and Other Places

1. Thomas Bender, "City Lite," *SacBee,* 12 Jan. 1997.

2. Bettuane Levine, "How *Sunset* Won the West," *LAT,* 1 May 1998.

3. Nancy Wride, "The Ultimate Material Girl," *LAT,* 8 May 1991.

4. Neal Pierce, "Mainstream Invades Suburbia," *WP,* 29 Nov. 1998.

5. E. Scott Reckard, "Homes with Attitude," *LAT,* 26 Apr. 1998.

6. Charles Burress, "War of Words in Berkeley," *SFCh,* 21 Aug. 1998.

7. Joseph Hanania, "From Mustard to Myanmar, West Hollywood Has an Opinion," *LAT,* 6 Oct. 1997.

8. Tom Gorman, "A City Wracked by Woe," *LAT,* 10 Oct. 1995.

9. Mark Arax, Mary Curtius, and Soraya Sarhaddi Nelson, "California Income Gap Grows amid Prosperity," *LAT,* 9 Jan. 2000.

10. Richard Rodriguez, "Are You Afraid to Go to Oakland?" *LAT,* 5 Apr. 1992.

11. April Lynch, "Oakland's Wave of Violence—A Shocking Toll," *SFCh,* 13 Mar. 1992.

12. Rick DelVecchio, "Jerry Brown Is Secure, Popular—and Having Fun," *SFCh,* 19 Jul. 1999.

13. Heather MacDonald, "Jerry Brown's No-Nonsense New Age for Oakland," *City Journal* (Autumn 1999), p. 40.

14. Adam Rogers, "A New Brand of Tech Cities," *Newsweek,* 30 Apr. 2001.

15. Martha Groves, "Oakland Military Charter School Okd," *LAT*, 7 Dec. 2000.

16. John Glionna, "Tour of Oakland Takes GOP Leaders to Political Terra Incognita," *LAT*, 14 Jul. 2001.

17. Carl Nolte, "Most-Changed City Is San Jose," *SFCh*, 2 Sept. 1999.

18. Morris Newman, "In San Jose, Hopes for a More Livable Downtown," *NYT*, 5 Sept. 1999.

PART VII / A Tale of Two Cities: Los Angeles and San Francisco

1. John Mitchell, "Home Screen Advantage," *LAT*, 14 Feb. 1998.

2. Bill Yankes, "One Person on Fire," *Humanist* (November-December 1992).

3. Jocelyn Stewart, "Our Town," *LAT Magazine*, 7 Jan. 2001.

4. Andrew Lam, "Hong Kong by the Bay," *LAT*, 26 Aug. 2001.

5. "Can LA Still Make It?" *Economist*, 27 Jul. 1991.

6. Roger Boas, "SF Must Counter Loss of BofA," *SFCh*, 28 Apr. 1998.

7. Peter Sinton, "BofA CEO May Reap $30 Million," *SFCh*, 15 Aug. 1998.

8. Kristina Sauerwein and Allison Cohen, "Tattered Clothes of Poverty Prove Costly in Classroom," *LAT*, 20 Feb. 2000.

9. Douglas Shuit, Claire Spiegel, and Irene Wielawski, "Hospitals Walk-In Powder Kegs," *LAT*, 10 Feb. 1993.

10. John L. Mitchell and Shawn Hubler, "Patient at County-USC Shoots 3 Doctors, Gives Up in Standoff," *LAT*, 9 Feb. 1993.

11. Bob Howard, "Homeward Bound: States Top Builder Sees a Great Need for Affordable New Housing," *LAT*, 16 June 1998.

12. Carla Hall, "The Prince and the Pauper: LA's Homeless Get the Royal Treatment from Prince Edward," *LAT*, 11 Dec. 1993.

13. Mary Curtius, "In San Francisco, Liberal vs. Ultraliberal," *LAT*, 26 Nov. 1999.

14. Elizabeth Mehren, "Do We Want to Stay in LA?" *LAT*, 11 May 1992.

15. Paul Robinson, "The Danger of Defending the Denny Acquittals," *WSJ*, 27 Oct. 1993.

16. Kathleen Decker and Sheryl Stolberg, "Half of Americans Disagree with Verdict," *LAT*, 4 Oct. 1995.

17. Robert A. Jones, "Mirroring a Deep Divide Among Us," *LAT*, 4 Oct. 1995.

18. George Will, "A Wrong Road to Self-Esteem in the Bay Area," *SFCh*, 11 May 1998.

19. Maria La Ganga, "Pot Candidate: High Hopes, High Visibility," *LAT*, 3 Apr. 1998.

20. Nanette Asimov, "SF High Schools to Get Diverse Authors List," *SFCh*, 21 Mar. 1998.

21. Jason Johnson and Edward Epstein, "SF Welfare Cuts Unleash Rage," *SFCh*, 21 Apr. 1998.

22. David Freed, "Hollywood's Shooting, and Not Just Films," *LAT*, 21 May 1992.

23. Philip Hager, "LAPD Losing Public Support, Judge Says," *LAT*, 8 May 1992.

24. Marc Lacey and James Rainey, "Riordan Calls for Mediator in LAPD Sick-Out," *LAT*, 1 June 1994.

25. Tracy Lovejoy as told to Robert Scheer, "It's like a Third World Country," *LAT*, 9 May 1994.

26. Larry Gordon, "New Life Planned for Old Downtown Buildings," *LAT*, 27 Sept. 1993.

27. Ann Marsh, "In LA Dating Is No Game," *LAT*, 18 May 2001.

28. Mimi Avins, "A Place with Every Single Thing—and More," *LAT*, 13 Aug. 2000.

29. Ambrose Clancy, "A Wild Colonial in England," *LAT,* 7 May 2001.

30. Cynthia Robins, " 'Mad Dog' Ellroy Sounds Off," *SFEx,* 4 Oct. 1992.

PART VIII / Growth and the Environment

1. Dan Smith, "Fresno County's Growing Pains," *[Riverside] Press Enterprise,* 15 Oct. 1996.

2. Mary Lynne Vellinga, "Surprise! West Isn't the Leader in Suburban Sprawl, Study Finds," *SacBee,* 11 Jul. 2001.

3. Connie Koenenn, "The Challenger," *LAT,* 28 Aug. 1991.

4. David Lazarus, "A Town Diseased and Torn," *SFCh,* 31 Mar. 2000.

5. Tony Perry, "Orphan Whale JJ Begins Long Journey Home," *LAT,* 1 Apr. 1998.

6. Paul Rogers, "Logging Fight Comes Down to the Wire," *Times-Picayune* (New Orleans), 15 Sept. 1996.

7. Jane Kay, "Pacific Lumber Cutting Virgin Forest; 'Salvage Logging' of Redwoods Near Headwaters Grove," *SFEx,* 8 Oct. 1996.

8. Bonnie Hayes, "The Eucalyptus Revolt," *LAT,* 28 Apr. 1998.

9. Gary Polakovic, "State Sues to Block Off-Shore Oil Leases," *LAT,* 17 Nov. 1999.

10. Kenneth R. Weiss, "Lords of the Dunes Battle for Their Patch of Sand," *LAT,* 9 June 2001.

11. Scott Gold, "Officials Invite Violence over Pact, Group Says," *LAT,* 23 Jul. 2001.

12. Mark Arax, "Packard Foundation Puts Its Faith, Funds in the Central Valley," *LAT,* 24 Oct. 1999.

13. John Johnson and Kenneth Weiss, "Speculator Ratchets Up Coastal Costs," *LAT,* 22 Jul. 2001.

14. Shelby Grad, "Turf War Pits Sports Groups vs. Wildlife Backers," *LAT,* 30 Mar. 1998.

15. Associated Press, "LA Subway Opens Its Doors Tomorrow," *SFCh,* 29 Jan. 1993.

16. Mark Stein, "Rail Commuter Era Begins in LA," *LAT,* 27 Oct. 1992.

17. Tim Ferguson, "Who Said Anything About Transportation?" *Forbes,* 4 Dec. 1995.

18. Mike Davis, "Runaway Train Crushes Buses," *Nation,* 18 Sept. 1995.

19. James Moore, Harry Richardson, and Peter Gordon, "The MTA Makes a Right Turn: Will It Stay on Course?" *LAT,* 28 Dec. 1997.

PART IX / Back on the Edge

1. CNN.com, "Clinton Passed the Hat in California," 26 Oct. 1998.

2. BBC News On Line, "Streisand Attacks 'Destructive' Bush," 3 Apr. 2001.

3. Ann O'Neill, "City of Angles," *LAT,* 26 Sept. 2001.

4. David Streitfeld, "The Industry Standard No Longer," *LAT,* 17 Aug. 2001.

5. Shawn Hubler, "Jobless, but Busy, Busy, Busy," *LAT,* 7 Aug. 2001.

6. Amy Chance, "Campaigns See Education Emerging as Central Issue in 1998," *SacBee,* 10 Nov. 1997.

7. Erin Riches, "How We Got to Where We Are Today: A Deregulation Timeline," *The California Budget Project,* 5 June 2001.

8. Emily Bazar, "State to Borrow Up to $5 Billion to Buy Energy," *SacBee,* 20 June 2001.

9. Stuart Leavenworth and Chris Bowman, "Power Crunch," *SacBee,* 28 Jan. 2001.

10. Karen Tumulty and Michael Weisskopf, "Has Bush Seen the Light?" *Time,* 25 June 2001.

11. Carla Marinucci and Lynda Gledhill, "Bush Facing Davis' Heat Over Energy," *SFCh*, 29 May 2001.

12. Ibid.

13. Kenneth Reich and Eric Malnic, "Man Held in Religious Hate Crimes," *LAT*, 7 Nov. 2001.

14. Teresa Watanabe, "At Mosque, Relief and Thanks," *LAT*, 14 Dec. 2001.

15. Teresa Watanabe, "Feeling like the Enemy Within," *LAT*, 20 Sept. 2001.

16. Maria La Ganga, "100 Protesting Cartoon Stage Sit-In at Student Newspaper," *LAT*, 20 Sept. 2001.

17. William Lobdell, "Teachers Terrorism Remarks Stir Academic Freedom Debate," *LAT*, 30 Sept. 2001.

18. Howard Rosenberg, "A Love Note to New York," *LAT*, 4 Jan. 2002.

EPILOGUE / Déjà Vu All Over Again

1. Tom Stienstra, "Invasive Northern Pike Just Won't Die," *SFCh*, 29 Jan. 2003.

2. Suzanne Herel, "Regal Condor Killed in the Wild," *SFCh*, 21 Feb. 2003.

SOURCES

I was privileged to spend the 1990s as a professor at the University of Southern California, a state official, a writer on California topics, and a contributing editor to the Opinion section of the *Los Angeles Times*. I was thus able to track the trends and developments addressed in this book from a variety of perspectives. I was also during this period a voracious consumer of books, pamphlets, government reports, promotional handouts, and assorted other ephemera dealing with California during a roller-coaster decade edging into the millennium. Most importantly, I was able to track the developing story of California in the 1990s through an equally voracious reading of state and national newspapers. Journalistic reports and assorted publications therefore constitute the factual foundation for what I have written in this book. Limitations of space prevent me from listing every newspaper article that has affected my judgment, nor does space allow me to document the hundreds of conversations I had throughout the 1990s that also helped shape my story and conclusions.

Journalism, it has been said, is history in a hurry. Even in this abbreviated list of sources, therefore, I wish to pay tribute to the first-rate journalists who throughout the decade provided me not only with the factual record of what was happening, but the more intriguing challenge of asking myself what, in the long run, of all the things that were happening, history would eventually remember.

PART I / Coast of Dreams

Surf's Up!

The Coast
Herbert Gold, "California in the '80s," *This World (SFCh)*, 31 Aug. 1981.
Jerry Hulse, "To Sir, with Love," *LAT*, 12 May 1991.
Post Ranch Inn at Big Sur, promotional brochure with inserts, 1992.
Susan Spano, "Making Sense of Elusive Malibu," *NYT*, 5 Jan. 1992.
Matthew Jaffe, "Malibu, Naturally," *Sunset* (March 1992).
Richard Paddock, "Playground for the Rich: New Resort at Big Sur Is Seen as a Symbol of the Transformation of an Area Once Known for Free Spirits," *LAT*, 21 Apr. 1992.
Charles Davis, "Big Sur Surprise: Post Ranch Inn, Hotel with View to the Environment," *Monterey County Herald*, 3 May 1992.
Sally Ogle Davis, "Mr. Post Builds His Dream Hotel," *LAT Magazine,* 24 May 1992.
Susan Benner, "Just Across the Golden Gate," *NYT,* 29 Nov. 1992.
Daniel Lewis, "Point Reyes: Paradise Retouched," *NYT,* 29 Nov. 1992.
Michael Konik, "A Pacific Coast Sampler: From San Francisco Bay to Malibu," *Newsday,* 15 Jan. 1995.

Jesus Sanchez, "Transamerica to Sell Posh Ventana Inn," *LAT*, 6 Dec. 1997.
Susan Spano, "California Dreamin'," *LAT*, 14 June 1998.

Surfing
J. M. Fenster, "Catching the Endless Wave," *NYT*, 2 Apr. 1989.
C. R. Stecyk III, "The Player," *Surfers' Journal* (Spring 1993).
Emily Yoffe, "Is Kary Mullis God? Nobel Prize Winner's New Life," *Esquire* (July 1994).
John M. Glionna, "The Evolution of Beach-Going Etiquette," *LAT*, 4 May 1997.
Paul McHugh, "Breaking Waves, Breaking Hearts," *SFCh*, 29 Jan. 1998.
Russ Stanton, "K2 Is Newest Surf Apparel Dude in Town," *LAT*, 19 Mar. 1998.
Rose Apodaca Jones, "Suave Surfer Stokes New Style," *LAT*, 30 Apr. 1998.
Leslie Earnest, "Surf 'n Turf," *LAT*, 26 June 1998.
Michael Quintanilla, "Sauntering into Summer," *LAT*, 25 May 2001.

Zen California

Health/Fitness
Scott Brown, "Pursuit of Perfection," *Time*, 18 Nov. 1991.
Jacqueline Metcalfe, "Healthy Hiatus," *Essence* (April 1997).
Carol Ness, "Gays Find Worship of Beauty a Beast," *SFEx*, 14 Dec. 1997.
Max Vanzi and Carl Ingram, "Lifting Smoking Ban Faces Tough Fight," *LAT*, 30 Jan. 1998.
Tara Aronson, "Working Out While Staying In," *SFCh*, 20 May 1998.
Herbert Gold, "Beyond the Golden Door," *SFEx Magazine*, 12 Jul. 1998.

High-Tech Sports
Beverly Bayette, "Downhill Thrills," *LAT*, 26 Sept. 1990.
Sally Donnelly, "Hot House of Champions," *Time*, 18 Nov. 1991.
Carol Emert, "Sporting an Attitude," *SFCh*, 4 Apr. 1998.
William Abeel, "Baywatch," *American Wind Surfer* (1998).

The Religious Impulse
Kevin Brass, "Gothic Temple Stirs a Debate," *NYT*, 21 Apr. 1991.
Lynn Smith, "Schuller's Son Steps In to Keep the Ministry's Message Flowing," *LAT*, 12 Oct. 1991.
Bill Lindelof, "His Text Is Scripture," *SDUT*, 29 Mar. 1996.
John Dart, "Poll Studies Chinese-Americans, Religion," *LAT*, 5 Jul. 1997.
Larry B. Stammer, "Diverse Adherents Await Bartholomew I," *LAT*, 6 Nov. 1997.
Debora Vrana, "Designing a Mall-Like Ambience for Worship," *LAT*, 8 Nov. 1997.
Patrice Apodaca, "Southland: Television's Bible Belt," *LAT*, 12 Jan. 1998.
"Spiritual Quests in Silicon Valley," *SFCh*, 5 Feb. 1998.
Karen Robinson-Jacobs, "Church Construction Is Looking Up," *LAT*, 17 Feb. 1998.
Larry B. Stammer, "Vote Planned on Fate of Historic Temple," *LAT*, 28 Mar. 1998.
John M. Glionna, "A Path Less Traveled," *LAT*, 16 Mar. 1998.
Alan Abrahamson, "Area's Jewish Population Held Steady by Migration," *LAT*, 4 Jul. 1998.
Margaret Ramirez, "A Day of Devotion Downtown," *LAT*, 15 Sept. 1999.
Rick Lyman, "A Sleeper Movie Awakened by a Hungry Audience," *NYT*, 25 Oct. 1999.
Kathleen Pender, "Praying for Stock Options," *SFCh*, 3 May 2000.
Mary Rourke, "Religious Studies, Left Coast Style," *LAT*, 27 May 2001.
Teresa Watanabe, "Global Convention Testifies to Pentecostal Revival," *LAT*, 31 May 2001.

Joanna Corman, "Hindus Gather in Pomona for Reading of Early Epic," *LAT*, 30 June 2001.
Teresa Watanabe, "Cheering Religious Diversity," *LAT*, 7 Jul. 2001.
Roy Rivenburg, "Heaven Can't Wait," *LAT*, 8 Jul. 2001.
Teresa Watanabe, "Reaching Out past a Taboo," *LAT*, 8 Jul. 2001.

New Age
Molly O'Neill, "Roman Catholic Rebel Becomes a Cause Celebre," *NYT*, 17 Mar. 1993.
Roy Rivenburg, "A True Conversion?" *LAT*, 21 Mar. 1993.
Bob Sipchen, "Tracking the Mystical Traveler," *LAT*, 1 Nov. 1994.
Dianne Weddington, "Another Split in Matthew Fox's Cosmos," *National Catholic Reporter*, 1 Nov. 1996.
Mary Rourke, "The Renegade Reverend," *LAT*, 11 Dec. 1996.
Don Lattin, "Prayer Party—Techno Mass Rocks Religious in Oakland," *SFCh*, 25 Feb. 1997.
Katherine Seligman, "Lawsuits Shed Light on Yuba 'Church,' " *SFEx*, 12 Oct. 1997.
Geoff Boucher, "Dancing Until Dawn," *LAT*, 30 Sept. 1999.

Zen Buddhism
Gary Snyder, *No Nature: New and Selected Poems* (1992).
Rosanne Keynan, "Southern California File," *LAT*, 6 May 1995.
John Taylor, "Buddhists Turn Out for Monk," *FBee*, 28 May 1995.
Kathy Bryant, "Deborah Barrett's Life Is Startlingly Simple. And Startlingly Complex," *LAT*, 5 Apr. 1996.
John Dart, "Southland Faithful Celebrate Buddha's Life," *LAT*, 5 May 1997.
John Dart, "Buddhists Plan to Revive Order of Nuns," *LAT*, 24 May 1997.
David DeVoss, "Tibet Makes the Bigtime as the Dalai Lama Tours America," *Asia Times*, 11 June 1997.
Bill Higgins, "Tibetan Monks Get in the Spirit of Benefit Tour," *LAT*, 25 Aug. 1997.
John Krich, "From Tibet to Tinseltown," *SFEx*, 22 Oct. 1997.
Susan Pack, "As Monks in Training, Boys Find Peace, Purity," *SDUT*, 26 Dec. 1997.
"Party Draws 20,000 for Buddha's Birthday," *SFEx*, 28 Apr. 1998.
Teresa Watanabe, "Dalai Lama, Humble Man Inspires Awe," *LAT*, 11 Oct. 1999.
Teresa Watanabe, "Dalai Lama Calls for a New Era of Ethics," *LAT*, 14 Oct. 1999.
Orville Schell, "Dalai Lama in Lotus Land," *SFEx*, 6 Apr. 2000.
Margaret Ramirez, "A Lofty Vision," *LAT*, 17 Feb. 2001.
Elaine Woo, "Rev. Julius Goldwater; Convert to Buddhism Aided WWII Internees," *LAT*, 23 June 2001.

Mind Games

The San Diego Scene
Eric Bailey, "Torrey Pines Research Park Plan Approved," *SDUT*, 5 Dec. 1989.
Ann Gibbon, "The Salk Institute at a Crossroads," *Science* (July 1990).
Tom Gorman, "Business of Biotech Comes of Age in San Diego," *LAT*, 26 May 1991.
Gerald Schultz, "City Looks to High-Tech Community," *National Real Estate Investor* (June 1992).
Herbert Muschamp, "Art and Science Politely Disagree," *NYT*, 16 Nov. 1992.
Sheryl Stolberg, "A Hero with Something to Prove," *LAT*, 7 Mar. 1993.
Herbert Muschamp, "Altering the Salk: Architects' Protest Grows," *NYT*, 6 May 1993.
Michael Granberry, "Salk Defends Construction of Institute Annex," *LAT*, 12 May 1993.

Lewis Wolpert, "Edelman's Thought Factories," *Independent* [*London*], 1 Dec. 1996.
John Krich, "From Tibet to Tinseltown," *SFEx,* 22 Oct. 1997.
Robert Berwick, "The Doors of Perception," *LAT Book Review,* 15 Mar. 1998.
Robert Sanders, "Brain Plan: Imagining a New Center for Neuroscience," *Berkeley Magazine* (Fall 1998).

Wired
Guy Kawasaki, *Selling the Dream* (1991).
David Wharton, "The New Age Meets the PC Age in Mondo 2000," *LAT,* 24 Jan. 1992.
Alexander Besher, "Flying High over the Rim of the Future," *SFEx,* 25 Sept. 1994.
Michael Ybarra, "The User-Friendly Manual to the World of PC Clones," *LAT,* 25 Mar. 1997.
Lois Kazakoff, "Adventure Capitalist," *SFCh,* 11 Dec. 1997.
Jonathan Marshall, "Silicon Valley Tunes In to Cable TV," *SFCh,* 11 Dec. 1997.
Jonathan Marshall, "Wired for the Future," *SFCh,* 29 Jan. 1998.
Kara Swisher, "Oh, What a Tangled Web Silicon Valley Moguls Weave," *WSJ,* 5 Mar. 1998.
Greg Miller, "Pretenders to the Silicon Valley Crown," *LAT,* 8 Mar. 1998.
James Smith, "Salsa and Chips," *LAT,* 8 Mar. 1998.
Karen Kaplan, "Tech Coast," *LAT,* 9 Mar. 1998.
Patrice Apodaca, "A Higher Degree of Demand for 'Techno-MBAs,' " *LAT,* 19 Mar. 1998.
Joel Kotkin, "The Award for the Most Cutthroat Industry Goes to . . . ," *WSJ,* 23 Mar. 1998.
Bobby McGill, "Java Battle Is Brewing," *SFEx,* 26 Mar. 1998.
Greg Miller, "Intuit Gets to It," *LAT,* 6 Apr. 1998.
Melinda Fulmer, "Investing in Bonds," *LAT,* 25 Apr. 1998.
Alan T. Saracevic, "Good Old-Fashioned Wired," *SFEx,* 6 May 1998.
Greg Miller, "Wired Magazine Is Sold to NY Publishing Firm," *LAT,* 9 May 1998.
Gary Chapman, "Counterculture Is Over—Is a Backlash Next?" *LAT,* 25 May 1998.
Jamie Beckett and Tom Abate, "Rock 'n Roll Fantasy," *SFCh,* 23 June 1998.
Jon Swartz, "Tech's High-Flier Soars Again," *SFCh,* 2 Jul. 1998.
Mylene Mangalindan, "Yahoo's Founder Becomes Billionaire," *SFCh,* 3 Jul. 1998.

Heaven's Gate
Gustav Niebuhr, "On the Furthest Fringes of Millennialism," *NYT,* 28 Mar. 1997.
Gustav Niebuhr, "Death in a Cult," *NYT,* 30 Mar. 1997.
Staff Writers, "Web of Death," *Newsweek,* 7 Apr. 1997.

Bon Appétit

Cuisine
Joan Cook, "A Pound of Brie, a Jug of Wine, and Bargains," *NYT,* 5 Jul. 1987.
Coleman Andrews, "An Epicure's Night Out in LA," *NYT,* 2 Apr. 1989.
Laurie Ochoa, "Hot Cuisine—Who Turned Off the Heat?" *LAT Calendar,* 18 Oct. 1992.
Ruth Reichl, "The Lost Art of the Meal," *LAT Calendar,* 18 Oct. 1992.
Leah Garchik, "Cuisine a la Alice Waters at the Louvre," *SFCh,* 13 May 1998.
Michael Bauer, Robin Davis, Janet Fletcher, and Karola Saekel, "Dining Along the Wine Road," *SFCh,* 20 May 1998.
Zillah Bahar, "Savoring Allende's Memoir," *SFEx,* 21 May 1998.
Michele Anna Jordan, "Serving Werner Herzog's Shoe and Other Savory Moments at Chez Panisse," *San Francisco Focus* (August 1996).

Wine

Gerald Lubenow and Annetta Miller, "A New Wave of Winemakers Invades the Napa Valley," *Newsweek,* 24 Aug. 1987.

Anthony Dias Blue, "French Vintner Adds Some American Sparkle," *OCR,* 7 Dec. 1988.

Clifford Carlsen, "Stock Swap Lets French Vintner Expand Business," *San Francisco Business Times,* 13 Mar. 1989.

Anthony Dias Blue, "A Foretaste of Hybrids to Come?" *The Record [Bergen County, NJ],* 19 Mar. 1989.

Anthony Dias Blue, "Another French Vintner Expands into California," *The Record [Bergen County, NJ],* 7 May 1989.

Melanie Wells, "Gallo Savors Its Upscale Wine Options," *SacBee,* 8 May 1997.

Dan Berger, "Pinot Noir Finds a Home in the Russian River Valley," *FBee,* 20 Aug. 1997.

Maria Cianci, "Lunch in the Vineyards," *SFCh,* 3 Sept. 1997.

Dan Berger, "The Wine King," *LAT,* 17 Sept. 1997.

Sandra Ann Harris, "Wines Newest Frontier," *SFEx,* 8 Feb. 1998.

Myrna Oliver, "Jack Davies, 75, Pioneer Winemaker," *The Record [Bergen County, NJ],* 12 Mar. 1998.

Peter Sinton, "California, Italian Wineries Joining Together in Industry Renaissance," *SFCh,* 24 Apr. 1998.

Dumbing Down

Film and Television

Jerry Carroll, "Hollywood Spews Poison, Critic Says," *SFCh,* 23 Oct. 1992.

"The New Baby Moguls," *Buzz* (March 1995).

Sharon Waxman, "Fireballs! Twisters! Upside-Down F-18s!" *International Herald Tribune,* 6 Jul. 1996.

Francis Hamit, "Inside Imaging R & D at Industrial Light & Magic," *Advanced Imaging* (July 1997).

Mick LaSalle, "That Sinking Feeling," *SFCh,* 19 Dec. 1997.

Chuck Philips, " 'Suge' Knight's Rap," *LAT,* 22 Jan. 1998.

Kenneth Turan, "You Try to Stop It," *LAT,* 21 Mar. 1998.

AP, "Jim Cameron Blasts LA Times Film Critic," *SFEx,* 1 Apr. 1998.

Amy Wallace and Marla Matzer, "Lucas Cuts Deal with Fox for Next 'Star Wars,' " *LAT,* 3 Apr. 1998.

Music Industry

Mary Rourke, "Street Savvy," *LAT,* 19 Sept. 1990.

Dennis Hunt and Daniel Cerone, "MTV's Big Surprise," *LAT,* 7 Sept. 1991.

Chuck Philips, "Anita Hill of Music Industry Talks," *LAT,* 5 Mar. 1992.

Chuck Philips, "Ice-T Pulls 'Cop Killer' Off the Market," *LAT,* 29 Jul. 1992.

Sheila Rule, " 'Cop Killer' to Be Cut from Ice-T Album," *NYT,* 29 Jul. 1992.

Charisse Jones, "Rap's Bad Rep," *LAT,* 2 May 1993.

John Seabrook, "The Many Lives of David Geffen," *The New Yorker,* 23 Feb. and 2 Mar. 1998.

Veronica Chambers, "Now He's the Top Dog," *Newsweek,* 15 June 1998.

Ocean Park

John Russell, "Diebenkorn's Stunning Achievement," *NYT,* 5 Dec. 1976.

Hilton Kramer, "Diebenkorn's Mastery," *NYT,* 12 June 1977.

Harry Waters, "Amazing Grace," *Newsweek,* 20 June 1977.

Roberta Smith, "A California Conceptualist Prods the Viewer," *NYT,* 19 Jul. 1991.

Sheila Benson, "Umbrellas of Christo," *LAT,* 23 Apr. 1991.

Kristine McKenna, "Lonely Scenes of Isolation from Bechtle," *LAT,* 23 Apr. 1991.

David Colker, "Christo's Latest Eye-Opener," *LAT Calendar,* 6 Oct. 1991.

David Colker, "Christo's Umbrellas—A Golden Forest Opens," *LAT,* 10 Oct. 1991.

Christopher Knight, "The Umbrellas of Christo," *LAT,* 11 Oct. 1991.

Michael Kimmelman, "A Life Outside," *NYT Magazine,* 13 Sept. 1992.

William Wilson, "Richard Diebenkorn: Still Life with Emotion," *LAT,* 28 Oct. 1992.

Susan Sward, "Sculptor Robert Arneson Dies of Cancer," *SFCh,* 4 Nov. 1992.

Julian Machin, "Richard Diebenkorn: A Rare Interview," *SFCh,* 17 Nov. 1992.

David Hockney, *That's the Way I See It* (1993).

Dan Levy, "Abstract Artist Richard Diebenkorn Dies," *SFCh,* 31 Mar. 1993.

Kenneth Baker, "Diebenkorn: Master of Abstract," *SFCh,* 31 Mar. 1993.

Jeffrey Herr, *John Register, Southern California Paintings* (Los Angeles Municipal Art Gallery, 27 Apr. 1993).

Mark Swed, "John Cage," *The Contemporary (Museum of Contemporary Art, Los Angeles)* (August 1993).

Jane Livingston, *The Art of Richard Diebenkorn* (1997).

Cynthia Robbins, "Art Comes Out to Play," *SFEx,* 12 Mar. 1998.

Diane Haithman, "Ceramist Beatrice Wood, the 'Mama of Dada,' Dies," *LAT,* 13 Mar. 1998.

Mark Swed, "Hindered Vision," *LAT,* 17 Apr. 1998.

Frank's Kids

Leon Whiteson, "Gehry: Quite the Man About Town," *LAT,* 21 Feb. 1988.

William Wilson, "The Undisputed Arrival of Frank Gehry," *LAT Calendar,* 21 Feb. 1988.

Pico Iyer, "Is It Really That Whacky?" *Time,* 18 Nov. 1991.

Carol Vogel, "Western Civilization," *NYT Magazine,* 8 Dec. 1991.

Diane Dorrans Saeks, photographs by John Vaughan, *California Country* (1992).

Jerry Carroll, "Pillar of Design," *SFCh,* 20 Jan. 1993.

Judy Fayard, "The New American Center: Gehry's Gem on the Seine," *WSJ,* 7 June 1994.

Diana Ketcham, "For Frank Israel, History Is There to Be Created," *NYT,* 17 Aug. 1995.

Nicolai Ouroussoff, "After the Crash-and-Burn '80s, LA Architecture Has Found Salvation with a Return to Essentials," *LAT Magazine,* 6 Apr. 1997.

Calvin Tomkins, "The Maverick: Why Is Frank Gehry a Genius Everywhere but in His Own Home Town?" *The New Yorker,* 7 Jul. 1997.

Janice Ross, "Lawrence Halprin: Landscape as Experience," *SFEx Magazine,* 10 Aug. 1997.

E. Scott Reckard, "If You're Ready to Move Way Up, Hurry," *LAT,* 3 Oct. 1997.

Zahid Sardar, "Frank Gehry, Modern Master," *SFEx Magazine,* 15 Feb. 1998.

Nicolai Ouroussof, "The Mechanics of Jones' Ideas," *LAT,* 18 Feb. 1998.

Morris Newman, "Shades of Dark, Ironic Humor Seen in Eye-Wear Maker's Headquarters," *LAT,* 31 Mar. 1998.

Brad Dunning, "Preserving the Optimism of Mid-Century Modern Design," *LAT,* 28 June 1998.

Nicolai Ouroussof, "I'm Frank Gehry, and This Is How I See the World," *LAT Magazine,* 25 Oct. 1998.

Nicolai Ouroussof, "A Messiness in Creating Masterworks," *LAT,* 18 May 2001.

Richard Fausset, "Owners Seeking Preservation Zone for Eichler Homes," *LAT,* 2 Jul. 2001.

PART II / Catastrophe

Earthquake, Fire, and Flood

Earthquake

Sandra Blakeslee, "Quake Theory Attacks Prevailing Wisdom on How Faults Slip and Slide," *NYT*, 14 Apr. 1992.

Paul Feldman, "Fear of the Unknown Is Rattling," *LAT*, 27 Jul. 1992.

"Hearts of LA: How the Quake of '94 Rocked Our Spirits and Changed Our Lives," Special Report, *LAT*, 30 Jan. 1994.

Sara Rimer, "Quake Brings Down Walls, and Neighborhood Emerges," *NYT*, 30 Jan. 1994.

Rob Haeseler, "Hidden Pockets of Quake Damage," *SFCh*, 7 Feb. 1994.

Kenneth Reich, "Quake Boosts Stress on Faults in LA Basin," *LAT*, 25 Feb. 1994.

Harold Johnson, "Aftershocks Jar Santa Monica's Rent Controllers," *WSJ*, 17 Mar. 1994.

Los Angeles Times Writers, "Still Shaken, A Resilient Los Angeles Seeks to Retrieve Its Future: A Special Quake Report One Year Later," *LAT*, 15 Jan. 1995.

Kevin Fagan, "No Fear on the Faultline," *SFCh*, 14 Oct. 1997.

Tom Gorman and Mitchell Landsberg, "7.0 Earthquake in Mojave Desert Rocks Southland," *LAT*, 17 Oct. 1999.

Robert Lee Hotz, Diana Marcum, and Kenneth Reich, " 'Inactive' Fault Blamed for 7.0 Earthquake," *LAT*, 18 Oct. 1999.

Jennifer Mena, "New Fault Is Found in Southern Orange County," *LAT*, 1 Nov. 1999.

Geoffrey Mohan, "4.2 Temblor Jolts Nerves in Southland," *LAT*, 10 Sept. 2001.

Kenneth Reich, "Quake Occurred Along Fault Said to Be Among Area's Most Dangerous," *LAT*, 11 Sept. 2001.

Fire

Dan Morain and Jenifer Warren, "Fire Declared Out: Death Toll at 24," *LAT*, 24 Oct. 1991.

Dan Morain and Jenifer Warren, " '70s Study Warned of Fire Threat," *LAT*, 25 Oct. 1991.

Richard Paddock, "Oakland's Elite Lose Irreplaceable History," *LAT*, 25 Oct. 1991.

Gerald Adams, " 'Priceless': 200 Historic Homes Lost in the Fire," *SFEx*, 10 Nov. 1991.

Los Angeles Times Writers, "The Southland Fires," *LAT*, 29 Oct. 1993.

J. Michael Kennedy, "For Firefighters, It Was a Wednesday from Hell Inferno," *LAT*, 31 Oct. 1993.

Mark Platte, David Haldane, and Leslie Earnest, "Laguna Fire Victims Seek Help," *LAT*, 31 Oct. 1993.

George Melloan, "California Again Is a 'Natural Burn' Victim," *WSJ*, 1 Nov. 1993.

Agence France-Presse, "Hollywood's Rich and Famous Burned Out of House and Home," 3 Nov. 1993.

Mike Bygrave, "Malibu: A Muddied Paradise with Four Disastrous Seasons," *Sunday Telegraph* (London), 13 Feb. 1994.

Tom Gorman and Greg Hernandez, "Fires Continue to Scorch Southland," *LAT*, 2 Sept. 1998.

AP, "Ferocious Wildfire Worst in Memory in Riverside County," *SFCh*, 3 Sept. 1998.

Carla Rivera, "Last of 5 Wildfires Contained; 75,000 Acres Burn in All," *LAT*, 6 Sept. 1999.

Eric Bailey and Terry McDermott, "2,500 Flee, 100 Homes Burn in N. California," *LAT*, 18 Oct. 1999.

Matthew Stannard and Chuck Squatriglia, "Raging Sierra Fire Burns 17,000 Acres," *SFCh*, 19 June 2001.

Flood

Robert Reinhold, "New California Storm Brings Worst Floods in Decades," *NYT,* 13 Feb. 1992.

Mario Camposeco, Tom Philp, and Sam Stanton, "One Person Killed; Rivers Run Wild; Thousands Flee," *SacBee,* 10 Jan. 1995.

Cynthia Hubert, Kimberly Moy, and Andy Furillo, "Storm Swamps Capital Streets," *SacBee,* 10 Jan. 1995.

Deborah Blum, "El Niño Blamed for Wet Weather," *SacBee,* 11 Jan. 1995.

Henry Chu and Tim Rutten, "California Deluge: Travelers Spin Their Wheels or Just Sit Still," *LAT,* 11 Jan. 1995.

Kenneth R. Weiss and Mark Arax, "Powerful Storm Pounds State," *LAT,* 11 Jan. 1995.

Steve Wiegand, "Merciless Rains Take Huge Toll," *SacBee,* 11 Jan. 1995.

Timothy Egan, "California Storm Brings Rethinking of Development," *NYT,* 15 Jan. 1995.

Zachary Coile and Malcolm Glover, "Big Storm Socks Bay; Flood Peril Looming," *SFEx,* 2 Feb. 1998.

Stephanie Simon and Mary Curtius, "2 Bruising Storms Cause Evacuations, 1 Death," *LAT,* 4 Feb. 1998.

Kevin Fagan, Jim Doyle, and Christopher Heredia, "It's Only Going to Get Worse, Forecasters Say," *SFCh,* 5 Feb. 1998.

Jane Kay, Emily Gurnon, and Zachary Coile, "Bay Area Braces for Next El Niño Deluge," *SFEx,* 5 Feb. 1998.

Maria Gaura, Torri Minton, and Edward Lempinen, "Thousands Flee Winter's Worst," *SFCh,* 6 Feb. 1998.

Marianne Costantinou, "Wet, Windy, and Worrisome," *SFEx,* 7 Feb. 1998.

Stephanie Simon and Daryl Kelley, "New Storms Lash Southland, with More Rains on Way," *LAT,* 7 Feb. 1998.

Eric Brazil, "Storm Pulls Out All Stops," *SFEx,* 8 Feb. 1998.

Tyra Mead, Ramon McLeod, and Kevin Fagan, "Storm Respite Expected but Not til Next Week," *SFCh,* 13 Feb. 1998.

Larry Hatfield, "Soaked State Readies for More," *SFEx,* 15 Feb. 1998.

Nicholas Riccardi, "A Rare Ray of Sunshine Lets State See Task Ahead," *LAT,* 16 Feb. 1998.

Stephanie Simon, Kate Folmar, and David Reyes, "Storm Kills 6, Inflicts Severe Damage in State," *LAT,* 25 Feb. 1998.

Marc Lacey, "Senate to Vote on Aid for State's Storm Damage," *LAT,* 26 Mar. 1998.

Bob Pool, "Driving Us Mad," *LAT,* 26 Mar. 1998.

David Reyes, "El Niño Brings Lingering Peril to Beaches," *LAT,* 27 Mar. 1998.

Mudslide

Arthur Louis, "Landslide Insurance Offered," *SFCh,* 6 Feb. 1998.

Michael Dougan, "Midnight Mudslide Clobbers Rio Nido," *SFEx,* 8 Feb. 1998.

Anastasia Hendrix, "Two Seacliff Homes Slipping," *SFEx,* 12 Feb. 1998.

Eric Malnic and T. Christian Miller, "Slide Threat Increases as 3 Storms Approach," *LAT,* 14 Feb. 1998.

Mary Curtius, "Rio Nido Teeters in a Landslide Limbo," *LAT,* 19 Feb. 1998.

Tini Tran and Robert Ourlian, "Hillside Residents Fear More Rain," *LAT,* 5 Mar. 1993.

Benjamin Pimentel and Torri Minton, "Pacific Getting $1.5 Million to Build Seawall," *SFCh,* 6 Mar. 1998.

Tini Tran and Shelby Grad, "Laguna Beach Family Copes with Impact of Losing Home," *LAT,* 10 Mar. 1998.

Robert Ourlian and Frank Messina, "Laguna Niguel Slide Destroys 7 Dwellings," *LAT,* 20 Mar. 1998.

Robert Ourlian, "Third House Collapses in Laguna Niguel," *LAT,* 21 Mar. 1998.

Mary Curtius, "Some Go Home to Rio Nido," *LAT,* 2 Apr. 1998.

Martin Kasindorf, "California Dreams Don't Die Easily," *USA Today,* 8 Apr. 1998.

Robert Ourlian, "Developers Knew of Landslide Risks, Lawsuit Contends," *LAT,* 13 Apr. 1998.

Examiner Staff Report, "7 Houses Demolished in Pacifica," *SFEx,* 7 May 1998.

Robert Ourlian, "Hill Collapses Near San Juan Capistrano Homes," *LAT,* 22 May 1998.

Scene of the Crime

Edmund Newton and Denise Hamilton, "Clash of Images: Some in S. Pasadena See Slayings of 3 Teenage Girls as Sign of a Subculture of Troubled Youth," *LAT,* 16 Apr. 1991.

Laurie Becklund, "Rage and Alienation Mark Suspects in Mall Murders," *LAT,* 22 Sept. 1991.

Richard Paddock, "Oakland Mayor Calls for Action to Stem Violence," *LAT,* 25 Mar. 1992.

Edmund Newton, " 'Dude, We Smoked 'Em All,' " *LAT Magazine,* 5 Apr. 1992.

Leslie Berger and Henry Chu, "Party Crashers Blamed in Gunfight," *LAT,* 7 Apr. 1992.

Paul Avery, "Carjacking Epidemic Perils SF Drivers," *SFEx,* 23 Oct. 1992.

Rick DelVecchio, "UC Berkeley Student Slain by Holdup Man," *SFCh,* 23 Oct. 1992.

Don Martinez, "Oakland Pizza Man Shot Down in Cold Blood," *SFEx,* 22 Feb. 1993.

Somini Sengupta, "Customs Inspector Pleads Guilty to Taking $1.7 Million in Bribes," *LAT,* 3 Mar. 1993.

Edmund Newton, "2 Get Maximum Terms in Pasadena Triple Murder," *LAT,* 11 Mar. 1993.

Juliet Tamaki, "Woman Dies After Being Stabbed in Carjacking," *LAT,* 2 Apr. 1993.

Edmund Newton, "3 Charged in Fatal Jewelry Store Holdup," *LAT,* 8 Apr. 1993.

Mark Arax, "Gunman Kills 7 in Fresno Bar," *LAT,* 17 May 1993.

Anthony Duignan-Cabrera, "Police Say Woman Takes Robber's Gun, Kills Him," *LAT,* 16 June 1993.

John M. Glionna and Scott Glover, "Robbers Kill Woman as Her Son, 9, Watches," *LAT,* 17 Sept. 1993.

Sara Catania and Mack Reed, "Body of Nurse Apparently Found," *LAT,* 27 Sept. 1993.

Faye Fiore, "Parole Sought in Slaying of Man After Shooting Dog," *LAT,* 1 Oct. 1993.

Shawn Hubler, "When the Music Stops: Choirmaster Slain in Holdup," *LAT,* 26 Apr. 1994.

Kenneth Reich, "Carjackers Slay Father of 3 to Steal Glitzy Auto," *LAT,* 16 May 1994.

Marcus Nieto, Roger Dunstan, and Gus Koehler, *Fire-Related Violence in California: Incidence and Economic Costs* (CRB, October 1994).

Los Angeles Times News Service, "Recycler Slain by Man Who Stole His Beer," *SFCh,* 1 Nov. 1994.

"Arrest Made in Ennis Cosby Slaying," *WP,* 13 Mar. 1997.

"Russian Émigré Held in Slaying of Cosby's Son," *WP,* 14 Mar. 1997.

Michael Krikorian, "Paying Tribute to a Son Who Died Too Young," *LAT,* 27 Sept. 1997.

Carl Ingram, "Violent Felons Barred from Jobs at Schools," *LAT,* 1 Oct. 1997.

"Nurse Shot to Death on 60 Freeway," *LAT,* 21 Oct. 1997.

Nicholas Riccardi and Jose Cardenas, "Nurse Slain on Freeway Recalled as Caring, Dauntless," *LAT,* 22 Oct. 1997.

Marcus Nieto, *Concealed Handgun Laws and Public Safety* (CRB, November 1997).

Ronald Ostrow, Matt Lait, and Daryl Kelley, "LA Crime Rate Falls 15% in FBI Midyear Figures," *LAT,* 23 Nov. 1997.

Tracy Wilson, "Haun Gets Life Term in Woman's Killing," *LAT,* 25 Nov. 1997.

Tracy Wilson, "Killer Ordered to Pay for Her Defense," *LAT,* 10 Dec. 1997.

Patricia Jacobus, "Woman Confesses in Kidnap-Slaying, Police Say," *SFCh,* 11 Dec. 1997.

Patricia Jacobus, "Slain Woman's Family and Friends Gather in Sorrow," *SFCh,* 13 Dec. 1997.

Patricia Jacobus and Christopher Heredia, "Rape-Murder Suspect's Jekyll-Hyde Life," *SFCh,* 19 Dec. 1997.

Robert Ourlian, "Freeway Chase Ends in Shooting," *LAT,* 19 Jan. 1998.

Nicholas Riccardi, "Freeway Shots Kill One Woman, Injure Another," *LAT,* 16 Feb. 1998.

Jim Zamora, "Black Murder Rate High in SF," *SFEx,* 16 Feb. 1998.

Deborah Belgum, "Armored Truck Hijacked, Robbed of $3 Million," *LAT,* 28 Mar. 1998.

Deborah Belgum, "2 Die in Shooting near Courthouse," *LAT,* 31 Mar. 1998.

AP, "2 Robbers Kill Hostage, Selves in Standoff," *LAT,* 29 Apr. 1998.

Alan Abrahamson and Miles Corwin, "Man Kills Self as City Watches," *LAT,* 1 May 1998.

Richard Simon, "MTA Settles Suit over Rider's Death," *LAT,* 1 May 1998.

Alan Abrahamson and Matt Lait, "Videotape: 'I'm a Dead Man . . . See Ya!,' " *LAT,* 2 May 1998.

Andrew Blankstein, "Suspect's Novel Is Evidence in Arson Case," *LAT,* 9 June 1998.

Sam Richards and John Simerman, "10 Shot, Spurring Fair Riot," *Contra Costa Times,* 5 Jul. 1998.

NYT Wire Service, "Fewer Drugs, Guns, Credited in Crime Drop," *SFCh,* 28 Dec. 1998.

Reefer Madness

Elizabeth Venant, "Two Families in Recovery," *LAT,* 6 Nov. 1991.

"Ex-Giants Outfielder Nabbed in Coke Bust," *SFEx,* 26 Apr. 1992.

Lynn Smith, "Testament to the Downward Spiral of Drugs and Teen Angst," *LAT,* 16 Feb. 1994.

Yvonne Chiu, "Drug Suspect Killed in Raid," *SacBee,* 16 Apr. 1997.

Trish Donnally, "Novelist Steel Says Son Battled Depression," *SFCh,* 23 Sept. 1997.

Jerry Bier, "Heroin Bust Called a Valley Record," *FBee,* 4 Oct. 1997.

Robert Welkos, "Actor Robert Downey Jr. Given 6-Month Jail Term," *LAT,* 9 Dec. 1997.

Bill Wallace, "14 Indicted in Methamphetamine Ring," *SFCh,* 21 Mar. 1998.

Tini Tran and Bonnie Hayes, "Family Says Teen's Work as Informant Led to Death," *LAT,* 23 Mar. 1998.

Michael Wagner and Davan Maharaj, "Scrutiny Grows over Use of Young Informants," *LAT,* 26 Mar. 1998.

Bonnie Hayes, "Slain Youth's Work as Informant Detailed," *LAT,* 2 Apr. 1998.

Erin McCormick and Marsha Ginsburg, "From Heroin to Heartbreak," *SFEx,* 10 Jan. 1999.

Sue Fox, "The Last Days of Nick Markowitz," *LAT,* 10 Dec. 2000.

Evelyn Nieves, "Illicit Drug Lab Grows in Fertile California Valley," *NYT,* 13 May 2001.

Tony Perry, "Charges Filed in Poisoning Case," *LAT,* 28 June 2001.

AP, "Millionaire Financed Large-Scale Methamphetamine Operation," *SFCh,* 3 Jul. 2001.

Mai Tran and Jack Leonard, "Two Men Detail Night of Rapes, Beatings," *LAT,* 17 Jul. 2001.

Peter Hecht, "Pilots' Deaths End in Arrest," *SacBee,* 29 Aug. 2001.

Monte Morin, "Huge Marijuana Farm Found in Cleveland National Forest," *LAT,* 31 Aug. 2001.

Monte Morin, "Marijuana Farm Nearly Invisible on Terraced O.C. Mountain Slope," *LAT,* 1 Sept. 2001.

Homeboys

Tracy Wilkinson, and Stephanie Chavez, "Elaborate Death Rites of Gangs," *LAT,* 2 Mar. 1992.
Jesse Katz, "An Ethic Dies with Gang Chief," *LAT,* 14 Apr. 1992.
Luis Rodriguez, "La Vida Loca, 'The Crazy Life': Two Generations of Gang Members," *LAT,* 21 June 1992.
Jesse Katz, "County's Yearly Gang Toll Reaches 800," *LAT,* 19 Jan. 1993.
Floyd Salas, "Leaving the Gang Behind," *LAT Book Review,* 7 Mar. 1993.
Julia Scheeres, "Man Dies in Gang Shooting; Youth Held," *LAT,* 17 Jul. 1993.
Michiko Kakutani, "Illuminating Gang Life in Los Angeles," *NYT,* 23 Jul. 1993.
Greg Krikorian, "Study Ranks Joblessness Top Factor in Gang Toll," *LAT,* 27 Oct. 1997.
Miles Corwin, "Police Arrest Fugitive Gang Member Turned Author," *LAT,* 29 May 1996.
Bill Wallace, "SF Arrests Show Gang's Resurgence," *SFCh,* 27 Apr. 1998.
Tom Gorman, "4 Are Indicted in Temecula Attack on Black Man," *LAT,* 18 Aug. 1999.
Evelyn Larrubia, "Skinhead Convicted of Killing Black Man," *LAT,* 5 Nov. 1999.

Asian Gangs
James Willwerth, "From Killing Fields to Mean Streets," *Time,* 18 Nov. 1991.
Daniel Yi and Greg Krikorian, "Three Men Convicted of Killing Ngor," *LAT,* 17 Apr. 1998.
Evelyn Larrubia, "Jury Selection Gets Underway in Asian Gang Slaying Case," *LAT,* 21 Sept. 1998.

Continuing Violence
Stephanie Chavez, "Mother's Mission Ends with Sentencing of 5 Killers," *LAT,* 1 Feb. 1992.
Jesse Katz, "Torment Drove Man Who Joined Slain Son in Death," *LAT,* 19 Feb. 1992.
Rick DelVecchio, "UC Berkeley Student Slain by Holdup Man," *SFCh,* 23 Oct. 1992.
John M. Glionna, " 'This Bus Is Plain Crazy,' " *LAT,* 25 Oct. 1992.
Peter Fimrite, "Gangs Grow in Alameda County Suburbs," *SFCh,* 26 Oct. 1992.
Andrea Ford, "Suspected Gang Members Held in Slayings of 2 Men," *LAT,* 6 Jan. 1993.
Ken Ellingwood, "Life Can Turn Ugly, Even on the Venice Boardwalk," *LAT,* 18 May 1993.
David Colker, "A Long, Painful Goodbye," *LAT,* 23 Aug. 1993.
Robert Lopez, "Black on Brown Crime," *LAT,* 5 Sept. 1993.
Jim Crogan, "Trapped by the Terror of a Venice Street War," *LAT,* 18 June 1994.
Susan Ferriss, " Teen Gangs: The Crazy Life Sweeping Sonoma County," *SFEx,* 30 Mar. 1997.
Glen Martin, "Gangs Get a Foothold in the Wine Country," *SFCh,* 16 June 1997.
Maria Gaura, "Blood Brothers," *SFCh,* 29 June 1997.
Hector Tobar, "Gang Carnage Yields Few Clues," *LAT,* 30 Aug. 1997.
Sue McAllister, "Oakwood Tries to Cope with Rash of Gang Violence," *LAT,* 16 Sept. 1997.
Michael Krikorian, "Gang Member Known as City's Most Violent Is Sentenced to Death," *LAT,* 13 Dec. 1997.
John M. Glionna, "The Fatal Shot That Woke LA," *LAT,* 30 Jan. 1998.
Tracy Johnson, "Police Roundup Suspects in Stolen Goods Sting," *LAT,* 3 Apr. 1998.
Tracy Johnson, "Special Delivery," *LAT,* 28 Apr. 1998.
Henry Weinstein, "Man Held in Shooting of Two at Baby Shower," *LAT,* 26 May 1998.
Steve Berry, "Markhasev Is Found Guilty of Cosby Murder," *LAT,* 8 Jul. 1998.

Robert Lopez and Rich Connell, "A Notorious Swath of Drugs and Violence," *LAT*, 14 Aug. 1998.

"Casino Killer Gets Sentence of Life in Prison," *SFCh*, 15 Oct. 1998.

Michael Krikorian, "Big Evil's Ride to Death Row," *LAT Magazine*, 29 Nov. 1998.

Douglas P. Shuit and Jack Leonard, "Deputies Thwart Courtroom Attack," *LAT*, 2 Dec. 1998.

"Suspect Calls I-80 Shootings 'Practice Run,' " *SFCh*, 7 Jan. 1999.

Tony Perry, "Drifter Sentenced to Die in Slaying of Boy," *LAT*, 5 Nov. 1999.

Michael Krikorian, "Escalating Gang Battle Plagues Northeast Valley," *LAT*, 4 Jul. 2001.

Sue Fox, "FBI Offers $20,000 in West Hills Boy's Death," *LAT*, 10 Jul. 2001.

Jean Guccione, "Family of Slain Boy Files Suit Against 32 People," *LAT*, 10 Aug. 2001.

Holly Wolcott, Tina Dirmann, and Daryl Kelley, "Gunman Kills 3 in Simi Valley Home, Then Flees," *LAT*, 6 Sept. 2001.

Eric Bailey, "Temple Arson Pleas Clear the Way for Murder Trial," *LAT*, 8 Sept. 2001.

Steve Chawkins and Timothy Hughes, "Man Sought in Rampage Kills Himself," *LAT*, 8 Sept. 2001.

John Johnson, "2 Suburbs See Shootings as Aberrations," *LAT*, 10 Sept. 2001.

Maria La Ganga, "4 Found Shot to Death in San Francisco Home," *LAT*, 10 Sept. 2001.

Margaret Talev and Eric Bailey, "5 Killed; Heavily Armed Man Sought," *LAT*, 10 Sept. 2001.

Eric Bailey and Robin Fields, "Shootout Vowed in Chilling Video," *LAT*, 11 Sept. 2001.

Hip-Hop and Gang Chic

Louis Sahagun, "Graffiti Tally Finds 6,900 Walls in LA Are Marred," *LAT*, 29 Oct. 1991.

John M. Glionna, "Leaving Their Mark," *LAT*, 10 Mar. 1993.

Richard Colvin, "Teaming Up on Taggers," *LAT*, 13 Apr. 1993.

Berkley Hudson, "Scrawl of the Wild," *LAT*, 24 Apr. 1993.

Blunt Graphics, *Fall '93 T-Shirt Designs* (Sales Catalog, 1993).

Ri' Chard Magee, "Hip Hop's Calling Shots in the NBA," *SFEx*, 30 Dec. 1997.

Mexican Mafia and Other Peacemakers

Andrea Ford and Carla Rivera, "Hope Takes Hold as Bloods, Crips Say Truce Is for Real," *LAT*, 21 May 1992.

John Mitchell, "No Letup in Random Violence During Gang Truce," *LAT*, 23 Aug. 1992.

Jesse Katz, "Film Leaves a Legacy of Fear," *LAT*, 13 June 1993.

Jesse Katz and Robert Lopez, "Mexican Mafia's Impact on Gangs Questioned," *LAT*, 28 Sept. 1993.

Leslie Berger, "San Fernando Valley Gangs Maintain Precious Peace," *LAT*, 27 Sept. 1994.

Scott Collins, "A Tenuous Truce," *LAT*, 27 Sept. 1994.

Michael Krikorian, "Ex-Gang Members Work to Bring Peace to Streets," *LAT*, 26 Jan. 1998.

Gangbusters

Gangs Versus Police

David Ferrell and Roxana Kopetman, "Two Compton Officers Slain in Traffic Stop," *LAT*, 24 Feb. 1993.

Miles Corwin and Roxana Kopetman, "Compton Officers Were Killed Execution-Style," *LAT*, 25 Feb. 1993.

Andrea Ford, "Key Suspect Surrenders in Slaying of Two Officers," *LAT*, 7 Apr. 1993.

Jean Merl and Nieson Himmel, "Gang Control Officer Shot," *LAT*, 29 Sept. 1993.

John Mitchell and Teresa Ann Willis, "Suspect Arrested in Shooting of LAPD Officer," *LAT*, 30 Sept. 1993.

Stuart Creque, "Officer Died, but We Blame Police," *WSJ*, 29 Dec. 1993.

Bill Boyarsky, "In the Line of Fire," *LAT*, 23 Feb. 1994.

Sam Enriquez and Josh Meyer, "Teen-Ager Kills Father, Officer, and Himself," *LAT*, 23 Feb. 1994.

Matt Lait, "Suspect Pleads Not Guilty in Officer's Death," *LAT*, 15 Aug. 1998.

Hector Tobar, "Thousands Join Officer's Family at Funeral," *LAT*, 15 Aug. 1998.

Steve Hochman, "Rap Artist Is Jailed over Anti-Police Lyrics," *LAT*, 4 Mar. 1998.

Legal Redress

Shawn Hubler, "Grand Jury to Investigate Shootings," *LAT*, 20 Sept. 1991.

Patrick McDonnell, "Plan to Ban Gangs from LA Parks Protested," *LAT*, 17 May 1993.

Felicia Cousart, "Computer Database Will Help Track Gangs," *FBee*, 23 May 1996.

Robert Lopez and Rich Connell, "Court Order Against LA Gang Expanded," *LAT*, 30 Aug. 1997.

Hugo Martin, "Funds Sought to Draft More Injunctions Against Gangs," *LAT*, 23 Sept. 1997.

Mark Arax, "In Fresno, Agencies Fight Gangs with MAGEC," *LAT*, 2 Feb. 1998.

Jeffrey L. Rabin, "Officials Seek Injunction Against 92 Gang Members," *LAT*, 4 May 1998.

Police Get Rough, Form Gang of Their Own

Staff and Wire Reports, "Shots Kill Man at Funeral for Boy Slain in Jail," *LAT*, 29 Dec. 1992.

Tom Gorman, " 'High Five' Called Officers' Sign of Relief," *LAT*, 26 Mar. 1993.

Steve Berry and Scott Glover, "Bank Robber Bled to Death Unnecessarily," *LAT*, 21 Apr. 1998.

Matt Lait and Scott Glover, "Ex-Officer Says He Shot Unarmed Man," *LAT*, 16 Sept. 1999.

Scott Glover and Matt Lait, "Second LAPD Shooting Targeted as Corruption Probe Widens," *LAT*, 17 Sept. 1999.

Tina Daunt and Anne-Marie O'Connor, "Survivor of 2nd Shooting Says He Was Framed," *LAT*, 18 Sept. 1999.

Matt Lait and Scott Glover, "Investigation Now Targets Beating at Rampart Station," *LAT*, 18 Sept. 1999.

Rich Connell and Robert Lopez, "Rampart Probe May Put Gang Injunction at Risk," *LAT*, 19 Sept. 1999.

Scott Glover and Matt Lait, "Ex-Officer Calls Corruption a Chronic 'Cancer,' " *LAT*, 21 Sept. 1999.

Jim Newton and Ann O'Neill, "Captain Under Fire as Rampart Probe Expands," *LAT*, 21 Sept. 1999.

Rich Connell and Robert Lopez, "Anti-Gang Arrests Reviewed to See If Discredited Officers Played Role," *LAT*, 22 Sept. 1999.

Ann O'Neill and Nicholas Riccardi, "Garcetti, Supervisors Dispute Funding for Reviving Officer-Involved Shooting Unit," *LAT*, 22 Sept. 1999.

Robert Lopez and Rich Connell, "Targets of Gang Injunctions Were Named by Officers in Police Probe," *LAT*, 23 Sept. 1999.

Jim Newton, "Ex-Rampart Commander a Focus of Probe, Sources Say," *LAT*, 24 Sept. 1999.

Nicholas Riccardi and Beth Shuster, "DA to Review Unit That Investigates Police Shootings," *LAT*, 29 Sept. 1999.

Matt Lait and Scott Glover, "Grand Jury to Probe Rampart Allegations," *LAT,* 5 Oct. 1999.

Matt Lait, Scott Glover, and Robert Lopez, "Rampart Officers Face Additional Accusations," *LAT,* 9 Oct. 1999.

Scott Glover and Matt Lait, "Man Freed amid Probe of LAPD Sues City," *LAT,* 14 Oct. 1999.

Matt Lait and Scott Glover, "7 Shootings, New Allegations Part of Growing LAPD Probe," *LAT,* 22 Oct. 1999.

Matt Lait and Scott Glover, "4th Inmate Is Expected to Be Freed," *LAT,* 30 Nov. 1999.

Henry Weinstein, "Rampart Scandal Figure Accused in Civil Suit of Planting Drugs," *LAT,* 8 Dec. 1999.

Scott Glover and Matt Lait, "10 More Rampart Cases Voided," *LAT,* 26 Jan. 2000.

Scott Glover and Matt Lait, "A 2nd Rampart Officer Tells of Corruption," *LAT,* 28 Jan. 2000.

Scott Glover and Matt Lait, "Convictions of 9 More Voided in Scandal," *LAT,* 2 Feb. 2000.

Tina Daunt, "Ramparts Settlements Could Hit $125 Million," *LAT,* 3 Feb. 2000.

Matt Lait and Scott Glover, "Insignia of Rampart Anti-Gang Unit Raises Concerns," *LAT,* 8 Feb. 2000.

Matt Lait and Scott Glover, "Police in Secret Group Broke Law Routinely, Transcripts Say," *LAT,* 10 Feb. 2000.

Matt Lait and Scott Glover, "Shooting Scenes Rigged, Perez Says," *LAT,* 10 Feb. 2000.

Matt Lait and Scott Glover, "4 Officers Back Tales of Parties After Shootings," *LAT,* 12 Feb. 2000.

Sue Fox, "Officers Used Valley 'Crash Pad,' Perez Says," *LAT,* 13 Feb. 2000.

Patrick McGreevy and Tina Daunt, "Council OKs $400,000 for Two Alleged Police Victims," *LAT,* 6 Apr. 2000.

Edward Boyer, "Cases Against 10 More Defendants in Rampart Cases Dismissed," *LAT,* 14 Apr. 2000.

Hugo Martin, "Inmate Freed in Ramparts Scandal Files Lawsuit," *LAT,* 7 June 2000.

Tom Gorman, "Man Police Shot Enters Plea Deal," *LAT,* 31 Aug. 2001.

Steve Berry, Scott Glover, and Matt Lait, "DA Says No New Charges Expected in Rampart Probe," *LAT,* 8 Nov. 2001.

Doing Time

Criminal Justice System

Jocelyn Stewart, "A Bleak Cycle," *LAT,* 11 Feb. 1993.

Marcus Nieto, *The 1994 Violent Crime Control and Law Enforcement Act Today* (CRB, 10 Apr. 1995).

Marcus Nieto, *Boot Camps: An Alternative Punishment Option for the Criminal Justice System* (CRB, 17 Apr. 1995).

Marcus Nieto, *Community Correction Punishments: An Alternative to Incarceration for Non-violent Offenders* (CRB, May 1996).

Dan Walters, "Second Chance on 3 Strikes," *SacBee,* 23 June 1996.

Dan Morain, "Democrats Offer Rival 3 Strikes Bill," *LAT,* 19 Jul. 1996.

Dan Lungren, "Three Cheers for 3 Strikes," *Journal of American Citizenship Policy Review* (November/December 1996).

Marcus Nieto, *The Changing Role of Probation in California's Criminal Justice System* (CRB, July 1996).

Andy Furillo, "Reforms for Parole System Urged," *SacBee,* 9 Feb. 1998.

Maura Dolan, "Court Says Act of Crime Can Get Separate Strikes," *LAT*, 15 May 1998.

Marcus Nieto, *Health Care in California State Prisons* (CRB, June 1998).

The Death Penalty

Larry Hatfield, Lance Williams, and Scott Winokur, "Executed," *SFEx*, 21 Apr. 1992.

Katherine Bishop, "After Long Night of Legal Battles, California Carries Out Execution," *NYT*, 22 Apr. 1992.

Dan Morain and Tom Gorman, "Harris Dies After Judicial Duel," *LAT*, 22 Apr. 1992.

David Savage, "Execution a Rarity amid State's Legal Quagmires," *LAT*, 31 May 1998.

Ralph Brave, "Death by the Numbers," *Sacramento News & Review*, 2 Jul. 1998.

Maria La Ganga, "Executions Eliciting a Growing Indifference," *LAT*, 5 May 1999.

Prisons

Daniel Akst, "New Prison Blunts Old Depression's Sting," *LAT*, 16 Apr. 1991.

Kenneth Reich, "Block Gets Ready for the Worst," *LAT*, 22 Apr. 1993.

John Hurst and Dan Morain, "A System Strains at Its Bars," *LAT*, 17 Oct. 1994.

Dan Morain, "California's Prison Budget: Why Is It So Voracious?" *LAT*, 19 Oct. 1994.

Maura Dolan, "Judge Orders End to Brutality at High-Tech Prison," *LAT*, 12 Jan. 1995.

Peter H. King, "Worst of the Worst," *LAT*, 18 Jan. 1995.

Fox Butterfield, "New Prisons Cast Shadow over Higher Education," *NYT*, 12 Apr. 1995.

Sheryl Stolberg, "School's Out for Convicts," *LAT*, 14 Sept. 1995.

Dan Morain, "1 Inmate Killed, 13 Hurt in Prison Fight," *LAT*, 28 Sept. 1996.

Marc Lifsher, "Legislators to Renew Push to Bar Expensive Prisons," *WSJ*, 20 Nov. 1996.

Anthony Lewis, "Abroad at Home," *NYT*, 25 Mar. 1996.

Louise Steinman, "Releasing the Artist Within," *LAT*, 8 Jul. 1997.

AP, "Prisons Crowded Despite Expansion," *SFCh*, 15 Jan. 1998.

Jenifer Warren, "Inmates Serving 26 to Life Is State's Top Literacy Tour," *LAT*, 9 Mar. 1998.

Darryl Fears, " 'Like Living in Hell,' " *LAT*, 27 Mar. 1998.

Kevin Fagan and Charlie Goodyear, "Sex Predator Arrested in New Rape," *SFCh*, 5 Sept. 1998.

Mark Arax and Mark Gladstone, "Inmate's Suicide Indicates Prison's Ongoing Problems," *LAT*, 19 Dec. 1998.

Erin McCormick, "Number of State Prisoners Soared in '90s," *SFCh*, 9 Aug. 2001.

Corcoran

Robert Gunnison and Greg Lucas, "Guard Union's Clout Impeding Prison Investigation, Critics Say," *SFCh*, 18 Mar. 1998.

Mark Arax, "FBI Probes Deaths at 2 More State Prisons," *LAT*, 19 Mar. 1998.

Mark Arax, "Ex-Guard Tells of Brutality, Code of Silence at Corcoran," *LAT*, 6 Jul. 1998.

Pamela Podger, "Witnesses Say Probe Hindered by Guards," *SFCh*, 5 Aug. 1998.

Mark Arax and Mark Gladstone, "Ex-Chief Says He Didn't Know of Violence at Prison," *LAT*, 19 Aug. 1998.

Pamela Podger, "Prison Rapist Marked Man, Hayden Says," *SFCh*, 21 Aug. 1998.

Editorial, "Corcoran's Shame," *LAT*, 23 Aug. 1998.

Mark Arax, "Stakes High as Prison Guards Go on Trial," *LAT*, 4 Oct. 1999.

Mark Arax, "Ex-Guard Says 4 Men Set Up Rape of Inmate," *LAT*, 14 Oct. 1999.

Mark Arax, "Tearful Victim Testifies on Prison Rape," *LAT*, 20 Oct. 1999.

Mark Arax and Richard Chon, "4 Guards Acquitted of Setting Up Prison Rape," *LAT*, 9 Nov. 1999.

A Lost Generation

A Violent Environment

Brian Cahill, "Help Children At Risk," *LAT*, 30 Jul. 1989.

Jane Gross, "San Franciscans to Vote for the Sake of Children," *NYT*, 23 Sept. 1991.

David Freed, "Guns, Violence Exact a Toll on LA's Youngest Victims," *LAT*, 21 May 1992.

Charles Stewart Mott Foundation, *A Fine Line: Losing American Youth to Violence* (Annual Report, 1994).

Ann O'Neill, "Shock Haunts Children Who See Parent's Slaying," *LAT*, 5 Oct. 1995.

David Foster and Farrell Kramer, "Kids as Young as 4 Found at Work in US," *LAT*, 14 Mar. 1997.

Leslie Helm, "Making a Killing," *LAT*, 26 Jan. 1998.

Tom Schultz, "Working More, Learning Less," *LAT*, 18 Mar. 1998.

Lynn Smith, "Unhappily Ever After," *LAT*, 26 May 1998.

Kids Get Killed

George Ramos, "Girl's Gang Friendship Is Fatal," *LAT*, 22 Apr. 1991.

John Johnson and Julio Moran, "Hard Work, Success, and a Brutal Death," *LAT*, 11 Dec. 1991.

Jesse Katz, "Fire Adds to Misery of Slain Child's Family," *LAT*, 21 Oct. 1992.

Ann O'Neill and Julio Moran, "Officer Kills Father Holding Screwdriver to Son's Throat," *LAT*, 29 Sept. 1993.

Sandy Close, "The Death of 'America's Child,' " *Baltimore Sun*, 19 Dec. 1993.

Ken Ellingwood and Adrian Maher, "Gunshots Again Rake Venice; 2 Youths Die," *LAT*, 11 June 1994.

J. Michael Kennedy and Stephanie Simon, "Shooting of Young Athlete Ends a Life Full of Promise," *LAT*, 12 Apr. 1995.

Peter H. King, "Maybe the Judges Can Judge!" *LAT*, 23 June 1996.

Bettina Boxall, "Father of Slain Girl, 6, Wants Shooting to Stop," *LAT*, 1 Jan. 1998.

Solomon Moore and Scott Glover, " 'Road Rage'-Type Crash Kills Two," *LAT*, 15 Jan. 1998.

Peter Hong, "Family of 4 Found Shot to Death in La Puente Home," *LAT*, 30 Jan. 1998.

Stacy Finz, Jaxon Van Derbeken, and Manny Fernandez, "Slain Girls' Mother Left Notes, Cops Say," *SFCh*, 25 Mar. 1998.

Ray Delgado, "Sanity Defense for Mom?" *SFEx*, 26 Mar. 1998.

Stacy Finz and Manny Fernandez, "Slain Girls' Mother Charged with Murder," *SFCh*, 26 Mar. 1998.

Patrick McDonnell and Douglas P. Shuit, "Sequence of 5 Slayings in Artesia Is Established," *LAT*, 29 Apr. 1998.

Jeff Leeds, Solomon Moore, and T. Christian Miller, "Mother Arrested in 4 Girls' Deaths, Fire," *LAT*, 3 Jul. 1998.

Christopher Heredia, "Little Girls Buried," *SFCh*, 17 Jul. 1998.

Alan Abrahamson and Hugo Martin, "Father of 3 Kills Wife, Children, Self," *LAT*, 5 Aug. 1998.

Stacy Finz and Carolyne Zinko, "Woman Dies After Hurling Self, Son in Front of Train," *SFCh*, 15 Aug. 1998.

Joseph Trevino, "Shooting Victim Dies of Wounds," *LAT*, 1 Sept. 1998.

Joseph Trevino and James Rainey, "Family Recalls Slain Boy as a Young Hero," *LAT*, 5 Sept. 1998.

Stacy Finz and Michael Taylor, "Palo Alto Murder-Suicide Blamed on Money Worries," *SFCh*, 24 Sept. 1998.

Larry Hatfield, Eric Brazil, and Jacob Fries, "Exec Kills Wife, Son, Self," *SFEx,* 24 Sept. 1998.

Joe Mozingo, "Aliso Village Violence Claims 2 New Victims," *LAT,* 1 Oct. 1998.

Tony Perry, "Mother Kills 4 Children, Wounds Herself," *LAT,* 28 Oct. 1997.

Nicholas Riccardi, "County Seeks to Seal Case Files on 2 Slain Children," *LAT,* 9 Nov. 1998.

Joseph Trevino and Jack Leonard, "Five Die in Grim Hour of Gunfire," *LAT,* 12 Nov. 1998.

Jack Leonard and Phil Willon, "Few Clues in Deaths of Father, Son," *LAT,* 17 Nov. 1998.

AP, "Drifter Blamed for Boy's Death," *Pasadena Star-News,* 18 Nov. 1998.

Nora Zamichow, "Antonovich Asks Family Services Agency to Review Adoption Policies," *LAT,* 21 Oct. 1999.

Jenifer Warren, "Financial, Cultural Tensions Preceded Sacramento Tragedy," *LAT,* 6 Dec. 1999.

Sue Fox, "Jurors Convict 1st Defendant in Kidnap-Slaying of Valley Teen," *LAT,* 21 Nov. 2001.

Kids Get Hit by Cars

Edward Boyer, "Baby Girl Critically Hurt in Gang Attack with Car, Police Say," *LAT,* 23 Apr. 1992.

Matea Gold, "Boy's Death Renews Call for Traffic Light," *LAT,* 22 Oct. 1997.

Jose Cardenas and Roberto Manzano, "A Christmas Tragedy Claims Teenager," *LAT,* 20 Dec. 1997.

Jose Mozingo, "Family Struck by Hit-and-Run Driver," *LAT,* 28 Jan. 1998.

George Ramos, "2 Hit-Run Drivers Strike Boy, Who Dies," *LAT,* 11 Oct. 1999.

Kids Encounter Violence in Schools

Hector Tobar and Michelle Fuetsch, "School Assaults Bring Tragedy to Compton," *LAT,* 25 Apr. 1991.

Eric Shepard and Nieson Himmel, "2 Teens Hurt in Shooting at High School Football Game," *LAT,* 5 Oct. 1991.

Eric Shepard, "Schools Study Tighter Security at Games," *LAT,* 6 Oct. 1991.

Charisse Jones and Lois Timnick, "Students at Dorsey Disappointed by Cancellation of Game; Defend School," *LAT,* 31 Oct. 1991.

Gary Libman, "On the Front Lines of War Against Gangs," *LAT,* 5 Nov. 1991.

Paul Feinberg, "Semi-Toughs: Gangs Spell Trouble for Dorsey Football," *LA Weekly,* 22 Nov. 1991.

Michael Connelly, "Gang Sends a School Back into Mourning," *LAT,* 1 Oct. 1992.

Sharon Bernstein and Josh Meyer, "4 Arrested in Racial Melee at High School," *LAT,* 27 Oct. 1992.

Stephanie Chavez and Sharon Bernstein, "Superintendent Acts as School Fights Spread," *LAT,* 28 Oct. 1992.

Somini Sengupta, "Farewell to a Friend," *LAT,* 29 Jan. 1993.

David Colker and Sam Enriquez, "Student Shot, Dies at Reseda High," *LAT,* 23 Feb. 1993.

Beth Shuster, "Violence on School Campus Eludes Solutions," *LAT,* 20 Feb. 1994.

Vicki Torres and Kenneth Reich, "Killings at San Marino Party Blamed on Gangs," *LAT,* 7 June 1994.

Ken Ellingwood, "Six Graduates Hurt as Gunfire Erupts at Party," *LAT,* 8 June 1994.

Jeff Leeds and Nicholas Riccardi, "Murder-Suicide Creates Frenzy at High School," *LAT,* 23 Oct. 1997.

Michael Krikorian, "Man Killed Trying to Settle Teens' Dispute," *LAT,* 7 Mar. 1998.

"Reward Offered in College Student's Slaying," *LAT,* 26 Mar. 1998.

Abigail Goldman, "Culver City School Calm in Wake of Shootings," *LAT,* 24 Apr. 1998.

"Two Teenagers Killed, One Wounded in Shooting," *LAT,* 1 May 1998.

Daniel Yi, "A Closer Look at Campus Fights," *LAT,* 4 May 1998.

Andrew Blankstein and Jon Steinman, "Summer Student Fatally Stabbed at Burbank High," *LAT,* 11 Jul. 1998.

Charles Wear Simmons, Elias Lopez, Joel Cohen, Patricia de Cos, and Marcus Nieto, *California Adolescents Ages 11–18: A Fact Sheet* (CRB, October 1999).

Nanette Asimov and Meredith May, "Drugs, Violence Increase in California Schools," *SFCh,* 1 Mar. 2000.

H. G. Reza and Matthew Ebnet, "Santee School Shootings," *LAT,* 8 Mar. 2001.

H. G. Reza, " 'He Never Said a Word,' Guard Recalls," *LAT,* 9 Mar. 2001.

Tony Perry, "Boy Killed in Rampage Recalled as Cheerful Youth," *LAT,* 11 Mar. 2001.

Jessica Garrison, "El Cajon School Shootings," *LAT,* 23 Mar. 2001.

Curt Streeter, "Girl, 16, Dies After Being Shot While Crossing Street," *LAT,* 6 June 2001.

Duke Helfand, "A Lonely Battler for Students," *LAT,* 9 June 2001.

Martha Groves, "Finding a Haven from Cliques and Other Annoyances," *LAT,* 20 June 2001.

Tony Perry, "Shooter in School Rampage Hangs Himself in Jail," *LAT,* 30 Oct. 2001.

Kids Get Neglected and/or Sexually Abused

Tracey Kaplan, "A Secret Is Their Shroud," *LAT,* 24 Mar. 1993.

"The Orphanage," *Newsweek,* 12 Dec. 1994.

David Early, "The Information Age: Has It Run Amok When Children Can Call Up Pornography at the Public Library?" *West Magazine, SJMN,* 12 Oct. 1997.

Sonia Nazario, "Orphans of Addiction," *LAT,* 16 and 17 Nov. 1997.

Paul Hefner, "State to Dump Child-Support Computer System," *Daily News,* 21 Nov. 1997.

Scott Harris, "A Call from Claudia: She's OK and the Crazy Life Is Over," *LAT,* 31 Jan. 1998.

AP, "Suicide Rate Rising for Black Kids," *SFCh,* 20 Mar. 1998.

Diana Griego Erwin, "It's a Tragedy, but Not a Trend," *SacBee,* 26 Mar. 1998.

Josh Meyer, "Child Abuse Deaths Increase for 2nd Year," *LAT,* 31 Mar. 1998.

Lynn Smith, "The $200 Question," *LAT,* 3 Apr. 1998.

Lynn Smith, "Effect of Parents' Split on Children Is Divided," *LAT,* 12 Apr. 1998.

Jenifer Warren, "No Fault Divorce Under Fire in State, Nation," *LAT,* 12 Apr. 1998.

Daniel Yi, "Boy Found in Grave Is Expected to Survive," *LAT,* 18 May 1998.

AP, "Groups Call Abandoned Babies a Common and Growing Problem," *SFCh,* 21 May 1998.

Tracy Weber, "Dependency Court: Lives in the Balance," *LAT,* 22 May 1998.

Nicholas Riccardi, "County Counsel's Children's Unit Criticized," *LAT,* 13 Nov. 1998.

Jonathan Curiel, "Stripper Charged After Show for Teen Girls in Pleasanton Home," *SFCh,* 26 Nov. 1998.

Cynthia Hubert, "Alarming Rise in Youth Suicides," *SacBee,* 3 Jan. 1999.

Jennifer Mena, "A Place Even Unwanted Children Could Call Home," *LAT,* 26 Sep. 1999.

Darragh Johnson, "Homeless Teens' Hopes Blossom in Spring," *SacBee,* 2 Nov. 1999.

Robin Fields, " 'Married with Children' Still Fading as a Model," *LAT,* 15 May 2001.

Oscar Johnson, "Being There for the Kids of Skid Row," *LAT,* 22 and 23 Jul. 2001.

Kids Commit Crimes

T. Christian Miller, "Accused Boys Stay in Custody," *SFCh,* 23 Oct. 1992.

Eric Malnic and Duke Helfand, "2 Teen-Agers Arrested in Race Killings," *LAT,* 10 June 1994.

Mary Curtius, "Life of Tears and Hope for Beaten Baby's Family," *LAT,* 2 Nov. 1997.

AP, "Teenager Fatally Shot Boy, 4, for Refusing to Get Cigarettes, Police Say," *LAT*, 20 Jan. 1998.

AP, "Youth Held as Suspect in Slaying of His Sister," *SFCh*, 27 Jan. 1998.

Charlie Goodyear, "11-Year-Old Convicted of Manslaughter," *SFCh*, 11 Aug. 1998.

Posses

John M. Glionna, "Posse Power," *LAT*, 26 Feb. 1993.

David Ferrell, " 'Spur Posse' Goes on the Defensive," *LAT*, 20 Mar. 1993.

Roy Rivenburg, " 'Get It If You Can,' " *LAT*, 25 Mar. 1993.

Jane Gross, "Where 'Boys Will Be Boys,' and Adults Are Bewildered," *NYT*, 29 Mar. 1993.

Somini Sengupta, "Spur Posse Youth Pleads No Contest in Girl's Assault," *LAT*, 27 Apr. 1993.

Joan Didion, "Trouble in Lakewood," *The New Yorker*, 26 Jul. 1993.

David Ferrell, "Skateboard Pros: Life on the Edge," *LAT*, 6 Mar. 1994.

Max Vanzi, "Bill Aims to Treat More Young Sex Offenders," *LAT*, 16 Feb. 1998.

Teenage Pregnancy

Maia Davis, "Crowning Touch," *LAT*, 23 Oct. 1992.

Laurie Becklund, "A Cry for Love," *LAT*, 15 Mar. 1993.

Laurie Becklund, "Opening a Closed Door," *LAT*, 16 Mar. 1993.

Shari Roan, "Painting a Bleak Picture for Teen Girls," *LAT*, 8 June 1993.

Charles Murray, "Does Welfare Bring More Babies?" *Public Interest* (Spring 1994).

Sara McLanahan, "The Consequences of Single Motherhood," *American Prospect* (Summer 1994).

Diane Levitt, *Teen Families and Welfare Dependency in California* (CRB, December 1994).

R. Meredith Burke, "Culture Clash Equals a Tide of Teenage Births," *LAT*, 2 Sept. 1997.

Kathryn Bold, "Home Maker," *LAT*, 29 Sept. 1997.

Carla Rivera, "A Couple's Rocky Road to Welfare Reform," *LAT*, 30 Sept. 1997.

Bob Pool, "Gifts and Hope for Teenage Parents," *LAT*, 10 Dec. 1997.

"Latinas Exceed Blacks in Teen Births," *SFCh*, 13 Feb. 1998.

Proposition 21

Margaret Ramirez, "Mahony Leads Protest Against Youth Crime Initiative," *LAT*, 13 Jan. 2000.

Ann Kim, "Study Finds Race Disparity in Juvenile Justice System," *LAT*, 3 Feb. 2000.

Bobby Cuza, "Felony Juvenile Arrest Rate Has Fallen, Group Says," *LAT*, 3 Mar. 2000.

Evelyn Nieves, "California Proposal Toughens Penalties for Young Criminals," *NYT*, 6 Mar. 2000.

Daniel Wood, "With Initiatives, California Tilts Conservative," *Christian Science Monitor*, 9 Mar. 2000.

Tracy Wilson, "Probation Officer Warns of Costs of New Juvenile Crime Measure," *LAT*, 26 Mar. 2000.

Maura Dolan, "Justices Curb Law on Prosecution of Youths as Adults," *LAT*, 8 Feb. 2001.

Tony Perry and Greg Krikorian, "Appeal Planned on Right to Try Juveniles as Adults," *LAT*, 16 Feb. 2001.

California Youth Authority

CYA, *Student Handbook* (February 1997).

Nancy Price, "CYA Dedicates School to Dedicated Teacher," *Stockton Record*, 8 Sept. 1997.

Jevon Swanson, "Teacher Never Afraid to Show Felons Who Is Boss," *Manteca Bulletin*, 8 Sept. 1997.

CYA, *Naming Ceremony: Johanna Boss High School* (dedication program pamphlet, 9 Sept. 1997).

Yvonne Chiu, "CYA's New Strategy a Costly Bust, Counties Say," *SacBee*, 19 Jan. 1998.

Mark Gladstone and James Rainey, "Abuse Reports Cloud Youth Authority," *LAT*, 24 Dec. 1999.

Jill Leovy, "Push to Educate Youthful Inmates Is Hard on Teachers," *LAT*, 8 Sept. 2001.

Send In the Marines

An Armed Camp

David Freed, "LA County: Armed and Dangerous," *LAT*, 17 May 1992.

David Freed, "Sales Put LA Under the Gun," *LAT*, 18 May 1992.

David Freed, "Many Nonfatal Shootings Get Scant Police Attention," *LAT*, 20 May 1992.

Los Angeles on Verge of Riots

Tom Shales, "The Decline and Fall of Los Angeles," *This World (SFCh)*, 5 Jul. 1987.

UPI, "Violence over the Weekend Takes 15 Lives," *LAT*, 22 Apr. 1991.

David Ferrell, "Window on Psyche of LA," *LAT*, 27 Apr. 1991.

Eric Malnic, "Concerns Linger at LAX Months After Crash," *LAT*, 8 Sept. 1991.

Jesse Katz and Richard Serrano, "Segregated Housing Sought at Jordan Downs," *LAT*, 10 Sept. 1991.

Bob Pool, "Sharp Edge: Mayor Proclaims 'Freddy Krueger Day' but Not Everyone Is Celebrating," *LAT*, 13 Sept. 1991.

Daniel Fromstein, " 'Bogeyman' Overkills," *Daily Trojan*, 17 Sept. 1991.

Frank Clifford, "Coalition Looks for Ties That Bind a Diverse City," *LAT*, 26 Oct. 1991.

Stuart Silverstein and Nancy Rivera Brooks, "Shoppers in Need of Stores," *LAT*, 24 Nov. 1991.

Stuart Silverstein, "Some Merchants Turn Stores into Urban Fortresses," *LAT*, 25 Nov. 1991.

Suzanne Muchnic, "Art in the City of Angels and Demons," *LAT*, 26 Jan. 1992.

Laurie Becklund, "Gang Suspects Shoot at Autos from Rooftop," *LAT*, 29 Mar. 1992.

Jeffrey L. Rabin, "Zoo Still Assailed for Elephant's Death," *LAT*, 29 Mar. 1992.

Sheryl Stolberg, "Judge Karlin's Race Is Closely Watched," *LAT*, 27 May 1992.

The Riots

Los Angeles Times for 1–6 May 1992.

San Francisco Chronicle for 1–6 May 1992.

Nora Zamichow, "Were All Deaths in Toll Really Riot-Related?" *LAT*, 6 May 1992.

Ted Rohrlich and Richard Serrano, "Criticism over Use of Force Inhibited Police, Gates Says," *LAT*, 7 May 1992.

Rich Connell, Richard Serrano, and Ted Rohrlich, "Gates Denies Riot Planning of LAPD Brass Was Lacking," *LAT*, 9 May 1992.

Seth Mydans, "4 Held in Attack at Riot's Outset," *NYT*, 13 May 1992.

Lou Cannon, *Official Negligence: How Rodney King and the Riots Changed Los Angeles and the LAPD* (1998).

PART III / Diversity

General Studies

James Allen and Eugene Turner, *The Ethnic Quilt: Population Diversity in Southern California* (Center for Geographical Studies, CSU Northridge, 1997).

Belinda Reyes, editor, *A Portrait of Race and Ethnicity in California: An Assessment of Social and Economic Well-Being* (Public Policy Institute of California, February 2001).

James Allen and Eugene Turner, *Changing Faces, Changing Places: Mapping Southern Californians* (California State University, Northridge, 2002).

Elias Lopez, *Census 2000 for California: A Friendly Guide* (CRB, July 2002).

Viva Mexico!

Bettijane Levine and Beth Ann Krier, "Of Carts and Corners," *LAT,* 26 Jan. 1992.

Luis Rodriguez, "Border States," *LAT,* 28 Feb. 1993.

Robert Lindsey, "Cesar Chavez, Founder of Union for Farm Workers, Is Dead at 66," *NYT,* 24 Apr. 1993.

Patt Morrison and Mark Arax, "For the Final Time, They Marched for Chavez," *LAT,* 30 Apr. 1993.

Elena Oumano and Enrique Lopetegui, "The Hottest Sound in LA is . . . *Banda,*" *LAT,* 1 May 1993.

John Mitchell and Shawn Hubler, "Apartment Fire Kills 9 in LA's Westlake Area," *LAT,* 4 May 1993.

Margaret Usdansky, "Census Shows Diversity of Hispanics in USA," *USA Today,* 23 Aug. 1993.

Patrick McDonnell, "New Urban Flight—to *El Norte,*" *LAT,* 22 Sept. 1993.

Carla Marinucci, "Treated like an Animal for Years," *SFEx,* 26 Sept. 1993.

Glenn Garvin, "America's Economic Refugees," *Reason,* November 1993.

William Greider, "Up Against the Drywall," *Rolling Stone,* 11 Nov. 1993.

George Sanchez, *Becoming Mexican-American: Ethnicity, Culture, and Identity in Chicano Los Angeles, 1900–1945* (1994).

Robert Lopez, "Just Whose Sidewalks Are They, Anyway?" *City Times, LAT,* 27 Feb. 1994.

World Cup USA, *Soccer Watch '94* (April 1994).

Los Angeles Times Special Report, "World Cup '94," 18 Jul. 1994.

Seth Mydans, "A New Wave of Immigrants on Farming's Lowest Rung," *NYT,* 24 Aug. 1995.

Gregory Rodriguez, *The Emerging Latino Middle Class* (Pepperdine University Institute for Public Policy, October 1996).

Jane Ganahal, "Former Farmworker Writes Himself into a Field of Dreams," *SFEx,* 10 Nov. 1996.

Deborah Guadan, " 'Café' Serves Up Vivid Characters, Surroundings," *Daily News,* 23 Mar. 1997.

Nancy Cleeland, "A Village's Odyssey: From Granjenal to Santa Ana," *LAT,* 3–4 Aug. 1997.

Kevin Baxter, "Re-discovering Roots Through Her Writing," *LAT,* 28 Oct. 1997.

Mark Arax, "10 People, Baby Die When Truck Hits Van," *LAT,* 17 Nov. 1997.

Patrick McDonnell, "Mexican Arrivals Seek New Frontiers," *LAT,* 1 Jan. 1998.

Debora Vrana, "Central Financial Provides a Vital Service to the Growing Number of Latino Immigrants, but the Price Isn't Cheap," *LAT,* 18 Jan. 1998.

Anne-Marie O'Connor, "LA County Is Hub of Nation's Largest Latino Market by Far, Survey Finds," *LAT,* 3 Aug. 1998.

Joseph Trevino and Jeffrey Gettleman, "Caught Flat-Footed Without Enough Soccer Fields," *LAT,* 1 Oct. 1999.

Maria Elena Fernandez, "Southland Churches Face Shortage of Latino Priests," *LAT,* 31 Oct. 1999.

Jesse Katz, "The Sport of Exiles," *LAT Magazine,* 5 Dec. 1999.

Hugo Martin, "Feathered Pets Give Wing to Comforting Memories of Home," *LAT,* 26 Aug. 2000.

Jill Leovy, "Tijuana Uses PR Firm to Polish Image," *LAT,* 10 June 2001.

Monte Morin and Ana Beatriz Cholo, "Soccer League Weighs Penalties After Brawl," *LAT,* 28 June 2001.

Asian Attitudes

Psyche Pascual, "Filipinos Find Nursing a Passport to America," *LAT,* 10 Mar. 1991.

Claudia Puig, "Radio Tunes-In Korean," *LAT,* 15 Apr. 1991.

Sherry Jo, "Back to the Nest," *LAT,* 28 Oct. 1991.

Teresa Watanabe, "Japan First to Help Fund LA Museum," *LAT,* 29 Nov. 1991.

Tania Azores-Gunter, "Filipino-Americans: Getting It Together, Raising Their Profile," *LAT,* 7 Dec. 1992.

Daniela Deane, "Have Job, Will Travel," *LAT,* 31 Mar. 1993.

Jason DeParle, "Last of the Manongs," *NYT,* 11 May 1993.

Uli Schmetzer, "Millionaire Wants to Be Cambodia's Ross Perot," *SFEx,* 22 May 1993.

Ling-Chai Wang, "Chinese Just Part of New Global Migration," *Oregonian,* 17 June 1993.

Randal Archibold, "Filipino-Americans Start to Reach for Reins of Power," *LAT,* 20 Aug. 1993.

Andrew Lam, "In Reality, Vietnam Is Not Free from Guilt," *Chicago Tribune,* 12 Jan. 1994.

Michael Quintanilla, "The 1.5 Solution," *LAT,* 12 Jan. 1996.

Lilly Dizon, "Aiming to Put OC Koreatown on Map," *LAT,* 16 Sept. 1996.

K. Connie Kang, "Korean-Americans Dream of Crimson," *LAT,* 25 Sept. 1996.

Nicholas Lemann, "Banana Man: Korean-American Columnist in Los Angeles," *Atlantic Monthly* (October 1996).

John Horton, "The Chinese Suburban Immigration and Political Diversity in Monterey Park, California," *Social Justice* (Fall 1996).

Karla Bruner, "Essay in Local Best-Seller Outrages Fresno Hmong," *FBee,* 28 Nov. 1996.

Stephen Magagnini, "New Light Shed on Pioneering Filipino American," *FBee,* 28 Dec. 1996.

Min Zhou, *The Politics of Diversity: Immigration, Resistance, and Change in Monterey Park, California* (1997).

John Horton, "Review of Min Zhou, *The Politics of Diversity,*" *Journal of American Ethnic History* (Spring 1997).

Heesun Wee, "For a New Culture," *Daily News,* 5 Jul. 1997.

Peter Hong, "In San Gabriel, a Redefined Chinatown Springs from Success," *LAT,* 20 Sept. 1997.

Michael Harris, "When Cultures Collide," *LAT,* 20 Oct. 1997.

Wendy Tanaka, "HMOs Get the Point," *SFEx,* 14 Dec. 1997.

Dan DeLuca, "Asian Chic," *Houston Chronicle,* 5 Jan. 1998.

Rose Dosti, "The Crimson Door Closes," *LAT,* 11 Feb. 1998.

Anne Fadiman, "Hmong Odyssey," *Via* (March–April 1998).

John Shea, "American Pastime, Japanese Star," *SFCh,* 3 Jul. 2001.

Valerie Gutierrez, "Pacific Swell," *LAT,* 7 Jul. 2001.

Multiple Identities

Assyrians and Armenians

Michael McCabe, " 'Caught Between West and Iraq,' Assyrians in Central Valley Deal with War," *SFCh,* 21 Feb. 1991.

Cyndee Fontana, "Armenians Gather to Bless Grapes," *FBee,* 11 Aug. 1997.

Islamic California

Somini Sengupta, "A Time to Celebrate," *LAT,* 25 Mar. 1993.

Edward Norden, "Allah in LA," *American Spectator* (December 1993).

John Dart, "Muslims Gather for Early Morning Prayers," *LAT,* 17 Feb 1996.

John Dart, "Muslims Protest Studio's New Film," *LAT,* 12 Mar. 1996.

Henry Weinstein, "Appeals Court Deals Setback," *LAT,* 11 Jul. 1996.

Ibrahim Sajid Malick, "New Americans: The Overlooked $400 Billion Market," *Marketing News,* 15 Jul. 1996.

John Dart, "Islamic Leader Urges Aid to the Needy," *LAT,* 27 Dec. 1997.

H. G. Reza, "Marines Invite Muslims to Base for Ramadan," *LAT,* 23 Jan. 1998.

Slavic California

Noelle Knox, "He'll Be Premier There, in Arrears Here," *LAT,* 11 Jul. 1992.

Immigration and Los Angeles

Kurt Andersen, Benjamin Cate, and the Los Angeles Bureau, "The New Ellis Island," *Time,* 13 June 1983.

Eric Heikkila, "Los Angeles: A Macrocosm of the Pacific Rim" (ms. draft report, December 1990).

Richard Simon, "Los Angeles County: The Census Story," *LAT,* 6 May 1991.

Fred Alvarez, "Legal Immigrants Find Refuge, Prosperity in LA," *LAT,* 23 Nov. 1993.

Diane Seo, "Space We're like the Ellis Island of Los Angeles,' " *City Times, LAT,* 20 Feb. 1994.

Christina Duff, "Most of the Nation's Ten Largest Cities Retain Crowns, Thanks to Immigration," *WSJ,* 19 Nov. 1997.

Immigration and San Francisco

Frank Viviano and Sharon Silva, "The New San Francisco," *San Francisco Focus* (September 1986).

Laura Jamison, Gary Kamiya, Shirley Fong-Torres, Donald George, and Corey Andrews, "Global Village: The Worlds of San Francisco," *Image, SFEx,* 27 June 1993.

Multiple Identities

Ashley Dunn, "Tension Grips Project in Aftermath of Fire," *LAT,* 9 Sept. 1991.

Elaine Woo, "2 Men Wounded in Robbery of Lynwood Store," *LAT,* 19 Sept. 1991.

Kim Kowsky, "Students Seek Causes of Brawl," *LAT,* 23 Nov. 1991.

Dexter Waugh, "Teacher Force is 82 Percent White, but Minorities Make Up 54 Percent of State Students," *SFEx,* 1 Dec. 1991.

Denise Hamilton, "A Long Lesson in Hate," *LAT,* 23 Apr. 1992.

Marty Graham, "Neighbors Block Construction of Monastery," *SFEx,* 26 Apr. 1992.

Jack Miles, "Blacks vs. Browns: The Struggle for the Bottom Rung," *Atlantic* (October 1992).

Leslie Berger, "Racial Tensions Flare Up at Hearing on Break-Up of LA District," *LAT,* 13 Mar. 1993.

Kevin Weston, "Laughing Through 'Schindler's List,' " *Minneapolis Star Tribune,* 16 Feb. 1994.

Teresa Ann Willis and Sam Enriquez, "Clashing Symbols," *LAT,* 27 Apr. 1994.

Laura Mecoy, "Ethnic Quilt Woven with Conflict," *SacBee,* 27 Oct. 1997.

John Wildermuth, "Racial Incidents Rock Carlmont High School," *SFCh,* 28 Oct. 1997.

James Sterngold, "For Asian-Americans, Political Power Can Lead to Harsh Scrutiny," *NYT,* 3 Nov. 1996.

John Dart, "Islamic Groups Protest Museum Exhibits," *LAT,* 13 Dec. 1997.

Henry Chu, "Council Lightens Leaf-Blower Penalties," *LAT,* 18 Dec. 1997.

Michael Preston, Bruce Cain, and Sandra Bass, editors, *Racial and Ethnic Politics in California* (1998).

Matea Gold, "Fast Tests Strength of Gardeners," *LAT,* 8 Jan. 1998.

Matea Gold and Jim Newton, "Fast Ends with Accord on Blowers," *LAT,* 10 Jan. 1998.

Jill Leovy, "Leaf Blowers Ban Backers Gird to Fight Bill," *LAT,* 21 Feb. 1998.

Roberto Suro, "Campaign Donor to Cooperate in Probe," *SFCh,* 6 Mar. 1998.

Greg Krikorian and Jodi Wilgoren, "Rep. Kim Sentenced to Serve Home Detention," *LAT,* 10 Mar. 1998.

Nicholas Riccardi and Richard Winton, "Kim Returns to Congress amid Doubts About Political Future," *LAT,* 11 Mar. 1998.

Emelyn Cruz, "Asians Sue SF Housing Authority," *SFEx,* 12 Mar. 1998.

PART IV / Wedge Issues

Backlash

Immigrants and Population Growth

Charles Wollenberg, *The New Immigrants and California's Multiethnic Heritage* (UC Berkeley Graduate School of Education pamphlet, 1989).

Nancy Gibbs, "Shades of Difference," *Time,* 18 Nov. 1991.

David Foster, "The West Is Fastest-Growing Region in the Nation—and It's Filling Up," *LAT,* 26 Jan. 1992.

John Wildermuth, "Immigrants Boost State Population to 31.3 Million," *SFCh,* 16 Feb. 1993.

Ben Wildavsky, "Americans Still Slow to Settle Down," *SFEx,* 10 Mar. 1993.

Daniel Weintraub, "Report Predicts 60 Million in State by 2040," *LAT,* 14 Apr. 1993.

Hans Johnson, *Immigrants in California: Findings from the 1990 Census* (CRB, September 1993).

Peter Morrison, "Goodbye Past, Hello Future: California's Demographic Shift," *LAT,* 13 Sept. 1993.

"The Great Divide: Immigration in the 1990s," *LAT,* 14–30 Nov. 1993.

Demographic Research Unit, State Department of Finance, *Race/Ethnic Population Estimates: Components of Change by Race, 1990–1995* (March 1997).

Heather Knight, "US Immigrant Level at Highest Peak Since '30s," *LAT,* 9 Apr. 1997.

Elias Lopez, "California's 21st Century: Demographic Profile' " (CRB, May 1997).

"California's Changing Demographics," *SacBee,* 27 Oct. 1997.

Pro-Immigrant Arguments

Thomas Fleming, "Immigrant Values Challenge American Ideals," *LAT,* 31 Dec. 1989.

Tim Ferguson, "California's Fertile Immigration Debate," *WSJ,* 29 Feb. 1992.

Tim Ferguson, "The Sleeper Issue of the 1990s Awakens," *WSJ,* 23 June 1992.

Julian Simon, "The Nativists Are Wrong," *WSJ,* 4 Aug. 1993.

Richard Rodriguez, "Reborn LA, Immigrant City," *WSJ,* 20 Jan. 1994.

"California Immigrants Make Fast Economic Gains, Study Finds," *NYT,* 5 Nov. 1995.

Joel Millman, *The Other Americans: How Immigrants Renew Our Country, Our Economy and Our Values* (1997).

Joseph Boyce, "Nonwhites Wake to 'American Dream,' " *WSJ,* 7 Oct. 1997.

Anti-Immigrant Arguments

Border Watch, newsletter of the American Immigration Control Foundation, 1984, 1986.

Glaister and Evelyn Elmer, *Sociobiology and Immigration: The Grim Forecast for America* (American Immigration Control Foundation, 1984).

B. A. Nelson, *The Coming Triumph of Mexican Irredentism* (American Immigration Control Foundation, 1984).

John Lukacs, *Immigration and Migration—A Historical Perspective* (American Immigration Control Foundation, 1986).

AICF Report, newsletter of the American Immigration Control Foundation, 1986–1987.

Howard Van Zandt, *Japan's "No Immigration" Policy—An Important Factor in Its Economic Success,* (American Immigration Control Foundation Special Report, 1986).

Brent Nelson, *Assimilation: The Ideal and the Reality* (American Immigration Control Foundation, 1987).

Peter Schuck, "America and the New Immigrant Experience," *LAT,* 5 May 1991.

David Rieff, "Coming Apart," *LAT,* 5 May 1991.

David Rieff, "The New Face of LA: Is This City Becoming a Universopolis or a Basin of Babel?" *LAT Magazine,* 15 Sept. 1991.

Otis Graham and Roy Beck, "To Help Inner City, Cut Flow of Immigrants," *LAT,* 19 May 1992.

Georges Vernez, *Mexican Labor in California's Economy: From Rapid Growth to Likely Stability* (RAND Corporation, 1993).

Harold Gilliam, "Bursting at the Seams," *This World (SFCh),* 21 Feb. 1993.

Louis Freedberg, "Immigration Now a Security Concern," *SFCh,* 23 June 1993.

Vlae Kershner, "Calculating the Cost of Immigration," *SFCh,* 23 June 1993.

Robert Reinhold, "A Welcome for Immigrants Turns to Resentment," *NYT,* 25 Aug. 1993.

Georges Vernez, *Undocumented Immigration: An Irritant or Significant Problem in US-Mexico Relations?* (RAND Corporation, 1994).

Patrick McDonnell, "Immigration Study Urges New Curbs and Criteria," *LAT,* 15 Sept. 1997.

Ramon McLeod, "State Warned of Immigrant Saturation," *SFCh,* 16 Sept. 1997.

Tucker Carlson, "The Intellectual Roots of Nativism," *WSJ,* 2 Oct. 1997.

Frank Clifford, "Immigration Vote Divides Sierra Club," *LAT,* 16 Mar. 1998.

Illegals

The Border

Larry Rohter, "Bustling Tijuana Lives Down Hooch and Honky-Tonk Past," *NYT,* 2 Aug. 1989.

John Phillip Santos, "My Berlin Wall: The Rio Grande," *NYT,* 18 Dec. 1989.

Larry Rohter, "In US-Mexico Town, What Border?" *NYT,* 17 Feb. 1990.

National Human Rights Commission, *Report on Human Rights Violations of Mexican Migratory Workers* (1991).

Seth Mydans, "Border near San Diego Is Home to More Violence," *NYT,* 9 Apr. 1991.

Susan Paterno, "Young and Alone," *LAT,* 10 Sept. 1991.

Sebastian Rotella, "Neighborhood's Nerves Tested by Border Crossings," *LAT,* 28 Apr. 1992.

Sebastian Rotella and Patrick McDonnell, "Truck Fleeing Border Agents Kills 5 in Crash," *LAT,* 3 June 1992.

Luis Alberto Urrea, *Across the Wire: Life in Hard Times on the Mexican Border* (1993).

Sebastian Rotella, "Desolation, Danger Haunt Children of the Border," *LAT,* 3 Apr. 1993.

Sebastian Rotella and Patrick McDonnell, "Calls Increase for Border Patrol Reforms," *LAT,* 24 Apr. 1993.

Joseph Treaster, "Huge Drug Tunnel from Mexico into US Is Found," *NYT,* 3 June 1993.

Sebastian Rotella, "Tijuana Battles for Respect," *LAT,* 22 Apr. 1994.

"Emerging Mexico, A Special Issue," *National Geographic* (August 1996).

Anne-Marie O'Connor, "Traditions Collide at Halloween," *LAT,* 31 Oct. 1997.

Smuggling Immigrants

Pamela Burdman, "Huge Boom in Human Smuggling—Inside Story of Flight from China," *SFCh,* 27 Apr. 1993.

Pamela Burdman, "How Gangsters Cash In on Human Smuggling," *SFCh,* 28 Apr. 1993.

Pamela Burdman, "American Dream Sours in NY," *SFCh,* 29 Apr. 1993.

Eric Brazil, "Chinese Shipmates Tell Tale of Hope, Peril," *SFEx,* 26 May 1993.

Jim Doyle, Pamela Burdman, and Ken Hoover, "Seized Ship's Link to Smuggling Ring Being Investigated," *SFCh,* 26 May 1993.

Clarence Johnson, Ken Hoover, and Susan Sward, "2 More Smuggling Boats Seized," *SFCh,* 3 June 1993.

Sebastian Rotella and Lee Romney, "Smugglers Use Mexico as Gateway for Chinese," *LAT,* 21 June 1993.

Vicki Torres, "2 Men Tell of Torture at Hands of Smugglers," *LAT,* 3 Oct. 1993.

"The Profits of Sin: Immigration," *Economist,* 12 Aug. 1995.

Kenneth Noble, "Manufacturers Fined in Sweatshop Inquiry," *NYT,* 16 Aug. 1995.

James Sterngold, "Raids Link Organized Crime to Sweatshops," *NYT,* 25 Aug. 1995.

AP, "Employers Named in False-Imprisonment Suit," *NYT,* 7 Sept. 1995.

James Sterngold, "Agency Missteps Put Illegal Aliens at Mercy of Sweatshops," *NYT,* 21 Sept. 1995.

Aurelio Rojas, "Growers Hire Illegals with Impunity," *SFCh,* 19 Mar. 1996.

Aurelio Rojas, "Boomtowns Count on Illegals," *SFCh,* 20 Mar. 1996.

AP, "4 Draw Prison Terms in Sweatshop Case," *NYT,* 8 May 1996.

Stuart Silverstein, "Government Berates Guess over Ads on Labor Practices," *LAT,* 10 Dec. 1997.

Diversity and Crime

Tammerlin Drummond, "Green Card: Real-Life Drama Is a Cat-and-Mouse Game," *LAT,* 21 Apr. 1991.

Daniel Yi, "Nation's Borders Don't Stop Special LAPD Unit," *LAT,* 16 Mar. 1993.

Andrew Meier, "From Russia, Without Love: Crime, Soviet-Style, Hits the US," *Image, SFEx,* 5 Dec. 1993.

Matt Lait, "4 Charged in Plot to Kill Federal Agent," *LAT,* 25 Sept. 1997.

Richard Serrano, "Mexican Drug Cartels Target US Heartland," *LAT,* 10 Dec. 1997.

Rising Tensions

Lines in the Sand

Seth Mydans, "Clash of Cultures Grows amid American Dream," *NYT,* 26 Mar. 1990.

Joan Walsh, "The Frontiers of White Flight," *Image, SFEx,* 17 Nov. 1991.

Gordon Smith, "Struggling in a State of Flux, Influx," *SDUT,* 14 Jan. 1993.

Carlos Ball, "Zoe Baird: The View from 'El Barrio,' " *WSJ,* 22 Jan. 1993.

Adela de la Torre, "Underneath California's Economy," *LAT,* 24 Feb. 1993.

Tom Abate, "Foreigners Take Jobs on Shaky Visas," *SFEx,* 7 Mar. 1993.

"The Great Divide," *LAT,* 14–30 Nov. 1993.

Lynell George and David Ferrell, "LA's Veneer Stripped to Show Blemishes," *LAT,* 10 Oct. 1995.

Dale Maharidge, *The Coming White Minority: California's Eruptions and America's Future* (1996).

Ariana Cha, "California—Balkanization Is Predicted by 2040," *Arizona Republic,* 13 Sept. 1997.

Manny Fernandez, "Hate Crimes Jump 17% in California," *SFCh,* 10 Jan. 1998.

Toward Political Action

Daryl Kelley, "Curb on US Citizenship Proposed," *LAT,* 24 Oct. 1991.

Robert Reinhold, "In California, New Discussion on Whether to Bar the Door," *NYT,* 3 Dec. 1991.

Dianne Feinstein, "We Can Get a Grip on Our Borders," *LAT,* 16 June 1993.

Vlae Kershner, "California Leads in Immigration—and Backlash," *SFCh,* 21 June 1993.

Vlae Kershner, "Why Immigration Laws Are So Hard to Change," *SFCh,* 21 June 1993.

Alan Nelson, "A Governor's Brave Stand on Illegal Aliens," *NYT,* 23 Aug. 1993.

Dianne Klein, "Majority in State Are Fed Up with Illegal Immigration," *LAT,* 19 Sept. 1993.

Wedge Issues

Jeffrey Rosen, "The War on Immigrants: Why the Courts Can't Save Us," *New Republic,* 30 Jan. 1995.

Philip Martin, "Proposition 187 in California," *International Migration Review* (Spring 1995).

Lloyd Krieger, "Illegal Aliens, Dirty Jobs," *NYT,* 28 Aug. 1995.

Richard Rayner, "What Immigration Crisis?" *NYT Magazine,* 7 Jan. 1996.

Steven Holmes, "California Governor Sues US for Cost of Imprisoning Aliens," *NYT,* 6 Mar. 1996.

Eric Schmitt, "Panel Votes for Worker Visas for 250,000," *NYT,* 6 Mar. 1996.

Michael Doyle, "Toughest Border Plan Yet," *SacBee,* 22 Mar. 1996.

Kenneth Noble, "Videotape of Beating by Authorities Jolts Los Angeles," *NYT,* 3 Apr. 1996.

Tim Golden, "California Governor Cuts Off Aid for Illegal Immigrants," *NYT,* 28 Aug. 1996.

Sandra Hernandez, "After the Storm, Quiet," *Los Angeles Weekly,* 29 Nov. 1996.

Patrick McDonnell, "Immigrants Not Lured by Aid, Study Says," *LAT,* 29 Jan. 1997.

Marcus Stern, "5 Million Illegal Immigrants Now Call US Home," *SDUT,* 8 Feb. 1997.

Pamela Podger and Robert Rodriguez, "Rural Schools See Enrollment Drop," *FBee*, 28 May 1997.

Walter Goodman, "One Stacked Deck Against Another," *NYT*, 1 Jul. 1997.

"Fake Licenses Tied to Bribes in California," *NYT*, 3 Aug. 1997.

Kevin Baxter, "Panic and Confusion over a Deadline to Leave," *LAT*, 22 Oct. 1997.

Jodi Wilgoren and Patrick McDonnell, "INS Deportations Soar as Crackdown Proceeds," *LAT*, 31 Oct. 1997.

Dave Lesher, "Deadlock on Prop. 187 Has Backers, Governor Fuming," *LAT*, 8 Nov. 1997.

"Cut-Off of Prenatal Care for Illegal Immigrants Allowed," *LAT*, 13 Nov. 1997.

Editorial, "Proposition 187 Backers Should Call It Quits," *LAT*, 17 Nov. 1997.

"100 Stage Protest over Backlog in Citizenship Cases," *LAT*, 22 Nov. 1997.

Patrick McDonnell, "Judge Upholds Wilson's Prenatal Care Ban," *LAT*, 13 Dec. 1997.

Jodi Wilgoren, "INS' Border Focus Is Shifting to Other States," *LAT*, 11 Mar. 1998.

Affirmative Action

The Debate

Richard Epstein, "Diversity Yes—but Without Coercion," *WSJ*, 22 Apr. 1992.

Ward Connerly, "With Liberty and Justice for All: A Warranty on Our Future," *Vital Speeches*, 1 May 1996.

Robert Novak, "Rising Stars," *National Review*, 23 Dec. 1996.

William Spohn, "Negative Action in California: A Gospel Perspective," *America*, 22 Feb. 1997.

"Negative Action," *Economist*, 12 Apr. 1997.

Michael Kelly, "The Great Divider," *New Republic*, 7 Jul. 1997.

Peter Hecht, "Jackson Takes Anti-209 Fight to UC Davis," *SacBee*, 27 Oct. 1997.

Larry Hatfield, "High Court: 209 Stands," *SFEx*, 4 Nov. 1997.

Reynolds Holding, "US Top Court Lets 209 Stand," *SFCh*, 4 Nov. 1997.

Tony Mauro and Gary Fields, "Affirmative Action Ban Upheld," *USA Today*, 4 Nov. 1997.

David Savage, "High Court Allows Prop. 209 Repeal of Affirmative Action," *LAT*, 4 Nov. 1997.

Annie Nakao, "Bay Area Is 209 Battleground," *SFEx*, 5 Nov. 1997.

Carol Morello, "Controversial Measure Proves Difficult to Enforce," *USA Today*, 17 Nov. 1997.

Marla Dickerson, Lee Romney, and Vicki Torres, "Despite Wilson Order, Goals for Diversity Thrive Elsewhere," *LAT*, 13 Mar. 1998.

UC, CSU, and Affirmative Action

Dexter Waugh, "Asians Enrich Berkeley Campus," *SFEx*, 29 Mar. 1993.

Norimitsu Onishi, "Affirmative Action: Choosing Sides," *NYT*, 31 Mar. 1996.

Mark Lasswell, "The Fall of an Affirmative Action Hero," *WSJ*, 27 Aug. 1997.

Randal Archibold and Richard Lee Colvin, "UC Urged to Drop SATs as Admission Criteria," *LAT*, 19 Sept. 1997.

Editorial, "Dropping SAT Is No Cure For Latinos' UC Problem," *LAT*, 24 Sept. 1997.

Editorial, "Harvard Bound," *WSJ*, 25 Sept. 1997.

Frank del Olmo, "The Affirmative Action Case Isn't Closed," *LAT*, 9 Nov. 1997.

Jocelyn Stewart, "Black Colleges Woo Students Alienated by Prop. 209," *LAT*, 25 Nov. 1997.

Mark Gladstone, "UC Applications at Record High," *LAT*, 29 Jan. 1998.

Katherine Seligman, "Novel UC Plan to Boost Diversity," *SFEx*, 12 Feb. 1998.

Brad Hayward, "SAT Test Still UC's Standard of Choice," *SacBee,* 17 Feb. 1998.
Peter Schrag, "UC Admissions: Is Podunk High School World Class?" *SacBee,* 18 Feb. 1998.
Kenneth R. Weiss, "UC Panel Backs Use of SATs for Admissions," *LAT,* 20 Feb. 1998.
Pamela Burdman, "Minority Admissions Drop at UC Schools," *SFCh,* 18 Mar. 1998.
Richard Atkinson, "Diversity at UC Must Equal Quality," *SFCh,* 1 Apr. 1998.
Steve Stecklow, "Minorities Fall at Universities in California," *WSJ,* 1 Apr. 1998.

Hasta La Vista!

James Crawford, *Hold Your Tongue: Bilingualism and the Politics of English Only* (1992).
Julian Guthrie, "When Language Hinders Learning," *SFEx,* 11 May 1997.
Alice Callaghan, "Desperate to Learn English," *NYT,* 15 Aug. 1997.
"Separate and Unequal," *Economist,* 30 Aug. 1997.
George Skelton, "A Lawmaker's Firsthand View of the Bilingual Issue," *LAT,* 23 Oct. 1997.
George Skelton, "Don't Hold Your Breath for Polite Bilingual Debate," *LAT,* 27 Oct. 1997.
Gregory Rodriguez, "An Opportunity for Latino Lawmakers to Take the Lead," *LAT,* 30 Nov. 1997.
Eric Wahlgren, "Glendale Training Homegrown Teachers for Linguistic Diversity," *Daily News,* 22 Dec. 1997.
Jennifer Kerr, "Bilingual Issue: Pressure Mounts," *SFEx,* 5 Jan. 1998.
Eric Bailey and Nick Anderson, "Democrats Make New Bid to Save Bilingual Ed," *LAT,* 27 Jan. 1998.
Frank del Olmo, "Take High Road in Bilingual Debate," *LAT,* 15 Feb. 1998.
Amy Pyle, "Opinions Vary on Studies That Back Bilingual Classes," *LAT,* 2 Mar. 1998.
Nick Anderson, "State Overhauls Rules on Bilingual Education," *LAT,* 13 Mar. 1998.
David Lesher, "Governor Candidates Avoid Bilingual Issue," *LAT,* 28 Mar. 1998.
Russell Schoch, "A Conversation with Eugene Garcia," *California Monthly* (April 1998).
Eric Bailey, "Assembly Panel Advances Bilingual Education Bill," *LAT,* 2 Apr. 1998.
Carl Ingram, "Board of Education Reaffirms Local-Control Bilingual Stance," *LAT,* 9 Apr. 1998.
Nick Anderson, "Bilingual Education Backers Go on the Offensive," *LAT,* 17 Apr. 1998.
William Booth, "In California Classrooms, a Troubled Transition," *Washington Post,* 4 Aug. 1998.
Fred Alvarez and Jennifer Hamm, "No Habla Espanol," *LAT,* 6 Sept. 1998.
Richard Lee Colvin, "A Crusader Well-Schooled in Education," *LAT,* 2 Oct. 1998.
Don Terry, "Bilingual Education Lives After All," *NYT,* 3 Oct. 1998.
Lisa Richardson, "Many Santa Ana Parents Seeking English-Only Waivers," *LAT,* 4 Oct. 1998.
Kate Folmar, "Word Getting Out on Bilingual Class Waivers," *LAT,* 8 Oct. 1998.
Richard Lee Colvin, "Prop 227 Delays Reading Lessons in English," *LAT,* 9 Oct. 1998.
Tina Nguyen, "At One School, a Third Opt for Bilingual Classes," *LAT,* 13 Oct. 1998.
Douglas Lasken, "The Battle over Prop 227 Is Far from Over," *LAT,* 15 Oct. 1998.
Harry Pachon, "Measure's Flaws Make It Hard to Implement," *LAT,* 15 Oct. 1998.
Editorial, "Resisting the Law," *WSJ,* 19 Oct. 1998.
Nick Anderson and Louis Sahagun, "Bilingual Classes Still Thriving in Wake of Prop 227," *LAT,* 22 Oct. 1998.
Nick Anderson and Louis Sahagun, "Hundreds Wait for Bilingual Education, Requests Often Fall Short of the Number Needed to Form a Class," *LAT,* 23 Oct. 1998.
Hugo Martin, "The ABC's of Helping Youngsters Achieve Literacy," *LAT,* 22 Nov. 1998.

Accommodations

Struggle for Reconciliation

Mark Ridley Thomas, Manuel Pastor, and Stewart Kwoh, "The 'New Majority' Wants Its Share," *LAT,* 12 Oct. 1989.

Paul Gray, "Whose America?" *Time,* 8 Jul. 1991.

William Cellis, "In Truth, Hispanic Groups Aim to Rewrite History," *NYT,* 31 Jul. 1991.

Robert Reinhold, "Class Struggle," *NYT Magazine,* 29 Sept. 1991.

Dennis Prager, "Fear and Loathing in Los Angeles," *Crisis* (September 1992).

Gordon Smith, "Racial Harmony Will Lead Goals," *SDUT,* 15 Jan. 1993.

Planning for Prosperity in the San Diego Baja Region (San Diego Dialogue, 30 Sept. 1993).

L. A. Murillo, *Spanish Pronunciation: A Key* (California Highway Patrol, LAPD, Sheriff's Department of LA County, 1994).

Roger Deitz, "Five Hispanic PhDs in SFSU Biology Department," *Hispanic Outlook in Higher Education,* 13 June 1997.

Amy Pyle, "Through the Front Door at USC," *LAT,* 7 Sept. 1997.

David Friedman, "The Numbers Game," *LAT,* 21 Sept. 1997.

Jodi Wilgoren and Patrick McDonnell, "Immigration Panel Urges Focus on Unity," *LAT,* 1 Oct. 1997.

Duane Noriuki, "His Own Path to a Life's Dream," *LAT,* 3 Oct. 1997.

Duane Noriuki, "Where Everybody Knows Your Name," *LAT,* 5 Nov. 1997.

Douglas P. Shuit, "In Nod to Latinos, Long Beach Names Park for Cesar Chavez," *LAT,* 20 Nov. 1997.

Denise Gellene, "In Their Own Images: TV Ad Seeks to Broaden How Latinos Are Viewed," *LAT,* 2 Apr. 1998.

Dorothy Korber, "Immigration Shapes State," *SacBee,* 23 May 2001.

Todd S. Purdum, "California Census Confirms Whites Are in Minority," *NYT,* 30 Mar. 2001.

Culture and the Arts

Nancy Nusser, "The Role Madonna Wants," *SFCh,* 31 Oct. 1990.

Tracy Wilkinson, "Beyond Borders," *LAT,* 15 Sept. 1991.

Susan Freudenheim, "Art That Crosses the Line," and John Phillip Santos, "Rediscovering America in 1991," *LAT Calendar,* 20 Oct. 1991.

David Kirp, "The Many Masks of Richard Rodriguez," *Image, SFEx,* 15 Nov. 1992.

Russell Schoch, "A Conversation with Richard Rodriguez," *California Monthly* (December 1992).

Marjorie Miller, "North of the Border," 29 Dec. 1992.

Virginia Postrel, "A Man of Two Heritages," *WSJ,* 17 Feb. 1993.

Don Shirley, "Ramona: Hit and Myth Affair," *LAT,* 22 Apr. 1993.

Richard Rodriguez, "True West: Relocating the Horizon of the American Frontier," *Harper's* (September 1996).

Lewis Segal, "Fine-Tuning the Authentic," *LAT Calendar,* 31 Aug. 1997.

Diane Haithman, "LA Museum Will Get Trove of Mexican Art," *SacBee,* 3 Oct. 1997.

Diane Haithman, "Mexico's Masters: LA Museum Acquires the $25 Million Lewin Collection of Modernist Works," *LAT,* 3 Oct. 1997.

Christopher Knight, "Artists in 2 Border Cities Blast Away at Artificial Barriers," *LAT,* 4 Oct. 1997.

Jan Breslauer, "Into Unchartered Waters," *LAT Calendar,* 5 Oct. 1997.

Mark Swed, "A Savvy but Sketchy 'Florencia,' " *LAT,* 7 Oct. 1997.

Christopher Knight, "Mixed Blessings," *LAT,* 24 Nov. 1997.

Richard Rodriguez, "Where Have Parents Gone?" *LAT,* 21 Dec. 1997.

Dorothy Korber, "Counting America: No Place like Home," *SacBee,* 15 May 2002.

PART V / Turnaround

For the Good Times

"California Leads the Nation in Major Business Growth," *News from California* (California Department of Commerce, 4 Mar. 1985).

"California Leads the Nation in Attracting Major Business Growth," *News from California* (Department of Commerce, 19 Feb. 1986).

"California Leads Nation in Business Growth," *Bear Tracks: News of the Californias* (Department of Commerce, Spring 1986).

California, the Nation State (Department of Commerce, March 1986).

"Industrial Expansion Pace Continues Through First Quarter," *News from California* (Department of Commerce, 8 May 1986).

"Second Quarter Industrial Expansions Top 100," *News From California* (Department of Commerce, 23 Jul. 1986).

Free Fall

1991

Robert Reinhold, "California's Fiscal Crisis Tests Government's Role," *NYT,* 3 Apr. 1991.

Dean Takahashi, "Northrop Loss Means 21,000 Lost Jobs," *LAT,* 24 Apr. 1991.

Ralph Vartabedian and Melissa Healy, "Lockheed Wins Fighter-Jet Pact," *LAT,* 24 Apr. 1991.

Jesus Sanchez, "State's Long-Term Jobless Corps Grows 50% in Year," *LAT,* 8 Sept. 1991.

Nancy Rivera Brooks, "New Group Tries to Fight LA Flight," *LAT,* 31 Oct. 1991.

Robert Reinhold, "Amid Cuts, California Is Curtailing College Dreams," *NYT,* 10 Nov. 1991.

George White, "Taiwan Group's Leader Is Symbol of High-Tech Shift," *LAT,* 22 Nov. 1991.

James Flanigan, "McDonnell Deal May Buy Stake in Asia's Future," *LAT,* 24 Nov. 1991.

Ralph Vartabedian, "McDonnell Douglas' Bumpy Ride," *LAT Magazine,* 1 Dec. 1991.

Sheryl WuDunn, "McDonnell's Rich Taiwanese Backer," *NYT,* 2 Dec. 1991.

Ralph Vartabedian, "Defending the Douglas Deal," *LAT,* 4 Dec. 1991.

1992

Robert A. Jones, "Bond Now, Let Others Pay Later," *LAT,* 29 Jan. 1992.

Daniel Weintraub, "California Bond Rating Lowered," *LAT,* 11 Feb. 1992.

Tim Deady, "Grand Jury Investigates LA Companies' Exodus," *Los Angeles Business Journal,* 13 Apr. 1992.

David Littmann, "The Cost of Regulation, Counted in Jobs," *WSJ,* 21 Apr. 1992.

Larry Gordon, "CSU Plans to Lay Off 2,200 Unless State Helps," *LAT,* 6 June 1992.

Robert Reinhold, "Stunned by Reality, California Mingles Despair and Hope," *NYT,* 31 Jul. 1992.

William Eaton and Susan Moffat, "Senate Bows to Bush, OKs 20 B-2 Bombers," *LAT,* 20 Sept. 1992.

Ralph Vartabedian, "Mayday for Aerospace," *LAT,* 22 Nov. 1992.

Steven Capps, "Death, Destruction—and Some Hope: 1992 the Year That Was," *SFEx*, 28 Dec. 1992.

1993

Jesus Sanchez, "Times Mirror Reports Loss of $66.6 Million for 1992," *LAT*, 4 Feb. 1993.
Nancy Rivera Brooks, "Northrop Will Slash 2,400 Jobs," *LAT*, 10 Mar. 1993.
James Gertstenzang, "Feds Forecast for California: Bleak," *LAT*, 11 Mar. 1993.
Donna Walters, "Down but Not Out," *LAT*, 14 Mar. 1993.
Ralph Vartabedian, "Hughes to Close Missile Facility in Canoga Park," *LAT*, 30 Mar. 1993.
Ken Stegmann, "Seagate Cutting 3,400 Workers," *SFCh*, 20 Apr. 1993.
Reuters, "US May Dump C-17 Jet Program," *SFCh*, 12 May 1993.
Leslie Guevarra, "1,478 Layoffs Called For in SF Budget," *SFCh*, 1 June 1993.
Ralph Vartabedian, "McDonnell Will Shut Down Its Torrance Plant," *LAT*, 6 June 1992.
Gregg Fields, "Textile Firm Moving from LA to Dade," *Miami Herald*, 27 Jul. 1993.
Frederick Rose, "Can an Entire State Have an Identity Crisis? Yes, If It's California," *WSJ*, 16 Nov. 1993.
Patt Morrison, "Payloads, Paydays, Palm Trees," *LAT*, 5 Dec. 1993.

1994

Ralph Vartabedian, "Northrop to Cut 3,000 from Work Force," *LAT*, 25 Mar. 1994.

A Beleaguered Middle Class

Michael McCabe, "Fed-Up Californians Flee to Colorado," *SFCh*, 4 Nov. 1992.
Richard Stern and Toddi Gutner, "A Helluva Place to Have a Business," *Forbes*, 21 Dec. 1992.
Frederick Rose, "Moving On: Americans Who Seek a Future in California Find Others Departing," *WSJ*, 19 Jan. 1993.
Jim Carlton, "Exodus from California Is Bringing Pains and Gains to Other Western States," *WSJ*, 22 Mar. 1993.
Sam Enriquez, "Data Shows Largest Exodus from LA This Century," *LAT*, 2 Oct. 1993.
Jonathan Marshall, "Income Gap Widens Fast in California," *SFCh*, 15 Jul. 1996.
Kenneth Howe, "Levi's Plans Big Cutback," *SFCh*, 14 Nov. 1997.
Ralph Vartabedian, "Raytheon Plans to Cut As Many As 10,000 Jobs," *LAT*, 20 Jan. 1998.
Karen Kaplan, "Job Cuts Jolt, but Aerospace Still Aloft," *LAT*, 24 Jan. 1998.

Turnaround

1992: Efforts at Recovery

Douglas P. Shuit, "Kathleen Brown, the Brown Charm Continued: But She's on the Hot Seat Now," *LAT*, 2 Feb. 1992.
Catherine Gewertz, "Ueberroth Begins New Challenge," *LAT*, 3 Feb. 1992.
Joel Kotkin, "Ueberroth's Breath of Fresh Economic Air," *LAT*, 26 Apr. 1992.
Staff Reports, "100 Best Performing Companies in California," *LAT*, 28 Apr. 1992.
Alvin Rabushka, *Reversing California's Decline* (Howard Jarvis Taxpayer's Foundation, May 1992).
Vlae Kershner, "Economist Urges Making Parents Pay for Schools," *SFCh*, 15 May 1992.

1993: Turnaround Begins

Gordon Smith, "State's Economy Strives to Change with the Times," *SDUT*, 16 Jan. 1993.
James Flanigan, "Defense Cuts Mean Work for LA Firm," *LAT*, 3 Feb. 1993.

Constance Sommer, "Leading Indicators Up 1.9%, Best in Decade," *LAT*, 3 Feb. 1993.

Staff Reports, "100 Best Performing Companies in California," *LAT*, 27 Apr. 1993.

Tim Ferguson, "Enterprising Answers to California's Continuing Crisis," *WSJ*, 18 May 1993.

California Business Higher Education Forum, *Forum Notes* (Summer 1993).

Tim Ferguson, "Familiar California Scene: A Hot Tax Vote," *WSJ*, 20 Jul. 1993.

Donald Woutat, "LA Left Behind As State Revs Up," *LAT*, 25 Dec. 1993.

1994: Recovery in Sight

"Ready to Take On the World," *Economist*, 15 Jan. 1994.

Staff Reports, "100 Best Performing Companies in California," *LAT*, 26 Apr. 1994.

Rosa Maria Moller, *California Economic Update* (CRB, October 1994).

Immigrants to the Rescue

Bad News Bears

Dan Walters, "State's Economy Is Hit With a Triple Whammy," *SacBee*, 23 Dec. 1991.

Paul Starobin, "Is the Dreamin' Over?" *National Journal*, 26 Sept. 1992.

Richard Hylton, "It Will Get Worse in California," *Fortune*, 19 Apr. 1993.

Immigrant Entrepreneurs

Joel Kotkin, "Why California's Economy Should Never Go Nativist," *LAT*, 8 Mar. 1992.

Joel Kotkin, "Immigrants Lead a Recovery," *WSJ*, 22 Apr. 1994.

Robin Berger, "Investing in Tomorrow," *Los Angeles Business Journal*, 27 June 1994.

Joel Kotkin, *The Next Act: Southern California's New Economy* (Center for the New West, Fall 1994).

David Friedman, "The Incredible Shrinking Recession," *Los Angeles Downtown News*, 1 May 1995.

Joel Kotkin, "A Recovery That's Creating High-Wage Jobs," *LAT*, 26 Nov. 1995.

Joel Kotkin, "New Fuel for California's Engine," *WSJ*, 25 Mar. 1996.

James Flanigan, "Low-Income Neighborhoods Prove They Can Drive Markets," *LAT*, 10 Apr. 1996.

K. Oanh Ha, "Latino Bus Firm Succeeds by Taking Its Own Route," *WSJ*, 8 Oct. 1997.

Dave Lesher, "Facts, Instinct Guide State's Economic Seer," *LAT*, 27 Oct. 1997.

Joel Kotkin, "A Union's War on Workers," *WSJ*, 9 Dec. 1997.

James Flanigan, "Immigrant Banks: A Model for Asia, a Boon to Us," *LAT*, 14 Jan. 1998.

Denise Hamilton, "Worlds Together: Knowledge of US, India, Helps Tech Firm Grow," *LAT*, 28 Jan. 1998.

Swords into Ploughshares

Tim Ferguson, "LA Lets Fly with New Grounds for Aerospace," *WSJ*, 24 Mar. 1992.

"Post-Cold War Retooling," *National Journal*, 26 Sept. 1992.

Ralph Vartabedian, "LA County Gets Grant for Defense Conversion," *LAT*, 10 Nov. 1992.

Christopher Reed, "Los Angeles Goes Back to the Future," *Guardian*, 19 Feb. 1993.

James Bornemeier and Glenn Bunting, "State Officials Mount Attack to Save Bases," *LAT*, 9 Mar. 1993.

Greg Lucas, "Aspin Promises to Consider Keeping Alameda Base Open," *SFCh*, 9 Mar. 1993.

Carl Hall, "A Potential Disaster for Shipyards," *SFCh*, 13 Mar. 1993.

Greg Lucas, "How Bay Area Bases Lost Out," *SFCh*, 13 Mar. 1993.

Carl Nolte, "Navy Has Been in Bay Area from the Beginning," *SFCh*, 13 Mar. 1993.

Gerald Adams, "Base Close May Free Bay Treasure," *SFEx*, 21 Mar. 1993.

Joel Kotkin and David Friedman, "Clinton's Troubling Welfare Plan for the State—Defense Conversion," *LAT*, 21 Mar. 1993.

Don Martinez, "Alameda Base May Avoid Ax, Official Says," *SFEx*, 22 Apr. 1993.

James Bornemeier, "Long Beach Spared by Bases Panel," *LAT*, 27 June 1993.

Brendan Riley, "Longtime Navy Town Fighting to Survive," *LAT*, 26 Sept. 1993.

Tim Ferguson, "Converting California, in Spite of Aid," *WSJ*, 7 Dec. 1993.

Mike Allen, "Defense Conversion Eludes Some, but Not All," *San Diego Business Journal*, 22 May 1995.

Lynn Graebner, "McClellan's Incubator for Electric Cars Moves Along," *Sacramento Business Journal*, 1 Jan. 1996.

Mike Sturman, "Import Trade Sales Center Proposed," *[Riverside] Press-Enterprise*, 12 Jan. 1996.

John McCloud, "A California City Is Attracting Short-Term Leases to a Naval Shipyard While It Works On a Long-term Plan," *NYT*, 31 Jan. 1996.

James Flanigan, "Two Success Stories in Trenches of Defense Conversion," *LAT*, 21 Feb. 1996.

Luis Monteagodo, "Long Beach Naval Shipyard Goes Commercial," *[Long Beach] Press-Telegram*, 3 Jul. 1996.

Onell Soto, "California Air Base Re-Use Group Weighs Military, Commercial Use," *[Riverside] Press-Enterprise*, 5 Jul. 1996.

Onell Soto, "Firm to Market Inland California Base as Commercial Cargo Airport," *[Riverside] Press-Enterprise*, 8 Aug. 1996.

Clint Swett, "Business Flying at Sacramento Mather Airport," *SacBee*, 23 Sept. 1996.

Onell Soto, "California Airbase Redevelopers Must Overhaul Electric, Phone Service," *[Riverside] Press-Enterprise*, 5 Dec. 1996.

Bill Hillburg, "Post–Cold War Recovery Blueprint Is Mired in a Nationwide Controversy," *[Long Beach] Press-Telegram*, 20 Mar. 1997.

Sheila Muto, "Real-Estate Investors Plan Attack on State's Former Military Bases," *WSJ*, 26 Mar. 1997.

Andrea Siedsma, "Conversion of Naval Training Center to Civilian Uses Now Begins," *San Diego Business Journal*, 31 Mar. 1997.

Joseph Ascenzi, "California Base Reuse Group Starts Joint Marketing," *[Ontario] Business Press*, 5 May 1997.

Robert Celaschi, "McClellan Enters the Home Stretch," *Sacramento Business Journal*, 12 May 1997.

Bob White, "Pacific Bell Opens Center on Former Air Force Base," *Modesto Bee*, 28 June 1997.

Gray Scott, "Victorville May Sell Former Base," *[Ontario] Business Press*, 7 Jul. 1997.

Karen Kaplan, "G.I. Joystick," *LAT*, 6 Oct. 1997.

The Comeback Kid

Good Times Back

Junius Ellis, "With Profits of 50% in Sight, I Wish My Picks All Could Be California Stocks," *Money* (June 1996).

Thad Seligman, "Southern California's Reawakening," *Mortgage Banking* (July 1996).

Robert Edelstein, "Assessing the Reemerging California Economy," *Real Estate Finance* (Fall 1996).

"The West Is Best Again," *Economist*, 9 Aug. 1997.

Don Lee, "Golden State's Economy Will Shine, Predict UCLA Analysts," *LAT*, 17 Sept. 1997.

Dave Lesher, "Wilson Signs $1 Billion Cut in Income Taxes," *LAT*, 2 Oct. 1997.

Don Lee, "State's Economy Robust, Most in Southland Believe," *LAT*, 24 Nov. 1997.

Don Lee, "Jobless Rate in California Hits 7-Year Low," *LAT*, 20 Dec. 1997.

Jodi Wilgoren, "Population Hike in State Outpaces US Growth," *LAT*, 1 Jan. 1998.

Art Pine, " '97 Employment Figure Strongest Since 1973," *LAT*, 10 Jan. 1998.

Staff Writer, "Home Prices Turn Up—Finally—in '97," *LAT*, 18 Jan. 1998.

Michael Benson, "Who's Knocking at the State Door?" *WSJ*, 21 Jan. 1998.

Patrice Apodaca, "State Gains 40,600 Jobs in December," *LAT*, 24 Jan. 1998.

Don Lee, "UCLA Raises Jobs Estimate but Expects Slowing in 2000," *LAT*, 22 Sept. 1999.

AP, "LA County Leads Way in Growth of Business, Employees," *LAT*, 5 Oct. 1999.

Rone Tempest, "In Marin County Plenty a Poverty of Service Workers," *LAT*, 25 Oct. 1999.

James Flanigan, "Taking Back the Aerospace Industry," *LAT*, 17 Nov. 1999.

Dan Morain, "$2.6 Billion State Budget Surplus Is Predicted," *LAT*, 18 Nov. 1999.

Entertainment Does Its Part

David Fox, "The Invasion of the Screens," *LAT*, 4 Dec. 1991.

Sallie Hofmeister and Jane Hall, "Disney to Buy Cap Cities/ABC for $19 Billion, Vault to No. 1," *LAT*, 1 Aug. 1995.

Bill Montague, "California Comeback Hollywood Sparks Revival in Golden State," *USA Today*, 6 May 1996.

Morris Newman, "14 Sound Stages Will Be Built on Speculation Southwest of Downtown Los Angeles," *NYT*, 8 Jan. 1997.

Sallie Hofmeister, "Universal Sells Most of Its TV Assets to Diller," *LAT*, 21 Oct. 1997.

Sallie Hofmeister, "Wheeler Diller," *LAT*, 25 Oct. 1997.

Bob Howard, "Tinsel Comes to Town," *LAT*, 5 Nov. 1997.

James Bates, "Hollywood as Southland Superstar," *LAT*, 18 Jan. 1998.

James Flanigan, "TV Deals' Message? The World Needs Entertainment," *LAT*, 18 Jan. 1998.

James Bates, "Making Movies and Moving On," *LAT*, 19 Jan. 1998.

James Bates, "Devastating Downturn for Hollywood Is Unlikely," *LAT*, 20 Jan. 1998.

Editorial, "Movies as a Job Engine," *LAT*, 25 Jan. 1998.

Claudia Eller, "Full Speed Ahead," *LAT*, 27 Jan. 1998.

James Flanigan, "Sound Stages Signal Commercial Real Estate Revival," *LAT*, 28 Jan. 1998.

Valley Talk

"Microchip Blues," *National Journal*, 26 Sept. 1992.

Tom Abate, "Zschau Takes the Helm at Adstar," *SFEx*, 27 Apr. 1993.

Michael Malone, "Nerds' Revenge," *NYT*, 18 Feb. 1996.

Robert X. Cringely, *Accidental Empires: How the Boys of Silicon Valley Make Their Millions, Battle Foreign Competition, and Still Can't Get a Date* (1997).

Po Bronson, *The First $20 Million Is Always the Hardest* (1997).

James Flanigan, "Large and Small Team for Technology," *LAT*, 29 Jan. 1997.

Edward Rothstein, "Heroes of a New Genre Seek Their Fortunes in the Kingdom of Silicon Valley," *NYT*, 31 Mar. 1997.

Melinda Fulmer, "A Growing Spectrum," *LAT*, 18 May 1997.

Joel Kotkin, *Southern California in the Information Age* (Pepperdine University Institute for Public Policy, June 1997).

Randall Stross, "Employers Beg for Techie Help in the Valley," *Fortune*, 21 Jul. 1997.

Po Bronson, "Silicon Valley, the Workers' Paradise," *WSJ*, 25 Aug. 1997.

"How the West Kicked Butt," *Forbes*, 25 Aug. 1997.

Tom Wolfe, "Robert Noyce and His Congregation," *Forbes ASAP*, 25 Aug. 1997.

Greg Miller, "In Search of Stability," *LAT*, 22 Sept. 1997.

AP, "High Tech Millionaires Proliferate," *SFEx*, 23 Sept. 1997.

"Richest List Has Gates at No. 1, Plus 83 Californians," *LAT*, 27 Sept. 1997.

Greg Miller, "Sun Accuses Microsoft of Violating Java Pact," *LAT*, 8 Oct. 1997.

David Einstein, "McKenna Is Selling Himself," *SFCh*, 20 Nov. 1997.

David Einstein, "Sun Serving More Than Just Java," *SFCh*, 12 Dec. 1997.

Martha Groves, "Asset Values Shifting as Firms Begin to Account for Employee Brainpower," *LAT*, 18 Jan. 1998.

Brian Taylor, "Growing Pains: The Stunting of Silicon Valley's Growth," *Reason* (February 1998).

Po Bronson, "Silicon Valley Searches for an Image," *WSJ*, 9 Feb. 1998.

Greg Miller, "Web Page Turner," *LAT*, 29 June 1998.

Karen Kaplan, "Another Incubator Is About to Hatch," *LAT*, 12 Oct. 1998.

Charles Piller, "Sitting on Top of the WWWorld," *LAT*, 12 Oct. 1998.

Peter Sinton, "High-Tech Pied Piper," *SFCh*, 22 Sept. 1999.

James Flanigan, "A 21st Century Vision for LA Means Work," *LAT*, 27 Oct. 1999.

Kenneth R. Weiss, "Netscape Co-Founder Gives $150 Million to Stanford," *LAT*, 27 Oct. 1999.

Meredith May, "Silicon Valley Crowns Its Goddess," *SFCh*, 22 June 2001.

Genes to Work

Map and text, *The World of Biotechnology* (Gilead Sciences, 1989).

Gilead Sciences, *Annual Report*, 1993.

Gilead Sciences, *Annual Report*, 1994.

Christian Tyler, "The Famous DNA Double Act," *Financial Times*, 2 Jul. 1994.

Gus Koehler, *Bioindustry: A Description of California's Bioindustry and Summary of the Public Issues Affecting Its Development* (CRB, April 1996).

Diane Seo, "Building Up for Bionic Success," *LAT*, 1 Oct. 1997.

David Pescovitz, "Growth Factor," *LAT*, 1 Dec. 1997.

Jerry Shay, "Scientists Discover Way to Prolong Life of Cells," *WP*, 14 Jan. 1998.

Frances Hong, "The Business of Biotech," *SFEx*, 15 Jan. 1998.

Carl Hall, "Genentech Shines Again," *SFCh*, 22 Jan. 1998.

Julio Laboy, "California's Biomedical Industry Is Larger Than Thought, Study Says," *WSJ*, 15 Jul. 1998.

Paul Jacobs, "California Fights to Stay atop the Heap in the Biotech Industry," *LAT*, 2 Aug. 1998.

Paul Jacobs, "Chiron to Sell Diagnostics Unit to Bayer," *LAT*, 18 Sept. 1998.

Brenda Moore and John Hechinger, "Heard in California: Money Manager Advises Biotechs," *WSJ*, 23 Sept. 1998.

Richard Atkinson, "It Takes Cash to Keep Ideas Flowing," *LAT*, 25 Sept. 1998.

Elaine Gale, "An 'A' for Improvement: Irvine Campus Is Shifting from 'Second Choice' to Top Notch Series," *LAT*, 19 Oct. 1998.

Paul Jacobs, "Geron's Stock Spikes on Sell Growth News," *LAT*, 7 Nov. 1998.

Morris Newman, "A $4 Billion Mix of Uses Is on Tap for San Francisco," *NYT*, 9 Jan. 2000.

Robert Lee Hotz, "Issues and Trends Affecting Science, Medicine, and the Environment," *LAT,* 6 Jul. 2000.

Margaret Talev, "With Amgen at Center, a Growing Role Is Expected for Biotechnology in County," *LAT,* 13 Aug. 2000.

John Markoff, "California Sets Up Three Centers for Basic Scientific Research," *NYT,* 8 Dec. 2000.

Foreign Trade

Japan-Bashing

Teresa Watanabe, "We Should Listen to Japanese, Trade Expert Says," *LAT,* 7 Oct. 1991.

Karl Schoenberger, "Could It Happen Again?" *LAT,* 7 Dec. 1991.

David E. Sanger, "A Top Japanese Politician Calls US Work Force Lazy," *NYT,* 21 Jan. 1992.

Joseph Lieberman, "Here's a Way to Fight Japan," *NYT,* 22 Jan. 1992.

Robert Reinhold, "LA Cancels Huge Contract with a Japanese Maker of Rail Cars," *NYT,* 23 Jan. 1992.

Amy Harmon, "A Sales Pitch Made in USA," *LAT,* 24 Jan. 1992.

James Fallows, "A Plea for Truth-in-Bashing," *NYT,* 10 Feb. 1992.

Steven R. Weisman, "Japanese Leaders Taken to Task by Political Boss for Bashing US," *NYT,* 13 Feb. 1992.

Mark Stein, "County to Buy 15 Rail Cars from Sumitomo," *LAT,* 6 Oct. 1992.

Joel Kotkin, "The Rail Deal That Thrusts LA into the 21st Century," *LAT,* 11 Oct. 1992.

Carl Irving, "Ron Brown Talks Tough on Japan and Trade," *SFEx,* 27 Apr. 1993.

Martin D. Beresford, "California Dreams, Asian Markets," *WSJ,* 8 Aug. 1993.

Doing Business

Martha Groves, "A Port in Peril," *LAT,* 22 Sept. 1991.

Carl Schoenberger, "Safe Harbor," *LAT,* 25 Oct. 1992.

Gordon Smith, "San Diego Turns to Foreign Trade and High Tech," *SDUT,* 16 Jan. 1993.

Michael Parks, "Partners in Trade: California and Israel," *LAT,* 7 May 1993.

Roger Dunstan and Rosa Maria Moller, *Overview of California's Exports* (CRB, 22 June 1994).

Karen Thuermer, "California Rebuilds Economy, Image with the Help of Exports," *World Trade* (April 1996).

Karen Thuermer, "Moving and Growing," *World Trade* (February 1997).

"World Trade Week—Southern California, the Granddaddy of Them All," *Business America* (May 1997).

Dave Lesher, "Golden and Global California," *LAT,* 18 Jan. 1998.

Patrice Apodaca, "Exports Linked to 14% of Jobs in Southland," *LAT,* 16 Jan. 1998.

Dan Morain and Evelyn Iritani, "Davis Fires Three Overseas Trade Officers," *LAT,* 28 Apr. 1999.

Dave Lesher, "Davis Plans to Expand State's Role as a Major Player in World Trade," *LAT,* 6 June 1999.

Stuart Silverstein, "States Quarterly Exports Rise 17.5%," *LAT,* 8 June 2000.

David Savage, "Justices Ban Many City, State Boycotts," *LAT,* 20 June 2000.

Jock O'Connell, "Is California Seeking to Fashion Its Own Foreign Policy?" *LAT,* 20 Aug. 2000.

Jock O'Connell, "Foreign-Trade Offices Are More Politics than Business," *LAT,* 12 Nov. 2000.

A Postmodernist Economy

Lester Thurow, "The Post-Industrial Era Is Over," *NYT,* 4 Sept. 1989.

Bob Drogin, "Cartoons Are No Longer Made in USA," *SFCh,* 8 Apr. 1993.

Dick Meister, "The Dollar-a-Day Workers Who Produce Michael Jordan's $200 Nike Shoes," *SFEx,* 16 Jun. 1993.

Collaborating to Compete in the New Economy: An Economic Strategy for California (California Trade and Commerce Agency, 1996).

California: A Twenty-First Century Prospectus (Center for the New West, 28 Feb. 1996).

Jeffrey Sachs, "The Limits of Convergence," *Economist,* 14 June 1997.

The Rim

Joel Kotkin, "Los Angeles: The Next Capital of the Pacific Rim," *Best of Business Quarterly* (Fall 1993).

Frank Viviano, "The Age of the Pacific," *San Francisco* (August 1982).

Pacific Rim 2010 (Futures Research Division, Security Pacific National Bank, 1984).

Facts on the Pacific Rim (California Department of Commerce, Office of Economic Research, June 1985).

George White, "Changing Asia's Landscape," *LAT,* 22 Apr. 1991.

Martha Groves, "Rolling On: GM-Toyota Plant Prospers amid Auto Industry Slump," *LAT,* 10 Dec. 1991.

George Melloan, "China's Miracle Workers Mostly Live Elsewhere," *WSJ,* 8 Mar. 1993.

"Pacific Rim Trade," *LAT* Special Section, 7 June 1994.

New United Motor Manufacturing (Corporate Brochure, September 1997).

Matt Nauman, "What's New from NUMI?" *SJMN,* 10 Oct. 1997.

Henry Chu, "Jiang Talks Up Sino-LA Ties," *LAT,* 3 Nov. 1997.

NAFTA

Sergio Munoz, "Mexican Businesses Are Coming," *LAT,* 19 Apr. 1991.

Juanita Darling, "On the Ground Floor of Mexico's Privatization," *LAT,* 10 Sept. 1991.

Carlos Fuentes, "Can Mexico Be Mexico?" *LAT,* 6 Oct. 1991.

"Mexico: Progress and Promise," *LAT* Special Section, 22 Oct. 1991.

Juanita Darling, Larry B. Stammer, and Judy Pasternak, "Can Mexico Clean Up Its Act?" *LAT,* 17 Nov. 1991.

Judy Pasternak, "Firms Find a Haven from US Environmental Rules," *LAT,* 19 Nov. 1991.

J. Michael Kennedy, "On Texas Border, Outlook for Air Quality Is Murky," *LAT,* 20 Nov. 1991.

Editorial, "Getting NAFTA Back on Course," *SFCh,* 3 May 1993.

Don Newquist, "Perot Is Dead Wrong on NAFTA," *NYT,* 10 May 1993.

Juanita Darling, "The Great Trade War," *LAT,* 18 May 1993.

Editorial, "After NAFTA," *National Review,* 24 May 1993.

Michael Doyle, "Mexico Spends Millions to Push for US Approval," *SacBee,* 31 May 1993.

James Gerstenzang, "Free-Trade Pact Blocked," *SFCh,* 1 Jul. 1993.

Chris Kraul, "Samsung to Build Major TV Tube Plant in Tijuana," *LAT,* 9 Apr. 1994.

"The Melding Americas," *LAT,* Special Edition, 27 Sept. 1994.

Chris Kraul, "From Border City to Boom Town (No, Not Tijuana)," *LAT,* 5 Oct. 1997.

Dave Lesher and Mary Beth Sheridan, "Davis's Trip to Mexico Will Seek to Mend Rifts," *LAT,* 31 Jan. 1999.

Editorial, "Making Up with Mexico," *LAT,* 1 Feb. 1999.

Howard LaFranchi, "Davis Meets with Zedillo in Mexico," *Christian Science Monitor*, 2 Feb. 1999.

Todd S. Purdum, "Governor Seeks Compromise on Aid to Illegal Immigrants," *LAT*, 16 Apr. 1999.

Editorial, "Davis Takes Squishy Path," *LAT*, 18 Apr. 1999.

Dan Morain, "Bustamante to Try to Block Prop. 187 Mediation Request," *LAT*, 22 Apr. 1999.

Mike Clough, "UC's Role in California's Developing Foreign Policy," *LAT*, 25 Apr. 1999.

Dave Lesher, "Zedillo Begins Historic Tour of State," *LAT*, 18 May 1999.

William Booth, "In 'State' Visit, Zedillo Signals Mexico-California Thaw," *WP*, 19 May 1999.

Mary Beth Sheridan and Dave Lesher, "Zedillo Courts LA's Latino Community," *LAT*, 20 May 1999.

Dave Lesher and Henry Weinstein, "Prop. 187 Backers Accuse Davis of Ignoring Voters," *LAT*, 30 Jul. 1999.

Mexico Transforming (Pacific Council on International Policy, January 2000).

Stuart Silverstein, "State's Quarterly Exports Rise 17.5%," *LAT*, 8 June 2000.

Patrick McDonnell and James Smith, "LA Welcomes Next President of Mexico," *LAT*, 10 Nov. 2000.

James Smith, "Gov. Davis, Mexico's Fox Explore New Ways to Boost Cooperation," *LAT*, 11 Nov. 2000.

Kevin Sullivan and Mary Jordan, "Fox Inauguration Ends Mexico's One-Party Rule," *WP*, 2 Dec. 2000.

James Smith and Dan Morain, "Fox's California Visit a Sign of Improved Ties," *LAT*, 21 Mar. 2001.

James Smith and Miguel Bustillo, "Fox Urges State to Ease Tuition Residency Rules," *LAT*, 22 Mar. 2001.

James Smith and Ken Ellingwood, "Border Pact to Target Safety," *LAT*, 23 June 2001.

Chris Kraul, "Economic Downturn Deepens in Mexico," *LAT*, 1 Jul. 2001.

James Smith and Esther Schrader, "Mexico, US Ties Warm in New Era," *LAT*, 7 Jul. 2001.

PART VI / Cities, Suburbs, and Other Places

How Should We Live?

"Census Notes Populations Shifts," *USA Today*, 28 Jan. 1991.

Eric Bailey, "Wealthy Enclaves Turn Gray," *LAT*, 10 Apr. 1991.

Wendy Steiner, "Calling For a Return to Sanity in Architecture," *NYT*, 19 May 1991.

Greg Smith, "California Still Most Urban State in Country," *SFEx*, 18 Dec. 1991.

Joel Kotkin, "Commuting via Information Superhighway," *WSJ*, 27 Jan. 1994.

Peter Gordon and Harry Richardson, "The Communications City," *Urban Land* (September 1997).

Joel Kotkin, *Back to the Renaissance? A New Perspective on America's Cities* (Pepperdine University Institute for Public Policy, September 1997).

Summerset Life (Summerset Active Adult Communities, September/October 1997).

Larry Greenberg, "Jane Jacobs Sounds Off, Again," *WSJ*, 8 Oct. 1997.

Devorah Knaff, "Senior Power: Leisure World Residents Unite to Form a City," *Chicago Tribune*, 2 June 1999.

Myron Orfield and Thomas Luce, *California Metropatterns* (Metropolitan Area Research Corporation, April 2002).

Holy Land or Plains of Id?

Jon Matthews, "Fast Grow Forecast for County, Area," *SacBee*, 20 May 1986.

John McCloud, "Sacramento Suburbs to Try 'Pedestrian Pockets,' " *NYT*, 4 Mar. 1990.

Gus Lee, "Moreno Valley, Home of the Y-Chop," *Time* (18 Nov. 1991).

Daniel Akst, "Developer Learns How Costly It Can Be to Build a Better Suburb," *LAT*, 26 Nov. 1991.

Steve Lowery, "Val Talk Takes on the World," *SFCh*, 3 Apr. 1992.

Scott Harris, "A Mall to Call Home," *LAT*, 9 Feb. 1993.

Peter Gordon and Harry Richardson, *Are Compact Cities a Desirable Planning Goal?* (USC Lusk Center Research Institute, April 1995).

Alex Barnum, "Pro-Growth vs. Slow Growth, Culture Clash as Sprawl Nears Sierra," *SFCh*, 27 May 1996.

Peter Gordon and Harry Richardson, *The Southern California Economy: Suburbanization and Growth* (USC Lusk Center Research Institute, September 1996).

Ryan McCarthy, "Foothills Growth Boom of 1970s Spelled End to Small-Town Atmosphere," *SacBee*, 17 Oct. 1996.

Duffy Hurley, "From the Ground Up," *SacBee*, 13 Feb. 1997.

Dale Kasler, "Fears Somewhat Doused, Natomas Growth Nears," *SacBee*, 16 Mar. 1997.

Washington Bureau, "Several Foothill Counties Buck State's Slow-Growth Trend," *SacBee*, 25 Mar. 1997.

Tony Bizjak, "Natomas Cleared for Home Building," *SacBee*, 30 Apr. 1997.

Jan Ferris, "Natomas Plans Bring 'Turf War' over Schools," *SacBee*, 10 Jul. 1997.

John Wildermuth, "Gold Rush or Fool's Gold?" *SFCh*, 10 Aug. 1997.

Bob Walter, "Major Builder Buys 474 acres in N. Natomas," *SacBee*, 3 Sept. 1997.

Loretta Kalb, "Surge in Sales of New Homes Could Hit Double Digits," *SacBee*, 19 Sept. 1997.

Melinda Fulmer, "Small Malls Suffer as Consumers Shop for Trendier Alternatives," *LAT*, 10 Dec. 1997.

Alan Ehrenhalt, "The View from Suburbia," *WSJ*, 5 Mar. 1998.

Morris Newman, "Working the Crowd," *LAT*, 5 May 1998.

Carol Emert, "Emeryville Aims Upscale," *SFCh*, 7 May 1998.

Kristine Carber, "Window Shopping in Walnut Creek," *SFEx*, 27 May 1998.

Barbara Marsh, "Bio-Burg," *LAT*, 15 June 1998.

Daryl Kelley, "As Suburbs Change, They Still Satisfy," *LAT*, 19 Oct. 1999.

Evan Halper, "New Vitality Seen in 'Boomburbs,' " *LAT*, 12 Jul. 2001.

Staying Time

Palm Springs Life, 1990–2003.
Santa Barbara, 1990–2003.

The Upper Left

Ira Eisenberg, "Berkeley's Answer to Begin," *NYT*, 19 Sept. 1991.

Daniel Akst, "Berkeley Offers a Rent-Control Lesson for SF," *LAT*, 29 Oct. 1991.

Patricia Holt, "More Than a Bookstore," *SFCh*, 27 Sept. 1992.

Belinda Taylor, "Welcome to the New Berkeley," *San Francisco Focus* (August 1996).

Matea Gold, "Is Santa Monica Ready for a Face-Lift?" *LAT*, 26 Feb. 1997.

Sam Hurwitt, "Don't Call It Beserkley," *SFEx*, 23 Jul. 1997.

Opinion, *LAT,* 6 Oct. 1997.

Charles Burress, "Berkeley Is Moved to Action," *SFCh,* 20 Nov. 1997.

Charles Burress, "With Food Show, Berkeley Cooks Up Another First," *SFCh,* 16 Feb. 1998.

Jess Bravin, "Booksellers Pin Hopes on State Laws," *WSJ,* 8 Apr. 1998.

Kenneth R. Weiss, "Berkeley Accepts Rebellious Past, $3.5 Million Donation," *LAT,* 30 Apr. 1998.

Laura Hamburg, "Berkeley Strips Sea Scouts of Free Berths at Marina," *SFCh,* 17 May 1998.

Kevin Fagan, "Hippie Heaven," *SFCh,* 5 Jul. 1998.

Robert Selna, "Berkeley's Blooming Meters," *SFEx,* 8 Jul. 1998.

Charles Burress, "Berkeley Council OKs Clothed Street People," *SFCh,* 9 Jul. 1998.

Charles Burress, "War of Words in Berkeley," *SFCh,* 21 Aug. 1998.

Sally McGrane, "Café Culture," *SFCh,* 23 Sept. 1998.

Mary Curtius, "Listeners Besiege Berkeley Station After Staff Arrests," *LAT,* 15 Jul. 1999.

Michael Taylor, "Berkeley Gets Radical Over KPFA Lockout," *SFCh,* 17 Jul. 1999.

Ilene Lelchuk and Marianne Costantinou, "Fans Rally Through the Night for Station," *SFEx,* 19 Jul. 1999.

Philip Elwood, "Baez Blasts from Past for KPFA," *SFEx,* 21 Jul. 1999.

Charles Burress, "KPFA Staff Gets Call to Return to Work," *SFCh,* 29 Jul. 1999.

Charles Burress, "KPFA's Air Attack," *SFCh,* 6 Aug. 1999.

Veronique de Turenne, "A Pedal Policy in Berkeley," *LAT,* 15 May 2001.

Booming Places

"North County Focus, News of Northern San Diego County," *LAT,* Special Section, 1 Apr. 1990.

Bruce Kelley, "Eastward, Ho! Southern Californians Are Headed Inland," *LAT Magazine,* 15 Mar. 1992.

Tracey Kaplan, "Far-Out City," *LAT,* 16 Apr. 1992.

Jonathan Peterson, "Plight of Cities Again on US Back Burner," *LAT,* 26 Oct. 1992.

Tom Gorman, "A City Wracked by Woe," *LAT,* 10 Oct. 1995.

Erik Ingram and George Snyder, "Five Anti-Sprawl Measures Pass in Sonoma County," *SFCh,* 7 Nov. 1996.

David Friedman, "Two Worlds," *LAT,* 26 Oct. 1997.

Dade Hayes, "Santa Clarita Thriving on 'Local Control,' " *LAT,* 14 Dec. 1997.

Irene Vasquez, "Kaufman & Broad Still No. 1," *LAT,* 15 Mar. 1998.

Faye Fiore, "4 Area Counties Among Population Gain Leaders," *LAT,* 18 Mar. 1998.

Haya el Nasser, "Population Moves Deeper into Suburbs," *USA Today,* 18 Mar. 1998.

Michael Hytha and Patricia Jacobus, "Developers Yank Plan to Build 5,300 Homes in Contra Costa County," *SFCh,* 19 May 1998.

Michael Hytha and Patricia Jacobus, "Saga of a Valley," *SFCh,* 20 May 1998.

Michael Hytha and Patricia Jacobus, "How Developers' Dream Died in Contra Costa," *SFCh,* 26 May 1998.

Mary Curtius, "Anxiously, City of Napa Braces for Jolt of Prosperity," *LAT,* 28 May 1998.

Miguel Bustillo, "Board Puts Growth Control Measure on Ventura County Ballot," *LAT,* 17 June 1998.

Pamela Podger, "Owners Opposed Zoning Plan in Sonoma County," *SFCh,* 22 June 1998.

Richard Winton, "Stiff Laws Keep San Marino Tidy," *LAT,* 1 Dec. 1998.

Jesus Sanchez, "LA County's Growth Spurt Pushes North," *LAT,* 23 Nov. 1999.

Stuart Leavenworth, "Suburbia's New Toy Room: Four Car Garage," *SacBee,* 12 Jan. 2000.

Tough Love

Martha Groves, "A Port in Peril," *LAT,* 22 Sept. 1991.

Patt Morrison, "Jerry Brown, Insurgent and Enigma," *LAT,* 22 Mar. 1992.

John Boudreau, "Kindred Spirit," *LAT,* 10 Apr. 1992.

Charles Hardy, "Oakland Slow to Heal from Quake, Fire," *SFEx,* 11 Oct. 1992.

Ken Coupland, "Bold Designs Forged from Fire," *SFEx,* 28 Feb. 1993.

Julian Guthrie, "Still High on the Hog, a Conversation with Sonny Barger," *SFEx,* 22 Apr. 1993.

Bob Sipchen, "The Rough Rider," *LAT,* 14 Dec. 1994.

Ann Brown, "The Soul of a City: Revisiting Oakland," New America News Service, 17 June 1997.

Michael Clough, "Can the Raiders Lead Oakland into 21st Century?" *LAT,* 14 Sept. 1997.

Mark Barabak and Maria La Ganga, "Jerry Brown Enters Race for Oakland Mayor," *LAT,* 29 Oct. 1997.

Stacey Wells, "Brown Takes Plunge, Vies for Mayor's Seat," *Oakland Tribune,* 29 Oct. 1997.

Ben Patterson, "Looking Up," *SFEx,* 4 Nov. 1997.

Bill Press, "Mayoral Candidate Jerry Brown Is No Stranger to Oakland," *SacBee,* 5 Dec. 1997.

Rick DelVecchio, "Oakland's First Black Mayor Dies," *SFCh,* 29 Jan. 1998.

Rick DelVecchio, "In Oakland, Jerry Brown Finds All Politics Is Local," *SFCh,* 20 Jan. 1998.

Rick DelVecchio, "The Flighty Fancies of Jerry Brown," *SFCh,* 17 Feb. 1998.

Carolyn Said, "Claremont Hotel Deal in the Works," *SFCh,* 4 Apr. 1998.

Rick DelVecchio, "Candidate Jerry Brown Seeks to Inspire Others," *SFCh,* 22 May 1998.

Rick DelVecchio, "Oakland Poll Puts Brown Way Ahead," *SFCh,* 27 May 1998.

Maria La Ganga, "Brown Eclipses Challengers in Oakland Mayor's Race," *LAT,* 27 May 1998.

Rick DelVecchio, "Blacks and Brown," *SFCh,* 16 Aug. 1998.

Rick DelVecchio and Debra Levi Holtz, "The Oracle of Oakland," *SFCh,* 5 Nov. 1998.

Sarah Yang, "New Oakland Police Chief Faces Pressures," *LAT,* 2 Jul. 1999.

Janine DeFao, "Public Military Academy for Oakland Is in Governor's Budget," *SFCh,* 12 Jan. 2000.

Eric Bailey, " 'He's Made Them Proud of Oakland,' " *LAT,* 10 Feb. 2000.

Paul van Slambrouck, "Philosopher Mayor Seeks Deep Thoughts," *Christian Science Monitor,* 6 Sept. 2000.

Patricia Leigh Brown, "Intellectual Forum Brings Jerry Brown to the Table," *NYT,* 17 Sept. 2000.

Wire Reports, "City Settles Harassment Claim for $50,000," *LAT,* 22 June 2001.

Sheila Muto, "Status Seeker: Oakland Tries to Build Reputation," *WSJ,* 27 June 2001.

John M. Glionna, "Oakland's In-Your-Face Ads Invade San Francisco," *LAT,* 9 Jul. 2001.

Downtown

Judie Telfer, "New SJ Chief Was Very Sought After," *SJMN,* 2 Oct. 1976.

Bill Romano and Judie Telfer, "New Chief Pledges Closer Public Ties," *SJMN,* 19 Oct. 1976.

Robert Lindsey, "Chief in San Jose Battles Gun Lobby," *NYT,* 8 June 1986.

John Flinn, "Conservative Bastion's Bulletproof Liberal," *SFCh,* 6 Oct. 1991.

Peter H. King, "San Jose Swings for the Big Time," *LAT,* 21 Jan. 1992.

Joseph McNamara, "To Rebuild Trust, LAPD Must Join the Community," *SJMN,* 11 Oct. 1995.

Michael Marois, "In the Land of High-Tech Suburbs, an Agency Steers the Action Downtown," *Bond Buyer,* 29 Aug. 1997.

John McCloud, "US Shopping Centers Thrive as Hubs of Entertainment," *National Real Estate Investor* (May 1999).

"Special Issue: The Best of Everything!" *San Jose, the Magazine for Silicon Valley* (September/October 1999).

Shari Weiss, "Cities That Sizzle: San Jose, California," *Nation's Restaurant News* (January 2001).

Play Ball!

Chris Kraul and Barry Horstman, "City, Hughes Form Jobs Task Force," *LAT*, 4 Aug. 1992.

Michael Granberry, "Affluent Area of San Diego Battles Plan for 'Tent City,' " *LAT*, 4 Sept. 1992.

Chris Kraul, "Once Immune, San Diego Now Suffers Economic Ills," *LAT*, 10 Jan. 1993.

Chris Kraul, "Convair Plant in San Diego to Close by 1996," 2 Jul. 1994.

Chris Kraul, "As California Heals, Defense-Reliant San Diego Is Still in Acute Pain," *LAT*, 3 Oct. 1994.

Tony Perry, "A Symbol for the Decline of Aerospace," *LAT*, 9 Jul. 1995.

Tony Perry, "Huge Auction Marks Decline of Aerospace," *LAT*, 16 Nov. 1995.

Tony Perry, "San Diego Symphony Is Back on Its Feet, but Still Unsteady," *LAT*, 5 Apr. 1996.

Tony Perry, "Concession Made in Stadium Dispute," *LAT*, 19 Feb. 1997.

Tony Perry, "Judge Rejects Bid to Halt San Diego Stadium Expansion," *LAT*, 21 Feb. 1997.

Tony Perry, "Hoping to Be a Hit with Voters," *LAT*, 12 Oct. 1997.

T. J. Simers, "Super Bowl XXXII," *LAT*, 21 Jan. 1998.

Elizabeth Douglass, "The Tech Coast," *LAT*, 9 Mar. 1998.

Tony Perry, "San Diego Deal to Build Baseball Park Is Reached," *LAT*, 15 Jul. 1998.

Tony Perry, "San Diego Symphony Making Modest Return," *LAT*, 24 Jul. 1998.

Bill Madden, "Boss Tears Down SD Park," *New York Daily News*, 21 Oct. 1998.

Tony Perry, "Padre Euphoria Could Sway Stadium Vote," *LAT*, 24 Oct. 1998.

Tony Perry, "Padres Threaten to Halt New Ballpark," *LAT*, 20 Sept. 2000.

Tony Perry, "Controversy Clouds Legacy as San Diego Mayor Leaves Office," *LAT*, 4 Dec. 2000.

Ross Newhan, "No Calm in San Diego Forecast," *LAT*, 17 Dec. 2000.

Chris Kraul and Elizabeth Douglass, "San Diego Benefiting from Qualcomm's Good Fortune," *LAT*, 6 Jan. 2001.

Tony Perry, "Councilwoman in San Diego Pleads Guilty and Resigns," *LAT*, 30 Jan. 2001.

"Judge Rejects More Penalties for Ex-Official," *LAT*, 6 Feb. 2001.

Tony Perry, "Stadium Foe Refuses to Play Ball with City," *LAT*, 11 Nov. 2001.

Christopher Reynolds, "San Diego Symphony Receives Record Donation," *LAT*, 11 Jan. 2002.

AP, "San Diego Symphony Gets $100 Million Gift," *WP*, 12 Jan. 2002.

Tony Perry, "San Diego Losing Its Football Team Spirit," *LAT*, 11 May 2002.

Sam Farmer, "LA Suitors Are Many," *LAT*, 16 May 2002.

PART VII / A Tale of Two Cities: Los Angeles and San Francisco

People

Children and Dogs

Katherine Seligman, "Children in Exodus," *SFCh*, 30 May 2001.

Maria La Gagna, "A City Losing Its Children," *LAT*, 7 June 2001.

John Mitchell, "LA Gets Middling Grade on Children's Quality of Life," *LAT,* 21 Aug. 2001.
Tanya Schevitz, "SF Is Kid-Friendly, to Those Who Can Afford to Stay," *SFCh,* 22 Aug. 2001.
Ilene Lelchuk, "SF Rated Top Spot to Hang Your Leash," *SFCh,* 8 Sept. 2001.

Sex and the City
Susan Sward, "DA Renews Plea for Regulation of Sex Trade," *SFCh,* 14 Oct. 1997.
Cynthia Robins, "Usual Suspects Show Up for Hookers' Ball," *SFEx,* 4 Nov. 1997.
Johnny Brannon, "Hooker Sting Clears Polk Corridor," *Independent [San Francisco],* 31 Mar. 1998.

The Gay Scene
Frederick Muir and Charisse Jones, "Police on Horseback Break Up Gay Protest," *LAT,* 24 Oct. 1991.
Lon Daniels, "Sisters Bring Message to Europride," *SFEx,* 28 June 1992.
Maitland Zane, "Marines Threaten to Sue over Tattoo in AIDS Ad," *SFCh,* 29 Sept. 1992.
Steve Heilig, "A Hospital at War with the AIDS Virus," *SFCh,* 6 Dec. 1992.
Carol Ness, "Attacks on Gays Reach Record High," *SFEx,* 11 Mar. 1993.
Kevin Allman, "Dressed to Excess," *LAT,* 25 Apr. 1993.
Mark Swed, "A Life Custom-Made for Opera," *LAT Calendar,* 15 Jan. 1995.
Bill Richards, "In San Francisco, Big Halloween Bash Is Becoming a Drag," *WSJ,* 30 Oct. 1995.
David Perlman, "Study Shows Flaws of New AIDS Drugs," *SFCh,* 30 Sept. 1997.
Mary Curtius and Michael Ybarra, "Gay Party Tour: More Harm Than Good?" *LAT,* 13 Oct. 1997.
Beth Shuster, "Gay Men's Sex Club Closes, Citing Exhausting Fight with City," *LAT,* 22 Nov. 1997.
Thomas Maugh, "AIDS Deaths Down 44 Percent in US," *LAT,* 3 Feb. 1998.
Wendy Koch, "Senator Torpedoes Hormel Nomination," *SFEx,* 12 Feb. 1998.
Bill Higgins, "Gala AIDS Fund-Raiser Is Sedate but Still Starry," *LAT,* 16 Feb. 1998.
Tyche Hendricks, "Same-Sex Couples Tie the Knot En Masse in City Ceremony," *SFEx,* 26 Mar. 1998.
Ray Delgado, "Transsexual Battles City Hall to Be a Cop," *SFEx,* 27 Mar. 1998.
C. S. B. Huntington and Gregory Lewis, "Gay Activist Named Supervisor," *SFEx,* 1 Apr. 1998.
Maria La Gagna and Stephanie Simon, "Judge Backs SF Law on Partners' Benefits," *LAT,* 11 Apr. 1998.
Elaine Herscher, "Castro's Change," *SFCh,* 12 May 1998.
AP, "Viagra, 'Poppers' Fatal Combination," *SFCh,* 23 June 1998.
Jane Kay, "Gay Pride, Bride and Vroom," *SFEx,* 29 June 1998.
David Perlman, "AIDS Discovery Scientists," *SFCh,* 1 Jul. 1998.
Cliff Rothman, "The Well-Heeled Crowd," *SFCh,* 1 Jul. 1998.
Don Lattin, "Rift Widens Between Religious Charities, SF," *SFCh,* 10 Jul. 1998.
Louis Freedberg, "Hormel Nomination Dies as Senate Fails to Vote," *SFCh,* 16 Oct. 1998.
Jenifer Warren, "Initiative Divides a Family," *LAT,* 4 Nov. 1999.
Alexander Cockburn, "Blacks and Gays, a Future Mayor and a Late President," *LAT,* 22 Nov. 1999.
Erica Goode, "With Fears Fading, More Gays Spurn Old Preventive Message," *NYT,* 19 Apr. 2001.

"Life in the Gay Area," *San Francisco*, Special Issue (June 2001).

Angelica Pence, "Puckish, Prideful, Queerific," *SFCh*, 25 June 2001.

Dorothy Korber, "Census Takes First Count of Same-Sex Households," *SacBee*, 8 Aug. 2001.

Carol Ness, "SF Upstaged as Gay Mecca," *SFCh*, 8 Aug. 2001.

Robin Fields, "Gay Male Couples Partial to City Life," *LAT*, 11 Sept. 2001.

Magical Urbanism

Ruben Martinez, "Why LA's Street Vendors Won't Be Swept Away," *LA Weekly*, 12 Dec. 1991.

Bill Higgins, "Doughnuts and Mariachis to Go," *LAT*, 22 Nov. 1992.

Latino Coalition for a New Los Angeles, *Latinos and the Future of Los Angeles: A Guide to the Twenty-first Century* (Latino Futures Research Group, 1993).

Joel Kotkin, "Can Pico Union Become like NY's Lower East Side?" *LAT*, 28 Sept. 1997.

Ben Ehrenreich, "The Latino Metropolis," *LA Weekly*, 7 Jul. 2000.

Daniel Hernandez, "Some Street Signs Get a Little Squiggle of Linguistic Respect," *LAT*, 21 Aug. 2001.

Soul Train

Woody Strode and Sam Young, *Goal Dust, an Autobiography* (1990).

Seth Mydans, "Walking a Narrow Line and Praying for Calm in a Riot-Torn City," *NYT*, 13 Sept. 1992.

Laurie Ochoa, "The First Family of Barbecue," *LAT*, 27 May 1993.

Jonathan Gold, "Cruising for 'Cue," *LAT*, 27 May 1993.

Myrna Oliver, "Jesse Robinson: Pioneering Black Civic Leader," *LAT*, 16 June 1993.

Lisa Dillman, "They're in Vogue," *LAT*, 28 May 1998.

Eleanor Yang, "Bringing a New Cool to the Pool," *LAT*, 10 Nov. 1998.

Evelyn Nieves, "Blacks Hit by Housing Costs Leave San Francisco Behind," *NYT*, 2 Aug. 2001.

Herbert Sample, "Bayview's Worries," *SacBee*, 13 Aug. 2001.

Diane Pucin, "A Williams Is Certain to Win the US Open," *LAT*, 8 Sept. 2001.

Koreatown

K. Connie Kang, "Koreans Prepare for Unrest," *LAT*, 3 Apr. 1993.

K. Connie Kang, "Fear of Crime Robs Many of Dreams in Koreatown," *LAT*, 21 June 1993.

Diane Seo, "Hard Choices," *LAT*, 12 Dec. 1993.

Can We All Get Along?

Jill Sharer, "New Neighbors, Bad Blood: Venice II Society," *LA Weekly*, 7 Oct. 1993.

Lynell George and David Ferrell, "LA's Veneer Stripped to Show Blemishes," *LAT*, 10 Oct. 1995.

David Ferrell and Robert Lee Hotz, "Ethnic Pockets amid a Vast Fabric of English," *LAT*, 23 Jan. 2000.

White Guys

San Francisco Gael, for the decade.

The Irish Herald [San Francisco], for the decade.

Reed Johnson, "Bittersweet Memories of Working-Class LA," *LAT*, 21 Aug. 2001.

Asian Times

Peter Waldman and Leslie Chang, "Paper Chase, the Rise of the Fangs: From Menu Printers to
    Backroom Kingpins," *WSJ*, 21 June 2000.
Ryan Kim, "Asians Seek United State," *SFCh*, 3 Aug. 2001.
Ryan Kim, "Pilgrimage: UC to Asia," *SFCh*, 5 Aug. 2001.
K. Connie Kang, "Bridge Builder for Immigrants," *LAT*, 11 Sept. 2001.

Payday

San Francisco Takeovers

Mark Dowie and Fran Smith, "How to Succeed in Banking Without Really Trying," *West*,
    SJMN, 12 Jan. 1992.
Gavin Power, "New Store Closures at Macy's, I. Magnin," *SFCh*, 2 Mar. 1993.
Gavin Power, "Catalog Company Buys Gumps," *SFCh*, 2 May 1993.
Edward Iwata, "Embarcadero Center Sold," *SFEx*, 12 May 1998.
Carol Emert, "Why Hal Riney Decided Time Was Ripe to Sell," *SFCh*, 12 May 1998.
Arthur Louis, "Stagecoach to Stay in SF," *SFCh*, 9 June 1998.

Bye, Bye, BofA!

Kenneth How and Ilana DeBare, "How BofA's Megadeal Will Hurt SF," *SFCh*, 14 Apr. 1998.
Arthur Louis, "Deal Will Marry Longtime Rivals," *SFCh*, 14 Apr. 1998.
Kenneth Howe, "BofA Finally Makes Its Dream Come True," *SFCh*, 14 Apr. 1998.
Thomas Mulligan and Debora Vrana, "BofA Outlines Plans for Merger with NationsBank,"
    LAT, 14 Apr. 1998.
Steve Rubenstein, "Charlotte Has Real Interest in Banks," *SFCh*, 17 Apr. 1998.
Peter Sinton, "It's West vs. East," *SFCh*, 17 Apr. 1998.
AP, "Head of BofA Unit First to Exit Amidst Merger," *LAT*, 20 Apr. 1998.
Peter Sinton, "Another BofA Executive to Bail Out," *SFCh*, 28 May 1998.
Debora Vrana, "Charlotte: A New US Behemoth of Banking," *LAT*, 28 May 1998.
Victoria Colliver, "The Softest of Landings," *SFEx*, 15 Aug. 1998.
Sam Zuckerman, "BankAmerica Profits Take Huge Drop," *SFCh*, 15 Oct. 1998.
Sam Zuckerman, "BofA Boss Seeks to Assuage Critics," *SFCh*, 9 Jan. 1999.

Los Angeles Takeovers

Douglas Frantz and John Medearis, "Encino Bank Ordered Sold," *LAT*, 8 May 1991.
Victor Zonana and Leslie Helm, "Japanese Will Pay $1 Billion for Stake in Time Warner,"
    LAT, 30 Oct. 1991.
The Planning Institute, USC, *Los Angeles: At an Economic Crossroads* (Los Angeles Head-
    quarters City Association, January 1992).
James Bates, "BankAmerica Takes Over at Security Pacific," *LAT*, 22 Apr. 1992.
Henry Weinstein, "Financial Scams Are on Rise in Region," *LAT*, 23 June 1993.
Joel Kotkin, "The Powers That Will Be," *LAT*, 14 Dec. 1997.
Scott Herhold, "Glendale Fed Joins Cal Fed," *SJMN*, 6 Feb. 1998.
Roger Altman, "Mergers Unlimited, Inc.," *LAT*, 12 Apr. 1998.

Rebuild LA

Jonathan Peterson, "Ueberroth Does Balancing Act as Rebuild LA Chief," *LAT*, 18 May 1992.
Tim Ferguson, "What's Shaken in LA? Not the Governing Complacency," *WSJ*, 7 Jul. 1992.
Jube Shiver, "Red Tape, Weak Economy Cast Pall over Rebuilding," *LAT*, 29 Aug. 1992.

Henry Weinstein, "Rebuild LA Struggles to Establish Its Role," *LAT,* 4 Nov. 1992.

Kenneth Garcia, "After Years of Boom, Los Angeles Hits Skids," *SFCh,* 21 Dec. 1992.

Robert Hilburn, "Garth Raises $1 Million, Modestly," *LAT,* 1 Feb. 1993.

John Mitchell, "A Day-Brightener," *LAT,* 8 Apr. 1993.

Miles Corwin, "How Good a Student Is LA?" *LAT,* 12 Apr. 1993.

Patrick Lee, "LA Refocuses on Basics, Rebuilding the Inner City," *LAT,* 22 Apr. 1993.

Stuart Silverstein and Alexei Varrionuevo, "Firms Lag in Keeping Vow to Hire More Minorities," *LAT,* 5 May 1993.

Carla Rivera and Dean Murphy, "Ueberroth Quits Rebuild LA Post," *LAT,* 22 May 1993.

Henry Weinstein and Nancy Rivera Brooks, "Resignation May Help RLA Rebuild Itself," *LAT,* 22 May 1993.

Carla Rivera and Dean Murphy, "Ueberroth Quits Job with Rebuild LA," *LAT,* 23 May 1993.

Rebuild LA, *Progress Report,* for 1993, 1994, 1995.

Poor

Down and Out in LA

Jane Fritsch, "4 Die, 2 Hurt in Arson at LA Housing Project," *LAT,* 8 Sept. 1991.

Frank Clifford, "Rich-Poor Gulf Widens in State," *LAT,* 11 May 1992.

Shawn Hubler, "South LA's Poverty Rate Worse than '65," *LAT,* 11 May 1992.

Bob Sipchen, "Living Close to the Edge," *LAT,* 27 June 1993.

Ronald White, "An Interview with Robert Kemp," *LAT,* 15 Feb. 1998.

Larry Gordon, "Doing Its Home Work," *LAT,* 21 Aug. 1998.

Dan Gordon, "Get Me to the Job on Time," *LAT,* 17 June 2001.

County/USC Hospital

Irene Wielawski, "County-USC Patients Left in Public Halls on Gurneys," *LAT,* 21 Jan. 1992.

Andrea Ford, "Easygoing Doctors Were Suited to a Difficult Job," *LAT,* 10 Feb. 1993.

Sheryl Stolberg, "Not Surprised, Says Doctor Shot at Hospital," *LAT,* 11 Feb. 1993.

Jeffrey L. Rabin, "Latino Leaders Demand Larger Hospital, Warn of Bailout Woes," *LAT,* 21 Oct. 1999.

Ted Rohrlich and Nicholas Riccardi, "Delays Put Lives at Risk at County-USC," *LAT,* 26 June 2001.

David Ferrell, "Beneath the Hospital, a Bewildering Labyrinth," *LAT,* 28 June 2001.

Homeless in San Francisco

Art Agnos, *Beyond Shelter: A Homeless Plan for San Francisco* (Draft for Public Review, August 1989).

Peter Marin, "The Prejudice Against Men: Chronic Homelessness Essentially Problem of Single Adult Men," *The Nation,* 8 Jul. 1991.

John Roszak with Rick Clogher, photography by Jock McDonald, "Why They're Still Homeless," *San Francisco Focus* (November 1991).

Marc Sandalow and Ben Wildavsky, "SF's New Homeless Director," *SFCh,* 3 Feb. 1993.

April Lynch, "Tenants Decry Life in Residential Hotels," *SFCh,* 18 Mar. 1993.

"Homeless Ask Court to Halt City Crackdown," *NYT,* 26 Nov. 1993.

Aurelio Rojas, "Governor Won't Fund Armories as Shelters," *SFCh,* 21 Aug. 1997.

Jean Lee, "From Doctor to Destitute: Retired Physician Lives on the Street," *LAT,* 28 Sept. 1997.

Glen Martin, "Penthouse for Pets," *SFCh,* 14 Apr. 1998.

Mary Curtius, "Presidio's First and Only Battle Is over Fair Housing," *LAT,* 5 May 1998.
Katherine Seligman, "Sharp Rise in SF Evictions," *SFEx,* 8 May 1998.
Kevin Fagen, "Homeless Best Friends," *SFCh,* 11 Jul. 1998.
Ray Delgado, "Closed Shelter's Legacy of Woe," *SFEx,* 12 Sept. 1999.
Eric Bailey, "Minimum Wage Isn't a Living in San Francisco," *LAT,* 18 Oct. 1999.
Corrie Anders, "Just 11% in City Can Afford a Home," *SFEx,* 12 Jan. 2000.
Maria L. La Ganga, "Hard News," *LAT,* 23 Jul. 2001.

Homeless in LA
Penelope McMillan, "Super Shelter," *LAT,* 22 Jan. 1992.
"A Far Cry from Skid Row," *City Times, LAT,* 3 Oct. 1993.
Marilyn Martinez and James Rainey, "Santa Monica Targets Promenade Loiterers," *LAT,* 22 Aug. 1996.
Steve Appleford, "Leaving Santa Monica," *New Times Los Angeles,* 6 Mar. 1997.
Beth Shuster and Henry Weinstein, "US Judge Blocks Law Against Begging," *LAT,* 31 Oct. 1997.
Sue McAllister and Karima Haynes, "Out in the Cold," *LAT,* 1 Apr. 1998.
Matea Gold, "Vacant Buildings Spark Debate," *LAT,* 3 Apr. 1998.

Deteriorating Quality of Life, San Francisco
Marc Sandalow, "SF Won't Jail Homeless Accused of Petty Crime," *SFCh,* 22 Jan. 1992.
Mary Curtius, "SF Seeks Parking for Homeless' 'Homes,' " *LAT,* 27 Sept. 1997.
Rachel Gordon, "Park Campers: What to Do?" *SFEx,* 28 Sept. 1997.
Johnny Brannon, "Mayor Signals New Get Tough Policy," *The Independent,* 21 Oct. 1997.
Ken Garcia, "Devastation of Golden Gate Park Hits Nerve—Cleanup of Camps in Works," *SFCh,* 4 Nov. 1997.
Carla Marinucci and Alex Barnum, "Mayor Says Park Tirade Was Wrong," *SFCh,* 6 Nov. 1997.
Jim Herronzamora, "GG Park Strategy Won't Fly for Now," *SFEx,* 11 Nov. 1997.
Kathleen Sullivan, "Young, Homeless, and Displaced," *SFEx,* 20 Nov. 1997.
Michael Dougan, "Panhandlers Face Grim Christmas," *SFEx,* 14 Dec. 1997.
Emily Soares, "Local Merchants Strive to Mitigate Panhandling," *The Independent,* 17 Mar. 1998.
Jonathan Curiel, "No Room at the Plazas," *SFCh,* 25 Jan. 1999.
Ilene Lelchuk, "Mayor Brown Defends Cleanliness of City by the Bay," *SFCh,* 11 Aug. 2001.
John M. Glionna, "SF Offers Cautionary Tales on Pay Toilets," *LAT,* 20 Aug. 2001.
Mark Simon, "Last Rites for City That Forgot How," *SFCh,* 4 Sept. 2001.
Ken Garcia, "Readers Give Bronx Cheer to Mayor: Nearly 200 Respond About Civic Hygiene," *SFCh,* 7 Sept. 2001.
Mark Simon, " 'Who Cares' Attitude on SF Decay," *SFCh,* 7 Sept. 2001.

Housing Crunch
Bridge Housing Corporation Annual Reports, 1985–2002.
Frank Viviano, "Making Housing Affordable," *SFCh,* 6 Feb. 1989.
Brad Breithhaupt, "$100 Million Project Proposed for Marin City," *Marin Independent Journal,* 23 Dec. 1989.
"Affordable California Hill Town," *Architectural Record* (July 1990).
Witold Rybczynski, "Down-Sizing the American Dream," *This World (SFCh),* 21 Apr. 1991.

Joseph Simon, "Eviction Notice: There Goes the Neighborhood," *SFEx,* 26 Sept. 1997.

Penny Skillman, "SF Landlords Will Oust 2700 Tenants This Year," *SFEx,* 26 Sept. 1997.

George Raine, "No Living Room," *SFEx,* 5 Oct. 1997.

Peter Sinton, "Surfing for Home Loans," *SFCh,* 12 Jan. 1998.

Sue Hutchison, "Teachers Must Tighten Belts to Work Here," *SJMN,* 10 Feb. 1998.

Corrie Anders and Frances Hong, "Home Prices Go Through the Roof," *SFEx,* 12 Feb. 1998.

Vivian Marino, "Housing Market Hot for Sellers," *SFEx,* 20 Mar. 1998.

E. Scott Rechard, "New Homes Are in Short Supply in OC," *LAT,* 14 Apr. 1998.

Arthur Louis, "When Money Isn't Enough," *SFCh,* 11 May 1998.

AP, "Auction Pulls in $13.6 Million for SF's Priciest Vacant Lot," *LAT,* 13 May 1998.

Jesus Sanchez, "State's Housing Prices and Sales Rate Continue to Climb in April," *LAT,* 27 May 1998.

Don Lee, "Home Prices Catch Fire, Lighting Up Economy," *LAT,* 7 June 1998.

Ted Rohrlich, "Affordable Housing Gap Seen Widening," *LAT,* 16 Jul. 1998.

Victoria Colliver and Corrie Anders, "Hot Housing Market Is in a Frenzy," *SFEx,* 30 May 1999.

James Flanigan, "Affordable Housing's Challenge," *LAT,* 24 Nov. 1999.

Ilene Lelchuk, "Proposed Live-Work Loft Ban in SF," *SFCh,* 7 Aug. 2001.

Daryl Strickland, "Housing Prices Soar at Low End," *LAT,* 21 Aug. 2001.

Timothy Hughes, "Scores of Ventura Homes for Sail," *LAT,* 1 Sept. 2001.

Politics

Post-Riot Malaise

Mack Reed, "Signs Point to Another Flight from LA?" *LAT,* 11 May 1992.

Robert Reinhold, "At Riot's Epicenter, Housing Market Is Thriving," *NYT,* 5 Sept. 1993.

Darryl Fears, "To Stay or Not to Stay in LA," *LAT,* 4 Dec. 1998.

Second King Trial

Seth Mydans, "Their Lives Consumed, Los Angeles Officers Await Trial," *NYT,* 2 Feb. 1993.

Seth Mydans, "Second Police Beating Trial Begins with Hurdle of Jury Selection," *NYT,* 4 Feb. 1993.

Steven Lucas and Eric Rose, "Getting Ready for Acquittal in Rodney King II," *LAT,* 16 Feb. 1993.

Carla Rivera, "Unveiling of Unity Sign Reveals Tensions in City," *LAT,* 27 Feb. 1993.

Henry Weinstein, "Rough and Tumble Trail in Court of Public Opinion," *LAT,* 15 Mar. 1993.

Carla Rivera, "LA Stepping Lightly as It Braces for Threat of Riots," *LAT,* 17 Mar. 1993.

Michael Taylor, "CHP Gets Ready for Urban Riots," *SFCh,* 31 Mar. 1993.

Robert Reinhold, "An Edgy Los Angeles Awaits a Jury's Verdict," *NYT,* 11 Apr. 1993.

Yumi Wilson, "Edgy LA Awaits King Verdict," *SFCh,* 12 Apr. 1993.

Jim Newton, "Rumors Fly as King Jury Meets for 7½ Hours," *LAT,* 13 Apr. 1993.

Jim Newton, "How the Case Was Won," *LAT Magazine,* 27 June 1993.

Reginald Denny Trial

David Ferrell and Richard Serrano, "12 Attacks by Denny Beating Suspects Alleged," *LAT,* 29 May 1992.

Jim Newton, "DA Videotapes Supporters of Denny Suspects, *LAT,* 20 June 1992.

Paul Lieberman, "Riot Violence in Venice Has Echoes of Denny Case," *LAT,* 14 Sept. 1992.

Lou Cannon, "Two Beating Verdicts May Be LA's Trial by Fire," *WP,* 31 Jan. 1993.

Edward Boyer, "Denny Assault Case Moved Back 2 Weeks," *LAT*, 27 Feb. 1993.

Edward Boyer, "Judge Delays Trial in Denny Case Until July," *LAT*, 8 Apr. 1993.

Edward Boyer, "Tough Law, Tough Cases," *LAT*, 24 Sept. 1993.

Edward Boyer and Ashley Dunn, "Williams, Watson Meant to Kill Denny, Prosecutor Says," *LAT*, 29 Sept. 1993.

Edward Boyer, "Attorney Depicts Williams as a Scapegoat for the Riots," *LAT*, 30 Sept. 1993.

Seth Mydans, "Jury Acquits 2 on Most Charges in Beatings in Los Angeles Riots," *NYT*, 19 Oct. 1993.

O. J. Simpson Trial

Jim Newton and Andrea Ford, "Simpson Lawyers Move to Suppress Evidence," *LAT*, 30 June 1994.

Jim Newton and Andrea Ford, "Simpson Attorneys Ask Judge to Bar Newest Prosecutor," *LAT*, 16 Nov. 1994.

Robert A. Jones, Lynell George, and Al Martinez, "Taking It Personally: Reflections on the Verdicts, the City, and Ourselves," *LAT*, 4 Oct. 1995.

Jim Newton, "Simpson Not Guilty," *LAT*, 4 Oct. 1995.

Andrea Ford and Greg Krikorian, "Simpson Talks of Trial, Criticizes 'Misconceptions,' " *LAT*, 5 Oct. 1995.

Paul Feldman and Kay Hwangbo, "Ministers Urge Harmony After Trial," *LAT*, 9 Oct. 1995.

"Obsession. Did the Media Overfeed a Starving Public?" *LAT*, Special Report, 9 Oct. 1995.

"Twist of Fate: How the Case Changed the Lives of Those It Touched," *LAT*, Special Report, 11 Oct. 1995.

Riordan vs. Woo

Robert Reinhold, "Fear Gives Los Angeles Race an Edge," *LAT*, 7 Apr. 1993.

Frank Clifford, "Clinton Endorses Woo, but Also Lauds Riordan," *LAT*, 19 May 1993.

Ted Rohrlich, "Riordan Discloses Third Alcohol-Related Arrest," *LAT*, 29 May 1993.

Frank Clifford, "Riordan, Woo in Dead Heat," *LAT*, 1 June 1993.

Frank Clifford, "Political Tale of 2 Cities in LA, NY Mayoral Races," *LAT*, 5 June 1993.

Faye Fiore and Frank Clifford, "And Now for Something Completely Different: Defining the Style of Dick Riordan, the Untested Tycoon Who Wants to Run Los Angeles," *LAT Magazine*, 11 Jul. 1993.

The Riordan Style

Ted Rohrlich, "Elected to Make the Little Decisions," *LAT*, 3 Nov. 1997.

Jim Newton, "Summit Impressed by Mayor's Venture Capitalist Instincts," *LAT*, 25 Nov. 1997.

Michael Krikorian, "Mayor's Diner Allowed to Reopen," *LAT*, 28 Nov. 1997.

Jim Newton, "Mayor Plans Valentine's Day Wedding," *LAT*, 11 Feb. 1998.

Carla Hall, "Mahony Rues Mayor's Plans to Remarry," *LAT*, 12 Feb. 1998.

Jim Newton, "LA's Chief of Airports Is Ousted," *LAT*, 9 May 1998.

"Mayor Goes to the Mat to Try Out New Club," *LAT*, 10 June 1998.

Jim Newton, "Mayor's Interest: Is It Flagging or Evolving?" 22 June 1998.

Jim Newton and Louis Sahagun, "Confusion Plagues Mayor's Education Plan," *LAT*, 18 Sept. 1998.

Mark Gladstone, "LA Evolves into Capitol Away from State Capitol," *LAT*, 23 Mar. 1999.

Jim Newton, "LA's Inner Circle Is Mostly Rich Rich, Enormously Powerful," *LAT*, 28 Nov. 1999.

Michael Finnegan, "Officeholders Neglecting Poor, Riordan Charges," *LAT,* 15 May 2001.

David Freedman, "Someone of Stature and Integrity," *LA Downtown News,* 18 June 2001.

Sue Laris, "A Picnic with the Mayor," *LA Downtown News,* 18 June 2001.

Kathryn Maese, "Riordan Reflected," *LA Downtown News,* 18 June 2001.

Michael Finnegan, "A Library Names 'Riordan,' " *LAT,* 19 June 2001.

Jim Newton, "Riordan Leaves a Better LA, but His Legacy Is Mixed," *LAT,* 1 Jul. 2001.

Kevin Roderick, "The Big Break-Up," *LAT Magazine,* 22 Jul. 2001.

Los Angeles Unified School District

Sam Enriquez, "Board Shelved Report on Averting Violence," *LAT,* 24 Feb. 1993.

Eddie Rivera, "Belmont Fiasco Gets the Stamp of Reality," *LA Downtown News,* 20 Sept. 1999.

Louis Sahagun, "Zacarias Fights Legality of Naming Miller CEO," *LAT,* 15 Oct. 1999.

Richard Lee Colvin, "How LA Unified Got into This Fix," *LAT,* 17 Oct. 1999.

Louis Sahagun, "Zacarias Vows Not to Go Voluntarily," *LAT,* 17 Oct. 1999.

Jocelyn Stewart, "Belmont Risks Can Be Controlled, Expert Says," *LAT,* 17 Oct. 1999.

Tom Hayden, "We're a City in Denial About Race," *LAT,* 19 Oct. 1999.

Doug Smith and Louis Sahagun, "Board Members Warn Zacarias to Cooperate," *LAT,* 19 Oct. 1999.

Ted Rohrlich and Antonio Olivo, "Groups Press District to Rescind Zacarias Move," *LAT,* 20 Oct. 1999.

Louis Sahagun and Antonio Olivo, "500 Rally at School District Offices to Support Zacarias," *LAT,* 23 Oct. 1999.

Ted Rohrlich and Antonio Olivo, "Anger at Zacarias Issue May Have Ripple Effect," *LAT,* 24 Oct. 1999.

Agustin Gurza, "Turning a School Crisis into an Ethnic Injustice," *LAT,* 26 Oct. 1999.

Louis Sahagun and Jim Newton, "Compromise Elusive in LA Schools Crisis," *LAT,* 26 Oct. 1999.

Louis Sahagun, "Zacarias Releases Plan to Reorganize School District," *LAT,* 27 Oct. 1999.

Louis Sahagun and Doug Smith, "School Board Majority Plans to Oust Zacarias," *LAT,* 28 Oct. 1999.

Doug Smith and Louis Sahagun, "Board Votes to Begin Zacarias Buyout Talks," *LAT,* 29 Oct. 1999.

Al Martinez, "Sundown for Zacarias," *LAT,* 31 Oct. 1999.

Gregory Rodriguez, "Sitting at the Table," *LAT,* 31 Oct. 1999.

Richard Lee Colvin and Louis Sahagun, "Board Buys Out Zacarias; Interim Chief Is Cortines," *LAT,* 5 Nov. 1999.

Doug Smith and Richard Lee Colvin, "Board Seized the Moment in Forcing a Change at the Top," *LAT,* 14 Nov. 1999.

Kaye Kilburn, "Don't Use Kids as Canaries at Belmont," *LAT,* 15 Nov. 1999.

Steven Windmueller, "Schools Dispute May Be Lesson in Finding Common Ground," *LAT,* 15 Nov. 1999.

Other Latino Matters

Beth Shuster and Matea Gold, "Contrasts Mark Hernandez's Council Return," *LAT,* 8 Oct. 1997.

Beth Shuster, "Hernandez Question Splits Angry Council," *LAT,* 25 Oct. 1997.

Greg Krikorian and Beth Shuster, "Mayor Joins Call for Hernandez to Quit Council," *LAT,* 28 Oct. 1997.

Beth Shuster, "Organizers Drop Bid to Recall Hernandez," *LAT,* 17 Jan. 1998.
Ted Rohrlich, "1st District's Plight Hinders Recall Efforts," *LAT,* 2 Feb. 1998.
Beth Shuster, "Hernandez Adhering to Recovery Plan, Judge Says," *LAT,* 13 Mar. 1998.
Beth Shuster, "Hernandez to Leave Politics After Council Term," *LAT,* 13 June 1998.
Gregory Rodriguez, "A Pyrrhic Victory in the Valley," *LAT,* 21 June 1998.
Hugo Martin, "Katz Rejects Alarcon's Apology over Flyer," *LAT,* 30 June 1998.
Gary Greenebaum and Arturo Vargas, "Jews, Latinos Need to Forge Coalition, Not Engage in Conflict," *LAT,* 1 Jul. 1998.
Beth Shuster, "Mike's Remake," *LAT Magazine,* 6 Feb. 2000.

People's Republic of San Francisco
Joan Smith, "The Lion and the Lioness," *SFEx,* 15 Mar. 1992.
Ralph King, "Discrimination Molds a Real Estate Tycoon into a Tough Survivor," *WSJ,* 1 June 1993.
Carla Marinucci, "Steamed at Supervisors, Mayor Thanks Colin Powell," *SFCh,* 26 Nov. 1997.
Stephen Schwartz, "Medical Marijuana Clubs Illegal," *SFCh,* 13 Dec. 1997.
Dave Murphy, "Blinding Brilliance and Staggering Stupidity," *SFEx,* 1 Mar. 1998.
Mary Curtius, "SF Schools Consider Non-White Writer Quota," *LAT,* 12 Mar. 1998.
Michael Dougan, "School Chief: No Quota," *SFEx,* 12 Mar. 1998.
Maria L. La Ganga, "SF School Board OKs Accord on Reading List," *LAT,* 21 Mar. 1998.
Anastasia Hendrix, "Williams to Step Down as Pastor," *SFEx,* 19 May 1998.
Maura Dolan and Edmund Sanders, "Judge Blocks Laws Banning ATM Surcharges," *LAT,* 16 Nov. 1999.

Da Mayor
Marc Sandalow, "Gays Celebrate 'Lavender Sweep' in San Francisco Election," *SFCh,* 8 Nov. 1990.
Anastasia Hendrix, "Security for Brown Unusually Extreme," *SFEx,* 16 Jan. 1998.
F. J. Gallagher, "Changes Ahead for SF Taxis," *The Independent,* 24 Feb. 1998.
Johnny Brannon, "Airport Taxi Glut," *The Independent,* 17 Mar. 1998.
Harriet Chiang and Manny Fernandez, "Judge Strikes Down Housing Moratorium," *SFCh,* 4 Apr. 1998.
F. J. Gallagher, "Playing Hard Ball," *The Independent,* 21 Apr. 1998.
Nina Siegal, "Renter Beware!" *San Francisco Bay Guardian,* 6 May 1998.
Glen Martin, "SF May Use Health Dept. in Pot War," *SFCh,* 29 May 1998.
Aurelio Rojas, "Cab Hits Cable Car in Latest MUNI Mishap," *SFCh,* 30 June 1998.
Chuck Finnie, "Brown Already Off and Running," *SFEx,* 8 Jul. 1998.
Edward Epstein, Lynda Gledhill, and Julie Lynem, "MUNI Confident Chaos Won't Be Back," *SFCh,* 1 Sept. 1998.
Edward Epstein and Steve Rubenstein, "Mayor Walks, MUNI Runs," *SFCh,* 4 Sept. 1998.
Elizabeth Fernandez, "N-Judah: 3 Stops with a Driver," *SFEx,* 6 Sept. 1998.
Erin McCormick, "SF Spending Spree," *SFEx,* 20 June 1999.
Erin McCormick, "$100K Club Swells at City Hall," *SFEx,* 22 June 1999.
Mary Curtius, "Ammiano Will Face Brown in SF Runoff," *LAT,* 5 Nov. 1999.
Mary Curtius, "GOP Leaders Forced to Weigh Lesser Evil in SF Mayor Runoff," *LAT,* 10 Nov. 1999.

San Francisco Confidential

Leslie Goldberg, "OMI: A Tale of Drugs, Urban Decay," *SFEx*, 28 Feb. 1993.

John O'Connor and Paul Avery, "Clashes Wreck Holiday Mood," *SFEx*, 3 May 1993.

Steve Rubenstein, "Poisoning of Pigeons Spreading," *SFCh*, 22 Apr. 1998.

Susan Sward, "101 California—Legacy of Horror," *SFCh*, 30 June 1998.

Elizabeth Fernandez, "Mayor Joins Ranks of Pied Pols," *SFEx*, 8 Nov. 1998.

Manny Fernandez and Michael Taylor, "Rampaging SF Revelers Trash Streets," *SFCh*, 2 Jan. 1999.

Daniel Hernandez and Maria L. La Ganga, "Puppies with a Deadly Lineage," *LAT*, 4 Aug. 2001.

Jaxon Van Derbeken, "Killer Dog's Owners Seek to Move Trial," *SFCh*, 14 Aug. 2001.

AP, "Dog Attack Suspects Plead for Lower Bail," *LAT*, 1 Sept. 2001.

Jaxon Van Derbeken, "Owner of Killer Dog, 7 Others Indicted," *SFCh*, 6 Sept. 2001.

AP, "Pair's Views on Attack Dogs Revealed," *LAT*, 19 Sept. 2001.

Los Angeles Confidential

Ashley Dunn and Jesse Katz, "Numbed LA Takes Grim Note of 27 Slain in Weekend," *LAT*, 25 Aug. 1992.

Beth Shuster, "Movie Makers Exempted from City Gun Law," *LAT*, 10 Dec. 1997.

Solomon Moore, "Lawyer Held in Alleged Prostitution Operation," *LAT*, 19 Feb. 1998.

Greg Krikorian, "Trial Starts in Spielberg Stalker Case," *LAT*, 20 Feb. 1998.

"Socialite Sentenced for Selling Cocaine," *LAT*, 22 Mar. 1998.

Scott Martelle and Bonnie Hayes, "Socialite Known for Compassion Is Drug Suspect," *LAT*, 13 Apr. 1998.

John M. Glionna, "Beverly Hills Steps Up Patrols to Stop Cruising," *LAT*, 29 May 1998.

Joe Monzingo, "Drug Smuggler, 73, Killed in Cocaine Deal, Police Say," *LAT*, 15 Jan. 2000.

Beth Shuster, "Jail Escape Explained: 'Dr. Doolittle Did It,' " *LAT*, 14 Jul. 2001.

Josh Meyer, "Surprise Plea Ends Lurid Case," *LAT*, 11 Sept. 2001.

Hector Becerra, "Suspect Held in Slaying of 2 Brothers," *LAT*, 4 Oct. 2001.

Mark Magnier and Miles Corwin, "Entrepreneur from Japan Shot to Death," *LAT*, 4 Oct. 2001.

Jill Leovy and Mark Magnier, "Slain Entrepreneur Recalled as Kind, Dynamic," *LAT*, 6 Oct. 2001.

LAPD Rules!

Jane Fritsch, "Head of Police Panel Resigns," *LAT*, 8 May 1991.

Leslie Berger, "City Worker Claims Brutality by LAPD," *LAT*, 27 Aug. 1991.

John Gregory Dunne, "Law & Disorder in Los Angeles," *New York Review of Books*, 10 Oct. 1991.

John Gregory Dunne, "Law & Disorder in Los Angeles: Part II," *New York Review of Books*, 24 Oct. 1991.

Hector Tobar and Elliott Almond, "Police Slaying of Man Mars LA Marathon," *LAT*, 2 Mar. 1992.

Sheryl Stolberg, "2 Inmates May Be Innocent and Freed After 17 Years," *LAT*, 9 Mar. 1992.

Sheryl Stolberg, "Judge Apologizes, Frees 2 Men in 1973 Murder," *LAT*, 26 Mar. 1992.

Daryl F. Gates, with Diane K. Shah, *Chief, My Life in the LAPD* (1992).

Bill Boyarsky, "Why He Does What He Does," *LAT Book Review*, 24 May 1992.

Jimmy Breslin, "LA's Top Gun," *LAT Book Review*, 24 May 1992.

Jim Herron Zamora, "Volunteers Give LA Police Extra Eyes in the Night," *LAT*, 18 Mar. 1993.

Richard Serrano and Kenneth Reich, "Chief Will Deploy Officers at Start of Jury Deliberations," *LAT*, 7 Apr. 1993.

Richard Serrano, "Show of Force to Be Biggest in LA History," *LAT*, 8 Apr. 1993.

Joe Domanick, *To Protect and to Serve: The LAPD's Century of War in the City of Dreams* (1994).

Mark Lacey and Jim Newton, "Police Union Rejects Mayor's Mediation Plan," *LAT*, 2 June 1994.

Mark Lacey and Jim Newton, "New Offer Presented to City by Police Union," *LAT*, 3 June 1994.

Mark Lacey, "Mayor Ready to Declare LAPD Impasse," *LAT*, 14 June 1994.

Stephen Braun, "Pushed by Change, Pulled by the Past," *LAT*, 10 Oct. 1995.

Matt Lait, "Panel Backs Strong Role for Police Watchdog," *LAT*, 18 Dec. 1998.

Jim Newton, "LAPD Corruption Probe May Be Test for City Leaders," *LAT*, 20 Sept. 1999.

Tina Daunt, "City Attorney Backs Civilian Police Panel," *LAT*, 21 Sept. 1999.

Jim Newton, "Delegates Arrive in LA Prepared for Best, Worst," *LAT*, 13 Aug. 2000.

Scott Martelle and Nicholas Riccardi, "95 Arrested as Protesters and Police Make a Day of It," *LAT*, 16 Aug. 2000.

Joe Domanick, "Can the LAPD Reform Itself?" *LAT*, 24 Sept. 2000.

Jim Newton, "The US-City Police Reform Deal: Monument to a Year of Upheaval," *LAT*, 31 Dec. 2000.

Tina Daunt, "Consent Decree Gets Federal Judge's OK," *LAT*, 16 June 2001.

Place

Metropolitan Regions

Frank Clifford, "LA's Past May Be Part of Its Future," *LAT*, 25 Dec. 1989.

"LA County's 86 Cities," *LAT*, 27 Dec. 1989.

William Fulton, "Can Anything Stop Los Angeles?" *WSJ*, 8 May 1990.

Mike Davis, "The Dark Side of Development," *LAT*, 29 Sept. 1991.

Carol Tucker, "Los Angeles: City of the Future," *USC Trojan Family Magazine* (Spring 1992).

Gerald Adams, "Major Renewal Plan for SF in Works," *SFEx*, 8 Mar. 1993.

Richard Rodriguez, "Slouching Towards Los Angeles," *LAT*, 11 Apr. 1993.

Jill Stewart, "East Side, West Side," *LAT Magazine*, 23 Jan. 1994.

John King, "Expansion of Bay Area Just Won't End," *SFCh*, 28 Apr. 1998.

Jim Newton, "City Considers Billion-Dollar Bond Measure," *LAT*, 1 Jul. 1998.

Todd S. Purdum, "Los Angeles Tests Its Limits in Quest to Grow," *NYT*, 13 Feb. 2000.

Redeveloping San Francisco

"A Railroad Heir's Legacy: Land Rich, Cash Poor," *NYT*, 1 Jan. 1993.

Zahid Sardar, "Rounding Off the Block," *SFEx Magazine*, 15 Jan. 1995.

Edward Epstein, "Going Downtown," *SFCh*, 7 Dec. 1997.

David Bush, "Field of Dreams Is Happening," *SFCh*, 12 Dec. 1997.

Johnson Fain Partners, *Mission Bay Land Use Plan* (Catellus Development Corporation, 6 Aug. 1998).

Alex Barnum, "Sweeping Vision for Presidio's Future," *SFCh*, 28 Apr. 1998.

Alex Barnum, "Bridge of the Future," *SFCh*, 11 May 1998.

Alex Barnum, "Bay Bridge Surprise—Suspension Plan Wins," *SFCh*, 30 May 1998.

Anastasia Hendrix, "Better than the Lottery," *SFEx*, 15 June 1998.

Gerald Adams, "Massive Waterfront Makeover to Begin," *SFEx,* 29 June 1998.

Dan Levy, "The Highrises Rise Again," *SFCh,* 9 Jul. 1998.

Dan Levy, "Face-Lift for an Aging Icon," *SFCh,* 11 Jul. 1998.

Rachel Gordon, "You Can't Beat City Hall," *SFEx,* 3 Jan. 1999.

Zahid Sardar, "Light Years," *SFEx Magazine,* 3 Jan. 1999.

John King, "Civic Pride," *SFCh,* 4 Jan. 1999.

Tyche Hendricks, "Lucas Wins 'Presidio Wars,' " *SFEx,* 15 June 1999.

Dan Levy, "Lucasfilm Signs Pact for 23-Acre Presidio Space," *SFCh,* 15 Aug. 2001.

Preserving Historic Los Angeles

Dave McCombs, "Bradbury's Revival," *Los Angeles Downtown News,* 23 Sept. 1991.

Amy Wallace, "Coffee Shops Modern," *LAT,* 1 Apr. 1993.

Barbara Hansen, "The Last Tea," *LAT,* 15 Apr. 1993.

Lynell George, "LA's Fatal Attraction," *LAT,* 17 Apr. 1995.

Todd S. Purdum, "A Swell, Swanky Emporium Turns Literary," *NYT,* 25 Sept. 1997.

Steve Harvey, "Touring LA, Confidentially," *LAT,* 27 Sept. 1997.

Tamara Hunt, "Ushering in a New Era," *Westside Weekly, LAT,* 3 Oct. 1997.

Larry Gordon, "Developer Has Option to Buy St. Vibiana's," *LAT,* 28 Oct. 1997.

Beth Shuster, "City Hall Renovation Offers a Lesson in Civic Archeology," *LAT,* 29 Nov. 1998.

Stephen Siciliano, "Lord Gilmore's Landmark," *Los Angeles Downtown News,* 1 Nov. 1999.

Larry Gordon, "St. Vibiana's Bought by Developer," *LAT,* 2 Nov. 1999.

Susan Freudenheim, "LA's Designing Woman," *LAT,* 10 June 2001.

Kenneth Reich, "Council Returns to Retrofitted City Hall," *LAT,* 29 June 2001.

Nicolai Ouroussoff, "More than Just Mortar," *LAT,* 6 Jul. 2001.

Cecilia Rasmussen, "City Hall Beacon to Shine Again," *LAT,* 9 Sept. 2001.

Wilshire, Hollywood, Playa Vista

Elaine Woo, "La Brea Goes from Frumpy to Fashionable," *LAT,* 21 Apr. 1991.

Bettina Boxall, "Miracle Riled," *LAT,* 22 Sept. 1991.

Susan Moffat, "Sheraton-Town House Is Latest Wilshire Landmark That May Be Doomed," *LAT,* 17 Mar. 1993.

Vicki Torres, "Battle Royal," *LAT,* 26 Mar. 1993.

Vicki Torres, "Millie's Owner Fails to Regain Silver Lake Café," *LAT,* 30 Mar. 1993.

Robin Rauzi, "A New Space for LACE," *LAT,* 27 Apr. 1993.

Lynell George, "Luring Lights Back to Wilshire," *LAT,* 6 June 1993.

Nicolai Ouroussoff, "Could It Be Magic—Again?" *LAT Calendar,* 23 Nov. 1997.

Jesus Sanchez, "High-Rising from Real Estate's Ashes," *LAT,* 23 Nov. 1997.

Ken Ellingwood, "Redemption for a Mall?" *LAT,* 27 Jan. 1998.

Dan Gordon, "NoHo Cool," *LAT,* 15 Feb. 1998.

Jim Newton, "Mayor Leads a Hurray for Hollywood," *LAT,* 3 Apr. 1998.

Editorial, "Hollywood's New Hurrah," *LAT,* 10 May 1998.

Bob Pool, "Tough Sell at the Market," *LAT,* 23 May 1998.

David Rosenzweig and Abigail Goldman, "Judge Orders Halt to Playa Vista Wetlands Project," *LAT,* 27 June 1998.

Larry Gordon, "Flashy Art for a Flashy Town," *LAT,* 8 Jul. 1998.

Greg Goldin, "Mall-Ywood," *LA Weekly,* 18 Dec. 1998.

Claudia Eller and Jim Bates, "Dreamworks Wakes Up to Reality," *LAT,* 13 Jul. 1999.

Mitchell Landsberg, "Hollywood May Finally Make Its Comeback," *LAT,* 24 Oct. 1999.

Patrick McGreevy and T. Christian Miller, "Heady Plans, Hard Reality," *LAT,* 30 Jan. 2000.

Laura Mecoy, "A Battle for the Hollywood Bowl," *SacBee,* 13 Aug. 2001.

Peter Hong, "Soboroff to Head Playa Vista Project," *LAT,* 11 Oct. 2001.

Maria Elena Fernandez, "Pied Piper of LA's Party Scene," *LAT,* 15 Oct. 2001.

George Ramos, "Trendy Night Spots Helping to Rejuvenate Hollywood," *LAT,* 15 Oct. 2001.

Mitchell Landsberg, "There's a New Buzz on Hollywood Blvd," *LAT,* 8 Nov. 2001.

Jesus Sanchez, "Hollywood's Star Yet to Shine," *LAT,* 7 May 2002.

LA Downtown

Jill Stewart, "Council OKs Huge Central City West Project," *LAT,* 30 Jan. 1991.

Barbara Isenberg, "Curtain Rises on Final Design for Disney Hall," *LAT,* 5 Sept. 1991.

Robert A. Jones, "An LA Kind of Place," *LAT,* 13 Oct. 1991.

Morris Newman, "Despite Doldrums, Downtown Los Angeles Bustles," *NYT,* 19 Jan. 1992.

Amy Wallace, "Like It's So LA! Not Really," *LAT,* 9 Feb. 1992.

Louis Sahagun, "Wide Expansion of Garment District Proposed," *LAT,* 6 Aug. 1992.

David Ferrell, "Life in the Underbelly of LA," *LAT,* 9 Nov. 1992.

Joseph Giovannini, "Wrapmaster Gehry and the New Culture Palace," *LAT Magazine,* 22 Nov. 1992.

Aaron Betsky, "Remaking LA," *LAT Magazine,* 13 Dec. 1992.

Herbert Muschamp, "Gehry's Disney Hall: A Matterhorn for Music," *NYT,* 13 Dec. 1992.

Sam Hall Kaplan, "A Concert Hall for Fantasyland," *LAT,* 21 Dec. 1992.

Marc Lacey, "Scene of the Crime: Often, It's City Hall," *LAT,* 26 Sept. 1993.

Leon Whiteson, "Dream Street," *LAT,* 31 Oct. 1993.

Diane Haithman, "When Disney's Done, What Then?" *LAT Calendar,* 10 Apr. 1994.

Christopher Knight, "Big 'Burb,' Architecture in Los Angeles," *Design Quarterly,* 22 Sept. 1994.

Joel Kotkin, "Los Angeles: Five Years Later," *WP,* 20 Apr. 1997.

Joel Kotkin, "How Cities Can Survive: Look to the Renaissance," *LAT,* 17 Aug. 1997.

Joel Wachs, "Sports Arena: Who Should Pay for It?" *LAT,* 2 Oct. 1997.

Melinda Fulmer, "Who Owns the Most," *LAT,* 5 Nov. 1997.

Michelle Rafter, "Spring Hopes Eternal," *LAT,* 5 Nov. 1997.

Mary Melton, "A Brief History of the Mini-Mall," *LAT Magazine,* 16 Nov. 1997.

Diane Haithman, "Disney Gives $25 Million to Downtown Concert Hall," *LAT,* 2 Dec. 1997.

Melinda Fulmer, "Comeback Stores: Downtown's Old Buildings," *LAT,* 14 Jan. 1998.

Melinda Fulmer, "Downtown Building Gets 'Lemon' Award," *LAT,* 10 Apr. 1998.

Joel Kotkin, " 'Everyone's Downtown,' " *LAT,* 4 June 1998.

Diane Haithman, "$20 Million in Gifts Meet Key Goal for Disney Hall," *LAT,* 21 Jul. 1998.

Frances Anderton, "The Global Village Goes Pop Baroque," *NYT,* 8 Oct. 1998.

Robert A. Jones, "The Pooh-Bahs Save Downtown," *LAT,* 25 Oct. 1998.

Robert A. Jones, "Like, Omigod, the Galleria Died," *LAT,* 31 Jan. 1999.

"Taking Center Stage," *LAT Magazine,* Special Issue, 10 Oct. 1999.

Geoff Boucher and Ted Rohrlich, "Madness on the Edge of Downtown," *LAT,* 18 Oct. 1999.

Nicolai Ouroussoff, "Picture This on Downtown's Doorstep," *LAT Calendar,* 24 Oct. 1999.

Joel Kotkin, "Keeping Life Downtown," *LAT,* 7 Nov. 1999.

Frank Gehry and Associates, Arata Isozaki and Associates, Jose Raphael Moneo, Olin Partnership, Stuart Ketchum, *The Music Center, the Performing Arts Center of Los Angeles County, Workshop Concept Plan* (December 2000).

Nicolai Ouroussoff, "A Grand Idea in Theory," *LAT Calendar,* 13 Dec. 2000.

Susan Salter Reynolds, "De-Malling the Mall," *LAT,* 18 Dec. 2000.

Elaine Woo, "Interview with Joanne Kozberg," *LAT,* 21 Jan. 2001.

Shashank Bengali, "Legend," *USC Trojan Family Magazine* (Summer 2001).

Usha Lee McFarling, "Beauty and the Beastly Project," *LAT,* 6 Aug. 2001.

Nicolai Ouroussoff, "Postcards from a City in Progress," *LAT Calendar,* 19 Aug. 2001.

Tina Daunt, "Development Plans for Staples Center Area OKd," *LAT,* 6 Sept. 2001.

Cry Me a River

Friends of the Los Angeles River, *Current News, the Voice of the River,* throughout the decade.

Richard Lee Colvin, "LA River Revival Effort Adrift, Officials Agree," *LAT,* 16 Oct. 1991.

Bob Pool, "River Rescue," *LAT,* 20 Apr. 1994.

Blake Gumprecht, *The Los Angeles River: Its Life, Death, and Possible Rebirth* (1999).

D. J. Waldie, "Changing a River's Course," *LAT,* 3 Oct. 1999.

Joe Mozingo, "New Urban Oases," *LAT,* 7 Nov. 2000.

Patt Morrison, *Rio LA, Tales from the Los Angeles River* (2001).

David Ferrell, "LA River Defies City in Nurturing Wildlife," *LAT,* 26 Jan. 2001.

Matea Gold, "State Plans 2 Parks by LA River," *LAT,* 22 Dec. 2001.

Talk of the Town

Baghdad by the Bay

"Fifty Years of the Caen Column," *SFCh,* 10 Jul. 1998.

"Herb Caen, Celebrating a Life, 1916–1997," *SFCh,* 3 Feb. 1997.

Susan Rivers, "Light in the Forest," *SFEx Magazine,* 14 Dec. 1997.

Jerry Carroll and William Carlsen, "Ex-Mayor Joe Alioto Dies at 81," *SFCh,* 30 Jan. 1998.

"Baylife '98, Past, Present, and Future," *SFEx,* Special Edition, 1 Mar. 1998.

Construing Los Angeles

Richard Meltzer, *LA Is the Capital of Kansas: Painful Lessons in Post–New York Living* (1988).

Ronald Brownstein, "LA in the Mind of America," *LAT Magazine,* 15 Jan. 1989.

David Reid, editor, *Sex, Death and God in LA* (1992).

Michael J. Dear, Eric Shockman, Greg Hise, *Rethinking Los Angeles* (1996).

Alan Scott, Edward Soja, editors, *The City: Los Angeles and Urban Theory at the End of the Twentieth Century* (1996).

William Fulton, *The Reluctant Metropolis* (1997).

Mike Davis, *Ecology of Fear: Los Angeles and the Imagination of Disaster* (1998).

David Fine, *Imagining Los Angeles: A City in Fiction* (2000).

William Alexander McClung, *Landscapes of Desire: Anglo Mythologies of Los Angeles* (2000).

Jim Newton, "LA Defined, Loosely," *LAT,* 13 Aug. 2000.

The Writing Life, San Francisco

Scott Winokur, "The Best and the Brightest," *Image, SFEx,* 29 Mar. 1992.

Cynthia Robins, "She's on a 'Suicide' Mission," *SFEx,* 7 Oct. 1992.

Cathy Hainer, "Keeping the Beat," *USA Today,* 4 Nov. 1997.

Edward Epstein, "SF Finds Its Voice," *SFCh,* 12 Aug. 1998.

Dana Gioia, "Fallen Western Star: The Decline of San Francisco as a Literary Region," *Denver Quarterly* (Fall 1998).
Penelope Rowlands, "La Dolce Vita," *SFEx Magazine*, 30 May 1999.
Laura Miller, "The Streetwalkers of San Francisco," *NYT*, 20 Aug. 2000.
Susan Carpenter, "The Father to a Popular Bunch of Orphans," *LAT*, 9 Sept. 2001.

The Writing Life, Los Angeles
Pamela Warrick, "Poetry in the Spin Cycle," *LAT*, 19 Apr. 1991.
Martin Booe, "The Making of a Sleuth," *LAT*, 22 Apr. 1992.
Edvins Beitiks, " 'Cheshire Moon' a Visible Winner," *SFEx*, 19 Feb. 1993.
Christopher Lehmann-Haupt, "Murders and Regrets in Southern California," *NYT*, 25 Feb. 1993.
Roy Rivenburg, "He's Angry, Raunchy, and Unapologetic," *LAT*, 8 Apr. 1993.
Nina Easton, "LA and Other Fictions," *LAT Magazine*, 5 Sept. 1993.
Meryl Ginsberg, "The LA Poetry Monde: Two Poets' Views," *UCLA Extension Writers' Program Quarterly* (Winter 1996).
Suzanne Lummis, "Charles Bukowski, 1920–1994," *LAT Book Review*, 10 Apr. 1994.
Susan Salter Reynolds, "A Literary Leap," *LAT*, 11 Nov. 1997.
Myrna Oliver, "James Robert Baker; Satiric Novelist, Cult Filmmaker," *LAT*, 15 Nov. 1997.
Bettijane Levine, "A Runaway Success," *LAT*, 20 Nov. 1997.
"A Guide: Literary LA," *LA Weekly*, 6 Feb. 1998.
"LA Lit (Does It Exist?), A Symposium," *LAT Book Review*, 25 Apr. 1999.
Lynell George, "Transcending the Genre," *LAT*, 24 Nov. 1999.
Lynell George, "To Have and Have Not in LA," *LAT*, 18 Jul. 2001.
Bettijane Levine, "A Harsh, Swift Clarity," *LAT*, 31 Jul. 2001.
D. J. Waldie, "Strangers in Paradise," *LAT Book Review*, 9 Sept. 2001.
Charlotte Innes, "Fightin' Words," *LAT*, 12 Sept. 2001.
"Sifting Through LA's Shadows, Interviews with Paula Woods and Karen Grigsby Bates," *LAT*, 10 Oct. 2001.
Lynell George, "Parody That's Personal," *LAT*, 16 Oct. 2001.
Mary Forgione, "Tribute to a Poet and Mentor," *LAT*, 31 Dec. 2001.

San Francisco Style
Elizabeth Fernandez, "Where Is Werner Erhard?" *SFEx*, 21 Apr. 1991.
Philip Elwood, "Impresario Lived Life at Center Stage," *SFEx*, 27 Oct. 1991.
Burr Snider, "Rock's Bill Graham Dies in Crash," *SFEx*, 27 Oct. 1991.
Harry Demoro, "SF Jazz Pianist John H. Cooper, 76," *SFCh*, 5 Dec. 1992.
"Best of the Beach," *North Beach Now* (June 1993).
Jerry Shriver, "San Francisco's Golden New Restaurants," *USA Today*, 18 Oct. 1996.
Dan Levy, "SOMA Wars," *SFCh*, 14 Apr. 1998.
Marianne Costantinou, "A Change in Attitude Mars Peaceful Haight Street Scene," *SFEx*, 12 June 1998.
David Bonetti, "Burned Out," *SFEx*, 19 Aug. 1998.
Sam Whiting, "The Hottest Burning Man in History," *SFCh*, 7 Sept. 1998.
Steven Winn, "All-Star 'Beach Blanket' Celebration," *SFCh*, 9 June 1999.
Louis Freedberg, "Coffee, Brewing a Cheaper Cup," *SFCh*, 5 Aug. 2001.
Rick Loomis, "A Hot Time," *LAT*, 7 Sept. 2001.
Carolyne Zinko, "A Bellissima Night of Wine and Roses," *SFCh*, 8 Sept. 2001.

Los Angeles Style
Duke Helfand, "Born to Be Chic," *LAT,* 9 Sept. 1991.
Mark Ehrman, "A Mating Ritual That Lasts," *LAT,* 11 Oct. 1992.
"LA Team Rolls with the Punches as It Smashes Record," *LAT,* 18 May 1993.
Robin Abcarian, "Standouts—Even in Venice," *LAT,* 16 June 1993.
Bob Sipchen, "Dueling Attitudes," *LAT,* 23 Sept. 1993.
Andrea Heiman, "Studies in Style," *LAT,* 24 Sept. 1993.
Jeannine Stein, "Dollars Today, Sense Tomorrow," *LAT,* 19 Nov. 1997.
Duane Noriyuki, "The Next Round," *LAT,* 10 Dec. 1997.
Alan Abrahamson, "A Latte Without Leaving Your Car—Life Is Good," *LAT,* 2 Feb. 1998.
Beverly Beyette, "Shark City, the Street," *LAT,* 8 Feb. 1998.
Steven Smith, "Catering to the Stars," *LAT,* 11 May 1998.
Amy Wallace, "The Talk of the Town," *LAT,* 10 Jul. 1998.
Heidi Siegmund Cuda, "All That Glitters," *LAT,* 29 Apr. 1999.
Tom Nolan, "Martinis & Mythology," *LAT Magazine,* 6 Feb. 2000.
Hilary MacGregor, "For Party-Goers, Tito's Hilltop Is a Spatial Odyssey," *LAT,* 7 May 2001.
Twila Decker, "At Zoo It's Crunching Dragon, Injured Editor," *LAT,* 11 June 2001.
Joe Mozingo, "Bite Boosts Zoo Fundraiser," *LAT,* 17 June 2001.
Claudia Rosenbaum, "*Oui,* the People Sing," *LAT,* 13 Aug. 2001.
Reed Johnson, "When Buff Ruled the Big Screen," *LAT,* 3 Sept. 2001.
Heseon Park, "A Feel-Good Favorite," *LAT Calendar,* 6 Sept. 2001.
Lina Lecaro, "A Born-Free Feeling," *LAT,* 27 Sept. 2001.
Heidi Siegmund Cuda, "Supper Clubs Redux," *LAT Calendar,* 11 Oct. 2001.

Arts and Architecture
Barbara Isenberg, "The Hot Wave from LA," *LAT Calendar,* 15 Sept. 1991.
William Wilson, "Don Bachardy: Drawings from a Deathwatch," *LAT,* 2 Oct. 1991.
Orville Clarke, "Of Murals, Messages and Memories," *LAT Magazine,* 13 Oct. 1991.
Suzanne Muchnic, "Forgotten Splendors," *LAT Calendar,* 16 Oct. 1991.
Bernard Weinraub, "Who Needs New York? New Films Show a Tougher Side of Los Ange-
     les," *NYT,* 3 Feb. 1992.
Aljean Harmetz, " 'Falling Down' Takes Its Cues from the Headlines," *NYT,* 21 Feb. 1993.
Kenneth Turan, "Everyman Can't Keep from 'Falling Down,' " *LAT Calendar,* 26 Feb. 1993.
Michael Webb, "Shapes with Shadows," *LAT Magazine,* 31 Oct. 1993.
Joseph Giovannini, "LA Architects: They Did It Their Way," *LAT Magazine,* 15 May 1994.
Lawrence Christon, "A Lasting Imprint," *LAT,* 15 Oct. 1995.
Anthony Vidler, "LA's Only Constant Is Change in Its Architecture," *LAT,* 5 Oct. 1997.
Mark Swed, " 'Flute' of Fancy," *LAT,* 16 Feb. 1998.
Sam Whiting, "Back in Their Sights," *SFCh,* 25 Mar. 1998.
Joseph Giovannini, "Showcase for the Emerging Voices of California Modern," *NYT,* 2 Apr.
     1998.
Jesse Hamlin, "Sculptured Vision of City," *SFCh,* 6 May 1998.
Ilana DeBare, "Art School Brushes Up Reputation," *SFCh,* 22 May 1998.
Allan Ulrich, "Family Reunion," *SFEx Magazine,* 6 Sept. 1998.
Elaine Dutka, "Orchestra's Outlook Is Sunny but Hazy," *LAT,* 14 Jan. 2000.
Mark Swed, "Determined to Be Daring," *LAT Calendar,* 16 Sept. 2001.
Carolyn Ramsay, "A Market-Fresh Look," *LAT,* 3 Jan. 2002.
Mark Swed, "Peter Hemmings, 67; LA Opera Founding Chief," *LAT,* 4 Jan. 2002.

The Getty

Suzanne Muchnic, "Plans for Getty Center Unveiled," *LAT,* 10 Oct. 1991.
Leon Whiteson, "Man, Nature, and the Getty," *LAT,* 13 Oct. 1991.
Suzanne Muchnic, "What the Getty Can't Buy: Time," *LAT,* 22 Oct. 1997.
Diane Haithman, "New Getty Attracting the World's Attention," *LAT,* 8 Nov. 1997.
Suzanne Muchnic, "Spending a Unique Inheritance," *LAT,* 30 Nov. 1997.
Nicolai Ouroussoff, "Realizing a Utopian Goal in Center That Doesn't Cohere," *LAT,* 1 Dec. 1997.
Jonathan Weber, "Center Pushes High-Tech Envelope," *LAT,* 8 Dec. 1997.
Larry Gordon, "Workers Built In Years of Pride," *LAT,* 9 Dec. 1997.
Betty Goodwin, "A-List Attends Getty's Opening Gala," *LAT,* 10 Dec. 1997.
Robert Smaus, "A Gardener's Getty," *LAT,* 14 Dec. 1997.
Paul Goldberger, "The People's Getty," *The New Yorker,* 23 Feb. and 2 Mar. 1998.
James Sterngold, "Avalanche of Visitors Flusters New Museum," *NYT,* 2 Apr. 1998.

Libraries and Newspapers

Joseph Giovannini, "Grandeur Central," *LAT Magazine,* 3 Oct. 1993.
Leon Whiteson, "More Is Less," *LAT,* 3 Oct. 1993.
Mary Lou Loper, "Central Library Opens Its Doors Again to LA," *LAT,* 4 Oct. 1993.
Paul Goldberger, "A Landmark Manages to Cheat the Wrecking Ball," *NYT,* 10 Oct. 1993.
Patrick Reilly, " 'Black Sheep' of Family Battles Kin for Control of Newspaper Dynasty," *WSJ,* 25 May 1995.
Seth Lubov, "Chandler vs. Chandler," *Forbes,* 20 Nov. 1995.
Johnny Brannon, "Library Usability to Get Long Look," *The Independent,* 7 Feb. 1998.
David Shaw, "An Uneasy Alliance of News and Ads," *LAT,* 29 Mar. 1998.
David Shaw, "Cooperation Within Times Viewed with Trepidation," *LAT,* 30 Mar. 1998.
Lisa Bannon, "The Publisher Plans New Type Faces for the LA Times," *WSJ,* 15 May 1998.
"Evaluation of SFPL Building Vindicates Staff Complaints," *Library Hotline,* 30 Aug. 1999.
Felicity Barringer, "Day of Contrition at the Los Angeles Times," *NYT,* 29 Oct. 1999.
"Crossing the Line," *LAT,* Special Report, 20 Dec. 1999.
William Carlsen and Reynolds Holding, "How Politics Tangled Up SF Newspaper Deals," *SFCh,* 27 Apr. 2000.

PART VIII / Growth and the Environment

Heartland

Central Valley

Ann Levin, "California's New Frontier," *SDUT,* 17 Mar. 1986.
Judy Pasternak, "Pollution Is Choking Farm Belt," *LAT,* 22 Apr. 1991.
Stephen Johnson, Gerald Haslam, and Robert Dawson, *The Great Central Valley, California's Heartland* (1993).
Michael Nava, "Where the Earth Abides," *LAT Book Review,* 6 June 1993.
Timothy Egan, "Urban Sprawl Strains Western States," *NYT,* 20 Dec. 1996.
Martha Groves, "Whole Lotta Encroachin' Goin' On," *LAT,* 21 Feb. 1997.
Great Valley Center, *Great Valley News,* from 1997 to 2002.
Kenneth Umbach, *A Statistical Tour of California's Great Central Valley—1998* (CRB, August 1998).

Mark Baldassare, *Special Survey of the Central Valley in Cooperation with the Great Valley Center* (Public Policy Institute of California, November 1999).
Gary Polakovic, "San Joaquin Valley Placed on List of Smoggiest Areas," *LAT,* 24 Oct. 2001.

Agribusiness
Keith Schneider, "Looking Abroad to Fill Our Bellies," *NYT,* 3 Aug. 1986.
Ellen Hawkes, *Blood and Wine: The Un-Authorized Story of the Gallo Wine Empire* (1993).
Donald Woutat, "What's In Store for Gallo Empire," *LAT,* 4 May 1993.
Michael Doyle, "Valley Cities See Boom in Exports," *SacBee,* 31 May 1996.

Heartland Cities
Robert Lindsey, "Rush Is to Interior as California Growth Shifts," *NYT,* 14 Jan. 1986.
Burton Swope, "Controversy No Stranger in Valley Town of Visalia," *LAT,* 3 Mar. 1991.
Morris Newman, "Bakersfield Is Making a Comeback," *Chicago Tribune,* 10 Nov. 1991.
Steve James, "Twangs for the Memories," *WP,* 28 Dec. 1995.
"Sacramento County," *SacBee,* 30 Jan. 1996.
Paul Schnitt, "Private Sector Job Gains Praised," *SacBee,* 27 Feb. 1996.
Paul Schnitt and Bob Walter, "Capital Jobs Outlook Brightens," *SacBee,* 28 Mar. 1996.
Eric Young, "Board Gives Initial OK to More Flexibility on Mather," *SacBee,* 12 June 1996.
Robert Davila, "Welfare-to-Work Outlook Called Good," *SacBee,* 8 Aug. 1996.
Jim Mikles, "19 Running for 4 Chico Council Seats," *SacBee,* 15 Aug. 1996.
Paul Schnitt, "6-Year Low for Area's Jobless Rate," *SacBee,* 21 Sept. 1996.
Leslie Layton, "Some Deep Pockets Fuel Hot Chico Council Race," *SacBee,* 2 Nov. 1996.
Paul Schnitt, "Capital Ports' Dreams of '63 Give Way to Anxiety in '96," *SacBee,* 15 Dec. 1996.
Eric Young and Tony Bizjack, "Cities Pay Price to Entice Business," *SacBee,* 30 Dec. 1996.
Leslie Layton, "Broker, Environmentalist Top Fund-Raisers in Chico Race," *SacBee,* 29 Apr. 1997.
Dan Walters, "Growth Is State's Ultimate Dilemma," *FBee,* 3 May 1997.
Leslie Layton, "Chico's Council Turning Right," *SacBee,* 8 May 1997.
Don McCormack, "Davis, Delightfully Off Center," *SFEx,* 15 Feb. 1998.

Poverty
Richard Steven Street, "Knife Fight City," *SJMN West,* 28 Jul. 1991.
Miles Corwin, "The Grapes of Wrath Revisited," *LAT,* 29 Sept. 1991.
John Hurst, "Invisible Poor—Whites," *LAT,* 11 Jul. 1992.
Mark Arax, "UFW Memorial Honors Lifelong Activist Fred Ross," *LAT,* 19 Oct. 1992.
Susan Ferris, "Fields of Broken Dreams," *Image, SFEx,* 18 Jul. 1993.
Deborah Leland, *Report Card for Rural California* (U.S. Department of Agriculture, 1995).
Shawn Garvey, *1996 Annual Report for California* (U.S. Department of Agriculture, 1996).
Virginia Ellis, "To Phase Out Aid, Farm Belt Needs New Crop of Jobs," *LAT,* 2 June 1997.
Alicia Bugarin and Elias Lopez, *Farmworkers in California* (CRB, July 1998).
Eric Lichtblau, "A Valley the Upturn Left Behind," *LAT,* 6 Nov. 1998.

Sprawl
Pamela Abramson, "Fresno's Dubious Distinction," *Newsweek,* 20 Aug. 1984.
Stephen Farber, "The Filming of 'Fresno' Upside-Down Dallas," *NYT,* 4 Aug. 1986.
Harry Waters, " 'Fresno': The Raisins of Wrath," *Newsweek,* 17 Nov. 1986.

Dan Morain, "Cultures Clashing Down on the Farm," *LAT,* 6 Oct. 1991.

Gary Wills, "Fresno, the Last Real California," *Time,* 18 Nov. 1991.

Dan Morain, "Fresno Plows Under Farm Town Roots for Suburbia," *LAT,* 25 Nov. 1991.

Vlae Kershner, "Valley Torn by Competing Forces," *SFCh,* 20 May 1992.

Mark Arax, "Sprawl Threatens Central Valley, Study Says," *LAT,* 26 Oct. 1995.

Mark Arax, "Trouble in California's Heartland," *LAT,* 6 Dec. 1995.

Dorsey Griffith, "Cultivating Peace Where Crops, Urbanites Meet," *SacBee,* 5 Dec. 1996.

Erik Vink, "Fighting Growth," *FBee,* 13 May 1997.

Donnell Alexander, "The Big Valley: Pavement Gets Out of Town," *LA Weekly,* 30 May 1997.

Mark Arax and Mark Gladstone, "Leading Fresno Developer Is Indicted on Corruption Charges," *LAT,* 21 Feb. 1998.

AP, "California's Vanishing Heartland," *SFCh,* 20 Aug. 1998.

Steve Chawkins, "Homes Sprouting, Farms Dying," *LAT,* 7 Feb. 1999.

Carl Nolte, "Sprawl, Clutter, Define Fresno," *SFCh,* 1 Sept. 1999.

Planning

Central Valley Planning Conference, *Workbook* (17 Mar. 1990).

"Planning Summit Held in Modesto," *Manteca Bulletin,* 18 Mar. 1990.

"Valley Master Plan Meeting Raises Issues," *Merced Sun-Star,* 19 Mar. 1990.

Bank of America, *Beyond Sprawl: New Patterns of Growth to Fit the New California* (January 1995).

American Farmland Trust, *Alternatives for Future Urban Growth in California's Central Valley: The Bottom Line for Agriculture and Taxpayers* (October 1995).

Dorsey Griffith, "Future Is Now, Regional Meeting Told," *SacBee,* 19 Jul. 1996.

Michael McFarland, "Stop It Now," *FBee,* 16 Nov. 1996.

University of California Division of Agriculture and Natural Resources, *The Challenge of Change, A Strategic Plan* (1997).

Jim Wasserman, "Great Valley's Center May Ward Off Another LA," *FBee,* 21 Sept. 1997.

Mark Grossi, "Policy-Making Center: Valley Under One Roof," *FBee,* 7 Oct. 1997.

California Council, the American Institute of Architects, *Housing the Next 10 Million* (1998).

Larry Gordon, "A Contest to Reshape Middle of California," *LAT,* 13 Mar. 1999.

Neal Pierce, "California Breakthrough: Smart Growth Meets Big Money," *WP,* 18 Jul. 1999.

Mark Arax, "Putting the Brakes on Growth," *LAT,* 6 Oct. 1999.

Eric Bailey, "Consensus Elusive on Central Valley Growth," *LAT,* 17 Nov. 1999.

The Great Valley Center, *The Economic Future of the San Joaquin Valley* (January 2000).

Peter H. King, "Sprawl Spills into Central Valley," *LAT,* 13 May 2000.

Waterworld

Gina Maranto, "A Once and Future Desert," *Discover* (June 1985).

"At the Crossroads," *LAT,* Special Report, 10 Dec. 1989.

Editorial, "Water: This Time It's Serious," *LAT,* 24 Dec. 1989.

Water Education Foundation, *Western Water,* for period 1990–2002.

Kevin Roderick and Frederick Muir, "Drought May Not End, Officials Say," *LAT,* 1 Apr. 1990.

"The People Who Live in a Desert," *Economist,* 12 May 1990.

"This Little Water Went to Market," *Economist,* 4 Aug. 1990.

"There's Another Desert War," *Economist,* 16 Feb. 1991.

Jane Gross, "California's Rice Growers Become Enemy in Drought," *NYT,* 7 Apr. 1991.

Jenifer Warren, "Water Shortages May Close Tap on Growth," *LAT,* 14 Apr. 1991.

Bill Stall, "Drought Users in a Dry Era," *LAT,* 21 Apr. 1991.

Jenifer Warren, "Underground Water Level Falling at a Dramatic Rate," *LAT,* 10 June 1991.

Oswald Johnston, "House OKs Changes in Water Policy," *LAT,* 21 June 1991.

Jenifer Warren and Virginia Ellis, "State's Water Bank Doing Fine—Except for Buyers," *LAT,* 22 June 1991.

Beth Hawkins, "Funds Sought for Desalination Research," *LAT,* 24 Jul. 1991.

Burton Gindler, "Enough Water to Keep Southland in Business," *LA Business Journal,* 21 Jul. 1991.

Frederick Muir, "Challenge to MWD's Old Ways," *LAT,* 11 Aug. 1991.

Ralph Frammolino, "Accord by MWD, Edison on Desalination Erodes," *LAT,* 29 Aug. 1991.

Virginia Ellis, "EPA Rejects Water Quality Plan for Delta," *LAT,* 4 Sept. 1991.

"Congress Enacts Key CVP Reforms," *Focus* (Metropolitan Water District of Southern California, no. 5, 1992).

Water Education Foundation, *Layperson's Guide to California Rivers and Streams* (1992).

Peter Passell, "Soaking Lawns, Not Taxpayers," *NYT,* 5 Feb. 1992.

"Is the Drought Over?" *SFEx,* 24 Feb. 1992.

Robert Reinhold, "Farmers in West May Sell Something More Valuable than Any Crop: Water," *NYT,* 6 Apr. 1992.

Vlae Kershner, "The Heartland: Water Wars Threaten Life on the Farms," *OCR,* 14 June 1992.

Glenn Bunting, "President Signs Major Western Water Measure," *LAT,* 1 Nov. 1992.

Dean Murphy, "Drought Is Over, Wilson Declares," *LAT,* 25 Feb. 1993.

"Pollution Solutions," *Focus* (Metropolitan Water District of Southern California, no. 1, 1993).

Water Education Foundation, *Lay Persons Guide to California Water* (1994).

Kenneth Umbach, *Agriculture, Water, and California's Drought of 1987–92: Background, Responses, Lessons* (CRB, April 1994).

Mark Arax, "Effort to Link Growth, Water Sparks Battle," *LAT,* 14 Aug. 1995.

Timothy Egan, "Great Dam: Life Saver, or a Big Boondoggle?" *NYT,* 9 June 1996.

Sue McClurg, "Building a Delta Consensus," *Western Water* (September/October 1996).

Jim Parsons, "The Age of Recycled Water," *Aqueduct 2000* (Metropolitan Water District, November 1996).

Kevin McLaughlin, "Narrowing the Choices," *Aqueduct 2000* (Metropolitan Water District, November 1996).

Jim Parsons, "The Ascension of Water Transfers," *Aqueduct 2000* (Metropolitan Water District, December 1996).

"Toast of the Tap," *Aqueduct 2000* (no. 2, 1997).

Water Education Foundation, *California Water MAP* (1997).

Monica Schwarze, "The Next Step," *Aqueduct 2000* (January/February 1997).

Elizabeth McCarthy, "Perspective on the New Year's Floods," *Western Water* (March/April 1997).

Elizabeth McCarthy, "CVP Improvement Act Update," *Western Water* (May/June 1997).

Jim Gogek, "The Quest for Water," *SDUT,* 7 Sept. 1997.

Joe Pomento, "Building the California Plan," *Aqueduct 2000* (no. 1, 1998).

"Mono Rising," *Aqueduct 2000* (no. 3, 1998).

Sue McClurg, "Delta Debate," *Western Water* (March/April 1998).

Glen Martin, "Freeing Napa from Floods," *SFCh,* 2 Mar. 1998.

Tony Perry, "Water Canal Plan, Debate Resurface," *LAT,* 17 Mar. 1998.

Dan Walters, "Peripheral Canal Idea Is Given Another Look," *FBee,* 17 Mar. 1998.

David Friedman, "The Divining Rod of Water Politics," *LAT,* 19 Apr. 1998.
George Skelton, "Taking the Plunge into Murky Waters," *LAT,* 19 Mar. 1998.
Marla Cone, "State Backs LA in Owens Valley Water Fight," *LAT,* 29 Apr. 1998.
Glen Martin, "Water-Rich Yuba County Fights for Its Liquid Asset," *SFCh,* 25 May 1998.
Dennis O'Connor, *The Governance of the Metropolitan Water District of Southern California: An Overview of the Issues* (CRB, August 1998).
Joe Pomento, "A Dusty End," *Aqueduct 2000* (no. 1, 1999).
David Carle, *Drowning the Dream: California's Water Choices at the Millennium* (2000).

Endangered Species

Rich Roberts, "Hunters Filling Catalina's Void," *LAT,* 6 Nov. 1991.
Marla Cone, "US Declares Gnatcatcher Threatened Southland Bird," *LAT,* 26 Mar. 1993.
Helen Roland, *California Endangered Species Act: Overview of Issue in the Reform Debate* (CRB, March 1996).
Nicholas Riccardi, "JPL's Toxic Waste Caused Cancer, Suit Says," *LAT,* 23 Sept. 1997.
Aurelio Rojas, "Hunters Point Health Problems Called an 'Epidemic,' " *SFCh,* 24 Oct. 1997.
Jim Doyle, "Oil Spill Shuts Humboldt Bay near Eureka," *SFCh,* 6 Nov. 1997.
Robert Smaus, "What's the Buzz? Honeybees, Vital Pollinators of Gardens and Crops, Are Disappearing," *LAT,* 23 Nov. 1997.
Paul McHugh, "Rare Otters Surface in SF Bay," *SFCh,* 17 Jan. 1998.
Jim Newton and Thomas Maugh, "Water Officials Suggest Prudence, Not Panic," *LAT,* 11 Feb. 1998.
Julia Scheeres and Abigail Goldman, "New Worry for Pregnant Women," *LAT,* 11 Feb. 1998.
Tony Perry, "J.J. Grows Up," *LAT,* 18 Mar. 1998.
AP, "Rescued Whale Going Home—but Will It Take Her In?" *SFCh,* 20 Mar. 1998.
AP, "Young Whale Returns to Sea," *SFCh,* 1 Apr. 1998.
Diana Marcum, "A Shell Game in Tortoise Count," *LAT,* 13 Apr. 1998.
Glen Martin, "Sierra Town in Distress," *SFCh,* 1 May 1998.
Daryl Kelley, "Nearby Crop Spraying Troubles Oxnard Teachers," *LAT,* 4 May 1998.
Maria L. La Ganga, "Wildlife Officials Charged in Lake Poisoning," *LAT,* 7 May 1998.
Michael McCabe, "Nitrate-Laced Water Sickens Town," *SFCh,* 12 May 1998.
Julia Scheeres, "El Niño Leaves Toxic Legacy in Bay," *LAT,* 22 May 1998.
Alex Barnum, "Sounding a Siren for the Sea," *SFCh,* 8 June 1998.
AP, "Wounded Condor May Not Fly Again," *SFCh,* 9 June 1998.
Richard Warchol, "Whale of a Chance," *LAT,* 10 June 1998.
Alex Barnum and Michael McCabe, "Clinton to Extend Ban on Drilling Until 2012," *SFCh,* 12 June 1998.
Cliff Rothman, "The Rescuers," *LAT,* 26 June 1998.
Bernadette Tansey, "Creating a Living Lake," *SFCh,* 1 Jul. 1998.
Michael Hytha and Bernadette Tansey, "Nuclear Rods Won't Sneak past Public," *SFCh,* 6 Jul. 1998.
Glen Martin, "White Abalone Poised on Brink of Extinction," *SFCh,* 7 Jul. 1998.
Patricia Jacobus, "Growing Hazards Emerge in Tire Fire," *SFCh,* 17 Aug. 1998.
Gary Polakovic, "Condors Flying High, but Not Out of Danger," *LAT,* 8 Nov. 1998.
Marla Cone, "New Tests Show Human Viruses in Beach Waters," *LAT,* 5 Sept. 1999.
Marla Cone, "Southland Runoff Remedies Will Be Complex, Costly," *LAT,* 6 Sept. 1999.
David Reyes and Louise Roug, "Beach Reopened After Needle Cleanup," *LAT,* 18 Sept. 1999.
James Rainey, "Sierra Trout Killed in Bid to Save Frogs," *LAT,* 22 Sept. 1999.

Jenifer Warren, "Tire Fire Spews Hazardous Smoke," *LAT,* 23 Sept. 1999.

Glen Martin, "A Puzzling Decline in Butterflies," *SFCh,* 22 Dec. 1999.

Manuel Pastor Jr., *Racial/Ethnic Inequality in Environmental-Hazard Exposure in Metropolitan Los Angeles* (University of California Policy Research Center, April 2001).

Maria L. La Ganga, "Jury Convicts Man Who Hurled Dog into Traffic," *LAT,* 20 June 2001.

Gary Polakovic, "Hinkley Faces New Chromium Threat," *LAT,* 1 Jul. 2001.

Geoffrey Mohan, "Family Faces Chromium Testing," *LAT,* 2 Jul. 2001.

Maria L. La Ganga, "Dog Killer Sent to Prison," *LAT,* 14 Jul. 2001.

Ann Marsh, "Life Lessons on the Ranch," *LAT,* 20 Jul. 2001.

Laura Mecoy, "Study: State Beaches Not So Balmy," *SacBee,* 9 Aug. 2001.

Kenneth R. Weiss, "Abalone Amore," *LAT,* 1 Oct. 2001.

Louis Sahagun, "Catalina Restoration Project Gaining Ground," *LAT,* 23 Nov. 2001.

North Coast Redwoods and Other Trees

Background Brief on Forests in California (CRB, 22 Jul. 1993).

Tom Knudson, "Sierra Logging Blueprint Attracts Critics," *SFEx,* 7 Feb. 1995.

"A 2,000-Year-Old Redwood Is a Precious Thing to Lose," *LAT,* 13 Sept. 1996.

David Brower, "Forest on the Verge," *NYT,* 15 Sept. 1996.

Mary Curtius, "The Fall of the 'Redwood Curtain,' " *LAT,* 28 Dec. 1996.

Tim Golden, "Setback in Deal to Preserve California Redwoods," *NYT,* 6 Feb. 1997.

"Logging Foes Sue over Use of Pepper Spray," *WP,* 31 Oct. 1997.

Richard Wilson, "A Forest to Conserve and Harvest," *Press Democrat [Santa Rosa],* 23 Nov. 1997.

Alex Barnum, "Possible Alterations to Headwaters Deal," *SFCh,* 13 Feb. 1998.

Susan Carpenter, "Fighting for Freedom," *LAT,* 20 Feb. 1998.

James Brooke, "Redwoods Still Inspire Sturdiest of Defenders," *NYT,* 28 Mar. 1998.

Marcia Meier, "Concern for Oaks Fuels Vintage Battle," *LAT,* 13 Apr. 1998.

AP, "Mapping of Oaks Planned in Disputed Wine Country," *SFCh,* 7 May 1998.

Lesley Wright, "Much-Loved Trees Are Trouble Too," *LAT,* 14 May 1998.

Marcia Meier, "Cambria's Pines Are Doomed, Experts Say," *LAT,* 26 May 1998.

Mary Curtius, "10 Months Later, Tree-Sitter Holding On," *LAT,* 22 Oct. 1998.

Todd Henneman, "SF Group Protects Huge Redwood Ranch," *SFCh,* 27 Oct. 1998.

Edwin Kiester, "A Town Buries the Axe," *Smithsonian* (July 1999).

Mary Curtius, "Tree-Sitter, Timber Firm Negotiating End of 2-Year Vigil," *LAT,* 8 Dec. 1999.

Mary Curtius, "Tree-Sitter, Lumber Firm Reach an Agreement," *LAT,* 18 Dec. 1999.

AP, "Protester Descends from Redwood," *LAT,* 19 Dec. 1999.

Glen Martin, "Tree-Sitter Recounts Life in the Clouds," *SFCH,* 20 Dec. 1999.

Blake Morrison, "Tree-Sitter Climbs Down to Earth," *USA Today,* 20 Dec. 1999.

Melinda Fulmer, "Imports Put Squeeze on California's Olive Growers," *LAT,* 23 Jan. 2000.

Glen Martin, "Vandals Slash Giant Redwood," *SFCh,* 28 Nov. 2000.

Glen Martin, "Tree Specialist Working Against Clock," *SFCh,* 29 Nov. 2000.

Bettina Boxall, "Tracking Down a Killer of Coastal Oaks," *LAT,* 20 May 2001.

Maria L. La Ganga, "Sudden Oak Death Fungus Found in Two More Counties," *LAT,* 23 Sept. 2001.

Going Green

Harold Gilliam, "Politics and the Soul," *SFCh, This World,* 24 May 1992.

Steve Proffitt, "Wallace Stegner Interview," *LAT,* 7 June 1992.

Sierra Business Council, *Planning for Prosperity: Building Successful Communities in the Sierra Nevada* (1997).

Jane Ganahl, "Stars Come Out to Help Green Party Salute David Brower," *SFEx,* 25 May 1997.

Dorsey Griffith, "Poor Policies Hurt Sierra, Study Says," *SacBee,* 10 Jul. 1997.

Ed Henry, "Earth First! Activists Invade Riggs's California Office," *Roll Call,* 27 Oct. 1997.

Jim Doyle, "Protest March Against Pepper Spray Use," *SFCh,* 14 Nov. 1997.

William Glaberson, "The Unabomber Case: The Overview," *NYT,* 23 Jan. 1998.

Dan Smith, "Ex-Congressman Plans Green Bid to Be Governor," *SacBee,* 14 Mar. 1998.

Mark Gladstone, "Unrepentant Unabomber Gets 4 Life Sentences," *LAT,* 5 May 1998.

Robert Selna, "Audie Bock Preparing for Second Campaign," *SFEx,* 21 May 1999.

John Johnson, "Conflicting Visions for 'Serengeti' of California," *LAT,* 13 May 2001.

Mark Gold, "A Looming Ecological Mistake," *LAT,* 9 Sept. 2001.

Miguel Bustillo and John Johnson, "Governor Gets Busy with His Green Pen," *LAT,* 14 Oct. 2001.

Kenneth R. Weiss, "Big Sur Deal Will Save Nearly 10,000 Acres," *LAT,* 10 May 2002.

Open Space

William Fulton, *Guide to California Planning* (1991).

Hunters Point Annex, Naval Station Treasure Island, *Environmental Clean-Up News* (no. 23, 18 June 1991).

Eugene Linden, "Gobbling Up the Land," *Time,* 18 Nov. 1991.

Manuel Pastor Jr. and Dennis Zane, editors, *The California Dilemma* (International and Public Affairs Center, Occidental College, February 1992).

Paul McHugh, "Reinventing the Map," *SFCh, This World,* 13 Sept. 1992.

Trish Reynales, "The Promised Land," *Santa Barbara Magazine* (May/June 1993).

William Stevens, "Disputed Conservation Plan Could Be Model for Nation," *NYT,* 16 Feb. 1997.

Michael McCabe, "Eastwood Donates Scenic Coastal Land," *SFCh,* 12 Dec. 1997.

George Brewster, Edith Pepper, and Michael Leccese, *Land Recycling and the Creation of Sustainable Communities* (California Center for Land Recycling, 1998).

Frank Clifford, "San Simeon Coast's Future Is Riding on Commission's Vote," *LAT,* 11 Jan. 1998.

Frank Clifford, "Family Assails Hearst Corp. Coast Plan," *LAT,* 16 Jan. 1998.

"Coast Panel Says No to Hearst Plan," *SacBee,* 16 Jan. 1998.

Peter H. King, "Just 18 Holes in Paradise," *LAT,* 18 Jan. 1998.

Frank Clifford and Louis Sahagun, "Land Use Plan Opens Window on Hearst Rift," *LAT,* 20 Jan. 1998.

Maria L. La Ganga, "Foundation Gives $175 Million to Save California Open Space," *LAT,* 11 Mar. 1998.

Deborah Belgum, "Creating Parks from Mountains to the City," *LAT,* 7 Apr. 1998.

Deborah Schoch, "Future Debated for Vast Piece of Open Space," *LAT,* 12 May 1998.

Barry Stavro, "A Hidden Mountain Treasure in the City," *LAT,* 19 May 1998.

Frank Clifford, "Mojave Park Feels Pressure of Growth," *LAT,* 23 June 1998.

Alan Abrahamson, "Waves of Change Taking Toll on Southland Beaches," *LAT,* 4 Jul. 1998.

Nancy Vogel, "Report: Shunned Toxic Sites Need State's Help," *SacBee,* 29 Sept. 1998.

George Raine, "Turning Brown into Green," *SFEx,* 30 Sept. 1998.

Robert A. Jones, "Ecotopia Comes South," *LAT,* 8 Nov. 1998.

T. Christian Miller, "A Growth Plan Run Amok," *LAT,* 27 Dec. 1998.

"An Abundant Land: The Story of West Marin Ranching," *Marin Agricultural Land Trust News* (Spring 1999).

Richard Simon and Tom Gorman, "Plan for Buying Desert Land Falters," *LAT,* 15 Oct. 1999.

Margaret Talev, "Ventura County Plan to Preserve Land on Hold," *LAT,* 1 June 2001.

Kenneth R. Weiss, "Hearst Hits Setback in San Simeon," *LAT,* 13 Jul. 2001.

Kenneth R. Weiss and John Johnson, "In Hearst Land Fight, Old Papers Are New Weapon," *LAT,* 22 Jul. 2001.

Kenneth R. Weiss, "State to Buy Malibu Open Space," *LAT,* 25 Sept. 2001.

Fixed Rail

Car Culture

"They Paved Paradise," *Economist,* 13 Oct. 1990.

John Chandler and Scott Harris, "14 Killed, 114 Hurt in I-5 Pileups," *LAT,* 30 Nov. 1991.

Marsha Ginsburg, "I-5 Pileup Deadliest in California's History," *SFEx,* 1 Dec. 1991.

Sharon Warzocha, "Affordable Housing, Good Schools, Long Drive," *LAT,* 12 Apr. 1992.

Haya El Nasser, "LA Subway Tough Sell to Car-Crazy Commuters," *USA Today,* 29 Jan. 1993.

Hugo Martin, "Traffic Report Card Goes from F to Worse," *LAT,* 9 Mar. 1993.

Randall Lane, "The Commuter Police," *Forbes,* 20 Dec. 1993.

Martin Miller, "The Stress-Free Way," *LAT,* 6 Oct. 1997.

USC Southern California Studies Center, *Sprawl Hits the Wall: Confronting the Realities of Metropolitan Los Angeles* (2001).

Douglas P. Shuit, "LA Leads the Nation in Survey of Worst Traffic," *LAT,* 8 May 2001.

Smog

Philip Verleger, "Clean Air Regulation and the LA Riots," *WSJ,* 19 May 1992.

Chang-Hee Christine Bae, "Air Quality and Travel Behavior: Untying the Knot," *Journal of the American Planning Association* (Winter 1993).

Buzz Breedlove, *Motor-Vehicle Inspection and Maintenance in California* (CRB, 24 Aug. 1993).

Marla Cone, "Southland Smog Drops to Lowest Level in Decades," *LAT,* 30 Oct. 1996.

Marla Cone, "LA Breathes Easier as It Hands Off Smog Title," *LAT,* 13 Oct. 1999.

Gary Polakovic, "State Losing Ground in War on Dirty Air," *LAT,* 17 Jul. 2001.

Gary Polakovic, "Southland on Course to Reclaim US Smog Title," *LAT,* 26 Sept. 2001.

Gary Polakovic, "California's Smog Story Is Tale of 2 States," *LAT,* 4 Nov. 2001.

Planning Fixed Rail

Frederick Rose, "Los Angeles Transit Agency Plans $184 Billion Program (Yes, Billion)," *WSJ,* 22 Apr. 1992.

Lewis MacAdams, "Nick Patsaouras Remakes LA," *LA Weekly,* 1 May 1992.

Southern California Rapid Transit District, *The Metro Red Line* (no date).

Metro Rail

Jeffrey Perlman, "Orange County Plan to Link Trains to Metro Rail Approved," *LAT,* 29 Oct. 1991.

Mark Stein, "12 Metrolink Double-Deckers Set to Roll," *LAT,* 25 Oct. 1992.

Construction

William Hamilton, "An Underground Railroad to Lure West Coast's Slaves of the Freeway," *WP*, 31 Jan. 1993.

Richard Simon and Jeffrey L. Rabin, "Subway Tunnel to Valley to Be Completed Today," *LAT*, 22 Oct. 1997.

Jeffrey L. Rabin, "Light of Acclaim Shines on Tunnelers," *LAT*, 23 Oct. 1997.

Problems and Meltdown

Richard Simon, "Rail Projects Face Further Delays, MTA Board Told," *LAT*, 15 Aug. 1997.

Richard Simon, "Review Finds MTA Budget 'Flawed' and 'Unrealistic,' " *LAT*, 20 Aug. 1997.

Larry Gordon, "MTA Plan to Replace Famed Stars Draws Fire," *LAT*, 21 Aug. 1997.

Richard Simon, "NY Transit Official Spurns Top MTA Job," *LAT*, 22 Aug. 1997.

Richard Simon, "MTA Names Crisis Expert as Interim CEO," *LAT*, 23 Aug. 1997.

Todd S. Purdum, "The Subway to Nowhere, No Time Soon," *NYT*, 28 Aug. 1997.

Jeffrey L. Rabin, "Lay-Offs Likely as MTA Lowers Expectations," *LAT*, 20 Oct. 1997.

Beth Barrett, "Going Broke," *Daily News*, 9 Nov. 1997.

Editorial, "MTA Must Face Reality," *LAT*, 14 Jan. 1998.

Richard Simon, "It's MTA's Day of Reckoning on Rail Projects," *LAT*, 14 Jan. 1998.

Richard Simon, "Cost Overruns for Hollywood Subway Hit $79.1 Million," *LAT*, 21 Jan. 1998.

Jeffrey L. Rabin, "MTA Borrowing Puts the Agency $7 Billion in Debt," *LAT*, 21 June 1998.

Editorial, "MTA: Saga of Bad Deals," *LAT*, 22 June 1998.

Jeffrey L. Rabin and Richard Simon, "MTA Budget Could Add to Its $7 Billion Debt," *LAT*, 24 June 1998.

Jeffrey L. Rabin and Richard Simon, "MTA Takes Steps to Put a Limit on Borrowing," *LAT*, 26 June 1998.

Jeffrey L. Rabin, "Voters Force a Detour for MTA Subway Builders," *LAT*, 27 Nov. 1998.

Richard Simon, "Senate OKs $3 Billion for State Transit," *LAT*, 5 Oct. 1999.

Jeffrey L. Rabin, "Hollywood Subway a Box Office Bust," *LAT*, 19 Mar. 2000.

Academic Critique

Peter Passell, "Transit Green, Gridlock Blues," *NYT*, 30 Oct. 1991.

Don Pickrell, "A Desire Named Streetcar: Fantasy and Fact in Rail Transit Planning," *Journal of the American Planning Association* (Spring 1992).

James E. Moore II, "Ridership and Cost on the Long Beach–Los Angeles Blue Line Train," *Transportation Research* (1993).

Frederick Rose, "Despite Huge Outlays, Transit Systems Fail to Lure Back Riders," *WSJ*, 29 June 1993.

Thomas A. Rubin and James E. Moore II, *Why Rail Will Fail: An Analysis of the Los Angeles County Metropolitan Authority's Long Range Plan* (Reason Foundation, Policy Study no. 209, July 1996).

Thomas A. Rubin and James E. Moore II, *Ten Transit Myths: Misperceptions About Rail Transit in Los Angeles and the Nation* (Reason Foundation, Policy Study no. 218, November 1996).

Thomas A. Rubin and James E. Moore II, *Rubber Tire Transit: A Viable Alternative to Rail* (Reason Public Policy Institute, August 1997).

Thomas A. Rubin and James E. Moore II, *Better Transportation Alternatives for Los Angeles* (Reason Public Policy Institute, September 1997).

Thomas A. Rubin, James E. Moore II, and Shin Lee, "Ten Myths About US Urban Rail Systems," *Transport Policy* (January 1999).

Pulling the Plug

Richard Simon, "MTA Board Votes to Suspend Work on 3 Rail Lines," *LAT*, 15 Jan. 1998.

Jeffrey L. Rabin, "Yaroslavsky Seeks to Stanch Subway Funds," *LAT*, 30 Mar. 1998.

Jeffrey L. Rabin and Matea Gold, "Yaroslavsky Plan Imperils Subway," *LAT*, 31 Mar. 1998.

Jeffrey L. Rabin and Richard Simon, "Becerra Calls for Halt to Subway," *LAT*, 9 Apr. 1998.

Richard Simon and Jeffrey L. Rabin, "MTA's Political Alliance Showing Some Cracks," *LAT*, 10 Apr. 1998.

Richard Simon, "Activists Demand Eastside Subway," *LAT*, 21 May 1998.

Jeffrey L. Rabin and Richard Simon, "State Must Rein in MTA, Official Says," *LAT*, 23 June 1998.

Richard Simon and Jeffrey L. Rabin, "Funding Panel Deals Setback to Subway," *LAT*, 9 Jul. 1998.

Jeffrey L. Rabin, "Anti-Subway Funding Measure Wins Easily," *LAT*, 4 Nov. 1998.

Martin Kasindorf, "LA Subway System Stopped in Its Tracks," *USA Today*, 6 Nov. 1998.

PART IX / Back on the Edge

Bill and Barbra

Ronald Brownstein, "Clinton Offers Views on Recovery," *LAT*, 5 May 1992.

Dennis Hunt, "The Presidential Hopeful as Musician: B-Minus," *LAT*, 5 June 1992.

Thomas Di Lorenzo, "The Economist on Clinton's Left," *WSJ*, 10 Sept. 1992.

Suzanne Garment, "Clinton and the Vietnam Draft: The Problem That Just Won't Die," *LAT*, 20 Sept. 1992.

Peter H. King, "Santa Bill Is Coming to Town," *LAT*, 18 Nov. 1992.

Ronald Brownstein, "Clinton to Mix Business, Pleasure in Southland," *LAT*, 27 Nov. 1992.

Jonathan Peterson, "Clinton's California Cure: Growth," *LAT*, 15 Dec. 1992.

Amy Harmon, "Clinton's Economic Plan: The Impact in California," *LAT*, 17 Feb. 1993.

"Clinton Is Streisand's Special Guest," *SJMN*, 13 May 1994.

Timothy K. Smith, "What Does Barbra Believe In, Anyway? 'Repair the World'—Washington's New Rising Star, Streisand Says She's Driven by a Key Childhood Lesson," *WSJ*, 14 May 1993.

Paul Richter and Greg Krikorian, "Sartorial Splendor May Cut Into Clinton's Image," *LAT*, 21 May 1993.

Danny Goldberg, "Slashing at Hollywood: East's Snobbery Turns Ugly," *LAT*, 23 May 1993.

James Perry, "Demographers Track Down the Cause of Clinton's Behavior: He's a Boomer," *WSJ*, 28 May 1993.

Paul Houston and Howard Libit, "Clinton Team Includes 73 Californians," *LAT*, 31 May 1993.

Glen Bunting, "Riordan Finds a Running Mate in Clinton," *LAT*, 24 June 1993.

Paul Richter, "Political Climate Cools for Clinton," *LAT*, 16 Jan. 1995.

Peter Warren, "Clinton California Tour to Include Santa Ana Stop," *LAT*, 16 Sept. 1995.

Jean Merl, "Riordan, President Share Compliments on Ride to Airport," *LAT*, 23 Sept. 1995.

John Schwada and Paul Richter, "Mayor Snubs President over LA Loss of Grant," *LAT*, 22 Dec. 1994.

Maria L. La Ganga, "Dole Charges That Clinton's Policies Have Failed California," *LAT,* 18 June 1996.

Alexander Cockburn, "Bankroll the President, Starring Streisand, Spielberg, and the Eagles," *New Statesman,* 20 Sept. 1996.

Martin Walker, "Princess of Tirades," *The Guardian [London],* 18 Nov. 1996.

Jim Newton, "Riordan, Clinton Alliance Faces Test," *LAT,* 14 Apr. 1997.

Jonathan Peterson and Nicholas Riccardi, "Clinton Arrives for Weekend of Fund-Raisers," *LAT,* 16 Nov. 1997.

Bob Pool, "Clinton Drops In on Church Congregation," *LAT,* 17 Nov. 1997.

Robert Welkos, "Washington Politicians Singing, 'Hooray for Hollywood,' " *SFEx,* 23 Nov. 1997.

Jeff Leen, "Conflicting Images of Lewinsky: Sweet Idealist, Spoiled Rich Kid," *SFCh,* 24 Jan. 1998.

"Clinton Decides to Fight Prop 227," *SFCh,* 27 Apr. 1998.

Elizabeth Shogren, "Hollywood Has Supporting Role in House Races," *LAT,* 3 May 1998.

Alex Barnum and Michael McCabe, "Clinton's Ocean Initiatives," *SFCh,* 13 June 1998.

Doyle McManus, "Clinton Strikes Middle Ground with Offshore Oil Ban," *LAT,* 13 June 1998.

John Wildermuth, "Bay Area Voters Back Clinton Despite Scandal," *SFCh,* 14 Sept. 1998.

Zachary Coile, "Loyalists Stand by Their Man," *SFEx,* 20 Sept. 1998.

Robert Welkos, "Hollywood's Loyalty to Clinton Put to Test," *LAT,* 25 Sept. 1998.

Richard Simon and Jeffrey L. Rabin, "Rallies Give Voice to Supporting Actors and Opposing Citizens," *LAT,* 17 Dec. 1998.

John J. Miller, "Celebrity Squares: Hollywood Swoons for Clinton," *National Review,* 25 Jan. 1999.

James Barnes, "Checking Out the Star Bucks," *National Journal,* 8 Mar. 1999.

David Friedman, "Dark Backdrop for Rag-Tag Presidential Protest," *Downtown News [Los Angeles],* 28 Mar. 1999.

Bill Higgins, "Prez, Benefit Aim High," *Variety,* 12 Dec. 1999.

Dana Thomas, "A Hollywood Job for Bill Clinton?" *The New Yorker,* 20 Dec. 1999.

"The End of the Affair: Valedictory Performance of Bill Clinton at Democratic Convention," *The Economist,* 19 Aug. 2000.

"Remarks at a Democratic National Committee Dinner in Los Angeles, California," *Administration of William J. Clinton,* 23 June 2000.

"Remarks at a Saxophone Club Reception in Hollywood, California," *Administration of William J. Clinton,* 23 June 2000.

"Remarks at a Hollywood Tribute to the President in Los Angeles," *Administration of William J. Clinton,* 12 Aug. 2000.

"Remarks at a California Democratic Party and Coordinated Campaign Reception in Los Angeles, California," *Administration of William J. Clinton,* 2 Nov. 2000.

"Remarks at a Get Out the Vote Rally in San Jose, California," *Administration of William J. Clinton,* 3 Nov. 2000.

"Remarks at a Get Out the Vote Rally in San Francisco, California," *Administration of William J. Clinton,* 3 Nov. 2000.

Harriet Chiang, "Stanford Graduation for Chelsea Clinton," *SFCh,* 18 June 2001.

Ann O'Neill, "Another Clinton Bash?" *LAT,* 22 June 2001.

Ann O'Neill, "Celebrities Go Online to Have Their Say About Terror Attacks," *LAT,* 26 Sept. 2001.

Robert Hilburn, "No Place like Home," *LAT,* 3 Nov. 2001.

Gina Piccalo and Louise Roug, "Barbra Berates Bush," *LAT,* 1 Oct. 2002.

Dot-Com Debacle

Martha Groves, "San Francisco's New Vision," *LAT,* 15 Jan. 1990.

Lisa Margonelli, "The Next Big Wave," *San Francisco* (December 1997).

Tom Innes, "Sales in December Set Record for Gap," *SFEx,* 10 Jan. 1998.

Arthur Louis, "Schwab Profits Rise 6%," *SFCh,* 15 Jan. 1998.

Tom Abate and Carolyn Said, "Study Finds SF Is New-Media Boomtown," *SFCh,* 3 Feb. 1998.

Arthur Louis, "Bay Area Office Squeeze Tightens," *SFCh,* 14 Feb. 1998.

Alan T. Saracevic, "Gap HQ Goes Before City Planners," *SFEx,* 20 Mar. 1998.

"Bay Area Top 100," *SFEx,* 27 Apr. 1998.

"The Chronicle 500," *SFCh,* 27 Apr. 1998.

"$1.7 Billion Bid Doesn't Excite Excite," *SFEx,* 22 May 1998.

Robert Berner, "Guys Fall Back into the Gap," *SFEx,* 23 June 1998.

Jonathan Marshall, "Telco Hotels Fill Up Fast," *SFCh,* 2 Jul. 1998.

Jesus Sanchez, "Telcom Invasion Rattles Downtown LA Boosters," *LAT,* 2 Nov. 1999.

Clint Swett and Dale Kasler, "Packard Bell, NEC Bailing Out," *SacBee,* 3 Nov. 1999.

Jesus Sanchez, "Demand for San Francisco Offices Plunges," *LAT,* 26 June 2001.

Elizabeth Douglass, "Net Bargains on Auction Block," *LAT,* 9 Jul. 2001.

Carol Emert, "Eating Their Losses," *SFCh,* 10 Jul. 2001.

Carrie Kirby, "Crash, Burn Calls E-Commerce into Serious Question," *SFCh,* 10 Jul. 2001.

Meredith May, "Bitter Ending for Workers," *SFCh,* 10 Jul. 2001.

Charles Piller, "Online Grocer Webvan Shuts Operations," *LAT,* 10 Jul. 2001.

Carolyn Said, "Webvan Runs Out of Gas," *SFCh,* 10 Jul. 2001.

Joseph Menn, "In Web Awards, the Nominees Are . . . Kaput," *LAT,* 16 Jul. 2001.

Maria L. La Ganga, "There's No Stopping Those Letterpresses," *LAT,* 17 Jul. 2001.

Joseph Menn, "Webby Awards: The Good, Badly Dressed, Bankrupt," *LAT,* 20 Jul. 2001.

Karen Alexander, "Irvine Research Park Hit by Tech Slump," *LAT,* 23 Jul. 2001.

Verne Kopytoff, "Cisco Earnings Slide 99%," *SFCh,* 8 Aug. 2001.

Shawn Hubler, "San Jose Almost Arrives," *LAT,* 14 Aug. 2001.

J. Michael Kennedy, "High-Tech Publications Are Dropping like Dot-Coms," *LAT,* 14 Aug. 2001.

Carolyn Said, "Webvan Asset Sale Won't Benefit Firm's Smarting Stockholders," *SFCh,* 14 Aug. 2001.

Jon Healey, "Excite at Home Warns SEC of Financial Peril," *LAT,* 21 Aug. 2001.

Jesus Sanchez, "Slump Hits San Francisco Hotels," *LAT,* 21 Aug. 2001.

Seth Hettena, "Gateway Reducing Staff by 25%," *SFCh,* 29 Aug. 2001.

Verne Kopytoff, "Internet Layoffs Seen Leveling Off," *SFCh,* 29 Aug. 2001.

Jesus Sanchez, "Ebb Tide for Marina Offices," *LAT,* 4 Sept. 2001.

Alan T. Saracevic, "HP, Compaq Plan Merger," *SFCh,* 4 Sept. 2001.

Joseph Menn, "Stakes Just Got Higher for Fiorina," *LAT,* 5 Sept. 2001.

Charles Piller, "HP Deal Could Trigger More Tech Mergers," *LAT,* 5 Sept. 2001.

David Streitfeld, "HP-Compaq Merger Gets No Raves," *LAT,* 5 Sept. 2001.

Christine Frey, "Hope Eclipsed," *LAT,* 6 Sept. 2001.

Christine Frey, "Wine.Com Is Going Out with an Auction Bang," *LAT,* 8 Sept. 2001.

Julie N. Lynem, "They're Outta Work but Not Outta Here," *SFCh,* 9 Sept. 2001.

Peter Sinton, "Merger Rhetoric Pales as Shares Plummet," *SFCh*, 9 Sept. 2001.

Chris Taylor, "Compaq: Fiorina's Folly or HP's Only Way Out?" *Time*, 17 Sept. 2001.

Maria L. La Ganga, "Dot.Com Dregs of a Tasty Sort," *LAT*, 30 Sept. 2001.

"Wine Auction Breaks One-Day Sales Record," *LAT*, 2 Oct. 2001.

Matt Richtel, "Promised Land No Longer," *NYT*, 10 Nov. 2001.

Elizabeth Douglass, "Global Crossing Shares Tumble 34%," *LAT*, 14 Dec. 2001.

John Markoff and Matt Richtel, "Down, but Not Out, in the Valley," *NYT*, 14 Jan. 2002.

Leslie Earnest, "Drexler to Step Down at Gap," *LAT*, 22 May 2002.

Report Card

K–12

David Smoller, "Learning Experience," *LAT*, 11 Mar. 1990.

Kim Kowsky and George Hatch, "Uneasy Calm Settles on Camp Day After Brawl, Four Arrests," *LAT*, 20 Apr. 1991.

Jane Gross, "A City's Determination to Rewrite History Puts Its Classrooms in Chaos," *NYT*, 18 Sept. 1991.

Gary Libman, "Genesis of a Dream," *LAT*, 22 Sept. 1991.

Vlae Kershner, "Educators Want to Keep School Choice Off Ballot," *SFCh*, 22 Jan. 1992.

Alicia Di Rado, "Math, Minus Escalante, Suffers," *LAT*, 23 Oct. 1992.

Howard Blume, "Students Protest Conditions at School," *LAT*, 26 Feb. 1993.

Vlae Kershner, "Assembly Panel Rebuffs Wilson on Schools Chief," *SFCh*, 20 Apr. 1993.

Through Our Eyes, Stories of a 6th Grade Class (Zellerbach Family Fund, 1996).

Ruben G. Rumbaut, "The New Californians: Assessing the Educational Progress of Children of Immigrants," *California Policy Seminar Brief* (April 1996).

California Youth: Their Access to Computers & Technological Readiness (Children's Partnership, July 1997).

Richard Lee Colvin, "Spurned Nobelists Appeal Science Standards Rejection," *LAT*, 17 Nov. 1997.

Phil Garcia, "Unz Keeps Focus on Bilingual Issue," *SacBee*, 19 Jan. 1998.

Bill Workman, "Learning Life Lessons in Class," *SFCh*, 29 Jan. 1998.

Anne-Marie O'Connor, "School Is Top Issue for 2 Immigrant Groups," *LAT*, 19 Mar. 1998.

John M. Glionna, "A Mission to Reclaim Lost Youths," *LAT*, 25 Apr. 1998.

Duke Helfand, "Third Time's the Charm for El Camino Real," *LAT*, 27 Apr. 1998.

Duke Helfand, "LAUSD Unveils $1.8 Billion Plan," *LAT*, 5 May 1998.

Les Birdsall, "A Golden Age of Education," *LAT*, 17 May 1998.

"Why Our Schools Are Failing," *LAT*, Special Report, 17 May 1998.

"Language, Culture: How Schools Cope," *LAT*, Special Report, 18 May 1998.

Janet Wilson and Michael Wagner, "Education Grants Target of US Probe," *LAT*, 18 May 1998.

"Little Training, Poor Oversight," *LAT*, Special Report, 19 May 1998.

James Rainey, "In Room 9, Rays of Hope amid Chaos," *LAT*, 31 May 1998.

Kenneth R. Weiss, "Full Mental Jackets," *LAT*, 10 June 1998.

Richard Lee Colvin and Nick Anderson, "Judge Blocks Release of State Test Scores," *LAT*, 26 June 1998.

Tanya Schevitz, Lori Olszewski, and Nanette Asimov, "Judge Suppresses Scores of Immigrant Students," *SFCh*, 26 June 1998.

Patricia L. de Cos, *Educating California's Immigrant Children* (CRB, June 1999).

"Girls Taking Math, Science Courses More Often than Boys," *LAT,* 28 Feb. 2001.
Solomon Moore, "Schools Told to Prepare for Cuts," *LAT,* 24 June 2002.

Failing Scores
Elizabeth Shogren and Ralph Frammolino, "State's Pupils Among Worst in Reading Test,"
  LAT, 16 Dec. 1993.
Elaine Woo, "Less than Third of Students Found Proficient in Science," *LAT,* 22 Oct. 1997.
Kenneth R. Weiss, "Almost Half of Cal State Freshmen Lack Skills," *LAT,* 27 Mar. 1998.
Nanette Asimov and Lori Olszewski, "State's Kids Score Low in School Test," *SFCh,* 1 Jul.
  1998.
Doug Smith, "30 LA School Principals Get Scores Warning," *LAT,* 3 Sept. 1998.
Martha Groves and Doug Smith, "County Ranks Poorly in Exit Test," *LAT,* 4 Oct. 2001.
Duke Helfand, "State Youths Flunk Fitness Exam," *LAT,* 11 Dec. 2001.
Doug Smith, "A Higher Learning Curve," *LAT,* 29 Dec. 2001.
Tanya Schevitz, "More Entering CSU Need Help to Stay," *SFCh,* 31 Jan. 2002.
Rebecca Trounson, "Cal State Ouster Rate Rises Slightly," *LAT,* 31 Jan. 2002.

An Inadequate Workforce
Edward Fiske, "Impending US Jobs 'Disaster': Work Force Unqualified to Work," *NYT,* 25
  Apr. 1989.
Joseph Berger, "Companies Step In Where the Schools Fail," *NYT,* 16 Sept. 1989.
Joel Kotkin, "A Shortage of Skilled Workers," *LAT,* 2 Nov. 1997.
Peter Sinton, "Milken, Doerr Share Their Ideas," *SFCh,* 17 Jan. 1998.
Jon Engellenner, "Welding a Future," *SacBee,* 17 Feb. 1998.

Reform Measures
Daniel Akst, "Jerome Porath Interview," *LAT,* 14 Mar. 1993.
David Illig, *Early Implementation of the Class Size Reduction Initiative* (CRB, April 1997).
Amy Pyle, "Drawn to Magnet Schools," *LAT,* 16 Jan. 1998.
Lori Olszewski, "More Kids Going to School After School," *SFCh,* 3 Feb. 1998.
Daniel Yi, "A Private School Builds Believers in Public Service," *LAT,* 25 Apr. 1998.
Dan Morain, "Wilson Expected to OK Bill on Charter Schools," *LAT,* 29 Apr. 1998.
Anne-Marie O'Connor, "Latino Students Fare Better in Catholic Schools," *LAT,* 3 Aug.
  1998.
Nanette Asimov, "Improve or Perish, 430 State Schools Told," *SFCh,* 2 Sept. 1999.
Richard Fausset, "Charter Schools and Wall of Separation," *LAT,* 27 Jan. 2002.

California State University
Charles B. Reed, "A Game Plan for Making Cal State an Education Powerhouse," *LAT,* 8 Oct.
  1997.
Joe Mozingo, "Young Scholars Find a Niche at Cal State LA," *LAT,* 3 Nov. 1997.
Pamela Burdman and Julia Angwin, "Cal State, High-Tech Industry Linking Up," *SFCh,* 1
  Dec. 1997.
Kenneth R. Weiss, "A Farewell Warning," *LAT,* 7 Jan. 1998.
Douglas P. Shuit, "Show Time at 'The Beach,' " *LAT,* 12 Jan. 1998.
Pamela Burdman, "High-Tech Venture by CSU Criticized," *SFCh,* 22 Jan. 1998.
Fred Alvarez, "Count Down to a New University," *LAT,* 4 Feb. 1998.

Kenneth R. Weiss and Leslie Helm, "Microsoft Dropped from University Partnership," *LAT,* 7 Apr. 1998.

Anne-Marie O'Connor, "Cal State LA, Its Alumni Mark 50 Years of Diversity," *LAT,* 20 May 1998.

Kenneth R. Weiss, "Big Man on Campus," *LAT Magazine,* 29 Nov. 1999.

Russell Contreras, "Some Illegal Immigrants Get to Pay In-State Tuition at State Colleges," *WSJ,* 7 Sept. 2001.

Zanto Peabody, "Faculty Union at Cal State Slams Hiring," *LAT,* 16 Oct. 2001.

Rebecca Trounson, "UC and Cal State Will Offer Joint Education PhDs," *LAT,* 9 Nov. 2001.

Diversity at UC

William Trombley, "UC Officials Among Elite in Pay," *LAT,* 16 Sept. 1991.

Carl Irving, "UC Predicts Higher Fees, Harder Entry Standards," *SFEx,* 16 Nov. 1991.

Larry Gordon, "Study Assails Secrecy, Pay, Perks of Top UC Executives," *LAT,* 30 Sept. 1992.

Louis Freedberg, "UC Whistle-Blower Ends Term as Regent," *SFCh,* 17 Feb. 1993.

"Facing 4th Year of Cuts, Berkeley Chancellor Leads Budget Revolt," *NYT,* 12 May 1993.

Larry Gordon, "UCLA Strikers End Fast; Compromise Reached," *LAT,* 8 June 1993.

Larry Gordon, "Berkeley Battles the Blues," *LAT Magazine,* 13 June 1993.

Amy Wallace and Dave Lesher, "UC Regents, in Historic Vote, Wipe Out Affirmative Action," *LAT,* 21 Jul. 1995.

Rene Sanchez, "Struggling to Maintain Diversity," *WP,* 11 Mar. 1996.

James Richardson, "UC Says It Gave Favors," *SacBee,* 15 Mar. 1996.

Mark Gladstone and Ralph Frammolino, "UC Chief Calls for Report on Admissions Favoritism," *LAT,* 19 Mar. 1996.

Ralph Frammolino, Mark Gladstone, and Henry Weinstein, "UCLA Gave Added Admissions Help to Well-Connected," *LAT,* 21 Mar. 1996.

Virginia Ellis and Ralph Frammolino, "UC Admissions Code of Ethics Is Proposed," *LAT,* 22 Mar. 1996.

Stephanie Simon and Ralph Frammolino, "Bruin Blues: Baffled by Rejection," *LAT,* 24 Mar. 1996.

Carl Ingram and Mark Gladstone, "Ban Sought on Political Clout at UC," *LAT,* 30 Mar. 1996.

Kenneth R. Weiss, "Tracking Affirmative Action," *LAT,* 8 Oct. 1997.

Dave Lesher and Kenneth R. Weiss, "Wilson Fights Benefits for Partners of UC Employees," *LAT,* 20 Nov. 1997.

Kenneth R. Weiss and Dave Lesher, "UC Regents Defy Wilson, OK Gay Partner Benefits," *LAT,* 22 Nov. 1997.

Julie Marquis, "Doctor Becomes Symbol in Affirmative Action Debate," *LAT,* 2 Dec. 1997.

Rebecca Trounson and Jill Leovy, "UC Ends Affirmative Action Ban," *LAT,* 17 May 2001.

Rebecca Trounson, "UC Admits Record Number of Community College Students," *LAT,* 1 June 2001.

Richard C. Atkinson, "The California Crucible: Demography, Excellence, and Access at the University of California" (Keynote Address, 2001 International Assembly of the Council for Advancement and Support of Education, San Francisco, 2 Jul. 2001, unpublished manuscript).

AP, "U of California Alters Admission Policy," *NYT,* 20 Jul. 2001.

Rebecca Trounson, "Critics, UC Are at Odds over SAT II," *LAT,* 23 Jul. 2001.

Tanya Schevitz, "UC Campuses Plan to Apply Admission Rules Differently," *SFCh,* 14 Nov. 2001.

Rebecca Trounson and Kenneth R. Weiss, "UC Admissions to Weigh 'Personal Achievement,' " *LAT,* 19 Nov. 2001.

Rebecca Trounson, "UC Faculty Panel Urges New Admissions Test," *LAT,* 31 Jan. 2002.

The Boys from Texas

Crisis Overview

Kenneth Howe, "Deregulation Sputtering," *SFCh,* 4 Mar. 1998.

California Power Exchange, *California's New Electricity Market: Great Expectations: What Happens When New Markets Open?,* 27 Mar. 1998.

George Raine, "Deflating Deregulation," *SFEx,* 29 Mar. 1998.

Nancy Rivera Brooks, "State Switches to Free Market for Electricity Today," *LAT,* 31 Mar. 1998.

Agis Salpukas, "Deregulation of Utilities in California," *NYT,* 2 Apr. 1998.

Mark Gladstone and Brandon Bailey, "State's Long Road to Current Problems," *SJMN,* 30 Nov. 2000.

Nancy Vogel, "How State's Consumers Lost with Electricity Deregulation," *LAT,* 9 Dec. 2000.

James C. Williams, *Energy and the Making of Modern California* (2001).

Alan Pasternak, "We're Paying the Price for Bad Energy Decisions of Years Past," *LAT,* 7 Jan. 2001.

"California Power Crisis: Blackouts and Lawsuits and No End in Sight," *WSJ,* 19 Jan. 2001.

Todd S. Purdum, "California's Power Crisis Replays a Familiar Theme," *NYT,* 25 Jan. 2001.

Timothy Egan and Sam Howe Verhovek, "How California Fell Prey to Power Sellers," *NYT,* 11 Feb. 2001.

Erin Riches, *How We Got to Where We Are Today: A Deregulation Timeline* (California Budget Project, 7 June 2001).

Robin Fields, "Demand Had Minor Role in Power Crisis," *LAT,* 25 June 2001.

Rebecca Smith, "The Lessons Learned: California Has Taught Us a Lot About the Do's and Don'ts of Deregulation," *WSJ,* 17 Sept. 2001.

William W. Hogan, "The California Meltdown," *Harvard Magazine* (September–October 2001).

Generators

Stuart Leavenworth and Chris Bowman, "All Kinds Have Foiled New Plants," *SacBee,* 28 Jan. 2001.

Scott Gold, "Communities $270-Million Power Line," *LAT,* 14 May 2001.

Tom Knudson, "Generator, Environmental Groups Strike Deal," *SacBee,* 16 May 2001.

Carla Marinucci, "Nuclear Power's Comeback," *SFCh,* 23 May 2001.

Matthew Ebnet, "Generator Idled by Fire Is Restarted," *LAT,* 2 June 2001.

Dan Morain, "Davis Eases Power Plant Pollution Rules," *LAT,* 12 June 2001.

Rachel Gordon, "Potrero Hill Power Plant Hit by 2 Lawsuits," *SFCh,* 20 June 2001.

Nicolai Ouroussoff, "A Much-Needed Park May Go Up in Smoke," *LAT,* 20 June 2001.

Joe Mozingo, "Energy Company Abandons Plans for Baldwin Hills Plant," *LAT,* 22 June 2001.

Joe Mozingo, "Pat Robertson's Oil Firm Seeks to Build Small Power Plant," *LAT,* 28 June 2001.

Scott Winokur, "SF Critiques Potrero Power Plant Proposal," *SFCh,* 4 Jul. 2001.

Bernadette Tansey, "Davis Opens Another New Power Plant," *SFCh,* 10 Jul. 2001.

Terence Monmaney, "Rush for Power Plant in Chino Raises Concerns," *LAT,* 24 Jul. 2001.

Carrie Peyton and Chris Bowman, "More Power, Cleaner Skies," *SacBee,* 5 Aug. 2001.

Robert Davila, "Power Plant Plans Ripped," *SacBee,* 29 Aug. 2001.

Chris Kraul, "Sempra Plans Major Energy Project in Baja," *LAT,* 5 Oct. 2001.

Blackouts

Miguel Bustillo and Nancy Vogel, "State to Issue Warnings of Power Outages," *LAT,* 22 May 2001.

Dan Morain and Nancy Vogel, "Davis Orders 3-Tiered Warnings of Blackouts," *LAT,* 25 May 2001.

Erin Hallissy, "Blackout Alert for Next Two Days," *SFCh,* 18 June 2001.

Jenifer Warren, "Blackout Forecasts' Dark Side," *LAT,* 20 June 2001.

Soaring Rates

Dan Smith, "Rate Hikes Bigger Worry than Blackouts, Poll Says," *SacBee,* 22 May 2001.

Marla Dickerson, Stuart Silverstein, and William Lobdell, "Power Customers Are Getting Shocked as They Open Bills," *LAT,* 30 June 2001.

Jerry Hirsch and Sam Kennedy, "High Power Prices Lit Fire Under Conservation," *LAT,* 14 Jul. 2001.

Tim Reiterman and Nancy Vogel, "PUC May Cede Control over Electricity Rates," *LAT,* 19 Jul. 2001.

AP, "Rate Proposal for Electricity in California," *NYT,* 20 Jul. 2001.

Tim Reiterman and Jerry Hirsch, "Rate Hike Will Cover Power Costs, State Says," *LAT,* 23 Jul. 2001.

Nancy Vogel, "Customers Keep Paying Price of Energy Deregulation Fiasco," *LAT,* 7 Oct. 2001.

Conservation

Burton Richter, "The Key: Reduce Demand," *LAT,* 20 May 2001.

John Hill, "New Views Emerging on Power," *SacBee,* 23 May 2001.

Sarah Hale, "Outdoor Lights Still Burning," *LAT,* 26 May 2001.

Stuart Leavenworth, "Lodi Just Says No to Powers That Be," *SacBee,* 29 May 2001.

Dave Wilson, "Energy Drain," *LAT,* 31 May 2001.

Mitchell Landsberg, "Summer Starts, Power Doesn't Stop," *LAT,* 21 June 2001.

Ruth Stroud, "Energy Efficient Living," *LAT,* 23 June 2001.

Robert A. Masullo, "The Cost of Cool," *SacBee,* 25 June 2001.

Paul Krugman, "Turning California On," *NYT,* 27 June 2001.

Joseph Menn, "Rule May Spur Firms to Waste Energy," *LAT,* 2 Jul. 2001.

Twila Decker, "Californians Cut Energy Use 12.3% from Last Year," *LAT,* 2 Jul. 2001.

David Perlman, "Davis Asks PUC to Let Utilities Cut Voltage," *SFCh,* 4 Jul. 2001.

Nancy Vogel, "Davis Urges Drop in Voltage to Stave Off Blackouts," *LAT,* 4 Jul. 2001.

Amy Chance, "Energy Savings Slip a Bit," *SacBee,* 2 Aug. 2001.

Elizabeth Shogren, "Calif. Orchestrating Energy Efficiency, but It's a One-Man Band," *LAT,* 19 Aug. 2001.

Mireya Navarro, "Lights Off Is New Policy for Coping in California," *NYT,* 26 Aug. 2001.

Harriet Chiang, "Californians Throttle Down Power Use," *SFCh,* 3 Sept. 2001.

PG&E

Tim Reiterman, Dan Morain, and Mitchell Landsberg, "PG&E Declares Bankruptcy; State's Crisis Plans Collapse," *LAT,* 7 Apr. 2001.

David Lazarus, "PG&E Wants to Double Its Top Executives Pay," *SFCh*, 30 May 2001.

Edie Lau, "3 Million Due Power Rebate," *SacBee*, 3 Aug. 2001.

George W. Bush Energy Plan

James Flanigan, "Bush's Plan Redraws Lines of Power Politics," *LAT*, 17 May 2001.

Richard Simon, Greg Miller, and James Flanigan, "Bush Energy Plan Seeks More Nuclear Power, Aid for Poor," *LAT*, 17 May 2001.

Edwin Chen and Richard Simon, "Bush Details Energy Plan, Calls for Boost in Supplies," *LAT*, 18 May 2001.

William Schneider, "California Left Twisting in the Political Wind," *LAT*, 20 May 2001.

George Skelton, "Davis Says Bad Guys Went Thataway to Texas," *LAT*, 21 May 2001.

Bush Visits California

Dan Morain and James Gerstenzang, "Governor to Stress Price Caps to Bush," *LAT*, 29 May 2001.

James Gerstenzang and Dan Morain, "Bush, Davis Collide over Energy Policy," *LAT*, 30 May 2001.

Carla Marinucci, "Bush, Davis, Spar over Energy Crisis," *SFCh*, 30 May 2001.

Matier & Ross, "Davis Steals Bush's Thunder," *SFCh*, 30 May 2001.

George Skelton, "Bush Blunders into Equal Footing with Davis," *LAT*, 31 May 2001.

Caps

Nancy Vogel and Dan Morain, "State Renews Demand for Power Price Relief," *LAT*, 26 May 2001.

Lynda Gledhill and Robert Salladay, "Davis Says He'll Sue Regulators over Cost," *SFCh*, 30 May 2001.

Amy Chance, " 'Soft Cap' a Win for Davis, Cover for GOP," *SacBee*, 19 June 2001.

Carolyn Lochhead, "Electricity Price Caps Imposed in West," *SFCh*, 19 June 2001.

Dan Walters, "Great California Energy Crisis May Be Heading Toward a Climax," *SacBee*, 19 June 2001.

David Whitney, "New FERC Limit on Power Costs," *SacBee*, 19 June 2001.

Borrowing Money

Mitchel Benson and Rebecca Smith, "California Governor Expected to Sign Bill to Allow Bond Sale to Pay Energy Costs," *WSJ*, 10 May 2001.

Debora Vrana and Miguel Bustillo, "State Offers Details on Electricity Bond Issue," *LAT*, 18 May 2001.

Greg Lucas, "Davis OKs Stopgap Loan," *SFCh*, 20 June 2001.

"State Closes on $4.3-Billion Interim Loan to Buy Power," *LAT*, 27 June 2001.

David Lazarus, "The $12.5 Billion Pitch," *SFCh*, 3 Aug. 2001.

Rebecca Smith, "California's Plan for $12.5 Billion of Bonds to Cover Electricity Costs Runs into Snags," *NYT*, 7 Sept. 2001.

Miguel Bustillo, "Cost of State's Energy Loan Getting Higher," *LAT*, 31 Oct. 2001.

Demanding a Refund

Richard Simon, "Davis Asks for Energy Refund Help," *LAT*, 21 June 2001.

Marc Sandalow, "Davis Winning Washington PR Battle," *SFCh*, 22 June 2001.

Doug Smith, Robert J. Lopez, and Rich Connell, "Estimates of Power Profits Disputed," *LAT*, 22 June 2001.

Doug Smith, Carl Ingram, and Rich Connell, "Duke Shaped Power Market, 3 Tell Panel," *LAT*, 23 June 2001.

Lynda Gledhill and Christian Berthelsen, "$9 Billion Dollar Showdown over Power," *SFCh*, 25 June 2001.

Zachary Coile, "Power Refund Talks Start—Trade-Off Urged," *SFCh*, 26 June 2001.

Ricardo Alonso-Zaldivar and Megan Garvey, "California May Not Deserve Utility Refund, Referee Says," *LAT*, 10 Jul. 2001.

Zachary Coile and Christian Berthelsen, "State's Refund Demand Rejected," *SFCh*, 10 Jul. 2001.

Emily Bazar, "Davis Repeats Threat to Sue FERC to Get Full Refund," *SacBee*, 11 Jul. 2001.

Nancy Vogel, "FERC Orders Refunds by 4 Power Firms," *LAT*, 9 Oct. 2001.

Nancy Vogel, "Energy Providers Accuse State of Unfair Practices," *LAT*, 19 Oct. 2001.

Tim Reiterman, "State Disputes Long-Term Power Pacts," *LAT*, 25 Feb. 2002.

James Sterngold, "California Tries to Have Energy Deals Renegotiated," *NYT*, 25 Feb. 2002.

9/11

Is California a Target? — no

LAX Millennium Plot

Josh Meyer, "Terrorist to Be Star Witness at Trial," *LAT*, 25 June 2001.

Josh Meyer, "Origins of LAX Plot Reportedly Detailed," *LAT*, 28 June 2001.

Josh Meyer, "Terrorist Says Plans Didn't End with LAX," *LAT*, 4 Jul. 2001.

Josh Meyer, "Man Charged as Bomb Plot Mastermind," *LAT*, 16 Jul. 2001.

Is California a Target?

Nita Lelyveld and Kenneth Reich, "Authorities Downplay Rumors of an Attack on LA," *LAT*, 22 Sept. 2001.

Seema Mehta, "Rethinking Security at San Onofre," *LAT*, 28 Oct. 2001.

John M. Glionna and Dan Morain, "Davis Warns of Threat to Bridges," *LAT*, 2 Nov. 2001.

Larry D. Hatfield, Steve Rubenstein, and Ray Delgado, "Tight Security on Bay Bridges," *SFCh*, 3 Nov. 2001.

Dan Morain, "Davis Defends Warning of Bridge Attack," *LAT*, 3 Nov. 2001.

Kenneth Reich, "Study to Seek Ways to Protect LA's Major Buildings from Terrorism," *LAT*, 18 Dec. 2001.

State of California, Little Hoover Commission, *Be Prepared: Getting Ready for New and Uncertain Dangers* (January 2002).

War and Peace

Maria L. La Ganga and John M. Glionna, "Storm Greets Lone Dissenter in Vote to Broaden Bush's Powers," *LAT*, 18 Sept. 2001.

John M. Glionna, "Berkeley's Removal of US Flags from Firetrucks Sparks Outrage," *LAT*, 21 Sept. 2001.

Shawn Hubler, "Berkeley Is Reeling over Anti-War Vote," *LAT*, 26 Oct. 2001.

Charles Burress, "Berkeley City Council to Vote on Helping Conscientious Objectors," *SFCh*, 11 Dec. 2001.

Islamic California Under Duress

Ken Ellingwood and Nicholas Riccardi, "Arab-Americans Enduring Hard Stares of Other Fliers," *LAT*, 20 Sept. 2001.

Larry B. Stammer, "Turbans Make Sikhs Innocent Targets," *LAT,* 20 Sept. 2001.

Mitchell Landsberg and David Rosenzweig, "Plane Suspect Denies Threat to Americans," *LAT,* 29 Sept. 2001.

Tony Perry and Phil Willon, "Bahraini Aristocrat, Ex-Marine Split Up," *LAT,* 29 Sept. 2001.

H. G. Reza and Rich Connell, "Sometimes-Hostile Scrutiny Difficult for San Diego's Muslim Community," *LAT,* 5 Oct. 2001.

William Lobdell, "Sept. 11 Terrorist Attacks Delay Completion of O.C. Mosque," *LAT,* 31 Oct. 2001.

Beverly Beyette, "Suddenly, Under Suspicion," *LAT,* 9 Dec. 2001.

William Lobdell, "Professor at Center of Debate Reinstated," *LAT,* 12 Dec. 2001.

Ken Ellingwood and Rebecca Trounson, "10 Held as INS Targets Visa Abuses," *LAT,* 13 Dec. 2001.

H. G. Reza and Ken Ellingwood, "Man Freed in Terror Probe Back in State," *LAT,* 15 Dec. 2001.

Greg Miller, "CIA Looks to Los Angeles for Would-Be Iranian Spies," *LAT,* 15 Jan. 2002.

Hate Crimes

Tamar Lewin, "Sikh Owner of Gas Station Is Fatally Shot in Rampage," *NYT,* 17 Sept. 2001.

Joe Mozingo, "Slain Egyptian Was a Fixture in San Gabriel," *LAT,* 19 Sept. 2001.

Kenneth Reich and Patrick McGreevy, "Police Agencies Crack Down on Hate Crimes," *LAT,* 20 Sept. 2001.

H. G. Reza, "San Diego Muslims Criticize Mayor's Response to Pleas," *LAT,* 12 Oct. 2001.

Greg Krikorian and Richard Winton, "JDL Leader Accused in Mosque Bomb Plot," *LAT,* 13 Dec. 2001.

Nita Lelyveld, "Jailed Jewish Militant Protector or Terrorist?" *LAT,* 22 Jan. 2002.

Support of Islamic California

Denny Walsh, "Services OK'd for Muslim Inmates," *SacBee,* 3 Aug. 2001.

Evelyn Nieves and Patricia Leigh Brown, "Group Struggling to Shed Association with Terrorism," *NYT,* 18 Sept. 2001.

Solomon Moore, "Expressions of Support Surprising to Muslims," *LAT,* 26 Sept. 2001.

David Kelly, "Afghan Rug Sellers Report Business Has Soared Since the Fighting Began," *LAT,* 15 Oct. 2001.

Mary Rourke, "A Stronger Voice for Muslims," *LAT,* 29 Oct. 2001.

William Lobdell and H. G. Reza, "For Ramadan, Signs of Muslims' Good Faith," *LAT,* 16 Nov. 2001.

Kimi Yoshino, "14,000 Muslims Turn Out for Celebration in Orange County," *LAT,* 17 Dec. 2001.

Marin Talib

Kevin Fagan, Pamela J. Podger, and Edward Epstein, "A Father's Fear for Taliban Son Held by US," *SFCh,* 5 Dec. 2001.

Editorial, "Sons of Liberty," *WSJ,* 7 Dec. 2001.

Don Lattin and Kevin Fagan, "John Walker's Curious Quest," *SFCh,* 13 Dec. 2001.

Eric Lichtblau, "US Talib Is Charged with Conspiracy," *LAT,* 16 Jan. 2002.

Richard A. Serrano, "American Talib in US Jail Awaiting Conspiracy Trial," *LAT,* 24 Jan. 2002.

Kevin Fagan and Edward Epstein, "Charges Mount for Marin Taliban," *SFCh,* 6 Feb. 2002.

Garrison State
Tony Perry, "San Diego Mood Tense as Military Gears Up," *LAT*, 7 Oct. 2001.
Tim Reiterman, "Disarming Biological Weapons," *LAT*, 22 Oct. 2001.
Peter Pae, "From Dune Buggy to Combat Vehicle," *LAT*, 24 Nov. 2001.
Marla Dickerson, "Ceradyne Stock Gains Ground with Army Deal," *LAT*, 26 Nov. 2001.
Kristina Sauerwein, "1000 Mourn Soldier Killed in War," *LAT*, 14 Dec. 2001.
AP, " 'Friendly Fire' Victim Is Buried at Arlington," *LAT*, 18 Dec. 2001.
Peter Pae, "Future Is Now for Creator of Predator," *LAT*, 3 Jan. 2002.

Economy Tanks
James Flanigan, "Terrorism, State Woes Cast Pall Over Cities," *LAT*, 4 Oct. 2001.
Claudia Eller, "Studios in Quandary Over Timing," *LAT*, 5 Oct. 2001.
Dale Kasler, "The Recession and Sept. 11 Take Wind Out Of S.F.'s Sails," *SacBee*, 28 Nov. 2001.
Fred Alvarez, "Terrorist Attacks Add to Woes of California's Farm Economy," *LAT*, 23 Dec.
    2001.

LAX On Hold
Jennifer Oldham, "Hahn Seeks to Shift Flights to Ontario Airport," *LAT*, 28 Aug. 2001.
Jennifer Oldham, "LAX Plan to Shift Focus to Security Issues," *LAT*, 26 Sept. 2001.
Jennifer Oldham, "Some Skycaps Back at LAX; Private Vehicles May Be Next," *LAT*, 2 Oct.
    2001.
Peter Y. Hong, "LA, SF Airports to Get National Guard," *LAT*, 5 Oct. 2001.
Peter Y. Hong, "Troops Posted at LAX, SF Airport," *LAT*, 6 Oct. 2001.
Jennifer Oldham, "Mayor Subs Security for LAX Growth," *LAT*, 8 Oct. 2001.
Jennifer Oldham, "LAX to Restore Private Vehicle Access," *LAT*, 14 Dec. 2001.

Terrorist Chic and New York Envy
"Changed Lives: Americans Redefine Their Futures in the Aftermath of September 11. How
    Will the Arts Respond? Our Critics Look for Signs of Courage," *LAT Magazine*, Special
    Issue, 21 Oct. 2001.
Paul Brownfield, "In Late Night, the Contrasts Grow Stark," *LAT*, 21 Dec. 2001.
Reed Johnson, "Architects Ask, 'What Did I Do to Cause This?,' " *LAT*, 21 Dec. 2001.
Tina Daunt and Geoffrey Mohan, "Hahn Picks Bratton to Lead Police Force," *LAT*, 3 Oct.
    2002.
Michael Finnegan, "Giuliani Talks Up a Sagging Simon," *LAT*, 14 Oct. 2002.
Roger Vincent, "Giving the Big Apple a Taste of LA's Core," *LAT*, 11 Nov. 2002.

EPILOGUE

Déjà Vu All Over Again

Things Can Go Wrong
Tom Stienstra, "Invasive Northern Pike Just Won't Die," *SFCh*, 29 Jan. 2003.
Sabin Russell, "Shuttle Tragedy," *SFCh*, 4 Feb. 2003.
Don Thompson, "Pike Seem Unfazed by Blast," *SFCh*, 20 Mar. 2003.

Crime
Henry Lee, "SF Teen Shot Dead," *SFCh*, 15 Feb. 2003.
Janine DeFao, "Jerry Brown's About-Face on Criminal Sentencing," *SFCh*, 18 Feb. 2003.

Robert Jablon, "South Central LA Now South LA," *SFCh,* 10 Apr. 2003.
Joshunda Sanders, "Young and Worried," *SFCh,* 20 Apr. 2003.

Displacement and Discontent
Glen Martin, Nanette Asimov, and Jim Zamora, "Raider Rage," *SFCh,* 27 Jan. 2003.
Steve Rubenstein, "Raider Fans Get Stood Up," *SFCh,* 1 Feb. 2003.
Rick DelVecchio, "Bill Walsh Kicks Off Raiders' Testimony," *SFCh,* 16 Apr. 2003.

Law and Order
Jaxon Van Derbeken, Rachel Gordon, Jim Herron Zamora, and Patrick Hoge, "SF Police
    Chief, Aides Step Aside," *SFCh,* 4 Mar. 2003.
Dean Murphy, "Police Dept. Indictments Rattle San Francisco," *NYT,* 5 Mar. 2003.
Jaxon Van Derbeken, Jim Herron Zamora, and Patrick Hoge, "Top Cops Hear Details of
    Charges," *SFCh,* 5 Mar. 2003.
Anastasia Hendrix, Pamela Podger, and Steve Rubenstein, "Huge, Peaceful Crowd Protests
    Stance on Iraq," *SFCh,* 17 Feb. 2003.
Mark Simon, "Joan Baez's Long March to Peace," *SFCh,* 20 Feb. 2003.
Wyatt Buchanan, "Photos Show 65,000 at Peak of SF Rally," *SFCh,* 21 Feb. 2003.
Joe Garofoli, "Rush-Hour Rally," *SFCh,* 15 Mar. 2003.
Nanette Asimov, Michael Cabanatuan, and Chuck Squatriglia, "Racing into Iraq—Rage in SF
    Streets," *SFCh,* 21 Mar. 2003.

Domestic Issues
Rachel Gordon, " 'Care Not Cash' Thrown Out," *SFCh,* 9 May 2003.
Katherine Seligman, "Street Attack Stuns Visiting Doctors," *SFCh,* 23 May 2003.
Patrick Hoge, "SF Welfare Chief Halts 'Care Not Cash' Plan," *SFCh,* 10 June 2003.
Jason Johnson, "Asthma Epidemic Sickens Thousands of Bay Area Kids," *SFCh,* 11 Feb.
    2003.
Ilene Lelchuk, "Bid to Stop SF's Child Prostitution," *SFCh,* 13 Feb. 2003.
Carolyn Lochhead, "Sex Trade Uses Bay Area to Bring In Women, Kids," *SFCh,* 26 Feb. 2003.

Murmurs in the Forest
Eric Bailey, "Activists Press for Ballot Measure to Save Old Trees," *LAT,* 29 Jan. 2003.
Glen Martin, "DA Hits Timber Firm with Fraud Charges," *SFCh,* 26 Feb. 2003.
Suzanne Herel and Andrew Edwards, "Standoff High in Redwood Forest," *SFCh,* 15 Mar.
    2003.
Chuck Squatriglia, "Sitters Climb Back Up in Trees," *SFCh,* 19 Mar. 2003.
Jane Kay and Suzanne Herel, "Northern Logging Plan Tossed," *SFCh,* 20 May 2003.

Pot
Bob Egelko, "Judge Keeps Tight Rein on Pot Trial," *SFCh,* 31 Jan. 2003.
Bob Egelko, "Jurors Say They Were Duped," *SFCh,* 5 Feb. 2003.
Harriet Chiang, "Judge Just Followed Law in Pot Trial, Experts Say," *SFCh,* 6 Feb. 2003.

Good News
Tyche Hendricks, "State's Latino Birthrate Surpasses 50 Percent," *SFCh,* 6 Feb. 2003.
Dean Murphy, "New Californian Identity Predicted by Researchers," *NYT,* 17 Feb. 2003.
Nanette Asimov, "English-Only Students Do Better on State Test," *SFCh,* 26 Mar. 2003.

Bad News

Stuart Silverstein, "CSU Ousts 8.2 Percent over Weak Skills," *LAT*, 29 Jan. 2003.

Sam Zuckerman, "Job Losses in State Twice as Bad as Thought," *SFCh*, 19 Feb. 2003.

Nanette Asimov, "Budget Crisis Killing State's Small Classes," *SFCh*, 11 Apr. 2003.

Larry Slonaker, "Oakland's Ailing Schools Come Under State Control," *SJMN*, 3 June 2003.

Even More Bad News

Todd Wallack and Harriet Chiang, "Top SF Dot.Com Law Firm to Close," *SFCh*, 31 Jan. 2003.

Carolyn Said, "After the Fall," *SFCh*, 5 May 2003.

Sam Zuckerman, "UCLA Scales Back Forecast for California's Resurgence," *SFCh*, 5 June 2003.

Energy Crisis

Christopher Weare, *The California Electricity Crisis: Causes and Options* (Public Policy Institute of California, 2003).

Mark Martin, " 'Proof' of Energy Scam," *SFCh*, 3 Mar. 2003.

Christian Berthelsen and Mark Martin, "How Wheeling, Dealing Raised Energy Prices," *SFCh*, 27 Mar. 2003.

Zachary Coile, "Energy Overcharge $3.3 Billion," *SFCh*, 27 Mar. 2003.

Budget Crisis

Lynda Gledhill and Greg Lucas, "Davis Against Vehicle Fee Increase," *SFCh*, 4 Feb. 2003.

Lynda Gledhill, "Davis Splits with Party on Budget," *SFCh*, 5 Feb. 2003.

Andres Martinez, "The Disintegration of the Golden Era in the Golden State," *NYT*, 9 Feb. 2003.

Greg Lucas, "Moody's Lowers California's Credit Rating," *SFCh*, 11 Feb. 2003.

Pamela Podger, "Journalists Get a Look at Death Row," *SFCh*, 12 Feb. 2003.

Mark Martin, "State Treasurer Calls For Increase in Business Taxes," *SFCh*, 14 Feb. 2003.

Greg Lucas and Lynda Gledhill, "Davis Budget Plan Faulted," *SFCh*, 20 Feb. 2003.

Mark Martin, "Demo Opposition Rises on Davis Plan for New Death Row," *SFCh*, 20 Feb. 2003.

Edward Epstein, "Davis Joins Governors at Capital in Plea for Funds," *SFCh*, 24 Feb. 2003.

"State Senate OKs Big Budget Cuts," *SFCh*, 25 Feb. 2003.

Greg Lucas, "GOP Budget Plan Axes $25 Billion," *SFCh*, 27 Feb. 2003.

Gregg Jones, "Davis Asks for a Bigger Cut from Casinos," *LAT*, 1 Apr. 2003.

Lynda Gledhill, "Davis Tells Agencies to Create Layoff Plans," *SFCh*, 4 Apr. 2003.

Robert Salladay, "Swarm of State Fees Proposed," *SFCh*, 13 Apr. 2003.

Lynda Gledhill, "State Piling Up Debt to Deal with Deficit," *SFCh*, 6 May 2003.

Greg Lucas, "Deficits Predicted for State," *SFCh*, 20 May 2003.

Lynda Gledhill and Christian Berthelsen, "State Strains to Find Budget Solution," *SFCh*, 9 June 2003.

Michael Taylor and Lynda Gledhill, "Layoffs Possible at CHP," *SFCh*, 12 June 2003.

Recall

Lynda Gledhill, "Campaign to Recall Davis Gets off Ground," *SFCh*, 12 Feb. 2003.

Lynda Gledhill, "Cost of Davis Recall Election: $25 Million," *SFCh*, 18 Feb. 2003.

John Wildermuth, "State GOP Backs Davis Recall Effort," *SFCh*, 24 Feb. 2003.

Carla Marinucci, "Davis Recall Effort Beset by Troubles," *SFCh*, 5 Mar. 2003.

Robert Salladay, "Recall Picks Up Steam," *SFCh*, 11 June 2003.

Carla Marinucci and John Wildermuth, "Candidates Hear Loud Knock of Opportunity," *SFCh*, 12 June 2003.

Robert Salladay, "Almost Half of Voters in Favor of Governor's Recall," *SFCh*, 12 June 2003.

Carla Marinucci and John Wildermuth, "Huge Win for Schwarzenegger," *SFCh*, 8 Oct. 2003.

Jerry Schwartz, "Schwarzenegger: From Mr. Universe to Governor," *SacBee*, 9 Oct. 2003.

Robert Salladay and Carla Marinucci, "Schwarzenegger's Vow: 'Miracle of Sacramento,' " *SFCh*, 18 Nov. 2003.

Hendrik Hertzberg, "Uncrazy California," *The New Yorker*, 21 Nov. 2003.

Larry N. Gerston and Terry Christensen, *Recall! California's Political Earthquake* (2004).

INDEX